The Knights
of England

The Knights of England

A Complete Record from the Earliest Time to the Present Day of the Knights of all the Orders of Chivalry in England, Scotland, and Ireland, and of Knights Bachelors

BY

WM. A. SHAW, Litt.D.

Editor of the Calendar of Treasury Papers at H.M. Record Office; Author of the History of the English Church under the Commonwealth; Author of the History of Currency; etc.

INCORPORATING
A Complete List of Knights Bachelors dubbed in Ireland

Compiled by

G. D. BURTCHAELL, M.A., M.R.I.A.

Barrister-at-Law, Office of Arms, Ireland
Author of Genealogical Memoirs of the Members of Parliament for Kilkenny

Vol. II.

Originally Printed and Published 1906 for the
CENTRAL CHANCERY OF THE ORDERS OF KNIGHTHOOD,
Lord Chamberlain's Office, St. James's Palace

LONDON

The Naval & Military Press Ltd

Published by

The Naval & Military Press Ltd
Unit 10 Ridgewood Industrial Park,
Uckfield, East Sussex,
TN22 5QE England

Tel: +44 (0) 1825 749494
Fax: +44 (0) 1825 765701

www.naval-military-press.com
www.military-genealogy.com

In reprinting in facsimile from the original, any imperfections are inevitably reproduced and the quality may fall short of modern type and cartographic standards.

1346, July 13.
> The king, Edward III., landed at La Hogue in his expedition to France, and there on the shore he knighted the Black Prince and made him Prince of Wales. Thereupon the said Black Prince immediately made the following knights:—

ROGER DE MORTIMER, afterwards earl of March.
WILLIAM DE MONTACUTE, lord Montacute, afterwards earl of Salisbury.
WILLIAM DE ROS, lord Ros.
et cum illis etiam fuerunt alii consimiliter ad ordinem promoti militarem.

1346, Aug. 26.
> Grants of annuity ordered to the following to support the order of knighthood which they have taken from the King (that is to say recently in the campaign in France).

ROBERT DE MAULE.
GUY DE BRIANE.
JOHN DE RAVENSHOLM.
PETER DE BREWESE.
THOMAS DE LANCASTRE.
HENRY DENGAYNE.
JOHN, son of GILES DE BELLO CAMPO.

1346, Aug. 26. Sir JOHN DE LISLE, of Rougemont, raised to the rank of a banneret by a writ of this date, being the date of the battle of Creecy.

1346, Aug. 26. RALPH DE SHELTON, knighted whilst in the king's retinue at Creecy.

1347. *Knights made by Edward III. at the Seige of Calais in France.**

FITZWALTER.
JOHN FOURNEYS.
RIC CORNERD.
EDW. MOLYN *alias* Montermer.
WILLIAM WALKINGTON.
WILLIAM WAUTOR *alias* Aches.
WILLIAM BLUNT.
THOMAS BLOWNT.
BASTARD GRAY.
GILES DE BEAUCHAMP.
NICOLAS LANGFORD.
ROGER HERHAM.
CHRISTOFER DE LANGFORD.
JO CREWES.
WILLIAM DE WATENALD.
JOHN TRACY.
NORMAN DARCY.

---
* This list of knights made in 1347 is contained in Harl. MS. 1156, fo. 82.

Knights Bachelors

1257, May 18. HENRY PLANTAGENET, 2nd son of Richard earl of Cornwall (knighted on the day of his father's coronation as king of the Romans at Aachen).

1272, Oct. 13. EDMUND PLANTAGENET, 5th son of Richard earl of Cornwall (knighted on the occasion of his marriage with Margaret, sister of the earl of Clare. He was made earl at the same time).

1272, Oct. 13. HENRY DE LACY (knighted and made earl of Lincoln, same occasion).

1272, Oct. 13. GEORGE DE CANTELUPE (same occasion), and many others, nobles of the kingdom of England, some of them knighted ('militiae cingulum susceperunt') by the King himself, others by the aforesaid earls.

1336.
> On Monday after St. Matthew's day the king, Edward III., made his eldest son (the Black Prince) earl of Chester and duke of Cornwall, and after making six other earls the same day the king made 20 knights, to wit:—

EDWARD DE MONTAGUE (Montacute).
THOM DE SWINNERTON.
JOH DE ISLE.
JOH DARCY.
RIC DAMMORY.
JO DE PULTENEY.
JO DE MERE.
ROGER BAVENT.
ROGER HILLARY.
JO DE BOLINGBROKE.
JO LUTERELE.
SYMON DE SWANLOND.
WILL STOT.
WILL BASSET.
ROB DE SADYNGTON.
WILL DE ZOUSCH.
JO DE COGESHALE.
ROGER DANNGERVILE.
THOM DEL MORE.
JO STRACCHE.

[Anno 1347.]
    JOHN DARCY.
    JOHN LYMBURNE.
    JOHN SAMBIE.
    HENRY FITZHENRY.
    RIC PIERS.
    REYNOLD MOYNE.
    CHRISTOFER DE LUDLOWE.
    JO STORMYE.
    JOHN DE LISLE.
    WARREN DE LISLE.
    OLIVER DYNHAM.
    THO. DE RACHESE.
    WILLIAM FERRERS.
    ROBERT FERRERS.
    RALPHE HASTINGS.
    HUGH COURTNEY.
    JO MORDAKE.
    RICHARD HEKYN.
    ROBERT DE BARCHHAILE.
    WILLIAM COZANS.
    HENR GLASTINGBUR.
    ROB BAYNTON.
    WILLIAM WOLTON.
    RIC CORNTCALL.
    JO HUSSEY.
    JO DE BELLUSE.
    JO POYNINGES.
    CHRISTOFER DE POYNINGES.
    JO BOALOR.
    WILLIAM MORTYMER.
    —— KIRKELOTS.
    JO TRUSSELL.
    ROG SWYNTON.
    WILLIAM LOVELL.
    PIERS DE LA WARE.
    FITZWILLIAM GAWRE.
    SIMON LE ZOWCHE.

[Anno 1347.]
    William le Zowche.
    William Frator [Vaire].
    William Boothe.
    Jo Dacton.
    John de Clivdon.
    Robert de Nevor.
    Warrein Latyne [? Lakyne].
    Otes de Guson.
    —— de Stafford.
    John Verdon.
    Christofer de Verdon.
    William de Gerdeston.
    William Francks.
    Robert Bowser.
    Christofer de Bourne.
    John de Mereworth.
    John de Sutton.
    John de Norweche.
    John Bafford.
    William de la Warre.
    Tho. de Halwton.
    John Daynwell.
    Tho. de Engayne.
    Jo de Engayne.
    John Paveley.
    John Cunstable.
    Jeoffrey de Gray.
    Ric de Were.
    John de Leyborne.
    Roger Corbet.
    Walter Paveley.
    Christofer de Layton.
    Robert Willowby.
    —— Trussell.
    Seigneur le Stratton.
    Robert de Rokeby.
    Simon de Sennyle.

KNIGHTS BACHELORS

[Anno 1347.]
- John Fitzsymond.
- John de Sirmone.
- —— Porchester.
- Talbot de Bashall, in Lanc.
- Roger Feldbrigge.
- John de Sullay.
- Christofer de Chawerth.
- John de Codington.
- —— Robsert.
- John Byron le fils.
- John de Palie.
- William Banestre.
- —— Timperley.
- John Dawbeney
- John Wallum.
- Piers de Thorneton.
- —— Ripleighe.
- John Backuse.
- John Talbot.
- Walter de Chirkingham.
- John Descurs.
- Christofer de Beckeringe.
- John Darderne.
- Walter Pechay.
- —— Layborne.
- —— Hartlewe.
- —— Langton.

Knights made by the Black Prince in the South West of France during the campaign which culminated in the battle of Poitiers.

- 1355, Oct. 11. Janekinus de Berefort, et alii milites.
- 1355, Oct. 13. Gilotus de Strattone, et quidam alii.
- 1355, Oct. 17. Adam de Lowches (probably a misreading for Zouche).
- 1355, Nov. 3. The son of the lord de Libreto.
- 1355, Nov. 3. Ralph Basset, lord Basset de Drayton.
- 1355, Nov. 3. Rolandus Daveys.
- 1355, Nov. 3. et plures alii ad ordinem militarem promovebantur.
- 1355, Nov. 12. Theodoricus Dale, ostiarius camere domini principis.

About April, 1360.

> ROGER (LE WARR), sire de la Warr (by Edward III., near Paris, France, on volunteering to lead a sally towards Paris).
>
> JOHN (FITZ-WALTER), sire de Fitz-Walter (same occasion).
>
> THUMAS BALASTRE (same occasion).
>
> GUILLAUME DE TROUSIAUS (same occasion).
>
> THUMAS LE DESPENSIER (same occasion).
>
> JEHAN DE NEUFVILLE (same occasion).
>
> RICHARD STURI (? STURMY) (same occasion).
>
> et plusieurs sultre.

Before 1362, Nov. 20.   RICHARD DE LA BERE, sheriff of Hereford.

Before 1372, Oct.   JOHN BOTILLER, sheriff of Lancashire.

Before 1377, June 22.   THOMAS BOKELOND, sheriff of Hampshire.

Before 1377, June 22.   JOHN DE CARESWELL, sheriff of Shropshire and Stafford.

About July, 1380.

> *The day the duke of Buckingham came before St. Omer he made several new knights, viz.:—*
>
> RAOUL DE NOEFVILLE.
>
> le fils au signeur messire BETREMIEU BOURSIER.
>
> le fils au signeur messire THUMAS CAMOIS.
>
> FOUKE COURBET.
>
> THUMAS D'ANGAIN (D'ANGLURI).
>
> RAOUL DE PIPPE.
>
> LOEIS DE SAINT-OBIN.
>
> JEHAN PAULLE.

KNIGHTS BACHELORS

After 1399, Aug. 22. JOHN BERKELEY, sheriff of Warwick and Leicester.

Before 1399, Sept. 30. THOMAS CLANVOWE, sheriff of Hereford.

Before 1399, Sept. 30. WILLIAM FYENS or FENYS, sheriff of Surrey and Sussex.

After 1399, Oct. 2. JOHN DAUNTESEY, sheriff of Wilts.

After 1399, Nov. 3. WILLIAM SHARESHULL, sheriff of Staffordshire.

After 1400, Nov. 24. HENRY NEVYLL, sheriff of Warwick and Leicester.

After 1401, Nov. 8. THOMAS MAUREWARD, sheriff of Warwick and Leicester.

1403, July 21. RICHARD DE SANDFORD (on the morrow of the battle of Shrewsbury) with at least two others.

After 1406, Nov. 5. ROBERT LYSLE, sheriff of Northumberland.

[1409, Aug. 4.]
Knights dubbed by king Henry IV. at the coming in of [Jean de Werchin], seneschal of Hainault, with other gentlemen to do feats of arms in Smithfield [on a challenge previously sent by them to the Order of the Garter], where these gentlemen did acquit themselves well, and were made knights [? at Windsor], viz.:—

JOHN CHEYNEY'S son and heir.
WILLIAM PORTER.
JOHN STANDISH.

After 1413, Nov. 6. JAMES HARYNGTON, sheriff of Cumberland.

After 1414, Nov. 10. JOHN HEVENYNGHAM, sheriff of Norfolk and Suffolk.

After 1416, Nov. 30. THOMAS WYKEHAM, sheriff of Hampshire.

1426, May 19.
After the battle of Verneuil (1424, August), the Duke of Bedford came over into England and on Whitsuntide in 1426 at Leicester [at a Parliament there] he dubbed King Henry VI. knight and forthwith the said King

KNIGHTS BACHELORS

>dubbed 44 knights. See the list of these knights supra pp. 130—2, where the names of the knights who may be presumed to have been made bachelor knights merely are printed in italics.

After 1427, Nov. 7. STEPHEN POPHAM, sheriff of Hampshire.

1439, May 15. HENRY, son of the earl of Huntingdon (at Kenyngton).

1439, May 15. HENRY, son of the earl of Arundel (*ibid.*).

1439, May 15. LEWYS JOHN (*idid.*).

1439, May 15. WILLIAM ESTEFYLDE, merchant of London (*ibid.*).

After 1441, June 10. FRANCIS DE SURIENNE, called l'Arragonois, received a grant of money to support the dignity of knighthood.

After 1449, Sept. 25. NICOLAS BYRON, sheriff of Lancashire.

After 1452, Nov. 8. RICHARD FENYS, sheriff of Surrey and Sussex.

1456, before July 15. A squire of the king of Denmark lately came to England and received the military order at Windsor.

1460, July 10.
>*Knights made at the battle of Northampton.*
>HENRY STAFFORD.
>THOMAS DYMMOKE.
>WILLIAM TYRELL.
>WILLIAM TYRELL, of the Beche (Bey).
>THOMAS STANLEY (STRANLEY).
>WILLIAM NORRYS.
>JOHN OF ASHETON.
>HENRY LEWYS (LOYS).
>THOMAS THORPE.

1460, Dec. 30.
>*Knights made at the battle of Wakefield.*
>Lord CLIFFORD (by the hands of Henry, duke of Somerset).
>JAMES LUTTERELL (by same).
>ROBERT WHITTINGHAM (by same).
>—— LATYMER, of Somersetshire (by same).
>RICHARD PERCY (by the hands of his brother, the earl of Northumberland).
>WILLIAM GASCOIGNE (by same).
>THOMAS METHAM (by same).
>WILLIAM BERTRAM (by same).
>RICHARD ALBOROUGH (by same).
>THOMAS ELDRETON (by same).
>JOHN MALEVER (by same).
>WILLIAM ST. QUYNTIN (by same).
>JOHN COURTENEY (by the hands of his brother, the earl of Devonshire).

1460, Dec. 30.
> THOMAS FULFORDE (by same).
> ALEXANDER HOODY (by same).
> RICHARD CARY (by same).
> ROGER CLIFFORD (by the hands of his brother, lord Clifford).
> RICHARD TEMPEST (by same).
> HENRY BELLINGHAM (by same).
> THOMAS BABTHORPE (by the hands of lord Roos).

1460–1, Feb. 17.
> *Knights made at the second battle of St. Albans.*
> *The King knighted his son Edward on the spot, and that young prince thereupon conferred that dignity on the earl of Shrewsbury and some thirty others, including:*
> THOMAS ROOS.
> ANDREW TROLLOPE (being the first that he made).
> —— WHYTYNGAM (who came next).
> —— TRESHAM (who came next).
> JOHN GRAY, and 12 more knights the same day.
> JOHN DONE.
> WILLIAM TALBOYS.
> SYMOND HAMMYS.

1461, Mar. 29.
> *Knights made by king Edward IV. at the battle of Towton.*
> WILLIAM HASTYNGES.
> WALTER DEVEREUX.
> HUMFREY STAFFORD.
> THOMAS MONTGOMERY.
> JOHN HOWARD, sheriff of Norfolk and Suffolk.
> THOMAS WALGRAVE.

1461, June 27.
> *Knights made the day before the Coronation of Edward IV.*
> JOHN FOGGE, made a knight of the Carpet.
> JOHN SCOTT, made a knight of the Carpet.

After 1461, Nov. 7.   GEORGE LOMLEY, sheriff of Northumberland.
After 1464, Nov. 5.   JAMES BASKERVILLE, sheriff of Hereford.

KNIGHTS BACHELORS

Before 1466, Easter.   LAWRENCE REYNFORD, sheriff of Essex and Herts.

Before 1465, April.   THOMAS UVEDALE, sheriff of Surrey and Sussex.

After 1465, Easter.   GEORGE DARELL, sheriff of Wilts.

1471, May 4.

> *Knights made by Edward IV. in the field of Grafton (Garton) beside Tewkesbury after the battle of Tewkesbury, on the field of battle.*

Lord JOHN COBHAM.
GEORGE NEVILL, son and heir to lord Abergavenny.
THOMAS WINGEFIELD.
HENRY WINGFIELD.
PHILIPPE COURTENEY, sheriff of Devonshire.
HENRY BEAUMONT, sheriff of Staffordshire.
MAURICE BERKELEY, sheriff of Hampshire.
RICHARD HASTINGES, called by his wife lord Welles.
RAUF HASTINGES.
ROBERT HARRINGTON.
THOMAS GREY, sheriff of Cambridge and Huntingdon.
JAMES TYRELL.
HENRY FERRERS.
JOHN APARRE (PARR).
HENRY PERPOYNT, sheriff of Notts and Derby.
JOHN DONE (DONNE, DOWNE).
ROGER KYNASTON (KINASTON, KINGESTON), sheriff of Shropshire.
RICHARD CROFTE, senior, sheriff of Hereford.
JOHN PILKINGTON.
JOHN LYNGEYNE.
JOHN HARLEY.
WILLIAM BOTTELLER.
CHRISTOPHER MORESBY.
JOHN CLAY.
ROBERT GREENE.

KNIGHTS BACHELORS

[1471, May 4.]

JOHN WILLOUGHBY [*de jure* lord Latimer].
ROGER REED (REE, RED).
JOHN SAVAGE (HAVAGE).
THOMAS STRICKLAND.
GEORGE BROWNE.
WILLIAM MOTTON.
JOHN CROKER.
—— SKERNE, of Essex.
JAMES CROWMER.
WILLIAM SANDES (SANDALLE).
JOHN DEVEREUX.
HENRY GREY.
JOHN SEYNTLOE.
EDWARD WOODHOUSE.
WILLIAM BRANDON.
RICHARD BEAUCHAMP.
THOMAS CORNEWALL (CROMWELL).
ROGER COUBETT.
HUMPHREY BLOUNT.
—— POOLE.
JOHN FERES.
JOHN BYNGHAM.
RICHARD RADCLYFFE.
JOHN SAUNDES.
NICHOLAS LANGFORD.

[1471, between May 4 and May 21.]

Knights Banneret made by Edward IV. on that voyage and late journey; whose pennons and standards (in the difference of pennons) were rent by the King's commandment.

THOMAS GREY.
RICHARD HASTINGES, afterwards lord Welles.
JOHN COURTENEY.
NICHOLAS LATYMER (LAWRENCE).

KNIGHTS BACHELORS

 RAUF HASTINGS, sheriff of Northamptonshire. May 5.
 ROGER TOKETTS (ROGERS).
 JOHN STANLEY.
 SYMON MOUNTFORD.
 JOHN HENNINGHAM.
 WILLIAM STANLEY.
 THOMAS DERING.
 WILLIAM STAMFORD.
 —— ABERDENNY.

1471, May 21.

 Knights made by Edward IV. outside the City Gates between Islington and Shoreditch when he entered London in state after the city had beaten off the Bastard Falconbridge.

 JOHN STOCKTON, lord mayor of London.
 JOHN CROSBY, sheriff of London.
 THOMAS URSWICK (HORSWYKE), recorder of London.

[1471, May 21.]

 RALPH VERNEY [alderman of London].
 RICHARD LEE [alderman of London].
 JOHN YONGE [alderman of London].
 WILLIAM TAYLOR [alderman of London].
 GEORGE IRELAND [alderman of London].
 JOHN (WILLIAM) STOKER (STOCKER) [alderman of London].
 MATHEW PHILIP (PHILIPPE) [alderman of London].
 WILLIAM HAMPTON [alderman of London].
 THOMAS STALBROKE [alderman of London].
 BARTHOLOMEW JAMES [alderman of London].

Between 1471, Oct., and 1472, July.

 Knights made in Granado by Sir Edward Woodville [? Anthony Woodville, Earl Rivers], warring on the infidels [? or by Sir Edward, styled Lord Woodville, in Brittany, in 1488].

 EDWARD WYNGFEILDE.
 CANTELUPE.

KNIGHTS BACHELORS

1472, JOHN PARR, sheriff of Westmoreland.

1476–7, Jan. 18. THOMAS HAWARD, or HOWARD, sheriff of Norfolk and Suffolk.

after 1480, Nov. 15. ROBERT WILLOUGHBY, sheriff of Devon.

after 1481, Sept. 29. GILES DAUBENEY, sheriff of Somerset and Dorset.

after 1481, Nov. 5. HUMPHREY STANLEY, sheriff of Staffordshire.

1482, July 24 (St. James's Eve).

> *Bannerets made in Scotland by the duke of Gloucester [probably on the conclusion of the Treaty between the duke of Gloucester, the duke of Albany, and the Scottish Nobles near Edinburgh].*
>
> EDWARD WYDEVILL (WOODVILE), banneret.
> WALTER HERBERT, banneret.
> HERBERT GREYSTOKE, banneret.

[1482, July 24.]

> JOHN ELRINGTON, banneret.
> HENRY PERCY, banneret.
> WILLIAM GASCOIGNE, banneret.
> EDMOND HASTINGS, banneret.
> JAMES TYRELL, banneret.
> JAMES DANBY, banneret.
> HUGH HASTINGES, banneret.
> RAUF ASHETON, banneret.
> WILLIAM REDMAN, banneret.
> RICHARD RADCLIF, banneret.
> THOMAS MALYVERER, banneret.
> BRYAN STAPLETON, banneret.
> JOHN SAVAGE, banneret.
> WILLIAM EVERS, banneret.
> PIERS MIDDELTON, banneret.
> CHRISTOPHER WARDE, banneret.
> STEPHEN HAMERTON, banneret.
> THOMAS TEMPEST, banneret.

KNIGHTS BACHELORS

[1482, July 24.]

John Everingham, banneret.
Robert Harrington, banneret.
Thomas Broughton, banneret.
John Aske, banneret.
Thomas Grey, of Warke, banneret.
Rauf Woderington, banneret.
Roger Thorneton, banneret.
Thomas Molyneux, banneret.
Alexander Houghton, banneret.
Piers A. Legh, banneret.
Edward Stanley, banneret.
John Grey, of Wilton, banneret.
Richard Hodleston, banneret.

Knights made the same day by the same duke of Gloucester.

William Nevill, of Thorneton Bridge.
Richard Hawte.
John Woderington (Widrington).
William Ingleby (Engelby),
Thomas Gowre.
Randolf Pygott.
John Darrell.
William Houghton.
William Parker, of London.
Roger Cotton.
Thomas Bowles.
Thomas (John) Bridges (Bergyll).
Alexander Baynham.
Sandy Jarden (Jurden), a Scot.

Knights made the same day in the Englishmen's Camp by Alexander, duke of Albany.

Adam Murrey.
Thomas Lyndsey.
John Coningham.
John Rotherford.

KNIGHTS BACHELORS

Knights made the same day by the earl of Northumberland in Scotland [at the same place].

JOHN PENYNGTON.
ROBERT PLOMPTON.
MARTIN, of the Sea.

Knights made the same day, at the same place by lord Stanley, steward of the King's House.

CHRISTOPHER SOUTHWORTH.
RICHARD LANGTON.
WILLIAM STANLEY.
JOHN BOWTHE.
GEORGE HOLFORDE.
RICHARD BOLDE.

[1482, July 24.]

RICHARD TOWNLEY.
JAMES LAWRENCE.
THOMAS TALBOTT.
HENRY TARBOCKE.
JOHN TALBOTT.
ALEXANDER STANDISHE.
CHRISTOPHER STANDISHE.
WILLIAM FARRINGTON.
HENRY KYGHLEY.

1482, Aug. 22.

Bannerets and Knights made by Richard, duke of Gloucester, in Scotland at Hoton Field beside Berwick [? at the surrendering of Berwick to the English, which took place on the 24th Aug., 1482].

Knights.

FRAUNCYS, lord Lovell.
[RICHARD], lord Fitz-Hugh.
[THOMAS], lord Scroop of Masham.
—— GREYSTOKE.

[1482, Aug. 22.]

    George, lord Lumley.

Bannerets.
- Thomas Pilkington.
- Robert Ryder.

Other Knights and Bannerets.
- William Darcy.
- John Melton.
- John Savell.
- Rauf Bulmer.
- Rauf Bigod.
- Rauf Bowes (Bowyer).
- John Constable, of Holderness.
- James Strangways.
- Robert Middelton.
- William Fitz William.
- Thomas Fitz William.
- Thomas Wortley.
- James Danby.
- Thomas Malyverer.
- Rauf Fitz Randall.
- Charles Pilkington.
- Robert Waterton.
- John Nevill, of Liverseege.
- Richard Coigners, of Cowton.
- William Beckwithe.

Knights, dubbed by the earl of Northumberland on the field of Sefford the same time.

- Marmaduke Constable.
- Christopher Warde.
- Roger Heron.
- Thomas Grey.
- William Malory.
- Piers Middelton.
- Stephen Hamerton.
- Robert Hilyard (Helyarde).

KNIGHTS BACHELORS

[1482, Aug. 22].
> RAUF WODRINGTON.
> RAUF HARBOTTELL.
> JOHN EVERINGHAM.
> JOHN ASKE.
> RAUF BABTHORPE.
> ROGER THORNETON.
> CHRISTOPHER CURWEN.
> JOHN SALVEYN, of Duflett.
> THOMAS GREY, of Horton.
> THOMAS TEMPEST.

? 1482–3, Jan. 6. THOMAS THWAYTES.

1482–3, after Feb. 18.
> *Knights dubbed after the Parliament was ended.*
> JOHN WOOD, speaker of the Parliament.
> WILLIAM CATESBY, justice.

1483, Saturday, July 5.
> *Knights made by Richard III., the day before his Coronation.*
> ROBERT DYMMOKE, the King's champion at the Coronation.
> WILLIAM HOPTON.
> ROBERT PERSAY (PERCYE).
> WILLIAM JENNEY, justice [of the King's Bench].
> GERVASE CLYFTON, sheriff of Notts and Derby.

[? 1483, July 12.]
> HUMPHREY STARKEY, chief baron of the Exchequer (on Saturday after [? the Coronation] in the Tower.

1483, Sept. 8.
> *Knights made at York by Richard III. on the procession through the city and the repetition of the Coronation.*
> GEFFEREY DE SASIOLA, ambassador from Spain, in testimony whereof he gave him letters patent dated at York the same day.
> RICHARD, of Gloucester, the King's natural son.
> And many other Northern Gentlemen.

KNIGHTS BACHELORS

[? 1484, the 13th day of   .]

    WILLIAM, lord Crichton of Crichton, a Scottishman, before dinner.

    THOMAS HYLL, mayor of London, after dinner.

before Easter, 1485. ROBERT BRACKENBURY, sheriff of Kent.

[before 1485, August.] CHARLES SOMERSET, made knight by Philip, archduke of Austria [in Flanders.]

1485, Aug. 7.

    Knights made at the landing of Henry, earl of Richmond (afterwards Henry VII.), at Milford Haven.

    EDWARD COURTENEY, afterwards earl of Devonshire.
    JOHN WELLES, afterwards viscount Welles.
    PHILIBERT DE CHANDÉE, afterwards earl of Bath.
    JOHN CHENEY (CHEINY).
    RICHARD GUILDFORD.
    EDWARD PONYINGES.
    JAMES BLOUNT.
    DAVY OWEN.
    CHARLES SOMERSET.
    JOHN FORTESCU, sheriff of Essex and Herts.
    JOHN HALIWEL (HALWYN).
    JOHN RYSELEY.
    WILLIAM BRANDON.
    *THOMAS MILBORN (MELBOURNE).
    *WILLIAM TYLER.
    JOHN TREURY (TERURY).

1485, Aug. 25.

    Knights made at the Battle of Redmore or Bosworth by Henry VII.

    JOHN TALBOTT.
    JOHN (ROGER) MORTEMER.
    WALTER HUNGERFORDE.

---

* In Ashmolean MS. 1121, p. 433, these names are given as made at the battle of Redmore.

KNIGHTS BACHELORS 23

1485, Aug. 25.

> ROBERT POINTZ.
> HUMFREY STANLEY.
> WILLIAM WYLOUGHBY.
> JOHN TURBERVILLE.
> RES (RICE) AP THOMAS.
> HUGH PERSALL.
> RICHARD EDGCOMBE.

[? 1485, Aug. 25.]

> [*At the same time or between the Battle of Bosworth and the Coronation of Henry VII.*]
> EDMUND CAREW.
> JOHN BICKENELL (BRIKENELL, KYKENELL).
> WILLIAM COURTENEY.

1485–6 (or 1486–7), Jan. 6.

> *Knights of London made twelfth day anno primo (? secundo) Henry VII., the King keeping his estate at Whitehall being crowned.*
>
> HENRY COLLETT, mayor of London.
> JOHN FENKELL (FENKYLL).
> JOHN BROWNE.
> WILLIAM CAPELL.
> [? *At the same time.*]
> NICHOLAS [ROBERT] BILLESDON.

1486, before Whitsuntide. JOHN BYRON, sheriff of Notts and Derby (as the King came from York).

1486, at Whitsuntide. ROGER TOWNESENDE (at Worcester, in the King's chamber).

after 1486, Nov. 5. JOHN LYNGEYN, sheriff of Hereford.

1486–7 [? Jan. 6].

> WILLIAM HODIE, chief baron of the Exchequer.
> JOHN SWYLIARD (SULIARD), judge of the King's Bench.

1487, June 16.

> *Knights Banneret made by Henry VII. at the Battle of Stoke-on-Trent whereof the first three were made before the battle and the other eleven after.*

GILBERT TALBOTT.
JOHN CHEYNY.
WILLIAM STOUNER.
JOHN ARUNDELL.
THOMAS COKESEY, *alias* Grevell.
EDMONDE BEDINGFEILDE (BENINGFIELD).
JOHN FORTESCUE.
HUMFREY STANLEY.
JAMES BLOUNT.
RICHARD DELABERE.
JOHN MORTEMER.
WILLIAM TROUTBECKE.
RICHARD CROFTS.
JAMES BASKERVILLE.

> *Knights made at the abovesaid battle.*

JAMES AWDELEY.
THOMAS POOLE (POALL).
ROBERT CLYFFORD.
EDWARD ABOROUGH (BOROUGH).
GEORGE HOPTON, of Swillington.
EDWARD NORRYS (MORYS).
WILLIAM TYRWHIT, of Kettleby.
THOMAS GREEN (GREY).
HENRY WILOUGHBY.
JOHN MUSGRAVE.
EDWARD PYKERINGE.
WILLIAM SANDES.
THOMAS (GREGORY) LOVELL.
JAMES PARKER (PICKS).

KNIGHTS BACHELORS

[1487, June 16.]

ANTHONY BROWNE.
MAURICE BARKLEY.
WILLIAM CAREW.
RICHARD FITZ LEWES (FITZ HEWS).
JOHN PASTON.
RICHARD POOLE (POLLE).
ROGER BELLINGHAM (BELINGHAM, BILLINGHAM).
EDWARD DARELL.
THOMAS HANSARD.
THOMAS, of Walton.
ROBERT, of Broughton.
THOMAS BLOUNT.
WILLIAM VAMPAGE, the first knight that was dubbed in the field that day.
HUMFREY SAUVAGE.
JOHN SABCOTTS (SAPPACOTTIS).
GREGORY LOVELL.
NICHOLAS VAULX.
WILLIAM TROWTBEKE [see on previous page].
JOHN DEVENISHE.
AMYAS POULET.
HENRY BOULDE.
WILLIAM REDMEYLL (REDMILL).
ROBERT CHEINEY.
JOHN WYNDHAM.
GEORGE NEVILL, the bastard.
RAUF SHIRLEY.
ROBERT BRANDON.
JOHN DIGBY.*
WILLIAM LITTILTON.
CHRISTOPHER WROUGHTON.
WILLIAM NORRYS.†
JAMES PARKER.
THOMAS LIEN (LINN, LYN).

---

* Harl MS. 5177, says :—"at Canterbury when the King went to Calais." This would mean Oct. 1492 But Digby occurs as already a Knight in 1488 in Gairdner's "materials for the History of Hy. VII.' Vol. II., p. 385.

† Occurs as an esquire in Sept. 1496, and as a Knight in Feb. 1487. Gairdner (*ibid*) pp. 35, 89.

[1487, June 16.]

> MAURICE ABAROW (A BAROW).
> THOMAS MANYNGTON (was dubbed as he says, but   ).
> JAMES HARINGTON.‡
> JOHN LONGVILLE.
> THOMAS TYRELL (TERELL).
> GEORGE HERBERT.
> RAUF LANGFORTH.*

1487 [? June 8]. THOMAS OULEY, merchant (at Coventry the same summer, the King's banner yet displayed. He was of the same town a burgess).

1487 [? Aug. 1–5]. RICHARD TODDE, mayor of York (dubbed by the King at York).

1487 [? Aug. 1–5]. RICHARD YORKE, mayor of the Staple (*ibid*).

1487 [Aug. 8]. RICHARD SALKYLD (by the King at Durham).

1487, Aug. 9. RICHARD CLERVAUX (at Croft, by the King on St. Laurence Eve).

1487, Aug. 24. JOHN WAREN (by the King at Ripon on St. Bartholomew's Day).

1487. Aug. 24. THOMAS ASHTON (HASHETON) (*ibid*).

1487 [? Nov. 3]. WILLIAM HORN, mayor of London (by the King in Hornsey Park at the King's return to London).

1487 [? Nov. 3]. JOHN PERSEVALL (*ibid*).

1487 [? Nov. 3]. THOMAS FITZ WILLIAM, recorder of London (? *Ibid*.).

[? 1487] Dec. 11. ARNOLD HAKE VAN SOTT, ge. nat. van Tyrell of Almaigne, dubbed by the King the same year on Friday after the conception of our Lady.

---

‡ Occurs as already a Knight in August 1486. Gairdner (*ibid*) p. 29.

* It is not easy to decide whether the whole of this list from Sir James Awdeley to Sir Rauf Langforth is, or is not, a homogeneous list of knights created at the same time, viz. :—At the battle of Stoke. Some patent descrepancies are noticed in the footnotes. In Harl MS. 5177, the list is arranged in a different order, viz. :—(1) Those who have paid their fees to the College of Arms ; (2) Those who have only paid part ; (3) Those who have not paid at all.

KNIGHTS BACHELORS

[?1487]. *These three following came from High Almaigne to see this realm and to receive the order of knighthood of the King, as they did.*

>   BALTHEZAR CANHAUSER.
>   CHRISTOPHER VAN SILBERMERG.
>   ADRYAN VAN GREKNECKE.

1488 [? Dec. 21., or between Easter and Michaelmas, 1489].

>   RICHARD NANFANT, sheriff of Cornwall, dubbed by the King before Christmas, who sent him on embassade into Spain. He was dubbed on the way towards Kingston.

[? Early in 1489.]

>   THOMAS STAFFORD (dubbed by the King at the sea side when he sent his army into Brittany).
>   JOHN HOLDILSTON (HODESTON) *(ibid.)*.

[?1489, August .] ALBRIGHT , brother to the Chancellor of Denmark.

? 1489 [between March and August, or ? 1490, August—September].
>   SAMPSON NORTON, dubbed in Brittany by Robert, first lord Willoughby de Broke.

after 1489, Nov. 5.   CHRISTOPHER THROGMARTON, sheriff of Gloucester.

[?1492, Oct.]

>   LEWYS CAERLION (CARLION) (dubbed by the King at Guines).
>   [GILBERT TALBOT]* [shield only].
>   [? —— NEVILL] [shield only].
>   [? —— BENSTEAD] [shield only].
>   [Shield only, unidentified. Per pale purpure and azure, three lucies' heads erased and erect or, in the mouth of each a spear head argent.]
>   [? —— SAVAGE] [shield only].
>   [Shield only, unidentified. Quarterly 1, Gules, a fesse dancettée argent; 2, Azure, an eagle displayed or, a bendlet gules; 3, or on a chief gules two hands couped argent, the one dexter the other sinister; 4, gules, three lucies in pale argent.]

---

* After the name of Sir Lewis Carleon, the MS. (Cott. Claud C. III.) gives the trickings of twelve shields without names. The conjectural identification of the bearers of these arms is given here on the authority of Metcalfe alone ("Book of Knights" pp. 22-3). The only reason for including these twelve knights under the date ?1492, Oct., is the fact that they follow Sir Lewys Carleon without any indication of break n the MS. The same is the case with the succeeding eleven knights.

[? 1492, Oct.]

[?   PICKERING] [shield only].
GEORGE DARELL.
[?—— STANLEY] [shield only].
[?—— COURTENEY] [shield only].
[?—— VERE] [shield only].
[?   FITZ WARYN] [shield only].
ROBERT CURSON.
—— GASCOIGNE.
—— BEAMONT.
WILLIAM BROWNE.
—— EVERS.
WILLIAM HAWTE.
[?—— MENCE] [shield only].
—— BREERTON.
—— STRANGE.
—— HUNGERFORD.
[—— —— Shield only, unidentified. Azure, a fesse dancettée between three falcons or, belted proper.]

1494, Jan. 6.*

RAUF OSTRICHE (ASTRY), mayor of London (in the King's Chamber at Westminster).
WILLIAM DE MARTIN, late lord mayor of London *(ibid.)*.
NICHOLAS, lord Howth, of Ireland *(ibid.)*.
Lord SLANE *(ibid.)*.

1494, Nov. 9. JOHN LEVESQUE (LANESQUE), a Breton (dubbed by the King on the day of the tournament after the creation of prince Henry as duke of York).

1497, June 17.

Knights Bannerets made at the Battle of Blackheath.

THOMAS LOVELL (LOVETT).
CHARLES SOMERSETT.
REIGNALD BRAY.
RICHARD GUYLFORDE.
ROBERT HARECOURT.

* Cott MS., Claud C. III. Harl MS. 5177. Harl MS. 6068. In the last of these MSS. these four names occur amongst the Knights made at the Coronation of Queen Elizabeth, wife of Henry VII.

KNIGHTS BACHELORS

[1497, June 17.]

RES AP THOMAS.
HENRY WILOUGHBY.
RICHARD LEWIS or FITZ LEWES.
JOHN SEINT JOHN.
THOMAS GREENE.
ROBERT [EDWARD] BROUGHTON.
NICHOLAS VAUX.
WILLIAM TYRWHITE.
THOMAS TYRELL (TYRETT, TYRWHIT).

Knights made at the same battle of Blackheath.

EDWARD BLOUNT.
WILLIAM DE LA POOLE, called lord William of Suffolk, brother to Edmond de la Pole, earl of Suffolk.
THOMAS BRANDON.
JOHN [EDWARD] SAVAGE, sheriff of Worcester.
THOMAS CORNEWALL, baron of Burford.*
JOHN SEYMER, of Wiltshire.*
ROBERT DRURY.*
CHARLES A. BRUGES (A. BRUGES).
EDWARD STANHOPE.
ROBERT LOVELL.
ROBERT TYRELL (TYRETT, TERELL).
JOHN FERRERS (FERRES).
HENRY TAY.*
JOHN HUSSEE (HUSE).
JOHN RODNEY (? UDNEY).
JOHN MONTGOMERY.
RICHARD PUDSEY (PUESEY).
JOHN DARELL (BARREL), of Calehill, in Kent.
EDMOND ARONDELL, of the West.
WILLIAM MERYNGE.
JOHN PECHE.
THOMAS DIGBY.*

* Occurs in Harl MS. 5177, under the heading of Knights dubbed at the Bridge foot on the King's entering London.

KNIGHTS BACHELORS

[1497, June 17.]

> Robert Payton.
> George Talboys.
> Philippe Calthorpe.
> John Greene, of Essex.*
> Roger Wentworthe.
> Robert Constable.*
> John Skipwith, of Co. Lincoln.
> John Williams.
> Rouland de Veyllevylle.

[after 1497, June 17.]

> *Knights dubbed at the Bridge Foot on the King's entering London after the Battle of Blackheath.*
>
> John H . . . . .
> Morgan . . . . .
> John Hungerforde.
> John Fyneulx (Fyneux), chief justice of the King's Bench.
> John Raynsforde.
> Bryan Sandforde.
> [Shield only; Argent, a chevron Gules.]
> John Langforde.
> Thomas Bryan.
> John Tate, lord mayor of London.
> John Shaa [Shawe], sheriff of London.
> Richard Haddon, sheriff of London.
> Robert Sheffield, recorder of London.
> John Dunham.
> Thomas Rotherham.
> John Awdeley, of Suffolk.
> Philippe Cooke.
> John Bruerton (Brereton).
> Thomas Lawne (de la Launde).
> Richard Lovelace.
> Thomas Salisbury.
> Richard [John] Carewe (Carn).

* Occurs in Harl. MS. 5177 under the heading of Knights dubbed at Bridge foot on the king's entering London.

KNIGHTS BACHELORS

(No place or date.)

> ANDREW DE TREVISANO.
> LAURENCE AYLMER.

[On or before 1497, Sept. 30.]

> *Knights Bannerets made in Scotland by Thomas, earl of Surrey, the King's Lieutenant.*
>
> WILLIAM GASCOIGNE.
> JOHN NEVILL.
> JOHN HASTINGES.
> THOMAS DARCY.
> WALTER GRYFFITH.
> RAUF RYDER.
> THOMAS WORTLEY.
> ROGER BELLINGHAM.
> WILLIAM TYLER.
> EDWARD PYKERINGE.
>
> *Knights made in Scotland by same at same time.*
>
> THOMAS, lord Howard, the earl of Surrey's son.
> EDWARD HOWARD, the earl of Surrey's son.
> HENRY SCROOPE.
> WILLIAM COGNYERS (CONNYERS).
> WILLIAM BULMER.
> GEORGE MANNERS.
> RAUF EVERS.

[? 1497, Sept. 30.]

> EDWARD SAVAGE.
> ROGER HOPTON.
> JOHN WARBRETON.
> RANDOLPH BRUERTON.
> ANDREW BRUERTON.
> ROBERT ASKE.
> JOHN HOTHOM.
> HENRY BOYNTON.

KNIGHTS BACHELORS

[? 1497, Sept. 30.]

 Robert Bellingham.
 Richard Woodrofe.
 Thomas Ilderton.
 John Wandisford.
 Roger Hastings.
 John Roclyff.
 Richard Cholmondeley.
 John Normanvile.
 Richard Aldeburgh.
 Richard Calverley.
 William Skargill.
 Richard Myrfeilde.
 Raulf Ellercar.
 William Calverley.
 John Gower.

 Other Knights made in Scotland by George, lord Strange, being there with Thomas, earl of Surrey.

 John Irelande.
 William Bowthe.
 Richard Asheton.
 John Townley.
 William Terbuke.
 Henry Halsall.
 Roger Pylston.
 Edward Hanmore.
 Humphrey Lysley (Lyll).

Before Easter, 1499. John Hothom, sheriff of Yorkshire.

[? 1500]. —— Brampton, son of Sir Edward Brampton, merchant, of London and Portugal (at Winchester).

Before 1501, Sept. 29. Edward Radclyff, sheriff of Northumberland.

1501, Nov. 14.

 Knights of the Sword (or Carpet) made at the marriage of prince Arthur.

 John Danvers, of Dauncy.
 John Cottysmore.

KNIGHTS BACHELORS

1501, Nov. 14.
>   HUMFREY CATISBY (CATESBY).
>   JOHN VAVASOUR, justice of Common Pleas.
>   JOHN POUNDE.
>   JOHN FOGGE (FOOG).
>   LEWES BAGOTT.
>   WILLIAM CLOPTON.
>   WILLIAM PEROTT.
>   JAMES AP OWEN.
>   EDMOND JENNY.
>   THOMAS BARNESTON.
>   THOMAS KNIGHT.
>   RAUF VERNEY.
>   PHILIPPE TILNEY.
>   THOMAS DANVERS.
>   DEDO DE AZEVEDO, a Spaniard.
>   FERDINAND DE VILLA LOBOS (LOGES), a Spaniard.
>   THOMAS WOODE, chief justice of Common Pleas.
>   ROBERT READE, justice of the King's Bench.
>   THOMAS TREMAYLE, justice of the King's Bench.
>   WILLIAM DANVERS, justice of Common Pleas.
>   JOHN TYMPERLEY.
>   JOHN CHAMPERNOUN.
>   JOHN VILLERS (VILLIERS).
>   ROBERT TANFELDE.

1502, May 18. FRANCISCUS DE CAPELLO.
 [?] A. P. DANE (DAVE), of Islande, a Scot.

1502, Xmas. THOMAS FROWYKE, chief justice of Common Pleas (at Richmond).

1503, between Easter and Whitsuntide. At Baynards Castle in the King's Chamber.
>   BARTHOLOMEW REDE, mayor of London.
>   KEY VAN ANVYLL.
>   JOHN FISHER.
>   EDMOND LUCY.
>   —— COTTON, of Cambridge.
>   GILBERT DEBBENHAM.

1503–4, Feb. 18.

> *Knights of the Sword dubbed at the creation of prince Henry as prince of Wales.*

*JOHN (GREY), 4th viscount Lisle.
THOMAS (DACRE), 3rd lord Dacre of the North.
BRYAN STAPLETON.
RAUF GREY.
MILES BUSSY.
EDWARD POMEREY.
JOHN MORDANT.
JAMES HUBERT.
RICHARD EMSON.
DAVY PHILIPPE.
HUGH VAUGHAN.
EDMOND HAMPDEN.
NICHOLAS WADDAM.
WILLIAM PERPOYNT.
JOHN SOUTHWORTHE.
ADRIAN FORTESCU.
JOHN LYNGEYN.
JOHN EVERINGHAM.
JOHN CONSTABLE, of Holderness.
HENRY WYDERINGTON.
THOMAS TRENCHARD.
WILLIAM GYFFORDE.
THOMAS SUTTON.
JOHN LYSLE: of Throkston, in Wiltshire.
THOMAS FETYPLACE.
JOHN CUTTE.
ROBERT SOUTHWELL.
HENRY STAFFORDE.

[?] JOHN WILTSHIRE, dubbed by the duke of Juliers at the command of the king of the Romans.

After 1505, Dec. 1. JOHN GAWYN, sheriff of Wilts.

1508. WILLIAM TREVANYON, sheriff of Cornwall.

---

* The first eight names in this list are given as Knights of the Bath, *supra* vol. i. p. 147.

Before Easter, 1509. EVERARD FYLDYNG, sheriff of Rutland.

1509, May 14. Charter by king James IV. of Scotland granting the dignity of knighthood to CHRISTOPHER GALIACE, of San Severino (dated St. Michael's Castle, Stirling, Scotland).

1509, June 23. STEPHEN JENNYNS, mayor of London (on the day of the King's Coronation).

After 1510, Nov. 9. RICHARD KNYGHTLEY, sheriff of Northamptonshire.

[? 1510-11, Feb. 12.] HUGH ODONELL, dubbed at the banquet at Westminster: anno secundo.

1511, Sept. 15.

 HENRY GUILDEFORDE, dubbed by the king of Aragon at Bruges [Burgos] in Castile.*
 WYSTAN (WESTON) BROWNE *(ibid.).*†

1512, Mar. 30.†

 HENRY GUILDEFORDE (at Westminster, the last day of the Parliament).
 CHARLES BRANDON *(ibid.).*

1512, Apr. 18. GUYOT DE HENLE, Sieur de la Mote (At Greenwich).

(?) 1512, Apr. 18. HENRY SHERBOURNE (? *ibid.*).

(?) 1512, Apr. 18. THOMAS LUCY (? *ibid.*).

(?) 1512, Apr. 18. JOHN BURDETT (? *ibid.*).

(?) 1512, Apr. 18. ROBERT MORTON (? *ibid.*).

[1512, between April and December.]

 WILLIAM SIDNEY (made in Brittany by the duke of Norfolk, lord admiral).

[? 1512]. ANTHONY UTREIGHT [UGHTRED] (made at Eltham).

---

* Lansd MS., Claud C. III., says 1511. Harl MS. 5177 says 1509.
† Claud C. says 1511, as does Harl 5177.

KNIGHTS BACHELORS

[?1513, Aug. 16.] *Possibly at the Battle of Spurs in France. Knights Bannerets.*

    JOHN PECHE (PEACHY).
    ROBERT BRANDON.
    HENRY GUILDFORD.
    EDWARD POYNINGES.
    ANDREW WYNDESORE, treasurer of the King's Middleward of battle.
    JOHN REYNSFORD.
    HENRY WYATT.
    JOHN SEYMOUR.
    JOHN AWDELEY.
    RICHARD CAREW.
    ANTHONY UTRIGHT *(see supra)*.
    THOMAS WEST.
    ROBERT DYMOKE, treasurer of the King's Rearward.
    JOHN HUSEE (HUSSEY).
    JOHN ARUNDELL, of the West.
    RICHARD WENTWORTHE.
    RANDOLF BRERETON, marshal of the Rearward.
    PIERS EDGECOMBE.
    HENRY CLYFFORDE.
    THOMAS CORNEWALL.
    THOMAS LEIGHTON.
    THOMAS BLOUNT.
    JOHN ASTON.
    WILLIAM PERPOUNT.
    HENRY SACHEVERELL.
    GEORGE HOLFORDE (HALLFORTH).
    HENRY HALSALL.
    GEORGE (JOHN) WARBLETON.

[?]   THOMAS DARCUS (DARUS) *alias* Denys, of Devonshire.*   , in

* Harl MS. 5177 says *anno* 5, 6

1513, Sept. 9.

> *Knightes made at the battaill on Bramston Moore, otherwise called Flodden Field, which field was faughten the IX day of September, in the yere of our Lord God 1513, being the fifte yere of the reign of king Henry the eight betweene the king of Scottes and his people to the number of 60,000 on the one partie, and the erle of Surrey, thresurer and marshall of England and lieutenant generall in the North Partes, and certain nobles and subjectes of the kinge of England to the number of 30,000 on the other partie. At what time the Scottish king and divers of his noblemen were slayne.*

The lord Scrope, of Upsall.
EDMUND HOWARD.
WILLIAM PERCY.
GEORGE DARCY.
WILLIAM MIDDLETON.
WILLIAM MAULIVERER.
THOMAS BERKLEY.
MARMADUKE CONSTABLE.
CHRISTOPHER DACRES.
JOHN HOTHOM.
NICHOLAS APPLEYARD.
EDWARD GORGE.
RAUF ELLERKAR, the younger.
JOHN WILLOUGHBY.
EDWARD ECHINGHAM.
WILLIAM PENINGTON.
JOHN STANLEY, the bastard.
WALTER STONNER.
VYVYAN MARKYNFELD.
RAUF BOWES.
BRYAN STAPLETON.

KNIGHTS BACHELORS

[1513 Sept. 9.]

    Guy Dawney.
    William Gascoigne, the younger.
    Rauf Salvayn.
    Richard Mauleverer.
    William Constable, of Hatfield.
    William Constable, of Carethorp.
    Christopher Danby.
    Thomas Burgh.
    William Ross.
    William Newton.
    Roger Grey.
    Robert Colyngwod.
    Roger Farewell.
    Thomas Stranguishe.
    John Bulmer.

1513, Sept. 25.

*Knights made at Tournay, in the church after the King came from Mass under his banner in the church.**

    John, lord Awdeley.
    [Thomas], lord Cobham.
    Lord Richard Grey.
    Lord Edward Grey.
    Henry Poole.
    Anthony Wingefelde.
    Thomas Tirrell (of Gyppynge).
    Thomas Bourough (Borough).
    Thomas Tyrrell, of Heron.
    Thomas Fairefax.
    Thomas Lovell (junior).
    John Veer.
    Henry Longe.
    John Marney.
    John Markham.

---

* Harl MS. 5177, Harl MS. 6069 f. 120, printed by Brewer, S.P. Hy. VIII., Vol. I. p. 676. Cott MS. Claud C. III. and Harl 6063, say Dec. 25, *anno* 5. Harl MS. 6069, says Dec. 25.

KNIGHTS BACHELORS

[1513, Sept. 25.]

JOHN SAVAGE.
JOHN RAGLANDE.
JOHN NEVILL (of Leversege).
WILLIAM HANSARDE.
JOHN SHARPPE.
JOHN MAINWARING.
EDWARD GUYLFORDE.
EDWARD BELKNAPP.
EDWARD HUNGERFORDE.
EDWARD STRADLING.
EDWARD NEVILE.
EDWARD DOON (DUN).
EDWARD FERRERS.
WILLIAM COMPTON.
WILLIAM EVERS.
WILLIAM HUSSE (HUSEE).
WILLIAM FITZWILLIAM.
WILLIAM BRERTON.
WILLIAM ESSEX.
WILLIAM GRYFFYTH.
WILLIAM A PARRE.
WILLIAM TYLER.
RAUF (EDWARD) CHAMBERLAYN.
RIC SACHEVERELL.
RIC TEMPEST.
WILLIAM ASCU.
RIC JERNYNHAM (JERMINGHAM).
ROB TYRWHYT.
RAUF EGERTON.
GYLES CAPELL.
GEOFFREY GATES.
CHRISTOPHER WILLOUGHBY.
JOHN GYFFORDE.
CHRISTOPHER GARNEYS.
OWEN PERROT.
HENRY OWEN.

KNIGHTS BACHELORS

[1513, Sept. 25.]

    JAMES FREMLINGHAM (FRAMLINGHAM).
    LEWIS ORELL.

[? 1513, Oct. 13. *? During the reception of prince Charles and Margaret of Savoy by Henry VIII. at Tournay.*]

    JOHN GLEYMHAM.
    ARTHUR PLANTAGENET, dubbed the 14th day of October.
    SYMON HARECOURT.
    JOHN ZOWKETT, de Germania.
    LEWES DE WALDENCOURTE, de Hannonia.
    RAUF VERNEY.
    RICHARD WALDEN.
    JAMES DARELL.
    ANTHONY HUNGERFORDE.
    WILLIAM KINGESTON.

[? at same time.]

    PETER VAVASOUR.
    EDWARD WADHAM.
    JOHN HAMPDEN.
    JOHN TALBOT.
    EDWARD GREY.
    WILLIAM BARANTINE.
    NICHOLAS BARINGTON.
    JOHN BRUGES.
    WILLIAM FYNCHE.
    GEORGE HARVY.
    NICHOLAS HEYDON.
    LYONELL DYMOKE.
    EDWARD BENSTED.
    WILLIAM SMYTHE.
    JOHN DAUNCE.
    THOMAS CLYNTON.
    RICHARD WHETHILL.
    WILLIAM THOMAS.
    JOHN WYSEMAN.

KNIGHTS BACHELORS

1513, Oct. 13.

> *Of the lord chamberlain's Ward at the same time, the 13th [? 14] day of October anno [quinto] were made knights* [these following :—]

[JOHN] LA ZOUCHE, son and heir of lord Zouche.
[JOHN] SUTTON, son and heir of lord Dudley.
ARTHUR HOPTON.
EDMOND BRAY.
GEORGE SAINTLEGER.
WILLIAM MORGAN.
EDWARD GREVILLE.
THOMAS PHILIPPS.
THOMAS GAMAGE.
RICHARD HERBERT.
WILLIAM MATHEW.
CHRISTOPHER BAYNHAM.
RICHARD VAUGHAN.
CHRISTOPHER ASCU.
ANDREW BYLISBY.
THOMAS HANMER (HAMER).
JOHN THIMBILBY.
SYMON FITZ RICHARD.
WILLIAM BAWDRYPPE.

1513, Oct. 14.

> *Knights dubbed at Lille the 14th day of October anno [quinto].*

[JOHN] NEVILL, son and heir to lord Latimer.
GILBERT TALBOTT.
SYMON DE FERRATO.
THOMAS FUCHS.
PAUL ARMESDROFFER.
WILLIAM DE NOUYON.
JOHN DE LA ZOUCHE.
JOHN LEYKE.
EDWARD CROFT.

[1513, Oct. 14.]

    WILLIAM GRYSLEY (GRISLE).
    THOMAS COKAYN.
    RICHARD BASSETT.
    JOHN MAYNWERINGE, of Ightfield.
    RICHARD BOSSUM.
    JOHN CRESSENOR.
    ALEXANDER RADCLYFF.
    WILLIAM STANLEY.
    WILLIAM POOLE.
    WILLIAM LEYLONDE.
    ALEXANDER ORBASTON.
    JOHN HOLFORDE.
    EDWARD BELYNGHAM.
    ROBERT NEVYLL, of Leversege.
    WILLIAM LYSLE.
    WALTER CALVERLEY.
    THOMAS WENTWORTH.
    JOHN RODNEY.
    JOHN BURTON.
    THOMAS ROKELEY.
    THOMAS KYNARDESTON.
    JOHN TREMAYLE.

after 1513, Nov. 9. WALTER RODNEY, sheriff of Oxfordshire.

after 1513, Nov. 9. EDWARD CROFTES, sheriff of Hereford.

1513, Dec. 25. WILLIAM COMPTON, sheriff of Hampshire.

[? 1513, ? at Flodden.]

    [—— WALSINGHAM] (shield only, sable a chevron argent between three cinquefoils pierced or).
    ROBERT (OGLE), 4th lord Ogle.
    EDMOND WALSINGHAM.
    THOMAS WEST.
    JOHN DAWTREY.

before Easter, 1515. EDWARD GORGE, sheriff of Somerset and Dorset.

KNIGHTS BACHELORS

[? 1515] WILLIAM BUTLER (BOTELER), lord mayor of London.
WILLIAM FITZ WILLIAM, of Geynspark Hall, in Essex.

Before 1516, Easter. JOHN SCROOPE, sheriff of Wiltshire.

After Easter, 1516. WILLIAM HERBERT, of Troy, sheriff of Hereford.

After 1517, Nov. 9. GILES STRANGWISSHE, sheriff of Somerset and Dorset.

1517-8, Jan. 3.
    JOHN HEYRON (HERON), dubbed at Windsor.
    RICHARD WESTON *(ibid).*

[? 1518]
    THOMAS DYNHAM.
    THOMAS EXMEW, lord mayor of London.

Before Easter, 1519. THOMAS BURGH, sheriff of Leicestershire.

[? 1519] JAMES YERFORDE [YARFORD], lord mayor of London.

1520, June.
    THOMAS SEYMOUR (dubbed by the King at Calais).
[?]   LAWRENCE STAYBER, of Noremberge, in High Almaigne.
    WILLIAM GASCOIGNE, of Cardington, Co. Beds.
    EDMONDE TAME.
    WILLIAM DENYS, sheriff of Gloucester.
    EDWARD DEYMER.

Before Easter, 1522. WILLIAM GYFFORD, sheriff of Hampshire.

Before Easter, 1522. EDWARD CROFT, sheriff of Hereford.

1523. *Knights made in Scotland by the Duke of Norfolk, lord treasurer of England* [between 1522-3, Feb., and 1523, Nov].
    ARTHUR (ANTHONY) DARCY.
    THOMAS CLYFFORDE.
    PHILIP DACRES.
    RICHARD BREERETON.

---

* Harl. MS. 6063 says simply "at Sefforth." Harl. 6069 says "at Sefforth in the 15 year of Henry VIII. at Blaykasne."

[1523.]

WILLIAM OGLE.
RAUF FENWYKE.
WILLIAM CARY.
JOHN HARBEY.
EDWARD GREY, of Fyllynham.
NICHOLAS RYDDELEY.
WILLIAM ELDRECARE.
WILLIAM TRENAYLL [? *ibid.*].
WILLIAM HERON.
JOHN HERON.
JOHN DE LA WAYLL.
THOMAS FOSTER.
WILLIAM BOWMER, of Morton.
RAPH HEDWORTH.
RICHARD HOWYCHEKE.
EDWARD KNOWILL, of Buckinghamshire.
THOMAS SOWNORTH.
RAFE BOULMER, of Maryke.
RAUF (NEVILL), 4th earl of Westmorland.
WILLIAM BARON, of Grayflesh.
JOHN DENNET.

Knights made at Jedworth the 25th day of September, in the reign of our king aforesaid.

Lord WILLIAM HOWARD [? *ibid.*]
CHRISTOPHER CONYERS.
WALTER STRICKLAND.
THOMAS HILTON.
MARMADUKE CONSTABLE.
THOMAS TEMPEST.
WILLIAM MUSGRAVE.

1523, July 1.

Knights made by the Lord Admiral after the taking of Morlaix "for their hardiness and noble courage."

FRANCIS BRYAN.
ANTHONY BROWNE.

KNIGHTS BACHELORS

[1523, July 1.]

 RICHARD CROMWELL.
 HENRY MORE.
 GILES HUSSEY.
 JOHN RUSSELL.
 JOHN RAYNSFORD.
 GEORGE COBHAM.
 JOHN CORNWALLIS.
 EDWARD RIGLEY.
 And divers others.

After 1523, Sept. 29. JOHN ROGERS, sheriff of Somerset and Dorset.

1523, Oct. 31.

Knights made by Charles, duke of Suffolk, in France, at a town called Roye, in the time of war, he being the King's lieutenant.

 HENRY, Lord HERBERT, son and heir to the earl of Worcester.
 EDWARD (GREY).
 Lord POWIS.
 ARTHUR POOLE, brother to lord Montagu.
 OLYVER MANERS, brother to lord Roos.
 THOMAS WENTWORTHE.
 RICHARD CORBETT.
 WILLIAM STOURTON.
 RICHARD SANDES.
 EDMONDE BENINGFEILDE (BEDINGFIELD).
 EDWARD SEYMOUR.
 GEORGE WARHAM.
 WILLIAM MANTELL (MARTELL).
 ROBERT JERNINGHAM.

Item: The said duke of Suffolk at the same tyme made these two knights on the river of Somme.

 JOHN DUDLEY.
 ROBERT UTREIGHT.

1523, Dec. 3.

> *Item: At Valenciennes the said duke of Suffolk made these two knights.*

WILLIAM PENYNGTON.
BARTHOLOMEW TATE.

[?1523.] THOMAS BALDRY, lord mayor of London.

After 1524, Nov. 10. THOMAS CORNEWALL, sheriff of Shropshire.

[?1524.] THOMAS WRYOTHESLEY, Garter King-at-Arms (dubbed by Don Ferdinando, archduke of Austria, at Nuremburg, Germany).

1525. WILLIAM BAYLY, lord mayor of London (by the King at Bridewell).

[?] —— FITZ JAMES.
—— FITZ HERBERT.
FOWKE GREVILL.

After 1527, Nov. 16. THOMAS PULTENEY, sheriff of Warwick and Leicester.

1527. ROGER MAYNORS, dubbed at Windsor on Corpus Christi day.

[?] THOMAS ELYOTT.
JOHN PORTE.
JAMES STRANGEWAYES.
THOMAS WHARTON.
EDWARD GOWER.
WILLIAM FAYRFAX.
ROBERT SKARGYLL.
HUMFRYE FORSTER.
ROGER LAMPELOWE.
GEORGE LAWSON.
EDWARD BOUGHTON, of Woolwich in Kent.
THOMAS SPEKE (SPOKE).
JAMES METCALFE.
GEORGE CAREW.

KNIGHTS BACHELORS

[After 1529, Nov. 3.]

Knights made by the King at York Place, now called Whitehall, in the Parliament time 1529.

WILLIAM HUSSEE.
GEOFFREY POOLE.
JOHN MILTON.
ROBERT PAYTON.
RICHARD GREENFEILDE.
RICHARD PAGE.
PHILIPPE BUTLER, of Hertfordshire.
THOMAS STRAUNGE.
JOHN RUSSELL.
ROBERT CHEYFFELDE.
RAUF DODMERE, mayor of London [mayor in 1529].
[THOMAS] PARGETER, mayor of London [mayor in 1530].
JAMES STRANGUISCHE.
JAMES SPENCER.
THOMAS DE CURTON.
[ROBERT] DE NORWYCHE, justice of Common Pleas.
[WILLIAM] SHELLEY, justice of Common Pleas.
JOHN RUDSTONE.
JOHN MUNDY.
JOHN ALLEN (ALEYN).
BRYAN TYKE.
ROBERT LEGHE.
JOHN CLERKE.
JOHN DAUNET.
EDWARD PYKERINGE.
OSBURNE ECHINGHAM.
WILLIAM PONDRE.
LYONELL NORRES.
JOHN CHAMOUN.
THOMAS SPERT (SPORTE).
HENRY FARMOUR.
WILLIAM STRETTON.
RAUF LANGFORDE.

[After 1529, Nov. 3.]

    ANTHONY BABINGTON.
    —— BASSETT, of Blowre.
    —— SMYTHE, of Chester.
    JAMES LEYBOURNE.
    RICHARD LAMPLEY, at Wolton.
    RICHARD CLEMENT.

After 1529, Nov. 9. ANDREW BYLESBY, sheriff of Lincolnshire.

After 1530, Nov. 11. GILES ALYNGTON, sheriff of Cambridge and Huntington.

After 1530, Nov. 11. CUTHBERT RADCLYFF, sheriff of Northumberland.

After 1531, Nov. 9. HENRY FERMOUR, sheriff of Norfolk and Suffolk.

After 1531, Nov. 9. JOHN VILLIERS, sheriff of Warwick and Leicester.

After 1531, Nov. 9. NICHOLAS FAYREFAX, sheriff of Yorkshire.

1532, Nov. 1.

    Knights made at Calais [after the interviews between Henry VIII. and Francis I.].

    THOMAS DARCY.
    HUMFREY FORSTER, sheriff of Oxfordshire.

[? Nov. 10.]. JOHN ACKETT, of Waterton in Ireland.

    GEORGE SOMERSETT, of Northampton.
    GEORGE GRYFFITH, of Staffordshire.
    WILLIAM NEWEMAN, of Northampton.
    EDMOND ASTON, of Staffordshire.
    THOMAS PALMER, Captain of Newnham Bridge: dubbed by the King the 10th of November.

After 1532, Nov. 16. EDMUND TRAFFORD, sheriff of Lancashire.

After 1532, Nov. 20. THOMAS LAKYN, sheriff of Shropshire.

KNIGHTS BACHELORS

Before 1532, Dec. 31. HUGH TREVANION, sheriff of Cornwall.

1533, May 24.

> *Knights made at Greenwich before the Coronation of queen Anne Boleyn on the Sunday before Whit-Sunday.*

CHRISTOPHER DANBY.
CHRISTOPHER HYLYARDE.
BRYAN HASTINGS.
THOMAS METHAM.
WILLIAM WALGRAVE.
WILLIAM FELDYNGE.
THOMAS BUTTELER.

1533, June 1.

> *Knights made with the Sword at the Coronation of Queen Anne Boleyn.*

JOHN WILUGHBY.
GEORGE CALVELEY.
ANDREW (RANDOLPH) BRERETON.
JOHN CHAWORTHE.
GEORGE GRESLEY.
JOHN CONSTABLE.
THOMAS UMPTON.
THOMAS RUSSHE.
JOHN SEINTCLERE.
ANTHONY WYNDESORE.
MARMADUKE TUNSTALL.
HENRY FARINGTON.
THOMAS HALSALL.
EDWARD FYTTON.
EDWARD MADESON.
RICHARD LYGON.
ROBERT NEDHAM, sheriff of Shropshire.
GEORGE COGNIERS.
HUMFREY FERRERS.

[1533, June 1.]
—— LONGFORD.
WILLIAM VENABLES, baron of Kynderton.

Before Easter, 1536. WALTER HUBBERD, sheriff of Norfolk and Suffolk.

1536, Apr. 20. HUGH POLLARD, sheriff of Devon.

1536, after July 18.
THOMAS LORD CROMWELL (at the breaking up of the Parliament).
—— POWLETT (at the same time).

1536, Oct. 16.
GEORGE SPEEKE (at Windsor).
THOMAS CAREWE *(ibid.)*.

1536 (after 1534, Nov.). WILLIAM WEST, sheriff of Essex and Herts.

1536, May-Aug. RICHARD RICH, chancellor of the Augmentations.

1536–7, Mar. 18 (? Apr. 1).
THOMAS WYATT (on Easter day).
—— DE LA MOYTE.

1537, Oct. 18.
Knights made at the creation of the earls of Hertford and of Southampton.
THOMAS HENNAGE.
THOMAS SEYMOUR.
RICHARD LONGE.
WILLIAM COFFYN.
MICHAEL LYSTER.
ROBERT DORMER.

[? after 1538, Nov. 15.] JOHN WILLIAMS, sheriff of Oxfordshire.
HENRY KNYVETT.
HUGH POWLET.
STEPHEN PECOCKE.

KNIGHTS BACHELORS

[? after 1538, Nov. 15.]

    EDWARD MONTAGU.
    HUMFREY BROWNE.
    GERVASE CLYFTON.
    ROBERT BOWES.
    RAUF EVERS.
    EDWARD WYNDHAM.
    CHRISTOPHER MORRYS.
    RAUF WARREN.
    ROGER CHOLMELEY.
    RICHARD GRESHAM.
    PERCYVALL HARTE.
    RAUF VERNEY.
    THOMAS WRYOTHESLEY.
    ROBERT SOUTHWELL.
    NICHOLAS HARE.
    ANTHONY KYNGESTON.
    RICHARD CROMWELL.
    THOMAS POPE.
    JOHN ARUNDELL.
    JOHN BAKER.
    NICHOLAS FORMAN.
    WILLIAM HOLLYES.
    JOHN GRESHAM.
    ANTHONY LEGHE.
    MARTIN BOWES.
    HENRY HOWARD [styled] earl of Surrey.
    WILLIAM, lord Parr.*
    JOHN VERNON, of Staffordshire.
    ANTHONY KNYVET, porter of Calais.
    RICHARD MANNERS.
    ROBERT NEVILL.
    THOMAS BOROUGH.
    RAUF SADLER, of Stondon, Herts.

* *sic* in MS. William Lord Parr of Horton was knighted 25 December, 1513 and created Lord Parr 23rd December, 1543. The person referred to in the list is his nephew Sir William Parr, who was created Lord Parr and Ros of Kendal 9th March, 1539, Earl of Essex 23 December, 1543, and Marquess of Northampton 16th February, 1547.

KNIGHTS BACHELORS

[? after 1538, Nov. 15.]

    Edmond Knightley.
    Christopher More, of Hampshire.
    James Foulchampe.
    John Gostwyke.
    John Gascoigne.
    Humfrey Wyngefeilde.
    Rauf Lane.
    Edward Carne.
    —— Partriche.
    Richard Pollard.
    Michael Dormer.

After 1540, Nov. 17. William Fermor, sheriff of Norfolk and Suffolk.

Knights living in Ireland in 1541 dubbed before that date.

Walter Bellew, of the Roche, Co. Louth.
Walter Chevers, of Maston, Co. Meath.
Walter de la Hyde, of Moyglare, Co. Meath.
Gerald FitzJohn FitzGerald *alias* MacShane, of Cloncurry, Co. Kildare.
John Grace, of Grace Court, Co. Kilkenny.
Oliver Plunket, of Kilsaran, Co. Louth.
John Plunket, of Bewley, Co. Louth.
Thomas Plunket, of Rathmore, Co. Meath.
John White, constable of the Castle of Dublin (1535, Aug. 28).
Thomas Butler, of Cahir, Co. Tipperary (at Clonmel, 1535, Sept., by lord Leonard Grey, lord deputy).
Ulick Bourke, captain of Clanrickard (at Galway, 1538, July 13, by same).
James FitzSimon, mayor of Dublin (at Belsho, 1539, Aug., by same).
Michael Courcy, mayor of Drogheda (at Belsho, 1539, Aug.).
Gerald Aylmer, lord chief justice of the King's Bench (*ibid.*, 1539, Aug.).
Thomas Talbot, of Malahide (*ibid.*, 1539, Aug.).
Thomas Cusack, chancellor of the Exchequer (1540).
James Dowdall, of Ballyscanlon, Co. Louth.

KNIGHTS BACHELORS

GERALD FLEMYNG, natural son of lord Slane.

PATRICK GERNON, of Gernonstown, Co. Louth.

THOMAS LUTTRELL, of Luttrellston, Co. Dublin, chief justice of Common Pleas.

PATRICK WHITE, 2nd baron of the Exchequer.

WILLIAM BIRMINGHAM, of Dunfert, Co. Kildare.

GERALD FITZJOHN FITZGERALD, of Dromany, Co. Waterford.

DONAL O'BRIEN.

TURLOGH O'BRIEN.

1542. RICHARD SOUTHWELL (dubbed at the Parliament anno 33, "who with these three following are placed in the original before Sir Richard Edgecombe ").

EDMUND MARVYN.
EDWARD NORTH.
WILLIAM DENHAM.
RICHARD EDGECOMBE.
JOHN GUILDEFORDE.
JOHN HARINGTON.
WILLIAM WILOUGHBY.
THOMAS MOYLE, of Kent.
WALTER HERBERT.
THOMAS JOHANES.
WILLIAM VAUGHAN.
ROBERT ACTON.
EDMOND (RICHARD) PECKHAM, cofferer of the Household.
ROWLAND HYLL.
GEORGE COTTON.
REIGNOLD SCOTTE, of Kent, sheriff of Kent.
JOHN CANDYSHE.

1541–2, Feb. 2. JOHN DAWNEY, of Yorkshire.

1542, Oct. 1. DONUGANS MACAMYCE [MAGENIS], of Ireland (at Greenwich).

1542, Oct. 1. ARTHUR MAKENYCE [MAGENIS], of Ireland *(ibid.)*.

After 1542, Nov. 22. RICHARD CATESBY, sheriff of Northamptonshire.

KNIGHTS BACHELORS

[?1542.] JOHN ARONDELL, of Trerice.
JOHN COTES, mayor of London.

1543. WILLIAM HERBERT.
ROBERT TYRWHITE.
WILLIAM PETER.
JOHN FOGGE.

[?1543–4.] WILLIAM PAGET, of Bromley, Co. Stafford (afterwards lord Paget de Beaudesert).
FOULKE GREVELL.
RICHARD MANNERS.
EDWARD STRADLINGE.
RAUF ELLERCAR.

1544, May 11. On Sunday, at Leith.

Knights made in Scotland by the Earl of Hertford, the King's lieutenant, 1544, at the burning of Edinburgh, Leith and others.

[? EDWARD] (CLINTON), lord Clinton *
JOHN (CONYERS), 3rd lord Conyers.
WILLIAM WROUGHTON.
THOMAS VENABLES (made knight at Edinburgh).
THOMAS LEIGHT (LEE), *alias* Doctor.
EDWARD DARRELL.
JOHN LUTTERELL.
GEORGE BOWES (of the Bishopric).
RAFE BULLMER.
THOMAS HOLCROFT.
WILLIAM BREERTON.
HUGH CHOLMELEY.

[1544, May 11.]

EDWARD WARREN.
BRIAN LAYTON (of Lancashire).
PETER LEE.
JOHN CONSTABLE (of Yorkshire).

---

* Edward, lord Clinton, is referred to as "chevalier" in April, 1536, when he was summoned to Parliament. The knight in the text could not possibly be his son Henry, as this latter was only about 4 years old in 1544. Possibly lord Edward Clinton was made a knight banneret in 1544.

KNIGHTS BACHELORS

EDMOND TRAFFORD (of Lancashire).
HUGH CALVELY.
JOHN ATHERTON.
THOMAS GERRAT (GERARD).
RICHARD LEE (of St. Albans).
RICHARD CHOMLEY (of Yorkshire).
THOMAS WATERTON (of Yorkshire).
WILLIAM VAVASOUR.
RICHARD SHIRBORNE.
PETER FRETCHWELL (FRECHEVILLE) (of Staveley, Co. Derby).
THOMAS COKIN (COKER, COKEYN) (of Ashburne, Co. Derby).
ROBERT STAPLETON.
RICHARD EGERTON.
LAURENCE SMYTH.
WILLIAM RATCLIFF (RADCLIFFE) (of Ordsall).
THOMAS MALEVERAY (MALYVERER) (of Alderton in Yorkshire).
ROBERT WORSELEY.
THOMAS TALBOTT (of Bashall).
RICHARD HOLLAND.
JOHN LEE (LEGH) (of Booth).
THOMAS CLEIR (CLERE), (of Norfolk).
ANTHONY NEVILL.
LEONARD BECKWITH.
JOHN JENNINGS (JENYNS) (of London, spinner).
THOMAS HOLT.

1544, on Tuesday, May 13, at Leith [by same].

CHARLES HOWARD.
GEORGE BLOUNT.
WILLIAM WOODHOWSE (? not a knight).
GEORGE (ROGER) BREERTON.
ERRYNGE (URYAN) BREERTON.
PHILIP EGERTON.

1544, on Sunday, May 18, at Butterden [by same].

WILLIAM DAMPORT (DAVENPORTE).
RAUFF LAYSTER (LEYCESTER).

EDMOND SAVAGE.
JOHN MASSEY.
JOHN NEVILL.
HEW WYLLOUGHBY.
EDWARD WARNER.
PETER MEWTAS.
ROBERT (THOMAS) CONSTABLE (of Yorkshire).
HUMFRY (THOMAS) BRAIDBURIE (BRADBOURNE).
FRANCIS HOTHOME (of Yorkshire).

1544, Sept. 30.

Knights made by the King at Bologne after the conquest of the town.

HENRY (MANNERS), 3rd earl of Rutland.
Lord NEVILL.
[THOMAS RADCLIFFE] lord FITZWALTER [afterwards earl of Essex].
[JOHN] (BRAY), 2nd lord Bray.
Lord JOHN GREY.
Lord EDWARD GREY.
PIERS, lord LE POWER [POER].*

1544, Oct. 1.   HUMPHREY STILE, sheriff of Kent.

[?] 1544–5, Jan. 20, or 1544, Sept. 30, or some other date.

INGRAM CLYFFORDE.
ANTHONY DENNY.
THOMAS CARDEN (COORDENNE).
PHILIPPE HOBBY.
THOMAS PASTON.
JOHN BARKELEY.
CHARLES BRANDON.
FRANCIS ASKUE (AWSKAME), of Lincolnshire, sheriff of Lincolnshire.
RAUF VANE.
RICHARD WYNYBANKE.
NICHOLAS WENTWORTHE, of Essex.

---

* After Lord Le Power the MS. reads "Sir Henry Dudley, dubbed by the King at Boulogne the 20th of January, *anno* 36, *i.e.* 1545. King Henry left Boulogne on the 30th of Sept., 1544. As there must be an error here, I have thought it best to relegate this Dudley to a footnote and to continue the list with Ingram Clyfforde with the addition of the query as to the date.

RAUF HOPTON.
JOHN POWLETT, afterwards 2nd marquess of Winchester.
THOMAS MORGAN, of Wales.
ROBERT STAFFORDE.
WILLIAM BLOUNT.
ANDREW FLAMOCKE (FLEMOK).
RICHARD WYNGEFIELDE.
ANTH SLAMNOTH.
MAURICE BARKLEYE.
JOHN WELLISBOURNE.

? 1545, Feb. 7. WILLIAM LAXTON, at the Palace of Westminster, on Sunday, the 7th of February, anno 37, he being then mayor of London [? an erratum for anno 36. Laxton was mayor of London from Nov., 1544, to Nov. 1545].

[? 1545, Apr. 5.] WILLIAM CAVENDISH, treasurer of the Chamber (dubbed Easter day, anno 37).

1545, May 31. ROBERT TOWNSHENDE, of Norfolk (dubbed on Trinity Sunday, anno 37).

1545, Sept. 23.

Knights made in Scotland by the Earl of Hertford, the King's lieutenant, being then encamped by our Lady Church by Norham Castle on his coming home after he had been in Scotland 15 days.

JOHN (NEVILL), 4th lord Latimer.*
THOMAS WHARTON, son and heir to lord Wharton.
JOHN TEMPEST.
GEORGE RADCLYFFE.
FRANCYS HASTYNGS.
WILLIAM SEINT QUINTIN.
CHRISTOPHER METCALF.
THOMAS DACRES.
WILLIAM STAFFORDE.
THOMAS GREY, of Horton.
WILLIAM CALVERLEY.
WILLIAM INGLEBY.
ROGER FENWYKE.
RICHARD CANDYSHE, Captain of Blackness.

---

* John, lord Latimer is styled "chivaler" from at least 1543, June 14, in the writs summoning him to Parliament. Possibly he was made a knight banneret in 1545.

After 1545, Nov. 22. JOHN DAWTRIE, sheriff of Surrey and Sussex.

[After 1545, Nov. 23.] THOMAS BROMLEY, justice of the King's Bench (dubbed at the Parliament, anno 1537).

[After 1545, Nov. 23.] JOHN HINDE (HYNDE), justice of the Common Pleas *(ibid.)*.

? 1545. MICHAEL STANHOPE (at Hampton Court, anno 37).
    RICHARD REDE, doctor, de Redbourn, juxta St. Albans (anno 37).
    JOHN PERPENT, of Hertfordshire (anno 37).
    FRANCIS BARNARDE, a Venetian (anno 37).
    JOHN PAKINGTON (anno 37).

[?] WILLIAM BUTTES.
    GEORGE BAYNHAM.
    FRANCIS LEYKE.
    JOHN HYLSTON.
    —— HOGAN.

1545–6, Mar. WILLIAM BRABAZON, vice-treasurer of Ireland (dubbed in Ireland).

[1546, after March.] GEORGE CORNWALL (dubbed at Boulogne by the earl of Hertford).

[1546.] WALTER BROWNE, of Mulbranken, Co. Wexford, 1546 (dubbed in Ireland).

[1546.] THOMAS NUGENT, of Carlanstown, Co. Westmeath *(ibid)*.

[? 1546.] PETER GAMBOW, a spaniard (dubbed by the King at York Place, anno 38).

[?] WILLIAM FARMOUR, of Norfolk.
    HUMFREY ACTON.
    THOMAS PALMER.

1546–7, Feb. 6.
    On Sunday King Edward the VI. was made knight by Edward, earl of Hertford, his uncle, lord Protector, and the same time the said King* dubbed the two following:—
    HENRY HOUBLETHORNE (HABARTHORNE), lord mayor of London (at the Tower).
    JOHN PORTMAN, justice of the King's Bench *(ibid)*.

---

* Harl MS. 5177, says His Highness [*i.e.*, the Lord Protector].

KNIGHTS BACHELORS

1546–7, Feb. 20.

> *Knights dubbed by the King on Sunday, the day of his Coronation, being crowned, to the number of 40, in lieu of [being knighted by] the Bath, which then could not be performed according to all ceremonies thereto belonging, the time for that purpose being too short.**
> (See these names supra vol. i. p. 150-2, under Knights of the Bath.)

1546–7, Feb. 22.

> *Knights of the Carpet dubbed by the King on Tuesday after the Coronation, being Shrove Tuesday.†*

JOHN RADCLYFFE.
WILLIAM STANLEY.
Lord [?] THOMAS GREY.
JOHN BUTLER, of Gloucestershire (of Hertfordshire).
ANTHONY AUCHER (AUGER) (AGER).
JOHN SHELTON, of Suffolk.
EDWARD SABCOTTES (SAPCOTS).
RICHARD COTTON.
JOHN MASON.
THOMAS NEWNAM (NEWMAN).
JOHN WYNDHAM.
PHILIPPE CALTHORPE
JOHN VAUGHAN, of Wales.
MAURYCE DENYS, of Gloucestershire.
ANTHONY HENYNGHAM.
ROWLAND MORETON (MOURTON).
JOHN WENTWORTHE, of Essex, father to the lady Maltravers.
THOMAS DYER.
JOHN GODSALVE.
THOMAS BARNESTON (BARMSTON).
THOMAS GYFFORDE (GILFORD).
ROGER GYFFORDE, of Devonshire.

---

* In Harl. MS. 6063, the list is headed "Coronation of Ed. VI. Knights of the Bath." In Strype's "Ecclesiastical Memorials," II., II., p. 328, these knights are styled Knights of the Carpet. I have, however, deliberately preferred to rank them as Knights of the Bath in view of the King's actual intention.

† Cott MS. Claud C III. Harl MS. 6063. Harl MS. 5177. This list is printed by Strype (Eccles. Memorials II., II., 327-8), from a MS. Ex. Offic Armor, No. 1, 7, under the title "The Knights of the Carpet, dubbed by the King on Shrove Tuesday, in the morning viz. : some of them the same day, and the rest of them during the utas of the abovesaid whole solemnization, being 55 in number."

KNIGHTS BACHELORS

JOHN SAVAGE.
EDWARD ROGERS.
WALTER (WILLIAM) BUCLER (BUTLER).
ROGER BLEWETT.
HUMFREY STAFFORD.
JOHN HERSEY (HERCY), of Nottinghamshire.
JOHN PERPOUNT (PERPOINT) of Nottinghamshire.
FRANCYS ENGLEFEILDE.
THOMAS FITZHERBERT.
JOHN SPRYNGE.
THOMAS HAMNARE (HANMER).
JOHN GREVILL.
JOHN BROKETT.
THOMAS BELL, of Gloucestershire.
JOHN HORSEY.
RES GRYFFYTHE, of Wales.
JOHN SALISBURY, of Wales.
THOMAS GRAVENER.
WILLIAM HOLLEYS, the younger.
THOMAS HOLLEYS, elder brother to the above.
WILLIAM RAYNSFORDE.
THOMAS WROTHE.
WILLIAM PYKERINGE.
JOHN CARY.
HENRY DOYLE.
URYAN BRERETON.
WILLIAM DRURY.
GEORGE HARPER.
THOMAS KEMPE.
JOHN NORTON, of Kent.
ROBERT LANGLEY.
THOMAS NEVILL.
JOHN APRICE (AP RES, DEPRICE).
WALTER MYLDMAY.
CLEMENT SMYTHE.

1547, Sept. EDWARD BELLINGHAM, marshal of the army (dubbed in Ireland).

[1547, between the 18th and 25th of September.]

> *Knights Bannerets and Bachelor Knights made in the camp beside Roxburgh, in Scotland, in the first year of Edward VI.'s reign by the hands of the high and mighty Prince Edward, duke of Somerset, Lieutenant General of all the King's armies by land and sea, and Governor of his Royal person and Protector of all his realms, dominions and subjects.*

FRANCYS BRYAN, banneret.
RAUF SADLER, banneret.
RAUFE VANE, banneret.
WILLIAM (GREY), 13th lord Grey of Wilton.*
Lord EDWARD SEYMOUR.
Lord WALDECK, a mercenary captain, served in England 1549–50.
THOMAS DACRES.
JOHN THYNE (BOTEVILLE *alias* Thynne).
JOHN GRESHAM.
MILES PARTRIGE.
FRANCYS FLEMYNGE.
CHARLES (STOURTON), 8th lord Stourton.
EDMONDE (EDWARD) BRUGES.
NICHOLAS STRANGE.
JOHN TALBOT, of Grafton.
FRANCYS SALVEYN (? TALBOYN).
JOHN SOUTHWORTHE.
THOMAS DANBY, of Yorkshire.
JOHN FOSTER.
JOHN HORSELEY.
RAUF BAGNALL.
Lord THOMAS HOWARD.
RICHARD CONWAY.
GYLES POOLE.
OLYVER LAWRENCE.
HENRY GATES.

---

* William, lord Grey of Wilton, is described as chivaler in the writs summoning him to Parliament from 1529, November onwards. Possibly he was made a knight banneret in 1547.

KNIGHTS BACHELORS

Edward Hastinges.
William Skipwithe.
William Buttes.
George Blage.
William Fraunces.
Francys Knolles.
William Thorneborough.
George Howarde.
James Wylforde.
Rauf Copynger.
Thomas Wentworth.
John Mervyn.
Hugh Ascue.
Richard Towneley.
Marmaduke Constable.
George Awdeley.
John Holcrofte.
—— Barteville, a Frenchman.
Andrew Dudley.
Christopher Dyes.
Thomas Chaloner.
Rowland Clerke.
Peter Negro.
Alonnce de Ville Serge (Seige).
Oliver Wallop.

[? 1547, Sept. 18.]

Nicholas Throckmorton (by the king (?) in London).

1547, Oct. 1.

Knights made at Newcastle the 1st day of October in anno primo by the hands of Edward, duke of Somerset, lord protector.

Walter Bonham.
Henry Hussee (Hussey).
Robert Branlyn.
Jaques Granado.

KNIGHTS BACHELORS 63

1547, Oct. 3.
> *Knights made at Berwick by the hands of John, Earl of Warwick, Lieutenant of the King's army in anno primo in Scotland.*
> RICHARD BUCKLEY.
> ANTHONY STRELLEY.
> ARTHUR MANWERYNGE.
> JOHN RYBANDE (dubbed at Newcastle?).
> ANDREW CORBET (dubbed at Newcastle?).
> THOMAS NEVILL, second son to Rauf, earl of Westmorland.

[? 1547, Nov.] JOHN JERMYN, of Suffolk.

1547, Nov. 24 *
> JAMES BASCARVILLE (at Westminster).
> JAMES CROFTES *(ibid.).*
> ANTHONY COPE *(ibid.).*

1547. ROBERT CURSON, of Norfolk.

[1547]. RICHARD BUTLER, of Ballyraggett, Co. Kilkenny (dubbed in Ireland).

1548, Aug. JAMES GERNON, of Killencoole, Co. Louth (dubbed at Navan, in Ireland, by Sir Edward Bellingham).

[? 1548, Dec.] HENRY WHARTON (? dubbed at Westminster).

1548, Dec. 1.†
> WILLIAM COBHAM (at Westminster).
> THOMAS CORNWALLES *(ibid).*
> RICHARD CORBETT *(ibid).*

[1548]. PATRICK HUSSEY, baron of Galtrim, Co. Meath (dubbed in Ireland).
? DOMYNIKE BOLLONUS, ambassador from Venice (dubbed in England by the King).
? HENRY AMCOTTES, lord mayor of London.

1549, March 3.
> WILLIAM LOCKE, sheriff of London (by the king at Whitehall).
> [JOHN] AWLYF (ALYF, AYLYF), sheriff of London.
> JOHN CUT, of Essex. [See *supra* vol. i. p. 152.]

---
* Harl MS. 5177 says 1549, Nov. 24, for these three Knights.
† Harl MS. 5177 says 1549, Dec. 1st, for these three Knights.

KNIGHTS BACHELORS

? THOMAS GARGRAVE, of Yorkshire.
? RICHARD SAKEVILLE, chancellor of the Augmentation Court.
[? 1549, Nov.] JOHN YORKE, sheriff of London.

1549, Nov. 10.
    JOHN DE LA ZOUCHE (at Westminster).
    JOHN POLLARDE *(ibid)*.
    ARTHUR CHAMPERNOUN *(ibid)*.
    GYLES STRANGUISHE [STRANGWAYES] *(ibid)*.
    JOHN MORE (MOORE), *(ibid)*.
    THOMAS WOODHOUSE *(ibid)*.
    WILLIAM HERBERT *(ibid)*.
    WALTER HERBERT *(ibid)*.

After 1549, Nov. 12. EDMUND WYNDHAM, sheriff of Norfolk and Suffolk.

1549, Nov. 17.
    The DUKE OF LUNINBOROUGH [LÜNEBURG] (at Westminster).
    JOHN (BOURCHIER), styled lord Fitz Warine, son and heir to the earl of Bath *(ibid)*.
    NICHOLAS PELHAM, sheriff of Surrey and Sussex *(ibid)*.
    AMBROSE DUDLEY, second son to the earl of Warwick *(ibid)*.
    JOHN PARRETT *(ibid)*.
    THOMAS RUSSELL *(ibid)*.

[?·after] 1549.
    THOMAS ESSEX.
    CHRISTOPHER HEYDON, of Norfolk.
    THOMAS POMEREY.
    JOHN SYDNAM.
    JOHN POLLARD [? 1553, Oct. 2.]
    JOHN MOWNE.
    HENRY BEDINGFEILDE.
    ROGER VAUGHAN.
    THOMAS GOLDYNGE.
    JOHN SAINTLOE.
    PAULE BAPTIST SPYNOLA, of Genoa.
    NICHOLAS ARNOLDE.
    WILLIAM ALLERTON.
    FRANCYS JOBSON.

KNIGHTS BACHELORS

ANTHONY GWYDOTT.
THOMAS SAUNDERS.
HENRY HUSSEY.
RICHARD BLOUNT (BLUNT).
ANDREW JUDDE.
GILBERT DETHIKE, Garter King of Arms (on Tuesday in Easter week, *anno* 5, 1551).
WILLIAM CECILL, secretary [1551, Oct. 11].
JOHN CHEKE [1551, Oct. 11].
HENRY NEVILL.
HENRY SIDNEY [1550, Oct. 11, with Sir W. Cecill *sic* ? for 1551].
WILLIAM WALDERTON.
WILLIAM FITZ WILLIAM, of Ireland, of the Privy Chamber to the king.
ROBERT CHESTRE, of Royston (dubbed at Waltham).
ROBERT OXENBRIDGE.
JOHN BROWNE.
GEORGE BARNES, lord mayor of London [lord mayor in 1552].
—— COURTPENY.
RICHARD DOBBES, lord mayor of London [lord mayor in 1551].
RAUF ELLERCAR.
JAMES STUMPES.
THOMAS SMYTH, secretary [? 1548, Oct.].
THOMAS STRADLINGE [1549, Feb. 17].
THOMAS WYATT, the younger.
JAMES DYER, sergeant-at-law [1552, ? Nov.].
JOHN SENTLEGER.

after 1550, Nov. 11. RICHARD PEXALL, sheriff of Hampshire.

[1550.] FRANCIS HARBERT, of Dublin (dubbed in Ireland).

1550, Dec. JOHN TRAVERS, Master of the Ordnance *(ibid)*.

[1551.] CHRISTOPHER BARNEWALL, of Crickstown, Co. Meath *(ibid)*.

[1551.] JOHN BELLEW, of Bellewstown, Co. Louth *(ibid)* see p. 69 *infra*.

[1551.] WILLIAM SENTLOWE, constable of the Castle of Wexford *(ibid)*.

1551–2. PATRICK BARNEWALL, of Gracedieu, Co. Dublin, Master of the Rolls *(ibid)*.
1551–2. THADY or TEIGE O'CARROLL, of Ely, Co. Tipperary *(ibid)*.
1552, Nov. NICHOLAS BAGENAL, marshall of the army *(ibid)*.
1552–3. MAURICE FITZ GERALD, of Lackaghe, Co. Kildare *(ibid)*.
1552–3. GERALD NUGENT, of Ballybretnagh, Co. Westmeath *(ibid)*.

1553, Oct. 2.

Knights [Bachelors] made the day after the coronation of queen Mary, being Monday, 2nd of Oct., at Westminster. in the presence of the queen, in her Presence Chamber, by the earl of Arundel, lord steward of the Household, who had commission to knight the following.*

Lord [FITZGERALD] GARRET.†
[WILLIAM] (BURGH), 4th lord Burgh.
[EDWARD] (SUTTON *alias* Dudley), 8th lord Dudley.
THOMAS STANLEY.
EDMONDE (EDWARD) WYNDESORE.
HENRY RADCLYFFE.
THOMAS HASTINGES.
EDWARD WALDEGRAVE.
JOHN BOORNE (BOURNE), secretary.
RAUFE CHAMBERLAIN.
JOHN TIRRELL, of Gippinge.
JOHN HUDDLESTON.
ROBERT PECKHAM.
JOHN BRAND (BRENT).
HENRY LEE (LEY).
CHRISTOPHER ALLEN.
RICHARD FRESTON.
WILLIAM KELLAWAY.
HENRY GASCON (GASCOIGNE) (GARTON).
JOHN TREGONNELL.
AMBROSE JERMIN.
LEONARD CHAMBERLEYN.

---

* Harl 6063. Cott, Claud C. III. Harl 5177. This has been printed in the Diary of Henry Machyn (Camden Soc. o. s. 42, p. 334), from an MS. in the College of Arms I y. f. 74.
† A late hand has inserted in the MS., Harl 5177, Lord Mayor Garret. This is undoubtedly incorrect, as Sir William Garret, or Gerard, was not Lord Mayor of London till 1555. For the evidence of the existence of a Lord Fitzgerald Garret, see Acts of the Privy Council, New Series, Vol. IV., pp. 31, 388.

1553, Oct. 2.
    THOMAS GERRARD.
    [DAVID] BROKE [BROOKE], chief baron of the Exchequer.
    [RICHARD] MORGAN, chief justice of Common Pleas.
    GEORGE GIFFORD (GEFFORD).
    THOMAS PAKENTON (PAKINGTON).
    THOMAS LOVELL.
    JOHN SPENCER.
    JOHN (WILLIAM) FITZWILLIAM (FITZWILLIAMS).
    THOMAS ANDREWES.
    WILLIAM COURTNEY.
    WILLIAM GRYSELEY (GRESLEY).
    THOMAS CAVE.
    EDWARD LITTLETON.
    PHILIP PARRYS (PARIS).
    THOMAS WHITE, master of the Requests.
    THOMAS METHAM (METTAM).
    RICHARD LEWSON (LAWSON) (LASEN).
    THOMAS DAWNEY.
    ROBERT WINGFIELD.
    THOMAS KNIVETT.
    ROGER WOODHOWSE (WODOWES).
    FRANCYS STONNER.
    JOHN à LEE (LYE, LEIGH).
    RICHARD TATE.
    EDWARD GREENE.
    ROBERT LANE.
    RICHARD STAPLETON.
    WILLIAM DENSELL (DAMSELL).
    JOHN CHICHESTER.
    HENRY CRIPPS.
    THOMAS PALMER.
    HENRY ASHLEY (ASHELEY).
    RICHARD STRANGEWAIES.
    GEORGE MATHIEU (MATHEW).
    JOHN COTTON.
    GEORGE (JOHN) POLLARD (PAWLETT *alias* Pollard).
    JOHN WERBERTON.

KNIGHTS BACHELORS

1553, Oct. 2.

    JOHN FARMOUR (FERMOUR).
    JOHN (THOMAS) BENGAR (BERENGAR).
    JOHN CONSTABLE.
    EDWARD (SUTTON *alias* Dudley), 8th lord Dudley.
    GER (GEORGE) STANLEY (inserted by a later hand in Harl MS., 6063, as a correction for the preceding item).
    ROWLAND STANLEY.
    RAUF EGARTON.
    RICHARD MALIVERY (? MOLINEUX).
    THOMAS HESKETT.
    THOMAS WAYNEMAN.
    JOHN CROFTS.
    EDWARD (EDMOND) MAULEVERER (MALEVERY).
    THOMAS TYNDALL.
    THOMAS THROGMORTON.
    EDWARD GREVILE.
    HENRY STAFFORD.
    THOMAS FINCHE.
    RICHARD BRAYE.
    WILLIAM LAWSON.

1553, Oct. 19.

    Knights made Oct. 19 primo Mariæ.
    RICHARD BRUGES (BRUGYS).
    JAMES FITZJAMES.
    THOMAS VERNEY.
    JAMES (THOMAS) WILLIAMS.
    RAUF (WILLIAM) MERINGE.
    EDMOND PINSON (PYLSON).
    EDWARD FITTON.
    WILLIAM WIGSTONE.
    HENRY JONES (JOANES, JAMES).
    JOHN BRUSE (BREWSE).
    ROBERT WHITNEY (WYTNEY).
    ROGER (RICHARD) CHUDLEY.
    THOMAS BASKERVILLE.
    THOMAS TYNDALL.

1553, Oct. 20.
> Knights made the next day following.
> WILLIAM WARRAM (WARHAM).
> RICHARD WALLWYN.
> THOMAS WHITE, lord mayor of London.

1554–5, Jan. 27.
> Knights made by King Philip in his chamber upon Sunday, the 27th of January.
> JOHN LYON (LYONS), lord mayor of London.
> ROBERT BROKE, lord chief justice of Common Pleas.
> EDWARD SAUNDERS, justice of Common Pleas.
> JOHN WHIDDON, justice of the King's Bench.
> WILLIAM STAIMFORD (STAUNFORD), justice of Common Pleas.
> CLEMENT HYGHAM (HIGHAM) [speaker of the House of Commons and afterwards chief baron of the Exchequer.]

(1555). THOMAS BARNEWALL, of Trimblestown, Co. Meath (dubbed in Ireland.
(1555). PETER BUTLER, of Cahir, Co. Tipperary *(ibid)*.
(1555). NICHOLAS DEVEREUX, of Balmagir, Co. Wexford *(ibid)*.
(1555). THOMAS NANGLE, baron of Navan, Co. Meath *(ibid)*.
(1555). OLIVER NUGENT, of Drumcree, Co. Westmeath *(ibid)*.
(1555). RICHARD TUITE, of Tuitestown, Co. Westmeath *(ibid)*.
[? 1555]. WILLIAM GARRET [GERARD], lord mayor of London (in England).
? OLIVER LEADER (LEDER), sheriff of Cambridge and Huntingdon, knighted some time after 1554, Nov. 14.
> EDWARD GAGE.
> ROBERT DENYS.

1556, May 26. JOHN BELLEW, of Bellewstown and The Roche, Co. Louth (dubbed in Ireland). See p. 65 *supra*.
1556, May 26. MAURICE FITZGERALD, of Bever, Co. Cork *(ibid)*.
(1556, May). CHRISTOPHER CHEVERS, of Maston, Co. Meath *(ibid)*.
1556 (July). GERALD PETIT, of Irishton, Co. Meath *(ibid)*.
1556–7. OLIVER PLUNKET, of Rathmore, Co. Meath *(ibid)*.
1556–7. THOMAS TYRELL, of Fertullagh, Co. Westmeath *(ibid)*.
1556–7, Feb. 7. THOMAS OFFELEY [OFFLEY], lord mayor of London (in England by the King).

1556–7, Feb. 7. WILLIAM CHESTER [alderman of London].
1557, Aug. DONAL MACDONELL, of Antrim (dubbed in Ireland by the earl of Essex, lord lieutenant).*
[? 1557]. THOMAS CURTEYS [CURTEIS], lord mayor of London (in England).
  [?] THOMAS PERCY, afterwards 8th earl of Northumberland.
  HENRY PERCY.
  WILLIAM CORDELL, solicitor general.
  JOHN SULYARD.
  EDWARD GREY.
  WILLIAM BELLOWS.

1558, June 26. DONAL MACCARTIE MORE (at Limerick on Sunday).
1558, Nov. 30. GERALD FITZGERALD, earl of Desmond (at Waterford).
1558, Nov. 30. MAURICE FITZGERALD, of Decies, Co. Waterford (*ibid*).
1558 [? Nov.–Dec.]
  THOMAS PARRY, of Wales, treasurer of the Household (in England).
  HENRY CAREY, afterwards baron Hunsdon.
  THOMAS LEIGH, lord mayor of London.
  NICHOLAS BACON, lord keeper of the Great Seal.
[? 1558–9, Jan.] ROBERT CATELYNE (CATLYN), chief justice of the Queen's Bench.
[1558–9 ? after Jan.] THOMAS GRESHAM.
1559. WILLIAM HEWET, lord mayor of London.
1559. ANTHONIE STANDEN.
1559–60, Jan. 2. EDMUND BUTLER, brother to the earl of Ormonde (dubbed in Ireland).
1559–60, Jan. 2. EDWARD STANLEY, brother to the earl of Derby (*ibid*).
1559–60, Jan. 2. THOMAS MANNERS (*ibid*).
1559–60, Jan. 2. JAMES FITZ GERALD, of Desmond (*ibid*).
1560 [? Feb. 27] on St. George's Day. GEORGE BOWES (at Berwick by the duke of Norfolk, when the armies returned from the seige of Leith).
1560, July 18. ARTHUR GREY, afterwards lord Grey of Wilton (*ibid* by same).

* In 1557 knighthood was offered to John Challoner, mayor of Dublin; but was declined.

KNIGHTS BACHELORS

1560, July 18. BERNABY FITZPATRICK, of Ireland (*ibid* by same).
1560, July 18. EDWARD BRAY (*ibid* by same).
1560, July 18. WILLIAM MALLORY (*ibid* by same).
1560, July 18. EDWARD LITLETON (*ibid* by same).
1560, July 18. WILLIAM BABTHORPE (*ibid* by same).
1560, July 18. JOHN CONWAY, of Warwickshire (*ibid* by same).
1560, July 18. WALTER ASTON, of Staffordshire (*ibid* by same).
1560, July 21. RICHARD NEWPORTE (*ibid* by same).
1560, July 21. WILLIAM FAYRFAX, of Gilling (*ibid* by same).
1560, July 24. RICHARD FULMERSTON (*ibid* by same).
after 1560, Nov. 12. EDWARD CAPELL, sheriff of Essex and Herts.
1561. WILLIAM BUTLER.
1561, Aug. 12. OWEN HOPTON (at Smalbridge, Sir William Waldgrave's house in Essex).
1561. HENRY LEA.
1561. JOHN PERROTT.
? 1560–1 (1562–3), Feb. 15. WILLIAM HARPER, lord mayor of London (at Westminster the 15th day of Feb., 1562 [*sic*? for 1560–1].
after 1561, Nov. 8. THOMAS TYNDALE, sheriff of Norfolk and Suffolk.
1562–3, Mar. 8. THOMAS LODGE, lord mayor of London (at Westminster).
1562–3, Mar. 8. ADRYAN POYNINGES.
1563. JOHN WHITE, lord mayor of London.
1563. HENRY CHEYNY (by the Queen's own hands).
1564 [Aug. 10]. [HENRY] WILLIAMS, *alias* Cromwell, of Huntingdonshire (by same).
1564. EDWARD CAPELL.
1564, Sept. 2. THOMAS FITZGERALD, *alias* O'Desmond, brother to the earl of Desmond. *See* p. 74 *infra*.
1564–5, Feb. 18. RICHARD MALLORY, lord mayor of London (at Westminster the 18th of Feb., 1564 [? 1563–4]).
1564–5. OWIN OSWILIFANT (ASSWILLIAN), of Ireland.
1565, June 23 (? 19). JAMES HARINGTON (by the earl of Leicester, at the Queen's command).
1565, July. OWEN O'SULLIVAN BEARE (dubbed in Ireland).
1565, July. WARHAM ST. LEGER *(ibid)*.
1565, Aug. 21. HENRY DARCY (at Kenilworth, by the earl of Leicester).
1565, Aug. 21. RICHARD KNIGHTLEY (*ibid* by same).

1565, Aug. 21. GEORGE HASTINGS *(ibid)*.
1565, Aug. 21. WILLIAM DEVEREULX *(ibid)*.
1565, Aug. 21. JOHN THROGMORTON, recorder of Coventry *(ibid)*.
1565, Aug. 21. FOULKE GREVILL *(ibid)*.
1565, Aug. 21. JOHN LITLETON, *(ibid)*.
1565 (1566), Aug. 21. GEORGE TURPYN, sheriff of Warwick and Leicester *(ibid)*.
1565, Aug. 21 (? after Aug. 21). THOMAS LUCY (in his own house in Warwickshire).
1565, Aug. 21 (? after Aug. 21). EDMOND BRUDENELL (at Thomas Lucy's house, by the earl of Leicester).
1565. PETER MANNERINGE.
1565. GEORGE STANLEY.
1565–6, Feb. 17. RICHARD CHAMPYON, lord mayor of London (at Greenwich by Thomas, earl of Sussex, the 17th of Feb., 1565, [? 1564–5].
[1565–6], Mar. 10 (Sunday). THOMAS HOBBY (at Greenwich).
1566, July. CHRISTOPHER NUGENT, baron of Delvin (at Drogheda by Sir Henry Sydney, lord deputy general of Ireland).
1566, July. ROBERT BARNEWELL, baron of Tremeleston *(ibid by same)*.
1566, July. THOMAS PLUNKET, baron of Louth *(ibid by same)*.
1566, July. CHRISTOPHER BARNEWALL, of Turvey and Gracedieu, Co. Dublin *(ibid)*.
1566, July. PATRICK BARNEWALL, of Stackallan and Crickstown, Co. Meath *(ibid)*.
1566, July. THOMAS FITZWILLIAM, of Merrion, Co. Dublin *(ibid)*
1566, July. NICHOLAS HERON *(ibid)*.
1566, Sept. 6. HENRY NORREYS (at Rycott at his own house by the Queen).
1566, Sept. 6. RICHARD WAYNEMAN *(ibid)*.
1566. CHRISTOPHER BROWNE (at Bradname).
1566, Nov. 16. WILLIAM SARSFIELD, of Lucan, mayor of Dublin (dubbed in Christchurch, Dublin, for service against Shan O'Neale).
1566, Nov. 27. JOHN ARUNDELL (at the Court at the Tower).
1566–7, Feb. 2. ANTHONY BROWNE [afterwards], justice of the Common Pleas (at the Parliament House at Westminster, the 2nd of Feb. (Jan.), 1566, by Thomas, earl of Essex).

1566-7, Feb. 10. HENRY COMPTON (CORUPTON), (at Arundell House, London, by Robert, earl of Leicester).

1556-7, Feb. 14. THEOBALD BUTLER, of Cahire (in the church of Clonmell by Sir Henry Sydney, lord deputy of Ireland).

1566-7, Feb. 16 (Sunday). CHRISTOPHER DRAPER, lord mayor of London (at Westminster on Sunday, Feb. 16th, 1566 [? 1565-6].

1567, Mar. 30. JAMES FITZRICHARD (BARRY), viscount Buttevant (at Limerick by Sir Henry Sydney, the lord deputy).

1567, Mar. 30. DAVID (ROCHE), 5th viscount Roche of Fermoy *(ibid* by same).

1567, Mar. 30. DERMOT MACCARTIE, lord of Muskerry, Co. Cork *(ibid* by same).

1567, Mar. 30. WILLIAM O'CARROLL (OCKERVILL), lord of Ely, Co. Tipperary *(ibid)*.

1567, Mar. 30. GERALD COURCY, lord Courcy *(ibid)*.

1567, Mar. 30. THOMAS (FITZMAURICE), 16th lord of Kerry and baron of Lixnaw *(ibid)*.

1567, Mar. 30. DONOGH (DENISE) MACCARTIE REAGH *(ibid)*.

1567, Mar. 30. JOHN FITZGERALD, of Desmond *(ibid)*.

1567, Mar. 31. WILLIAM BOURKE (at Limerick in the afternoon).

1567, Apr. 4. HUGH O'DONNEL (at Balliloughrea, the earl of Clanricarde's house, by Henry Sydney, knt., lord deputy).

1567, Apr. 4. (DONAL) O'CONNOR SLIGAGH *(ibid* by same).

1567, Apr. 4. RORY O'SHAUGHNESSY (O'SHAGHNES) *(ibid)*.

1567, June 8. THOMAS SACKVILLE (at Westminster, by the duke of Norfolk, and the same day created baron of Buckhurst).

1567, June 23. THOMAS MYLDMAY (at Richmond, by Robert, earl of Leicester).

1567, Sept. BRIAN MACPHELIM O'NEALE (at Carrickfergus).

1567, Dec. JOHN PLUNKET, of Dunsoghly, Co. Dublin, lord chief justice of the Queen's Bench (in Ireland).

1567, Dec. ROBERT DILLON (DE LION), of Newtown, Co. Meath, lord chief justice of Common Pleas *(ibid)*.

1567-8, Mar. 14. ROGER MARTIN, lord mayor of London (at Westminster the 14th March, 1567 [? 1566-7] by Robert, earl of Leicester).

1568, Aug. 7. GEORGE PENRODOCKE, sheriff of Herts. (at Hatfield by Robert, earl of Leicester).

1568, Aug. (?). LEWES MORDANT, of Northampton.

1568, Aug. EDWARD MONTAGU, of Northampton.

KNIGHTS BACHELORS

1568, Aug. RICHARD FENYS (FYNES), [of] Oxford, sheriff of Oxford
after 1568, Nov. 18. CUTHBERT MUSGRAVE, sheriff of Cumberland.
1569, Aug. or Sept. HENRY WALLOPE (at Basing).
1569, Aug. or Sept. WILLIAM KINGESMYTH *(ibid)*.
1569, Sept. 11. THOMAS FITZGERALD, of Desmond (in the church at Limerick on Sunday). *See supra* p. 71.
1569, ? Oct. 28. THOMAS ROWE, lord mayor of London (at Westminster).
1569–70, Jan. 1. HUMPHREY GILBERT (at Drogheda).
1569–70, Jan. 13. CHRISTOPHER ST. LAWRENCE, lord baron of Howthe (at Drogheda by Sir Henry Sydney, knt., lord deputy).
1569–70, Feb. 5. WILLIAM WEST (at Hampton Court, and was then created lord de la Warr).
1570, May 11. WILLIAM DRURY, of Suffolk (at Berwick by Thomas. earl of Sussex).
1570, May 11. THOMAS MANNERS *(ibid* by same).
1570, May 11. ROBERT CONSTABLE *(ibid* by same).
1570, May 11. GEORGE CARY *(ibid* by same).
1570, Aug. 28. VALENTYNE BROWNE (at Carlisle, by Thomas, earl of Sussex).
1570, Aug. 28. EDWARD HASTINGS, of Leicester *(ibid* by same).
1570, Aug. 28. FRANCIS RUSSELL, of Bedford *(ibid* by same).
1570. Aug. 28. WILLIAM HYLTON, baron of Hilton *(ibid* by same).
1570, Aug. 28. SIMON MUSGRAVE *(ibid* by same).
1570, Aug. 28. HENRY GRAY, of Warke, Co. Northumberland *(ibid* by same).
1570, Aug. 28. HENRY CURWEN, of Workington *(ibid* by same).
1570, Aug. 28. ROBERT STAPLETON *(ibid* by same).
1570, Aug. 28. JEROME BOWES, of Staffordshire *(ibid* by same).
1570. JOHN GOODEWYNE (at Eythorpe in Waddesdon, Bucks., at William Dormer's house by the earl of Leicester, at the Queen's command).
1570. EDMUND ASHFIELD *(ibid)*.
1570. GEORGE PECKHAM *(ibid)*.
1570, ? July–Aug. ROBERT WHITNEY (at Windsor).
1570, ? July–Aug. EDWARD ASTON.
1570, ? July–Aug. ALEXANDER AVENON, lord mayor of London 1569 (at Somerset House, 1570 [doubtless an erratum for 1569].

1570. ROWLANDE HAYWARDE, of Wales, lord mayor of London (*ibid*).
1570. THOMAS SCOTT, of Kent, (*ibid*).
1570. CUTHBERT COLLINGBOURNE.
1570. JOHN MACCOGHLAN (dubbed in Ireland).
1571 [after Sept. 5]. JOHN CUTTE (CUTTES) (at Mr. Altham's, in Essex, by the earl of Leicester).
1571 [after Sept. 5]. THOMAS LUCAS (*ibid*).
1571 [? Oct.]. THOMAS BARRINGTON (at Greenwich).
1571 [? Oct.]. GEORGE CALVELEY (CALVERLEY), of Calveley.
1571 [? Oct.]. JOHN GILBERT (at Westminster).
1571 [? Oct.]. WILLIAM ALLEN, lord mayor of London.
1572. WALTER WALLER.
1572, ? Aug. WILLIAM FITZ WILLIAM, of Northamptonshire.
1572, ? Aug. EDWARD MAUNCELL (MANSFIELD), of Monmouthshire.
1572–3, Jan. CORMAC MAC TEIG MAC CARTIE, of Muskerry (in Ireland by Sir William Fitz Williams).
1572–3, Jan. CHARLES SOMERSET, of Wales (on the   of Jan.).
1572–3, Feb. 2 (Candlemas Day). LIONELL DUCKETT, lord mayor of London (at Greenwich [? *sic*. for 1571–2]).
1573, Apr. 26. JAMES FITZ GERALD of Decies, of the House of Dromaney (in Christchurch, Dublin, by Sir William Fitz Williams).
1573, Aug. 12. THOMAS GUILDEFORDE (at Rye).
1573, Aug. 12. ALEXANDER COLEPEPER (*ibid*).
1573, Aug. 12. THOMAS SHIRLEY (*ibid*).
1573, Aug. 12. THOMAS WALSINGHAM (*ibid*).
1573, Aug. 12. THOMAS PALMER of Angmering, sheriff of Surrey and Sussex (*ibid*).
1573, Aug. 12. JOHN PELHAM (*ibid*).
1573, Aug. 31. RICHARD BAKER, of Sisingherst (at Dover).
1573, Aug. 31. THOMAS VANE, sen., of Tunbridge, sheriff of Kent (*ibid*).
1573, Sept. WILLIAM WYNTER (at Gillingham).
1573, Sept. JAMES HALES (at Cobham Hall).
1573, ? Sept. or Oct. THOMAS (JOHN) HERBERT (at Greenwich).
1573, Oct. EDWARD STRADLINGE (*ibid*).
1574, May 2. JOHN RIVERS, lord mayor of London [lord mayor in 1573] (at Greenwich, 1574, May 2).
1574, Aug. 21. RICHARD BARKLEY (at Bristol).

1574, Aug. 21. JOHN TRACY *(ibid)*.
1574, Aug. 21. THOMAS PORTER (PARLER) *(ibid)*.
1574, Aug. 21. JOHN YONGE, of Somerset *(ibid)*.
1574, Aug. 21. WILLIAM MORGAN, of Wales *(ibid)*.
1574, Aug. 21. JOHN SIDNAM (SIDENHAM) *(ibid)*.
1574, Aug. 23. JOHN STOWELL, of Somersetshire (at Mr. Bonham's house).
1574, Aug. 23. JOHN HORNER, of Somersetshire *(ibid et tunc)*.
1574 [Aug. 23 ?]. GEORGE ROGERS, of Somersetshire [? *ibid*].
1574 [Aug. 23 ?]. HENRY PORTMAN [? *ibid*].
1574, Aug. 23. JOHN CLIFTON, of Somersetshire *(ibid et tunc)*.
1574, Sept. 9. EDWARD HERBERT (at Salisbury).
1574, Sept. 9. JOHN HORSEY [? *ibid*].
1574, Sept. JOHN HUNGERFORDE, [of] Oxfordshire [? *ibid*].
1574, Sept. HENRY KNYVET, of Wilts [? *ibid*].
1574, Sept. JAMES MERVIN (MARTIN), of Wilts [? *ibid*].
1574. THOMAS WROUGHTON, of Wilts [? *ibid*].
1574. JOHN DANVERS, of Wilts *(ibid)*.
1574, HENRY SHERRINGTON, of Wilts *(ibid)*.
1574. MATHEW ARONDELL, of Dorset.
1574. EDWARD BAYNTON, of Wilts.
1574. JOHN NORTON (MORTON), of Yorkshire.
1574. WILLIAM BABINGTON.
1574. JOHN HUBAND (HUBBERT), of Warwickshire, sheriff of Herefordshire.
1574. WILLIAM DRURY.
1574. EDWARD STRADLING.
1574, Nov. 6. CHRISTOPHER WRAY, lord chief justice of the King's Bench (at Hampton Court).
1575. JAMES HAWES, lord mayor of London [1574].
1575, July 18. HENRY BROOKE, *alias* Cobham, brother to lord Cobham (at Kenilworth).
1575. THOMAS CECIL (SIKSALT, SCISSALL) (son and heir to the lord treasurer), of Lincolnshire *(ibid)*.
1575. THOMAS STANHOP, of Co. Nottingham, sheriff of Notts *(ibid)*.
1575. ARTHUR BASSETT, of Cornwall *(ibid)*.
1575. THOMAS TRESHAM, of Northamptonshire *(ibid)*.
1575, ? Aug. FRANCYS WYLUGHBY, of Co. Nottingham (at Mydelton in his own house).
1575, ? Aug. WILLIAM CATESBY, of Co. Northampton *(ibid)*.

1575, ? Sept. JOHN FETYPLACE, of Berks (at Woodstock).
1575, Sept. EDMOND FETYPLACE (his cousin) *(ibid)*.
1575, Sept. GERARD CROKER, of Oxfordshire *(ibid)*.
1575. GEORGE HASTINGS.
1575, Sept. LUCAS DILLON (DE LION), lord chief baron of the Exchequer (in the church at Drogheda by Sir Henry Sydney, lord deputy).
(1575, ? Sept.) OWEN MACTOOLE O'GALLAGHER, sometimes erroneously called Owen O'Toole (by Sir Henry Sydney, lord deputy).
(1575, ? Sept. HUGH O'MAGENIS *(ibid)*.
1575, Oct. AMYAS POWLET, of Wilts (at Windsor).
1575–6, Feb. 19. AMBROSE NICHOLAS, lord mayor of London [in 1575] (at Whitehall 1575–6, Feb. 19, in the Parliament time).
1576, Mar. 25 (Sunday). RICHARD ROGERS, of Dorset (at Westminster on Sunday).
1576, Mar. 25. JOHN KELLIGREWE, of Cornwall *(ibid)*.
1576, Mar. 25. WILLIAM COURTENEY, of Devonshire.
1576, Apr. JOHN MAC OLIVERIUS (BOURKE), MAC WILLIAM EIGHTER (at Athlone by Sir Henry Sydney, lord deputy).
1576, Apr. 23. HENRY COLLEY (COULKE), of Castle Carbery, Co. Kildare (at Dublin, in Christ Church, on St. George's day, by Sir Henry Sydney lord deputy).
1576, May 14. WILLIAM MOORE, of Surrey (at Pirford, in Surrey, the seat of Sir John Wolley, by the earl of Leicester).
1576. FRANCIS CAREW, of Surrey.
1576. THOMAS BROWNE, of Betchworth Castle, Surrey.
1576, ? Aug. 5, 1577. WILLIAM DRURY, deputy lieutenant of Co. Bucks.
1576, ? Aug. WILLIAM WALDEGRAVE, of Essex (Suffolk).
1576. JOHN PETER, of Essex, sheriff of Essex and Herts.
1576. ROBERT D'OYLEY (DOYLE), of Oxford.
1576. WILLIAM HERBERT, of Wales.
1576. JOHN SMITHE, of Essex.
1576, Oct. 7. NICHOLAS MALBY, chief of the commissioners of Connaught (at Athlone).
1576–7, Jan. ROBERT BELL, of Norfolk, chief baron of the Exchequer.

KNIGHTS BACHELORS

1576–7, Feb. 17. (Shrove Sunday) RICHARD BULKELEY (BARKLEY), of Anglesea (of Co. Cheshire), at Whitehall the day before his marriage.

1576–7, Mar. JOHN LANGLEY, lord mayor of London [in 1576] (at Westminster).

1577 (? 1576), Mar. OWEN ARLYE [ARTYE] see 1579, May.

1577, May (18–23). JOHN BROCKET, of Herts (at Gorhambury, Herts, the house of Sir Nicholas Bacon, lord keeper of the Great Seal).

1577, May. HENRY COCKE, of Herts *(ibid)*.

1577, May. HENRY BOTELER, of Lancs. *(ibid)*.

1577, May. RAUF BREERTON, of Cheshire *(ibid)*.

1577, May. WILLIAM BOUTHE, of Co. Lincoln. [? Lancs.] *(ibid)*.

1577, Oct. JOHN GEOFFREY (JEFFERY), chief baron of the Exchequer (at Windsor).

1577. RICHARD GRENEVILLE, of Cornwall *(ibid)*.

1577, Nov. FRANCIS WALSINGHAM, principal secretary *(ibid)*.

1577, Nov. CHRISTOPHER HATTON, vice chamberlain and captain of the Guard *(ibid)*.

1577, Nov. THOMAS HENEAGE, of Essex, treasurer of the Chamber *(ibid)*.

1577, Dec. EDWARD HORSY, of Dorsetshire, captain of the Isle of Wight (at Hampton Court).

1577–8, Jan. THOMAS BOYNTON, of Aclam, Yorks. *(ibid)*.

1578, Feb. (on Shrove Tuesday). JOHN RADCLIFF, of Ordsall, Lancs. *(ibid)*.

1578. EDWARD LONGE, of Wilts.

1578. FRANCYS HYNDE, of Co. Cambridge.

1578, Apr. 24. HENRY HARRINGTON (at Dublin, in Christ Church).

1578, Apr. 24. HENRY BAGENAL (BAGNOL) *(ibid)*.

1578, May 1. THOMAS RAMSEY, lord Mayor of London [in 1577] at Greenwich).

1578, May 4. CHRISTOPHER HYLYARD (HILLYARD), of Yorkshire *(ibid)*.

1578, May 25. EDMOND TRAFFORD, of Lancashire.

1578, Aug. 1. GEORGE COLT, of Graysor Candish (at his house called Colts Hall in Suffolk).

1578, Aug. 5. (Saturday) PHILIP PARKER (at Bury St. Edmunds).

1578, Aug. 5. ARTHUR HEVENINGHAM (HEYGHAM), of Barrow *(ibid)*.

1578, Aug. 5. ROBERT JERMYN, of Rushbroke *(ibid)*.

1578, Aug. 5. WILLIAM SPRINGE, of Lavenham, Suffolk, sheriff of Suffolk *(ibid)*.
1578, Aug. 5. THOMAS KIDSON (RITSON), of Hengrave Hall, near Bury *(ibid)*.
1578, Aug. 5. THOMAS BERNARDESTON *(ibid)*.
1578, Aug. 22. RAUF SHELTON, of Shelton, Norfolk (at Norwich).
1578, Aug. 22. EDWARD CLEERE *(ibid)*.
1578, Aug. 22. WILLIAM PASTON, of Paston, Norfolk *(ibid)*.
1578, Aug. 22. NICHOLAS BACON, son to the lordkeeper *(ibid)*.
1578, Aug. 22. THOMAS KNYVET (KNEVET), of Ashwell Thorpe, Norfolk *(ibid)*.
1578, Aug. 22. ROBERT WOODE, mayor of Norwich *(ibid)*.
1578, Aug. 22. ? THOMAS GREEN, of Harpham, or FRANCIS GREEN, of Wilby Norfolk.
[1578, Aug. 22 ?] HENRY KNYVETT (? REVET).
1578, Aug. 26. (Tuesday) THOMAS GAWDY, of Gaudy Hall, Norfolk (at Woodrysing).
1578, Aug. 27. (Wednesday) ROGER WOODHOUSE (at Sir Edward Cleere's house in Thetford Blickling).
1578, Aug. 27. HENRY WOODHOUSE *(ibid)*.
1578, Nov. 15. ROGER MANWOODE, chief baron of the Exchequer (at Richmond).
1578. RICHARD PIPE, lord Mayor of London.
1578, Dec. 21 (Sunday). WILLIAM HERBERT (at Richmond on St. Thomas Day).
1578. ROBERT CLARKE, baron of the Exchequer [an erratum].
1578. ROWLAND CLARKE.
1578. WILLIAM CLARKE.
1578. JAMES WHITNEY.
1579, May. THOMAS FAYRFAX, of Yorkshire (at Westminster).
1579, May. THOMAS BROMLEY, of Shropshire, lord chancellor *(ibid)*.
1579, May. THOMAS LAYTON (LEIGHTON), of Shropshire *(ibid)*.
1579, May 28. BRIAN O'RORKE (O'ROWRWERKE) (at Dublin, in Christ Church, on Ascension day).
1579, May. OWEN MACCARTIE REAGH (dubbed in Ireland at Kilkenny), see 1577, Mar.
1579, June. HUGH CONOLAGH O'REILLY (dubbed in Ireland).
1579, July 5. GILBERT GERARD, of Lancs., attorney general (at Greenwich).
1579, Sept. DREWE DREWRY, of Norfolk (at Wanstead, in Essex).

KNIGHTS BACHELORS

1579, Sept. JOHN HIGHAM, of Suffolk (at Mulsham, Sir Thomas Mildmay's house in Essex).

1579, Sept. HENRY (EDMOND) HUDLESTON, of Cambridge, sheriff of Essex *(ibid)*.

1579, Sept. 14. WILLIAM PELHAM (by the Rt. Hon. Sir William Drurye, lord justice of Ireland).

1579, Sept. GEORGE BOURCHIER (by same in the field near Arklow, Tipperary).

1579, Sept. WILLIAM STANLEY (by same).

1579, Sept. PETER CARUE (CAREWE), the younger, of Laghlin (by same).

1579, Sept. EDWARD MOORE, of Melivant (by same).

1579, Sept. GEORGE (? WILLIAM) GORGES (by same).

1579, Sept. THOMAS PERROTT (by same).

1579, Sept. PATRICKE WALSHE, mayor of Waterford (by same at Waterford).

1579, Oct. 11. WILLIAM GERARD (GERALD), lord chancellor of Ireland (dubbed in Ireland by Sir William Pelham, lord justice).

1579, Oct. 11. EDWARD FITTON, the younger *(ibid)*.

1579. JOHN GODOLPHIN, of Cornwall.

1579. ARTHUR BASSET.

1579. WILLIAM RUSSELL.

1579. WILLIAM ZOUCH.

1579–80, Jan. 24 (Sunday). GEOFFREY FOULGIAM (FOULIAMBE), of Co. Derby (at Westminster).

1579–80, Jan. 24. JOHN BYRON, of Notts. *(ibid)*.

1579–80, Feb. 7. NICHOLAS WOODROFFE, lord mayor of London [in 1579] *(ibid)*.

1579–80, Feb. 7 (or 14). JOHN CHICHESTER, of Devon (at Westminster).

1579–80, Feb. 14. —— RYVET (RYVE) *(ibid)*.

1580, June 3. (Friday) GEORGE BROMLEY, of Salop, attorney to the Duchy of Lancaster (at Nonsuch).

1580 [after June 3]. HENRY WODERINGTON (WIDDRINGTON, WITHERINGTON), of Northumberland.

1580, Nov. 20. (Sunday) FRANCIS GODOLPHIN, of Cornwall (at Richmond).

1580, Nov. 20. (Sunday) —— SAINCTPOLL (ST. PAULE, SAMPOLE), of Lincolnshire (at Richmond).

1580. WILLIAM CAVENDISH.

1580, Nov. 30. JOHN DAWNAY, of Yorkshire (at Richmond, on Wednesday, being St. Andrew's day).

1580–1, Feb. 5. JOHN BRANCHE, lord mayor of London [in 1580] (at Westminster, on Shrove Sunday).

1581, Apr. 4. FRANCIS DRAKE (at Deptford, near Greenwich, on Tuesday, by the Queen's Majesty, being on the ship the "Golden Hind," wherewith he had travelled about the world).

1581, Apr. 4. GEORGE HART, son and heir of Sir Percival Hart, of Kent (at St. James's, near Westminster).

1581. THOMAS HUMFREY.

1581. JAMES HALES, of Kent.

1581, Sept. 10. WILLIAM RUSSELL (at St. Patrick's Church, Dublin, by lord Grey de Wilton, lord deputy of Ireland).

1581, Sept. 16. MCWILLIAM BOURKE (RICHARD AN IARAIN) (by same in Dublin Castle).

1581, Nov. 17. ROBERT DILLON, of Riverston, chief justice of Common Pleas (by same on Coronation day, an erratum for Accession day).

1581 (? 1583), Dec. 31. CHARLES FRAMLINGHAM, of Suffolk (at Westminster on Sunday).

1582, May 3. EDMOND ANDERSON, chief justice of Common Pleas (at the Court at Greenwich on Thursday).

1582, May 6. JAMES HERVY, lord mayor of London [in 1581] (at the Court at Greenwich on Sunday).

1582, May 22. EDWARD HOBBY (at Somerset Place in London on Tuesday, the day after his marriage with the baron of Hunsdon's daughter).

1582, July. JOHN SELBY, knight porter of Berwick (at Nonsuch).

1582, Sept. 6 or 7. ANTHONY COLCLOUGH, of Tinterne, Co. Wexford (in Ireland by the lords justices).

1582. CHARLES CAVENDISH, of Derby.

1582. CLOPTON GARGRAVE.

1582–3, Feb. 11 (12). THOMAS (ANTHONY) SANDᴌS (SANDE), of Throwley, Kent (at Barn Elmes, near Fulham, at Shrovetide).

[? after 1582–3, Feb. 12.] FRANCIS WILLOUGHBY, of Walterton.

1583, May 6. THOMAS BLANKE, lord mayor of London [in 1582] (at Greenwich on Sunday).

1583, May 5. JOHN BOURKE, baron of Leitrim (by the lords justices of Ireland in St. Patrick's Church on Rogation Sunday).

KNIGHTS BACHELORS

1583, May 5. THOMAS FLEMINGE, baron of Slane (by the same).

1583, May 5. *PATRICKE (PETER) BARNEWELL, baron of Tremleston (by the same).

1583, May 13. JAMES (? WILLIAM) DOWDALL (dubbed in Ireland).

1583, June 16 (Sunday). WILLIAM MOHUN.

1583. TYRLOW (TYRELAGH) O'BRIAN, of the House of Towmont, in Ireland (at Oatlands, by lord Hunsdon).

1583. JOHN ORELLY, of the Brenne, in Ireland (*ibid* by same or by the Queen).

1583, Oct. (? 5). EDMOND STAFFORD (at Oatlands on his going as ambassador resident to France).

1583, Nov. 3. WILLIAM HAYDON, of Norfolk (by the earl of Leicester at St. James's on Sunday).

1583, Nov. 3. PHILIP BOTELLER, of Co. Herts (*ibid* by same).

1583, Nov. RICHARD MACOLIVERIUS BOURKE, MacWilliam Eighter (dubbed in Ireland).

1583, Dec. 8 (? 1584, Jan. 8). GEORGE HENNEAGE, of Lincolnshire (at St. James's on Sunday).

1583, Dec. 8 (? 1584, Jan. 8). ROBERT (JAMES) SAVELL, bastard son of Sir Henry Savell (*ibid* or Westminster).

1583. FRANCIS FLEMING?

1583. DONOUGH OLIVER?

1583–4, Jan. 9 (? 15). JOHN (HENRY) HARINGTON, sheriff of Warwick (at Sir Thomas Henneage's house in London, by Sir Henry Sidney).

1583–4, Feb. 2. EDWARD OSBOURN (OSBORNE), lord mayor of London [in 1583] (at Westminster on Candlemas Day).

1583–4, Feb. 16 (? Jan. 9). RICHARD MALIVERER (at lord Lumley's house on Tower Hill, or at Westminster).

1583–4, Mar. 1. GEORGE SYDENHAM (at Whitehall).

1583–4, Mar. 5 (6, ? 16). RAUF BURGHCHIER (BOWSER), of Yorkshire (at Westminster, Whitehall) [Harl 6063, dates it 1585].

1583–4. JOHN BERHAM.

1584, May 17 (? Mar. 17, 1584–5). GEORGE CHAWORTH, of Wyverton, Co. Notts (at Greenwich on Sunday).

1584, June 9. EDWARD (MANNERS), 4th earl of Rutland (at (Greenwich).

*M.S. addit. 4763 reads Sir John Burgh, Sir Barnewall Fleming, and Sir Patrick Bar. of Tremleston.

1584, June 21. JAMES DOWDALL, of Knock, chief justice of Her Majesty's Bench (by Sir John Perrott, lord deputy general of Ireland).
1584, June 21. EDWARD WATERHOWES (by same in St. Patrick's Church).
1584, June 21. RICHARD BINGHAM (by same).
1584, June 21. NICHOLAS WHITE, master of the rolls (by same).
1584, Aug. THOMAS LESTRANGE (by same).
1584, Aug. WILLIAM COLLYER (by same).
1584, Aug. THOMAS JONES (by same).
1584, Aug. 18. EDWARD DYMOKE, of Lincolnshire.
1584. JOHN MCCOSTLY. [? *See* John MacCoghlan, p. 75 *supra*.]
1584–5, Jan. 6. WALTER RAWLEY [RALEIGH] (at Greenwich on Twelfth Day).
1584–5, Feb. 14. THOMAS [EDWARD] PULLYSON, lord mayor of London [in 1584] (at Somerset House).
1584–5, Mar. 7. MOYLE FYNCHE, of Kent (at Greenwich).
[1584–5 ? 1583–4, Mar. 7 or after]. HENRY BERKLEY, of Stoke, Co. Somerset.
1585, Apr. 4. RICHARD DYER, son and heir to the late lord chief justice of the Common Pleas.
1585. COTTON GARGRAVE, of Yorkshire, sheriff of Yorkshire.
1585, Apr. 13. THOMAS SCROOPE, son and heir to the lord Scrope (at Greenwich).
1585, May 1. ARTHUR O'NEILL (NELE) (in Ireland by the lord deputy).
1585, May 1. CHARLES O'CARROLL, of Ely (by same).
1585, May 1. MOROGH NE DOE O'FLAHERTY (by same).
1585, May 6. ANTHONY THOROLD, of Lincolnshire.
1585, May 16. HUBERT BOURKE, *alias* McDavie (at Dublin by Sir John Perrott, knight, lord deputy of Ireland).
1585, May 16. CUCONAGHT MAGUIRE (MCSKRINE) (in Ireland by the lord deputy).
1585, May 16. ROSSE MACMAHON *(ibid)*.
1585, May 16. CON OGE O'NEILL *(ibid)*.
1585, May 16. JOHN O'DOHERTY *(ibid)*.
1585, May 16. FINEEN (FLORENCE) O'DRISCOLL MORE *(ibid)*.
1585, May 16. THOMAS BARRY OGE *(ibid)*.
1585, June 18. ROBERT SOUTHWELL (at Theobalds, on Friday, on the removing day).
1585, June 18. HENRY CONINGESBY *(ibid)*.

1585, Oct. 14. JOHN ARONDELL, of Tolverne (at Richmond).
1585, Nov. 27. PIERCE FITZJAMES FITZGERALD, of Ballysonan, Co. Kildare (by the lord deputy of Ireland).
1585-6, Jan. 9. BERNARD DRAKE (at Greenwich, on Sunday).
1585-6, Feb. 6. WOLSTAN DIXIE, lord mayor of London [in 1585] (*ibid* on Sunday).
1585-6. WILLIAM BOWES, of Stretham, in the bishopric of Durham (at Greenwich).
1585-6, Feb. 24. JOHN TYRRELL, of the Pass, Co. Westmeath (by the lord deputy of Ireland).
1585-6, Feb. 28. GEORGE CAREWE (in Christ Churche by same).
1585-6, Feb. 28. PATRICK BARNEWALL, of Gracedien and Turvey, Co. Dublin (by same).
1585-6, Mar. 2. ANDREW NOEL, of Dalby, Co. Leicester (at Greenwich on Wednesday).
1585-6. CHRISTOPHER WANDESFORD, of Kirtlington, Co. York (*ibid*).
1586, June 24. RICHARD MOLYNEULX, of Sefton, Co. Lancs. (*ibid*, on Midsummer Day, being Thursday).
1586, June 24. JOHN MONSON, of Lincolnshire (*ibid*) [Harl MS. 6063 says 1585].
1586 (? 1588), July 23. JOHN OWGAN (of Beleston) (by the lord deputy of Ireland).
1586. ANTHONY SPILLMAN.
1586. EDWARD WINGFIELD, of Kimbolton.
1586. HENRY CONSTABLE.
1586. THOMAS GORGES.
1586. RICHARD MALORY.
1586. MARTIN SKINKE, a Dutchman (in the Low Countries by the earl of Leicester).
1586. JOHN NORRYS (in Holland by Robert, earl of Leicester).
1586. ROBERT (DEVEREUX), 19th earl of Essex (*ibid* by same).
1586. GEORGE (TUCHET), 11th lord Audley (*ibid* by same).
1586. WILLIAM RUSSELL (*ibid* by same).
1586. HENRY PALMER (*ibid* by same).
1586. EDWARD DENNY (*ibid* by same).
1586. WILLIAM HATTON (*ibid* by same).
1586. HENRY UMPTON (UNTON), (in Holland by Robert, earl of Leicester).
1586. HENRY NORRIS (*ibid* by same).
1586. HENRY NOELL (*ibid* by same).

KNIGHTS BACHELORS

1586 (? Oct. 7). ROBERT SYDNEY (*ibid* by same).
1586. JOHN BORRUGH (BURROWES) (*ibid* by same).
1586. HENRY GOODYEAR (*ibid* by same).
1586. GEORGE FARRER (FARMOUR) (*ibid* by same).
1586. JOHN WINGFIELD (*ibid* by same).
1586. GEORGE DIGBY (*ibid* by same).
1586. PHILLIP BUTLER (*ibid* by same).
1586. THOMAS DENNYS (*ibid* by same).
1586. ROGER WILLIAMS (*ibid* by same).
1586. WILLIAM READ (*ibid* by same).
1586. EDWARD STANLEY (*ibid* by same).
1586. EDWARD NORRIS (*ibid* by same).
1586. THOMAS HORSEY (*ibid* by same).
1586. RICHARD DYER (*ibid* by same).
1586. EDWARD (EDMOND) CARY (*ibid* by same).
1586. JOHN PASTON (PAYTON or PAYNTON) (*ibid* by same).
1586. WILLIAM KNOWLES (*ibid* by same).
1586. BARTHOLOMEW BAFFORD (BAMPFORD), a Scot (*ibid* by same).
1586. ALEXANDER STEWARD, a Scot (*ibid* by same).
1586. ROWLAND YORK (*ibid* by same. This name is given in Ashmolean M.S. 840 (fo. 161) but is erased).
1586. HENRY NORTH (*ibid* by same).
1586. THOMAS GEORGE (*ibid* by same).
1586. HENRY YARTLEY (*ibid* by same).
1586. EVAN LLOYD (*ibid* by same).
1586. HENRY JONES (*ibid* by same).
1586. JOHN LLOYD (FLOYD) (*ibid* by same).
1587. HENRY NOWELL, of Leicester.
1587. GEORGE BOND, lord mayor of London.
1587. LEWIS DYVE.
1587. JOHN MANNERS.
1587. JOHN ROPER.
1587. HENRY POOLE, at Richement (Richmond).
1587, June 11. GEORGE BARNES, lord mayor of London (on Sunday by the lord chamberlain).
1587, June 18. GEORGE SAVELL (on Sunday, at Greenwich).
1587, June 18. THOMAS THROGMORTON (*ibid*).
1587, July (?) 10. WALTER LEWSON (LEVESON), sheriff of Staffordshire (at Theobald's).

KNIGHTS BACHELORS

1587. —— MORYSON.

1587, Nov. 11 (12). HENRY GREY (on Sunday).

1587, Nov. 11. HORATIO PALAVICHINI (PALEVESYN) (on Sunday).

1587, Nov. 17. THOMAS WILLIAMS (by Sir John Perrott, lord deputy of Ireland).

1587, Nov. 17. OGHY O'HANLON (by same).

1587, Nov. 21. JOHN PAGINGTON (PACKINGTON), (on Tuesday at the lord admiral's).

1587, Dec. 7. THOMAS MORGAN (by the earl of Leicester at his embarking at Flushing on Thursday).

1587, Dec. 7. EDWARD WINGFELD (*ibid* by same).

1587, Dec. 7. HUGH CHOLMELEY (*ibid* by same).

1587, Dec. 7. CHARLES BLOUNT (*ibid* by same).

1587, Dec. 7. FRANCYS KNOLLES (*ibid* by same).

1587, Dec. 7. THOMAS WEST (*ibid* by same).

1588, Apr. (May) 14. EDWARD BARKLEY (*ibid* by same).

1588, May 1.* NICHOLAS ST. LAWRANCE, son and heir to lord Houth (*ibid* by same).

1588, May 1 (? June 30). WILLIAM BRERETON † (?), of Brereton in Cheshire (*ibid* by same).

1588, July 4. GEORGE CLYVE, of Cheshire (by Sir William Fitz Williams, knt., lord deputy general of Ireland, who received the sword the last day of June, 1588).

1588, July 25. THOMAS HOWARD, lord Howard (at sea, on board the "Ark," by the admiral, lord Howard of Effingham).

1588, July 25. JOHN HAWKINS (*ibid* by same).

1588, July 25. MARTIN FROBISHER (*ibid* by same).

1588, ? July. Lord EDM. SHEFFIELD (at sea by same).

1588, ? July. ROGER TOWNSEND (*ibid* by same).

1588, ? July. GEORGE BEESTON, of Chester (*ibid* by same).

1588, Oct. 6. THOMAS NORRYS, armiger, vice regent of Munster (in the Cathedral Church of Dublin by same). The lord deputy took his journey into Ulster for Connaught the 4th of November, and came home the 23rd of December, in which time he made four knights, viz.:—

1588. GEORGE BYNGHAM, of Ballemote, in the County of Sligo, brother to the chief justice of Connaught (by same).

1588. THOMAS MASTERSON (by same).

1588. HENRY DUKE (by same).

---

* Addit. 4763 reads 1588, Sir Murthowne do offard before Sir Nicholas Lawrence. *See* 1585, May 1.

† M.S. addit. 4763 adds Sir John Ougan, Sir Thomas Johnes (the Coronation day), Sir Edw. Varlett.

KNIGHTS BACHELORS

1588. TIRLOUGH LENAGH O'NELE (by same).
1588. THOMAS WILFORD (in the Low Countries by the lord Willoughby).
1588. FRANCIS VERE (*ibid* by same).
1588. JOHN POOLEY (*ibid* by same).
1588. JOHN POINTZ (PORE) (*ibid* by same).
1588. NICHOLAS PARKER (*ibid* by same).
1588. THOMAS KNOWLES (KNOLLES) (*ibid* by same).
1588. JOHN SCOTT (*ibid* by same).
1588. EDWARD UVEDALL (*ibid* by same).
1588. CHARLES DANVERS (*ibid* by same).
1588. CHRISTOPHER BLOUNT (*ibid* by same).
1588. EDWARD ASTON.
1588. PAUL BACKES, governor of Bergen, by lord Willoughby.
1588. THOMAS BASKERVILLE.
1588. MARTIN CALTHORPE, lord mayor of London.
1588. GEORGE (CLIFFORD), 3rd earl of Cumberland.
1588. ANTHONY MANEY, of Kent.
1588. JOHN SPENCER.
1588. GEORGE TRENCHARD.
1588-9, Jan. 5. GEFFERY FENTON, secretary (by the lord deputy of Ireland).
1588-9, ? Jan. 5. NICHOLAS LESTRANGE (by same).
1589, Aug. 12. RICHARD SHEE, of Kilkenny (at Kilkenny, by Sir William Fitz Williams, lord deputy of Ireland).
1589, Oct. 26. EDWARD DENNY, of Walton Abay, in the County of Essex (by same).
1589, Oct. 26. THOMAS SHIRLEY (at Kilkenny by same).
1589. WALTER LONGE, of Wracksall, in Wiltshire (by same).
1589. THOMAS SHIRLEY, jun.
1589. WILLIAM BEVILL.
1589. WILLIAM LEIGH.
1589. JOHN LEVESON.
1589. THOMAS LLOYDE, *alias* Fludd.
1589 (? 1588). RICHARD MARTIN, lord mayor of London [an erratum, Martin was not lord mayor till 1593. ? Read afterwards lord mayor].
1589. WILLIAM SACKVILL.

1590–1, Jan. 14 (24). HUGHE MAGWIER (in Trinity Church, Dublin, by the Rt. Hon. Sir William Fitz Williams, knight, lord deputy general of Ireland.
1590–1. MICHAEL BLOUNT.
1590–1. EDWARD FERRERS.
1590–1. JOHN HART, lord mayor of London [in 1589].
1590–1. RALPH HORSEY.
1590–1. JOHN HUNGERFORD.
1590–1. RICHARD WELCHE.
1591. JOHN ALLOT, lord mayor of London [in 1590].
1591, Apr. 4. GEORGE DELVES (dubbed in Ireland on Easter day by the lord deputy).
1591, May 20. ROBERT CECILL (? at Theobalds).
1591. CONYERS CLIFFORD.
1591 (1592). ANTHONY COPE.
1591. WALTER COVERT.
1591. FRANCIS DARCY.
1591. ROBERT GARDINER.
1591. HENRY GUILDFORD, of Bennenden, Kent.
1591. WALTER HARCOURT.
1591. JOHN HICKFORD.
1591. CLEMENT (JOHN) HIGHAM.
1591. HENRY KILLEGREW.
1591. EDWARD LAYTON.
1591. RICHARD PAWLETT.
1591. WALTER SANDES.
1591. ANTHONY SHELLEY.
1591. JOHN SEYMOUR.
1591. THOMAS WEST.
1591, July 1. NICHOLAS DEVEREUX, of Co. Wexford (dubbed in Ireland).
1591, Aug. 21. GEORGE BROWNE (2nd son of Viscount Montagu) (at Cowdray, by the lord admiral).
1591, Aug. 21. ROBERT DORMER (*ibid* by same).
1591, Aug. 21. HENRY GORING (*ibid* by same).
1591, Aug. 21. HENRY GLEMHAM (*ibid* by same).
1591, Aug. 21. JOHN CARRELL (*ibid* by same).
1591, Aug. 21. NICHOLAS PARKER (*ibid* by same).
1591, ? Sept. THOMAS CHALLONER (by the French King).

1591, Sept. DEVEREUX POOLE (by same).
1591, Sept. CHRISTOPHER LYDCOTE (by same).
1591, Sept. THOMAS WILKES (by same).
1591, Sept. ? 27 (1592, Oct. 8).
    CHARLES PERCY (before Rouen by Robert, earl of Essex).
    WILLIAM (EDWARD) BROOKE (*ibid* by same).
    THOMAS CONISBYE (*ibid* by same).
    THOMAS GERRARD (*ibid* by same).
    JOHN TRACY (*ibid* by same).
    JOHN WOOTTON (*ibid* by same).
    RICHARD ACTON (*ibid* by same).
    HENRY JONES (*ibid* by same).
    FRANCIS ALLYN (ALLEN) (*ibid* by same).
    EDWARD (EDMOND) YORKE (*ibid* by same).
    MATHEW MORGAN (*ibid* by same).
    THOMAS FAIRFAX (*ibid* by same).
    NICHOLAS CLIFFORD (*ibid* by same).
    ROBERT DRURY (*ibid* by same).
    THOMAS JERMYN (*ibid* by same).
    WILLIAM WOODHOWSE (*ibid* by same).
    WILLIAM DAWTREY (HAWTRY) (*ibid* by same).
    GRIFFIN MARKHAM (*ibid* by same).
    HENRY DANVERS of Dantsey, Wilts (*ibid* by same).
    EDWARD HASTINGS (*ibid* by same).
    FERDINAND GORGE (*ibid* by same).
1591, Oct. 24. THOMAS COLECLUGH, of Tintern, Co. Wexford (by Sir William Fitz Williams, lord deputy of Ireland).
1591-2, Feb. MICHAEL MOLINES (dubbed in Ireland by the lord deputy).
1592, Sept. JOHN HIGFORD (HICKFORD), lord of the manor of Alderton (by the Queen in the Progress? at Alderton).
1592. WILLIAM BRIDGES.
1592. WILLIAM BRINKERD (BRUNKARD).
1592. HENRY BROMLEY, sheriff of Worcester.
1592. CHRISTOPHER EDMONDS.
1592. WILLIAM EYRE.
1592, Sept. JOHN FORTESCUE.
1592. HUMFREY FOSTER of Aldermaston, Berks.

KNIGHTS BACHELORS

1592. RICHARD FYNES.
1592. FRANCIS HASTINGES.
1592. THOMAS LUCY, jun.
1592. HENRY NEWTON.
1592. WILLIAM PERIAM.
1592. JOHN POPHAM.
1592. JOHN PUCKERINGE.
1592. THOMAS READ.
1592. WILLIAM SPENCER.
1592. WILLIAM WEBB, lord mayor of London [in 1591].
1592. HENRY WINSTON.
1592. JOHN WOOLLEY, of Pirford.
1592. EDWARD WOTTON.
1593, May 28. THOMAS MOORE, of Crohan, in King's County (dubbed in Ireland by the lord deputy).
1593. THOMAS NAPPER.
1593. WILLIAM ROWE.
1593. ANTHONY ST. LEGER.
1593. WILLIAM WESTON.
1593, June 17. EDWARD KYNASTON DE OTLEY, in Salop (by the lord deputy of Ireland).
1593, June 17. ANTHONY MANEY (MANE), of Biddenden, in Kent (by same).
1593, June 17. GEORGE VILLIERS (WILLERS) (by same).
1593, July. EDWARD FITZ GERALD, of Tecroghan (by same).
1593, Oct. 15. JOHN HOLLES, of Haughton, in Nottingham (by same).
1593, Nov. 9 or 11. ROBERT SALISBURIE (by same).
1593, Nov. 17. RAPHE LANE (by same).
1593, Nov. 17. GEORGE COLLEY, of Edendere, *alias* Colleiston, in King's Co. (by same).
1593. HENRY OUGHTRED (by same).
1593, Dec. 2. DUDLEY LOFTUS (by same).
1593, Dec. 2. EDWARD HERBERT, of Monaster Orys, in King's Co. (by same).
1594, May 19. JOHN DOWDALL, of Kilfinny, Co. Limerick (by same on Whit Sunday).
before 1594, May 30. EDWARD RATCLYFFE, afterwards 13th earl of Sussex.

1594, July 7. THOMAS POSTHUMUS HOBY (in Ireland by the lord deputy).
1594, Aug. 11. STEPHEN THORNEHURST (by same).
1594, Aug. 30. Prince HENRY of Scotland (by his father, at his baptism).
1594, Aug. 30. WILLIAM STEWART, of Houston (by king James of Scotland at the baptism of his son).
1594, Aug. 30. ROBERT BRUCE, of Clackmannan (by same).
1594, Aug. 30. JOHN BOSWELL, of Balmowrow (by same).
1594, Aug. 30. JAMES SCHAW, of Salquhy (by same).
1594, Aug. 30. JOHN MURRAY, of Ethilstoun (by same).
1594, Aug. 30. WILLIAM MONTEITH, of Kerse (by same).
1594, Aug. 30. ALEXANDER FRASER, of Fraserburgh (by same).
1594, Aug. 30. JOHN LINDSAY, of Dunrod (by same).
1594, Aug. 30. GEORGE LEVINGSTON, of Ogilface (by same).
1594, Aug. 30. JAMES FORESTER, of Torwood-head (by same).
1594, Aug. 30. ANDREW BALFOURE, of Strathour (by same).
1594, Aug. 30. WALTER DUNDAS, of Over Newlistoun (by same).
1594, Aug. 30. JOHN BOSWEL, of Glasemont (by same).
1594, Aug. 30. GEORGE ELPHINGSTOUN, of Blytherhood (by same).
1594, Aug. 30. WILLIAM LEVINGSTON, of Darnechester (by same).
1594, Aug. 30. DAVID MELDRUM, of New-hall (by same).
1594, Sept. 1. WILLIAM CLARKE (upon a hill near Enniskillen, which was then distressed: by Sir William Russell, kt., lord deputy of Ireland).
1594, Sept. 1. ROBERT NEEDHAM (by same).
1595, Apr. 20. EDWARD MONINS (by the Rt. Hon. Sir William Russell, kt., lord deputy general of Ireland, at Mone).
after 1595, May 22. JOHN CONYERS, of Sockbourne, sheriff of Durham.
1595, Aug. 24. EDWARD BRABAZON, of Estwell, in Leicestershire (in Christchurch by Sir William Russell lord deputy of Ireland).
1595, Aug. 24. WILLIAM WALDEGRAVE, of Smallbrige, in Suffolk (*ibid* by same).
1595, Nov. 9. RICHARD WINGFIELD, of Northamptonshire (*ibid* by same).
1595 (1593). GEORGE MANNERING.
1595. WILLIAM READ.
1595. JOHN SPENCER, lord mayor of London [in 1594].
1595. EDWARD WINTER.

1595–6, Jan. 4. HENRY WARREN (in Christchurch by the Rt. Hon. Sir William Russell, knt., lord deputy general of Ireland).
1596, Apr. 11. JOHN NORTH, son and heir to the lord North (*ibid* by same).
1596, ? June ? 22.

    ROBERT (RADCLYFFE) 12th earl of Sussex (at Cadiz, 1596, by the lord admiral and the earl of Essex).

    DON CHRISTOFERO (*ibid* by same).

    Count LODOVICK (*ibid* by same).

    Lord HERBERT (*ibid* by same).

    Lord BURKE (*ibid* by same).

    SAMUEL BAGNALL (*ibid* by same).

    ARTHUR SAVAGE (*ibid* by same).

    WILLIAM HOWARD (*ibid* by same).

    GEORGE DEVEREUX (*ibid* by same).

    HENRY NEVILL (*ibid* by same).

    EDWIN RICH (*ibid* by same).

    ANTH. ASHLEY (*ibid* by same).

    Monsieur LAVINS (*ibid* by same).

    Monsieur EDMARKER (EGMORLES) (*ibid* by same).

    HENRY LEONARD (*ibid* by same).

    RICHARD LEWSON (LEVESON) (*ibid* by same).

    HORATIO VERE (*ibid* by same).

    ARTHUR THROGMORTON (*ibid* by same).

    MILES CORBET (*ibid* by same).

    EDWARD CONWAY, (*ibid* by same).

    OLIVER LAMBERT (*ibid* by same).

    ANTHONY COOKE (*ibid* by same).

    JOHN TOWNSEND (*ibid* by same).

    CHRISTOPHER HAIDON (HEYDON) (*ibid* by same).

    FRANCIS POPHAM (*ibid* by same).

    PHILIP WOODHOWSE (*ibid* by same).

    ALEXANDER CLIFFORD (*ibid* by same).

    MORIS BARKLEY (*ibid* by same).

    CHARLES BLOUNT (*ibid* by same).

    GEORGE GIFFORD (*ibid* by same).

    ROBERT CROSSE (*ibid* by same).

    JOHN SCUDAMOUR (*ibid* by same).

    WILLIAM (JOHN or PIERRE) LEIGH (*ibid* by same).

KNIGHTS BACHELORS 93

1596, ? June ? 22.
    JOHN LEA (at Cadiz by the earl of Essex).
    RICHARD WAYNMAN (*ibid* by same).
    RICHARD WESTON (*ibid* by same).
    JAMES WOOTTON (*ibid* by same).
    RICHARD RANDALL (RUDDALL) (*ibid* by same).
    ROBERT MANSFIELD (MANSELL) (*ibid* by same).
    WILLIAM MOUNSON (*ibid* by same).
    JOHN BOWLLES (BAILLES, BOLLES) (*ibid* by same).
    EDWARD BOWES (*ibid* by same).
    HUMFRY DREWELL (*ibid* by same).
    AMYAS PRESTON (*ibid* by same).
    ROBERT REMINGTON (*ibid* by same).
    JOHN BUTTS (BUCKE) (*ibid* by same).
    JOHN MORAN (MORGAN) (*ibid* by same).
    JOHN ALDRIGG (ALDRICH) (*ibid* by same).
    JOHN SHELTON (*ibid* by same).
    WILLIAM ASHENDON (*ibid* by same).
    MATHEW BROWNE (*ibid* by same).
    THOMAS ACTON (*ibid* by same).
    THOMAS GATES (*ibid* by same).
    WILLIAM (GELLIAN) MERRICK (*ibid* by same).
    THOMAS SMYTH (*ibid* by same).
    WILLIAM POLEY (POOLEY) (*ibid* by same).
    THOMAS PALMER (*ibid* by same).
    ROBERT LOVELL (*ibid* by same).
    JOHN STAFFORD (*ibid* by same).
    JOHN GILBERT (*ibid* by same).
    WILLIAM HARVY (*ibid* by same).
    JOHN GRAY (*ibid* by same).
    BALDWIN MEDKIR (MEDKERKE, METHKIRK) (*ibid* by same).
    GERRAT HARVY, of Co. Bedford (*ibid* by same).
1596. HENRY BILLINGSLEY, lord mayor of London.
1596 (1595). ARTHUR CHICHESTER.
1596. OCHEMACH DRINIR.
1596. ROBERT DUDLEY.
1596. EDWARD DYER.
1596. —— GUILFORD.

KNIGHTS BACHELORS

1596. RICHARD LEVER, a stranger.
1596. BARENTINE MOLINES, junr.
1596. JOHN PEYTON.
1596. JOHN STANHOP.
1596. WILLIAM WRAY.
1596–7, Mar. 4. JOHN CHICHESTER, of Devonshire (in the Glynes, where that traytor, Feogh Mac Hugh, some tyme remayned; by the Rt. Hon. Sir William Russell, knt., lord deputy general of Ireland).
1597, Mar. 27. WILLIAM LANE, of Horton, in the County of Northampton (in St. Patrick's Church by same).
1597, May 8. CALISTENES BROOKE, of Sutton, in the County of Kent (in the Glynes by same).
1597, May 8. RICHARD TREVOR, of Trevallin, in the County of Denbigh (*ibid* by same).
1597, May 8. THOMAS MARIA WINGFIELD (*ibid* by same).
1597, July 19. THOMAS WALLER, of Branchele, in the County of Kent (at the Fort of the Blackwater by Thomas Lord Burgh, lord deputy of Ireland).
1597, Aug. 15. CHRISTOPHER PLUNKETT (at his manor house of Donsoghly by same).
1597, Sept. 24. HENRY BROUNKER, of Westham, in the County of Essex (at Drogheda by same).
1597, Oct. 30. NICHOLAS WALSHE (by Sir Thomas Norreys, lord justice of Ireland).
1597, Oct. 30. WARHAM ST. LEGER (by same).
1597. BASSINGBOURNE GAWDY.
1597. ARTHUR GORGES.
1597. HUGH JAMES (MAC JAMES).
1597. RICHARD SALTINGSTALL (SALTINGSTONE), lord mayor of London.
1597. ANTHONY WINGFIELD.
1597. HENRY (WRIOTHESLEY), 4th earl of Southampton (at the Azores [by the earl of Essex]).
1597. THOMAS EGERTON (*ibid* by same).
1597. THOMAS VAVASOR (*ibid* by same).
1597. LODOVICK GREVILL (*ibid* by same).
1597–8, Jan. 22. WALTER BUTLER, son and heir to John Butler, third brother to the earl of Ormond (in St. Patrick's Church by Adam Loftus, archbishop of Dublin, and Sir Robert Gardiner, knt., chief justice of the Queen's Bench, Ireland, joint lords justices of Ireland).

KNIGHTS BACHELORS 95

1597-8, Jan. 22. JAMES BUTLER, of Lismalin (in St. Patrick's Church by the same).

1597-8, Feb. JONATHAN TRELANY (at Whitehall on Shrove Tuesday).

1597-8, Feb. WILLIAM STROWDE *(ibid)*.

1597-8, Feb. GEORGE MORE, of the West *(ibid)*.

1597-8, Feb. 28 ? 29. GEORGE CARY, of Cockington (at Whitehall, the last day of February).

1598, May 25. THOMAS VANE, of Kent.

1598, June 17. GARRETT AYLMER (in Christ Church, by Adam Loftus, archbishop of Dublin, and Sir Robert Gardiner, knt., chief justice of the Queen's Bench, Ireland, joint lords justices of Ireland).

1598, June 18. MICHILL SANDS (SONDS) (at Greenwich).

1598, June 18. THOMAS RERESBY *(ibid)*.

1598, July. HENRY (BROOKE), 11th lord Cobham (at Nonsuch).

1598, Sept. 24. RICHARD PERCY (in Christ Church, by Adam Loftus, archbishop of Dublin, and Sir Richard Gardiner, *ut supra)*.

1598, Sept. 24. ROBERT ASHEFIELD *(ibid* by same).

1599, Mar. 25. RENALD MOHUN.

1599, Apr. 8. JOHN EGERTON (in Christ Church, by Adam Loftus, archbishop of Dublin, and Sir Robert Gardiner, *ut supra*).

1599, Apr. 25. STEPHEN SOHAM (SOAME, SOME), lord mayor of London [in 1598] (at Greenwich).

1599, May 5. THOMAS MOSTEN (at Dublin, by Robert, earl of Essex, lord lieutenant of Ireland).

1599, May 9. THOMAS TASBOROUGH, of Harwich, in the county of Buckingham (at Dublin by same).

1599, May 17. FRANCIS RUSHE (at Maryborough, the Fort of Lease, by same).

1599, May 22. TERENCE O'DEMPSY (at Kiltenan, in Mounster, by same).

1599, May 30. ROGER (MANNERS), 6th earl of Rutland (at Caluri Castle by same).

1599, June 12. FRANCIS BARKLEY (at Asketon by same).

1599, June 19. GEORGE THORNTON (at Killmallocke by same).

1599, June 20. JAMES DEVEREUX (at Sir John Colley's Towne by same).

KNIGHTS BACHELORS

1599, June 30. RICHARD MASTERSON (at his own house at Fernes by the earl of Essex, lord lieutenant of Ireland).
1599, July 12. THOMAS (GREY), 15th lord Grey, of Wilton (at Dublin by same).
1599, July 12. Lord MOUNTEAGLE (*ibid* by same).
1599, July 12. THOMAS WEST (*ibid* by same).
1599, July 12. ROBERT VERNON (*ibid* by same).
1599, July 12. HENRY CARY (*ibid* by same).
1599, July 12. ARTHUR CHAMPERNOUN (*ibid* by same).
1599, July 12. WILLIAM CONSTABLE (*ibid* by same).
1599, July 12. JOHN DAVYS (*ibid* by same).
1599, July 12. JOHN POOLEY (POLEY) (*ibid* by same).
1599, July 12. CAREY (CAREW) REYNELL (RAYNOLDES, REGINALD) (*ibid* by same).
1599, July 12. GEORGE MANNERS (*ibid* by same).
1599, July 12. EDWARD (CROMWELL), 4th lord Cromwell (*ibid* by same).
1599, July 13. WILLIAM GODOLPHIN (*ibid* by same).
1599, July 13. WILLIAM COURTNEY (*ibid* by same).
1599, July 13. FRANCIS LACON (*ibid* by same).
1599, July 15. ROBERT BASSETT (*ibid* by same).
1599, July 22. ROBERT CONSTABLE (*ibid* by same).
1599, July 22. EDWARD WARREN (*ibid* by same).
1599, July 22. CUTHBERT HALSELL (*ibid* by same).
1599, July 24. HEWETT OSBURNE (in Meath by same).
1599, July 24. HUGH O'CONNOR DUNE (in the camp at the meeting with Sir Conyers Clifford, who fought well the day before, by same).
1599, July 24. JOHN MACCOGHLAN (*ibid* by same).
1599, July 24. MULLMORE MACSWINE A DOE (*ibid* by same).
1599, July 24. THEOBALD DILLON (*ibid* by same).
1599, July 30. JOCELIN PERCY (at the rising of the camp, after the fight in Ophaley, by same).
1599, July 30. THOMAS BOURKE (BURGH) (by same).
1599, July 30. WILLIAM WARREN (by same).
1599, July 30. HENRIE LINDLEY (by the earl of Essex, lord Lieutenant of Ireland, at the rising of the camp after the fight in Ophaley).
1599, July 30. THEOPHILUS FINCH (by same).
1599, July 30. JOHN VAUGHAN (by same).

KNIGHTS BACHELORS

1599, July 30.   WILLIAM LOVELACE (by same).
1599, July 30.   JOHN HARRINGTON (by same).
1599, July 30.   WILLIAM GASCOIGNE (by same).
1599, Aug. 4.   ROBERT DIGBY (at Dublin by same).
1599, Aug. 4.   EDWARD BLUNT (BLOUNTE) (*ibid* by same).
1599, Aug. 5.   HENRY GOODEARE (*ibid* by same).
1599, Aug. 5.   EDWARD ESSEX (*ibid* by same).
1599, Aug. 5.   WILLIAM CORNEWALLYS (*ibid* by same).
1599, Aug. 5.   RICHARD LOVELACE (*ibid* by same).
1599, Aug. 5.   EDWARD READ (*ibid* by same).
1599, Aug. 5.   RICHARD (EDWARD) MORGAN (*ibid* by same).
1599, Aug. 5.   HENRY CAREWE (*ibid* by same)
1599, Aug. 5.   RICHARD MORISON (*ibid* by same).
1599, Aug. 5.   JOHN HAYDON (*ibid* by same).
1599, Aug. 5.   FRANCIS MERRICKE (*ibid* by same)..
1599, Aug. 5.   CHARLES WILLMOTE (*ibid* by same).
1599, Aug. 5.   EDWARD MICHELBORNE (*ibid* by same).
1599, Aug. 6.   GEORGE LESTER (LEYCESTER) (at Dublin Castle by same).
1599, Aug. 6.   JOHN CROFTES (at Dublin by same).
1599, Aug. 6.   HENRY WALLOP (*ibid* by same).
1599, Aug. 6.   JOHN SAMES (by same).
1599, Aug. 6.   HENRY FOOKES (FOULXE) (by same).
1599, Aug. 6.   WILLIAM BOUSTRED (BOWLSTRAD) (by same).
1599, Aug.   SIMON WESTON (by same).
1599, Aug. 31.   JOHN DRAYCOTT (by same).
1599, Aug. 31.   WILLIAM CLOVELL (by same).
1599, Aug. 31.   JOHN BROCKETT (by same).
1599, Sept. 6.   CHARLES MANNORS (by same).
1599, Sept. 6.   FULKE CONWAY (by same).
1599, Sept. 6.   HENRY FOLLIOTT (by same).
1599, Sept. 6.   JOHN CHAMBERLAINE (by same).
1599, Sept. 6.   ROBT. YAXELEY (by same).
1599, Sept. 6.   GERRATT MOORE (by same).
1599, Sept. 6.   JOHN TALBOT (by same).
1599, Sept. 10. JONATHAN PETTO (by same).
1599, Sept. 10. ROBART BROOKE (by same).

G

1599, Sept. 24. ROBERT OSBURNE (at Sir Robte Gardiner's house in Dublin by same).
1599, Sept. 24. JOHN POOLEY (*ibid* by same).
1599, Sept. 24. JOHN RATCLIFF (on the sandes by same).
1599, Sept. 24. THOMAS LOFTUS (*ibid* by same).
1599, Sept. 24. EDWARD LOFTUS (*ibid* by same).
1599, Sept. 24. EDWARD BAYNHAM (*ibid* by same).
1599. EDWIN SANDES (by Adam Loftus, archbishop of Dublin, and Sir George Cary, knt., treasurer at war, Ireland, and joint lords justices of Ireland).
1599 (1591). EDWARD BROOKE.
1599. GEORGE BOOTH.
1599 (1601). RICHARD FETIPLACE.
1599. PETER LEE, of Ireland.
1599 [? 1596, 1600]. RICHARD LEE (? 1596, Peter Lee, jun.).
1599. JOHN LYNE.
1599. JOHN SAVAGE.
1599. FRANCIS STAFFORD.
1599 [?]. RICHARD CHAMPERNON.
[1599–1600], Jan. RICHARD HAUGHTON.
[1599–1600], Jan. RICHARD (THOMAS) LASSELLS.
[1599–1600], Jan. EDM. WITHEPOLE.
1599–1600, Feb. 28. OLIVER ST. JOHN (in Christchurch by Charles, lord Mountjoy, lord deputy of Ireland).
1600, Apr. 6. FRANCIS SHANE (*ibid* by same).
1600, May 1. JAMES FITZPIERCE FITZGERALD (at Dublin Castle by same).
1600, Aug. NICHOLAS MOSELEY, lord mayor of London [in 1599].
1600, Aug. ? RICHARD LEWKENOR.
1600, Aug. ? THOMAS RIDGWAY.
[?] 1600, Aug. FRANCIS LEAKE.
1600, Aug. ? EDWARD MORE.
1600, Aug. ? ROBERT OXENBRIDGE.
1600, Nov. 17. WILLIAM FORTESCUE (at Drogheda by Charles, lord Mountjoy, lord deputy of Ireland).
1600, Nov. 17. JOHN ROTHERHAM (*ibid* by same).
1600, Nov. 17. JAMES DILLON (*ibid* by same).
1600, Nov. 19. BENJAMIN BERRY (at Dublin Castle by same).
1600, Nov. 19. RICHARD GRAHAM (GREIME, GREAME) (by same).
after 1600, Nov. 24. THOMAS MEADE, sheriff of Essex.

KNIGHTS BACHELORS

1601, June. PERCIVALL HART.
[?]. WILLIAM RYDER, lord mayor of London [in 1600].
1601, Sept. 14 (? Nov.). EDWARD CECIL (2nd son to lord Burghley) (at Basing, at the marquis of Winchester's by the Queen).
1601, Sept. 14. EDWARD HUNGERFORD (next heir to lord Hungerford) (*ibid* by same).
1601, Sept. 14. EDWARD BAINTON (*ibid* by same).
1601, Sept. 14. W. KINGSMIL (*ibid* by same).
1601, Sept. 14. CAREW RAWLEIGH (*ibid* by same).
1601, Sept. 14. FRANCIS PALMER (then sheriff of the shire) (*ibid* by same).
1601, Sept. 14. BENJAMIN TICHBOURNE (*ibid* by same).
1601, Sept. 14. HAMDEN PAULET (*ibid* by same).
1601, Sept. 14. RICHARD NORTON, of Hampshire (*ibid* by same).
1601, Sept. 14. FRANCIS STONER, of Oxfordshire (*ibid* by same).
1601, Sept. 14. EDMUND LUDLOW (LUTLOW), of Wilts (*ibid* by same).
1601, Sept. 15 or 16. RICHARD WHITE (in his house at Farnham by same).
1601, Sept. 15 or 16. RICHARD MILL (? *ibid* by same).
1601, Sept. 15. WILLIAM UDALL (? *ibid* by same).
1601, Sept. EDWIN GOODWIN, of Bishops Wooburn, Bucks. (probably son of John Goodwin and either the father or elder brother of Sir Francis, sheriff in 21 king James I.) (at Causham, at Mr. Comptroller while there at dinner, by the Queen).
1601, Sept. EDWARD FETTIPLACE (an ancient Bedford family) (*ibid* by same).
1601, Sept. RICHARD WARDE (*ibid* by same).
1601, Sept. [? end of]. RICHARD STAFFORD (at Englefield House—Sir Edward Norris's house—at Ricott by the Queen).
1601, Sept. [? end of]. JOHN NORRIS (*ibid* by same).
1601, Oct. 31 (the last of). THOMAS SAVAGE (by Charles, lord Mountjoy, lord deputy of Ireland).
1601, Nov. —— LEIGH.
1601, Dec. 24. RICHARD BOURKE, 4th earl of Clanricarde (at Tyrone's overthrow at the battle of Kinsale by the lord deputy of Ireland).
1601-2, Mar. 11. JOHN FITZ EDMOND FITZ GERRALD, of Clone (by Charles, lord Mountjoy, lord deputy of Ireland).
1601-2, Mar. 14. TEGUE (TIRLAUGH) O'BRIAN, uncle to the earl of Thomond (by same).
1601-2, Mar. 18. JOHN FITZGERALD (at Waterford by same).

1601–2, Mar. 18. EDWARD GOUGH *(ibid* by same).
1602, Apr. 29 (19). HENRY SLINGSBY (in Dublin Castle by same).
1602, Apr. 29. MYLES FLEETWOODE (by same).
1602, May 13. RICHARD AILWARD (by same).
1602, May 13. EDWARD NOELL (by same).
1602, May 13. NEALE GARVE O'DONELL (by same).
1602, May 13. CAHIRE O'DOGHERTIE (by same).
1602, May 13. RANDAL MCDONELL MCSORLEY (MCSAWERLY), BOY (by same).
1602, Dec. 5. RANDOLFE MANNERING (at Trim by same).
1602–3, Jan. 4. THEOBALD BOURKE, *alias* ne Long (by same).

Knights dubbed by King James.

1603, Mar. 28. JOHN PEYTON (PAYTON), of Wells, Norfolk (at Edinburgh).
1603, Apr. 6. WILLIAM SELBY, of Northumberland (at Berwick).
1603, Apr. 8 (6). RAFE GREY, of Northumberland *(ibid)*.
1603, Apr. 9. ROBERT DUDLEY, mayor of Newcastle (at Widdrington).
1603, Apr. 9. HENRY WIDERINGTON, of Northumberland *(ibid)*.
1603, Apr. 9. NICHOLAS FORSTER, of Northumberland *(ibid)*.
1603, Apr. 9. WILLIAM FENWICKE, of Northumberland *(ibid)*.
1603, Apr. 9. EDWARD GORGES, of Northumberland *(ibid)*.
1603, Apr. 9. NICHOLAS SCRIVEN (at Newcastle, ? not knighted).
1603, Apr. 13. ROBERT DELAVALL, of Northumberland (at Newcastle).
1603, Apr. 13. CHRISTOPHER LOWTHER, of Cumberland *(ibid)*.
1603, Apr. 13. NICHOLAS CURWEN, of Cumberland *(ibid)*.
1603, Apr. 13. JAMES BELLINGHAM, of Westmorland *(ibid)*.
1603, Apr. 13. NICHOLAS TUFTON, of Kent *(ibid)*.
1603, Apr. 13. ROBERT ANDERSON, mayor of Newcastle.
1603, Apr. 13. JOHN CONYERS, of Durham *(ibid)*.
1603, Apr. 13. BERTRAM BULMER *(ibid)*.
1603, Apr. 17. WILLIAM CECIL, lord Burghley (at York).
1603, Apr. 17. EDMOND TRAFFORD, of Lancashire *(ibid)*.
1603, Apr. 17. THOMAS HOLCROFT, of Lancashire *(ibid)*.
1603, Apr. 17. JOHN MALLORY, of Yorkshire *(ibid)*.
1603, Apr. 17. WILLIAM INGLEBY, of Yorkshire *(ibid)*.
1603, Apr. 17. PHILIP CONSTABLE, of Durham *(ibid)*.
1603, Apr. 17. CHRISTOPHER HILLYARD (HAWARD, HELLYARD), of Yorkshire *(ibid)*.

1603, Apr. 17. ROBERT SWIFT, of Yorkshire (at York).
1603, Apr. 17. RICHARD WORTLEY, of Yorkshire *(ibid)*.
1603, Apr. 17. HENRY BELLASIS, of Yorkshire *(ibid)*.
1603, Apr. 17. THOMAS FAIRFAX, of Yorkshire *(ibid)*.
1603, Apr. 17. HENRY GRIFFITH, of Yorkshire *(ibid)*.
1603, Apr. 17. FRANCIS BOYNTON, of Yorkshire *(ibid)*.
1603, Apr. 17. HENRY CHOLMLEY, of Yorkshire *(ibid)*.
1603, Apr. 17. RICHARD GARGRAVE, of Yorkshire *(ibid)*.
1603, Apr. 17. MARMADUKE GRIMSTON, of Yorkshire *(ibid)*.
1603, Apr. 17. LANCELOT ALFORD, of Yorkshire *(ibid)*.
1603, Apr. 17. RALPH ELLERKER (ILLERKER), of Yorkshire *(ibid)*.
1603, Apr. 17. GEORGE FREVIL (FREWIL), of Durham *(ibid)*.
1603, Apr. 17. MAUGER VAVASOR, of Yorkshire *(ibid)*.
1603, Apr. 17. RALPH BABTHORPE, of Yorkshire *(ibid)*.
1603, Apr. 17. RICHARD LOUTHER *(ibid)*.
1603, Apr. 17. WALTER CRAPE.
1603, Apr. 18 (17). ROBERT WALTER, lord mayor of York (at York).
1603, Apr. 18. ROGER ASTON, of Cheshire (at Grimstone).
1603, Apr. 18. THOMAS ASTON, of Cheshire *(ibid)*.
1603, Apr. 18. THOMAS HOLT, of Cheshire *(ibid)*.
1603, Apr. 18. JAMES HARRINGTON, of Rutland *(ibid)*.
1603, Apr. 18. CHARLES MONTAGUE, of Northamptonshire *(ibid)*.
1603, Apr. 18. THOMAS DAWNEY, of Yorkshire *(ibid)*.
1603, Apr. 18. WILLIAM BAMBROUGH, of Yorkshire *(ibid)*.
1603, Apr. 18. FRANCIS LOVELL, of Harling, Norfolk *(ibid)*.
1603, Apr. 18. THOMAS (FRANCIS) BEAUFIELD.
1603, Apr. 18. THOMAS GERRARD, of Byrn, Co. Lancs. *(ibid)*.
1603, Apr. 18. RALPH CONESBIE (CONINGSBY), of Herts *(ibid)*.
1603, Apr. 18. RICHARD MUSGRAVE, of Yorks. *(ibid)*.
1603, Apr. 20. HENRY LEIGH (by the lord deputy of Ireland at Dublin Castle).
1603, Apr. 20. JARMAN POOLE (by same, *ibid*).
1603, Apr. 21. JOHN MANNERS, of Derbyshire (by the King at Worksop).
1603, Apr. 21. HENRY GREY, of Co. Bedford *(ibid)*.
1603, Apr. 21. EDWARD LORAYN (LOCKRANE), of Co. Derby *(ibid)*.
1603, Apr. 21. HENRY PERPOINT (PIERREPONT), of Co. Notts. *(ibid)*.
1603, Apr. 21. FRANCIS NEWPORT (DAVENPORT), of Salop *(ibid)*.
1603, Apr. 21. HENRY BEAUMONT, of Co. Leicester *(ibid)*.

KNIGHTS BACHELORS

1603, Apr. 21. WILLIAM SKIPWITH, of Co. Leicester
(By the King at Worksop).
1603, Apr. 21. HUGH SMITH, of Somerset *(ibid)*.
1603, Apr. 21. WALTER COPE, of Co. Oxford *(ibid)*.
1603, Apr. 21. EDMOND LUCY (LACY), of Co. Warwick *(ibid)*.
1603, Apr. 21. EDMOND COCKAYN, of Co. Derby *(ibid)*.
1603, Apr. 21. JOHN HARPER, of Co. Derby *(ibid)*.
1603, Apr. 21. THOMAS GRESLEY, of Co. Notts *(ibid)*.
1603, Apr. 21. JOHN BIRON, of Co. Notts *(ibid)*.
1603, Apr. 21. PERCIVALL WILLOUGHBY, of Co. Linc. *(ibid)*.
1603, Apr. 21. PETER FRESCHVILE (FRESHWELL), of Co. Derby *(ibid)*.
1603, Apr. 21. RICHARD THEKESTON (CHECKSTONE, SEXTON), of Co. York *(ibid)*.
1603, Apr. 21. THOMAS STANLEY, of Co. Derby *(ibid)*.
1603, Apr. 22. JOHN PARKER, of Sussex (at Newark Castle).
1603, Apr. 22. ROBERT BRETT, of Devon *(ibid)*.
1603, Apr. 22. LEWIS LEWKNOR, of Sussex *(ibid)*.
1603, Apr. 22. RICHARD MOMPESSON, of Bucks *(ibid)*.
1603, Apr. 22. FRANCIS DUCKET, of Salop *(ibid)*.
1603, Apr. 22. RICHARD WARBURTON, of Cheshire *(ibid)*.
1603, Apr. 22. RICHARD WYGMORE, of Co. Hereford *(ibid)*.
1603, Apr. 22. EDWARD (EDMOND) FOXE, of Salop *(ibid)*.
1603, Apr. 22 (21). WILLIAM DAVENPORT (DAMPORT), of Cheshire *(ibid)*.
1603, Apr. 22. ROGER AYSCHUE (ASKEWE, ASKOTH), of Cheshire (upon the way to Belvoir Castle).
1603, Apr. 22. WILLIAM SUTTON, of Co. Notts *(ibid)*.
1603, Apr. 22. JOHN STANHOP, of Co. Derby *(ibid)*.
1603, Apr. 22. BRIAN LASSELLS, of Co. Yorks *(ibid)*.
1603, Apr. 23. OLIVER MANNERS, of Co. Lincoln (at Belvoir Castle).
1603, Apr. 23. WILLIAM WILLOUGHBY, of Co. Lincoln *(ibid)*.
1603, Apr. 23. THOMAS WILLOUGHBY, of Co. Lincoln *(ibid)*.
1603, Apr. 23. GREGORY CROMWELL, of Co. Hants *(ibid)*.
1603, Apr. 23. GEORGE MANNERS, of Co. Lincoln *(ibid)*.
1603, Apr. 23. HENRY HASTINGS, of Co. Leicester *(ibid)*.
1603, Apr. 23. WILLIAM PELHAM, of Co. Lincoln *(ibid)*.
1603, Apr. 23. PHILIP TIRWHITT, of Co. Lincoln *(ibid)*.
1603, Apr. 23. VALENTINE BROWN, of Co. Lincoln *(ibid)*.

KNIGHTS BACHELORS 103

1603, Apr. 23. ROGER DALYSON, of Co. Lincoln (at Belvoir Castle).
1603, Apr. 23. THOMAS GRANTHAM, of Co. Lincoln *(ibid)*.
1603, Apr. 23. ANTHONY MARKHAM, of Co. Oxford *(ibid)*.
1603, Apr. 23. WILLIAM CARRE, of Co. Lincoln *(ibid)*.
1603, Apr. 23. JOHN THOROLD, of Co. Lincoln *(ibid)*.
1603, Apr. 23. EDWARD AYSCUE (AYSCOUGH), of Co. Lincoln *(ibid)*.
1603, Apr. 23. HENRY PAGENHAM, of Co. Lincoln *(ibid)*.
1603, Apr. 23. EDWARD (EDMUND) BUSSY (BUSHEY), of Co. Lincoln *(ibid)*.
1603, Apr. 23. EDWARD TIRWHIT, of Co. Lincoln *(ibid)*.
1603, Apr. 23. EDWARD CARRE, of Co. Lincoln *(ibid)*.
1603, Apr. 23. EVERARD DIGBY, of Co. Rutland *(ibid)*.
1603, Apr. 23. WILLIAM ERMYNE (AYRMINE), of Co. Lincoln *(ibid)*.
1603, Apr. 23. NICHOLAS SANDERSON, of Co. Lincoln *(ibid)*.
1603, Apr. 23. RICHARD OGLE, of Co. Lincoln *(ibid)*.
1603, Apr. 23. HUGH WHICHCOT (SWYTHCOATE), of Lincoln *(ibid)*.
1603, Apr. 23. EDWARD ROSSETER, of Co. Lincoln *(ibid)*.
1603, Apr. 23. WILLIAM HYCKMAN, of Co. Lincoln *(ibid)*.
1603, Apr. 23. THOMAS BEAUMONT, of Co. Leicester *(ibid)*.
1603, Apr. 23. WILLIAM JEPSON, of Hants. *(ibid)*.
1603, Apr. 23. THOMAS CAVE, of Co. Leicester *(ibid)*.
1603, Apr. 23. PHILIP SHERRARD, of Co. Leicester *(ibid)*.
1603, Apr. 23. WILLIAM SKEFFINGTON, of Co. Leicester *(ibid)*.
1603, Apr. 23. WILLIAM FAWNT (FAUNT), of Co. Leicester *(ibid)*.
1603, Apr. 23. BASIL BROOK, of Shropshire (Lubbenham, Co. Leicester. *(ibid)*.
1603, Apr. 23. WILLIAM TURPIN, of Co. Leicester *(ibid)*.
1603, Apr. 23. WILLIAM LAMBERT.
1603, Apr. 23. JOHN ZOUCHE, of Co. Derby *(ibid)*.
1603, Apr. 23. JOHN THORNHAUGH (THORNEY, THORNIX), of Co. Nott. *(ibid)*.
1603, Apr. 23. EDWARD SWYFT, of Co. Yorks. *(ibid)*.
1603, Apr. 23. PHILIP (? GEORGE) STIRLEY (? STRELLEY, SHIRLEY), of Co. Leicester *(ibid)*.
1603, Apr. 23. JOHN FERRERS, of Co. Warwick *(ibid)*.
1603, Apr. 23. EDWARD LITTLETON, of Co. Salop *(ibid)*.
1603, Apr. 23. WILLIAM FIELDING, of Co. Warwick *(ibid)*.
1603, Apr. 23. JOHN WENTWORTH, of Co. Essex *(ibid)*.
1603, Apr. 23. WALTER CHUTE, of Kent *(ibid)*.

KNIGHTS BACHELORS

1603, Apr. 23. EDWARD CONYERS (COMMES, COMINES)
(at Belvoir Castle).
1603, Apr. 23. WILLIAM FAIRFAX, of Co. York. *(ibid)*.
1603, Apr. 23. JOHN TYRELL, of Essex *(ibid)*.
1603, Apr. 23. HUMFREY CONISBY *(ibid)*.
1603, Apr. 23. EDWARD CLEARE *(ibid)*.
1603, Apr. 23. HAMOND SOUTHCOTE *(ibid)*.
1603, May 7. WILLIAM KILLIGREW, of Cornwall (Berks) (at Theobalds).
1603, May 7. MICHAEL (NICHOLAS) STANHOPE, of Suffolk *(ibid)*.
1603, May 7. FRANCIS BARRINGTON, of Essex *(ibid)*.
1603, May 7. ROWLAND LITTON, of Knebworth, Herts *(ibid)*.
1603, May 7. WILLIAM PETER (PETERS), of Essex *(ibid)*.
1603, May 7. JOHN BROGRAVE, attorney general of the Duchy of Lancaster, of Essex (Herts) *(ibid)*.
1603, May 7. WILLIAM COOKE, of Essex *(ibid)*.
1603, May 7. HENRY (? ARTHUR) CAPELL, of Haddon, Herts *(ibid)*.
1603, May 7. HERBERT CROFT (CROFTS), of Co. Hereford *(ibid)*.
1603, May 7. EDWARD GREVILL, of Wilcot, Co. Warwick *(ibid)*.
1603, May 7. HENRY BUTLER (BOTYLAR), of Bramfield, Herts *(ibid)*
1603, May 7. HENRY MAYNARD, of Essex *(ibid)*.
1603, May 7. RICHARD SPENCER, of Herts. *(ibid)*.
1603, May 7. JOHN LEVENTHORP, of Shingle Hall, Herts *(ibid)*.
1603, May 7. THOMAS POPE BLUNT, of Tittenhanger, Herts *(ibid)*.
1603, May 7. RICHARD CLIFFORD *(ibid)*.
1603, May 7. THOMAS MEDCALFE, of Co. York *(ibid)*.
1603, May 7. HENRY FANSHAW, of Ware, Herts *(ibid)*.
1603, May 7. GAMALIEL CAPEL, of Rookwood Hall, Essex *(ibid)*.
1603, May 7. WILLIAM SMITH, of Thoydon Mount, Essex *(ibid)*.
1603, May 7. JOHN FERRERS, of Mackiat, Herts *(ibid)*.
1603, May 7. ROBERT BITTON.
1603, May 7. RICHARD BAKER, of Kent *(ibid)*.
1603, May 7. VINCENT SKINNER, of Enfield, Middlesex *(ibid)*.
1603, May 7. HUGH BEESTON, of Cheshire.
1603, May 7. JOHN LEE (LEIGH).
1603, May 7. THOMAS BISHOP, of Parham, Sussex *(ibid)*.
1603, May 7. GERVASE ELLYS (ELVIS, ELWYS, ELWES), lieutenant of the Tower *(ibid)*.
1603, May 7. EDWARD LEWIS, of Glamorgan *(ibid)*.

KNIGHTS BACHELORS 105

1603, May 11. CHARLES HOWARD (HAWARD), of Sheffield, Sussex (at the Charterhouse).
1603, May 11. AMBROSE WILLOUGHBY, of Co. Lincoln *(ibid)*.
1603, May 11. EDWARD HOWARD (HAWARD), of Surrey *(ibid)*.
1603, May 11. HENRY HASTYNGS, of Co. Leicester *(ibid)*.
1603, May 11. GYLES ALLINGTON, of Horsheath, Co. Cambridge *(ibid)*.
1603, May 11. WILLIAM HYNDE, of Co. Cambridge *(ibid)*.
1603, May 11. RICHARD VERNEY, of Compton Maddock, Co. Warwick *(ibid)*.
1603, May 11. JOHN THINNE, of Longleat, Co. Wilts *(ibid)*.
1603, May 11. WILLIAM FITZWILLIAMS, of Co. Lincoln (Dostrap, Co. Northampton) *(ibid)*.
1603, May 11. EDWARD (WILLIAM) CARELL, of Sussex *(ibid)*.
1603, May 11. EDWARD BACON, of Suffolk *(ibid)*.
1603, May 11. FRANCIS ANDERSON, of Co. Beds. *(ibid)*.
1603, May 11. JOHN POULTNEY (POUNTNEY), of Co. Notts (Misterton, Co. Leicester *(ibid)*.
1603, May 11. EDWARD DARCY, of Co. Yorks *(ibid)*.
1603, May 11. JOHN SYDENHAM, of Co. Somerset *(ibid)*.
1603, May 11. JOHN TUFTON, of Hothfield, Kent *(ibid)*.
1603, May 11. THOMAS GRIFFIN, of Co. Northampton *(ibid)*.
1603, May 11. VALENTINE KNIGHTLEY, of Fausley, Co. Northampton *(ibid)*.
1603, May 11. RAFE WISEMAN, of Ravens Hall, Essex *(ibid)*.
1603, May 11. WILLIAM AYLOFF (AYLIFF), of Braxted, Essex *(ibid)*.
1603, May 11. EDWARD WATSON, of Co. Northampton *(ibid)*.
1603, May 11. JAMES CROMER, of Kent *(ibid)*.
1603, May 11. THOMAS CHEEK, of Pirgo, Essex *(ibid)*.
1603, May 11. THOMAS ROUSE, of Suffolk (Norfolk) *(ibid)*.
1603, May 11. JOHN RODNEY.
1603, May 11. HENRY VAUGHAN.
1603, May 11. JOHN SMITH, of Osterhanger, Kent *(ibid)*.
1603, May 11. CHARLES (THOMAS) CORNWALLIS, of Suffolk *(ibid)*.
1603, May 11. JOHN HUNNAM (HANNAM, HAMMAN), of Cheshire *(ibid)*.
1603, May 11. THOMAS MEDE (MEADE), of Kent *(ibid)*.
1603, May 11. EUSEBIUS ISHAM, of Co. Northampton *(ibid)*.
1603, May 11. ARTHUR (JOHN) COOPER, of Surrey *(ibid)*.

1603, May 11. ROBERT WINGFIELD, of Co. Northampton (Suffolk) (at the Charterhouse).
1603, May 11. THOMAS JOSSELING (JOSSELINE), of Herts (Kent) *(ibid)*.
1603, May 11. HENRY GOODERICK (GOODRIKE), of Co. Yorks. *(ibid)*.
1603, May 11. MAXIMILIAN DALISON (DALLISON), of Kent *(ibid)*.
1603, May 11. WILLIAM COPE (COAPE), of Co. Northampton *(ibid)*.
1603, May 11. GEORGE FLEETWOOD, of Co. Bucks (Beds) *(ibid)*.
1603, May 11. PETER EVENS (EVERS), of Co. Lincoln (Yorks) *(ibid)*.
1603, May 11. HENRY CLARE (CLEERE), of Co. Norfolk *(ibid)*.
1603, May 11. EDWARD FRANCIS.
1603, May 11. FRANCIS WOLLEY, of Co. Lincoln *(ibid)*.
1603, May 11. ARTHUR MANWARING (MANNERING), of Cheshire *(ibid)*.
1603, May 11. EDWARD WATERHOUSE, of Co. Yorks *(ibid)*.
1603, May 11. WILLIAM TWISDEN, of Kent *(ibid)*.
1603, May 11. HATTON CHEEK *(ibid)*.
1603, May 11. HENRY GORING, of Sussex *(ibid)*.
1603, May 11. RICHARD (WALTER) SANDS, of Kent *(ibid)*.
1603, May 11. ROBERT COTTON, of Connington, Co. Huntingdon *(ibid)*.
1603, May 11. OLIVER LUKE, of Co. Beds. *(ibid)*.
1603, May 11. THOMAS KNIVETT (KNEVET), of Norfolk (? Wilts) *(ibid)*.
1603, May 11. HENRY SECKFORD (SACKFORD), of Suffolk *(ibid)*.
1603, May 11. EDWIN SANDES, of Kent *(ibid)*.
1603, May 11. JOHN ASHLEY, of Kent *(ibid)*.
1603, May 11. WILLIAM (MILES) FLEETWOOD, of Co. Beds. (Middlesex) *(ibid)*.
1603, May 11. WALTER MILDMAY, of Essex *(ibid)*.
1603, May 11. ARTHUR ATYE (ATEY), of Kilburn, Midds. *(ibid)*.
1603, May 11. EDWARD LEWKENOR, of Denham Hall, Suffolk *(ibid)*.
1603, May 11. MILES SANDS, of Wimbleton, Ely, Co. Camb. *(ibid)*.
1603, May 11. WILLIAM KINGSMILL, of Hants *(ibid)*.
1603, May 11. THOMAS KEMP, of Wye, Kent *(ibid)*.
1603, May 11. EDWARD TIRRELL (TERRILL), of Thornton, Bucks *(ibid)*.
1603, May 11. THOMAS RUSSELL, of Co. Strensham, Worcester *(ibid)*.

KNIGHTS BACHELORS

1603, May 11. RICHARD TICHBORNE, of Hants (at the Charterhouse).
1603, May 11. THOMAS CORNWALL, of Salop (baron of Burford, Cheshire) *(ibid)*.
1603, May 11. JOHN CUTTS, of Co. Cambridge *(ibid)*.
1603, May 11. RICHARD FARMER (FERMOR), of Co. Northampton (of Swinerton, Oxford) *(ibid)*.
1603, May 11. THOMAS (WILLIAM) AYLOFF (AYLIFF), of Essex (Gloucester) *(ibid)*.
1603, May 11. JOHN TASBOROUGH (TASBURGH), of Suffolk *(ibid)*.
1603, May 11. JOHN SHIRLEY (SHURLEY), of Ifield, Sussex *(ibid)*.
1603, May 11. THOMAS PRESTON, of Dorset *(ibid)*.
1603, May 11. WILLIAM STAFFORD, of Co. Huntingdon (Blotherwick, Northampton) *(ibid)*.
1603, May 11. THOMAS CARRELL, of Sussex *(ibid)*.
1603, May 11. EDWARD CARRELL, of Sussex *(ibid)*.
1603, May 11. THOMAS PALMER, of Wingham, Kent *(ibid)*.
1603, May 11. ROBERT (JOHN) NEWDIGATE, of Co. Beds. *(ibid)*.
1603, May 11. GEORGE RAWLEY (RAWGHLEY), of Essex *(ibid)*.
1603, May 11. THOMAS BEAUFOE, of Co. Warwick *(ibid)*.
1603, May 11. WILLIAM LOWER, of Cornwall *(ibid)*.
1603, May 11. THOMAS (CHARLES) FAIRFAX, of Denton, Co. Yorks. *(ibid)*.
1603, May 11. HENRY SIDNEY, of Norfolk *(ibid)*.
1603, May 11. PECKSALL BROCAS (BROCKHURST), of Hants *(ibid)*.
1603, May 11 (1604, Nov. 16). WALTER TICHBORNE.
1603, May 11. HENRY CRIPPS (CRIPS), or CRISPE, of Kent *(ibid)*.
1603, May 11. GEORGE HARVY (HERVEY), of Rumford, Essex *(ibid)*.
1603, May 11. JOHN HEVENINGHAM, of Norfolk *(ibid)*.
1603, May 11. WILLIAM BOWYER, of Denham, Bucks. *(ibid)*.
1603, May 11. JEROM WESTON, of Skreene, Essex *(ibid)*.
1603, May 11. EDMOND BOWYER, of Camberwell, Surrey *(ibid)*.
1603, May 11. NICHOLAS HASELWOOD (HALSWELL, HASELWELL), of Northampton *(ibid)*.
1603, May 11. JOHN JENNINGS, of Co. Worcester (Church Hill, Surrey) *(ibid)*.
1603, May 11. AMBROSE TURVILE (TURWELL), of Co. Lincoln *(ibid)*.
1603, May 11. JOHN LUKE (LUCK), of Co. Beds.
1603, May 11. JOHN (WILLIAM) DORMER, of Bucks. *(ibid)*.
1603, May 11. RICHARD (NICHOLAS) SAUNDERS (SANDERS), of Co. Lincoln *(ibid)*.

KNIGHTS BACHELORS

1603, May 11. JOHN SHIRLEY (SHEARLEY), of Sussex (Devon) (at the Charterhouse).
1603, May 11. THOMAS WAYNMAN, of Co. Oxford *(ibid)*.
1603, May 11. GODDARD PEMBERTON (PEMPTON) *(ibid)*.
1603, May 11. THOMAS METHAM (METTAME), of Co. Yorks. *(ibid)*.
1603, May 11. EDWARD (EDMOND) BILLINGHAM (BELLINGHAM), of Cumberland *(ibid)*.
1603, May 11. JOHN HARRINGTON, of Yorks. *(ibid)*.
1603, May 11. EDWARD HARRINGTON, of Yorks. (Ridlington, Rutland) *(ibid)*.
1603, May 11. WILLIAM DYER, of Somerset, Great Houghton, Hunts. *(ibid)*.
1603, May 11. JOHN (WILLIAM) WENTWORTH, of Somerset *(ibid)*.
1603, May 11. WALTER MONTAGU, of Somerset (Northampton) *(ibid)*.
1603, May 11. GUY PALMES, of Ashwell, Co. Rutland *(ibid)*.
1603, May 11. HENRY ASHLEY, of Surrey (Berks.) *(ibid)*.
1603, May 11. THOMAS BAKER *(ibid)*.
1603, May 11. THOMAS VACHILL, alias VACATHELL, of Colley, Berks. *(ibid)*.
1603, May 11. THOMAS BASKERVILLE *(ibid.)*.
1603, May 11. THOMAS STUKLEY, of Sussex *(ibid)*.
1603, May 11. WILLIAM LEEK (LEAKE).
1603, May 11. HUGH LOOSSE (LOSSE), of Middlesex *(ibid)*.
1603, May 11. WILLIAM LYGON, of Worcester *(ibid)*.
1603, May 11. EDWARD LYGON *(ibid)*.
1603, May 11. THOMAS GROSSE (LEGROSSE), of Norfolk *(ibid)*.
1603, May 11. THOMAS FOWLER, of Islington, Middlesex *(ibid)*.
1603, May 11. EUSEBIUS ANDREW (ANDREWES), of Co. Northampton *(ibid)*.
1603, May 11. EDWARD ANDREW.
1603, May 11. ROBERT LUCY, of Co. Warwick *(ibid)*.
1603, May 11. WILLIAM WALTER *(ibid)*.
1603, May 11. RICHARD BLOUNT, of Co. Oxford (Devon) *(ibid)*.
1603, May 11. ANTHONY DERING, of Pluckley, Kent *(ibid)*.
1603, May 11. JOHN CAREW, of Somerset *(ibid)*.
1603, May 11. EDWARD APSLEY, of Worminghurst, Sussex *(ibid)*.
1603, May 11. BARTRAM BOOMER.
1603, May 11. WILLIAM ALFORD, of Co. Yorks. *(ibid)*.
1603, May 11. ROBERT LEE (LEIGH), of Co. Lincoln (Sussex) *(ibid)*.

KNIGHTS BACHELORS

1603, May 11. THOMAS BEAUMONT (BEAMOND), of Co. Leicester (at the Charterhouse).
1603, May 11. ROBERT MARKHAM, of Co. Oxford *(ibid)*.
1603, May 11. FRANCIS CASTILION, of Co. Bucks. (Benhall Valence, Berks.) *(ibid)*.
1603, May 11. GEORGE MARKHAM (MARTHAM).
1603, May 11. JOHN MASHALL (MARSHALL).
1603, May 11. ROBERT MARSHALL *(ibid)*.
1603, May 11. GEORGE SAVILE, of Co. Yorks. *(ibid)*.
1603, May 11. ROBERT CLEVELAND *(ibid)*.
1603, May 11. ROBERT TOWNESEND, of Salop (Norfolk) *(ibid)*.
1603, May 13. ROBERT MACKLARAND (MAICKLAND, MACKLAND, MARKEHAM), of Co. Oxford (at the Tower).
1603, May 13. GEORGE MORTON (MORETON, NORTON), of Dorset. *(ibid)*.
1603, May 13. EDMOND BELL (BOLT), of Norfolk *(ibid)*.
1603, May 13. THOMAS PEYTON (PARTON), of Kent *(ibid)*.
1603, May 13. DAVID FOWLIS, of Ingleby, Yorks. *(ibid)*.
1603, May 13. WILLIAM GARDNER, of Surrey *(ibid)*.
1603, May 13. JOHN DEANE (DENIE), of Essex *(ibid)*.
1603, May 13. JOHN TREVOR (TREAVOR, TRAVER), of Flint *(ibid)*.
1603, May 13. THOMAS SMITH, of Kent *(ibid)*.
1603, May 13. THOMAS HUBERT (HOBART, HUBART, HUBBARDE), of Norfolk *(ibid)*.
1603, May 13. WILLIAM DETHICK, Garter King of Arms, of Surrey *(ibid)*.
1603, May 20. JULIUS CAESAR, of London, master of requests (at Greenwich).
1603, May 20. ROGER WILBRAHAM, of Cheshire, master of requests *(ibid)*.
1603, May 20. WILLIAM WADE (WAAD), of Middlesex, a clerk of the Council *(ibid)*.
1603, May 20. THOMAS SMITH, of Berks, a clerk of the Council *(ibid)*.
1603, May 20. THOMAS EDMONDES, of Devon, a clerk of the Council *(ibid)*.
1603, May 20. THOMAS LEAKE (LAKE), of Co. Derby, a clerk of the Signet *(ibid)*.
1603, May 20. JOHN WOOD, of Co. Cambridge, a clerk of the Signet *(ibid)* see p. 116 *infra*.
1603, May 22. ROBERT LEE (LEIGH), lord mayor of London *(ibid)*.

1603, May 22. JOHN CROOK (CROKE), of Co. Oxford (Chilton, Bucks), recorder of London (At Greenwich).

1603, May 22. EDWARD COKE, of Co. Norfolk, attorney general *(ibid)*.

1603, May 22. JOHN MORRYS (NORRYS, NORRIS), of Essex *(ibid)*.

1603, May 22. EDWARD SEYMORE, of Devon *(ibid)*.

1603, May 22. WARWICK HELE, of Devon *(ibid)*.

1603, May 22 (June 3). THOMAS ARUNDELL, of Cornwall *(ibid)*.

1603, May 29. EDWARD BLAYNEY (by the lord deputy of Ireland at Dublin Castle, which day the lord lieutenant departed into England).

1603, June 10 (3). WILLIAM SELBY, of Kent (by the King at Greenwich).

1603, June ? 6 [after 23]. NICHOLAS THROGMORTON, of Bedington, Surrey (at Beddington, at Sir Francis Carew's).

1603, ? 6 [? after June 23]. EDWARD GORGES, of Co. Somerset (Langford, Wilts) *(ibid)*.

1603, 6 [? after June 23]. ALEXANDER BRETT, of Co. Somerset (Devon) *(ibid)*.

1603, 9 [? after June 23]. WILLIAM FLEETWOOD, of Bucks (at Hendon (? Kensington), at Sir John Fortescue's).

1603, 7 [? after June 23]. THOMAS HESKETH, of Lancashire, attorney of the wards *(ibid)*.

1603, June 23 (?). EDMOND HERRICK *(ibid)*.

1603, June 8. WILLIAM NORTON, of Hants (at Sion House).

1603, June 8 (23). ROBERT WROTHE (WORTHIE), of Loughton, Essex *(ibid)*.

1603, June 8 (23). THOMAS TIRRINGHAM *(ibid)*.

1603, June 8 (23). MARMADUKE WYVELL, of Constable Burton, Co. Yorks *(ibid)*.

1603, June 8 (23). FRANCIS (ROBERT) MORE, of Berks (Losely, Surrey *(ibid)*.

1603, June 11. EDMUND CONQUEST, at Sir John Fort's.

1603, June 25 (? 24). THOMAS GARDNER (GARDENER, GOODNES), of Surrey (at Hanworth).

1603, June 25 (? 24). THOMAS GRYMES (CRIMES, GORGES), of Peckham, Surrey *(ibid)*.

1603, June 14 (? 24). WILLIAM WELSH (WALSH), of Worcester *(ibid)*.

1603, June 11 (? 24). JOHN TOWNSEND, of Salop *(ibid)*.

1603, June 25 (? 24). GEORGE TRENCHARD, of Dorset *(ibid)*.

1603, June 25 (? 24). JOHN FOLIOTT (TALBOT), of Worcester *(ibid)*.

1603, June 25 (? 24). HENRY POOLE, of Oaksey, Wilts (at Hanworth).
1603, June 25 (? 24). JOHN PAWLETT, of Wilts *(ibid)*.
1603, June 25 (? 24). THOMAS CROMPTON (COMPTON), of Hereford *(ibid)*.
1603, June 11 (? 24). JOHN LANGTON, of Lancashire *(ibid)*.
1603, June 13 (? 27). HATTON FERMOR (FARMER), of Bucks (? of Easton Neston, Northampton) at Easton Neston, Sir George Fermor's).
1603, June 13 (? 27). EDWARD LEE *(ibid)*.
1603, June 13 (? 27). THOMAS WOODHOUSE, of Norfolk *(ibid)*.
1603, June 27. FRANCIS CURSON, of Salop *(ibid)*.
1603, June 27 (July 14). RICHARD CONQUEST, of Co. Beds. (Haughton Conquest, Northampton) *(ibid)*.
1603, June 27 (July 14). RAFE (RICHARD) TEMPEST, of Co. Yorks. *(ibid* or at Sir William Fleet's).
1603, June 27 (July 14). EDWARD RANDALL, of Albury, Surrey *(ibid)*.
1603, June 27. ANTHONY CHESTER, of Co. Hereford *(ibid)*.
1603, June 27. WALTER VAUGHAN, of Hereford *(ibid)*.
1603, June 28. WILLIAM DUNCHE, of Berks (at Salden House, Sir John Fortescue's).
1603, June 28. JOHN DYVE (DYVES), of Beds. *(ibid)*.
1603, June 28. GERRARD THROCKMORTON, of Co. Gloucester *(ibid)*.
1603, June 28. JOHN CROOK (CROKE), of Co. Oxford (Bucks) *(ibid)*.
1603, June 28. RICHARD CHEETWOOD (CHETWOOD), of Co. Northampton *(ibid)*.
1603, June 28. ROBERT HAREWELL (HARTWELL), of Preston, Co. Northampton *(ibid)*.
1603, June 28. RICHARD PRYCE, of Co. Huntingdon *(ibid)*.
1603, June 28. JAMES HAYDON (HEYDON), of Norfolk *(ibid)*.
1603, June 28. THOMAS SNAGGE, of Beds (Bucks) *(ibid)*.
1603, June 28. FRANCIS CHENEY, of Bucks *(ibid)*.
1603, June 28. HENRY LONGFEILD (LONGVILE), of Bucks *(ibid)*.
1603, June 28. HENRY DRURY, of Bucks *(ibid)*.
1603, June 28. WILLIAM BURLACY, of Bucks *(ibid)*.
1603, June 28. THOMAS DENTON, of Hillesden, Bucks *(ibid)*.
1603, June 28. ANTHONY TIRRINGHAM, of Thurringham, Bucks *(ibid)*.
1603, June 28. JOHN SANDES (SAMS, SANDS), of Bucks *(ibid)*.
1603, June 28. RICHARD HINTLEY (HUNTLEY) *(ibid)*.

1603, June 28.   THOMAS HYLL (HILL), of Kent (at Salden House).
1603, June 28.   THOMAS CAVE, of Stanford, Northampton *(ibid)*.
1603, June 28.   EDMUND CONQUEST.
1603, June 28.   JOHN CARRELL, of Sussex *(ibid)*.
1603, June 28 (14).   HENRY BILLINGSLEY, of London *(ibid)*.
1603, June 28.   ADRIAN SCROOP, of Co. Lincoln *(ibid)*.
? 1603, June 28.   ROBERT STRICKLAND *(ibid)*.
? 1603, June 28.   EDMUND HORRELL *(ibid)*.
? 1603, June 28.   JOHN LANGTON *(ibid)*.
? 1603, June 28.   THOMAS TEMPLE, of Stow, Bucks *(ibid)*.
1603, after June 28 (July 18).   WILLIAM SMITH, of Co. Leicester (at Aylesbury, at Sir John Packington's).
1603, ? after June 28.   ALEXANDER HAMPDEN (at Great Hampden, Bucks, the seat of said Sir Alexander).
1603, after June 28 (July 12).   HENRY BARKER, of Berks *(ibid)*.
1603, after June 28 (July 12).   WILLIAM WILLOUGHBY, of Bucks *(ibid)*.
1603, after June 28 (July 12).   EDWARD PYNCHON, of Essex *(ibid)*.
1603, after June 28 (? July ? 12, 14).   WILLIAM PAWLET, of Wilts (at Great Missenden, the seat of Sir William Fleetwood).
1603, after June 28 (June 14).   THOMAS EVERSFIELD, of Sussex *(ibid)*.
1603, after June 28 (June 14).   ARTHUR PORTER, of Co. Gloucester *(ibid)*.
1603, after June 28 (June 14).   GERRARD FLEETWOOD, of Bucks *(ibid* or at Sir George Fermor's).
? ? ?   THOMAS MONKE, of Powderwick, Devon (at Sir William Fleetwood's).
1603, after June 28 (June 14).   THOMAS SOMERFIELD (SOMERVILE) *(ibid)*.
1603, after June 28 (June 14).   FRANCIS HARRIS *(ibid)*.
1603, after June 28 (June 14).   EDWARD HALLES (HALES), of Kent *(ibid)*.
1603, after June 28 (June 14).   RICHARD SAUNDERS *(ibid)*.
1603, after June 28 (June 14).   JAMES PARRETT (PERROTT) *(ibid)*.
1603, after June 28 (June 14).   WILLIAM SOUTHLAND *(ibid)*.
1603, after June 28 (June 14).   WILLIAM FOSTER (FORSTER), of Surrey *(ibid)*.
1603, after June 28 (June 14).   WILLIAM WALSH (WELSH), of Worcester *(ibid)*.

KNIGHTS BACHELORS

1603, July 9. THOMAS (NICHOLAS, RICHARD) TEMPEST, of Bucks (at Worcester).
1603, July 9. JOHN ROPER, of Kent *(ibid)*.
1603, July 9. WILLIAM WOGAN, of Co. Pembroke (Salop) *(ibid)*.
1603, July 9. JOHN WOGAN, of Co. Pembroke *(ibid)*.
1603, July 9. RICHARD CHOLMLEY, of Whitby, Co. Yorks *(ibid)*.
1603, July 9. JOHN YORK, of Co. York *(ibid)*.
1603, July 9. JOHN CHAMBERLEYN, of Co. Oxford (Prestbury. Gloucester) *(ibid)*.
1603, July 9. FRANCIS TRAPPES, of Co. York *(ibid)*.
1603, July 9. WILLIAM HILLARD (HILLIARD), of Co. York *(ibid)*.
1603, July 9. THOMAS BELLASIS, of Co. York *(ibid)*.
1603, July 9. RICHARD LOWTHER (CHRISTOPHER LOWDER), of Cumberland *(ibid)*.
1603, July 9. EDWARD PLOMPTON (PLUMPTON), of Uflet, Co. York *(ibid)*.
1603, July 9. BRYAN (GEORGE) PALMES, of Hants (Naborn, Yorks) *(ibid)*.
1603, July 9. MATHEW REDMAN, of Co. York *(ibid)*.
1603, July 9. MATHEW TENANT.
1603, July 9. THOMAS SAMFORD (SANDFORD), of Westminster *(ibid)*.
1603, July 9. STEPHEN (RICHARD) TEMPEST, of Co. York *(ibid)*.
1603, July 9. WILLIAM PADDY, of Co. Oxford *(ibid)*.
1603, July 9. JOHN BABFORD (HENRY BABTHORPE) *(ibid)*.
1603, July 9. AMYAS BAMFIELD, of Poltmore, Devon *(ibid)*.
1603, July 9 (21). FRANCIS STIDOLFE, of Mickleham, Surrey.
1603, July 9. THOMAS BROWNE, of Devon *(ibid)*.
1603, July 9. MARTIN GAMMON, of Devon *(ibid)*.
1603, July 9. THOMAS PRESTON, of Dorset *(ibid)*.
1603, July 9 (21). MICHAEL GREEN, of Co. Oxford *(ibid)*.
1603, July 9 (21). WILLIAM GREEN, senior.
1603, July 9. EDWARD STODDER, of Surrey *(ibid)*.
1603, July 20. JOHN GAMMES, of Co. Radnor (at Hampton Court).
1603, July 20. WILLIAM CAVE, of Co. Oxford *(ibid)*.
1603, July 23.* JOHN BENNET, of London (in the Royal garden at Whitehall before the King's Coronation).
1603, July 23. FRANCIS GAWDY, of Norfolk, judge of the King's Bench *(ibid)*.
1603, July 23. EDWARD FENNOR, of Middlesex, judge of the King's Bench *(ibid)*.

* 1603, July 17, general summons for all persons that had £40 in lands to come and receive the honour of knighthood or compound (Rymer xvi. 560). This list of July 23 must be in response to this. The majority attended according to the summons.

1603, July 23. CHRISTOPHER YELVERTON, of Norfolk, judge of the King's Bench (In the Royal Garden at Whitehall before the King's Coronation).

1603, July 23. THOMAS WALMESLEY, of Lancs., judge of the Common Pleas *(ibid)*.

1603, July 23. PETER WARBERTON, of Cheshire, judge of the Common Pleas *(ibid)*.

1603, July 23. GEORGE KINGSMILL, of Hants., judge of the Common Pleas *(ibid)*.

1603, July 23. ROBERT CLARK, of Essex, baron of the Exchequer *(ibid)*.

1603, July 23. JOHN SAVILE, of Co. Yorks., baron of the Exchequer *(ibid)*.

1603, July 23. WILLIAM DANIEL, of London, baron of the Exchequer *(ibid)*.

1603, July 23. DAVID WILLIAMS, serjeant-at-law *(ibid)*.

1603, July 23. JOHN HELE, of Devon, serjeant-at-law *(ibid)*.

1603, July 23. EDWARD HERON (HERNE), of Co. Lincoln, serjeant-at-law *(ibid)*.

1603, July 23. EDWARD PHILIPPS, of Somerset, serjeant-at-law *(ibid)*.

1603, July 23. HENRY HUBERT (HOBART), of Norfolk *(ibid)*.

1603, July 23. CHRISTOPHER PARKINS (PERKINS) (Northampton), of Kent, LL.D. *(ibid)*.

1603, July 23. DANIEL DUNNE, of London, LL.D. *(ibid)*.

1603, July 23. THOMAS CROMPTON, of London, LL.D. *(ibid)*.

1603, July 23. MATHEW CAREW, of London *(ibid)*.

1603, July 23. JOHN TYNDALL, of Norfolk, master in Chancery *(ibid)*.

1603, July 23. JOHN GYBSON, of Co. York., master in Chancery *(ibid)*.

1603, July 23. EDWARD STANHOP, of Co. York (Northampton), LL.D. *(ibid)*.

1603, July 23. RICHARD SWALE, of Swale, Co. York. LL.D. *(ibid)*.

1603, July 23. JOHN HARRIS, of Essex *(ibid)*.

1603, July 23. THOMAS FLEMYNG, of Hants. (Dorset), solicitor-general *(ibid)*.

1603, July 23. HENRY MONTAGUE, of Co. Northampton. *(ibid)*.

1603, July 23. FRANCIS BACON, of Herts. *(ibid)*.

1603, July 23. GEORGE COPPIN (COPPEN), of Norfolk, clerk of the Crown *(ibid)*.

1603, July 23. RICHARD CUNNISBY (CONESBIE, CONINGSBIE), of London, gentleman usher *(ibid)*.

KNIGHTS BACHELORS 115

1603, July 23. JOHN DROMMOND, gentleman usher, a Scotchman (in the Royal Garden at Whitehall before the Coronation of the King).
1603, July 23. JOHN (THOMAS) CONWAY, of London, gentleman usher *(ibid)*.
1603, July 23. JOHN WILLOUGHBY, of Co. Lincoln *(ibid)*.
1603, July 23. JOHN TYRRELL, of Essex *(ibid)*.
1603, July 23. PHILIP SCUDAMORE, of Co. Hereford. *(ibid)*.
1603, July 23. THOMAS DABRIDGECOURT, of Stratfield, Hants. *(ibid)*.
1603, July 23. RAFE BOSWELL (BOSVILL), of Kent *(ibid)*.
1603, July 23. WILLIAM ROPER, of Eltham, Kent *(ibid)*.
1603, July 23. ANTHONY ROPER, of Farningham, Kent *(ibid)*.
1603, July 23. CHRISTOPHER ROPER, of Kent *(ibid)*.
1603, July 23. THOMAS BRIDGES, of Co. Gloucester. *(ibid)*.
1603, July 23. THOMAS SMITH, of Cheshire *(ibid)*.
1603, July 23. JOHN GILBERT, of Suffolk *(ibid)*.
1623, July 23. FRANCIS VINCENT, of Stoke Dabernon, Surrey *(ibid)*.
1603, July 23. JOHN COTTON, of Lanwade, Co. Cambridge *(ibid)*.
1603, July 23. ROBERT LANE, of Co. Warwick (Barford, Northampton) *(ibid)*.
1603, July 23. ROBERT EDWARDS, of Kent *(ibid)*.
1603, July 23. NICHOLAS GILBORNE, of Charing, Kent *(ibid)*.
1603, July 23. SAMUEL SANDES, of Co. Worcester. *(ibid)*.
1603, July 23. THOMAS MILDMAY, of Co. Hereford (Moulsham, Essex *(ibid)*.
1603, July 23. THOMAS HANMER (HAMMOND), of Cheshire *(ibid)*.
1603, July 23. JOHN WHITTON (WHIDDON), of Berks. *(ibid)*.
1603, July 23. ALEXANDER CAVE, of Bograve, Leicester *(ibid)*.
1603, July 23. JOHN (RICHARD) TRACY, of Co. Gloucester. *(ibid)*.
1603, July 23. THOMAS (RICHARD) SALTONSTALL (SALTINGSTON), of London *(ibid)*.
1603, July 23. ROBERT VARNAM (VARNON), of Cheshire *(ibid)*.
1603, July 23. THOMAS PENRUDDOCK, of Wiltshire *(ibid)*.
1603, July 23. EDWARD COOKE (COKE), of Giddy Hall, Essex *(ibid)*.
1603, July 23. RAFE LAWSON, of Kent *(ibid)*.
1603, July 23. WILLIAM MEREDITH, of Glamorgan *(ibid)*.
1603, July 23. GEORGE SELBY, of Northumberland *(ibid)*.
1603, July 23. THOMAS HUMPHREY, of Sweptston, Leicester. *(ibid)*.
1603, July 23. THOMAS WINDEBANCK, of Berks. *(ibid)*.

1603, July 23. THOMAS CLARKE, of Essex (in the Royal Garden at Whitehall before the King's Coronation).
1603, July 23. JOHN WOOD, of Essex (clerk of the Signet *(ibid)*. See p. 109 *supra*.
1603, July 23. LEWIS MANSFIELD (MANSELL, MAUNSELL), of Co. Glamorgan. *(ibid)*.
1603, July 23. RICHARD HAWKYNS, of Kent *(ibid)*.
1603, July 23. JOHN ROGERS *(ibid)*.
1603, July 23. ROBERT ALEXANDER, of Herts. *(ibid)*.
1603, July 23. JOHN BROWN, of Frampton, Dorset. *(ibid)*.
1603, July 23. RICHARD SKIPWITH, of Co. Leicester. *(Ibid)*.
1603, July 23. THOMAS BARNARDESTON, of Witham, Essex *(ibid)*.
1603, July 23. WILLIAM GERRARD (GARRARD, GARRETT), of Dorney, Bucks. *(ibid)*.
1603, July 23. THOMAS PALMER, of Kent (Parham, Sussex) *(ibid)*.
1603, July 23. RICHARD ASTON, of Cheshire *(ibid)*.
1603, July 23. WILLIAM (JOHN) THORNY (THORNEGH), of Co. Nottingham. *(ibid)*.
1603, July 23. FRANCIS BOYLDEN (BALDWINE, BALDEN, BAYLDON), of Co. York. *(ibid)*.
1603, July 23. EDWARD DUNTON (DUNCOMBE), of Beds.
1603, July 23. WILLIAM HARMAN (HANMER), of Cheshire (Flint) *(ibid)*.
1603, July 23. HENRY LONGFEILD (LONGVILE), of Bucks. *(ibid)*.
1603, July 23. JOHN MERES (MEERES), of Kent (Amborn, Leicester) *(ibid)*.
1603, July 23. CHARLES DIMMOCK (DYMOCKE), of Co. Lincoln. *(ibid)*.
1603, July 23. VALENTYNE BROWN, of Co. Lincoln. *(ibid)*.
1603, July 23. JOHN READ, of Co. Lincoln. (Leicester) *(ibid)*.
1603, July 23. JOHN LEE (LEIGH), of Co. Lincoln. *(ibid)*.
1603, July 23. GEORGE REYNELL, of Devon. *(ibid)*. See p. 117 *infra*.
1603, July 23. EDWARD PYTTS (PITTS), of Curweer, Co Worcester. *(ibid)*.
1603, July 23. THOMAS ROE (ROW), of London *(ibid)*.
1603, July 23. HENRY SAVYLE, of Methley, Co. York. *(ibid)*.
1603, July 23. WALTER TREADWAY, of Co. Northampton. *(ibid)*.
1603, July 23. GEORGE KNIGHTON, of Co. Notts. *(ibid)*.
1603, July 23. EDWARD PEINTER (PAINTER) *(ibid)*.
1603, July 23. HENRY JONES *(ibid)*.

KNIGHTS BACHELORS

1603, July 23. ANTHONY EVERARD, of Waltham, Essex (in the Royal Garden at Whitehall before the King's Coronation).
1603, July 23. STEPHEN BOOD (BOARDE), of Cuckfield, Sussex *(ibid)*.
1603, July 23. THOMAS MAY, of Mayfield, Sussex *(ibid)*.
1603, July 23. JOHN BEDELL (BEEDLE), of Hamerton, Co. Huntingdon. *(ibid)*.
1603, July 23. THOMAS BEDELL (BEAKE), of Co. Huntingdon., son of the foregoing *(ibid)*.
1603, July 23. HENRY DAY, of Norfolk, ignoble *(ibid)*.
1603, July 23. HENRY ROWLEY (HAWLEY), of Essex *(ibid)*.
1603, July 23. FRANCIS SMYTH, of Ashley Folvill, Leicester *(ibid)*.
1603, July 23. HENRY DRURY, of Norfolk *(ibid)*.
1603, July 23. GEORGE CHOWNE, of Kent *(ibid)*.
1603, July 23. ARTHUR ACKLAND, of Devon. *(ibid)*.
1603, July 23. THOMAS REYNELL (REYNOLLES), of Devon. *(ibid)*.
1603, July 23. GEORGE REYNELL, of Devonshire *(ibid)*. See p. 116 *supra*.
1603, July 23. WILLIAM BARNES, of Wolwich, Kent *(ibid)*.
1603, July 23. WALTER RICE, of Co. Lincoln. *(ibid)*.
1603, July 23. ROBERT MONSON, of Burton, Co. Lincoln *(ibid)*.
1603, July 23. HENRY AYSCUE (ASKEWE, ASKOUGH), of Santon. Lincoln *(ibid)*.
1603, July 23. CHARLES HUSSY (HUSSEY), of Co. Lincoln. *(ibid)*.
1603, July 23. JAMES PITTS, of Co. Worcester. *(ibid)*.
1603, July 23. THOMAS HENEAGE, of Co. Lincoln. *(ibid)*.
1603, July 23. EDWARD (EDMUND) THOROLD, of Co. Lincoln. *(ibid)*.
1603, July 23. WALTER (WILFRED) LAWSON (LUSON), of Westmorland *(ibid)*.
1603, July 23. EDMOND MONTFORD (EDWARD MOUNTFORD), of Norfolk (Warwick) *(ibid)*.
1603, July 23. JOHN MONTFORD *(ibid)*.
1603, July 23. WILLIAM RIGDEN (RIGDON), of Co. Lincoln. *(ibid)*.
1603, July 23. JOHN THORNBOROWE (THORNBERY), of Co. Lincoln. *(ibid)*.
1603, July 23. FRANCIS ZOUCHE (SOWTH), of Co. Lincoln. *(ibid)*.
1603, July 23. WILLIAM SOMERVILE (SOMERFELD), of Somerset. *(ibid)*.
1603, July 23. NICHOLAS COTES (COOTE), of Barking (Essex).
1603, July 23. AMBROSE (HENRY) COPPINGER, of Co. Middl. *(ibid)*.
1603, July 23. HENRY BLOMER, of Co. Gloucester. (Bucks) *(ibid)*.
1603, July 23. EDMOND (EDWARD) THIMBLETHORP (THEMILTHORP), of Norfolk *(ibid)*.

1603, July 23. NICHOLAS LASHER (LUSHER), of Sholand, Surrey in the Royal Garden at Whitehall, before the King's coronation).
1603, July 23. ROBERT PHILLIPPS, of Somerset. *(ibid)*.
1603, July 23. ROBERT HYDE, of Co. Cambridge. *(ibid)*.
1603, July 23. JOHN PHILPOT, of Hants. *(ibid)*.
1603, July 23. THOMAS NEVILL, of Berks. (Leicester) *(ibid)*.
1603, July 23. CHRISTOPHER ROPER, of Kent *(ibid)*.
1603, July 23. ROBERT CHICHESTER (CHESTER), of Devon. *(ibid)*.
1603, July 23. CHRISTOPHER (EUSTACE) HART, of Kent *(ibid)*.
1603, July 23. JOHN NEWDIGATE, of Co. Beds. (of Orbey, Warwick.) *(ibid)*.
1603, July 23. EDWARD GORGE (GEORGE), of Somerset. *(ibid)*.
1603, July 23. MARTIN BARNHAM, of Kent *(ibid)*.
1603, July 23. WILLIAM DORRINGTON, of Dorset. (Hants.) *(ibid)*.
1603, July 23. EDWARD GILES, of Devon. *(ibid)*.
1603, July 23. RICHARD ELDERTON (ELDRINGTON, ETHERINGTON) *(ibid)*.
1603, July 23. ANTHONY CULPEPER (COLEPEPER), of Sussex *(ibid)*.
1603, July 23. RICHARD COOPER (COOP ROPER), of Surrey, sergeant porter *(ibid)*.
1603, July 23. JOHN GRANGER, of Co. Middl. *(ibid)*.
1603, July 23. WILLIAM READE, of Co. Middl. (Suffolk) *(ibid)*.
1603, July 23. HENRY RAYNSFORD, of Surrey (Gloucester) *(ibid)*.
1603, July 23. JOHN CHAMBERLAIN, of Oxford. *(ibid)*.
1603, July 23. RICHARD LECHFORD, of Kent (Lee, Surrey) *(ibid)*.
1603, July 23. THOMAS HARFLEET, *alias* Septuans, of Kent *(ibid)*.
1603, July 23. THOMAS DUTTON, of Cheshire *(ibid)*.
1603, July 23. THOMAS ROBERTS, of Kent *(ibid)*.
1603, July 23. FRANCIS DOWSE, of Somerset, Nether Wallep, Hants. *(ibid)*.
1603, July 23. HENRY WILLIAMS *(ibid)*.
1603, July 23. HENRY BOWYER, of London (of Cookfield, Sussex) *(ibid)*.
1603, July 23. THOMAS DUCKETT, of Berks. *(ibid)*.
1603, July 23. THOMAS DARRELL, of Co. Lincoln *(ibid)*.
1603, July 23. ROBERT ASHBY, of Essex *(ibid)*.
1603, July 23. THOMAS (EDWARD) CULPEPPER, of Sussex *(ibid)*.
1603, July 23. EDWARD AVERY (ALVEY, AWBRAY), of Co. Gloucester. *(ibid)*.
1603, July 23. GEORGE SOMMERS, of Dorset. *(ibid)*.
1603, July 23. RICHARD PORTMAN (POTMAN), of Kent *(ibid)*.

KNIGHTS BACHELORS 119

1603, July 23. THOMAS HUNT, of Norfolk (London) (in the Royal Garden at Whitehall before the King's coronation).
1603, July 23. JOHN MORLEY, of London *(ibid)*.
1603, July 23. JOHN WILDGOSE, of Kent *(ibid)*.
1603, July 23. GEORGE PETER (PEETERS), of Essex *(ibid)*.
1603, July 23. SYMON STEWARD, of Co. Cambridge. *(ibid)*.
1603, July 23. NICHOLAS GASCOYNE, of Surrey *(ibid)*.
1603, July 23. BARNARD WHETSTONE, of Co. Lincoln (Woodford Hall, Essex) *(ibid)*.
1603, July 23. THOMAS CLARK, of Essex *(ibid)*.
1603, July 23. GEORGE WALDEGRAVE, of Suffolk *(ibid)*.
1603, July 23. WILLIAM BARROW, of Suffolk *(ibid)*
1603, July 23. JOHN WENTWORTH, of Suffolk (Norfolk) *(ibid)*.
1603, July 23. RICHARD SMITH, of Kent *(ibid)*.
1603, July 23. WILLIAM SLYNGSBY, of Co. York *(ibid)*.
1603. July 23. ARNOLD LYGON, of Worcester. *(ibid)*.
1603, July 23. EDWARD ALLAMY (ALBAINE) *(ibid)*.
1603, July 23. GEORGE YOUNG, of Somerset. *(ibid)*.
1603, July 23. JOHN SKYNNER, of Essex (Cambridge) *(ibid)*.
1603, July 23. CONYERS DARCY, of Co. Yorks. *(ibid)*.
1603, July 23. WILLIAM HARMAN, of Chester *(ibid)*.
1603, July 23. ANTHONY BROWNE, of Essex (Elson, Norfolk) *(ibid)*.
1603, July 23. NICHOLAS POYNTZ, of Co. Gloucester. *(ibid)*.
1603, July 23. OWEN OGLETHORPE, of Co. Oxford. *(ibid)*.
1603, July 23. GEORGE WILMORE (WALMORE), of Co. Notts. *(ibid)*.
1603, July 23. GREGORY WILMORE (WOLMORE), of Co. Lincoln. *(ibid)*.
1603, July 23. GEORGE BUCK, of Co. Lincoln, Master of the Revels *(ibid)*.
1603, July 23. JOHN BUCK, of Co. Worcester. (Hornby Grange, Lincoln) *(ibid)*.
1603, July 23. THOMAS CONEY (CONNEY), of Bassingham, Co. Lincoln. *(ibid)*.
1603, July 23. THOMAS PERNY (BERNEY), of Co. Norfolk. *(ibid)*.
1603, July 23. MARK STEWARD, of Ely, Cambridge *(ibid)*.
1603, July 23. MATHEW GAMBLE, of Co. Lincoln. (Spalden, Holland) *(ibid)*.
1603, July 23. JOHN GAMBLE, of Co. Lincoln. *(ibid)*.
1603, July 23. RICHARD WESTON, of Surrey *(ibid)*.
1603, July 23. THOMAS (HENRY) MAY, of Sussex *(ibid)*.

KNIGHTS BACHELORS

1603, July 23. LEONARD HASSELL (in the Royal Garden at Whitehall before the King's Coronation).
1603, July 23. FRANCIS BARNHAM, of Kent *(ibid)*.
1603, July 23. GEORGE FANE, of Hunton, Kent *(ibid)*.
1603, July 23. ANTHONY ROPER, of Farningham, Kent *(ibid)*.
1603, July 23. HENRY STONER (STEWARD), of Oxford. *(ibid)*.
1603, July 23. JOHN CARUS (CAROWSE).
1603, July 23. LEONARD HYDE (HIDE), of Herts. (Cambridge) *(ibid)*.
1603, July 23. CHARLES MORGAN, of Co. Hereford. *(ibid)*.
1603, July 23. ROWLAND MORGAN, of Co. Hereford. *(ibid)*.
1603, July 23. THOMAS HARDRES (HARDES), of Kent *(ibid)*.
1603, July 23. RICHARD BEAUMONT, of Co. Leicester. (Whitley, Yorks.) *(ibid)*.
1603, July 23. HENRY CHOLMLEY, of Cheshire (Yorks.) *(ibid)*.
1603, July 23. EDWARD PEACOCK, of Co. Middl. *(ibid)*.
1603, July 23. DREW DRURY, of Polsby, Norfolk. *(ibid)*.
1603, July 23. CHRISTOPHER YELVERTON, of Norfolk. *(ibid)*.
1603, July 23. CHARLES YELVERTON, of Norfolk. *(ibid)*.
1603, July 23. WILLIAM (RICHARD) GRESHAM, of Norfolk. *(ibid)*.
1603, July 23. HENRY ROLLE (ROWLE), senior, of Stevenston, Devon. *(ibid)*.
1603, July 23. HENRY ROLLE, junior, of Devon. *(ibid)*.
1603, July 23. JOHN HACKER *(ibid)*.
1603, July 23. WILLIAM BLACKSTON, of Durham. *(ibid)*.
1603, July 23. THOMAS MILDMAY, of Essex, *(ibid)*.
1603, July 23. ROWLAND LACY, of Co. Oxford. *(ibid)*.
1603, July 23. WILLIAM GOODYERE, of Berks. *(ibid)*.
1603, July 23. TIMOTHY LOWE, of Kent *(ibid)*.
1603, July 23. THOMAS WANTON (WAUTON), of Essex *(ibid)*.
1603, July 23. JULIAN (GIDEON) HANSON (ANSAM, AWNSHAM), of Middl. *(ibid)*.
1603, July 23. THOMAS SKYNNER, of Essex *(ibid)*.
1603, July 23. JAMES CROFT (CROFTES), of Co. Hereford. *(ibid)*.
1603, July 23. WILLIAM WORLINGTON (WORTHINGTON), of Essex *(ibid)*.
1603, July 23. JOHN DORRINGTON (DODINGTON), of Co. Notts. *(ibid)*.
1603, July 23. ANTHONY DENTON, of Bucks. *(ibid)*.

KNIGHTS BACHELORS 121

1603, July 23. JOHN NEEDHAM (KEEDHAM), of Co. Northampton. (in the Royal Garden at Whitehall before the King's Coronation).
1603, July 23. EDWARD ONLEY, of Co. Catesby, Northampton. *(ibid)*.
1603, July 23. THOMAS SEYMORE (SEIMORE), of Somerset. *(ibid)*.
1603, July 23. HENRY HELMES, of Norfolk. (Northampton) *(ibid)*.
1603, July 23. WILLIAM LAYTON (LATON, LEIGHTON), of Salop. *(ibid)*.
1603, July 23. WILLIAM MYNNE, of Co. Rutland. *(ibid)*.
1603, July 23. JAMES STONHOWSE, of London *(ibid)*.
1603, July 23. MARK IVE (IVES), of Essex *(ibid)*.
1603, July 23. THOMAS HORWOLLE (HORWOOD).
1603, July 23. WILLIAM (JAMES) THOMAS, of Co. Carnarvon. *(ibid)*.
1603, July 23. WILLIAM MORRIS, of Co. Carnarvon. *(ibid)*.
1603, July 23. EDWARD CAPEL, of Herts. *(ibid)*.
1603, July 23. MAURICE COOPER, of Herts.
1603, July 23. MORRIS GRIFFITH *(ibid)*.
1603, July 23. ANDREW ASHLEY, of Writtle, Essex *(ibid)*.
1603, July 23. EDWARD SULIARD, of Suffolk *(ibid)*.
1603, July 23. BENJAMIN PELLET, of Bolney, Sussex *(ibid)*.
1603, July 23. ANDREW PASCHALL, of Springfield, Essex *(ibid)*.
1603, July 23. EDWARD RALEIGH, of Co. Warwick. *(ibid)*.
1603, July 23. RICHARD EDGECOMBE, of Devon. *(ibid)*.
1603, July 23. RICHARD VAUGHAN, of Co. Hereford. *(ibid)*.
1603, July 23. WILLIAM COB (COBBE), of Norfolk *(ibid)*.
1603, July 23. NICHOLAS GASCOIGN, of Surrey *(ibid)*.
1603, July 23. FRANCIS CLEER (CLEARE), of Norfolk *(ibid)*.
1603, July 23. GEORGE FORSTER *(ibid)*.
1603, July 23. JAMES CALTHROPP, of Norfolk *(ibid)*.
1603, July 23. THOMAS DARREL *(ibid)*.
1603, July 23. THOMAS ROBERTS *(ibid)*.
1603, July 23. HENRY DISNEY, of Co. Lincoln. *(ibid)*.
1603, July 23. GILFORD (WILLIAM) SLINGSBY, of Co. Yorks. *(ibid)*.
1603, July 23. JOHN SULIARD, of Suffolk *(ibid)*.
1603, July 23. PHILIP CONNISBY (CONESBIE), of Co. Hereford. *(ibid)*.
1603, July 23. GEORGE COTTON, of Cambridge. *(ibid)*.
1603, July 23. JOHN GILBERT, of Suffolk *(ibid)*.

1603, July 23. EDWARD BUTLER, of Herts. (in the Royal Garden at Whitehall before the King's Coronation).
1603, July 23. HENRY THYNNE, of Wilts. *(ibid)*.
1603, July 23. RICHARD EGERTON, of Stafford. *(ibid)*.
1603, July 23. EDWARD (HENRY) ASHFORD *(ibid)*.
1603, July 23. RALPH GIBBS, of Co. Lincoln. (Warwick) *(ibid)*.
1603, July 23. JOHN GUNBERT (GUNTER) *(ibid)*.
1603, July 23. JOHN (HENRY) JENKINS, of York. *(ibid)*.
1603, July 23. WILLIAM BOUCHIER *(ibid)*.
1603, July 23. WILLIAM DE GREY (GRAY), of Martyn, Norfolk. *(ibid)*.
1603, July 23. ROBERT DINLEY (DYNLEY), of Yorks. *(ibid)*.
1603, July 23. DANIEL NORTON, of Southwick, Hants. *(ibid)*.
1603, July 23. GEORGE GILL, of Herts. *(ibid)*.
1603, July 23. CLIPESBY GAWDY, of Suffolk *(ibid)*.
1603, July 23. WILLIAM WYTHERINGTON, of Co. Northampton. *(ibid)*.
1603, July 23. WILLIAM WYTHENS, of Eltham, Kent *(ibid)*.
1603, July 23. INGLEBY DANIEL, of Co. Yorks. *(ibid)*.
1603, July 23. HUGH WYRALL (WORRALL), of Co. Yorks. *(ibid)*.
1603, July 23. RICHARD SALTONSTALL, of London *(ibid)*.
1603, July 23. ROBERT (ROGER) HORTON (HALTON).
1603, July 23. VINCENT FULNETBY (FOWNETBY).
1603, July 23. FRANCIS EGEOCK, of Co. Worcester. *(ibid)*.
1603, July 23. PHILIP KIGHLEY (KEIGHLEY) *(ibid)*.
1603, July 23. WILLIAM HARRIS, of Shenfield, Essex *(ibid)*.
1603, July 23. THOMAS DALLISON, of Co. Lincoln. *(ibid)*.
1603, July 23. JOHN DORMER, of Bucks. *(ibid)*.
1603, July 23. WILLIAM BOND, of London *(ibid)*.
1603, July 23. FRANCIS TANFIELD, of Norfolk. (Gayton, Northampton) *(ibid)*.
1603, July 23. GEORGE BELGRAVE, of Co. Lincoln. (Belgrave, Leicester) *(ibid)*.
1603, July 23. CLEMENT SPILMAN, of Norfolk (Oxford) *(ibid)*.
1603, July 23. EDWARD SHEFFIELD, of Co. Yorks. *(ibid)*.
1603, July 23. CALTHROP PARKER, of Suffolk *(ibid)*.
1603, July 23. EDWARD MARBURY, of Co. Lincoln *(ibid)*.
1603, July 23. JOHN DANNSEY (DAUNCIE), of Cheshire *(ibid)*.

KNIGHTS BACHELORS 123

1603, July 23. RICHARD TRACY, of Co. Gloucester. (in the Royal Garden at Whitehall before the King's Coronation).
1603, July 23. JOHN POWELL *(ibid)*.
1603, July 23. ROBERT EDOLFE, of Henxhall, Kent *(ibid)*.
1603, July 23. DAVID WOODROFFE, of Poyl, Surrey *(ibid)*.
1603, July 23. MANWOOD PENRUDDOK, of Wilts. *(ibid)*.
1603, July 23. THOMAS HARWELL (HARTWELL, HORWOLL), of Co. Worcester. *(ibid)*.
1603, July 23. THOMAS BIGGES, of Co. Worcester. *(ibid)*.
1603, July 23. EDWARD (THOMAS) BLENERHASSET, of Norfolk *(ibid)*.
1603, July 23. ROBERT WELSH, of Sussex *(ibid)*.
1603, July 23. GEORGE SNELLING, of Portslade, Sussex *(ibid)*.
1603, July 23. JOHN (EDWARD) CLAXTON, of Durham *(ibid)*.
1603, July 23. RICHARD MANWARING, of Cheshire *(ibid)*.
1603, July 23. GEORGE PARKINS, of Kent (Bunny, Notts.) *(ibid)*.
1603, July 23. RALPH MADDISON, of Kent *(ibid)*.
1603, July 23. RICHARD WYVER *(ibid)*.
1603, July 23. ROBERT STAMFORD (STANFORD), of Co. Stafford. *(ibid)*.
1603, July 23. ROBERT CHESTER, of Herts. *(ibid)*.
1603, July 23. THOMAS GRESHAM, of Titsey, Surrey *(ibid)*.
1603, July 23. HENRY WARNER, of Suffolk *(ibid)*.
1603, July 23. THOMAS HAYES.
1603, July 23. HENRY ASHLEY, of Kent *(ibid)*.
1603, July 23. ROBERT WYNDE (WINDEY, WINDE), of Norfolk (Gloucester) *(ibid)*.
1603, July 23. EDWARD CLAYBORNE (CLEYBORNE), of Notts. *(ibid)*.
1603, July 23. FRANCIS CURSON, of Salop *(ibid)*.
1603, July 23. ANTHONY ROWSE, of Haulten, Cornwall *(ibid)*.
1603, July 23. WILLIAM REYNARD *(ibid)*.
1603, July 23. WILLIAM STEED, of Havesham, Kent *(ibid)*.
1603, July 23. WILLIAM AP RICE (PRICE AP RHEIS), of Washoughly, Co. Huntingdon. *(ibid)*.
1603, July 23. THOMAS STANDISH, of Co. Lincoln. *(ibid)*.
1603, July 23. WALTER DEVEREUX, of Suffolk (Castle Bromwich, Warwick) *(ibid)*.
1603, July 23. WILLIAM HUDSON, of Northumberland *(ibid)*.
1603, July 23. EDWARD PYNCHON, of Essex *(ibid)*.

KNIGHTS BACHELORS

1603, July 23. THOMAS FREAK, of Sherborn, Dorset. (in the Royal Garden at Whitehall before the King's Coronation).
1603, July 23. ROBERT MILLER, of Dorset. *(ibid)*.
1603, July 23. THOMAS PRIDEAUX, of Devon. *(ibid)*.
1603, July 23. FLEETWOOD DORMER, of Shipton Lee, Bucks. *(ibid)*.
1603, July 23. HENRY MAXEY, of Bradwell, Essex *(ibid)*.
1603, July 23. HENRY BUCKINGHAM (BOKENHAM), of Norfolk (Suffolk) *(ibid)*.
1603, July 23. WILLIAM SAMUEL, of Northampton *(ibid)*.
1603, July 23. JOHN ACTON, of Devon. *(ibid)*.
1603, July 23. BARTHOLOMEW SAMBORNE, of Somerset. *(ibid)*.
1603, July 23. THOMAS ROOKBY (ROCKLEY), of Co. Yorks. *(ibid)*.
1603, July 23. ALEXANDER BARLOW, of Lancs. *(ibid)*.
1603, July 23. ROGER PORTINGTON, of Co. Yorks. (Everton, Notts.) *(ibid)*.
1603, July 23. HENRY WHITEHEAD, of Herts. (Normans Court, Southants) *(ibid)*.
1603, July 23. REYNOLD (REGINALD) SCRYVEN, of Salop. *(ibid)*. Not knighted.
1603, July 23. FRANCIS HILLESLEY, of Co. York. *(ibid)*.
1603, July 23. RICHARD PELL, of Hants. (Silk Willoughby, Lincoln) *(ibid)*.
1603, July 23. THOMAS BARTLET, of Co. Gloucester. (Berks.) *(ibid)*.
1603, July 23. ANTHONY IREBY, of Boston, Co. Lincoln. *(ibid)*.
1603, July 23. ANTHONY PELHAM *(ibid)*.
1603, July 23. THOMAS SOUTHWELL, of Norfolk *(ibid)*.
1603, July 23. EDWARD PARHAM, of Co. Lincoln. *(ibid)*.
1603, July 23. JOHN BENTLEY, of Co. Derby (Birdsall Park, Devon) *(ibid)*.
1603, July 23. THOMAS LAMBERT, of Co. Derby *(ibid)*.
1603, July 23. EDWARD SOWTHE, of Co. Somerset. *(ibid)*.
1603, July 23. JOHN HUBERT (HUBBERT), of Norfolk. *(ibid)*.
1603, July 23. THOMAS FOWLER, junior, of Middl. *(ibid)*.
1603, July 23. CHARLES KELK, of Co. Lincoln. *(ibid)*.
1603, July 23. WALTER AYSCOUGH, of Co. Lincoln. *(ibid)*.
1603, July 23. RICHARD CONQUEST, of Co. Lincoln. (York) *(ibid)*.
1603, July 23. JOHN BYNNE (BYNDE) *(ibid)*.
1603, July 23. GILES HOWLAND, of London *(ibid)*.
1603, July 23. FRANCIS VENTRICE, of Co. Northampton. *(ibid)*.
1603, July 23. HENRY BUNBURY, of Stanny, Co. Cheshire *(ibid)*.
1603, July 23. THOMAS EDEN, of Suffolk *(ibid)*.

KNIGHTS BACHELORS

1603, July 23. HENRY JAMES, of Smarden, Kent (in the Royal Garden at Whitehall before the King's Coronation).
1603, July 23. EDWARD AWBREY, of Co. Pembroke. *(ibid)*.
1603, July 23. WILLIAM AWBREY, of Co. Pembroke. *(ibid)*.
1603, July 23. GEORGE FORSTER *(ibid)*.
1603, July 23. WILLIAM HOWSON, of Co. Lincoln. *(ibid)*.
1603, July 23. WILLIAM WRAY, of Cornwall (Glentworth, Lincoln) *(ibid)*.
1603, July 23. RICHARD MICHELBORNE, of Suffolk (Broadhurst, Sussex *(ibid)*.
1603, July 23. ISAAC APPLETON, of Essex (Waldingfield, Suffolk) *(ibid)*.
1603, July 23. TOBIE CHANCY (CHAUNCIE), of Co. Northampton. *(ibid)*.
1603, July 23. WILLIAM CHANCY, of Co. Northampton. *(ibid)*.
1603, July 23. THOMAS VARNAM (VERNAN), of Co. York. *(ibid)*.
1603, July 23. CHRISTOPHER HODSON, of Co. Bucks. *(ibid)*.
1603, July 23. JOHN LOCKTON, of Co. Lincoln. *(ibid)*.
1603, July 23. JOHN PAWLET, of Wilts. *(ibid)*.
1603, July 23. CHARLES BARNABY (BARNEBY), of Co. Yorks. *(ibid)*.
1603, July 23. THOMAS DREW, of Devon. *(ibid)*.
1603, July 23. GEORGE SOWTHCOT, of Devon. *(ibid)*.
1603, July 23. ROBERT BROWN, of Dorset. *(ibid)*.
1603, July 23. ANTHONY DRURY, of Norfolk *(ibid)*.
1603, July 23. WILLIAM HARRIS, of Crixey, Essex *(ibid)*.
1603, July 23. HUGH BRAWNE, of London *(ibid)*.
1603, July 23. HENRY WINDHAM, of Norfolk *(ibid)*.
1603, July 23. ROBERT DRURY, of Rougham, Suffolk *(ibid)*.
1603, July 23. JOHN PRETYMAN, of Suffolk *(ibid)*.
1603, July 23. WILLIAM PAWLET, of Wilts. *(ibid)*.
1603, July 23. JOHN AYLMER (ELMER), of Co. Lincoln. *(ibid)*.
1603, July 23. THOMAS HANMER, of Co. Flint *(ibid)*.
1603, July 23. JASPER MOORE *(ibid)*.
1603, July 23. WILLIAM CRAFORD (CRAYFORD), of Kent *(ibid)*.
1603, July 23. ROBERT STANFORD, of Co. Stafford. *(ibid)*.
1603, July 23. ROBERT COTTON, of Co. Huntingdon. *(ibid)*.
1603, July 23. GEORGE GRENVILE (GREINFELD), of Cornwall *(ibid)*.
1603, July 23. GEORGE GILBY (SELBEE), of Co. Lincoln. *(ibid)*.

1603, July 23. RICHARD FETIPLACE, of Berks. (in the Royal Garden at Whitehall before the King's Coronation).
1603, July 23. JEROM (JEREMY), HORSEY, of Bucks. (Lincoln) *(ibid)*.
1603, July 23. FRANCIS GOLDSMITH, of Crayford, Kent *(ibid)*.
1603, July 23. THOMAS ELLIOT, of Surrey (Newland Hall, Writtle, Essex *(ibid)*.
1603, July 23. ROBERT PRIDEAUX, of Devon. *(ibid)*.
1603, July 23. NICHOLAS STODDER (STODDARD), of Mottingham, Eltham, Kent *(ibid)*.
1603, July 23. ROBERT PENRUDDOK, of Wilts. *(ibid)*.
1603, July 23. THOMAS BEAKE.
1603, July 23. —— LEICESTER.
1603, July 23. EDWARD WINGFEILD.
1603, July 23. ROBERT STROUDE.
1603, July 23. JOHN WINDHAM.
1603, July 23. JOHN FITZ.
1603, July 23. LEWIS STUKELEY.
1603, July 23. THOMAS HARRIS, of Malden, Essex.
1603, July 23. HENRY BOULE ? see Rolle *supra*, p. 120.
1603, July 23. SAMUEL (SAMPSON) LENNARD, of Kent.
1603, July 23. THOMAS MARVIN.
1603, July 23. THOMAS BLENNERHASSET.
1603, July 23. THOMAS HARTGILL, of Herts.
1603, July 23. THOMAS HAREWOOD.
1603, July 23. —— WYATT.
1603, July 23. WILLIAM GAINSFORD.
1603, July 23. NICHOLAS SMITHE.
1603, July 23. EDWARD PENRUDDOCKE.
1603, July 23. WILLIAM MORGAN, of Tredegar, Glamorgan.
1603, July 23. —— FITZWILLIAMS.
1603, July 23. PHILIP ANESLIE (ANNESLEY).
1603, July 23. WESTON BROWN.
1603, July 23. JOHN OTELEY.
1603, July 23. THOMAS BROMLEY.
1603, July 23. —— RUDYARD.
1603, July 23. —— SHERBORNE.
1603, July 23. EDWARD FILMORE.

KNIGHTS BACHELORS

1603, July 23. —— BUCKMORE.
1603, July 23. JOHN THORNEY.
1603, July 23. JAMES BUGGES.
1603, July 23. THOMAS INGHAM, of Goodneston, Kent *(ibid)*.
1603, July 23. THOMAS VERNEY *(ibid)*.
1603, July 23. THOMAS PHILLIPS, of Sommerset *(ibid)*.
1603, July 23. CHARLES PERSHALL *(ibid)*.
1603, July 23. THOMAS CROWE *(ibid)*.
1603, July 23. ROBERT KELLIGREW (at Hanworth, June 5, *sic?* for Whitehall).
1603, July 24. BAPTIST HICKS, alderman (at Whitehall).
1603, July 24. RICHARD BROWN, of Essex *(ibid)*.
1603, July 24. MARMADUKE DARRELL (DOREL), of Fulmere, Bucks. *(ibid)*.
1603, July 24. RAFE WELDON, of Kent *(ibid)*.
1603, July 24. HENRY COCK, cofferer, of Broxborne, Herts.
1603, July 24 (23). RICHARD COCKS, clerk comptroller of the Household (at Whitehall).
1603, July 24. BARTHOLOMEW FULKS (FOWKES), of Herts. *(ibid)*.
1603, July 24. ROBERT VERNAM (VERNON, VARNAM), of Cheshire *(ibid)*.
1603, July 25. RALPH BINGLEY (in Christ Church, Dublin, by Sir George Carey, lord deputy, on St. James's day, being Coronation day).
1603, July 25. THOMAS WILLIAMS *(ibid)*.
1603, July 25. EDMUND FETTEPLACE *(ibid)*.
1603, July 25. TOBY CALFIELD *(ibid)*.
1603, July 25. JOHN TYRRELL, mayor of Dublin *(ibid)*.
1603, July 25. THOMAS COOCHE (at Dublin Castle by same after dinner).
1603, July 25. FERDINANDO FRECKLETON *(ibid)*.
1603, July 25. GEORGE GREAME (GRYMES) *(ibid)*.
1603, July 25. MULRONY O'CARROLL *(ibid)*.
1603, July 25. THOMAS ASH *(ibid)*.
1603, July 25. WILLIAM USSHER *(ibid)*.
1603, July 25. RICHARD BOYLE *(ibid, after supper)*.
1603, July 25. LAURENCE ESMOND *(ibid)*.
1603, July 25. PETER MANWOOD, sheriff of Kent.
1603, July 26 (24). THOMAS BENNETT, alderman of London (at Whitehall).

1603, July 26 (24). THOMAS LOWE, alderman of London (at Whitehall).
1603, July 26 (24). LEONARD HALIDAY (HOLIDAY), alderman of London *(ibid)*.
1603, July 26 (24). JOHN WATTS, alderman of London *(ibid)*.
1603, July 26 (24). RICHARD GODDARD, alderman of London *(ibid)*.
1603, July 26 (24). HENRY ROWE, alderman of London *(ibid)*.
1603, July 26 (24). EDWARD HOLMDEN (HAMDAINE), alderman of London *(ibid)*.
1603, July 26 (24). ROBERT HAMPSON, alderman of London *(ibid)*.
1603, July 26 (24). HUMPHREY WELD (WILDE), alderman of London
1603, July 26 (24). THOMAS CAMBELL, alderman of London *(ibid)*.
1603, July 26 (24). WILLIAM CRAVEN, alderman of London *(ibid)*.
1603, July 26 (24). HENRY ANDERSON, alderman of London *(ibid)*.
1603, July 26 (24). WILLIAM GLOVER, alderman of London *(ibid)*.
1603, July 26 (24). JAMES PEMBERTON, sheriff of London *(ibid)*).
1603, July 26 (24). JOHN SWYNERTON, sheriff of London *(ibid)*.
1603, July 26 (24). WILLIAM ROMNEY (RUMNEY), alderman of London *(ibid)*.
1603, July 26 (24). THOMAS MIDDLETON, alderman of London *(ibid)*.
1603, July 26 (24). THOMAS HAYES, alderman of London *(ibid)*.
1603, July 26 (24). WILLIAM CRANLEY, alderman of London *(ibid)*.
1603, Aug. 5. THOMAS BECKINGHAM of Beckingham, end, Essex (at Hampton Court).
1603, Aug. 5. JAMES MURREY, of Scotland *(ibid)*.
1603, Aug. 5. JOHN FERON (FEARNE) *(ibid)*.
1603, Aug. (13–16). RICHARD WHITE, of Hants. (at South Warnborough).
1603, Sept. 4. RICHARD WILBRAHAM (at Christ Church, Dublin, by Sir George Carey, lord deputy of Ireland).
1603, Sept. 16. THOMAS ROPER *(ibid* by same).
1603, Sept. 18 (21). WILLIAM WINDSOR *(ibid* by same).
1603, Sept. 29. RODERICK (ROREY) O'DONNELL, created earl of Tyrconnel and knighted (at Dublin Castle by same).
1603, Sept. 29. FRANCIS ROE (ROWE), (at Dublin Castle by the earl of Tyrconnel).
1603, Sept. 29. HENRY CROFTES *(ibid* by same).
1603, Sept. 29. RAFE CONSTABLE *(ibid* by same).
1603, Sept. 29. RICHARD NUGENT, lord Delvin *(ibid* by same).

KNIGHTS BACHELORS 129

1603, Sept. 29. RALPHE SYDLY
    (at Dublin Castle by the earl of Tyrconnel).
1603, Sept. 29. JAMES GOUGH (GOGHE) *(ibid by same)*.
1603, Sept. 29. JOHN MACNAMARA *(ibid by same)*.
1603 [Sept. 20–Oct. 4]. JOHN GEFFERY (JEFFERY), of Co. Worcester. (at Southampton by the King).
1603 [Sept. 20–Oct. 4]. JAMES OUCHTERLONY (at Winchester).
1603. WILLIAM RICHARDSON, of Co. Worcester *(ibid)*.
1603, Oct. 2. JAMES LANCASTER, of Herts. *(ibid)*.
1603, Oct. 2. WILLIAM HARPOLE (by Sir George Carey, lord deputy of Ireland).
1603, Oct. 2. EDWARD FISHER *(ibid by same)*.
after 1603, Dec. 1. WILLIAM RAYNER, sheriff of Notts.
1603, Dec. 9. (Oct. 8). JAMES LEA (LEY), of Devon (Westbury Wilts) (at Wilton by the King).
1603, Dec. 9 (Nov.–Oct. 18). MOUNS. DAVELI. (DOVALLE) *(ibid)*.
1603, Dec. 18. (10 ? Nov. 18). RICHARD COOK, of Bucks. (at Woodstock).
1603, Dec. 18. JOHN JEPHSON (at Dublin Castle by Sir George Carey, lord deputy of Ireland).
1603, Dec. 18. JOHN DAVIS *(ibid by same)*.
1603, Feb. 22. WILLIAM BRABAZON, son and heir to Sir Edward Brabazon (at Reban by same).
1603-4, Mar. 9. FRANCIS KINGSMILL *(ibid by same)*.
1603-4, Mar. 12. ELIAS JONES *(ibid by same)*.
1603-4, Mar. 14 (? 15). LAWRENCE TANFIELD, of Co. Oxford (at the Tower by the king).
1603-4, Mar. 14. GEORGE BLOUNT, of Devon *(ibid)*.
1603-4, Mar. 14. GEORGE (GARRET) KEMP *(ibid)*.
1603-4, Mar 14. NICHOLAS BROWN *(ibid)*.
1603-4, Mar. 14. NICHOLAS TEMPEST, of Kent (? Durham) *(ibid)*.
1603-4, Mar. 14. WILLIAM BROWN, of Sussex, lieut. gov. of Flushing *(ibid)*.
1603-4, Mar. 14. TIMOTHY WHITTINGHAM, of Bucks. (? Durham) *(ibid)*.
1603-4, Mar. 14. ANTHONY BROWN, of Essex (at the Tower).
1603-4, Mar. 14. JOHN ASHBORNHAM, of Sussex *(ibid)*.
1603-4, Mar. 14. EDWARD BELLINGHAM.
1603-4, Mar. 14. GEORGE YOUNG.
1603-4, Mar. 14. HAMON LE STRANGE, of Norfolk *(ibid)*.
1603-4, Mar. 14. GILBERT WAKERING, of Sussex *(ibid)*.

1603–4, Mar. 14. ROBERT DALINGTON (At the Tower).
1603–4, Mar. 14. JOHN KERN *(ibid)*.
1603–4, Mar. 14. THOMAS MULLYNS *(ibid)*.
1603–4, Mar. 14. ALEXANDER TEMPLE, of Kent *(ibid)*.
1603–4, Mar. 14. THOMAS HORSMAN, of Co. Lincoln. *(ibid)*.
1603–4, Mar. 14. WILLIAM BILSBY, of Co. Lincoln. *(ibid)*.
1603–4, Mar. 14. JOHN (EDWARD) BOYS of Kent *(ibid)*.
1603–4, Mar. 14. JOHN WILLIAMS, of Northampton *(bid)*.
1603–4, Mar. 14. THOMAS LEWSEY *(ibid)*.
1603–4, Mar. 14. JUSTINIAN LEWEN (LOWEN), of Kent *(ibid)*.
1603–4, Mar. 14. STEPHEN PROCTOR, of Co. York. *(ibid)*.
1603–4, Mar. 14. CHRISTOPHER MARTYN, of Cambridge *(ibid)*.
1603–4, Mar. 14. JOHN COLLYMORE, of Kent *(ibid)*.
1603–4, Mar. 14. JOHN CONWAY, of Co. Flint *(ibid)*.
1603–4, Mar. 14. EDMOND ASHFIELD, of Bucks. *(ibid)*.
1603–4, Mar. 14. JOHN ACKLAND (ACKLAM), of Devon, (Yorks.) *(ibid)*.
1603–4, Mar. 14. THOMAS STANLEY, of Co. Derby (Fittleworth, Sussex) *(ibid)*.
1603–4, Mar. 14. WILLIAM WEBBE, of Wilts. (Melcomb, Dorset) *(ibid)*.
1603–4, Mar. 14. JOHN HAMDEN, of Sussex *(ibid)*.
1603–4, Mar. 14. CAVALLERO MAYCOTT (MACOTT), of Kent *(ibid)*.
1603–4, Mar. 14. THOMAS CULPEPPER, of Sussex *(ibid)*.
1603–4, Mar. 14. JOHN HALL, of Hants. *(ibid)*.
1603–4, Mar. 14. HARBOTTLE GRYMSTON, of Suffolk (Bradfield, Essex) *(ibid)*.
1603–4, Mar. 14 (1604, Aug. 20). EDWARD MANSFIELD (MANSELL) *(ibid)*.
1603–4, Mar. 14. RICHARD STROUDE *(ibid)* [? see 1603, July 23].
1603–4, Mar. 14. HENRY ST. BARBE, of Devon. *(ibid)*.
1603–4, Mar. 14. WILLIAM THOROLD, of Co. Lincoln *(ibid)*.
1603–4, Mar. 14. CLEMENT (*recte* HENRY) SPILMAN, of Co. Oxford (Norfolk) *(ibid)*.
1603–4, Mar. 14. HENRY CONSTABLE, of Co. York *(ibid)*.
1603–4, Mar. 14. JOHN HEDWORTH, of Durham (at the Tower).
1603–4, Mar. 14. JOHN WEBBE, of Wilts *(ibid)*.
1603–4, Mar. 14. PETER GARTON, of Sussex *(ibid)*.
1603–4, Mar. 14. HENRY JENKINSON, of York *(ibid)*.
1603–4, Mar. 14. FRANCIS VERNEY, of Cheshire *(ibid)*.

KNIGHTS BACHELORS 131

1603–4, Mar. 14. JOHN RHODES, of Co. Derby (At the Tower).
1603–4, Mar. 14. FRANCIS LEAKE, of Co. York. (Sutton, Derby) *(ibid)*.
1603–4, Mar. 14. THOMAS KNIVETT, of Co. Wilts. *(ibid)*.
1603–4, Mar. 14. NICHOLAS BLUNT *(ibid)*.
1603–4, Mar. 14. ROBERT DONALT *(ibid)*.
1603–4, Mar. 14. THOMAS MONTFORD, of Warwick *(ibid)*.
1603–4, Mar. 14. ROBERT VERNEY *(ibid)*.
1604, Mar. 25. JOSIAS BODLEY (at Reban by Sir George Carey, lord deputy of Ireland).
1604, Mar. 25. JOHN OWESLEY *(ibid by same)*.
1604, Mar. 25. WILLIAM TAAFE *(ibid by same)*.
1604, Apr. 1. RICHARD GROBHAM (GRUBHAM), of Wilts, Herts., (at Royston by the King).
1604, Apr. 1. GEORGE GUNTER, of Sussex *(ibid)*.
1604, Apr. 1. RICHARD HYDE, of Cambridge. *(ibid)*.
1604, Apr. 1. CHARLES NORWYCH, of Northampton. *(ibid)*.
1604, Apr. 1. DAVID CONINGHAM, of Coningham *(ibid)*.
1604, Apr. 17. TEIGE O'ROURKE (at Reban by Sir George Carey, lord lieutenant of Ireland).
1604, Apr. 17. DONNOGH O'CONNOR SLIGAH *(ibid)*.
1604, Apr. 17. TIRLOGHE McHENRY O'NEALE *(ibid)*.
1604, Apr. 18. ROBERT BRETT, of Devon. (at Whitehall by the King).
1604, Apr. 18. THOMAS NEAL, of Hants *(ibid)*.
1604, Apr. 18. GEORGE CONYERS, of Co. York (Soackburn, Durham) *(ibid)*.
1604, Apr. 18. ROBERT DOLMAN, of Berks (Yorks.) *(ibid)*.
1604, Apr. 18. FRANCIS FITCHE (FITZ), of Co. Yorks. (Essex) *(ibid)*.
1604, Apr. 18 ? THOMAS BODLEY (at Whitehall).
1604, Apr. 18. JOHN OSBORNE *(ibid)*.
1604, Apr. 18. THOMAS WISEMAN, of Essex *(ibid)*.
1604, Apr. 18. WILFORD LAWSON, of Cumberland (at Whitehall).
1604, Apr. 18. THOMAS PIGOTT, of Bucks. *(ibid)*.
1604, Apr. 18. ALEXANDER TUTT, of Wilts. *(ibid)*.
1604, Apr. 18. NORTON KNATCHBULL, of Kent. *(ibid)*.
1604, Apr. 18. ROBERT YOUNG, of Somerset, Haselbury (Herts.) *(ibid)*.
1604, Apr. (? 18). MICHAEL DORMER, of Bucks. *(ibid)*.
1604, Apr. (? 18). RICHARD GREENWAY, of Sussex (London *(ibid)*.

1604, Apr. (? 18). THOMAS DILKES, of Warwick (At Whitehall).
1604, Apr. (? 18). GEORGE THROCKMORTON, of Co. Gloucester. *(ibid)*.
1604, Apr. (? 18). RICHARD INGOLSBY (INGLEBY), of Bucks. *(ibid)*.
1604, May 1. BASIL BROOK, of Madeley, Shropshire (at Sir William Cornwallis's at Highgate).
1604, May 5. LYONELL GUEST (at Lexlipp by Sir George Carey, lord deputy of Ireland).
1604, May 8. PARR LANE *(ibid* by same).
1604, May 8. GEORGE BEVERLY *(ibid* by same).
1604, May 12. FRANCIS EVERS (EWERS), of Co. York. (by the King at Whitehall).
1604, May 12. MARTIN CULPEPPER, of Co. Oxford. *(ibid)*
1604, May 12. EDWARD BOYS, of Kent *(ibid)*.
1604, May 12. THOMAS POWER (GOWER), of Stitnam, Co. York. *(ibid)*.
1604, May 12. BARTHOLOMEW MICHEL, of Co. Notts. *(ibid)*.
1604, May 12. MATTHEW BAMFEILD, of Devon. (Wilts.) *(ibid)*.
1604, May 12. ROGER (ROBERT) WOODROFF *(ibid)*.
1604, May 12. WOLSTON DIXIE, of Co. Leicester. *(ibid)*.
1604, May 12. WILLIAM GRATWICKE (GREATWICK), of Sussex *(ibid)*.
1604, May 12. ADOLPHUS CAREW (RODOLPHUS CARIE) *(ibid)*.
1604, May 12. JOHN BOWYER, of London *(ibid)*.
1604, May 12. EDMOND CRIPPES (CRISPE), of Kent *(ibid)*.
1604, May 12. EDWARD HEXT (HEX), of Devon *(ibid)*.
1604, May 12. NICHOLAS STALAGE, of Sussex *(ibid)*.
1604, May 30. CUTHBERT PEPPER, of Co. Lincoln. (Yorks.) (at Whitehall).
1604, May 30. ROBERT OSBORN, of Co. Northampton. *(ibid)*.
1604, May 30. WILLIAM (GILBERT) PRINCE, of Wilts. (at Whitehall).
1604, May 30. WYMOND CAREW, of Norfolk *(ibid)*.
1604, May 30. ROGER OWEN, of Essex, sheriff of Shropshire *(ibid)*.
1604, May 30. GABRIEL POYNTZ, of London *(ibid)*.
1604, May 30. RICHARD WILLIAMSON, of the Council at York *(ibid)*.
1604, May 30. JOHN JACKSON, of the Council at York *(ibid)*.
1604, May 30. WILLIAM GEE, of the Council at York. *(ibid)*.
1604, May 30. HUGH BETHEL, of Co. York. *(ibid)*.
1604, May 30. THOMAS BLAND, of Co. York. *(ibid)*.
1604, May 30. CHARLES EGERTON (EVERTON), of Co. Stafford. *(ibid)*.

KNIGHTS BACHELORS 133

1604, May 30. JOHN FERON (FERNE), of Co. York. *(ibid ?* at Hampton Court, June 10).
1604, May 30. WILLIAM BERWICK (BARWICKE), of Suffolk *(ibid ?* at Hampton Court, June 10).
1604, June 2. JOHN SPECOT (SPECOTT), of Devon (at Greenwich).
1604, June 12. ADAM SPRATLING, of Kent *(ibid)*.
1604, June 12. GEORGE SMYTH, of Devon *(ibid)*.
1604, June 12. THOMAS HONYWOOD, of Kent *(ibid)*.
1604, June 12. RICHARD GRAVES (GREEVES), of Co. Herts (Worcester) *(ibid)*.
1604, June 12. CHARLES HOLLIS (HOLES, HALES), of Kent, Warwick *(ibid)*.
1604, June 12. JOHN WHETBROOK (WHITBROKE), of Salop *(ibid)*.
1604, June 12 (14). JOHN CLAYPOOLE *(ibid)*.
1604, June 16. RICHARD TRACY, son and heir of Paul Tracy, of Stanway, Gloucester (at Leighton).
1604, June 16. WILLIAM STONE, of London (Leighton, Beds.) (at Ruckholts, the seat of Michael Hickes at Leyland (Leighton), Essex (Beds).
1604, June 16. DAVID WOOD *(ibid)*.
1604, June 29. ROBERT HITCHMAN (HITCHAM), of Suffolk (attorney to queen Anne, sergeant-at-law (at Whitehall).
1604, June 29. HENRY TOWNSEND, of Salop, chief justice of Chester *(ibid)*.
1604, June 29. THOMAS EDEN, of Suffolk *(ibid)*.
1604, June 30 (July 3). WILLIAM HUTTON, of Cumberland (at Greenwich by the King).
1604, July 1. RICHARD GRYMES (at Lexlipp by Sir George Carey, the lord deputy of Ireland).
1604, July 1 (10). DANIEL O'BRIEN *(ibid by same)*.
1604, July 1 (10). NICHOLAS MORDANTE *(ibid by same)*.
1604, July 3 (21). WILLIAM FORD (FORTH), at Suffolk (at Greenwich).
1604, July 3. WILLIAM HALL, of Bibrook, Kent (at Greenwich).
1604, July 3. EDMOND PELHAM (PEKHAM), of Sussex *(ibid)*.
1604, July 4. FRANCIS HOWARD, of Surrey (at Chatham).
1604, July 4. SECKFORD TREVOR, of Flint. *(ibid)*.
1604, July 4. FRANCIS CORNWALL, of Salop *(ibid)*.
1604, July 4. GEORGE CURSON *(ibid)*.
1604, July 4. STEPHEN (JOHN) RIDELSDON (RYDELSTON), of Co. York. *(ibid)*.
1604, July 4. ROGER NEVESON, of Kent *(ibid)*.

1604, July 4. THOMAS BLUDDER, of Essex (Surrey) (at Chatham).
1604, July 4. JOHN LEWIS, of Glamorgan *(ibid)*.
1604, July 4. WALTER GORE, of Wilts. *(ibid)*.
1604, July 4. WILLIAM LOWRE (LOWER), of Cornwall *(ibid)*.
1604, July 4. PETER BUCK, of Kent *(ibid)*.
1604, July 4. WALTER CHETWYND, of Co. Stafford. *(ibid)*.
1604, July 4. FRANCIS CHERRY, of London *(ibid)*.
1604, July 4. WILLIAM CHETWYND, of Co. Stafford. *(ibid)*.
1604, July 4. WILLIAM PAGE, of Kent *(ibid)*.
1604, July 4. WILLIAM HORWOOD, of Co. Stafford. *(ibid)*.
1604, July 4. ROBERT JAUDRELL, of Co. Cambridge. *(ibid)*.
1604, July 4. JOHN SCORY (STORY) *(ibid)*.
1604, July 4. WILLIAM HILL, of Kent *(ibid)*.
1604, July 4. ANTHONY AUGER (AUCHER), of Kent *(ibid)*.
1604, July 4. JEREMIAH TURNER, of Surrey *(ibid)*.
1604, July 4. EDWARD BROMLEY, of Salop *(ibid)*.
1604, July 4. EDWARD (THOMAS) STODDER (STUDDER), of Bucks. *(ibid)*.
1604, July 4. JOHN RAWLINSON, of Essex *(ibid)*.
1604, July 4. GEORGE WRIGHT, of Kent *(ibid)*.
1604, July 7. THOMAS FORSTER, of Herts. (at Whitehall).
1604, July 8. JAMES DEAN, of London *(ibid)*.
1604, July 8. ROGER JONES, of London *(ibid)*.
1604, July 10 (? 11). JOHN LINWRAY, of Somerset. *(ibid)*.
1604, July 10. EDWARD MUSGRAVE, of Cumberland *(ibid)*.
1604, July 10. ROBERT JOHNSON, of Bucks. *(ibid)*.
1604, July 15. GEORGE LYNNE (HAME) (at Oatlands).
1604, July 15. ARTHUR ASTON, of Co. Staff. *(ibid)*.
1604, July 15. GEORGE KEER, of Caithness *(ibid)*.
1604, July 21. GILBERT HOUGHTON (HAUGHTON), of Co. Lancs. *(ibid* or at Whitehall).
1604, July (? after 21). PHILIP HOWARD of Herts (at Oatlands).
1604, July (? after) 21. WILLIAM FORD (FORTH), of Suffolk *(ibid)*.
1604, July (? after) 21. NATHANIEL (FRANCIS) BACON, junr., of Norfolk *(ibid)*.
1604, July (? after) 21. MARTYN STUTVILE, of Suffolk *(ibid)*.
1604, July (? after) 21. JAMES BACON, of Suffolk *(ibid)*.
1604, July (? after) 21. HENRY BENINGFIELD, of Suffolk *(ibid)*.

KNIGHTS BACHELORS

1604, July (? after) 21. WILLIAM WISEMAN, of Essex (at Ware, ? Whitehall, in the King's bedchamber).

1604, Aug. 2. AMBROSE FOORD (FORTH) (at Lexlipp by Sir George Carey, lord deputy of Ireland).

1604, Aug. 6. MICHAEL HICKS, of Essex (at Theobalds).

1604, Aug. 6. STEPHEN POWLE, of Essex *(ibid)*.

1604, Aug. 6. THOMAS DACRES, of Co. Yorks. (Herts.) *(ibid)*.

1604, Aug. 6. CHRISTOPHER PIGOT, of Bucks. *(ibid)*.

1604, Aug. 6. GEORGE HEYWARD (HAWARD, HAYWOOD), of London (Salop) *(ibid)*.

1604, Aug. 6. ARTHUR DAKYNS, of Co. York. *(ibid)*.

1604, Aug. 18. OLIVER BUTLER (BOTELER), of Sharnbrook, Co. Beds. (Kent) (at the King's passage through Ware).

1604, Aug. 15. JOHN SYDNEY (at Lexlipp by Sir George Carey, lord deputy of Ireland).

1604, Aug. 20. THOMAS STEWARD, of Co. Cambridge. (at Whitehall by the King).

1604, Aug. 20. THOMAS THINNE, of Wilts. *(ibid)*.

1604, Aug. 20. JAMES WINGFIELD, of Co. Northampton. *(ibid)*.

1604, Aug. 20. GEORGE WAUTON (WALTON), of Co. Huntingdon. *(ibid)*.

1604, Aug. 20. PHILIP CROMWELL, of Co. Huntingdon. *(ibid)*.

1604, Aug. 20. ANTHONY FORREST, of Co. Huntingdon. *(ibid)*.

1604, Aug. 27. BRYAN McHUGH OGE McMAHOUNE (at Lexlipp by Sir George Carey, lord deputy of Ireland).

1604, Aug. 28. PATRICK M'ART MOYLE (MACMAHON) *(ibid by same)*.

1604, Aug. 30. JOHN SYDNEY *(ibid by same)*.

1604, Sept. 21. HENRY SAVILE, of Bucks., provost of Eton (at a banquet at Eton College, by the King).

1604, Oct. 11. HENRY OGE O'NEALE (at Lexlipp by Sir George Carew, lord deputy of Ireland).

1604, Oct. 11. RICHARD HANSARD *(ibid by same)*.

1604, Nov. 1. ARTHUR MAGENNIS *(ibid by same)*.

before 1604, Nov. 5. JOHN BEDELL, sheriff of Cambridge and Huntingdon.

1604, Nov. 6. RICHARD BULKLEIGH (BUCKLEY), of Cheshire (Beaumaris, Anglesey) (by the King at Whitehall).

1604, Nov. 6. HUMFREY ORME, of Co. Lincoln. (Northampton) *(ibid)*.

1604, Nov. 6. GEORGE SYMONS, of Devon. *(ibid)*.

1604, Nov. 6. RICHARD HOPTON, of Hereford (At Whitehall).
1604, Nov. 6. WILLIAM HAMBDEN (HARPDEN, HUMDAINE), of Co. Notts. (Gloucester *(ibid)*.
1604, Nov. 6. JOHN DRURY, of Essex *(ibid)*.
1604, Nov. 11. JOHN DAWSON (LAWSON), of Co. York. (Cumberland) *(ibid)*.
1604, Nov. 16. FRANCIS CLARE, of Somerset. *(ibid)*.
1604, Nov. 16. CLEMENT FYSHER, of Co. Warwick. *(ibid)*.
1604, Nov. 16. WALTER TICHBORN, of Hants. *(ibid)*.
1604, Nov. 20. ROBERT JERMIN, of Suffolk (at Royston).
1604, Nov. 24. AUGUSTINE PALGRAVE, of Norfolk (at Sir Oliver Cromwell's at Hinchinbrook).
1604, Dec. 7. GAWEN HARVEY (at Lexlipp by Sir George Carey, lord deputy of Ireland).
1604, Dec. 17 (?). JAMES CARNEGIE, of Scotland (at Whitehall).
1604, Dec. 17. JOHN SHARP, of Scotland *(ibid)*.
1604, Dec. 17. JOHN LERMENT (LARMANT) *(ibid)*.
1604, Dec. 17. JOHN SKINNER (SKINNE) *(ibid)*.
1604, Dec. 17. ROBERT LOWRESTON (LOWESTON) *(ibid)*.
1604, Dec. 18. RICHARD HUSSEY, of Salop. (at Royston).
1604, Dec. 18. ISAAC JERMYN, of Suffolk *(ibid)*.
1604, Dec. 19. EDWARD BUSHELL, of Co. Gloucester. *(ibid)*.
1604, Dec. 25. CHRISTOPHER NUGENT (on Christmas Day by Sir George Carey, lord deputy of Ireland).
1604, Dec. 25. ADAM LOFTUS (at Christchurch, Dublin, by same).
1604-5, Jan. 17. JOHN ROUSE, of Norfolk (by the King at Royston).
1604-5, Jan. 18. JOHN FENWICK, of Northumberland *(ibid)*.
1604-5, Jan. 22. THOMAS MUSCHAMP, of Surrey *(ibid)*.
1604-5, Jan. 22. JOHN HUET (HEWETT), of London *(ibid)*.
1604-5, Jan. 30. EDWARD RADCLIFFE, of Co. Cambridge (Dilston, Northumberland) (at Sir Oliver Cromwell's at Hinchinbrook).
1604-5, Feb. 3. GEORGE (THOMAS) SNIGGE (SNAGGE, SNEGG), of Somerset., baron of the Exchequer (at Whitehall).
1604-5, Feb. 3. JOHN PORTMAN, of Somerset *(ibid)*.
1604-5, Feb. 10. THOMAS ROTHERAM (at Dublin Castle by Sir Arthur Chichester, lord deputy of Ireland).
1604-5, Feb. 10. JOHN EVERARD *(ibid* by same).
1604-5, Feb. 10. DOMINICK SARSFEILD, 2nd justice of the King's Bench, attorney of Munster *(ibid* by same).

KNIGHTS BACHELORS

1604–5, Feb. 14. RICHARD WELSH (WEALCH), of Co. Worcester, sheriff of Worcester. (at Whitehall by the king).
1604–5, Feb. 19. PETER YOUNG, of Angus *(ibid)*.
1604–5, Feb. 20. EDWARD DYMMOCK, of Co. Lincoln. *(ibid)*.
1604–5, Feb. 26. EDWARD FRANCIS (at Newmarket).
1604–5, Feb. 26. RICE GRIFFIN, of Co. Warwick. *(ibid)*.
1604–5, Feb. 26. FRANCIS FULFORD, of Devon. *(ibid)*.
1604–5, Feb. 27. THOMAS FLEMING, of Hants. *(ibid)*.
1604–5, Feb. 27. ROBERT CRANE, of Suffolk *(ibid)*.
1604–5, Feb. 27. THOMAS HUGGON, of Norfolk *(ibid)*.
1604–5, Feb. 27. HENRY COLT, of Suffolk *(ibid)*.
1604–5, Mar. 23. PHILIP CAREW, of Herts. (at Greenwich).
1604–5, Mar. 23. JOHN SHEFFIELD, of Co. York. *(ibid)*.
1604–5, Mar. 23. HENRY KNOLLES, of Berks. *(ibid)*.
1604–5, Mar. 23. JOHN GUEVARA, of Co. Lincoln. (at Greenwich).
1604–5, Mar. 23. JOHN EYRE, of Wilts. *(ibid)*.
1604–5, Mar. 23. THOMAS ROWE, of Gloucester. *(ibid)*.
1604–5, Mar. 24 (Feb. 10). CHARLES CALTHORPE, attorney-general (by Sir Arthur Chichester, lord deputy of Ireland).
1605, Apr. 2. WILLIAM HERRICK, of London, goldsmith *(ibid)*.
1605, Apr. 9. THOMAS CORNWALLIS, of Norfolk *(ibid)*.
1605, Apr. 9. JOHN SEYMORE, of Somerset. *(ibid)*.
1605, Apr. 9. WILLIAM THOMAS UVEDALL, of Hants. *(ibid)*.
1605, Apr. 9. GEORGE ALDRIDGE, of Somerset. *(ibid)*.
1605, Apr. 9. FRANCIS CALTON, of Surrey *(ibid)*.
1605, Apr. 9. GEORGE IVE, of Bristol, Somerset. *(ibid)*.
1605, Apr. 14. CLEMENT SCUDAMORE, of London *(ibid)*.
1605, Apr. 21. CHRISTOPHER CLEVE (CLEIVE), of Kent *(ibid)*.
1605, Apr. 21. THOMAS GLOVER, of London *(ibid)*.
1605, Apr. 21 (12). RICHARD BUTLER (at Dublin Castle by Sir Arthur Chichester, lord deputy of Ireland).
1605, Apr. 29. ROBERT BANYSTER, of Salop, master of the King's Household (at Greenwich by the King).
1605, May 4. JOHN SELBY, of Co. Northampton. *(ibid)*.
1605, May 4. GEORGE FLOWER, of Devon. *(ibid)*.
1605 May 14 (15). THOMAS FOLJAMBE, of Co. Derby. (at Richmond).
1605, May 14. ROGER DELAVALE (DAVILL, D'EIVIL), of Co. York. *(ibid)*.
1605, May 15 (14). HUGH POLLARD, of Devon. *(ibid)*.

1605, May 15. HUGH MONTGOMERY (at Richmond).
1605, May 16. THOMAS HENLEY (HENDLEY), of Kent *(ibid)*.
1605, May 16. JOHN BUCKLEY (BUNKLEY, BULCKLEY, BANCKLEY), of Co. Derby. (Chester) *(ibid)*.
1605, May 17. ROBERT WRIGHT, of Surrey *(ibid)*.
1605, May 22 (17). JOHN MEUX (MEWSE, MONOX), of Hants. (At Greenwich, ? Richmond).
1605, May 22. WILLIAM KIRKHAM (KIRTHAM), of Devon (at Greenwich).
1605, May 22. JOHN FITZ WILLIAMS, of Co. Bedford. *(ibid)*.
1605, May 22. ROBERT PAYN, of London (Medlow, Hunts.). *(ibid)*.
1605, May 22. HUGH PLATT, of London *(ibid)*.
1605, May 22. EDWARD COPE, of Northampton (at Greenwich).
1605, May 22. HENRY MALLORY, of Co. Cambridge. *(ibid)*.
1605, May 22. NICHOLAS HALL (HALSE), of Devon. *(ibid)*.
1605, May 22. ANNESLEY (ANSELM) WILDEGOS, of Sussex *(ibid)*.
1605, May 22. JOHN LEE (LEIGH), of Surrey *(ibid)*.
1605, May 22. WILLIAM COBHAM, of Devon. *(ibid)*.
1605, May 22. AMBROSE BUTTON, of Wilts. (Hants.) *(ibid)*.
1605, May 22. ROBERT ALBANY, of Surrey *(ibid)*.
1605, May 25. JOHN SPELMAN (SPILMAN), of London (of Dartford, Kent, Dutch) (at Dartford).
1605, May 25. HENRY MILDMAY (at Dublin Castle by Sir Arthur Chichester, lord deputy of Ireland).
1605, May 26. DAVID MURRAY (by the King at Greenwich).
1605, May 29 (4 or 7). GEORGE CHAWORTH, of Co. Derby. *(ibid)*.
1605, May 29 (7). GILBERT KINGSTON (KNIVETON, KNIGHTON, KNIFTON), of Co. Notts. *(ibid)*.
1605, June 5. FRANCIS SLINGSBIE (at Dublin Castle by Sir Arthur Chichester, lord deputy of Ireland).
1605, June 5. ALLEN APSLYE *(ibid by same)*.
1605, June 9. ROBERT NEWCOMEN *(ibid by same)*.
1605, June 19. JOHN BINGHAM *(ibid by same)*.
1605 (? 1606), July 5. WILLIAM BUTTON (HUTTON), of Wilts. (by the King at Whitehall).
1605, July 18. EDMOND WAYNEMAN (at Dublin Castle by Sir Arthur Chichester, lord deputy of Ireland).
1605, July 27. GEORGE PERIAM, of Co. Oxford. (at Luton by the King).
1605, Aug. 23. CORMACK MCBARON O'NEALE (at Dublin Castle by Sir Arthur Chichester, lord deputy of Ireland).
1605, Aug. 23. THOMAS FITZWILLIAMS, of Merion *(ibid by same)*.

1605, July (Aug.) 30. WILLIAM SIDLEY (SYDLEY), of Kent (at Oxford).
1605, July (Aug.) 30. GEORGE RIVERS, of Kent (ibid).
1605, July (Aug.) 30. GEORGE TIPPIN (TYPPIN, TAPPIN), of Co. Oxford (upon the way the same day).
1605, Sept. CHARLES DE CAMBRAY, of France (at Huntingdon).
1605, Sept. 20. CHRISTOPHER BELLEW or BEDLOWE, of Castleton (at Dublin Castle by Sir Arthur Chichester, lord deputy).
1605, Oct. 5 (3). THOMAS BURTON (at Howth by same).
1605, Oct. 13. HUGH OWEN (ibid by same).
1605, Oct. (? Aug.). THOMAS HOSKINS (HOPKINS), of Surrey (at Windsor).
1605, Oct. (? Aug. 14). PETER SALTONSTALL (SALTINGSTOWE), of London (ibid).
1605, Nov. 24. THOMAS HUNCKES (in the Castle, Dublin, by Sir Arthur Chichester, lord deputy).
1605 [end of Nov. or begin. of Dec.]. JOHN SMYTH, of Essex (at Royston).
1605, Dec. THOMAS HAWARD, alias Hewer, of Norfolk (at Hinchinbroke).
1605, Dec. 16. RICHARD WHITE, of Hants. and the Isle of Wight (at Whitehall).
1605, Dec. 16. PHILIP STANHOP, of Co. Leicester. (ibid).
1605, Dec. 16. AMBROSE GREY, of Co. Leicester. (ibid).
1605-6, Jan. 14. ROBERT NUGENT, of the Disert (in Dublin Castle by Sir Arthur Chichester, lord deputy of Ireland).
1605-6, Jan. 23. NICHOLAS DE MOLLIN (MOLINE), Venetian ambassador (at Whitehall).
1605-6, Feb. 2. FRANCIS KETTELBY, of Co. Leicester. (ibid).
1605-6, Feb. 2. WILLIAM TATE (TATT), of Northampton. (ibid).
1605-6, Feb. 2. ROBERT PURSELL (PURSLEY), of Salop (ibid).
1605-6, Feb. 16. TIMOTHY HUTTON, of Co. York. (ibid).
1605-6, Feb. 16. JOHN THROGMORTON, of Co. Lincoln. (ibid).
1605-6, Mar. 8 (? May 14). JOHN DIGBY, of Co. Warwick. (ibid).
1605-6, Mar. 18.. HENRY MOODY, of Wilts. (ibid).
1606, May 14. JOHN WYNN, of Co. Carnarvon. (ibid).
1606, May 14-21. THOMAS BROOKE, of Co. Northampton. (Leicester) (at Theobalds).
1606, May 14-21 (? Mar. 14). HENRY PEYTON, of Suffolk (at Royston).
1606, May 14-21 (May 20). WILLIAM LISLE (LISLEY), of the Isle of Wight (at Whitehall).

- 1606, May 23. GEORGE MARBURY (MERBURY), of Co. Lincoln. (at Greenwich).
- 1606, May 23. ROGER MOSTON, of Co. Flint. *(ibid)*.
- 1606, May 25. HENRY MIDDLETON, of Cheshire *(ibid)*.
- 1606, June 1. EDMOND WALSH (at Christchurch by Sir Arthur Chichester, lord deputy of Ireland).
- 1606, June 7. WILLIAM GLYNN (at Dublin Castle by same).
- 1606, June 19. THOMAS DALE, of Surrey, governor of Virginia (by the King at Richmond).
- 1606, June 22. WILLIAM SYNNOTT, of Bolefernock, in Co. Wexford (at Dublin Castle by Sir Arthur Chichester, lord deputy of Ireland).
- 1606, July 5. JOHN BURLACY, of Suffolk (at Greenwich by the King).
- 1606, July 13. THOMAS WINGFEILD *(ibid)*.
- 1606, July 15. HENRY BAKER, of Kent (at Oatlands).
- 1606, July 15. ARTHUR HARRIS, of Essex *(ibid)*.
- 1606, July 23. JOHN JOLLES (JOWLES), of London (at Greenwich).
- 1606, Aug. 17 (? July 19). THOMAS GLOVER, ambassador into Turkey (at Hampton Court).
- 1606, Aug. 17. REYNOLD (REGINALD) ARGALL (ARGOLL), of Essex *(ibid)*.
- 1606, Aug. (?) THOMAS JORDAIN (at Windsor).
- 1606, Aug. 24. GEORGE ERSKINE (at Farnham Castle, the bishop of Winchester's residence).
- 1606, Aug. 30. JOHN LEIGH, of the Isle of Wight (at Beaulieu, the earl of Southampton's residence).
- 1606, Sept. WILLIAM OGLANDER, of the Isle of Wight (at Hampton Court).
- 1606, Sept. GEORGE PHILPOT, of Co. Hants. *(ibid)*.
- 1606, Oct. 17. NICHOLAS HAYES, of Co. Hants. (at Newmarket).
- 1606, Oct. 18. WILLIAM HEWET, of London *(ibid)*.
- 1606, Oct. 19. THOMAS PLATERS (PLAYTER), of Suffolk, sheriff of Suffolk (at Newmarket).
- 1606, Oct. 19. EDWARD LEWKENOR, of Suffolk *(ibid)*.
- 1606, Oct. 20. HENRY CHENEY, of Co. Cambridge. (Oxford) (at Royston).
- 1606, Oct. 20. JOHN LEIGH *(ibid)*.
- 1606, Nov. 1. EDWARD TARBOCK (TURBOCKE), of Lancs. at Whitehall).
- 1606, Nov. 5. JOHN GREY (GRAYES), *(ibid)*.
- 1606, Nov. 5. WILLIAM WRIGHT, of Suffolk *(ibid)*.

KNIGHTS BACHELORS 141

1606, Nov. 13. NICHOLAS PRIDEAUX, of Cornwall (at Richmond).
1606, Nov. 22. ROBERT LOVET (LOVERTT), of Bucks. (at Whitehall).
1606, Nov. 28. GEORGE SHERLOCK (at Dublin Castle by Sir Arthur Chichester, lord deputy of Ireland).
1606, Dec. 1. EDMOND FITZJOHN FITZGERALD (at Drogheda by same).
1606, Dec. 5. JOHN FLEMING (FLAMING), of Co. Denby. (by the King at Enfield).
1606, Dec. 6. ISAAK SYDLEY (SEDLEY), of Kent *(ibid)*.
1606, Dec. 11. GEORGE FULWOOD, of Co. Derby (Warwick) (at Whitehall).
1606, Dec. 11. ANTHONY HUNGERFORD, of Co. Gloucester *(ibid)*.
1606, Dec. 15. WILLIAM BUTTON, of London *(ibid)*.
1606, Dec. 23. THOMAS PALMER, of Kent (Angmerin, Sussex) *(ibid)*.
1606–7, Jan. 3. GEORGE FITZWILLIAMS, of Co. Lincoln *(ibid)*.
1606–7, Jan. 20. JOHN MILLISENT, of Co. Cambridge. (at Royston).
1606–7, Feb. 8. JOHN RYVES, of Dorset. (at Whitehall).
1606–7, Feb. 15 (9). JAMES ALTHAM, of London *(ibid)*.
1606–7, Feb. 15. WILLIAM (JOHN) POOLE, of Devon. *(ibid)*.
1606–7, Feb. 17. HENRY OXENDEN, of Kent *(ibid)*.
1606–7, Feb. 17. JOHN (AUGUSTINE) NICHOLS (NICHOLAS) *(ibid)*.
1606–7, Mar. 1. THOMAS BOWLES (BOLLES), of Lancs. *(ibid)*.
1606–7, Mar. 2. THOMAS PANTON, of Co. Denbigh. *(ibid)*.
1606–7, Mar. 4. THOMAS CROMPTON (COMPTON), of Co. Warwick. *(ibid)*.
1606–7, Mar. 4. WILLIAM FIELDING (FEILDINGES), of Co. Warwick. *(ibid)*.
1606–7, Mar. (?) (1607, Apr. 14). ROBERT TIRRELL, of Essex (at Royston).
1606–7, Mar. (?) (1607, Apr. 14). ROGER (GEORGE) MILLISENT, of Co. Cambridge. *(ibid)*.
1606–7, Mar. (?) (1607, Apr. 14). GEORGE FITZJEFFREY (FITZGEFFREY) *(ibid)*.
1606–7, Mar. 24. ROGER JONES (at Drogheda by Sir Arthur Chichester, lord deputy of Ireland).
1606–7, Mar. 24. THOMAS PHILLIPS *(ibid by same)*.
1606–7, Mar. 24. JOHN MORE, of Croghan *(ibid by same)*.
1607, Mar. 30. FRANCIS RUSSELL, of Co. Beds. (at Whitehall by the King).
1607, Mar. 30. ROBERT BUTLER, of Herts. *(ibid)*.
1607, Apr. 14 (5–12). THOMAS TYRRELL (at Royston).

1607, Apr. 15 (16). EDWARD VERE, of Essex (at Newmarket).
1607, Apr. 15 (16). JOHN VERE, of Essex (at Newmarket).
1607, Apr. 16. JOHN GIBSON, of Co. Yorks. (at Royston).
1607, Apr. 29. THOMAS CHICHLEY, of Co. Cambridge (at Whitehall ? Royston).
1607, Apr. 29 (24). DUDLEY DIGGS, of Kent *(ibid)*.
1607, Apr. 29 (24). GEORGE HENEAGE, of Co. Lincoln. *(ibid)*.
1607, Apr. 29 (24). GEORGE WANDESFORD (MANSFORD), of Co. Yorks. *(ibid)*.
1607, May 3 (Apr. 29). EDWARD GOSTWICK, of Co. Beds. *(ibid)*.
1607, May 7 (14). CHARLES EGERTON, of Co. Stafford. (at Whitehall).
1607, May 24. JOHN BOWYER *(ibid)*.
1607, May 27. JOHN KEYES (KAYES), of Co. York. *(ibid)*.
1607, May 27. RICHARD CONQUEST, of Co. Beds. *(ibid)*.
1607, May 28. WILLIAM DILLON, of Devon. *(ibid)*.
1607, May 28. CHARLES WRENNE (WRINNER), of Co. York. *(ibid)*.
1607, May 30. HENRY LEGH (LEE), of Co. Middl. *(ibid)*.
1607, June 4. JOHN STANHOP, of Co. Derby. *(ibid)*.
1607, June 7 (? Apr. 30). CHRISTOPHER HARRIS, of Devon. *(ibid)*.
1607, June 11. GEORGE SAYER, of Stanway (? Aldham), Essex *(ibid)*.
1607, June 19. HENRY MILDMAY, of Essex *(ibid)*.
1607, June 26. WILLIAM MEWES (MEUX), of the Isle of Wight *(ibid)*.
1607, June 26. GEORGE DALTON (DALSTON), of Westmorland *(ibid)*.
1607, June 26 (27). FRANCIS FREEMAN, of Co. Northampton. (at Richmond).
1607, June 26. GEORGE PAWLETT (at Slane by Sir Arthur Chichester, lord deputy of Ireland).
1607, June 28. DONELL O'CATHAN (at Slane by Sir Arthur Chichester, lord deputy of Ireland).
1607, June 28 (27). RALPH WYNWOOD, secretary of State (at Richmond by the King prior to being sent ambassador to Holland with Sir Richard Spencer).
1607, June 29. JOHN PETTUS (PETHOUSE), alderman of Norwich (at Whitehall).
1607, July 5. JOHN DODRIDGE, of London, on his becoming the King's principal serjeant-at-law (at Whitehall).
1607, July 5. CHRISTOPHER PICKERING, of Co. York. *(ibid)*.
1607, July 5. HENRY FRANKLIN (FRANKLAND), of Cumberland *(ibid)*.
1607, July 5. JOHN WYLDE, of Kent *(ibid)*.
1607, July 5. GEORGE PAULE, of Surrey *(ibid)*.

KNIGHTS BACHELORS

1607, July (5–10). JOHN ROWSE, of Co. Worcester. (at Greenwich).
1607, July (5–10). JOHN BUTLER (BOTELAR), of Co. Beds. (Hatfield Woodhall, Herts.).
1607, July 10. GEORGE DOUGLAS, a Scotchman (*ibid* or Theobalds).
1607, July 10. JARVIS PRICE, of Wales *(ibid)*.
1607, July 10. VINCENT CORBET, of Salop *(ibid)*.
1607, July 19. EDWARD WALGRAVE, of Norfolk *(ibid)*.
1607, July 20. THOMAS NORTON, of Kent (at Oatlands).
1607, July 20 (Oct. 2). EDWARD DENNIS, of the Isle of Wight *(ibid)*.
1607, Aug. 16. THOMAS CHICHESTER (at Slane by Sir Arthur Chichester, lord deputy of Ireland).
1607, Aug. 20 (23). BOWYER WORSLEY, of the Isle of Wight (at Sarum).
1607, Aug. 20 (23). EDWARD DUKE (DUCKE), of Kent *(ibid)*.
1607, Aug. 20 (23). THOMAS JARVIS (JERVOIS, IVERS), of Co. Hants. (Surrey) *(ibid)*.
1607, Aug. 26 (23). EDMOND UVEDALL (UDALL), of Wilts. *(ibid)*.
1607, Aug. 29 (23). EDWARD ESTCOURT (ESTOCKE, ESCOTT), of Salisbury *(ibid)*.
1607, Aug. 29 (23). GABRIEL PILE (PILLE), of Wilts. *(ibid)*.
1607, Sept. 8. EDWARD TYRRELL (at Windsor).
1607, Sept. 23. THOMAS DARRELL (DAYRELL, DORRELL), of Bucks. (at Theobalds).
1607, Oct. 5. FABIAN LEVENS (LEWENS), of Hampton Court (at Royston).
1607, Oct. 7 (Nov. 8 at Whitehall). JOHN CONSTABLE, of Co. Yorks. (at Royston).
1607, Oct. 27. HENRY LOVELL, of Essex *(ibid)*.
1607, Nov. 5. ROBERT JACOB, the King's solicitor-general (at Christchurch, Dublin by Sir Arthur Chichester, lord deputy of Ireland).
1607, Nov. 6 (8). THOMAS ESTCOURT (ERESCOURT), of Co. Gloucester. sheriff of Gloucester. (by the King at Whitehall).
1607, Nov. 17. WILLIAM DANVERS (DAVERS), of Wilts. (at Hampton Court).
1607, Nov. 29. THOMAS BROWNE, of the Hospital, Co. Limerick (at Dublin Castle by Sir Arthur Chichester, lord deputy of Ireland).
1607, Nov. ? 18 [after 29]. JAMES OXENDEN (OXENFORD), of Kent (by the King at Whitehall).
1607, Nov. ? 18 [after 29]. THOMAS WILFORD, of Kent *(ibid)*.

1607, Nov. 30. JOHN (JAMES) COLVILE, of Norfolk (at Theobald's).
1607, Nov. 30. RALPH SHELTON (SKELTON), of Norfolk *(ibid)*.
1607, Dec. 20. WILLIAM HAMOND (HAYMAN), of Kent (at Whitehall).
1607, Dec. 20. ROBERT COOK (COKE), son of Sir Edward, of London *(ibid)*
1607, Dec. 21. WILLIAM ST. JOHN (at Dublin Castle by Sir Arthur Chichester, lord deputy of Ireland).
1607, Dec. 23. JOHN THOMPSON, of Kent (by the King at Hampton Court).
1607, Dec. 23. CHARLES (GILES) BRAY, of Co. Oxford *(ibid)*.
1607, Dec. 23 (24). ROBERT CARRE (KARR), a Scotchman *(ibid)*.
1607–8, Jan. 7. WILLIAM POWELL, of Wales (at Whitehall).
1607–8, Jan. 15. FRANCIS CLARKE, of Surrey (at Theobalds).
1607–8, Jan. 17 (24). EDWARD FISHER, of Berks. *(ibid)*.
1607–8, Jan. 21. HENRY LILLE (LILLO), of Lillie (at Whitehall).
1607–8, Jan. 25. ROBERT LEWKNER, of Suffolk (Kent) *(ibid)*.
1607–8, Jan. 30. FERDINANDO FAIRFAX (at Theobalds).
1607–8, Feb. 1. RALPH DELAVALL (DALLIVALL) of Northumberland (at Whitehall).
1607–8, Feb. 11 (5). JOHN DAVIES, of London (at Theobalds).
1607–8, Feb. 11. MOLTON LAMBARD (LAMBERT), of Kent (at Theobald's).
1607–8, Feb. 13. WILLIAM ACKLAM, of Co. Yorks. (at Whitehall).
1607–8, Feb. 13 (15). ANTHONY HUNGERFORD, of Wilts. *(ibid)*.
1607–8, Feb. 15 (Mar. 5). HENRY GONTHERANT (GUNTHEROPE, GOUNTHROUT), a German (at Whitehall ? Newmarket).
1607-8, Mar. 5. WILLIAM CROMPTON (at Newmarket).
1607–8, Mar. 5 (4). EDWARD LEWKNER, of Suffolk *(ibid)*.
1607–8, Mar. 5 (4). ROBERT QUARLES, of Essex *(ibid)*.
1607–8, Mar. 5 (4). THOMAS SECKFORD (SACKFORD), of Co. Beds. *(ibid)*.
1608, Mar. 25. JOHN CROMPTON (at Whitehall).
1608, Mar. 25 (26). STEPHEN LISURES (LEESURES, LEISURE) *(ibid)*.
1608, Mar. 26. WILLIAM (FERDINANDO) FYTCH (FITCH), of Essex *(ibid)*.
1608, Mar. 26. JOHN ISHOM (ISHAM), of Co. Northampton. *(ibid)*.
1608, Mar. 26 (? 29). EDWARD HUSSEY, of Co. Lincoln. *(ibid)*.
1608, Mar. 30. ANTHONY BARKER, of Berks. *(ibid)*.
1608, Mar. 30. MERVYN TOUCHET, *alias* Audley (Dudley) *(ibid)*.
1608, Mar. 30. ROBERT DUTTON.
1608, Mar. 30. JAMES ALTHAM, of London *(ibid)*.

KNIGHTS BACHELORS

1608, Apr. 8. FRANCIS HARRIS, of Essex (at Newmarket).
1608, Apr. 17. EDWARD BARRETT, of Essex *(ibid)*.
1608, Apr. 26. EDWARD LEWES (LEWIS), of Wales (at Whitehall).
1608, Apr. 29. WILLIAM YOUNG, of Berks. *(ibid)*.
1608, Apr. 29. WILLIAM HARVEY, of St. Martins, Middlesex *(ibid)*.
1608, Apr. 30. THOMAS HERN (HARNE), of Norfolk *(ibid)*.
1608, May 2 (13). THOMAS WOTTON, of Kent *(ibid)*.
1608, May 7. WILLIAM HARVEY, of Suffolk *(ibid)*.
1608, May 8. WILLIAM SOUTH (CUTTS), of Co. Cambridge. *(ibid)*.
1608, May 8. FRANCIS SWANN, of Kent *(ibid)*.
1608, May 13. (OLIVER) PYTT (PITTES), of Surrey *(ibid)*.
1608, May 15 (? 13). JOHN STRADLING, of Salop (St. Donet's, Glamorgan) *(ibid)*.
1608, May 15 (? 13). SAMUEL (THO) PAYTON, of Knolton, Kent *(ibid)*.
1608, May 24 (22). THOMAS HOLLAND, of Norfolk (at Greenwich).
1608, May 24. ROTHERAM WILLOUGHBY *(ibid)*.
1608, May 24. ANTHONY PELL, of Co. Lincoln. *(ibid)*.
1608, May 27. EVERARD WHITNEY, of Co. Hereford *(ibid)*.
1608, May 29 (27). GEORGE GORING, of Sussex (at Greenwich).
1608, June 5. THOMAS HAWKINS, of Kent *(ibid)*.
1608, June 7 (3). JOHN BROWN, of Essex (Sussex) *(ibid)*.
1608, June 13. WARHAM ST. LEGER, of Kent *(ibid)*.
1608, June 13. RICHARD BULLER (BALLARY), of Cornwall *(ibid)*.
1608, June 13. ALEXANDER HAYES, a Scotchman *(ibid)*.
1608, June 19. THOMAS OVERBURY, of Co. Gloucester. *(ibid)*.
1608, July 6. ROBERT RIDGEWAY (near Dundalk by Sir Arthur Chichester, lord deputy of Ireland).
1608, July 19. HENRY GOODYEERE (by the King at Lamer, the seat of Sir John Gerrard in Wheathamsted, Co. Herts.).
1608, Aug. 1–3. CHARLES MORDEN (MORDANT) (at Grafton, Northampton).
1608, Aug. 1–3. RICHARD CATCHMAYD (CATSMAY) *(ibid)*.
1608, Aug. 1–3. THOMAS ROTHERAM, of Co. Beds. *(ibid)*.
1608, Aug. 1–3 (? 5). THOMAS TRESHAM, of Newton, Co. Northampton. *(ibid ? at Bletsoe)*.
1608, Aug. 1–3 (4). THOMAS (JOHN) CHENEY, of Bucks. (Sandown, Beds.) *(ibid)*.
1608, Aug. 1–3 (4). WILLIAM SANDERS, of Co. Northampton. *(ibid)*.
1608, Aug. 1–3 (4). THOMAS HASELRIG, of Co. Leicester. *(ibid)*.

K

1608, Aug. 4. HENRY ANDERSON, of London (at Holmby, Alderton, Sir Thomas Haselrig's house).

1608, Aug. 5 (July 10). ANTHONY ST. JOHN, third son of Oliver, lord St. John (at Bletsoe, the seat of said lord St. John).

1608, Aug. 5. ALEXANDER ST. JOHN, fourth son of said lord St. John *(ibid)*.

1608, Aug. 6. RICHARD HARPER (HARPUR), of Co. Derby., sheriff of Derby. (at Holmby).

1608, Aug. 19 (8). SEYMOUR KNIGHTLEY, of Co. Northampton. (at Grafton).

1608, Aug. 19 (8). EDWARD GRIFFIN, of Co. Northampton. *(ibid)*.

1608, Aug. 19 (8). LEWIS WATSON, of Co. Northampton. *(ibid)*.

1608, Aug. 19 (8). RICHARD MERWOOD (MARWOOD), of Co. Yorks. *(ibid)*.

1608, Aug. 19 (8 ? 3). THOMAS BUTLER *(ibid ?* at Grafton).

1608, Aug. 20 (29). EDWARD LENTHALL (at Windsor).

1608, Aug. 20 (29). ROBERT LEE (at Windsor).

1608, Aug. 20 (29). THOMAS LEE (LEIGH), of Stoneley, Warwick. *(ibid)*.

1608, Sept. (end of) (Oct. 2). WILLIAM BODENHAM (BODRINGHAM) (at Hampton Court).

1608, Oct. 1 (2). PHILIP FAIRFAX, of Co. Yorks. *(ibid)*.

1608, Oct. 1 ? (28). JUSTINIAN CLARKE (at Whitehall).

1608, Oct. 4 (28). FRANCIS HEALE, of Somerset (at Royston).

1608, Oct. 4 (28). GEORGE CHAWORTH, of Co. Yorks. *(ibid)*.

1608, Oct. 4 (28). JOHN PEYTON, of Suffolk (Island, Cambridge) *(ibid)*.

1608, Oct. 14. GEORGE CHEWTE, of Stockwell, in Surrey (at Christchurch, Dublin, by Sir Arthur Chichester, lord deputy of Ireland).

1608, Nov. 1. GEORGE JUSTINIANUS, Venetian ambassador (at Whitehall).

1608, Nov. 5. BARNARD GRENVILE (GREENEFEILDE), of Stowe, in Cornwall (at Christchurch, Dublin, by Sir Arthur Chichester, lord deputy of Ireland).

1608, Nov. 7 (6). CHARLES VAUGHAN (WANGHAM), of Co. Hereford. (at Whitehall).

1608, Nov. 10. JOHN MOLINEUX, of Co. Notts. *(ibid)*.

1608, Nov. 13 (14). ROWLAND COTTON, of Salop *(ibid)*.

1608, Nov. 13 (14). WILLIAM SWANN, of Kent (at Whitehall).

1608–9, Jan. 2. FRANCIS NEALE, of Hants. *(ibid)*.

KNIGHTS BACHELORS 147

1608–9, Jan. 6. ROBERT OGLETHORPE, 2nd baron of the Exchequer (in the Presence Chamber at Dublin Castle by Sir Arthur Chichester, lord deputy of Ireland).

1608–9, Jan. 8. THOMAS FINCH, of Kent (by the King at Whitehall).

1608–9, Jan. 9. ROBERT BROOKE, of London (Cocfield, Suffolk *(ibid)*.

1608–9, Feb. 1. RICHARD BARNABY (BURNABY), of Co. Northampton. (at Theobalds).

1608–9, Feb. 1. JOHN ANDREWES, of Co. Gloucester. (Bucks.) *(ibid)*.

1608–9, Feb. 2. JOHN ST. JOHN, of Lidiard Tregoos, Wilts. (at Whitehall).

1608–9, Feb. 2. PETER PETTESWORTH (BETTESWORTH), of Milland, Sussex *(ibid)*.

1608–9, Feb. 2 (7). HENRY WHETTENHALL, of Kent *(ibid)*.

1608–9, Feb. 2 (7). WILLIAM WEBB, of London *(ibid)*.

1608–9, Feb. 2 (7). GEORGE LE HUNT, of Suffolk *(ibid)*.

1608–9, Feb. 7 (12). ROBERT DOUGLAS, of Scotland *(ibid* or at Royston).

1608–9, Feb. 14. JOHN ELIOT, 3rd baron of the Exchequer (at Dublin Castle by Sir Arthur Chichester, lord deputy of Ireland).

1608–9, Mar. 3 (5). JOHN DAVERS (DANVERS), of Co. Gloucester. (at Whitehall).

1608–9, Mar. 7. WILLIAM CAVENDISH, of Co. Derby. *(ibid)*.

1608–9, Mar. 7. WILLIAM (EDMUND) PASTON, of Norfolk *(ibid)*.

1608–9, Mar. 7. HUMPHREY BASKERVILLE, of Co. Hereford. *(ibid)*.

1608–9, Mar. 7. WILLIAM MAYNARD, of Essex *(ibid)*.

1608–9, Mar. 7. LEVENTHORPE FRANCK, of Essex *(ibid)*.

1608–9, Mar. 7. THOMAS EDOLPH, of Kent *(ibid)*.

1608–9, Mar. 7. HENRY SAMBORNE, of Co. Oxford. (Moulsford, Berks.) *(ibid)*.

1608–9, Mar. 7. THOMAS AWBERY (AUBREY), of Co. Hereford *(ibid)*.

1608–9, Mar. 7. JAMES BOGG, of Co. Lincoln. *(ibid)*.

1608–9, Mar. 22. GEORGE BOSTON (BESTON, BEESTON), of London (Cheshire) *(ibid)*.

1609, Mar. 30. HENRY NEVILL, of Berks. *(ibid)*.

1609, Apr. 18 (13 ? Mar. 30). THEODORE NEWTON, of Somerset. *(ibid)*.

1609, Apr. 18 (? Mar. 30). JOHN CROOK (CROKE), of Co. Oxford. *(ibid)*.

1609, Apr. 21 (27, 29). THOMAS GAINSFORTH, of Co. Surrey *(ibid)*.

1609, Apr. 29. WILLIAM ERSKINE, a Scotchman *(ibid)*.

1609, Apr. 29 (May 8). HENRY BARTLETT (BERKLEY), of Somerset. (Gloucester) (At Whitehall).

1609, May 23. ANTHONY GAWDY, of Norfolk (at Greenwich or Whitehall).

1609, May 28. JOHN DENHAM, of Berks. (at Greenwich).

1609, May 28. FRANCIS AUNGIER (ANGER), of Surrey (Cambridge) *(ibid)*.

1609, June 2 (May 23). JOHN BOUCHIER (BOWCER), of Co. York. (at Whitehall ? Greenwich).

1609, June 24. JOHN CAGE, of Co. Cambridge., sheriff of Cambridge. and Huntingdon. (at Greenwich).

1609, June 24. EDWARD SOUTHCOT *(ibid)*.

1609, June 24. ADRIAN MANMAKER, of Middleburg, Zeland *(ibid)*.

1609, June (July) 25. CORNELIUS HOFFMAN, of Antwerp *(ibid)*. See p. 623.

1609, June 26. ROBERT FISHER, of Co. Warwick. (*ibid* or Whitehall).

1609, July 2 (June 29). GEORGE (JOHN) HOLLIS (at Greenwich).

1609, July 2. THOMAS COTTEL (CUTTEAL), a German (Dutch denizen merchant) *(ibid)*.

1609, July 3 (2). THOMAS HERNE (HORNE, HARNE), of Norfolk *(ibid)*.

1609, July 5 (3). EDWARD BULLOCK (at Richmond).

1609, July 7. JOHN KING, of Abbey O'Boyle, Ireland (at Whitehall).

1609, July 9. BRIAN CAVE, of Co. Leicester. *(ibid)*.

1609, July 10. THOMAS DELVES, of Cheshire *(ibid)*.

1609, July 18. HENRY SKIPWITH, of Lincoln. (Prestwould, Leicester) *(ibid)*.

1609, July 23 (29). JOHN HEYWARD (HAYWARD), of Salop (Kent) (at Windsor).

1609, July 23. HENRY MINNE (MEENE, MYNN), of Rutland (Norfolk) *(ibid)*.

1609, Aug. 2. THOMAS TRACY, of Gloucester (at Salisbury).

1609, Aug. 13. ANTHONY MAYNEY, of Kent (at Basing).

1609, Sept. 20. WILLIAM LOVELACE, of Kent (at Theobalds).

1609, Sept. 30. NICHOLAS WHITE (at Loghroer by Sir Arthur Chichester, lord deputy of Ireland).

1609, Sept. 30. JAMES CARROLL (*ibid* by same).

1609, Sept. 30. ROBERT PIGOTT, of Disert in Leix (*ibid* by same).

1609, Oct. 3. HENRY GOSTERY (GOSTRY, GOSTRO) (by the King at Hampton Court).

1609, Oct. 3. JOHN LIDCOTT, of Co. Oxford (Sussex) *(ibid)*.

KNIGHTS BACHELORS

1609, Oct. 3. JOHN KIDERMINSTER (KEDERMINSTER), of Bucks. *(ibid)*.
1609, Oct. 3. JOHN BLENERHASSET, of Norfolk *(ibid)*.
1609, Nov. 11. ANTHONY TERRILL (at Whitehall).
1609, Nov. 14. JAMES HAMILTON, a Scotchman (at Royston).
1609, Nov. 27. HENRY BOWYER, of Bucks. (at Theobalds).
1609-10, Jan. 6. WILLIAM ST. CLERE (at Whitehall).
1609-10, Jan. 7. CHARLES JONES, of Monmouth *(ibid)*.
1609-10, Jan. 9. WILLIAM LYGON, of Co. Worcester. *(ibid)*.
1609-10, Jan. 9. JAMES ALTHAM, of Essex (London) *(ibid)*.
1609-10, Jan. 9. HENRY DAVIES, of Hants. *(ibid)*.
1609-10, Jan. 9. JOHN HORTON, of Cheshire (Gloucester) *(ibid)*.
1609-10, Jan. 10. JOHN FORD, of Essex (at Theobalds) (? confusion with next item).
1609-10, Jan. 20. JOHN LUNSFORD, of Sussex (at Theobalds).
1609-10, Jan. 20 (16). GEORGE FARWELL, of Somerset *(ibid)*.
1609-10, Jan. 26 (23). HENRY TANCRED, of Co. Yorks. (at Royston).
1609-10, Jan. 26 (23). JOHN LAWRENCE, of London (Iver, Bucks) *(ibid)*.
1609-10, Feb. 25 (26). EDWARD (EDMUND) DOWSE, of Hants. (at Whitehall).
1609-10, Feb. 26 (1610, Mar. 25). EDWARD BROMLEY, of Shropshire (at Whitehall).
1609-10, Mar. 24. WILLIAM POWER (at Dublin Castle by Sir Arthur Chichester, lord deputy of Ireland).
.1610, May 17. ALBERT JOACKIMY, deputy of Zealand in the Assembly of the United Provinces and councillor of Goes; an ambassador from the United Provinces (by Letters Patent).
1610, May 17. HELIAS AB OLDENBARNEVELT, doctor of law, lord in Middlehern, syndic and councillor of Rotterdam, and ambassador as above (by same).
1610, May 17. JOHN BERK, doctor of law, lord in Godschalkoor, syndic and chief councillor of Dort, and ambassador as above (by same).
1610, May 17. ALBERT DE VEER, doctor of law, syndic and chief councillor of Amsterdam, and ambassador as above (by same).
1610, June 25. THOMAS CESAR, a baron of the Exchequer (at Whitehall).

1610, Aug. 9 (? 15–20). DUDLEY CARLETON, of Surrey (at Holdenby on his audience of leave on going ambassador to Venice ? at Windsor, July 2).

1610. —— MURRAY *(ibid)*.

1610, Oct. 30. FRANCIS WILLOUGHBIE (at Dublin Castle by Sir Arthur Chichester, lord deputy of Ireland).

1610, Dec. 20. JACOB VAN DER EYNDEN, prefect and governor of Woerdam (by patent dated at Westminster).

1610–11, Jan. 7. PETER OSBORN (by the King at Whitehall).

1610–11, Jan. 7. EDWARD (EDMUND) VERNEY, of Bucks., knight marshal *(ibid)*.

1610–11, Jan. 8. WILLIAM SIDNEY, of Kent *(ibid)*.

1610–11, Jan. 8. JOHN LEEDES, of Surrey (Sussex) *(ibid)*.

1610–11, Jan. 8. RICHARD LEA, of Salop (Cheshire) *(ibid)*.

1610–11, Jan. 10. RICHARD NORTON, of Hants. (at Hampton Court).

1610–11, Jan. 10. THOMAS BRERETON, of Cheshire *(ibid)*.

1610–11, Jan. 10. CORNELIUS HOOFTMAN, of Belgium. See p. 621.

1610–11, Jan. 15. FRANCIS WORTLEY, of Co. Yorks. (at Theobalds).

1610–11, Jan. 22. ADAM LOFTUS, eldest son of Sir Dudley (at Dublin Castle by Sir Arthur Chichester, lord deputy of Ireland).

1610–11, Feb. 3 (10). HENRY CROFTS (at Whitehall).

1610–11, Feb. 4. EDWARD PEYTO, of Co. Warwick. *(ibid* ? at Newmarket, Mar. 5).

1619–11, Feb. 8. RICHARD WORSELEY *(ibid* ? at Richmond, Feb. 13.

1610–11, Feb. 8 (4). THOMAS MEWTAS (MEUTIS) *(ibid)*.

1610–11, Feb. 8 (4). THOMAS ERSKINE *(ibid)*.

1610–11, Feb. 8 (13). BERNARD DEWHURST (DIAS, DYOSE, DEMSTURT) *(ibid)*.

1610–11, Feb. 8 (4). HENRY KINGSMILL *(ibid)*.

1610–11, Feb. 12 (5). FRANCIS PRINCE, of Salop. (at Theobalds).

1610–11, Feb. 12 (5). WILLIAM SPRINGE, of Suffolk *(ibid)*.

1610–11, Feb. 16 (6). HENRY PALLAVICIN, of Co. Cambridge. (at Newmarket).

1610–11, Feb. 16 (6). CHARLES HOWARD *(ibid)*.

1610–11, Mar. (early). ROBERT BELL, of Norfolk (at Greenwich).

1610–11, Mar. 14 (5). HENRY FANE (VANE), of Kent (at Newmarket).

1610–11, Mar. 24. JOHN BOURCHIER (at Dublin Castle by Sir Arthur Chichester, lord deputy of Ireland).

1611, Apr. 13. JOHN STEWARD (at Royston ? at Whitehall, Apr. 25).

KNIGHTS BACHELORS

1611, Apr. 25. THOMAS WHARTON (at Whitehall).
1611, May 5. The Venetian Ambassador (at Greenwich).
1611, ? Aug. 3. OTTO STARCHEDELL, president of Hessia and in the retinue of prince Otto of Hesse.
1611, ? Aug. 3. GASPER WIDMARKTER, a colonel in the retinue of prince Otto of Hesse.
1611, Oct. 6. FRANCIS COOKE (at Dublin Castle by Sir Arthur Chichester, lord deputy of Ireland).
1611, Oct. 6. MATHEW CAREW (*ibid* by same).
1611, Oct. 6. THOMAS STAFFORD (*ibid* by same).
1611, Nov. 10. JOHN HOBART, of Co. Norfolk (by the King at Whitehall).
1611, Nov. 10. RICHARD BINGLEY, of Co. Flint. *(ibid)*.
1611, Nov. 10. LAWRENCE STOUGHTON, of Surrey *(ibid)*.
1611, Nov. 10. GILBERT PICKERING, of Co. Northampton. (at Whitehall).
1611, Nov. 10. EDWARD WHORWOOD (HORWOOD, HARWOOD), of Co. Stafford. *(ibid)*.
1611, Nov. 10. JOHN HUNT, of Co. Leicester. *(ibid)*.
1611, Dec. 6 (2). THOMAS WENTWORTH, of Co. Yorks. (at Royston).
1611, Dec. 6 (2). AUGUSTINE PETTUS (PETHOUSE), of Norfolk *(ibid)*.
1611, Dec. 20 (5). FERDINANDO HEBBURN, of Midds. (at Theobalds).
1611, Dec. 20 (5). JOHN (JAMES) LEVESON, of Kent *(ibid)*.
1611, Dec. 20 (5). HENRY LEE (LEIGH) *(ibid)*.
1612, Apr. 4 (9). THOMAS BRUDENELL, of Co. Northampton, a baronet who had not before received the honour of knighthood (at Whitehall).
1612, Apr. 4 (9). LEWIS TRESHAM, of Co. Northampton, a baronet who had not before received the honour of knighthood, *ut supra (ibid)*.
1612, Apr. 4 (9). JOHN SHELLEY, of Sussex, a baronet who had not before received the honour of knighthood, *ut supra (ibid)*.
1612, Apr. 9. WILLIAM METHWOLD, chief baron of the Exchequer, Ireland (at Theobalds ? 1611-12, Mar. 16, at Whitehall).
1612, May (Mar.) 24. LYONELL TALMACHE, of Suffolk, a baronet who had not previously received the honour of knighthood (at Whitehall).
1612, May 24 (June 8). THOMAS SPENCER, of Oxford, a baronet, etc., as above *(ibid)*.
1612, June 3. JOHN MOLINEUX, of Notts., a baronet, etc., as above *(ibid)*.
1612, June 3. THOMAS PUCKERING, of Herts., a baronet, etc., as above *(ibid)*.

1612, June 5. JOHN HACKET (at Eltham).

1612, July 21. ROBERT SANDY *alias* NAPPER or NAPIER, of Co. Beds. (at ? Wrest, the seat of the earl of Kent).

1612, Aug. 19 (July 24). EDWARD DEVEREUX, of Co. Warwick. (at Leicester).

1612, Aug. 30 (? 31). ROBERT EATON (at Rycott).

1612, Sept. (? June 3, ? Oct. 11). ROBERT (GEORGE) GRESLEY (GREDISLEY), of Co. Derby, a baronet who had not previously received the honour of knighthood (on the King's return to Whitehall ? at Royston).

1612, Sept. (? June 7, ? Oct. 11). JOHN WRAY, of Co. Lincoln. (at Whitehall).

1612, Sept. (? Oct. 11). CHARLES HOWARD (at Whitehall, ? at Royston).

1612, Nov. ? 15. —— GABELLINE, a banker (at Whitehall on the agents of Savoy taking their leave prior to the King's going to Theobalds).

1612, Dec. 2. WILLIAM VAN DER RYT (RIT), of Brodchen, general of horse of the United Netherlands (by especial patent dated at Westminster, enrolled on the French Roll 201, membrane 38, Record Office).

? 1612. THOMAS BURKE, of Ballyloughmask and Newtown, Co. Mayo (dubbed in Ireland).

? 1612. WILLIAM BURKE, of Kilcowley, Co. Galway *(ibid)*.

1612-3, Jan. 10 (12). ROBERT KNOLLES (KNOWLES) (at Theobalds).

1612-3, Jan. ? 13 (after 14). HUMPHREY MAY, of Sussex (at Newmarket).

1612-3, Jan. ? 13 (after 14). FRANCIS (OLAVE) LEIGH, of Co. Warwick. *(ibid)*.

1612-13, Jan. ? 13 (after 14). ROBERT WINGFIELD *(ibid)*.

1612-13, Jan. 15 (after 14). EDMOND WYLD *(ibid)*.

1612-3, Jan. (after 14). EDWARD AYSCOUGH (ASKEWE) *(ibid)*.

1612-3, Jan. (after 14). JOSEPH KILLEGREW *(ibid)*.

1612-13, Jan. 15 (after 14). EDWARD UNDERHILL, of Co. Warwick. (? Hants.), late proctor of Oxford *(ibid)*.

1612-3, Jan. 15 (after 14). NEVILL POOLE *(ibid)*.

1612-3, Feb. 2 (5). WILLIAM PORDAGE, of Kent (at Whitehall).

1612-3, Mar. 21. EDWARD ALTHAM (At Royston).

1612-3, Mar. 21. WILLIAM TRESHAM, of Northumberland (Northamptonshire) *(ibid)*.

1612-3, Mar. 21. JOHN WOODWARD *(ibid)*.

KNIGHTS BACHELORS 153

1612–3, Mar. 21. JOHN TEMPLE (At Royston).

1612–3, Mar. 21. ROGER JAMES (JEAMES) of Surrey *(ibid)*.

1612–3, Mar. 21. EDMOND COCKETT, of Norfolk *(ibid)*.

1612–3, Mar. 22. THOMAS GOURNEY, of London (at Theobalds).

1612–3, Mar. 22 (1613. Mar. 30, May 19). JOHN WYNN, of Carnarvon. (*ibid* ? at Whitehall).

1613, Mar. 27. RICHARD MOLINEUX (at Whitehall).

1613, Apr. 21 (Mar. 30 ? May 19). ROBERT HOUGHTON, justice of the King's Bench (at Whitehall).

1613, Apr. 22. RICHARD ALDWORTH, provost marshal of Munster (at Dublin Castle by Sir Arthur Chichester, lord deputy of Ireland).

1613, June 27. HENRY APLETON (APULTON), of Essex (at Greenwich by the King).

1613, July 4. LYONEL CRANFEILD, of London (at Oatlands).

1613, July 9. ARTHUR INGRAM, of London (at Theobalds).

1613, July 20. EDWARD MOORE, eldest son of Sir Garret Moore, of Melifont (at Dublin Castle by Sir Arthur Chichester, lord Deputy of Ireland).

1613, Aug. 1. GAMALIEL CAPELL (*ibid* by same).

1613, Oct. 9 (20 or 6). CHARLES CAESAR (by the king at Theobalds).

1613, Oct. 22 (? 23). FRANCIS SEYMOUR (at Royston).

1613, Oct. 22. HENRY WARDELER (WARDLAW), a Scotchman *(ibid)*.

1613, Oct. 22. EDWARD BAYNTON, of Wilts. *(ibid)*.

1613, Oct. 25. GERRARD HERBERT (HARBERT ? HARFORD) *(ibid)*.

1613, Oct. 25. THOMAS BILSON, of Hants. *(ibid)*.

1613, Oct. 29 (? 24). HUMPHREY LYNE (LYNDE), of Surrey *(ibid)*.

1613, Oct. 29. ROBERT CLARKE *(ibid)*.

1613, Nov. 8. HENRY YELVERTON, of London, solicitor general (at Whitehall).

1613, Nov. 11 (12). THOMAS WROTH (at Theobalds).

1613, Nov. 13. WILLIAM STEWARD, a Scotchman (at Royston).

1613, Nov. 19. WILLIAM UVEDALL (UDALL) of Wickham, Hants. *(ibid)*.

1613, Nov. 26 (20). WILLIAM SELBIE, of Northumberland *(ibid)*.

1613, Nov. 26 (20). THOMAS BROOK (BROOKES), of Co. Leicester *(ibid)*.

1613, Nov. 26 (20). ROBERT BELL, of Norfolk *(ibid)*.

1613, Nov. 26 (21). CHARLES GAWDIE, of Norfolk (at Royston).
1613, Nov. 26 (22). THOMAS WALSINGHAM, of Kent *(ibid)*.
1613, Nov. 26 (22). JOHN GILL, of Somerset.
1613, Dec. 15 (14). THOMAS TRENCHARD, of Dorset (at Theobalds).
1613, Dec. 15. THOMAS HEWET, of London (shire clerk, of Worsop, Notts.) *(ibid)*.
1613–4, Jan. 16 (18). HUMPHREY TUFTON, of Kent (at Royston).
1613–4, Jan. 16. JOHN CLAVERING, of Co. Northampton (Calely, Northumberland) *(ibid)*.
1613–4, Feb. 20 (9). MICHAEL EVERARD (EVERED) *(ibid)*.
1613–4, Mar. 4. JOHN STEEDE, of Kent (at Theobalds).
1613–4, Mar. 4. WILLIAM CLOPTON, of Norfolk (Kentwell, Suffolk) *(ibid)*.
1614, Apr. 1. ROBERT DARRELL (DORRELL), of Kent *(ibid)*.
1614, Apr. 1. HENRY ROBINSON *(ibid)*.
1614, May 3 (5). TIMOTHY THORNHILL, of Kent *(ibid)*.
1614, May 29. EDWARD RODNEY (at Somerset House).
1614, June 8. RANDOLPH CREW, of Cheshire, speaker of the late House of Commons (at Whitehall).
1614, June 13. JOHN MERRICK, of London (at Greenwich).
1614, June 13. WILLIAM CROSSE (CROFT, CROFTS) *(ibid)*.
1614, July 7. JOHN HORNER, of Somerset (at Windsor).
1614, July 18. JAMES SCORDECK (SCORDICKE), a Belgian (at the Rye in Hatfield Broad Oak). *See infra.*
1614, July 19. PAUL BANNING (BAYNING), of London (Little Bentley, Essex, a baronet) (at Audley End).
1614, Aug. 25 (18). HENRY LEE, bart., of Quarrendon, Bucks. (at Woodstock).
1614, Oct. 2. JOHN FRANKLIN, of Co. Midds. (at Theobalds or the Tower).
1614, Nov. 5. JOHN SMITH, of Flechamsted, Warwick. (by lord Chichester, lord deputy of Ireland).
1614, Nov. 5. ROWLAND RIDGLEY *(ibid by same)*.
1614, Nov. 7. LAWRENCE HYDE, the queen's attorney (at Whitehall by the king).
1614, Nov. 21 (20). WILLIAM SOME, of Great Thurlow, Suffolk (at Newmarket).
1614, Nov. 21. JOHN REPINGDON (REPPINGTON), of Co. Warwick *(ibid)*.
1614, Dec. 29. JAMES SCHOORDICK, of Renounwen, Netherlands. Letters patent dated at Westminster; enrolled on French Roll 201, membrane 38, Record Office. *See supra.*

1614, Dec. 31. EDWARD MOSELEY, of Grays Inn, attorney of the Duchy of Lancaster (at Whitehall).
1614–5, Jan. 19. DUDLEY NORTON, secretary, Ireland, at his going over into Ireland (at Newmarket).
1614–5, Jan. 30. JOHN SAVAGE *(ibid)*.
1614–5, Feb. 3. ROBERT ANSTROTHER, a Scotchman *(ibid)*.
1614–5, Feb. 12. OLIVER SHORTALES, of Ballilorkan, Co. Kilkenny (by lord Chichester, lord deputy of Ireland).
1614–5, Feb. 15. ROBERT DILLON (by the king at Theobalds).
1614–5, Feb. 21. CHRISTOPHER DILLON, eldest son of Sir Theobald (in Ireland by lord Chichester, lord deputy of Ireland).
1614–5, Feb. 26. JOHN BLAGRAVE (BLAUGRAVE), of Berks. (by the King at Whitehall).
1614–5, Feb. 26. JOHN GARRETT (GARRARD), of Lamer, Herts. *(ibid)*.
1614–5, Mar. 2. EDMOND WHEELER, of Datchet, Bucks. (at Theobalds).
1614–5, Mar. 2. CHARLES NOWELL (NOELL) *(ibid)*.
1614–5, Mar. 17. WILLIAM LAMPTON (at Newmarket).
1614–5, Mar. 19. (NICHOLAS) CLAUDIUS FOSTER (FORSTER) of Bamborough Hall, Northumberland *(ibid)*.
1614–5, Mar. 21. THOMAS GERRARD (at Royston).
1614–5, Mar. 23. THOMAS WHITE, of Farnham, Surrey (at Theobalds).
1615, Mar. 30 (Apr. 3). ROBERT VERNON, the Avener (at Woking).
1615, Apr. 13 (9). FULKE GREVILLE (at Whitehall or Greenwich).
1615, Apr. 13 (9). EDWARD BANESTER (BANISTER) of Hants. *(ibid)*.
1615, Apr. 13 (9). DAVID BAFFORD (BAFORE), *(ibid)*.
1615, Apr. 24. GEORGE VILLIERS, of Co. Leicester. (at Somerset House).
1615, Apr. 25. THOMAS LAMPLOUGH, sheriff of Cumberland (at Theobalds).
1615, Apr. 25. JOHN OFFLEY, of Madeley, Stafford *(ibid)*.
1615, Apr. 25. SAMUEL TRYON, of London (Essex) (at Newmarket ? May 20 at Greenwich).
1615, Apr. 30. PIERCE BUTLER, of Lismalin, Co. Tipperary (in Ireland by lord Chichester, lord deputy of Ireland).
1615, May 26 (20). RICHARD CARRELL (by the King at Greenwich).
1615, June 2. ROGER MANNERS, of Whitwell, Derby (at Theobalds).
1615, June 2. RICHARD NEWPORT *(ibid)*.
1615, June 3. JOHN ASHFIELD, of Netherall, Suffolk *(ibid)*.

1615, June 10. THOMAS BLACKSTONE (BLACKISTON), baronet (at Greenwich ? Theobalds).
1615, June 13. THOMAS CAVE, of Co. Northampton. *(ibid)*.
1615, June 13. HENRY COWLEY *(ibid)*.
1615, June 22. WILLIAM ELWAYS (ELWISS) *(ibid)*
1615, June 22. THOMAS WINNE (at Wanstead ? Greenwich).
1615, June 22. WILLIAM ZOUCHE *(ibid)*.
1615, June 26. THOMAS ELLIOTT (at Greenwich).
1615, July 2. WILLIAM LISTER, of Co. York. (at Oatlands).
1615, July 11. —— PORTER (in Ireland by lord Chichester, lord deputy of Ireland).
1615, July 13. GODFREY RODES, of Co. York. (by the King at Havering).
1615, July 16. WILLIAM GARWAY (GARRAWAY), of London, the chief of the Customers (at Theobalds).
1615, July 19. HENRY SOUTHWELL *(ibid)*.
1615, July 21. THOMAS SOUTHWELL (at Whitehall).
1615, July 21. THOMAS SMITH, of Cheshire *(ibid)*.
1615, July 21. BARNABY BRYAN, of Ireland *(ibid)*.
1615, July 22. THOMAS BELLEY, of Hunts. (at Bagshot).
1615, July 23. WILLIAM COLLEY, of Edendery (in Ireland, in camp, by lord Chichester, lord deputy of Ireland).
1615, July 23. HENRY BELINGE, of Killussy *(ibid* by same).
1615, Aug. 5. JOHN SAMWELL (CAMMELL, SAMRILL, LAMVILL) (by the King at Salisbury).
1615, Aug. 15. JOHN FITZJAMES (at Lulworth Castle, in Co. Dorset., the seat of Viscount Bindon).
1615, Aug. 19. JOHN BEARE, serjeant-at-law (in Ireland by lord Chichester, lord deputy).
1615, Aug. 27. JOHN RICHARDS, of the Isle of Wight (at Broadlands, the seat of the family of St. Barbe adjoining the town of Romsey).
1615, Aug. 29. HENRY CLARKE (at Tichborne, the seat of Sir Benjamin Tichborne).
1615, July 29. JOHN MACDOWGAL, a Scotchman *(ibid)*.
1615, July 31. JOHN DINGLEY, of the Isle of Wight (at Farnham Castle, the Episcopal Palace of the see of Winchester).
1615, Sept. 7. ROBERT NAUNTON, master of the Court of Wards (at Windsor).
1615, Sept. 14 (21). FRANCIS THORNEY, of Co. Notts (at Theobalds).

KNIGHTS BACHELORS 157

1615, Oct. 6 (2). GEORGE MARSHALL (at Royston).
1615, Oct. 9. PATRICK MURRAY (MARREY) *(ibid)*.
1615, Oct. 14 (Sept. 14). WILLIAM HARINGTON *(ibid)*.
1615, Oct. 14 (July 4). EDWARD HINDE, of Cambridge *(ibid)*.
1615, Oct. 31. HENRY CROOK (at Theobalds).
1615, Nov. 5. GEORGE HASTINGS (at Whitehall ? Theobalds).
1615, Dec. 1. WILLIAM BARDES (BARDESIUS), lord of Warmenhuysen (letters patent dated at Westminster, enrolled on French rolls 201, membrane 38, Record Office).
1615, Dec. 1. WILLIAM DE HERTOGHE, lord of Ormaele, Steen, and Steenorkersel (same).
1615, Dec. 1. JAMES MAGNUS, lord of Amers, Arentsberg, Berchambacht, and Melissant (same).
1615, Dec. 1. JOHN AB ARSEN, governor of Breda (same).
1615, Dec. 4. WILLIAM BROUNCKER (BRUNKARD), (at Newmarket).
1615, Dec. 4. THOMAS (JOHN) LEIGHTON *(ibid)*.
1615, Dec. 15. ALEXANDER MONCRIEFF (MUNCRIFE) *(ibid)*.
1615, Dec. 22. JOHN OGLANDER, of the Isle of Wight (at Royston).
1615, Dec. 23. ROBERT BROOKE (at Theobalds).
1615–6, Jan. 22. THOMAS PERYENT (PERRIANT) *(ibid)*.
1615–6, Jan. 22. ROBERT LEIGH, of Billesley, Warwick. *(ibid)*.
1615–6, Jan. 22. ROBERT OFFLEY *(ibid)*.
1615–6, Jan. 22. JOHN LEIGH *(ibid)*.
1615–6, Jan. 22. JOHN SUCKLING *(ibid)*.
1615–6, Feb. 27. THOMAS BLAND, of Co. York. (at Newmarket).
1615–6, Mar. 16 (22). GILES WATERFLEET, a Belgian, in the retinue of the ambassador (at Theobalds).
1615-6, Mar. 16 (22). CORNELIUS WATERFLEET, a Belgian, in the retinue of the ambassador *(ibid)*.
1615–6, Mar. 21 (24). JOHN FINETT, of Kent, master of the ceremonies (at Whitehall).
1616, Apr. 4. FRANCIS HENDERSON (HINDERSHAM), a Scotchman (at Theobalds).
1616, Apr. 20. JOHN HUYSSEY, lord of Catterdyke, in the Netherlands, a lord of Zeeland. Letters patent dated at Westminster, enrolled on French Roll 201, membrane 39, Record Office.
1616, Apr. 24. ANTHONY MARBURY, of Surrey (at Whitehall).
1616, Apr. 25. THOMAS RIDELL (BEDELL), of Newcastle (at Theobalds).
1616, Apr. 25. WALTER SMITH *(ibid)*.

KNIGHTS BACHELORS

1616, May 4. WALTER EARLE (at Thetford).
1616, May 8. HENRY DOYLEY *(ibid)*.
1616, May 9. EDMUND GAWSELL (GOWSHILL) *(ibid ? Newmarket)*.
1616, May 14. STEPHEN BOTELER (BUTLER) (at Newmarket).
1616, May 18. THOMAS CHAMBERLAINE (at Greenwich ? at Newmarket).
1616, June 3. JOHN DACOMBE, on his being made chancellor of the Duchy of Lancaster *(ibid)*.
1616, June 6. EDWARD BAESH (BASHE), of Co. Herts. (at Theobalds).
1616, June 6. THOMAS BRAYTHWAITE, of Westminster *(ibid)*.
1616, June 8. WILLIAM COCKAINE (at Alderman Cockaine's house).
1616, June 15. GERRARD SAMS (SAMNES), of London, Lankford Hall, Essex (at Theobalds).
1616, June 15. JOHN BENNET, of London *(ibid)*.
1616, June 16. THOMAS TILDESLEY, of Lancs. (at Greenwich).
1616, June 16. RICHARD WYNNE, of Co. Carnarvon. *(ibid)*.
1616, June 20. HENRY FINCH, of Kent (at Whitehall).
1616, June 20. CONOR MACGWIRE, of Ireland *(ibid)*.
1616, June 26. ROBERT WISEMAN, of London (at Greenwich ? Whitehall).
1616, June 26. HENRY FOX *(ibid)*.
1616, June 27. THEOBALD GORGES (GEORGE), of Wilts. *(ibid)*.
1616, June 28. PATRICKE FOX, of Ireland *(ibid)*.
1616, June 30. JOHN VILLIERS (VILLERS), of Co. Leicester. (at Oatlands).
1616, June 30. ROBERT GORGES (GEORGE), of Wilts. *(ibid)*.
1616, July 3 (2). JOHN SEDLEY (SIDLEY), of Kent *(ibid)*.
1616, July 3 (2). THOMAS WISEMAN, of Norfolk *(ibid)*.
1616, July 3. GEORGE STOUGHTON *(ibid)*.
1616, July 3 (4). THOMAS MILDMAY *(ibid)*.
1616, July 10. HUMPHREY MILDMAY, of Essex (at Whitehall).
1616, July 10 (15). GEORGE SMITH, of Co. Hereford. (at Theobalds).
1616, July 16. HENRY LEVESTON, a Scotchman *(ibid)*.
1616, July 16. CHARLES SNELL, of Wilts. (at Theobalds).
1616, July 17. SEBASTIAN HARVY (HARPER), of London *(ibid)*.
1616, July 17. PEIRCE CROSBIE (CORBY), of Ireland *(ibid)*.
1616, July 18. EDWARD CHICHESTER, of Devon. *(ibid)*.
1616, July 18. FRANCIS ANNESLOWE (ANNESLEY) *(ibid)*.
1616, July 18. ARTHUR BASSET *(ibid)*.

KNIGHTS BACHELORS 159

1616, July 18. EDWARD DORRINGTON (DODDINGTON, CARINGTON) (At Theobalds).
1616, July 18. WILLIAM HENTON (FENTON) *(ibid)*.
1616, July 19. RICHARD LUMLEY, of Sussex *(ibid)*.
1616, July 19. ROBERT LLOYD *(ibid)*.
1616, July 20. ARCHIBALD NAPPER, a Scotchman (at Royston).
1616, July 20. JAMES CRAGGE, a Scotchman *(ibid)*.
1616, July 20. SIDNEY MONTAGU, of Co. Northampton., master of the Requests *(ibid)*.
1616, July 26. THOMAS HATTON, of Co. Cambridge. (at Bletsoe).
1616, Aug. 6. FRANCIS BODENDEN, BODENDINE, or BODENHAM (at Burley on the Hill).
1616, Aug. 17. THOMAS CAVE, of Co. Leicester. (at Dingley).
1616, Aug. 18. JAMES WARE, of Somerset. (at Holdenby).
1616, Aug. 28. JOHN BURGH or BURKE, of Ireland (at Woodstock).
1616, Aug. 28. FRANCIS ROGERS, of Somerset. *(ibid)*.
1616, Aug. 28. WILLIAM POPE, of Co. Oxford. *(ibid)*.
1616, Aug. 28. RICHARD CECILL, of Co. Northampton. *(ibid)*.
1616, Aug. 29. JOHN DENHAM (at Rycott).
1616, Aug. 30. ANDREW GREY, a Scotchman (at Bisham ? Bletso).
1616, Aug. 30. THOMAS BUTTON, of Larenny, Co. Pembroke., and captain of the King's ship "Phœnix" (in Ireland by Sir Oliver St. John, lord deputy of Ireland).
1616, Sept. 7. EDWARD VILLIERS (VILLERS), of Co. Leicester (at Windsor).
1616, Sept. 7. HENRY BUTLER, of Herts. *(ibid)*.
1616, Sept. 7. JOHN DRAKE, of Devon. *(ibid)*.
1616, Sept. 17. GILES BRIDGES (BRUGES), of Co. Gloucester. (at Theobalds).
1616, Sept. 23. FRANCIS CONINGESBY (CONESBY), of Herts. (at Enfield).
1616, Sept. 23 (29). WILLIAM PLOMER (PLUMER), of Surrey (at Enfield).
1616, Sept. 28. RICHARD ST. GEORGE, Norroy King of Arms (at Hampton Court).
1616, Oct. 2. ROBERT TRACY, of Co. Gloucester. (at Theobalds).
1616, Oct. 11. GEORGE SEXTON (at Royston).
1616, Oct. 12 (22). GEORGE HAMILTON (HAMBLETON), a Scotchman (at Hinchinbroke).
1616, Nov. 5. WILLIAM SEGAR, Garter King of Arms (at Whitehall).

KNIGHTS BACHELORS

1616, Nov. 5. CHARLES COOTE, provost marshal of Connaught (in Ireland by Sir Oliver St. John, lord deputy of Ireland).

1616, Nov. 11. RICHARD ROBERTS, of Cornwall (at Whitehall).

1616, Nov. 12. GEORGE NEWMAN, of Kent (at Theobalds).

1616, Nov. 12. CHARLES BOWLES (BOLLES), of Co. Lincoln. *(ibid)*.

1616, Nov. 14. JOHN LENTHALL, of Oxford, keeper of the King's Bench prison (at Royston).

1616, Nov. 18. GILES MOMPESSON, of Wilts. (at Newmarket).

1616, Nov. 20. WILLIAM PELHAM, of Co. Lincoln. *(ibid)*.

1616, Nov. 25. MOSES (MOYSES) HILL *(ibid)*.

1616, Nov. 28. HUNTINGDON COLBY, of Suffolk *(ibid)*.

1616, Nov. 28. FERDINANDO KNIGHTLEY, of Co. Northampton. *(ibid)*.

1616, Nov. 29 (20). ROBERT OXENBRIDGE, of Hants. *(ibid)*.

1616, Nov. 29. ROBERT BROWN *(ibid)*.

1616, Dec. 6. CHARLES LE GROSSE *(ibid)*.

1616, Dec. 6. HENRY RADLEY (RODLEY), of Co. Lincoln. *(ibid)*.

1616, Dec. 6. SAMUEL SOMESTER, of Devon. *(ibid)*.

1616, Dec. 6. RICHARD SANDFORD, of Westminster *(ibid)*.

1616, Dec. 12. RICHARD WALDRON (at Newmarket).

1616, Dec. 14. PATRICK MONEYPENNY *(ibid)*.

1616, Dec. 16. GEORGE LAMPLOUGH *(ibid)*.

1616, Dec. 16. THOMAS WENTWORTH (*ibid* or Theobalds, Dec. 20).

1616, Dec. 21. HENRY MARTIN, of Berks. (at Theobalds).

1616, Dec. 21 (31). THOMAS LEIGH (at Whitehall).

1616–7, Jan. 16. WILLIAM MARTIN, of Essex (at Hampton Court).

1616–7, Jan. 31. JOHN HARBERT (HERBERT) (at Theobalds).

1616–7, Feb. 1. JOHN GRESHAM, of Surrey *(ibid)*.

1616–7, Feb. 2. BASIL BROOKE (in Ireland by Sir Oliver St. John, lord deputy of Ireland, "in the presence on Sunday being Candlemas Day").

1616–7, Feb. 2. JOHN VAUGHAN *(ibid)*.

1616–7, Feb. 8. OWEN SMITH, of Norfolk (by the King at Hampton Court).

1616-7, Feb. 10. THOMAS MIDLETON, of London (at Whitehall).

1616-7, Feb. 14. ROGER O'SHAGHNES (in Ireland by Sir Oliver St. John, lord deputy of Ireland).

1616–7, Feb. 16. FRANCIS HOWARD (by the King at Whitehall).

1616–7, Feb. 19. —— NETEOF (NEETENS, NEETESE), a Dutchman (at Theobalds ? Whitehall).

KNIGHTS BACHELORS

1616–7, Feb. 22. THOMAS DACRES (DAKERS), of Cumberland (at Theobalds).
1616–7, Feb. 22. THOMAS NORCLIFFE, of Co. Yorks. *(ibid)*.
1616–7, Feb. 23. PHILIP CARTWRIGHT (CARTERET) (at Whitehall).
1616–7, Feb. 28. JOHN SMITH *(ibid)*.
1616–7, Mar. 1. JOHN HOWLAND (at Theobalds).
1616–7, Mar. 1. WILLIAM ACCLOM (ACHLAM, ASKAM), of Co. Yorks. (Andescott, Oxford) *(ibid)*.
1616–7, Mar. 6. THOMAS SAVILE (at Whitehall).
1616–7, Mar. 6 (? 10). GEORGE BLUNDELL *(ibid)*.
1616–7, Mar. 9. JOHN LEMAN, lord mayor of London *(ibid)*.
1616–7, Mar. 12. ROBERT HATTON, of Co. Northampton *(ibid)*.
1616–7, Mar. 12. THOMAS FISHER, of Middlesex *(ibid)*.
1616–7, Mar. 12. JOHN WOLSTENHOLME *(ibid)*.
1616–7, Mar. 12. FRANCIS JONES *(ibid)*.
1616–7, Mar. 12. THOMAS WATSON *(ibid)*.
1616–7, Mar. 12. NICHOLAS SALTER *(ibid)*.
1616–7, Mar. 12. WILLIAM JONES *(ibid)*.
1616–7, Mar. 14. ROWLAND EGERTON, of Cheshire *(ibid)*.
1616–7, Mar. 16. THOMAS COVENTRY, solicitor general (at Theobalds).
1616–7, Mar. 16. PHILIP PAKENHAM (DECKHAM) *(ibid)*.
1616–7, Mar. 17. FRANCIS MOORE (at Theobalds, in the King's progress).
1616–7, Mar. 17. JOHN (JAMES) POYNTZ (POYNES), of Essex *(ibid)*.
1616–7, Mar. 18. EDWARD FIENNES (at Royston).
1616–7, Mar. 18. FRANCIS SWIFT, of Essex (at Royston).
1616–7, Mar. 20 (21). THOMAS HUTCHINSON (HUCHENSON), of Co. Notts (at Hinchinbroke).
1616–7, Mar. 20 (21). WILLIAM BIRD, LL.D. *(ibid)*.
1616–7, Mar. 24. BEVERLEY NEWCOMEN, eldest son of Sir Robert Newcomen (in Ireland by Sir Oliver St. John, lord deputy of Ireland).
1617, Mar. 26. JAMES EVINGTON, of Co. Lincoln. (by the King at Burley on the Hill).
1617, Mar. 26. RICHARD CONWAY (CONNYE, CONNER), sheriff of Rutland *(ibid)*.
1617, Apr. 4. HENRY BRETTON (BRITTON), of Surrey (at Lincoln).
1617, Apr. 4. THOMAS WILLOUGHBY *(ibid)*.
1617, Apr. 4. JOHN BUCK, of Co. Lincoln. *(ibid)*.

KNIGHTS BACHELORS

1617, Apr. 4. WILLIAM WILMER (WILLMORE), of Co. Northampton. *(ibid ? at Newark).*

1617, Apr. 7. GEORGE PECKHAM, of Co. Derby (at Newark ? York).

1617, Apr. 7. HENRY HERBERT, a captain *(ibid).*

1617, Apr. 11. WILLIAM ELLIS, of Co. Lincoln. (at York).

1617, Apr. 11. WILLIAM INGRAM *(ibid).*

1617, Apr. 11 (? 12). FERDINANDO LEGH (LEIGH), of Co. Yorks. *(ibid).*

1617, Apr. 11. WILLIAM SHEFFIELD, of Co. Yorks. *(ibid).*

1617, Apr. 11. WILLIAM HUNGATE, of Co. Yorks. *(ibid).*

1617, Apr. 11. PETER MIDLETON, of Co. Yorks. *(ibid).*

1617, Apr. 11. JOHN HOTHAM, of Co. Yorks. *(ibid).*

1617, Apr. 11. RICHARD DARLEY, of Co. Yorks. *(ibid).*

1617, Apr. 11. WALTER BETHELL (BYTHELL), of Co. Yorks. *(ibid).*

1617, Apr. 12. EDWIN SANDES *(ibid).*

1617, Apr. 13. ROBERT ASCOUGH (ASKWITH), lord mayor of York *(ibid).*

1617, Apr. 13. RICHARD HUTTON, recorder of York *(ibid).*

1617, Apr. 14. RICHARD HARPER, of Co. Derby. (at Sheriff Hutton Park).

1617, Apr. 14. JOHN HIPPESLEY (HEPSLEY) *(ibid).*

1617, Apr. 14. WILLIAM BELLASIS, of Co. Durham (at Sheriff Hutton Park).

1617, Apr. 15. WILLIAM CHATER (CHATOR, CHAREM), of Co. Yorks. (at York).

1617, Apr. 15. THOMAS ELLIS, of Grantham, Co. Lincoln. *(ibid).*

1617, Apr. 15. GEORGE RERESBY (RISBIE), of Co. Yorks. *(ibid).*

1617, Apr. 16. JOHN VAVASOR, of Co. York. (at Ripon).

1617, Apr. 16. MICHAEL WHARTON (WARTON), sheriff of Co. York. *(ibid).*

1617, Apr. 18. JOHN STANHOPE, of Co. Yorks. (by the King at Bishop Auckland, in Durham).

1617, Apr. 18. THOMAS MERRY, clerk comptroller *(ibid).*

1617, Apr. 19. ARTHUR GRAY (GREY), of Co. Northumberland *(ibid).*

1617, Apr. 19. MARMADUKE WIVELL, of Co. Yorks. *(ibid).*

1617, Apr. 23 (24). GEORGE TONGE, of Durham Bishopric (at Durham ? at Auckland).

1617, Apr. 23. WILLIAM BLAKISTON (BLACKSTONE), of the same *(ibid).*

1617, Apr. 23. TALBOT BOWES, of the same *(ibid).*

KNIGHTS BACHELORS

1617, Apr. 23. RALPH CONYERS, of the same (*ibid*).
1617, Apr. 23. MATTHEW FORSTER, of the same *(ibid)*.
1617, Apr. 23. JOHN CALVERLEY, of the same *(ibid)*.
1617, Apr. 23. WILLIAM WRAY, of the same *(ibid)*.
1617, Apr. 23 (24). WILLIAM KENNET (KNEVITT), of Newcastle (at Newcastle).
1617, Apr. 27. JOHN FITZGERALD, grandson of Sir John Fitz-Edmond FitzGerald (in Ireland by Sir Oliver St. John, lord deputy of Ireland).
1617, May 1. HENRY BABINGTON, of Northumberland (at Hexham).
1617, May 4. PETER RIDDELL, of Newcastle (at Newcastle).
1617, May 4. JOHN DELAVALL, of Newcastle *(ibid)*.
1617, May 9. EDMUND (EDWARD) GRAY, of Newcastle (at Chillingham).
1617, May 11. ANTHONY WELDON, of Kent, clerk of the Kitchen (at Berwick).
1617, May 11 (12). WILLIAM MUSCHAMP, of Northumberland (at Berwick).
1617, May 13. ROBERT JACKSON, of Northumberland (Berwick) *(ibid)*.
1617, May 14 (24, 29). WILLIAM FENWICK, of Northumberland (at Cavers in Co. Roxburgh).
1617, June 8. THOMAS LAKE, of Middlesex (at Edinburgh).
1617, June 29 (July 2). ROGER GREY (GRAY), of Northumberland (by the King at Edinburgh).
1617, June 29. THOMAS SAVAGE, of Cheshire *(ibid)*.
1617, June 29. JOHN CAESAR, of Herts. *(ibid)*.
1617, June 29. JOHN KINGSMILL (in Ireland by Sir Oliver St. John, lord deputy of Ireland).
1617, July 17 (23). ARTHUR TIRRINGHAM,* one of the gentlemen pensioners attending the King into Scotland (at St. Andrews).
1617, July 17 (27). JOHN BRAND, a same *(ibid)*.
1617, July 17 (27). RALPH SIDENHAM (SANDERS), a same *(ibid)*.
1617, July 17 (27). EDWARD GORING, a same *(ibid)*.
1617, July 17 (27). SANDERS DUNCOMBE, a same *(ibid)*.
1617, July 17 (27). RICHARD GREEN, clerk of the band of gentlemen pensioners *(ibid)*.
1617, July 17 (27). EDWARD FOWLER, of Kent, a gentleman pensioner *(ibid)*.

* Chamberlain to Sir Dudley Carleton dated June 4th, 1617. "All our pensioners that went with the King are knighted there that were undubbed before, and all the Gentlemen of Yorkshire ... and the Order [of Knighthood] is descended somewhat lower even to Adam Hill that was the Earl of Montgomery's barber and to one Green husband to the Queen's laundress an host [innkeeper] of Doncaster and to another that lately kept an inn at Rumford ... all the mean officers of the household are likewise said to be knighted.'

1617, July 17 (27). ARNOLD HERBERT, a gentleman pensioner (at St. Andrews).

1617, July 17 (27). HENRY RYVE (REVE, REEVE, KEENE), a same *(ibid)*.

1617, July 17 (27). THOMAS EVELYN, a same *(ibid)*.

1617, July 17 (27). JOHN HALES, a same *(ibid)*.

1617, July 17 (27). WILLIAM FRYER, a same *(ibid)*.

1617, July 17 (27). EDWARD BURNELL, a same *(ibid)*.

1617, July 17 (27). EDWARD GILBORN, a same *(ibid)*.

1617, July 17 (27). JOHN FARMER (FARWELL, FAREWELL), of Kent, a same *(ibid)*.

1617, July 29. GEORGE TREVELLIAN (in Ireland by Sir Oliver St. John, lord deputy of Ireland).

1617, Aug. 6. RICHARD FLETCHER, of Cockermouth (at Carlisle ? at Bruin or Brougham Castle, at the King's return out of Scotland).

1617, Aug. 6. HENRY BLENCOW (BLYNKHOWE), of Cumberland *(ibid)*.

1617, Aug. 6. WILLIAM MUSGRAVE, of Holme, sheriff of Cumberland *(ibid)*.

1617, Aug. 6 (8). FRANCIS BRANDLYN (BRANDLING), of Newcastle (at Brougham Castle, a mansion of the earl of Cumberland).

1617, Aug. 8. HENRY TROTTER, of Co. Yorks. *(ibid)*.

1617, Aug. 8. WILLIAM THOROLD, of Co. York (Lincoln) *(ibid)*.

1617, Aug. 8. THOMAS HUTTON (HATTON), of Co. York *(ibid)*.

1617, Aug. 8. CHRISTOPHER DALSTON, of Westmorland *(ibid)*.

1617, Aug. 8. PHILIP MOUNTENEY (MONCKTON), of Co. York. *(ibid)*.

1617, Aug. 8. GEORGE BOWES, of Durham *(ibid)*.

1617, Aug. 8. DAVID DROMOND, a Scotchman *(ibid)*.

1617, Aug. 9. HENRY MILDMAY, sewer to the King, master of the Jewels (at Kendal).

1617, Aug. 9. GEORGE SPENCER, sewer to the King *(ibid)*.

1617, Aug. 9. FRANCIS KNIGHTLEY, cupbearer *(ibid)*.

1617, Aug. 9. —— ——, a Scotchman (in the Park [near Brougham castle] the earl of Cumberland's).

1617, Aug. 12 (11). CHARLES GERARD (GARRETT), of Co. Middl. (at Ashton Hall in Lancashire, a mansion of lord Gerard's).

1617, Aug. 12. THOMAS WALMESLEY, of Co. Lancs. *(ibid)*.

1617, Aug. 18. ARTHUR LAKE, of Co. Middl. (at Houghton Tower).

1617, Aug. 18. CECIL TRAFFORD, of Co. Lancs. *(ibid)*.

1617, Aug. 20. WILLIAM MASSEY, of Co. Lancs. (Puddington, Cheshire) (at Lathom House, the seat of the earl of Derby).
1617, Aug. 20. ROBERT BINDLOSSE (BENDLOES), of Lancs. *(ibid)*.
1617, Aug. 20. GILBERT (GERVAS) CLIFTON, of Lancs. *(ibid)*.
1617, Aug. 20. JOHN TALBOT, of Preston *(ibid)*.
1617, Aug. 20. GILBERT IRELAND, of the Hut *(ibid)*.
1617, Aug. 20. EDWARD OSBALDSTON (OLBASTON, OSBERSTON) of Lancs. *(ibid)*.
1617, Aug. 21. THOMAS IRELAND (at Bewsy Hall, his house).
1617, Aug. 21. LEWIS PEMBERTON, of Herts. *(ibid)*.
1617, Aug. 23. GEORGE CALVELY (CALVERLEY) (at his own house, Leigh or Lea Hall, near Alford).
1617, Aug. 24 (23). HENRY LEY (LEIGH), of Cheshire *(ibid*, or at Vale Royal).
1617, Aug. 24. RICHARD GROSVENOR, of Cheshire *(ibid)*.
1617, Aug. 25. JOHN DONE, chief forester of Delamere (at his own house of Utkinton).
1617, Aug. 25. ANDREW CORBET, of Co. Salop *(ibid)*.
1617, Aug. 26. HUGH WROTESLEY, of Wrottesley, Stafford (at Nantwich).
1617, Aug. 26. WILLIAM OWEN, of Condover, Co. Salop *(ibid)*.
1617, Aug. 26. JOHN DAVENPORT, of Davenport, sheriff of Cheshire *(ibid)*.
1617, Aug. 28. ROGER PULESTON, of Co. Flint. (at Gerard's Bromley).
1617, Aug. 28. THOMAS WOLSELEY, of Co. Stafford. *(ibid)*.
1617, Aug. 28. RICHARD LIDDALL, of Berks. *(ibid)*.
1617, Sept. 1. HENRY AGARD, sheriff of Co. Derby. (at the last bounds of the shire of Derby).
1617, Sept. 2. WALTER DEVEREUX, base brother to the earl of Essex (at Ashby de la Zouch).
1617, Sept. 2. MATTHEW SAUNDERS, of Co. Leicester. *(ibid)*.
1617, Sept. 2. JOHN BALE (BALL), of Co. Leicester *(ibid)*.
1617, Sept. 2. WILLIAM HARTOP, of Co. Leicester. *(ibid)*.
1617, Sept. 2. FRANCIS ASHBY, of Middl. *(ibid)*.
1617, Sept. 2. THOMAS TRENTHAM, of Co. Stafford. *(ibid)*.
1617, Sept. 5 (4). WILLIAM BOWYER (at Warwick ? Coventry).
1617, Sept. 5. HENRY SNELGROVE, pensioner *(ibid)*.
1617, Sept. 5. WILLIAM CADE, of Co. Herts., a gentleman pensioner *(ibid)*.
1617, Sept. 5. JOHN BODLEY, of Surrey *(ibid)*.

1617, Sept. 5. FRANCIS CRANE, secretary to the Prince, chancellor of the Order of the Garter) (at Warwick ? Coventry).
1617, Sept. 5. WILLIAM BURLACIE, of Bucks. *(ibid)*.
1617, Sept. 5. HUMPHREY FERRERS, of Co. Warwick. *(ibid)*.
1617, Sept. 5 (6). ARTHUR (WILLIAM) MAXEY, of Co. Warwick *(ibid ?* at Compton).
1617, Sept. 5. RICHARD SAMWELL (SAMUEL), of Co. Northampton *(ibid* at Compton Wingate, the seat of lord Compton).
1617, Sept. 5. HENRY GIBBES, of Co. Warwick *(ibid)*.
1617, Sept. 6. WILLIAM SOMERFIELD (SOMERVILLE), of Warwick. *(ibid)*.
1617, Sept. 6. HERCULES UNDERHILL, of Co. Warwick. *(ibid)*.
1617, Sept. 10. THOMAS GLENHAM (GLEMHAM), of Suffolk (at Woodstock).
1617, Sept. 10. THOMAS WAYNEMAN, of Co. Oxford. *(ibid)*.
1617, Sept. 10. HENRY ROWE, of Middl. *(ibid)*.
1617, Sept. 11. ROBERT DORMER, of Co. Oxford. (at Rycot).
1617, Sept. 11. ARTHUR (ANTHONY) VINCENT, of Surrey *(ibid)*.
1617, Sept. 11. JOHN CULPEPER, of Sussex *(ibid)*.
1617, Sept. 15. ANTHONY BENN, recorder of London (at Hyde Park on the King's entering London after his return from Scotland).
1617, Sept. 15. RALPH FREEMAN, of London *(ibid)*.
1617, Sept. 16. ALEXANDER DENTON, of Bucks. (at Whitehall).
1617, Sept. 23. ARTHUR CAPELL, of Co. Herts. (at Enfield).
1617, Sept. 29. CLEMENT EDMONDS, of Co. Northampton., a clerk of the Council (at Hampton Court).
1617, Sept. 29. GEORGE CALVERT, of Co. Yorks., a clerk of the Council *(ibid)*.
1617, Sept. 29. ALBERT MORTON, of Kent, a clerk of the Council *(ibid)*.
1617, Oct. 1. GREVILL VERNEY (at Whitehall).
1617, Oct. 3. NICHOLAS KEMP, of London (at Theobalds).
1617, Oct. 22. RICHARD INGOLDSBY, of Bucks. (at Sir Oliver Cromwell's, at Hinchinbroke, ? at Theobalds).
1617, Oct. 28. GEORGE AYLOFF, of Essex (Grettenham, Wilts) (at Royston).
1617, Nov. 5. EDWARD TREVOR (in Ireland by Sir Oliver St. John, lord deputy of Ireland).
1617, Nov. 5. WILLIAM COLE (in Ireland by Sir Oliver St. John, lord deputy of Ireland).
1617, Nov. 8. JOHN KILLIGREW (by the King at Whitehall).

KNIGHTS BACHELORS

1617, Nov. 8. NATHANIEL RICH, of London (at Hatton House).
1617, Nov. 8. WILLIAM WYTHIPOLE, of Suffolk *(ibid)*.
1617, Nov. 8. FRANCIS NEEDHAM, of Suffolk *(ibid)*.
1617, Nov. 8. PETER CHAPMAN *(ibid)*.
1617, Nov. 11. JOHN WILD (WELD) (at Theobalds).
1617, Nov. 12. EDWARD GRESHAM, of Surrey *(ibid)*.
1617, Nov. 12. THOMAS PARKER (PORTER), of Ratton, Sussex *(ibid)*.
1617, Nov. 12. CHRISTOPHER BUCKLE, of Essex (Bansted, Surrey) *(ibid)*.
1617, Nov. 12. GABRIELL DOWSE, of Hants. *(ibid)*.
1617, Nov. 17. ROBERT DIGBY (at Newmarket).
1617, Nov. 24. THOMAS MOORE, eldest son to the lord Moore (in Ireland by Sir Oliver St. John).
1617, Nov. 27. WILLIAM FISH (FITCH) (by the King at Newmarket).
1617, Nov. 30. WILLIAM SARSFIELD (in Ireland by Sir Oliver St. John, lord deputy of Ireland).
1617, Dec. 3. CHARLES HUSSEY (by the King at Newmarket).
1617, Dec. 6. RICHARD SALTONSTALL (SALTINGSTALL, SALTINSTONE), of London *(ibid)*.
1617, Dec. 14. JOHN SKITT (SKEPT, SKEYETE), ambassador out of Russia (ambassador from the King of Sweden) *(ibid)*.
1617-8, Jan. 7. RICHARD YOUNG, of London (Surrey) (at Whitehall).
1617-8, Jan. 8. RICHARD LUCY, of Co. Warwick (Broxbourn, Herts.) *(ibid)*.
1617-8, Jan. 10 (20). EDWARD FLEETWOOD (at Theobalds).
1617-8, Jan. 10. ROWLAND VAUGHAN *(ibid)*.
1617-8, Jan. 10. JOHN BINGLEY, of the Exchequer *(ibid)*.
1617-8, Jan. 30. FRANCIS BLUNDELL, of Ireland (at Newmarket).
1617-8, Feb. 3. SIMON NORWICH, of Co. Northampton. *(ibid)*.
1617-8, Feb. 7. MICHAEL LONGEVILL, of Bucks. *(ibid)*.
1617-8, Feb. 8. JASPER HERBERT *(ibid)*.
1617-8, Feb. 23. HENRY YELVERTON, of Gray's Inn (at Newmarket).
1617-8, Feb. 25. JAMES HALES (HALLES), of Kent (at Theobalds).
1617-8, Feb. 26. WALTER SCOTT *(ibid)*.
1617-8, Mar. 16. HUGH CLOTWORTHY, of Devon. (at Whitehall).
1617-8, Mar. 18. EDWARD BROUGHTON (at Hampton Court).
1617-8, Mar. 20. HENRY MANWARING, of Surrey (at Woking).
1617-8, Mar. 23. GABRIELL LOWE, of Co. Gloucester. (at Whitehall).
1617-8, Mar. 24. JOHN DOWDALL (in Ireland by Sir Oliver St. John, lord deputy of Ireland).

1618, Mar. 25. EDWARD CONWAY (by the King at Whitehall).
1618, Mar. 28. HENRY PALMER, of Kent (at Theobalds).
1618, Mar. 31 (30). BENJAMIN RUDIARD, surveyor of the Court of Wards (at Whitehall).
1618, Apr. 3. JOHN MANWOOD *(ibid)*.
1618, Apr. 6. RALPH BURCHINSHAW (BIRKENSHAWE), of Ireland *(ibid)*.
1618, Apr. 12 (10). THOMAS STEPNEY (at Theobalds).
1618, Apr. 12 (10). THOMAS GARTON (GERTON) *(ibid)*.
1618, Apr. 22. THOMAS BLUDDER (at Whitehall).
1618, Apr. 22. JOHN TRACY *(ibid)*.
1618, Apr. 25. WILLIAM ST. LEGER *(ibid)*.
1618, Apr. 28. JAMES REYNOLDS (at Theobalds).
1618, Apr. 29. WILLIAM RUSSELL, of Chippenham, Cambridge *(ibid)*.*
1618, Apr. 30. ROBERT JENKINSON, of London *(ibid)*.
1618, May 3. CHRISTOPHER SIBTHORPE (in Ireland by Sir Oliver St. John, lord deputy of Ireland).
1618, May 3. GARRET LOWTHER *(ibid* by same).
1618, May 4. THOMAS HAWKINS, of Kent (by the King at Whitehall).
1618, May 6. WILLIAM ANDREWES, of Bucks. *(ibid)*.
1618, May 9. MATTHEW BOYNTON, of Co. Yorks. *(ibid)*.
1618, May 18 (13, 10). JOHN ELIOT *(ibid)*.
1618, May 19. HENRY LEE (in Ireland by Sir Oliver St. John, lord deputy of Ireland).
1618, May 20. HENRY BOSVILE, of Kent (by the King at Theobalds ? 1620 at Whitehall).
1618, May 21 (14). FRANCIS BEAUMONT (at Whitehall).
1618, May 26. ANDREW HUME, a Scotchman (at Greenwich).
1618, May 31. GEORGE BOWLES (BOLLES), lord mayor of London *(ibid)*.
1618, June 8. FRANCIS WAINEMAN (WEYNMAN), of Co. Oxford *(ibid)*.
1618, June 8. WILLIAM CAULFIELD (in Ireland by Sir Oliver St. John, lord deputy of Ireland).
1618, June 16. WILLIAM HALTON (HOUGHTON, HAUGHTON), (by the king at Theobalds).
1618, June 16. ROGER NORTH, of Suffolk *(ibid)*.

* 1618, April 20. Chamberlain to Sir Dudley Carleton, "I hear also that the King hath knighted one Russel, a Muscovy merchant, who is in speech with Sir Robert Mansfield (Mansel) to buy his place of Treasurer of the Navy."

KNIGHTS BACHELORS

1618, June 22. FRANCIS MEDCALFE, of Co. Yorks. (at Greenwich).
1618, June 23. WILLIAM FORD (at Greenwich).
1618, June 25. THOMAS WATSON, of Kent (at Halstead in Kent, said Watson's residence).
1618, June 26. WILLIAM CAMPION, of Kent (at Greenwich).
1618, June 29. WILLIAM BARNES, of Kent *(ibid)*.
1618, June 30. JOHN STEPNEY, of Pembroke (at Oatlands ? at Greenwich).
1618, July 4. EDMOND SCORY *(ibid)*.
1618, July 4. CHARLES BLUNT (BLOUNT), son and heir of Sir Robert Blount of Mapledurham (in Ireland by Sir Oliver St. John, lord deputy of Ireland).
1618, July 4. RICHARD BOLTON *(ibid)*.
1618, July 5. FRANCIS ASHLEY, of Dorset (by the King at Windsor).
1618, July 6. JAMES KIRTON, of Somerset *(ibid)*.
1618, July 6. EDWARD MORLEY *(ibid)*.
1618, July 7. FRANCIS WYATT, of Kent *(ibid)*.
1618, July 8. CHARLES NORTH *(ibid)*.
1618, July 15. WILLIAM WENDY, of Cambridge, sheriff of Cambridge and Huntingdon (at Theobalds ? at Windsor).
1618, July 15. JOHN PRICE *(ibid)*.
1618, July 19. RICHARD CALVELEY (in Ireland by Sir Oliver St. John, lord deputy of Ireland).
1618, July 20. THOMAS WILSON (by the King at Whitehall).
1618, July 20. EDWARD WARDOUR *(ibid)*.
1618, July 20. HENRY SPILLER *(ibid)*.
1618, July 21. CHARLES PLEYDELL (at Halstead ? at Woking).
1618, Aug. 1. RAWLYN RAGHLEY BUSSEY (BUSHEY) (at Bruncham or Bromham, at Brampton).
1618, Aug. 10. GEORGE WROUGHTON (at Salisbury).
1618, Aug. 10. ANTHONY BUGG (BUGGES) *(ibid)*.
1618, Aug. 14. HERCULES PAWLETT (at Cranborne, in Dorset, the seat of the earl of Salisbury).
1618, Aug. 29. THOMAS TIMPERLEY, of Suffolk (at Tichborne).
1618, Sept. 2. (? Aug. 29). BENJAMIN TICHBORNE, third son of Sir Benjamin Tichborne (at Aldershot ? at Tichborne).
1618, Sept. 2. (? Aug. 29). JOHN CHAPMAN (at Aldershot ? at Tichborne).
1618, Sept. 2. RICHARD UVEDALE, of Hants. (at Aldershot).
1618, Sept. 22. JOHN SMITH (at Whitehall).

1618, Sept. 30. WILLIAM DRURIE (DREWRY) (at Hampton Court).

1618, Oct. 1. GREGORY (GEORGE) FENNER *(ibid* or Whitehall or Royston).

1618, Oct. 3 (8). THOMAS CLARKE, of Kent (at Theobalds).

1618, Oct. 31 (Nov. 3). EDWARD STAFFORD (at Whitehall or at Theobalds).

1618, Nov. 5. THOMAS HIBBOTTS (in Ireland by Sir Oliver St. John, lord deputy of Ireland).

1618, Nov. 9 (3). THOMAS LITTLETON, a baronet (at Whitehall).

1618, Nov. 11 (9). EDWARD SULYARD (at Theobalds or Whitehall).

1618, Nov. 12 (11). SHILSTON CALMADY *(ibid)*.

1618, Nov. 22 (24, 30). GEORGE YARDLEY, the new governor of Virginia (at Newmarket).

1618, Nov. 23 (12). RICHARD SALTONSTALL (SALTINGSTONE) *(ibid* or at Theobalds).

1618, Nov. 23. GEORGE ELLIS, of Co. Yorks. *(ibid)*.

1618, Nov. 23. ROBERT KEMP, of Norfolk *(ibid)*.

1618, Nov. 24 (23). BENJAMIN THORNBORROW (at Newmarket).

1618, Nov. 30 (24). NATHANIEL NAPPER *(ibid)*.

1618, Dec. 1 (Nov. 30). THOMAS DERHAM (DEERHAM), of Norfolk *(ibid)*.

1618, Dec. 4 (1). JOHN HARE *(ibid)*.

1618, Dec. 5 (4). PHILIP BEDINGFIELD *(ibid)*.

1618, Dec. 11 (5). ROBERT WILLOUGHBIE *(ibid)*.

1618, Dec. 12 (11). FRANCIS LEIGH, of Co. Warwick. *(ibid)*.

1618, Dec. 15 (12). JOHN BREWSE (BRUSE, BRASE), *(ibid)*.

1618, Dec. 21 (15). NATHANIEL BARNARDISTON (at Newmarket or Theobalds).

1618, Dec. 21. STEPHEN SOAME (SOHAM) *(ibid)*.

1618-9, Jan. 1 (1618, Dec. 21). FRANCIS KYNASTON (at Whitehall or Theobalds).

1618-9, Jan. 2 (1). WALTER HEVENINGHAM (at Whitehall).

1618-9, Jan. 2. ROBERT MORDANT, of Norfolk *(ibid)*.

1618-9, Jan. 4 (? Dec. 18). BARTHOLOMEW PEEL *(ibid)*.

1618-9, Jan. 8. ROBERT BAYNARD, of Norfolk (at Theobalds).

1618-9, Jan. 9. FRANCIS VIVYAN *(ibid)*.

1618-9, Jan. 9. JOHN LANE (LAMM, LAMBE) *(ibid)*.

1618-9, Jan. 21. ROBERT (JOHN) LACY, of Oxford (at Newmarket).

1618-9, Jan. 21. JOHN MILLER *(ibid)*.

1618-9, Jan. 22 (9). EDWARD DERING, of Kent *(ibid)*.

1618-9, Jan. 24 (22). ROBERT FILMER, of Kent *(ibid)*.

KNIGHTS BACHELORS

1618–9, Feb. 1. THOMAS POLHILL (POLLEY), of Kent (at Theobalds).
1618–9, Feb. 2. NICHOLAS FORTESCUE, "one of the commissioners that are employed about the matters of the Household and Navy" *(ibid)*.
1618–9, Feb. 2. JOHN OSBORNE, a commissioner as above *(ibid)*.
1618–9, Feb. 2. FRANCIS GOFTON, of Surrey, a commissioner as above *(ibid)*.
1618–9, Feb. 2. RICHARD SUTTON, of Essex, a commissioner as above *(ibid)*.
1618–9, Feb. 2. WILLIAM PITT (PITTS), a commissioner as above *(ibid)*.
1618–9, Feb. 16 (10). GEORGE ETHERINGTON (at Whitehall).
1618–9, Feb. 16. GEORGE HORSEY *(ibid)*.
1618–9, Feb. 16. ROBERT SEYMOUR (SEAMOR) *(ibid)*.
1618–9, Feb. 16. ISAACK WAKE *(ibid ?* Apr. 9 at Royston).
1618–9 Feb. 16. RICHARD WISEMAN *(ibid)*.
1618–9, Feb. 19 (17). THOMAS MUSGRAVE (at Theobalds).
1618–9, Feb. 19. HENRY ROSWELL *(ibid)*.
1618–9, Feb. 21. EDWARD HARRIS (DAVIES) (in Ireland by Sir Oliver St. John, lord deputy of Ireland).
1618–9, Feb. 26. THOMAS FLEETWOOD (at Newmarket).
1618–9, Mar. 24. JAMES BLUNT (BLOUNT) (in Ireland by Sir Oliver St. John, lord deputy of Ireland).
1619, Apr. 19 (10). HENRY MARVYN (MERVINE) *(ibid)*.
1619, Apr. 19. JOHN JACKSON, of Co. Yorks. *(ibid)*.
1619, Apr. 20. HENRY HUNGATE, of Co. Leicester. (Surrey) *(ibid)*.
1619, Apr. 24. CHARLES RICH, of London (at Theobalds).
1619, Apr. 26. ROBERT KNOLLES (KNOWLES) *(ibid)*.
1619, Apr. 27. PETER WROTHE, of Kent *(ibid)*.
1619, May 10. JOHN WINGFEILD *(ibid)*.
1619, May 18. CHARLES CHIBBORNE (CHYBORN, CHEBBORNE), of Essex (at Greenwich).
1619, May 18. JOHN WALTER *(ibid)*.
1619, May 18. THOMAS (JOHN) TREVOR, of London *(ibid)*.
1619, May 21. CHARLES (CHRISTOPHER) HARFLEET, of Kent *(ibid)*.
1619, May 24. ALEXANDER MUNCRIFE, a Scotchman *(ibid)*.
1619, June 1. NICHOLAS LOWER (at Whitehall).

1619, June 8. MILES SANDES (at Greenwich).
1619, June 9. JOHN WHITE *(ibid)*.
1619, June 10. JOSEPH HAYES *(ibid)*.
1619, June 11. ROBERT BENNETT *(ibid)*.
1619, June 13. ROBERT GORGES *(ibid)*.
1619, June 13. SAMPSON DARRELL (DORRELL) *(ibid)*.
1619, June 18. JOHN HONYWOOD, of Kent (at Wansted).
1619, June 22 (20). NICHOLAS FULLER *(ibid)*.
1619, June 24. THOMAS RIDLEY (at Greenwich).
1619, June 28. CHARLES SMITH *(ibid)*.
1619, June 28. SAMUEL ROLLES (RODES) (at Wimbledon).
1619, June 29. JAMES WOLVERIDGE (WOLRICH), master in Chancery (at Greenwich).
1619, June 29. RICHARD MOOR (MORE), master in Chancery *(ibid)*.
1619, June 29. EWBALL THELWALL, master in Chancery *(ibid)*.
1619, June 29. ROBERT RICH, master in Chancery *(ibid)*.
1619, July 1. THOMAS HINTON (at Oatlands).
1619, July 1. BAPTISTA JONES *(ibid)*.
1619, July 7. THOMAS (JOHN) TREVOR (at Windsor).
1619, July 7. ALEXANDER HUME *(ibid)*.
1619, July 7. JOHN HOWELL, of Kent (at Windsor).
1619, July 8. ROBERT VAUGHAN *(ibid)*.
1619, July 9. EDWARD WIDNALL (WIGNALL, WIGGENHALL), of Surrey (at Wanstead).
1619, July 13 (19). JOHN DE GOCH (JOHN COCHRE, COKER, GOCHE, GOOCHE), consul of Zutphen, a commissioner from the United Provinces (at Theobalds).
1619, July 13 (19). EWALD VAN DER DUSSEN (EDMUND VANDERDUFFIN), consul of Delft, a commissioner as above *(ibid)*.
1619, July 13 (19). JOACHIM LYNES (LIENS), syndic of Tholen, a commissioner as above *(ibid)*.
1619, July 13. JOHN TUNSTALL, of Surrey *(ibid)*.
1619, July 15. JOHN CLARKE, of Kent *(ibid)*.
1619, July 15. EDWARD INGHAM (ENGHAM), of Kent *(ibid)*.
1619, July 19. NICHOLAS TROT *(ibid)*.
1619, July 19. JAMES CHISSELME (CHISHEALME) *(ibid)*.
1619, July 19. GEORGE CRAYFORD (CRAFFORD) *(ibid)*.
1619, July 19. WILLIAM PARKHURST, of Kent *(ibid)*.
1619, July 19. JAMES ST. LOW (SANDELOWE) *(ibid)*.
1619, July 21. THOMAS READE, of Herts. (at Royston).

KNIGHTS BACHELORS

1619, July 24 (22). HENRY ST. JOHN, brother of lord St. John (at Bletsoe, the seat of lord St. John).

1619, July 24 (22). BEAUCHAMP ST. JOHN, brother of the said lord St. John *(ibid)*.

1619, July 25. CORNELIUS VANCHELIN (VANSCHENLIN) (at Castle Ashby, the seat of the earl of Northampton.)

1619, July 27. FRANCIS BROWNE *(ibid)*.

1619, July 28. EDWARD WATSON, son of Sir Lewis Watson (at Rockingham Castle, seat of the said Sir Lewis Watson).

1619, July 29. WILLIAM BEECHER (at Kirkby, the seat of Sir Christopher Hatton).

1619, July 29. ROBERT CHARNOCK *(ibid)*.

1619, Aug. 3. WILLIAM ROBERTS, sheriff of Co. Leicester. (at Belvoir Castle).

1619, Aug. 6. JAMES BUCHANAN (BUCKHANNON), a Scotchman (at Belvoir Castle ? at Welbeck).

1619, Aug. 10. SUTTON CONEY (CONNY, CUNNYE), of Co. Lincoln. (at Welbeck, the seat of Sir William Cavendish).

1619, Aug. 10. CHARLES CAVENDISH, brother of Sir William Cavendish *(ibid)*.

1619, Aug. 10. EDWARD RICHARDSON, of Bucks. *(ibid)*.

1619, Aug. 10. WILLIAM CARNABY, of Northumberland (Northampton) *(ibid)*.

1619, Aug. 12. RALPH HANSBY, of Co. Lincoln. (Tickill Castle, Yorks.) (at Nottingham).

1619, Aug. 12. JOHN RAMSDEN, of Co. Derby. (Longley, Yorks.) *(ibid)*.

1619, Aug. 13. WILLIAM (PHILIP) BALFOUR (BAFORD), a Scotchman *(ibid)*.

1619, Aug. 13. THOMAS BARTON, sheriff of Notts. *(ibid)*.

1619, Aug. 17. FRANCIS COOK (at Tutbury).

1619, Aug. 17. WILLIAM POWELL *(ibid)*.

1619, Aug. 19 (? 18). THOMAS SCRIMSHIRE, sheriff of Stafford (in the fields in Staffordshire).

1619, Aug. 20. PHILIP EATON, of Eaton, Salop (at Tamworth).

1619, Aug. 21. BARTHOLOMEW HALES (HALE), of Co. Warwick. (at Warwick).

1619, Aug. 21. RICHARD BROWN (BRAWN), of Warwick *(ibid)*.

1619, Aug. 25. HECTOR PAWLET (at Woodstock).

1619, Aug. 27. WILLIAM GUISE, of Co. Gloucester (in the fields at Rycot).
1619, Aug. 27. EDMUND (EDWARD) FENNER, sheriff of Oxford *(ibid)*.
1619, Aug. 27. FRANCIS DUNCOMBE, of Northampton (Brickhill, Bucks. *(ibid)*.
1619, Aug. 27. JOHN CATCHER, of London *(ibid)*.
1619, Sept. 5. ANTHONY THOMAS, of London (at Windsor).
1619, Sept. 19. FRANCIS NETHERSOLE, of Kent (at Theobalds).
1619, Sept. 23 (21). JOHN FOWLE, of Kent *(ibid* ? at Alderman Jaye's house).
1619, Sept. 23. THOMAS CULPEPER, of Kent *(ibid)*.
1619, Sept. 23. THOMAS HOORD (HOODE), of Salop (at Alderman Jaye's house).
1619, Sept. 23. SAMUEL THWAITES, of Essex (at Whitehall).
1619, Oct. 10 (? 13). WILLIAM STEWARD (at Royston).
1619, Oct. 13. EDWARD SKERNE, of Co. Lincoln. *(ibid)*.
1619, Oct. 14. WILLIAM LEWIS, of Hants. *(ibid)*.
1619, Oct. 19. HENRY GRIMSTON, of Kent (at Sir Oliver Cromwell's, at Hinchinbroke).
1619, Oct. 19. JOHN PICKERING *(ibid)*.
1619, Nov. 3. GEORGE HASTINGS, of Grays Inn (at Whitehall).
1619, Nov. 4. THOMAS (GEORGE) HUGHES, of Gray's Inn and of Somerset *(ibid)*.
1619, Nov. 5 (? 4). JOHN BRUEN *(ibid)*.
1619, Nov. 5 (4). EDWARD LAWRENCE *(ibid)*.
1619, Nov. 5. ROBERT LOFTUS (in Ireland by Sir Oliver St. John, lord deputy of Ireland).
1619, Nov. 5. JOHN BELLEW, of Bellewston *(ibid* by same).
1619, Nov. 5. EDWARD BUTLER *(ibid* by same).
1619, Nov. 5. EDMUND TUITE, of Tuiteston *(ibid* by same).
1619, Nov. 5. WILLIAM HILL, of Allenston *(ibid* by same).
1619, Nov. 5. MAURICE GRIFFITH *(ibid* by same).
1619, Nov. 8. EDWARD VOWELL (FOWELL) (at Greenwich).
1619, Nov. 8. JOHN (RICHARD) CARNSHAW (CARVESHAW, CRANSHAW), of Co. Lincoln *(ibid)*.
1619, Nov. 9. JOHN AMY (AMIE), LL.D., of Great Abington, Cambridge (at Whitehall).
1619, Nov. 9. JAMES HUSSEY, LL.D. *(ibid)*.
1619, Nov. 9. JOHN HAYWARD (HEYWARD), LL.D., of Salop *(ibid)*.
1619, Nov. 9. JOHN MICHELL, of Surrey, master of Chancery *(ibid)*.

KNIGHTS BACHELORS

1619, Nov. 9. EDWARD LAWLEY, of Herts. (Salop) (At Whitehall).
1619, Nov. 10. WILLIAM REEVES (at Theobalds).
1619, Nov. 10. JOHN THORNHILL, of Kent *(ibid)*.
1619, Nov. 11. JOHN BOURCHIER *(ibid)*.
1619, Nov. 11. RICHARD ROBERTS *(ibid)*.
1619, Nov. 21. WILLIAM SPARKE (in Ireland by Sir Oliver St. John, lord deputy of Ireland).
1619–20, Mar. 2. GEORGE SHERLEY (SHIRLEY), chief justice of Ireland (at Whitehall by the King).
1619–20, Mar. 24. CHARLES MCCARTY (in Ireland by Sir Oliver St. John, lord deputy of Ireland).
1620, Mar. 31 (Apr. 1). ARCHIBALD ACHESON, a Scotchman (at Theobalds by the King).
1620, Apr. 11. GEORGE ABERCROMIE (at Hampton Court).
1620, Apr. 13 (15). ARCHIBALD BETON, a Scotchman *(ibid)*.
1620, Apr. 19. LEWIS DIVE (at Whitehall).
1620, May 1. ALLAN ZOUCH, of Greenwich (at Greenwich).
1620, May 13. —— RAMSEY *(ibid)*.
1620, May 31. HENRY BELLINGHAM, of Westmoreland, a baronet (at Theobalds).
1620, June 1. ROGER TWISDEN (at Greenwich).
1620, June 7. WILLIAM PARSONS (in Ireland by Sir Oliver St. John, lord deputy of Ireland).
1620, June 18 (1). CLIPSBY CREW (at Theobalds ? Greenwich by the King).
1620, July 4. DANIEL DELYNE (DE LIGNE) (of Henault) of Harlaxton, Co. Lincoln. (at Oatlands).
1620, July 4. ANTHONY HYNTON *(ibid)*.
1620, July 4. ROBERT TINTE (in Ireland by Sir Oliver St. John, lord deputy of Ireland).
1620, July 8. SAMUEL AWBREY, of Co. Hereford (in the Western progress).
1620, July 8. STAFFORD WILMOT (in same).
1620, July 8. ANDREW BOYD (in same).
1620, July 10. PAUL PINDAR (PENDAR) (in same).
1620 (?) JOHN HEYDON (in same).
1620 (?) THOMAS MENZIES, of Durn, provost of Aberdeen, delegated to the Court in England on a mission concerning some civic affairs of Aberdeen.
1620, Oct. 2. THOMAS LAMBERT (at Theobalds or Royston).
1620, Oct. 4. JAMES WHITLOCK, of Bucks. *(ibid)*.

1620, Nov. 5. HENRY STRADLING (at Theobalds).
1620, Nov. 5. HENRY (WILLIAM) YELVERTON *(ibid)*.
1620, Nov. 5 (12). DAVID WATKINS *(ibid)*.
1620, Nov. 5. JOHN DILLON (in Ireland by Sir Oliver St. John, lord deputy of Ireland).
1620, Nov. 26. LAWRENCE PARSONS *(ibid* by same).
1620, Dec. 3. FRANCIS MICHELL (MYCHILL) (at Newmarket ? Theobalds; degraded June, 1621).
1620, Dec. ALEXANDER NORTON (at Theobalds).
1620, Dec. 5. GILBERT CORNWALL *(ibid)*.
1620, Dec. 26. CLEMENT COTTERELL, groom porter (at Whitehall at Xmas).
1620, Dec. 26 (31). HENRY CARVELL, of Norfolk *(ibid* ? at Nonsuch).
1620-1, Jan. 23 (22). JERVIS HOLLIS (at Theobalds or Whitehall).
1620-1, Jan. 28. ROBERT HEATH (at Whitehall).
1620-1, Feb. 1. WILLIAM ELLIOT, of Surrey *(ibid)*.
1620-1, Feb. 13. RICHARD BROOK *(ibid)*.
1621, Mar. 25. THOMAS RICHARDSON, speaker of the Parliament *(ibid)*.
1621, Apr. 2. PETER SCOTT, of Kent *(ibid)*.
1621, Apr. 8. JACOB DE WINGAREDEN (WYNGAERDEN), lord of Benthus, an ambassador from the states of the Low Countries (at Whitehall).
1621, Apr. 8. JOHN CAMERLYN, syndic of Delft, a same *(ibid)*.
1621, Apr. 8. ALBERTUS SUCHE (SOUCK), consul of Horne, a same *(ibid)*.
1621, Apr. 8. ALBERTUS BRUGUING (BRUYENINCK BRUNNING), a same *(ibid)*.
1621, Apr. 8. JACOB DE SCHOTTE, consul of Middelburg, a same *(ibid)*.
1621, Apr. 8. FREDERICK DE VERVER (VERVON), from Martuahniss, a same *(ibid)*.
1621, Apr. 8. PAUL DE GRENN, lieut. gov. of the Forces of the United Netherlands.
1621, Apr. 10 (20). CHARLES WILLIAMS (at Theobalds).
1621, Apr. 24. LEONARD BOSVILE (BOSWELL), of Kent (at Whitehall).
1621, May 11. WILLIAM HULL, captain in Ireland (at Theobalds).
1621, May 13. JAMES BAYLY (at Greenwich).
1621, May 16. FRANCIS GLANVILE *(ibid)*.
1621, May 18. ALEXANDER CHAULKE *(ibid)*.

KNIGHTS BACHELORS

1621, May 18 (23). ANTHONY HASELWOOD (At Greenwich).
1621, May 18. ROBERT JOSELYNE *(ibid)*.
1621, May 31. WILLIAM NUCE (at Theobalds).
1621, June 2. PETER HAYE (at Theobalds).
1621, June 2. PATRICK HAY *(ibid)*.
1621, June 18. NICHOLAS TEMPEST, of Co. Durham *(ibid)*.
1621, June 22. THOMAS SPRINGETT (at Wanstead).
1621, June 24 (28). WILLIAM WHITMORE (at Greenwich).
1621, July 9. HENRY CAMPION, of Kent (at Windsor).
1621, July 13. ROBERT PYE (at Theobalds).
1621, July 16. ARTHUR INGRAM *(ibid)*.
1621, July 16. THOMAS LEVESON *(ibid)*.
1621, July 16. THOMAS EVERSFIELD, of Sussex *(ibid)*.
1621, July 19. JOHN FENNER (at Royston).
1621, July 19. RICHARD ROGERS *(ibid)*.
1621, July 21. WILLIAM CRAWFORD (CRAYFORD) (at Ampthill).
1621, July 21. ROBERT COOK, of Essex *(ibid)*.
1621, July 21. EDWARD SALTER, of Bucks. *(ibid)*.
1621, July 24. FRANCIS STANTON, of Beds. (at Bletsoe).
1621, July 26. JOHN LAMBE (at Castle Ashby).
1621, Aug. 4. ANTHONY COLLY, sheriff of Rutland (at Burley on the Hill).
1621, Aug. 6. EDWARD WORTLEY, of Co. York. (at Belvoir Castle).
1621, Aug. 6. THOMAS SAVAGE *(ibid)*.
1621, Aug. 12. THOMAS WALDRON (in Ireland by viscount Grandison, lord deputy of Ireland).
1621, Aug. 19. ROBERT KING (by the King at Tutbury).
1621, Aug. 19. HERCULES LANGFORD (in Ireland by viscount Grandison, lord deputy of Ireland).
1621, Aug. 20. HENRY MARNY (MERRY), of Barton Bakeping, Derby. (at Whitehall).
1621, Aug. 21. EDMOND (EDWARD) WINDSOR, sheriff of Stafford (at Tamworth, the seat of Sir Humphrey Ferrers).
1621, Aug. 22. NICHOLAS OVERBURY, of Barton, Gloucester. (at Warwick).
1621, Aug. 22. EDWARD LITTLETON *(ibid)*.
1621, Aug. 28 (26). STEPHEN (RICHARD) HAWKESWORTH (at Woodstock).
1621, Aug. 31. RICHARD HARRISON, of Hurst, Berks. (at Easthampstead).

1621, Sept. 9. EDWARD LEACH, of Cheshire (at Windsor).
1621, Sept. 11. MAURICE BERKLEY, of Hannam, Gloucester. (at Whitehall).
1621, Sept. 18. ARTHUR GORGES (at Theobalds).
1621, Nov. 5. PETER VANLORE (at Whitehall).
1621, Nov. 9. HENRY BOURCHIER (at Theobalds).
1621, Nov. 19. ALEXANDER CULPEPER (at Newmarket).
1621, Dec. 8. THOMAS LIDDELL (LYDALL), of Newcastle *(ibid)*.
1621, Dec. 17. ROBERT CRESSIE (in Ireland by viscount Grandison, lord deputy of Ireland).
1621, Dec. 22. THOMAS FERNEFOLD (FERNEFOLL, FARNFIELD), of Essex (Sussex) (by the King at Theobalds).
1621, Dec. 31. FRANCIS GODOLPHIN, of Cornwall (at Whitehall).
1621–2, Jan. 5. THOMAS STANLEY, of Essex *(ibid)*.
1621–2, Jan. 5. JOHN BOTELER (BUTLER), of Kent *(ibid)*.
1621–2, Jan. 11. TRACY (NEDHAM) SMART, of Kent (at Theobalds).
1621–2, Jan. 11. THOMAS NUGENT, of Moyrath (in Ireland by viscount Grandison, lord deputy of Ireland).
1621–2, Jan. 14. JOHN CULPEPER, of Kent (at Theobalds by the King).
1622, Jan. 17. WILLIAM WASHINGTON, of Northampton (at Theobalds).
1622, Jan. 28. JOHN MEADE (in Ireland by viscount Grandison, lord deputy of Ireland).
1622, Feb. 2. DANIEL LEIGH, bart. *(ibid* by same).
1622, Feb. 7. JAMES BARRET *(ibid* by same).
1622, Feb. 12. GEORGE HAYES (at Newmarket by the King).
1622, Feb. 21. THOMAS BARKER, of Suffolk *(ibid)*.
1622, Mar. 31. JOHN PARSONS (in Ireland by viscount Grandison, lord deputy of Ireland).
1622, Apr. 6. MATHEW BRAND, of West Moulsey, Co. Middl. (at Hampton Court by the King).
1622, Apr. 7. MARMADUKE LLOYD, of Masluellyn, Co. Cardigan. (at Whitehall).
1622, Apr. 13. ROBERT (JOHN) SHARPEY (SHARPEIGH), of Kent or Westminster (at Theobalds).
1622, Apr. 18. THOMAS GEE, of Mildenhall, Suffolk (at Whitehall).
1622, Apr. 28. RANDALL CLEYTON (in Ireland by viscount Grandison, lord deputy of Ireland).
1622, May 1. HENRY HOLCROFT, of London (by the King at Whitehall).

1622, May 4. WILLIAM TEMPLE (in Ireland by viscount Grandison, lord deputy of Ireland).
1622, May 4. ROGER HOPE (*ibid* by same, which day the lord viscount Grandison embarqued for England).
1622, May 13. —— PRESTON, a Scotchman (at Whitehall).
1622, May 14.* PAUL BOWLE, a Dutchman *(ibid)*.
1622, May 22. THOMAS SHIRLEY, of Betlebrig, Rutland (Hunts.) (at Whitehall).
1622, May 31. WILLIAM COURTEEN (at Greenwich or Whitehall).
1622, June 5. PETER MORTON (MUTTON), of Slenny, Co. Denbigh. (at Whitehall).
1622, June 8. THOMAS ALLEN, bart. (in Ireland by Sir Adam Loftus and viscount Powerscourt, lords justices).
1622, June 8. CHARLES O'CONNOR, bart. (*ibid* by same).
1622, June 11 (22). JERONIMO (SERCOMIUS) LANDO, the Venetian ambassador (with a patent of augmentation of his arms given by His Majesty) (at Greenwich).
1622, June 12. THOMAS SACKVILL, one of His Majesty's gentlemen ushers, daily waiters (at Whitehall).
1622, June 16. EDWARD BARKHAM, lord mayor of London (at Greenwich).
1622, June 18. FRANCIS LOWER, fourth son of Sir Thomas Lower, of St. Wynow, in Cornwall (at Wanstead).
1622, June 20. WILLIAM WALLER, of Brenchley, Kent *(ibid)*.
1622, June 26. SAMUEL ARGALL, of East Sutton, Essex (Kent), governor of Virginia (at Rochester).
1622, July 3 (23). WILLIAM SHERRARD, of Greenwich (at Oatlands).
1622, July 10. JOHN COWPER, of Rockburne, in Hampshire (at Windsor).
1622, July 10 (13). JOHN PRESCOT, of Hoxon, Suffolk (at Windsor ? at Wansted).
1622, July 13. FRANCIS IRELAND, of Westhull, Co. York. *(ibid)*.
1622, July 14. WILLIAM HOBBY, of Hales, in Gloucester (at Wanstead).
1622, July 15. HUMPHREY HANDFORD, sheriff of London (at his residence, The Hearts, in Woodford Row).
1622, July 23. RICHARD REYNELL, of Devon. (at Theobalds).
1622, July 25. THOMAS HOLLAND, of Berrow, Anglesea (at Whitehall).
1622, July 27. RICHARD WESTON, of Sutton, Surrey (at Guildford).
1622, July 27. ROBERT SPILLER, of Sutton, Surrey *(ibid)*.

* 1622, May 14. Philpot p. 84. "Here came the Privy Seal from his Majesty and a proclamation followed the same." See introduction p. xlix.

1622, Aug. 6. JOHN MELDROM, a Scotchman (at Windsor).

1622, Aug. 10. FRANCIS INGLEFIELD (ENGLEFIELD), of Shelley, Co. Leicester (Wootton Basset, Wilts.) (at Easthampstead).

1622, Aug. 11. HUMPHREY STILES (STYLE), of Kent (at Farnham).

1622, Aug. 12. THOMAS HOLMEDEN (HAMSDEN), of Tinchley, Surrey (at Holt).

1622, Aug. 12. JOHN COMPTON, of Priors Dean, Hampshire *(ibid)*.

1622, Sept. 5. THOMAS GREVE (GREEVE, GREEN), of Bobbing, Kent (at Windsor).

1622, Sept. 5. FRANCIS POONEY (PERNDY ? a duplication of Biondi) (at Windsor).

1622, Sept. 6. FRANCIS BIONDI (BYONDY), an Italian (at Windsor).

1622, Sept. 7 (17). THOMAS HILLERSDEN, of Elstow (Ampthill), Co. Beds. (at Theobalds).

1622, Sept. 8. CARY LAMBERT (in Ireland by viscount Falkland).

1622, Sept. 25. SAMUEL SMYTH *(ibid* by same).

1622, Oct. 13. JOHN CUNNINGHAM *(ibid* by same).

1622, Oct. 21. CHARLES HARBERT (HERBERT), of London (at Royston).

1622, Nov. 7. PERCY HERBERT (at Theobalds).

1622, Nov. 8. —— BALLANTINE, a Scotchman (at Royston).

1622, Nov. 16. WILLIAM BEECHER, of London, clerk of the Council (at Newmarket).

1622, Nov. 29. VALENTINE BLAKE (in Ireland by viscount Falkland).

1622, Dec. 3. GILES ESTCOURTE, of Sarum (Newton), Wilts. (at Newmarket).

1622, Dec. 3. WILLIAM MAISTERS (MASTER), of Cirencester, Gloucester. *(ibid)*.

1622, Dec. 8. NICHOLAS ARTHUR (in Ireland by the viscount Falkland).

1622, Dec. 9. JOHN MADISON (WADESON), of Co. York. (at Newmarket).

1622, Dec. 11. THOMAS WAUTON (WAUGHTON), a Scotchman *(ibid)*.

1622, Dec. 13. PETER BEELEN (BELING), of the Hague *(ibid)*.

1622, Dec. 15. WILLIAM BROWNLOW (in Ireland by viscount Falkland).

1622, Dec. 18. WALTER WALLER, of Kent (at Theobalds).

1622, Dec. 24. HENRY PEIRCE, bart. (in Ireland by viscount Falkland).

1622–3, Jan. 1. THEODORE DOCWRA *(ibid* by same).

1622–3, Jan. 1. EDWARD LOFTUS *(ibid* by same).

KNIGHTS BACHELORS

1622–3, Jan. 24. —— STAVENETS, one of the States ambassadors, prior to taking leave (at Whitehall).

1622–3, Feb. 1. HENRY BATTEN (BATTEY) (*ibid*, or at Theobalds).

1622–3, Feb. 1. PHILIBERT A TUYLL, a Serooskercke, Thienhouse, a lord of Zealand (letters patent dated at Westminster, with an augmentation of arms. Enrolled on the French Roll 201, membrane 46, Record Office).

1622–3, Feb. 1. VERE A CATS, of Maelsted, a lord of Zealand (same).

1622–3, Feb. 1. PHILIBERT A TUYLL, Serooskercke, and Popkensburg, lord of Zealand (same).

1622–3, Feb. 1. HENRY A TUYLL, lord of Serooskercke, Stanenissen and Rynhus, a lord and councillor of Zealand and maritime Prefect of Middleburg (same).

1622–3, Feb. 10 (12). JOHN PROUD, of Canterbury, Kent (at Theobalds).

1622–3, Feb. 12. WILLIAM MONSON, of Kennersley, Surrey *(ibid)*.

1622–3, Feb. 21 (12). JOHN WASHINGTON, of Co. Northampton. (at Newmarket).

1622–3, Mar. 2. JOHN MEADE, of Lofts, Essex *(ibid)*.

1622–3, Mar. 12. THOMAS SANDERS, of Agmondisham, Bucks. *(ibid)*.

1623, Mar. 25. THOMAS (JOHN) SYMONS, of Buckerell (Brightwell), Oxford (at Newmarket).

1623, Apr. 17 (27). RICHARD HIGHAM, of East Ham, Essex (at Hampton Court).

1623, Apr. 17. WILLIAM DORRINGTON, of Bremer, Southampton *(ibid)*.

1623, Apr. 29. CHARLES HOWARD, son of the earl of Nottingham *(ibid)*.

1623, Apr. 30. ROBERT NAPPER (NAPIER), of Lawton (Beds.) (at Whitehall).

1623, Apr. CHARLES MOORE (in Ireland by viscount Falkland).

1623, May 4. JOHN BURGH (BURGHOWER, BURROWES), of Stowe, Lincoln (at Greenwich).

1623, May 6. CHRISTOPHER YELVERTON, of Maudit, Northampton. *(ibid)*.

1623, May 9 (29). HENRY AUDLEY, of Barton Benchurch, Essex (at Theobalds).

1623, May 28. —— SPOTT, a Dutchman (*ibid* ? at Wansted).

1623, June 2. PAUL FLEETWOOD (at Greenwich).

1623, June 8. PETER PROBY, lord mayor of London *(ibid)*.

1623, June 15. ERASMUS DE LA FOUNTAIN, of Kirkby Bellers, Co. Leicester *(ibid)*.

1623, June 19. —— ——, a Dutchman (at Wanstead). *See* Spott *supra*.

1623, June 22. HENEAGE FINCH, of Kent, recorder of London (at Wansted or Greenwich).

1623, June 29. GEORGE CROOK (CROKE), of Waterstock, Oxford (at Greenwich).

1623, June 30. EDWARD BARKHAM, of Southam, Norfolk, baronet (*ibid* ? Theobalds).

1623, June 30 (July 18). THOMAS CANNON, of Haverford West, Pembroke *(ibid)*.

1623, July 13 (18, 12). RICHARD LECHFORD, of Selwood, Surrey (at Wanstead ? Theobalds).

1623, July 18 (3). THOMAS CECIL (at Theobalds).

1623, July 21. RANDALL CRANFIELD, of London (at Whitehall).

1623, Aug. 7. HENRY HERBERT, master of the Revels (at Wilton, the earl of Pembroke's).

1623, Aug. 7. THOMAS MORGAN, of Glamorgan, steward to the Lord Chamberlain (at Wilton, the earl of Pembroke's).

1623, Aug. 8. JOHN EVELYN, of Westdean, Wilts. (at Salisbury).

1623, Aug. 8. THOMAS SADLER, of Salisbury *(ibid)*.

1623, Aug. 8. MILES HOBART (HOBERD), of Halford, Bucks. *(ibid)*.

1623, Aug. 8. AUGUSTIN SOTHERTON, of Davers, Norfolk *(ibid)*.

1623, Aug. 8. WILLIAM BROWN, of Ireland *(ibid)*.

1623, Aug. 10. PETER FRENCH (in Ireland by viscount Falkland).

1623, Aug. 19 (14). JOHN BATH, of Ireland (at Cranborne).

1623, Aug. 26. CHARLES BERKLEY, of Bruton, Somerset (at Beaulieu, seat of the earl of Southampton).

1623, Aug. 29. HENRY TICHBORNE, of Hampshire (of Ireland) (at Tichborne).

1623, Sept. 3. BEVIS THELWALL, of Easthampstead (at Easthampstead).

1623, Sept. 4. JOHN HOME, earl Home (in Ireland by viscount Falkland).

1623, Sept. 4. RICHARD SOUTHWELL *(ibid* by same).

1623, Sept. 7. RICHARD KINGSMILL (at Windsor).

1623, Sept. 12. WILLIAM PLATER (PLAITERS) of Soterby, Suffolk (at Wanstead).

1623, Sept. 13. HENRY SPOTTESWORTH (in Ireland by viscount Falkland).

1623, Sept. 29. CHRISTOPHER DARCY (at Hampton Court).

1623, Oct. 3. SIMON HARVY, remembrancer of the Household (at Theobalds).

1623, Oct. 4. JAMES HILDERSTON (HILLERSDON), a Scotchman *(ibid)*.

1623, Oct. 4. JOHN COTTON, one of the serjeants at arms (at Hampton Court).
1623. Oct. 4. HUGH CULLUM (in Ireland by viscount Falkland).
1623, Oct. 10. TOBY MATHEW, of Co. Yorks. (at Royston).
1623, Oct. 23. EDMUND BLANCHVILE (in Ireland by viscount Falkland).
1623, Oct. 28. KENELM DIGBY, of Gotehurst, Bucks. (at Hinchinbroke).
1623, Nov. 8. NICHOLAS WALSH (in Ireland by viscount Falkland).
1623, Nov. 12. CHRISTOPHER WRAY, of Kent (at Theobalds).
1623, Nov. 12. JASPER FOWLER, of Dover *(ibid)*.
1623, Nov. 17. THOMAS CREW, of Stean, Co. Northampton, a serjeant-at-law (at Whitehall).
1623, Nov. 17. THOMAS HEDLEY (HETLEY), of Brampton, Co. Huntingdon, a serjeant-at-law *(ibid)*.
1623, Nov. 22. THOMAS MOSTON (MOISTEN), of Flint (at Theobalds).
1623, Nov. 27. THEOBALD ROCHE (in Ireland by viscount Falkland).
1623, Dec. 1 (Nov. 23). GILES OVERBURY, of Burton, Co. Gloucester. (at Theobalds).
1623, Dec. 1. JOHN STRODE (STROUDE), of Chantmarell, Co. Dorset. *(ibid)*.
1623, Dec. 2. WILLIAM SMITH, of Hill Hall, Essex *(ibid)*.
1623, Dec. 3. THOMAS LONGVILL, of Cannons, Berks. *(ibid)*.
1623, Dec. 7. JOHN BRIDGEMAN, of Nymphsfield (Mirfield), Co. Gloucester, a serjeant-at-law (at Whitehall).
1623, Dec. 8. THADY DUFFE, mayor of Dublin (in Ireland by viscount Falkland).
1623, Dec. 8. WILLIAM HOWARD, son of lord William (at Whitehall).
1623, Dec. 16. EDWARD WINGFIELD (in Ireland by viscount Falkland).
1623–4, Jan. 6. ARTHUR BLUNDELL *(ibid by same)*.
1623–4, Jan. 11 (1). JOHN LLOYD (FLUID), of Keyswin, Co. Merioneth. (at Whitehall).
1623–4, Jan. 15. EGREMONT THINN, of Braxborne, Co. Herts., a serjeant-at-law (at Theobalds).
1623–4, Feb. 8. HENRY O'NEALE (in Ireland by viscount Falkland).
1623–4, Feb. 12. WALTER COVERT, of Vintners, Maidstone, Kent (at Whitehall).
1623–4, Feb. 22. PETER CURTEEN (COURTEEN), a Dutchman, of Belgium and London *(ibid)*.
1623–4, Feb. 22. ROBERT CAREW (in Ireland by viscount Falkland).

1623–4, Feb. 25. WILLIAM INGRAM, of York. (at Hampton Court).

1624, Feb. 26. ARTHUR SMITHES (SMITHIES), of Obden (Olden), Co. Gloucester. (at Hampton Court).

1624, Mar. 4. THOMAS CROOKE, of Carbery, Ireland (at Theobalds).

1624, Mar. 11 (10). RALPH CANTRELL, of Hemmington, Suffolk (at Woking).

1624, Mar. 23. WILLIAM DOVE, of Upton, son of the bishop of Peterborough, Co. Northampton. (at Whitehall).

1624, Apr. 2. CHARLES HOWARD, son to the earl of Nottingham (at Theobalds).

1624, Apr. 9. CORNELIUS BALTIS (BALTRIS), of Tregose, in Zealand *(ibid)*.

1624, Apr. 19. JOHN SAUNDERS, of Marston Moretaine, Co. Beds. *(ibid)*.

1624, May 7. WALTER ROBERTS, of Glastonbury, Kent (at Greenwich).

1624, May 9. JOHN BRERETON (in Ireland by viscount Falkland). *See infra.*

1624, May 18. WILLIAM ROBERTS, of Willesden, Co. Middl. (at Greenwich).

1624, May 19 (20). JOHN BRERETON, of Brereton, Cheshire *(ibid)*. *See supra.*

1624, May 23. MARTIN LUMLEY, lord mayor of London *(ibid)*.

1624, June 1. JOHN DANVERS, of Culworth, Co. Northampton. (at Theobalds).

1624, June 2. ANTHONY IRBY, of Whaplode, Co. Lincoln. *(ibid)*.

1624, June 2. RICHARD ONSLOWE, of Knoll Cranley, Surrey *(ibid)*.

1624, June 6. ROGER JONES, of Sligo (in Ireland by viscount Falkland).

1624, June 10. LUCAS DILLON, of Ireland (at Greenwich).

1624, June 10. THOMAS COUNY (CUNNY), of Hescomblind (Wisholme), Co. Rutland. *(ibid)*.

1624, June 13. PETER GLEEN (GLEAN), of Norwich, alderman *(ibid)*.

1624, June 14 (15). JOHN HUIZON (HUSSEYN), of Middelburg, in Zealand (at Theobalds).

1624, June 15. WILLIAM COBBE, of Adderbury, Co. Oxford. *(ibid)*.

1624, June 17. HUMPHREY DAVENPORT, of Cheshire, a serjeant at law (at Greenwich).

1624, June 19. WILLIAM THECKSTON (at Wanstead).

1624, June 23. EDWARD HAWLEY, of Buckland, Co. Somerset. (at Wanstead).

1624, July 2. GEORGE (GREGORY) WINTER, of Durham, Co. Gloucester. (at Oatlands).
1624, July 4. ROBERT CRAYFORD (CRAFORD), of St. Margarets by Rochester, Kent (at Windsor).
1624, July 7 (9). RALPH DONE, of Duddon, Cheshire (*ibid* ? Whitehall).
1624, July 9. FRANCIS BINDLOSS (BENLOSS), of Kendington, Co. Lancs. (at Kensington).
1624, July 10. THOMAS WHORWOOD, of Sandwell, Co. Stafford, (at Wanstead).
1624, July 10. WILLIAM LEIGH, of Oldesthorpe, Co. Gloucester. *(ibid).*
1624, July 13. CHRISTOPHER O'DEMPSIE (in Ireland by viscount Falkland).
1624, July 14. THEODORE MAYHERN, the King's Physician (at Theobalds).
1624, July 14. THOMAS CONWAY, senr. *(ibid).*
1624, July 14. THOMAS CONWAY, junr. *(ibid).*
1624, July 17. JOHN BORROUGH (BOROUGHS), Norroy King of Arms *(ibid).*
1624, July 17. JOHN CONYERS, captain, of Co. Worcester *(ibid).*
1624, July 17. JACOB ASTLEY (ASHLEY), of Norfolk *(ibid).*
1624, July 18. PETER LE MAIER, of London (at Royston).
1624, July 19. CLEMENT SCUDAMORE, sheriff of Herts. (in the highway between Royston and Houghton Lodge).
1624, July 20. WILLIAM FLEETWOOD, cupbearer (at Houghton Lodge).
1624, July 20. SAMUEL LUKE, of Woodend, Co. Beds. *(ibid).*
1624, July 23. FRANCIS CLARKE, of Houghton Conquest, Co. Beds., sheriff of Beds. (in the way between Bletsoe and Castle Ashby).
1624, July 24. LUKE FITZGERALD (in Ireland by viscount Falkland).
1624, July 25. WILLIAM LYTTON, of Knebworth, Herts. (at Castle Ashby, the seat of the earl of Northampton).
1624, Aug. 3. GEORGE QUARLES (at Burley on the Hill, the seat of the duke of Buckingham).
1624, Aug. 3. JOHN TAAFFE (in Ireland by viscount Falkland).
1624, Aug. 4. JOHN BALE, of Carlton Curleiw, sheriff of Co. Leicester. (at Belvoir).
1624, Aug. 5. Six Frenchmen of the retinue of the French ambassador who pursued the Royal footsteps throughout the progress (at Belvoir).

1624, Aug. 7. JOHN SAVAGE, son and heir to viscount Savage (at Belvoir).

1624, Aug. 7. JOHN WINTER, of Lydney, Gloucester. *(ibid)*.

1624, Aug. 7. JOHN THIMBLEBY, of Co. Lincoln. *(ibid)*.

1624, Aug. 7. JOHN MEDLICOT *(ibid)*.

1624, Aug. 8. THOMAS HARTOP, of Burton Lazars, Co. Leicester. (at Newmarket).

1624, Aug. 8. RICHARD BLAKE, of Galway (in Ireland by viscount Falkland).

1624, Aug. 10. JOHN FITZHERBERT, of Norbury, Co. Derby. (at Welbeck, the seat of Sir W. Cavendish).

1624, Aug. 10. JOHN FITZHERBERT, of Tissington, Co. Derby. *(ibid)*.

1624, Aug. 14. MATHEW PALMER, of Southwell, sheriff of Notts. (at Nottingham).

1624, Aug. 16. ROGER COOPER, of Thurgarton, Co. Notts. (at Derby).

1624, Aug. 17. HENRY RAINSFORD, of Clifford Chambers, Co. Gloucester. (at Tutbury).

1624, Aug. 18. EDWARD VERNON, of Sudbury, Co. Derby *(ibid)*.

1624, Aug. 18. GERVAISE CUTLER, of Stoynborough, Co. Yorks. *(ibid)*.

1624, Aug. 19. JOHN SKEFFINGTON, of Skeffington, Co. Leicester., sheriff of Stafford (at Tamworth).

1624, Aug. 20. RICHARD SKEFFINGTON, of Fisherwick, Co. Staff. (at Bastwell Hall, ? Berkswell or Balsall).

1624, Aug. 21. SIMON ARCHER, of Tamworth, Co. Warwick. (at Warwick Castle).

1624, Aug. 24. ARTHUR HYDE (in Ireland by viscount Falkland).

1624, Aug. 28. JOHN REPINGTON, of Atherston, Co. Warwick. (at Woodstock).

1624, Aug. 28. RALPH DUTTON, of Standish, Co. Gloucester. *(ibid)*.

1624, Aug. 29. TIMOTHY TIRRELL (at Shotover Lodge, Sir Timothy Tirrell's Lodge in Oxfordshire).

1624, Aug. 29. JOHN FARMER (FERMER), of Swinerton, Co. Oxford. *(ibid)*.

1624, Aug. 30. RICHARD BOYLE, viscount Dungarvan (in Ireland by viscount Falkland).

1624, Aug. 30. RICHARD SMYTH *(ibid* by same).

1624, Aug. 30. GEORGE BOYLE *(ibid* by same).

1624, Sept. 9. PETER AYLWARD *(ibid* by same).

KNIGHTS BACHELORS

1624, Sept. 9. JOHN COOK, of Hall Court, Co. Herts., master of requests (at Whitehall).

1624, Sept. 13. JOHN COPPINGER (in Ireland by viscount Falkland).

1624, Sept. 19. THOMAS FANSHAW, of Jenkins, Co. Essex (at Theobalds).

1624, Sept. 19. —— VALERESSO, the Venetian ambassador *(ibid* on his farewell audience).

1624, Sept. 23. WILLIAM TERRY (TIRREY), of London (at Enfield).

1624, Sept. 26. ANTHONY BROWNE, of Kingston, Surrey (at Hampton Court).

1624, Sept. 26. —— ——, a Scotchman *(ibid)*.

1624, Oct. 3. EDWARD CARRE, senior, of Hillingdon, Co. Surrey (at Theobalds).

1624, Oct. 3. EDWARD CARRE, junior, a gentleman pensioner *(ibid)*.

1624, Oct. 5. HENRY GIBB (GILL) *(ibid)*.

1624, Oct. 29. WILLIAM GOURDON, a Scotchman (at Royston). See p. 188 *infra*.

1624, Nov. 6. WILLIAM MAJOR (MAJON, MAYON, MASON), of Bering, a Dutchman (at Chesterford Park).

1624, Nov. 19. PHILIP PARKER, of Arwerton (Annerton), Suffolk (at Newmarket).

1624, Dec. 2. ALEXANDER BRETT (at Newmarket).

1624, Dec. 10. WALTER COPPINGER (in Ireland by viscount Falkland).

1624, Dec. 14. BRIAN IANSON *(ibid* by same).

1624, Dec. 19. ROBERT ROKEWOOD, of Coldham Hall, Suffolk (at Royston).

1624, Dec. 23 (29). ROBERT HUDSON (HODGSON) (at Whitehall).

1624, Dec. 25. Two Scotch captains

1624, Dec. 27. ARCHIBALD DOUGLAS (at Whitehall).

1624, Dec. 29. Four Frenchmen *(ibid)*.

1624, Dec. 30. ROBERT DALLINGTON, master of Sutton's Hospital *(ibid)*.

1624, Dec. 30. JAMES ST. CLERE, a Scotchman *(ibid) see infra*.

1624–5, Jan. 3. PATRICK DRUMMOND, a Scotchman *(ibid)*.

1624–5, Jan. 4. —— BOSWELL, a Scotchman *(ibid)*.

1624–5, Jan. 4 (29). —— ST. CLEER (Singler), a Scotchman *(ibid) see supra*.

1624–5, Jan. 29. JAMES REY (ROYE), a Scotchman (at Theobalds).

1624–5, Feb. 8. THOMAS SWINBORNE, of Northumberland (at Newmarket).

1624–5, Feb. 15. NICHOLAS MARTIN, of Devon. *(ibid)*.

1624–5, Feb. 20. THOMAS CULPEPER, of Kent (of Tegington, Sussex) *(ibid)*.

1624–5, Feb. 24. ROGER THORNTON, of Swainwell, Co. Cambridge. (at Newmarket).

1624–5, Feb. 24. EDMOND SAWYER, an auditor of the Exchequer Court, London (at Chesterford Park).

1624–5, Feb. 28. RICHARD BETTENSON, of Essex (at Royston).

1625, Apr. 12. MORRIS ABBOT, merchant, alderman of London (at Whitehall).

1625, Apr. 22. ABRAHAM WILLIAMS, agent for the queen of Bohemia, clerk of the Signet *(ibid)*.

1625, Apr. 25. JAMES (JOHN) LESLEY a Scot. *(ibid)*.

1625, Apr. 30. PAUL HARRIS, of Boreatton, Salop. *(ibid)*.

1625, May 6. JOHN MILLER (MELLER), of Little Bredy, Dorset. *(ibid)*.

1625, May (?) CHARLES GLEMHAM, master of the Household *(ibid)*.

1625, May 15. EDWARD CLERK, of Reading, Berks. *(ibid)*.

1625, May 20. EDWARD GRIFFIN, of Braybrook Castle, Co. Northampton. *(ibid)*.

1625, May 24. JOHN HALES, of Kent *(ibid)*.

1625, May 26. WALTER LONG, of Wraxhall, Wilts. *(ibid)*.

1625, May (?) THURSTON (TRUSTON) SMITH, of Walpole, Sussex (Suffolk) *(ibid)*.

1625, June 9. GEORGE MALBY (in Ireland by viscount Falkland).

1625, June 15. CHRISTOPHER MAN, of Canterbury (at Canterbury).

1625, June 15. JOHN FINCH, of Kent *(ibid)*.

1625, June 15. ROBERT HONIWOOD, of Pet (Charing), Kent *(ibid)*.

1625, June 18. THOMAS POWER, of Newcastle (at Whitehall).

1625, June 20. HUGH STUCKLEY (STEWKLY), of Hinton, Hants. *(ibid)*.

1625, June 25. ROBERT TRAVERS (in Ireland by viscount Falkland).

1625, June 27 (18). ROGER MARTIN, of Long Melford, Sussex (at Whitehall).

1625, July 4. WILLIAM GOURDON, a Scotchman *(ibid)* see p. 187 *supra*.

1625, July 9. MARTIN LYSTER (BISTER) (at Hampton Court).

1625, July 10. MORRIS DRUMMOND, a Scotchman *(ibid)*.

KNIGHTS BACHELORS

1625, July 16. NICHOLAS ROW, of Muswell Hill, Middlesex (at Windsor).
1625, July 17. RICHARD HUTTON, of Goldsborough, Yorks. *(ibid)*.
1625, July 19. MORGAN RANDALL (RANDEL), of Oxenford, Co. Surrey (at Woking).
1625, Aug. 2 (? 3). THOMAS POPE, of Wroxton, Co. Oxford. (at Woodstock).
1625, Aug. 7. THOMAS MORTON, of Eastnor, Kent *(ibid)*.
1625, Aug. 7. THOMAS YORK, of Brackley, Northamptonshire *(ibid)*.
1625, Aug. 8. THOMAS BAKER *(ibid)*.
1625, Aug. 11. FRANCIS ACKLAND (in Ireland by viscount Falkland).
1625, Aug. 15. HENRY KILLIGREW (at Woodstock).
1625, Aug. 25. RICHARD WHITBURNE (in Ireland by viscount Falkland).
1625, Aug. 25. WILLIAM BISHOPPE, mayor of Dublin *(ibid* by same).
1625, Aug. 31. WILLIAM SAUNDERSON, of Co. Lincoln. (at Albury).
1625, Aug. 31. THOMAS BRODERICK (BORDERY, BRODERY), of Arnbury, Co. Wilts. *(ibid)*.
1625, Sept. 4. WILLIAM MORLEY (at Titchfield).
1625, Sept. 12. JOHN ASHBURNHAM, of Bromham, Sussex *(ibid)*.
1625, Sept. 13. EDWARD BARKLEY, of Bruton, Somerset. (at Bruton).
1625, Sept. 15. RICHARD REYNEL, of East Ogwell, Devon. (at Ford).
1625, Sept. 15. THOMAS REYNEL, brother of abovesaid Sir Richard *(ibid)*.
1625, Sept. 15. JOHN YONG (YOUNG) *(ibid)*.
1625, Sept. 16. JOHN CHICHESTER, of Devon. (at Plymouth).
1625, Sept. 17. JOHN CAREW, of Devon. *(ibid)*.
1625, Sept. 19. JAMES BAGG, of Plymouth (at Salcombe).
1625, Sept. 26. SIMON LEECH, of Cadley, Devon. (at Ford).
1625, Sept. 27. FRANCIS DODDINGTON (DORRINGTON), of Doddington, Somerset. (at Hinton).
1625, Sept. 27. THOMAS (AMYAS) PAWLET, of Somerset. *(ibid)*.
1625, Sept. 28 (? 23). THOMAS THORNIX (THORNHURST), of Kent (at Plymouth).
1625, Sept. 28. WILLIAM COURTNEY, of Devon. *(ibid)*.
1625, Sept. 28. HENRY SPRYE, of Devon., captain *(ibid)*.
1625, Sept. 28. JAMES (THOMAS) SCOT, captain *(ibid)*.

1625, Sept. 28. SHEFFIELD (JOHN) CLAPHAM (at Plymouth)

1625, Sept. 28 (23). JOHN GIBSON, captain *(ibid)*.

1625, Sept. 28. HENRY (FRANCIS) WILLOUGHBY, captain *(ibid)*.

1625, Sept. 28. THOMAS LOVE, captain *(ibid)*.

1625, Sept. 28. MICHAEL GEAR (GERE), captain *(ibid)*.

1625, Sept. 28. JOHN WATTS, captain *(ibid)*.

1625, Sept. 28. JOHN CHIDLEY (CHUDLEIGH), captain, of Devon. *(ibid)*.

1625, Oct. 3. THOMAS JAY, of Netherhaven, Wilts. (at Wilton).

1625, Oct. 18. ROBERT COCK, clerk of the check (at Salisbury).

1625, Oct. 31. RICHARD SHELDEN, solicitor general (at Hampton Court).

1625, Nov. 3. EDWARD BATHURST, of Horton Kirby, Kent (at Nonsuch).

1625, Nov. 22. JOHN NETTERVILE (in Ireland by viscount Falkland).

1625, Dec. 18. EDWARD BISHOP, of Parham, Sussex (at Hampton Court).

1625, Dec. 27. EDWARD SPENCER, filius domini Spencer, of Baston, Co. Middl. *(ibid)*.

1625, Dec. (? Sept.), 29. PETER KILLIGREW *(ibid)*.

1625-6, Feb. 2. BRIAN MAGUIRE (in Ireland by viscount Falkland).

1626, Mar. 27 (Coronation day). LUCIUS CARY *(ibid by same)*.

1626, Mar. 27. EDWARD BRABAZON *(ibid by same)*.

1626, Mar. 27. HENRY BLANEY *(ibid by same)*.

1626, Mar. 27. ANTHONY BRABAZON *(ibid by same)*.

1626, Apr. 12. DODMORE COTTON (at Whitehall).

1626, May 12. WILLIAM KILLIGREW, son of Sir Robert *(ibid)*.

1626, May 19. HUGH CHOLMONDELEY, of Whitby Abbey, Yorks. *(ibid)*.

1626, June 4. CHARLES COOTE, junior, (in Ireland by viscount Falkland).

1626, June 6. JOHN LOWTHER (LODER), of Loder, Westmorland (at Whitehall).

1626, June 14 (4). JOHN GORE, late lord mayor of London *(ibid)*.

1626, June 14 (4). ALLEN COTTON, then lord mayor of London *(ibid)*.

KNIGHTS BACHELORS 191

1626, June 26. MARMADUKE WHITECHURCH (in Ireland by viscount Falkland).

1626, July 2. FRANCIS HARVEY, of Cotton End, Co. Northampton. (at Whitehall).

1626, July 9. EDWARD DENNY (in Ireland by viscount Falkland).

1626, July 11. THOMAS HARRIS *(ibid* by same).

1626, July 22. JOHN UNDERHILL (at Oatlands).

1626, Sept. 7. WILLIAM GARDNER, of Peckham, Surrey (at Hampton Court).

1626, Nov. 26. JOHN CLOTWORTHY (in Ireland by viscount Falkland).

1626, Nov. 26. JAMES DILLON *(ibid* by same).

1626, Nov. 27. GEORGE KNEVIT (CENIT, KEVITT, KERRIT), a captain (at Whitehall).

1626, Nov. 30. THOMAS HUNCKS *(ibid)*.

1626, Dec. 2. THOMAS RICHARDSON, of Thorpmarket, Co. Norfolk *(ibid)*.

1626, Dec. 3. WALTER LEECH, of Cadley, Co. Devon. *(ibid)*.

1626, Dec. 6. SIMONDS D'EWES, of Stow Langloft, Suffolk *(ibid)*.

1626, Dec. 9. MILES SANDS (SANDYS), of Wilburton, Co. Cambridge. *(ibid)*.

1626, Dec. 11. RICHARD MINSHULL, of Cheshire *(ibid)*.

1626, Dec. (?) ROBERT SANDS, brother of aforesaid Sir Miles *(ibid)*.

1626, Dec. 16. PETER WICHE, of London, ambassador to Constantinople *(ibid)*.

1626-7, Jan. 28. NICHOLAS HIDE, lord chief justice, of Marlborough, Wilts. *(ibid)*.

1626-7, Feb. 8. FRANCIS CLARK, of Hitcham, Bucks. *(ibid)*.

1626-7, Feb. 11 (21). GEORGE KEMP, of Pentlow, Essex *(ibid)*.

1626-7, Mar. 4. WILLIAM CRAVEN, afterwards lord Craven, of London (at Newmarket).

1626-7, Mar. 6. WILLIAM CARR, son of Sir Robert *(ibid)*.

1626-7, Mar. (? May) 21 [? 1627-8]. WILLIAM PESHAL (PELSHULL) *(ibid)*.

1626-7, Mar. 22. WILLIAM ALEXANDER (at Whitehall).

1627, Apr. 9. CHRISTOPHER TRENTHAM, of Co. Stafford *(ibid)*.

1627, Apr. 10. EDWARD SEABRIDGE (SEBRIGHT), of Besford, Co. Worcester *(ibid)*.

1627, Apr. 14. ROBERT BARKLY, one of the King's serjeants-at-law, of Spetchley, Worcester. (At Whitehall).

1627, Apr. 19. THOMAS KELLEYON (KELLION, KELLEY), of Scotland *(ibid)*.

1627, Apr. 21. TOBY CAGE, of Woodford Bridge *(ibid)*.

1627, Apr. 21. EDWARD BAGSHAW (in Ireland by viscount Falkland).

1627, Apr. 29. JOHN HANBERY, of Kellmarsh, Co. Northampton. (at (Whitehall).

1627, Apr. 29. WILLIAM BRYERS, of Co. Bedford *(ibid)*.

1627, May 20. CUTHBERT HACKET, lord mayor of London *(ibid)*.

1627, May 23 (28). MARTIN SNOUCKAERT (SNOWKART), of Scanbergh, Flanders *(ibid)*.

1627, June 20 (21). RICHARD GREENVILLE (GRENVYLE), a captain going the voyage with the duke of Buckingham (at Portsmouth).

1627, June 20 (21). THOMAS FRYER, a captain as above *(ibid)*.

1627, June 20 (21). WILLIAM CUNNINGHAM, a captain as above *(ibid)*.

1627, June 20 (21). JOHN TALCARN (TOLCARN), a captain as above *(ibid)*.

1627, June 21. CON MAGENIS (in Ireland by viscount Falkland).

1627, June 22. DANIEL NORTON (at Southwich, Hants., seat of the said Sir Daniel).

1627, June 22. JOHN SAVILL, of Lupset, Co. Yorks. *(ibid)*.

1627, June 26. SIMON HARCOURT (HARECOURT), captain (at Whitehall).

1627, July 7. ROBERT HONIWOOD, servant to the queen of Bohemia (at Oatlands).

1627, July 17. DREW DEAN, of Dineshall, Essex (at Theobalds).

1627, July 22. GEORGE (JOHN) RUSSEL, of Richmonds, Co. Beds. (at Ampthill).

1627, July 23. HENRY AUSTREY, of Woodend *(ibid)*.

1627, July 24. MATTHEW DE RENZI (in Ireland by viscount Falkland)

1627, July 29. LAURENCE WASHINGTON (at Alderton).

1627, Aug. 5. GEORGE ST. GEORGE (in Ireland by viscount Falkland).

1627, Aug. 5. RICHARD BUTLER, of Knocktofer *(ibid* by same).

1627, Aug. 7. EDWARD CLARK, of Arlington, Berks. (at Bisham).

1627, Aug. 22. COPE DOYLEY, of Greenland, Bucks. (at Windsor).

1627, Sept. 23.
> These six Knights following were knighted by the king of Sweden at Darsaw, in Prussia, in the midst of his whole army in the King's tent with great honour and triumph, the King himself at the same time receiving the Order of the Garter, being upon Sunday, Sept. 23. The first two of these six Knights were sent with the said Order of the Garter as ambassadors from the king of England to the king of Sweden; who likewise gave to each of them as a perpetual badge of honour the arms of the kingdom of Sweden to be joined with their own arms for ever.

    PETER YONG, gentleman usher and daily waiter to the King of England, a Scotchman.
    HENRY ST. GEORGE, Richmond herald, of Cambridge.
    PATRICK (PALMER) RUTHIN, colonel, a Scotchman.
    ALEXANDER LESLEY, colonel, a Scotchman.
    THOMAS MUSCHAMP, colonel, of Co. Northampton.
    JOHN HEYBRON (HEBRON), lieutenant colonel, a Scotchman.

1627, Oct. 8.   HENRY MORISON, of Tuly Park, Co. Leicester. (at Whitehall).
1627, Oct. 13.   WILLIAM BLAKE, of Kensington, Middlesex *(ibid)*.
1627, Oct. 13.   GARRET RAINSFORD *(ibid)*.
1627, Oct. 31.   WILLIAM DENNEY, of Norwich, one of the King's Counsel-at-law *(ibid)*.
1627, Dec. 5.   JOHN TUFTON, son to lord Tufton *(ibid)*.
1627, Dec. 7.   ANTHONY ST. LEGER (in Ireland by viscount Falkland).
1627, Dec. 9.   THOMAS GOUGH, of Waterford (*ibid* by same).
1627, Dec. 23.   GEORGE VERNON, of Hassington, a baron of the Exchequer (at Whitehall).
1627-8, Jan. 20.   FRANCIS RATCLIFF, of Newcastle, Northumberland *(ibid)*.
1627-8, Jan. 26.   JAMES CUTSEUS, syndic of Dordrecht.
1627-8, Jan. 27.   JOHN TERRIL (TIRRELL), of Essex (at Whitehall).
1627-8, Feb. 1.   PHILIP OLDFIELD, of Somerford, Cheshire *(ibid)*.
1627-8, Feb. 5.   MARMADUKE LANGDALE, of Peghall, Co. Yorks. *(ibid)*.
1627-8, Feb. 13.   ROBERT FORTH (in Ireland by viscount Falkland).
1627-8, Feb. 15.   WHITE BECONSHAW, of Moyl's Court, Hants. (at Whitehall).

1627-8, Feb. 17. CHRISTOPHER GARVEY (in Ireland by viscount Falkland).

1627-8, Feb. 18. BASIL DIXWELL, of Folkestone, Kent (at Whitehall).

1627-8, Feb. 20. WILLIAM MAYNARD (in Ireland by viscount Falkland).

1627-8, Mar. 11. HENRY ACHESON (*ibid* by same).

1628, Mar. 21. WILLIAM PESHALL, of Cannell, Staffs. (at Whitehall).

1628, Mar. 26. EDWARD CARY (in Ireland by viscount Falkland).

1628, Apr. 1. TIMOTHY FEATHERSTON (FEATHERSTONHALGH), of Northumberland (at Whitehall).

1628, Apr. 1. LEWIS BOYLE, viscount Kinalmeakie (dubbed in Ireland).

1628, Apr. 1. ROGER BOYLE, lord Boyle of Broghill (*ibid* by same).

1628, Apr. 14. THOMAS LUCAS, of Colchester (at Whitehall).

1628, Apr. 16. JOHN SACKVIL, of Suddlescomb, Sussex (*ibid*).

1628, Apr. 29. THOMAS LEWIS, of Penmalk, Co. Glamorgan. (*ibid*).

1628, May 12. CHARLES CROFTS, of Bardwell, Suffolk (*ibid*).

1628, May 20. EDWARD RICHARDS (RICHARD), of Southampton (*ibid*).

1628, May 21. ALEXANDER MACDONELL, bart. (dubbed in Ireland).

1628, May 23. JOHN LYSTER, of Lincel (Linell ? Linton), Co. Yorks. (at Whitehall).

1628, May 25. HUGH BETHEL, of Alne, Yorks. (*ibid*).

1628, June 3. ROBERT MORTON, of Easture, Kent (*ibid*).

1628, June 4. THOMAS HOPE, of Scotland (*ibid*).

1628, June 8. HUGH HAMMERSLEY, lord mayor of London (*ibid*).

1628, June 10. THOMAS CARY (dubbed in Ireland).

1628, June 29. THOMAS GERRARD (GARRET), of Ashby de la Zouch (at Whitehall).

1628, June 29. JOHN TRELAWNEY, of Trelawney, Cornwall (*ibid*).

1628, June (?) WALTER LANGDON, of Keverel, Cornwall (*ibid*).

1628, July 11 (? June 12). JOHN FOTHERBY, of Canterbury (*ibid*).

1628, July 11. JOHN ROWTH, of Romiley, Derbyshire (*ibid*).

1628, July 12. WILLIAM HOPKINS, of Coventry (*ibid*).

1628, July 27. WILLIAM VAUGHAN (dubbed in Ireland).

1628, Aug. 5. JOHN MILLS, of Devington, Kent (at Bewley).

1628, Aug. 6. THOMAS STAPLES, bart. (dubbed in Ireland).

1628, Aug. 6. CYPRIAN HORSFALL (*ibid*).

KNIGHTS BACHELORS 195

1628, Aug. 16.   THOMAS ESMOND (ISMOND), captain, of Ireland (at Bewley or Southwick).
1628, Aug. 16.   JOHN CROSBY, captain *(ibid)*.
1628, Aug. 16.   ROBERT GRISE (LE GRIS), captain *(ibid)*.
1628, Aug. 16 (? Aug. 1).   JOHN LANGWORTH, captain *(ibid)*.
1628, Aug. 16.   JOHN HARVEY, captain *(ibid)*.
1628, Sept. 1.   JOHN LEIGH, of Newport, in the Isle of Wight *(ibid)*.
1628, Sept. 8.   THOMAS CULPEPPER, of Sussex (at Farnham).
1628, Sept. 9.   CHRISTOPHER BELLEW (dubbed in Ireland).
1628, Sept. 23 (13).   GEORGE (JOHN) WILMOT, of Charlton, Berks (at Windsor).
1628, Sept. 24.   LODOVICK AB ALTEREN, a Dutchman *(ibid)*.
1628, Sept. 25.   CORNELIUS FAIRMADOW, a gentleman pensioner, of Fulham, Middl *(ibid)*.
1628, Oct. 29.   EDWARD DODSWORTH, of Troutsdale, Yorks. (at Whitehall).
1628, Nov. 2.   WILLIAM SALTER, of Ritchking, Co. Bucks. *(ibid)*.
1628, Nov. 8.   JERVIS NEVIL, of Haddington, of Co. Gloucester. (Lincoln.) *(ibid)*.
1628, Dec. 4.   ROWLAND DE LA HYDE (dubbed in Ireland).
1628, Dec. 6.   WILLIAM CATCHMAY, of Brixweer, Co. Gloucester. (at Whitehall).
1628, Dec. 9 (19).   WILLIAM ASHTON, of Tingery, Co. Beds. (at Theobalds).
1628, Dec. 9.   GEORGE GRIMES (CRIMES), of Peckham, Surrey *(ibid)*.
1628, Dec. 10.   WILLIAM QUADRING, of Iraby, Co. Lincoln. (at Whitehall).
1628, Dec. 10.   CHEYNEY CULPEPPER, of Hollingborn, Kent *(ibid)*.
1628, Dec. 14.   TEGUE MCMAHON, bart. (dubbed in Ireland).
1628, Dec. 23.   JAMES HARRINGTON, of Merton, Co. Oxford. (at Whitehall).
1628–9, Jan. 1.   JOHN BRACKEN (BRACKING), of Eaton, Co. Beds., cupbearer *(ibid)*.
1628–9, Jan. 6.   CORNELIUS VERMUYDEN, of Hadfield, Co. Yorks. *(ibid)*.
1628–9, Jan. 7.   JOHN HEYDON, of Baconsthorp (Barkenslop), Co. Norfolk *(ibid)*.
1628–9, Jan. 9.   RICHARD GRAHAM (GRIMES), of Eske, Cumberland *(ibid)*.
1628–9, Jan. 22.   WILLIAM ROWE, of Higham Hill, Essex *(ibid)*.

1628–9, Jan. 27. RICHARD MANLEY, one of the Board of Greencloth (at Whitehall).
1629, Mar. 25. LEWIS MORGAN, son of Sir Thomas *(ibid)*.
1629, Apr. 20 (26). JERVIS ELWIS (ELWES), of Co. Notts (? Northampton) *(ibid)*.
1629, Apr. 28. WILLIAM DALTON, of York city *(ibid)*.
1629, May 3. ROBERT DE VERE, earl of Oxford (at Greenwich).
1629, May 31. RICHARD DEAN, lord mayor of London *(ibid)*.
1629, May 31. WILLIAM ACTON, sheriff of London *(ibid)*.
1629, June 11. WILLIAM CALLEY, of Burdrop, Wilts. *(ibid)*.
1629, June 11. [CAPTAIN] BALTHEZER (BALTHAZAR), a Dutchman [one of the retinue of the Queen] *(ibid)*.
1629, June 21. CRANMER HARRIS, of Creeksea, Essex *(ibid)*.
1629, June 28. JOHN LEE, of Lawshal, Suffolk *(ibid)*.
1629, June 28. JOHN WILSON (dubbed in Ireland).
1629, July 6. HARDRESSE WALLER, of Kent (at Nonsuch).
1629, July 19. ANTHONY MANSEL, of Bretton Ferry, Co. Gloucester., Glamorgan (at Greenwich).
1629, Aug. 11. POPHAM SOUTHCOT, of Mohun's Awtry, Devon. (at Oatlands).
1629, Aug. 14. HENRY CASON, of Peyton, Suffolk (at Bagshot).
1629, Aug. 18. CHARLES WISEMAN, of Steventon, Berks. (at Barton).
1629, Aug. 19. JOHN YATE (YATES), of Buckland, Berks. *(ibid)*.
1629, Aug. 23. NATHANIEL BRENT, doctor at law, warden of Merton College, Oxford (at Woodstock).
1629, Aug. 27. WILLIAM SPENCER, of Yarnton, Co. Oxford. (at Oxford).
1629, Aug. 28. JOHN (WILLIAM) STONEHOUSE, of Radley, Berks. (at Abingdon).
1629, Sept. 5. WILLIAM ANDERSON (dubbed in Ireland).
1629, Sept. 24. THOMAS WORTELEY (at Hampton Court).
1629, Oct. 3. VALENTINE BLAKE (dubbed in Ireland).
1629, Oct. 4. THOMAS WARNER, captain of the ship "St. Christopher" (at Hampton Court).
1629, Oct. 16. CHRISTOPHER ABDY, of Belgat, Kent *(ibid)*.
1629, Oct. (?). JOHN PESHALL *(ibid)*.
1629, Oct. 18. JOHN BOWEN (dubbed in Ireland).
1629, Oct. 23. WILLIAM GILBERT *(ibid)*.
1629, Oct. 26. ROSSE CARY *(ibid)*.
1629, Oct. 29. JOHN VEEL *(ibid)*.

KNIGHTS BACHELORS

1629, Nov. 15. EDWARD POVEY (in Ireland by viscount Loftus and the earl of Cork, lords justices of Ireland).
1629, Dec. 9. LEONARD FERBY (FEERBY), of Pauls Cray, Kent (by the King at Whitehall).
1629, Dec. 9. EDMOND MOULFORD (MONDEFORD, MOUNTFORD), of Feltwal, Norfolk *(ibid)*.
1629, Dec. 9. THOMAS GAWDY, of Gawdy Hall, Norfolk *(ibid)*.
1629–30, Jan. 17. PERCY SMITH (in Ireland by viscount Loftus and the earl of Cork, lords justices of Ireland).
1629–30, Feb. 6. FERDINANDO CAREY (at Whitehall by the King).
1629–30, Feb. 7 (21, 27). RALPH BLACKSTONE, of Blackstone, Yorks. *(ibid)*.
1629–30, Feb. 11. THOMAS THORNBOROUGH, of Elmley, Worcester. *(ibid)*.
1629–30, Feb. 12. NICHOLAS BIRON, of Norfolk *(ibid)*.
1629–30, Feb. 15. EDMUND SCOT, of Lambeth, Surrey *(ibid)*.
1629–30, Feb. 21. PETER PAUL RUBENS, ambassador from the Archduchess.
1629–30, Feb. 28. DUDLEY LOFTUS (in Ireland by viscount Loftus and the earl of Cork, lords justices of Ireland).
1629–30, Feb. 28. JAMES WARE *(ibid* by same).
1629–30, Mar. 1. DUDLEY CARLETON, of Holcombe, Co. Oxford. (at Newmarket by the King).
1629–30, Mar. 12. JOHN BROWNE (in Ireland by viscount Loftus and the earl of Cork, lords justices of Ireland).
1629–30, Mar. 21. GEORGE HERBERT, of Dorrow, Ireland (at Whitehall by the King).
1630, Apr. 17. LAURENCE DE LA CHAMBRE, of Rodmell, Sussex (at Somerset House).
1630, Apr. 25. GEORGE WENTWORTH, of Whalley, Yorks. (at Whitehall).
1630, May 1. JOHN MORLEY, of Chichester *(ibid)*.
1630, May 3. OLIVER NICHOLAS, of Manningford Bruce, Wilts. (at Somerset House).
1630, May 23. JAMES CAMBELL, lord mayor of London (at Whitehall).
1630, May 25. PHILIP STAPLETON, of Walter, Co. Yorks. *(ibid)*.
1630, June 1. WILLIAM FAIRFAX, of Co. Yorks. *(ibid)*.
1630, June 4. ROBERT NEEDHAM (at St. James's).
1630, June 6. PHILIP LANGDON (LANGTON), of Handleby (Haldenby), Co. Lincoln. (at Whitehall).
1630, June 7. EDWARD MASTERS, of East Handon (Langdon), Kent *(ibid* or St. James's).

1630, June 13. CHARLES POINTZ (dubbed in Ireland).
1630, June 24. THOMAS GOWER, of Sittenham, Yorks. (at Whitehall).
1630, June 24. WILLIAM STRICKLAND, of Hildingley, Co. Yorks. *(ibid)*.
1630, June 27. JERVIS SCROOP, of Cockrington, Co. Lincoln. *(ibid)*.
1630, June 28. EDWARD LLOYD, of Berthloyd, Montgomery. *(ibid or St. James's)*.
1630, June ? (July) (29). WALTER PYE, of the Minde, Co. Hereford. (at Whitehall).
1630, June (29). JAMES STUART, duke of Lennox *(ibid or St. James's)*.
1630, July 4. STEPHEN SCOT, of Hayes, Kent (at Whitehall).
1630, July (4 ?). JOHN HARPER, of Swarson (Swarkston), Derbyshire *(ibid)*.
1630, July 7. JAMES MONTGOMERY, a Scotchman *(ibid)*.
1630, July 9. RICHARD PIGOT, of Dothersol, Bucks. (at Theobalds).
1630, July 15. CHRISTOPHER FORSTER, mayor of Dublin (in Ireland by viscount Loftus and the earl of Cork, lords justices of Ireland).
1630, July 15. JAMES MOORE *(ibid by same)*.
1630, July 15. THOMAS MEREDYTH *(ibid by same)*.
1630, July 15. WALSINGHAM COKE *(ibid by same)*.
1630, July 19. THOMAS BOWES, of Much Bromley Hall, Essex (at Nonsuch by the King).
1630, Aug. ROBERT EATON (in Ireland by viscount Loftus and the earl of Cork, lords justices of Ireland).
1630, Sept. 4 (14). JOHN THOROWGOOD, of London (at Moor Park by the King).
1630, Sept. (? Dec.) 19. JOHN SUCKLING, of Whitton in Twickenham, Co. Middl. (at Theobalds).
1630, Sept. 27. HENRY DAWTREY, of Moor in Petworth, Sussex (at Hampton Court).
1630, Sept. (? Dec. 27). HENRY ATKINS, son and heir of Henry Atkins, doctor of physic and one of His Majesty's physicians-in-ordinary, of London (at Whitehall).
1630, Oct. 16 (6). THOMAS CARLTON (CHARLTON), of Charlton, Cumberland (at Hampton Court).
1630, Dec. 2. FREDERICK CORNWALLIS, of Bromhall, Suffolk (at Whitehall).
1630, Dec. 2 (7, 27). WALTER ALEXANDER, of St. James's *(ibid)*.
1630, Dec. 14. ROGER LANGFORD (in Ireland by viscount Loftus and the earl of Cork, lords justices of Ireland).
1630, Dec. 25. EDMUND PLOWDEN *(ibid by same)*.

KNIGHTS BACHELORS

1630–1, Jan. 11 (13). THOMAS SWAN, of Southfleet, Kent (at Theobalds by the King).

1630–1, Feb. 13. VINCENT GOOKIN (in Ireland by viscount Loftus and the earl of Cork, lords justices of Ireland).

1630–1, Feb. 15. ARTHUR ROBINSON, of Deighton, Yorks. (at Whitehall by the King).

1631, Apr. 25. MARTIN BARNHAM (BRANHAM, BARHAM), of Hollingborn (at Whitehall).

1631, May 21. JAMES WESTON, a baron of the Exchequer, of Castle Camp, Co. Cambridge (at Greenwich).

1631, June 5. ROBERT DUCY, bart., lord mayor of London *(ibid)*.

1631, June 7. JOHN BANKS, attorney general to the Prince, of Gray's Inn (at St. James's).

1631, June 12. ROBERT YELVERTON, servant to the queen of Bohemia *(ibid)*.

1631, Oct. 13. WILLIAM POLEY (POOLEY), of Bickstead, Suffolk (at Hampton Court).

1631, Oct. 30. JOHN CASWELL, a captain with the king of Sweden (at St. James's).

1631, Nov. 5. SAMUEL MAYART (in Ireland by viscount Loftus and the earl of Cork, lords justices of Ireland).

1631, Nov. 9. GERRARD LOWTHER *(ibid by same)*.

1631, Nov. 21. EDWARD POWEL, bart., master of requests (at St. James's by the King).

1631, Nov. 27 (21). THOMAS WINDHAM of Kentsford (Rensford), Somerset. *(ibid)*.

1631, Nov. 27. JOHN PHILPOT, in Ireland by viscount Loftus and the earl of Cork, lords justices of Ireland.

1631, Dec. 4. LANCELOT LOWTHER (in Ireland by viscount Loftus and the earl of Cork, lords justices of Ireland).

1631, Dec. 11. JOHN (THOMAS) SHERLOCK *(ibid by same)*.

1631–2, Feb. 2. WILLIAM PIERS *(ibid)*.

1631–2, Feb. 6. SORANZO, the Venetian Ambassador (by the King at St. James's).

1631–2, Mar. 19 (18). WILLIAM WITHERINGTON, of Widdrington, Northumberland (at Newmarket).

1631–2, Mar. 22. GEORGE DEVEREUX, of Sheldon, Warwick. (at Theobalds).

1632, Apr. 30. FRANCIS ASTLEY, of Hill Morton, Warwick. (at Whitehall).

1632, May 6. JOHN SOMERSET, of Pontley Court, Co. Gloucester. *(ibid)*.

1632, May 23. RICHARD PRIME (PRINCE), of Shrewsbury (Salop) (at Greenwich).

1632, May 27. GEORGE (? WILLIAM) WHITMORE, lord mayor of London *(ibid)*.

1632, June 3. GEORGE FLEETWOOD, a colonel to the king of Sweden *(ibid)*.

1632, June 6. GEORGE CARNEGIE, a Scotchman *(ibid)*.

1632, June 18. FRANCIS WINDEBANK, of Middlesex, secretary of state *(ibid)*.

1632, June 22. FRANCIS RAINSFORD, a captain (at Theobalds).

1632, July 2. JAMES CARMICHAEL, a Scotchman (at Oatlands).

1632, July 3. GEORGE CAREY, of Bradford, Devon., son of Sir Edward (at Greenwich).

1632, July 5. ANTHONY VANDYKE (at St. James's).

1632, July 29. JOHN HALL (at Oatlands).

1632, Aug. 4. ROBERT PAIN, of Barton Stacy, Hants., sheriff of Hampshire (at Bagshot Hill).

1632, Aug. 24. NICHOLAS SLANNING, of Devon. (at Nonsuch).

1632, Sept. 11. JOHN MELTON, of Co. Yorks. (at Wanstead).

1632, Sept. 30. HENRY ATKINS, D.Ph., of London (at Whitehall).

1632, Nov. 4. FRANCIS CRAWLEY, of Luton, Beds. *(ibid)*.

1632, Nov. 22. THOMAS HONIWOOD, of Mark Hall, Essex (at Hampton Court).

1632, Dec. 8. EDWARD ALFORD, of Offington, Sussex (at Whitehall).

1632-3, Feb. 24 (13, 18). WILLIAM BROCKMAN, of Bilchborow (Richborow) *(ibid)*.

1632-3, Mar. 4 (? Feb. 24). ARNOLD WAI EING, of Sivington, Bucks. *(ibid)*.

1632-3, Mar. (? 4). JOHN COLT (COULT), of Rickmansworth, Herts. *(ibid)*.

1633, Apr. 21. HENRY KNOWLIS (KNOLLES), of Grove Place, clerk comptroller of the King's House *(ibid)*.

1633, Apr. 21. JOHN RAMSEY *(ibid)*.

1633, May 2. ALEXANDER HALL, of Allemer Hall, Northumberland *(ibid)*.

1633, May 5. NICHOLAS RAINTON, lord mayor of London *(ibid)*.

1633, May 8. JOHN WOLSTENHOLM, of London *(ibid)*.

1633, May (? 8). ABRAHAM DAWES, of Putney *(ibid)*.

1633, May (? 8). JOHN JACOB, of Stansted, Essex (London) *(ibid)*.

1633, May 22. GEORGE DOUGLAS, a Scotchman (at Worksop).

KNIGHTS BACHELORS

1633, May 26. WILLIAM ALLENSON, lord mayor of York (at York).
1633, May 26. WILLIAM BELT, of Overton, recorder of York *(ibid)*.
1633, May 27. PAUL NEILE, of Hutton Bonvile, York, son of the archbishop of York (at Bishopsthorpe).
1633, June 4. LIONEL MADDISON (MATTESON), mayor of Newcastle, of Northumberland (at Newcastle).
1633, June 17. WILLIAM ROBINSON (RIDDELL), of Newcastle (of Newby, Topcliff, Yorks.) (at Edinburgh).
1633, July 4.* EDMUND BOWYER, of Camberwell (at Dunfermline).
1633, July 16. PELHAM CARY, son of the earl of Dover (at Innerwick).
1633, July 16. JOHN COKE, son to Sir John Coke, deceased, principal secretary of State *(ibid)*.
1633, July 16. PATRICK ABERCROMY, one of the band of gentlemen pensioners (knighted by the King in Master James Maxwell's house at Innerwick).
1633, July 16. THOMAS HOPTON, a gentleman pensioner *ut supra (ibid)*.
1633, July 16. THOMAS ASTON, a gentleman pensioner (knighted in Master James Maxwell's house at Innerwick).
1633, July 16. WILLIAM EYRE, a same *(ibid)*.
1633, July 16. JAMES ACHMUTY, a same *(ibid)*.
1633, July 16. FRANCIS SIDENHAM, a same *(ibid)*.
1633, July 16. ROBERT WOOD, a same *(ibid)*.
1633, July 16. MATTHEW HOWLAND, a same *(ibid)*.
1633, July 16. GEORGE THEOBALDS, a same *(ibid)*.
1633, July 16. JOHN SALTINGSTON, a same *(ibid)*.
1633, July 16. GEORGE WINDHAM, a same *(ibid)*.
1633, July 16. DAVID KIRK, a same *(ibid)*.
1633, July 16. THOMAS TRESS, a same *(ibid)*.
1633, July 16. JOHN THOROWGOOD, a same *(ibid)*.
1633, July 16. NICHOLAS SERVIN (SELWIN), a same *(ibid)*.
1633, July 16. JOHN TEMPLE, a same *(ibid)*.
1633, July 16. ROGER HIGS, a same *(ibid)*.
1633, July 17. THOMAS DAKERS, of Cumberland (at Berwick).
1633, July 17. WILLIAM RIDDAL, of Northumberland (at Newcastle).
1633, July 25. WILLIAM BOSWELL, resident for the King of Great Britain with the States of the United Provinces; was made knight by the lord Vere of Tilbury and other commissioners named in His Majesty's letters patent of 1633, June 8 (in the army of the said States at Buckstal, near Balduck, in Brabant, the same day that the Prince Elector Palatine received the Order of the Garter).

*˸For the Scotch knights bachelors made by Charles in Scotland between June 13 and July 16, 1633, see Introduction, vol. i. pp. lxii.—lxiii.

KNIGHTS BACHELORS

1633, July 25. GEORGE WENTWORTH, fifth brother to the lord deputy (at Dublin Castle by viscount Wentworth, lord deputy of Ireland).

1633, July 25. THOMAS DANBY, of Leighton, Co. York. (*ibid* by same).

1633, July 25. THOMAS REMINGTON, of Lund, Co. York. (*ibid* by same).

1633, Aug. 4. RICHARD PLOMLEY, captain of the King's ship called the "Antelope" (*ibid* by same).

1633, Aug. 5. RICHARD HOBART, of London, groom porter (at Greenwich by the King).

1633, Aug. 5. SELWIN PARKER, of Eastford, Sussex, a gentleman pensioner *(ibid)*.

1633, Aug. 27. THOMAS COGHIL, of Bletchington, Co. Oxford, sheriff of Oxfordshire (at Woodstock).

1633, Aug. 27. FRANCIS NORRIS, of Weston, Co. Oxford. (at Abingdon).

1633, Nov. 1. GEORGE RADCLIFFE, eldest son of Nicholas Radcliffe, of Overthorpe, Co. York. (at Dublin Castle by lord Wentworth, lord deputy of Ireland).

1633–4, Feb. 4. THOMAS DAYREL (DARRELL), of Lillingstone Dayrell, Bucks. (at Whitehall by the King).

1634, Mar. 27. LORENZO CARY (at Dublin Castle by lord Wentworth, lord deputy of Ireland).

1634, Apr. 2. WILLIAM BOSWELL, see *supra* p. 201.

1634, Apr. 14 (24). JOHN (THOMAS) PENNINGTON, vice admiral (aboard the "Unicorn," by the King).

1634, Apr. 23. WILLIAM LE NEVE, of Aslacton, Norfolk, norroy king of arms (at Whitehall).

1634, Apr. 27. ARTHUR LOFTUS (at Dublin Castle by lord Wentworth, lord deputy of Ireland).

1634, June 1. THOMAS MOULSON, lord mayor of London (at Greenwich by the King).

1634, July 13. PHILIP MAINWARING (at Dubliin Castle by lord Wentworth, lord deputy of Ireland).

1634, July 17. ANTHONY CAGE, of Stow, Co. Cambridge., sheriff of Cambridge and Huntingdon (at Wentridge, Herts., by the King).

1634, July 25. EDWARD HARTOP, of Buckminster, Co. Leicester. (at Belvoir).

1634, Sept. 22. ROBERT DIXON, mayor of Dublin (at the mayor's house at Dublin, by lord Wentworth, lord deputy of Ireland).

1634, Nov. 5. ROBERT FARRER (*ibid* by same).

1634, Nov. 24. JOHN BRAMSTON, of Margraling, Essex, chief justice of the King's Bench (by the King at Whitehall).

1635, Apr. 18 (Mar. 8).
These four gentlemen who came over with the Swedish Ambassador.
JACOB SKITTEE, younger son of said ambassador.
JOHN KRUS, a Swede.
GUSTAVUS BANIR (BANIZ), a Swede.
GABRIEL OXENSTERN, a Swede.

1635, Apr. 18. NATHANIEL CATLYNE, speaker of the House of Commons (in Ireland by lord Wentworth, lord deputy of Ireland).

1635, May 10. JOHN SKITTIE (SKYTTE), junior, baron of Dudeor, a gentleman of His Majesty's Privy Chamber and colonel of a regiment of Scots in Sweden (at Greenwich).

1635, May 24. ROBERT PARKHURST, lord mayor of London *(ibid)*.

1635, June 6. EDWARD LITTLETON, of Henley, Salop, solicitor general (at Whitehall).

1635, June 28. WILLIAM WENTWORTH, eldest son to the lord deputy (in Ireland by lord Wentworth, lord deputy of Ireland).

1635, June 28. EDWARD RHODES, brother to the lady Wentworth (*ibid* by the same).

1635, June 30. RICHARD SCOTT (*ibid* by same).

1635, Aug. 11. DOMINICK BROWNE, mayor of Galway (at Galway by same).

1635, Sept. 6. ROBERT MEREDITH, chancellor of the Exchequer (at Dublin by same).

1635, Sept. 13. RICHARD DYETT, of Lichfield, in England (*ibid* by same).

1635, Sept. 23. JOHN, lord POULETT of Hinton St. George (by the earl of Lindsay, on board his Majesty's royal ship the "Marie Honor").

1635, Sept. 23. JOHN POULETT, son to the said lord Poulett (*ibid* by same).

1635, Sept. 23. JAMES DOUGLAS, son to the earl of Morton (*ibid* by same).

1635, Sept. 23. JOHN DIGBY, brother to Sir Kenelm (*ibid* by same).

1635, Sept. 23. CHARLES HOWARD, son and heir to Sir Francis Howard, of Bookham, Surrey (*ibid* by same).

1635, Sept. 23. ELIAS (ELLIS) HICKS, one of the gentlemen pensioners to his Majesty, on board the "Marie Honor" by the earl of Lindsay.

1635, Oct. 4. RALPH WHITFIELD, of Tenterden, Kent, his Majesty's serjeant at law (at Hampton Court).

1635, Oct. 11 (12). THOMAS CORBET, of Sprouston, Norfolk (at Royston).

1635, Dec. 7. RICHARD WESTON, a baron of the Exchequer, of Co. Stafford (at Whitehall).

1635-6, Jan. 13. JOHN SHERLOCK (at Dublin by lord Wentworth, lord deputy of Ireland).

1635-6, Jan. 14 (8) (? 1635, June 14). JOHN DALTON, of West Wratting, Cambridge. (by the King at St. James's).

1635-6, Jan. 16. JOHN GYFFORD (at Dublin by lord Wentworth, lord deputy of Ireland).

1635-6, Feb. 2. EDWARD BOLTON, the King's solicitor (*ibid* by same).

1635-6, Mar. 1. RICHARD VIVIAN, of Trelotoren (Trelawaren), Cornwall (by the King at Whitehall).

1635-6, Mar. 6. LEONARD BLENERHASSETT (at Dublin by lord Wentworth, lord deputy of Ireland).

1635-6, Mar. 8. HENRY CALTHORP, attorney of the Court of Wards, of Cockthorpe, Norfolk (by the King at St. James's).

1636, Mar. 28. WILLIAM SHELLEY, of Michelgrove, Sussex *(ibid)*.

1636, Apr. 3. JOHN GIBSON, eldest son of Sir John Gibson, of Co. York. (at Dublin by lord Wentworth, lord deputy of Ireland).

1636, May 26. WILLIAM USHER (*ibid* by same).

1636, May 29. CHARLES HERBERT (HARBORD), of Moor, Herts. (by the King at Hampton Court).

1636, June 2. PAUL DAVIS, clerk of the Council (at Dublin by lord Wentworth, lord deputy of Ireland).

1636, June 2. PHILIP PERCIVAL, clerk of the Lords' House of Parliament and clerk of the Court of Wards and Liveries (*ibid* by same).

1636, Aug. 30. SIMON BASKERVILE, of Fleet Street, London, doctor of physic (at Oxford by the King).

1636, Oct. 11. MATTHEW LYSTER, of London, physician in ordinary to his Majesty (at Oatlands).

1636, Oct. 16. THOMAS INGRAM, of Co. Yorks. (at Newmarket).

1636, Nov. 27. JOHN SOUTH, of Kilstirne, Co. Lincoln. (at Dublin by lord Wentworth, lord deputy of Ireland).

1636, Nov. 27. HENRY FRANKLAND, eldest son of William Frankland, of Thirkleby, Co. York. (*ibid* by same).

KNIGHTS BACHELORS

1636–7, Jan. 15. CHRISTOPHER CLITHEROE (CLETHERO), lord mayor of London (by the King at Hampton Court).

1636–7, Feb. 3. WILLIAM ELVERTON (ELVESTON), a Scotchman (at Whitehall).

1636–7, Feb. 7. WILLIAM HOWARD, of Bravor, Co. Yorks. *(ibid).*

1637, Apr. 9. RICHARD OSBALDESTON, the King's attorney (at Dublin by lord Wentworth, lord deputy of Ireland).

1637, June 4. EDWARD BROMFIELD, lord mayor of London (by the king at Whitehall).

1637, July 23. WILLIAM WENTWORTH, 2nd brother to the lord deputy (at Dublin by lord Wentworth, lord deputy of Ireland).

1637, Aug. 7. CHARLES MORDANT, of Massingham, Norfolk (by the King at Oatlands).

1637, Aug. 28. DOMINICK WHITE, mayor of Limerick (at Limerick by lord Wentworth, lord deputy of Ireland).

1637, Dec. 4. JOB HARVEY (HARBEY), of London (Aldenham, Herts.) one of the farmers of the Customs (by the King at Whitehall).

1637–8, Feb. 2 (20). ARTHUR HOPTON, of Witham, Somerset *(ibid).*

1637–8, Feb. 12. ROWLAND WANDSFORD, of Haddegly, Co. Yorks., an attorney of the Court of Wards and Liveries *(ibid).*

1637–8, Mar. 24. THOMAS MILWARD (MILDWARD), of Eaton Dovedale, Derbyshire *(ibid).*

1638, Apr. 22. MAURICE WILLIAMS (at Dublin by lord Wentworth, lord deputy of Ireland).

1638, Apr. 29. ROBERT PARKHURST *(ibid by same).*

1638, May 8. JOHN BARRINGTON, of Barrington, Essex (by the King at Whitehall).

1638, May 8. JOHN LUCAS, near Colchester *(ibid).*

1638, May 20. CHARLES, prince of Wales.

1638, May 20. ROBERT (DEVEREUX), 20th earl of Essex (at Windsor on the occasion of the prince of Wales's installation as Knight of the Garter).*

1638, May 20. ULICK (BOURKE), 2nd earl of St. Albans *(ibid* on same occasion).

1638, May 20. THOMAS (BRUCE), 1st earl of Elgin *(ibid* on same occasion).

1638, May 20. WILLIAM (VILLIERS), 2nd viscount Grandison *(ibid* on same occasion).

---

* For an account of the knighthood of the Prince and his 4 companions see the documents in Appendix lxxxii. and lxxxiii. of Anstis's Essay upon the Knighthood of the Bath. These documents prove so conclusively that the knighthood conferred on this occasion was knighthood by the Bath, and not a mere Bachelor knighthood that I have entered the five names, *supra* p. 163 vol. i. in the lists of the Bath.

1638, May 27. RICHARD FEN, lord mayor of London (at Whitehall).
1638, June 23. THOMAS BEDDINGFIELD, of Holborn, Midds. (at Greenwich).
1638, June 27. ANGELO CORRARIO, Venetian ambassador.
1638, Oct. 2. BALTHAZAR GERBIER (at Hampton Court).
1638–9, Jan. 8. EDMUND WILLIAMS, of London (at Whitehall).
1638–9, Mar. 17. RANDALL MACDONELL, earl of Antrim (at Dublin by lord Wentworth, lord deputy of Ireland).
1638–9, March 17. PHELIM O'NEALE *(ibid* by same).
1638–9. MAURICE EUSTACE, serjeant-at-law (dubbed in Ireland).
1639, Mar. 26. ARTHUR JERMY (JENNY), of Knowdshall, Suffolk (at Whitehall by the King).
1639, Mar. 26. RICHARD ALLEN *(ibid)*.
1639, Mar. 26. GILLAM MERRICK *(ibid)*.
1639, Apr. 1. ROGER JACQUES, lord mayor of York (at York).
1639, Apr. 1. THOMAS WIDDRINGTON, recorder of York *(ibid)*.
1639, Apr. 1 (30). ALEXANDER DAVISON, of Blackstone, Co. Durham *(ibid)*.
1639, Apr. 1. THOMAS RIDDAL, of Tunstal, Durham *(ibid)*.
1639, June 23. JOHN HELE (HEAL), of Wembworthy, Devon. (at Berwick).
1639, June 23. JAMES THIN (THYNNE), of Wilts. *(ibid)*.
1639, June 23. BEVIL GRENVILE, of Stow, Cornwall *(ibid)*.
1639, June 23 (26). EDWARD SAVAGE, of Westminster *(ibid)*.
1639, June 23 (26) WILLIAM DARCY, of Witton Castle, Co. Durham (at Berwick).
1639, June 26. WILLIAM BELLASIS, of Co. Durham *(ibid)*.
1639, July 6. CHARLES GAWDY, of Cross Hall, Suffolk (at Newcastle).
1639, July 7. ANDREW BARRETT (at Dublin by lord Wentworth, lord deputy of Ireland).
1639, July 26. WILLIAM SELBY, of Twisle, Co. Northumberland (at Berwick by the King).
1639, July 27 (26). VIVIAN MOLINEUX (MULLENEUX), lieutenant colonel *(ibid)*.
1639, July 27 (26). JOHN PAWLET *(ibid)*.
1639, July 27. HUMPHREY SIDENHAM, a major *(ibid)*.
1639, July 27. PEREGRINE BERTIE, son to Robert, earl of Lindsey *(ibid)*.
1639, July 27. CHARLES HOWARD, of Croglin, Cumberland, son to William, lord Howard *(ibid)*.
1639, July 27. RICHARD BELLARS, sheriff of Durham *(ibid)*.

KNIGHTS BACHELORS   207

1639, July 27 (26). JOHN MORLEY, mayor of Newcastle (at Berwick, by the King).
1639, July 27 (26). WILLIAM GUN, a Scotchman *(ibid)*.
1639, July 27 (26). CHARLES LUCAS, of Essex *(ibid)*.
1639, July 27 (26). MICHAEL EARNLEY, a sergeant major *(ibid)*.
1639, July 27. —— DOUGLAS *(ibid)*.
1639, July 27. JOHN BARKLEY, brother to Sir Charles Barkley, of Bruton *(ibid)*.
1639, July 27. WILLIAM BARKLEY, brother to Sir John *(ibid)*.
1639, Sept. 4. THOMAS KNOT (NOTT), of Obden, Co. Worcester. (at Whitehall).
1639, Sept. 4 (24, 26). JERVIS (JACOB) EYRE, of Rampton, Co. Notts. *(ibid)*.
1639, Sept. 4 (26, 29). WILLIAM CRAVEN, of Combe Abbey, Co. Warwick. (at Whitehall).
1639, Sept. WILLIAM SAMBACH (at Dublin Castle by lord Wentworth, lord deputy of Ireland).
1639, Oct. 12. EDMOND REVE, of Stratton, Norfolk (at Whitehall by the King).
1639, Dec. 31. THOMAS DAWS, of Putney *(ibid)*.
1639–40, Jan. 1. NICHOLAS CRISPE, of London *(ibid)*.
1639–40, Jan. 1. JOHN NULLS (? NEELLS), of the Custom House, London (at Whitehall).
1639–40, ? ? (30). ROBERT FORSTER, of Forsters, in Egham, Surrey *(ibid)*.
1639–40, Feb. 26. JAMES DILLON, eldest son of lord Dillon and grandson of the earl of Roscommon (dubbed in Ireland by lord Dillon and Christopher Wandesforde, lords justices).
1639–40, Mar. 21. HENRY BLUNT (BLOUNT), of Co. Herts. (at Whitehall).
1640, Mar. 31. THOMAS FOTHERLY, of Essex *(ibid)*.
1640, Apr. 2. GEORGE SAYER, of Bewsers Hall, Essex *(ibid)*.
1640, May 12. NATHANIEL FINCH, serjeant-at-law, of Ash, Kent *(ibid)*.
1640, May 31. HENRY GARRAWAY, lord mayor of London *(ibid)*.
1640, June 23. HENRY VANE, junr., son of Sir Henry Vane, secretary of State *(ibid)*.
1640, June 30. THOMAS ASTON (ASHTON), of Weathill, Co. Beds. (Lancs.) *(ibid)*.
1640, Aug. ROBERT BELT, lord mayor of York (at York).
1640, Aug. THOMAS WRIGHTINGTON, of Co. Yorks. *(ibid)*.

1640, Aug. JAMES BARRY, one of the barons of the Exchequer (at Dublin by Christopher Wandesford, deputy to the earl of Strafford, lieutenant general of Ireland).

1640, Oct. 11. THOMAS HARRISON, of Co. York. (at York by the King).

1640, Nov. 22. GEORGE VANE, second son of Sir Henry Vane (at Whitehall).

1640, Dec. 24. HENAGE PROBY *(ibid)*.

1640, Dec. 30. THOMAS TEMPEST, the King's attorney (at Dublin by lord Dillon and Sir William Parsons, lords justices).

1640-1, Jan. 4. JOHN HARRISON, of Herts., farmer of the customs (at Whitehall by the King).

1640-1, Jan. 9. MARTIN LUMLEY, of Essex, knight and baronet *(ibid)*.

1640-1, Jan. 25. JOHN GORE, of Co. Hertford. *(ibid)*.

1640-1, Jan. 28 (18). THOMAS FAIRFAX, of Co. Yorks. *(ibid)*.

1640-1, Jan. 28. EDWARD HERBERT, attorney general (at Whitehall).

1640-1, Feb. 1. ROBERT WILDGOOSE, of Sussex *(ibid)*.

1640-1, Feb. 11. SIMON FANSHAW, of Herts. *(ibid)*.

1640-1, Feb. 11. NICHOLAS COLE, bart., of Durham *(ibid)*.

1640-1, Feb. 15. ARTHUR ASHTON, of Lancashire *(ibid)*.

1640-1, Feb. 16. JOHN WITTERONG, of Herts. *(ibid)*.

1640-1, Feb. 25. THOMAS MEAUTIS, of Gorhambury, Herts. *(ibid)*.

1640-1, Feb. 26. WILFRID LAWSON, bart., of Northumberland *(ibid)*.

1640-1, Mar. 8. RALPH VERNEY, son of Sir Edmund, of Co. Bucks. *(ibid)*.

1640-1, Mar. 21. NICHOLAS MILLER, of Kent *(ibid)*.

1641, Mar. 26. RICHARD HOWEL, of Norfolk *(ibid)*.

1641, Apr. 18. WILLIAM PALMER, of Co. Beds. *(ibid)*.

1641, Apr. 19. WILLIAM POLE (POOL), of Wilts. *(ibid)*.

1641, Apr. 27. EDMUND (? EDWARD) PYE, of Leckhampsted, Bucks. *(ibid)*.

1641, Apr. 30. PETER RICAUT (RICOTT, RICKHARD), of Kent *(ibid)*.

1641, May 13. SAMUEL OLDFIELD (OWFIELD), of Co. Lincoln. *(ibid)*.

1641, May 24. JOHN KEY (KAY), of Woodsom Hall, Co. Yorks. *(ibid)*.

1641, May 29. WILLIAM BUTLER, of Kent (Bedford) *(ibid)*.

1641, May 31. NICHOLAS KEMIS (KEMYS, KEYMICH), of Keven Mably, Co. Glamorgan. *(ibid)*.

KNIGHTS BACHELORS

1641, June 1. ROBERT THOROLD, of Co. Lincoln (At Whitehall).
1641, June 4. SIMON EVERY, of Co. Derby. *(ibid)*.
1641, June 4. JOHN WORLEY (WYRLEY), of Co. Stafford. *(ibid)*.
1641, June 4. GEORGE WINTER *(ibid)*.
1641, June 5. ROGER FIELDING, of Barnacle, Co. Warwick. *(ibid)*.
1641, June 6. PETER TEMPLE, of Bucks. *(ibid)*.
1641, June 18. HERBERT WHITFIELD, son of Sir Ralph *(ibid)*.
1641, June 19. THOMAS DIKE (DYKE), of Sussex *(ibid)*.
1641, June 20. EDMUND WRIGHT, lord mayor of London *(ibid)*.
1641, June 23. GEORGE COURTHOPE, of Sussex *(ibid)*.
1641, June 23. ROBERT DE GREY, of Norfolk *(ibid)*.
1641, June 23. CHRISTOPHER ATHOWE (ATHOE), of Beechamwell, Norfolk *(ibid)*.
1641, June 24. THOMAS CAVE, of Co. Northampton *(ibid)*.
1641, June 25. JOHN EVELYN, of Surrey *(ibid)*.
1641, June 26. JOHN COTTON, serjeant-at-arms *(ibid)*.
1641, June 28. THOMAS WHITMORE, of Apley, Salop *(ibid)*.
1641, June 28. JOHN PALGRAVE, of Barningham Norwood, Norfolk *(ibid)*.
1641, June 29. VINCENT CORBET, of Salop *(ibid)*.
1641, June 29. JOHN MAYNEY (MAIN), of Kent *(ibid)*.
1641, June 29. GEORGE (GERARD) NAPPER, of Dorset. *(ibid)*.
1641, June 30. ROWLAND BARKLEY, of Co. Worcester. *(ibid)*.
1641, July 2. VALENTINE PELL, of Norfolk *(ibid)*.
1641, July 4. WILLIAM BUTLER, of Co. Beds. (Teston, Kent) *(ibid)*.
1641, July 4. ANTHONY AUCHER (AUGHER), of Borns, Kent *(ibid)*.
1641, July 4. RICHARD NAPPER, of Bucks. *(ibid)*.
1641, July 4. THOMAS BERNARDISTON, of Suffolk *(ibid)*.
1641, July 6. THOMAS MALLET, a justice of the King's Bench *(ibid)*.
1641, July 8. THOMAS ABDY, of Essex *(ibid)*.
1641, July 8. SAMUEL SLEIGH (SLY), of Co. Derby. *(ibid)*.
1641, July 9. WILLIAM DOYLY (DOYLE), of Norfolk *(ibid)*.
1641, July 9. THOMAS GUIBON (GIBBON), of Norfolk *(ibid)*.
1641, July 10. THOMAS HEWIT, of Herts. *(ibid)*.
1641, July 11. EDWARD DUKE, of Suffolk *(ibid)*.
1641, July 13. ROGER SMITH, of Co. Leicester. *(ibid)*.
1641, July 14. ROBERT LITTON, of Co. Warwick. *(ibid)*.
1641, July 14. WILLIAM DRAKE, of Bucks. *(ibid)*.

1641, July 18. ROGER BURGOYN, of Co. Beds (At Whitehall).
1641, July 19. JOHN NORWICH (HERWICH), of Co. Northampton. *(ibid)*.
1641, July 21 (23). THOMAS GODFREY, of Kent *(ibid)*.
1641, July 21. PETER GODFREY, of Kent *(ibid)*.
1641, July 22. THOMAS WOOLRIDGE, of Salop *(ibid)*.
1641, July 23. THOMAS EVERSFIELD, of Sussex *(ibid)*.
1641, July 26. HENRY PRATT, bart., of Co. Berks and alderman of London *(ibid)*.
1641, July 27. JOHN HENDEN, of Kent *(ibid)*.
1641, July 27. JOHN GORE, of Herts. *(ibid)*.
1641, July 29. JOHN WILDE, of Salop *(ibid)*.
1641, July 29. THOMAS BRIDGES, of Somerset. *(ibid)*.
1641, July 30. NORTON KNATCHBULL, of Kent *(ibid)*.
1641, July 30. GEORGE STROUD, of Kent *(ibid)*.
1641, July 31. WILLIAM DALSTON, bart., of Cumberland *(ibid)*.
1641, July 31. EDWARD PARTRIDGE, of Kent *(ibid)*.
1641, Aug. 5. JOHN CURSON, of Co. Derby. *(ibid)*.
1641, Aug. 5. ROBERT BARKHAM, of Co. Middl. *(ibid)*.
1641, Aug. 7. ROBERT KEMP, of Essex (bart. of Gissing, Norfolk) *(ibid)*.
1641, Aug. 7. SAMPSON EURE, of Gately, Hereford, a serjeant-at-law *(ibid)*.
1641, Aug. 7. HENRY HAMOND (HEYMAN, HAYMAN), of Kent *(ibid)*.
1641, Aug. 7. JOHN GLANVILE, of Wilts. *(ibid)*.
1641, Aug. 8. THOMAS HAMERSLY, son to Sir Hugh, alderman of London *(ibid)*.
1641, Aug. 9. JOHN ROLT, of Co. Beds. *(ibid)*.
1641, Aug. 9. GEORGE ASCOUGH *(ibid)*.
1641, Aug. 9. FRANCIS WILLIAMSON, serjeant-at-arms *(ibid)*.
1641, Aug. 9. ROBERT FEN, clerk comptroller of the King's House *(ibid)*.
1641, Aug. 9. MICHAEL HUTCHINSON, a pensioner *(ibid)*.
1641, Aug. 9. ISAAC SIDNEY (SIDLEY), of Kent *(ibid)*.
1641, Aug. 9. FRANCIS RHODES, bart., of Co. Derby. *(ibid)*.
1641, Aug. 9. ROBERT CROOK, of Co. Oxford. *(ibid)*.
1641, Aug. 9. JOHN POTTS (PETS), of Norfolk *(ibid)*.
1641, Aug. 9. THOMAS BISHOP, of Co. Lincoln. (Sussex) *(ibid)*.
1641, Aug. 10. HUGH OWEN, of Co. Pembroke. *(ibid)*.
1641, Aug. 10. HUGH WINDHAM, bart., of Dorset *(ibid)*.

KNIGHTS BACHELORS

1641, Oct. 23. JOHN HOYE (at Dublin by Sir John Borlace and Sir William Parsons, lords justices).

1641, Nov. 1. JOHN BORLACE, eldest son and heir of Sir John *(ibid by same)*.

1641, Nov. 1. WILLIAM COURTENAY, eldest son and heir of George Courtenay, of Newcastle, Co. Limerick *(ibid by same)*.

1641, Nov. PATRICK WEMYS, of Dunfert, Co. Kilkenny (at Edinburgh by the King ?).

1641, Nov. 21. ROBERT BARWICK (at York).

1641, Nov. 22 (? 1642, Apr. 21). THOMAS NORTHCLIFFE (NOTCLIFF) (at York by the King).

1641, Nov. 25. RICHARD GURNEY, lord mayor of London (at Kingsland).

1641, Nov. 25. THOMAS GARDNER, recorder of London *(ibid)*.

1641, Nov. 25. JOHN PETTUS, of Norfolk, bart, (at the Guildhall).

1641, Nov. 29 (26, 30). EDWARD NICHOLAS, of Wilts., principal secretary of State (at Whitehall).

1641, Dec. 3. JOHN CORDELL (at Hampton Court).

1641, Dec. 3. THOMAS SOAME, alderman of London *(ibid)*.

1641, Dec. 3. JOHN GAYER (GAIR), alderman of London *(ibid)*.

1641, Dec. 3. JACOB GERRARD, alderman of London *(ibid)*.

1641, Dec. 3. JOHN WOLLASTON, alderman of London *(ibid)*.

1641, Dec. 3. GEORGE GARRET, alderman of London *(ibid)*.

1641, Dec. 3. GEORGE CLARK, sheriff of London *(ibid)*.

1641, Dec. 5. EDWARD ASTLEY, brother of Sir Isaac (Sir Francis) (at Whitehall).

1641, Dec. 8 (5). ANTHONY PERCIVAL, of Kent *(ibid)*.

1641, Dec. 12. THOMAS TREVOR, of Middlesex, bart. *(ibid)*.

1641, Dec. 18. JOHN SPELMAN, of Norfolk *(ibid)*.

1641, Dec. 20. JOHN ROBERTS, of Kent *(ibid)*.

1641, Dec. 21. JOHN TUFTON, of Kent *(ibid)*.

1641, Dec. 23. JOHN MALLORY, of Co. York. *(ibid)*.

1641, Dec. 27. HENRY CHOLMLEY, brother of Sir Hugh *(ibid)*.

1641, Dec. 28. THOMAS LUNSFORD, of Sussex *(ibid)*.

1641-2, Jan. 5. THOMAS MARTIN, of Co. Cambridge. (? Cumberland) *(ibid)*.

1641-2, Jan. 5 (8). RICHARD HALFORD (HOLFORD), of Co. Leicester. *(ibid)*.

1641–2, Jan. 12. JOHN DORREL (DAREL), of Kent, son of Sir Robert (at Windsor).

1641–2, Jan. 21. ISAAC ASTLEY, of Melton Constable, Norfolk, son to Sir Jacob, the famous general (*ibid* or Whitehall). See *infra* on p. 215.

1641–2, Jan. (?) JOHN RAINEY (RAYNEY), of Kent *(ibid)*.

1641–2, Feb. (? Jan.) 10. WILLIAM SPRINGATE, of Kent (at Hampton Court).

1641–2, Feb. 10. JOHN JENNET (JENNY, JERMY), of Suffolk *(ibid)*.

1641–2, Feb. 14. HENRY PALMER, of Kent (on His Majesty's journey towards Dover).

1641–2, Feb. 15. EDWARD PHILMER (FILMER) (on same journey at Canterbury).

1641–2, Feb. (?) HENRY STRADLING, of Co. Glamorgan. (at Dover).

1641–2, Feb. JOHN MENYS (MINNES, MENNES), vice-admiral *(ibid)*.

1641–2, Feb. WILLIAM MAN, of Kent *(ibid)*.

1641–2, Feb. MARTIN VAN TROMP, admiral, of Holland (*ibid* on the 20th of May following he received by letters patent from the king a grant of supporters in addition to the honour of knighthood).

1641–2, Mar. 1. WILLIAM COOPER, of Cathrincork, Kent (at Theobalds ? Dover).

1641–2, Mar. 2. WILLIAM CAWLEY (CALEY) (*ibid* ? Dover).

1641–2, Mar. 12 (16). JOHN READ, of Herts., second son to Sir Thomas (at Newmarket).

1641–2, Mar. 12. ROBERT CROMPTON, of Middlesex *(ibid)*.

1641–2, Mar. 13. JOHN FORTESCUE, of Suffolk *(ibid)*.

1641–2, Mar. 14. RICHARD STONE, of Co. Huntingdon. (at Huntingdon).

1641–2, Mar. 20. EDMUND COOPER, lord mayor of York (at York).

1642, Apr. 18. JAMES, duke of York *(ibid)*.

1642, Apr. 18. ROBERT (DORMER), 1st earl of Carnarvon *(ibid)*.

1642, Apr. 18. GEORGE or CHARLES (STUART), lord AUBIGNY *(ibid)*.

1642, Apr. 18. Lord JOHN STUART *(ibid)*.

1642, Apr. 18. Lord BARNARD STUART *(ibid)*.

1642, Apr. 21. BRIAN PALMES, of Astwell, Co. Rutland. (at ? York).

1642, Apr. 23 (? June or July). PATRICK DRUMMOND (at Durham, ? at Nottingham, or ? 2 different men).

1642, Apr. 23 (21). THOMAS NORCLIFF (NORTCLIFF) (at Durham), of Co. York.

KNIGHTS BACHELORS 213

1642, Apr. 24. JAMES (THOMAS) PENNYMAN, of Ormsby, Co. York. (at York ? Durham).
1642, May 1. FRANCIS BUTLER, of Herts. *(ibid)*.
1642, May 2. THOMAS BOSWELL (BOSVILE), of Kent *(ibid)*.
1642, May 2. JORDAN METHAM, of Co. York. *(ibid)*.
1642, May 21. RICHARD TANKARD, of Wixley, Co. York. (at York ? Durham).
1642, June 6. JOHN GIRLINGTON (GARLINGTON), of Co. York. ? Lancs. *(ibid)*.
1642, June 7. THOMAS WILLIAMSON, of East Markham, Co. Notts. *(ibid)*.
1642, June 25. INGRAM HOPTON, of Leathley, Co. Yorks. *(ibid)*.
1642, June 25. FRANCIS MONKTON, of Cavel, Co. Yorks. *(ibid)*.
1642, June 26. GEORGE MIDDLETCN, of Leighton, Co. Yorks. ? Lancs. *(ibid)*.
1642, June 27. EDMOND DUNCOMBE, of Co. Yorks., sergeant major of the Trained Bands *(ibid)*.
1642, June 28. PETER COURTNEY, cf Cornwall *(ibid)*.
1642, July 12. JOHN DIGBY, of Mansfield Woodhouse,, high sheriff of Notts., Co. Notts. (at Newark).
1642, July 14. CHARLES DALLISON, recorder of Lincoln (at Lincoln ? Newark).
1642, July 14. WILLIAM CONEY (CONNY), of Sturton, Co. Lincoln. *(ibid)*.
1642, July 14. ROBERT TREDWAY, of Hoffe (Haugh), Co. Lincoln *(ibid)*.
1642, July 14. RICHARD WINGFIELD, of Ticken, Co. Lincoln. ? Rutland. *(ibid)*.
1642, July 14 (15). JOHN BURRELL, of Dowsby, Co. Lincoln. *(ibid)*.
1642, July 14. JORDAN CROSLAND, of Co. York. *(ibid)*.
1642, July 26. EUSEBY PELSANT, of Cadeby, Co. Leicester. (at Leicester).
1642, July 28. GEORGE BINNION, of London (at Beverly).
1642, July 28. ANTHONY ST. LEGER (SELLENGER), of Oakham, Kent *(ibid)*.
1642, July 30. FRANCIS COB, of Beverly, Yorks. *(ibid)*.
1642, Aug. 8. WILLIAM CLARK, of Ford Place, Kent (at York).
1642, Aug. 9. EDMOND FORTESCUE, of Fallapit, Devon. *(ibid)*.
1642, Aug. 13 (9). EDWARD GARRET (JARRET), colonel (at York).
1642, Aug. 19. GEORGE THYNNE (THEAM, THEIM), (at Leicester).

1642, Aug. 21. ROBERT LEIGH, of Co. Warwick. (at Stoneleigh Abbey).

1642, Aug. 22. THOMAS LEIGH, of Hamstal Ridware, Co. Stafford. *(ibid)*.

1642, Aug. 24 (22). JOHN MIDDLETON, of Stockel, Co. Yorks. (at Nottingham).

1642, Sept. 7. HENRY JONES, of Albemarle, Co. Carmarthen. *(ibid)*.

1642, Sept. 13. ROBERT STAPLETON, of Co. York. *(ibid)*.

1642, Sept. 19 (21). JOHN WILDE, of Wolly, Salop, sheriff of Salop (at Wellington).

1642, Sept. 21. FRANCIS OTLEY (OTTLEY, OATLEY), of Pitchford, Salop (at Shrewsbury).

1642, Sept. 22. JOHN WILDE, junr., of Wolly, Salop *(ibid)*.

1642, Sept. (? 22). WALTER WROTTESLEY, of Co. Stafford *(ibid)*.

1642, Sept. 25. HUGH CALVELEY, of Ley, Cheshire (at West Chester).

1642, Sept. 26. RICHARD CRANE, a captain (lieutenant colonel) of Prince Rupert's troop (regiment) of Horse *(ibid)*.

1642, Sept. 27 (28). THOMAS BIRON, colonel of prince Charles's regiment of Horse (at Shrewsbury).

1642, Sept. 29. ARNOLD DE LILLE (LISLE), a Frenchman *(ibid)*.

1642, Sept. 29. THOMAS SCRIVEN, of Co. Denbigh (Salop), in the field at the head of his company *((ibid)*.

1642, Oct. 1. RICHARD WYLLIS, brother to Sir Thomas, of Fen Ditton *(ibid)*.

1642, Oct. 1. THOMAS LISTER, of Salop *(ibid)*.

1642, Oct. 1 (Sept. 29). RICHARD BYRON *(ibid)*.

1642, Oct. 7 (3). RICHARD LLOYD, of Denbigh (at Wrexham).

1642, Oct. 9. GARRET (GERARD) EATON, of Co. Derby. (Denbigh) (at Shrewsbury).

1642, Oct. 11. THOMAS EATON (EYTON), of Co. Salop *(ibid)*.

1642, Oct. 21. ANTHONY MORGAN, of Co. Northampton (at Southam).

1642, Oct. 22. RICHARD SHUGBOROUGH, of Shugborough, Co. Warwick. (at Edgecot).

1642, Oct. 24. JOHN SMITH, a captain, at Edgehill fight, brother to Sir Charles; he recovered the King's great banner which the rebels had taken in battle the day before (at Edgehill or Edgcott).

1642, Oct. 25. ROBERT WELCH (WALSH), an Irishman (? *ibid*).

1642, Nov. 2. WILLIAM PALMER (at Oxford).

1642, Nov. 7 (8). WINGFIELD BODENHAM, of Co. Rutland (at Reading).
1642, Nov. 9 (8). EDWARD SIDENHAM, of Essex, knight marshal *(ibid)*.
1642, Nov. 10. HENRY HENE, of Folly John Park, Berks. (at Maidenhead ? Reading).
1642, Nov. 12. JOHN TYRRINGHAM, of Bucks. (at Coalbrook).
1642, Nov. 29. THOMAS MANWARING, recorder, of Reading (at Reading).
1642, Dec. 27. THOMAS BLACKWELL, of Mansfield Woodhouse, Co. Notts. (at Oxford).
1642–3, Jan. 1. HENRY HUNCKS, lieutenant colonel (? *ibid*).
1642–3, Jan. 9. EDWARD CHESTER, of Herts. (? *ibid*).
1642–3, Jan. 10. ROBERT MURRAY, a Scotchman (? *ibid*).
1642–3, Jan. 14. HENRY VAUGHAN, lieutenant colonel. (? *ibid*).
1642–3, Feb. 1. WILLIAM MALLORY, captain (? *ibid*).
1642–3, Feb. 3. WILLIAM NEAL, Scoutmaster, upon bringing to the King the news of the taking of Cicester *(ibid)*.
1642–3, Feb. 6. GEORGE VAUGHAN, of Wilts. *(ibid)*.
1642–3, Feb. 22. EDWARD HYDE, chancellor of the Exchequer *(ibid)*.
1642–3, Feb. 22. HENRY HELYE, privy councillor (? see Hene *supra* 1642, Nov. 10).
1642–3, Feb. 23. ISAAC (JOHN) ASTLEY, son of Sir Jacob *(ibid)*. See *supra* on p. 212.
1642–3, Feb. 24 (? Feb. 5, ? Mar. 5). JOHN PENRUDDOCK, of Wilts. (Southampton) *(ibid)*.
1642–3, Feb. 26. JOHN WINFORD, of Astley, Co. Worcester. *(ibid)*.
1642–3, Mar. 2 (Feb. 24). HENRY HUNLOCK (HUNLOKE), of Wingermouth, Co. Derby. *(ibid)*.
1642–3, Mar. 5 (4). THOMAS BAD (BAUD), of Caims Oysels, Co. Hants. (at Oxford).
1642–3, Mar. 5. JOHN PENRUDDOCK *(ibid)*.
1642–3, Mar. (? Feb.) 22. JOHN SCUDAMORE, of Ballingham (Bullingham), Co. Hereford. *(ibid)*.
1642–3, Mar. (? Feb.) 24. WALTER LLOYD, of Co. Cardigan *(ibid)*.
1642–3, Mar. 24. FRANCIS LLOYD, of Co. Carmarthen (Cardigan) *(ibid)*.
1643, Apr. 12. WILLIAM BLAKESTON (BLACKSTON), of Newton. Durham *(ibid)*.
1643, Apr. 23. LEWIS KIRK, of Bridgenorth, Salop., a gentleman pensioner *(ibid)*.

1643, May 17. EDWARD LAURENCE, of Dorset. sheriff of Dorset. (at Oxford).

1643, June 1. JAMES MURRAY, a Scotchman *(ibid)*.

1643, June 13 (30). CHARLES KEMISH (KEMYS), of Keven Mabley, Co. Glamorgan. *(ibid)*.

1643, June 13. EDWARD STRADLING, of St. Donats, Co. Glamorgan. *(ibid)*.

1643, June 13. JOHN URREY (VERPEY), a Scotchman *(ibid)*.

1643, June 24. HUMBLE WARD, of Co. Stafford. *(ibid)*.

1643, July 15. [? EDMUND] BUTLER, an Irishman *(ibid)*.

1643, Aug. 3. CHARLES MOHUN, of Putmoghan, Co. Cornwall (at Bristol).

1643, Aug. 3 (4). JOHN GRANVILE (GRENFIELD), son to Sir Bevil *(ibid)*.

1643, Aug. 3. SAMUEL COSWORTH (COLAWARTH), of Cosworth, Co. Cornwall *(ibid)*.

1643, Aug. 3. CHRISTOPHER WRAY, of Trebigh, Cornwall *(ibid)*.

1643, Aug. 15. RICHARD (HENRY) CHOMLEY, eminent in the law, of Whitby, Co. York. (in the army by Sudeley).

1643, Sept. 8. WILLIAM MORTON (MERTON), of Winchcombe, Co. Oxford. (at Sudeley Castle).

1643, Sept. 9. WILLIAM HOWARD (HAYWARD), of Surrey *(ibid)*.

1643, Sept. (?) WILLIAM DAVENANT, poet laureate (at Gloucester).

1643, Sept. 22 (21). MICHAEL WOODHOUSE, governor of Ludlow (at Newbury).

1643, Sept. 24. TIMOTHY TIRREL, of Co. Oxford. (Bucks.) (at Oxford).

1643, Sept. 28. GEORGE AP ROBERTS (PROBERT), of Pautlacy (Penalt), Co. Monmouth. *(ibid)*.

1643, Sept. 30. EDWARD ALSTON, of Allvercot, Co. Oxford. (Northampton) *(ibid)*.

1643, Oct. 4. EDWARD FORD, of Harting, Co. Sussex *(ibid)*.

1643, Oct. 7. PETER BALL, of Devon., the Queen's attorney *(ibid)*.

1643, Oct. 26 (20). FRANCIS CHOCK (CHOKE), of Abington, Berks. *(ibid)*.

1643, Nov. 9. ARTHUR BLANY, of Co. Montgomery *(ibid)*.

1643, Nov. 10. —— OTLEY *(ibid)*.

1643, Oct. 11. JOSEPH SEAMORE (LEAMORE), of Devon. *(ibid)*.

1643, Nov. 17 (? 1642, Nov. 17). ORLANDO BRIDGMAN, of Westchester, attorney general *(ibid)*.

1643, Nov. 22. HENRY BARD, colonel *(ibid)*.

1643, Nov. 24. EDWARD VAUGHAN, of Cornwall (Caermarthen) (at Oxford).

1643, Nov. (? Dec. 28). THOMAS PERT, colonel *(ibid)*.

1643, Dec. 6. ROBERT BREREWOOD, recorder of Chester *(ibid)*.

1643, Dec. 9. EDMUND VERNEY, 2nd son to Sir Edmund Verney, Knight Marshal *(ibid)*.

1643, Dec. 12. CHARLES COMPTON, a brother to the earl of Northampton *(ibid)*.

1643, Dec. 12. WILLIAM COMPTON, a same *(ibid)*.

1643, Dec. 12. SPENCER COMPTON, a same *(ibid)*.

1643, Dec. 20 (28). MARMADUKE RAWDON (ROYDON), of Hodsden (Herts.) *(ibid)*.

1643–4, Jan. 4. RICHARD LANE, attorney general to the Prince afterwards chief baron of the Exchequer *(ibid)*.

1643–4, Jan. 9. WILLIAM MANWARING, of West Chester *(ibid)*

1643–4, Jan. 19 (27). ROBERT HOLBORN, attorney to the Prince *(ibid)*.

1643–4, Feb. 5 (Jan.) 5. JOHN REED (READ), a Scotchman *(ibid)*.

before 1643–4, Mar. THOMAS ARMSTRONG (in Ireland by the earl of Ormonde).

1644, Mar. 25. THOMAS GARDNER, captain of a troop of horse, son to the solicitor-general (at Oxford, knighted by the King whilst he sat at dinner upon delivery of the news of prince Rupert's success against the rebels that had besieged Newark).

1644, Apr. 2. HUGH CARTWRIGHT, of Southwell, Notts. (at Oxford).

1644, Apr. 9. WILLIAM COURTNEY *(ibid)*.

1644, Apr. 16. HENRY WOOD, clerk comptroller *(ibid)*.

1644, Apr. 19. THOMAS CHEDLE (CHEDDLE), of Anglesea, governor of Beaumaris *(ibid)*.

1644, Apr. 24. GEORGE VILLIERS, brother to lord Grandison *(ibid)*.

1644, Apr. (? Aug.) 25. FRANCIS GAMULL, of Cheshire *(ibid)*.

before 1644, May. THEOPHILUS JONES (in Ireland by the earl of Ormonde).

1644, May 6. WILLIAM GODOLPHIN, of Spergor, Co. Cornwall (at Oxford).

1644, May 12. ROBERT BYRON, brother to lord Byron *(ibid)*.

1644, May 12. GEORGE PARREY, D.C.L., recorder of Exeter *(ibid)*.

1644, June 18. BARNARD ASTLEY, son of Sir Jacob (at Burford).

1644, June 18. MARTIN SANDES (at Worcester).

1644, June 18. DANIEL TYAS (TYERS), mayor of Worcester *(ibid)*.

1644, June (?) JOHN KNOTSFORD, of Studley, Co. Warwick. (at Evesham).

1644, June 29 (July 2). ROBERT HOWARD, a younger son to the earl of Berks. (at Cropredy Bridge for taking Wemes, the Scot, general of Sir William Waller's artillery).

1644, June 29. THOMAS HOOPER (at Williamscot).

1644, July 27. HUGH CROCKER, mayor of Exeter (at Exeter).

1644, July 30. THOMAS BASSETT, general of the ordnance to prince Maurice (at Crediton).

1644, July 30. RICHARD CHOLMELEY, younger son of Sir Richard Cholmeley, of Whitby (ibid at the taking of Exeter).

? 1644, July 30. JAMES SMITH (? ibid).

1644, July 30. FRANCIS BASSETT, of St. Michael's Mount, brother of Sir Thomas (at Crediton).

1644, July 30 (? 28). JOSEPH WAGSTAFF, major general to the army under prince Maurice in the West (ibid).

1644, July 30. HENRY CAREY (ibid).

1644, Aug. (July 5). CHARLES TREVANIAN, of Cornwall (at Boconnoc).

1644, Aug. (? 3, July 9). JOHN ARUNDEL, of Cornwall (ibid ? at Liskeard).

1644, Aug. JAMES COBB (ibid).

1644, Aug. 3 (July 11). JOHN GRILLS, sheriff of Cornwall (at Liskeard).

1644, Aug. 8 (? 25). FRANCIS GAMULL, of Cheshire (at Boconnoc).

1644, Sept. 1. EDWARD (ROBERT) BRETT, captain of the Queen's troop (in the field at the pursuit of Essex's army).

1644, Sept. 1. SACKVIL GLENHAM (GLEMHAM), son of Sir Thomas (ibid).

1644, Sept. 1. THOMAS PRESTWICH, of Lancashire (ibid or at Oxford).

1644, Sept. 1. WILLIAM RATCLIFF (ibid or at Oxford).

1644, Oct. 22. JOHN BOYS, governor of Donnington Castle (upon Redheath at Read Hall near Newbury).

1644, Oct. (?). JOHN CAMPSFIELD (CANSFIELD) (near Newport Pagnell).

1644, Nov. 1. HENRY GAGE, governor of Oxford (at Oxford).

1644, Nov. 1. CHARLES LLOYD, of Co. Cardigan., governor of Devizes, quarter-master general (ibid).

1644, Nov. 2. PETER BROWN, of Co. Oxford. (ibid).

1644, Nov. 3. ANTHONY GREENE, of Co. Oxford (ibid).

1644, Nov. 3. CHARLES WALDRON, captain (ibid).

KNIGHTS BACHELORS

1644, Nov. 7. WILLIAM CAMPION, of Cooly, Kent, governor of Boistall House (at Oxford).
1644, Dec. 17. JOHN OWEN, colonel, of Cornwall *(ibid)*.
1644, Dec. 17. WILLIAM ROLLOCK, a Scotchman *(ibid)*.
1644, Dec. 18. CHRISTOPHER LEWKENOR, colonel, recorder of Chichester *(ibid)*.
1644, Dec. 18. JAMES CROFT, the pensioner *(ibid)*.
1644 (Dec. or 1644–5, Jan.). LEWIS LEWKENOR, colonel.
1644–5, Jan. 14 (4). GILBERT TALBOT, colonel, the King's agent at Venice *(ibid)*.
1644–5, Jan. 17. ARTHUR (CAPELL), lord CAPEL *(ibid)*.
1644–5, Jan. 17. HENRY lord SEYMOUR *(ibid)*.
1644–5, Jan. 23. HENRY CHICHLEY, of Co. Cambridge., lieut. col. to Sir Richard Willes *(ibid)*.
1644–5, Jan. 27. RICHARD HATTON (HALTON), of Co. Northampton. *(ibid)*.
1644–5, Jan. 30. GEORGE BUCKLEY (BUNCKLE, BUNCKLY), of Greenwich, lieutenant governor of Oxford *(ibid at Christ Church)*.
1644–5, Feb. 1. THOMAS D'ABRIGECOURT *(ibid)*.
1644–5, Feb. 2 (?9). EDWARD WALKER, garter king-at-arms *(ibid)*.
1644–5, Feb. 3 (? Jan. 21). STEPHEN HAWKINS, colonel *(ibid)*.
1644–5, Mar. 20 (19). THOMAS REEVES (RIVES), the King's advocate *(ibid)*.
1644–5, Mar. 21 (6). CHARLES COTTEREL, master of the ceremonies *(ibid)*.
1644–5, Mar. 21. RICHARD BRAHAM (BREAM, BREYM) *(ibid)*.
1645, Mar. 28 (27). RICHARD MALEVERER (MALEVERY), of Co. Yorks. *(ibid)*.
1645, Mar. 28. ROBERT PEAKE, lieutenant colonel *(ibid)*.
1645, Mar. 28. WILLIAM MASON *(ibid)*.
1645, Apr. 3. JOHN (WILLIAM) RATCLIFF *(ibid)*.
1645, Apr. 29. LODOWICK WYER (WIER), a German *(ibid)*.
1645, May 5. BARTHOLOMEW LA ROCHE, a Frenchman, principal fire worker to the King *(ibid)*.
1645, May 14. EDWARD BARRET (BAROGH), of Droitwich, Co. Worcester (at Droitwich).
1645, June 2. RICHARD PAGE, colonel (at the countess of Devon's house near Leicester).
1645, June 2. WILLIAM BRIDGES, sergeant major to Sir Richard Page *(ibid)*.
1645, June 2. MATTHEW APPLEYARD, colonel *(ibid)*.

1645, June 4. EDWARD HOPTON, colonel (at Leicester).
1645, June 4 (25). DUDLEY WYAT, commissary general (at Hereford ? Leicester).
1645, July 6 (31). HENRY LINGEN, colonel, of Co. Hereford. (at Hereford ? Leicester).
1645, July 6. HENRY LUNSFORD, governor of Monmouth (at Monmouth).
1645, July 10. EDMOND PEIRCE, LL.D., and colonel of horse, of Greenwich (at Ragland Castle).
1645, July 31. JOHN WALPOLE, of Co. Lincoln., cornet to the King's troop (at Cardiff Castle).
1645, Sept. 5. WILLIAM LAYTON, colonel, lieutenant colonel to the King's regiment of Guards (at Hereford).
1645, Sept. 5. BARNABY SCUDAMORE, of Hereford, governor *(ibid)*.
1645, Sept. 15. HENRY WROTH, a gentleman pensioner (at Hereford or ? Chirk Castle).
1645, Sept. 23. JOHN WATTS, governor of Chirk Castle (at Chirk Castle).
1645, Oct. 27. THEOPHILUS GILBY, colonel (at Newark ? Chirk Castle).
1645, Dec. 20. EDWARD COOPER, a gentleman pensioner (at Oxford).
1645, Dec. 21. GEORGE LISLE (LYLE), colonel and master of the King's Household *(ibid)*.
1645, Dec. 21. FERDINANDO FISHER *(ibid)*.
1645, Dec. 25 (28). CHARLES LEE (LEIGH), brother to Sir Robert *(ibid)*.
1645–6, Feb. 2. JOHN OGLE, son to Sir John *(ibid)*.
1645–6, Feb. 4. ANTHONY WILLOUGHBY *(ibid)*.
1645–6, Feb. 16. ALLEN BUTLER, colonel, of Bourney, Co. Bucks. *(ibid)*.
1645–6, Feb. 17. JOHN SOUTHCOTE (SURCOT) *(ibid)*.
1645–6, Feb. 25. THOMAS SHIRLEY, lieutenant colonel, of Sussex *(ibid)*.
1645–6, Feb. 25. WILLIAM BYRON, brother to lord Byron *(ibid)*.
1646, Apr. 2. GEORGE AGLIONBY (EGLANDBY), lieutenant colonel of horse *(ibid)*.
1646, Apr. 4. FRANCIS ROUSE, scout master general *(ibid)*.
1646, Apr. 8. JAMES BRIDGEMAN, colonel *(ibid)*.
1646, Apr. 11. EDMUND POOLEY, of Badley, Co. Suffolk *(ibid)*.
1646, Aug. ROBERT ROTHE, mayor of Kilkenney (at Kilkenny by the marquess of Ormonde).
1646, Oct. HENRY TALBOT (by same).

The King went from Oxford the 27th of April, 1646.

Knights made [by Charles I.], but the dates not known.

1646. THOMAS LONGUEVILLE.
      EDWARD BATHURST, of Lechlade.
1646. EDMUND (EDWARD) BRAY.
1646. EDWARD PRIDEAUX.
1646. ALLEN ZOUCH.
1646. ALLEN APSLEY.
1646. EDWARD CLARK, of Berks.
1646. GEORGE PROBAT.
1646. WILLIAM MORGAN.
1646. EDWARD WALGRAVE (? MULGRAVE).
1646. HENRY JONES.
1646, Apr. 11. JOHN NORRIS, of Northamptonshire.
1646. GAMALIEL DUDLEY.
      JOHN WALCOT, of Sherborn, Co. Dorset.
1646. JOHN DUNCOMB, of Battelsden, Co. Beds. (in the Isle of Wight).
      JOHN CHIESLEY, of Scotland *(ibid)*.

Knights made in Ireland by the earl of Ormonde.

1648, before Oct. WALTER BLAKE.
1648, Nov. 12. ROBERT STERLING (at Cork).
1648-9, Jan. GEORGE MONROE (at Kilkenny).
1649, Nov. JOHN WALSH, mayor of Waterford (at Waterford).
1649-50, Jan. NICHOLAS COMYN, mayor of Limerick (at Limerick).
1650, Apr. OLIVER FRENCH (at Galway).
1650, May 6. DERMOT O'SHAUGHNESSY (at Galway).
1650, May 6. JOHN BURKE, of Derrymaclaghny.

*Knights [incorrectly stated to have been] made in 1649, by the Speaker of the House of Commons, by recommendation of the House.**

---

* A draft Act exists among the State Papers Domestic Commonwealth (ii. 3) dated 1649, June 6, to authorise the Speaker to knight Thomas Andrews, the Lord Mayor, and Isaac Pennington and Thomas Atkins, aldermen of London. This was doubtless with a view to the feast in the city on the following day (June 7). But the bill did not pass the House and the ceremony was not performed. (See Commons Journals, vi. 225-6; Whitelock's *Memorials*, iii. 46-7; Somers' *Tracts*, vii. 57.)

Knights made by Charles II. abroad.

1649. JOHN SAYER, lieutenant colonel to colonel Robert Sydney (at Breda).
1649. WILLIAM SWAN, a captain in Holland *(ibid)*.
1650. ROBERT KILLEGREW, son and heir of Sir William *(ibid)*.
1650. ROBERT STARESMORE, younger son of —— Staresmore of Staresmore, Co. Leicester. *(ibid)*.
1650. ANTHONY JACKSON, of the middle Temple *(ibid)*.

Knights made by Charles II. in Scotland in 1650–1.

1650, July 10. THOMAS NICOLSON, His Majesty's Advocate (at Falkland).
1650, Oct. PHILIP ANSTRUTHER, of Anstruther (at Perth).
1650, Nov. GEORGE SETTONE, of Hailles *(ibid)*.
1650–1, Jan. 2. LAWRENCE OLIPHANT, of Gask (at Scone).
1650–1, Jan. 2. JAMES DRUMMOND, of Machany *(ibid)*.
1650–1, Jan. 2. GEORGE HAY, junr., of Megginch *(ibid)*.
1650–1, Jan. 2. JOHN KER, of Lochtower *(ibid)*.
1650–1, Jan. 3. JAMES RICHARDSON, of Synton (at Perth).
1650–1, Jan. 3. ALEXANDER BLAIR, of Balthayock *(ibid)*.
1650–1, Jan. 8. ARCHIBALD DOUGLAS, junior, of Cavers, sheriff of Teviotshire *(ibid)*.
1650–1, Feb. 14. DAVID ACHMUTY (at the earl of Wemys's house).
1650–1, Feb. 14. THOMAS GOURLEY, of Kincraig *(ibid)*.
1650–1, Feb. 14. WALTER SCOTT, of Whitsted, base son to Walter, first earl of Buccleuch and colonel of a regiment of horse (at Largo Sands, the same day when the King ran at the glove).
1650–1, Feb. 14. GILBERT ELLET, of Stobs (? *ibid*).
1650–1, Feb. 14. ALEXANDER SETON, second son to George, earl of Wintoun (? at Largo Sands).
1650–1, Feb. 21. JAMES DURHAM, eldest son to the laird of Pittcarrow (at Dundee).
1650–1, Feb. 22. JAMES HAY, brother's son to the earl of Tweeddale.
1650–1, Feb. PATRICK LESLEY, former provost of Aberdeen (at Aberdeen).
1650-1, Feb. ROBERT FARQUHAR, provost of Aberdeen *(ibid)*.
1650-1, Feb. —— MOWAT, son to Mr. Roger Mowat, of Baquhaley, advocate.
1650–1, Mar. THOMAS MUDIE, provost of Dundee (at Dundee).
1651, Mar. CECIL (WILLIAM) HOWARD, third son of lord Howard of Escrick (at Breda).

KNIGHTS BACHELORS

Knights made by Oliver Cromwell.

HENRY CROMWELL, his son.

1653-4, Feb. 8. THOMAS VINER, lord mayor of London (at Grocers' Hall, London).

1653 or 1654. WILLIAM BOTELER.

1655, June 1. JOHN COPPLESTON, sheriff of Devon. (at Whitehall).

1655, June 11. JOHN REYNOLDS, commissary general in Ireland, son of Sir James, of Essex, drowned 1657 *(ibid)*.

1655, Sept. 20 (23). CHRISTOPHER PACKE, lord mayor of London *(ibid)*.

1655-6, Jan. 17. THOMAS PRIDE, colonel (at Whitehall).

1655-6, Jan. 19. JOHN BARKSTEAD, lieutenant of the Tower and major general, of Middlesex *(ibid)*.

1656, May 3. PETER JULIUS COYET, ambassador from the King of Sweden *(ibid)*.

[1656], July 26 (25). [GUSTAVUS DU VALE], one of the chief gentlemen attending the Swedish ambassador.

1656, July. ANTHONY MORGAN (at Whitehall, on being sent over especially from Ireland to inform the protector of the state of Ireland) ? an erratum see *infra* under date 1658, July 26, also see p. 232 *infra*.

1656, Aug. RICHARD COMBE, of Combe, Co. Herts. (at Whitehall).

1656, Sept. 15. JOHN DETHICK ,lord mayor of London *(ibid)*.

1656, Sept. 15. GEORGE FLEETWOOD, of Co. Bucks. *(ibid)*.

1656, Dec. 10. WILLIAM LOCKHART, colonel, His Highness's resident in France *(ibid)*.

1656, Dec. 10. JAMES CALTHORP, sheriff of Suffolk *(ibid)*.

1656, Dec. 15. ROBERT TITCHBORNE, lord mayor of London *(ibid)*.

1656, Dec. 15. LISLEBONE LONG, recorder of London *(ibid)*.

1656-7, Jan. 6. JAMES WHITELOCK, colonel, son and heir of Sir Bolstrode *(ibid)*.

1656-7, Mar. 3. THOMAS DICKENSON, alderman of York *(ibid)*.

1657, June 11. RICHARD STAINER, commander of the frigate "Speaker."

1657, July 16. JOHN CLAYPOLE, bart. *(ibid)*.

1657, Aug. 26 (20). WILLIAM WHEELER, of Channel Row, Westminster (at Hampton Court).

1657, Nov. 7 (2). EDWARD WARD, sheriff of Norfolk.

1657, Nov. 14. THOMAS ANDREWS, alderman and mayor of London in 1650 (at Whitehall).

1657, Dec. 5. THOMAS FOOTE.
1657, ? ? JOHN HEWSON.
1657–8, Jan. 6. JAMES DRAX.
1657–8, Feb. 1. HENRY PICKERING.
1657–8, Feb. 1. PHILIP TWISTLETON.
1657–8, Mar. 2 (? 22, 9). JOHN IRETON (at Whitehall).
1657–8, Mar. 9. JOHN LENTHALL.
1657–8, Mar. 22. RICHARD CHEVEDON (CHIVERTON), lord mayor of London (at Whitehall).
1658, July 17. HENRY JONES.
? THOMAS WHITGRAVE.
? WILLIAM ELLIS [see 1671, Apr. 10].
? THOMAS ATKINS, alderman and mayor of London in 1653.
? JOHN CARTER, of Wales.
? JOHN STRODE, sheriff of Dorset.

Knights made in Ireland by Henry Cromwell, lord deputy of Ireland.

1657, Nov. 24. MATHEW THOMLINSON (at Dublin in the Council Chamber).
1658, May 3. ROBERT GOODWIN *(ibid)*.
1658, June 7. MAURICE FENTON (in the forenoon at Cork House).
1658, June 7. JOHN KING (in the afternoon in the Council Chamber).
1658, July 21. WILLIAM BERRY (BURY) (at Dublin Castle).
1658, July 22. JOHN PERCIVALL *(ibid)*.
1658, July 26. ANTHONY MORGAN *(ibid)*.
1658, July 26. THOMAS HERBERT *(ibid)*.
1658, Nov. 16. HIEROME SANKY *(ibid)*.
1658, Nov. 16. DANIEL ABBOTT *(ibid)*.
1658, Nov. 30. HENRY PIERS *(ibid)*.
1658, Dec. 20. WILLIAM PEN *(ibid)*.
1658–9, Jan. 24. THOMAS STANLEY *(ibid)*.
1658–9, Feb. 23. OLIVER ST. GEORGE *(ibid)*.

Knights made by Richard Cromwell, Protector.

1658, Nov. 26. JOHN MORGAN.
1658, Dec. 6. RICHARD BEKE.

KNIGHTS BACHELORS

Knights made by Charles II. abroad prior to his Restoration.

1656–7, Mar. HENRY BENNETT, second son of Sir John, of Uxbridge (at Bruges).

1656–7, Mar. 17–27. GEORGE LANE, of Tulsk, clerk of the Council *(ibid)*.

1657, Mar. 31 (Apr. 9). CONNELL O'FARRELL, of Ireland (at Ghent).

1657, June 14–24. ARTHUR SLINGSBY, of Kent (at Brussels).

1657. GODFREY LLOYD, a captain in Holland and engineer *(ibid)*.

1657–8, Jan. JOHN STEPHENS, governor of Dublin Castle (at Bruges).

1659. ANTHONY DEMARIAS, a French gentleman servant to the duke of York (at Antwerp).

1659, Apr. ELLIS LEIGHTON, servant to the duke of York (at Brussels).

Knights made by Charles II.

1660, Apr. RICHARD FANSHAW, master of requests (at Breda).

1660, May 8–18. THOMAS CLARGES, muster master general *(ibid)*.

1660, May 10–20. THOMAS WOODCOCK, of Lewes, governor of Windsor Castle *(ibid)*.

1660, May 10–20 (? 16–26). SAMUEL MORLAND *(ibid)*.

1660, May 16–26. JAMES BUNCE, alderman of London, commissioner from the City to present the address to Charles II. (at the Hague on the reception of the commissioners from the Parliament and the City).

1660, May 16–26. JOHN LANGHAM, alderman of London, a commissioner as above *(ibid)*.

1660, May 16–26. JOHN ROBINSON, alderman of London, a commissioner as above *(ibid)*.

1660, May 16–26. WILLIAM THOMPSON, alderman of London, a commissioner as above *(ibid)*.

1660, May 16–26. THOMAS ADAMS, alderman of London, a commissioner as above *(ibid)*.

1660, May 16–26. WILLIAM WILDE, recorder of London, a commissioner as above *(ibid)*.

1660, May 16–26. ANTHONY BATEMAN, alderman of London, a commissioner as above *(ibid)*.
1660, May 16–26. WILLIAM WALE, alderman of London, a commissioner as above *(ibid)*.
1660, May 16–26. THEOPHILUS BIDDULPH, of London, a commissioner as above *(ibid)*.
1660, May 16–26. RICHARD FORD, of London, a commissioner as above *(ibid)*.
1660, May 16–26. WILLIAM VINCENT, of London, a commissioner as above *(ibid)*.
1660, May 16–26. THOMAS BLUDWORTH (BLOODWORTH or BLUDDER), a commissioner as above *(ibid)*.
1660, May 16–26. WILLIAM BATEMAN, of London and of Charlton, Kent, a commissioner as above *(ibid)*.
1660, May 16–26. JOHN LEWIS, of Ledstone, Yorks., master chamberlain of London, a commissioner as above *(ibid)*.
1660, May 16–26. LAURENCE BROMFIELD, of London, a commissioner as above *(ibid)*.
1660, May (? 16–26). CYRIL WYCH, of Hockwold, Co. Norfolk (at the Hague).
1660, May (? 16–26). JAMES LANGHAM, of London, eldest son of John Langham, alderman of London *(ibid)*.
1660, May 20. GEORGE CATHCART *(ibid)*.
1660, May 20. THOMAS CHAMBERLAINE *(ibid)*.
1660, May 21. GEORGE DOWNING, English resident in Holland *(ibid)*.
1660, May 27 (? 26). WILLIAM MORRICE, of Werrington, Co. Devon., secretary of state (at Canterbury).
1660, May 27. EDWARD MASSEY, major general *(ibid)*.
1660, May 27. EDWARD ROSSITER, of Somersby, Co. Lincoln. *(ibid)*.
1660, May 27. PHILIP HOWARD, brother of Charles, earl of Carlisle *(? ibid)*.
1660, May 27. ROBERT PASTON, of Oxnede, Norfolk *(ibid)*.
1660, May 27. THOMAS STEWKELEY (STUTELEY), of Alton, Co. Devon. *(ibid)*.
1660, May 27. DANIEL HARVEY, of Combe Park, Surrey *(ibid)*.
1660, May 27. ELIAB HARVEY, of Chigwell, Essex *(ibid)*.
1660, May 27. THOMAS INGHAM, of Goodnestone, Kent *(ibid)*.
1660, May 27. GEORGE KINNAIRD (KENART), of Scotland *(? ibid)*.
1660, May 27. ARNOLD BRAHAMS, of Bridge, E. Kent *(ibid)*.
1660, May 27. ROBERT MOYLE, of Buckswell, Kent *(ibid)*.

KNIGHTS BACHELORS

1660, May 27. RALP BANKES, of Corfe Castle, Dorset (at Canterbury).
1660, May 28. BAYNHAM THROCKMORTON, of Tortworth, Co. Gloucester. (at Rochester).
1660, May 28. WILLIAM SWAN, of Denton, Kent *(ibid)*.
1660, May 28. FRANCIS CLARKE, of Rochester, Kent *(ibid)*.
1660, May 28. GEORGE REEVE, of Thwaite, Suffolk *(ibid)*.
1660, May 29. THOMAS ALLEYNE, lord mayor of London (at the King's entry into the city of London) (at London).
1660, May 30. RICHARD BROWNE, senior, alderman, the succeeding mayor of London.
1660, May 30. RICHARD BROWNE, junior, son of Alderman Browne (at Whitehall).
1660, May 31. ROBERT TOWNSEND *(alias* Agborough), of Hem House, near Holt, Denbigh. *(ibid)*.
1660, May 31. JOHN WARRE, of Hestercombe, Somerset. *(ibid)*.
1660, May 31. GEORGE NORTON, of Abbots Leigh, Somerset. *(ibid)*.
1660, June 2. ROBERT HYDE, justice of common pleas *(ibid)*.
1660, June 2. EDWARD AYSCOUGH, of South Kelsey, Co. Lincoln. *(ibid)*.
1660, June 2. CAPELL LUCKYN, of Messinghall, Co. Essex *(ibid)*.
1660, June 2. JOHN DAWNEY, of Cowick, Co. York. *(ibid)*.
1660, June 4. WILLIAM PULTENEY, of St. James's *(ibid)*.
1660, June 4. ROBERT REYNOLDS, of Elvetham, Hants. *(ibid)*.
1660, June 5 (? 4). ROBERT ABDY, of St. Albans *(ibid)*.
1660, June 5. ROGER MOSTYN, of Mostyn, Co. Flint. *(ibid)*.
1660, June 5. JOHN KING, of Abbey Boyle, Co. Roscommon. *(ibid)*.
1660, June 5. PHILIP HARCOURT, of Stanton Harcourt, Co. Oxford. *(ibid)*.
1660, June 5. JAMES (? JOHN) DRAKE, of Ashe, Devon. *(ibid)*.
1660, June 5. WILLIAM HOVELL, of Hillington, Norfolk *(ibid)*.
1660, June 5. WILLIAM DALTON, of Hawkeswell, York. *(ibid)*.
1660, June 6. JOHN TALBOT, of Lacock, Wilts *(ibid)*.
1660, June 6. LANCELOT LAKE, of Canons, in Edgeworth, Middl. *(ibid)*.
1660, June 6. WILLIAM WRAY, of Ashby, Lincoln *(ibid)*.
1660, June 6. HENRY CONINGSBY (CONYSBY), of North Mimms Herts. (at Whitehall).
1660, June 7. JOHN MAYNARD, of Tooting, Surrey (? *ibid*).
1660, June 7. JOHN CARTER, of Kinmell, Denbigh. *(ibid)*.
1660, June 7. CHARLES CLEAVER, of Bygrave, Herts. *(ibid)*.
1660, June 7. JOHN CLOBERY, of Bradstone, Devon. *(ibid)*.

1660, June 8. CHRISTOPHER CLAPHAM, of Clapham, Yorkshire (at Whitehall).
1660, June 8. FRANCIS GERARD, son of Sir Gilbert Gerard, of Harrow, Middlesex *(ibid)*.
1660, June 9. ROBERT BERNARD, serjeant-at-law.
1660, June 9. ROBERT BROOKE, of Cockfield Hall, Suffolk *(ibid)*.
1660, June 9. ANDREW KING, of London *(ibid)*.
1660, June 9. HENRY OXENDEN, of Dene, in Wingham parish, Kent *(ibid)*.
1660, June 9. THOMAS HEBLETHWAYT, of Norton, Yorks. *(ibid)*.
1660, June 9. . WILLIAM PENN, commissioner of Admiralty and Navy *(ibid)*.
1660, June 9. ROBERT PARKHURST, of Porford, Surrey *(ibid)*.
1660, June (? 9). JOHN PRESCOTT, of Radwinter, Essex.
1660, June 11. RICHARD ATKINS, of Clapham, Surrey (at Whitehall).
1660, June 11. THOMAS MEERS, of Kirton, Lincoln. *(ibid)*.
1660, June 13. ARTHUR CAYLEY, of Newlands, in Coventry, Warwick. *(ibid)*.
1660, June 13. BRIAN BROUGHTON, of Broughton, Staffs. *(ibid)*.
1660, June 14. RICHARD FRANKLYN, of Moor Park, Herts.
1660, June 14. HENRY MAYNARD, of Estaines.
1660, June 15. THOMAS TIPPING, of Wheatfield, Oxon. *(ibid)*.
1660, June 15. WALTER RAWLEIGH, of West Horsley, Surrey *(ibid)*.
1660, June 15 (? or Aug. 23). FRANCIS SALKELD, of Whitehall and of Salkeld, Cumberland.
1660, June 16. GILBERT IRELAND, of Holt, Lancaster *(ibid)*.
1660, June 16. JOHN YORKE, of Gouldthwayte, Yorks. *(ibid)*.
1660, June 17. JOHN LAURENCE, alderman of London (at Sir Thomas Alleyn's house when he entertained the King).
1660, June 17. WILLIAM LEECH, of Squerries, Kent *(ibid)*.
1660, June 17. JOHN CUTLER, of London, merchant *(ibid)*.
1660, June 17. CHARLES COOTE, son of the earl of Mountrath (? *ibid*).
1660, June 18. CLEMENT ARMIGER, of Bloomsbury, Co. Middlesex and North Creek, Norfolk.
1660, June 18. JAMES DRAX, of Deresalt, York., of London and Barbados.
1660, June 18. ROGER BRADSHAIGH, of Haigh, Lancs.
1660, June 18. EMANUEL SORRELL, of Ipswich, Suffolk.
1660, June 19. JOHN COVERT, of Slaugham, Sussex.
1660, June 19. WILLIAM HARTOPP, of Rotherby, Leicester.
1660, June 21. RICHARD OTTLEY, of Pitchford, Salop.

KNIGHTS BACHELORS 229

1660, June 21. RICHARD WISEMAN, of Thoralds Hall, Essex.
1660, June 23. PHILIP EGERTON, of Egerton Hall, Co. Chester.
1660, June 24. JOHN GODSHALL, of Aldeston, Worcester.
1660, June 24. WILLIAM WISEMAN, of Rivenhall, Essex.
1660, June 25. JOHN HALE, of Stagenhoe, Herts.
1660, June 25. THOMAS OVERBURY, of Burton-on-the-Hill, Gloucester.
1660, June 25. ROBERT COTTON, of Combermere, Cheshire.
1660, June 25. MILES STAPLETON, of Carleton, York.
1660, June 25. GEORGE HORNER, of Cloford, Somerset.
1660, June 26. JOHN FREDERICK, alderman of London.
1660, June 27. ROWLAND LYTTON, of Knebworth, Herts.
1660, June 27. THOMAS BEAUMONT, of Whitby, York. (at Whitehall).
1660, June 27. NICHOLAS STRODE, of Westerham, Kent.
1660, June 30. GEORGE BROWNE, of Radford, Warwick.
1660, July 1. JOHN MARSHAM, of Whornes Place, Kent (at Whitehall).
1660, July 2. THOMAS TWISDEN, of Bradbourne, in East Malling, Kent, judge of King's Bench.
1660, July 2. THOMAS WENTWORTH, of Bretton, Yorks.
1660, July 2. EDWARD ATKYNS, of Hensington, Oxon., baron of the Exchequer.
1660, July 4. JOHN ALDER, of St. Martin's-in-the-Fields, Westminster.
1660, July 5. ABRAHAM REYNARDSON, alderman of London (at the Guildhall).
1660, July 5. JASPER CLAYTON, alderman of London *(ibid)*.
1660, July 5. THOMAS PLAYER, senr., chamberlain of London *(ibid)*.
1660, July 5. THOMAS PLAYER, junr. *(ibid)*.
1660, July 7. THOMAS NUTT, of Lewes, Sussex.
1660, July 7. EDWARD TURNOR, of Parendon, Essex, afterwards Speaker of the House of Commons.
1660, July 7. HENRY CÆSAR, of Bennington, Herts.
1660, July 7. WILLIAM BASSETT, of Clofferton, Somerset.
1660, July 8. JOHN CREMER, of Siechy, Norfolk.
1660, July 9. JOHN ARDERN, of Ardern, Chester.
1660, July 9. JOHN FITZ-JAMES, of Leweston, Dorset.
1660, July 10. ANDREW RICCARD, merchant, of London.
1660, July 11. THOMAS STEPHENS, of Sodbury, Gloucester.
1660, July 11. GEORGE CHUTE, of Streatham, Surrey.

1660, July 11. JAMES BEVERLEY, of Begurney, in Eaton Socon, Co. Bedford.

1660, July 11. OLIVER ST. GEORGE, of Drumrusk, Leitrim.

1660, July 11. GOBART BARRINGTON, of Toftes, in Little Baddow, Essex.

1660, July 13. ROBERT JENNINGS, of Ripon, Yorks.

1660, July 13. STEPHEN WHITE, of London.

1660, July 14. EDWARD FARMER, of Holbeck, Lincoln.

1660, July 15. THOMAS OGLE, of Pinchbeck, Lincoln, and of Wykyn, Suffolk.

1660, July 15. WILLIAM THOROLD, of Hough, Lincoln.

1660, July 16. RALPH ASSHETON, of Middleton, Lancs.

1660, July 16. CHRISTOPHER TURNER, of Milton Ernest, Co. Bedford., baron of the Exchequer.

1660, July 16. THOMAS TYRRELL, of Hanslope and Castle Thorpe, Bucks.

1660, July 17. THOMAS GARDINER, of Tollesbury, Essex.

1660, July 17. ANDREW RAMSEY, of Abbots Hall, Scotland.

1660, July 19. WILLIAM NUTT, of Chigwell, Essex, and London, merchant.

1660, July 19. AUDLEY MERVIN, of Castle Mervin, Co. Tyrone.

1660, July 21. ANDREW HENLEY, of Henley, Somerset, and of Bramshill, Hants.

1660, July 21. COMBE WAGSTAFF, of Tachbrook, Warwick.

1660, July 24. PETER BROOK, of Mere, Co. Chester.

1660, July 24. THOMAS RANT, of Bramshill, Hants., and of Broomhill, Norfolk.

1660, July 24. JOSEPH PAYN, mayor of Norwich.

1660, July 25. RICHARD SANDYS, of Northbourne, Kent.

1660, July 25. WILLIAM TREDENHAM, of Philleigh, Cornwall.

1660, July 28. JOHN SHAW, commissioner of Customs.

1660, July 30. HUMPHRY GORE, of Geldeston, Herts.

1660, July 30. CONRAD GILDENSHORNE, of Vlaburg, Sweden.

1660, July 30. NATHANIEL POWELL, of Ewhurst, Sussex.

1660, July 30. WILLIAM HUGESON, of Linsted, Kent.

1660, July 30. THOMAS DAVISON, of Blakston, Durham, sheriff of Durham.

1660, Aug. 1. THOMAS VINOR, of Lombard Street, London, goldsmith.

1660, Aug. 1. ALLEN BRODERICK, of Wandsworth, Surrey.

KNIGHTS BACHELORS 231

1660, Aug. 1 (or 31). WILLIAM DOMVILLE, of Fryern Barnet, Middlesex.
1660, Aug. 3. GABRIEL LOWE, of Newark, Gloucester.
1660, Aug. 5. JOHN ROTH, of Utrecht, Holland.
1660, Aug. 6. JOHN STAPELEY, of Patcham, Sussex.
1660, Aug. 7. ROBERT CARY, of Clovelly, Devon.
1660, Aug. 9. JOHN HANMER, of Whittingham Hall, Co. Suffolk.
1660, Aug. 14. HERBERT PERROTT, of Harroldston, Co. Pembroke.
1660, Aug. 16. THOMAS MEADOWS (MEDOWES), of Yarmouth, Co. Norfolk.
1660, Aug. 17. FRANCIS KYNASTON, of Oateley, Salop.
1660, Aug. 18. JEROME ALEXANDER, of Dublin, judge of common pleas.
1660, Aug. 18. ARTHUR CHICHESTER, of Dungannon, Ireland.
1660, Aug. 18. JOHN GORE, of Sacombe.
1660, Aug. 19 (or ? 18 or 16). EDWARD CROPLEY, of Clerkenwell, London.
1660, Aug. 25. ROBERT SMITH, of Upton, West Ham, Essex.
1660, Aug. 26 (or Sept. 7). STEPHEN TEMPEST, of Broughton, Yorks.
1660, Aug. 29. GIDEON SCOTT, of High Chester, Co. Roxburgh.
1660, Aug. 29. WILLIAM FLOURE, of Ireland.
1660, Aug. 29 (? Aug. 30 or Sept. 28). RICHARD KENNEDY, a judge in Ireland).
1660, Aug. 31. EDWARD MINSHULL, of Minshull, Cheshire.
1660, Sept. 1. RICHARD HOPKINS, of Coventry, Warwick, sergeant-at-law.
1660, Sept. 2. SAMUEL JONES, of Courteenhall, Northampton.
1660, Sept. 3 (or Oct. 24). JOHN ROLLE (ROLLES), of Bicton, Devon.
1660, Sept. 3. PURBECK TEMPLE, of Croydon, Surrey.
1660, Sept. 3 (?) EDWARD ALSTON, M.D., of London and Edwardstone, Suffolk.
1660, Sept. 11. CLEMENT THROCKMORTON, of Haseley, Warwick.
1660, Sept. 19. JOHN CLENCK, of Amsterdam.
1660, Sept. 21. GEORGE SMITH, merchant, of London.
1660, Sept. 24. JOHN LAWSON, vice admiral, of Ashford, Essex.
1660, Sept. 24. RICHARD STAYNER, rear admiral, of Greenwich, Kent.
1660, Sept. 26. THOMAS CREW, of Steen, Northampton.
1660, Sept. 28. WILLIAM ASTON, a judge in Ireland.
1660, Sept. 29. GEORGE PRETTYMAN, of Loddington, Leicester.

1660, Oct. 10. WILLIAM LANGDALE, of Longthorpe, York.
1660, Oct. 20. HENRY PIGOT, of Nether Gravenhurst, Beds.
1660, Oct. 25. THOMAS BURTON, of Stockerston, Leicester.
1660, Oct. 27 (? 23). LAURENCE SMYTH, of Bramley, Surrey.
1660, Nov. 6 (? 5). EDWARD CATER, of Kempston, Beds.
1660, Nov. 8 (? 7). GEORGE CROOKE, of Waterstock, Oxon.
1660, Nov. 16. JOHN GLYNN, King's Sergeant, of Henley Park, Surrey.
1660, Nov. 16. JOHN MAYNARD, sergeant-at-law, of Gunnersbury, Middl.
1660, Nov. 16. WILLIAM BEECHER, of Howbury, Beds.
1660, Nov. 19. EDWARD HARLEY, second son of Sir Robert Harley, of Brampton Bryan, Co. Hereford.
1660, Nov. 19. ANTHONY MORGAN (at Whitehall) see *supra* p. 705.
1660, Nov. 20. WILLIAM HEWYTT, of Breckles, Norfolk.
1660, Nov. 22. JOHN ATKINSON, of Stowell, Co. Gloucester.
1660, Nov. 24. WILLIAM GAGE.
1660, Nov. 26. JOHN POLY (POOLEY), of Boxted, Suffolk.
1660, Dec. 1. WILLIAM AYSCOUGH, of Osgodby, Co. York.
1660, Dec. 3. WILLIAM FORSTER, of Bamburgh Castle, Northumberland.
1660, Dec. 4. SAMUEL BROWNE, a justice of the King's Bench, of Arlesey, Beds.
1660, Dec. 4. WADHAM WINDHAM, a justice of the King's Bench, of Salisbury (at Whitehall).
1660, Dec. 5. WILLIAM STRODE, of Northington, Devon.
1660, Dec. 6. WALTER PLUNKETT, of Rathbeale, Co. Dublin, Ireland.
1660, Dec. 10. THOMAS FANSHAW, of Jenkins, in Barking, Essex.
1660, Dec. 14. HENRY HATTON, of Mitcham, Surrey.
1660, Dec. 15. THOMAS GRUBHAM HOWE, of Kempley, Gloucester.
1660, Dec. 22. JAMES SHANE, of Dublin.
1660, Dec. 30 (? 31). HENRY TEYNT (TYNTE, TAYNT), of Bally Crevan, Co. Cork.
1660–1, Jan. 18 (? 8). WILLIAM COBB, of Beverley, Yorks.
1660–1, Jan. 26. WILLIAM BURY (in Ireland by the lords justices).
1660–1, Jan. 27. WILLIAM JUXON, of Albourne, Sussex (in England by the King).
1660–1, Feb. 2. THOMAS DOLEMAN, of Shaw, Berks.
1660–1, Feb. 4. JOSEPH THROCKMORTON, of London, merchant (on board his own ship at Blackwall.

KNIGHTS BACHELORS

1660–1, Feb. 5. RICHARD COMBE (COMBES), of Hemel Hempstead.
1660–1, Feb. 16. ARTHUR DENNY (in Ireland by the lords justices).
1660–1, Feb. 16. BOYLE MAYNARD (*ibid* by same).
1660–1, Feb. 19. JOHN PONSONBY (*ibid* by same).
1660–1, Feb. 21. HUMPHRY HOOKE (HOOKES), alderman, of Bristol (in England by the King).
1660–1, Feb. 21. HUBERT ADRIAN-VERVEER, mayor of Dublin (in Ireland by the lords justices).
1660–1, Feb. 22. RICHARD LANE (*ibid* by same).
1660–1, Mar. 2. THOMAS ESTCOURT, of Sherston Pinkney, Wilts., a master in Chancery (in England by the King).
1660–1, Mar. 12. JAMES CUFFE, of Ballinrobe, Ireland.
1660–1, Mar. 12. WILLIAM RYDER, alderman, of London.
1660–1, Mar. 13. JOHN ROWLEY, of Castle Row, Co. Londonderry (in Ireland by the lords justices).
1660–1, Mar. 14. NICHOLAS PURDON, of Ballyclogh, Co. Cork *(ibid* by same).
1660–1, Mar. 15. PETER COURTHOP, of Little Island, Co. Cork *(ibid* by same).
1660–1, Mar. 16. WILLIAM KING, of the Hospital, Co. Limerick (*ibid* by same).
1660–1, Mar. 18. RALPH WILSON (*ibid* by same).
1660–1, Mar. 18. GILBERT GERARD, second son of Sir Gilbert Gerard, of Harrow-on-the-Hill, Co. Middl. (in England by the King).
1660–1, Mar. 19. JOHN BABER, physician-in-ordinary to the King.
1660–1, Mar. 19. ISAAC THORNTON, of Snailwell, Co. Cambridge.
1660–1, Mar. 19. FRANCIS FOULKE (in Ireland by the lords justices).
1660–1, Mar. 20. ST. JOHN BRODRICK (*ibid* by same).
1661, Mar. 27. THOMAS CLAYTON, master of Merton College, Oxon., regius prof. of medicine (in England by the King).
1661, Apr. 1. FRANCIS PRIDGEAN (*alias* Prugean, *alias* Privian), M.D., of London and of Hornchurch, Essex.
1661, Apr. 8. THOMAS BYDE, of Shoreditch, Middl., and of Ware Park, Herts., a brewer.
1661, Apr. 9. ROBERT MASON, of King's Cleere, Hants. (at Whitehall).
? 1661, Apr. 9. RICHARD MASON, of Bishops Castle and Ednop, Co. Salop, Avener.
1661, Apr. 10. EDWARD DYMOCK, of Scrivelsby, Lincoln., King's Champion at the Coronation of Charles II.

1661, Apr. 11. WILLIAM PETTY, M.D., of London, surveyor-general of Ireland.
1661, Apr. 12. WILLIAM WARREN, of Wapping, shipbuilder.
1661, Apr. 13. JOHN DETHICK, alderman of London.
1661, Apr. 17. GEORGE COURTHORPE (of Wylegh in Sussex) a gentleman pensioner (at Windsor).
1661, Apr. 17. GEORGE BLUNDELL, of Cardington, Co. Bedford., a gentleman pensioner *(ibid)*.
1661, Apr. 17. EDMUND BARKER, of Sibton, Suffolk, a gentleman pensioner *(ibid)*.
1661, Apr. 18. WALTER WALKER, D.C.L., of Bushey Hall, Herts. (at Whitehall).
1661, Apr. 19. JOHN LOWE.
1661, Apr. 20. EDWARD BYSSHE, of Byssche Court, Surrey, Clarenceux king-of-arms.
1661, Apr. 20. NICHOLAS PELHAM, of Lewes, Sussex.
1661, Apr. 20. GEORGE CONY, of Gray's Inn, sergeant-at-law.
1661, Apr. 23. JAMES DONELLAN, chief justice of the Common Pleas (in Ireland by the lords justices).
1661, Apr. 23. WILLIAM TITCHBORNE (*ibid* by same).
1661, Apr. 23. WILLIAM DIXON (*ibid* by same).
1661, Apr. 25. SAMPSON WHITE, mayor of Oxford (in England by the King).
1661, Apr. 26. JOHN MORLEY, of Chichester, Sussex.
1661, Apr. 28. THOMAS LEIGH, of Addington, Surrey.
1661, Apr. 28. JAMES WILFORD, of Olding, Kent (at Whitehall).
1661, Apr. 30. BERNARD HYDE, of Bore Place, Kent.
1661, May 8. FRANCIS GORE (in Ireland by the lords justices).
1661, May 9. ROBERT WISEMAN, D.C.L., King's advocate-general (in England by the King).
1661, May 10. CHARLES UMFREVILL, of Langham, Essex.
1661, May 11. JOSEPH CRADOCK, commissary of Richmond, Co. Yorks.
1661, May 12. WILLIAM CHILD, of Kinlet, co. Salop, a master in chancery.
1661, May 12. JUSTINIAN LEWYN (LEWEN), of Heybam, Essex, a master in chancery.
1661, May 12. MUNDEFORD BRAMSTON (BRAMPSTON), of Little Baddow, Essex, a master in chancery.
1661, May 12. WILLIAM GLASCOCK, D.C.L., of Wormeley, Herts., a master in chancery.

KNIGHTS BACHELORS 235

1661, May 12. THOMAS BIRD (BYRD), of Chancery Lane, Co. Middl., a master in chancery.
1661, May 12. NATHANIEL HOBART, of Chancery Lane, a master in Chancery.
1661, May 12. TOBY WOOLRICH, of Cowling, Suffolk, a master in Chancery.
1661, May 14. FRANCIS CLINTON, of Stourton Castle, Co. Lincoln.
1661, May 19. RICHARD KYRLE (KEARLES) (in Ireland by the lords justices).
1661, May 25. THOMAS IVY (IVEY), of Malmesbury, Wilts, (in England by the King).
1661, May 29. GEORGE ST. GEORGE (in Ireland by the lords justices).
1661, May 30. JOHN FARRINGTON, of Chicester (in England by the King).
1661, June 10. JOHN FINCH, ambassador to Constantinople.
1661, June 14. ANTHONY CRAVEN, of Sparsholt, Berks.
1661, June 25. JOHN BUSBY, of Addington, Bucks.
1661, July 10. JOHN DORMER, of Lee Grange, Bucks. (at Whitehall).
1661, Aug. 21 (? 24). THOMAS BENNETT, a master in chancery *(ibid)*.
1661, Sept. 27. THOMAS BLADWELL, of Swanington, Norfolk.
1661, Oct. 3. AUGUSTINE CORONEL or COLLONEL, agent for the king of Portugal (at Whitehall).
1661, Oct. 23. WILLIAM THROCKMORTON, son of Sir William *(ibid)*.
1661, Sept. 24. JOHN SHAW, of Colchester, Essex *(ibid)*.
1661, Sept. 25. JOHN BERNARD, of Abingdon, Northampton.
1661, Nov. 8. WILLIAM MERICK, judge of the Prerogative Court (at Whitehall).
1661, Nov. 10. JOHN FLOSWICK, of Amsterdam *(ibid)*.
1661, Nov. 23. WILLIAM CALEY (CALLEY), of Burderope, Wilts. *(ibid)*.
1661, Nov. 24 (? Oct. 24). GEORGE OXENDEN, of Dean, Kent *(ibid)*.
1661, Nov. 29 (? Oct. 29). HANS HAMILTON, of Hamiltons Hall, Armagh, Ireland *(ibid)*.
1661, Dec. 9. WILLIAM BLOIS (BLOYS), of Yoxford, Suffolk *(ibid)*.
1661, Dec. 10. JAMES AUSTIN, of Southwark.
1661, Dec. 16. RICHARD BISHOP, of Bridgetown, Warwick, senior sergeant-at-arms.

1661, Dec. 22. St. John Moore, of Fawley, Berks. (at Whitehall).
1661, Dec. 27. Clifford Clifton, of Clifton, Notts. *(ibid)*.
1661, Dec. 27. Francis Compton, of Hamerton, Hunt. *(ibid)*.
1661, Dec. 30. William Lowther, of Swillington, Yorks.
1661-2, Jan. 2. Thomas Tomkins (Thompkins), of Monington, Hereford. *(ibid)*.
1661-2, Jan. 7. Robert Christopher, of Alford, Co. Lincoln. *(ibid)*.
1661-2, Jan. 9. Henry Vaughan, of Derwydd, Carmarthen. *(ibid)*.
1661-2, Jan. 16. Nathaniel Napier, eldest son of Sir Gerard Napier, of Middlemarsh Hall, Dorset. *(ibid)*.
1661-2, Jan. 17. John Lort, of Stackpole, Co. Pembroke. *(ibid)*.
1661-2, Jan. 21 (? 16). John Keling, of Southill, Beds., sergeant-at-law *(ibid)*.
1661-2, Jan. 22. William Craven, of Elston, Glouc., gentleman usher to the queen of Bohemia *(ibid)*.
1661-2, Jan. 23. Thomas Cookes, of Stanton, Worcester. *(ibid)*.
1661-2, Jan. 29. Jervase Cutler, of Stansborough, Yorks. *(ibid)*.
1661-2, Jan. 30. Mathew Hale, of Alderley, Co. Gloucester., lord chief baron *(ibid)*.
1661-2, Jan. 31. Charles Hamilton *(ibid)*.
1661-2, Feb. 13. Edward Winter (Wintour), of Lidney, Co. Gloucester., and of the East Indies, a sea captain *(ibid)*.
1661-2, Feb. 17. Drayner Massingberd, of South Ormesby, Linc. *(ibid)*.
1661-2, Feb. 23. Walter Littleton, of Lichfield *(ibid)*.
1661-2, Feb. 23 (? 24). Thomas Monpesson.
1661-2, Mar. 3. Francis Goodrick, of Manby, Linc. *(ibid)*.
1661-2, Mar. 4. Jeoffry Shakerley, of Shakerley, Lancs.
1661-2, Mar. 14. Job Charlton, of Ludford, Co. Hereford, chief justice of Chester.
before 1661-2, Mar. 19. John Harbert, sheriff of Breconshire.
1662, Apr. 22. Robert Canne, of Bristol.
1662, Apr. 26. Thomas Daniell, of Beswick, Yorks., a captain of the Foot Guards.
1662, May 24. Henry Peckham, of Chichester (at Portsmouth).
1662, June 16. Edmund Hoskins, sergeant-at-law (at Whitehall).
1662, June 24. John Rogers, of Langton, Dorset (at Hampton Court).
1662, July 5. Thomas Beverley, of Lincoln's Inn *(ibid)*.

KNIGHTS BACHELORS

1662, July 6. JOHN CLOPTON, of Clopton, near Stratford-on-Avon, Warwick.

1662, July 19. WILLIAM TURNER, alderman of London.

1662, Aug. 3. JAMES WEYMES (in Ireland by the duke of Ormonde, lord lieutenant of Ireland).

1662, Aug. 3. WILLIAM DAVIS (*ibid* by same).

1662, Aug. 3. GEORGE CARR (*ibid* by same).

1662, Aug. 24. NICHOLAS LOFTUS (*ibid* by same).

1662, Sept. 2. MARTIN NOELL, of London, scrivener (at Whitehall by the King).

1662, Sept. 7. TOBY POYNTZ (in Ireland by the duke of Ormonde, lord lieutenant of Ireland).

1662, Sept. 30. GEORGE GILBERT, mayor of Dublin (*ibid* by same).

1662, Sept. 30. DANIEL BELLINGHAM, alderman of Dublin (*ibid* by same).

1662, Oct. 11 (? 1). NEVILL CATELYNE, of Kirby Cane, Norfolk (at Somerset House by the King).

1662, Nov. 14. JOHN BIRKENHEAD, D.C.L., M.P. for Wilton, Master of Requests (at Whitehall).

1662, Nov. 14 (? 16). JOHN DAVIES, of Pangbourne, Berks.

1662, Nov. 16. HENRY WADDINGTON (in Ireland by the duke of Ormonde, lord lieutenant of Ireland).

1662, Nov. 22. EDWARD NORREYS, of Weston on the Green, Oxon. (in England by the King).

1662, Nov. 24. PHILIP MEDOWES, of Bentley, Suffolk (at Whitehall).

1662, Dec. 18. JOHN WHATTON, of Newarke, Leicester. *(ibid)*.

1662-3, Jan. 28. JOHN FETTIPLACE, of Colne St. Edwins, Gloucester. *(ibid)*.

1662-3, Feb. 13. THOMAS GORE, of Barrow, Somerset *(ibid)*.

1662-3, Feb. 14. CHARLES PYM, of Brymore, Somerset *(ibid)*.

1662-3, Feb. 28. WILLIAM EYRE.

1662-3, Mar. 11. SCROPE HOWE, of Langar, Notts. *(ibid)*.

1662-3, Mar. 14. JOHN EUSTACE, of Gray's (Lincoln's) Inn *(ibid)*.

1662-3, Mar. 14 (1662, Nov.). MAURICE EUSTACE, of Lincoln's Inn *(ibid)*.

1662-3, Mar. 16. JEFFRY BURWELL, of Rougham, Suffolk *(ibid)*.

1662-3, Mar. 16. JOHN HUXLEY, of Eaton Park, Beds. *(ibid)*.

1662-3, Mar. 23. JOHN WYNN, of Rhiwgoch (Ryworth) Merioneth. *(ibid)*.

1663, Mar. 30. PETER PETT, judge of the Admiralty (in Ireland by the duke of Ormonde, lord lieutenant of Ireland).
1663, May 8 (? 2). THOMAS YARBOROUGH, of Snaith, Yorks. (at Whitehall by the King).
1663, May 8. GEORGE WYNNEVE (WYNYEVE), of Brettenham, Suffolk *(ibid)*.
1663, May 15. JOHN REA, of Richmond, Surrey *(ibid)*.
1663, May 30. JOHN HEBDON, of London, merchant, agent for the emperor of Russia *(ibid)*.
1663, June 1. GEORGE JUXON, of Canterbury *(ibid)*.
1663, June 2. JOHN MUSTERS, of Hornsey, Middl. *(ibid)*.
1663, June 3. ROBERT COTTON, of Hatley St. George, Cambridge. *(ibid)*.
1663, June 9. ROBERT HENLEY, of the Grange, Somerset, chief clerk for enrolling pleas in the King's Bench *(ibid)*.
1663, June 17. THOMAS HIGGINS (HIGGONS), of Gruell, Hants. *(ibid)*.
1663, June 24. GEORGE VINOR, eldest son of Sir Thomas Vinor *(ibid)*.
1663, June 30. JOHN HEWLEY, of York City *(ibid)*.
1663, July 1. JOHN STAWELL (STOWELL), of Bovey Tracy, Devon. *(ibid)*.
1663, July 7. EDWARD WALPOLE, of Pinchbeck, Lincolnshire *(ibid)*.
1663, July 23. FREDERICK HYDE (HIDE), sergeant-at-law *(ibid)*.
1663, July 26. JOHN PAYNE, steward of the Charter House *(ibid)*.
1663, Aug. 15. JOHN TEMPLE, solicitor general (in Ireland by the duke of Ormonde, lord lieutenant of Ireland).
1663 ? ? THOMAS FORTESCUE (*ibid* by same).
1663, Sept. 5. WILLIAM CANN, alderman of Bristol (at Bristol by the King).
1663, Sept. 5. HENRY CRESWICK, alderman of Bristol *(ibid)*.
1663, Sept. 5. JOHN KNIGHT, burgess for Bristol *(ibid)*.
1663, Sept. 5. ROBERT ATKYNS, junr., of Saperton, Co. Gloucester., son of Sir Robert Atkyns, the lord chief justice (at Bristol).
1663, Sept. 7. ROBERT YEOMANS, alderman of Bristol (at Bath).
1663, Oct. 1 (? Nov. 9). WILLIAM PEAKE, alderman of London (at Whitehall).
1663, Oct. 6. DOWSE FULLER, of Chamberhouse, Berks. *(ibid)*.
1663, Oct. 11. WILLIAM BOLTON, alderman of London.

KNIGHTS BACHELORS

1663, Oct. 12. RICHARD CHIVERTON, alderman of London (at Whitehall).
1663, Oct. 12. RICHARD RYVES, sheriff of London *(ibid)*.
1663, Dec. 2. JAMES DRAX, of London *(ibid)*.
1663, Dec. 4. JOHN ARCHER, justice of Common Pleas *(ibid)*
1663, Dec. 10. JOHN BRIDGES, of Kainsham, Co. Gloucester *(ibid)*.
1663, Dec. 18. RICHARD CHAWORTH, of Richmond, Surrey *(ibid)*.
1663-4, Jan. 10. WILLIAM DELAUNE (DE LAUNE), of London, merchant *(ibid)*.
1663-4, Jan. 22. WINSTON CHURCHILL, of Minterne, Dorset. *(ibid)*.
1663-4, Jan. 24. EDMUND TURNER, of Lincoln's Inn Fields, London *(ibid)*.
1663-4, Feb. 4. WALTER MOYLE, of St. Germains, Cornwall *(ibid)*.
1663-4, Feb. 6. EDWARD TURNOR, son of Sir Edward Turnor, Speaker of the House of Commons *(ibid)*.
1663-4, Feb. 16. GEORGE DALSTON, eldest son of Sir W. Dalston, of Dalston, Cumberland, bart.
1663-4, Feb. 16. JOHN DALSTON, second son of the above Sir W. Dalston.
1663-4, Feb. 26. WILLIAM TURNER, of Richmond, Surrey (at Whitehall).
1663-4, Mar. 3. SAMUEL TUKE, of Cressing, Essex *(ibid)*.
1663-4, Mar. 9. HENRY BOSVILE, of Aynsford, Kent *(ibid)*.
1663-4, Mar. 25. GILES SWEIT, dean of the arches *(ibid)*.
1663-4, Mar. 31. EDMOND FORTESCU, of Fallowpit, Devon. (at Whitehall).
1664, Apr. 30. WILLIAM D'OYLY, son of Sir W. D'Oyly of Shottisham *(ibid)*.
1664, May 13. HENRY ONSLOW, of Warnham, Sussex *(ibid)*.
1664, May 27. JOHN HEATH, of Brasted, Kent *(ibid)*.
1664, June 5. THOMAS HARMAN (in Ireland by the earl of Ossory, lord deputy of Ireland).
1664, June 5. HENRY BROOKE (BROOKES) (*ibid* by same).
1664, June 27. JOHN POLEY, of Boxted, Suffolk (at Whitehall by the King).
1664, June 27. ROBERT SEWSTER, of Great Ranby, Hunts. *(ibid)*.
1664, June 29. ROBERT YALLOP, of Bowthorpe, Norfolk *(ibid)*.
1664, July 15. JOHN BROWNE, of Pinchbeck, Co. Lincoln. *(ibid)*.
1664, July 30. MICHAEL HENEAGE, of Gray's Inn *(ibid)*.
1664, Aug. 7. FRANCIS PEISLEY (PEASLEY) (in Ireland by the earl of Ossory, lord deputy).

1664, Aug. 8. PAUL PAYNTER, of Muswell Hill (at Whitehall by the King).
1664, Aug. 8. JOHN COLLADON, of St. Martins-in-the-Fields, a physician to the Queen Consort (at Somerset House).
1664, Sept. 11 (4). THOMAS WORSOP (WORSSOP) (in Ireland by the earl of Ossory, lord deputy of Ireland).
1664, Oct. 11. WILLIAM BRODNAX (BRODNIX), of Godmersham, Kent (at Whitehall by the King).
1664, Oct. 25. PETER HARVEY, of Dublin *(ibid)*.
1664, Nov. 5. ARTHUR INGRAM, of London, merchant *(ibid)*.
1664, Nov. 17. JOHN CLAYTON, of the Inner Temple *(ibid)*.
1664, Nov. 19. CHRISTOPHER EYRE, of Harrow on the Hill, Middl. *(ibid)*.
1664, Dec. 29. ROBERT WORSLEY, eldest son of Sir Henry Worsley, of Appuldurcomb, Isle of Wight *(ibid)*.
[? 1664–1672]. TRISTRAM BERESFORD (in Ireland by the lord deputy of Ireland).
1664–5, Jan. 2. JOHN GRIFFITH, captain of the fort at Gravesend (at Whitehall by the King).
1664–5, Jan. 16. THEODORE DE VAUX, of Middl. and Guernsey *(ibid)*.
1664–5, Jan. 20. EDMUND BEAUCOCK, of Finchinfield, Essex *(ibid)*.
1664–5, Feb. 11. WILLIAM ADAMS, of Scawesby, Yorks. *(ibid)*.
1664–5, Feb. 11. THOMAS BATHURST, of Franks in Horton (Kirby), Kent *(ibid)*.
1664–5, Feb. 11. THOMAS FOSTER, of Egham, Surrey *(ibid)*.
1664–5, Mar. 1. FRANCIS ROLLE, of East Titherley, Hants, sheriff of Hampshire (at Portsmouth).
1664–5, Mar. 3. WILLIAM COVENTRY, secretary to the duke of York.
1664–5, Mar. 8. HENRY THOMPSON, alderman of York (at Whitehall).
1664–5, Mar. 10. PHILIP FROWDE, of London and Kent *(ibid)*.
1664–5, Mar. 18. SAMUEL MICO (MICAULT), alderman of London *(ibid)*.
1665, Apr. 15. GEORGE ENT, M.D., president of the College of Physicians (at the College of Physicians).
1665, Apr. 22. EDWARD THURLAND, of Ryegate, Surrey, solicitor to the duke of York.
1665, Apr. 27. THOMAS BONFOY, alderman of London.
1665, May 2. THOMAS TURBERVILLE, of Bere Regis, Dorset. (at Whitehall).
1665, May 10. DEMETRIUS JAMES, of Ightam, Kent.

KNIGHTS BACHELORS

1665, May 12. MATTHEW (MARTIN) HOLWORTHY, London (at Whitehall).
1665, May 14. JOHN JAMES, of Crishall, Essex *(ibid)*.
1665, May (? Apr.) 16. PAUL WHICHCOTE, of Hendon, Middlesex *(ibid)*.
1665, May (? Apr.) 19. ROWLAND OKEOVER, of Okeover, Stafford. *(ibid)*.
1665, May 31. FRANCIS CLARKE, of London *(ibid)*.
1665, May 31. JOHN COELL, of Depden, Suffolk, a master in Chancery *(ibid)*.
1665, June 10. GEORGE WATERMAN, sheriff of London *(ibid)*.
1665, June 10. CHARLES DOE, sheriff of London *(ibid)*.
1665, June 22. HENRY CODONY, gentleman usher of the Privy Chamber to the Queen *(ibid)*.
1665, June 22. JEROME SMITH, captain R.N.
1665, June 24. ROBERT VINER (VINOR, VYNER), alderman and goldsmith of London *(ibid)*.
1665, June 24. EDWARD SPRAGG, captain R.N.
1665, June 24. THOMAS ALLIN (ALLEN), captain R.N.
1665, June 27. CHRISTOPHER MINNES (MYNNES, MINGS).
1665, July 1. THOMAS TEDDIMAN, captain R.N.
1665, July 1. JOSEPH JORDAN, captain R.N.
1665, July 1. ROGER CUTTINGS, captain R.N.
1665, July 1. STEPHEN FOX, paymaster of the Guards, etc. (at Whitehall).
1665, July 4. WILLIAM LISLE, of the Middle Temple and of Wootton, Isle of Wight.
1665, July 4. WILLIAM OGLANDER, of Nunwell, Isle of Wight.
1665, Oct. 14. JOHN ELWES, of Barton Court, Berks. (at Oxford).
1665, Nov. MARTIN NOELL, son of Sir Martin Noell.
1665, Nov. (?) JOHN ERNLE, of Wheatham, Co. Wilts.
1665, Dec. 21. ROBERT SOUTHWELL, a clerk of the Council.
1665, Dec. 21 (?) EDWARD HOOPER.
1665 (?) CLEMENT FARNHAM.
[1665]. LUKE DOWDALL (dubbed in Ireland).
[1665]. THOMAS HUME *(ibid)*.
1665-6, Feb. 1. ROBERT HANSON, sheriff of London (in England by the King).
1665-6, Feb. 1. WILLIAM HOOKER, sheriff of London.

1665–6, Feb. 24. JOHN POYNTZ, of Iron Acton, Gloucester. (at Whitehall).
1665–6, Feb. 28. RICHARD PIGOTT (PYGOTT), of London, and of Woodford, Essex *(ibid)*.
1665–6, Mar. 6. THOMAS CHAMBERS, of Bromley, Middl. *(ibid)*.
1665–6, Mar. 6. RICHARD BELLINGS (BEELING), principal secretary and master of requests to the Queen.
1666, Mar. 27. ROBERT HOLMES, captain of H.M.S. "Defiance" (at Deptford).
1666, Apr. 28. CHARLES TUFTON, of Coston, Co. Gloucester.
1666, June 18. EDWARD MASTER, of Canterbury.
1666, June 30. MILES (MICHAEL) WHARTON (WARTON), of Beverley, Yorks. (at Whitehall).
1666, July 10. EDWIN RICH, of Lincoln's Inn, and of Mulbarton, Norfolk.
1666, July 24. ROBERT FAUNCE, of Cliffe, Kent.
1666, Sept. EDMONDBURY GODFREY, of St. Martins in the Fields (at Whitehall).
1666, Oct. 8. JOHN ST. LOE, of Knighton, Wilts. *(ibid)*.
1666, Oct. 23. JOSEPH SHELDON, sheriff of London *(ibid)*.
1666, Nov. 4. THOMAS LANGTON, of Bristol *(ibid)*.
1666, Nov. 10. THOMAS GERY, of Lincoln's Inn *(ibid)*.
? 1666, Nov. 10. JOHN GONNING, alderman of Bristol.
1666, Nov. 18. THOMAS WODEHOUSE (WOODHOUSE, of Kimberley Hall, Norfolk (at Whitehall).
[1666]. EDWARD ORMSBY (dubbed in Ireland).
1666–7, Feb. 20. JOHN MALET, of St. Anderry's, Somerset. (at Whitehall).
1666–7, Feb. 20 (?) NICHOLAS MYLLET, of Battersea, Surrey.
1667, Apr. 13 PHILIP CARTERET, son of Sir Geo. Carteret, of Hawnes (at Whitehall).
1667, May 8. JOHN WENTWORTH, of Elmes Court, or Elmhall, Yorkshire *(ibid)*.
1667, Oct. 21. SAMUELL STERLING (STARLING), alderman of London *(ibid)*.
1667, Oct. 23. THOMAS DAVIES, sheriff of London (at the Royal Exchange when Charles II. laid the foundation-stone).
1667, Oct. 23. DENNIS GAUDEN, sheriff of London (at the Royal Exchange as above).
1667, Nov. 20. GEORGE CURTES, of Otterden, Kent (at Whitehall).
1667–8, Jan. 6 (? 7) JOHN SPARROW, of Corbets Tey, Essex, and of the Inner Temple, counsel at law.

KNIGHTS BACHELORS 243

1667–8, Jan. 10. RICHARD KNIGHT, of Chawton, Hants. (at Whitehall).
1667–8, Feb. 18. RALPH RATCLIFFE, of Hitchen, Herts.
1668, Apr. 9. WILLIAM HOSKYNS, of Oxted, Surrey (at Windsor).
1668, May 15. ROBERT BOOTH (at Whitehall).
1668, May 19. JOHN VAUGHAN, of Trescoed, Co. Cardigan., lord chief justice of Common Pleas *(ibid)*.
1668, May 30. WILLIAM CONSTANTINE, of the Inner Temple *(ibid)*.
1668, July 18. ROGER HILL, of the Inner Temple, and of Denham, Bucks. *(ibid)*.
1668, July 18 (? 21). ROGER PRATT, of Riston, Norfolk *(ibid)*.
1668, July 21 (? 29). JOHN HOWELL, recorder of London *(ibid)*.
1668, Aug. 28. WILLIAM GODOLPHIN.
1668, Sept. 2. WILLIAM DRAKE, of Shardeloes, Bucks. *(ibid)*.
1668, Oct. 16. HENRY TOMPSON, alderman of York (at Newmarket).
1668, Nov. 24. WILLIAM GOSTWICK, of Willington, Beds. (at Whitehall).
1668, Dec. 8. THOMAS CROFT (CROFTS), a master in Chancery *(ibid)*.
1668. ROBERT HARTPOLE (dubbed in Ireland).
1668. RICHARD ALDWORTH *(ibid)*.
1668–9, Feb. 12. WILLIAM JESSON, of Coventry.
1668–9, Feb. 26. JOHN HAMBY, of Tathwell, Linc. (at Whitehall).
1668–9, Mar. 19. RALPH WARTON, of Beverley, Yorks. (at Newmarket).
1669, Apr. 19. JAMES WORSLEY, of Apuldercombe, Pylewell, Hants. (at Whitehall).
1669, Apr. 21. CLEMENT HARBY, of London *(ibid)*.
1669, May 11. FRANCIS THEOBALD, of Barking, Suffolk *(ibid)*.
1669, May 25. JOSEPH COLSTON, of Pudding Norton, Norfolk *(ibid)*.
1669, June 1. THOMAS ST. GEORGE, of Bexley, Kent, Somerset Herald *(ibid)*.
1669, June 2. MATHEW (MARTIN) PIERSON, of Lowthorpe, Yorks. *(ibid)*.
1669, Aug. 4. THOMAS CLUTTERBUCK, consul at Leghorn and merchant in London *(ibid)*.
1669, Aug. 12. THOMAS LEIGH, of Testwood, Hants. *(ibid)*.
1669, Aug. 14. CHARLES SCARBOROUGH, M.D. (at Durdans, lord Berkeley's house at Epsom, Surrey).
1669, Sept. 14. CHARLES MEREDITH (dubbed in Ireland).

1669, Oct. 9. WILLIAM HASLEWOOD, of Maydwell, Co. Northampton. (at Whitehall).
1669, Oct. 29. SAMUEL MARROW, of Barkswell, Warwickshire *(ibid)*.
1669, Dec. 6. EDWARD BARNARD, of North Dalton, Yorks. *(ibid)*.
1669, Dec. 6 (? 18). THOMAS STRINGER, of Gray's Inn *(ibid)*.
1669, Dec. 17. JOHN MORDAUNT, deputy governor of Tangiers *(ibid)*.
[1669]. WILLIAM FITZGERALD (dubbed in Ireland).
1669-70. ALEXANDER BENCE *(ibid)*.
1669-70, Jan. 7. LEOLINE JENKINS, judge of the Admiralty and Prerogative Courts (at Whitehall).
1669-70, Jan. 11. JOHN MAY, of Raymere, Sussex *(ibid)*.
1669-70, Jan. 20. BENJAMIN TICHBORNE, of Aldershot, Hants. *(ibid)*.
1669-70, Jan. 28. GABRIELL SYLVIUS.
1669-70, Mar. 2. SIMON DEGGE, judge of South Wales *(ibid)*.
1669-70, Mar. 2. WILLIAM WISE, of Beverley, Yorks. *(ibid)*.
1670, Apr. 5. BARROW FITCH, of Woodham Walters, Essex *(ibid)*.
1670, May 14. JOHN HALSEY, of Great Gadsden, Herts., a master in Chancery *(ibid)*.
1670, May. JOHN KEMPTHORNE, of Ashford, Essex, rear admiral.
1670, June 2. THOMAS CHICHELEY, of Wimple, Cambridge *(ibid)*.
1670, June 24. TIMOTHY TOURNER (TOURNEUR, TURNOUR) of Shrewsbury, a serjeant-at-law *(ibid)*.
1670, June 26. ROBERT SHAFTO, recorder of Newcastle-upon-Tyne *(ibid)*.
1670, June 28. HUGH WINDHAM, of Pilsdon Court, Dorset, a baron of the Exchequer *(ibid)*.
1670, June 28. JAMES HAYES, of Beckington, Somerset.
1670, July 8. JOHN SMITH, sheriff of London *(ibid)*.
1670, July 8. FRANCIS BREWSTER, alderman of Dublin *(ibid)*.
1670, July 10. TIMOTHY BALDWYN, of Stoake Castle, Salop, a master in Chancery *(ibid)*.
1670, July 10. ROBERT STEWART, of Wisbech, Cambridgeshire, a master in Chancery *(ibid)*.
1670, July 12. ROBERT PEYTON, of East Barnet, Herts. *(ibid)*.
1670, July 26. JOHN DARRELL, of Calehill, Somerset *(ibid)*.
1670, Aug. 12 (? 18). JOHN CHURCHILL, of Churchill, Somerset, afterwards master of the rolls *(ibid)*.
1670, Sept. 12. JOHN JAMES, of Heston, Middlesex *(ibid)*.
1670, Sept. 20. WILLIAM BUCKNELL, of Oxey, Herts. *(ibid)*.

KNIGHTS BACHELORS 245

1670, Oct. 26. THOMAS NORTCLIFFE (NORTHCLIFFE, NORCLIFFE), of Langton, Yorks. (at Whitehall).
Before 1670, Nov. FRANCIS CHAPLIN, alderman of London.
1670, Nov. 5. JAMES EDWARDS, of Islington, Middl., alderman of London *(ibid)*.
1670, Nov. 21 (? 20) HENRY ARCHBOLD, of Lichfield *(ibid)*.
1670, Dec. 1. EDWARD RICH, of Lincoln's Inn *(ibid)*.
1670, Dec. 3. THOMAS LYNCH (LINCH), of Rixton Hall, in Great Sankey, Lancs., governor of Jamaica *(ibid)*.
1670, Dec. 4. THOMAS LAKE, of Canons, near Edgware, Middlesex *(ibid)*.
[1670]. ALBERT CONYNGHAM (dubbed in Ireland).
[1670]. ROBERT HAMILTON *(ibid)*.
[1670]. THOMAS NEWCOMEN *(ibid)*.
[1670]. ROBERT WARD *(ibid)*.
[1670]. ABRAHAM YARNER *(ibid)*.
1670-1, Jan. 16. ANDREW HACKETT, a master of Chancery (at Whitehall).
1670-1, Jan. 22. JOHN CAW, of Zeeland, one of the gentlemen to the prince of Orange, son to the Baliue of Flushing, commander of Isingdike *(ibid)*.
1670-1, Jan. 29. JOHN TREVOR, of the Inner Temple *(ibid)*.
1670-1, Feb. 12. WILLIAM BEVERSHAM, of Holbrook, Suffolk, a master of Chancery *(ibid)*.
1670-1, Feb. 18. HUMPHRY FERRERS, of Tamworth, Co. Warwick. *(ibid)*.
1670-1, Mar. 2. GILBERT CLERKE (CLARK), of Somershall, Derby. *(ibid)*.
1670-1, Mar. 22. JOHN SABINE, of Eyne, Beds. *(ibid)*.
1671, Mar. 25. ROBERT COLE, of Ballymachey, Co. Tipperary *(ibid)*.
1671, Mar. 27. RICHARD BARKER, doctor of physic *(ibid)*.
1671, Apr. 24. EDWARD CHISNALL (CHESNALL, CHESENHALL), of Chesnal, Lancs. *(ibid)*.
1671, Apr. 30. WILLIAM ELLIS, of Grantham, Lincoln. serjeant-at-law *(ibid)*.
1671, May 16 (? June 16). WILLIAM RANT, of Thorpe Market, Norfolk *(ibid)*.
1671, May 21. [Some days before the 23rd] FRANCIS NORTH, solicitor general *(ibid)*.
1671, May 25. WILLIAM WALROND (WALDRON), of Bradfield, Devon. (at Whitehall ? at Bedford).
1671, May 30 (? June 30). ANDREW OWEN, of Dublin *(ibid)*.

1671, June 29. TIMOTHY LITTLETON, a baron of the Exchequer (at Whitehall).
1671, July 6. WILLIAM PAUL, of Bray, Berks. (at Windsor).
1671, July 15. WILLIAM JONES, of Gray's Inn, attorney-general (at Berkshire House, Middlesex).
1671, July 18. THOMAS BERRY, of Devon. (at Plymouth).
1671, July 21. THOMAS CAREW, of Barley, Devon. (at Dartmouth).
1671, July 23. BENJAMIN OLIVER, mayor of Exeter (at Exeter).
1671, July 28. JOHN COCKS, of Northey, Gloucester. (at Whitehall).
1671, Sept. 22. JOHN MYNNE, of Lincoln's Inn *(ibid)*.
1671, Sept. 27. JOHN BLODWELL, of Swannington, Norfolk (at Yarmouth).
1671, Sept. 27 (? 28). ROBERT BALDOCK (BOLDOCK), of Tacolnestone, Norfolk, recorder of Yarmouth *(ibid)*.
1671, Sept. 28. JAMES JOHNSON, of Yarmouth *(ibid)*.
1671, Sept. 28. GEORGE ENGLAND, of Yarmouth, Norfolk *(ibid)*.
1671, Sept. 29. HENRY HOBART, of Blickling, Norfolk (at Blickling).
1671, Sept. 29. THOMAS BROWNE, M.D., of Norwich (at Norwich).
1671, Sept. 29. EDWARD MASSEY, of Hodgsdon, Middx. (at Sir Robert Paston's house at Oxnead, Norfolk).
1671, Oct. 4. CHARLES CAESAR, of Benington, Herts. (at Cambridge).
1671, Oct. 26. THOMAS JONES, of Shrewsbury, serjeant-at-law (at Whitehall).
1671, Oct. 30. JONATHAN DAWES, sheriff of London (at the Guildhall).
1671, Oct. 30. ROBERT CLAYTON, sheriff of London *(ibid)*.
1671, Nov. 28. DERRICK POPELY, of Bristol (at Whitehall).
1671, Dec. 1. FRANCIS LEIGH, of Bexley, Kent *(ibid)*.
1671, Dec. 11. EDWARD NEVILL, of Grove, Notts. *(ibid)*.
1671, Dec. 14. WILLIAM LANGHAM, sheriff of Co. Northampton. *(ibid)*.
1671, Dec. 14. GEORGE NORTON, of Abbots Leigh, Somerset. *(ibid)*.
1671, Dec. 23. JAMES MORTON, son of Sir William Morton *(ibid)*.
[1671]. GEORGE INGOLDSBY (dubbed in Ireland).
1671-2, Jan. 17. EDWARD AYSCOUGH, of South Kelsey, Lincoln.
1671-2, Jan. 24. JOSEPH WILLIAMSON, a clerk of the Council *(ibid)*.
1671-2, Feb. 29. NICHOLAS PEDLEY, of Abbotsley, Hunt., a former reader of Lincoln's Inn (at a dinner at Sir Francis Goodrick's at Lincoln's Inn).
1671-2, Feb. 29. RICHARD STOTE, of Joemond Hall, Northumberland, a former reader of Lincoln's Inn *(ibid)*.

KNIGHTS BACHELORS

1671-2, Feb. 29. JAMES BUTLER, of Lincoln's Inn, an illegitimate son of James, duke of Ormonde (at Lincolns Inn)
1671-2, Feb. 29. FRANCIS DAYRELL (DORREL), of Lincoln's Inn, and of Lillingstone Dayrell, Bucks. *(ibid).*
1671-2, Mar. 13. STEPHEN LANGHAM, of Quinton, Northampton.
1671-2, Mar. 20. EDWARD BASH, of Stanstedbury, Herts. (at Whitehall).
1671-2, Mar. 22. JAMES OXENDEN, of Dene, Kent.
1672, Mar. 30. STRAFFORD BRAITHWAITE, of Catherick, Yorks. (at Whitehall).
1672, Apr. 7. JOHN TOTTY, mayor of Dublin (in Ireland by the lord deputy).
1672, Apr. 30. FRANCIS WINGATE, of Harlington, Beds. (at Whitehall by the King).
1672, May 10. JAMES RUSSELL, late governor of Nevis *(ibid).*
1672, May 13. JOHN MOORE, sheriff of London *(ibid).*
1672, May 24. THOMAS BAYNES or BAINE, M.D. *(ibid).*
1672, about end of May. JOHN BERRY, captain R.N.
1672, June 20. ALEXANDER WALDRON, of Barbados *(ibid).*
1672, July 6. JOHN PLATT, of Westbrook Place, Surrey *(ibid).*
1672, July 20. HENRY FORD, of Bagtor, Devon., secretary to his Excellency the earl of Essex, lord lieutenant of Ireland *(ibid).*
1672, July 21. JOHN EDGEWORTH, captain of the Guards in Ireland *(ibid).*
1672, Aug. 14. JOHN ONEBY, gentleman of the Privy Chamber *(ibid).*
1672, Sept. 20. DAWES WYMONDESOLD, of Putney, Surrey *(ibid).*
1672, Oct. 28 (? 23). WILLIAM PRICHARD, sheriff of London *(ibid).*
1672, Oct. 29. JAMES SMITH, sheriff of London *(ibid).*
1672, Dec. 7. LAURENCE DE BUSTIE, merchant, London.
1672, Dec. 10. EDWARD CHALONER, of Guisbrough, Yorks.
1672, Dec. 17. FRANCIS WINNINGTON, of Bewdley, Worcester, solicitor general to the duke of York.
1672, Dec. 19 (? 9). PERCIVAL HART, of Lullingstone, Kent (at Whitehall).
1672-3, Jan. 13. HENRY OSBORNE, esquire of the Body in Ordinary *(ibid).*
1672-3, Jan. 21. WILLIAM PARGITER, of Greatworth, Northampton, a master in Chancery *(ibid).*
1672-3, Jan. 21. EDWARD LOWE, a master in Chancery *(ibid).*
1672-3, Jan. 28. JONAS MOORE, surveyor of the Ordnance *(ibid).*

1672–3, Feb. 5. SAMUEL BALDWYN, of Stoke Castle, Salop, and of the Inner Temple (at Whitehall).

1672–3, Feb. 22. SAMUEL CLARKE, of West Haddon, Northampton. *(ibid)*.

1672–3, Feb. JOHN DAVYS (dubbed in Ireland by the earl of Essex, lord lieutenant).

1672–3, Mar. 15 (? 5). RICHARD LANGLEY, son of alderman Langley, of London (at Whitehall).

1673, Mar. 28. JAMES BRADSHAW, of Aspull, Lancs.

1673, Apr. 13 (? 3). JOHN CREW, of Utkinton, Chester *(ibid)*.

1673, Apr. JOHN POVEY, lord chief justice of the King's Bench (dubbed in Ireland).

1673, May 14 (? 24). WILLIAM HUSTLER, of Aclam, Co. Yorks. (at Whitehall).

1673, May 29. THOMAS SKIPWITH, of Grantham, Lancs. serjeant-at-law *(ibid)*.

1673, May 29. CHARLES DYMOCK, of Scrivelsby, Co. Linc. *(ibid)*.

1673, June 16 (? 6). LACON WILLIAM CHILD, of Kinlet, Salop *(ibid)*.

1673, June 20. JOHN OTWAY, of Gray's Inn *(ibid)*.

1673, June 24. WILLIAM HALFORD, of Welham, Co. Leicester.

1673, June 26. STEPHEN THOMPSON, of York. *(ibid)*.

1673, Aug. 2. EDWARD ABNEY, of Willesley, Co. Derby *(ibid)*.

1673, Sept. 22. JAMES STANSFIELD, a commissioner for managing the estates of the duke of Monmouth *(ibid)*.

1673, Sept. 30. JOHN NARBOROUGH, rear admiral.

1673, Oct. 29. ROBERT JEFFERIES, sheriff of London (at the Guildhall).

1673, Oct. 29. HENRY (? WILLIAM) TULSE, sheriff of London *(ibid)*.

1673, Nov. 15 [Oct. 21]. FRANCIS BRIDGEMAN, 3rd son of lord keeper Orlando Bridgman (at Whitehall).

1673, Nov. 20. CHRISTOPHER WREN, surveyor of His Majesty's Works *(ibid)*.

1673, Dec. 6. RICHARD MUNDEN (MUNDY), captain, for services in the retaking St. Helens, also the three Dutch East India Prizes *(ibid)*.

1673. MICHAEL COLE (dubbed in Ireland).

1673. CHARLES FIELDING (dubbed in Ireland).

1673. RICHARD REYNELL, second serjeant-at-law *(ibid)*.

KNIGHTS BACHELORS 249

1673–4, Jan. 25. MILES COOKE, a master in Chancery (at Whitehall).

1673–4, Feb. 21. WILLIAM SOAME, of Haughley, Suffolk *(ibid)*.

1674, May 17. RICHARD LLOYD, of Hallum, Co. Notts. *(ibid)*.

1674, May 19. WILLIAM HEVENINGHAM, of Heveningham, Suffolk, and of Ketteringham, Norfolk *(ibid)*.

1674, May 29. JOSHUA ALLEN, lord mayor [of Dublin] (in Ireland by the lord lieutenant).

1674, May 29. ARTHUR JONES *(ibid by same)*.

1674, July 10. NICHOLAS WILMOT, of Osmaston, Co. Derby., serjeant-at-law (at Hampton Court by the King).

1674, Aug. 9. NATHANIEL HERNE, of London, merchant (at Windsor Castle).

1674, Aug. 24. HUMPHREY SYDENHAM, of Cholworthy House, Somerset. *(ibid)*.

1674, Sept. 15. THOMAS ESCOURT, of Lincoln's Inn, a master in Chancery (at Whitehall).

1674, Sept. 18. PHILIP LLOYD, one of the clerks of the Council *(ibid)*.

1674, Sept. 26. CHARLES CROFTS ROAD, of Bradwell, Suffolk *(ibid)*.

1674, Sept. 29. HERBERT EVANS, of Nethe, Glamorgan. *(ibid)*.

1674, Sept. 29. JOHN LETHIEULLIER, sheriff of London (at the Guildhall, London).

1674, Nov. 5. DIDRIGH TULP, meestersknaep of Holland and West Friesland, and director of the Dutch East India Company (in His Majesty's bedchamber at Whitehall).

1674, Nov. 5. JOHN CAW (CAU, CAWE), commissary of the Musters to the States General *(ibid)*.

1674, Nov. 7. WILLIAM YORKE, of Burton Pedwardine, Lincoln. (at Whitehall).

1674, Nov. 8. ISAAC GIBSON, of Combe Abbey, Co. Warwick. *(ibid)*.

1674, Nov. 9. DUNCOMBE COLCHESTER, of Abenhall, Co. Gloucester. and of Gloucester City *(ibid)*.

1674, Dec. 10. JOHN KING, solicitor general to the duke of York *(ibid)*.

1674, Dec. 13. JOHN CHAMPANTE (in Ireland by the lord lieutenant).

1674, Dec. 15. CHRISTOPHER NEVILL, of Aubourn, Lincoln. (at Whitehall by the King).

1674, Dec. 27. HUMPHREY DOLEMAN, of Shawe, Berks. *(ibid)*.

1674–5, Jan. 15 (? 25). PETER APSLEY *(ibid)*.

1674–5, Feb. 2. ROBERT HARDINGE, of Bramcott, Notts., and of King's Newton, Derby. *(ibid)*.

1674–5, Feb. 12. ROBERT ROBINSON (ROBERTSON), captain, late commander of the *Monmouth* frigate (at Whitehall for good services).

1674–5, Feb. 16 ? THOMAS WARNER, of the Inner Temple, and of Barbados, attorney general of Barbados, son of Sir Thomas Warner, knt. (at Whitehall).

1674–5, Feb. 16. JOHN BIGGS, of Petersfield, Hants., recorder of Portsmouth *(ibid)*.

1674–5, Feb. 22. Letters patent containing a testimonial of the honour of knighthood granted to ANGELL DE RUYTER, of Holland, at Whitehall (Crown Office Docquet Book).

1674–5, Feb. 24. LESTRANGE CALTHORPE, of West Barsham and the Middle Temple *(ibid)*.

1675, Apr. 13. KENDRICK EYTON, of Eyton, Denbigh. *(ibid)*.

1675, Apr. 13. PALMES FAIRBORNE, major, for services at Tangiers *(ibid)*.

1675, Apr. 14. RICHARD ROOTH, captain *(ibid)*.

1675, Apr. 16. MATHEW ANDREWS, of Walton-upon-Thames (on board an East India ship).

1675, Apr. 19. PHILIP SKYPPON, of Stratton, Suffolk (at Whitehall).

1675, May 9. RICHARD BLAKE, of the Strand, Middlesex, the King's tailor *(ibid)*.

1675, June 18. JOHN MOLESWORTH, of Pencarrow, Cornwall, vice-admiral of Cornwall.

1675, July. RICHARD HADDOCK, a commissioner of the Navy.

1675, Aug. 30. WILLIAM FRANKLYN, of Mavern, Beds. (at Whitehall).

1675, Sept. 19 (? 9). THOMAS PAGE, provost of King's College, Cambs. *(ibid)*.

1675, Oct. 6. FRANCIS PEMBERTON, serjeant-at-law *(ibid)*.

1675, Oct. 29. PATIENCE WARD, alderman of London (at the Guildhall, London).

1675, Oct. 29. THOMAS GOLD, sheriff of London *(ibid)*.

1675, Oct. 29. JOHN SHORTER, sheriff of London *(ibid)*.

1675, Nov. 12 or 14. JOHN FRANKLIN, a master of Chancery (at Whitehall).

1675, Nov. 23. THOMAS EXTON, of Doctor's Commons *(ibid)*.

1675, Dec. 7 (? 3). MARK GUYON, of Dynes Hall, Essex *(ibid)*.

1675, Dec. 14. THOMAS MIDDLETON, of Stansted Montfichet *(ibid)*.

1675, Dec. 24 (? 4). HENRY CALVERLEY, of Eryholm *(ibid)*.

1675–6, Jan. 12. JAMES RUSSELL *(ibid)*.

KNIGHTS BACHELORS 251

1675–6, Jan. 19. RICHARD BULSTRODE, king's agent with the governor of the Spanish Netherlands, appointed resident in that Court (at Whitehall).

1675–6, Jan. 24. JOHN HOSKYNS (HOSKINS), a master in Chancery *(ibid)*.

1675–6, Feb. 14. ROBERT RICH, of Stondon, Essex *(ibid)*.

1675–6, Mar. 15 (? 10). GREGORY (GEORGE) HAWKMORE (or HOCKMORE), of Buckland, Co. Devon. *(ibid)*.

1676, May 17. THOMAS HARDRESSE (or HARDY), serjeant-at-law *(ibid)*.

1676, May 17. GEORGE STRODE, of Lee Weston, Dorset., a serjeant-at-law *(ibid)*.

1676, June 6. HENRY BEAUFOY, of Emscote, Co. Warwick. (at Whitehall).

1676, June 26. RALPH CARR, of Cockin, Co. Durham *(ibid)*.

1676, Aug. 12. RICE WILLIAMS, of Rhydodwin, Carnarvon. *(ibid)*.

1676, Aug. 22. CHARLES PITTFIELD, of Hoxton, Middl. *(ibid)*.

1676, Sept. 13. ROBERT KNIGHTLEY, of Ashstead, Co. Surrey, a merchant in London, sheriff of Surrey (at Worcester Park, Surrey).

1676, Sept. 13. EDWARD EVELYN, of Long Ditton, Surrey *(ibid)*.

1676, Sept. 24. ROBERT RANDS, of London, merchant (at Whitehall).

1676, Oct. 2. JOHN PEAKE, sheriff of London *(ibid)*.

1676, Oct. 20. RICHARD GIPPS, of Whelnethan, Co. Suffolk (at Saxham, Suffolk).

1676, Oct. 24. BARRINGTON BOUCHIER, of Beningborough Grange, Yorks. (at Newmarket).

1676, Oct. 31. THOMAS STAMPE, sheriff of London (at the Guildhall, London).

1676, Nov. 2. MARMADUKE DALTON, of Hawkeswell, Yorks. (at Whitehall).

1676, Nov. 22. GEORGE WALKER, of Bushey Hall, Herts. *(ibid)*.

1676, Nov. 27. GILES HUNGERFORD, of Calne, Wilts. *(ibid)*.

1676, Dec. (? 1). WILLIAM CHIFFINCH (when the king dined with him at Windsor).

1676, Dec. 27. THOMAS HANMER, of the Inner Temple *(ibid)*.

1676. ROBERT COLVILL (dubbed in Ireland).

1676–7, Jan. 16. RICHARD LLOYD, of Salop, and Doctor's Commons, D.C.L. *(ibid)*.

1676–7, Feb. 2. JOHN JONES, of Funmon Castle, Glamorgan. *(ibid)*.

1676–7, Feb. 3. WILLIAM DOLBEN, of the Inner Temple *(ibid)*.

1676–7, Feb. 10. JOHN BOTELER, of Watton Woodhall, Herts. *(ibid)*.

1676–7, Mar. 5. HENRY BERNARD, of London, merchant (dubbed in Ireland).
1676–7, Mar. 18. THOMAS HEATH, comptroller of the house to archbishop Sheldon *(ibid)*.
1677, Apr. 10. ROBERT HATTON, of Thames Ditton, Surrey *(ibid)*.
1677, Apr. 17. JOHN MATHEWS, of Evesham and of London, merchant *(ibid)*.
1677, May 6. WILLIAM LYTTON, of Knebworth, Herts. *(ibid)*.
1677, May 18. RALPH JENISON, of Elswick, Co. Northumberland (at Whitehall).
1677, May 25. WILLIAM DUGDALE, Garter King of Arms *(ibid)*.
1677, May 25. HENRY ST. GEORGE, Norroy King of Arms *(ibid)*.
1677, July 18. HENRY DACRE (DACRES, DACERS), of Clerkenwell, agent for the East India Company at Bantam in India *(ibid)*.
1677, July 22 (? 23). THOMAS HUDSON, of Breemwich, near Doncaster, Yorks. *(ibid)*.
1677, July 25 [or 1678, Aug. 25]. CÆSAR CRANMER, of Whitehall, and of Astwood Bury, Bucks. *(ibid)*.
1677, Aug. 13. WILLIAM BASTARD, sheriff of Devon. *(ibid)*.
1677, Sept. 14. GEORGE JEFFERIES, common serjeant (at Whitehall).
1677, Oct. 17. ROBERT SAWYER, of the Inner Temple *(ibid)*.
1677, Oct. 19. EDWARD WALDO, of London, Mercer (at his own house in Cheapside).
1677, Oct. 19 (29). THOMAS BECKFORD, sheriff of London (at the Guildhall).
1677, Oct. 19. WILLIAM RAWSTORNE (ROYSTON), sheriff of London *(ibid)*.
1677, Nov. 23. ROBERT HACKETT, of Barbados (in the bedchamber, at Whitehall).
1677, Dec. 18. HENRY ROBINSON, of Cransley, Northampton *(ibid)*.
1677. JOHN DILLON (in Ireland by the duke of Ormonde, lord lieut.).
1677. THOMAS CROSBY (*ibid* by same).
1677–8, Jan. 14. GABRIEL ROBERTS, Dep. Gov. of the African Comp. (at St. James's by the King).
1677–8, Feb. 22. FRANCIS WATSON (at Whitehall).
1677–8, Feb. 26. JOHN SYMPSON, of the Inner Temple, serjeant-at-law (at Whitehall by the King).
1677–8, Mar. 13. JOHN LENTHALL, of Basselsleigh, Berks. *(ibid)*.
1677–8, Mar. 18. JONATHAN JENNINGS, of Ripon, Yorks. *(ibid)*.
1678, Apr. 7. HENRY GOUGH, of Perry Hall, Staffs. (at St. James's).

KNIGHTS BACHELORS 253

1678, June 5. JOHN BOYNTON, of Roecliffe, Yorks. (at Whitehall).
1678, July 13. FLEETWOOD DORMER, of Arle Court, Co. Gloucester. *(ibid)*.
1678, July 16. ROBERT OWEN, of Llewenny, Carnarvon.
1678, July 17. ROBERT GORING, of Coldeston (at Whitehall).
1678, July 22. WILLIAM BISHOP, of Bridgetown House, near Stratford-upon-Avon *(ibid)*.
1678, July 27. ROBERT TALBOR, physician-in-ordinary to the King *(ibid)*.
1678, Aug. 31. JOHN MEADE (dubbed in Ireland during the lord lieutenant's progress).
1678, Sept. RICHARD HULL *(ibid* same occasion).
1678, Sept. SAMUEL FOXEN, of Limerick *(ibid* came occasion).
1678, Oct. 2. CRESWELL LEVING, of Gray's Inn *(ibid)*.
1678, Oct. 28. RICHARD How, sheriff of London *(ibid)*.
? 1678, Oct. 28. JOHN CHAPMAN, sheriff of London *(ibid)*.
1678, Nov. 5. HENRY WEYMES (in Ireland by the duke of Ormonde, lord lieutenant).
1678, Nov. 24. WILLIAM ROBINSON, of London (at Whitehall by the King).
1678, Nov. 27. JOHN LLOYD, mayor of Bristol *(ibid)*.
1678, Nov. 27. CHARLES NEALE, of   , Co. Northampton. *(ibid)*.
1678. FRANCIS BRAMSTON, baron of the Exchequer (? when knighted).
1678-9, Jan. 7. JEREMIAH SNOW, of Lombard Street, goldsmith, London (at Whitehall).
1678-9, Feb. 23. ROBERT GORE (in Ireland by the duke of Ormonde, lord lieutenant).
1678-9, Feb. 23. JOHN PARKER *(ibid* by same).
1678-9, Feb. 23. JOHN TOPHAM *(ibid* by same).
1678-9, Feb. 27. RICHARD WESTON, a serjeant-at-law.
1678-9, Mar. 8. ROGER BRADSHAW, of the Haigh, Lancs. (at Whitehall).
1679, Mar. 26. FRANCIS MORTON, chancellor of the Island of Nevis *(ibid)*.
1679, Apr. 16. JOSEPH BRAND, of Edwardstone, Suffolk *(ibid)*.
1679, June 26. THOMAS RAYMOND, baron of the Exchequer *(ibid)*.
1679, June (or July) 26. EDWARD ATKYNS, a baron of the Exchequer *(ibid)*.
1679, July 26. WILLIAM GREGORY, a baron of the Exchequer *(ibid)*.

1679, Aug. 3. BENJAMIN NEWLAND, of London, merchant (at Titchfield House, Co. Southampton).

1679, Aug. 7. RICHARD STEPHENS, of Lincoln's Inn (at Portsmouth).

1679, Oct. 20. JONATHAN RAYMOND, of Barton Court and Kentbury, sheriff of London (at Whitehall).

1679, Oct. 20. SIMON LEWIS, linen draper, of Cornhill, sheriff of London *(ibid)*.

1679, Oct. 20. WILLIAM RUSSELL, of London, mercer *(ibid)*.

1679, Oct. 26. JOHN KELING, of Southill, Beds. *(ibid)*.

1679, Nov. 5. THOMAS OSBORNE (dubbed in Ireland).

1679, Nov. 5. HENRY PONSONBY *(ibid)*.

1679, Dec. 7. THOMAS FITCH, of Blackfriars, London (at Whitehall).

1679–80, Jan. 6. EDWARD DERING, of London, merchant *(ibid)*.

1679–80, Jan. 11. PETER LELY, of St. Paul's, Covent Garden, the King's painter *(ibid)*.

1679–80, Mar. 6 [or 8]. HENRY JOHNSON, of Blackwall, shipbuilder, M.P. for Aldborough (knighted in his own house).

1679–80, Mar. 6. THOMAS MILLINGTON, M.D., of York Buildings, Strand.

1679–80, Mar. 8. WILLIAM GULSTON (GOULSTON), of Whitechapel (at the lord mayor's).

1680, Apr. 3 (or 13). RICHARD DERHAM (DEREHAM), remembrancer of London (at Whitehall).

1680, Apr. 6. JOHN EDWARDS, of Heath House, Salop *(ibid)*.

1680, Apr. 7. EDWARD VILLIERS, knight marshal of the Household *(ibid)*.

1680, Apr. 16. THOMAS HOLT, recorder of Reading (at Windsor Castle).

1680, Apr. 18. WILLIAM DODSON, of St. Paul's Churchyard, London, woollen draper (at Whitehall).

1680, Apr. 18 (17). FRANCIS WYTHENS (WITHENS), of Eltham, Kent, dep. steward of Westminster and a J.P., Westminster, on presenting an address to the King from the grand inquest for the city of Westminster testifying their dislike and abhorrence of the late petition for a parliament *(ibid)*.

1680, Apr. 18. THOMAS CANN, of Bristol *(ibid)*.

1680, May 1. JEMMETT RAYMOND (at Skinner's Hall, London, the house of his father, Sir Jonathan).

1680, May 15. ROBERT WRIGHT, of Wangford, Suffolk (at Whitehall).

1680, May 28. ROBERT ADAMS, of London (at Windsor Castle).

1680, May 28. ROWLAND GWYN, of Llanelwa, Co. Radnor *(ibid)*.

KNIGHTS BACHELORS 255

1680, June 17. WILLIAM DAWSON, of Asterley, recorder of Ripon (at Windsor Castle).
1680, June 30. ADAM OTTLEY (OATLEY), a master of Chancery *(ibid)*.
1680, Aug. 1. JAMES HERBERT, of Colebroke, Co. Monmouth. (at Whitehall).
1680, Aug. 5. PHINEAS (PHINES) PETT, of Chatham, master shipwright of the King's yard at Chatham, comptroller of the stores (to be a principal officer and commr. of the Navy).
1680, Aug. 9. JONAS MOORE, surveyor of the Ordnance in the Tower (at Windsor Castle).
1680, Sept. 16 (? 14). HENRY BATHURST, of Edmonton, Middl. (at Mr. Coventry's Lodge in Enfield Chase).
1680, Oct. 27. RICHARD HART, mayor of Bristol (at Whitehall).
1680, Oct. 28. WILLIAM KINGSMILL, of Sydmonton, Hants. *(ibid)*.
1680, Nov. 5. JOHN MAGILL (in Ireland by the duke of Ormonde, lord lieutenant).
1680, Nov. 12. ROGER PULESTON, of Emrall, Flint. (at Whitehall by the King).
1680, Nov. 20. JOHN WETWANG, captain *(ibid)*.
1680, Dec. 3. MATHEW DEANE (in Ireland by the duke of Ormonde, lord lieutenant).
1680, Dec. 21. PHILLIPS COOTE *(ibid by same)*.
1680, (? Dec.) 28. NATHANIEL JOHNSON, commissioner of hearth money (at Whitehall by the King).
? 1680. GEORGE ETHEREDGE.
1680–1, Jan. 20. GEORGE TREBY, recorder of London, solicitor-general, 1689 *(ibid)*.
1680–1, Jan. 27. ROBERT NAPIER (NEPPIER, NAPER), of Puknoll, high sheriff of Dorset. *(ibid)*.
1680–1, Feb. 9. HENRY LANGLEY, of the Abbey, Shrewsbury *(ibid)*.
1680–1, Mar. 4. HUMPHRY NICHOLSON, of Mile End Green, Middl. *(ibid)*.
1680–1, Mar. 7. RICHARD TUFTON, of Westminster *(ibid)*.
1680–1, Mar. 14. GEORGE PUDSEY, of Elsfield, Oxon (at Oxford).
1680–1, Mar. 16. RICHARD CROKE (CROOKE), serjeant-at-law *(ibid)*.
1681, Apr. 7 (? 16). WILLIAM SCROGGS, of Gray's Inn and of St. Clement's Danes, Co. Middl. (at Whitehall).
1681, Apr. 17. THOMAS DEREHAM, resident at Florence *(ibid)*.
1681, May 1. RICHARD RYVES (REVES), recorder of Dublin (in Ireland by the duke of Ormonde, lord lieutenant).
1681, May 15. DANIEL FLEMING, of Rydal, Westmoreland (at Windsor Castle by the King).

KNIGHTS BACHELORS

1681, May 19. GEORGE WOODRUFFE, of Poyle, Surrey (at Hampton Court).

1681, May 19. EDMUND WISEMAN, of Paternoster Row, Mercer *(ibid)*.

1681, May 30. CHRISTOPHER PHILLIPSON (PHILLOPSON), of Colgarth, Westmoreland, and Creek Hall, Cumberland (at Windsor Castle).

1681, May 30. RICHARD MAY, recorder of Chichester *(ibid)*.

1681, May 31. JOHN FARINGTON, of Chichester *(ibid)*.

1681, June 1. THOMAS WALKER, of Exeter *(ibid)*.

1681, June 2. WILLIAM ELIOT (ELLIOT), of Godalming, Surrey (at Hampton Court).

1681, June 8. THOMAS STREET, a baron of the Exchequer (at Whitehall).

1681, June 10 (? 20). WILLIAM PERKINS, of Marston Jabbett, Co. Warwick., one of the six clerks of Chancery *(ibid)*.

1681, June 12. EDWARD NEVILL, recorder of Bath (at Windsor Castle).

1681, June 13. GEORGE SAVAGE, of Blackworth, Dorset. (at Windsor Castle).

1681, June 14. HENRY CHAUNCY, of Ardeley, Herts. *(ibid)*.

1681, June 14 (? 18). JOHN COLLINS, of Chute Lodge, Hants. *(ibid)*.

1681, June 18. JOHN BUCKWORTH, of London, merchant *(ibid)*.

1681, July 5. MICHAEL WENTWORTH, of Woodley, Yorks. *(ibid)*.

1681, July 23. THOMAS FOTHERBY, of the Bury, in Rickmansworth, Co. Herts. *(ibid)*.

1681, July 23. NICHOLAS MILLER, of Hyde Hall, Herts., sheriff of Herts. (at Windsor).

1681, July 23. THOMAS FIELD, of Stanstedbury, Norfolk *(ibid)*.

1681, Aug. 1. CHARLES RAWLEY, of Downton, Wilts. (at Windsor Castle).

1681, Aug. 3. JAMES CLARKE, of Moulsey, Surrey *(ibid)*.

1681, Aug. 3. JOHN MARSHALL, of Sculpuis in Finchingfield, Essex (at Windsor Castle).

1681, Aug. 5. CHRISTOPHER BUCKLE, of Bansted, Surrey *(ibid)*.

1681, Aug. 8 (6). ANDREW NOELL, of Pickwell, Leicester *(ibid)*.

1681, Aug. 12. RICHARD OSBALDESTON, of Hunmanby, York. *(ibid)*.

1681, Aug. 12. EDWARD DINGLEY, of Charlton, near Evesham *(ibid)*.

1681, Aug. 15 (? 18). THOMAS HASLEWOOD, of Wich (Wyke), Co. Worcester. (at Windsor).

KNIGHTS BACHELORS 257

1681, Sept. 6. GEORGE RAINSFORD (RAYNSFORD), of Lincoln's Inn Fields (son of the lord chief justice Raynsford) (at Whitehall).

1681, Oct. 18. RICHARD CRUMPE (CROMP), of Bristol, merchant *(ibid)*.

1681, Nov. 5. HUMPHREY JERVIS, lord mayor of Dublin (in Ireland by the duke of Ormonde, lord lieutenant).

1681, Nov. 6. GEORGE VERNON, major, of Farnham, Surrey (at Whitehall by the King).

1681, Nov. 11. EDMUND WARNEFORD, of Sevenhampton, Wilts. *(ibid)*.

1681, Nov. 18. RICHARD DOWNTON, of Isleworth, Middlesex *(ibid)*.

1681, Nov. 21. NICHOLAS TOKE, of Goddington, Kent *(ibid)*.

1681, Nov. 21. THOMAS WALLCOTT, of Bitterley, Salop., serjeant-at-law *(ibid)*.

1681, Dec. 4. THOMAS EARLE, mayor of Bristol *(ibid)*.

1681-2, Jan. 2. THOMAS GRIFFITH, of London, merchant *(ibid)*.

1681-2, Jan. 17. BENJAMIN BATHURST, deputy governor of the Royal Africa Company *(ibid)*.

1681-2, Jan. 31. JEREMIAH SAMBROOKE, merchant, of London (on board the earl of Berkeley's ship "Berkeley").

1681-2, Feb. 3. RICHARD BASSETT, of Beaupré, Glamorgan (at Whitehall).

1681-2, Feb. 17. JAMES ETHERIDGE, of the Inner Temple *(ibid)*.

1681-2, Feb. 25. THOMAS CUTLER, of Lechlade, Gloucester. *(ibid)*.

1681-2, Mar. 2. NICHOLAS BUTLER, of London, merchant *(ibid)*.

1681-2, Mar. 3 (? 8). WILLIAM WILSON, of Leicester town *(ibid)*.

1681-2, Mar. 12. JOHN KNIGHT, sheriff of Bristol (at Newmarket).

1681-2, Mar. 17 (1681, Apr. 17). JOHN CHARDIN, a Frenchman, merchant and jeweller (at Whitehall).

1682, Apr. 26. CHARLES SKRYMSHIRE (SKRYMSHAW), of Norbury, Staff., high sheriff of the County of Staffordshire (at Windsor Castle).

1682, June 4. ROBERT DASHWOOD, of London, merchant, and of Northbroke, Co. Oxford. *(ibid)*.

1682, June 7. THOMAS BLOODWORTH (BLUDWORTH), of London and of Leatherhead, merchant *(ibid)*.

1682, June 13. RAPHAEL COTES (COOTS), of Bruges, in Flanders *(ibid)*.

1682, June 19. FRANCIS GUIBON, of Thursford, Norfolk *(ibid)*.

1682, June 28. JOHN BRATTLE, assay master of the mint (at Whitehall).

1682, June 29. ROBERT LEGARD, of Anlaby, Yorkshire, master in Chancery (at Whitehall).
1682, July 13. Two Ambassadors were knighted, from the king of Bantam.
1682, July 23. WILLIAM HILL, of Teddington, Middl. (at Windsor Castle).
1682, Aug. 18. CORNWALL BRADSHAW, of London, one of the farmers of the hearth money (at Windsor Castle).
1682, Aug. 18. ORLANDO GEE, of St. Martin's-in-the-Fields (steward to the earl of Northumberland, and registrar to the Court of Admiralty) *(ibid)*.
1682, Sept. 1 (? 11). GEORGE WHEELER, of Odiam, Herts. (at Winchester).
1682, Oct. 1. THOMAS ROULT, of London, merchant (at Whitehall).
1682, Oct. 12. ROBERT KING, bart. (dubbed in Ireland).
1682, Nov. 5. MARTIN BENTLY, of Barbados (at Whitehall).
1682, Nov. 12. WILLIAM BOOTH, a captain in the Navy.
1682, Nov. 27. RICHARD GIPPS (GIBBS), of Gray's Inn, and of Horninger Hall, master of the Revels (at Whitehall).
1682, Nov. 29 (? 25). WILLIAM GLASSCOCK, of Farnham, Surrey, sheriff of Essex *(ibid)*.
1682–3, Jan. 6. EDWARD SHERBURNE, clerk of the Ordnance in the Tower *(ibid)*.
1682–3, Jan. 15. HUMPHRY MACKWORTH, of the Middle Temple *(ibid)*.
1682–3, Jan. 15. CHARLES ADDERLEY, of Lea.
1682–3, Jan. 21. EDMUND SAUNDERS, chief justice of the King's Bench *(ibid)*.
1682–3, Jan. 29. THOMAS ATKINS (in Ireland by the earl of Arran, lord deputy).
1682–3, Feb. 11. DUDLEY NORTH, sheriff of London (at Whitehall by the King).
1682–3, Feb. 19. JAMES (LAMER) WARD, of London, merchant (at Deptford).
1682–3, Feb. 21. THOMAS DAVALL (DE VALL), of London, merchant (at Whitehall).
1682–3, Mar. 17. HENRY ALLNUTT, of Abston, Bucks. (at Newmarket).
1682–3, Mar. 17. HENRY MARTIN, of Longworth.
1682–3, Mar. 17. JOHN WELD, of Willey.
1682–3, Mar. 17. JOHN CHURCHMAN, of Illington.
1683, Apr. 12. EDWARD SELWYN, of Friston, Sussex, sheriff of Sussex (at Whitehall).
1683, Apr. 21. JAMES LEIGH (in Ireland by the earl of Arran, lord deputy).
1683, May 6. THOMAS DUPPA, gentleman usher of the Black Rod (in England by the King).

KNIGHTS BACHELORS

1683, May 17. ROBERT FENWICK, of Bywell, Northumberland (at Windsor Castle).
1683, May 20. JOHN IVORY, of New Ross, Ireland *(ibid)*.
1683, May 24. RICHARD HOLLOWAY, of Oxford City *(ibid)*.
1683, June 17. ABRAHAM JACOB, of Dover, governor of Walmer Castle *(ibid)*.
1683, July 26. WILLIAM STANHOPE, of Shelford, Notts., gentleman usher daily waiter to the Queen *(ibid)*.
1683, Aug. 7. PAUL BARRETT, recorder of Canterbury *(ibid)*.
1683, Aug. 14. EDWARD WIGLEY, of Whitwell, Rutland *(ibid)*.
1683, Aug. 14. WILLIAM HOLFORD (HALFORD), of Welham, Co. Leicester. *(ibid)*.
1683, Sept. 6. GEORGE BROWNE, of Wolverton, Hants. (at Portsmouth).
1683, Oct. 4. THOMAS JENNER, recorder of London (at Whitehall).
1683, Nov. 19. MATHEW JENNISON, of Newark-upon-Trent, Notts *(ibid)*.
1683, Nov. 20. JAMES ASTRY, master in Chancery *(ibid)*.
1683, Nov. 27. WILLIAM CLUTTERBUCK, mayor of Bristol *(ibid)*.
1683, Nov. 28. ANDREW MACDOWGALL, of Scotland *(ibid)*.
1683, Nov. 29. HENRY WALDGRAVE, of Chiswick, Middlesex, doctor of physic (at St. James's).
1683, Dec. 3. JOHN BRISCO, of Harrowden, Co. Northampton. (at Whitehall).
1683, Dec. 8. SAMUEL ASTRY, of Henbury, Gloucester., clerk of the Crown in the King's Bench *(ibid)*.
1683-4, Feb. 10 (? 1683, Dec. 10). WILLIAM INWOOD, of Cobham, Surrey, sheriff of Surrey *(ibid)*.
1683-4, Feb. 19 (? 1683, Dec. 19). EDWARD HERBERT, of the Middle Temple, chief justice of Chester *(ibid)*.
1683-4, Feb. 24. RICHARD DIXON (in Ireland by the earl of Arran, lord deputy).
1684, Apr. 6. RICHARD CARNEY, Ulster king-of-arms (under the canopy in the Presence Chamber, Dublin Castle, by same).
1684, Apr. 13. WILLIAM BOWES, of Streatham, Northumberland (at Windsor Castle by the King).
1684, Apr. 13. PETER DANIEL, sheriff of London *(ibid)*.
1684, Apr. 13. SAMUEL HUSBANDS, of Shalford, Essex *(ibid)*.
1684, Apr. 23. ELIAS BEST, lord mayor of Dublin (in Christ Church at the foot of the stairs by the earl of Arran, lord deputy).
1684, Apr. 29. HERBERT WHALEY, of Broyle, Surrey (at Windsor Castle by the King).

1684, May 20. THOMAS TRAVELL, of Jermyn Street, Westminster (at Windsor Castle).
1684, June 15. RICHARD SHUTTLEWORTH, of Forcett, Yorks. (at Windsor Castle).
1684, June 22. RICHARD ATHERTON, of Busey (Bushby), Co. Leicester. *(ibid)*.
1684, June 30. SIMON TAYLOUR, of Lynn Regis, Norfolk *(ibid)*.
1684, June 30. JOHN TURNER, of Lynn Regis, Norfolk *(ibid)*.
1684, July 13. ROBERT CLARKE (CLERKE), junr., of Twickenham, of Long Buckby, Co. Northampton. *(ibid)*.
1684, July 30. SAMUEL DASHWOOD, sheriff of London *(ibid)*.
1684, Sept. 26. WILLIAM GOSLYN (GOSLING), sheriff of London (at Whitehall).
1684, Sept. 26. PETER VANDEPUT (VANDERPUTT), sheriff of London *(ibid)*.
1684, Nov. 13. ABELL RAM, lord mayor of Dublin (in the Tolsell, Dublin, by the duke of Ormonde, lord lieutenant).
1684, Nov. 14. HENRY BEDINGFIELD, a serjeant-at-law (at Whitehall by the King).
1684, Nov. 14. EDWARD LUTWICHE, a serjeant-at-law *(ibid)*.
1684, Nov. 21. WILLIAM TRUMBULL, of Doctor's Commons, D.C.L. *(ibid)*.
1684, Nov. 26. WILLIAM DUTTON COLT *(ibid)*.
1684, Dec. 1. JOHN CLERKE, of Twickenham *(ibid)*.
1684, Dec. 15. EDMUND WORCUP (WARCOP), of Northmere, Co. Oxon. *(ibid)*.
1684–5, Jan. 1. WILLIAM CREAGH, of Newcastle-upon-Tyne *(ibid)*.
1684–5, Jan. 7. WILLIAM DOMVILL (in Dublin Castle by the duke of Ormonde, lord lieutenant).
1684–5, Jan. 24. JOHN FLOYER, of Lichfield, doctor of physic (at Whitehall by the King).
? 1684–5, Jan. 24. RICHARD RAINSFORD, de Dallington.
? 1684–5, Jan. 24. JOHN YOUNGE, de Escot, of Great Mitton, Oxfordshire.
? 1684–5, Jan. 24. JOHN BOOTHE, de Woodford, near Over.
? 1684–5, Jan. 24. JOHN STRATFORD, de Nuneaton.
1684–5, Feb. 14. PETER RICH, of Southwark, alderman of London *(ibid)*.
1684–5, Feb. 13 (? 18). WILLIAM WALKER, mayor of Oxford *(ibid)*.
1684–5, Feb. 25. EDWARD FREWEN, of Northiam, Sussex *(ibid)*.
1684–5, Feb. 25. ROBERT WYMONDESOLD, of Putney, Surrey *(ibid)*.
1684–5, Mar. 8. THOMAS VERNON, of London, Turkey merchant *(ibid)*.
1684–5, Mar. 8. WILLIAM HEYMAN, mayor of Bristol *(ibid)*.
1684–5, Mar. 13. WILLIAM DRAKE, of Ashe, Devon. *(ibid)*.
1684–5, Mar. 13 or 18. HENRY JOHNSON, shipbuilder, of Blackwall.
1684–5, Mar. 17. JOHN SOUTHCOTT, of   , Co. Devon. *(ibid)*.

KNIGHTS BACHELORS 261

1684–5, Mar. 19. EDWARD DES BOUVERIE, of London, merchant (on board a ship).
1684–5, Mar. 20. MATHIAS VINCENT, of London, merchant (at Whitehall).
1684–5, Mar. 20 (? Feb. 20). WILLIAM WREN, of Wilberton, Isle of Ely *(ibid)*.
1684–5, Mar. 22. MARMADUKE DAYRELL, of Castle Camps, Co. Camb. *(ibid)*.
1685, Apr. 1. RICHARD VARNEY, of Compton, Warwick. *(ibid)*.
1685, May 20. JOHN LEIGH, of Addington, Surrey *(ibid)*.
1685, June 5. HENRY SELBY, a serjeant-at-law *(ibid)*.
1685, before July. JOHN KID (by the duke of Monmouth during his rebellion, near Taunton).
1685, July 9. JOHN COTTON, of Bottreaux Castle *(ibid)*.
1685, July 9. ROWLAND LACY, of Pudlicott, Oxon. *(ibid)*.
1685, July 11 (? 1684, July 11). SEBASTIAN SMYTH, of Cuddesden, Oxon. *(ibid)*.
1685, July (? 20). HENRY SHERE, surveyor of the Ordnance, commanded the Artillery against the Monmouth rebellion.
1685, Aug. 3. JOHN FRIEND, a brewer in the Minories (at Whitehall).
1685, Aug. (Oct.) 23. BENJAMIN THOROWGOOD, of Cornhill, linen draper, of London (at Windsor Castle).
1685, Aug. 23. THOMAS KINSEY, sheriff of London, vintner, kept the Crown Tavern in Bloomsbury (at Windsor).
1685, Sept. 7. GEORGE STROUDE [*see* under date 1676, May 17].
1685, Oct. 8. PAUL RICOTT (RICAUT), of London, chief secretary to the lord lieutenant of Ireland (at Whitehall).
1685, Dec. 12 (13). ROBERT NIGHTINGALE, sheriff of Norfolk *(ibid)*.
1685–6, Jan. 25 (? Feb. 28). CHARLES PORTER, of the Middle Temple *(ibid)*.
1685–6, Feb. 2. EDWARD (EDMUND) KING, M.D., of Hatton Garden, physician-in-ordinary to the late King (*ibid* in the King's bedchamber).
1685–6, Feb. 6. JOHN FLEMING (in Dublin Castle by the earl of Clarendon, lord lieutenant).
1685–6, Feb. 6. JOHN KNOX, lord mayor of Dublin (Christ Church at the foot of the stairs by same).
1685–6, Feb. 9. JOHN HOLT, of Gray's Inn, recorder of London (at Whitehall by the King).
1685–6, Feb. 23. JOHN BUCKNELL (BUCKNALL), of London, merchant, and of Oxlie, Herts. *(ibid)*.
1685–6, Mar. 20. MARTIN BECKMAN, major, of the Tower of London, his Majesty's chief engineer *(ibid)*.
1686, Apr. 11. AMBROSE PHILLIPS, serjeant-at-law *(ibid)*.

1686, Apr. 23. MICHAEL CREAGH (in Dublin Castle by the earl of Clarendon, lord lieutenant).
1686, Apr. 25. CHRISTOPHER MILTON, a baron of the Exchequer (at Whitehall by the King).
1686, Apr. 25. JOHN POWELL, of Broadway, Carmarthen, a justice of the Common Pleas *(ibid)*.
1686, Apr. 25. THOMAS POWYS, solicitor-general *(ibid)*.
1686, Apr. 26. WILLIAM TURNOR, of Barton, Co. Lincoln. *(ibid)*.
1686, May 13. JOHN LYTCOTT *(ibid)*.
1686, May 25. THOMAS MANBY, of Bawds Farm, South Weald, Essex *(ibid)*.
1686, May 28. BEVILLE GRANVILLE, captain (at the head of the earl of Bath's (his uncle) regiment, at the camp on Hounslow Heath).
1686, June 5. JOHN COGHILL, master of Chancery (in Dublin by the earl of Clarendon, lord lieutenant).
1686, July 4. THOMAS PINFOLD, of Doctors Commons, D.C.L. (at Windsor Castle by the King).
1686, July 11. THOMAS JEFFREYS, of Alicante, Spain *(ibid)*.
1686, Aug. 6. THOMAS RAWLINSON, sheriff of London (at Windsor).
1686, Aug. 22. THOMAS MONTGOMERY, of the Middle Temple *(ibid)*.
1686, Aug. 26 or 26. GEORGE WILLOUGHBY, of Bishopstone, Wilts. (at Marlborough).
1686, Aug. 27. CHARLES WINTER (WINTON), of Lydney, Co. Gloucester., high sheriff of Gloucester. (at Bristol).
1686, Aug. 27. WILLIAM MERRICK, sheriff of Bristol *(ibid)*.
1686, Aug. 27. EDMUND THOMAS, of Glamorganshire *(ibid)*.
1686, Sept. 26. THOMAS FOWLE, of London, goldsmith, an alderman and sheriff of London (at Windsor Castle).
1686, Oct. 22. RICHARD ALLIBOND (ALLEBONE, ALIBON), of Gray's Inn, a King's council-at-law.
1686, Oct. 22. RICHARD HEATH, of Hatsland, Surrey, a baron of the Exchequer (at Whitehall).
1686, Nov. 29. RICHARD NEALE, of Plessy, Co. Northumberland, high Sheriff of the county of Northumberland *(ibid)*.
1686, Dec. 1. EDMUND GARDNER (GARDINER), deputy recorder of Bedford (in His Majesty's Bedchamber, *ibid*).
1686, Dec. 13 (? 18). RICHARD REYNES (RAINES), Dr. of Doctors Commons, a judge of the Admiralty and Prerogative Courts *(ibid)*.
1686-7, Jan. 1. FRANCISCUS KNUYDYT, of Rotterdam *(ibid)*.
1686-7, Jan. 1. JOHN CASTLETON, lord mayor of Dublin (in Christ Church by the lord lieutenant).

KNIGHTS BACHELORS 263

1686–7, Jan. 14. JAMES TILLEY (TILLIE), of Pillaton Castle, Co. Cornwall (at Whitehall by the King).

1686–7, Feb. 18. CHARLES COTTERELL (COTTRELL), junr., master of the Ceremonies *(ibid)*.

1686–7, Feb. 20. RICHARD NAGLE, attorney general, Ireland (in the earl of Limerick's house by the earl of Tyrconnel, lord lieutenant).

1687, May 1. THOMAS POWELL, of Lleckwedd Derris, Co. Cardigan, a baron of the Exchequer (at Whitehall by the King).

1687, May 12. JOHN TATE, recorder of London *(ibid)*.

1687, May 13. GRIFFITH JEFFREYS, of Acton, Co. Denbigh *(ibid)*.

1687, May 14. BARTHOLOMEW SHOWER (SHORE), deputy recorder of London *(ibid)*.

1687, May 28. EDWARD VAUDRY (VAUDREY), of Whitehall (at Windsor Castle).

1687, June 19. PETER PALLAVICINI (PALAVICINE or PARAVICINI), of London, merchant *(ibid)*.

1687, June 28. WILLIAM PHIPPS, captain, governor of Massachusetts Bay; for good services in a late expedition, bringing considerable treasure home that had lain in the sea 44 years *(ibid)*.

1687, July 3. JOHN SPARROWE, clerk-comptroller of the Honourable His Majesty's Board of Green Cloth (at Windsor).

1687, Aug. 2. BASIL FIREBRACE, sheriff-elect of London (at Windsor Castle).

1687, Aug. 15. RICHARD HAWKINS, scrivener in the Old Bailey *(ibid)*.

1687, Aug. 15. JOHN PARSONS, sheriff-elect of London, a brewer in St. Katherine's *(ibid)*.

1687, Aug. 15. JOHN EYLES, merchant, of London *(ibid)*.

1687, Aug. 21. STEPHEN RICE, lord chief baron of the Exchequer, Ireland (in the Castle of Dublin by the earl of Tyrconnel, lord lieutenant).

1687, Oct. 25. CHARLES CARTERET (at Whitehall by the King).

1687, Oct. 31 (? Aug.). JOHN BAUDING, alderman of London *(ibid)*.

1687, Oct. 31 (? Aug.). WILLIAM ASHURST, alderman of London *(ibid)*.

1687, Oct. 30. THOMAS HACKETT, lord mayor of Dublin (in the Castle of Dublin under the canopy in the Presence Chamber, by the earl of Tyrconnel, lord lieutenant).

1687, Nov. 1. JOHN BARNEWALL, recorder of Dublin (at the lord mayor's house by same).

1687, Nov. 17. HENRY DERING, a commissioner of wine licences (at Whitehall by the King).
1687, Nov. 18. HUMPHRY EDWYN, of London, merchant *(ibid)*.
1687, Dec. 11. WILLIAM WILLIAMS, of Anglesea, and Gray's Inn, solicitor general *(ibid)*.
1687–8, Mar. 6. WILLIAM HEDGES (*alias* Lacy), of London, merchant *(ibid)*.
1688, Mar. 13. ANTHONY MULLEDY, of Robertstown (in the Castle of Dublin, by the earl of Tyrconnel, lord lieutenant).
1688, June 10. WILLIAM WALDEGRAVE, Her Majesty's physician (by the King at Her Majesty's bedside soon after her delivery).
1688, June 15. MATHEW BRIDGES, who brought news to Ireland of the Prince's birth (in Dublin Castle by the earl of Tyrconnel, lord lieutenant, "but went immediately after for England without paying any fees at all").
1688, June 28. THOMAS GIFFORD (JEFFORD), mayor of Exeter (at Whitehall by the King).
1688, July 13 (? 16 or 19). JOHN ROTHERHAM, baron of the Exchequer *(ibid)*.
1688, July 13 (? 30). CHARLES INGLEBY, a baron of the Exchequer
1688, July 14. THOMAS ELMES, of Lilford, Co. Northampton. (at Whitehall).
1688, July 30. THOMAS LANE, of St. Laurence Lane, in Cheapside.
1688, Aug. 12. SAMUEL GERARD (in His Majesty's bedchamber).
1688, before Oct. 6. S. THOMSON, sheriff of London.
1688, Oct. between 11 and 13. JOHN FLEET, a cooper or a sugar baker, sheriff of London (at Whitehall).
1688. WILLIAM ELLIS (dubbed in Ireland by the earl of Tyrconnel, lord lieutenant).
1688, FRANCIS WHEELER, admiral.
1688–9, Mar. 5. ANTHONY KECK, a commissioner of the Great Seal (at Whitehall by the King).
1688–9, Mar. 5. WILLIAM RAWLINSON, serjeant-at-law, a commissioner of the Great Seal *(ibid)*.
1688–9, Mar. 5. HENRY POLLEXFEN, attorney general *(ibid)*.
1688–9, Mar. 12. CHARLES SEDLEY, natural son of Sir Charles Sedley, of South Fleet, in Kent, bart. *(ibid)*.
1689, Apr. 10. THOMAS PILKINGTON, lord mayor of London (at Whitehall by the King).
1689, Apr. 10. WILLIAM WHITLOCK, of the Middle Temple *(ibid)*.
1689, Apr. 12. ROBERT HARRISON, mayor of Oxford *(ibid)*.
1689, May 16. JOHN ASHBY, captain of the "Defiance" (at Portsmouth on the Admiral's ship).
1689, May 16. CLOUDESLEY SHOVELL, captain of the "Edgar" *(ibid)*.
1689, June 4. CHARLES HEDGES, LL.D., of Doctors Commons, and of Wanborough, Wilts., and Richmond, Surrey, judge of the Admiralty.

KNIGHTS BACHELORS 265

1689, June 4. EDWARD MOSELEY (MOSLEY), of Hulme, Lancs. (at Whitehall).

1689, after July. THEOBALD BUTLER, solicitor general, Ireland (in Ireland by king James II., who landed at Kinsale, Mar. 12).

1689, (? Aug. 20). JAMES FORBES, clerk of the Green Cloth (at Hampton Court).

1689, (? Aug. 20). WILLIAM FORESTER, of Watling Street, clerk of the Green Cloth *(ibid)*.

1689, Aug. 27. FRANCIS BLAKE, of Ford Castle, Co. Northumberland *(ibid,* in His Majesty's bedchamber).

1689, Aug. 27. CHARLES O'HARA, of St. Martin's in the Fields.

1689, Oct. 24. RALPH BOX, of London, druggist, citizen, and mercer, chief warden of the grocers' company (at Whitehall).

1689, Oct. 29. CHRISTOPHER LETHEUILLIER, merchant, sheriff of London *(ibid)*.

1689, Oct. 29. JOHN HOUBLON, merchant, sheriff of London *(ibid)*.

1689, Oct. 29. EDWARD CLARK, alderman of London *(ibid)*.

1689, Oct. 29. FRANCIS CHILD, of London, goldsmith *(ibid)*.

1689, Oct. 31. NICHOLAS LECHMERE, a baron of the Exchequer *(ibid)*.

1689, Oct. 31. THOMAS ROKEBY, judge of the Common Pleas *(ibid)*.

1689, Oct. 31. GILES EYRE, judge of the King's Bench *(ibid)*.

1689, Oct. 31. PEYTON VENTRIS, judge of the Common Pleas *(ibid)*.

1689, Oct. 31. JOHN TURTON, a baron of the Exchequer *(ibid)*.

1689, Oct. 31. GEORGE HUTCHINS, a serjeant-at-law *(ibid)*.

1689, Oct. 31. WILLIAM WOGAN (WOGHAM), a serjeant-at-law *(ibid)*.

1689, Oct. 31. JOHN TREMAIN,, a serjeant-at-law *(ibid)*.

1689, Oct. 31. WILLIAM THOMPSON, a serjeant-at-law *(ibid)*.

1689, Oct. 31. JOHN TRENCHARD, a serjeant-at-law, *(ibid)*.

1689, Oct. 31. JOHN SOMERS, solicitor-general *(ibid)*.

1689, Dec. 1 (? Nov. 25 or 26). JAMES DE SANTIAGO DEL CASTELLO (CASTILLO), a Spaniard, commissary general from the king of Spain to reside at Jamaica *(ibid)*.

1689, Dec. 14. WILLIAM CRANMER, of London, merchant *(ibid)*.

1689, Dec. 23. THOMAS MILLER, of Chichester *(ibid)*.

1690, Apr. 10. PURY CUST, of Stamford *(ibid)*.

1690, Apr. 17. WILLIAM HUSSEY, of London, merchant, deputy governor of the Turkey Company, ambassador at the Ottoman Port of Constantinople *(ibid)*.

1690, May 14. TERENCE MCDERMOT, lord mayor, Dublin (in Ireland by James II.).
1690, May 17. TEIGUE O'REGAN (*ibid* by same).
? 1690. DANIEL ARTHUR (? by same).
? 1690. JAMES MOCLER (? by same).
? 1690. GEORGE ST. LEGER (? by same).*
? 1690. JOHN KIRWAN (? by same).
1690, May 31. RALPH DELAVALL, admiral (by the King, confirmed 1690, June 31).
1690, June 11. WILLIAM GLEGG (at his own house, Gayton, Cheshire, the King having lain there the night before embarking for Ireland).
1690, July 1. ROBERT ADAIR (by William III. at the battle of the Boyne).
1690, Sept. 15. JOSEPH HERNE, of London, merchant, governor of the East India Company (at Kensington).
1690, Sept. 15. THOMAS COOK, of London, goldsmith, deputy governor of East India Company *(ibid)*.
1690, Sept. 15. JOHN DUDDLESTON, of Bristol, merchant (at Bristol).
1690, Oct. 9. GEORGE MEGGOTT, of Horseleydown, Co. Surrey, brewer, high sheriff of Surrey (at Kensington).
1690, Oct. 14. STEPHEN EVANCE, of London, goldsmith *(ibid)*.
1691, Aug. (? Apr.) 30. ABSTRUPUS DANBY, of Masham, Yorks. (at Kensington).
1691, Oct. 18 (new style). HENRY FOURNES (FURNACE), of London, merchant (at the Hague, on Sunday, in the king's bedchamber, for carrying the news of the defeat of the Irish at Limerick).
1691, Oct. 22. RICHARD LEVET, sheriff of London (at Kensington).
1691, Nov. 4. JOHN POWELL, a baron of the Exchequer (at Whitehall).

---

* By the courtesy of the Marquis de Ruvigny I am permitted to reprint here (from his "Jacobite Peerage," pp. 191-2) the following list of knights dubbed by the Stuarts in exile.
1705, before April 16. Toby Bourke, afterwards first Baron Bourke.
1707, before March 21. Timon Connock.
1709, June 15. James Sarsfield of Nantes.
1710, before Nov. 12. Captain George Colgrave.
1713, before Sept. 13. Thomas Higgons.
1714, before Dec. 9. John Forrester, afterwards first Baronet.
1715, Dec. 29. Patrick Bannerman, Provost of Aberdeen.
1716, Jan. (?). Henry Crawford, Portioner of Crail, Fifeshire.
1717, Jan. (?). John Walkinshaw of Burrowfield, Lannockshire.
1717, Jan. (?). George Jerningham.
1717, before Dec. 20. Peter Redmond, afterwards first Baron Redmond.
1719, June . Richard Gaydon, Knight of St. Louis, major in Dillon's regiment.
1719, June . John Missett, captain in Dillon's regiment.
1719, June . Edward O'Toole, Ensign in Dillon's regiment.
1722, before July 6. Luke O'Toole.
1728, before June 28. John Hely, afterwards first Baronet.
1734, before Jan. 22. Mark Forstal, afterwards first Baronet.
1747, before April 17. John William O'Sullivan, afterwards first Baronet.

KNIGHTS BACHELORS

1691, Nov. 14 (? Dec.). RICHARD HARRIS, recorder of Winchester (at Kensington).
1691–2, Feb. 8. JOHN GOLDSBOROUGH, commissary general to the East India Company *(ibid)*.
1691–2, Mar. 3. GODFREY KNELLER, principal painter in ordinary to His Majesty *(ibid)*
1692, Sept. 5. MICHAEL MITCHELL, lord mayor of Dublin (in Ireland by viscount Sidney, lord lieutenant).
1692, Sept. 23. RICHARD LEVINGE, solicitor general, Ireland *(ibid by same)*.
1692, Oct. 21. THOMAS TREVOR, solicitor general (at Kensington by the King).
1692, Oct. 21. SALATHIEL LOVEL, serjeant-at-law, recorder of London *(ibid)*.
1692, Oct. 29. JOHN WYLDMAN, alderman of London (at the Guildhall).
1692, Oct. 29. WILLIAM GORE, alderman of London *(ibid)*.
1692, Oct. 29. JAMES HOUBLON, alderman of London *(ibid)*.
1692, Oct. 29. LEONARD ROBINSON, chamberlain of London *(ibid)*.
1692, Oct. 29. ROWLAND AINSWORTH, of London, Turkey merchant, of Basinghall Street, London *(ibid)*.
1692, Oct. 29. WILLIAM SCAWEN, of London, merchant *(ibid)*.
1692, Oct. 29. JOSIAH CHILD (eldest son of Sir Josiah Child, bart.)
1692, Oct. 29. JOHN FOCHE, of London, scrivener *(ibid)*.
1692, Oct. 30. WILLIAM BEESTON, colonel, lieutenant governor and commander-in-chief of Jamaica (kissed hands on going) (at Whitehall, ? at Kensington).
? before 1692, Nov. SAMUEL THOMPSON, sheriff of Bedford.
1692, Nov. 5. RICHARD PYNE, lord chief justice of the Common Pleas in Ireland (at Dublin in the presence chamber by viscount Sidney, lord lieutenant).
1692, Nov. 5. JOHN HELY, lord chief baron of the Exchequer, Ireland *(ibid by same)*.
1692, Nov. 5. RICHARD COX, justice of Common Pleas, Ireland *(ibid by same)*.
1692, Nov. 5. JOHN LYNDON, justice of the Chief Place, Ireland *(ibid by same)*.
1692, Nov. 5. HENRY ECHLIN, justice of the Chief Place, Ireland *(ibid by same)*.
1692, Nov. 5. JOHN JEFFREYSON, justice of Common Pleas, Ireland *(ibid by same)*.
1692, Dec. 4. LITTLETON POWYS (at Whitehall by the King).

1692–3, Jan. 22. EDWIN STEDE (STEED), of Stede Hill, Kent, late governor of Barbados (at Whitehall).

1692–3, Jan. 26. CHRISTOPHER GREENFIELD, *alias* GRENVILE (GREENVILLE), of Preston, Lancs., chamberlain of Chester *(ibid)*.

1692–3, Feb. 20. GEORGE ROOKE, admiral (at Portsmouth).

1692–3, Feb. 24. THOMAS WAGSTAFF, of Tachbrook, Warwick (at Kensington).

1692–3, Mar. 18. JOHN GAYER, of London *(ibid)*.

1693, Mar. 26. ISAAC REBOW (REBOES, RELOE), of Colchester, merchant (at Harwich).

1693, May 12. THOMAS PAKENHAM (PACKENHAM), prime serjeant-at-law (in Ireland by viscount Sidney, lord lieutenant).

1693, June 12. JOHN ROGERSON, lord mayor elect of Dublin *(ibid by same)*.

1693, Oct. 30. EDWARD WARD, attorney general (at Kensington by the King).

1693, Nov. 2. THOMAS ABNEY, sheriff of London (at Whitehall).

1693, Nov. 24. CHARLES LLOYD, of Maesyfelin, Cardigan. (at Kensington).

1693, Dec. 2. JOHN BUCKWORTH, of London (at Sir Henry Furnes' house at Petersham, Surrey).

1693–4, Feb. 22. SAMUEL EYRE (EYRES), a serjeant-at-law (in the bedchamber, Whitehall, on his appointment as a judge of King's Bench).

1693–4, Feb. 22. HENRY GOULD (GOOLD, GOLD), serjeant-at-law, appointed a King's serjeant (at Whitehall).

1694, Mar. 28. HENRY TITCHBOURNE (in Ireland by the lords justices).

1694, Apr. 22. FLEETWOOD SHEPPARD, gentleman usher of the Black Rod (at Whitehall by the King).

1694, Nov. 12. JOHN SWEETAPPLE, of London, goldsmith, sheriff of London *(ibid)*.

1694, Nov. 12. WILLIAM COLE (COLES), sheriff of London *(ibid)*.

1694, Nov. 28. THOMAS DAY, mayor of Bristol (at Kensington).

1694, Nov. 28. WILLIAM DANES, sheriff of Bristol *(ibid)*.

1694–5, Feb. 14. ISAAC PRESTON, of Beeston, Norfolk, and of Lincoln's Inn (at Whitehall).

1695, Oct. 14. EDWARD WILLS (WILES), sheriff of London (at Kensington).

1695, Oct. 14. OWEN BUCKINGHAM, sheriff of London (congratulating the King on his safe return and success) *(ibid)*.

1695, Oct. 23 (Wednesday). JOHN COMBES, of Daventry, Northampton, chief justice of Chester.

KNIGHTS BACHELORS 269

1695, Nov. 2. GILBERT METCALFE, mayor of York (knighted at the duke of Newcastle's house at Welbeck, Co. Notts., where the King lay in his progress).

1695, Nov. 28 (? 21). RICHARD HOLFORD, a master in Chancery.

1695, Nov. 28. JOHN HAWLES (HAWLIS), of Lincoln's Inn, and of Salisbury, Wilts., solicitor general.

1695–6, Jan. 26 (? 1695, Nov. 28). JOHN COPE, of Kensington (at Kensington).

1695–6, Feb. 6. WILLOUGHBY CHAMBERLAYNE, colonel, of Barbados and Chelsea *(ibid)*.

1695–6, Mar. 22. HENRY PEACHEY, of Sussex *(ibid)*.

1695–6, Mar. 22. CHARLES TURNOR (TURNER), of Wareham, Norfolk, M.P. for Lynn Regis (at Kensington at the delivery of the Association for Norfolk).

1695–6, Mar. 24 (? 1695, Nov. 28). EDWARD SEAWARD (SEYWARD), of Exeter (at Kensington).

1695–6, Mar. 24. JOSEPH TYLEY, of Exeter, and of Bromley, Co. Middlesex *(ibid)*.

1696, Mar. 29. ALEXANDER RIGBY *(ibid;* on delivery of the Association of the mayor and corporation of Wigan, Lancs.).

1696, Apr. 12 (? 1695, Nov. 28). WILLIAM MYLORD (MILLARD), of Houghton Regis, Co. Bedford., sheriff of Beds. (on presentation of the Address from the Association of Co. Bedford.).

1696, Apr. 20 (22). CHARLES MORLEY, of Droxford, Hants. (in the bedchamber at Kensington on the presentation of the Association for Co. Wilts.).

1696, Apr. 27. GEORGE HANGER, of Driffield, Co. Gloucester., high sheriff of Gloucester. (at Kensington).

1696, Apr. 28. JOHN ELWILL, of Exeter *(ibid)*.

1696, Apr. 30. JOSEPH SMART, draper, alderman of London (at Kensington).

1696, May 1. (Signor) LORENZO SORENZO (SORANZO), the eldest of the ambassadors from the Republic of Venice (at Kensington at his audience of leave and had the sword wherewith the King knighted him, as the ambassadors claimed).

1696, May 1. DEWEY BULKELEY, of Nether Burgate (at Kensington).

1696, May 1. THEODORE JANSSEN, of London, merchant *(ibid)*.

1696, May 1. JOHN ROBINSON, of Sudbury, Suffolk *(ibid* on the delivery of the Association).

1696, Oct. 8 (7). JOHN JOHNSON, goldsmith in Cheapside, alderman of London *(ibid)*.

1696, Oct. 8. JOHN WOLFE (WOOLFE), sheriff of London *(ibid)*.

1696, Oct. 8. SAMUEL BLEWET, sheriff of London *(ibid)*.

? 1696–7, Jan. 5. NATHAN WRIGHT, serjeant-at-law, recorder of Leicester (at Kensington).

1696–7, Jan. 29. PATRICK DUN (DUNN), president of the King's and Queen's College of Physicians (in Ireland by the lords justices).

1696–7, Mar. 9. THOMAS MAY, of Rawmore, near Chichester (at Kensington by the King).

1696–7, Mar. 18. RICHARD BLACKMORE, M.D., physician-in-ordinary to His Majesty *(ibid* in the bedchamber).

1696–7, Mar. 24. JOSEPH TRILBY, of Bow, Middlesex.

1697, Apr. 16. CHARLES ISAAC, an officer of the Green Cloth (at Kensington).

1697, Apr. 23. ROBERT MURRAY, of Scotland *(ibid)*.

1697, Apr. 23. BARRINGTON BOUCHIER, of Beningborough, Yorks. *(ibid)*.

1697, Apr. 23. LAMBERT BLACKWELL, shortly afterwards knight harbinger and envoy to Genoa *(ibid)*.

1697, June 17. WILLIAM BILLINGTON, lord mayor of Dublin (in Ireland by the marquess of Winchester, the earl of Galway and viscount Villiers, lords justices of Ireland).

1697, Nov. (Oct.) 17. BARTHOLOMEW GRACEDIEU, of London, salter, sheriff of London (in the bedchamber at Kensington by the King).

1697, Nov. 17. JAMES COLLETT, sheriff of London *(ibid)*.

1697, Nov. 18. THOMAS CUDDON (CUDDEN) chamberlain of London (at Kensington).

1697, Nov. 18. ROBERT BEDINGFIELD, woollen draper, alderman of London *(ibid)*.

1697, Dec. 12. JOHN BLINCOW, justice of Common Pleas (in the bedchamber at Kensington).

1697, Dec. 12. HENRY HATSELL, a baron of the Exchequer (at Kensington).

1697, Dec. 12. WILLIAM SIMPSON, cursitor baron of the Exchequer *(ibid)*.

1697, Dec. 12. JOSEPH JEKYLL, chief justice of Chester *(ibid)*.

1697–8, Feb. 26. JOHN JERMAYNE (created a baronet immediately after *(ibid)*.

1698, July 20. JOHN MASON, mayor of Waterford (at Waterford by the marquess of Winchester, the earl of Galway and viscount Villiers, lords justices of Ireland).

KNIGHTS BACHELORS

1698, Dec. 5. DAVID MITCHELL, an admiral and usher of the Black Rod (at Kensington by the King).

1698, Dec. 6 or 7. JACOB BANKS, a Swede by birth, of Milton Abbas, captain of the "Russell" man-of-war *(ibid)*.

1698, Dec. 14. STREYNSHAM MASTER, of London, merchant, a director of the New East India Company (in the drawing room at Kensington).

1698, Dec. 14. JAMES BATEMAN, of London, merchant, a director of the New East India Company *(ibid)*.

1698, Dec. 14. EDMUND HARRISON, of London, merchant, a director of the New East India Company *(ibid)*.

1698-9, Jan. 15. EDWARD LITTLETON, of London, merchant, president of Bengal for the New East India Company (at Kensington).

1698-9, Feb. 8. WILLIAM PHIPARD, of Poole, Dorset. *(ibid)*.

1699, Apr. 2. NICHOLAS WAITE, of London, merchant *(ibid)*.

1699, May 15. EDWARD HASEL, of Dalmaine, Co. Cumberland *(ibid)*.

1699, May 31. JONATHAN ANDREWS, of London, an East India merchant *(ibid)*.

1699, June 1. JOHN DARNELL, of the Inner Temple, serjeant-at-law *(ibid)*.

1699, Oct. 20. CHARLES DUNCOMBE, sheriff of London (in the bedchamber at Kensington).

1699, Oct. 20. JEFFRY JEFFERIES, sheriff of London *(ibid)*.

1699, Oct. 20. WILLIAM WITHERS, linen draper in Cheapside (at Kensington).

1699, Nov. 12. GEORGE GOURDON, tutor to the marquess of Huntley *(ibid)*.

1699, Dec. 17. CHARLES EYRE, of London, president of the Old East India Company at Bengal, on his appointment to be governor of Fort William *(ibid)*.

1699, Dec. 30. ANDREW FOUNTAINE, of Narford, Norfolk (at Hampton Court).

1699-1700, Jan. 6. ANTHONY PERCY, lord mayor of Dublin (under the canopy in the Great Dining Room of the Castle, by the lords justices of Ireland).

1699-1700, Jan. 6. WILLIAM HANDCOCK, recorder of Dublin *(ibid)*.

1699-1700, Jan. 9. ROGER JENNYNS (JENYNS), of Ely, Co. Cams. (at Kensington).

1699-1700, Feb. 1 (? 1699, Apr. 2). RICHARD WALTER *(ibid)*.

1699-1700, Feb. 21. THEODORE COLLYDON, a walloon physician to Chelsea Hospital *(ibid)*.

1700, June 23. SOLOMON DE MEDINA, of London and Middlesex, a Jew (at Hampton Court).

? 1700, June 23. GAUDENTIUS DE CAPELL (CAPOL).

1700, Oct. 24. ROBERT BEACHCROFT, sheriff of London *(ibid)*.

1700, Dec. 23. PHILIP MEDOWES, knight marshal of the Household *(ibid)*.

1700, Dec. 26. JOHN MEERES (MERES), one of the clerks in Chancery, eldest son of Sir Thomas Meres (at Kensington).

1700–1, Jan. 21. NICHOLAS VANAKER, of London, merchant (presently after made a baronet) *(ibid)*.

1700–1, Feb. 6. EDWARD LAURENCE, collector of Customs at Shoreham, Sussex, usher of His Majesty's chamber *(ibid)*.

1700–1, Feb. 16. THOMAS BURY, a baron of the Exchequer *(ibid)*.

1701, before Apr. MARK RANSFORD, lord mayor of Dublin (in Dublin by the lords justices).

1701, May 21 (? 30). JOHN COOKE, king's advocate (at Kensington).

1701, June 18. JOHN ST. LEGER, of Ireland (brother of the first viscount Doneraile *(ibid)*.

1701, June (? July) 18. ROBERT SUTTON, late resident at Vienna, ambassador to Turkey *(ibid)*.

1701, June 27. BENJAMIN POOLE (POULE), of Amsterdam, merchant (in the bedchamber at Hampton Court, for good services done abroad).

1701, June 29. PETER FLOYER, refiner and goldsmith, sheriff elect of London (at Hampton Court).

1701, July 1. JOHN MUNDEN, of Chelsea, admiral (on board the "William and Mary" yacht).

1701, Nov. STAFFORD FAIRBORNE, rear admiral (on board his own ship when he brought king William over from Ireland).

1701, Nov. ROBERT CONSTABLE, sheriff of Yorkshire (at Hampton Court).

1702, Apr. (? 1701–2, Mar. 14). JOHN LEIGH, of Addington, Surrey (at St. James's).

1702, Apr. 24. WILLIAM CLAXTON (CLACKSON), mayor of Oxford *(ibid* the day after the coronation? or the coronation day itself, Apr. 23).

1702, June 1. EDWARD NORTHEY, attorney-general (at St. James's).

1702, June 1. SIMON HARCOURT, solicitor general *(ibid)*.

1702 (? 1701), June 19. WILLIAM ROBINSON, of Dublin, receiver general [of Ireland] (at St. James's).

1702, July 3. THOMAS WINFORD, of Glashampton, Worcestershire, second prothonotary in the Court of Common Pleas.

1702, Aug. 27. SAMUEL ECKLEY (ECCLYE), sheriff of Gloucester. (at Mr. Master's house in Cirencester, Co. Gloucester.).

1702, Sept. 3. JOHN HAWKINS, mayor of Bristol (at Sir Thomas Day's house in Bristol).

1702, Oct. 31. THOMAS HARDY, captain, R.N. (at Windsor for bringing the news of the burning of the French fleet in Vigo Bay).

1702, Oct. 29. JAMES EYTON, of London, merchant, a linen draper in Cheapside (at the Guildhall on the Queen's driving there on lord mayor's day).

1702, Oct. 29. GILBERT HEATHCOTE, alderman of London (*ibid* on the same occasion).

1702, Oct. 29. FRANCIS DASHWOOD, of London, and of Wanstead, Essex, silk merchant, brother to the lord mayor (*ibid* on the same occasion).

1702, Oct. 29. RICHARD HOARE, of London, alderman, goldsmith (*ibid* on the same occasion).

1702, Nov. 29. THOMAS HOBSON (at St. James's for his good service at Vigo in breaking the boom).

1702–3, before Feb. 9 [or 13]. ANDREW LEAKE (LAKE), captain, R.N. (*ibid* for his service at Vigo).

1702–3, Feb. 9 or 13. THOMAS CRISP, of Dornford or Dransford, Co. Oxford (at St. James's).

1703, Apr. 3. DAVID HAMILTON, one of Her Majesty's physicians-in-ordinary *(ibid)*.

1703, Aug. 1. DALBY THOMAS, of Essex and London, general, and chief director for the Royal Africa Company (at Windsor Castle).

1703, Aug. 30 (? 12). WILLIAM LEWIS (LOUIS), (at the Bath).

1703, Nov. 11. THOMAS DOLEMAN, of Shaw, Berks. (at St. James's, the Queen having dined at his house on her return from the Bath).

1703–4, Feb. 3. JOHN LEAKE, admiral (for his good service in the relief of Gibraltar).

1703–4, Feb. DAVID NEARNE (NAIRN), a Scotchman (at St. James's and constituted recorder of the order of St. Andrew in Scotland).

1703–4, Feb. 6. DANIEL GAHAN (in the Presence Chamber, Dublin Castle, by the duke of Ormonde, lord lieutenant).

1703–4, Mar. 23. WILLIAM MATHEWS, governor of the Leeward Islands (at St. James's).

1704, Apr. 5. CHARLES THOROLD, alderman of London (at St. James's Palace).

1704, Sept. 6. JOSEPH WOLFE (WOOLFE), sheriff of London (at St James's).

1704, Sept. 7. GEORGE MATHEWS, of London, captain of a company of (at St. James's Palace).
1704, Oct. 22. GEORGE BYNG, admiral of the Red (at St. James's, for services against the French in the Mediterranean).
1704, Oct. 22. THOMAS BROMSELL (BROMSALL), of Biggleswade, Beds., justice of the peace (at St. James's Palace, being presented to the Queen by the earl of Kent, the lord chamberlain).
1704, Oct. 24. THOMAS DILKES, rear admiral of the White (*ibid* for services against the French in the Mediterranean).
1704, Oct. 24. JAMES WISHART, captain R.N. (*ibid* for services against the French in the Mediterranean).
1704, Oct. 24. JOHN JENNINGS, commander of H.M.S. " St. George" (*ibid* for the like).
1704, Oct. 26. WILLIAM HUMPHREYS, sheriff of London, an oilman in the Poultry (at St. James's).
1704, Nov. 21 (? 24). WILLIAM JUMPER, of Leeds Abbey, Kent, commander of H.M.S. " Lennox " (at St. James's for many good services performed against the French).
before 1704, Dec. HUMPHREY FOSTER (FORSTER), sheriff of Berks.
? 1704, Dec. EDWARD WHITAKER, captain R.N. (at St. James's Palace for good services done at Gibraltar, in Spain).
1704–5, Feb. 6. FRANCIS STOYTE, lord mayor of Dublin (dubbed in Dublin Castle by the duke of Ormonde, lord lieutenant).
1704–5, Feb. 22. WILLIAM WHETSTONE, rear admiral of the White, and commander-in-chief of the Squadron designed for the West Indies, captain of H.M.S. " Montagu " (at St. James's for great services done at sea).
1705, Apr. 16. JOHN ELLIS, M.D., master of Caius College, commonly called the Divel of Keys or vice-chancellor of Cambridge (at Trinity College on the Queen visiting the University).
1705, Apr. 16. JAMES MONTAGU, queen's counsel, son of George Montagu, sixth son of the earl of Manchester (*ibid* on the same occasion).
1705, Apr. 16. ISAAC NEWTON, president of the Royal Society, master and worker of the Mint (*ibid* on the same occasion).
1705, July 9. CHARLES HOBBY, of New England, merchant (at Windsor Castle for good service done in New England).
1705, July 9. THOMAS PARKER, a serjeant-at-law (at Windsor Castle).
1705, July 27. WILLIAM READ, Her Majesty's oculist in ordinary *(ibid)*.
1705, July 29. EDWARD HANNES, first physician to the Queen *(ibid)*.

KNIGHTS BACHELORS 275

1705, Sept. 6. JOHN GIBSON, a Scotsman, deputy governor of Portsmouth (at Winchester).

1705, Sept. 6. WILLIAM GIFFORD, commissioner of the dock at Portsmouth, and M.P. for Portsmouth *(ibid)*.

1705, Nov. 25. JOHN NORRIS, captain of H.M.S. "Britannia" (at St. James's, being sent express by Sir Clowdisley Shovell to inform the Queen of the taking of Barcelona).

1705, Dec. 18. WILLIAM MILMAN, of the Inner Temple, and of Ormond Street, Red Lion Square (at St. James's).

1705–6, Feb. 22 (? 1705, Dec. 18). SAMUEL STANIER (STANNIER), sheriff of London *(ibid)*.

1706, June 3. GEORGE NEWLAND, of London, and Gatton, Surrey, a scrivener in Smithfield and deputy lieutenant for London (at Windsor Castle, on the presentation of the London address).

1706, June 3. WILLIAM FAZAKERLY, of London, merchant, and of Totteridge, Herts., chamberlain of London, a deputy lieutenant for London (at Windsor Castle on the presentation of the above address).

1706, July 10 (? 7). JOHN BENNETT, serjeant-at-law, steward of the Marshalsea of the Household, and judge of the Palace Court (at Windsor on the delivery of the address from the county of Middlesex).

1706, July 24 (? 14). THOMAS CLERK (CLARK), of Brickendonbury, Herts. (at Windsor Castle).

1706, Oct. THOMAS COLE, captain of Sir Clowdisley Shovell's ship (at Kensington).

1706, Dec. 8. WILLIAM BENSON, of Bromley, Middlesex, a sheriff of London (at St. James's).

1706–7, Jan. 1. AMBROSE CROWLEY, sheriff of London (at St. James's in the bedchamber).

1707, May 11. WILLIAM THORNTON, of the city of York *(ibid* on his presenting the address from that county about the union of the two kingdoms).

1707, July 16. JAMES HALLETT, of London, goldsmith in Cheapside, one of the commissioners for the lieutenancy of London (at Windsor Castle).

1707, July 16. CHARLES PEERS, of London, merchant, one of the commissioners for the lieutenancy of London *(ibid)*.

1707, Nov. 16 (Sunday). BENJAMIN GREENE, a brewer in Leather Lane, Holborn, a sheriff of London and Middlesex (at St. James's).

1707-8, Mar. 18. ISAAC SHARD, of Horsleydown, Southwark, a deputy lieutenant for London (at Windsor Castle on presenting the address from the city).

1707-8, Mar. 18. JAMES CLARKE, of Moulsey, Surrey (*ibid* on the same occasion).

1707-8, Mar. 18. GEORGE THOROLD (THORALD), of London, merchant (*ibid* on the same occasion).

1707-8, Mar. 18. JOHN SCOTT, of London, soap boiler, and of Enfield (*ibid* on the same occasion).

1707-8, Mar. 20. THOMAS JOHNSON, of Liverpool, merchant and M.P. for Liverpool (at Westminster, in the Prince's Chamber, immediately after the Queen returned out of the House of Lords on his presenting the address from Liverpool).

1707-8, Mar. 20. DANIEL WRAY, of London, high sheriff of Essex, soap boiler in Little Britain just without Aldersgate (at St. James's, on his presenting the address from Essex).

1708, July 18. THOMAS BURY, of Exeter, citizen and merchant (at Windsor Castle, on Sunday).

1708, July 26. ROBERT DUNKLEY, of Westminster, ironmonger, a deputy lieutenant for London (*ibid* on delivering the address to the Queen on the victory of Oudenarde).

1708, July 26. RANDOLPH KNIPE, Turkey or Russia merchant (*ibid* on same occasion).

1708, Aug. 2. GODFREY WEBSTER, merchant, of London, and of Nelmes, Co. Essex, a packer by trade, one of the commissioners for the lieutenancy of London (at Windsor).

? 1708, Aug. 2. RICHARD HUTCHINSON.

1708, Sept. 12. PETER KING, recorder of London (at Windsor Castle).

1708-9, Feb. 21 (? 22). SAMUEL DANIEL, of Over Tabley, Co. Chester (at St. James's within the verge of the bedchamber).

1708-9, Mar. 21. WILLIAM DODWELL, of Sevenhampton, Co. Gloucester. (at St. James's).

1709, May 17. WILLIAM FOWNES, lord mayor of Dublin (dubbed in Ireland by the earl of Wharton, lord lieutenant).

1709, Sept. 7 (12). CHARLES HOPSON, sheriff of London, joiner to the Queen (on attending the Queen concerning the congratulatory address from the city on the victory of Malplaquet).

1709, Sept. 7. RICHARD GUY [GREY], sheriff of London (on the same occasion).

1709, Sept. 17. EDWARD GOULD, of Highgate, Middlesex, justice of the peace, one of the commissioners of the lieutenancy of London (at Windsor on the occasion of presenting a congratulatory address on the late victory).

KNIGHTS BACHELORS

1709, Sept. 21. CHARLES COX, of Southwark, brewer, a magistrate for Surrey.

1709, Dec. 8. CHARLES WAGER, admiral (for his services in taking the galleons in the West Indies).

1709-10, Jan. 18. THOMAS DUNKE (DANCK), sheriff of London.

1709-10, Jan. 18. ANDREW (AMBROSE) CHADWICK, gentleman pensioner.

1710, May 6. ROBERT EYRE, solicitor general, one of the managers of the trial against Dr. Sacheverell (on his appointment as a judge of the Queen's Bench).

1710, May 29. NATHANIEL LLOYD, LL.D., of Doctors Commons, King's advocate in the Court Military.

1710, June 4 (Sunday). WILLIAM OLDES (OWLDS), gentleman usher of the Black Rod.

1710, June 6. NICHOLAS TREVANION.

1710, July 24. CLEMENT COTTERELL, master of the ceremonies (at Kensington).

1710, Oct. 20. ROBERT RAYMOND (RAYMUND), solicitor general (at Whitehall).

1710, Dec. 12. CONSTANTINE PHIPPS, of the Middle Temple, lord Chancellor of Ireland *(ibid)*.

1711, April 5. HOVENDEN WALKER.

1711-2, Feb. 16. MAURICE CROSBIE (dubbed under the Canopy in the Castle, by Sir Constantine Phipps, lord justice of Ireland).

1712, June 14. JOHN CASS, alderman and sheriff of London (at St. James's).

1712, June 14. WILLIAM STEWART, sheriff of London, a barber surgeon, president of the Blue Coat Hospital *(ibid)*.

1712, June 14. SAMUEL CLARKE, of London, merchant and sheriff *(ibid)*.

1712, June 21. WILLIAM STEVENS (STEAVENS), of Rotherhithe, on the presentation of an address from Surrey on the subject of the peace (at Westminster).

1712, July 6. PETER SEAMAN, of Norwich, on the presentation of an address from Norwich on the subject of the Peace (probably at Kensington).

1712, July 7. THOMAS GERY, a master in Chancery, M.P. for Coventry.

1712, July 13. PETER MEWS (MEWES), LL.D., chancellor of Winchester, M.P., for Christchurch, Hants.

1712, July 22. JOSEPH MARTIN, of London, a Turkey merchant (at Whitehall).

1712, Dec. 17. WILLIAM LEWEN (LEWYN), sheriff of London *(ibid)*.

1712–3, Jan. 16. SAMUEL COOKE, lord mayor of Dublin (under the canopy in the Dining Room of the Castle, by the lords justices of Ireland).

1713, Apr. 15. GEORGE MERTTINS, alderman and goldsmith (at St. James's on presenting the address about the Peace).

1713, Apr. 27. ANTHONY STURT, of Heckfield, Co. Hants. (at St. James's on presenting the address from the County of Southampton on the subject of the Peace).

1713, June 3. WILLIAM BANASTRE (BANISTER), a baron of the Exchequer.

1713, June 7. JOHN CHESHIRE, serjeant-at-law.

1713, June 7. NICHOLAS HOOPER, a serjeant-at-law, M.P. for Barnstaple, Co. Devon.

1713, June 17. THOMAS DAVALL, of Burr Street, Wapping, M.P. for Harwich (at Kensington).

1713, June 17. RALPH CRESSFIELD, of Colchester *(ibid)*.

1713, June 23. SAMUEL ONGLEY, of London, merchant, linen draper in Cornhill, director of the South Sea Company, of Oldwarden, Co. Beds. (at Kensington on presenting the address from the South Sea Company).

1713, June 23. CHRISTOPHER BOUVERIE (DESBOUVRIE), a director of the South Sea Company (*ibid* on the same occasion).

1713, June 23. JOHN WILLIAMS, of London, merchant, a director of the South Sea Company (*ibid* on the same occasion).

1713, July 3. RICHARD OLDNER (ODNER), sheriff of Surrey.

1713, July 11. JOHN SUFFIELD, of Portsmouth.

1713, Aug. [10 or 7 ?]. WILLIAM PENDARVES, of Pendarves, Co. Cornwall (probably at Hampton Court [before or on the 10th] or Windsor after the 10th?).

1713, Oct. 6. Marquis DE DRESNAY, captain of a French man-of-war and gentleman of the bedchamber to the king of Spain (at Windsor).

1713, Dec. 30. FRANCIS FORBES, sheriff of London *(ibid)*.

1713, Dec. 30 (20). JOSHUA SHARPE, sheriff of London, stationer *(ibid)*.

? 1713. GRIMANI, the Venetian ambassador.

1713–4, Mar. 23. RICHARD CARTER, appointed attorney general.

1714, Apr. 10. DUNCAN CAMPBELL, of Scotland.

1714, June 18. JOHN STATHAM, of Wigwell, Co. Derby., a deputy lieutenant and justice of the peace of Derby.

1714, July or August. JAMES BARLOW, lord mayor elect of Dublin (in Dublin by the lords justices of Ireland).

KNIGHTS BACHELORS 279

1714, Sept. 18. WILLIAM SANDERSON, of Greenwich, Kent, commander of the Peregrine yacht, which brought over the King (knighted in the yacht immediately before the King landed).

1714, Sept. 19. JOHN VANBRUGH, Clarenceux king of arms, and comptroller of works and surveyors of gardens (at Greenwich House).

1714, Sept. 23 (? 25). ROBERT CHILD, alderman of London (at St. James's).

1714, Sept. 23 (? 25). PETER DELME, alderman of London *(ibid)*.

1714, Sept. 25. [THOMAS SNELLING], of Deptford, Kent, brewer, one of the gentlemen who accompanied the lord Rockingham on the delivery of the address from Kent.

1714, Sept. 25. JOSEPH LAURENCE, alderman of London.

1714, Sept. 25. THOMAS SCAWEN, alderman of London, governor of the Bank of England.

1714, Sept. 25. JOHN WARD, alderman of London.

1714, Sept. 25. GERARD CONIERS (CONYERS), alderman of London.

1714, Oct. 4. WILLIAM CHAPMAN, of London, director of the South Sea Company.

1714, Oct. 4. JAMES DOLLYFFE (DOLIFF, D'OLIVE), of London, merchant, director of the South Sea Company (at St. James's).

1714, Oct. 4. HARCOURT MASTERS, alderman of London.

1714, Oct. 5. DAVID HETCHETTER (HOCHSTETTER, HECHSTETTER), of London, merchant, a director of the Merchant Adventurers Company.

1714, Oct. 9. PETER MEYER, of London, director of the Africa Company (at St. James's).

1714, Oct. 11. SAMUEL DOD, councillor-at-law, shortly after made a serjeant-at-law, etc. (at St. James's).

1714, Oct. 11. JOHN PRATT, serjeant-at-law.

1714, Oct. 10. SAMUEL GARTH, M.D. (the poet), physician-in-ordinary to the King (at St. James's).

1714, Oct. 11. ROBERT BREEDON, sheriff of London.

1714, Oct. 15. PHILIP JACKSON; high sheriff of Co. Hereford (at St. James's, on presenting an address from Co. Hereford).

1714, Oct. 20. WILLIAM PERKINS, of Chertsey, Co. Surrey.

1714, Oct. 20. BARNHAM RIDER, of Kent.

1714, Oct. 20. DANIEL WEBB, mayor of Oxford.

1714, [? Oct., ? 21]. RICHARD LANE, sheriff of Co. Worcester.

KNIGHTS BACHELORS

1714. Oct. 25. CHARLES NORTON, a gentleman of the Honourable Band of Gentlemen Pensioners (at Whitehall).

1714, Oct. 25. THOMAS SAUNDERS, a gentleman of the Honourable Band of Gentlemen Pensioners *(ibid)*.

1714, Nov. 16. JOHN ECCLES, alderman of Dublin (at St. James's).

1714–5, Jan. 1. MATHEW KIRWOOD, of London, goldsmith.

1714–5, Jan. 8. THOMAS HEATH.

1714–5, Jan. 8. RICHARD GOUGH, of London, merchant, M.P. for Bramber (at St. James's, on the occasion of an address from the city on the advantage to the country by the accession of His Majesty).

1714–5, Jan. 8. WILLIAM JOLIFFE, of London, director of the Bank of England and a Turkey merchant *(ibid* on same occasion).

1714–5, Jan. 21. FRANCIS PAGE, serjeant-at-law.

1714–5, Feb. 17. NATHANIEL MEAD, serjeant-at-law.

1714–5, Mar. 4. HENRY NEWTON, LL.D., judge of the Admiralty, formerly envoy extraordinary to the great duke of Tuscany and the Republic of Genoa.

1715, Apr. 9. GEORGE COOKE, prothonotary of Common Pleas.

1715, Apr. 9. ROBERT THORNHILL, of Lincoln's Inn.

1715, Apr. 9. RICHARD STEELE, of Bloomsbury Square.

1715, May 15. JAMES MISSON, of Great Ealing, Middlesex (at Whitehall).

1715, June 9. THOMAS MOLINEUX.

1715, June 9. THOMAS MOORE, of Chertsey, Surrey.

1715, June 18. JOHN SHADWELL, M.D., physician to queen Anne and king George I., son to the poet laureat (at St. James's).

1715, June 19. WILLIAM JOHNSTON, of Gilford, Co. Down, Ireland (dubbed in England).

1715, July 10. NATHANIEL WHITWELL, of Dublin (at St. James's).

1715, July 18. WILLIAM THOMPSON, recorder of London.

1715, July 29. PETER EATON, of Woodford, Essex.

1715, July 29. RICHARD HOUBLON, of Woodford, Essex.

1715, Aug. 9. CHARLES FARNABY, of Kipington, Kent.

1715, Aug. 21. HUMPHRY HOWARTH (HOWORTH), of Lewis, Radnor., sheriff of Radnor. (at St. James's on the presentation of an address from Co. Radnor.).

1715, Sept. 13. THOMAS JONES, of Boswell Court, Lincoln's Inn, barrister, secretary to the Society of Antient Britain (at St. James's on the presentation of an address from the said society).

1715, Nov. 15. HENRY PENRICE, LL.D., judge of the Admiralty.

KNIGHTS BACHELORS 281

1716, June 22. JOHN COLBATCH, doctor of physic (? St. James's).
1717, Jan. 24. JOHN FORTESCUE-ALAND, a baron of the Exchequer.
1717, Jan. 24. CHARLES COOKE, sheriff of London and Middl. (at St. James's).
1717, Jan. 24. WILLIAM BOYS, doctor of physic at Canterbury *(ibid)*.
1717, Mar. 4. HENRY BATEMAN, of Queen Square *(ibid)*.
1717, Aug. 3 [July 6]. NICHOLAS LAWES, appointed governor of Jamaica (at Hampton Court).
1717, Oct. 27. TIMOTHY LANNOY, on the occasion of a deputation from the governors of the Turkey Company, together with several merchants trading to the Levant *(ibid)*.
1717, Oct. 27. PHILIP JACKSON *(ibid* on some occasion).
1717, Oct. 27. WILLIAM HAMMOND *(ibid* on same occasion).
1717, Oct. 27. JOHN LOCK, director of the South Sea Company and of the East India Company, a Turkey merchant, sometime a residen at Ispahan *(ibid* on same occasion).
1717, Oct. 27. JOHN BULL *(ibid* on same occasion).
1717, Oct. 27. CHARLES VERNON *(ibid* on same occasion).
1718, Jan. 14. THOMAS BRAND, gentleman usher of the Green Rod and gentleman usher daily waiter to the King.
1717–8, Feb. 10. GEORGE CASWELL, of London, banker, and of the South Sea Company.
1717–8, Feb. 10. JACOB JACOBSON, of London, merchant, director of the South Sea Company.
1718, Apr. ADOLPHUS OUGHTON, of Tachbrook.
1718, May 11. PATRICK STRAHAN (STRACHAN), of Glenkindy, Scotland, barrack master general in Scotland, in consideration of his loyal and acceptable services during the late rebellion.
1718, July 7. WILLIAM SMYTH, high sheriff of the County of Bedford (at Whitehall).
1718–9, Jan. 2. JOHN ASKEW, of Lydiard Millicent, Wilts., sheriff of Wilts.
1719, Apr. 3. RICHARD WYNNE.
1719, May 1. THOMAS PENGELLY, serjeant-at-law.
1719, May 1. GEORGE HOWELL (on presenting an address of the high sheriff of Glamorgan, cte., at St. James's).
1719, May 9. THOMAS AMBROSE.
1719, Nov. 16. JOHN TASH, sheriff of London.
1719, Nov. 16. GEORGE LUDLAM, chamberlain of London.
1719, Nov. 21. THOMAS HEWET, surveyor of the Board of Works.
? 1719–20, Jan. 21. ROBERT JOHNSON, captain of a man-of-war.
1720, Apr. BENJAMIN WRENCH, M.D., of Norwich.
1720, May 2. JAMES THORNHILL, serjeant painter.

1720, June 11. NICHOLAS DOVIGNI, an engraver.

1720, June 11. PHILIP YORKE, solicitor-general (at Whitehall).

1720, Oct. 8. GEORGE SAUNDERS, captain, R.N.

1720, Oct. 8. LUKE SCHAUB, a Hanoverian.

1720–1, Jan. 1. WALTER SINSERFF, of Amsterdam.

1720–1, Jan. 15. GEORGE WALTON, R.N.

1721, Mar. 26. WILLIAM SAVAGE, of Barbados, solicitor-general in Barbados.

1721, Apr. 14. NATHANIEL GOULD, M.P., of London, merchant, director of the Bank of England.

1721, Sept. 8. ROGER HUDSON, director of the South Sea Company (at Kensington on the address from said Company thanking the King for the treaty with Spain.

1721, Sept. 8. THOMAS FREDERICK, director of the South Sea Company (*ibid* on same occasion).

1721, Nov. 4. CHAMBERLAIN WALKER (in the Presence Chamber, Dublin Castle, by the duke of Grafton, lord lieutenant).

1721–2, Feb. 18. RICHARD MANNINGHAM, M.D., of London.

1722, May 9. EDWARD BECHER (BEECHER), alderman and sheriff of London (on the occasion of an address from the city of congratulation on the subject of the Pretender's conspiracy).

1722, May 14. JOHN GONSON, of the Inner Temple (at Whitehall).

1722, May 19. ISAAC TILLARD, of London.

1722, May 19. DANIEL DOLLINS, of Hackney.

1722, July 25. RICHARD HOPKINS, of London, merchant, a director of the South Sea Company (at Kensington on presentation of an address from said Company).

1722 Aug. 31. EDWARD HILL, of Wanborough, sheriff of Wilts.

1722, Aug. 31. ISAAC TOWNSEND, commissioner of the Navy (at Spithead on the Royal progress).

1722, Aug. 31. JACOB ACKWORTH, surveyor of the Navy (*ibid*).

1722, Aug. 31 (?) THOMAS PECKHAM, sheriff of Essex (at Stanstead, on the Royal progress).

1722–3, Jan. 26. SYDENHAM FOWKE, of Westowe, Suffolk (at Whitehall).

1723, Apr. 11. GERARD ROETIERS, of London, a Dutch merchant.

1723, May. CHALLONER OGLE, captain, R.N.

1723, May. THOMAS RENTON, the rupture doctor.

1723, Dec. 2. FELIX FEAST, sheriff of London (at St. James's on an address from the Corporation congratulating the King on his safe return from the Continent).

1723–4, Feb. 4. CLEMENT WEARGE, solicitor general (at Whitehall).
1723–4, Mar. JOHN DARNELL, serjeant-at-law.
1724, Apr. MOORE MOLYNEUX, of Losely, near Guildford, Surrey.
1724, Apr. JAMES CAMPBELL, of Edinburgh.
1724, May 4. LAWRENCE CARTER, king's serjeant.
1724, Sept. 24. JOHN RUSH, high sheriff of Berks.
1724, Dec. 9. JOSEPH EYLES, M.P., sheriff of London (at St. James's).
1724–5, Jan. 7. JEFFERY GILBERT, baron of the Exchequer.
1724–5, Mar. 6. THOMAS MASTERS, of London.
1725, May 1. CONRADE JOACHIM SPRENGELL, M.D., member of the College of Physicians and fellow of the Royal Society, physician to king William III. and King George I. (at Whitehall).
1725–6, Jan. 11. FRANCIS PORTEN, sheriff of London (at St. James's on the occasion of an address from the city to congratulate the King on his safe arrival from Hanover).
1725–6, Jan. 11. JEREMIAH MURDEN, sheriff of London (*ibid* on same occasion).
1725–6, Jan. 16. BERNARD HALE, a baron of the Exchequer.
1725–6, Jan. 20. JOHN DIMSDALE, M.D., of Hertford.
1726, Nov. 8 (15). EDMUND PROBYN, judge of the King's Bench (at Whitehall).
1726, Nov. 8. JOHN COMYNS, a baron of the Exchequer *(ibid)*.
1726–7, Jan. 31. WILLIAM BILLERS, F.R.S., alderman of London.
1726–7, Jan. 31. EDWARD BELLAMY, alderman of London.
1726–7, Jan. 31. JOHN THOMPSON, alderman of London.
1726–7, Jan. 31. WILLIAM OGBORNE, sheriff of London.
1726–7, Feb. 24. NATHANIEL HODGES, colonel of the 2nd-Regiment of the Tower Hamlets.
1726–7, Mar. 22. PHILIP HALL, of Upton, sheriff of Essex.
1726–7, Mar. 24. WILLIAM ROOKE, of Leeds, Yorks.
1727, Apr. 29. THOMAS STEVENS (STEAVENS), sheriff of Surrey, a timber merchant.
1727, May 18. CHARLES DALTON, gentleman usher of the Black Rod.
1727, June 16. ROBERT BAYLISS (BAYLIS), alderman of London, a commissioner of Customs (at Leicester House).
1727, July 8. JOHN GROSVENOR, sheriff-elect of London (at St. James's on an address of sympathy and congratulation on the occasion of the accession).
1727, July 8. THOMAS LOMBE, sheriff-elect of London (*ibid* same occasion).

1727, Oct. 11.   MULTON LAMBARD, colonel, represented the duke of Aquitain at the Coronation of George II., lieutenant governor of Tilbury Fort (at Whitehall).
1727, Oct. 11.   GEORGE WALTERS, represented the duke of Normandy at the Coronation of George II. *(ibid)*.
1727, Oct. 11.   WILLIAM WYNNE, gentleman pensioner *(ibid)*.
1727, Oct. 11.   JOHN TAYLOR, gentleman pensioner *(ibid)*.
1727, Oct. 13.   JOHN BOYCE, mayor of Oxford (at the Coronation of George II.).
1727, Oct. 13.   OLIVER GREENWAY, alderman of Oxford (same occasion).
1728, Apr. 26.   PHILIP RYLEY (RILEY), surveyor of woods.
1728, Oct. 13.   CHARLES PAYNE, governor of the Leeward Islands (at Windsor Castle).
1729, Apr. 15.   JOHN DE LANG, merchant of Holland, and F.R.S.
1729, May 14.   JAMES SHEPHARD, serjeant-at-law.
1729, May 14.   WILLIAM CHAPELL (CHAPPLE), serjeant-at-law, a justice of the King's Bench.
1729, Aug. 16.   JOHN EMERTON (EMMERSON or ERNESTON), of Holland (deputy governor of the Merchants Adventurers) (at Lüneburg).
1729, Sept. 13.   RICHARD BROCAS, sheriff of London.
1730, July 16 (14).   Rt. Hon. PIETER VERDOEN, lord mayor of Dublin (at his house in Dawson Street, Dublin, by their excellencies the lords justices).
1731–2, Mar. 10.   EDWARD LOVET PEARCE, captain, surveyor of works, Ireland, and architect of the Parliament House (by the duke of Dorset, lord lieutenant, in his robe room in the Parliament House).
1732, Sept. 26.   CHARLES HARDY, commander of the "Carolina" yacht.
1732, Sept. 28.   FRANCIS CHILD, lord mayor of London (at Kensington).
1732, Sept. 28.   HENRY HANKEY, sheriff of London *(ibid)*.
1732, Sept. 28.   JOHN BARNARD, alderman of London *(ibid)*.
? 1732.   JOHN RANDOLPH, of Virginia.
1732–3, Feb.   HUGH CLOPTON, of Stratford-on-Avon.
1733–4, Mar. 19.   HENRY HICKS, of Deptford, sheriff of Kent.
1734.   MALTIS RYALL, of Southwark, sheriff of Surrey.
1735.   MATTHEW SKINNER, of Oxfordshire, serjeant-at-law.
1735, Oct. 3.   EVERARD FAWKENER, merchant of London, appointed ambassador to the Ottoman Porte, Constantinople (at Hanover).
1735, Oct. 31.   JOHN SALTER, alderman of London (at St. James's on the occasion of an address from the lord mayor and court of aldermen, etc., congratulating the King on his safe return from Hanover).
1735, Oct. 31.   ROBERT GODSCHALL, alderman and sheriff of London *(ibid* same occasion).

KNIGHTS BACHELORS

1735, Dec. 23. THOMAS ABNEY, judge of the Marshalsea (at Whitehall).

1735–6, Jan. 25. THOMAS REEVES (REEVE), one of the judges of His Majesty's Court of Common Pleas, appointed lord chief justice of same Court (at Whitehall) (? not knighted).

1735–6, Jan. 31. ROBERT COWAN, late governor of Bombay (at Whitehall).

1736, May 6. RICHARD GRATTAN, lord mayor of Dublin (dubbed in Ireland by the duke of Dorset, lord lieutenant).

1736–7, Jan. 18. WILLIAM ROUS, sheriff of London (at St. James's on the occasion of an address from the lord mayor and Court of Aldermen of the City of London congratulating the King upon his safe return from Helvoetsluys).

1736–7, Jan. 18. JOHN LEQUESNE, alderman of London *(ibid)*.

1736–7, Jan. 18. GEORGE CHAMPION, alderman of London *(ibid)*.

1736–7, Jan. 18. BENJAMIN RAWLINS, sheriff of London *(ibid)*.

1736–7, Jan. 23. JOHN WILLES, attorney general, appointed lord chief justice of the Court of Common Pleas (at Whitehall).

1736–7, Jan. 26. JAMES DARCY LEVER, LL.D., of Alkington, Lancaster, high sheriff of Lancaster.

1737, June 8. WILLIAM LEE, chief justice of the King's Bench.

1737, Aug. 4. JOSEPH HANKEY, alderman of London (at Hampton Court on the presentation of an address congratulating the King on the birth of a princess to Her Royal Highness the Princess of Wales, from the lord mayor and Court of Alderman of the City of London).

1737, Sept. 9. JAMES SOMERVELL, lord mayor of Dublin (dubbed in Ireland by the duke of Devonshire, lord lieutenant).

1738, June 9. ROBERT KENDALL CATER [or KENDALL-CATER], sheriff of London (at Kensington on an address from the lord mayor, aldermen, and commons of the City of London of congratulation of the birth of a prince).

1739, May 30. ROBERT WILMOT, of Osmaston, Co. Derby.

1740, May 12. DUDLEY RYDER, attorney general (at Whitehall).

1740, May 12. JOHN STRANGE, solicitor general *(ibid)*.

1742, Dec. 4. THOMAS PARKER, chief baron of the Exchequer.

1743, Apr. 27. CHARLES MOLLOY, captain, R.N.

1743–4, Jan. 24. WILLIAM RICHARDSON, justice of the peace, of Surrey (at St. James's, on the presentation of an address from the lord lieutenant, high sheriff, etc., etc., for the County of Surrey, of congratulation on his safe arrival, the recovery of the duke of York, and marriage of the princess Louisa and the birth of a prince).

1743–4, Jan. 24. ABRAHAM SHARD, of Kennington, Surrey (on the same occasion (at St. James's).

1743–4, Feb. 1. THOMAS DENNY (dubbed in Ireland by the duke of Devonshire, lord lieutenant).

1743–4, Feb. 18. WILLIAM CALVERT, sheriff of London (at St. James's, on the presentation of an address from the lord mayor, aldermen, and council of the City of London, on the threatened invasion of the pretender's son).

1743–4, Feb. 18. DANIEL LAMBERT, alderman of London, M.P. (*ibid* on same occasion).

1743–4, Feb. 18. ROBERT LADBROOKE, (LADBROKE), sheriff of London (*ibid* on same occasion).

1743–4, Feb. 18. SIMON URLING (URLIN), serjeant-at-law, recorder of London (*ibid* on same occasion).

1743–4, Feb. 18. Right Hon. ROBERT WESTLEY, lord mayor of London (at St. James's on presentation of an address from the lord mayor, alderman, and common council of the City of London on the threatened invasion of the Pretender's son).

1743–4, Feb. 18. ROBERT WILMOT (WILLIMOTT), alderman of London (*ibid* on same occasion).

1743–4, Feb. 21. CHARLES EGGLETON, deputy lieutenant of Middlesex (at St. James's on presentation of an address from the commissioners of lieutenancy for the City of London on the threatened invasion of the Pretender's son).

1743–4, Feb. 21. WILLIAM SMITH, deputy lieutenant of Middlesex (*ibid* on same occasion).

1743–4, Feb. 21. JAMES CREED, deputy lieutenant of Middlesex, director of the East India Company (*ibid* on same occasion).

1743–4, Mar. 5. THOMAS HEAD, sheriff of Berks. (at St. James's on presenting an address from the sheriff, justices of the peace, grand jury, etc., etc., of Berks. on the threatened invasion of the Pretender's son).

1743–4, Mar. 7. JEFFERY ELWES, of Hoddesdon, Herts. (*ibid* on the occasion of a like address from Co. Hertford).

1743–4, Mar. 7. RICHARD CHASE, of Much Hadham, Herts., sheriff of Hertford (*ibid* on same occasion).

1743–4, Mar. 13. EDWARD (WORSELEY) WORSLEY, of Gatcombe, Isle of Wight, sheriff of Hants. (at St. James's on presentation of an address from the high sheriff, grand jury, and justices of the peace on the threatened invasion of the Pretender's son).

1743–4, Mar. 13. THOMAS SNELL, of Upton, St. Leonards, sheriff of Gloucester.

KNIGHTS BACHELORS   287

1743–4, Mar. 13. SAMUEL GOWER, justice of Middlesex (at St. James's on the presentation of an address from the justices of the peace for the liberty of the Tower of London and precincts thereof on the threatened invasion of the Pretender's son).

1743–4, Mar. 13. CLIFFORD WILLIAM PHILLIPS (PHILIPS), a deputy lieutenant of the Tower Hamlets (at St. James's on presentation of same address).

1743–4, Mar. 13. THOMAS DE VEIL, justice of the peace (*ibid* on same occasion).

1743–4, Mar. 21 or 13. THOMAS RYDER (RIDER), of Boughton Monchelsea, one of the grand jury, and son of Sir Barnham Rider (at St. James's on presentation of an address of the high sheriff and grand jury of the County of Kent on the threatened invasion of the Pretender's son).

1744, May. JOHN BALCHEN, admiral of the White, and governor of Greenwich Hospital.

1744, June 8. PETER DAVENPORT, of Macclesfield, Cheshire, receiver general of land tax for Cheshire.

1745, Apr. 21. MICHAEL FOSTER, justice of the King's Bench.

1745, Sept. 5. HENRY MARSHAL (MARSHALL, lord mayor of London, president of St. Bartholomew's Hospital, M.P. for Agmondesham, Co. Bucks. (at Kensington).

1745, Sept. 5. SAMUEL PENNANT, sheriff of London *(ibid)*.

1745, Sept. 5. JOHN BOSWORTH, chamberlain *(ibid)*.

1745, Sept. 9. THOMAS HANKEY, of London, a banker, a commissioner of lieutenancy for the City of London *(ibid)*.

1745, Oct. 31. RICHARD HOARE, lord mayor of London.

1745, Nov. 23. MARTIN WRIGHT, justice of the King's Bench (at St. James's).

1745, Nov. 23. JAMES REYNOLDS, a baron of the Exchequer *(ibid)*.

1745, Nov. 23. THOMAS BURNET, justice of Common Pleas *(ibid)*.

1745, Nov. 23. THOMAS DENNISON, justice of the King's Bench *(ibid)*.

1745, Nov. 23. THOMAS BOOTLE, chancellor to the prince of Wales *(ibid)*.

1745. Nov. 23. SAMUEL PRIME, serjeant-at-law *(ibid)*.

1745, Nov. 23. THOMAS BIRCH, serjeant-at-law (King's serjeant) *(ibid)*.

1745, Nov. 23. RICHARD LLOYD, King's counsel *(ibid)*.

1745, Nov. 27 (Dec. 3). PETER THOMPSON, of Bermondsey, sheriff of Surrey *(ibid)*.

1746. Aug. (Sept.) 20. THOMAS RIDGE, of Trotter, sheriff of Sussex.

1747, Jan. 30. WILLIAM BROWNE, of Lynn, M.D.
1747, Sept. 30. GEORGE RIBTON, lord mayor of Dublin (dubbed in Ireland by the earl of Harrington, lord lieutenant).
1748, Nov. 25. JOHN STRACEY, recorder of London.
1749, June 22. The Hon. HENRY BELLENDEN, gent. usher of the Black Rod.
1749-50, Jan. 9. CHARLES BURTON, alderman of Dublin (dubbed in Ireland by the earl of Harrington, lord lieutenant).
1750, Nov. 7. SYDNEY STAFFORD SMYTH, a baron of the Exchequer.
1750, Nov. 10. JOSEPH ALLEN, surveyor of the Navy.
1750. JAMES STUART, on being appointed admiral.
1751, Nov. 18. THOMAS SALUSBURY, of Offley Place, Herts., LL.D., judge of the Admiralty.
1752, Feb. 12. GEORGE LEE, LL.D., treasurer to the princess dowager of Wales, dean of the arches, and judge of the Prerogative Court of Canterbury, and a member of the Privy Council.
1752, Nov. 22. CRISPE GASCOIGNE, lord mayor of London (at St. James's).
1752, Nov. 22. RICHARD ADAMS, recorder *(ibid)*.
1752, Nov. 22. CHARLES ASGILL, sheriff of London *(ibid)*.
1752, Nov. 22. RICHARD GLYNN, sheriff of London *(ibid)*.
1752, Nov. 22. THOMAS HARRISON, chamberlain of London *(ibid)*.
1753, Jan. 2. PERCY BRETT, captain R.N.
1753, Feb. 9. EDWARD CLIVE, justice of Common Pleas.
1753. WILLIAM ANNE STEPHENSON, of Oxfordshire.
1753. WILLIAM BENTLEY, of Mount's Mill, Cornwall (at Kensington).
1753. WILLIAM MAY, of Knighton, Essex.
1754, Apr. 9. WILLIAM BURNABY, of Broughton, Oxford.
1754, May 25. THOMAS CLARKE, a king's counsel-at-law, appointed master of the rolls (at Whitehall).
1755, Jan. 31. JOHN GLANVILLE, of Catchfrench, sheriff of Cornwall.
1755, Feb. 3. JOHN EARDLEY WILMOT, of the Inner Temple, appointed one of the judges of the King's Bench (at Whitehall).
1755, Apr. 20. CHARLES HARDY, governor of New York, afterwards admiral.
1755, May 28. WILLIAM EVANS MORRES, mayor of Kilkenny (at Kilkenny by the marquess of Hartington, lord lieutenant).
1755, Sept. 19. WILLIAM MORETON, recorder of London, M.P. for Brackley (at Kensington on the occasion of an address from the lord mayor, aldermen, and commons of the City of London, congratulating the King on his safe return).
1755, Sept. 19. SAMUEL FLUDYER, sheriff of London (*ibid* same occasion).
1755, Sept. 19. JOHN TORRIANO, sheriff of London (*ibid* same occasion).

KNIGHTS BACHELORS

1756, Apr. 10. GEORGE MONTGOMERY METHAM, of North Cave, sheriff of Co. Yorks.
1756, Apr. 18. ELLIS CUNLIFFE, of Liverpool, M.P. for Liverpool.
1756, June 5. THOMAS REEVE, of New Windsor, sheriff of Berks.
1756, Oct. 29. ROBERT HENLEY, attorney general (at Whitehall).
1758, Dec. 5. CHARLES COTTERELL DORMER, master of the ceremonies *(ibid)*.
1759, June 8. MATHEW BLAKISTONE, alderman of London.
1759, June 8. THOMAS CHITTY, alderman of London.
1759, June 8. JAMES HODGES, town clerk of London.
1759, June 8. WILLIAM STEPHENSON, alderman of London.
1759, Sept. 20. JOHN BENTLEY, captain R.N.
1759, Oct. 5. THOMAS STANHOPE, captain R.N.
1759, Oct. 16. JAMES DOUGLAS, captain R.N.
1759, Nov. 12. JAMES BURROUGHES, vice-chancellor of Cambridge, and master of Gonville and Caius College.
1760, Jan. 21. THOMAS WILSON, of West Wickham, sheriff of Kent.
1760, May 17. FIELDING OULD, M.D. (in Ireland by the duke of Bedford, lord lieutenant).
1760, Oct. 16. ROBERT KITE, sheriff of London (at Kensington by the King).
1760, Oct. 16. WILLIAM HART, sheriff of London *(ibid)*.
1760, Oct. 28. THOMAS RAWLINSON, alderman of London.
1760, Oct. 28. FRANCIS GOSLING, banker, of London.
1760, Nov. 3. WILLIAM BAKER, alderman of Bassishaw Ward, London.
1760, Nov. 11. CLEMENT TRAFFORD, of Dunton Hall, high sheriff of Lincolnshire (at St. James's).
1760, Dec. 5. ROBERT BEWICKE, of Closehouse, sheriff of Northumberland (? at St. James's, on the occasion of the presentation of an address on the accession).
1760, Dec. 9 (? Nov. 3). LANCELOT ALGOOD (ALLGOOD), of Nunwick, Co. Northumberland *(ibid* on same occasion).
1760, Dec. 10. HENRY CHEERE, deputy lieutenant of the County of Middlesex and a justice of peace, Co. Middlesex (at St. James's).
1760, Dec. 17. ONESIPHORUS PAUL, of Woodchester, Co. Gloucester., sheriff of Gloucester. (at Whitehall).
1760, Dec. 22. JAMES HEREFORD, of Modiford, sheriff of Hereford.
1760, Dec. 23. THOMAS JONES, of Shrewsbury, and of Stanley, Co. Salop, sheriff of Shropshire.

1760, Dec. 24. WILLIAM BENNETT, of Fareham, sheriff of Hants.

1760, Dec. 24. HENRY ST. JOHN.

1760, Dec. 27 (1761, Jan. 3). WILLIAM DALSTON (DAULSTON), of Milrigge, sheriff of Cumberland (at Whitehall).

1761, Jan. 16. BENJAMIN TRUMAN (TRUEMAN), of Hatfield, sheriff of Herts.

1761, Jan. 21. JOHN VANHATTEN, of Dinton, Co. Bucks. (at St. James's in connection with coronation condolence and accession).

1761, Jan. 24. PHILIP VAVAZOR, of Wisbech, high sheriff of the County of Cambridge (at St. James's on same kind of address from Co. Cambridge).

1761, Feb. 9. THOMAS THOROWGOOD, of Kersey, sheriff of Suffolk (at Whitehall).

1761, Feb. 23. CHRISTOPHER TREISE, of Lavethan, late high sheriff of Co. Cornwall (at Whitehall).

1761, Mar. 4. CHARLES PRICE (PRYCE), of Rotherfield Peppard, sheriff of Oxford.

1761, Mar. 6. WILLIAM FARRINGTON, of Shaw Hall, sheriff of Lancashire (at St. James's).

1761, Mar. 18. SAMUEL GORDON, of Newark-upon-Trent, sheriff of Notts.

1761, Apr. 10. SEPTIMUS ROBINSON, gentleman usher of the Black Rod.

1761, Sept. 18. THOMAS CHURCHMAN, mayor of Norwich.

1761, Sept. 18 (before the coronation, probably Sept. 21 or 22) (? 22 or 23). THOMAS ROBINSON, of Rookby Park, Co. York, bart., representing the duke of Normandy at the coronation of king George III. (at Whitehall).

1761, Sept. 21 or 22 (previous to the coronation). WILLIAM BRETTON (BRETON))who represented the duke of Aquitaine at the coronation *(ibid)*.

1761, Sept. 24. THOMAS MUNDAY, mayor of Oxford.

1761, Sept. 24. PETER FENOUILHET, exon of the Yeomen of the Guard.

1761, Sept. 26 (after the coronation). JOHN BRIDGER (BRIDGE), of Combe Place, Sussex, standard bearer to the Band of Gentlemen Pensioners (at St. James's).

1761, Sept. 26. OWEN JONES, senior gentleman of the Band of Gentlemen Pensioners *(ibid)*.

1761, Sept. 26. CHARLES TOWNLEY, clarenceux king of arms *(ibid)*.

1761, Sept. 30. JOHN FIELDING, of Westminster, police magistrate.

KNIGHTS BACHELORS

1761, Oct. 5. WILLIAM FLEMING, of Norwich.

1761, Oct. 30. TIMOTHY ALLEN, lord mayor of Dublin (dubbed in Ireland by the earl of Halifax, lord lieutenant).

1761, Oct. 30. PATRICK HAMILTON, late lord mayor of Dublin (*ibid*).

1761, Nov. 2. HENRY GOULD, a baron of the Exchequer (by the King in England).

1761, Nov. 2 (9). NATHANIEL NASH, sheriff of London.

1761, Nov. 9. JOHN CARTWRIGHT, sheriff of London.

1761, Nov. 9. THOMAS FLUDYER, of London.

1761, Nov. 10. JOHN COTTERELL BROOKS, of Garnon, sheriff of Herefordshire (took the surname of Cotterell).

1761, Nov. 16. THOMAS WARD, of Guilsborough, sheriff of Northamptonshire.

1761, Dec. 28. CHARLES PRATT, chief justice of the Common Pleas.

1761, Dec. EDWARD SIMPSON, LL.D., dean of the arches and judge of the Prerogative Court, of Doctors Commons, M.P. for Dover.

1762, Jan. 25. FLETCHER NORTON, solicitor general.

1762, Jan. 26. THOMAS BLACKHALL, one of the sheriffs of Dublin (dubbed in Ireland by the earl of Halifax, lord lieutenant).

1762, Feb. 14. CLIFTON WINTRINGHAM, M.D., physician extraordinary to His Majesty (by the King in England).

1762, Aug. 25. ALEXANDER POWELL, deputy recorder of Salisbury.

1762, Sept. 3. THOMAS GATEHOUSE, sheriff of Hampshire.

1762, Sept. 8. JOHN MEREDYTH (MEREDITH), high sheriff of Brecon. (at St. James's on the occasion of an address from Co. Brecknock. on the birth of the prince of Wales).

1762, Sept. 17. SAMUEL HELLIER, of Woodhouse, high sheriff of Worcester.

1762, Sept. 22. ROBERT GOODYERE, lieutenant of the band of gentlemen pensioners.

1762, Sept. 29. GEORGE KELLEY, of Bishopsdown, Speldhurst, Kent, and sheriff of that county.

1762, Oct. 1. WILLIAM BRIDGES BALDWYN, of Wallington, high sheriff of Surrey (at St. James's on the occasion of an address from Co. Surrey on the birth of the prince of Wales).

1762, Oct. 4. HENRY BANKES, alderman of Cordwainers Ward, London, and sheriff of London and Middlesex.

1762, Oct. 4. THOMAS CHALLENOR, sheriff of London and alderman of Aldgate Ward.

1762, Oct. 26. THOMAS GUNSTON, of Upcott, Bishops-Hull, Co. Somerset., sheriff of Somersetshire (at St. James's).

1763, Mar. 25. Dr. JAMES JAY, of New York (*ibid* on an address of the governors of the King's College, New York).

1763, July 27. WILLIAM ERSKINE, of Torrie, Co. Fife, lieutenant colonel.

1763, Sept. 21. JAMES PORTER, minister at Brussels.

1763, Nov. 10. EDWARD NEWENHAM, high sheriff of Co. Dublin (dubbed in Ireland).

1763, Nov. 21. WILLIAM MCLEOD BANNATYNE (in England by the King).

1763, Dec. 16. JOSEPH YATES, judge of the King's Bench.

1763, Dec. 29. ROBERT FLETCHER, a major in the East India Company's service.

1764, Jan. 16. CHARLES COOTE, Knight of the Bath (dubbed in Ireland).

1764, Feb. 10. JOHN LINDSAY, captain R.N.

1764, Apr. 16. ROBERT BARKER, major of artillery at the Siege of Manila.

1764, Oct. 19. GEORGE MACARTNEY, ambassador at St. Petersburg.

1764, Nov. 30. THOMAS SEWELL, master of the Rolls.

1765, Apr. 19. RICHARD ASTON (late chief justice of the Common Pleas in Ireland), on being appointed a judge of the King's Bench in England.

1765, Apr. 20. JAMES DOUGLAS, consul general at Naples.

1765, Aug. 28. THOMAS HARRIS, sheriff of London, on the congratulatory address on the birth of a second prince (at St. James's).

1765, Sept. 18. FRANCIS MOLYNEUX, gentleman usher of the Black Rod.

1765, Sept. 30. JAMES TAYLOR, lord mayor of Dublin (in Ireland by the lord lieutenant) (at the Mansion House, Dublin, by the lords justices).

1765, Nov. 22. JOHN JOHNSON, son of Sir William Johnson, bart. (in England by the King).

1766, July 3. JAMES WRIGHT, British minister at Venice.

1766, Oct. 8. ROBERT DARLING, sheriff of London (at St. James's).

1766, Oct. 8. JAMES ESDAILE, alderman of Cripplegate Ward and sheriff of London (at St. James's).

1768, Jan. 27. THOMAS SLADE, surveyor of the Navy.

KNIGHTS BACHELORS 293

1768, Feb. 22. PETER FRANCIS LAURENT, of Grenada (then recently ceded by France, and the first native of the ceded islands on whom the honour was conferred) (at Whitehall).

1768, Apr. 28. TOMASO QUERINI, ambassador from Venice.

1768, Aug. 19. CHARLES WHITWORTH, M.P. for Minehead, and lieutenant governor of Tilbury Fort.

1768, Nov. 22. CHALONER OGLE, of Martyr Worthy, captain R.N., sheriff of Hants.

1769, Apr. 12. TIMOTHY WALDO, of Clapham, Co. Surrey.

1769, Apr. 12. RICHARD HOTHAM, of Merton, Co. Surrey, M.P. for Southwark, and founder of Hothampton, or Bognor, Sussex.

1769, Apr. 21. JOSHUA REYNOLDS, president of the Royal Academy.

1770, Feb. WILLIAM BLACKSTONE, judge of the King's Bench.

1770, June 22. WILLIAM HENRY ASHURST, judge of the King's Bench.

1770. ANTHONY KING, one of the sheriffs of Dublin (dubbed in Ireland).

1771, Jan. 27. GEORGE NARES, judge of Common-Pleas.

1771, Jan. 28. WILLIAM DE GREY, justice of the Common Pleas.

1771, July 15. WILLIAM DESSE, clerk of the cheque to the Band of Gentlemen Pensioners.

1771, Sept. 27. JOHN WILLIAMS, surveyor of the Navy.

1771, Oct. 16. THOMAS KENT, of Kingston, sheriff of Surrey.

1772, Jan. 31. JOHN CLERKE, captain R.N.

1772, June 5. GEORGE OSBORNE, bart., of Chicksands, Bedfordshire (on being appointed proxy for H.R.H. Frederick, duke of York, at the approaching installation of the Bath) (at St. James's).

1772, June 5. STANIER PORTEN, under-secretary of State, proxy for Sir George Macartney at the Installation of the Bath, 1772 *(ibid)*.

1772, June 5. THOMAS MILLS, town major of Quebec, proxy for Sir Ralph Payne (afterwards lord Lavington), at the installation of the Bath, 1772 *(ibid)*.

1772, June 10. PETER PARKER, captain, R.N., proxy for Sir John Moore, bart., at the installation of the Bath, 1772.

1772, June 10. HORATIO MANN, proxy for his uncle, Sir Horatio Mann, at the installation of the Bath, 1772.

1772, June 10. BASIL KEITH, captain, R.N., proxy for his brother, Sir Robert Murray Keith, at the installation of the Bath, 1772, subsequently governor of Jamaica.

1772, Sept. 10. JOHN HASLER (dubbed in Ireland by viscount Townshend, lord lieutenant).

1772, Oct. 22. JAMES EYRE, a baron of the Exchequer (in England by the King).
1772, Oct. 23. JOHN HAWKINS, chairman of the Middlesex Sessions (at St. James's).
1773, Feb. 5. WATKIN LEWES (LEWIS), alderman of Lime Street Ward, London, sheriff 1772.
1773, Feb. 5. THOMAS HALLIFAX, lord mayor of London.
1773, Mar. 10. JAMES BURROW, master of the Crown Office, and sometime president of the Royal Society (on presentation of the address of thanks from the Royal Society : at St. James's).
1773, June 22. JOHN CARTER, mayor of Portsmouth (at the governor's house, Portsmouth).
1773, June 24. THOMAS PYE, admiral of the Blue (on the quarter-deck of the "Barfleur" at Spithead, the king's standard then flying at the top mast head).
1773, June 24. RICHARD SPRY, rear admiral of the "White."
1773, June 24. JOSEPH KNIGHT, captain of the "Ocean," senior captain in the Fleet at Spithead *(ibid)*.
1773, June 24. RICHARD BICKERTON, captain of the "Augusta" yacht *(ibid)*.
1773, June 24. EDWARD VERNON, captain of the "Barfleur" *(ibid)*.
1773, Sept. MICHAEL CROMIE (dubbed in Ireland).
1773, Oct. 27. EDWARD HUGHES, captain, R.N., commander-in-chief of His Majesty's ships and vessels to be employed in the East Indies (at St. James's).
1773, Nov. 11. GEORGE HAY, D.C.L., principal of the Court of Arches, and judge of the Admiralty.
1774, Feb. 25. ROBERT HERRIES, a banker, (at St. James's).
1774, Mar. 4. WALTER RAWLINSON, alderman of London.
1774, Mar. 30. ELIJAH IMPEY, of Lincoln's Inn, chief justice of His Majesty's Supreme Court of Judicature at Fort William in Bengal (at St. James's).
1774, Apr. 8. JOHN BURLAND, appointed a baron of the Court of Exchequer, a serjeant-at-law *(ibid)*.
1774, July 21. BAPTIST JOHN SILVESTER, M.D., F.R.S., physician to the Army in the Low Countries.
1775, Jan. 27. GEORGE COLLIER, of Froyle, Co. Hants., captain, R.N. (at St. James's).
1775, Mar. 15. NOAH THOMAS, M.D., physician-in-ordinary to the King *(ibid)*.
1775, May 17. BEAUMONT HOTHAM, appointed a baron of the Exchequer *(ibid)*.
1775, Sept. 20. ROBERT AINSLIE, ambassador to the Ottoman Porte *(ibid)*.

1776, Mar. 29. TREVOR CORRY, consul at Dantzic.

1776, Apr. 3. RICHARD PERRYN, appointed a baron of the Exchequer (at St. James's).

1776, May 31. JOHN ELIOTT, of Peebles, M.D. *(ibid)*.

1776, June 4. ALEXANDER SCHOMBERG, captain of His Majesty's yacht "Dorset" (at Dublin Castle by earl Harcourt, lord lieutenant).

1776, June 4. FRANCIS JAMES BUCHANAN, major, usher of the Black Rod *(ibid)*.

1776, Sept. 30. PATRICK KING, sheriff of the County of Dublin *(ibid)*.

1776, Nov. 4. BOYLE ROCHE *(ibid* by same).

1777, Feb. 12. JAMES WALLACE, captain R.N. (at St. James's).

1777, May 2. PHILIP (? or PATRICK) CRAUFURD, conservator of the Privileges of Scotland at Campvere and other places in Zealand or elsewhere in the United Provinces, and resident there for the same *(ibid)*.

1777, June 7. ROBERT CHAMBERS, a puisné judge of the Supreme Court at Fort William in Bengal (by patent).

1777, June 18. JOHN DAY, judge advocate general in Bengal (at St. James's).

1777, Nov. 23. JOHN SKYNNER, appointed chief baron of the Exchequer *(ibid)*.

1778, Jan. 28. JOHN DURBIN, of Walton, Co. Somerset., mayor of Bristol *(ibid)*.

1778, Feb. 25. PHILIP AINSLIE, of Pilton, N.B., and lieutenant colonel of Horse Guards (at St. James's).

1778, Mar. 13. JAMES NAPIER, superintendent general of all the hospitals in Jamaica for the forces in North America *(ibid)*.

1778, May 10. GEORGE MASSY, captain (at Dublin Castle by his excellency the earl of Buckinghamshire, lord lieutenant).

1778, May 19. DIGBY DENT, captain R.N. (at St. James's).

1778, Sept. 28. JOHN DAVIS, brewer, captain of the West Kent Militia (first militia captain who had the honour of mounting the King's Guard) (at Winchester).

1778, Sept. 30. CHARLES VENTRIS FIELD, captain of the Bedfordshire Militia *(ibid)*.

1778, Oct. 9. JAMES MARRIOTT, LL.D., His Majesty's advocate general [on his appointment] to be official principal commissary general, etc., judge of the Admiralty Court (at St. James's).

1778, Nov. 4. WILLIAM BISHOP, mayor of Maidstone.
1778. ASHTON LEVER, of Alkrington, Co. Lancaster.
1778, Nov. 15. THOMAS BELL, M.D. (at Dublin Castle by the lord lieutenant).
1779, Jan. 15. ANDREW SNAPE HAMOND (HAMMOND), captain of His Majesty's ship "The Roebuck" (at St. James's).
1779, Apr. 21. HYDE PARKER, captain R.N.
1779, Apr. 30. GEORGE MUNRO, of Poyntzfield, Co. Cromarty, proxy for Sir Hector Munro, at the Installation of the Bath, 1779 (at St. James's).
1779, Apr. 30. JAMES DUFF, of Kinstoun (Kenstair), Aberdeenshire, N.B., proxy for Sir James Harris at the Installation of the Bath, 1779 *(ibid)*.
1779, May 5. THOMAS FOWKE, of Lowesby Hall, Co. Leicestershire, proxy for Sir Henry Clinton, K.B., at the Installation of the Bath, 1779, sometime groom of the bedchamber to Henry Frederick, duke of Cumberland *(ibid)*.
1779, May 5. CHARLES GOULD, of Ealing, Co. Middlesex, judge advocate general *(ibid)*.
1779, May 5. HEW WHITEFOORD DALRYMPLE, major of the Athol Regiment of Highlanders *(ibid)*.
1779, Oct. 15. CLEMENT COTTRELL DORMER, appointed master of the Ceremonies *(ibid)*.
1780, Apr. 19. RICHARD PEARSON, captain R.N. *(ibid)*.
1780, May 31. JOHN CUMMING, colonel in the Bengal Army *(ibid)*.
1780, Dec. THOMAS CHAPMAN (dubbed in Ireland).
1781, Mar. 19. WALTER STIRLING, captain R.N. (at St. James's).
1781, June 22. WADSWORTH BUSK, attorney general of the Isle of Man, a bencher of the Middle Temple *(ibid)*.
1781, June 22 (? 2). GEORGE MOORE, late speaker of the House of Keys in the Isle of Man *(ibid)*.
1781, July 6. PETER BURRELL, deputy lord great chamberlain *(ibid)*.
1781, Aug. 24. GEORGE YOUNGE (YOUNG), captain R.N. *(ibid)*.
1782, Jan. 5. JOHN TURTON, physician in ordinary to the Queen.
1782, May 24 (Apr. 12). ABRAHAM PITCHES, of Streatham, sheriff of Surrey *(ibid)*.
1782, May 12. WILLIAM PLOMER, alderman of London, lord mayor of London *(ibid)*.
1782, May 29. HENRY BLACKMAN, constable of Lewes, Co. Sussex, one of the chief magistrates of the borough of Lewes *(ibid)*.
1782, June 19. THOMAS KYFFEN, of Mayman, Co. Carnarvon *(ibid)*.
1782, June 19. WILLIAM FORTICK, high sheriff of Co. Dublin (dubbed in Ireland by the duke of Portland, lord lieutenant).

KNIGHTS BACHELORS 297

1782, July 29. HOPTON SCOTT, high sheriff of Co. Wicklow (at Dublin Castle by the lord lieutenant).

1782, July 29. JEROME FITZPATRICK, M.D. *(ibid)*.

1782, July 29. HENRY JEBB, M.D. *(ibid)*.

1782, July 29. ROBERT SCOTT, M.D. *(ibid)*.

1782, Sept. 4. SAMPSON WRIGHT, one of His Majesty's justices of the peace for the Cos. of Middlesex, Essex and Surrey (at St. James's).

1782, Sept. 8. JOHN MORELLA OLDMIXON, lieutenant of Dragoons, and one of the gentlemen-in-waiting on His Grace's Family (at Dublin Castle by the duke of Portland, lord lieutenant of Ireland).

1782, Sept. RICHARD WHEELER-DENNY-CUFFE (dubbed in Ireland by same).

1782, Sept. THOMAS ASHE, high sheriff of Co. Meath *(ibid)*.

1782, Nov. 29. ROGER CURTIS, captain R.N., for his services at the siege of Gibraltar (at St. James's).

1782, Dec. 20. WILLIAM FORDYCE, M.D., of London *(ibid)*.

1783, Feb. 26 (Jan. 25). ROBERT TAYLOR, sheriff of London, architect to the Bank of England, on the address of lord mayor, alderman and commons of the City of London, in common council assembled, "hoping the stipulations of the Treaty are such as will revive our injured trade and restore our commercial intercourse with our American brethren," etc., etc. *(ibid)*.

1783, Mar. 11. ROBERT TILSON (DEANE), 1st lord Muskerry (knighted at Dublin by earl Temple, lord lieutenant, at the first investiture of St. Patrick as the proxy for prince Edward Augustus. For the names of the knights of St. Patrick knighted on that occasion *see* supra, i. pp. 96-7).

1783, Mar. 17. ALEXANDER MUNRO, consul at Madrid (at St. James's).

1783, Mar. 17. WILLIAM HAWKINS, ulster king of arms (dubbed in Ireland by earl Temple, lord lieutenant, after the banquet at the first installation of the Knights of St. Patrick).

1783, Mar. 19. WILLIAM JONES, one of the judges of His Majesty's Supreme Court of Judicature at Fort William in Bengal (at St. James's).

1783, Apr. 7. JOSEPH SENHOUSE, mayor of the City of Carlisle *(ibid)*.

1783, May. WILLIAM SYNNOT, high sheriff of Co. Armagh (dubbed in Ireland by earl Temple, lord lieutenant).

1783, May. JOHN MEREDYTH, high sheriff of Co. Meath *(ibid)*.

1783, June 27. THOMAS DAVENPORT, serjeant-at-law (at St. James's).
1783, July 4. JOHN COLLINS, captain, R.N. *(ibid)*.
1783, Aug. 22. THOMAS HYDE PAGE, lieutenant, Royal Engineers *(ibid)*.
1784, Jan. 9. HENRY AUGUSTUS MONTAGU COSBY, lieutenant colonel, adjutant general in India 1773 (at St. James's).
1784, Jan. 16. BARNARD TURNER, sheriff of London *(ibid* on presentation of an address of concern at the "present alarming moment on a measure which tended to encroach on the rights of Your Majesty's Crown, to annihilate the chartered rights of the East India Company, etc., etc.").
1784, Feb. 23. BENJAMIN THOMPSON, colonel of His Majesty's Regiment of American Dragoons (at St. James's).
1784 (? 1783), Feb. 23. JAMES PATEY, sheriff of the County of Berks. *(ibid)*.
1784, Mar. 8. JOHN EDENSOR HEATHCOTE, of Longton, sheriff of Stafford. (at St. James's).
1784, Apr. 14. HENRY THOMAS GOTT, of Newlands, Co. Bucks. *(ibid)*.
1784, May 28. CHARLES BOOTH, of Stede Hill, of Harrietsham, sheriff of Kent *(ibid)*.
1784, June 2. RICHARD KING, captain, R.N., commodore in His Majesty's Fleet employed in the East Indies *(ibid)*.
1784, Aug. 11. FRANCIS WILLES, of Hampstead, Co. Middl, sometime under secretary of State *(ibid)*.
1785, Apr. 20. JAMES DOUGLAS, His Majesty's consul general at Naples *(ibid)*.
1785, May 14. RICHARD MCGUIRE (dubbed in Dublin by the duke of Rutland "as a mark of approbation for his undaunted courage and enterprising spirit in going up in the balloon").
1785, Sept. 13. JOHN TREACHER (at Oxford).
1785, Oct. 18. CHRISTOPHER KNIGHT, mayor of Limerick (at Limerick by the duke of Rutland, lord lieutenant).
1785, Oct. 25. HENRY MARR, captain, 47th Regiment (at Killarney).
1785, Oct. 28. JAMES CARTY, sovereign of Kinsale (at Kinsale).
1785, Oct. 31. RICHARD KELLETT (at Cork).
1785, Oct. 31. JOHN HALY, doctor of physic *(ibid)*.
? 1785, Nov. JOSEPH GRAY (dubbed in Ireland).
1785. PAUL BANKS, captain, 20th Regiment *(ibid)*.
1785, Nov. JOHN ALCOCK, mayor of Waterford *(ibid)*.
1785, Nov. SIMON NEWPORT, one of the sheriffs of Waterford *(ibid)*.

KNIGHTS BACHELORS

1786, Jan. JOHN FRANKLIN, mayor of Cork (at Dublin Castle).

1786, Feb. 13. JOHN CRICKLOE (CRICHLOE) TURNER, of Great Stukeley, sheriff of Cambridge and Huntingdon (at St. James's).

1786, June 2. ISAAC HEARD, garter king of arms.

1786, Aug. 11. BENJAMIN HAMMETT, alderman of Portsoken Ward, London (at St. James's on presentation of an address from the lord mayor, aldermen, etc., of congratulation on the late escape of the King from an attack endangering his life).

1786, Aug. 13. RICHARD TAWNEY, senior alderman of Oxford City (at Oxford).

1786, Aug. 15. CHARLES NOURSE, of Oxford, surgeon *(ibid)*.

1786, Aug. 18. WILLIAM HILLMAN, mayor of the City of Winchester, clerk of the Board of Green Cloth (at St. James's).

1786, Aug. 18. ALEXANDER HAMILTON, of Topsham, sheriff of Devon. *(ibid)*.

1786, Aug. 18. STEPHEN NASH, sheriff of Bristol *(ibid)*.

1786, Aug. 23. CHARLES MARSH, of Reading, Berks *(ibid)*.

1786, Aug. 25. MICHAEL NOWELL, of Falmouth, sheriff of Cornwall *(ibid)*.

1786, Aug. 30. WILLIAM APPLEBY, of the City of Durham *(ibid)*.

1786, Sept. 6. ISAAC POCOCK, of Biggin, Northamptonshire, and of Maidenhead Bridge, sheriff of Northamptonshire *(ibid)*.

1786, Sept. 6. LAWRANCE COX, of the City of Westminster *(ibid)*.

1786, Sept. 13. WILLIAM ALTHAM, of the Borough of Thetford, mayor of Thetford, Co. Norfolk, and of Mark Hall, Essex

1786, Sept. 13. JONATHAN PHILLIPPS, of St. Stephens, near Launceston, in the County of Cornwall, sometime M.P. for Camelford *(ibid)*.

1786, Oct. 6. WILLIAM WATSON, of the City of London, M.D., and trustee of the British Museum *(ibid)*.

1786, Oct. 6. JAMES SANDERSON (SAUNDERSON), alderman of London *(ibid)*.

1786, Oct. 13. JAMES HAMILTON, high sheriff of the County of Monaghan (at Dublin Castle by the lord lieutenant).

1786, Nov. 15. JOHN WILSON, one of the justices of His Majesty's Court of Common Pleas *(ibid)*.

1786, Dec. 22. RICHARD ARKWRIGHT, of Wirksworth, Co. Derby. *(ibid* on the occasion of presenting the King with an address of congratulation from the wapentake of Wirksworth on the King's escape from assassination by Margaret Nicholson).

1787, Jan. 5. ROBERT STRANGE, an eminent engraver, of Great Queen Street, Westminster *(ibid)*.

1787, Jan. 19. GEORGE CHETWYND, of Brockton Hall, Co. Stafford, clerk of the Privy Council in ordinary (at Dublin Castle).

1787, Feb. 7. ALEXANDER THOMPSON (THOMSON), of Lincoln's Inn, a baron of the Exchequer *(ibid)*.

1787, Feb. 9. NASH GROSE, a judge of the King's Bench, serjeant-at-law *(ibid)*.

1787, May 23. JOHN FENN, of East Dereham, Co. Norfolk *(ibid)*.

1787, July 12. WILLIAM O'DOGHERTY, alderman of Drogheda (at Drogheda by the duke of Rutland, lord lieutenant).

1787, July 22. GEORGE ATKINSON, doctor of physic, deputy recorder of Hillsborough (at Hillsborough by same).

1787, Aug. 1. COSLET STOTHARD, of Dromore, Co. Down (at Dromore by the lord lieutenant).

1787, Aug. JAMES BRISTOW, of Belfast (by same).

1787, Aug. WILLIAM KIRK, mayor of Carrickfergus (at Carrickfergus).

1787, Aug. 25. WALTER HUDSON, of Enniskillen (at Castle Coole).

1787, Sept. 6. WILLIAM BOYD, doctor of physic, of Castlebar (at Castlebar).

1787, Sept. JAMES SHEE, of Galway (at Galway).

1787, Oct. 26. PAUL JODRELL, M.D., physician to the nabob of Arcott (at St. James's).

1787. THOMAS CUFFE, innkeeper, of Kilbeggan (dubbed in Ireland).

1787, JOHN TRAILE, high sheriff of Co. Dublin *(ibid)*.

1788, Feb. 21. CHICHESTER FORTESCUE, Ulster king-of-arms *(ibid* by the marquess of Buckingham, lord lieutenant).

1788, May 9. JAMES CAMPBELL, colonel (at St. James's).

1788, June 18. RICHARD PEPPER ARDEN, master of the Rolls *(ibid)*.

1788, June 27. ARCHIBALD MACDONALD, attorney general *(ibid)*.

1788, June 27. JOHN SCOTT, solicitor general, of the Middle Temple *(ibid)*.

1788, Aug. 6. CHARLES SCRIBSHAW WITHERS, of Worcester. (at Worcester).

1788, Sept. 3. WILLIAM SCOTT, doctor of laws, king's advocate general (Letters Patent).

1788, Sept. 24. WILLIAM WYNNE, LL.D., official principal of the Court of Arches, and master of the Prerogative Court of Canterbury (at St. James's).

1789, Aug. 26. THOMAS BYARD, captain of the "Impregnable," R.N. (at Plymouth).

1789, Sept. 13. ANDREW SNAPE DOUGLAS, captain R.N. (at Weymouth).

1789, Oct. 28. ASHTON WARNER BYAM, attorney general for the Island of Grenada. (at St. James's).

1790, Mar. 21. SAMUEL ROWLAND, alderman of the City of Cork (at Dublin Castle, on Sunday the 21st, at noon, by the earl of Westmorland, lord lieutenant, in the Presence Chamber and under the Canopy of State).

1790, Oct. HENRY WILKINSON, recorder of Kilkenny (dubbed in Ireland by the earl of Westmorland, lord lieutenant).

1790, Oct. 8. HENRY BROWN HAYES, one of the sheriffs of Cork (at Mitchellstown, Co. Cork).

1790, Nov. 24. RICHARD CARR GLYNN, sheriff of London and alderman of Bishopsgate Ward (at St. James's, on presentation of an address upon the agreeable prospect of a continuance of established peace by the Convention with Spain).

1790, Nov. 24. JOHN WILLIAM ROSE, recorder of London (*ibid* same occasion).

1791, Mar. 18. WILLIAM DUNKIN, one of the judges of the Supreme Court of Judicature at Fort William in Bengal *(ibid)*.

1792, July 30. WILLIAM CLARKE, one of the sheriffs elect of Cork (at Cork).

1792,* Aug. 1. ERASMUS GOWER, captain R.N. (at St. James's).

1792, Oct. 12. JOHN HOPKINS, lord mayor of London, alderman of Castle Baynard Ward (at St. James's on presentation of an address of congratulation on the glorious and important advantages gained in the East Indies).

1792, Oct. 12. BENJAMIN TEBBS, sheriff of London (*ibid* on same occasion).

1792, Nov. 26. JOHN (FANE) 16th earl of Westmorland (Letters Patent).

1792, Dec. 19. EDMUND (EDMOND) LACON, of Great Yarmouth (Letters Patent).

1792. CHARLES BLAGDEN.

1793, Feb. 1. THOMAS COXHEAD, of Epping, Co. Essex (at St. James's).

1793, Feb. 15. JOHN MITFORD, solicitor general.

---

* In the *Gazette*, dated for May 16th, 1792 (p. 317), there is an account of George III. investing Sir William Sidney Smith with the insignia of the Royal Swedish Order of the Sword. The *Gazette* adds in a footnote, "not knighted on this occasion, that ceremony having been performed by the late Swedish King in the field under the royal banner." Townend considers him entitled to the rank of a Knight Bachelor of England in consequence of this recognition of his foreign knighthood having been thus marked at a date prior to the Regulation of 1812, relative to Foreign Orders. I cannot follow the reasoning, and in accordance with the rigorous plan of the present book I have omitted him and all other such foreign made knights from my lists whether they had or had not obtained the royal licence to accept such foreign order or knighthood.

For this same reason I have omitted Peter Francis Bourgeois, a member of the Royal Academy of London, who on the 16th April, 1791, received the King's allowance of the knighthood conferred upon him by the King of Poland by diploma, dated at Warsaw, 16th February, 1791. Townend on the contrary ranks him as a knight bachelor of England.

1793, Mar. 15. JOHN TURNER DRYDEN, of Canons Ashby, Co. Northampton, sheriff of Northampton (at St. James's).

1793, Mar. 20. JOHN HENSLOW, surveyor of the Navy *(ibid)*.

1793, Mar. WILLIAM DILLON, of Mannanstown, Co. Meath (dubbed in Ireland by the earl of Westmorland, lord lieutenant).

1793, June 28. EDWARD PELLEW, captain R.N. (afterwards viscount Exmouth) (letters patent).

1793, July 16. EWEN BAILLIE, major, of Ross-shire, North Britain (at Dublin Castle by the earl of Westmorland, lord lieutenant).

1793, July. JOHN ST. LEGER GILLMAN *(ibid)*.

1793, Nov. 6. JAMES SAUMAREZ (SAUMARETZ), captain R.N. (at St. James's by the King).

1793, Nov. 13. GILES ROOKE, appointed a judge of Common Pleas, a serjeant-at-law *(ibid)*.

1794, Mar. 12. SOULDEN LAWRENCE, judge of the King's Bench, a serjeant-at-law, appointed one of the justices of His Majesty's Court of Common Pleas *(ibid)*.

1794, May 16. JOSHUA COLLES MEREDITH, of the City of Dublin (at Dublin Castle by the earl of Westmorland, lord lieutenant).

1794, May 19. ROBERT BAXTER *(ibid)*

1794, June 23. ST. GEORGE O'KELLY, high sheriff of the County of Dublin *(ibid)*.

1794, June 27. WILLIAM RULE, surveyor of the Navy (in England by the King).

1794, July 23. HENRY WILSON (afterwards WRIGHT-WILSON), captain 1st Life Guards (letters patent).

1795, Feb. 9. PATRICK O'CONOR, of the City of Cork (dubbed in Ireland by earl FitzWilliam, lord lieutenant).

1795, Apr. 15. JOHN EAMER, alderman of Langbourn Ward and sheriff of London and Middlesex (at St. James's).

1795, Apr. 15. ROBERT BURNETT, sheriff of London and Middlesex *(ibid)*.

1795, Apr. 22. THOMAS PICKERING, mayor of Arundel *(ibid)*.

1795, Apr. 22. GEORGE PICKNELL (PECKNELL), mayor of Arundel *(? ibid)*.

1795, May 8. ROBERT MACKRETH *(ibid)*.

1795, May 27. EDWARD HARRINGTON, mayor of Bath *(? ibid)*.

1795, June 10. JAMES WATSON, serjeant-at-law *(ibid)*.

1795, July 15. THOMAS SAUMAREZ, major in the Army *(ibid)*.

KNIGHTS BACHELORS

1795, Aug. DAVID PERRIER, late one of the sheriffs of Cork (at Dublin Castle, by earl Camden, lord lieutenant).

1795, Aug. 27 (26). WILLIAM PARSONS, Mus.D., master and conductor of His Majesty's Band of Music at St. James's (*ibid* by same).

1795, Nov. 6. RICHARD GLODE, of Mayfield Place, near Orpington, Kent, a sheriff of London (at St. James's by the King on presentation of an address of congratulation at the escape of the King from an assault on his way to and from Parliament).

1795, Nov. 18. SAMUEL STANDIDGE, sometime Mayor of Kingston-upon-Hull (at St. James's).

1795, Dec. 2. ISAAC PENNINGTON, regius professor of medicine in the University of Cambridge *(ibid)*.

1795, Dec. 9. CUTHBERT SHAFTO, of Basington, sheriff of Northumberland *(ibid)*.

1795, Dec. 9 (2). JOHN BULKELEY *(ibid)*.

1795, Dec. 16. THOMAS BONSALL, of Tronfraith, sheriff of Cardigan. *(ibid)*.

1795, Dec. 30. RICHARD HODGSON, mayor of Carlisle *(ibid)*.

1795. JOSEPH EYLES, captain R.N.

1795. EDMUND NAGLE, captain R.N.

1796, Mar. 18. CHARLES MITCHELL, captain E.I.C.S., knighted [on his return from the East Indies] for an action in the Straits of Molucca with a French frigate, he being then captain of the "William Pitt," East Indiaman (at St. James's).

1796, Mar. 23. WILLIAM WATSON *(ibid)*.

1796, Apr. 6. GEORGE POWELL (POWNALL), His Majesty's secretary of the Province of Lower Canada (letters patent).

1796, Apr. 29. JOHN MACARTNEY, of Dublin (at Ringsend, Dublin, by earl Camden, lord lieutenant).

1796, May 11. FRANCIS D'IVERNOIS (at St. James's by the King).

1796, July 13. THOMAS WILLIAMS, captain, R.N. *(ibid)*.

1796, Sept. 30. WILLIAM WORTHINGTON, alderman, late lord mayor of Dublin (at Dublin Castle by earl Camden, lord lieutenant).

1796, Oct. 26. STEPHEN LANGSTONE, alderman of Bread Street Ward, and sheriff of London (dubbed in England).

1796, Oct. 26. WILLIAM STAINES (STAINE), sheriff of London.

1796, Dec. 21. STEPHEN COTTRELL, master of the ceremonies (letters patent).

1797, Jan. 11. WILLIAM HERNE, alderman of Castle Baynard Ward (at St. James's, on presentation of an address to thank the King on the measures adopted by His Majesty on the recent manifesto of the Court of Madrid, abruptly declaratory of an unprovoked war with Great Britain, etc.).

1797, Mar. 3. ROBERT CALDER, captain, R.N. (at St. James's).

1797, May 10. HENRY RUSSELL (RUSSEL), a judge of the Supreme Court of Judicature at Fort William, in Bengal *(ibid)*.

1797, May 31. GEORGE BUGGIN *(ibid)*.

1797, Oct. HENRY TROLLOPE, captain, R.N.

1797, Oct. 4. JOHN ANSTRUTHER, on his appointment as chief justice of the Supreme Court of Judicature at Bengal (at St. James's).

1797, Sept. or Oct. VESIAN PICK, late mayor of Cork (at Cork by earl Camden, lord lieutenant).

1797. WILLIAM ADDINGTON, chief magistrate of the police (dubbed in England).

1797. GEORGE FAIRFAX, captain, R.N., captain of the "Venerable" at the Battle of Camperdown.

1798. SIMON LE BLANC, judge of the King's Bench.

1798. WILLIAM SEYER.

1798, Mar. 14. THOMAS ANDREW STRANGE, sometime chief justice of Madras (at St. James's).

1798, May 9. WILLIAM BEECHY (BEECHEY), R.A. *(ibid)*.

1798, July 18. JAMES BONTEIN, lieutenant colonel (Letters patent).

1798, Oct. 31. JOHN NICHOLL, LL.D., king's advocate general (same).

1798, Dec. 12. EDWARD BERRY, captain, R.N. of the "Vanguard" at the Battle of the Nile (at St. James's).

1799, Feb. 13. THOMAS BOULDEN THOMPSON, captain, R.N. *(ibid)*.

1799, Mar. 13. JAMES DURNO, of Atrochie, N.B., late His Majesty's consul general at Memel *(ibid)*.

1799, Apr. 3. GEORGE BOLTON, preceptor to the princesses in writing, geography, etc. *(ibid)*.

1799, May 10. THOMAS HAYWARD, of Carswell, Berks., clerk of the cheque to the Band of Gentlemen Pensioners *(ibid)*.

1799, June 19. EDWIN JEYNES (JOYNES), banker, of Gloucester. *(ibid)*.

1799. Rt. Hon. WILLIAM GRANT, D.C.L., solicitor general.

1799, June 26. CHRISTOPHER PEGGE, M.D., regius professor of anatomy in the University of Oxford (at St. James's).

1799, Dec. 3. ECCLES NIXON, major general *(ibid)*.

KNIGHTS BACHELORS

1799. CHARLES HAWLEY VERNON, chamberlain to the lord lieutenant (dubbed in Ireland).

1799 (?) WILLIAM JACKSON HOMAN *(ibid)*.

? 1800. ALAN CHAMBRE, judge of Common Pleas (in England by the King).

1800, Feb. 1. EDWARD HAMILTON, captain, R.N., and commander of His Majesty's ship the "Surprize" (letters patent dated Feb. 3).

1800, Feb. 11. WILLIAM OUSELEY (by the marquess Cornwallis, lord lieutenant of Ireland).

1800, May 30. JOHN ARUNDEL.

1800, Apr. 2. JOHN DOUGLAS, major, late commander of a party of marines serving on board H.M.S. "The Tigre" (at St. James's).

1800, June 11. RICHARD HETLEY, of Alwalton, Co. Huntingdon, sheriff of the Counties of Huntingdon and Cambridge (at St. James's).

1800, June 19. ROGER KERRISON, of Brooke and Norwich, banker, sheriff of Norfolk *(ibid)*.

1800, June 19. SAMUEL CHAMBERS, of Woodstock House, sheriff of Kent (at Mote Park on the occasion of George III. reviewing the Kentish Volunteers there).

1800, June 19. JAMES EARLE, surgeon (at St. James's).

1800, June 19. MATTHEW BLOXHAM (BLOXAM), M.P., alderman of Bridge Ward Within *(ibid)*.

1800, June 19. ROBERT BURTON, a bencher of Gray's Inn, formerly M.P. for Wendover *(ibid)*.

1800, June 19. WILLIAM LEIGHTON, alderman of Billingsgate Ward, London *(ibid)*.

1800, June 19. JOHN BRAZIER (afterwards ARUNDEL), mayor of Huntingdon (took the surname of Arundel by Royal Sign Manual 16, Feb., 1801) *(ibid)*.

1800, June 19. THOMAS CARR, of Bedingham, Co. Sussex, sheriff of Sussex *(ibid)*.

1800, June 19. JOHN EVERITT (EVERETT), of Westoning, sheriff of Bedfordshire *(ibid)*.

1800, June 19. ALEXANDER GORDON *(ibid)*.

1800, June 19. ROBERT GRAHAM, baron of the Exchequer *(ibid)*.

1800, June 19. WILLIAM BEAUMARIS RUSH *(ibid)*.

1800, July 2. GABRIEL POWELL, of Capel Thydis, sheriff of Carmarthen *(ibid)*.

1801, Feb. 20. EDWARD LAW, attorney general *(ibid)*.

1801, Feb. JOHN WHITE, late high sheriff of Co. Dublin (dubbed in Ireland by the marquess Cornwallis, lord lieutenant).

1801, June 16. ROBERT BARLOW, captain R.N., knighted for the capture of the "Africane," French frigate (at the Queen's house).

1801, June 24. CODRINGTON EDMUND CARRINGTON, of the Middle Temple, barrister, D.C.L., and chief justice of the Supreme Court of Judicature of Ceylon *(ibid)*.

1801, June 30. JOHN ROYDS, one of the judges of the Supreme Court at Bengal (Letters patent dated July 15).

1801, June 30 (July 16). HENRY GWILLIM, one of the judges of the Supreme Court at Bengal (same).

1801, June 30. BENJAMIN SULLIVAN, one other of the judges of the Supreme Court at Madras (same).

1801, Nov. JOHN FERNS, one of the sheriffs of Dublin (dubbed in Ireland by the earl of Hardwicke, lord lieutenant).

1801, Dec. 16. RICHARD FORD, chief magistrate of the police (same).

1801. JOHN ESDAILE, banker [an erratum for Joseph Esdaile, lieutenant of the band of gentlemen pensioners, knighted on resigning that office].

1801. R. POCKLINGTON.

1802, Feb. 10. ALEXANDER MACKENZIE (at St. James's).

1802, May 13 (22). WILLIAM RAWLINS, sheriff of London *(ibid)*.

1802, May 19. THOMAS MANNERS SUTTON, solicitor general *(ibid)*.

1802, May 19 (22). JOHN PINHORN, of Ningwood House, Isle of Wight *(ibid)*.

1802, June 2. JOHN LESTER, of Poole, Co. Dorset.

1802, June 2 (? June 16). DANIEL WILLIAMS, chief magistrate of Lambeth Street Post Office.

1803, Feb. 2. CHARLES HOLLOWAY, major of the Royal Engineers (at St. James's).

1803, Mar. 2. RICHARD WELCH, sheriff of London.

1803, Mar. 2. JAMES ALEXANDER, sheriff of London.

1803, Mar. 16. SAMUEL WATHEN, of Woodchester, sheriff of Gloucestershire (at St. James's).

1803, Mar. 16. HENRY PROTHERO *(ibid)*.

1803, Mar. 16. WILLIAM PAXTON *(ibid)*.

1803, Mar. 16. CHARLES BLICKE, surgeon *(ibid)*.

KNIGHTS BACHELORS 307

1803, Mar. 16. WILLIAM BLIZARD (BLIZZARD), surgeon to Their Royal Highnesses, the duke and duchess of Gloucester, a vice-president, one of the curators of the Museum, and honorary professor of anatomy and surgery, in the College of Surgeons (At St. James's).

1803, Mar. 30. FRANCIS SEARLE, of Kingston-upon-Thames, Co. Surrey *(ibid)*.

1803, Mar. 30. JOHN DUMARESQ, of Guernsey *(ibid)*.

1803, Mar. 30. JAMES DUBERLY (DUBERLEY), of Gains Hall, Huntingdonshire, sheriff of Cambridge and Huntingdon. *(ibid)*.

1803, May 4. WILLIAM BULKELEY HUGHES *(ibid)*.

1803, May 4. CHARLES GREEN, colonel, major general *(ibid)*.

1803, May 4. FRANCIS JOHN HARTWELL, proxy for lord Keith at the installation of the Bath, 1803.

1803, May 4. SAMUEL AUCHMUTY (AUTCHMOUTTY), knighted as proxy for Sir Robert Abercrombie at the installation of the Bath, 1803 (at St. James's).

1803, May 18. JAMES MURRAY PULTENEY, bart., lieutenant general, proxy for Sir William Medows at the installation of the Bath, 1803 (at St. James's).

1803, May 18. RICHARD HANKEY, proxy for Sir Andrew Mitchell at the installation of the Bath, 1803 *(ibid)*.

1803, May 18. WILLIAM (ROBERT) BOLTON, captain, R.N. *(ibid)*.

1803 May 18. FRANCIS WHITWORTH, lieut. col. Royal Artillery *(ibid)*.

1803, May 18. RUPERT GEORGE, proxy for Sir Thomas Graves at the installation of the Bath, 1803 *(ibid)*.

1803, Dec. 21. JAMES MACKINTOSH, professor of general polity and the laws in the East India College *(ibid)*.

1803. JOHN ANDREW STEVENSON, Mus.D. (dubbed in Ireland by the earl of Hardwicke, lord lieutenant).

1804, Jan. 29. DAVID OGILBY (dubbed in Ireland).

1804, May. JAMES MANSFIELD, chief justice of the Common Pleas (*note in "London Gazette," May 12, 1804:* "The Rt. Hon. Sir James Mansfield, knight, lord chief justice of the Common Pleas, was sworn of the Honble. Privy Council and took his place at the Board.")

1804, June 19 (Aug. 18). DAVID BAIRD, major general, for services in India and Egypt (letters patent dated June 19).

1804, June 20 (Aug. 18). JOHN STUART, major general, for services in the late glorious campaign in Egypt (letters patent dated June 20).

1805, Feb. 20. VICARY GIBBS, solicitor general (at St. James's).

1805, Feb. 21. JOHN GORE, captain, R.N.

1805, Mar. 11. NATHANIEL DANCE, captain in the Naval Service of the East India Company.

1805, Apr. 21. JOSEPH SYDNEY YORKE, captain, R.N. (at Windsor).

1805, Apr. 23. JOHN BURTON, of Soho Square *(ibid)*.

1805, May 9. JAMES LIND, captain, R.N. (at St. James's).

1805, Dec. 26. WILLIAM CHAMBERS BAGSHAW, of the Oaks, sheriff of Derbyshire (formerly Darling—took the surname of Bagshaw 1801) (at the Queen's Palace).

1806, Feb. 12. SAMUEL ROMILLY, solicitor general (at St. James's).

1806, Feb. 12. ARTHUR PIGOTT (PIGGOTT), attorney general *(ibid)*.

1806, Apr. 16. MORIS XIMENES, of Bear Place, Berks., sheriff of Berks. (at the Queen's Palace).

1806, May 21. CHARLES MONTAGU ORMSBY (at St. James's).

1806, June 11. BUSIC (BUSICK) HARWOOD, M.D., professor of anatomy and of medicine in Downing Street, of Emanuel College, Cambridge (at the Queen's Palace).

1806, Sept. 17. STEPHEN SHAIRP, consul general in Russia *(ibid)*.

1806 (? 1808), Dec. 9. JOHN CARR, of the Middle Temple (dubbed in Ireland by the duke of Bedford, lord lieutenant).

1807, Mar. 11. EDMUND STANLEY, chief justice of Madras (in England by the King).

1807, Apr. 7. CHARLES BRISBANE, captain in the Royal Navy (letters patent dated Apr. 10).

1807, Apr. 15. THOMAS PLUMER (PLOMER), solicitor general (at the Queen's Palace).

1807, Apr. 22. JONATHAN MILES, sheriff of London *(ibid)*.

1807, Apr. 22. JAMES BRANSCOMB, sheriff of London, a stockbroker and lottery contractor *(ibid)*.

1807, May 13. JONAH BARRINGTON, D.C.L., judge of the High Court of Admiralty in Ireland *(ibid)*.

1807, July 16 (? 1806, June). RICHARD HARTE, mayor of Limerick (dubbed in Ireland).

1807, Sept. 16. GEORGE RALPH COLLIER, captain R.N. (at the Queen's palace).

1807, Dec. 9. GEORGE SMITH, lieutenant colonel and aide-de-camp to the King.

KNIGHTS BACHELORS 309

1807. GEORGE WOOD, on his appointment as a baron of the Exchequer (At the Queen's Palace).

1807. CHARLES IMHOFF, lieutenant general.

1808, Mar. 11. CHARLES SHIPLEY, brigadier general: of the Royal Engineers (letters patent).

1808, Mar. 30. RICHARD PHILLIPS, sheriff of London (at the Queen's Palace).

1808, Apr. 27. JAMES GAMBIER, consul general in the Portuguese Dominions in South America *(ibid)*.

1808, May 11. JOHN BAYLEY, appointed a judge of the King's Bench *(ibid)*.

1808 (? 1809), Dec. 9. HUGH MASSEY, of Limerick (dubbed in Ireland).

1809, Feb. 6. CHRISTOPHER ROBINSON, LL.D., King's advocate general (at the Queen's Palace).

1809, Mar. 10. FRANCIS JOHN HASSARD, recorder of Waterford (dubbed in Ireland).

1809, Mar. 10. JOHN BATEMAN, of the City of Waterford *(ibid)*.

1809, Mar. 21 (? Mar. 21, 1810). JAMES FELLOWES (FELLOWS), M.D., physician to the Forces (at the Queen's Palace).

1809, Apr. 26. THOMAS COCHRANE, commonly called lord Cochrane.

1809, Aug. 30. MARK ANTHONY GERARD, captain, Royal Marines (in Ireland by the lord lieutenant).

1809, Sept. 2. NICHOLAS BRITLIFFE SKOTTOWE, one of the sheriffs of Waterford *(ibid)*.

1809, Sept. 4. RICHARD JONES, of Clonmell *(ibid* by same).

1809, Sept. 7. WILLIAM VASCHELL, of the City of Waterford *(ibid)*.

1809, Sept. ANTHONY PERRIER, one of the sheriffs of Cork *(ibid)*.

1809, Sept. CHARLES THOMAS JONES, of Montgomery, Wales, lieutenant R.N. *(ibid)*.

1809, Oct. 25. EDWARD STANLEY, one of the sheriffs of Dublin *(ibid)*.

1809, Oct. 25. JAMES RIDDALL, one of the sheriffs of Dublin *(ibid)*.

1809, Nov. 1. JAMES ATHOLL WOOD, captain R.N. (at the Queen's Palace).

1809, Nov. 1. WILLIAM PLOMER, alderman of London *(ibid)*.

1809, Nov. 1. FRANCIS MACNAUGHTEN (MACNAGHTEN), judge of the Supreme Court of Judicature at Madras *(ibid)*.

1809, Nov. 1. ALEXANDER JOHNSTON, chief justice of the Supreme Court of Judicature in Ceylon *(ibid)*.

1809, Nov. 22. JEREMIAH HOMFRAY, of Llandaff House, Co. Glamorgan *(ibid)*.

1809, Dec. 6. THOMAS STAINES, captain, R.N. *(ibid)*.

1810, Mar. 30. JAMES DUNBAR, of Boath, N.B., captain R.N.

1810, Apr. 17. JOHN HENRY NEWBOLT, of Portswood House, Hants., appointed one of the judges of the Supreme Court of Judicature at Madras, 1810, Apr. 16.

1810, May 2. WILLIAM WYNN, captain in the Army and governor of Sandown Fort (at the Queen's Palace).

1810, June 20. JAMES LUCAS YEO, captain R.N. *(ibid)*.

1810, Oct. 9. GEORGE ALLEY, M.D., of Fermoy (dubbed in Ireland).

1810, Nov. THOMAS MORIARTY, M.D. *(ibid)*.

1810, Dec. 24. JOHN JAMES BURGOYNE, provost of Strabane *(ibid by the lord lieutenant)*.

1810. THOMAS SEVESTRE.

1811, Feb. 20. JOHN ROUSSELET WHITEFOORD (at Dublin Castle by the lord lieutenant).

1811, Feb. 22. GEORGE THOMAS SMART, Mus.D., organist to His Majesty (in Ireland by same).

1811, Mar. 7. ARTHUR CLARKE, M.R.C.S. *(ibid by same)*.

1811, June 18. WILLIAM AUGUSTUS SMITH, captain R.N. *(ibid by same)*.

1811, June 18. Revd. JOHN READ, of Moynoe House, Co. Clare, clerk *(ibid by same)*.

1811, June 18. JOHN PURCELL, of Charleville, Co. Cork *(ibid by same)*.

1811, Sept. 9. WILLIAM ALEXANDER FLETCHER, of Londonderry *(ibid by same)*.

1811, Sept. 17. CHARLES THOMAS MORGAN, M.D. (at Baronscourt by same).

1812, Apr. 9. SAMUEL TOLLER, advocate general at Madras (at Carlton House by H.R.H. the Prince Regent).

1812, Apr. 9. GEORGE EYRE, captain R.N. *(ibid)*.

1812, Apr. 9. HUMPHRY DAVY, LL.D., secretary to the Royal Society, professor of Chemistry to the Royal Institution and Board of Agriculture, F.R.S.E., M.R.I.A., etc., etc. *(ibid)*.

1812, Apr. 18. RICHARD FLETCHER, lieutenant colonel of the Royal Engineers, and chief engineer with the Army in the Peninsula (letters patent dated Apr. 25).

1812, Apr. 21. JOHN HULLOCK.

1812, May 8. ROBERT HUGH KENNEDY, commissary general to the Forces (at Carlton House by H.R.H. the Prince Regent).

KNIGHTS BACHELORS 311

1812, May 8. THOMAS TYRWHITT, member of the present Parliament for the borough of Plymouth and lord warden of the Stannaries in the Duchy of Cornwall, gentleman usher of the Black Rod (at Carlton House by H.R.H. the Prince Regent).

1812, May 22. PAUL BAGHOTT (formerly Wathen), of Lypiatt Park, Co. Gloucester., proxy for viscount Strangford at the installation of the Bath, 1812, took the surname of Baghott by Royal Sign Manual, 1812, May 19 *(ibid)*.

1812, May 22. DAVID DAVIDSON, of Cantray, N.B., major in the local militia for the County of Nairn *(ibid)*.

1812, May 22. GEORGE ADAM WOOD, major general, lieutenant colonel in the Royal Artillery, proxy to Sir J. C. Sherbrooke at the installation of the knights of the Bath, 1812 *(ibid)*.

1812, May 22 (? Dec. 14). JOHN MAXWELL TYLDEN, major, proxy for Sir Samuel Auchmuty, at the installation of the Bath, 1812 *(ibid)*.

1812, May 22. JOHN POO BERESFORD, post captain, R.N., M.P. for Coleraine, proxy for Sir William Carr Beresford, at the installation of the Bath, 1812 *(ibid)*.

1812, May 22. ALEXANDER HOOD, proxy for his uncle, Sir Samuel Hood, at the installation of the Bath, 1812.

1812, May 29 (? 27). Hon. CHARLES GORDON, captain in the Army and brother of the earl of Aberdeen, proxy for the Rt. Hon. Sir John Hope, at the installation of the Bath, 1812 *(ibid)*.

1812, May 29. CHARLES WILLIAM FLINT, proxy for the Rt. Hon. Sir Henry Wellesley, at the installation of the Bath, 1812

1812, May 29. CHARLES HENRY COLVILLE, proxy for Sir Thomas Graham, at the installation of the Bath, 1812 *(ibid)*.

1812, May 29. CHRISTOPHER COLE, post captain, R.N., proxy for Sir Richard Goodwyn Keats, at the installation of the Bath, 1812 *(ibid)*.

1812, May 29. THOMAS JOHN COCHRANE, post captain, R.N., proxy for his father, Sir Alexander Forester Cochrane, at the installation of the Bath, 1812 (at Carlton House by the Prince Regent).

1812, May 29. THOMAS SYDNEY BECKWITH, colonel in the Army, proxy to his brother, Sir George Beckwith, at the installation of the Bath, 1812 *(ibid)*.

1812, May 29. ROBERT CHAMBRE HILL, lieutenant colonel in the Army, proxy for his brother, Sir Robert Hill *(ibid)*.

1812, May 29. ALEXANDER CAMPBELL, lieutenant general, proxy for the earl of Wellington, at the installation of the Bath, 1812 *(ibid)*.

1812, June. EDWARD HITCHINS, mayor of Oxford.

1812, June (July) 17. FELIX AGAR *(ibid)*.

1812, July 14. WILLIAM BETHAM, deputy ulster king of arms (in Ireland, by the lord lieutenant).

1812, July 17. WILLIAM GARROW, solicitor general (at Carlton House, by the Prince Regent).

1812, July 18 (17). LAUCHLAN (LACHLAN), MACLEAN, M.D., alderman of Sudbury *(ibid)*.

1812, Dec. 11. CHRISTOPHER SWEEDLAND (SWEELAND), of Lambeth *(ibid)*.

1812, Dec. 14. SAMUEL WHITCOMBE, of Thornton House, Greenwich, Kent *(ibid)*.

1812, Dec. 15. JOHN MALCOLM, lieutenant colonel, E.I.C.S., late envoy and plenipotentiary from the Supreme Government in India to the Court of Persia, to be permitted to wear the insignia of the Royal Persian Order of the Lion and Sun, conferred by the King of Persia, and as a further mark of Royal favour the prince Regent was pleased this day to confer the honour of knighthood upon him (at Whitehall).

1813, Feb. 26. EDWARD HYDE EAST, chief justice of the Supreme Court of Judicature at Fort William in Bengal (at Carlton House, by H.R.H. the prince Regent).

1813, Mar. 30. ALEXANDER ANSTRUTHER, recorder of the Court of Judicature at Bombay (letters patent dated Apr. 8).

1813, Apr. 2. ROBERT KER PORTER (at Carlton House by H.R.H. the prince Regent).

1813, May 6. EDWARD TUCKER, a post captain in the R.N. *(ibid)*.

1813, May 10. ALEXANDER WILSON, M.D., of Bath (at Dublin Castle by the lord lieutenant).

1813, May 19. ROBERT DALLAS, solicitor general (at Carlton House, by H.R.H. the prince Regent).

1813, May 19. JOHN DOWNIE, commissary general and brigadier general in the Portuguese Service *(ibid)*.

1813, May 19. JOHN JAMIESON (JAMISON), M.D. *(ibid)*.

1813, May 19. LUDFORD HARVEY, late examiner of the College of Surgeons *(ibid)*.

1813, June 24. THOMAS BERTIE (formerly Hoar), took the surname of Bertie 1788, rear admiral of the Red Squadron, permitted to accept the Royal Swedish order of the Sword from the king of Sweden and it was commanded that the said Royal concession be registered in the College of Arms, and the Prince Regent was this day further pleased to confer upon him the honour of knighthood (Letters patent).

KNIGHTS BACHELORS 313

1813, July 15. JOHN HAMILTON, lieutenant general (at Carlton House by the Prince Regent).

1813, July 15. HENRY DAMPIER, one of the justices of the Court of King's Bench *(ibid)*.

1813, Nov. 11. NATHANIEL CONANT, on being appointed chief magistrate of the police at the public office, Bow Street (Letters patent).

1813, Nov. 11 (13). GEORGE ELDER, colonel, a knight of the Royal Portuguese Order of the Tower and Sword (at Carlton House by H.R.H. the Prince Regent).

1813, Nov. 25. GEORGE NAYLER, York Herald, genealogist of the most Honourable and Military Order of the Bath and Blanch Coursier *(ibid)*.

1813, Dec. 10. JOHN HUNTER, on his return to Spain as His Majesty's Consul General *(ibid)*.

1813, Dec. 10. GEORGE BURGMAN, British commissioner under a Convention with the emperor of Russia and king of Prussia, concluded September 30th last *(ibid)*.

1814, Jan. 4. Rev. JOHN THOROTON.

1814, Apr. 16 (26). JOHN WILSON, brigadier general in the Portuguese Service, lieutenant colonel in the Regiment of Royal York Rangers (Letters patent dated May 11).

1814, Apr. 16 (? Aug. 24). JOHN BROWNE, lieutenant colonel in the Army, colonel in the Portuguese Service (Letters patent).

1814, Apr. 26. HUDSON LOWE, colonel of the Corsican Rangers (at Carlton House by H.R.H. the Prince Regent).

1814, Apr. 28. ARCHIBALD CAMPBELL, lieutenant colonel.

1814, May 11. RICHARD RICHARDS, late solicitor general, on his appointment as a baron of the Court of Exchequer (at Carlton House).

1814 [? 1813], May 11. HENRY BRIDGES (BRYDGES), of Ewell, late sheriff of Surrey *(ibid* by H.R.H. the Prince Regent).

1814, May 11. WILLIAM GELL, upon his return from the Ionian mission, under the patronage of His Royal Highness the Prince Regent *(ibid* by same).

1814, May 11. WILLIAM ADAMS (afterwards RAWSON), oculist extraordinary to His Royal Highness, on presenting the official report of the directors of Greenwich Hospital of the superior success of his new and improved modes of effecting the cure of the various species of cataract, and the Egyptian ophthalmia *(ibid* by same).

1814, May 11. SAMUEL SHEPHERD, a serjeant-at-law, and late solicitor general to the Prince of Wales, upon his appointment as His Majesty's solicitor general (at Carlton House by the Prince Regent).

KNIGHTS BACHELORS

1814, about May ?   ALBERT GLEDSTANES, lieutenant general.
1814, June 13.   WILLIAM ELIAS TAUNTON, town clerk of Oxford (at Oxford by H.R.H. the Prince Regent).
1814, June 13 (? June 14).   JOSEPH LOCK, mayor of Oxford *(ibid)*.
1814, June 25.   FREEMAN BARTON, captain 2nd Foot or Queen's Own (at Portsmouth by H.R.H. the Prince Regent).
1814, June 25.   HENRY PEAKE, surveyor of the Navy *(ibid)*.
1814, June 25.   GEORGE MARTIN, vice admiral *(ibid)*.
1814, June 25.   HENRY WHITE, mayor of Portsmouth *(ibid)*.
1814, June 29.   THOMAS EDLYNE TOMLINS, of the Inner Temple, barrister-at-law (at Carlton House by H.R.H. the Prince Regent).
1814, July 13.   CHARLES SUTTON, lieutenant colonel in the Army and colonel of the 9th Portuguese regiment of Infantry *(ibid)*.
1814, July 28.   CUTHBERT SHARP, mayor of Hartlepool *(ibid)*.
1814, July 28.   GREGORY HOLMAN BROMLEY WAY, lieutenant colonel of His Majesty's 29th Regiment of Foot.
1814, July 28 (29).   PATRICK WALKER, gentleman usher of the White Rod and hereditary usher of Scotland *(ibid)*.
1814, July 28.   TOMKYNS HILGROVE TURNER, lieutenant general and lieutenant governor of Jersey, and groom of the Bedchamber, colonel of the 19th (or the 1st Yorkshire, North Riding) Regiment of Foot *(ibid)*.
1814, July 28.   JAMES EDWARD SMITH, M.D., of Norwich, president of the Linnean Society, fellow of the Royal Society *(ibid)*.
1814, July 28.   ARTHUR DAVIES OWEN, of Glansevern, Co. Montgomery, adjutant general in the East Indies and colonel in the Army *(ibid)*.
1814, July 28.   JAMES MCGRIGOR (GREGOR), M.D., inspector general of Hospitals (at Carlton House by the Prince Regent).
1814, July 28.   WILLIAM LONG, mayor of Bedford *(ibid)*.
1814, July 28.   JAMES JELF, alderman of Gloucester *(ibid)*.
1814, July 28.   THOMAS NOEL HILL, lieutenant colonel, colonel in the 1st Portuguese Regiment of Infantry *(ibid)*.
1814, July 28.   JOHN MILLEY DOYLE, lieutenant colonel in the Army, colonel of the 19th Regiment of Portuguese Infantry *(ibid)*.
1814, Oct. 7.   NEIL CAMPBELL, colonel in the Army and sometime colonel of the Corsican Rangers, major in the 55th (or West Norfolk) Regiment of Foot (Letters patent dated Oct. 29).

KNIGHTS BACHELORS 315

1814, Nov. 10. CHARLES FELIX SMITH, lieutenant colonel Royal Engineers (at Carlton House by H.R.H. the Prince Regent).
1814, Nov. 10. CHARLES DALRYMPLE, commissary general to the Army under the duke of Wellington *(ibid)*.
1814. JAMES WYLIE, M.D., councillor of State and first physician to the emperor of Russia (at Ascot Races, 1814) (not gazetted).
1815, Jan. 5. EDWARD KERRISON (not gazetted).
1815, Jan. 15. LOFTUS WILLIAM OTWAY, major general (not gazetted).
1815, Feb. 23. JOHN HAWKER ENGLISH, surgeon to the king of Bavaria (at Carlton House by the Prince Regent on obtaining permission to accept and wear the insignia of the Royal Swedish Order of Gustavus Vasa).
1815, Feb. 23 (? Feb. 26). ARTHUR BROOKE FAULKENER (FAULKNER), M.D., fellow of the Royal College of Physicians, and physician to the Forces (*ibid* by same).
1815 (? 1816), Feb. 23. HENRY PYNN (at Carlton House by the Prince Regent on obtaining permission to accept and wear the insignia of a Commander of the Royal Portuguese Military Order of the Tower and Sword).
1815, Feb. 23 (26). JOSEPH GILPIN, M.D., for his services at Gibraltar and in the West Indies (at Carlton House by the Prince Regent).
1815, Mar. 7. JAMES STOPFORD (in Ireland by the lord lieutenant).
1815, Mar. 9. JOHN CAMPBELL, lieutenant colonel in the British service and colonel of the 4th Regiment of Portuguese Cavalry (at Carlton House by H.R.H. Prince Regent).
1815, Apr. 20. VICTOR VON ARENTSCHILDT, lieutenant colonel of Portuguese Regiment of Artillery (at Carlton House by the Prince Regent upon receiving the Royal licence to accept and wear the insignia of Knight of the Royal Portuguese Order of the Tower and Sword).
1815, Apr. 20. RICHARD VAUGHAN, of Bristol and of Redland Court, Co. Gloucester. (*ibid* by same).
1815, Apr. 20 (? Apr. 22). WILLIAM JOHN STRUTH, mayor of Bristol (*ibid* by same).
1815, Apr. 20 (22). THOMAS LAWRENCE, president of the Royal Academy, principal painter in ordinary to His Majesty (*ibid* by same).
1815, May 3. SAMUEL FORD WHITTINGHAM, colonel, aide-de-camp to His Royal Highness the Prince Regent, lieutenant general in the Spanish Armies (*ibid* by same).
1815, May 10 (? May 13). DIGGORY FORREST, of Plymouth, Co. Devon. (*ibid* by same).

1815, May 25. JOHN SEWELL, LL.D., of Pembroke College, Oxford, late judge of His Majesty's Vice Admiralty Court of Malta (*ibid* by same).

1815, May 25. WILLIAM OSBORNE HAMILTON, of the 8th Royal Veteran Battalion, lieutenant colonel and late governor of Heligoland, for meritorious services (*ibid* by same).

1815, May 25 (? May 27). WILLIAM COKE (COOKE), judge of the Supreme Court of Ceylon (*ibid* by same).

1815, May 25. ROBERT MENDS, captain, R.N. (at Carlton House by the Prince Regent on obtaining permission to wear the Order of Charles III. of Spain).

1815, June 6. MATTHEW (AYLMER, afterwards WHITWORTH-AYLMER), 5th lord Aylmer (in Ireland by the lord lieutenant).

1815, June 20 (29). DANIEL BAYLEY, His Majesty's consul general in Russia (at Carlton House by the Prince Regent).

1815, July 27. WARREN MARMADUKE PEACOCK, major general (at Carlton House by the Prince Regent on obtaining permission to accept and wear the insignia of an Honorary Knight Commander of the Royal Military Order of the Tower and Sword).

1815 (? 1816), Sept. 23. JAMES BRISBANE, captain R.N.

1815, Nov. 3. SKEARS REW, of Coventry.

1815, Nov. 27. THOMAS READE, lieutenant colonel, deputy adjutant general at St. Helena.

1815, Dec. 4. HUGH GOUGH, colonel, permission to wear Portuguese Order K.T.S. granted 1815, Aug. 28, without the style of Knight Bachelor (? not a Knight Bachelor of England).

1815, Dec. 11. BENJAMIN BLOOMFIELD, major general, clerk marshal and chief equerry to H.R.H. the Prince Regent, and one of the representatives in Parliament for Plymouth (at Carlton House by the Regent).

1815. CHARLES WILLIAM DOYLE, lieutenant general.

1815, Dec. 22. ROBERT LE POER TRENCH (at Dublin Castle by the lord lieutenant).

1815, Dec. 22. JOSEPH CARNCROSS, lieutenant colonel (*ibid*).

1816, Jan. 4. HENRY RYCROFT, knight harbinger (not gazetted).

1816, Feb. 4. JOHN ROWLAND EUSTACE, captain, 19th Dragoons (in Dublin Castle by the lord lieutenant).

1816, Mar. 6. JOHN SCOTT LILLIE, major in the Army (in England by the Prince Regent) [an erratum: he was an Irish knight and made in Ireland by the lord lieutenant, 1817, Jan. 21, see *infra*, p. 318].

1816, Apr. 20. ROBERT BARCLAY, colonel, of the East India Company's service (*ibid*).

1816, Apr. 20. STEPHEN EDWARD MAY, of Belfast (in Ireland by the lord lieutenant).
1816, Apr. 23. ANTHONY BULLER, on being appointed one of the judges in Bengal (at Carlton House by H.R.H. the Prince Regent).
1816, Apr. 29. THOMAS BELL, sheriff of London *(ibid)*.
1816, Apr. 30. GEORGE COOPER, judge at Madras *(ibid)*.
1816, May 29. WILLIAM BARTON, recorder of Liverpool.
1816, May 14. GEORGE SOWLEY HOLROYD, one of the judges of the Court of King's Bench *(ibid)*.
1816, May 14. CHARLES ABBOTT, one of the judges of the Court of King's Bench *(ibid* by same*)*.
1816, May 14. JAMES BURROUGH, one of the judges of the Court of Common Pleas *(ibid* by same*)*.
1816 (? 1815), May 14. WILLIAM PARKER CARROLL (CARROL), lieutenant colonel in the British Army, and a major general in the service of His Catholic Majesty *(ibid* by same*)*.
1816, May 14. PHILIP KEATING ROCHE, lieutenant colonel in the British Army, and lieutenant general in the service of His Catholic Majesty *(ibid* by same*)*.
1816, May 14. JAMES ALLEN PARK (PARKE), one of the judges of the Court of Common Pleas (at Carlton House by the Prince Regent).
1816, May 29. HENRY MATTHIAS, of Fern Hill, high sheriff of Pembroke, upon presenting an address of congratulation on the marriage of the princess Charlotte with the duke of Saxe *(ibid* by same*)*.
1816, July 1. THOMAS ARBUTHNOT, colonel *(ibid* by same*)*.
1816, July 1. ROBERT LAWRENCE DUNDAS, lieutenant colonel *(ibid)*.
1816, July 5 (? July 6). JOHN CHETHAM (CHEETHAM) MORTLOCK, lieutenant colonel, mayor of Cambridge (upon presenting an address of congratulation on the marriage of the princess Charlotte with the duke of Saxe *(ibid* by same*)*.
1816, July 5. GEORGE ALLAN MADDEN, major general (Portuguese service), of Cole Hill House, Fulham, Middlesex *(ibid* by same*)*.
1816, July 5. JOHN WOODFIELD COMPTON, LL.D., late judge of the Vice-Admiralty Court at Barbados *(ibid* by same*)*.
1816, July 5. HENRY (HARRY) NIVEN LUMSDEN, on presenting an address of congratulation from Aberdeen on the marriage of the princess Charlotte with the duke of Saxe, etc. *(ibid* by same*)*.
1816, July 5 (15). JOHN COTGREAVE, mayor of Chester, on presenting a like address *(ibid* by same*)*.

1816, July 5. ALEXANDER CROKE, of Studley Priory, Co. Oxon., LL.D., late judge of the Vice-Admiralty Court at Halifax, Nova Scotia (at Carlton House by the Prince Regent).

1816, July 15. ROBERT HALL, post captain R.N. and commodore on the lakes of Canada (*ibid* by same).

1816, Aug. 13 (? Aug. 17). WILLIAM COX, lieutenant colonel in the Army, major general in the Portuguese service (*ibid* by same).

1816, Sept. 18. ALEXANDER BRYCE, brigadier general and colonel of Royal Engineers (at Carlton House by the Prince Regent).

1816, Sept. 23. JAMES BRISBANE, post captain, R.N., captain of His Majesty's ship "Queen Charlotte" (*ibid* by same).

1816, Nov. 22 (Sept. 6). JAMES LITTLE, of the Island of Teneriffe (by patent dated Nov. 22).

1816, Nov. 25 (? Nov. 30). JOHN MEADE, M.D., deputy inspector of Hospitals for eminent services in Hanover (at Carlton House by H.R.H. the Prince Regent).

1816, Nov. 25. DUDLEY ST. LEGER HILL, lieutenant colonel in the Army, colonel in the Portuguese service (*ibid* by same).

1816. JOHN BETTON, mayor of Shrewsbury (never gazetted).

1816. JOHN BUCHAN, colonel in the Army (never gazetted).

1817, Jan. JOHN LEACH, chief justice of Chester and privy councillor.

1817, Jan. 18. HENRY WATSON, lieutenant colonel in the Army and colonel of the 1st Portuguese Cavalry (Letters patent).

1817, Jan. 21. JOHN SCOTT LILLIE, of Drimdoe, Co. Roscommon, captain in the Army and late colonel in the service of the king of Portugal: in consideration of his highly distinguished and meritorious services during the whole of the late campaigns in the Peninsula (see under date 1816, Mar. 6, *supra* p. 316).

1817, Feb. 6. ROBERT JOHN HARVEY, lieutenant colonel (at Carlton House by H.R.H. the Prince Regent).

1817, Feb. 20. ROBERT BOLTON, major general (*ibid* by same).

1817, Feb. 26. ROBERT STEELE, lieutenant of the Royal Marines, lieutenant colonel in the Spanish service (*ibid* by same).

1817, Mar. 6. PETER DE HAVILAND (HAVILLAND), bailiff of the Island of Guernsey (*ibid* by same).

1817, Mar. 6. ROBERT JONES ALLARD KEMEYS (KEMYS), lieutenant colonel, of Ynisarwed, Co. Glamorgan., and of Malpas and Panteague, Co. Monmouth. (*ibid* by same).

KNIGHTS BACHELORS   319

1817, Mar. 6. CHARLES PHILLIPS, major general (at Carlton House by the Prince Regent on obtaining permission to accept and wear the Grand Cross of the Royal Sicilian Order of St. Janarius, conferred by the king of the two Sicilies).

1817, Mar. 6. SAMUEL SPICER, of Portsea, Hants. (*ibid* by same).

1817, Mar. 13. ARCHIBALD WILLIAM CRICHTON (at Carlton House by the Prince Regent).

1817, Mar. 21. JOHN SALUSBURY PIOZZI SALUSBURY (formerly PIOZZI), of Bynbella, near Denbigh, North Wales (*ibid* by same).

1817, Mar. 21. ROBERT SHAFTO HAWKS, of Gateshead, Co. Durham (*ibid* by same).

1817, May 14 (? July 11). THOMAS BURDON, of Newcastle-upon-Tyne, brother-in-law of the earl of Eldon (*ibid* by same).

1817, May 29. FRANCIS JOHN WILDER, major general, M.P. for Arundel (*ibid* by same).

1817, May 29. RALPH RICE, recorder of Prince of Wales Island (*ibid* by same).

1817, May 29. THOMAS STAMFORD RAFFLES, lieutenant governor of Java and its dependencies (*ibid* by same).

1817, May 29. ROBERT GIFFORD, solicitor general (*ibid* by same).

1817, May 29. RICHARD BASSETT, mayor of Newport, Isle of Wight (*ibid* by same).

1817, July 1. JOHN EVANS, of Erbistock Hall, Hendreforfydd, sheriff of Merionethshire (*ibid* by same).

1817, July 1. SPIRIDION FORESTI (FORESTER), His Majesty's English resident at Corfu, minister in the Ionian Islands (*ibid* by same).

1817, July 2. WILLIAM HENRY ROBINSON, commissary general to the Forces in Canada (Letters patent dated Aug. 7).

1817, Oct. 10. THOMAS WILLIAM STUBBS, major general in the Portuguese Service, commanding the second division of the Portuguese Army (at Carlton House by the Prince Regent).

1818, Feb. 12. FRANCIS baron DE ROTTENBURG, major general (*ibid* by same).

1818, Apr. 17. GEORGE ALDERSON, sheriff of London (*ibid* by same).

1818, Apr. 17. FRANCIS DES ANGES (DESANGES), sheriff of London (*ibid* by same).

1818, Apr. 17. HENRY TUCKER MONTRESOR, lieutenant general (at Carlton House by the Prince Regent).

1818, May 5 (7). ROBERT WIGRAM, eldest son of Sir Robert Wigram, bart., of Connaught Place, Co. Middlesex, and of Belmont Lodge, Co. Worcester., one of the representatives in Parliament for Fowey, Cornwall (*ibid* by same).

1818, May 28. MURRAY MAXWELL, captain R.N.

1818, June 5. THOMAS BERNERS PLESTOW, of Watlington Hall, Co. Norfolk, and of Berners St., Co. Middlesex (not gazetted) (*ibid* by same).

1818, June 5 (? 6). ROBERT CHESTER, on being nominated by His Royal Highness Master of the Ceremonies to the King (*ibid* by same).

1818, June 5. CHARLES BROWN, M.D., of Margaretta Farm, Co. Norfolk, late first physician to the Prussian Court and Army. (*ibid* by same).

1818, Nov. 8 (? Nov. 15). JOHN D. FOWLER, bailiff of Burton-upon-Trent (never gazetted).

1819, Jan. 30 (? Feb. 2). WILLIAM WEBBER DOVETON, late one of the Council of the Island of St. Helena, and lieutenant colonel of the St. Helena Volunteers (at the Pavilion, Brighton, by H.R.H. the Prince Regent).

1819, Jan. 26. FREDERICK WATSON, major in the Army and lieutenant colonel in Portugal (in Ireland by the lord lieutenant).

1819, Mar. 18. JAMES ROBERT GRANT, M.D., inspector general of Hospitals and chief of the Medical Department of the Army, lately employed in France and the Netherlands (at Carlton House by H.R.H. the Prince Regent).

1819, Apr. 28. FREDERICK ARMSTRONG, captain in the Army and major in Portugal (in Ireland by the lord lieutenant).

1819, June 3. JOHN RICHARDSON, on being appointed one of the judges of the Court of Common Pleas (at Carlton House by H.R.H. the Prince Regent).

1819, June 3. WILLIAM DRAPER BEST, chief justice of Chester, on his being appointed one of the judges of the Court of King's Bench (at Carlton House by H.R.H. the Prince Regent).

1819, June 20. HENRY HEATHCOTE, captain, R.N. (not gazetted).

1819, July 20. ALEXANDER KEITH, on his appointment as Knight Marshal of Scotland (*ibid* by same).

1819, Aug. 17. ROBERT SEPPINGS, surveyor of the Navy (knighted on board the "Royal George" yacht, under sail and the Royal Standard flying) (not gazetted).

1819, Oct. JOHN SINGLETON COPLEY, solicitor general.

KNIGHTS BACHELORS 321

1819, Oct. 30. THOMAS GREY, M.D., F.R.S., and F.L.S., of Slane Castle, Co. Meath (at the Office of Arms, Dublin, by the lord lieutenant).
1819. HARDINGE GIFFARD, chief justice of Ceylon (not gazetted).
1819. FRANCIS THOMAS HAMMOND, general.
1819. Rt. Hon. GEORGE HENRY ROSE.
1820, Feb. 23. ALEXANDER WOOD.
1820, Mar. 22. GARRETT NEVILLE, high sheriff of Dublin (at Carlton House).
1820, Mar. 22. RICHARD OTTLEY, judge of the Island of Ceylon *(ibid)*.
1820, Apr. 20. JOHN CONNELL, procurator of the Church of Scotland, and judge of the High Court of Admiralty, Scotland *(ibid)*.
1820, Apr. 28. GEORGE LEMAN TUTHILL, physician to Bridewell and Bethlehem Hospitals *(ibid)*.
1820, May 6. WILLIAM HUTCHINSON, maj. gen., lieut. gov. of Malta *(ibid)*.
1820, May 10. WILLIAM DAVID EVANS, recorder of Bombay *(ibid)*.
1820, May 10. ROBERT BAKER, chief magistrate at Bow Street *(ibid)*.
1820, May 10 (? 11). JOHN TOBIN, mayor of Liverpool *(ibid)*.
1820, May 10. THOMAS MANTELL, mayor of Dover *(ibid)*.
1820, May 10. GEORGE SMITH GIBBES (GIBBS), of Bath, physician-in-ordinary to her late Majesty, Queen Charlotte (at Carlton House).
1820, May 10. FRANCIS SACHEVERELL DARWIN, M.D., senior bailiff of Lichfield *(ibid)*.
1820, May 11. GREGORY ALLNUTT LEWIN, lieutenant, R.N. (dubbed in Ireland by earl Talbot, lord lieutenant).
1820, May 17. FRANCIS MOLYNEUX OMMANEY, of Norfolk Street, London, navy agent, and late M.P. for Barnstaple (at Carlton House).
1820, May 17. CHARLES EDWARD GREY, a judge of the Supreme Court, Madras *(ibid)*.
1820, June 28 (? July 28). ARCHIBALD CHRISTIE, commandant general of Army Hospitals at Chatham, colonel of the 1st Royal Veteran Battalion.
1820, July 12. RICHARD GRANT, captain R.N. (at the Viceregal Lodge by the lord lieutenant).
1820, Sept. 27. GEORGE GARRETT, of Portsmouth (on board His Majesty's yacht the "Royal George," Spithead, after the presentation to His Majesty of the address of the inhabitants of Portsmouth).

w

1820, Nov. 22. CHARLES LYRAGH MACCARTHY, colonel, captain general and governor in chief of Sierra Leone, and colonel of the staff commanding the Forces on the Western Coast of Africa (at Carlton House by the King).

1820, Dec. 19. GEORGE AIREY, major general (*ibid* by same on his appointment as Knight Commander of the Order of the Guelphs).

1820, Feb. 24. ALEXANDER WOOD [made K.C.M.G. in the same year]

1821, Jan. 26. ANDREW HALLIDAY, M.D., physician to the duke of Clarence (at Carlton House).

1821, Feb. 23. JOHN WEBB, director general of the Ordnance Medical Department, Woolwich *(ibid)*.

1821, Mar. 1. ALEXANDER CRICHTON, M.D., first physician-in-ordinary to the emperor of Russia (at the Pavilion, Brighton).

*1821, Mar. 30. JOHN HOPE, lieutenant general.

1821, July 19. FENWICK BULMER, senr., gentleman of the band of gentlemen pensioners.

1821, July 19. GEORGE BARTHOLOMEW POCOCK, standard bearer of the band of gentlemen pensioners.

1821, July 24. ANTHONY CARLISLE, M.R.C.S. (never gazetted).

1821, July 25. CHARLES WEBB DANCE, major of the 2nd Life Guards (at Carlton House).

1821, July 25 (? Sept. 29). HENRY ASKEW, major general *(ibid)*.

1821, Aug. 8. JOSEPH HUDDART, of Brynkir, Carnarvon, high sheriff of Carnarvon. *(ibid)*.

1821, Aug. 20. THOMAS NORTH (GRAVES), lord Graves (knighted by George IV. as proxy for the duke of Cumberland at the investiture of the knights of St. Patrick).

1821, Aug. 20. THOMAS PAKENHAM, admiral (knighted in Ireland by George IV.).

1821, Aug. 23. JONAS GREENE, recorder of Dublin (at the Mansion House, Dublin, by same).

1821, Aug. 23. GEORGE WHITFORD, one of the sheriffs of Dublin (*ibid* by same).

---

* The *London Gazette* of 1821, May 5, contains the following notice :—

Carlton House, 1821, May 4.

The following is a copy of an order from His Majesty to the Marquess of Winchester, Groom of the Stole, which in obedience to His Majesty's commands has been communicated by his Lordship to the Lords of the Bedchamber:

"The honour of Knighthood having in two recent instances been surreptitiously obtained at the levée, His Majesty, for the purpose of effectually guarding against all such disgraceful practices in future, has been pleased to direct that henceforth no person shall be presented to His Majesty at the levée by the Lord in Waiting, to receive the honour of Knighthood, unless His Majesty's pleasure shall have been previously signified in writing to the Lord in Waiting by one of His Majesty's principal Secretaries of State."

The two individuals who practised this disgraceful trick on the King were Francis Columbine Daniel and Charles Aldis.

Townend considered that as a matter of course they were not to be included in the list of Knights. I cannot see on what principle, for, however obtained from the King, the honour, if once conferred, remains until the death or degradation of the recipient.

KNIGHTS BACHELORS 323

1821, Aug. 23. NICHOLAS WILLIAM BRADY, one of the sheriffs of Dublin (at the Mansion House, Dublin, by George IV.).

1821, Aug. 30. CHRISTOPHER MARRETT, mayor of Limerick (in Ireland by George IV.).

1821, Aug. 30. JOHN MAGENIS, M.D., mayor of Londonderry (*ibid* by same).

1821, Aug. 30. EDWARD SMITH LEES, secretary general of the Post Office, Ireland (*ibid* by same).

1821, Sept. 17. RICHARD BIRNIE, chief magistrate at Bow Street (at Carlton House).

1821, Dec. 8. GEORGE AUGUSTUS QUENTIN, lieutenant colonel of the 10th Light Dragoons (at the Pavilion, Brighton by the King).

1821, Dec. 12. WILLIAM SMITH, sheriff of Dublin (in Ireland by lord lieutenant).

1821, Dec. 12. THOMAS WHELAN, sheriff of Dublin (*ibid* by same).

1821, Dec. 12. JOHN PHILLIMORE, captain R.N. (*ibid* by same).

1821, Dec. 29. JOHN KINGSTON JAMES, lord mayor of Dublin *(ibid* by the marquess Wellesley, lord lieutenant).

1821. SAMUEL HULSE, general, treasurer of the Household (in England by the King).

1822, Mar. 16. FREDERICK GEORGE HERRIOTT [an erratum, he was not knighted but only appointed C.B. on that day].

1822, Apr. 19. ROBERT HENRY BLOSSET (on his appointment as chief justice in Bengal).

1822, Apr. 19. CHARLES KER, M.D., of Gateshaw, Roxburgh, late of the Army Medical Board (at Carlton House).

1822, Apr. 19. JAHLEEL BRENTON, bart. *(ibid)*.

1822, Apr. 19. WILLINGHAM FRANKLIN (on his appointment as justice of the Supreme Court, Madras).

1822, June 12. JOHN WILLIAM HEAD BRYDGES, of Wootton Court, Kent, captain of Sandgate Castle (at Carlton House).

1822, June 12. RICHARD CHURCH, lieutenant colonel.

1822, June 12. EDWARD BANKS, of Mile Town, near Sheerness (at Carlton House).

1822, June 12 (or 19). GEORGE FARRANT, of Northsted House, Chelsfield, Kent *(ibid)*.

1822, June. JAMES WEDDERBURN.

1822, July 4. JOHN WILLIAM PHILLIPS MARSHALL, captain in the Royal Navy.

1822, July 5. EDWARD WEST, recorder of Bombay *(ibid)*.

1822, Aug. 22. THOMAS PATE HANKIN, lieutenant colonel of the Scots Greys (at Holyrood House).

1822, Aug. 27. MICHAEL BENIGNUS CLARE, M.D., of Spanish Town, Jamaica (order for letters patent. Letters patent dated 1822, Sept. 14).

1822, Aug. 29. ADAM FERGUSON, deputy keeper of the regalia of Scotland (at Edinburgh).

1822, Aug. 27. HENRY RAEBURN, of Stockbridge, president of the Academy and first portrait painter to the King in Scotland *(ibid)*.

1822, Dec. 3. Hon. CHARLES PAGET, captain, R.N. (not gazetted).

1823, Apr. 21. WILLIAM FRANKLIN, M.D., principal inspector of the Army Medical Department (at Carlton House).

1823, Apr. 21. JOHN HULLOCK, a baron of the Exchequer *(ibid)*.

1823, Sept. 30. GEORGE RICH, chamberlain of the Household (in Ireland by the lord lieutenant).

1823, Oct. 28. CHRISTOPHER PULLER, on his appointment as chief justice of Bengal (at Windsor Castle by the king).

1823, Nov. 18 (? 12). JOHN CHAPMAN, late mayor of Windsor *(ibid)*.

1823, Nov. 18. GIFFIN WILSON, recorder of Windsor *(ibid)*.

1823, Nov. 21. WILLIAM MACLEOD BANNATYNE, late judge of the Court of Session, Scotland (at Carlton House).

1823, Nov. 21. FRANCIS BAYLEY, recorder of the Prince of Wales's Island *(ibid)*.

1823, Nov. 21. CHARLES HARCOURT CHAMBERS, a judge of the Supreme Court, Bombay *(ibid)*.

1823, Dec. 4. JAMES HENRY REYNETT, lieutenant colonel, military secretary and equerry to the duke of Cambridge *(ibid)*.

1823, Dec. 11. JOHANNES ANDREAS TRÜTER, late senior justice at the Cape of Good Hope (Letters patent).

1824, Jan. 19. The Hon. WILLIAM ALEXANDER, lord chief baron of the Exchequer Court (at Brighton by the king).

1824, Mar. 10. CHARLES WETHERALL, solicitor general (at Carlton House).

1824, Apr. 7. GEORGE AUGUSTUS WESTPHALL, captain, R.N. *(ibid)*.

1824, Apr. 7. PETER LAURIE, sheriff of London *(ibid)*.

1824, Apr. 7. JAMES WILLIAMS, of The Gothic, Kentish Town *(ibid)*.

1824, Apr. 28. JAMES BRABAZON URMSTON, president of the Select Committee of supercargoes of the East India Company, at Ceylon (order for Letters patent).

1824, June 9. JOSEPH LITTLEDALE, a justice of the King's Bench (at Carlton House).

1824, Sept. 3. WILLIAM DAVISON, aide-de-camp and equerry to the duke of Cambridge (at the king's lodge, Windsor).

1824, Nov. 24. AUGUSTUS WEST, M.D., brevet deputy inspector of hospitals, a physician-in-ordinary to the king of Portugal (at Carlton House).

1824, Nov. 24. RALPH PALMER, judge at Madras.

1824, Dec. 15. JOHN HARVEY, lieutenant colonel (at the King's Lodge, Windsor).

1824. FRANCIS WASKETT MYERS.

1825, Feb. 9. ROBERT BUCKLEY COMYN, a judge at Calcutta (at Carlton House).

1825, Mar. 23. GEORGE WILLIAM RICKETTS, a judge of the Supreme Court of Madras *(ibid)*.

1825, Apr. 16 (? 11). WINDSOR EDWIN BAYNTON SANDYS (at the Lord Chamberlain's Office).

1825, Apr. 20. GABRIEL WOOD, commissary general (at Carlton House).

1825, Apr. 20. HENRY JARDINE, King's remembrancer of the Exchequer, Scotland *(ibid)*.

1825, Apr. 20. CHARLES DASHWOOD, late captain of H.M.S. "Windsor Castle" *(ibid)*.

1825, Apr. 20. THOMAS LE BRETON, lieutenant, bailly of the Island of Jersey *(ibid)*.

1825, Apr. 20. JOHN FRANKS, a judge of the Supreme Court of Bengal *(ibid)*.

1825, Apr. 20. BENTINCK CAVENDISH DOYLE, late captain of H.M.S. "Glasgow" *(ibid)*.

1825, Apr. 20 (? Apr. 25). ROBERT MOUBRAY, of Cockairney, Fife, lieutenant colonel *(ibid)*.

1825, Apr. 27. STEPHEN GAZELEE, judge of the Common Pleas.

1825, Apr. 27. JAMES MONK, late chief justice in Canada.

1825, May 29. THOMAS JOHN COCHRANE, captain in the Royal Navy.

1825, Sept. 30. JOHN THOMAS CLARIDGE, recorder of Prince of Wales's Island (at Windsor Castle).

1825. HENRY FREDERICK COOKE, colonel, and M.P. for Camelford (not gazetted).

KNIGHTS BACHELORS

1826, May 29. WILLIAM LEWIS HERRIES, lieutenant colonel, quartermaster general in the Mediterranean, and registrar of the Order of the Bath, and a comptroller of Army Accounts (at Carlton House).

1826, July 27. THOMAS HENRY BROWNE, lieutenant colonel.

1826, July 27. JOHN STODDART, LL.D., president of the High Court of Appeal, and judge of the Vice-Admiralty Court at Malta.

1826, Sept. 30. CHARLES MALCOLM, captain R.N., commander of the yacht in attendance on the lord lieutenant (in Ireland by the lord lieutenant).

1826, Sept. 30. RICHARD HUNTER, M.D., one of the gentlemen of the bedchamber and physician to the lord lieutenant).

1826, Nov. 27. NICOLAS CONYNGHAM TINDAL, solicitor general (at St. James's Palace by the King).

1826, Nov. 27. JOHN FRASER, lieutenant general *(ibid)*.

1826, Nov. 27. EDWARD MILES, lieutenant colonel *(ibid)*.

1826, Nov. 27. EDWARD RYAN (on his appointment as judge to the Supreme Court at Calcutta) *(ibid)*.

1826, Dec. 16. JOSEPH FULLER, lieutenant general *(ibid)*.

1827, Mar. 9. JOHN EDMUND DE BEAUVOIR, eldest son of Sir John Edmund Browne, bart. (in Ireland by the lord lieutenant).

1827, Apr. 30. ANTHONY HART (on being appointed vice-chancellor of England) (at St. James's Palace by the King).

1827, Apr. 30. JAMES SCARLETT, attorney general *(ibid)*.

1827, May 18 (? 16). FREDERICK BEILBY WATSON, master of the Household *(ibid)*.

1827, May 23. SAMUEL ST. SWITHIN BURDEN WHALLEY, of Farzebrook House, Devon *(ibid)*.

1827, June 30. HENRY WILLOCK, major *(ibid)*.

1827, June 30. NESBIT JOSIAH WILLOUGHBY, captain, R.N. (at St. James's Palace at the instance of the duke of Clarence, then lord high admiral. By a blunder of the King's was again knighted 1832, Aug. 21, on his investiture as K.C.H.).

1827, June 30. JOHN PETER GRANT, a judge at Bombay (at St. James's Palace).

1827, June 30. JOHN WYLDE, LL.D., chief justice at the Cape of Good Hope.

1827, Aug. 17 (? 16). JOHN CONROY, captain, equerry and private secretary to the Duchess of Kent (at Windsor Castle).

1827, Aug. 29. THOMAS ANBUREY, lieutenant colonel in the East India Company's service (order for Letters patent. The letters patent passed on the 27th March, 1829).

1827, Aug. 29. ALEXANDER MCLEOD, lieutenant colonel in the East India Company's service (Letters patent).

KNIGHTS BACHELORS

1827, Oct. 31. Rt. Hon. WILLIAM HENRY FREEMANTLE, treasurer of the Household (at Windsor).

1827, Nov. 16. LANCELOT SHADWELL, appointed vice-chancellor of England, Oct. 31, took seat at Privy Council as Sir Lancelot Shadwell Nov. 16.

1827, Dec. 1. THOMAS CHARLES YEATES, one of the sheriffs of Dublin (in Ireland by the lord lieutenant).

1827, Dec. 1. RICHARD WILCOCKS, late inspector of police in Munster (*ibid* by same).

1827, Dec. 5. FRANCIS MACDONNELL, of Dunferth Castle, Co. Kildare (*ibid* by same).

1827, Dec. 6 (7). WILLIAM ROBERT SYDNEY, of Woolwich, Co. Kent (*ibid* by same).

1827, Dec. 19. JOHN THEOPHILUS LEE, of Brompton, Middlesex (in Ireland by the lord lieutenant).

1828, Feb. 13. THOMAS (EDWARD) FELLOWES, captain, R.N. (in England by the King).

1828, Mar. 1. EDMOND NUGENT, lord mayor of Dublin (in Ireland by the marquess of Anglesey, lord lieutenant).

1828, Mar. 22. DAVID CHARLES ROOSE, one of the sheriffs of Dublin (*ibid* by same).

1828, Mar. 27. JOHN MACRA, lieutenant colonel, military secretary to the late marquess of Hastings (at St. James's Palace by the King).

1828, June (? Feb.) 28. HERBERT JENNER (afterwards Jenner-Fust), on his appointment as king's advocate general *(ibid)*.

1828, Nov. 24. The Hon. ROBERT CAVENDISH SPENCER, captain, R.N. (at Windsor Castle on being invested K.C.H.)

1828, Nov. 24. JOHN VAUGHAN, a baron of the Exchequer Court (at Windsor Castle).

1828, Dec. 1. JAMES PARKE, a justice of the King's Bench *(ibid)*.

1828, Dec. 9. JEFFERY WYATVILLE *(ibid)*.

1829, Jan. 4. JOHN WHALE, of North Down House, Co. Kent (in Ireland by the marquess of Anglesey, lord lieutenant).

1829, Jan. 18. JAMES EGLINTON ANDERSON, M.D., physician to the lord lieutenant (in Ireland by the lord lieutenant).

1829, Apr. 15. JAMES DEWAR, chief justice of the Supreme Court of Judicature at Bombay (Letters patent).

1829, Apr. 23. RALPH HAMILTON, colonel, of Olivestob, North Britain (at Dublin Castle by the duke of Northumberland, lord lieutenant).

1829, Apr. 29. WILLIAM ANGLIN SCARLETT, chief justice of Jamaica (at St. James's Palace).
1829, Apr. 29. WILLIAM EDWARD PARRY, captain, R.N., late commander of the expeditions for the discovery of a North-West passage *(ibid)*.
1829, Apr. 29. WILLIAM CAMPBELL, chief justice of Upper Canada *(ibid)*.
1829, Apr. 29. WILLIAM SEYMOUR, a judge of the Supreme Court of Bombay *(ibid)*.
1829, Apr. 29. JOHN FRANKLIN, captain, R.N., late commander of the Northern Lands Expedition *(ibid)*.
1829, Apr. 29. WILLIAM RICHARD COSWAY, of Bilsington, Kent, late secretary to vice-admiral lord Collingwood *(ibid)*.
1829, June 10. EDWARD BURTENSHAW SUGDEN, solicitor general *(ibid)*.
1829, Aug. 12. ALBERT CONYNGHAM, secretary to H.M. Legation at Berlin (at Windsor).
1829, Sept. 16. JOHN HAYES (HAYS), commodore in the East India Company's marine service (Letters patent dated Nov. 18).
1829, Sept. 16. ROBERT HENRY CUNLIFFE, lieutenant colonel commandant in the East India Company's service (same of same date).
1829, Sept. 16. JEREMIAH BRYANT, lieutenant colonel in East India Company's service (same of same date).
1829, Sept. 30. CHARLES SCUDAMORE, M.D., F.R.S. (by the lord lieutenant at Dublin).
1829, Nov. 17. JOHN MCDONALD, lieutenant colonel in East India Company's service and envoy extraordinary from the Government of India to H.M. the Shah of Persia (Letters patent).
1830, Feb. 2. WILLIAM BOLLAND, a baron of the Exchequer (at Windsor Castle).
1830, Feb. 2. JOHN BERNARD BOSANQUET, Hon., a judge of the Common Pleas (at Windsor Castle).
1830, June 18. JOHN WITHER AWDRY, of Notton, Co. Wilts., a judge of the Supreme Court, Bombay (Letters patent dated July 22).
1830, July 17. WILLOUGHBY COTTON, major general (at St. James's Palace).
1830, July 21. WILLIAM PYM, M.D., inspector of Army Hospitals *(ibid)*.
1830, July 21. MARTIN ARCHER SHEE, president of the Royal Academy *(ibid)*.
1830, July 21. GEORGE DRINKWATER, mayor of Liverpool *(ibid)*.

KNIGHTS BACHELORS

1830, July 21. WILLIAM HENRY RICHARDSON, sheriff of London (At St. James's).
1830, July 21 (? Aug.). JAMES SOUTH, F.R.S., of the Observatory at Kensington (Letters patent).
1830, July 28. FRANCIS AUGUSTUS COLLIER, captain R.N. (at St. James's Palace).
1830, Aug. 4. JAMES EYRE, mayor of Hereford *(ibid)*.
1830, Aug. 4. AUGUSTUS CLIFFORD, captain R.N. *(ibid)*.
1830, Aug. 4. GEORGE BALLINGALL, regius professor of Military Surgery, Edinburgh *(ibid)*.
1830, Aug. 4. OCTAVIUS CAREY, colonel *(ibid)*.
1830, Sept. 11. DAVID ERSKINE, of Dryburgh Abbey, Merionethshire (at the Pavilion, Brighton).
1830, Oct. 5. EDMUND MASSENBERG BELLINGER SKOTTOWE, mayor of Waterford (at Waterford by the lord lieutenant).
1830, Oct. 5. JOHN KINGSMILL, colonel of the Battle Axe Guards *(ibid* by same).
1830, Oct. 8. CHARLES WITHAM, lieutenant R.N. (at Cork by same).
1830, Oct. 9. THOMAS DEANE, one of the sheriffs of Cork *(ibid* by same).
1830, Oct. 27. DANIEL KEYTE SANDFORD, professor of Greek, Glasgow (at St. James's Palace).
1830, Oct. 27. EDWARD WILLIAM CORRY ASTLEY, captain R.N. *(ibid)*.
1830, Oct. 27. JAMES LEIGHTON, M.D., physician to the Navy.
1830, Nov. 17. EDWARD HALL ALDERSON, a justice of Common Pleas *(ibid)*.
1830, Nov. 17. WILLIAM ELIAS TAUNTON, a justice of the King's Bench *(ibid)*.
1830, Nov. 17. JAMES (? JOHN) PATTESON, a justice of the King's Bench *(ibid)*.
1830, Oct. 24. WILLIAM HORNE, solicitor general *(ibid)*.
1830, Nov. 24. THOMAS DENMAN, attorney general *(ibid)*.
1830. GEORGE HOSTE, colonel.
1830. AUGUSTUS FREDERIC D'ESTE.
1831, Feb. 4. JAMES CHARLES DALBIAC, major general, colonel of the 3rd Dragoon Guards.
1831, Mar. 2. JOHN DE VEULLE, bailiff of the Island of Jersey (at St. James's Palace).
1831, Mar. 2. CHARLES WADE THORNTON, major general.
1831, Mar. 9 (? Mar. 2). CHAPMAN MARSHALL, sheriff of London *(ibid)*.
1831, Mar. 9. Major Gen. JAMES CAMPBELL *(ibid)*.

1831, Mar. 9 (? Mar. 2). WILLIAM HENRY POLAND, sheriff of London (At St. James's).
1831, Mar. 20. Maj. Gen. H. WHEATLEY.
1831, Mar. 23. Captain GEORGE FRANCIS SEYMOUR.
1831, Mar. 23. Maj. Gen. Benj. CHARLES STEPHENSON.
1831, Mar. 28. JOHN HALL, consul general for Hanover.
1831, Mar. 30. HERBERT ABINGDON DRAPER COMPTON, late chief justice at Bombay.
1831, Apr. 13. GEORGE HARRISON.
1831, May 3. WILLIAM GOSSETT, lieutenant colonel, under secretary to the lord lieutenant in Ireland (in Ireland by the lord lieutenant).
1831, May 11. JOSEPH WHATLEY, groom of the bedchamber.
1831, May 25. WILLIAM BURNETT (BURNET), medical commissioner of H.M. Navy (at St. James's Palace).
1831, May 25. WILLIAM BEATTY, physician, of Greenwich Hospital (at St. James's Palace).
1831, June 8. STEPHEN REMNANT CHAPMAN, commander-in-chief of the Bermudas *(ibid)*.
1831, June 8. Rt. Hon. ROBERT WILMOT HORTON, governor and commander-in-chief of Ceylon *(ibid)*.
1831, Aug. 3. Hon. EDWARD CUST, lieutenant colonel.
1831, Aug. 3. GEORGE BAILLIE HAMILTON, secretary of Legation at Berlin.
1831, Aug. 10. Lieut. Gen. JOHN SMITH.
1831, Aug. 10. JOHN RENNIE, of Whitehall Place *(ibid)*.
1831, Aug. 17. RICHARD DOBSON, surgeon of the Royal Hospital, Greenwich *(ibid)*.
1831, Aug. 31. JOHN HILL, captain, R.N., and resident commissioner of the Victualling Board at Deptford *(ibid)*.
1831, Sept. 13. ALEXANDER ANDERSON, colonel.
1831, Sept. 13. JOHN MARK FREDERICK SMITH, colonel.
1831, Sept. 13. FRANCIS BOND HEAD, major, of Sutton, Surrey *(ibid)*.
1831, Sept. 13. HENRY BROMLEY HINRICH, lieutenant of the Band of Gentlemen Pensioners *(ibid)*.
1831, Sept. 13. HENRY CIPRIANI, senior exon of the Yeoman of the Guard *(ibid)*.
1831, Sept. 13. ROBERT GILL (GYLL), lieutenant of the Yeoman of the Guard *(ibid)*.
1831, Sept. 13. THOMAS BRANCKER (BRANKER), mayor of Liverpool *(ibid)*.
1831, Sept. 13. RICHARD BURTON, senior member of the Band of Gentlemen Pensioners (at St. James's Palace).
1831, Sept. 13. Maj. Gen. AMOS GODSILL R. NORCOT.
1831, Sept. 13. Col. NEIL DOUGLAS, 79th foot.
1831, Sept. 13. Capt. WILLIAM HOWE MULCASTER, R.N.

KNIGHTS BACHELORS 331

1831, Sept. 16. GEORGE MAGRATH, M.D., of Plymouth, surgeon in the Royal Navy (Letters patent dated Sept. 26).
1831, Sept. 18. WILLIAM DE TUYLL, baron de Tuyll, major general.
1831, Sept. 21. Col. MICHAEL MACCREAGH.
1831, Sept. 21. Col. ROBERT DICK, A.D.C.
1831, Sept. 21. Maj. Gen. GEORGE BULTEEL FISHER.
1831, Sept. 21. JOHN SOANE, of Lincoln's Inn Fields (at St. James's Palace).
1831, Sept. 21. LEWIS GRANT, major general, governor of Trinidad, and colonel of the 96th Regiment.
1831, Sept. 28. GEORGE POWNALL ADAMS, lieutenant general.
1831, Sept. 28. RICHARD ARMSTRONG, colonel, for military services).
1831, Oct. 5. THOMAS CHARLES FRANCIS DOWNMAN, major general.
1831, Oct. 12. NICHOLAS HARRIS NICOLAS.
1831, Oct. 12. CHARLES BELL, F.R.S.
1831, Oct. 12. JOHN FREDERICK WILLIAM HERSCHEL, of Slough, Bucks.
1831, Oct. 19. ARCHIBALD MACLAINE, colonel.
1831, Oct. 19. JOHN HOLLAMS, mayor of Deal, Kent (ibid).
1831, Oct. 21 (? Oct. 12). GEORGE HEAD, deputy knight marshal of H.M. Household.
1831, Dec. 7. RALPH BIGLAND, garter king of arms.
1831, Dec. 7. GEORGE ROSE, a judge of the Court of Bankruptcy (ibid).
1831, Dec. 7. JOHN CROSS, a judge of the Court of Bankruptcy (ibid).
1831, Dec. 7. ALBERT PELL, a judge of the Court of Bankruptcy (ibid).
1831. GEORGE COCKBURN, general (at Brighton).
1831. THOMAS USSHER, captain R.N. [? not a Knight Bachelor of England: only a K.C.H.].
1831. JAMES MAXWELL WALLACE, colonel.
1832, Jan. 26. JOSIAH CHAMPAGNÉ, general, colonel of the 17th Foot (at the Pavilion, Brighton).
1832, Feb. 6. CHARLES BULKELY EGERTON, lieutenant general (at St. James's Palace).
1832, Feb. 22. DAVID BARRY, M.D., deputy inspector general of Hospitals (ibid).
1832, Feb. 22. JOHN HARRISON YALLOP, mayor of Norwich (ibid).
1832, Feb. 22. JOHN GURNEY, a baron of the Exchequer Court (ibid).
1832, Feb. 22. WILLIAM AUGUSTUS MONTAGU (MONTAGUE), captain, R.N. (at St. James's Palace).
1832, Feb. 22. SIGISMUND SMITH, major general (ibid).
1832, Feb. 22. JAMES HAY, lieutenant general, colonel of 2nd Dragoon Guards (ibid).
1832, Feb. 22. WILLIAM PATERSON, major general (ibid).

1832, Feb. 22. FREDERICK TRENCH, colonel, A.D.C. to the King (At St. James's).
1832, Feb. 22. LEONARD GREENWELL, colonel, commissioner of the garrison at Chatham *(ibid)*.
1832, Feb. 22. SAMUEL RUSH MEYRICK, LL.D., of Goodrich Court, Hereford *(ibid)*.
1832, Feb. 22. GEORGE WHITMORE, colonel, R.E. *(ibid)*.
1832, Feb. 22. WILLIAM OLDNALL RUSSELL, chief justice of the Supreme Court of Bengal *(ibid)*.
1832, Feb. 22. ROBERT SMIRKE, of Stratford Place *(ibid)*.
1832, Feb. 22. HENRY EDMUND AUSTEN, of Shalford House, Surrey, a gentleman of the Privy Chamber in Ordinary *(ibid)*.
1832, Feb. 22. JOHN GIBNEY, physician to the Sussex County Hospital *(ibid)*.
1832, Feb. (? Mar.) 29. JOSHUA ROWE, chief justice of Jamaica *(ibid)*.
1832, Mar. 5. GEORGE CAMPBELL, of Edenwood, Fife (Letters patent dated Mar. 17).
1832, Mar. 8. DAVID BREWSTER (at St. James's Palace).
1832, Mar. 22. MARTIN HUNTER, general *(ibid)*.
1832, Apr. 12. WILLIAM WOODS, clarenceux king of arms *(ibid)*.
1832, June 24. JOHN WOODFORD, colonel (at Windsor Castle).
1832, June 27. JOHN LESLIE, of Coates, professor of Natural Philosophy at Edinburgh (at St. James's Palace).
1832, June 27. JOSEPH STRATON, major general *(ibid)*.
1832, June 27. FREDERICK WILLIAM MULCASTER, major general R.E. *(ibid)*.
1832, June 27. EDWARD THOMASON, of Birmingham (at St. James's Palace).
1832, July 4. HENRY BETHUNE, of Kilconquhar, Fife *(ibid)*.
1832, July 4. JOHN HANBURY, major general *(ibid)*.
1832, July 4. JOHN MARSHALL, captain *(ibid)*.
1832, July 4. JOHN MACLEOD, major general *(ibid)*.
1832, July 14. DAVID XIMENES, colonel (Letters patent dated July 27).
1832, July 17. CHARLES MARSHALL, chief justice of the Supreme Court in Ceylon (at St. James's Palace).
1832, Aug. 1. MICHAEL CREAGH, lieutenant colonel *(ibid)*.
1832, Aug. 24. WILLIAM NICOLAY, major general, governor of Mauritius *(ibid)*.
1832, Aug. 24. JOHN DEAS THOMSON *(ibid)*.

KNIGHTS BACHELORS

1832, Aug. 31. FRANCIS PALGRAVE (at St. James's Palace).
1832, Sept. 5. FREDERICK ADAIR ROE, chief magistrate of Bow Street *(ibid)*.
1832, Sept. 12. GEORGE JACKSON, His Majesty's commissary judge at Rio de Janeiro *(ibid)*.
1832, Oct. 12. CHARLES EURWICKE DOUGLAS, king-of-arms of the Order of St. Michael and St. George *(ibid)*.
1832, Oct. 31. FRANCIS GEARY GARDNER LEE *(ibid)*.
1832, Nov. 6. JOHN BISSETT *(ibid)*.
1832, Nov. 6. CHARLES CONYNGHAM, rear admiral *(ibid)*.
1832, Nov. 6. THOMAS BROWNE, lieutenant general *(ibid)*.
1832, Dec. 3. JOHN CAMPBELL, solicitor general *(ibid)*.
1832, Dec. 3. The Hon. COURTENAY BOYLE, rear admiral *(ibid)*.
1832, Dec. 15. JOHN NICOLL ROBERT CAMPBELL, captain in the East India Company's service, and envoy from the governor general of India to the Court of Persia (Letters patent dated Dec. 22).
1832. WILLIAM WHYMPER, M.D.
1832. ANDREW PELLATT GREEN, captain, R.N.
1833, Jan. 22. EDWARD DURNFORD KING, rear admiral (at the Pavillion, Brighton).
1833, Feb. 4. Rt. Hon. CHARLES RICHARD VAUGHAN (at St. James's Palace).
1833, Feb. 22. FREDERICK AUGUSTUS WETHERALL, of Castlebar, Great Ealing, Middlesex *(ibid)*.
1833, Feb. 22. DAVID LATIMER TINLING WIDDRINGTON, lieutenant general *(ibid)*.
1833, Feb. 22. JOHN BOSCAWEN SAVAGE, colonel Royal Marines *(ibid)*.
1833, Feb. 22. HENRY ELLIS, principal librarian of the British Museum *(ibid)*.
1833, Feb. 22. RICHARD SPENCER, captain R.N. *(ibid)*.
1833, Mar. 13 (? Feb. 13). HENRY JOHN CUMMING, lieutenant general *(ibid)*.
1833, Mar. 13 (? Feb. 13). FREDERICK MADDEN, of the British Museum *(ibid)*.
1833, Mar. 26. GEORGE TEESDALE, colonel *(ibid)*.
1833, May 1. JOHN WILLIAM JEFFCOTT, chief justice of the Court of Vice-Admiralty, Sierra Leone *(ibid)*.
1833, May 3. JAMES STIRLING, R.N.

1833, June 27. THOMAS ISAAC HORSLEY CURTEIS, senior exon of the Yeomen of the Guard (At St. James's).

1833, June 27. CHARLES WILKINS *(ibid)*.

1833, July 18 (? June 27). GRAVES CHAMNEY HAUGHTON *(ibid)*.

1833, July 23. SAMUEL ROBERTS, captain R.N. (in Ireland by the lord lieutenant).

1833, Aug. 8. JOHN ORMSBY VANDELEUR, lieutenant general (at St. James's Palace).

1833, Sept. 26. WILLIAM WAINWRIGHT FAWCETT-LYNAR, captain 18th Regiment, one of the sheriffs of Dublin (in Ireland by the lord lieutenant).

1833, Sept. 26. GEORGE PRESTON, one of the sheriffs of Dublin *(ibid* by same).

1833, Sept. 26. JAMES MURRAY, M.D., physician to the lord lieutenant *(ibid* by same).

1833, Sept. 30. DRURY JONES DICKINSON, one of the sheriffs of Dublin *(ibid* by same).

1833, Sept. 30. RICHARD BAKER, one of the sheriffs of Dublin *(ibid* by same).

1833, Nov. 5. PHINEAS RIALL, lieutenant general (at the Pavilion, Brighton, by the King).

1833, Nov. 15. ARTHUR FARQUHAR, captain R.N. *(ibid)*.

1833. HENRY WILLOUGHBY ROOKE.

1834, Jan. 17. HENRY BAILY, lieutenant general, colonel of the 8th Foot, 2nd son of Col. Nicholas Bayly *(ibid)*.

1834, Jan. 29. SAMUEL TREVOR DICKENS, major general R.E. *(ibid)*.

1834, Feb. 21. SALUSBURY PRYCE HUMPHREYS, of Bramhall Hall, Chester, captain R.N. (at St. James's Palace [? not a Knight Bachelor of England: only a K.C.H.].

1834, Feb. 21. JAMES VINEY, major general of the Royal Artillery *(ibid)*.

1834, Feb. 21. JAMES KEARNEY, major general, late of the 2nd Dragoon Guards *(ibid)*.

1834, Feb. 21. EVAN LLOYD, lieutenant general of the 17th Lancers *(ibid)*.

1834, Feb. 21. THOMAS GAGE MONTRESOR, lieutenant general *(ibid)*.

1834, Feb. 21. SALUSBURY PRYCE DAVENPORT, rear admiral.

1834, Feb. 26. CHARLES CHRISTOPHER PEPYS, solicitor general *(ibid)*.

1834, Mar. 5. EATON STANNARD TRAVERS, captain R.N. *(ibid)*.

1834, Mar. 12. CHARLES EDMUND NUGENT, admiral *(ibid)*.

KNIGHTS BACHELORS

1834, Mar. 19. LORENZO MOORE, major general (at St. James's).
1834, Mar. 26. JAMES NICHOLL MCADAM, of Whitehall, and of Tindon End, Essex *(ibid)*.
1834, Mar. 27. JOHN WOOLMORE, captain, deputy master of Trinity House (at Windsor Castle).
1834, Apr. 16. JOHN WILLIAMS, a baron of the Exchequer (at St. James's Palace).
1834, May 3. JOHN FERRIS DEVONSHIRE, rear admiral, of Alwington House, Davon. (Letters patent dated May 21).
1834, May 27. The Hon. ALEXANDER DUFF, lieutenant general.
1834, May 27. JOSEPH MACLEAN, major general, commandant at Woolwich (at St. James's Palace).
1834, June 5. HUMPHREY LE FLEMING SENHOUSE, captain R.N. *(ibid)*.
1834, June 5. HENRY KING, colonel *(ibid)*.
1834, June 18. HUGH PIGOT, captain R.N. *(ibid)*.
1834, July 9. ARETAS WILLIAM YOUNG *(ibid)*.
1834, Aug. 6. EDWARD JOHN GAMBIER, recorder of Prince of Wales Island *(ibid)*.
1834, Aug. 13. SAMUEL THOMAS SPRY, of Place, Cornwall, M.P., *(ibid)*.
1834, Aug. 20. DAVID JAMES HAMILTON DICKSON, physician to the Royal Naval Hospital at Plymouth *(ibid)*.
1834, Aug. 20. Rt. Hon. ROBERT GRANT, governor of Bombay *(ibid)*.
1834, Sept. 17. SAMUEL RAYMOND JARVIS, of Fair Oak Park, Hants. *(ibid)*.
1834, Oct. 8 (? 3). THOMAS STEPHEN SORELL (SORRELL), lieutenant colonel, H.M. consul general to the Austrian States in Italy *(ibid)*.
1834, Oct. 29 (? 24). JOHN DODSON, LL.D., His Majesty's advocate general *(ibid)*.
1834, Dec. 15. The Hon. HENRY DUNCAN, captain *(ibid)*.
1834, Dec. 22. WILLIAM WEBB FOLLETT, solicitor general *(ibid)*.
1834, Dec. 24. JOHN Ross, captain R.N. *(ibid)*.
1834, Dec. 29. JONATHAN FREDERICK POLLOCK, attorney general (at the Pavilion, Brighton).
1835, Jan. 23. EDMUND LYONS, captain R.N. *(ibid)*.
1835, Feb. 18. JAMES LIMOND, colonel (at St. James's Palace).
1835, Feb. 18. JOSEPH O'HALLORAN, colonel *(ibid)*.
1835, Feb. 18. THOMAS BLIGHT ST. GEORGE, major general *(ibid)*.
1835, Feb. 25. CHARLES BULLEN, captain R.N. *(ibid)*.
1835, Mar. 18. THOMAS PEARSON, major general *(ibid)*.

1835, Mar. 25. WILLIAM O'MALLEY, ensign 14th Regiment, eldest son of Sir Samuel O'Malley, bart. (in Dublin Castle in the closet by the lord lieutenant).

1835, Apr. 1. HENRY JOHN LEEKE, captain R.N. (at St. James's Palace).

1835, Apr. 2. CHARLES HOLLAND HASTINGS, colonel, steward of the Household to His Excellency (in Ireland by the lord lieutenant).

1835, Apr. 15. RALPH OUSELEY, major general in Portugal (*ibid* by same).

1835, May 6. ROBERT MONSEY ROLFE, solicitor general (at St. James's Palace).

1835, May 20. JOHN ACKWORTH OMMANNEY, rear admiral (*ibid*).

1835, June 5. THOMAS HASTINGS, of Titley Court, Co. Hereford, captain R.N. (by the lord lieutenant of Ireland).

1835, June 10. WHITELAW AINSLIE, M.D. (at St. James's Palace).

1835, June 24. GEORGE GIPPS, captain, Royal Engineers (*ibid*),

1835, June 24. WILLIAM HENRY DILLON, captain R.N. (*ibid*).

1835, July 1. FRANCIS CHANTREY, member of Royal Academy of Arts (*ibid*).

1835, July 22. ALEXANDER FERRIER, consul at Rotterdam.

1835, July 23 (24). CHARLES ROUTLEDGE O'DONNELL, lieutenant colonel (in the Phœnix Park by the lord lieutenant of Ireland).

1835, July 31. ROBERT CHERMSIDE, M.D. (at St. James's Palace).

1835, Aug. 4. WILLIAM WHITE, one of the sheriffs of Cork (at Cork by the lord lieutenant of Ireland).

1835, Aug. 4. ROBERT HAGAN, commander, R.N. (*ibid* by same).

1835, Aug. 5. SAMUEL WARREN, captain, R.N. (at St. James's Palace).

1835, Aug. 12. DAVID DUNN, captain, R.N. (*ibid*).

1835, Aug. 15. WILLIAM ROWAN HAMILTON, astronomer royal of Ireland and Andrews' professor of astronomy (in the Library Trinity College, Dublin, by the lord lieutenant of Ireland).

1835, Sept. 2. RALPH DARLING, lieutenant general, governor-in-chief of New South Wales (at St. James's Palace).

1835, Sept. 25. HORATIO GEORGE POWYS TOWNSHEND.

1835, Oct. 28. WILLIAM CHARLES ELLIS, M.D., of Hanwell, Middl. (*ibid*).

1835, Nov. 7. WILLIAM NORRIS, chief justice of the Supreme Court of the Island of Ceylon (Letters patent dated Nov. 21).

KNIGHTS BACHELORS

1835, Nov. 18. ROBERT LEWIS FITZ-GERALD, rear admiral (at the Pavilion, Brighton).
1835. JOHN TAYLOR COLERIDGE, Rt. Hon., justice of Queen's Bench.
1835. MAURICE CHARLES O'CONNELL, major general.
1835. LOVE PARRY JONES PARRY, major general.
1836, Feb. 23. WILSHIRE WILSON, major general (at St. James's Palace).
1836, Feb. 23. JAMES JOHN GORDON BREMER, captain, R.N. *(ibid)*.
1836, Feb. 23. The Hon. JAMES ASHLEY MAUDE, captain, R.N. *(ibid)*.
1836, Feb. 23. JOHN STRUTT PEYTON, captain, R.N. *(ibid)*.
1836, Feb. 23. HENRY HART, captain, R.N. *(ibid)*.
1836, Feb. 23. CHARLES WILLIAM MAXWELL, major general *(ibid)*.
1836, Mar. 16. The Hon. FLEETWOOD BROUGHTON REYNOLDS PELLEW, captain, R.N.
1836, Mar. 16. DANIEL JONES, colonel, of Brockville, Johnstown, Upper Canada *(ibid)*.
1836, Mar. 16 (? Mar. 23). WILLIAM GABRIEL DAVY, major general *(ibid)*.
1836, Mar. 16. GEORGE FRANCIS HAMILTON SEYMOUR *(ibid)*.
1836, Apr. 20. WILLIAM JACKSON HOOKER, LL.D., Regius Prof. of botany in the University of Glasgow *(ibid)*.
1836, May 4. EDWIN PEARSON, lieutenant of the Yeomen of the Guard *(ibid)*.
1836, June 8. JOHN SIMPSON, lord mayor of York *(ibid)*.
1836, June 15. WARWICK HELE TONKIN, major *(ibid)*.
1836, June 15. DAVID WILKIE, royal academician, principal painter to the King *(ibid)*.
1836, June 15. WILLIAM SYMONDS, captain R.N., and surveyor of His Majesty's Navy *(ibid)*.
1836, July 11. THOMAS CAREW, captain R.N. (at Wexford by the lord lieutenant).
1836, July 21. WILLIAM DANIEL, commander Royal Navy, inspecting commander of the Coast Guard (at Cove of Cork by same).
1836, July 21. HENRY ESCH ATKINSON, commander in the Royal Navy, inspecting commander of Coast Guard (at Youghal by same).
1836, July 24. WILLIAM PARKE, of Dunally, lieutenant colonel (at Sligo by same).
1836, Aug. 10. BENJAMIN MORRIS, late captain 25th Foot, one of the sheriffs of Waterford (in the Town Hall, Waterford, by same).

1836, Aug. 10. PATRICK LINDESAY, colonel (at St. James's Palace).
1836, Aug. 19. CHARLES LYON HERBERT, M.D. *(ibid)*.
1836, Aug. 22. JOHN GRAHAM DALYELL, of Edinburgh, advocate (Letters patent dated Sept. 3).
1836, Aug. 26. EDWARD BRACKENBURY, major (at St. James's Palace).
1836, Oct. 1. WILLIAM HENRY PIERSON, captain R.N., of H.M.S. "Madagascar" (by the lord lieutenant of Ireland).
1836. RICHARD O'CONNOR, rear admiral.
1837, Jan. 9. THOMAS BAUCUTT MASH (at the Pavilion, Brighton).
1837, Mar. 1. ROBERT BARTON, lieutenant general (at St. James's Palace).
1837, Mar. 1. THOMAS HAWKER, major general *(ibid)*.
1837, Mar. 1. EDWARD CHETHAM (afterwards CHETHAM-STRODE), captain R.N. *(ibid)*.
1837, Mar. 1. THOMAS MANSELL, captain R.N. *(ibid)*.
1837, Mar. 1. WOODBINE PARISH, late consul general, plenipotentiary and chargé d'affaires at Buenos Ayres *(ibid)*.
1837, Mar. 1. THOMAS COLTMAN, a justice of Common Pleas (at St. James's Palace).
1837, Mar. 1. ADAM DRUMMOND, vice admiral of the Blue *(ibid)*.
1837, Mar. 1. AUGUSTUS DE BUTTS, R.E. *(ibid)*.
1837, Mar. 8. ALEXANDER HALKETT, lieutenant general *(ibid)*.
1837, Mar. 8. HENRY GEORGE MACLEOD, lieutenant colonel, lieutenant governor of the Island of St. Christopher *(ibid)*.
1837, Mar. 8. THOMAS FINLAY, late high sheriff of Co. Cavan (by the lord lieutenant of Ireland).
1837, Mar. 8. FRANCIS WILLIAM SMITH, M.D., surgeon-in-ordinary to the lord lieutenant (by same).
1837, Mar. (May) 31. WILLIAM MACBEAN GEORGE COLEBROOKE, lieutenant colonel, governor and commander-in-chief of the Leeward Islands (at Windsor Castle).
1837, Apr. 5. JAMES DUKE, sheriff of London and Middlesex (at St. James's Palace).
1837, Apr. 5. FRANCIS FORBES, chief justice of New South Wales *(ibid)*.
1837, Apr. 26. CHARLES GORDON, of Drimnin, secretary to the Highland and Agricultural Society of Scotland *(ibid)*.
1837, Apr. 26. CHARLES HOPKINSON, lieutenant colonel, of the East India Company's service *(ibid)*.
1837, Apr. 26. EPHRAIM STANNUS, colonel *(ibid)*.

KNIGHTS BACHELORS

1837, Apr. 26 (? June 5). CHARLES AUGUSTUS FITZROY, lieutenant governor of Prince Edward Island, in the Gulf of St. Lawrence (At St. James's Palace).

1837, Apr. 27. JAMES MACDONELL, major general, first equerry to Her Majesty *(ibid)*.

1837, May 3. JOHN WENTWORTH LORING, rear admiral of the White *(ibid)*.

1837, May 10. JOHN GUSTAVUS CROSBIE, general *(ibid)*.

1837, June 5. SIMON HEWARD, chief of the medical staff of the Madras Army during the whole of the Burmese War (Letters patent).

1837, July 14. His Serene Highness CHARLES WILLIAM FREDERIC EMICON, prince of Leiningen (at St. James's Palace).

1837, July 19. JOHN BICKERTON WILLIAMS, of Shrewsbury, LL.D., F.S.A. *(ibid* at the request of the duke of Sussex, being the first (?) knight made by Queen Victoria after her accession).

1837, July 19. WATKIN OWEN PELL, captain, R.N. *(ibid)*.

1837, July 19. JOHN JACOB HANSLER, of Tavistock Square, a deputy lieutenant for Co. Essex *(ibid)*

1837, July 19. AUGUSTUS WALL CALLCOTT, of Kensington Gravelpits, royal academician *(ibid)*.

1837, July 19. JAMES SPITTAL, lord provost of the City of Edinburgh *(ibid)*.

1837, July 19. WILLIAM JOHN NEWTON, miniature painter in ordinary to the Queen Dowager *(ibid)*.

1837, July 19. DAVID DAVIES, M.D., physician-in-ordinary to the Queen Dowager *(ibid)*.

1837, July 19. RICHARD WESTMACOTT, royal academician, Hon. D.C.L., Oxford *(ibid)*.

1837, July 19. Col. GEORGE ARTHUR.

1837, July 19. WILLIAM ELLIOTT, captain, R.N. *(ibid)*.

1837, Aug. 7. WILLIAM HENRY ROUGH, sergeant at law, chief justice of the Supreme Court at Ceylon (Letters patent).

1837, Nov. 13. GEORGE CARROLL, sheriff of London and Middlesex (at St. James's Palace).

1837, Nov. 13. MOSES MONTEFIORE, sheriff of London and Middlesex *(ibid)*.

1837, Dec. 13. JAMES PITCAIRN, M.D., deputy inspector general of hospitals (at Cork by the lord lieutenant of Ireland).

1838, Feb. 14. JOHN DORATT, M.D. (at St. James's Palace).

1838, Feb. 14. JOHN HAMPET, doctor of physic, Fellow of the Royal Society of London, one of the medical commission employed in 1831 in the North of Germany during the cholera *(ibid)*.

1838, Feb. 14. GEORGE STEPHEN, of Collins, Princes Risborough, Co. Bucks *(ibid)*.

1838, Feb. 21. ISAAC WILSON, M.D. (at St. James's Palace).

1838, Feb. 21. SAMUEL BROWN, commander, R.N. *(ibid)*.

1838, Feb. 21. SPENCER LAMBERT HUNTER VASSALL, captain, R.N. *(ibid)*.

1838, Feb. 21. JOHN ROBISON, secretary of the Royal Society, Edinburgh *(ibid)*.

1838, Feb. 21. WILLIAM BLACKBURNE, major general *(ibid)*.

1838, Mar. 21. HENRY WILMOT SETON, a judge of the Supreme Court of Bengal *(ibid)*.

1838, Mar. 21. ALLAN NAPIER McNAB, colonel of militia of the province of Upper Canada (Letters patent).

1838, Mar. 2. JOHN GASPARD LE MARCHANT, major (at St. James's Palace).

1838, May 2. WILLIAM COLLINGS, colonel, and jurat of the Royal Court of Guernsey *(ibid)*.

1838, May 2 (? 1837, May 2). FORTUNATUS DWARRIS, of the Middle Temple, barrister-at-law, a master of the Court of Queen's Bench *(ibid)*.

1838, May 8. WILLIAM EDWARD LEESON, chamberlain to the lord lieutenant (by the lord lieutenant of Ireland).

1838, June 20. THOMAS NEWLEY REEVE, standard bearer of the Gentlemen at Arms (at St. James's Palace).

1838, June 20. BENJAMIN SMITH, senior member of the Gentlemen at Arms *(ibid)*.

1838, June 20. GEORGE [? WILLIAM CHARLES] HOULTON, ensign of the Yeomen of the Guard.

1838, July 18. DUNCAN MACDOUGALL, late lieutenant colonel of the 79th Regiment of Highlanders (at St. James's Palace).

1838, July 18. HENRY BAYLY, major *(ibid)*.

1838, July 18. WILLIAM LLOYD, major of the East India Company's Service *(ibid)*.

1838, July 18. CHARLES SHAW. *(ibid)*.

1838, July 18. CHARLES FREDERICK WILLIAMS, of Lennox Lodge, Hayling, Hants., and Upper Bedford Place, Middl. *(ibid)*.

1838, July 18. EDWARD JOHNSON, of Greenhill, Weymouth, Co. Dorset *(ibid)*.

1838, July 18. JOHN KIRKLAND, of Hampton and Pall Mall, Middl. *(ibid)*.

1838, July 18. WILLIAM NEWBIGGING, F.R.C.S. and R.S. of Edinburgh *(ibid)*.

1838, July (? June) 18. WILLIAM HYDE PEARSON, F.R.S., of Clapham, Surrey *(ibid)*.

KNIGHTS BACHELORS 341

1838, July 18. EDWARD ALEXANDER CAMPBELL, of the Bengal Cavalry *(ibid)*.

1838, July 18. JEFFERY PRENDERGAST, major general in Hon. East India Company's service and late military auditor general at Madras *(ibid)*.

1838, July 18. ALEXANDER MORISON, M.D., of Mid Lothian, N.B. and Cavendish Square, Middl., late president of the Royal College of Physicians of Edinburgh *(ibid)*.

1838, Aug. 6. ALEXANDER BURNES, captain in the 21st regiment of Bombay Native Infantry, on a mission to the chiefs of Afghanistan (Letters patent).

1838, Aug. 15. Capt. GEORGE BACK, R.N.

1838, Aug. 15 (? Mar. 18). JAMES EDWARD ALEXANDER, captain, lieutenant-colonel in the Portuguese service (at St. James's Palace).

1838, Nov. 19. GEORGE TYLER, captain R.N., lieutenant governor of the Island of St. Vincent (Letters patent).

1838, Nov. 26 (1839, Jan. 19). JAMES EDWARD DOWLING, chief justice of New South Wales (Letters patent).

1838, Nov. 26 (1838, Dec. 19). JOHN LEWIS PEDDER, B.C.L., chief justice of Van Diemen's Land (same).

1838. JOHN MORILLYON WILSON, colonel.

1839, Feb. 15. BURTON MACNAMARA, captain R.N. (in the Presence Chamber, Dublin Castle, at the levée, by the lord lieutenant of Ireland).

1839, Feb. 15. THOMAS ROSS, commander R.N. *(ibid* by same).

1839, Mar. 6 (? 1838). HENRY ROPER, a judge of the Supreme Court of Judicature at Bombay (at St. James's Palace).

1839 [Mar.]. WILLIAM HENRY MAULE [a baron of Exchequer].

1839, Apr. 17. THOMAS LIVINGSTON MITCHELL, major, surveyor general of New South Wales (at St. James's Palace).

1839, Apr. 24. JOHN ARCHIBALD MURRAY, of Edinburgh, a judge of the Supreme Court of Scotland, lord advocate of Scotland *(ibid)*.

1839, June 5. THOMAS HASTINGS, of Titley House, Co. Hereford, captain, R.N *(ibid)*.

1839, June 5. WILLIAM WARRE, colonel, commandant of the garrison at Chatham *(ibid)*.

1839, Aug. 7. ANTHONY OLIPHANT, chief justice of the Supreme Court at Ceylon (Letters patent).

1839, Aug. 26. JOHN GARDNER WILKINSON, fellow of the Royal Society (at Buckingham Palace).

1839, Sept. 7. MICHAEL MACTURK, of British Guiana (Letters patent).

1839, Dec. 9. THOMAS PHILLIPS, late mayor of Newport, Co. Monmouth. (at Windsor Castle).

1839, Dec. 11. CLAUDE MARTINE WADE, lieutenant colonel, East India Company military service, political resident at Loodiana (Letters patent).

1840, Feb. 19. THOMAS WILDE, solicitor general and a serjeant at law (at St. James's Palace).

1840, Feb. 19. WILLIAM MARTINS, gentleman usher of the Sword of State, and one of Her Mjaesty's gentlemen ushers daily waiters *(ibid)*.

1840, Feb. 19. The Hon. EDWARD BUTLER, lieutenant of Her Majesty's Honourable Corps of Gentlemen at Arms *(ibid)*.

1840, Mar. 6. THOMAS MARRABLE, secretary to the Board of Green Cloth *(ibid)*.

1840, Mar. 18. RICHARD HENRY BONNYCASTLE, major, R.E. *(ibid)*.

1840, Mar. 20. ROBERT BOUCHIER CLARKE, solicitor general in the Island of Barbados (Letters patent).

1840, July 1. WILLIAM STEPHENSON CLARK, lord mayor of York City (at St. James's Palace, on presentation of addresses from the City of York).

1840, July 1 (? July 11). JOSHUA WALMSLEY, of Wavertree Hall, Co. Palatine of Lancaster, mayor of the borough of Liverpool, and magistrate, Co. Palatine *(ibid)*.

1840, July 1. WILLIAM LOWTHROP, mayor of Hull *(ibid)*.

1840, July 1. JOHN WESTLEY WILLIAMS, F.R.S., mayor of Portsmouth *(ibid)*.

1840, July 1. THOMAS POTTER, mayor of Manchester, and a magistrate for Co. Palatine of Lancaster *(ibid)*.

1840, July 1. JACOB ADOLPHUS, M.D., inspector general of Army Hospitals, and physician general to the Militia Forces in the Island of Jamaica *(ibid)*.

1840, July 1. ALEXANDER MACKENZIE DOWNIE, M.D., physician to her late Royal Highness the Landgravine of Hesse Hombourg *(ibid)*.

1840, July 1. JOHN HARE, of Springfield, Co. Somerset., and of the City of Bristol *(ibid)*.

1840, July 1. RALPH PENDLEBURY, alderman, and late mayor of Stockport, Co. Chester (At St. James's Palace).

1840, July 1. JOHN FIFE, late mayor of Newcastle *(ibid)*.

KNIGHTS BACHELORS 343

1840, Aug. 7. JAMES JOHN REID, chief justice of the United States of the Ionian Islands (at Buckingham Palace).

1840, Aug. RICHARD FRANKLIN, M.D., mayor of Limerick (by the lord lieutenant of Ireland).

1840, Nov. 5. JOHN JEREMIE, captain general, and governor in chief of the Colony of Sierra Leone and its dependencies (at Windsor Castle).

1840. CHARLES CHICHESTER, lieutenant-colonel.

1841, Jan. 22. RICHARD MORRISON, architect, vice-president of the Royal Institute of Architects in Dublin (by the lord lieutenant of Ireland on presenting an address from the said Institute).

1841, Jan. 25. GEORGE SIMPSON, governor of the Hudson's Bay Company's Settlements (at Buckingham Palace).

1841, Jan. 25. ROBERT MARSH HORSFORD, solicitor general of Antigua *(ibid)*.

1841, Feb. 11. THOMAS ERSKINE PERRY, a judge of the Supreme Court of Judicature at Bombay *(ibid)*.

1841, Mar. 22. RANDOLPH ISHAM ROUTH, commissary general to Her Majesty's Forces in Canada (by Letters patent).

1841, Mar. 24. JOSEPH DOUGLAS, captain, late of the ship "Cambridge" (at St. James's Palace).

1841, Mar. 24. ISAMBART MARC BRUNEL (at Buckingham Palace).

1841, Mar. 24. ARNOLD JAMES KNIGHT, M.D., of Sheffield, Co. York. *(ibid)*.

1841, Apr. 24 (28). THOMAS NOEL HARRIS, a groom of the Privy Chamber (at St. James's Palace).

1841, Apr. 28. EDWARD SAMUEL WALKER, mayor of Chester *(ibid)*.

1841, Apr. 28. WILLIAM WIGHTMAN, a justice of the King's Bench *(ibid)*.

1841, Apr. 28. ISAAC MORLEY, for public services as mayor of Doncaster (At St. James's Palace).

1841, May 6. GEORGE MORRIS, lieutenant colonel, one of the commissioners of paving the city of Dublin, on being invested as Usher of the Black Rod of the Order of St. Patrick (by the lord lieutenant of Ireland).

1841, May 12. SAMUEL HANCOCK, senior exon of the Yeomen of the Guard (at Buckingham Palace).

1841, Aug. 21. GEORGE LE FEVRE, M.D., physician to Her Majesty's Embassy at the Court of St. Petersburg (Letters patent).

1841, Aug. 21. GEORGE ROSE SARTORIUS, captain R.N. (at Windsor Castle).
1841, Aug. 21. RICHMOND CAMPBELL SHAKESPEAR, lieutenant of the Bengal Artillery *(ibid)*.
1841, Aug. 21. RICHARD LA SAUSSAYE *(ibid)*.
1841, Sept. 8. FRANCIS COCKBURN, colonel, governor of the Bahamas (Letters patent).
1841, Sept. 9. NICHOLAS FITZSIMON, of Broughal Castle, King's County, one of the divisional magistrates of the Metropolitan District (at Dublin Castle by the lord lieutenant).
1841, Oct. 9. HENRY HUNTLEY, commander in Her Majesty's Navy (Letters patent).
1841, Nov. 27. RICHARD DOHERTY, lieutenant-colonel (same).
1842, Jan. 27. JOHN DAVID NORTON, puisne judge of the Supreme Court of Judicature at Madras (same).
1842 [Jan.]. Rt. Hon. JAMES LEWIS KNIGHT BRUCE, a vice-chancellor.
1842 [Jan.]. Rt. Hon. JAMES WIGRAM.
1842, Feb. 14. JAMSETJEE JEEJEEBHOY, of Bombay, in the East Indies (Letters patent).
1842, Apr. 13. JAMES CAMPBELL, lord provost of the City of Glasgow (at St. James's Palace).
1842, Apr. 13. HENRY THOMAS DE LA BECHE, F.R.S., director of the Ordnance Geological Survey of Great Britain and of the Museum of Economic Geology Department of Woods, etc. (at St. James's Palace).
1842, Apr. 13. WILLIAM DRYSDALE, of Pittuchar, Co. Fife *(ibid)*.
1842, Apr. 13. GEORGE GUN MUNRO, major of the Rosshire Militia, and of the Poyntzfield, Co. Cromarty, N.B.
1842, May 4. CRESSWELL CRESSWELL, a justice of the Common Pleas *(ibid)*.
1842, May 18. LAURENCE PEEL, chief justice at Fort William, in Bengal (Letters patent).
1842, June 1. GEORGE HAYTER, member of the Academies of Rome, Florence, Bologna, Parma and Venice, etc., painter-in-ordinary to the Queen (at St. James's Palace).
1842, June 1. WILLIAM ALLAN, president of the Royal Academy of Scotland and Her Majesty's limner for Scotland *(ibid)*.
1842, June 1. WILLIAM CHARLES ROSS, A.R.A., miniature painter to the Queen *(ibid)*.
1842, June 1. HENRY ROWLEY BISHOP, of Albion Street, Hyde Park *(ibid)*.

KNIGHTS BACHELORS

1842, Aug. 27. CHARLES GEORGE YOUNG, on his investiture as Garter Principal King at Arms (at Windsor Castle).
1842, Nov. 23. JASPER ATKINSON, of Portman Square, Middl. (Letters patent).
1843, Jan. 21. EDWARD BELCHER, captain R.N. (same).
1843, Apr. 1. THOMAS MAITLAND, captain R.N. (same).
1843, Apr. 20. ROBERT OLIVER, captain R.N., superintendent of the Indian Navy (same).
1843, May 18. HENRY VASSALL WEBSTER, lieutenant-colonel (same).
1843, Aug. 19. JAMES DOMBRAIN, inspector general of Coast Guard in Ireland (knighted by the lord lieutenant of Ireland, on board a cruiser in Kingstown Harbour, after an inspection of the Irish squadron of revenue cruisers at Kingstown, Dublin, erroneously supposed to have been a knight banneret in consequence of having been knighted under the Royal Standard).
1843, Oct. 30. JAMES WYLLIE, M.D., in attendance on H.I.H. the Grand Duke Michael of Russia (at Windsor Castle).
1843, Nov. 22. ANTHONY PERRIER, Her Majesty's consul at Brest (Letters patent).
1844, Mar. 13. JAMES CLARK ROSS, F.R.S., captain R.N. (at St. James's Palace).
1844, Mar. 13. CHARLES FERGUSSON FORBES, M.D., fellow of the Royal College of Physicians, deputy inspector general of Army Hospitals *(ibid)*.
1844, Mar. 13. GEORGE PHILIP LEE, lieutenant of the Yeomen of the Guard *(ibid)*.
1844, Mar. 13. ROBERT NICKLE, colonel *(ibid)*.
1844, Mar. 20. WILLIAM BAIN, master in the Royal Navy *(ibid)*.
1844, Apr. 17. WILLIAM CHALMERS, colonel, of Glenericht, Co. Perth (Letters patent).
1844, Apr. 25. THOMAS HERBERT MADDOCK, of the Bengal Civil Service (same).
1844, May 13. JAMES ANNESLEY, of the Madras medical establishment (same).
1844, May 23. FREDERIC THESIGER, solicitor general (at Buckingham Palace).
1844, May 24. JOHN MACNEILL, LL.D., civil engineer (by the lord lieutenant of Ireland, on the opening of the railway from Dublin to Drogheda).
1844, June 7. WILLIAM CORNWALLIS HARRIS, major in the Bombay Corps of Civil Engineers (Letters patent).
1844, Nov. 18. WILLIAM WESTBROOKE, puisne judge of the Supreme Court of Judicature at Madras (same).

1844, Dec. 26. ROBERT SCHOMBURGH, chevalier, recently at the head of the expedition for exploring the boundaries of the Colony of British Guiana (Letters patent).

1845, Mar. 5. JOHN HAMILTON, captain, late of Her Majesty's packet service (at St. James's Palace).

1845, Mar. 12. JAMES COCHRANE, chief justice of Gibraltar *(ibid)*.

1845, Apr. 23. WILLIAM ERLE, a judge of the Common Pleas *(ibid)*.

1845, Apr. 23. THOMAS JOSHUA PLATT, a baron of the Exchequer *(ibid)*.

1845, May 7. JOHN MACPHERSON BRAKENBURY, late consul at Cadiz *(ibid)*.

1845, May 7. CHARLES FELLOWS, of Russell Square *(ibid)*.

1845, May 7. HENRY ROBINSON, lieutenant of Her Majesty's Honourable Corps of Gentlemen at Arms *(ibid)*.

1845 [? July] JAMES EMERSON TENNENT (on his appointment as civil secretary to the Colonial Government of Ceylon).

1845, Aug. 8. Rt. Hon. FITZROY KELLY, solicitor general (at Buckingham Palace).

1845, Oct. 30. JOHN AUGUSTUS FRANCIS SIMPKINSON, a Queen's counsel, and treasurer of Lincoln's Inn (at St. James's Palace).

1846, Feb. 11. JOHN RICHARDSON, R.N., F.R.S., medical inspector of Hospitals and Fleets *(ibid)*.

1846, Feb. 11. RODERICK IMPEY MURCHISON, fellow of the Royal Society, V.P.G.S., and R.G.S., member of the Imperial Academy of Sciences at St. Petersburgh, corresponding member of the Institute of France, etc., etc. *(ibid)*.

1846, Mar. 12. ROBERT JOHN KANE (by the lord lieutenant of Ireland at a meeting of the Royal Society of Dublin).

1846, Aug. 1. JOHN JERVIS, attorney general (at Buckingham Palace).

1846, Aug. 1. WILLIAM THOMAS DENISON, captain, of the Royal Engineers, lieutenant governor of Van Diemen's Land *(ibid)*.

1846, Aug. 19. ALFRED STEPHEN, chief justice of New South Wales (Letters patent).

1846, Sept. 2. DAVID POLLOCK, chief justice of the Supreme Court of Judicature at Bombay (Letters patent).

1846, Sept. 16. EDWARD PINE COFFIN, commissary general of Her Majesty's Forces (same).

1847, Feb. 4. EDWARD VAUGHAN WILLIAMS, a judge of Common Pleas (at Windsor Castle).

1847, Feb. 12. THOMAS LE BRETON, colonel of the Royal Jersey Militia (at St. James's Palace).
1847, Feb. 12. HENRY EDWARD FOX YOUNG, lieutenant governor of the eastern districts of the Colony of the Cape of Good Hope *(ibid)*.
1847, Feb. 24. DAVID DUNDAS, solicitor general *(ibid)*.
1847, Feb. 24. CHRISTOPHER RAWLINSON, recorder of Prince of Wales Island, Singapore and Malacca *(ibid)*.
1847, Apr. 28. WILLIAM SNOW HARRIS, F.R.S. *(ibid)*.
1847. WILLIAM YARDLEY, on his appointment as puisne judge, Bombay.
1848, May 17. JOHN ROMILLY, M.P., solicitor general (at St. James's Palace).
1848, May 17. JOHN LIDDELL, M.D., F.R.S., medical inspector of Fleets and Hospitals, Royal Hospital, Greenwich *(ibid)*.
1848, May 17. WILLIAM BELLAIRS, captain, senior exon of the Yeomen of the Guard *(ibid)*.
1848, May 17. MATTHEW WYATT, lieutenant of the Hon. Corps of Gentlemen at Arms *(ibid)*.
1848 [? July]. ARTHUR WILLIAM BULLER, on his appointment as a judge of the Supreme Court, Calcutta (at Osborne).
1848, Sept. 19. CHARLES LYELL, junr., F.R.S., late president of the Geological Society (at Balmoral).
1848, Dec. 9. Rt. Hon. JAMES WILLIAM COLVILE, puisne justice of the Supreme Court of Judicature at Calcutta (Letters patent).
1849, Jan. 31. ELKANAH ARMITAGE, later mayor of Manchester (at Buckingham Palece).
1849, Feb. 22. GEORGE WILLIAM ANDERSON, governor of the Mauritius (at St. James's Palace).
1849, Feb. 28. THOMAS SEYMOUR SADLER, senior exon of Her Majesty's Bodyguard of Yeomen of the Guard *(ibid)*.
1849, June 29. WILLIAM WINNIETT, commander R.N., lieutenant governor of the Gold Coast (at Buckingham Palace).
1849, Aug. 4 (3). WILLIAM LYONS, mayor of Cork (knighted by the Queen on board H.M. frigate " The Fairy " yacht during Her Majesty's visit to Cork).
1849, Aug. 12. WILLIAM GILLILAN JOHNSON, mayor of Belfast (by the Queen on the occasion of Her Majesty's visit to Belfast).
1849, Aug. JAMES ANDERSON, lord provost of Glasgow (by the Queen on the occasion of Her Majesty's visit to Glasgow).
1849, Oct. 19. EDWARD MCDONNEL, merchant, of Dublin, chairman of the Great Southern and Western Railway of Ireland (knighted by the lord lieutenant of Ireland on the opening of the said railway to Cork).

1849, Dec. 29. WILLIAM JEFFCOTT, recorder of Prince of Wales Island, Singapore and Malacca (Letters patent).
1850, Jan. 30. THOMAS NOON TALFOURD, one of the judges of Common Pleas (at Windsor Castle).
1850, July 3. JOHN WATSON GORDON, limner to the Queen for Scotland, and president of the Royal Scottish Academy (at St. James's Palace).
1850, July 3. CHARLES HASTINGS, M.D. *(ibid)*.
1850, July 3. ROBERT CARSWELL, M.D., physician to the king of the Belgians *(ibid)*.
1850, July 3. EDWIN LANDSEER, royal academician *(ibid)*.
1850, July 12 (? Aug. 14). ALEXANDER JAMES EDMUND COCKBURN, on his appointment as solicitor general (at Buckingham Palace).
1850, Aug. 14. ROBERT STANFORD [of the Cape of Good Hope].
1850 Aug. 19. BENJAMIN FONSECA OUTRAM, of Hanover Square, Middlesex, M.D., retired inspector of Hospitals and Fleets (Letters patent).
1850, Oct. 14. FREDERICK ASHWORTH, major general (by the lord lieutenant of Ireland).
1850, Nov. 13. SAMUEL MARTIN, a baron of the Exchequer (at Windsor Castle).
1850, Nov. 13. CHARLES LOCK EASTLAKE, president of the Royal Academy *(ibid)*.
1851, Feb. 3. JAMES WILLIAM MORRISON, late dep. master and worker of the Mint (at Buckingham Palace).
1851, Feb. 3. ALEXANDER BANNERMAN, lieutenant governor of Prince Edward's Island *(ibid)*.
1851, Feb. 3. JAMES MEEK, late comptroller of the Victualling and Transport Services in the Admiralty *(ibid)*.
1851, Feb. 26. JOHN THOMAS BRIGGS, accountant general of the Navy (at St. James's Palace).
1851, Mar. 26. JOHN KERLE HABERFIELD, mayor of Bristol *(ibid)*.
1851, Apr. 14. GEORGE JAMES TURNER, a vice chancellor (at Buckingham Palace).
1851, Apr. 14. WILLIAM PAGE WOOD, M.P., solicitor general *(ibid)*.
1851, May 28. JAMES TYLER, lieutenant of Her Majesty's Hon. Corps of Gentlemen at Arms (at St. James's Palace).
1851, July 17. ROBERT WALTER CARDEN, sheriff of London and Middl. (at Buckingham Palace).
1851, July 17. GEORGE EDMUND HODGKINSON, sheriff of London and Middl. *(ibid)*.
1851, Aug. 7. JOHN HINDMARSH, captain R.N., lieutenant governor of Heligoland *(ibid)*.

1851, Aug. 28. Rt. Hon. WILLIAM JOHNSTON, of Kirkhill, lord provost of Edinburgh (at Holyrood Palace, on the occasion of the Queen's visit to Edinburgh).
1851, Oct. 9. JOHN BENT, mayor of Liverpool (at the Town Hall, Liverpool).
1851, Oct. 10. JOHN POTTER, of Buile Hill, Co. Lancs., mayor of Manchester (at Manchester).
1851, Oct. 23. Rt. Hon. RICHARD TORIN KINDERSLEY, a vice-chancellor (at Windsor Castle).
1851, Oct. 23. JAMES PARKER, a vice-chancellor *(ibid)*.
1851, Oct. 23. JOSEPH PAXTON, fellow of the Linnæan Society, Horticultural Society, and the Society of Arts *(ibid)*.
1851, Oct. 23. CHARLES FOX, of New Street, Spring Gardens, Co. Middl. *(ibid)*.
1851, Oct. 23. WILLIAM CUBITT, fellow of the Royal Society *(ibid)*.
1852, Feb. 11. CHARLES BARRY, architect, royal academician, fellow of the Royal Society, the Society of Arts, and the Institute of British Architects, etc., etc. *(ibid)*.
1852, Feb. 25. CHARLES NICHOLSON, M.D., and speaker of the Legislative Council of New South Wales (Letters patent).
1852, Feb. 26. CHARLES CROMPTON, a judge of the Queen's Bench (at St. James's Palace).
1852, Feb. 26. GEORGE GOODMAN, mayor of Leeds *(ibid)*.
1852, Mar. 24. JOHN DORNEY HARDING, D.C.L., advocate in Doctor's Commons, and of the Inner Temple, barrister-at-law, advocate general *(ibid)*.
1852, June 10. WILLIAM BARTHOLOMEW HACKETT, mayor of Cork (by the lord lieutenant of Ireland on the opening of the Irish National Exhibition of Industry in Cork).
1852, June 30. JOHN KINCAID, late captain in the Rifle Brigade, and senior exon of the Yeomen of the Guard (at Buckingham Palace).
1852, Nov. 19. WILLIAM A'BECKETT, chief justice of the Colony of Victoria (Letters patent).
1852, Dec. 2. CHARLES ROBERT MITCHELL JACKSON, puisne judge of the Supreme Court of Judicature at Bombay (Letters patent).
1853, May 12. JOHN BENSON, architect of the great Dublin Industrial Exhibition (by the lord lieutenant of Ireland on the opening of the said Exhibition).
1853, June 13. JOHN STUART, a vice-chancellor (at Buckingham Palace).
1853, June 13. RICHARD BETHELL, M.P., solicitor general *(ibid)*.

1853, June 13. JOSEPH FRANCIS OLLIFFE, M.D., physician to Her Majesty's Embassy at Paris (At Buckingham Palace).

1853, Aug. 8. JOHN FORBES, M.D., D.C.L., and F.R.S., physician to Her Majesty's Household, and physician extraordinary to H.R.H. the prince Albert *(ibid)*.

1853, Aug. 8. JAMES LOMAX BARDSLEY, M.D., of Manchester *(ibid)*.

1853, Oct. 31. CUSAC PATRICK RONEY, secretary of the Dublin Industrial Exhibition (by the lord lieutenant of Ireland on the occasion of the closing of the Dublin Industrial Exhibition).

1853, Nov. 25. STEPHEN BARTLETT LAKEMAN, captain, late commander of Lakeman's Waterkloof Rangers, Cape of Good Hope (at Windsor Castle).

1853, Dec. 9. ARCHIBALD BOGLE, lieutenant colonel of the East India Company's Bengal establishment, civil commissioner in the Tenasserim and Martaban Provinces (by Letters patent).

1854, Feb. 16. JOHN BOWRING, LL.D., governor, commander-in-chief and vice admiral of Hong Kong and its Dependencies, plenipotentiary and chief superintendent of British trade in China (at Buckingham Palace).

1854, Feb. 22. JOHN KINGSTON JAMES, of No. 8, Hertford Street, Mayfair, eldest son of Sir John Kingston James, bart. (at St. James's Palace).

1854, Feb. 22. JOHN BERNARD BURKE, Ulster king of arms (by the lord lieutenant of Ireland at Dublin Castle).

1854, May 3. RICHARD BUDDEN CROWDER, a judge of Common Pleas (at St. James's Palace).

1854, May 3. SAMUEL BIGNOLD, of Norwich, mayor of Norwich, deputy lieutenant and magistrate of Co. Norfolk
(At St. James's Palace).

1854, June 9. FREDERICK ABBOTT, lieutenant colonel, late of the Bengal Engineers, lieutenant governor of the East India Company's Military College at Addiscombe *(ibid)*.

1854, June 9. GEORGE MACLEAN, commissary general to Her Majesty's Forces *(ibid)*.

1854, June 9. ABRAHAM JOSIAS CLOËTE, colonel, deputy quartermaster general to the Forces, Cape of Good Hope *(ibid)*.

1854, Aug. 14. WILLIAM OGLE CARR, chief justice of the Supreme Court of Ceylon (Letters patent).

1854, Oct. 14. HENRY COOPER, mayor of Kingston-upon-Hull, M.D. of the University of London, and fellow of the Royal College of Surgeons (on the pier at Hull).

KNIGHTS BACHELORS 351

1854, Nov. 14. JOHN SPENCER LOGIN, of the East India Company's Bengal Medical Service, superintendent of His Highness the Maharajah Duleep Singh (at Windsor Castle).

1855, Feb. 28. RICHARD GRAVES MACDONNELL, captain general, and governor-in-chief of South Australia (at Buckingham Palace).

1855, May 1. HENRY MUGGERIDGE, sheriff of London and Middl. (at Buckingham Palace).

1855, May 1. CHARLES DECIMUS CROSLEY, sheriff of London and Middl. *(ibid)*.

1855, May 22. THOMAS TOBIN, president of the Athenæum (at Cork by the lord lieutenant of Ireland, on the occasion of the inauguration of the Athenæum of Cork).

1855, May 22. JOHN GORDON, mayor of Cork (same occasion by same).

1855, Aug. 14 (? 13). JAMES SHAW WILLES, a judge of Common Pleas (at Osborne).

1855, Nov. 21. ROBERT JOHN LE MESURIER MCCLURE, captain R.N. (at Windsor Castle for services in the Arctic regions).

1856, Jan. 30 (Feb. 28). GEORGE WILLIAM WILSHERE BRAMWELL, a baron of the Court of Exchequer (at Buckingham Palace).

1856, Jan. 30. WILLIAM CARPENTER ROWE, chief justice of Ceylon *(ibid)*.

1856, Jan. 30. MATTHEW R. SAUSSE, puisne judge at Bombay *(ibid)*.

1856, Jan. 30. WILLIAM EDMOND LOGAN, director of the Geological Survey of Canada *(ibid)*.

1856, Jan. 30. PETER BENSON MAXWELL, recorder of Prince of Wales Island *(ibid)*.

1856, Jan. 30. RICHARD BOLTON MCCAUSLAND, recorder of Singapore *(ibid)*.

1856, Feb. 20. THOMAS BLAIKIE, provost of the City of Aberdeen (at St. James's Palace).

1856, Mar. 12. WILLIAM MACARTHUR, of Camden Park, New South Wales (at St. James's Palace).

1856, Mar. 12. HUGH LYON PLAYFAIR, H.E.C.S., provost of St. Andrews *(ibid)*.

1856, Apr. 4. WILLIAM HENRY HOLMES, of the Civil Service, British Guiana, late special commissioner from British Guiana to the Paris Exhibition of 1855 (at Buckingham Palace).

1856, July 2. VALENTINE FLEMING, chief justice of the Supreme Court of Tasmania (Letters patent).

1856, July 2. DOMINICK DALY, lieutenant governor of Prince Edward Island (Letters patent).

KNIGHTS BACHELORS

1856, Nov. 28. WILLIAM HENRY WATSON, a baron of the Exchequer (at Windsor Castle).

1856, Nov. 28. HENRY DAVISON, of the Inner Temple, barrister-at-law *(ibid)*.

1856, Nov. 28. BENJAMIN CHILLEY CAMPBELL PINE, governor and commander-in-chief of Her Majesty's Forts and Settlements on the Gold Coast *(ibid)*.

1856, Nov. 28. WILLIAM BROOKE O'SHAUGHNESSY, F.R.S., surgeon in the Bengal Army *(ibid)*.

1856, Nov. 28. ROWLAND MACDONALD STEPHENSON, civil engineer, of Gloucester Terrace, Hyde Park and late of Calcutta (At Windsor Castle).

1857, June 18. CHARLES COOPER, chief justice of the Supreme Court of South Australia (at St. James's Palace).

1857, June 18. WILLIAM FRY CHANNELL, a baron of the Exchequer *(ibid)*.

1857, June 18. HENRY SINGER KEATING, solicitor general *(ibid)*.

1857, June 30. JAMES WATTS, Abney Hall, Co. Chester, mayor of Manchester (at Manchester).

1857, July 10. CHARLES JUSTIN MACCARTHY, colonial secretary of the Island of Ceylon (Letters patent).

1857, July 13. WILLIAM FOSTER STAWELL, chief justice of the Colony of Victoria (same).

1857, July 13. JAMES FREDERICK PALMER, president of the Legislative Council of the Colony of Victoria (same).

1857, July 13. DANIEL COOPER, speaker of the Legislative Assembly of New South Wales (same).

1858, Feb. 3. WILLIAM HODGES, chief justice of the Cape of Good Hope (at Buckingham Palace).

1858, Feb. 18. WILLIAM TOPHAM, of Her Majesty's Hon. Corps of Gentlemen at Arms (at St. James's Palace).

1858, Feb. 18. BENJAMIN TRAVELL PHILLIPS, major general, lieutenant of the Yeomen of the Guard *(ibid)*.

1858, Feb. 18. GEORGE DEAS, Hon., one of the senators of the College of Justice, sometime solicitor general for Scotland *(ibid)*.

1858, Feb. 18. ANDREW ORR, lord provost of the City of Glasgow *(ibid)*.

1858, Feb. 18. WILLIAM MONTAGU MANNING, LL.D., barrister of Lincoln's Inn, member of the Executive Council of New South Wales, and one of Her Majesty's counsed for that Colony *(ibid)*.

1858, Mar. 12. RICHARD DRY, late speaker of the Legislative Council of Tasmania (Letters patent dated Mar. 16).

KNIGHTS BACHELORS 353

1858, Mar. 17. HUGH MACCALMONT CAIRNS, solicitor general (at St. James's Palace).
1858, Apr. 14. JOHN BARNARD BYLES, a judge of Common Pleas *(ibid)*.
1858, Apr. 28. ADAM BITTLESTON, judge of the Supreme Court of Judicature of Madras *(ibid)*.
1858, May 7. HENRY WATSON PARKER, late first minister and principal secretary for New South Wales (at Buckingham Palace).
1858, June 11. WILLIAM RAE, M.D., inspector of Hospitals and Fleets, Royal Navy (at St. James's Palace).
1858, June 11. JAMES PRIOR, deputy inspector of Hospitals and Fleets, Royal Navy *(ibid)*.
1858, June 15. JOHN RATCLIFF, of Wyddrington, Co. Warwick., mayor of Birmingham (at the Town Hall, Birmingham).
1858, Aug. 30. FREDERIC HUGHES, late a captain in the 7th Regiment of Madras Light Cavalry (Letters patent).
1858, Sept. 2. JOHN WILLIAM FISHER, chief surgeon to the Metropolitan Police (at Osborne).
1858, Sept. 4. CHARLES TILSTON BRIGHT, C.E., engineer of the Atlantic telegraph (by the lord lieutenant of Ireland).
1858, Sept. 7. PETER FAIRBAIRN, of Woodsley House, Co. York., mayor of Leeds (at Leeds, on the occasion of the opening of the Town Hall, Leeds).
1858, Nov. 12. HENRY JOHN BROWNRIGG, inspector general of Constabulary in Ireland (at Dublin by the lord lieutenant of Ireland).
1858, Nov. 13. ETIENNE PASCHAL TACHÉ, colonel, of Montgomery, Canada (at Windsor Castle).
1858, Nov. 26. CHARLES CLIFFORD, speaker of the House of Representatives of the Colony of New Zealand (Letters patent).
1858, Dec. 13. WILLIAM ARRINDELL, chief justice of the Colony of British Guiana (same).
1858, Dec. 30. MORDAUNT LAWSON WELLS, judge of the Supreme Court at Calcutta (at Windsor Castle).
1859, Jan. 13. JAMES BUCHANAN MACAULAY, some time chief justice of Common Pleas for Canada, West (Letters patent dated Jan. 20).
1859, Feb. 2. JOSEPH ARNOULD, puisne judge of the Supreme Court at Bombay (at Buckingham Palace).
1859, Feb. 23. WILLIAM GEORGE ARMSTRONG, D.C.L., LL.D., F.R.S., engineer to the War Office for Rifled Ordnance; inventor of Armstrong gun.
1859, Apr. 13. BRENTON HALLIBURTON, chief justice of Nova Scotia (Letters patent dated Apr. 14).

Y

1859, Apr. 18. HUGH HILL, a judge of the Queen's Bench (at Buckingham Palace).
1859, May 26. BARNES PEACOCK, chief justice of the Supreme Court of Judicature at Calcutta (Letters patent dated May 30).
1859, June 25. ALEXANDER DUNDAS ARBUTHNOTT, vice admiral (at St. James's Palace).
1859, June 25. HERCULES GEORGE ROBERT ROBINSON, governor of Hong Kong *(ibid)*.
1859, June 25. STEPHENSON VILLIERS SURTEES, chief justice of the Island of Mauritius *(ibid)*.
1859, July 6. WILLIAM BYAM, president of the Council of Antigua (Letters patent dated July 11).
1859, July 6. WILLIAM SNAGG, chief justice of Antigua and Montserrat (Letters patent dated July 12).
1859, July 23. JOHN THOMAS, speaker of the House of Assembly of Barbados (Letters patent dated July 27).
1859, Aug. 22. EDWARD HAY DRUMMOND HAY, governor of the Island of St. Helena (Letters patent dated Sept. 2).
1859, Oct. 12. JAMES CARTER, chief justice of the Supreme Court of New Brunswick (Letters patent dated Oct. 18).
1859, Oct. 15. Rt. Hon. JOHN MELVILLE, lord provost of Edinburgh (at Holyrood Palace).
1859, Nov. 10. JOHN ARNOTT, mayor of Cork, M.P. (by the lord lieutenant of Ireland on the occasion of laying the foundation stone of the bridge over the Lee).
1859, Nov. 15. BRYAN EDWARDS, chief justice of Jamaica (Letters patent dated Nov. 21).
1860, Feb. 23. WILLIAM ATHERTON, M.P., solicitor general (at St. James's Palace).
1860, Feb. 23. FRANCIS LEOPOLD MCCLINTOCK, captain R.N., LL.D., commander of the Arctic (Fox) Expedition *(ibid)*.
1860, Mar. 28. HENRY JAMES, colonel, of the Royal Engineers, director of the Ordnance Survey and of the Topographical and Statistical Department of the War Office *(ibid)*.
1860, Mar. 28. EDWARD SHEPHERD CREASY, chief justice of Ceylon *(ibid)*.
1860, Apr. 24. COLIN BLACKBURN, one of the judges of the Queen's Bench *(ibid)*.
1860, Apr. 24. JAMES PLAISTED WILDE, a baron of the Exchequer *(ibid)*.
1860, May 24. WILLIAM MARTIN, late chief justice of New Zealand (Letters patent).
1860, May 24. FRANCIS BRADY, chief justice of Newfoundland (same).

KNIGHTS BACHELORS 355

1860, May 24. JAMES HURTLE FISHER, president of the Legislative Council, South Australia (same).

1860, May 24. CHRISTOFFEL JOSEPHUS BRAND, speaker of the House of Assembly of the Cape of Good Hope (same dated June 7).

1860, May 24. FRANCIS MURPHY, speaker of the House of Assembly of Victoria (same dated June 8).

1860, May 24. REDMOND BARRY, senior puisne judge of Victoria (same).

1860, May 24. THOMAS MACLEAR, astronomer royal at the Cape of Good Hope (same dated June 11).

1860, May 24. WALTER CURRIE, commandant of the Armed Mounted Police at the Cape of Good Hope (same dated June 12).

1860, June 13. GEORGE BURDETT L'ESTRANGE, gentleman usher of the Black Rod (by the lord lieutenant of Ireland).

1860, June 19. JOHN NODES DICKINSON, first puisne judge of the Supreme Court of New South Wales (Letters patent).

1860, June 20. WILLIAM LOCKYER FREESTUN, colonel (at St. James's Palace).

1860, June 20. JAMES RANALD MARTIN, F.R.S., physician to the Secretary of State for India in Council, and surgeon in the Bengal Army, retired *(ibid)*.

1860, Aug. 21. NARCISSE FORTUNAT BELLEAU, speaker of the Legislative Assembly of Canada (at the Parliament House, Quebec, by the prince of Wales, under authority of Letters patent granted for that purpose).

1860, Aug. 21. HENRY SMITH, speaker of the Commons House, Canada (*ibid* by same).

1860, Aug. 23. STUART ALEXANDER DONALDSON, formerly principal secretary to the Government of New South Wales (Letters patent).

1860, Oct. 26. CHARLES SARGENT, member of the Supreme Council of Justice of the Ionian Islands (at Windsor Castle).

1860, Dec. 10. JEAN EDOUARD RÉMONO, first puisne judge of the Supreme Court of the Island of Mauritius (Letters patent dated Dec. 18).

1860, Dec. 10. ANDREW SCOTT WAUGH, lieutenant colonel, Bengal Engineers, superintendent of Trigonometrical Survey, and surveyor general of India (Letters patent dated Dec. 19).

1861, Feb. 4. ARTHUR COTTON, colonel-commandant, Her Majesty's Madras Engineers (at Buckingham Palace).

1861, Feb. 14. RICHARD CHARLES KIRBY, late accountant general of the War Department (at St. James's Palace).

1861, Mar. 13. GEORGE EVEREST, colonel, F.R.S., of the Bengal Artillery, formerly superintendent of the Great Trigonometrical Survey, and surveyor general of India, on the retired list *(ibid)*.

1861, Mar. 13. COLLEY HARMAN SCOTLAND, chief justice of Madras *(ibid)*.

1861, Aug. 5. ROUNDELL PALMER, solicitor general (at Osborne).

1861, Aug. 9. EDWARD COEY, mayor of Belfast (by the lord lieutenant of Ireland, on his visit to the Botanical Gardens, Belfast).

1861, Nov. 14. PATRICK MACCHOMBAICH DE COLQUHOUN, LL.D., chief justice of the Ionian Islands (at Windsor Castle).

1862, Feb. 28. EDMUND GRIMANI HORNBY, judge of the Supreme Consular Court at Constantinople (Letters patent).

1862, May 30. WALTER FREDERIC CROFTON, captain, R.A., chairman of the Directors of Government Prisons (by the lord lieutenant of Ireland at the Vice-Regal Lodge).

1862, June 11. JOHN MELLOR, a justice of the Queen's Bench (Letters patent).

1862, July 18. GEORGE ALFRED ARNEY, chief justice of the Supreme Court of New Zealand (same).

1862, July 18. FRANCIS SMITH, judge of the Supreme Court of Tasmania (same).

1862, Sept. 16. CHARLES AUGUSTUS HARTLEY, the civil engineer employed by the European Commission for the improvement of the navigation of the Danube (same).

1862, Sept. 17. ROBERT JOSEPH PHILLIMORE, Q.C., Queen's advocate general (same).

1862, Oct. 31. GABRIEL PIERRE JULES FROPIER, of the Island of Mauritius (same).

1862, Dec. 11. LUKE SMITHETT, of Dover, Co. Kent, one of the justices of the peace for the borough of Dover (same).

1863, May 30. FRANCIS RICHARD SANDFORD (Letters patent dated June 8).

1863, June 30. JOHN GRAY, M.D., of Charleville House, Rathmines, Co. Dublin, chairman of the Waterworks Committee of the Dublin Corporation, "in special recognition of the indefatigable zeal and high ability evinced by the chairman of the Waterworks Committee throughout the whole progress of the undertaking" (by the lord lieutenant of Ireland).

KNIGHTS BACHELORS 357

1863, Aug. 10. JAMES COXE, of Kinellen, Co. Edinburgh, doctor of medicine, one of the commissioners of the General Board of Lunacy for Scotland (Letters patent).

1863, Aug. 10. GOLDSWORTHY GURNEY, of Bude, Co. Cornwall (same).

1863, Oct. 13. ALEXANDER ANDERSON, lord provost of Aberdeen (at Aberdeen on the occasion of unveiling the statue of prince Consort).

1863, Nov. 1. GILLERY PIGOTT, a baron of the Exchequer (Letters patent).

1863, Nov. 23. ROBERT PORRETT COLLIER, M.P., solicitor general (at Windsor Castle).

1863, Nov. 23. PETER STAFFORD CAREY, bailiff of Guernsey *(ibid)*.

1864, Jan. 28. WILLIAM ROBERT WILLS WILDE, fellow of the Royal College of Surgeons in Ireland, surgeon-oculist-in-ordinary to Her Majesty in Ireland, and vice-president of the Royal Irish Academy, "not so much in consideration of high professional reputation, which is European, as to mark the sense of services rendered to statistical science, especially in connection with the Irish Census" (by the lord lieutenant of Ireland).

1864, June 10. WILLIAM SHEE, a judge of the Queen's Bench (at Windsor Castle).

1864, Aug. 30. DAVID ROSS, lord provost of Perth (at Perth on the occasion of the unveiling the statue of prince Consort).

1864, Nov. 30. THOMAS HENRY, chief magistrate at Bow Street (at Windsor Castle).

1865, Feb. 11. ALEXANDER TAYLOR, doctor of medicine (Letters patent).

1865, Feb. 21. GEORGE CLENDINING O'DONNELL, eldest son of Sir Richard Annesley O'Donnell, bart., of Newport House, Co. Mayo (by the lord lieutenant of Ireland, the said knighthood having been claimed in accordance with a privilege pertaining to the heir of the said baronetcy under the terms of a clause in the patent of baronetcy granted in 1780 to Neale O'Donnell).

1865, May 18. MONTAGUE EDWARD SMITH, a justice of Common Pleas (at Windsor Castle).

1865, May 18. JOHN THWAITES, chairman of the Metropolitan Board of Works *(ibid)*.

1865, Aug. 14. JOHN HOWLEY, Q.C., the Queen's first serjeant in Ireland, late chairman of the County of Tipperary (by the lord lieutenant at the Vice-regal Lodge).

1865, Nov. 20. ROBERT LUSH, serjeant-at-law, a justice of Queen's Bench (at Windsor Castle).

1865, Nov. 20. EDWARD HILDITCH, M.D., inspector general of Hospitals and Fleets *(ibid)*.

1865, Nov. 20. JOHN CAMPBELL LEES, late chief justice of the Bahamas *(ibid)*.

1866, Feb. 10. DAVID MUNRO (MONRO), M.D., late speaker of the House of Representatives, New Zealand (Letters patent dated Feb. 13).

1866, Mar. 24. FRANCIS GRANT, president of the Royal Academy of Arts (at Buckingham Palace).

1866, June 13. RICHARD COUCH, chief justice of Her Majesty's High Court of Judicature at Bombay (Letters patent dated June 18).

1866, June 13. WALTER MORGAN, chief justice of Her Majesty's High Court of Judicature for the North-western Provinces of the Presidency of Fort William, in Bengal (Letters patent dated June 19).

1866, July 26. WILLIAM BOVILL, M.P., Q.C., solicitor general (at Osborne).

1866, Nov. 10. JOHN ROLT, attorney general (at Windsor Castle).

1866, Nov. 10. SAMUEL CANNING *(ibid)*.

1866, Nov. 10. WILLIAM THOMSON, LL.D., F.R.S., professor of Natural Philosophy in the University of Glasgow *(ibid)*.

1866, Nov. 10. JAMES ANDERSON, captain *(ibid)*.

1866, Nov. 10. SAMUEL WHITE BAKER *(ibid)*.

1866, Nov. 26. RICHARD ATWOOD GLASS (Letters patent).

1866, Nov. 30. JOHN MORRIS, mayor of Wolverhampton (at Wolverhampton).

1866, Dec. 12. WILLIAM HACKETT, recorder of Prince of Wales Island (at Windsor Castle on his appointment as chief justice for Penang).

1866, Dec. 28. JOHN BURGESS KARSLAKE, solicitor general (at Osborne).

1866, Dec. 28. BENJAMIN SAMUEL PHILLIPS, alderman and late lord mayor of London *(ibid)*.

1867, Feb. 2. RICHARD MALINS, a vice-chancellor *(ibid)*.

1867, Mar. 26. HENRY MANGLES DENHAM, rear-admiral, F.R.S. (at Windsor Castle).

1867, Mar. 26. GEORGE HARVEY, president of the Royal Scottish Academy *(ibid)*.

1867, Mar. 26. CHARLES HENRY PENNELL *(ibid)*.

1867, Mar. 26. JOSEPH NOEL PATON, R.S.A., Her Majesty's Limner for Scotland *(ibid)*.

KNIGHTS BACHELORS 359

1867, July 27. WILLIAM MITCHELL, editor and proprietor of the "Shipping and Mercantile Gazette" (Letters patent).
1867, Aug. 3. HENRY THOMPSON, F.R.C.S. (at Osborne).
1867, Aug. 3. WILLIAM HENRY BODKIN, assistant judge of the Court of Sessions, Middl. *(ibid)*.
1867, Aug. 3. JOHN ILES MANTELL, late chief justice of Her Majesty's settlements in the Gambia *(ibid)*.
1867, Aug. 3. WILLIAM ANDERSON ROSE, alderman of the City of London *(ibid)*.
1867, Aug. 3. SYDNEY HEDLEY WATERLOW, of Fairseat House, Highgate, alderman and sheriff of London and Middlesex (at Osborne).
1867, Aug. 3. FRANCIS LYCETT, sheriff of London and Middlesex *(ibid)*.
1867, Aug. 3. CHARLES JASPER SELWYN, M.P., solicitor general *(ibid)*.
1867, Aug. 19. HARRY ST. GEORGE ORD, colonel, lieutenant colonel in the Corps of Royal Engineers, governor and commander-in-chief of the Straits Settlements (Letters patent).
1867, Aug. 31. JOHN BROWN, of Endcliffe Hall, parish of Sheffield, West Riding of Co. York (same).
1867, Aug. 31. JOSEPH NEALE MCKENNA, of Ardo House, parish of Ardmore, Co. Waterford (same).
1867, Nov. 4. TRAVERS TWISS, D.C.L., advocate general (at Windsor Castle).
1867, Dec. 11. JOHN PAUL HOPKINS, major, governor of the Military Knights of Windsor *(ibid)*.
1867, Dec. 11. JOHN HENRY COOKE, lieutenant colonel, lieutenant of the Yeomen of the Guard *(ibid)*.
1867, Dec. 20. ARTHUR EDWARD KENNEDY, governor-in-chief of the West African Settlements (at Osborne).
1868, Jan. 17. CHARLES LANYON, of the Abbey, White Abbey, Co. Antrim, a justice of the Peace, Co. Antrim, M.P. for Belfast, president of the Royal Institute of the Architects of Ireland, and a Royal Hibernian Academician (by the lord lieutenant of Ireland).
1868, Jan. 17. RICHARD JOHN THEODORE ORPEN, president of the Incorporated Society of Attorneys and Solicitors of Ireland (by same).
1868, Jan. 30. CHARLES WHEATSTONE, F.R.S. (at Osborne).
1868, Feb. 29. WILLIAM BALIOL BRETT, M.P., solicitor general *(ibid)*.
1868, May 14. Rt. Hon. GEORGE MARKHAM GIFFARD, a vice-chancellor (at Windsor Castle).

1868, May 14. JAMES HANNEN, one of the justices of Her Majesty's Court of Queen's Bench (At Windsor Castle).
1868, May 14. Rt. Hon. WILLIAM CARROLL, M.D., lord mayor of Dublin *(ibid)*.
1868, July 7. THOMAS TILSON, of Clapham Park *(ibid)*.
1868, July 7. WILLIAM CHARLES HOOD, M.D. *(ibid)*.
1868, Aug. 29. ANDREW FAIRBAIRN, of Woodsley House, Leeds, West Riding, Co. York., mayor of Leeds (Letters patent).
1868, Aug. 29. FREDERICK ARROW, of Pilgrims Hall, Co. Essex, deputy master of the Trinity House, London (Letters patent).
1868, Aug. 29. EDWARD WILLIAM WATKIN, of Northenden, Co. Palatine of Chester (same).
1868, Nov. 3. JAMES LUMSDEN, of Arden, Co. Dumbarton., lord provost of the City of Glasgow (same).
1868, Nov. 13. JOHN BARRINGTON, a deputy lieutenant for the county of the City of Dublin, and lord mayor of that city in the year 1865 (by the lord lieutenant of Ireland).
1868, Nov. 13. EDWARD REID, of The Elms, Londonderry, mayor of that city (by same).
1868, Dec. 1. CHARLES HENRY FIRTH, of Heckmondwike, near Leeds, West Riding, Yorks (Letters patent).
1868, Dec. 5. PETER TAIT, of South Hill, Limerick, mayor of Limerick in the years 1866, 1867, and 1868, and a deputy lieutenant of the said city (by the lord lieutenant of Ireland).
1868, Dec. 7. PHILIP FRANCIS, judge of the Supreme Consular Court at Constantinople (Letters patent).
1868, Dec. 9. ANTHONY CLEASBY, a baron of the Exchequer (at Windsor Castle).
1868, Dec. 9. RICHARD BAGGALLAY, solicitor general *(ibid)*.
1868, Dec. 9. LOUIS MALLET, assistant secretary to the Board of Trade *(ibid)*.
1868, Dec. 9. GEORGE HAYES, one of the justices of Her Majesty's Court of Queen's Bench *(ibid)*.
1868, Dec. 12. JOHN DUKE COLERIDGE, M.P., solicitor general *(ibid)*.
1869, Jan. 14. MATTHEW DIGBY WYATT, (at Osborne).
1869, Feb. 4. WILLIAM MILBOURNE JAMES, a vice-chancellor *(ibid)*.
1869, Feb. 8. WILLIAM YOUNG, chief justice and president of the Legislative Council of the Province of Nova Scotia (Letters patent).
1869, Feb. 13. HUGH WILLIAM HOYLES, chief justice of the Colony of Newfoundland (same).

KNIGHTS BACHELORS 361

1869, Mar. 7. ROBERT HODGSON, chief justice of the Island of Prince Edward (Letters patent).

1869, Apr. 1. CHARLES FARQUHAR SHAND, chief justice of the Island of Mauritius (Letters patent dated Apr. 3).

1869, Apr. 14. MICHAEL COSTA (at Windsor Castle).

1869, May 4. JAMES MARTIN, late first minister and attorney general in the Colony of New South Wales (Letters patent dated May 5).

1869, May 4. ROBERT OFFICER, speaker of the House of Assembly of the Colony of Tasmania (Letters patent dated May 7).

1869, May 4. TERENCE AUBREY MURRAY, president of the Legislative Council of the Colony of New South Wales (Letters patent dated May 6).

1869, July 9. WILLIAM TITE, M.P., F.R.S. (at Windsor Castle).

1869, July 9. THOMAS DUFFUS HARDY, deputy keeper of the Public Records *(ibid)*.

1869, July 9. JAMES MEEK, sometime lord mayor of York *(ibid)*.

1869, July 9. RICHARD DAVIES HANSON, chief justice of the Colony of South Australia *(ibid)*.

1869, July 9. JOSEPH HERON, town clerk of Manchester *(ibid)*.

1869, July 9. PETER COATS, of Paisley, N.B. *(ibid)*.

1869, July 29. JAMES COCKLE, chief justice of the Supreme Court of the Colony of Queensland (Letters patent).

1869, Aug. 7. WILLIAM WRIGHT, of Sigglesthorne Hall, chairman of the directors of the Dock Company at Hull (at Osborne).

1869, Sept. 6. WILLIAM RICHARD DRAKE, of Oatlands Lodge, Co. Surrey (Letters patent).

1869, Oct. 9. SIDNEY SMITH BELL, chief justice of the Supreme Court of the Colony of the Cape of Good Hope (Letters patent).

1869, Nov. 11. ALBERT WILLIAM WOODS, Garter Principal King of Arms (at Windsor Castle).

1869, Nov. 11. JAMES ALDERSON, M.D., F.R.S., president of the Royal College of Physicians *(ibid)*.

1869, Nov. 11. ROGER THERRY, many years a judge of the Supreme Court of New South Wales *(ibid)*.

1869, Nov. 11. THOMAS GIBBONS FROST, of Dolcorsllwyn, Cemmaes, Co. Montgomery, and of Redcliff, Co. Chester, late mayor of Chester *(ibid)*.

1869, Nov. 11. WILLIAM FOTHERGILL COOKE, for great and special services in connexion with the practical introduction of the electric telegraph *(ibid)*.

1869, Dec. 11. JOSEPH CAUSTON, alderman and sheriff of London and sheriff of Co. Middlesex (At Windsor Castle).

1869, Dec. 11. JAMES VALLENTIN, sheriff of the City of London and county of Middlesex *(ibid)*.

1870, Feb. 26. JOHN LUCIE SMITH, chief justice of the Island of Jamaica (Letters patent).

1870, Mar. 12. MICHAEL ROBERTS WESTROPP, chief justice of Her Majesty's High Court of Judicature at Bombay (Letters patent).

1870, Mar. 31. FRANCIS RONALDS, in consideration of his having been the original inventor of the electric telegraph (at Windsor Castle).

1870, Apr. 30. JOHN MORPHETT, president of the Legislative Council of the colony of South Australia (Letters patent).

1870, Apr. 30. GEORGE STRICKLAND KINGSTON, speaker of the House of Assembly of the Colony of South Australia (same).

1870, May 18. WILLIAM BROWN, late accountant general in the War Department (at Windsor Castle).

1870, June 4. JAMES MCCULLOCH, chief secretary to the Government in the Colony of Victoria (Letters patent).

1870, June 23. JOHN HENRY BRIGGS, late chief clerk of the Admiralty (at Windsor Castle).

1870, June 23. ANTONIO BRADY, late superintendent of contracts at the Admiralty *(ibid)*.

1870, Aug. 9. Rt. Hon. GEORGE MELLISH, a judge of the Court of Appeal in Chancery (at Osborne).

1870, Aug. 9. DANIEL ADOLPHUS LANGE *(ibid)*.

1870, Aug. 17. EDWARD SMIRKE, vice-warden of the Stannaries (at Windsor).

1870, Nov. 3. EDWARD KENNY, late president of the Privy Council of the Dominion of Canada (Letters patent).

1870, Nov. 29. JAMES PENNETHORNE, late architect to the Board of Works and of the Woods and Forests (at Windsor Castle).

1870, Nov. 29. LLEWELLYN TURNER, deputy constable of Carnarvon Castle *(ibid)*.

1871, Jan. 14. JAMES BACON, a vice-chancellor (at Osborne).

1871, Jan. 14. JOHN MACLEAN, of Pallingswick Lodge, Hammersmith, deputy auditor of the War Office *(ibid)*.

1871, Feb. 8. WILLIAM HARRISON WALKER, captain, senior professional member of the Harbour and Marine Department of the Board of Trade (at Windsor Castle).

1871, Feb. 13. CHARLES ROBERT TURNER, late senior master of Her Majesty's Court of Queen's Bench at Westminster (Letters patent).

KNIGHTS BACHELORS 363

1871, Mar. 6. MAURICE CHARLES O'CONNELL, president of the Legislative Council of the Colony of Queensland (Letters patent).

1871, Mar. 24. WILLIAM BOXALL, R.A., D.C.L., director of the National Gallery (at Windsor Castle).

1871, Mar. 24. GEORGE ELVEY, doctor of music *(ibid)*.

1871, Mar. 24. WILLIAM STERNDALE BENNETT, D.C.L., doctor of music *(ibid)*.

1871, Mar. 24. JULIUS BENEDICT (At Windsor Castle).

1871, June 21. FRANCIS HICKS, treasurer of St. Thomas's Hospital (on the occasion of the opening of said Hospital).

1871, June 29. JOHN WICKENS, a vice-chancellor (at Windsor Castle).

1871, July 24. HUGH ALLAN, of Ravenscrag, Co. Montreal, Canada (Letters patent).

1871, July 28. FRANCIS PETTIT SMITH, curator of the Patent Office Museum, South Kensington (at Osborne).

1871, July 28. JAMES JELL CHALK, barrister-at-law, secretary to the Ecclesiastical Commissioners for England *(ibid)*.

1871, Oct. 3.* ROBERT STUART, one of Her Majesty's counsel, chief justice of Her Majesty's High Court of Judicature for the North-Western Provinces of the Presidency of Fort William, in Bengal (Letters patent).

1872, Feb. 21. WILLIAM ROBERT GROVE, a judge of the Court of Common Pleas (at Osborne).

1872, Feb. 21. GEORGE JESSEL, solicitor general *(ibid)*.

1872, Feb. 21. OLIVER NUGENT, president of the Legislative Council of Antigua *(ibid)*.

1872, Feb. 28. ROBERT PRESCOTT STEWART, Mus. Doc, of Holyrood, Bray, Co. Wicklow, professor of music in the University of Dublin (by the lord lieutenant of Ireland at Dublin Castle before the levée).

1872, Mar. 14. JOHN COODE, chief engineer of the Portland Breakwater (at Buckingham Palace).

1872, Mar. 14. JOSEPH COWEN, M.P., alderman, of Newcastle-on-Tyne, in recognition of his services as chairman of the River Tyne Commissioners *(ibid)*.

1872, Mar. 14. PETER SPOKES, late mayor of Reading *(ibid)*.

1872, Mar. 14. JOHN ROSE CORMACK, M.D. of the Universities of Paris and Edinburgh, physician to the Hertford British Hospital of Paris, and late surgeon to the Ambulance Anglaise at Paris *(ibid)*.

* In August, 1871, knighthood was offered to John Campbell, of Dublin, on the occasion of the visit of the Prince of Wales, but was declined.

1872, Mar. 14. JOHN GILBERT, A.R.A., president of the Society of Painters in Water Colours (At Buckingham Palace).

1872, Mar. 14. FRANCIS WYATT TRUSCOTT, alderman of London and sheriff of London and Middlesex (*ibid* in commemoration of the Queen's visit to St. Paul's Cathedral, Feb. 27).

1872, Mar. 14. JOHN BENNETT, sheriff of London and Middlesex (*ibid* same occasion).

1872, Mar. 14. THOMAS CHAMBERS, Q.C., M.P., deputy recorder (*ibid*).

1872, Mar. 19. JOHN GOSS, composer for Her Majesty's Chapels Royal, and organist of St. Paul's Cathedral (at Windsor Castle).

1872, Apr. 11. ALBERT ABDALLAH DAVID SASSOON, of Bombay, member of the Council of the governor of Bombay for making Laws and Regulations (Letters patent).

1872, Apr. 22. JOHN RICHARD QUAIN, one of the justices of Her Majesty's Court of Queen's Bench at Westminster (at Windsor Castle).

1872, Apr. 22. THOMAS DAKIN, alderman (*ibid*).

1872, June 7. DANIEL BROOKE ROBERTSON, Her Majesty's consul at Canton (Letters patent).

1872, June 25. JAMES RAMSDEN, of Barrow-in-Furness (at Windsor Castle).

1872, June 7. WILLIAM PERRY, late Her Majesty's consul-general at Venice (Letters patent).

1872, June 27. COWASJEE JEHANGHIER READYMONEY, of Bombay, (Letters patent).

1872, Aug. 9. GEORGE GILBERT SCOTT, R.A. (at Osborne).

1872, Aug. 9. JOHN SAVAGE, mayor of Belfast (at Belfast by the lord lieutenant of Ireland).

1872, Aug. 9. JAMES HAMILTON, chairman of the Belfast Harbour Commission (*ibid* by same).

1872, Aug. 17. JOHN LE COUTEUR, colonel, late adjutant general of the Royal Jersey Militia, and one of Her Majesty's aides-de-camp, viscount of the Isle of Jersey (Letters patent).

1872, Nov. 30. JOSIAH MASON, of Norwood House, Erdington, near Birmingham, Co. Warwick. (same).

1872, Nov. 30. EDWARD LEE, manager of the Dublin Exhibition of Arts, Industries, and Manufactures (by the lord lieutenant of Ireland, on the occasion of the closing of the Dublin Exhibition of Arts, Industries, and Manufactures).

KNIGHTS BACHELORS 365

1873, Jan. 16. WILLIAM PALLISER, major, for his distinguished services in connection with Artillery (at Osborne).
1873, Feb. 5. THOMAS DICKSON ARCHIBALD, a justice of the Queen's Bench *(ibid)*.
1873, Feb. 5. CHARLES EDWARD POLLOCK, a baron of Her Majesty's Court of Exchequer *(ibid)*.
1873, Feb. 5. JOHN CORDY BURROWS, ex-mayor of Brighton *(ibid)*.
1873, Feb. 13. JOSEPH NEEDHAM, chief justice of the Island of Trinidad (Letters patent).
1873, Feb. 21. WILLIAM HAMILTON, Her Majesty's consul at Boulogne (Letters patent).
1873, Mar. 14. FRANCIS DILLON BELL, speaker of the House of Representatives of the Colony of New Zealand (Letters patent).
1873, Apr. 15. RALPH SMITH CUSACK, chairman of the Midland Great Western Railway Company of Ireland, clerk of the Hanaper in Ireland (by the lord lieutenant, on the occasion of the opening of the "Spencer" Dock at Dublin).
1873, May 5. JAMES HILL, chief commissioner of Charities for England and Wales (at Windsor Castle).
1873, May 10. SIDNEY SMITH SAUNDERS, late Her Majesty's consul general in the Ionian Islands (Letters patent).
1873, May 31. CHARLES GAVAN DUFFY, lately chief secretary of the Colony of Victoria and its Dependencies (Letters patent).
1873, June 26. ALEXANDER NISBET, doctor, honorary physician to Her Majesty and inspector general of Hospitals and Fleets, Royal Navy (at Windsor Castle).
1873, June 26. GEORGE BIDDLECOMBE, captain R.N. *(ibid.)*
1873, June 30. JOSEPH RITCHIE LYON DICKSON, M.D., physician to Her Majesty's Legation in Persia, in attendance on His Majesty the Shah *(ibid)*.
1873, Aug. 4. THOMAS WHITE, sheriff of London and Middlesex (at Osborne).
1873, Aug. 4. FREDERICK PERKINS, sheriff of London and Middlesex *(ibid)*.
1873, Aug. 31. JOHN HAWKSHAW (at Balmoral).
1873, Sept. 2. JAMES MILNE WILSON, late chief member of the Executive Government and colonial secretary of the Colony of Tasmania (Letters patent).
1873, Dec. 12. HENRY JAMES, Q.C., M.P., attorney general (at Windsor Castle).
1873, Dec. 12. WILLIAM GEORGE GRANVILLE VENABLES-VERNON-HARCOURT, Q.C., M.P., solicitor general *(ibid)*.
1873, Dec. 12. CHARLES HALL, a vice-chancellor *(ibid)*.

KNIGHTS BACHELORS

1873, Dec. 12. ARCHIBALD PAULL BURT, chief justice of the Colony of Western Australia *(ibid)*.

1873, Dec. 12. WILLIAM HENRY DOYLE, chief justice of the Bahama Islands *(ibid)*.

1874, Jan. 27. RICHARD PAUL AMPHLETT, a baron of the Exchequer (at Osborne).

1874, Jan. 27. JAMES WILLIAM MACKEY, of Clonsilla House, Co. Dublin (by the lord lieutenant of Ireland, for public services as J.P. and alderman of Dublin, lord mayor 1866 and 1873).

1874, Jan. 28. THOMAS SIDGREAVES, chief justice of the Straits Settlements (Letters patent).

1874, Jan. 31. JULIAN PAUNCEFOTE, chief justice of the Supreme Court of the Leeward Islands (Letters patent).

1874, Feb. 20. HENRY DONOVAN, J.P., Co. Kerry, and high sheriff, 1873; chairman of the Tralee Town Commissioners (by the lord lieutenant of Ireland).

1874, Feb. 21. CHARLES REED, M.P., LL.D., F.S.A., J.P. and D.L., chairman of the London School Board (at Windsor Castle).

1874, Feb. 21. CHARLES ALEXANDER WOOD, formerly one of Her Majesty's Commissioners of Emigration *(ibid)*.

1874, Mar. 2. JAMES WATSON, lord provost of Glasgow *(ibid)*.

1874, Mar. 17. JOHN SMALE, chief justice of the Colony of Hong Kong (Letters patent).

1874, May 12. JOSEPH WILLIAM BAZALGETTE, engineer to the Metropolitan Board of Works (at Windsor Castle).

1874, July 7. JOHN RICE CROWE, Her Majesty's consul general at Christiania *(ibid)*.

1874, July 7. JOHN GREEN, late Her Majesty's agent and consul general at Bucharest *(ibid)*.

1874, July 20. RICHARD FRANCIS MORGAN, Queen's advocate of the Colony of Ceylon (Letters patent).

1874, Aug. 6. MUTEE COOMÁRA SWÁMY, a member of the Legislative Council of Ceylon (at Osborne).

1874, Aug. 6. CHARLES WHETHAM, sheriff of London and Middlesex *(ibid)*.

1874, Aug. 6. JOHN HENRY JOHNSON, sheriff of London and Middlesex *(ibid)*.

1874, Sept. 16. GEORGE CAMPBELL ANDERSON, attorney general of the Bahama Islands (Letters patent).

1874, Dec. 12. JOHN HOLKER, M.P., Q.C., solicitor general (at Windsor Castle).

1874, Dec. 12. LUDLOW COTTER *(ibid)*.

KNIGHTS BACHELORS 367

1874, Dec. 29. MUNGULDASS NATHOOBHOY, of Bombay, member of the Council of the Governor of Bombay for making Laws and Regulations (Letters patent).
1875, Jan. 30. JOSEPH GEORGE LONG INNES, attorney general of the Colony of New South Wales (Letters patent).
1875, May 13. JOHN WALTER HUDDLESTON, a baron of the Exchequer (at Windsor Castle).
1875, May 13. NATHANIEL LINDLEY, a justice of the Court of Common Pleas (ibid).
1875, May 13. WILLIAM VENTRIS FIELD, a justice of the Queen's Bench (ibid).
1875, May 13. RICHARD GARTH, Q.C., chief justice of Bengal (ibid).
1875, May 13. WILLIAM HENRY WALTON, late senior master of the Court of Exchequer and Queen's Remembrancer (ibid).
1875, July 17. WILLIAM HENRY FANCOURT MITCHELL, president of the Legislative Council of the Colony of Victoria (Letters patent).
1875, Aug. 14. JOHN LARKINS CHEESE RICHARDSON, speaker of the Legislative Council of the Colony of New Zealand (same).
1875, Sept. 29. SAMUEL WILSON, of Ercildoun, near the town of Ballarat, in the Colony of Victoria (same).
1875, Sept. 29. CHARLES MACMAHON, speaker of the Legislative Assembly of the Colony of Victoria (same).
1875, Oct. 26. MATTHEW BAILLIE BEGBIE, chief justice of British Columbia (at Balmoral).
1875, Nov. 24. FRANK HENRY SOUTER, commissioner of police at Bombay (by the prince of Wales at the Government House, Bombay).
1875, Nov. 27. HARDINGE STANLEY GIFFARD, Q.C., solicitor general (at Windsor Castle).
1876, Jan. 5. STUART SAUNDERS HOGG, commissioner of police, Calcutta, in recognition of his services during the Royal visit (by the prince of Wales at the Government House, Calcutta).
1876, Mar. 24. EDMUND HAY CURRIE, chairman of the House Committee of the London Hospital (at Windsor Castle in connection with the Queen's recent visit to said Hospital).
1876, June 27. THOMAS HOWELL, late director of contracts, War Department (At Windsor Castle).
1876, June 27. GEORGE WEBBE DASENT, D.C.L., one of Her Majesty's civil service commissioners (ibid).
1876, June 27. CHARLES WYVILLE THOMSON, professor, director of the Civilian Scientific Staff of Her Majesty's ship "Challenger" (ibid).

1876, July 21. JAMES TAYLOR INGHAM, chief magistrate of the Police Courts of the Metropolis (at Osborne).

1876, July 21. HENRY ARTHUR HUNT, consulting surveyor to Her Majesty's Office of Works *(ibid)*.

1876, July 21. WILLIAM HENRY WYATT, a deputy lieutenant and magistrate for the County of Middlesex; chairman of the Committee of Management of Colney Hatch and Leavesden Asylums *(ibid)*.

1876, July 21. DANIEL MACNEE, LL.D., president of the Royal Scottish Academy *(ibid)*.

1876, July 21. DAVID PATRICK CHALMERS, Queen's advocate of the Gold Coast Colony *(ibid)*.

1876, Aug. 17. JOHN STEELL, R.S.A., sculptor to the Queen for Scotland (at Holyrood Palace, on the occasion of the unveiling of the memorial to Prince Consort in Edinburgh).

1876, Aug. 17. HERBERT STANLEY OAKELEY, doctor of music, professor of music in the University of Edinburgh *(ibid)*.

1876, Aug. 19. WILLIAM MILNE, president of the Legislative Council of South Australia (Letters patent).

1876, Aug. 19. LUKE SAMUEL LEAKE, speaker of the Legislative Council of Western Australia (same).

1876, Sept. 27. HENRY SCHOFIELD, Her Majesty's consul at Guatemala (same).

1876, Nov. 28. HENRY MANISTY, a judge of the High Court (at Windsor Castle).

1876, Nov. 28. HENRY HAWKINS, a judge of the Queen's Bench Division of the High Court *(ibid)*.

1876, Nov. 28. HENRY CHARLES LOPES, of Easthill, Somerset, a judge of the Common Pleas Division of the High Court *(ibid)*.

1876, Dec. 5. Rt. Hon. GEORGE BOLSTER OWENS, M.D., J.P., lord mayor of Dublin (at Dublin Castle by the lord lieutenant of Ireland, on the occasion of the presentation of the address from the Corporation of Dublin at his Grace's farewell reception).

1876, Dec. 5. GEORGE DEVONSHIRE PENROSE, mayor of Cork *(ibid by same)*.

1876, Dec. 5. WILLIAM MILLER, mayor of Londonderry 1875—77 *(ibid by same)*.

1877, Jan. 30. ROBERT BOAG, mayor of Belfast in 1876 (knighted at the duke of Marlborough's first levée held that day at Dublin Castle).

1877, Mar. 12. ALLEN YOUNG (at Buckingham Palace).

KNIGHTS BACHELORS

1877, Mar. 20. JAMES GELL, attorney general for the Isle of Man (at Windsor Castle).

1877, Mar. 20. WILLIAM LEECE DRINKWATER, first deemster of the Isle of Man *(ibid)*.

1877, Mar. 20. WALTER HENRY MEDHURST, late Her Majesty's consul at Shanghai *(ibid)*.

1877, Apr. 30. EDWARD FRY, a judge of the High Court *(ibid)*.

1877, Apr. 30. HERBERT BRUCE SANDFORD, colonel, R.A., acting assistant director, South Kensington Museum; in recognition of his services as commissioner for this country at the Philadelphia Exhibition *(ibid)*.

1877, July 11. Rt. Hon. HENRY COTTON, one of the lords justices of Appeal in Chancery *(ibid)*.

1877, Aug. 13. WILLIAM RICHARD HOLMES, late Her Majesty's consul for Bosnia (at Osborne).

1877, Aug. 13. ERASMUS OMMANNEY, admiral, F.R.S. *(ibid)*.

1877, Aug. 13. EDWARD AUGUSTUS INGLEFIELD, vice-admiral, F.R.S. (At Osborne).

1877, Aug. 13. GEORGE HENRY RICHARDS, vice-admiral, F.R.S. *(ibid)*.

1877, Aug. 14. HENRY WHATLEY TYLER, late a captain in Her Majesty's Corps of Royal Engineers, and late chief inspector of railways (Letters patent).

1877, Oct. 4. WILLIAM BUELL RICHARDS, chief justice of the Supreme Court of the Dominion of Canada (Letters patent).

1877, Oct. 4. ANTOINE AIMÉ DORION, chief justice of the Court of Queen's Bench for the Province of Quebec, in the Dominion of Canada (same).

1877, Oct. 4. JOHN HENRY DE VILLIERS, chief justice of the Supreme Court and speaker of the Legislative Council of the Colony of the Cape of Good Hope (same).

1877, Oct. 4. DAVID TENNANT, speaker of the Legislative Assembly of the Colony of the Cape of Good Hope (same).

1877, Oct. 4. GEORGE WIGRAM ALLEN, speaker of the Legislative Assembly of the Colony of New South Wales (same).

1877 Oct. 4. JOHN BUDD PHEAR, chief justice of the Supreme Court of Ceylon (same).

1877, Dec. 12. ANDREW BARCLAY WALKER, late mayor of Liverpool (at Windsor Castle).

1877, Dec. 12. BRYAN ROBINSON, late judge of the Supreme Court, Newfoundland *(ibid)*.

1877, Dec. 12. JAMES BAIN, of Crofthend, Cumberland, late lord provost of Glasgow, D.L., J.P., F.R.S., F.R.G.S. *(ibid)*.

1878, Jan. 8. JOHN PRESTON, mayor of Belfast (by the lord lieutenant of Ireland at Dublin Castle).

1878, Jan. 15. LEWIS WHINCOP JARVIS, D.L., of Middelton Towers, King's Lynn (at Osborne).

1878, Mar. 18. SAMUEL FERGUSON, LL.D., Q.C., deputy keeper of the Public Records in Ireland (by the lord lieutenant of Ireland at Dublin Castle).

1878, May 31. THOMAS ELDER, member of the Legislative Council of the Colony of South Australia (dubbed by the Queen, but at first intended to have been created by Letters patent).

1878, May 31. SALVATORE NAUDI, doctor of laws, judge of the Court of Appeal of the Island of Malta (Letters patent).

1878, May 31. EDWARD EYRE WILLIAMS, late puisne judge of the Supreme Court of the Colony of Victoria (dubbed by the Queen, but at first intended to have been created by Letters patent).

1878, July 30. EDWARD HERTSLET, F.R.G.S., librarian and keeper of the Papers of the Foreign Office (at Osborne, in recognition of his labours at the Congress of Berlin).

1878, Aug. 14. JAMES OLDKNOW, mayor of Nottingham, and chairman of the Committee of the Nottingham Castle Art Museum *(ibid)*.

1878, Aug. 16. JACOB DIRK BARRY, recorder of the High Court of the Province of Griqualand and West (Letters patent).

1878, Nov. 25. FREDERICK LEIGHTON, president of the Royal Academy of Arts (at Windsor Castle).

1878, Nov. 27. JAMES SALMON, M.D., inspector general of Hospitals and Fleets *(ibid)*.

1878, Nov. 27. BEN THOMAS BRANDRETH GIBBS *(ibid)*.

1878, Nov. 27. JOHN ANDERSON, LL.D., M.I.C.E. *(ibid)*.

1878, Nov. 27. THOMAS SCAMBLER OWDEN, alderman and late lord mayor of the City of London *(ibid)*.

1878, Nov. 27. JOHN MILTON, late accountant general of the Army War Department *(ibid)*.

1878, Dec. 20. ALFRED SANDISON, Oriental second secretary at Her Majesty's Embassy at Constantinople (Letters patent).

1879, Apr. 23. CHARLES ARTHUR TURNER, chief justice of Her Majesty's Court of Judicature at Madras (Letters patent).

1879, June 26. CHARLES SYNGE CHRISTOPHER BOWEN, one of the judges of Her Majesty's High Court of Justice (at Windsor Castle).

KNIGHTS BACHELORS 371

1879, June 26. HENRY BESSEMER, of Denmark Hill (at Windsor Castle in recognition of his services in the manufacture of malleable iron and steel and in numerous other inventions).

1879, June 26. HENRY EDWARD LANDOR THUILLIER, Royal Artillery, F.R.S. *(ibid)*.

1879, June 26. THOMAS BOUCH, M.I.C.E., chief engineer of the Tay Bridge *(ibid)*.

1879, July 29. WALTER EUGENE DE SOUZA, of Calcutta (Letters patent).

1879, Oct. 29. CHARLES PACKER, chief judge of the Island of Barbados (same).

1880, Jan. 5. HENRY CONNOR, LL.B., chief justice of the Supreme Court of the Colony of Natal (same).

1880, Feb. 24. THOMAS ALFRED JONES, president of the Royal Hibernian Academy, in recognition of his high professional standing as well as of the eminence of the Royal Hibernian Academy of Painting and Sculpture over which he had so long and so honourably presided (at Dublin Castle by the lord lieutenant of Ireland).

1880, Feb. 27. NICHOLAS GUSTAVE BESTEL, barrister at law, formerly senior puisne judge, and lately acting chief judge of the Supreme Court of the Island of Mauritius (Letters patent).

1880, Mar. 18. HENRY LUSHINGTON PHILLIPS, judicial commissioner of the High Court of Justice in Cyprus (Letters patent).

1880, Mar. 18. JOHN BRADDICK MONCKTON, town clerk of the City of London (at Windsor Castle).

1880, Mar. 18. WILLIAM THOMAS CHARLEY, D.C.L., M.P., common serjeant of the City of London *(ibid)*.

1880, Apr. 20. EDMUND STEPHEN HARRISON, deputy clerk of the Council *(ibid)*.

1880, Apr. 20. THOMAS JAMES NELSON, solicitor of the City of London *(ibid)*.

1880, Apr. 20. THOMAS CUPPAGE BRUCE, R.N., superintendent of packets, Dover *(ibid)*.

1880, Apr. 20. ALGERNON BORTHWICK (At Windsor Castle).

1880, Apr. 28. JOHN LENTAIGNE, of Tallaght, Co. Dublin, formerly one of the inspectors general of prisons in Ireland and now an honorary member of the General Prison Board, a commissioner of national education and inspector of Reformatory and Industrial Schools in Ireland, president of the Royal Zoological Society, and ex-president of the Statistical Society (at Dublin Castle by the lord lieutenant of Ireland).

1880, May 13. FARRER HERSCHELL, M.P., Q.C., solicitor general (at Buckingham Palace).

1880, May 31. ROBERT RIPON MARETT, bailiff of Her Majesty's Island of Jersey (Letters patent).

1880, July 12. GEORGE MAURICE O'RORKE, speaker of the House of Representatives of the Colony of New Zealand (same).

1880, July 31. PHILIP PROTHERO SMITH, mayor of Truro, for services on the occasion of the visit of the prince of Wales to Truro to lay the foundation stone of the new Cathedral (at Osborne).

1880, July 31. GEORGE HENRY CHAMBERS, chairman of the London and St. Katharine's Docks Company (ibid).

1880, Dec. 1. RUPERT ALFRED KETTLE, of Merridale, Wolverhampton (at Windsor Castle).

1880, Dec. 1. LOUIS STEUART JACKSON, late a judge of the High Court of Judicature at Fort William in Bengal (ibid).

1880, Dec. 1. WATKIN WILLIAMS, a judge of the Supreme Court (ibid).

1880, Dec. 1. GUSTAVUS HUME, lieutenant colonel, lieutenant of Her Majesty's Bodyguard of the Honourable Corps of Gentlemen at Arms (ibid).

1880, Dec. 16. WALTER WATSON HUGHES, of South Australia (ibid).

1880, Dec. 16. EDWARD BURROWES SINCLAIR, A.M., M.D., of Dublin, in recognition of his public services in training soldiers' wives as nurses (ibid).

1880, Dec. 16. EDWARD BAINES, late member of Parliament for Leeds (at Windsor Castle).

1881, Feb. 25. ARTHUR NEED, lieutenant colonel, lieutenant of Her Majesty's Royal Bodyguard of Yeomen of the Guard (at Buckingham Palace).

1881, Mar. 2. JAMES RISDON BENNETT, M.D., president of the Royal College of Physicians, F.R.S. (at Windsor Castle).

1881, Apr. 1. JAMES CHARLES MATHEW, one of the justices of Her Majesty's High Court of Justice (ibid).

1881, Apr. 1. LEWIS WILLIAM CAVE, one of the justices of Her Majesty's High Court of Justice (ibid).

1881, Apr. 1. CHARLES WILLIAM SIKES (ibid).

1881, May 2. EDWARD EBENEZER KAY, one of the justices of Her Majesty's High Court of Justice (ibid).

1881, May 24 (Nov. 1). WILLIAM JOHNSTON RITCHIE, chief justice of the Supreme Court and Exchequer Court of the Dominion of Canada (Letters patent to bear date 1881, May 24).

1881, Aug. 18. FREDERICK JOSEPH BRAMWELL, F.R.S. (at Osborne).

1881, Aug. 18. JAMES ALLANSON PICTON (ibid).

1881, Aug. 18. JOHN HUMPHREYS, senior coroner for the County of Middlesex (At Osborne).
1881, Aug. 18. HUGH OWEN *(ibid)*.
1881, Aug. 25. Rt. Hon. THOMAS JAMIESON BOYD, lord provost of Edinburgh, and lord lieutenant of the County of the City of Edinburgh (at Holyrood Palace).
1881, Aug. 26. WILLIAM COLLINS, ex-lord provost of Glasgow *(ibid)*.
1881, Nov. 1. JAMES PRENDERGAST, chief justice of the Supreme Court of New Zealand (Letters patent).
1881, Nov. 23. EDWARD PORTER COWAN, of Craig-a-vad, Belfast, and of Clintaugh House, Anahilt, Co. Down; mayor of Belfast (by the lord lieutenant of Ireland).
1881, Dec. 7. JOSEPH WILLIAM CHITTY, one of the justices of Her Majesty's High Court of Justice (at Windsor Castle).
1881, Dec. 7. FORD NORTH, one of the justices of Her Majesty's High Court of Justice *(ibid)*.
1881, Dec. 7. WILLIAM MACCORMAC, surgeon and lecturer on surgery, Saint Thomas's Hospital; consulting surgeon, French Hospital, and examiner in surgery, University of London; in consideration of his services in connection with the International Medical Congress *(ibid)*.
1881, Dec. 7. GEORGE CHRISTOPHER MOLESWORTH BIRDWOOD, M.D., late Bombay Medical Staff, special assistant in Revenue Statistics and Commerce Department of the India Office *(ibid)*.
1881, Dec. 7. ERASMUS WILSON, F.R.S., president of the Royal College of Surgeons of England *(ibid)*.
1881, Dec. 7. ANDREW CROMBIE RAMSAY, LL.D., F.R.S., director general of the Geological Survey of the United Kingdom *(ibid)*.
1881, Dec. 24. CHARLES LILLEY, chief justice of Queensland (Letters patent).
1882, Jan. 20. WILLIAM PATRICK ANDREW, of Saint Bernard's, and of Charlefield, both in the County of Midlothian (same).
1882, Feb. 27. WILLIAM HENRY WHITE, one of Her Majesty's Army Purchase Commissioners to carry into effect the provisions of the Regulation of the Forces Act, 1871 (at Windsor Castle).
1882, Apr. 8. JOHN GORRIE, chief justice of the Supreme Court of Fiji (Letters patent).
1882, May 17. WILLIAM FETTES DOUGLAS, president of the Royal Scottish Academy (at Windsor Castle).
1882, May 17. JOHN JONES JENKINS, M.P. *(ibid)*.

1882, June 29. REGINALD HANSON, alderman of London and sheriff of London and Middlesex (At Windsor Castle).

1882, June 29. WILLIAM ANDERSON OGG, sheriff of London and Middlesex *(ibid)*.

1882, June 29. RICHARD CAYLEY, chief justice of the Island of Ceylon *(ibid)*.

1882, June 29. JAMES MARSHALL, chief justice of the Gold Coast Colony *(ibid)*.

1882, June 29. HENRY JAMES BURFORD BURFORD-HANCOCK, chief Justice of the Supreme Court of the Leeward Islands *(ibid)*.

1882, June 29. ADAM GIB ELLIS, chief justice of the Supreme Court of Mauritius *(ibid)*.

1882, June 29. JOHN CHARLES DAY, one of the justices of Her Majesty's High Court of Justice *(ibid)*.

1882, June 29. JAMES NICHOLAS DOUGLASS, engineer-in-chief to the Trinity House *(ibid)*.

1882, June 29 (Nov. 30). GEORGE PRINGLE, secretary to the Ecclesiastical Commission *(ibid)*.

1882, July 20. GEORGE PHILLIPPO, chief justice of the Supreme Court of Hong Kong and its Dependencies (Letters patent).

1882, Nov. 30. JOSEPH COCKSEY LEE (at Windsor Castle).

1882, Nov. 30. RICHARD TEMPLE RENNIE, chief justice of the Supreme Court for China and Japan *(ibid)*.

1882, Nov. 30. JOHN PEARSON, one of the justices of Her Majesty's High Court of Justice *(ibid)*.

1882, Nov. 30. OSCAR MOORE PASSEY CLAYTON *(ibid)*.

1882, Nov. 30. ROBERT WILLIAM JACKSON, brigade surgeon *(ibid)*.

1882, Nov. 30. JACOB BEHRENS *(ibid)*.

1882, Dec. 7. JOHN PETER DE GEX, Q.C., treasurer of Lincoln's Inn *(ibid)*.

1882, Dec. 7. JOHN BLOSSET MAULE, Q.C., treasurer of the Inner Temple *(ibid)*.

1882, Dec. 7. FRANCIS ROXBURGH, Q.C., treasurer of the Middle Temple *(ibid)*.

1882, Dec. 7. WILLIAM ST. JAMES WHEELHOUSE, Q.C., treasurer of Gray's Inn *(ibid)*.

1882, Dec. 7. THOMAS PAINE, president of the Incorporated Law Society *(ibid)*.

1883, Jan. 30. DANIEL VINCENT O'SULLIVAN, late mayor of Cork (at Dublin Castle by the lord lieutenant).

1883, Apr. 20. CHARLES PARKER BUTT, one of the justices of Her Majesty's High Court of Justice (at Osborne).

1883, Apr. 20. ARCHIBALD LEVIN SMITH, one of the justices of Her Majesty's High Court of Justice *(ibid)*.

1883, Apr. 20. WILLIAM SIEMENS, D.C.L., LL.D., F.R.S. *(ibid)*.

1883, Apr. 20. FREDERICK AUGUSTUS ABEL, in recognition of his valuable services to the War Department and other departments of the Government in his capacity as chemist to the War Department *(ibid)*.

1883, Apr. 20. ABRAHAM WOODIWISS, councillor and sometime mayor of Derby *(ibid)*.

1883, Apr. 20. THOMAS BAKER, alderman and sometime mayor of Manchester *(ibid)*.

1883, Apr. 20. RICHARD HENRY WYATT, for the valuable services rendered by him to the Government during the last 25 years as Parliamentary agent to the Treasury *(ibid)*.

1883, Apr. 20. HENRY DARVILL, solicitor and town clerk of Windsor *(ibid)*.

1883, May 9. ALFRED BALLISTON, staff captain, R.N., commanding Her Majesty's Royal yacht "Alberta" (at Windsor Castle).

1883, May 22. GEORGE GROVE, D.C.L., director of the Royal College of Music *(ibid)*.

1883, May 22. GEORGE ALEXANDER MACFARREN, professor of music of the University of Cambridge and principal of the Royal Academy of Music *(ibid)*.

1883, May 22. ARTHUR SEYMOUR SULLIVAN, doctor of music of the Universities of Oxford and Cambridge *(ibid)*.

1883, June 16. HENRY THOMAS WRENFORDSLEY, chief justice of the Colony of Fiji (Letters patent).

1883, June 16. RODERICK WILLIAM CAMERON, commissioner for the Dominion of Canada to the Australian International Exhibition (same).

1883, June 16. ALFRED ROBERTS, honorary secretary and consulting surgeon to Prince Alfred Hospital, Sydney, New South Wales (same).

1883, July 19. JACOBUS PETRUS DE WET, acting chief justice of the Island of Ceylon (at Windsor Castle).

1883, July 19. WILLIAM BOWER FORWOOD, alderman of the City of Liverpool *(ibid)*.

1883, July 19. JOHN GILLESPIE, secretary to the Royal Company of Archers, the Queen's Body Guard for Scotland *(ibid)*.

1883, July 19. HENRY ALFRED PITMAN, M.D., registrar of the Royal College of Physicians *(ibid)*.

KNIGHTS BACHELORS

1883, July 19. EDWIN SAUNDERS, F.R.C.S., surgeon-dentist-in-ordinary to Her Majesty (At Windsor Castle).

1883, July 19. GEORGE HORNIDGE PORTER, surgeon-in-ordinary to Her Majesty in Ireland *(ibid)*.

1883, Aug. 23. JOSEPH DEVEREUX, mayor of Windsor, justice of the peace and alderman (at Osborne).

1883, Aug. 23. ROBERT RAWLINSON, chief engineering inspector of the Local Government Board *(ibid)*.

1883, Dec. 31. HENRY MORGAN VANE, secretary to the Charity Commission for England and Wales *(ibid)*.

1883, Dec. 31. WILLIAM HARDY, deputy keeper of the Public Records *(ibid)*.

1883, Dec. 31. FRANCIS JOHN BOLTON, C.E., of the Local Government Board *(ibid)*.

1883, Dec. 31. HENRY EDMUND KNIGHT, alderman and late lord mayor of the City of London *(ibid)*.

1884, May 20. JAMES JOSEPH ALLPORT, of Littleover, Derby. (at Windsor Castle).

1884, May 20. RICHARD DICKESON, late mayor of Dover *(ibid)*.

1884, May 20. FREDERICK WILLIAM BURTON, F.S.A., director of the National Gallery of London *(ibid)*.

1884, June 13. SAMUEL DAVENPORT, of South Australia (Letters patent).

1884, June 20. DAVID TAYLOR, mayor of Belfast (at Dublin Castle by the lord lieutenant of Ireland).

1884, Aug. 11. ELLIOT CHARLES BOVILL, chief justice of the Supreme Court of the Island of Cyprus (Letters patent).

1884, Aug. 11. Rt. Hon. GEORGE HARRISON, LL.D., lord provost of Edinburgh, and lord lieutenant of the County of the City of Edinburgh (at Osborne).

1884, Aug. 11. ALFRED WILLS, one of the justices of Her Majesty's High Court of Justice *(ibid)*.

1884, Aug. 26. WILLIAM CARTER HOFFMEISTER, M.D., of Clifton House, West Cowes *(ibid)*.

1884, Sept. 11. JOHN WILLIAM DAWSON, LL.D., principal and vice-chancellor of the McGill University, Montreal, in the Dominion of Canada (Letters patent).

1884, Sept. 11. WILLIAM COMER PETHERAM, Q.C., chief justice of the High Court of Judicature for the North-Western Provinces of India (same).

1884, Sept. 29. BRUCE LOCKHART BURNSIDE, chief justice of the Island of Ceylon (same).

KNIGHTS BACHELORS 377

1884, Oct. 27. SAMUEL LEE ANDERSON, crown solicitor for Waterford and Kilkenny, in recognition of his long and able services (at the Vice-Regal Lodge by the lord lieutenant of Ireland).

1884, Nov. 29. HENRY ENFIELD ROSCOE, LL.D. (Cambridge and Dublin), F.R.S., professor of Chemistry in the Victoria University of Manchester (at Windsor Castle).

1884, Dec. 22. RAJA SOURINDRO MOHUN TAGORE (Letters patent).

1885, June 6. CHARLES ALEXANDER CAMERON, M.D., medical officer of health and city analyst [of Dublin], in recognition of his services in the cause of sanitation and public health in Ireland; president of the Royal College of Surgeons, and vice-president of the Chemical Institute of Great Britain (at the Vice-Regal Lodge by the lord lieutenant of Ireland).

1885, June 6. GEORGE JOSEPH WYCHERLEY, M.D., high sheriff of the city of Cork (*ibid* by same).

1885, June 27. WILLIAM SQUIRE BARKER KAYE, LL.D., Q.C., assistant under-secretary to the lord lieutenant (at Dublin Castle by same).

1885, June 27. JOHN BALL GREENE, commissioner of valuation and boundary surveyor of Ireland (at Dublin Castle by the lord lieutenant).

1885, July 9. RICHARD EVERARD WEBSTER, Q.C., M.P., attorney general (at Windsor Castle).

1885, Aug. 1. JOHN ELDON GORST, Q.C., M.P., solicitor general.

1885, Aug. 1. WILLIAM WILLIS, late accountant general of the Navy, and comptroller of Navy Pay (at Osborne).

1885, Aug. 1. MICHAEL CONNAL, ex-chairman of the Glasgow School Board *(ibid)*.

1885, Aug. 1. EDWARD WALTER, captain, late 8th Hussars, founder and commanding officer of the Corps of Commissionaires *(ibid)*.

1885, Aug. 1. PETER EADE *(ibid)*.

1885, Aug. 1. GEORGE CLEMENT BERTRAM, bailiff of Jersey *(ibid)*.

1885, Aug. 1. JAMES DROMGOLE LINTON, president of the Royal Institute of Painters in Water Colours *(ibid)*.

1885, Aug. 1. JAMES PARKER DEANE, D.C.L., Q.C., Her Majesty's Admiralty Advocate *(ibid)*.

1885, Aug. 1. GEORGE HAYTER CHUBB *(ibid)*.

1885, Aug. 1. HENRY CHRISTOPHER MANCE, engineer and electrician to the Indian Government, Persian Gulf Telegraph Department *(ibid)*.

1885, Aug. 1. ARTHUR JOHN HAMMOND COLLINS, Q.C., chief justice of Madras (at Osborne).
1885, Aug. 7. ROBERT MCVICKER, mayor of Londonderry (by the lord lieutenant of Ireland at Dublin Castle).
1885, Sept. 14. ROPER LETHBRIDGE (Letters patent).
1885, Dec. 15. JAMES SAWYER, M.D., of Birmingham (same).
1885, Dec. 15. WILLIAM THOMAS LEWIS, of the Mardy, Aberdare (Letters patent).
1885, Dec. 29. ALBERT KAYE ROLLIT, LL.D. (at Osborne).
1885, Dec. 29. GEORGE WILLIAM MORRISON, town clerk of Leeds (ibid).
1885, Dec. 29. WILLIAM HARDMAN, chairman of Quarter Sessions for the County of Surrey, and recorder of the Borough of Kingston-on-Thames (ibid).
1885, Dec. 29. OSWALD WALTERS BRIERLY, F.R.G.S., R.W.S. (ibid).
1885, Dec. 29. Dr. WILLIAM ROBERTS, of Manchester, professor in the Victoria University (ibid).
1885, Dec. 29. HENRY EDWARDS, M.P.
1886, Jan. 18. WILLIAM BARTLETT DALBY, M.B., of Savile Row, (letters patent).
1886, Jan. 19. WILLIAM GRANTHAM, one of the justices of Her Majesty's High Court of Justice (at Osborne).
1886, Jan. 19. JAMES CRICHTON-BROWNE, M.D., LL.D., F.R.S. (ibid).
1886, Jan. 25. ANDREW SEARLE HART, LL.D., vice-provost of Trinity College (at Dublin Castle by the lord lieutenant).
1886, Jan. 25. ROBERT STAWELL BALL, LL.D., Astronomer Royal for Ireland (ibid by same).
1886, Feb. 15. RICHARD NICHOLSON, of Cleveland-gardens, Paddington, Co. Middlesex, and of Oak Hill, Hildenborough, Co. Kent; clerk of the Peace, and clerk of the Lieutenancy for the County of Middlesex (Letters patent).
1886, Mar. 8. CHARLES RUSSELL, M.P., attorney general (at Windsor Castle).
1886, Mar. 8. HORACE DAVEY, Q.C., solicitor general (ibid).
1886, Mar. 8. MONIER WILLIAMS, D.C.L., Boden professor of Sanskrit in the University of Oxford (ibid).
1886, Mar. 8. ROBERT GEORGE RAPER, of the City of Chichester (ibid).
1886, Mar. 8. HENRY EDMUND WATSON, of Shirecliffe Hall, Sheffield (ibid).
1886, Mar. 8. CHARLES DOUGLAS FOX, of Coombe Springs, Kingston-on-Thames, civil engineer (ibid).

1886, Mar. 8. WILLIAM TURNER, M.B., LL.D., F.R.S., professor of Anatomy in the university of Edinburgh *(ibid)*.
1886, May 8. JAMES BRUNLEES *(ibid)*.
1886, May 8. EDGAR MACCULLOCH, bailiff of Guernsey *(ibid)*.
1886, May 8. DYCE DUCKWORTH, M.D., treasurer of the Royal College of Physicians of London *(ibid)*.
1886, May 11. DAVID RADCLIFFE, mayor of Liverpool (at Liverpool).
1886, May 18. VINCENT HUNTER BARRINGTON KENNETT-BARRINGTON, M.A., L.L.M., of the Manor House, Dorchester, Oxon., and of the Inner Temple, barrister-at-law (at Windsor Castle).
1886, May 28. WILLIAM WHITE COOPER, F.R.C.S., surgeon-oculist-in-ordinary to the Queen (nominated for knighthood but died before dubbing. By royal warrant dated 1886, June 26, Mary Elizabeth, his widow, was granted the style and precedence of a widow of a knight bachelor).
1886, June 21. JAMES MACBAIN, president of the Legislative Council of the Colony of Victoria (Letters patent).
1886, June 21. ROBERT DALRYMPLE ROSS, speaker of the House of Assembly of the Colony of South Australia (same).
1886, June 21. WILLIAM COLLES MEREDITH, late chief justice of the Superior Court of the Province of Quebec in the Dominion of Canada (same).
1886, June 26. JOHN EDGE, Q.C., chief justice of the High Court of Judicature of the North-Western Provinces of India, at Allahabad (at Windsor Castle).
1886, July 9. ROBERT MOLESWORTH, lately a judge of the Supreme Court of the Colony of Victoria (Letters patent).
1886, July 30. JOHN TOMES, F.R.S., F.R.C.S., etc., L.D.S. (Eng.) (at Osborne).
1886, July 30. DOUGLAS MACLAGAN, M.D., professor of medical jurisprudence in the University of Edinburgh, and president of the Royal College of Physicians of Edinburgh *(ibid)*.
1886, July 30. THOMAS LONGMORE, surgeon general, C.B., professor of military surgery in the Army Medical School at Netley *(ibid)*.
1886, July 30. SAMUEL WILLIAM SAYER LEWES, late director of victualling for the Royal Navy *(ibid)*.
1886, July 30. RICHARD NICHOLAS HOWARD, mayor of Weymouth *(ibid)*.
1886, July 30. EDWARD HENRY SIEVEKING, M.D., LL.D., F.R.C.P., physician extraordinary to Her Majesty *(ibid)*.
1886, July 30. HORACE JONES, for distinguished services to the City of London as architect to the Corporation *(ibid)*.
1886, Aug. 2. EDWARD CHARLES BUCK *(ibid)*.

1886, Aug. 2. WILLIAM STOKES, M.D., president of the Royal College of Surgeons in Ireland (at the Vice-Regal Lodge by the lord lieutenant of Ireland).

1886, Aug. 3. THOMAS FRANCIS BRADY, J.P., inspector of Irish fisheries (*ibid* by same).

1886, Aug. 16. EDWARD GEORGE CLARKE, Q.C., M.P., solicitor general (at Osborne).

1886, Aug. 16. WILLIAM LAMBERT DOBSON, chief justice of the Supreme Court of Tasmania *(ibid)*.

1886, Aug. 19. JAMES GOWANS, lord dean of Guilds of the City of Edinburgh (at Holyrood Palace).

1886, Aug. 26. JOHN SIMON, serjeant at law (Letters patent).

1886, Oct. 21. CHARLES EDWARD KEITH KORTRIGHT, of Grosvenor Crescent, parish of St. George, Hanover Square, Co. Middl., and of Wherstead Park, Co. Suffolk (same).

1886, Nov. 11. ROWLAND FRANCIS NICHOL FANNING, late deputy inspector general of the Royal Irish Constabulary (by the lord lieutenant of Ireland at the Vice-Regal Lodge).

1886, Nov. 26. JAMES STIRLING, one of the justices of Her Majesty's High Court of Justice (at Windsor Castle).

1886, Nov. 26. ARTHUR KEKEWICH, Q.C., one of the justices of Her Majesty's High Court of Justice *(ibid)*.

1886, Nov. 26. JOSEPH DODGE WESTON *(ibid)*.

1886, Nov. 26. BALTHAZAR WALTER FOSTER, M.D., president of the Council of the British Medical Association *(ibid)*.

1886, Nov. 26. PHILIP MAGNUS, director and secretary of the City and Guilds of London Technical Institute *(ibid)*.

1886, Nov. 26. JOHN RICHARD SOMERS VINE *(ibid)*.

1886, Nov. 26. EDWARD BOSC SLADEN, M.S.C., late chief political officer with the Burma Expeditionary Force (at Windsor Castle).

1887, Feb. 14. ALEXANDER WILSON, sheriff of Calcutta (Letters patent dated Feb. 16).

1887, Feb. 14. RAMASWAMI MOODLIAR (MUDALIAR), sheriff of Madras (Letters patent dated Feb. 16).

1887, Feb. 14. DINSHAW MANEKJEE PETIT, sheriff of Bombay (Letters patent dated Feb. 16).

1887, Feb. 14. HENRY LELAND HARRISON, Bengal Civil Service, commissioner of Police and chairman of the Corporation of the Town of Calcutta (Letters patent dated Feb. 16).

1887, Feb. 14. HENRY MEREDYTH PLOWDEN, senior judge in the Chief Court of the Punjab (Letters patent dated Feb. 16).

1887, Mar. 25. THOMAS MARTINEAU, mayor of Birmingham (at Windsor Castle).

1887, May 9. MATTHEW CROOKS CAMERON, chief justice of the Common Pleas, of the Province of Ontario, in the Dominion of Canada (Letters patent).

1887, May 9. ANDREW STUART, chief justice of the Superior Court in and for the Province of Quebec, in the Dominion of Canada (same).

1887, May 9. FREDERICK MATTHEW DARLEY, chief justice of the Supreme Court of the Colony of New South Wales (same).

1887, May 14. JOHN ROGERS JENNINGS, master of the Drapers' Company (at the People's Palace for East London).

1887, June 1. EÙGENE PIERRE JULES LÉCLEZIO, chief judge of the Supreme Court of the Island of Mauritius (Letters patent).

1887, June 27. HENRY EDMUND CARTWRIGHT, of Magherafelt Manor, Co. Londonderry (at Dublin Castle by the lord lieutenant of Ireland).

1887, June 30. HENRY MORLAND, captain, of Her Majesty's Indian Marine (late Indian Navy), port officer and chairman of the Municipal Corporation of Bombay (at Windsor Castle).

1887, June 30. CHARLES ALLEN LAWSON, of London, in the County of Middlesex, England, and of Madras, in the East Indies *(ibid)*.

1887, June 23. HENRY LUNNON SIMPSON, mayor of Windsor *(ibid)*.

1887, July 4. JOHN CHARLES ROBINSON, of Newton Manor, parish of Swanage, Co. Dorset, surveyor of pictures in ordinary to Her Majesty *(ibid)*.

1887, July 6. PRYCE JONES, of Dolerw, parish of Llanllwchaiarn, Co. Montgomery. (Letters patent).

1887, July 28. JAMES WRIGHT, late engineer-in-chief to the Admiralty (same).

1887, July 28. WILLIAM CHRISTOPHER LENG, of Sheffield, West Riding, Co. York (same).

1887, Aug. 5. JOSEPH TERRY, of Hawthorn Villa, the Mount, York, lord mayor of York (at Osborne).

1887, Aug. 5. JAMES KING, of Campsie, Co. Stirling, LL.D., lord provost of Glasgow *(ibid)*.

1887, Aug. 5. BENJAMIN CHAPMAN BROWNE, mayor of Newcastle-on-Tyne, D.C.L., justice of the peace for Gloucestershire, Northumberland and Newcastle-on-Tyne, member of the Institute of Civil Engineers *(ibid)*.

1887, Aug. 5. WILLIAM DAVID KING, mayor of Portsmouth *(ibid)*.

1887, Aug. 5. HENRY STEPHENSON, mayor of Sheffield *(ibid)*.

1887, Aug. 5. GEORGE WILLIAM EDWARDS, mayor of Bristol.

1887, Aug. 5. HARRY BULLARD, of Hellesdon House, Norwich, mayor of Norwich, justice of the peace for the City of Norwich, and deputy lieutenant for the County of Norfolk (At Osborne).

1887, Aug. 5. EDWIN GAUNT, mayor of Leeds, a justice of the peace for the Borough of Leeds *(ibid)*.

1887, Aug. 5. JAMES POOLE, mayor of Liverpool *(ibid)*.

1887, Aug. 5. JAMES FARMER, of Hope House, Eccles, Lancashire, alderman and mayor of Salford *(ibid)*.

1887, Aug. 5. HENRY FOX BRISTOWE, Q.C., of the Cliffe, Nantwich, Vice-Chancellor of the County Palatine of Lancaster (at Osborne).

1887, Aug. 5. HENRY AARON ISAACS, alderman and sheriff of London and Middlesex *(ibid)*.

1887, Aug. 5. ALFRED KIRBY, lieutenant colonel, of Fairlawn, New Cross, justice of the peace, sheriff of London and Middlesex *(ibid)*.

1887, Aug. 5. WILLIAM JAMES FARRER, high bailiff of Westminster *(ibid)*.

1887, Aug. 5. ARNOLD WILLIAM WHITE, the Queen's solicitor *(ibid)*.

1887, Aug. 6. ALFRED BARING GARROD, of Harley Street, Parish of Marylebone, Co. Middlesex, doctor of medicine, fellow of the Royal College of Physicians of London (Letters patent).

1887, Aug. 12. HENRY DOULTON, of Woolpits, Ewhurst, Co. Surrey, a commissioner of lieutenancy for the City of London (at Osborne).

1887, Aug. 12. WILLIAM LAWRENCE, of Lancaster Gate, Co. Middl., and of Adelaide Crescent, Brighton, Co. Sussex, an alderman of London, in the commission of the peace for the County of Middlesex and City of Westminster, and a commissioner of lieutenancy for the City of London *(ibid)*.

1887, Aug 12. JOHN SMITH, of Parkfield, Derby, alderman and justice of the peace for the Borough of Derby *(ibid)*.

1887, Aug. 12. EDWIN EDWARD GALSWORTHY, of 18, Park Crescent, Portland-place, London, and the Chestnuts, Shepperton, a justice of the peace and deputy lieutenant for the County of Middlesex, chairman of the Metropolitan Asylums Board *(ibid)*.

1887, Aug. 12. ANDREW MACLEAN, of Viewfield House, Balshagray, Partick, chief magistrate Partick, N.B. *(ibid)*.

1887, Aug. 12. GEORGE HUSBAND BAIRD MACLEOD, F.R.S., Edinburgh, regius professor of surgery in the University of Glasgow, and surgeon-in-ordinary to Her Majesty in Scotland *(ibid)*.

KNIGHTS BACHELORS 383

1887, Aug. 12. JOHN NEILSON CUTHBERTSON, chairman of the School Board of Glasgow (At Osborne).
1887, Aug. 12. HENRY MITCHELL, a justice of the Peace, president of the Bradford Technical College *(ibid)*.
1887, Aug. 12. GEORGE MARTIN - HOLLOWAY, of Tittenhurst, Sunning Hill, Berks. *(ibid)*.
1887, Aug. 12. WILLIAM AITKEN, M.D., F.R.S., of Grove Cottage, Woolstone, Southampton, professor of Pathology, Army Medical School, Netley Hospital *(ibid)*.
1887, Aug. 12. WARINGTON WILKINSON SMYTH, M.A. (Cambridge), F.R.S., professor of Mining in the Normal School of Science and Royal School of Mines, chief inspector in the Department of Woods and Forests *(ibid)*.
1887, Aug. 12. HENRY WATSON PARKER, late president of the Incorporated Law Society *(ibid)*.
1887, Aug. 12. FRANCIS PITTIS, mayor of Newport, Isle of Wight *(ibid)*.
1887, Aug. 22. JAMES HORNER HASLETT, mayor of Belfast (at Dublin Castle by the lord lieutenant of Ireland).
1887, Aug. 22. THOMAS LECKY, mayor of Londonderry *(ibid* by same).
1887, Aug. 22. GEORGE MOYERS, LL.D., alderman of Dublin *(ibid* by same).
1887, Aug. 22. HENRY COCHRANE, alderman of Dublin, D.L. *(ibid* by same).
1887, Aug. 22. JAMES SPAIGHT, Esq., president of the Chamber of Commerce, Limerick, and chairman of the Waterford and Limerick Railway Company *(ibid* by same).
1887, Aug. 22. PATRICK MAXWELL, president of the Incorporated Law Society of Ireland *(ibid* by same).
1887, Aug. 22. ROBERT HERRON, chairman of Kingstown Town Commissioners *(ibid* by same).
1887, Aug. 22. HOWARD GRUBB, F.R.S. (at Dublin Castle by the lord lieutenant).
1887, Aug. 25. MORGAN MORGAN, of Cathedral road, Parish of St. John the Baptist, Cardiff, and of Hendrescythan, both in the County of Glamorgan, mayor of the Borough of Cardiff (Letters patent).
1887, Aug. 25. THOMAS RICHARD EDRIDGE, of the Elms, in the Parish of Croydon, Co. Surrey (same).
1887, Aug. 25. JOHN HENRY PULESTON, of Ffynogion, Parish of Llanfair Dyffryn Clwyd, Co. Denbigh. (same).
1887, Sept. 1. HARRY THOMAS ALFRED RAINALS, late Her Majesty's consul at Brest (same).

1887, Sept. 8. MORELL MACKENZIE, M.D., in recognition of his valuable services to the Queen's son-in-law, the Crown Prince of Germany (at Balmoral).
1887, Sept. 12. CHARLES JOHN PEARSON, of Drumshaugh Gardens, in the City of Edinburgh, procurator for the Church of Scotland (Letters patent).
1887, Sept. 12. THOMAS STOREY, mayor of Lancaster (at Balmoral).
1887, Nov. 28. ARTHUR CHARLES, Q.C., one of the justices of Her Majesty's High Court of Justice (at Windsor Castle).
1887, Dec. 20. ADAM WILSON, late chief justice of the Queen's Bench, of Ontario, in the Dominion of Canada (Letters patent).
1887, Dec. 29. HENRY COCKBURN MACANDREW, provost of Inverness (at Osborne).
1888, Feb. 7. WILLIAM TINDAL ROBERTSON, M.P., a member of the Royal Commission to enquire into the Education of the Blind, Deaf and Dumb *(ibid)*.
1888, Feb. 7. OWEN ROBERTS, M.A., F.S.A., of 48, Westbourne Terrace, Hyde Park, Middlesex, clerk to the Worshipful Company of Cloth Workers of the City of London *(ibid)*.
1888, Apr. 21. DOMINIC ELLIS COLNAGHI, Her Majesty's consul general at Florence (at Villa Palmieri, Florence).
1888, Apr. 30. Rt. Hon. WILLIAM THACKERAY MARRIOTT, Q.C., judge advocate general (Letters patent).
1888, Apr. 30. JOHN WILLIAM TYLER, M.D., F.R.C.S., L.R.C.P., L.M., and L.S.A. (London) (same).
1888, June 18. WILLIAM HENRY MELVILL, of Beaufort Gardens in the Parish of Brompton, Co. Middlesex, and of Lincoln's Inn, barrister-at-law, solicitor to the Board of Inland Revenue (same).
1888, June 18. THOMAS GALT, chief justice of the Common Pleas Division of the High Court of Justice, Ontario (Canada) (same).
1888, June 21. JAMES GEORGE LEE STEERE, speaker of the Legislative Council of Western Australia (same).
1888, July 10. CHARLES HALLÉ (at Windsor Castle).
1888, July 10. JOHN STAINER, Mus. Doc., late organist of St. Paul's *(ibid)*.
1888, July 10. JOHN JAMES HARWOOD, mayor of Manchester *(ibid)*.
1888, July 10. JOHN HASSARD, M.A., principal registrar of the Province of Canterbury, and registrar of the Diocese of Canterbury *(ibid)*.
1888, July 10. GEORGE BARCLAY BRUCE, president of the Institute of Civil Engineers *(ibid)*.
1888, July 10. GEORGE DAVID HARRIS, formerly member of the Executive Council of the Bahamas *(ibid)*.

KNIGHTS BACHELORS 385

1888, July 18. THEODORE THOMAS FORD, chief justice of the Straits Settlements (Letters patent).
1888, July 30. DANIEL WILSON, LL.D., president of the University of Toronto, Canada (same).
1888, Aug. 24. JAMES DAVID MARWICK, of Killermont House, Dumbartonshire, LL.D., of Glasgow University, F.R.S.E., formerly town clerk of the City of Edinburgh, and now town clerk of the City of Glasgow, and a justice of peace for Lanarkshire (at Blythswood).
1888, Aug. 24. WILLIAM MCONIE, of Heathbank, Pollokshields by Glasgow, and of Ballochneck, in the County of Stirling, lately lord provost of the City of Glasgow, a justice of the Peace for the Counties of Lanark and Renfrew (at Blythswood).
1888, Dec. 4. PETER HENRY EDLIN, Q.C., assistant judge of the Court of the Sessions of the Peace for the County of Middlesex (at Windsor Castle).
1888, Dec. 4. POLYDORE DE KEYSER, alderman, late lord mayor of the City of London *(ibid)*.
1889, Jan. 28. WILLIAM CONRAD REEVES, Q.C., chief justice of the Island of Barbados (Letters patent).
1889, Jan. 28. JOHN TURNEY, of Springfield, Alexandra Park, Nottingham, ex-mayor of Nottingham (at Osborne).
1889, Jan. 29. ALEXANDER EDWARD MILLER, of 11, Stone Buildings, Lincoln's Inn, one of Her Majesty's counsel, and late one of the railway commissioners (at Osborne).
1889, Jan. 29. MYLES FENTON, of South Nutfield, Surrey, lieutenant colonel of the Engineer and Railway Volunteer Staff Corps, general manager of the South-Eastern Railway, and a justice of the peace for the County of Surrey *(ibid)*.
1889, Jan. 29. CHARLES WATHEN, mayor of Bristol *(ibid)*.
1889, Feb. 4. JOHN CAMPBELL ALLEN, chief justice of the Province of New Brunswick (Letters patent).
1889, May 25. ANDREW REED, inspector general of the Royal Irish Constabulary (at the Vice-Regal Lodge, Dublin, by the lord lieutenant of Ireland).
1889, June 4. ARTHUR WILLIAM BLOMFIELD, A.R.A., M.A. (at Windsor Castle).
1889, June 4. JOSEPH CROSLAND, of Royd's Wood, Huddersfield *(ibid)*.
1889, June 4. WILLIAM HENRY CRUNDALL, mayor of Dover *(ibid)*.
1889, June 4. RICHARD CHARLES OLDFIELD, Indian Civil Service, late a puisne judge of the High Court of Judicature, North-Western Provinces *(ibid)*.

1889, June 4. AUBREY WALSH, J.P. and D.D., formerly chairman of the Justices of the Liberty of the Tower
(At Windsor Castle).

1889, June 4. JAMES ROBERTON, LL.D., professor of conveyancing in the University of Glasgow *(ibid)*.

1889, June 22. JAMES RUSSELL, chief justice of the Supreme Court of Hong Kong and its Dependencies (Letters patent).

1889, June 22. BENJAMIN BENJAMIN, mayor of the City of Melbourne, in the Colony of Victoria (same).

1889, June 22. WILLIAM MACLEAY, member of the Legislative Council of the Colony of New South Wales (same).

1889, June 22. CHARLES FREDERICK BLAINE, of Port Elizabeth, in the Colony of the Cape of Good Hope, for services rendered to the Cape of Good Hope (same).

1889, June 29. JACOB WILSON, honorary director of the Royal Agricultural Society of England, and fellow of the Highland and Agricultural Society of Scotland (at Windsor Castle).

1889, Aug. 27. EVAN MORRIS, of Roseneath, Wrexham, in the County of Denbigh, and 3, St. James's Place, S.W., mayor of Wrexham (at Palé, Llandderfel, North Wales).

1889, Aug. 30. C. C. CONNOR, mayor of Belfast was offered knighthood but declined (at a farewell levée while presenting the marquess of Londonderry with an address from the Belfast Corporation).*

1889, Nov. 18. EDMUND ARNOUT GRATTAN, late Her Majesty's consul general for Belgium (Letters patent).

1890, Jan. 20: MATTHEW HENRY DAVIES, speaker of the Legislative Assembly of the Colony of Victoria (same).

1890, Jan. 20. JOSEPH HICKSON, general manager of the Grand Trunk Railway of the Dominion of Canada (same).

1890, Feb. 8. RAYLTON DIXON, of Gunnersgate Hall, Middlesbrough (at Osborne).

1890, Feb. 8. ROBERT PALMER HARDING, chief official receiver of the Bankruptcy Department of the Board of Trade (at Osborne).

1890, Feb. 8. THOMAS SOWLER, of Victoria Park, Manchester *(ibid)*.

1890, Mar. 10. JOHN NUGENT, M.D., late inspector of lunatic asylums (at Dublin Castle by the lord lieutenant of Ireland).

1890, May 5. FRANK FORBES ADAM (Letters patent).

1890, May 5. JOHN BRIDGE, of Headley Grove, Headly, Surrey, chief magistrate of the Police Courts of the Metropolis (at Windsor Castle).

* On the same occasion Mr. James Musgrave, chairman of the Belfast Harbours Commissioners declined to be knighted.

KNIGHTS BACHELORS

1890, June 12. ROBERT JOHN PINSENT, D.C.L., senior puisne judge of the Supreme Court of the Colony of Newfoundland (Letters patent).

1890, June 23. HENRY LUDLOW, chief justice of the Leeward Islands (same).

1890, June 23. ROMESH CHUNDER MITTER, late a puisne judge of the Calcutta High Court (same).

1890, June 30. HENRY BEYER ROBERTSON, of Palé, Corwen, Merionethshire, and of Llantysilio Hall, Denbighshire (at Windsor Castle).

1890, June 30. WILLIAM ARROL, of Seafield, Ayr, contractor for the Forth Bridge *(ibid)*.

1890, June 30. HENRY TRUEMAN WOOD, secretary to the Society of Arts *(ibid)*.

1890, June 30. WILLIAM GRAY, of West Hartlepool and Greatham, in the County of Durham *(ibid)*.

1890, June 30. ROBERT STICKNEY BLAINE, of Summerhill, Bath *(ibid)*.

1890, June 30. REGINALD JOHN CUST, chief commissioner of the West Indian Incumbered Estates Court *(ibid)*.

1890, June 30. JOHN COMPTON LAWRANCE, one of the justices of Her Majesty's High Court of Justice *(ibid)*.

1890, June 30. ROLAND LOMAX VAUGHAN WILLIAMS, one of the justices of Her Majesty's High Court of Justice *(ibid)*.

1890, June 30. HORATIO LLOYD, one of the judges of Her Majesty's County Courts in England and Wales, chairman of the Quarter Sessions for Cheshire and Recorder of Chester *(ibid)*.

1890, June 30. FRANCIS GODSCHALL JOHNSON, chief justice of the Superior Court of the Province of Quebec in the Dominion of Canada (Letters patent).

1890, July 25. THARIA TOPAN, of Bombay (same).

1890, Aug. 29. THOMAS NEWENHAM DEANE, architect of the Museum of Science and Art and of the Library in Kildare Street, Dublin (at the said Museum by the lord lieutenant of Ireland on the occasion of the opening).

1890, Sept. 11. STEUART MACNAGHTEN, of Bittern Manor House, County of Southampton, and of the Middle Temple, barrister-at-law, chairman of the Southampton Dock Company (Letters patent).

1890, Nov. 22. ROBERT ROMER, a justice of the Queen's Bench Division of the High Court of Justice (at Windsor Castle).

1891, Jan. 12. JAMES GODFRAY, colonel commanding 2nd Regiment Royal Jersey Militia, Military Aide-de-Camp to Her Majesty, and of Grainville Manor, Jersey (at Osborne).

1891, Jan. 12. ALFRED HICKMAN, of Goldthorn Hill, near Wolverhampton (At Osborne).

1891, Jan. 12. GEORGE MURRAY HUMPHRY, M.D., F.R.S., professor of surgery in the University of Cambridge *(ibid)*.

1891, Jan. 12. GEORGE SAMUEL MEASOM, chairman of the Royal Society for the Prevention of Cruelty to Animals *(ibid)*.

1891, Jan. 12. HENRY JOHN WARING, of Osborne House, Plymouth, late mayor of Plymouth *(ibid)*.

1891, Jan. 19. FRANK RINGLER DRUMMOND HAY, late consul general in Tripoli (Letters patent).

1891, Jan. 19. JOSIAH REES, chief justice of the Bermudas or Somers Islands (same).

1891, Jan. 19. EDWARD LOUGHLIN O'MALLEY, chief justice of the Straits Settlements (same).

1891, Feb. 23. FRANCIS HENRY JEUNE, one of the justices of Her Majesty's High Court of Justice (at Windsor Castle).

1891, Mar. 20. WILLIAM PINK, mayor of Portsmouth, and of Shrover Hall, Cosham *(ibid)*.

1891, Mar. 20. ROBERT SAMUEL WRIGHT, one of the justices of Her Majesty's High Court of Justice *(ibid)*.

1891, May 21. ALFRED SEALE HASLAM, of North Lees and West Bank, in the County of Derby, liveryman and citizen of London, mayor of Derby (at Derby).

1891, June 28. HENRY BENNETT, of Westlands, Grimsby, and of Thorpe Hall, Louth, both in the County of Lincoln, mayor of the County Borough of Grimsby (Letters patent).

1891, July 13. WILLIAM CHARLES WINDEYER, puisne judge of the Supreme Court of the Colony of New South Wales (same).

1891, July 13. WALTER THOMAS WRAGG, puisne judge of the Supreme Court of the Colony of Natal, for services in Zululand (same).

1891, July 13. JULIAN EMANUEL SALOMONS, member of the Legislative Council of the Colony of New South Wales (same).

1891, July 30. ARCHIBALD GEIKIE, F.R.S., director general of the Geological Survey of the United Kingdom (at Osborne).

1891, July 30. HENRY READER LACK, comptroller general of the Patent Office *(ibid)*.

1891, July 30. GUSTAVUS NATHAN, Her Majesty's consul general at Vienna *(ibid)*.

1891, July 30. HENRY OAKLEY, general manager of the Great Northern Railway *(ibid)*.

1891, July 30. WALTER SHERBURNE PRIDEAUX, clerk of the Goldsmiths' Company *(ibid)*.

KNIGHTS BACHELORS 389

1891, July 30. ROBERT GILLESPIE, of Spring Hill, Douglas, Lanark, N.B., and of Brighton (At Osborne).
1891, July 30. WILLIAM FARMER, of Coworth Park, Sunningdale, and 40, Cornwall Gardens, sheriff of London (*ibid* for services on the occasion of the visit of the German Emperor and Empress to the Guild Hall).
1891, July 30. AUGUSTUS HENRY GLOSSOP HARRIS, of the Elms, Avenue Road, Regents Park, sheriff of London (*ibid* same occasion).
1891, Sept. 9. The Hon. RICHARD HENN COLLINS, a judge of the Probate, Divorce and Admiralty Division of the High Court of Justice (Letters patent: writ dated 1892, July 16; Gazette notice dated 1892, July 30, but the letters patent ordered to bear date 1891, Sept. 9).
1891, Nov. 28. ALFRED JEPHSON, captain R.N., honorary secretary of the Royal Naval Exhibition (at Windsor Castle).
1891, Nov. 28. EVAN COLVILLE NEPEAN, C.B., late director of contracts at the War Office *(ibid)*.
1891, Nov. 28. JOHN BOYD, late lord provost of the City of Edinburgh *(ibid)*.
1891, Dec. 3. GEORGE REID, president of the Royal Scottish Academy of Painting, Sculpture, and Architecture *(ibid)*.
1892, Jan. 18. WILLIAM HOLLINGWORTH QUAYLE JONES, chief justice of Sierra Leone (Letters patent).
1892, Jan. 22. Royal warrant granting to CATHERINE DE SOYSA, widow and relict of Charles Henry de Soysa, in the commission of the Peace for the Island of Ceylon, deceased, the style and precedence of a widow of a Knight Bachelor of Great Britain and Ireland as if her husband had been knighted.
1892, May 9. EDWARD CHARLES ROSS, colonel, Indian Staff Corps (at Windsor Castle).
1892, May 9. WILLIAM DUGUID GEDDES, doctor of laws, vice-chancellor and principal of the University of Aberdeen *(ibid)*.
1892, May 9. JOHN CHARLES SAMUEL GRENIER, attorney general for the Colony of Ceylon *(ibid)*.
1892, May 9. GEORGE BUCHANAN, M.D., F.R.S., late medical officer of the Local Government Board *(ibid)*.
1892, June 15. WILLIAM JAMES BELL, of Scatwell, in the Parish of Contin, Co. Ross., and of the Inner Temple, barrister-at-law, doctor of laws of the University of Cambridge (Letters patent).
1892, June 15. JOSEPH PALMER ABBOTT, speaker of the Legislative Assembly of the Colony of New South Wales (same).

1892, June 15. ALEXANDRE LACOSTE, chief justice of the Court of Queen's Bench for the Province of Quebec, Canada
(Letters patent).

1892, June 15. GEORGE CLARKE PILE, president of the Legislative Council of the Island of Barbados (same).

1892, July 5. FREDERIC BATEMAN, M.D., F.R.C.P., senior physician to the Norfolk and Norwich Hospital (at Windsor Castle).

1892, July 5. WILLIAM JAMES RICHMOND COTTON, chamberlain of the City of London *(ibid)*.

1892, July 5. JOHN GARDNER DILLMAN ENGLEHEART, clerk of the Council of the Duchy of Lancaster *(ibid)*.

1892, July 5. GEORGE FINDLAY, general manager of the London and North-Western Railway *(ibid)*.

1892, July 5. GEORGE JOHNSON, M.D., F.R.S., physician extraordinary to Her Majesty *(ibid)*.

1892, July 5. ROBERT MICKS, joint secretary to the Inland Revenue Board *(ibid)*.

1892, July 5. JOHN GORELL BARNES, one of the justices of Her Majesty's High Court of Justice *(ibid)*.

1892, Aug. 5. GAINSFORD BRUCE, D.C.L., one of the justices of Her Majesty's High Court of Justice (at Osborne).

1892, Aug. 5. JOSEPH BARNBY, precentor of Eton College, principal of the Guildhall School of Music, and conductor of the Royal Choral Society, Albert Hall *(ibid)*.

1892, Aug. 5. WILLIAM GEORGE CUSINS, master of Music to the Queen *(ibid)*.

1892, Aug. 5. WALTER PARRATT, organist of Her Majesty's Private Chapel, and of St. George's Chapel Royal, Windsor *(ibid)*.

1892, Aug. 5. ARTHUR DE CAPEL CROWE, Her Majesty's consul general, and late commissary judge at Havana, Cuba *(ibid)*.

1892, Aug. 6. PHILLIP CRAMPTON SMYLY, Esq., M.D., physician-in-ordinary to the Household of the lord lieutenant (at the Viceregal Lodge by the lord lieutenant of Ireland).

1892, Aug. 13. JOHN HARLEY SCOTT, Esq., high sheriff of the City of Cork *(ibid by same)*.

1892, Aug. 13. FRANCIS XAVIER FREDERICK MACCABE, Esq., M.D., commissioner of the Local Government Board *(ibid by same)*.

1892, Aug. 15. DANIEL DIXON, lord mayor of Belfast *(ibid by same)*.

1892, Aug. 15. SAMUEL BLACK, town clerk of Belfast *(ibid by same)*.

1892, Aug. 15. ROBERT SEXTON, alderman of Dublin *(ibid by same)*.

KNIGHTS BACHELORS 391

1892, Sept. 15. ELLIS ASHMEAD BARTLETT, of Grange House, Eastbourne, Co. Sussex, and of Grosvenor Street, in the Parish of St. George, Hanover Square, in the County of London (Letters patent).

1892, Nov. 26. WILLIAM RANN KENNEDY, one of the justices of Her Majesty's High Court of Justice (at Windsor Castle).

1892, Nov. 26. JOHN RIGBY, Q.C., M.P., Her Majesty's solicitor general *(ibid)*.

1892, Nov. 26. DOUGLAS STRAIGHT, late puisne judge of the High Court of Judicature of the North-West Provinces of India *(ibid)*.

1892, Nov. 26. CHARLES OPPENHEIMER, Her Majesty's consul general at Frankfort on Main *(ibid)*.

1892, Dec. 2. FORREST FULTON, Q.C., common serjeant of the City of London *(ibid)*.

1892, Dec. 2. JOHN BLUNDELL MAPLE, M.P. *(ibid)*.

1892, Dec. 2. JOHN BENJAMIN STONE, of Erdington, and Sutton Coldfield, Co. Warwick. *(ibid)*.

1892, Dec. 2. GEORGE IRWIN, of Cumberland Lodge, Headingly, Leeds *(ibid)*.

1892, Dec. 2. WILLIAM SMITH, D.C.L., LL.D. *(ibid)*.

1892, Dec. 2. WILLIAM RENNY WATSON, chairman of the Glasgow South-Western Railway Company *(ibid)*.

1892, Dec. 2. JOSEPH HENRY WARNER *(ibid)*.

1893, Jan. 2. JOHN TANKERVILLE GOLDNEY, chief justice of Trinidad (Letters patent).

1893, Jan. 19. DAVID HARREL, under secretary to the lord lieutenant (in Ireland by the lord lieutenant).

1893, June 26. SAMUEL HENRY STRONG, chief justice of the Supreme Court of the Dominion of Canada (Letters patent).

1893, June 26. JOHN MADDEN, chief justice of the Supreme Court of the Colony of Victoria (same).

1893, June 26. GEORGE SHENTON, president of the Legislative Council of the Colony of Western Australia (same).

1893, June 26. HENRY DIAS, late puisne judge of the Supreme Court of the Island of Ceylon (same).

1893, July 6. FRANCIS HENRY LAKING, M.D., M.R.C.P., London, surgeon-apothecary to Her Majesty (at Buckingham Palace).

1893, July 14. JOSEPH RENALS, alderman and sheriff of the City of London (at Windsor Castle).

1893, July 14. WALTER HENRY WILKIN, colonel, alderman and sheriff of the City of London *(ibid)*.

1893, Aug. 11. WILLIAM ROGER BROWN, of Highfield, Hilperton, Wilts (at Osborne).
1893, Aug. 11. WILLIAM DAVIES, of Scoveston, Pembrokeshire *(ibid)*.
1893, Aug. 11. WILLIAM HENDERSON, late lord provost of Aberdeen *(ibid)*.
1893, Aug. 11. SAMUEL GEORGE JOHNSON, town clerk and clerk of the peace of Nottingham *(ibid)*.
1893, Aug. 11. JOHN LENG, M.P., Dundee *(ibid)*.
1893, Aug. 11. GEORGE HENRY LEWIS *(ibid)*.
1893, Aug. 11. PATTESON NICKALLS, of Fallowfield, Chiselhurst, Kent *(ibid)*.
1893, Aug. 11. FRANCIS POWELL, R.W.S., president of the Royal Scottish Society of Painters in Water Colours *(ibid)*.
1893, Aug. 11. WILLIAM OVEREND PRIESTLEY, M.D., of 17, Hertford Street, May Fair, and of Sherrards, Welwyn, Herts. *(ibid)*.
1893, Aug. 11. HUGH GILZEAN-REID, first president of the Institute of Journalists incorporated by Royal Charter *(ibid)*.
1893, Aug. 11. BENJAMIN WARD RICHARDSON, M.D., F.R.S., of 25, Manchester Square, London *(ibid)*.
1893, Aug. 11. JOHN RICHARD ROBINSON, of Addison Crescent, Kensington *(ibid)*.
1893, Aug. 11. EDWARD RICHARD RUSSELL, of Liverpool *(ibid)*.
1893, Aug. 11. JOHN TENNIEL, R.I. *(ibid)*.
1893, Aug. 11. THOMAS WRIGHT, of Leicester *(ibid)*.
1893, Aug. 11. JOSEPH HENRY GILBERT, M.A., LL.D., F.R.S., of Harpenden, near St. Albans *(ibid)*.
1893,* Aug. 11. GEORGE AUGUSTUS PILKINGTON, of Belle Vue, Lord Street West, Southport, and of Swinithwaite Hall, Yorkshire, formerly mayor of Southport (twice), and at one time M.P. for the Southport Division of South-west Lancashire *(ibid)*.
1894, Feb. 1. DONALD HORNE MACFARLANE, of Portman Square, in the Parish of Saint Marylebone, in the County of London (Letters patent).
1894, Feb. 15. FIELDING CLARKE, LL.B., chief justice of the Supreme Court of the Colony of Hong Kong (same).
1894, Feb. 15. JOHN WINFIELD BONSER, chief justice of the Island of Ceylon (same).
1894, Feb. 15. HARTLEY WILLIAMS, senior puisne judge of the Supreme Court of the Colony of Victoria (same).
1894, Feb. 15. WILLIAM PATRICK MANNING, mayor of the City of Sydney, in the Colony of New South Wales (same).

* In November, 1893, Christopher Robinson, Q.C., of the Canadian Bar was offered knighthood in recognition of his services before the Behring Sea arbitration. He appears not to have accepted it.

1894, Mar. 12. WILLIAM LANE BOOKER, Her Majesty's consul general at New York (Letters patent).
1894, Apr. 5. THOMAS SALTER PYNE (same).
1894, May 21. ANTHONY MARSHALL, lord mayor of Manchester (at Manchester at the opening of the Manchester Ship Canal).
1894, May 21. WILLIAM HENRY BAILEY, mayor of Salford, of Sale Hall, Cheshire, and Glan-y-Mor, Beaumaris (*ibid* same occasion).
1894, May 24. THOMAS FARRELL, president of the Royal Hibernian Academy (in Ireland by the lord lieutenant).
1894, June 25. The Hon. FRANK SMITH, senator and member of the Government of the Dominion of Canada (Letters patent).
1894, June 25. LOUIS EDELMAR NAPOLEON CASAULT, senior puisne judge of the Superior Court of the Province of Quebec, in the Dominion of Canada (same).
1894, June 25. The Hon. ARTHUR RENWICK, M.D., commissioner for New South Wales at the recent Exhibition at Chicago; formerly minister of Mines, minister of Public Instruction, and now member of the Legislative Council of that Colony (same).
1894, June 25. JOHN JOSEPH GRINLINTON, member of the Legislative Council of the Island of Ceylon, commissioner for that Island at the recent Exhibition at Chicago (same).
1894, July 2. JOHN CHARLES BUCKNILL, of East Cliff House, in the Parish of Christchurch, Co. Southampton, doctor in medicine of the University of London, and fellow of the Royal College of Physicians of London (same).
1894, July 2. EDWARD LEADER WILLIAMS, of the Oaks, in the Parish of Dunham Massey, in the County Palatine of Chester (same).
1894, July 13. JOHN VOCE MOORE, alderman and sheriff of the City of London (at Windsor Castle).
1894, July 13. JOSEPH COCKFIELD DIMSDALE, alderman and sheriff of the City of London *(ibid)*.
1894, July 13. ALBERT JOSEPH ALTMAN, chairman of the Bridge House Estates Committee of the Corporation of London *(ibid)*.
1894, July 18. THOMAS ROE, M.P., of Litchurch, Derby *(ibid)*.
1894, July 18. ROBERT HUNTER, solicitor to the Post Office *(ibid)*.
1894, July 18. HENRY THOBY PRINSEP, judge, High Court, Calcutta *(ibid)*.
1894, July 18. JAMES ALEXANDER RUSSELL, Rt. Hon., lord provost of Edinburgh, and lord lieutenant of the County of the City of Edinburgh *(ibid)*.

1894, July 18. FRANCIS SEYMOUR HADEN, of Woodcote Manor, Alresford, Hants., founder and president of the Royal Society of Painter-Etchers (At Windsor Castle).
1894, July 18. PHILIP MANFIELD, M.P., of Redlands, Cliftonville, Northampton. *(ibid)*.
1894, July 18. JEROM MURCH, of Cranwells, Bath, ex-mayor of Bath *(ibid)*.
1894, July 18. JOHN HUTTON, chairman of the London County Council *(ibid)*.
1894, July 18. ISAAC PITMAN, of Bath *(ibid)*.
1894, July 18. THOMAS WEMYSS REID, of 26, Bramham Gardens, South Kensington *(ibid)*.
1894, July 18. THOMAS GRAINGER-STEWART, M.D., physician-in-ordinary to the Queen in Scotland, and professor of the Practice of Physic in the University of Edinburgh; deputy lieutenant of the City and County of Edinburgh *(ibid)*.
1894, July 18. RICHARD TANGYE, of Gilbertstone, Kingston Vale *(ibid)*.
1894, July 18. THOMAS THORNTON, of Thornton Castle, town clerk of Dundee *(ibid)*.
1894, July 18. THOMAS ROBINSON, M.P., of Maisemore Park, near Gloucester *(ibid)*.
1894, July 18. GEORGE WILLIAMS, of 72, Saint Paul's Churchyard, ,and of 13, Russell Square *(ibid)*.
1894, July 18. JOSEPH LEIGH, M.P. *(ibid)*.
1894, July 18. BOSDIN THOMAS LEECH, of Oakmount, Timperley, near Manchester, director of the Manchester Ship Canal and deputy mayor of Manchester *(ibid)*.
1894, July 18. ROBERT THRESHIE REID, Q.C., M.P., Her Majesty's solicitor general *(ibid)*.
1894, Nov. 30. FRANK LOCKWOOD, M.P., Q.C., Her Majesty's solicitor general, justice of the peace and deputy lieutenant for the North Riding of Yorkshire *(ibid)*.
1894, Nov. 30. FREDERICK WIGAN, of Clare Lawn, Upper Sheen, Surrey, high sheriff of Surrey and justice of the peace for Surrey and the County of London, and deputy lieutenant for Surrey *(ibid)*.
1894, Nov. 30. JAMES WEEKS SZLUMPER, of Glanteifi, Kew Gardens, Surrey, and of Aberystwyth, in the County of Cardigan. *(ibid)*.
1895, Feb. 4. JOHN MCINTYRE, Hon., member of the Executive Council and Legislative Assembly of the Colony of Victoria, and lately president of the Board of Land and Works, and commissioner of Crown Lands and Survey in that Colony (Letters patent).

KNIGHTS BACHELORS 395

1895, Feb. 27. JOHN BAKER, M.P., of North End House, Portsmouth (at Windsor Castle).

1895, Feb. 27. EDWARD ROBERT PEARCE EDGCUMBE, of Somerleigh Court, Dorchester *(ibid)*.

1895, Feb. 27. ISRAEL HART, of Ashleigh, Knighton, Leicester. *(ibid)*.

1895, Feb. 27. ALEXANDER CAMPBELL MACKENZIE, principal of the Royal Academy of Music *(ibid)*.

1895, Feb. 27. JOSEPH TURNER HUTCHINSON, chief justice of the Gold Coast Colony ,and chief justice designate of the Colony of Grenada *(ibid)*.

1895, Feb. 27. CHARLES SCOTTER, general manager of the South-Western Railway *(ibid)*.

1895, Feb. 27. JOHN JACKSON, contractor for public works, of 3, Victoria Street, Westminster *(ibid)*.

1895,Feb. 27. JAMES THOMAS WOODHOUSE, of Elloughton House, Brough, Yorkshire *(ibid)*.

1895, Apr. 1. WILLIAM HENRY RATTIGAN, barrister-at-law, Doctor-of-Laws of the university of the Punjab, and vice-chancellor of said university (Letters patent).

1895, July 4. (WILLIAM) THORNLEY STOKER, M.D., president of the Royal College of Surgeons in Ireland (in the Presence Chamber, Dublin Castle, by the lord lieutenant of Ireland).

1895, July 4. CHRISTOPHER JOHN NIXON, LL.D., M.D., physician-in-ordinary to His Excellency *(ibid* by same).

1895, July 15. ALEXANDER CAMPBELL ONSLOW, chief justice of the Colony of Western Australia (Letters patent).

1895, July 15. WILLIAM HALES HINGSTON, M.D., of Montreal, in the Province of Quebec, in the Dominion of Canada (same).

1895, July 15. ARTHUR SNOWDEN, mayor of the City of Melbourne, in the Colony of Victoria (same).

1895, July 18. ARTHUR ARNOLD, chairman of the London County Council, of 45, Kensington Park Gardens, W., and Hyde Hill, Dartmouth (at Windsor Castle).

1895, July 18. EDWARD TEMPERLEY GOURLEY, M.P., V.D., justice of the peace and deputy lieutenant for the County of Durham, of Roker-on-Sea, Sunderland, and Cleaden, County of Durham *(ibid)*.

1895, July 18. FREDERICK HOWARD, of the Abbey Close, Bedford *(ibid)*.

1895, July 18. JEHANGHIER COWASJEE JEHANGHIER, of Ready Money House, Malabar Hill, Bombay *(ibid)*.

KNIGHTS BACHELORS

1895, July 18. HENRY DUNCAN LITTLEJOHN, M.D., LL.D., of Edinburgh (At Windsor Castle).

1895, July 18. JAMES LOW, lord provost of Dundee *(ibid)*.

1895, July 18. CLARENCE SMITH, of the Hawthorns, Chislehurst *(ibid)*.

1895, July 18. WALTER BESANT, of Frognal End, Hampstead *(ibid)*.

1895, July 18. JOSEPH EWART, M.D., of Montpelier Hall, Brighton, and Holmhead, Bewcastle, Cumberland *(ibid)*.

1895, July 18. CHRISTOPHER FURNESS, merchant and ship owner *(ibid)*.

1895, July 18. WILLIAM MARTIN CONWAY, of 21 Clanricarde Gardens, W. *(ibid)*.

1895, July 18. NICHOLAS JOHN HANNEN, of Lake Lodge, Wargrave, Berks., chief justice of Her Majesty's Supreme Court for China and Japan, and consul general at Shanghai *(ibid)*.

1895, July 18. HENRY BROBRIBB IRVING, of the Lyceum Theatre *(ibid)*.

1895, July 18. WILLIAM WOLLASTON KARSLAKE, Q.C., of 8 Curzon Street *(ibid)*.

1895, July 18. JOSEPH FRANCIS LEESE, M.P., Q.C., of the Red House, Sidmouth, and of 12 Members' Mansions, Victoria Street; recorder of Manchester *(ibid)*.

1895, July 18. GEORGE CHARLES MASON, of Courtlands, Clapham Park, Surrey *(ibid)*.

1895, July 18. LEWIS MORRIS, of Penbryn, Carmarthenshire *(ibid)*.

1895, July 18. ROBERT PULLAR, of Tayside, Perth *(ibid)*.

1895, July 18. WILLIAM HOWARD RUSSELL, LL.D. *(ibid)*.

1895, Aug. 12. THOMAS ACQUIN MARTIN, agent of the Government of Afghanistan (at Osborne).

1895, Nov. 25. WILLIAM MCCAMMOND, lord mayor of Belfast (at the Viceregal Lodge by the lord lieutenant of Ireland).

1895, Dec. 12. ROBERT BANNATYNE FINLAY, Q.C., M.P., Her Majesty's solicitor general (at Windsor Castle).

1895, Dec. 12. HARRY BODKIN POLAND, Q.C., recorder of Dover, one of Her Majesty's Justices of the Peace for the County of London *(ibid)*.

1895, Dec. 12 (July 15). HENRY HICKS HOCKING, attorney general for the Island of Jamaica *(ibid)*.

1896, Jan. 6. PATRICK COLL, chief crown solicitor for Ireland (at the Viceregal Lodge by the lord lieutenant of Ireland).

KNIGHTS BACHELORS 397

1896, Jan. 6. THOMAS WILLIAM MOFFETT, LL.D., president of Queen's College, Galway (at the Vice-regal Lodge by the lord lieutenant of Ireland).

1896, Jan. 6. [JAMES] ACHESON MACCULLAGH, M.D., late mayor of Londonderry *(ibid* by same).

1896, Jan. 17. CHARLES EDWARD HOWARD VINCENT, M.P., L.C.C., commandant of the Queen's Westminster Volunteers, of 1 Grosvenor Square, London (at Osborn).

1896, Jan. 17. ROBERT MARTIN CRAVEN, F.R.C.S., of 14, Albion Street, Hull *(ibid)*.

1896, Jan. 17. WILLOUGHBY FRANCIS WADE, M.D., of Kilmurrey, Edgbaston *(ibid)*.

1896, Jan. 17. JOHN SMALMAN SMITH, late chief justice of the Colony of Lagos *(ibid)*.

1896, Jan. 17. JOHN SENHOUSE GOLDIE-TAUBMAN, speaker of the House of Keys, Isle of Man *(ibid)*.

1896, Jan. 20. JOSEPH PRESTWICH, of Darent Hulme, in the Parish of Shoreham, in the County of Kent (Letters patent).

1896, Jan. 23. SAMUEL LEWIS, barrister-at-law, unofficial member of the Legislative Council of the Colony of Sierra Leone, and first mayor of the City of Freetown (same).

1896, Jan. 23. WILLIAM JAMES SMITH, chief justice of the Supreme Court of the Island of Cyprus (same).

1896, Jan. 23. HENRY PERING PELLEW CREASE, on his retirement as senior puisne judge from the Bench of the Supreme Court of British Columbia, in the Dominion of Canada (same).

1896, Jan. 27. CHARLES FREDERIC HAMOND, of Lovaine Place, in the County and City of Newcastle-on-Tyne (same).

1896, Jan. 27. CHARLES FREDERICK FARRAN, chief justice of the High Court of Judicature, Bombay (same).

1896, Jan. 27. LYTTLETON HOLYOAKE BAYLEY, late puisne judge of the High Court, Bombay (same).

1896, Feb. 28. ALFRED GEORGE MARTEN, Q.C., one of the judges of Her Majesty's County Courts in England and Wales (at Windsor Castle).

1896, Apr. 25. JAMES CHARLES HARRIS, Her Majesty's consul for the Department des Alpes Maritimes, France, and for the Principality of Monaco (at Cimiez, Nice).

1896, June 6. DAVID STEWART, of Banchory Devenick, Kincardineshire (at Balmoral).

1896, June 18. WILLIAM RALPH MEREDITH, LL.D., chief justice of the Court of Common Pleas of the Province of Ontario, in the Dominion of Canada (Letters patent).

1896, June 18. WILLIAM HENRY LIONEL COX, chief justice of the Straits Settlements (Letters patent).
1896, June 19. VINCENT HENRY PENALVER CAILLIARD, president of the Council of Administration of the Ottoman Public Debt (at Balmoral).
1896, July 4. WILLIAM JOHN ANDERSON, chief justice of British Honduras (Letters patent).
1896, July 9. JOHN CASS, of Maylands, Bradford (at Windsor Castle).
1896, July 9. JOSHUA GIRLING FITCH, LL.D., of 13, Leinster Square, London, W. *(ibid)*.
1896, July 9. JOSEPH SEBAG MONTEFIORE, of 4, Hyde Park Gardens, London, and East Cliff Lodge, Ramsgate *(ibid)*.
1896, July 9. PETER LE PAGE RENOUF, of 46, Roland Gardens, London, S.W.
1896, July 9. ALLEN LANYON SARLE, secretary and general manager of the London, Brighton, and South Coast Railway *(ibid)*.
1896, July 9. CHARLES CECIL TREVOR *(ibid)*.
1896, July 9. The Hon. GEORGE ARTHUR PARKER, late judge of the High Court, Madras (Indian Civil Service, retired).
1896, Aug. 15. FREDERICK RICHARD FALKINER, Q.C., recorder of Dublin (at the Vice-Regal Lodge by the lord lieutenant of Ireland).
1896, Aug. 15. FRANCIS RICHARD CRUISE, M.D. *(ibid by same)*.
1896, Aug. 15. ARTHUR EDWARD VICARS, F.S.A., Ulster king of arms, registrar and knight-attendant on the Most Illustrious Order of St. Patrick *(ibid by same)*.
1896, Oct. 12. FRANCIS WILLIAM MACLEAN, Q.C., chief justice of Bengal (at Balmoral).
1896, Nov. 2. HENRY SPENCER BERKELEY, chief justice of Fiji, and chief judicial commissioner for the Western Pacific (Letters patent).
1896, Nov. 25. EDWARD JOHN POYNTER, president of the Royal Academy of Arts (at Windsor Castle).
1897, Jan. 9. OWEN RANDAL SLACKE, captain, divisional commissioner (in the drawing-room at the Vice-Regal Lodge by the lord lieutenant of Ireland).
1897, Jan. 9. WILLIAM HUFFINGTON FINDLATER, J.P., D.L., president of the Incorporated Law Society of Ireland *(ibid by same)*.
1897, Jan. 9. JOHN THOMAS GILBERT, F.S.A., LL.D., M.R.I.A., hon. librarian of the Royal Irish Academy, and hon. professor of antiquities in the Royal Hibernian Academy of Arts *(ibid by same)*.
1897, Jan. 9. [ROBERT] NEWMAN CHAMBERS, town clerk of Londonderry *(ibid by same)*.

KNIGHTS BACHELORS 399

1897, Jan. 25. The Hon. JOHN WORRELL CARRINGTON, D.C.L., LL.D., chief justice of the Supreme Court of the Colony of Hong Kong (Letters patent).

1897, Jan. 25. WILLIAM RAYMOND KYNSEY, principal civil medical officer and inspector general of hospitals of the Island of Ceylon (same).

1897, Jan. 25. JOHN WOODHEAD, mayor of the City of Capetown (same).

1897, Feb. 3. FREDERICK THOMAS EDRIDGE, of Addiscombe Court, Croydon (at Osborne).

1897, Feb. 3. RICHARD FARRANT, of 2, Park Square West, Regents Park, London *(ibid)*.

1897, Feb. 3. WILLIAM WEBB HAYWARD, mayor of Rochester *(ibid)*.

1897, Feb. 3. JAMES LAING, of Thornhill, Sunderland, and of Etal Manor, Northumberland *(ibid)*.

1897, Feb. 3. WILLIAM LAIRD, of No. 168, West George Street, Glasgow *(ibid)*.

1897, Feb. 3. THOMAS WARDLE, of Leek, and Swainsley, Warslow, Staffordshire, F.G.S., F.C.S.

1897, Feb. 3. WILLIAM BIRT, general manager of the Great Eastern Railway (at Osborne).

1897, Feb. 3. WILLIAM ARBUTHNOT BLAIN, of the Park, Nottingham *(ibid)*.

1897, Feb. 3. CAMPBELL CLARKE, of No. 116, Avenue des Champs Elysées, Paris *(ibid)*.

1897, Feb. 4. JAMES MACPHERSON LE MOINE, of Quebec, ex-president of the Royal Society of Canada (Letters patent).

1897, Mar. 29. The Hon. CHARLES ARTHUR ROE, chief judge of the Chief Court of the Punjab (same).

1897, May 14. EDMUND WIDDRINGTON BYRNE, one of the justices of Her Majesty's High Court of Justice (at Windsor Castle).

1897, May 14. EDWARD RIDLEY, one of the justices of Her Majesty's High Court of Justice *(ibid)*.

1897, July 9. GEORGE HENRY LONG, mayor of Windsor *(ibid)*.

1897, July 15 (? 16). The Hon. HENRY HUBERT JUTA, Q.C., speaker of the House of Assembly of the Cape of Good Hope (Letters patent).

1897, July 15. THOMAS NAGHTEN FITZ-GERALD, F.R.C.S., senior surgeon of the Melbourne Hospital, in the Colony of Victoria (same).

1897, Aug. 2. FREDERICK FITZ JAMES CULLINAN, a principal chief clerk in the secretary's office, Dublin Castle (by the lord lieutenant of Ireland at the Vice-regal Lodge).

1897, Aug. 2. GEORGE FREDERICK DUFFEY, M.D., president of the Royal College of Physicians of Ireland (*ibid* by same).

1897, Aug. 2. WILLIAM THOMSON, M.D., president of the Royal College of Surgeons in Ireland, surgeon in ordinary to his Excellency (*ibid* by same).

1897, Aug. 2. GERALD RICHARD DEASE, colonel, chamberlain to His Excellency the lord lieutenant of Ireland (at the Vice-regal Lodge by the lord lieutenant).

1897, Aug. 2. REGINALD ROBERT BRUCE GUINNESS, (*ibid* by same).

1897, Aug. 2. WILLIAM WATSON, chairman of the City of Dublin Steam Packet Company (*ibid* by same).

1897, Aug. 2. BENJAMIN WHITNEY, clerk of the Crown and peace for Co. Mayo (*ibid* by same).

1897, Aug. 3. HENRY HOWE BEMROSE, M.P. (at Osborne).

1897, Aug. 3. CHARLES WILLIAM CAYZER, M.P., of Ralston, Renfrewshire, N.B. (*ibid*).

1897, Aug. 3. THOMAS GEORGE FARDELL, M.P., of 26, Hyde Park Street, London, W. (*ibid*).

1897, Aug. 3. THOMAS RICHARDSON, M.P., of Kirklevington Grange, Yarm, Yorkshire (*ibid*).

1897, Aug. 3. JOHN ARCHIBALD WILLOX, M.P. (*ibid*).

1897, Aug. 3. ALEXANDER RICHARDSON BINNIE, chief engineer to the London County Council (*ibid*).

1897, Aug. 3. FREDERICK BRIDGE, Mus. Doc., organist of Westminster Abbey, and Gresham Professor of Music (*ibid*).

1897, Aug. 3. WILLIAM CROOKES, F.R.S., of 7, Kensington Park Gardens, London, W. (*ibid*).

1897, Aug. 3. WILLIAM RICHARD GOWERS, M.D., F.R.S. (*ibid*).

1897, Aug. 3. JOHN FOWKE LANCELOT ROLLESTON, of Glen Parva Grange, Leicester (*ibid*).

1897, Aug. 3. HENRY HARBEN, of Seaford Lodge, Hampstead (*ibid*).

1897, Aug. 3. JAMES VAUGHAN, a magistrate of the Police Courts of the Metropolis (*ibid*).

1897, Aug. 9. BENJAMIN ALFRED DOBSON, of Doffcockers, Heaton, in the Parish of Deane, Co. Lancs., mayor of Bolton (Letters patent).

1897, Aug. 18. CHARLES THOMAS SKELTON, deputy mayor of Sheffield (at Osborne).

1897, Aug. 18. SQUIRE BANCROFT BANCROFT, of No. 18, Berkeley Square (*ibid*).

KNIGHTS BACHELORS 401

1897, Aug. 18. FELIX SEMON, M.D. (At Osborne).
1897, Aug. 18. WYKE BAYLISS, president of the Royal Society of British Artists *(ibid)*.
1897, Aug. 18. JOHN DUNNE, deputy lieutenant and chief constable of Cumberland and Westmoreland *(ibid)*.
1897, Aug. 18. FELIX CALVERT MACKENZIE, of Forres, N.B. *(ibid)*.
1897, Aug. 18. GEORGE CLEMENT MARTIN, Mus.Doc., organist of St. Paul's Cathedral *(ibid)*.
1897, Aug. 18. HENRY HUGH OLDHAM, lieutenant of Her Majesty's Honourable Corps of Gentlemen at Arms *(ibid)*.
1897, Aug. 18. WILLIAM LUCIUS SELFE, one of the judges of Her Majesty's County Courts in England and Wales *(ibid)*.
1897, Aug. 18. GEORGE JOHN SMITH, of Treliske, Truro *(ibid)*.
1897, Aug. 18. JAMES THOMPSON, general manager of the Caledonian Railway *(ibid)*.
1897, Aug. 18. HORATIO PAGE VANCE, lieutenant colonel of Her Majesty's Royal Body Guard of Yeomen of the Guard *(ibid)*.
1897, Aug. 18. CHRISTOPHER ANNAKIN MILWARD, alderman, lord mayor of York *(ibid)*.
1897, Aug 18. JOHN GEORGE BLAKER, alderman, mayor of Brighton *(ibid)*.
1897, Aug. 18. CHARLES RACKHAM GILMAN, mayor of Norwich *(ibid)*.
1897, Aug. 18. RICHARD MOTTRAM, alderman, mayor of Salford *(ibid)*.
1897, Aug. 18. PATRICK PLAYFAIR, late president of the Bengal Chamber of Commerce *(ibid)*.
1897, Aug. 18. (ANDREW) CHARLES HOWARD, assistant commissioner of Metropolitan Police *(ibid)*.
1897, Aug. 18. JAMES SMITH, lord mayor of Birmingham *(ibid)*.
1897, Aug. 18. JAMES THOMSON RITCHIE, sheriff of the City of London *(ibid)*.
1897, Aug. 18. ROBERT HARGREAVES ROGERS, sheriff of the City of London *(ibid)*.
1897, Aug. 28. GEORGE COTTON, sheriff of Bombay, and president of the Bombay Municipal Corporation (Letters patent).
1897, Aug. 31. WILLIAM BURGESS GOLDSMITH, staff captain, R.N., on retirement from the command of the "Alberta," which he had held for the last fourteen years; (at Gosport, on the quarter-deck of Her Majesty's Royal yacht "Alberta").
1897, Sept. 15. GEORGE MONTGOMERIE JOHN MOORE, lieutenant colonel, R.A. (retired), president of the Madras Municipality (Letters patent).

BB

1897, Sept. 29. MELBOURNE MCTAGGART TAIT, Q.C., chief justice of the Superior Court of the Montreal District of the Province of Quebec, in the Dominion of Canada (Letters patent).

1897, Sept. 15. JOHN HAWKINS HAGARTY, D.C.L., late chief justice of the Province of Ontario, in the Dominion of Canada (same).

1897, Oct. 7. Rt. Hon. ANDREW MCDONALD, lord provost of Edinburgh (at Balmoral).

1897, Oct. 7. JOHN CHEYNE, Q.C., procurator of the Church of Scotland *(ibid)*.

1897, Oct. 22. THOMAS WARDLAW TAYLOR, Q.C., chief justice of the Province of Manitoba, in the Dominion of Canada (Letters patent).

1897, Nov. 25. CHARLES GEORGE WALPOLE, late chief justice of the Bahama Islands (at Windsor Castle).

1897, Nov. 25. JOHN CHARLES BIGHAM, one of the justices of Her Majesty's High Court of Justice *(ibid)*.

1897, Nov. 25. CHARLES JOHN DARLING, one of the justices of Her Majesty's High Court of Justice *(ibid)*.

1897, Nov. 25. ARTHUR MOSELEY CHANNELL, one of the justices of Her Majesty's High Court of Justice *(ibid)*.

1898, Jan. 5. EDMUND THOMAS BEWLEY, judge of the High Court of Justice in Ireland, land commissioner, on his retirement [at the Viceregal Lodge, by the lord lieutenant of Ireland].

1898, Jan. 15. HENRY THYNNE, deputy inspector general, Royal Irish Constabulary [by same].

1898, Jan. 17. WILLIAM BRANDFORD GRIFFITH, chief justice of the Gold Coast Colony (Letters patent).

1898, Jan. 25. HENRY ARTHUR WHITE, Her Majesty's solicitor (at Osborne).

1898, Jan. 25. GEORGE THOMAS BROWN, professor, consulting veterinary adviser to the Board of Agriculture (retired) *(ibid)*.

1898, Jan. 25. HERBERT BARNARD, chairman of the Public Works Loan Commission *(ibid)*.

1898, Jan. 25. ERNEST CLARKE, secretary to the Royal Agricultural Society of England *(ibid)*.

1898, Jan. 25. THOMAS HUGHES, alderman, late lord mayor of Liverpool *(ibid)*.

1898, Jan. 25. THOMAS JOHNSTONE LIPTON *(ibid)*.

1898, Jan. 25. ROBERT HENRY SYMES, mayor of Bristol *(ibid)*.

1898, Jan. 25. JOHN BATTY TUKE, M.D., president of the Royal College of Physicians, Edinburgh *(ibid)*.

KNIGHTS BACHELORS

1898, Jan. 25. JOHN STRUTHERS, M.D., LL.D., vice-president of the Royal College of Surgeons of Edinburgh (at Osborne).

1898, Jan. 25. EDWARD JAMES ACKROYD, late a puisne judge of the Supreme Court of the Colony of Hong Kong *(ibid)*.

1898, Feb. 23. GEORGE WILLIAM BURTON, chief justice of the Province of Ontario, in the Dominion of Canada (Letters patent).

1898, Apr. 28. LOUIS ADDIN KERSHAW, Q.C., chief justice of the High Court of Judicature at Allahabad (Letters patent).

1898, May 6. ROBERT BARET STOKES, captain (at the Viceregal Lodge by the lord lieutenant of Ireland).

1898, June 9. EDWARD KNOX, late member of the Legislative Council of the Colony of New South Wales (Letters patent).

1898, June 9. JAMES READING FAIRFAX, in recognition of services rendered to the Colony of New South Wales (same).

1898, June 9. JOHN LANGDON BONYTHON, in recognition of services rendered in the cause of Public Education in the Colony of South Australia (same).

1898, June 9. ORMOND DRIMMIE MALCOLM, Q.C., chief justice of the Bahama Islands (same).

1898, July 13. CHARLES HUBERT HASTINGS PARRY, D.C.L., Mus. Doc., M.A., of 17 Kensington Square, London, and Highnam Court, Gloucester (at Windsor Castle).

1898, Aug. 6. JOHN GUNN, of Cardiff, and Llandaff House, Llandaff (at Osborne).

1898, Aug. 6. AUGUSTUS FREDERICK GODSON, M.P., of Westwood Park, Worcestershire *(ibid)*.

1898, Aug. 6. ARTHUR WELLINGTON MARSHALL, colonel, of Buckden Towers, Huntington *(ibid)*.

1898, Aug. 6. MARCUS SAMUEL, one of the alderman of the City of London, of 20, Portland Place, London, and of the Mote, Kent *(ibid)*.

1898, Aug. 6. SWIRE SMITH, of Steeton Manor, near Keighley *(ibid)*.

1898, Aug. 6. HENRY CHARLES FISHER, of St. Heliers, Bromley, Kent *(ibid)*.

1898, Aug. 6. JAMES WILLIAM WHITTALL, of the Tower, Moda, Constantinople *(ibid)*.

1899, Jan. 5. WILLIAM CHRISTOPHER MACDONALD, merchant, of Montreal, in the Dominion of Canada (Letters patent).

1899, Jan. 12. JOHN CHUTE NELIGAN, Q.C., recorder of Cork (at the Vice-regal Lodge by the lord lieutenant).

1899, Jan. 12. JAMES HENDERSON, lord mayor of Belfast *(ibid* by same).

1899, Jan. 12. JOHN BARR JOHNSTON, mayor of Londonderry *(ibid* by same).

1899, Jan. 12. GEORGE PLUNKETT O'FARRELL, M.D., commissioner of Control and inspector of Lunatic Asylums *(ibid* by same).

1899, Jan. 14. ANDREW MURE, of Edinburgh, late senior puisne judge of the Supreme Court of the Colony of Mauritius (at Osborne).

1899, Jan. 14. JAMES FORTESCUE FLANNERY, M.P., of Gibson's Hill, Norwood, Surrey *(ibid)*.

1899, Jan. 14. JOHN FURLEY, of 14, Evelyn Gardens, London, commissioner to the National Aid Society *(ibid)*.

1899, Jan. 14. DAVID RICHMOND, lord provost of Glasgow, and Her Majesty's lieutenant of the County of the City of Glasgow *(ibid)*.

1899, Jan. 14. HERMANN WEBER, M.D., of 10, Grosvenor Street, London *(ibid)*.

1899, Jan. 14. THOMAS TOWNSEND BUCKNILL, Q.C., one of the justices of Her Majesty's High Court of Justice *(ibid)*.

1899, Jan. 30. ARTHUR STRACHEY, B.A., LL.B., chief justice of the High Court of Judicature for the North-Western Provinces of India (Letters patent).

1899, Mar. 1. EDWARD LAWRENCE, of the Grange, St. Michael's Hamlet, in the City of Liverpool, in the County Palatine of Lancaster, a justice of the Peace of the said city, and mayor 1864–5, of the borough of Liverpool (Letters patent).

1899, May 24. JOHN THOMAS SOUNDY, J.P., mayor of Windsor (at Windsor Castle).

1899, June 26. JAMES CREED MEREDITH, LL.D., secretary of the Royal University of Ireland (at the Vice-regal Lodge by the lord lieutenant).

1899, June 26. WALTER ARMSTRONG, director of the National Gallery of Ireland *(ibid* by same).

1899, June 26. JOHN EDMOND BARRY, president of the Chamber of Commerce, Dublin *(ibid* by same).

1899, June 26. ROBERT ALEXANDER TAYLOR, of Coleraine *(ibid* by same).

1899, June 30. JOHN FRANCIS ROTTON, Q.C., late legal adviser to the Local Government Board (at Windsor Castle).

1899, June 30. ALURED DUMBELL, judge of the Chancery Division of the High Court of Justice, and clerk of the Rolls for the Isle of Man *(ibid)*.

KNIGHTS BACHELORS 405

1899, June 30. HERBERT HARDY COZENS-HARDY, one of the justices of Her Majesty's High Court of Justice (At Wndsor Castle).

1899, June 30. LAWRENCE ALMA TADEMA, R.A., of 17, Grove End Road, N.W. *(ibid)*.

1899, June 30. WALTER MURTON, solicitor to the Board of Trade *(ibid)*.

1899, June 30. CHARLES BOWMAN LOGAN, deputy keeper of the Signet of Scotland *(ibid)*.

1899, June 30. WILLIAM POLLITT, general manager of the Great Central Railway *(ibid)*.

1899, June 30. JOHN SIBBALD, late lunacy commissioner in Scotland *(ibid)*.

1899, June 30. (HENRY) EVELYN OAKELEY, late chief inspector of schools, Education Department *(ibid)*.

1899, June 30. THOMAS MOREL, alderman, J.P., mayor of Cardiff *(ibid)*.

1899, June 30. WILLIAM MITCHELL BANKS, M.D., F.R.C.S., LL.D., of 28, Rodney Street, Liverpool *(ibid)*.

1899, Aug. 17. LAWRENCE HUGH JENKINS, chief justice of the High Court of Judicature, Bombay (Letters patent).

1899, Aug. 17. JOHN ALEXANDER BOYD, chancellor of the High Court of Justice of the Province of Ontario, in the Dominion of Canada (same).

1899, Aug. 17. THOMAS CROSSLEY RAYNER, chief justice of the Supreme Court of the Colony of Lagos (same).

1899, Aug. 17. MATTHEW HARRIS, mayor of the City of Sydney, in the Colony of New South Wales (same).

1899, Aug. 17. THOMAS JACKSON, chief manager at Hong Kong, of the Hong Kong and Shanghai Bank (Letters patent).

1899, Sept. 16. JOSEPH FRIZELLE, late chief judge of the Chief Court of the Punjab (same).

1899, Sept. 26. WILLIAM FISCHER AGNEW, recorder of Rangoon (same).

1899, Nov. 15. HERBERT ASHMAN, lord mayor of Bristol, justice of the peace (at Bristol).

1899, Nov. 28. GEORGE FARWELL, one of the judges of Her Majesty's High Court of Justice (at Windsor Castle).

1899, Nov. 28. FRANKLIN LUSHINGTON, chief magistrate of the Metropolitan Police Courts *(ibid)*.

1900, Jan. 22. The Hon. JOHN STOKELL DODDS, chief justice of the Supreme Court of the Colony of Tasmania (Letters patent).

1900, Jan. 22. FRANCIS HENRY LOVELL, surgeon general and member of the Executive and Legislative Councils of the Colony of Trinidad and Tobago (same).

1900, Jan. 22. MALCOLM DONALD MCEACHARN, mayor of the City of Melbourne, in the Colony of Victoria (Letters patent).

1900, Feb. 2. V. BHASHYAM AIYANGAR, diwan bahadur acting advocate general, Madras (same).

1900, Feb. 5. BHALCHANDRA KRISHNA BHATAWADEKAR, justice of peace, chairman of the Standing Committee of the Municipal Corporation, Bombay (same).

1900, Feb. 9. GERALD RAOUL DE COURCY-PERRY, Her Majesty's consul general at Antwerp for Belgium (at Osborne).

1900, Feb. 9. JAMES BALFOUR PAUL, Lyon King of Arms *(ibid)*.

1900, Feb. 9. THOMAS HENRY TACON, justice of peace, D.L., of the Red House, Eye, Suffolk *(ibid)*.

1900, Feb. 9. WILLIAM THEODORE DOXFORD, M.P., of Grindon Hall, Sunderland *(ibid)*.

1900, Feb. 9. WALTER THORBURN, M.P., of Glenbreck, Peebles, N.B. *(ibid)*.

1900, Feb. 9. THOMAS LAUDER BRUNTON, M.D., F.R.S. *(ibid)*.

1900, Feb. 17. GEORGE DALHOUSIE RAMSAY, of Manson Place. London (Letters patent).

1900, Mar. 3. HENRY BURTON BUCKLEY, Q.C., one of the judges of Her Majesty's High Court of Justice (at Windsor Castle).

1900, Mar. 5. OTTO JAFFÉ late lord mayor of Belfast (in the Throne Room at Dublin Castle, by the lord lieutenant of Ireland).

1900, Mar. 12. The Rt. Hon. SAMUEL JAMES WAY, of Montefiore, North Adelaide, and Kadlunga Mintar, both in the Colony of South Australia, lieutenant governor and chief justice of the Supreme Court of the said Colony, chancellor of the University of Adelaide, and member for the Australasian Colonies of the Judicial Committee of Her Majesty's Privy Council.

1900, Mar. 29. WILLIAM PURDIE TRELOAR alderman and sheriff of the City of London (at Windsor Castle).

1900, Mar. 29. ALFRED HENRY BEVAN, sheriff of the City of London *(ibid)*.

1900, May 15. WILLIAM MACPHERSON, judge of the High Court of Judicature at Fort William in Bengal *(ibid)*.

1900, May 25. DANIEL JOSEPH HEGARTY, lord mayor of Cork (in the Throne Room at Dublin Castle by the lord lieutenant of Ireland).

1900, May 25. WILLIAM M'LEARN, mayor of Londonderry (by same).

1900, May 25. JOSEPH DOWNES, high sheriff of the City of Dublin (*ibid* by same).

KNIGHTS BACHELORS 407

1900, May 25. ALFRED GRAHAM DOBBIN, high sheriff of the City of Cork at Dublin Castle by the lord lieutenant of Ireland)

1900, May 25. THOMAS HENRY CLEEVE, high sheriff of the City of Limerick (*ibid* by same).

1900, May 25. JOHN WILLIAM MOORE, M.D., president of the Royal College of Physicians, Ireland (*ibid* by same).

1900, May 25. THOMAS DREW, president of the Royal Institute of Architects of Ireland (*ibid* by same).

1900, May 25. JOHN MALCOLM INGLIS, president of the Dublin Chamber of Commerce (*ibid* by same).

1900, May 25. THOMAS WILLIAM ROBINSON, chairman of Kingstown Urban District Council (*ibid* by same).

1900, June 27. ARTHUR JAMES RICHENS TRENDELL, the assistant secretary of the Science and Art Department (at Windsor Castle).

1900, June 27. JOHN GROVES, formerly mayor of Weymouth from November, 1886, to November, 1889 *(ibid)*.

1900, June 27. JOHN GLOVER, justice of peace, chairman of the City Liberal Unionist Association, and of Lloyd's Registry of British and Foreign Shipping *(ibid)*.

1900, June 27. THOMAS GODFREY CAREY, the bailiff of Guernsey *(ibid)*.

1900, June 27. WILLIAM WILSON MITCHELL, member of the Legislative Council of Ceylon *(ibid)*.

1900, June 27. CHARLES ARNOLD WHITE, chief justice of Madras *(ibid)*.

1900, June 27. JAMES WILLIAMSON, director of Her Majesty's Dockyards *(ibid)*.

1900, June 27. WILLIAM WARD, Her Majesty's consul general at Hamburg *(ibid)*.

1900, June 27. ALLAN ARTHUR, of Calcutta, member of the Viceroy's Legislative Council *(ibid)*.

1900, June 30. HECTOR CLARE CAMERON, president of the Faculty of Physicians and Surgeons, Glasgow *(ibid)*.

1900, June 30. JOHN WATNEY, clerk of the Mercers' Company, honorary secretary of the City and Guilds of London Institute for the advancement of Technical Education *(ibid)*.

1900, June 30. (HENRY) HOMEWOOD CRAWFORD, of Guildhall, in the City of London, and of 3, West Bolton Gardens, South Kensington, S.W., solicitor of the Corporation of London *(ibid)*.

1900, June 30. GEORGE HARE PHILIPSON, M.D., of Newcastle-on-Tyne, president of the University of Durham College of Medicine *(ibid)*.

1900, June 30. CHARLES CLEMENT BOWRING, J.P., of Park Grange, Derby (At Windsor Castle).

1900, June 30. WILLIAM HASWELL STEPHENSON, alderman, City of Newcastle *(ibid)*.

1900, June 30. RICHARD CLAVERHOUSE JEBB, M.P., Regius Professor of Greek in the University of Cambridge *(ibid)*.

1900, June 30. COLIN GEORGE MACRAE, of Wellbank, Forfarshire, and writer to the Signet, Edinburgh, late chairman of the School Board of Edinburgh *(ibid)*.

1900, June 30. RILEY LORD, mayor of Newcastle-upon-Tyne *(ibid)*.

1900, June 30. JAMES CORNELIUS O'DOWD, formerly deputy judge advocate general *(ibid)*.

1900, June. Rt. Hon. EDWARD HENRY CARSON, Q.C., M.P., solicitor general *(ibid)*.

1900, July 16. WILLIAM BISSET BERRY, M.D., Q.C., speaker of the House of Assembly of the Colony of the Cape of Good Hope (Letters patent).

1900, July 16. DAVID PALMER ROSS, M.D., surgeon general of the Colony of British Guiana (same).

1900, Oct. 24. FRANCIS PRATT WINTER, chief judicial officer of the Possession of British New Guinea (Letters patent).

1900, Dec. 14. MATTHEW INGLE JOYCE, one of the justices of Her Majesty's Court of Justice (at Windsor Castle).

1901, Jan. 16. ARTHUR ROBERT WALLACE, D.L., principal chief clerk, Secretary's Office, Dublin Castle (at the Viceregal Lodge by the lord lieutenant).

1901, Jan. 16. EDWARD MATTHEW HODGSON, chairman of the Rathmines Urban District Council *(ibid* by same).

1901, Feb. 9. EDWARD HENRY BUSK, chairman of Convocation of the University of London (at Marlborough House).

1901, Feb. 9. ROBERT HARVEY, high sheriff of Cornwall *(ibid)*.

1901, Feb. 9. JOHN MARK, J.P., of Didsbury, Lancashire *(ibid)*.

1901, Feb. 9. EDWARD WOLLASTON KNOCKER, registrar of the Cinque Ports *(ibid)*.

1901, Feb. 9. ALFRED COOPER, of the Gables, Surbiton *(ibid)*.

1901, Feb. 9. HIRAM STEVENS MAXIM *(ibid)*.

1901, Feb. 9. JOSEPH SYKES RYMER, late lord mayor of York *(ibid)*.

1901, Feb. 11. The Hon. HENRY JOHN MILLER, speaker of the Legislative Council of the Colony of New Zealand (Letters patent).

1901, Feb. 11. HUGH ADCOCK, consulting physician-in-chief to His Imperial Majesty the Shah of Persia (Letters patent).
1901, Oct. 31. JOHN QUICK, LL.D., of Victoria (on the occasion of the visit of the duke and duchess of York to His Majesty's Dominion beyond the seas) (nominated Jan. 1).
1901, Oct. 31. JAMES GRAHAM, M.D., member of the Legislative Assembly of the State of New South Wales, mayor of the City of Sydney (on same occasion).
1901, Oct. 31. The Hon. SAMUEL GILLOTT, member of the Legislative Assembly of the State of Victoria, attorney general of that State, mayor of the City of Melbourne (same occasion).
1901, Oct. 31. LOUIS VICTOR DELAFAYE, chief judge of the Supreme Court of the Colony of Mauritius (on same occasion).
1901, Oct. 31. EBENEZER JOHN BUCHANAN, senior puisne judge of the Colony of the Cape of Good Hope (on same occasion).
1901, Oct. 31. BENJAMIN WESLEY GREENACRE, member of the Legislative Assembly of the Colony of Natal (on same occasion).
1901, Oct. 31. THOMAS GEORGE SHAUGHNESSY, president of the Canadian Pacific Railway Company (on same occasion).
1901, Nov. 4. ARTHUR RICHARD JELF, a judge of the High Court (at Marlborough House).
1901, Nov. 4. JOSEPH WALTON, a judge of the High Court *(ibid)*.
1901, Nov. 7. JOHN STANLEY, K.C., chief justice of the High Court of Judicature for the North-Western Provinces, India (Letters patent).
1901, Dec. 10. CHARLES SWINFEN EADY, one of the justices of His Majesty's High Court of Justice (at Marlborough House).
1901, Dec. 10. GEORGE GOUGH ARBUTHNOT, of Madras *(ibid)*.
1901, Dec. 10. GEORGE BULLOUGH, of Isle of Rum, Scotland *(ibid)*.
1901, Dec. 10. ANDERSON CRITCHETT, F.R.C.S., honorary surgeon oculist to His Majesty *(ibid)*.
1901, Dec. 10. GEORGE HUSSEY, mayor of Southampton *(ibid)*.
1901, Dec. 10. ARCHIBALD CAMPBELL LAWRIE, on retirement as late puisne justice of the Supreme Court of Ceylon *(ibid)*.
1901, Dec. 10. (JAMES) ERNEST SPENCER, M.P., of Warren Mount, Oxshot, Surrey *(ibid)*.
1901, Dec. 10. ALBERT DE RUTZEN, chief magistrate of the Metropolitan Police Courts *(ibid)*.
1901, Dec. 19. JOSEPH IGNATIUS LITTLE, chief justice of the Supreme Court of Newfoundland (Letters patent).
1901, Dec. 19. SAMUEL BROWNLOW GRAY, chief justice of the Bermuda Islands (same).

1902, Aug. 11. JOHN OLPHERT, gentleman usher to His Excellency (in the Throne Room, Dublin Castle, by the lord lieutenant).

1902, Aug. 11. JOHN HAMILTON FRANKS, secretary to the Irish Land Commission (*ibid* by same).

1902, Aug. 11. JOHN GEORGE BARTON, commissioner of Valuation (*ibid* by same).

1902, Aug. 11. JAMES BROWN DOUGHERTY, assistant under secretary to the lord lieutenant (*ibid* by same).

1902, Aug. 11. (FRANCIS) HENRY MILLER, mayor of Londonderry (*ibid* by same).

1902, Aug. 11. THOMAS MYLES, M.D., late president of the Royal College of Surgeons in Ireland (*ibid* by same).

1902, Aug. 11. VINCENT NASH, high sheriff of the city of Limerick (*ibid* by same).

1902, Aug. 11. GEORGE ROCHE, late president of the Incorporated Law Society of Ireland (*ibid* by same).

1902, Aug. 11. WILLIAM WHITLA, M.D. (*ibid* by same).

1902, Aug. 11. JAMES MURPHY, president of the Dublin Chamber of Commerce (*ibid* by same).

1902, Aug. 12. ROBERT LLOYD PATTERSON (*ibid* by same).

1902, Aug. 14. EDWARD ALBERT STONE, chief justice of the State of Western Australia (Letters patent).

1902, Aug. 14. The Hon. ARTHUR RUTLEDGE, K.C., attorney general of the State of Queensland (same).

1902, Aug. 14. The Hon. HENRY NORMAN MACLAURIN, LL.D., M.D., M.A., chancellor of the University of Sydney, and member of the Legislative Council of the State of New South Wales (same).

1902, Aug. 14. HENRI ELZÉAR TASCHEREAU, K.C., LL.D., puisne judge of the Supreme Court of the Dominion of Canada.

1902, Aug. 14. The Hon. ADYE DOUGLAS (THORPE-DOUGLAS), president of the Legislative Council of the State of Tasmania (same).

1902, Aug.14. JOHN LANCELOT STIRLING, LL.B., president of the Legislative Council of the State of South Australia (same).

1902, Aug. 14. The Hon. EDWARD D'ALTON SHEA, president of the Legislative Council of the Colony of Newfoundland (same).

1902, Aug. 14. The Hon. ROBERT BOAK, president of the Legislative Council of the Province of Nova Scotia, in the Dominion of Canada (same).

1902, Aug. 14. WILLIAM RUSSELL RUSSELL, member of the House of Representatives of the Colony of New Zealand (same).

KNIGHTS BACHELORS 411

1902, Aug. 14. JOHN LOGAN CAMPBELL, M.D., late mayor of Auckland, in the Colony of New Zealand (Letters patent).
1902, Oct. 2. The Hon. JAMES LIEGE HULETT, speaker of the Legislative Assembly of the Colony of Natal (same).
1902, Oct. 2. WILLEM VAN HULSTEYN, of Johannesburg (same).
1902, Oct. 24. JOHN CHARLES BELL, sheriff of the City of London (at Buckingham Palace).
1902, Oct. 24. HORACE BROOKS MARSHALL, sheriff of the City of London *(ibid)*.
1902, Oct. 24. WILLIAM ALLAN, M.P. *(ibid)*.
1902, Oct. 24. FRANCIS COWLEY BURNAND, B.A. *(ibid)*.
1902, Oct. 24. CASPAR PURDON CLARKE, F.S.A., F.R.I.B.A., director of the Victoria and Albert Museum (Art Museum), South Kensington *(ibid)*.
1902, Oct. 24. WILLIAM LAIRD CLOWES *(ibid)*.
1902, Oct. 24. WILLIAM JOB COLLINS, M.D., F.R.C.S. *(ibid)*.
1902, Oct. 24. ALFRED COOPER, F.R.C.S. *(ibid)*.
1902, Oct. 24. (JOHN) HALLIDAY CROOM, president of the Royal College of Surgeons (Edin.) *(ibid)*.
1902, Oct. 24. ARTHUR CONAN DOYLE, M.D., D.L. *(ibid)*.
1902, Oct. 24. WILLIAM EMERSON, past president of the Royal Institute of British Architects *(ibid)*.
1902, Oct. 24. Colonel AUBONE GEORGE FIFE, standard bearer of His Majesty's Bodyguard of the Honourable Corps of Gentlemen-at-Arms *(ibid)*.
1902, Oct. 24. JOSEPH THOMAS FIRBANK, M.P. *(ibid)*.
1902, Oct. 24. THOMAS RICHARD FRASER, F.R.S., M.D., president of the Royal College of Physicians of Edinburgh *(ibid)*.
1902, Oct. 24. WILLIAM HENRY HOLLAND, M.P. *(ibid)*.
1902, Oct. 24. SAMUEL HALL, K.C., vice-chancellor of the County Palatine of Lancaster *(ibid)*.
1902, Oct. 24. REGINALD HENNELL, colonel, lieutenant of the King's Bodyguard of Yeomen of the Guard *(ibid)*.
1902, Oct. 24. VICTOR ALEXANDER HADEN HORSLEY, F.R.S., F.R.C.S. *(ibid)*.
1902, Oct. 24. HENRY GREENWAY HOWSE, president of the Royal College of Surgeons *(ibid)*.
1902, Oct. 24. JOSEPH LAWRENCE, M.P. *(ibid)*.
1902, Oct. 24. RALPH DANIEL MAKINSON LITTLER, K.C. *(ibid)*.
1902, Oct. 24. GEORGE THOMAS LIVESEY *(ibid)*.
1902, Oct. 24. OLIVER JOSEPH LODGE, F.R.S. *(ibid)*.

1902, Oct. 24. HENRY BELL LONGHURST, honorary surgeon dentist to His Majesty (At Buckingham Palace).
1902, Oct. 24. JOHN HENRY LUSCOMBE, chairman of Lloyds *(ibid)*.
1902, Oct. 24. JOHN MCDOUGALL, chairman London County Council *(ibid)*.
1902, Oct. 24. WILLIAM MACEWEN, F.R.S. *(ibid)*.
1902, Oct. 24. WILLIAM MATHER, M.P. *(ibid)*.
1902, Oct. 24. ISAMBARD OWEN, M.D., senior deputy chancellor of the University of Wales *(ibid)*.
1902, Oct. 24. (HORATIO) GILBERT GEORGE PARKER, colonel, M.P., D.C.L. *(ibid)*.
1902, Oct. 24. PAYNTON PIGOTT, barrister-at-law, D.L., chief constable of the County of Norfolk *(ibid)*.
1902, Oct. 24. ARTHUR WILLIAM RÜCKER, D.Sc., LL.D., principal of the University of London *(ibid)*.
1902, Oct. 24. WILLIAM JAMESON SOULSBY *(ibid)*.
1902, Oct. 24. CHARLES VILLIERS STANFORD, Mus.Doc., D.C.L. *(ibid)*.
1902, Oct. 24. ALFRED THOMAS, M.P. *(ibid)*.
1902, Oct. 24. JOHN ISAAC THORNYCROFT, LL.D., F.R.S. *(ibid)*.
1902, Oct. 24. ERNEST ALBERT WATERLOW, A.R.A., president of the Royal Society of Painters in Water Colours *(ibid)*.
1902, Oct. 24. JOSEPH LOFTUS WILKINSON, general manager of the Great Western Railway *(ibid)*.
1902, Oct. 24. GUY DOUGLAS ARTHUR FLEETWOOD WILSON, assistant under secretary of State for War.
1902, Oct. 24. CHARLES WYNDHAM *(ibid)*.
1902, Oct. 24. CATCHICK PAUL CHATER, member of the Executive and Legislative Council, Hong Kong *(ibid)*.
1902,* Nov. 9. JOHN ELIJAH BLUNT (knighted at Malta by king Edward VII., 1903, April 16).
1902, Dec. 1. JAMES PERCY FITZPATRICK, of Johannesburg, in the Colony of the Transvaal (Letters patent).
1902, Dec. 2. GEORGE FARRAR, of the Transvaal (Letters patent).
1902, Dec. 4. EDWARD FLEET ALFORD, of the Boltons, in the Royal Borough of Kensington, in the County of London (Letters patent).
1902, Dec. 5. The Hon. WILLIAM ARBUCKLE, president of the Legislative Council of the Colony of Natal (Letters patent).
1902, Dec. 6. LEWIS LLOYD MICHELL, member of the House of Assembly of the Colony of the Cape of Good Hope, and late chairman of the Martial Law Board in that Colony (Letters patent).

* John Winthrop Hackett was gazetted a knight bachelor, 1902, Nov. 9, but declined the honour.

KNIGHTS BACHELORS

1902, Dec. 8. WILLIAM MEIGH GOODMAN, chief justice of the Supreme Court of the Colony of Hong Kong (Letters patent).
1902, Dec. 9. HENRY ALLEYNE BOVELL, chief justice of British Guiana (Letters patent).
1902, Dec. 10. The Hon. WILLIAM JUKES STEWARD, late speaker of the House of Representatives of the Colony of New Zealand (Letters patent).
1902, Dec. 18. THOMAS ROBERT DEWAR, M.P. (at Buckingham Palace).
1902, Dec. 18. CHARLES JOHN OWENS, lieutenant colonel, Engineer and Railway Volunteer Staff Corps *(ibid)*.
1902, Dec. 18. (CHARLES) FREDERICK HARRISON, lieutenant colonel, Engineer and Railway Volunteer Staff Corps *(ibid)*.
1902, Dec. 18. CHARLES HAMPDEN WIGRAM *(ibid)*.
1902, Dec. 18. HENRY HALL SCOTT, of Eilanreach *(ibid)*.
1902, Dec. 18. ROBERT HUDSON BORWICK, of Eden Lacy, Lazonby, Cumberland *(ibid)*.
1902, Dec. 18. THOMAS HENRY BROCKE-HITCHING, sheriff of the City of London *(ibid)*.
1902, Dec. 18. JOHN MOWLEM BURT *(ibid)*.
1902, Dec. 18. WILLIAM THOMAS DUPREE, mayor of Portsmouth *(ibid)*.
1902, Dec. 18. WALTER GRAY, late mayor of Oxford *(ibid)*.
1902, Dec. 18. ROBERT MITTON HENSLEY, chairman of the Metropolitan Asylums Board *(ibid)*.
1902, Dec. 18. JOHN HOLLAMS, of Dene Park, Kent, J.P. for Kent and D.L. London *(ibid)*.
1902, Dec. 18. JAMES HOY, LL.D., late lord Mayor of Manchester *(ibid)*.
1902, Dec. 18. EDWARD LETCHWORTH, F.S.A. *(ibid)*.
1902, Dec. 18. JOHN ROPER PARKINGTON, colonel, D.L., J.P., County of London *(ibid)*.
1902, Dec. 18. (EMIL HUGO OSCAR) ROBERT ROPNER, colonel, M.P. *(ibid)*.
1902, Dec. 18. JOHN SHERBURN *(ibid)*.
1902, Dec. 18. GEORGE WYATT TRUSCOTT, sheriff of the City of London *(ibid)*.
1902, Dec. 18. MAX LEONARD WAECHTER *(ibid)*.
1902, Dec. 18. CHARLES JOHN FOLLETT, solicitor of His Majesty's Customs *(ibid)*.
1902, Dec. 18. ROBERT ROWAND ANDERSON, LL.D. *(ibid)*.
1902, Dec. 18. WILLIAM JOHN CRUMP *(ibid)*.

KNIGHTS BACHELORS

1902, Dec. 18. EDWIN HUGHES, colonel, V.D. *(ibid)*.
1902, Dec. 18. HENRY SETON-KARR, M.P. *(ibid)*.
1902, Dec. 18. JAMES GILDEA, colonel *(ibid)*.
1902, Dec. 23. CHARLES BENT BALL, M.D., regius professor of surgery in the University of Dublin (in the Throne Room, Dublin Castle, by the lord lieutenant of Ireland).
1903, Jan. 1. MONTAGU CHARLES TURNER.
1903, Jan. 1. GEORGE WATT.
1903, Jan. 1. WILLIAM OVENS CLARK.
1903, Jan. 1. JAMES LEWIS WALKER, lieutenant colonel.
1903, Apr. 17. JAMES ACWORTH DAVIES, Indian Civil Service, judge of the High Court of Judicature, Fort St. George (Letters patent).
1903, Apr. 18. WILLIAM EARNSHAW COOPER, lieutenant colonel, commandant Cawnpore Volunteer Rifles (Letters patent).
1903, Apr. 20. HURKISONDAS NURROTUMDAS, sheriff of Bombay (Letters patent).
1903, May 12. ROBERT CRANSTON, colonel, treasurer of the City of Edinburgh (at Holyrood Palace, by the King).
1903, May 12. WILLIAM JOHN MENZIES, writer to the "Signet," agent of the Church of Scotland *(ibid)*.
1903, May 12. JAMES GUTHRIE, president of the Royal Scottish Academy *(ibid)*.
1903, May 14. JOHN SHEARER, convenor of the Parks and Galleries Committee of the Corporation of the City of Glasgow (at Glasgow).
1903, July 18. PATRICK HERON WATSON, LL.D., M.D., F.R.S.E., hon. surgeon to His Majesty in Scotland (at Buckingham Palace).
1903, July 18. ALFRED DOWNING FRIPP, surgeon-in-ordinary to His Majesty *(ibid)*.
1903, July 18. STEPHEN MACKENZIE, M.D., of 18, Cavendish Square, W. *(ibid)*.
1903, July 18. HIRAM SHAW WILKINSON, chief justice of H.M.'s Supreme Court for China and Corea *(ibid)*.
1903, July 18. WILLIAM ALFRED GELDER, mayor of Hull *(ibid)*.
1903, July 18. ALFRED ARNOLD, of Woodroyde, Halifax *(ibid)*.
1903, July 18. HENRY FLEMING HIBBERT, of Dalegarth, Chorley, Lancs. *(ibid)*.
1903, July 18. FRANCIS CHARLES GORE, solicitor to the Board of Inland Revenue *(ibid)*.
1903, July 18. GEORGE COLLARD, mayor of Canterbury *(ibid)*.

KNIGHTS BACHELORS 415

1903, July 18. EDWIN COOPER PERRY, M.D., F.R.C.P., physician to Guy's Hospital (at Buckingham Palace).

1903, July 18. ALEXANDER CARMICHAEL BRUCE, assistant commissioner of police of the Metropolis *(ibid)*.

1903, July 18. JOHN JOHNSON RUNTZ, first mayor of Stoke Newington *(ibid)*.

1903, July 18. WILLIAM GODSELL, of 18, Ridgway Place, Wimbledon *(ibid)*.

1903, July 18. GEORGE THOMAS LAMBERT, late director of Greenwich Hospital *(ibid)*.

1903, July 18. LEWIS TONNA DIBDIN, D.C.L., dean of Arches *(ibid)*.

1903, July 18. CHARLES SAMUEL BAGOT, late legal commissioner in lunacy and now an honorary commissioner in lunacy *(ibid)*.

1903, July 18. CHARLES PETRIE, late lord mayor of Liverpool *(ibid)*.

1903, Aug. 3. The Hon. CHARLES ABERCROMBIE SMITH, M.A., late controller and auditor general of the Colony of the Cape of Good Hope (Letters patent).

1903, Aug. 4. CHARLES PETER LAYARD, chief justice of the Island of Ceylon (Letters patent).

1903, Aug. 5. CHARLES JOHN DUDGEON, chairman of the Shanghai Branch of the China Association (Letters patent).

1903, Aug. 26. EYRE COOTE, high sheriff of Co. Dublin (at the Viceregal Lodge by the lord lieutenant of Ireland).

1903, Aug. 26. ROBERT ANDERSON, high sheriff of Belfast *(ibid)*.

1903, Aug. 26. ABRAHAM SUTTON, high sheriff of Cork *(ibid)*.

1903, Aug. 26. THOMAS BROWN, chairman of Kingstown Urban District Council *(ibid)*.

1903, Aug. 26. JAMES CARROLL, chairman of Queenstown Urban District Council *(ibid)*.

1903, Aug. 26. JAMES O'DONOHOE, chairman of Galway Urban District Council *(ibid)*.

1903, Aug. 26. LAMBERT HEPENSTAL ORMSBY, M.D., president of the Royal College of Surgeons in Ireland *(ibid)*.

1903, Aug. 26. AUGUSTINE FITZGERALD BAKER, president of the Incorporated Law Society of Ireland *(ibid)*.

1903, Nov. 9. ALAN REEVE MANBY, M.D., surgeon apothecary to the King's Household at Sandringham and to the prince of Wales (at Sandringham).

1903, Nov. 30. FRANCIS BATHURST SUTTOR, Hon., president of the Legislative Council of the State of New South Wales (Letters patent).

1903, Dec. 1. EDWARD DUNDAS HOLROYD, puisne judge of the Supreme Court of the State of Victoria (Letters patent).

1903, Dec. 18. THOMAS WILLIAM SNAGGE, a county court judge, of 14, Courtfield Gardens, S.W. (at Buckingham Palace).

1903, Dec. 18. JOHN GEORGE CRAGGS, of Claverley, Chislehurst *(ibid)*.

1903, Dec. 18. CHARLES HOLROYD, keeper of the National Gallery of British Art, Tate Gallery *(ibid)*.

1903, Dec. 18. AUGUST MANNS, of Gleasdale, 4, Harold Road, Norwood *(ibid)*.

1903, Dec. 18. HENRY ALEXANDER GIFFARD, K.C., of Braye du Valle, Guernsey, bailiff of Guernsey *(ibid)*.

1903, Dec. 18. JOHN MACDONELL, master of His Majesty's Supreme Court, of 31 Kensington Park Gardens, W. *(ibid)*.

1903, Dec. 18. HENRY KATZ DAVSON, of 20, Ennismore Gardens, S.W. *(ibid)*.

1903, Dec. 18. ERNEST FLOWER, M.D., of 6, Upper Phillimore Gardens, W. *(ibid)*.

1903, Dec. 18. Professor CLEMENT LE NEVE FOSTER, D.Sc., F.R.S., late one of His Majesty's inspectors of Mines, of 86 Coleherne Court, Earl's Court, S.W. *(ibid)*.

1903, Dec. 18. NATHANIEL NATHAN, of the Cottage, Edenbridge *(ibid)*.

1903, Dec. 18. ALFRED JAMES REYNOLDS, one of the sheriffs of the City of London, of Digswell, Welwyn, Herts. *(ibid)*.

1903, Dec. 18. ROBERT KENNAWAY DOUGLAS, of the British Museum *(ibid)*.

1903, Dec. 18. HARRY SIMON SAMUEL, M.P., of 7 Park Lane, W. *(ibid)*.

1903, Dec. 18. CHARLES SCARISBRICK, J.P., of Scarisbrick Lodge, Southport, Lancashire *(ibid)*.

1903, Dec. 18. WILLIAM HENRY VENABLES-VERNON, bailiff of Jersey, of St. Peter's House, Jersey *(ibid)*.

KNIGHTS BACHELORS

1903, Dec. 18. ARTHUR VERNON MACAN, M.B., president of the Royal College of Physicians of Ireland (at the Vice-regal Lodge by the lord lieutenant).
1904, Jan. 29. WALTER MYTTON COLVIN, barrister-at-law, of Allahabad (Letters patent).
1904, May 2. JAMES ALOYSIUS POWER, mayor of Waterford (at the South Railway Station, Waterford, by the King).
1904, June 7. THOMAS ROLLS WARRINGTON, justice (at the levée at St. James's).
1904, July 5. GEORGE BARHAM (at Buckingham Palace).
1904, July 5. THOMAS BARCLAY, 13 Old Square, Lincoln's Inn *(ibid)*.
1904, July 5. ALBERT À BECKETT, late assistant accountant general of the Army *(ibid)*.
1904, July 5. ARTHUR BIGNOLD, M.P. *(ibid)*.
1904, July 5. JOHN BRICKWOOD, of Brankesmere, Southsea, Hants. *(ibid)*.
1904, July 5. EDWARD TOWNSHEND CANDY, Indian Civil Service (retired), lately puisne judge of the High Court of Judicature at Bombay *(ibid)*.
1904, July 5. JAMES DEWAR, professor, F.R.S., Royal Institution, 21 Albemarle Street *(ibid)*.
1904, July 5. GEORGE DONALDSON, 4 Queen Anne Street, W. *(ibid)*.
1904, July 5. GEORGE DOUGHTY, M.P. *(ibid)*.
1904, July 5. EDWIN HARRIS DUNNING, of Stoodleigh Court, Stoodleigh, Devon *(ibid)*.
1904, July 5. EDWARD ELGAR, Mus. Doc., of Craig Lea, Wells Road, Malvern *(ibid)*.
1904, July 5. GEORGE STEGMANN GIBB, 31 Great George Street, Westmister *(ibid)*.
1904, July 5. THOMAS HEWITT, K.C., 9 Queen's Gate, S.W. *(ibid)*.
1904, July 5. JOHN EDWARD GRAY HILL, Law Society's Hall, Chancery Lane *(ibid)*.
1904, July 5. CONSTANTINE HOLMAN, 26 Gloucester Place, Portman Square *(ibid)*.
1904, July 5. FRANK THOMAS MARZIALS, late accountant general of the Army, 9 Ladbrooke Square, W. *(ibid)*.
1904, July 5. DAVID MUNRO, captain, late inspector of constabulary for Scotland, of Allan House, Fearn, Ross-shire *(ibid)*.
1904, July 5. WALTER RICHARD PLUMMER, M.P. *(ibid)*.
1904, July 5. WILLIAM HANDCOCK PILKINGTON, of Haggard, Carbury, high sheriff Co. Kildare *(ibid)*.

1904, July 5. ALEXANDER OLIVER RIDDELL, Craiglockhart, Slateford, Midlothian (At Buckingham Palace).

1904, July 5. WILLIAM PHILLIPS SAWYER, Draper's Hall, E.C. *(ibid)*.

1904, July 5. BENJAMIN SCOTT, Linden House, Stanwix, Carlisle *(ibid)*.

1904, July 5. EDWARD DAVID STERN, 4 Carlton House Terrace, S.W. *(ibid)*.

1904, July 5. THOMAS STEVENSON, M.D., scientific analyst to the Home Office *(ibid)*.

1904, July 5. HENRY TANNER, of the Office of Works *(ibid)*.

1904, July 5. THOMAS MARCHANT WILLIAMS, of Taff House, Cathedral Road, Cardiff *(ibid)*.

1904, July 5. WILLIAM LLOYD WISE, of 142 Inverness Terrace, Hyde Park, W. *(ibid)*.

1904, July 8. HUGH MONTAGU ALLAN, of Montreal, Canada (Letters patent).

1904, July 9. PETER NICOL RUSSELL, formerly of the City of Sydney, New South Wales (Letters patent dated July 9).

1904, July 11. POPE ALEXANDER COOPER, chief justice of Queensland (same, dated July 11).

1904, July 12. KENDALL MATHEW ST. JOHN FRANKS, M.D., of Johannesburg, Transvaal (same, dated July 12).

1904, July 13. ANDRIES FERDINAND STOCKENSTROM MAASDORP, chief justice of the Orange River Colony (same, dated July 12).

1904, July 14. WILLIAM HERBERT GREAVES, chief judge of Barbados (same, dated July 14).

1904, July 15. ALFRED SCOTT SCOTT-GATTY, on his investiture with the insignia of office as garter king of arms *(ibid* after the Council meeting).

1904, July 15. The Hon. EDWARD PATRICK MORRIS, minister of justice of Newfoundland, delegated to England on the fisheries question, 1899 and 1901 (same, dated July 15).

1904, July 16. WILLIAM THORNE, mayor of Capetown, Cape of Good Hope (same, dated July 16).

1904, July 18. GOOROO DASS BANARJEE, M.A., D.L., lately a puisne judge of the High Court of Judicature at Fort William, in Bengal (Letters patent, dated July 18).

1904, July 19. ROBERT ALFRED HAMPSON, alderman, mayor of Liverpool (at Liverpool, on the occasion of the laying of the foundation-stone of the new Cathedral).

1904, July 19. WILLIAM ROBERT BURKITT, Indian Civil Service, puisne judge of the High Court of Judicature for the North-Western Provinces (same, dated July 19).

1904, July 20. DAVID PARKES MASSON, V.D., lieutenant colonel and commandant of the 1st Punjab Volunteer Rifle Corps, a member of the Council of the lieutenant governor of the Punjab for making Laws and Regulations (same, dated July 20).

1904, July 20. GRIFFITH THOMAS, mayor of Swansea (at Swansea, on the occasion of the opening of a new a dock at Swansea).

1904, July 21. HALLEWELL ROGERS, mayor of Birmingham (at Rhayader, on the opening of the new waterworks of the City of Birmingham).

1904, Aug. 10. REGINALD MORE BRAY, recently appointed judge of the High Court (at Buckingham Palace after the Council meeting).

1904, Nov. 14. ALFRED TRISTRAM LAWRENCE, a justice of the High Court (at Buckingham Palace).

1904, Dec. 19. THEODORE VIVIAN SAMUEL ANGIER, of Hill Crest, Dyke Road, Brighton (at Buckingham Palace).

1904, Dec. 19. GEORGE WASHINGTON BAXTER, of Ashcliffe, Dundee *(ibid)*.

1904, Dec. 19. (RICHARD) MELVILL BEACHCROFT, of 11 Craven Hill, W. *(ibid)*.

1904, Dec. 19. JOSEPH ARTHUR BELLAMY, of Yalta, Mannamead, Plymouth *(ibid)*.

1904, Dec. 19. HENRY COOK, of 32 Eglington Crescent, Edinburgh *(ibid)*.

1904, Dec. 19. JOHN LOWE McCRAITH, of Park Terrace, Nottingham *(ibid)*.

1904, Dec. 19. ALFRED MAJOR, of Gibraltar Close, Cookham Dean, Cookham Rise, S.O., Berks. *(ibid)*.

1904, Dec. 19. CHARLES HAYES MARRIOTT, M.D., of Harcourt House, Kibworth, Leicester *(ibid)*.

1904, Dec. 19. SHIRLEY FOSTER MURPHY, of 9 Bentinck Terrace, Regent's Park, N.W. (At Buckingham Palace).

1904, Dec. 19. ALLAN PERRY, M.D., surgeon major, principal civil medical officer and inspector general of hospitals in the island of Ceylon, of 8 Draycott Place, S.W. *(ibid)*.

1904, Dec. 19. THOMAS PINK, of Thornton House, Clapham Park *(ibid)*.

1904, Dec. 19. WILLIAM JAPP SINCLAIR, professor of Obstetrics and gynæcology at the Victoria University of Manchester *(ibid)*.

1904, Dec. 19. (MATTHEW) HENRY STEPHEN, lately acting chief justice of the Supreme Court of New South Wales, London Joint Stock Bark, Gloucester Road, S.W. *(ibid)*.

1904, Dec. 19. JOSEPH WILSON SWAN, F.R.S., D.Sc., of 58 Holland Park *(ibid)*.

KNIGHTS BACHELORS

1904, Dec. 19. ASTON WEBB, R.A., of 19 Queen's Gate, S.W. *(ibid)*.

1904, Dec. 19. GEORGE HENRY JENKINS, clerk of the Parliaments and clerk of the Legislative Council of the State of Victoria (date of writ for letters patent. Letters patent dated Dec. 19).

1904, Dec. 19. The Hon. WILLIAM HENRY BUNDEY, late judge of the Supreme Court of South Australia (same).

1904, Dec. 19. The Hon. ALFRED SANDLINGS COWLEY, speaker of the Legislative Assembly of the State of Queensland (same).

1904, Dec. 19. STEPHEN HERBERT GATTY, chief justice of Gibraltar (same).

1904, Dec. 19. WILLIAM HENRY HORWOOD, chief justice of the Supreme Court of Newfoundland (same).

1904, Dec. 19. WALTER LLEWELLYN LEWIS, chief justice of the Colony of British Honduras (Letters patent).

Index

General Rules followed in the construction of this index.

(1) Sovereigns of England are indexed under their ruling title.

(2) Princes of Wales who succeeded to the throne are indexed under their ruling title as sovereigns. If they did not succeed to the throne they are indexed under WALES.

(3) Princes of the Blood Royal of England are indexed under their titles, *e.g.*, Cumberland, Cambridge, etc., etc.

(4) Peers of England, Scotland or Ireland are indexed under their family names. If any such peers occur in different parts of this work with different titles, representing their successive advancement in the peerage, they are here indexed consistently only under their final title, that is under the title which represents their highest step in the peerage.

(5) Foreign sovereigns are indexed under the countries over which they ruled.

(6) Foreign nobles are indexed under their title, not under their family name.

(7) Purely Mediæval names are indexed under the forms adopted by Palgrave in the index to the "Parliamentary Writs." In the text, the spelling of such names has been left in every case in the form in which it occurs in the original authority, whatever that authority may be. As a rule there will be no difficulty in identifying the form given in the index with that given in the text.

(8) Wherever there is an admixture of mediæval and modern forms of one and the same name, all the forms are brought together in the index under one head; the various forms are printed first in capitals, and all the items under those capitals are recessed in order not to disturb the strict alphabetical sequence. This is the plan adopted in the Parliamentary "Return of Members" and is the only feasible plan where such bewildering varieties of spelling occur in one and the same book.

(9) Purely modern names, that is where there is no admixture of mediæval names, are left in their exact modern forms.

(10) Compound names are indexed under the first element of the compound.

INDEX.

The numerals and figures at end of lines indicate volume and page respectively.

ABAROW, A BAROW, ABOROUGH, BOROUGH
Abarow (A Barow), Maurice, Kt.1487, II. 26
Aborough (Borough), Edward, Kt.1487, II. 24
ABBOTT, ABBOT
Abbott, Charles, Kt.1816, II. 317
Abbott, Charles S. A., lord Tenterden, K.C.B.1878, I. 286
Abbott, Daniel, Kt.1658, II. 224
Abbott, Frederick, Kt.1854, II. 350
Abbott, James, K.C.B.1894, I. 265
Abbott, John J. C., K.C.M.G.1892, I. 377
Abbott, Joseph P., Kt.1892, II. 389; K.C.M.G.1895, I. 380
Abbot, Morris, Kt.1625, II. 188
Abdelsadok, Abderrahman ben, K.C.V.O. 1903, I. 441
Abdy, Christopher, Kt.1629, II. 196
Abdy, Robert, Kt.1660, II. 227
Abdy, Thomas, Kt.1641, II. 209
A' Beckett, William, Kt.1852, II. 349
Abel, Frederick A., Kt.1883, II. 375; K.C.B.1891, I. 292; G.C.V.O.1901, I. 419
Abercorn, marquess and duke of. See Hamilton
ABERCROMBY, ABERCROMY, ABERCROMBIE
Abercromie, George, Kt.1620, II. 175
Abercromby, John, K.C.B.1815, I. 218; G.C.B.1815, I. 183
Abercromy, Patrick, Kt.1633, II. 201; lxiii.
Abercromby, Ralph, K.B.1795, I. 174
Abercromby, Ralph, lord Dunfermline, K.C.B.1851, I. 278
Abercromby, Robert, K.B.1792, I. 174; G.C.B.1815, I. 180
Aberdare, lord. See Bruce, H. A.
Aberdeen, earl of. See Gordon, G.; Hamilton-Gordon, J. C.
Aberdenny, —, Kt.1471, II. 16
Abergavenny or Bergavenny, lord (1376). See Beauchamp, W.

Abergavenny, lord, earl or marquess. See Nevill
Abernethie, Thomas, K.H.1834, I. 470
Abetot, Hugh, K.B.1327, I. 124
Abney, Edward, Kt.1673, II. 248
Abney, Thomas, Kt.1693, II. 268
Abney, Thomas, Kt.1735, II. 285
Abney, William de W., K.C.B.1900, I. 298
Aborough. See Abarow
Aboyne, earl of. See Gordon, G.
ABRICHECOURT, D'ABRICHECOURT, D'ABRIGECOURT, DABRIDGECOURT
Abrichecourt, John D', K.G.1412-3, I. 9
Abrichecourt, Sanchet D', K.G.1348, I. 2
Dabridgecourt, Thomas, Kt.1603, II. 115
D'Abrigecourt, Thomas, Kt.1644-5, II. 219
Abruzzi, Luigi Amadeo, duc d', G.C.V.O. 1903, I. 426
Abulkassim, khan, styled Nasr-ul-Mulk, K.C.M.G.1889, I. 374; G.C.M.G.1897, I. 345
Achard, Robert, K.B.1306, I. 117
Aches. See Wautor
ACHESON, AITCHISON
Acheson, Archibald, Kt.1620, II. 175
Acheson, Archibald, earl of Gosford, G.C.B.1838, I. 206
Acheson, Archibald, earl of Gosford, son of the preceding, K.P.1855, I.102
Acheson, Archibald B. S., earl of Gosford, K.P.1869, I. 103
Acheson, Henry, Kt.1627-8, II. 194
Aitchison, Charles U., K.C.S.I.1881, I. 322
Aitchison, John, K.C.B.1859, I. 245; G.C.B.1867, I. 195
Achmuty. See Auchmuty
Ackett, John, Kt.1532, II. 48
ACKLAM, ACCLOM, and see Ackland
Acklam, William, Kt.1607-8, II. 144
Acclom (Acklam, Askam), William, Kt.1616-7, II. 161
Ackland, Arthur, Kt.1603, II. 117
Ackland, Francis, Kt.1625, II. 189

INDEX

Acland, Henry W. D., K.C.B.1884, I. 289
Ackland (Acklam), John, Kt.1603–4, II. 130
Acland, Wroth, K.C.B.1815, I. 218
Ackroyd, Edward J., Kt.1898, II. 403
Ackworth, Jacob, Kt.1722, II. 282
A'Court, Charles A., K.H.1818, I. 463
A'Court, William, lord Heytesbury, G.C.B.,1819, I.205; Grand Master, K.P.1844, I. 94
Acton, Humfrey, Kt.1546, II. 58
Acton, Jo, d', Kt.1347, II. 8
Acton, John, Kt.1603, II. 124
Acton, lord. See Dalberg-Acton
Acton, Richard, Kt.1591, II. 89
Acton, Robert, Kt.1542, II. 53
Acton, Thomas, Kt.1596, II. 93
Acton, William, Kt.1629, II. 196
Adair, Charles W., K.C.B.1882, I. 259
Adair, Robert, Kt.1690, II. 266
Adair, Robert, G.C.B.1831, I. 206
Adam, Agenor M., count Goluchowski, G.C.V.O.1903, I. 428
Adam, Charles, K.C.B.1835, I. 233
Adam, Frank F., Kt.1890, II. 386
Adam, Frederick, K.C.B.1815, I. 228; G.C.M.G.1821, I. 332; G.C.B.1840, I. 188
Adams, Francis O., K.C.M.G.1886, 1. 370
Adams, George P., K.C.H.1831, I. 457; Kt.1831, II. 331
Adams, Henry W., K.C.B.1855, footnote I. 241
Adams, John W., K.C.B.1831, I. 232; G.C.B.1837, I. 188
Adams, Richard, Kt.1752, II. 288
Adams, Robert, Kt.1680, II. 254
Adams, Thomas, Kt.1660, II. 225
Adams, William, Kt.1664-5, II. 240
Adams (afterwards Rawson), William, Kt.1814, II. 313
Adcock, Hugh, Kt.1901, II. 409
Adderley, Augustus J., K.C.M.G.1886, I. 369
Adderley, Charles, Kt.1683, II. 258
Adderley, Charles B., lord Norton, K.C.M.G.1869, I. 355
Addington, William, Kt.1797, II. 304

Adolphus, Jacob, Kt.1840, II. 342
Adrian - Verveer, Hubert, Kt.1660-1, II. 233
Adye, John M., K.C.B.1873, I. 254; G.C.B.1882, I. 198

AFGHANISTAN
Afghanistan, Abdul Rahman, amir of, G.C.S.I.1885, I. 312; G.C.B.1893, I. 214
Shahzada Habibulla Khan, of, G.C.M.G.1896, I. 344
Shahzada Nasrulla Khan, of, G.C.M.G. 1896, I. 344

Agar, Felix, Kt.1812, II. 311
Agard, Henry, Kt.1617, II. 165
Ager. See Aucher
Agha Khan, of Bombay, G.C.I.E.1902, I. 403
Aglionby (Eglandby), George, Kt.1646, II. 220
Agnew, James W., K.C.M.G.1895, I. 380
Agnew Stair A., K.C.B.1895, I. 294
Agnew, William F., Kt.1899, II. 405
Aguilar, Charles L. D', K.C.B.1877, I. 256; G.C.B.1887, I. 199
Aguilar, George C. D', K.C.B.1852, I. 239
Ahmad Khan, K.C.S.I.1888, I. 324
Ailesbury, earl and marquess of. See Brudenell-Bruce
Ailsa, marquess of. See Kennedy
Ailward. See Aylward
Ainslie, Philip, Kt.1778, II. 295
Ainslie, Robert, Kt.1775, II. 294
Ainslie, Whitelaw, Kt.1835, II. 336
Ainsworth, Rowland, Kt.1692, II. 267

AIREY, AIRY
Airey, George, K.C.H.1820, I. 455; Kt.1820, II. 322
Airy, George B., K.C.B.1872, I. 285
Airey, James T., K.C.B.1877, I. 256
Airey, Richard, K.C.B.1855, I. 240; G.C.B.1867, I. 195

Airlie, earl of. See Ogilvy
Aitcheson. See Acheson
Aitken, William, Kt.1887, II. 383
Aiyangar, V. Bhashyam, Kt.1900, II. 406
Ajaigarh, Ranjor Singh, of, K.C.I.E. 1897, I. 409

INDEX

Ajudhya, Narayan Singh, of, K.C.I.E. 1895, I. 408
Akerman, John W., K.C.M.G.1887, I. 371
Akihito of Komatsu, prince, G.C.B.1890, I. 200
Alabaster, Chaloner, K.C.M.G.1892, I.377
Alava, Miguel D', K.C.B.1815, I. 228
Alba de Tormes, duke of, G.C.V.O.1902, I. 425
Albaine. See Allamy
Albany, duke Leopold G. D. A. of, K.G. 1869, I. 64; K.T. 1871, I. 86; G.C.S.I.1877, I. 311; G.C.M.G.1880, I. 339
Albany, duchess of (1784). See Stuart C.
Albany, Robert, Kt.1605, II. 138
Albemarle, earl of. See Keppel
Albemarle, duke of. See Monck
Albemarle, William de, K.B.1326, I. 123
ALBERT, prince consort, K.G.1839, I. 56; First and Principal G.C.B.1840, I. 188; K.T.1842, I. 83; K.P.1842, I. 101; G.C.M.G.1842, I. 334; Grand Master of the Bath (1843), I. 109; K.S.I.1861, I. 306
Alborough. See Aldeburgh
Albret, sire d'. See Libreto
Albright, —, Kt.1489, II. 27
Albuquerque, Joaquim A. M. de, K.C.M.G.1898, I. 384
Alcester, lord. See Seymour
Alcock, John, Kt.1785, II. 298
Alcock, Rutherford, K.C.B.1862, I. 282
ALDEBURGH, ALBOROUGH
Aldeburgh, Richard de, K.B.1332, I. 125
Alborough, Richard, Kt.1460, II. 12
Aldeburgh, Richard, Kt.1497, II. 32
Alder, John, Kt.1660, II. 229
Alderson, Charles H., K.C.B.1903, I. 301
Alderson, Edward H., Kt.1830, II. 329
Alderson, George, Kt.1818, II. 319
Alderson, Henry J., K.C.B.1891, I. 264
Alderson, James, Kt.1869, II. 361
Aldis, Charles, Kt.1821, footnote II. 322
ALDRICH, ALDRIDGE, ALDRIGG
Aldridge, George, Kt.1605, II. 137
Aldrigg (Aldrich), John, Kt.1596, I. 93

Aldworth, Richard, Kt.1613, II. 153
Aldworth, Richard, Kt.1668, II. 243
Alexander, Du Pre, earl of Caledon, K.P. 1821, I. 99
Alexander, James, Kt.1803, II. 306
Alexander, James, K.C.B.1871, I. 252
Alexander, James, earl of Caledon, K.P. 1897, I. 106
Alexander, James E., Kt.1838, II. 341
Alexander, Jerome, Kt.1660, II. 231
Alexander, Robert, Kt.1603, II. 116.
Alexander, Walter, Kt.1630, II. 198
Alexander, William, Kt.1626-7, II. 191
Alexander, William, Kt.1824, II. 324
ALEXANDRA, queen of England, Lady of the Garter 1901, I. 71
Alford, Edward, Kt.1632, II. 200
Alford, Edward F., Kt.1902, II. 412
Alford, Lancelot, Kt.1603, II. 101
Alford, William, Kt.1603, II. 108
Algood (Allgood), Lancelot, Kt.1760, II. 289
Ali Kuli Khan, of Persia, K.C.I.E.1892, I. 407
Alibon. See Allibond
Alison, Archibald, K.C.B.1874, I. 254; G.C.B.1887, I. 199
Allamy (Albaine), Edward, Kt.1603, II. 119
ALLAN, ALLEN, ALLIN, ALEYN, ALLYN, ALLEYNE.
Allen, Christopher, Kt.1553, II. 66
Allyn, Francis, Kt.1591, II. 89
Allen, George W., Kt.1877, II. 369; K.C.M.G.1884, I. 366
Allen, George W., K.C.I.E.1897, I. 409
Allan, Hugh, Kt.1871, II. 363
Allan, Hugh M., Kt.1904, II. 418
Alleyne, James, K.C.B.1897, I. 269
Allen, John, Kt.1529, II. 47
Allen, John C., Kt.1889, II. 385
Allen, Joseph, Kt.1750, II. 288
Allen, Joshua, Kt.1674, II. 249
Allen, Richard, Kt.1639, II. 206
Allen, Thomas, Kt.1622, II. 179
Alleyne, Thomas, Kt.1660, II. 227
Allin (Allen), Thomas, Kt.1665, II. 241
Allen, Timothy, Kt.1761, II. 291

INDEX

ALLEN
Allen, William, Kt.1571, II. 75
Allan, William, Kt. 1842, II. 344
Allan, William, Kt.1902, II. 411
Allard-Kemys. See Kemys
Allenson, William, Kt.1633, II. 201
Allercar, Rauf, Kt. after 1549, II. 65
Allerton, William, Kt.1549, II. 64
Alley, George, Kt.1810, II. 310
Aleyn. See Allen
Allibond (Allebone, Alibon), Richard, Kt.1686, II. 262
Allin. See Allan.
ALLINGTON, ALYNGTON
Allington, Gyles, K.B.1509, I. 148
Alyngton, Giles, Kt.1530, II. 48
Allington, Gyles, Kt.1603, II. 105
Allnutt, Henry, Kt.1682-3, II. 258
Allonville, Armand O. M. d', K.C.B.1856, I. 242
Allot, John, Kt.1591, II. 88
Allport, James J., Kt.1884, II. 376
Almeida, Antonio J. S. de, K.C.V.O.1903, I. 441
Alston, Edward, Kt.1643, II. 216.
Alston, Edward, Kt.1660, II. 231
Alston, Francis B., K.C.M.G.1886, I. 370
Altamont, earl of. See Browne, J. D.
Alten, Charles, baron and count, K.C.B. 1815, I. 226; G.C.B.1820, I. 185
Alteren, Lodovick ab, Kt.1628, II. 195
Altham, Edward, Kt.1612-13, II. 152
Altham, James, Kt.1607 or 1608 or 1610, II. 141, 144, 149
Altham, James, K.B.1661, I. 166
Altham, William, Kt.1786, II. 299
Altman, Albert J., Kt.1894, II. 393
Alwar, Mangal Sinh of, G.C.S.I.1886, I. 312
Alyngton. See Allington
Amar, Singh, K.C.S.I.1891, I. 324
Amaral, Francesco J. F. do, K.C.V.O. 1903, I. 441
Amaravati, Seshayya Sastri, K.C.S.I. 1902, I. 327
Amb, Akram Khan, of, K.C.S.I.1889, I. 324
Ambrose, Thomas, Kt.1719, II. 281
Amcotes, Richard, K.B.1603, I. 155

Amcottes, Henry, Kt.1548, II. 63
Amherst, Jeffery, lord Amherst, K.B. 1761, I. 170
Amherst, William P., earl Amherst, G.C.H.1834, I. 452.
Amir, Khan, sirdar, G.C.M.G.1897, I. 345
Amphlett, Richard P., Kt.1874, II. 366
Ampthill, lord. See Russell
Amy (Amie), John, Kt.1619, II. 174
Anburey, Thomas, Kt.1827, II. 326; K.C.B.1838, I. 236
Anderson, Alexander, Kt.1831, II. 330
Anderson, Alexander, Kt.1863, II. 357
Anderson, Edmond, Kt.1582, II. 81
Anderson, Francis, Kt.1603, II. 105
Anderson, George C., Kt.1874, II. 366
Anderson, George W., Kt.1849, II. 347; K.C.B.1850, I. 278
Anderson, Henry, Kt.1603, II. 128
Anderson, Henry, Kt.1608, II. 146
Anderson, Henry L., K.C.S.I.1867, I. 318
Anderson, Henry P., K.C.M.G.1885, I. 367; K.C.B.1890, I. 291
Anderson, J. Jocelyn, K.H.1837, I. 477
Anderson, James, Kt.1849, II. 347
Anderson, James, Kt.1866, II. 358
Anderson, James E., Kt.1829, II. 327
Anderson, John, Kt.1878, II. 370
Anderson, John, K.C.M.G.1901, I. 389
Anderson, Joseph, K.H.1835, I. 472
Anderson, Robert, Kt.1603, II. 100
Anderson, Robert, K.H.1836, I. 473
Anderson, Robert, K.C.B.1901, I. 298
Anderson, Robert, Kt.1903, II. 415
Anderson, Robert R., Kt.1902, II. 413
Anderson, Samuel L., Kt.1884, II. 377
Anderson, William, Kt.1629, II. 196
Anderson, William, K.C.B.1897, I. 295
Anderson, William G., K.C.B.1870, I. 285
Anderson, William J., Kt.1896, II. 398
Andoe, Hilary G., K.C.B.1902, I. 273
Andover, viscount. See Howard, T.
Andrew, Eusebius, Kt.1603, II. 108
Andrew, Edward, Kt.1603, II. 108
Andrew, William P., Kt.1882, II. 373
ANDREWS, ANDREWES
Andrews, Henry, K.H.1837, I. 477
Andrewes, John, Kt.1608-9, II. 147
Andrews, Jonathan, Kt.1699, II. 271

INDEX

ANDREWS
Andrews, Mathew, Kt.1675, II. 250
Andrewes, Thomas, Kt.1553, II. 67
Andrews, Thomas, Kt.1649, II. 221; Kt.1657, II. 223
Andrewes, William, Kt.1618, II. 168
Angain. See Engaine
Angelo, Edward A., K.H.1827, I. 465
Angely, Auguste M. E., count Regnault de Saint Jean d', G.C.B.1856, I. 192
Anger. See Aungier
Anges, Francis Des, Kt.1818, II. 319
Angier, Theodore V. S., Kt.1904, II. 419
Angle, Guichard D', earl of Huntingdon, K.G.1371-2, II. 4
Anglesey, marquess of. See Paget
Anhalt, prince Aribert J. A. of, G.C.B. 1891, I. 213
Anino, count Nicolo, K.C.M.G.1820, I. 350; G.C.M.G.1823, I. 332
Annaly, baron. See White, L.
Annandale, marquess of. See Johnston, W.
ANNESLEY, ANESLIE, ANNESLOWE
Annesley, James, Kt.1844, II. 345
Aneslie, Philip, Kt.1603, II. 126
Anneslowe, Francis, Kt.1616, II. 158
Ansam. See Awnsham
Anson, Archibald E. H., K.C.M.G.1882, I. 365
Anson, George, K.C.B.1815, I. 219; G.C.B.1833, I. 187
Anson, William, K.C.B.1815, I. 219
ANSTRUTHER, ANSTROTHER
Anstruther, Alexander, Kt.1813, II.312
Anstruther, John, Kt.1797, II. 304
Anstruther, Philip, Kt.1650, II. 222
Anstrother, Robert, Kt.1614-5, II. 155
Anstruther, William, K.B.1603, I. 154
Antelme, Célicourt A., K.C.M.G.1890, I. 375
Antoniadas, John, K.C.M.G.1887, I. 372
Antrim, earl and marquess of. See MacDonnell
Anvyll, Key van, Kt.1503, II. 33
Aosta, Emmanuel Philibert, etc., duke d', K.G.1902, I. 72
Ap Griffith, Ryce, K.B.1326, I. 123
Ap Meredith, Morgan, K.B.1306, I. 115

Ap Roberts. See Probert
Ap Rice. See Price
Ap Thomas Res, Kt.1485, II. 23
Ap Thomas William, K.B. (1426), I. 132
Appleby, William, Kt.1786, II. 299
Apleton, Henry, Kt.1613, II. 153
Appleton, Isaac, Kt.1603, II. 125
Appleyard, Matthew, Kt.1645, II. 219
Appleyard, Nicholas, Kt.1513, II. 37
Apslye, Allen, Kt.1605, II. 138
Apsley, Allen, Kt.1646, II. 221
Apsley, Edward, Kt.1603, II. 108
Apsley, Peter, Kt.1675, II. 249
Arbuckle, William, Kt.1902, II. 412
ARBUTHNOT, ARBUTHNOTT
Arbuthnot, Alexander D., Kt.1859, II. 354
Arbuthnot, Alexander J., K.C.S.I.1873, I. 319
Arbuthnot, Charles G., K.C.B.1881, I. 258; G.C.B.1894, I. 201
Arbuthnot, George G., Kt.1901, II. 409
Arbuthnott, Hugh, K.C.B.1862, I. 247
Arbuthnot, Robert, K.C.B.1815, I. 224
Arbuthnot, Thomas, K.C.B.1815, I. 224
Archibald, Adams G., K.C.M.G.1885, I. 367
Archibald, Edward M., K.C.M.G.1882, I. 365
Archibald, Thomas D., Kt.1873, II. 365
Archibald, Henry, Kt.1670, II. 245
Archer, John, Kt.1663, II. 239
Archer, Simon, Kt.1624, II. 186
Arcot, Ali Muhammad, of, K.C.I.E.1897, I. 409
Arcot, Azim Jah, prince of, G.C.S.I.1877, I. 311
Ardagh, John C., K.C.I.E.1894, I. 408; K.C.M.G.1902, I. 393
ARDEN, ARDERN
Ardern, John d', Kt.1347, II. 9
Arden, John, K.B. (1400), I. 129
Ardern, John, Kt.1660, II. 229
Ardern, Richard P., Kt.1788, II. 300
Arendrup, Christian H., G.C.V.O.1904, I. 429
Arentschildt, Frederick, baron de, K.C.B.1815, I. 226
Arentschildt, Victor von, Kt.1815, II. 315

INDEX

ARGALL, ARGOLL
　Argoll, Reynold, Kt.1606, II. 140
　Argall, Samuel, Kt.1622, II. 179
　Argyll, duke of. See Campbell
Arkwright, Richard, Kt.1786, II. 299
Arlington, earl of. See Bennet, H.
Arlye [Artye], Owen, Kt.1577, II. 78
Armesdroffer, Paul, Kt.1513, II. 41
Armiger, Clement, Kt.1660, II. 228
Armine. See Ermyne
Armitage, Elkanah, Kt.1849, II. 347
Armstrong, Alexander, K.C.B.1871, I. 253
Armstrong, Frederick, Kt.1819, II. 320
Armstrong, Richard, Kt.1831, II. 331; K.C.B.1852, I. 239
Armstrong, Thomas, Kt. before 1643-4, II. 217
Armstrong, Walter, Kt.1899, II. 404
Armstrong, William G., Kt.1859, II. 353
Arnaud, John, K.H.1833, I. 469
Arney, George A., Kt.1862, II. 356
Arnim, Ferdinand G. H. von, K.C.V.O. 1900, I. 439
Arnim, Gustav C. H. F. E. von, G.C.V.O. 1900, I. 424

ARNOLD, ARNOULD, ARNOLDE
　Arnold, Alfred, Kt.1903, II. 414
　Arnold, Arthur, Kt.1895, II. 395
　Arnold, Edwin, K.C.I.E.1888, I. 405
　Arnold, James R., K.H.1831, I. 465
　Arnold, John, K.C.B.1827, I. 230
　Arnould, Joseph, Kt.1859, II. 353
　Arnolde, Nicholas, Kt.1549, II. 64
Arnoso, Count d', K.C.V.O.1901, I. 439; G.C.V.O.1903, I. 426
Arnott, John, Kt.1859, II. 354
ARRAGON
　Alphonsus I., of, K.G.1450, I. 12
Arran, earl of. See Hamilton; see Gore
Arrindell, William, Kt.1858, II. 353
Arrol, William, Kt.1890, II. 387
Arrow, Frederick, Kt.1868, II. 360
Arsen, John ab, Kt.1615, II. 157
Arthur, Allan, Kt.1900, II. 407
Arthur, Daniel, Kt.1690, II. 266
Arthur, George, K.C.H.1837, I. 462; Kt. 1838, II. 339
Arthur, James, K.H.1837, I. 478
Arthur, Nicholas, Kt.1622, II. 180

Artye. See Arlye
ARUNDELL, ARONDELL, ARUNDEL, ARUNDELE, ARRUNDELL
　Arundell, earl of. See Fitz-Alan; see Howard
　Arundel, Arundel T., K.C.S.I.1904, I. 328
　Arundel, Edmund [John] de, K.B.1306, I. 111
　Arondell, Edmond, Kt.1497, II. 29
　Arundel, John, Kt.1800, II. 305
　Arundell, John, K.B.(1400), I. 129
　Arundelle, John, K.B.1465, I. 134
　Arundell, John, Kt.1487, II. 24
　Arundell, John, K.B.(1494), I. 144
　Arundel, John, K.B.1501, I. 145
　Arundell, John, Kt. 1513, II. 36
　Arundell, John, Kt.1538, II. 51
　Arondell, John, Kt.1542, II. 54
　Arundell, John, Kt.1566, II. 72
　Arondell, John, Kt.1585, II. 84
　Arundel, John, Kt.1644, II. 218
　Arundel, John, Kt.1800, II. 305
　Arondell, Mathew, Kt.1574, II. 76
　Arundell, Thomas, K.B.(1483), I. 139
　Arundell, Thomas, K.B.(1483), I. 141
　Arundell, Thomas, K.B.1533, I. 149
　Arundell, Thomas, Kt.1603, II. 110
　Arundel, William, K.G.1394-5, I. 6
Ascu. See Ayscough
Asgher Khan, Amin-es-Sultan, grand vizier to the shah of Persia, G.C.B. 1889, I. 213
Asgill, Charles, Kt.1752, II. 288
Asgill, Charles, G.C.H.1820, I. 449
ASH, ASHE
　Ash, Thomas, Kt.1603, II. 127
　Ashe, Thomas, Kt.1782, II. 297
ASHBURNHAM, ASHBORNHAM
　Ashburnham, Cromer, K.C.B.1882, I. 258
　Ashburnham, George, 3rd earl of Ashburnham, G.C.H.1827, I. 450; K.G.1829, I. 53
　Ashbornham, John, Kt.1603-4, II. 129
　Ashburnham, John, Kt.1625, II. 189
Ashby, Francis, Kt.1617, II. 165
Ashby, James W. M., K.C.B.1902, I. 274
Ashby, John, Kt.1689, II. [264]

INDEX

Ashby, Robert, Kt.1603, II. 118
Ashe. See Ash
Ashenden, William, Kt.1596, II. 93
ASHFIELD, ASHEFIELD
Ashfield, Edmund, Kt.1570, II. 74
Ashfield, Edmond, Kt.1603-4, II. 130
Ashfield, John, Kt.1615, II. 155
Ashefield, Robert, Kt.1598, II. 95
Ashford, Edward (Henry), Kt.1603, II. 122
ASHLEY, ASHELEY, ASTLEY
Ashley, Andrew, Kt.1603, II. 121
Ashley, Anth., Kt.1596, II. 92
Astley, Barnard, Kt.1644, II. 217
Astley, Edward, Kt.1641, II. 211
Astley, Edward W. C., Kt.1830, II. 329
Astley, Egidius de, K.B.1306, I. 118
Ashley, Francis, Kt.1618, II. 169
Astley, Francis, Kt.1632, II. 199
Ashley (Asheley), Henry, Kt.1553, II. 67
Ashley, Henry, Kt.1603, II. 123; Kt.1603, II. 108
Astley, Isaac, Kt.1642 or 1643, II. 212; II. 215
Astley (Ashley), Jacob, Kt.1624, II. 185
Astley, John, K.G.1461, I. 14
Ashley, John, Kt.1603, II. 106
Ashman, Herbert, Kt.1899, II. 405
ASHTON, ASTON, ASHETON, ASSHETON, HASHETON
Aston, —, K.B.1501, I. 146
Aston, Arthur, Kt.1604, II. 134
Ashton, Arthur, Kt.1640-1, II. 208
Aston, Arthur, G.C.B.1843, I. 207
Aston, Edmond, Kt.1532, II. 48
Aston, Edward, Kt.1570, II. 74
Aston, Edward, Kt.1588, II. 87
Ashton, John, K.B.1400, I. 128
Ashton, John of, Kt.1460, II. 12
Aston, John, Kt.1513, II. 36
Aston, John, K.B.1501, I. 145
Assheton, Ralph, Kt.1660, II. 230
Asheton, Rauf, Kt.1482, II. 17
Asheton, Richard, Kt.1497, II. 32
Ashton, Richard, Kt.1603, II. 116
Aston, Richard, Kt.1765, II. 292
Aston, Roger, Kt.1603, II. 101
Hasheton, Thomas, Kt.1487, II. 26

ASTON
Aston, Thomas, Kt.1603, II. 101
Aston, Thomas, Kt.1633, II. 201
Aston (Ashton), Thomas, Kt.1640, II. 207
Aston, Walter, Kt.1560, II. 71
Aston, Walter, afterwards 1st lord Aston of Forfar, K.B.1603, I. 155
Ashton, William, Kt.1628, II. 195
Aston, William, Kt.1660, II. 231
Ashton. See Aston
Ashurst, William, Kt.1687, II. 263
Ashurst, William H., Kt.1770, II. 293
Ashworth, Charles, K.C.B.1831, I. 231
Ashworth, Frederick, Kt.1850, II. 348
Askam. See Acclom
Aske or Askew. See Ayscough
Asman, Jah, K.C.I.E.1888, I. 405
Asswillian. See Oswilifant
Astley. See Ashley
Aston. See Ashton
Astry, James, Kt.1683, II. 259
Astry, Rauf, Kt.1494, II. 28
Astry, Samuel, Kt.1683, II. 259
ASTURIAS
Charles, prince of the, G.C.B.1903, I. 216
Atherton, John, Kt.1544, II. 55
Atherton, Richard, Kt.1684, II. 260
Atherton, William, Kt.1860, II. 354
Atholl, marquess and duke of. See Murray; see Stewart-Murray
Athowe (Athoe), Christopher, Kt.1641, II. 209
ATKINS, ATKYNS
Atkyns, Edward, Kt.1660, II. 229
Atkyns, Edward, Kt.1679, II. 253
Atkins, Henry, Kt.1630 or 1632, II. 198, 200
Atkins, Richard, Kt.1660, II. 228
Atkins, Robert, K.B.1661, I. 166
Atkyns, Robert, jun., Kt.1663, II. 238
Atkins, Thomas, Kt.1649, II. 221; Kt.1658, II. 224
Atkins, Thomas, Kt.1682-3, II. 258
Atkinson, George, Kt.1787, II. 300
Atkinson, Harry A., K.C.M.G.1888, I. 372
Atkinson, Henry E., Kt.1836, II. 337
Atkinson, Jasper, Kt.1842, II. 345

Atkinson, John, Kt.1660, II. 232
Aton, Gilbert de, K.B.1306, I. 119
Atye (Atey), Arthur, Kt.1603, II. 106
Aubigny, lord. See Stuart
Aubrey. See Awbrey, Avery

AUCHER, AUGER, AGER
Aucher (Auger, Ager), Anthony, Kt. 1547, II. 59
Auger (Aucher), Anthony, Kt.1604, II. 134
Aucher (Augher), Anthony, Kt.1641, II. 209

Auchinlech, William, Kt.1633, II. lxii.

AUCHMUTY, ACHMUTY, AUTCHMOUTTY
Achmuty, David, Kt.1650-1, II. 222
Achmuty, James, Kt.1633, II. 201, lxiii.
Auchmuty (Autchmoutty), Samuel, Kt. 1803, II. 307; K.B.1812, I. 178; G.C.B.1815, I. 181
Auchmuty, Samuel B., K.C.B.1857, I. 243; G.C.B.1861, I. 193

Auchterlony. See Ochterlony
Auckland, earl of. See Eden

AUDLEY, AWDELEY
Awdeley, George, Kt.1547, II. 62
Audley, Henry, Kt.1623, II. 181
Audley, James, K.G.1348, I. 2
Awdeley, James, Kt.1487, II. 24
Awdeley, John, Kt.1497, II. 30
Awdeley, John, Kt.1513, II. 36
Awdeley, John, lord, Kt.1513, II. 38
Audley, Thomas, lord Audley, K.G.1540, I. 23
Audley, lord. See Touchet, J.

Auersperg, prince Franz J. von, G.C.V.O. 1904, I. 429
Austen, Francis W., G.C.B.1860, I. 193
Auger. See Aucher
Aungier (Anger), Francis, Kt.1609, II.148

AUSTEN, AUSTIN
Austen, Francis W., K.C.B.1837, I. 233
Austen, Henry E., Kt.1832, II. 332
Austin, Horatio T., K.C.B.1865, I. 249
Austin, James, Kt.1661, II. 235
Austen, John, K.H.1837, I. 477

Austrey, Henry, Kt.1627, II. 192

AUSTRIA
Albert II. of, K.G.1438, I. 11

AUSTRIA
Charles, Archduke of, G.C.B.1834, I. 187
Francis I. of, K.G.1814, I. 51
Francis Joseph of, K.G.1867, I. 64
Franz Ferdinand, archduke of, G.C.B. 1901, I. 216
Franz Salvator, archduke of, G.C.V.O. 1903, I. 427
Frederick C., archduke of, G.C.B.1842, I. 189
Frederick M. A. W. C., duke of Teschen, of, G.C.B.1904, I. 204
Leopold S., archduke of, G.C.V.O1903, I. 427
Ludwig V., archduke of, G.C.V.O.1903, I. 427
Rainer, archduke of, G.C.V.O.1903, I. 428
Rudolph, etc., crown prince of, K.G. 1887, I. 68

AUSTRIA-ESTE
Francis Ferdinand, etc., archduke of, K.G.1902, I. 71

Avalos, Inigo d' count de Monte Odorisio K.G.1467, I. 15
Avenon, Alexander, Kt.1570, II. 74
Avery (Alvey, Awbray), Edward, Kt.1603, II. 118
Avila e Bolama, count, K.C.V.O.1903, I. 441
Avranches, count d', K.G.1445, I. 12

AWBREY, AUBREY, AWBERY
Awbrey, Edward, Kt.1603, II. 125
Awbrey, Samuel, Kt.1620, II. 175
Awbery (Aubrey), Thomas, Kt.1608-9, II. 147
Awbrey, William, Kt.1603, II. 125

Awdeley. See Audley
Awdry, John W., Kt.1830, II. 328
Awdry, Richard D., K.C.B.1902, I. 299
Awnsham, Julian, Kt.1603, II. 120
Ayers, Henry, K.C.M.G.1872, I. 356 G.C.M.G.1894, I. 344
Aylesford, Gerard de, K.B.1306, I. 119
Aylmer, Frederick W. W., lord Aylmer, K.C.B.1855, I. 241
Aylmer, Garrett, Kt.1598, II. 95
Aylmer, Gerald, Kt.1541, II. 52

INDEX

Aylmer (Elmer), John, Kt.1603, II. 125
Aylmer, Laurence, Kt.1497, II. 31
Aylmer (afterwards Whitworth-Aylmer), Matthew, 5th lord Aylmer, Kt.1815, II. 316; K.C.B.1815, I. 221
Aylmer. See Whitworth-Aylmer
AYLIFF, AYLOFF, AWLYF, ALYF, AYLYF
Ayloff, George, Kt.1617, II. 166
Awlyf (Alyf, Aylyf), John, Kt.1549, II. 63
Ayloff, Thomas (William), Kt.1603, II. 107
Ayloff, William, Kt.1603, II. 105
AYLWARD, AILWARD
Aylward, Peter, Kt.1624, II. 186
Ailward, Richard, Kt.1602, II. 100
AYSCOUGH, AYSCUE, AYSCHUE, ASCU, ASCUE, ASKE, ASKEWE, ASKUE, ASKOUGH, ASKOTH, ASKWITH, AWSKAME
Ascu, Christopher, Kt.1513, II. 41
Ayscue, Edward, Kt.1603, II. 103
Ayscough, Edward, Kt.1613, II. 152
Ayscough, Edward, Kt.1660, II. 227
Ayscough, Edward, Kt.1672, II. 246
Askue (Awskame), Francis, Kt.1545, II. 56
Ascough, George, Kt.1641, II. 210
Ayscue, Henry, Kt.1603, II. 117
Askew, Henry, Kt.1821, II. 322
Ascue, Hugh, Kt.1547, II. 62
Aske, John, Kt.1482, II. 21
Aske, John, Kt.1482, II. 18
Askew, John, Kt. 1719, II. 281
Ascough (Askwith), Robert, Kt.1617, II. 162
Aske, Robert, Kt.1497, II. 31
Ayschue (Askewe, Askoth), Roger, Kt. 1603, II. 102
Ayscough, Walter, Kt.1603, II. 124
Ascue, William, K.B.1501, I. 147
Ascu, William, Kt.1513, II. 39
Ayscough, William, Kt.1660, II. 232
Azevedo, Dedo de, Kt.1501, II. 33

B

Babbage, Charles, K.H.1831, I. 466
Baber, John, Kt.1661, II. 233
Babford, John, Kt.1603, II. 113
BABINGTON, BABYNGTON
Babyngton, —, K.B.(1483), I. 140
Babington, Anthony, Kt.1529, II. 48
Babington, Henry, Kt.1617, II. 163
Babington, William, K.B.(1426), I. 132
Babington, William or Henry, K.B. 1483, I. 141
Babington, William, Kt.1574, II. 76
BABTHORP, BAPTHORPE
Babthorpe, Henry, Kt.1603, II. 113
Babthorpe, Ralph, Kt.1603, II. 101
Babthorpe, Rauf, Kt.1482, II. 21
Babthorpe, Thomas, Kt.1460, II. 13
Bapthorpe, William, K.B.1547, I. 151
Babthorpe, William, Kt.1560, II. 71
Back, George, Kt.1838, II. 341
Backes. See Backhouse
BACKHOUSE, BACCUS, BACKES
Backhouse, John, Kt.1347, II. 9
Baccus, John, K.B.1626, I. 163
Backes, Paul, Kt.1588, II. 87
Bacon, Edward, Kt.1603, II. 105
Bacon, Francis, Kt.1603, II. 114
Bacon, James, Kt.1604, II. 134
Bacon, James, Kt.1871, II. 362
Bacon, Nathaniel, K.B.1626, I. 163
Bacon, Nathaniel, Junr., Kt.1604, II.134
Bacon, Nicholas, Kt.1558, II. 70
Bacon, Nicholas, Kt.1578, II. 79
Bacon, Nicholas, K.B.1661, I. 165
Bacon, Thomas, K.B.1332, I. 125
Bad (Baud), Thomas, Kt.1643, II. 215
Badcock, —, K.H.1835, I. 471
Badcock, Alexander R., K.C.B. 1902, I. 274
Baden-Powell, George S., K.C.M.G.1888, I. 372
Baesh. See Bash
BAFFORD, BAFORD, BAMPFORD, BAFORE
Bafford. See Balfour
Bampford, Bartholomew, Kt.1586, II. 85
Bafore, David, Kt.1615, II. 155
Bafford, John, Kt.1347, II. 8
BAGENAL, BAGNOL, BAGNALL
Bagenol (Bagnol), Henry, Kt.1578, II. 78

BAGENAL
Bagenal, Nicholas, Kt.1552, II. 66
Bagnall, Rauf, Kt.1547, II. 61
Bagnall, Samuel, Kt.1596, II. 92
Bagg, James, Kt.1625, II. 189
Baggallay, Richard, Kt.1868, II. 360

BAGOT, BAGOTT, BAGHOT
Bagot, Charles, G.C.B.1820, I. 205
Bagot, Charles S., Kt.1903, II. 415
Bagott, Lewes, Kt.1501, II. 33
Baghott, Paul, Kt.1812, II. 311
Bagot, Ralph, K.B.1306, I. 115
Bagshaw, Edward, Kt.1627, II. 192
Bagshaw, William C., Kt.1805, II. 308
Bahawalpur, nawab of, G.C.S.I.1880, I. 312
Baieux, Richard de, K.B.1329, I. 125
Baieux, William de, K.B.1306, I. 121

BAILLIE, BAYLY, BAYLEY, BAILY, BAILEY
Bayley, Daniel, Kt.1815, II. 316; K.H.1823, I. 464
Baillie, Ewen, Kt.1793, II. 302
Bayley, Edward C., K.C.S.I.1877, I. 321
Bayley, Francis, Kt.1823, II. 324
Bayly, Henry, G.C.H.1834, I. 452
Baily, Henry, Kt.1834, II. 334
Bayly, Henry, Kt.1838, II. 340; K.H.1835, I. 472
Bayly, James, Kt.1621, II. 176
Bayley, John, Kt.1808, II. 309
Bayley, Lyttleton H., Kt.1896, II. 397
Bayley, Stewart C., K.C.S.I.1878, I. 322
Bayly, William, Kt.1525, II. 46
Bailey, William H., Kt.1894, II. 393
Baillie-Hamilton, William A., K.C.M.G. 1897, I. 382
Baillie-Hamilton-Arden, George, earl of Haddington, K.T.1902, I. 89
Bain, Baine, Baines. See Baynes
Bainton. See Baynton
Bainbridge, Edmond, K.C.B.1903, I. 300
Bainbrigge, Philip, K.C.B.1860, I. 246
Baird, David, Kt.1804, II. 307; K.B. 1809, I. 177; G.C.B.1815, I. 181
Baird, John K. E., K.C.B.1890, I. 263
Baker, Augustine F., Kt.1903, II. 416

Baker, Benjamin, K.C.M.G.1890, I. 375; K.C.B.1902, I. 300
Baker, Henry, Kt.1606, II. 140
Baker, John, Kt.1538, II. 51
Baker, John, Kt.1895, II. 395
Baker, Richard, Kt.1573, II. 75
Baker, Richard, Kt.1603, II. 104
Baker, Richard, Kt.1833, II. 334
Baker, Richard C., K.C.M.G.1895, I. 380
Baker, Robert, Kt.1820, II. 321
Baker, Samuel W., Kt.1866, II. 358
Baker, Thomas, Kt.1603, II. 108
Baker, Thomas, Kt.1625, II. 189
Baker, Thomas, K.C.B.1831, I. 230
Baker, Thomas, Kt.1883, II. 375
Baker, Thomas D., K.C.B.1881, I. 257
Baker, William, Kt.1760, II. 289
Baker, William E., K.C.B.1870, I. 284
Baksh, Singh, K.C.I.E.1887, I. 399
Balastre, Thomas, Kt.1360, II. 10
Balchen, John, Kt.1744, II. 287
Baldock (Boldock), Robert, Kt.1671, II. 246
Baldry, Thomas, Kt.1523, II. 46

BALDWINE, BALDWYN
Baldwine, Francis, Kt.1603, II. 116
Baldwyn, Samuel, Kt.1672-3, II. 248
Baldwyn, Timothy, Kt.1670, II. 244
Baldwyn, William B., Kt.1762, II. 291
Bale, Henry, K.C.M.G.1901, I. 390
Bale (Ball), John, Kt.1617, II. 165
Bale, John, Kt.1624, II. 185
Balfour, Andrew, Kt.1594, II. 91
Balfour, George, K.C.B.1870, I. 284
Balfour (Baford), William (Philip), Kt.1619, II. 173
Balfour of Burghley, lord. See Bruce, A. H.
Ball. See Bale
Ball, Charles B., Kt.1902, II. 414
Ball, Peter, Kt.1643, II. 216
Ball, Robert S., Kt.1886, II. 378
Ballantine, —, Kt.1622, II. 180
Ballary, Richard, Kt.1608, II. 145
Ballingall, George, Kt.1830, II. 329
Balliston, Alfred, Kt.1883, II. 375
Balneavis, Henry, K.H.1836, I. 474
Balthezer (Balthazar), capt., Kt.1629, II. 196

INDEX

Baltis (Baltris), Cornelius, Kt.1624, II. 184
Baluchistan, Ghaus Bakhsh, chief of the Sarawans, K.C.I.E.1903, I. 412
Baluchistan, Shahbaz khan of, K.C.I.E. 1901, I. 410
Bambrough, William, Kt.1603, II. 101
Bamfield, Amyas, Kt.1603, II. 113
Bamfield, Matthew, Kt.1604, II. 132
Bamford. See Bafford
Bamra, Sudhal Deo of, K.C.I.E.1895, I. 408
Banarjee, Gooroo Das, Kt.1904, II. 418
Banastre. See Banister
Banbury, earl of. See Knollys, W.
Banckley. See Buckley
Bancroft, Squire B., Kt.1897, II. 400
Bandiera, Francis de, K.C.B.1841, I. 237
Banding, John, Kt.1687, II. 263
Bandon, earl of. See Bernard, J. F.
BANISTER, BANYSTER, BANASTRE, BANESTER, BANESTRE
Banester (Banister), Edward, Kt. 1615, II. 155
Banyster, Robert, Kt.1605, II. 137
Banastre, Thomas, K.G.1375, I. 4
Banestre, William, Kt.1347, II. 9
Banister, William, Kt.1713, II. 278
Banington (Barington), Henry [? William], K.B.(1483), I. 141
Banir (Baniz), Gustavus, Kt.1635, II. 203
BANKES, BANKS
Banks, Edward, Kt.1822, II. 323
Bankes, Henry, Kt.1762, II. 291
Banks, Jacob, Kt.1698, II. 271
Banks, John, Kt.1631, II. 199
Banks, John T., K.C.B.1889, I. 291
Banks, Joseph, K.B.1795, I. 174; G.C.B.1815, I. 205
Banks, Paul, Kt.1785, II. 298
Bankes, Ralph, Kt.1660, II. 227
Banks, William M., Kt.1899, II. 405
Bannatyne, Ja, Kt.1633, I. lxiii.
Bannatyne, William M., Kt.1763, II. 292
Bannatyne, William M., Kt.1823, II. 324
Bannerman, Alexander, Kt.1851, II. 348
Bannerman, Patrick, Kt.1715, footnote II. 266

Banning (Bayning), Paul, Kt.1614, II. 154
Bantam, two ambassadors from, Kt. 1682, II. 258
Bapu, Sahib, K.C.I.E.1887, I. 400
Bapu, Saheb, K.C.I.E.1895, I. 408
Barantine, William, Kt.1513, II. 40
Barbour, David M., K.C.S.I.1889, I. 324; K.C.M.G.1899, I. 387
Barchhaile, Robert de, Kt.1347, II. 7
Barclay. See Berkeley
Bard, Henry, Kt.1643, II. 216
Bardes (Bardesius), William, lord of Warmenhuysen, Kt.1615, II. 157
Bardolf, lord (1418). See Phelipp, W.
Bardolf, Thomas, K.B.1306, I. 113
Bardsley, James L., Kt.1853, II. 350
Barentino, Drogo de, nephews of, K.B. 1256, I. 110
Barham, George, Kt.1904, II. 417
Barham. See Barnham
Baring, Evelyn, earl of Cromer, K.C.S.I. 1883, I. 323; K.C.B.1887, I. 290; G.C.M.G.1888, I. 341; G.C.B.1895, I. 214
Baring, Thomas G., earl of Northbrook, Grand Master of Star of India, G.C.S.I., I. 305; G.C.S.I.1872, I. 310
Barington. See Barrington
Barker, Anthony, Kt.1608, II. 144
Barker, Christopher, K.B.1547, II. 151
Barker, Edmund, Kt.1661, II. 234
Barker, George D., K.C.B.1900, I. 271
Barker, George R., K.C.B.1859, I. 245
Barker, Henry, Kt.1603, II. 112
Barker, Richard, Kt.1671, II. 245
Barker, Robert, K.B.1603, I. 156
Barker, Robert, Kt.1764, II. 292
Barker, Thomas, Kt.1622, II. 178
Barkham, Edward, Kt.1622, II. 179
Barkham, Edward, Kt.1623, II. 182
Barkham, Robert, Kt.1641, II. 210
Barkstead, John, Kt.1656, II. 223
Barlee, Frederick, K.C.M.G.1883, I. 365
Barlow, Alexander, Kt.1603, II. 124
Barlow, George H., K.B.1806, I. 176; G.C.B.1815, I. 205
Barlow, James, Kt.1714, II. 278

D D

Barlow, Robert, Kt.1801, II. 306; K.C.B. 1820, I. 229; G.C.B.1842, I. 189
Barlow, Thomas, K.C.V.O.(1901), I. 433
Barnaby. See Barnby and Burnaby
Barnard. See Bernard
Barnardiston. See Bernardiston
BARNBY, BARNABY, BARNEBY, BURNABY
Barneby, Charles, Kt.1603, II. 125
Barnaby, Nathaniel, K.C.B.1885, I. 289
Barnaby (Burnaby), Richard, Kt. 1609, II. 147
Barnby, Joseph, Kt.1892, II. 390
Burnaby, William, Kt.1754, II. 288
Barnes, Edward, K.C.B.1815, I. 220; G.C.B.1831, I. 186
Barnes, George, Kt.1549, II. 65
Barnes, George, Kt.1587, II. 85
Barnes, Hugh S., K.C.S.I.1903, I. 328; K.C.V.O.(1903), I. 435
Barnes, James S., K.C.B.1831, I. 231
Barnes, John G., Kt.1892, II. 390
Barnes, William, Kt.1603, II. 117
Barnes, William, Kt.1618, II. 169
Barneston. See Bernardiston
BARNEWALL, BARNEWELL
Barnewall, Christopher, Kt.1551, II. 65
Barnewall, Christopher, Kt.1566, II. 72
Barnewall, John, Kt.1687, II. 263
Barnewall, Patrick, Kt.1552, II. 66
Barnewall, Patrick, Kt.1566, II. 72
Barnewell, Robert, baron of Tremleston, Kt.1566, II. 72
Barnewell, Patricke (Peter), baron of Tremleston, Kt.1583, II. 82
Barnewall, Patrick, Kt.1586, II. 84
Barnewall, Thomas, Kt.1555, II. 69
Barnham, Francis, Kt.1603, II. 120
Barnham, Martin, Kt.1603, II. 118
Barnham (Branham, Barham), Martin, Kt.1631, II. 199
BARODA
Khunde Rao, guicowar of, K.S.I.1861, I. 306; G.C.S.I.1866, I. 308
Sayaji Rao, gaekwar of, G.C.S.I.1887, I. 312
Barogh. See Barret

Baron, William, Kt.1523, II. 44
Barr, David W. K., K.C.S.I.1902, I. 327
Barrel, John, Kt.1497, II. 29
Barrera, Edouard P. A., K.C.V.O.1897, I. 438
BARRETT, BARRET
Barrett, Andrew, Kt.1639, II. 206
Barrett, Edward, Kt.1608, II. 145
Barret (Barogh), Edward, Kt.1645, II. 219
Barret, James, Kt.1622, II. 178
Barrett, Paul, Kt.1683, II. 259
Barrie. See Barry
BARRINGTON, BARINGTON, and see Banington
Barrington, Bernard E., K.C.B.1902, I. 299
Barrington, Francis, Kt.1603, II. 104
Barrington, Gobart, Kt.1660, II. 230
Barrington, John, Kt.1638, II. 205
Barrington, John, Kt.1868, II. 360
Barrington, Jonah, Kt.1807, II. 308
Barington, Nicholas, Kt.1513, II. 40
Barrington, Thomas, Kt.1571, II. 75
Barrington, William A. C., K.C.M.G. 1901, I. 389
Barrow, Edmund George, K.C.B.1901, I. 273
Barrow, William, Kt.1603, II. 119
Barry, Charles, Kt.1852, II. 349
Barry, David, Kt.1832, II. 331
Barry, Jacob D., Kt.1878, II. 370
Barry, James, Kt.1640, II. 208
Barry, James F., viscount Buttevant, Kt.1567, II. 73
Barry, John E., Kt.1899, II. 404
Barry, John W., K.C.B.1897, I. 295
Barry, Redmond, Kt.1860, II. 355; K.C.M.G.1877, I. 359
Barrie, Robert, K.C.H.1834, I. 460; K.C.B.1840, I. 236
Barry oge, Thomas, Kt.1585 II. 83
Barteville, —, Kt.1547, II. 62
Bartlett. See Berkeley
Bartley. See Berkeley
Barton, Alexander, K.H.1836, I. 474
Barton, Edmund, G.C.M.G.1902, I. 348
Barton, Freeman, Kt.1814, II. 314
Barton, John G., Kt.1902, II. 410

INDEX 15

Barton, Robert, K.C.H.1837, I. 461; Kt.1837, II. 338
Barton, Thomas, Kt.1619, II. 173
Barton, William, Kt.1816, II. 317
Barwick. See Berwick
BASH, BASHE, BAESH
Baesh (Bashe), Edward), Kt.1616, II. 158
Bash, Edward, Kt.1672, II. 247
Bash, Ralph, K.B.1661, I. 166
Bashall, Talbot de, Kt.1347, II. 9
Basinges, William de, K.B.1306, I. 115
BASKERVILLE, BASKERVILE, BASKERVYLE, BASCARVILE
Baskervile, Humphrey, Kt.1609, II. 147
Baskerville, James, Kt.1461, II. 13
Baskerville, James, Kt.1487, I. 24
Bascarville, James, Kt.1547, II. 63
Baskervile, Simon, Kt.1636, II. 204
Baskerville, Thomas, Kt.1553, II. 68
Baskerville, Thomas, Kt.1588, II. 87
Baskerville, Thomas, Kt.1603, II. 108
Baskervyle, Walter, K.B.1501, I. 145
Bass, Michael A., baron Burton, K.C.V.O. (1904), I. 437
BASSETT, BASSET
Bassett, —, of Blowre, Kt.1529, II. 48
Bassett, Arthur, Kt.1575, II. 76; Kt.1579, II. 80
Bassett, Arthur, Kt.1616, II. 158
Bassett, Francis, Kt.1644, II. 218
Bassett, John, K.B.1501, I. 145
Basset, Ralph, K.B.1306, I. 117
Basset, Ralph, lord Basset, K.G.1368, I. 3; Kt.1355, II. 9
Bassett, Richard, Kt.1682, II. 257
Basset, Richard, Kt.1513, II. 42
Bassett, Richard, Kt.1817, II. 319
Bassett, Robert, Kt.1599, II. 96
Bassett, Thomas, Kt.1644, II. 218
Basset, Will, Kt.1336, II. 5
Bassett, William, Kt.1660, II. 229
Bassingburn, Humfry, K.B.1306, I. 112
Bassingburn, John de, K.B.1306, I. 121
Bassingburn, Warin, K.B.1306, I. 114
Bastard, William, Kt.1677, II. 252
Bateman, Alfred E., K.C.M.G.1900, I. 388
Bateman, Anthony, Kt.1660, II. 226

Bateman, Frederic, Kt.1892, II. 390
Bateman, Henry, Kt.1717, II. 281
Bateman, James, Kt.1698, II. 271
Bateman, John, Kt.1809, II. 309
Bateman, William, Kt.1660, II. 226
Bateman, William, viscount Bateman, K.B.1732, I. 168
Bateman-Champain, John U., K.C.M.G. 1886, I. 368
Bates, Henry, K.C.B.1879, I. 256
Bath, earl of. See Bourchier; marquess of, see Thynne
Bath, John, Kt.1623, II. 182
Bath, Nathaniel de, K.B.1333, I. 125
Bathurst, Benjamin, Kt.1681-2, II. 257
Bathurst, Edward, Kt.1625, II. 190
Bathurst, Edward, Kt.1646, II. 221
Bathurst, Henry, Kt.1680, II. 255
Bathurst, Henry, earl Bathurst, K.G. 1817, I. 52
Bathurst, James, K.C.B.1831, I. 231
Bathurst, Thomas, Kt.1665, II. 240
Batten (Battey), Henry, Kt.1622-3, II. 181
Battenberg, Alexander Joseph of, prince of Bulgaria, G.C.B.1879, I. 211
Battenberg, Francis Joseph of, K.C.B. 1896, I. 294; G.C.V.O.1897, I. 423
Battenberg, Henry M. of, K.G.1885, I. 67
Battenberg, Louis A. of, K.C.B.1884, I. 288; G.C.B.1887, I. 212; G.C.V.O. 1901, I. 418
Baud. See Bad
Baudissin, count Frederick von, K.C.V.O. 1904, I. 443
Bavaria, Luitpold C. J. G. L., regent of, G.C.B.1901, I. 203
Bavent, Roger, Kt.1336, II. 5
Bavent, Roger de, K.B.1306, I. 118
Bawde, Thomas, K.B.(1494), I. 144
Bawdin, John, Kt.1687, II. 263
Bawdryppe, William Kt.1513, II. 41
Baxter, George W., Kt.1904, II. 419
Baxter, Robert, Kt.1794, II. 302
Bayley, Bayly. See Baillie
Bayliss (Baylis), Robert, Kt.1727, II. 283
Bayliss, Wyke, Kt.1897, II. 401
Baynard, Robert, Kt.1619, II. 170

BAYNES, BAIN, BAINE, BAINES
  Baines, Edward, Kt.1880, II. 372
  Baynes, Edward S., K.C.M.G.1833, I. 352
  Baynes, Henry, K.H.1837, I. 477
  Bain, James, Kt.1877, II. 369
  Baynes, Robert L., K.C.B.1860, I. 246
  Baynes or Baine, Thomas, Kt.1672, II. 247
  Bain, William, Kt.1844, II. 345
  Baynham, Alexander, Kt.1482, II. 18
  Baynham, Christopher, Kt.1513, II. 41
  Baynham, Edward, Kt.1599, II. 98
  Baynham, George, Kt.1545, II. 58
  Bayning. See Benning
BAYNTON, BAYNTUN, BAINTON, and see Boynton
  Baynton, Edward, Kt.1574, II. 76
  Bainton, Edward, Kt.1601, II. 99
  Baynton, Edward, Kt.1613, II. 153
  Baynton, Edward, K.B.1661, I. 165
  Bayntun, Henry W., K.C.B.1815, I. 220; G.C.B.1839, I. 188
  Bayntun, Rob, Kt.1347, II. 8
Bazalgette, Joseph W., Kt.1874, II. 366
Beachcroft, Robert, Kt.1700, II. 272
Beaconsfield, earl of. See D'Israeli
Beadon, Cecil, K.C.S.I.1866, I. 315
BEAKE, BEKE
  Beke, Richard, Kt.1658, II. 224
  Beake, Thomas, Kt.1603, II. 126, 117
Beamond, Beamont. See Beaumont
Beare, John, Kt.1615, II. 156
Beare, Owen O'S., Kt.1565, II. 71
Beatty, William, Kt.1831, II. 330
BEAUCHAMP, BEAUCHAMPE, DE BELLO CAMPO
  Beauchamp, earl. See Lygon
  Beauchampe, Gilbert, K.B.(1426), I. 132
  Beauchamp, Giles de, Kt.1347, II. 7
  Beauchamp, John de, K.B.1306, I. 117
  Bello Campo, John de, Kt.1346, II. 6
  Beauchamp, John, K.B.1478, I. 138
  Beauchamp, John, lord Beauchamp de Warwick, K.G.1344, I. 1
  Beauchamp, John, lord Beauchamp of Powyk, K.G.1441, I. 12
  Beauchamp, lord. See Seymour, E.

BEAUCHAMP
  Beauchamp, Richard, earl of Warwick, K.B.1399, I. 127
  Beauchamp, Richard, K.B.1471, I. 15
  Beauchamp, Richard, earl of Warwick, K.G.1403, I. 7
  Beauchamp, Richard, 6th lord St. Amand, K.B.(1475), I. 136
  Beauchamp, Thomas de, K.B.1306, I. 121
  Beauchamp, Thomas, earl of Warwick, K.G.1348, I. 1
  Beauchamp, Thomas, earl of Warwick, K.G.1373, I. 4
  Beauchamp, William, lord Bergavenny, K.G.1376, I. 4
  Beauchamp, Thomas, K.B.1400, I. 128
  Beauclerk, lord Amelius, K.C.B.1815, I. 220; G.C.H.1831, I. 451; G.C.B. 1835, I. 187
  Beauclerk, Charles, duke of St. Albans, K.G.1718, I. 41
  Beauclerk, Charles, duke of St. Albans, K.B.1725, I. 167; K.G.1740-1, I. 43
  Beaucock, Edmund, Kt.1665, II. 240
  Beaufield, Thomas (Francis), Kt.1603, II. 101
  Beaufort, duke of. See Somerset
  Beaufort, Edmund, duke of Somerset, K.G.1436, I. 11
  Beaufort, Francis, K.C.B.1848, I. 277
  Beaufort, John, marquess of Dorset, K.G.1396, I. 6
  Beaufort, John, duke of Somerset, K.G. 1439, I. 11
  Beaufort, Thomas, duke of Exeter, K.G. 1400, I. 7
BEAUFOU, BEAUFOY, BEAUFOE
  Beaufou, Henry, K.B.1306, I. 120
  Beaufoy, Henry, Kt.1676, II. 251
  Beaufoy, Roger de, K.B.1306, I. 112
  Beaufoe, Thomas, Kt.1603, II. 107
Beaulieu, earl of. See Hussey-Montagu
BEAUMONT, BEAMONT, BEAMOND, DE BELLO MONTE
  Beaumont, —, K.B.(1483), I. 138
  Beamont, —, Kt.1492, II. 28
  Beaumont, Francis, Kt.1618, II. 168

BEAUMONT

Beaumont, Henry, lord Beaumont, K.B.1399, I. 128
Beaumont, Henry, Kt.1471, II. 14
Beaumont, Henry, Kt.1603, II. 101
Beaumont, John, lord Beaumont, K.G. 1392-3, I. 6
Beaumont, John, viscount Beaumont, K.B.(1426), I. 131; K.G.1441, I. 12
Beaumont, Lewis A., K.C.M.G.1901, I. 390; K.C.B.1904, I. 276
Beaumont, Richard, Kt.1603, II. 120
Beaumont (Beamond), Thomas, Kt. 1603, II. 103, 109
Beaumont, Thomas, Kt.1660, II. 229
Beauvale, lord. See Lamb
Beauvoir, John E. de, Kt.1827, II. 326
Beche, Henry T. de la, Kt.1842, II. 344
Becher. See Beecher
Bechtolsheim, baron Anton von, G.C.V.O. 1903, I. 428
Beckering. See Bekering
Beckett, Albert à, Kt.1904, II. 417
Beckford, Thomas, Kt.1677, II. 252
Beckingham, Thomas, Kt.1603, II. 128
Beckman, Martin, Kt.1686, II. 261
Beconshaw, White, 1628, II. 193
Bective, earl of. See Taylour, T.
Beckwith, George, K.B.1809, I. 177; G.C.B.1815, I. 181
Beckwith, Leonard, Kt.1544, II. 55
Beckwith, Thomas S., Kt.1812, II. 311; K.C.B.1815, I. 221
Beckwith, William, Kt.1482, II. 20
Beckwith, William, K.H.1832, I. 466

BEDELL, BEEDLE

Bedell, Thomas, Kt.1616, II. 157
Bedell (Beake), Thomas, Kt.1603, II. 117
Beedle, John, Kt.1603, II. 117

Bedford, duke of. See Tudor, see Russell
Bedford, John, duke of, K.B.1399, I. 127; K.G.1400, I. 7
Bedford, earl of. See Couci, see Russell
Bedford, Frederick G. D., K.C.B.1894, I. 266; G.C.B.1902, I. 203

BEDINGFIELD, BEDINGFEILDE, BEDDINGFEILD, BENYNFELD, BENINGFIELD

Bedynfeld, —, K.B.(1483), I. 139
Beningefeld, Edmund, K.B.(1483), I. 141; Kt.1487, II. 24
Beninfeilde, Edmonde, Kt.1523, II. 45
Bedingfeilde, Henry, Kt.1549, II. 64
Beningfield, Henry, Kt.1604, II. 134
Bedingfield, Henry, Kt.1684, II. 260
Bedingfield, John, K.C.H.1831, I. 457
Bedingfield, Philip, Kt.1618, II. 170
Bedingfield, Robert, Kt.1697, II. 270
Bedingfield, Thomas, K.B.1509, I. 148
Beddingfield, Thomas, Kt.1638, II. 206
Bedlow, John, Kt.(1397), preface to Irish Kts., II. lx.
Bedlow. See Bellew

BEECHER, BECHER

Becher, Arthur M., K.C.B.1873, I. 253
Becher, Edward, Kt.1722, II. 282
Beecher, William, Kt.1619, II. 173; Kt.1622, II. 180
Beecher, William, Kt.1660, II. 232
Beechy (Beechey), William, Kt.1798, II. 304
Beedle. See Bedell

BEELING, BELLINGS, BELING, BEELEN

Belinge, Henry, Kt.1615, II. 156
Beelen (Beling), Peter, Kt.1622, II. 180
Bellings (Beeling), Richard, Kt.1666, II. 242

BEESTON, BESTON, BOSTON

Beeston, George, Kt.1588, II. 86
Boston (Beston, Beeston), George, Kt. 1609, II. 147
Beeston, Hugh, Kt.1603, II. 104
Beeston, William, Kt.1692, II. 267
Begbie, Matthew B., Kt.1875, II. 367
Behrens, Jacob, Kt.1882, II. 374
Beja, duc Manuel, etc., de, G.C.V.O.1904, I. 431
Beke. See Beake
Bekering, Christopher de, Kt.1347, II. 9

BELASYSE, BELLASIS, BELLASYSE

Bellasis, Henry, Kt.1603, II. 101
Belasyse, Henry, K.B.1661, I. 164
Bellasyse, Rowland, K.B.1661, I. 164
Bellasis, Thomas, Kt.1603, II. 113

INDEX

BELLASIS
Bellasis, William, Kt.1617, II. 162
Bellasis, William, Kt.1639, II. 206
Belcher, Edward, Kt.1843, II. 345; K.C.B.1867, I. 250
Belet, Ingelram, K.B.1306, I. 115
Belfast, earl of. See Chichester
BELGIUM
 Leopold I. King of, G.C.H.1816, I. 447; G.C.B.1816, I. 183
 Leopold II. of, K.G.1866, I. 63
 Leopold George F. of, K.G.1814, I. 52
Belgrave, George, Kt.1603, II. 122
Belhaver lord. See Hamilton
Belhouse, John de, K.B.1306, I. 122
Belhouse (Belluse), Jo de, Kt.1347, II. 7
Beling. See Beeling
Belknapp, Edward, Kt.1513, II. 39
Bell, Charles, K.H.1831, I. 466; Kt.1831, II. 331
Bell (Bolt), Edmond, Kt.1603, II. 109
Bell, Francis D., Kt.1873, II. 365; K.C.M.G.1881, I. 363
Bell, George, K.C.B.1867, I. 251
Bell, Henry, K.C.B.1815, I. 219
Bell, John, K.C.B.1852, I. 239; G.C.B. 1860, I. 193
Bell, John C., Kt.1902, II. 411
Bell, Joshua P., K.C.M.G.1881, I. 364
Bell, Robert, Kt.1577, II. 77
Bell, Robert, Kt.1611, II. 150, 153
Bell, Sidney S., Kt.1869, II. 361
Bell, Thomas, Kt.1547, II. 60
Bell, Thomas, Kt.1778, II. 296
Bell, Thomas, Kt.1816, II. 317
Bell, William, K.C.B.1867, I. 251
Bell, William J., Kt.1892, II. 389
Bellairs, William, Kt.1848, II. 347
Bellairs, William, K.C.M.G.1882, I. 364
Bellamont, earl of. See Coote
Bellamy, Edward, Kt.1727, II. 283
Bellamy, Joseph A., Kt.1904, II. 419
Bellars, Richard, Kt.1639, II. 206
Bellasis. See Belasyse
Belleau, Narcisse F., Kt.1860, II. 355; K.C.M.G.1879, I. 360
Bellegarde, count August, etc., K.C.V.O. 1903, I. 442
Bellenden, Henry, Kt.1749, II. 288

BELLEW, BELLEY, BEDLOWE
Bellew or Bedlowe, Christopher, Kt. 1605, II. 139
Bellew, Christopher, Kt.1628, II. 195
Bellew, John, Kt.1551, II. 65; Kt.1556, II. 69
Bellew, John, Kt.1619, II. 174
Belley, Thomas, Kt.1615, II. 156
Bellew, Walter, Kt.1541, II. 52
BELLINGHAM, BELYNGHAM, BELINGHAM, BILLINGHAM
Bellingham, Daniel, Kt.1662, II. 237
Belyngham, Edward, Kt.1513, II. 42
Bellingham, Edward, Kt.1547, II. 60
Billingham, Edward (Edmond), Kt. 1603, II. 108; Kt.1604, II. 129
Bellingham, Henry, Kt.1460, II. 13
Bellingham, Henry, Kt.1620, II. 175
Bellingham, James, Kt.1603, II. 100
Belingham, Roger, Kt.1487, II. 25
Bellingham, Roger, Kt.1497, II. 31
Bellingham, Robert, Kt.1497, II. 32
Bellings. See Beeling
Bellomont, earl of. See Coote
Bellows, William, Kt.1557, II. 70
Belluse. See Belhouse
Belmore, earl of. See Lowry-Corry
Belson, Charles P., K.C.B.1815, I. 223
Belt, Robert, Kt.1640, II. 207
Belt, William, Kt.1633, II. 201
Beltz, George F., K.H.1836, I. 475
Bemrose, Henry H., Kt.1897, II. 400
Benanges, vicomte de. See Grailly
Benares, Narain Singh of, K.C.S.I.1866, I. 316; G.C.S.I.1877, I. 311; K.C.I.E. I. 407
Benares, Prabhu maharaja of, G.C.I.E. 1898, I. 403
Benbow, Henry, K.C.B.1902, I. 274
Bence, Alexander, Kt.1670, II. 244
Benckendorf, count Paul, K.C.V.O.1896, I. 438; G.C.V.O.1896, I. 422
Bendemann, Felix R. E. E., G.C.M.G. 1902, I. 348
Bendloes. See Bindlosse
Benedict, Julius, Kt.1871, II. 363
Bengar (Berengar), John (Thomas), Kt. 1553, II. 68
Beningfield. See Bedingfield

INDEX

Benjamin, Benjamin, Kt.1889, II. 386
Benloes. See Bindlosse
Benn, Anthony, Kt.1617, II. 166
BENNETT, BENNET
Bennet, Charles, earl of Tankerville, K.T.1721, I. 77
Bennet, Charles, earl of Tankerville, K.T.1730, I. 77
Bennet, Henry, earl of Arlington, K.G.1672, I. 36
Bennett, Henry, Kt.1657, II. 225
Bennett, Henry, Kt.1891, II. 388
Bennett, James R., Kt.1881, II. 372
Bennet, John, Kt.1603, II. 113
Bennet, John, Kt.1616, II. 158
Bennet, John, K.B.1661, II. 166
Bennett, John, Kt.1706, II. 275
Bennett, John, Kt.1872, II. 364
Bennett, Robert, Kt.1619, II. 172
Bennet, Thomas, Kt.1603, II. 127
Bennett, Thomas, Kt.1661, II. 235
Bennett, William, Kt.1760, II. 290
Bennett, William H., K.C.V.O.(1901), I. 434
Bennett, William S., Kt.1871, II. 363
Benson, John, Kt.1853, II. 349
Benson, William, Kt.1706, II. 275
Benstead, —, Kt.1492, II. 27
Bensted, Edward, Kt.1513, II. 40
Bent, John, Kt.1851, II. 349
Bentheim and Steinfurth, prince Alexis, etc., of, G.C.V.O.1904, I. 428
Bentinck, Henry J. W., K.C.B.1855, I. 240
Bentinck, lord William Cavendish, K.B.1813, I. 178; G.C.B.1815, I. 181; G.C.H.1817, I. 448
Bentinck, William, earl of Portland, K.G.1697, I. 39
Bentinck, William, duke of Portland, K.G.1741, I. 44
Bentley, John, Kt.1603, II. 124
Bentley, John, Kt.1759, II. 289
Bentley, Martin, Kt.1682, II. 258
Bentley, William, Kt.1753, II. 288
Bere, de la. See Delabere
Berefort, Janekinus, Kt.1355, II. 9
Berengar. See Bengar

Beresford, lord Charles W., K.C.V.O.(1903), I. 435; K.C.B.1903, I. 276
Beresford, George de la, marquess of Waterford, K.P.1783, I. 96
Beresford, lord George T., G.C.H.1827, I. 450
Beresford, Henry de la P., marquess of Waterford, K.P.1806, I. 98
Beresford, Henry de la P., marquess of Waterford, K.P.1845, I. 101
Beresford, Henry de la P., marquess of Waterford, K.P.1902, I. 106
Beresford, John H. de la P., marquess of Waterford, K.P.1868, I. 103
Beresford, John P., Kt.1812, II. 311; K.C.B.1819, I. 229; G.C.H.1836, I. 453
Beresford, Tristram, Kt.1664, II. 240
Beresford, William, K.H.1832, I. 467
Beresford, William C., viscount Beresford, K.B.1810, I. 177; G.C.B.1815, I. 181; G.C.H.1818, I. 448
Beresford, William L. de la Poer, K.C.I.E.1894, I. 408
Bergne, John H. G., K.C.M.G.1888, I. 373; K.C.B.1903, I. 300
Bergyll, Thomas (John), Kt.1482, II. 18
Berham, John, Kt.1584, II. 82
Berk, John, Kt.1610, II. 149
BERKELEY, BERKLEY, BARTLETT, BARKLEY, BARTLEY, BARKELEY, BARCLAY, BARKLEYE
Berkeley, Augustus, earl of Berkeley, K.T.1739, I. 78
Berkley, Charles, Kt.1623, II. 182
Berkeley, Charles, earl of Berkeley, K.B.1661, I. 164
Berkeley, Edward, K.B.(1487), I. 142
Barkley, Edward, Kt.1588, II. 86
Barkley, Edward, Kt.1625, II. 189
Bartlett, Ellis A., Kt.1892, II. 391
Barkley, Francis, Kt.1599, II. 95
Berkeley, George, lord Berkeley, K.B.1616, I. 159
Berkley, George, K.C.M.G.1881, I. 363
Berkley, George, K.C.M.G.1893, I. 378
Berkeley, George C., K.B.1813, I. 178; G.C.B.1815, I. 181

INDEX

BARTLEY
Bartley, George C. T., K.C.B.1902, I. 300
Berkeley, George H. F., K.C.B.1815, I. 224
Berkeley, Henry, lord Berkeley, K.B. 1553, I. 152
Berkley, Henry, Kt.1584, II. 83
Bartlett, Henry, Kt.1609, II. 148
Barkly, Henry, K.C.B.1853, I. 279; G C.M.G.1874, I. 337
Berkeley, Henry S., Kt.1896, II. 398
Berkeley, James de, lord de Berkeley, K.B.(1426), I. 131
Berkeley, James, earl of Berkeley, K.G.1718, I. 42
Berkeley, John de, K.B.1303, I. 110
Berkeley, John, Kt.1399, II. 11
Barkeley, John, Kt.1545, II. 56
Berkeley, John, K.B.1559, I. 153
Barkley, John, Kt.1639, II. 207
Berkeley, Maurice, Kt.1471, II. 14
Barkley, Maurice, Kt.1487, II. 25
Barkeley, Morris, K.B.1509, I. 148
Barkleye, Maurice, Kt.1545, II. 57
Barkley, Moris, Kt.1596, II. 92
Berkley, Maurice, Kt.1621, II. 178
Berkeley, Maurice F. F., lord Fitzhardinge, K.C.B.1855, I. 241; G.C.B. 1861, I. 194
Barkley, Richard, Kt.1574, II. 75
Barkly, Robert, Kt.1627, II. 192
Barclay, Robert, K.C.B.1815, I. 227
Bartley, Robert, K.C.B.1842, I. 237
Barkley, Rowland, Kt.1641, II. 209
Berkley, Thomas, Kt.1513, II. 37
Berkeley, Thomas, K.B.1603, I. 153
Bartlet, Thomas, Kt.1603, II. 124
Barclay, Thomas, Kt.1904, II. 417
Berkeley, William, marquess of Berkeley, K.B.(1475), I. 137
Berkeley, William, K.B.(1483), I. 139, 140, 141
Berkeley, William, Kt.1576, II. 78
Barkley, William, Kt.1639, II. 207
Berkshire, earl of. See Norris, see Howard
Berlay, Richard de, K.B.1306, I. 119
Bernack, William, K.B.1306, I. 117

BERNARD, BARNARD, BARNARDE
Barnard, Andrew F., K.C.B.1815, I. 223; K.C.H.1819, I. 455; G.C.H. 1833, I. 452; G.C.B.1840, I. 189
Bernard, Charles E., K.C.S.I.1886, I. 323
Barnard, Charles L., K.C.B.1887, I. 261
Barnard, Edward, Kt.1669, II. 244
Barnarde, Francis, Kt.1545, II. 58
Barnard, Frederick, K.C.H.1828, 1. 456
Barnard, Henry W., K.C.B.1856, I. 243
Barnard, Herbert, Kt.1898, II. 402
Barnard, John, Kt.1732, II. 284
Bernard, Henry, Kt.1677, II. 252
Bernard, James F., earl of Brandon, K.P.1900, I. 106
Bernard, John, Kt.1661, II. 235
Bernard, Robert, Kt.1660, II. 228
BERNARDESTON, BERNARDISTON, BARNESTON, BARMSTON
Barnardiston, Nathaniel, Kt.1618, II. 170
Barneston, Thomas, Kt.1501, II. 33
Barneston (Barmston), Thomas, Kt. 1547, II. 59
Bernardeston, Thomas, Kt.1578, II. 79
Barnardeston, Thomas, Kt.1603, II. 116
Bernardiston, Thomas, Kt.1641, II. 209
Berners or Barnes, lord. See Bourchier
Berney. See Perny
Beron. See Byron
BERRY, BURY
Berry, Benjamin, Kt.1600, II. 98
Berry, Edward, Kt.1798, II. 304; K.C.B.1815, I. 222
Berry, Graham, K.C.M.G.1886, I. 369
Bury, Henry de, K.B.1306, I. 120
Berry, John, Kt.1672, II. 247
Berry, Thomas, Kt.1671, II. 246
Bury, Thomas, Kt.1701, II. 272
Bury, Thomas, Kt.1708, II. 276
Bury, viscount. See Keppel
Bury, William, Kt.1658, II. 224, 232

INDEX

BERRY
Berry, William B., Kt.1900, II. 408
Bertie, Albemarle, K.C.B.1815, I. 217
Bertie, Francis L., K.C.B.1902, I. 299;
 G.C.V.O.1903, I. 421; G.C.M.G.1904,
 I. 349
Bertie, Montagu, earl of Lindsey, K.B.
 1616, I. 160
Bertie, Montagu, earl of Lindsey, K.G.
 1661, I. 35
Bertie, Peregrine, K.B.1610, I. 158
Bertie, Peregrine, Kt.1639, II. 206
Bertie, Robert, earl of Lindsey, K.B.
 1605, I. 156; K.G.1630, I. 32
Bertie, Roger, K.B.1626, I. 162
Bertie (formerly Hoar), Thomas, Kt.
 1813, II. 312
Bertram, George C., Kt.1885, II. 377
Bertram, William, Kt.1460, II. 12
BERWICK, BARWICK
Berwick, duke of. See FitzJames
Barwick, Robert, Kt.1641, II. 211
Berwick (Barwicke), William, Kt.
 1604, II. 133
Besant, Walter, Kt.1895, II. 396
Bessborough, earl of. See Ponsonby
Bessemer, Henry, Kt.1879, II. 371
Best, Elias, Kt.1684, II. 259
Best, William D., Kt.1819, II. 320
Bestel, Nicholas G., Kt.1880, II. 371
Betham, William, Kt.1812, II. 312
BETHELL, BETHEL, BYTHELL
Bethel, Hugh, Kt.1604, II. 132
Bethel, Hugh, Kt.1628, II. 194
Bethell, Richard, Kt.1853, II. 349
Bethell (Bythell), Walter, Kt.1617, II.
 162
Bethune, Henry, Kt.1832, II. 332
Beton, Archibald, Kt.1620, II. 175
Bettenson, Richard, Kt.1625, II. 188
Bettesworth. See Pettesworth
Bettia, Kishor Singh of, K.C.I.E.1888,
 I. 406
Betton, John, Kt.1816, II. 318
Bevan, Alfred H., Kt.1900, II. 406
BEVERLEY, BEVERLY
Beverly, George, Kt.1604, II. 132
Beverley, James, Kt.1660, II. 230
Beverly, Thomas, Kt.1662, II. 236

Beversham, William, Kt.1671, II. 245
Bevill, Robert, K.B.1603, I. 155
Bevill, Robert, K.B.1626, I. 163
Bevill, William, Kt.1589, II. 87
Bewicke, Robert, Kt.1760, II. 289
Bewley, Edmund T., Kt.1898, II. 402
Bhadour, Atar Sing of, K.C.I.E.1888, I.
 406
Bhatawadekar, Bhalchandra Krishna,
 Kt.1900, II. 406
Bhaunagar, Jeswunt Singjee of, K.C.S.I.
 1866, I. 317
Bhaunagar, Bhavsinghji of, K.C.S.I.
 1904, I. 328
Bhaunagar, Tukht Singh of, K.C.S.I.
 1881, I. 322; G.C.S.I.1886, I. 312
Bhopal, Jahan, begum of, G.C.I.E.1904,
 I. 404
Bhopal, Nuwab Sekunder, begum of,
 K.S.I.1861, I. 307; G.C.S.I.1866, I.
 308
Bhopal, Shah Jehan, begum of, G.C.S.I.
 1872, I. 310
Bhownaggree, Mancherjee Merwanjee,
 K.C.I.E.1897, I. 409
Bhurtpore, Jaswant Sing maharaja,
 G.C.S.I.1877, I. 311
Bickbury, John de, K.B.1306, I. 115
Bickenell (Brikenell, Kykenell), John,
 Kt.1485, II. 23
Bickerton, Richard, Kt.1773, II. 294
Bickerton, Richard, K.C.B.1815, I. 217
Biddlecombe, George, Kt.1873, II. 365
Biddulph, Michael A. S., K.C.B.1879, I.
 256; G.C.B.1895, I. 201
Biddulph, Robert, K.C.M.G.1880, I. 362;
 G.C.M.G.1886, I. 341; K.C.B.1896,
 I. 267; G.C.B.1899, I. 202
Biddulph, Theophilus, Kt.1660, II. 226
Biddulph, Thomas M., K.C.B.1863, I.
 283
Bigge, Arthur J., K.C.B.1895, I. 294;
 G.C.V.O.1901, I. 419; K.C.M.G.1901,
 I. 391
BIGGES, BIGGS
Biggs, John, Kt.1675, II. 250
Bigges, Thomas, Kt.1603, II. 123
Bigham, John C., Kt.1897, II. 402
Bigland, Ralph, Kt.1831, II. 331

Bigland, Wilson B., K.H.1836, I. 475
Bignold, Arthur, Kt.1904, II. 417
Bignold, Samuel, Kt.1854, II. 350
Bigod, Rauf, Kt.1482, II. 20
Bigod, Roger, earl of Norfolk, K.B.1233, I. 109
Bigot, De St. Quentin, count Anatol, G.C.V.O.1904, I. 430
Bikanir, Gunga Singh of, K.C.I.E.1901, I. 410; K.C.S.I.1904, I. 328
Bilfinger, baron Herman von, G.C.V.O. 1904, I. 428
Biliotti, Alfred, K.C.M.G.1896, I. 381
Bille, Frants E., G.C.V.O.1904, I. 429
Billers, William, Kt.1727, II. 283
Billesdon, Nicholas [Robert], Kt.1486, II. 23
Billingham. See Bellingham
Billingsley, Henry, Kt.1596, II. 93
Billingsley, Henry, Kt.1603, II. 112
Billington, William, Kt.1697, II. 270
Bilsby, William, Kt.1604, II. 130
Bilson, Thomas, Kt.1613, II. 153
BINDLOSS, BENDLOES, BENLOSS
  Bindloss (Benloss), Francis, Kt.1624, II. 185
  Bindlosse (Bendloes), Robert, Kt.1617, II. 165
BINGHAM, BYNGHAM
  Byngham, George, Kt.1588, II. 86
  Bingham, George, earl of Lucan, K.P. 1898, I. 106
  Bingham, George C., earl of Lucan, K.C.B.1855, I. 240; G.C.B.1869, I. 195
  Bingham, George R., K.C.B.1815, I. 223
  Byngham, John, Kt.1471, II. 15
  Bingham, John, Kt.1605, II. 138
  Bingham, Richard, K.B.(1465), I. 134
  Bingham, Richard, Kt.1584, II. 83
Bingley, John, Kt.1618, II. 167
Bingley, Ralph, Kt.1603, II. 127
Bingley, Richard, Kt.1611, II. 151
Binnie, Alexander R., Kt.1897, II. 400
Binnion, George, Kt.1642, II. 213
BINNS, BYNNE, BYNDE
  Binns, Henry, K.C.M.G.1898, I. 385
  Bynne (Bynde), John, Kt.1603, II. 124

Biondi (Byondy), Francis, Kt.1622, II. 180
Birch, Arthur N., K.C.M.G.1886, I. 369
Birch, Richard J. H., K.C.B.1860, I. 281
Birch, Thomas, Kt.1745, II. 287
BIRD, BYRD
  Bird, George C., K.C.I.E.1898, I. 410
  Bird (Byrd), Thomas, Kt.1661, II. 235
  Bird, William, Kt.1617, II. 161
Birdwood, George C. M., Kt.1881, II. 373; K.C.I.E.1887, I. 400
Birkenhead, John, Kt.1662, II. 237
Birkenshaw. See Burchinshaw
BIRMINGHAM, BERMINGHAM
  Bermingham, Gilbert de, Kt.(1330), preface to Irish Kts., II. lix.
  Birmingham, Henry de, K.B.1306, I. 121
  Birmingham, John, Kt.(1317), I. lix.
  Birmingham, Walter, Kt.(1330), I. lix.
  Birmingham, William, Kt.1541, II. 53
  Birmingham, William, K.B.(1483), I. 139
  Birmingham, William de, K.B.1306, I. 113
Birnie, Richard, Kt.1821, II. 323
Biron. See Byron
Birt, William, Kt.1897, II. 399
BISHOP, BISHOPPE
  Bishop, Edward, Kt.1625, II. 190
  Bishop, Henry R., Kt.1842, II. 344
  Bishop, Peter, K.H.1837, I. 477
  Bishop, Richard, Kt.1661, II. 235
  Bishop, Thomas, Kt.1603, II. 104
  Bishop, Thomas, Kt.1641, II. 210
  Bishoppe, William, Kt.1625, II. 189
  Bishop, William, Kt.1678, II. 253
  Bishop, William, Kt.1778, II. 296
Bisset, John, K.C.H.1832, I. 459; Kt. 1832, II. 333; K.C.B.1850, I. 239
Bisset, John J., K.C.M.G.1877, I. 359
Bisset, William S. S., K.C.I.E.1897, I. 409
Bittleston, Adam, Kt.1858, II. 353
Bitton, Robert, Kt.1603, II. 104
Blachford, lord. See Rogers
Black, Samuel, Kt.1892, II. 390
Black. See Blake
Blackburn, Colin, Kt.1860, II. 354
Blackburne, William, Kt.1838, II. 340

INDEX 23

Blackhall, Thomas, Kt.1762, II. 291
Blackman, Henry, Kt.1782, II. 296
Blackmore, Richard, Kt.1697, II. 270

BLACKSTONE, BLACKISTON, BLACKSTON, BLAKISTONE, BLAKESTON
Blakistone, Mathew, Kt.1759, II. 289
Blackstone, Ralph, Kt.1630, II. 197
Blakiston, Thomas, Kt.1615, II. 156
Blackston, William, Kt.1603, II. 120
Blakiston, William, Kt.1617, II. 162
Blakeston (Blackston), William, Kt. 1643, II. 215
Blackstone, William, Kt.1770, II. 293
Blackwell, Lambert, Kt.1697, II. 270
Blackwell, Thomas, Kt.1642, II. 215
Blackwood. See Hamilton-Temple-Blackwood
Blackwood, Henry, K.C.B.1819, I. 229; G.C.H.1832, I. 452
Blackwood, Stevenson A., K.C.B.1887, I. 290
Bladwell, Thomas, Kt.1661, II. 235
Blagden, Charles, Kt.1792, II. 301
Blage, George, Kt.1547, II. 62

BLAGRAVE, BROGRAVE, BLAUGRAVE
Brograve, John, Kt.1603, II. 104
Blagrave (Blaugrave), John, Kt.1615, II. 155
Blaikie, Thomas, Kt.1856, II. 351
Blaine, Charles F., Kt.1889, II. 386
Blaine, Robert S., Kt.1890, II. 387
Blain, William A., Kt.1897, II. 399
Blair, Alexander, Kt.1651, II. 222
Blair, Robert, K.C.B.1815, I. 227
Blair, William, Kt.1633, II. lxiii.
Blair, Tho, Kt.1633, II. lxii.
Blair, Bryce, Kt.1633, II. lxiii.
Blake, Ernest E., K.C.M.G.1901, I. 391
Blake, Francis, Kt.1689, II. 265
Blake, Henry A., K.C.M.G.1888, I. 373; G.C.M.G.1897, I. 345
Blake, Richard, Kt.1624, II. 186
Blake, Richard, Kt.1675, II. 250
Blake, Valentine, Kt.1622, II. 180
Blake, Valentine, Kt.1629, II. 196
Blake, Walter, Kt.1648, II. 221
Blake, William, Kt.1627, II. 193

Blakeney, Edward, K.C.B.1815, I. 223; G.C.H.1836, I. 453; G.C.B.1849, I. 190
Blakeney, William, lord Blakeney, K.B. 1756, I. 170
Blaker, John G., Kt.1897, II. 401
Blakistone. See Blackstone

BLANC, BLANKE
Blanc, Henry J., K.C.V.O.(1901), I. 434
Blanc, Simon le, Kt.1798, II. 304
Blanke, Thomas, Kt.1583, II. 81
Blanchvile, Edmund, Kt.1623, II. 183
Bland, Thomas, Kt.1604, II. 132
Bland, Thomas, Kt.1616, II. 157

BLANEY, BLANY, BLAYNEY
Blany, Arthur, Kt.1643, II. 216
Blayney, Edward, Kt.1603, II. 110
Blaney, Henry, Kt.1626, II. 190
Blantyre, lord. See Stewart
Blaquiere, John, lord de Blaquiere, K.B. 1774, I. 172

BLENCOW, BLINCOW, BLYNKHOWE
Blencow (Blynkhowe), Henry, Kt.1617, II. 164
Blincow, John, Kt.1697, II. 270

BLENERHASSET, BLENNERHASSET
Blenerhasset, Edward (Thomas), Kt. 1603, II. 123
Blenerhasset, John, Kt.1609, II. 149
Blenerhassett, Leonard, Kt.1636, II. 204
Blennerhasset, Thomas, Kt.1603, II. 126
Blewett. See Bluet
Blicke, Charles, Kt.1803, II. 306
Bligh, John D., K.C.B.1856, I. 280
Bligh, Richard R., G.C.B.1820, I. 184
Bliss, Henry W., K.C.I.E.1897, I. 409
Blizard (Blizzard), William, Kt.1803, II. 307
Blodwell, John, Kt.1671, II. 246
Blois (Bloys), William, Kt. 1661, II. 235
Blomer, Henry, Kt.1603, II. 117
Blomfield, Arthur W., Kt.1889, II. 385
Bloomfield, Benjamin, lord Bloomfield, K.C.H.1815, I. 454; Kt.1815, II. 316; G.C.H.1819, I. 449; G.C.B. 1822, I. 206

Bloomfield, John, K.C.B.1867, I. 251; G.C.B.1873, I. 196
Bloomfield, John A. D., lord Bloomfield, K.C.B.1851, I. 278; G.C.B.1858, I. 208
Blomfield, Richard M., K.C.M.G.1904, I. 395
Blood, Bindon, K.C.B.1896, I. 266
Bloodworth. See Bludworth
Blosset, Robert H., Kt.1822, II. 323
Blouket (Bloucat, Plouket), Nicholas, K.B.(1426), I. 132

BLOUNT, BLUNT, BLOUNTE
  Blount, Charles, Kt.1587, II. 86
  Blount, Charles, Kt.1596, II. 92
  Blount, Charles, earl of Devonshire, K.G.1597, I. 29
  Blunt, Charles, Kt.1618, II. 169
  Blount, Christopher, Kt.1588, II. 87
  Blunt, Edward, Kt.1599, II. 97
  Blount, Edward le, K.B.1329, I. 125
  Blount, Edward, Kt.1497, II. 29
  Blount, Edward C., K.C.B.1888, I. 291
  Blount, George, Kt.1544, II. 55
  Blount, George, Kt.1604, II. 129
  Blunt, Henry, Kt.1640, II. 207
  Blount, Humphrey, Kt.1471, II. 15
  Blount, James, Kt.1485, II. 22
  Blount, James, Kt.1487, I. 24
  Blount, James, lord Mountjoy, K.B. 1553, I. 152
  Blunt, James, Kt.1619, II. 171
  Blount, John le, K.B.1306, I. 114
  Blount, John, lord Mountjoy, K.B. 1478, I. 137
  Blount, John, K.G.1417, I. 9
  Blunt, John E., Kt.1902, II. 412
  Blount, Michael, Kt.1591, II. 88
  Blunt, Nicholas, Kt.1604, II. 131
  Blount, Richard, Kt.1549, II. 65
  Blount, Richard, Kt.1603, II. 108
  Blount, St. John, K.B.1626, I. 162
  Blount, Thomas, Kt.1347, II. 6
  Blount, Thomas, Kt.1487, II. 25
  Blount, Thomas, Kt.1513, I. 36
  Blunt, Thomas P., Kt.1603, II. 104
  Blount, Walter, K.B.(1461), I. 133

BLOUNT
  Blount, Walter, lord Mountjoy, K.G. 1472, I. 15
  Blunt, William, Kt.1347, II. 6
  Blount, William, lord Mountjoy, K.B. 1509, I. 148; K.G.1526, I. 21
  Blount, William, Kt.1545, II. 57
Bloxham (Bloxam), Matthew, Kt.1800, II. 305
Bloyon, Ralph de, K.B.1327, I. 124
Blucher, prince Albert L. L., G.C.B.1815, I. 183
Bludder. See Bludworth

BLUDWORTH, BLOODWORTH, BLUDDER
  Bludder, Thomas, Kt.1604, II. 134
  Bludder, Thomas, Kt.1618, II. 168
  Bludworth (Bloodworth or Bludder), Thomas, Kt.1660, II. 226
  Bloodworth, Thomas, Kt.1682, II. 257

BLUETT, BLEWETT
  Bluett, Buckland S., K.H.1836, I. 475
  Blewett, Roger, Kt.1547, II. 60
  Blewet, Samuel, Kt.1696, II. 270
Blum, Pasha, K.C.M.G.1890, I. 376
Blundell, Arthur, Kt.1624, II. 183
Blundell, Francis, Kt.1618, II. 167
Blundell, George, Kt.1617, II. 161
Blundell, George, Kt.1661, II. 234
Blunt. See Blount
Blyth, Arthur, K.C.M.G.1877, I. 359
Boag, Robert, Kt.1877, II. 368
Boak, Robert, Kt.1902, II. 410
Boalor, Jo, Kt.1347, II. 7.
Boarde. See Bood
Bobbili, Vencatesveta of, K.C.I.E.1895, I. 408
Bock und Polach, Frederick W. C. von, G.C.V.O.1904, I. 430
Bocland, Thomas, Kt.1377, II. 10
Boden, Monier W., K.C.I.E.1887, I. 399

BODENHAM, BODENDEN, BODENDINE, BODRINGHAM
  Bodenden, Bodendine, or Bodenham, Francis, Kt.1616, II. 159
  Bodryngham, Henry, K.B.(1475), I. 136
  Bodenham, Roger, K.B.1603, I. 156

BODENHAM
  Bodenham (Bodringham), William, Kt.1608, II. 146
  Bodenham, Wingfield, Kt.1642, II. 215
Bodkin, William H., Kt.1867, II. 359
Bodley, John, Kt.1617, II. 165
Bodley, Josias, Kt.1604, II. 131
Bodley, Thomas, Kt.1604, II. 131
Bodringham. See Bodenham
Bogg, James, Kt.1609, II. 147
Bogle, Archibald, Kt.1853, II. 350
Bogue, John, K.H.1837, I. 477
Bohun, Humfrey de, K.B.1306, I. 115
Bohun, Humphrey de, earl of Hereford, K.G.1364, I. 3
Bohun, John de, earl of Hereford, K.B. 1327, I. 124
Bohun, William de, earl of Northampton, K.G.1349, I. 2
BOLDE, BOULDE
  Boulde, Henry, Kt.1487, II. 25
  Bolde, Richard, Kt.1482, II. 19
Boldock. See Baldock
BOLEYN, BOLAYNE, and see Bullen
  Bolayne, Thomas, K.B.(1483), I. 141
  Boleyn, Thomas, K.B.1509, I. 148
  Boleyn, Thomas, earl of Wiltshire, K.G.1523, I. 21
Bolingbroke, earl of. See St. John
Bolingbroke, Jo de, Kt.1336, II. 5
Bolland, William, Kt.1830, II. 328
Bolle, Bolles. See Bowle, Bowles
Bollonus, Domynike, Kt.1548, II. 63
Bolney, William, K.B.(1483), II. 139
Bologna, Brankaleo de, K.B.1306, I. 122
Bologna, count, Nicola S., K.C.M.G. 1868, I. 354
Bolt, Edmond, Kt.1603, II. 109
Bolton, duke of. See Powlett
Bolton, Edward, Kt.1636, II. 204
Bolton, Francis J., Kt.1883, II. 376
Bolton, George, Kt.1799, II. 304
Bolton, Richard, Kt.1618, II. 169
Bolton, Robert, K.C.H.1816, I. 454; Kt.1817, II. 318; G.C.H.1834, I. 452
Bolton, William, Kt.1663, II. 238
Bolton, William (Robert), Kt.1803, II. 307

Bonavita, Ignatius G., K.C.M.G.1836, I. 352; G.C.M.G.1856, I. 335
Bond, Edward A., K.C.B.1898, I. 296
Bond, George, Kt.1587, II. 85
Bond, Robert, K.C.M.G.1901, I. 391
Bond, William, Kt.1603, II. 122
Bonfoy, Thomas, Kt.1665, II. 240
Bonham, Samuel G., K.C.B.1850, I. 278
Bonham, Walter, Kt.1547, II. 62
Bonnici, Claudio V., K.C.M.G.1835, I. 352
Bonnycastle, Richard H., Kt.1840, II. 342
Bonsall, Thomas, Kt.1795, II. 303
Bonser, John W., Kt.1894, II. 392
Bontein, James, Kt.1798, II. 304
Bonville, William, lord Bonville, K.G. 1461, I. 13
Bonython, John L., Kt.1898, II. 403
Bood (Boarde), Stephen, Kt.1603, II. 117
Booker, William L., Kt.1894, II. 393
Boomer, Bartram, Kt.1603, II. 108
BOOTH, BOOTHE, BOWTHE, BOTHE, BOUTHE
  Booth, Charles, Kt.1784, II. 298
  Booth, George, Kt.1599, II. 98
  Booth, Henry, K.H.1835, I. 472
  Bowthe, John, Kt.1482, II. 19
  Boothe, John, Kt.1685, II. 260
  Bothe, Philip, K.B.1501, I. 147
  Booth, Robert, Kt.1668, II. 243
  Booth, William, Kt.1347, II. 8
  Bowthe, William, Kt.1497, II. 32
  Bouthe, William, Kt.1577, II. 78
  Booth, William, Kt.1682, II. 258
Booth-Wilbraham, Edward, earl of Lathom, G.C.B.1892, I. 213
Bootle, Thomas, Kt.1745, II. 287
Borden, Frederick W., K.C.M.G.1902, I. 392
Borgo, count Carlo A. P. de, K.C.B.1819, I. 228
Borlace. See Burlacy
Borough. See Burrow, see Abarow
Borthwick, Algernon, Kt.1880, II. 371
Borton, Arthur, K.C.B.1877, I. 255; G.C.M.G.1880, I. 339; G.C.B.1884, I. 198
Borwick, Robert H., Kt.1902, II. 413
Bosanquet, John B., Kt.1830, II. 328

Bosoun, Peter de, K.B.1306, I. 117
Bosquet, Pierre F. J., G.C.B.1856, I. 192
Bossett, Charles P. de, K.H.1818, I. 463
Bossum, Richard, Kt.1513, II. 42
Boston. See Beeston
BOSWELL, BOSWEL, BOSVILE, BOSVILL
   Boswell, —, Kt.1625, II. 187
   Bosvile, Henry, Kt.1618, II. 168
   Bosvile, Henry, Kt.1664, II. 239
   Boswell, John, of Balmowrow, Kt. 1594, II. 91
   Boswell, John, of Glasemont, Kt.1594, II. 91
   Bosvile, Leonard, Kt.1621, II. 176
   Boswell, Rafe, Kt.1603, II. 115
   Boswell, Thomas, Kt.1642, II. 213
   Boswell, William, Kt.1633, II. 201
   Boswell, William, Kt.1634, II. 202
Bosworth, John, Kt.1745, II. 287
Boteler. See Butler
Botetourt, Oto, K.B.1327, I. 124
Botetourte, Ralph de, K.B.1306, I. 114
Botetourte, William de, K.B.1303, I. 110
Bothe. See Booth
Bouat, Marie J. G., K.C.B.1856, I. 242
Boucaut, James P., K.C.M.G.1898, I. 384
Bouch, Thomas, Kt.1879, II. 371
Bouchier. See Bourchier
Bouët-Willaumez, Louis E., comte, K.C.B.1857, I. 244
Boughton, Edward, Kt.1527, II. 46
Boule, Henry, Kt.1603, II. 126
Boulmer. See Bulmer

BOURCHIER, BOUCHIER, BOURGCHIER, BOWSER, BOWCER, BOURSIER
   Bouchier, Barrington, Kt.1676, II. 251
   Bourchier, Barrington, Kt.1697, II. 270
   Boursier, Betremieu, Kt.1380, II. 10
   Bourchier, Edward, earl of Bath, K.B. 1610, I. 157
   Bourchier, George, Kt.1579, I. 80
   Bourchier, George, K.C.B.1872, I. 253
   Bourchier, Henry, Kt.1621, II. 178
   Bourchier, Henry, K.B.(1426), I. 131
   Bourchier, Henry, earl of Essex, K.G. 1450, I. 13
   Bourchier, Henry, earl of Essex, K.B. 1478, I. 137; K.G.1496, I. 19
   Bourchier, Humphry, K.B.(1461), I. 133
   Bourchier, John, lord Bourchier, K.G. 1392, I. 6
   Bourchier, John, lord Berners, K.G. 1459, I. 13
   Bourchier, John, lord Berners, K.B. 1478, I. 137
   Bourchier, John, lord FitzWarin, K.B. (1494), I. 144
   Bourchier, John, lord FitzWarine, Kt. 1549, II. 64
   Bouchier (Bowcer), John, Kt.1609, II. 148
   Bourchier, John, Kt.1611, II. 150
   Bourchier, John, Kt.1619, II. 175
   Bourchier, lord. See Robessart, see Stafford
   Burghchier (Bowser), Rauf, Kt.1584, II. 82
   Bouchier, Thomas, K.B.1478, I. 138
   Bourchier, Thomas, K.C.B.1842, I. 237
   Bouchier, William, Kt.1603, II. 122
Bourdieu, Arthur de, K.H.1836, I. 474
Bourdillon, James A., K.C.S.I.1904, I. 328
Bourgeois, Peter F., Kt.1791, II. footnote 301
Bourinot, John G., K.C.M.G.1898, I. 384
BOURKE, BURKE, BURGH, BURGHOWER
   Bourke, Dermot R. W., earl of Mayo, K.P.1904, I. 106
   Burgh, Henry de, earl Clanrickarde, K.P.1783, I. 96
   Bourke, *alias* McDavie, Hubert, Kt. 1585, II. 83
   Bourke, John MacO., Kt.1576, II. 77
   Bourke, John, baron of Leitrim, Kt. 1583, II. 81, 82
   Burgh, John, Kt.1616, II. 159
   Burgh (Burghower, Burrowes), John, Kt.1623, II. 181
   Burke, John, Kt.1650, II. 221
   Bourke, John, earl of Mayo, G.C.H. 1819, I. 449
   Burke, John B., Kt.1854, II. 350

INDEX 27

BOURKE
Bourke, McWilliam, Kt.1581, II. 81
Bourke, Richard MacO., Kt.1583, II. 82
Bourke, Richard, lord Bourke, Kt. 1596, II. 92
Bourke, Richard, earl of Clanricarde, Kt.1601, II. 99
Bourke, Richard, K.C.B.1835, I. 233
Bourke, Richard, earl of Mayo, K.P. 1869, I. 103; G.C.S.I.1869, I. 309; Grand Master Star of India, I. 305
Bourke, Robert, lord Connemara, G.C.I.E.1887, I. 401
Bourke, *alias* ne Long, Theobald, Kt. 1603, II. 100
Burgh, Thomas, Kt.1513, II. 38
Burgh, Thomas, Kt.1519, II. 43
Burgh, Thomas, lord Burgh, K.G. 1483, I. 17
Burgh, Thomas, lord Burgh, K.G. 1593, I. 28
Bourke (Burgh), Thomas, Kt.1599, II. 96
Burke, Thomas, Kt.1612, II. 152
Bourke, Toby, baron Bourke, Kt.1705, Jacobite, footnote II. 266
Bourke Ulick, Kt.1541, II. 52
Bourke, Ulick, 2nd earl of St. Albans, Kt.1638, II. 205; K.B.1638, I. 163
Burgh, Ulick J. de, marquess of Clanricarde, K.P.1831, I. 100
Burgh, Ulysses, lord Downes, K.C.B. 1815, I. 225; G.C.B.1860, I. 193
Burgh, William, K.B.1385, I. 126
Burgh, William, lord Burgh, Kt.1553, II. 66
Bourke, William, Kt.1567, II. 73
Burke, William, Kt.1612, II. 152
BOURNE, BOORNE, and see Burne
Bourne, Christopher de, Kt.1347, II. 8
Boorne, John, Kt.1553, II. 66
Bourne, Roger de, K.B.1326, I. 123
Boursier. See Bourchier
Boustred (Bowlstrad), William, Kt.1599, II. 97
Bouverie (Desbouvrie), Christopher, Kt. 1713, II. 278
Bouverie, Edward Des, Kt.1685, II. 261
Bouverie, Henry F., K.C.B.1815, I. 224; G.C.M.G.1836, I. 333; G.C.B.1852, I. 190
Bovell, Henry A., Kt.1902, II. 413
Bovill, Elliot C., Kt.1884, II. 376
Bovill, William, Kt.1866, II. 358
Bowater, Edward, K.C.H.1837, I. 462
Bowden-Smith, Nathaniel, K.C.B.1897, I. 269
Bowell, Mackenzie, K.C.M.G.1895, I. 380
Bowen, Charles S. C., Kt.1879, II. 370
Bowen, George F., K.C.M.G.1856, I. 353; G.C.M.G.1860, I. 335
Bowen, John, Kt.1629, II. 196
BOWER, BOWYER, and see Bowes, Boyer
Bowyer, Edmond, Kt.1603, II. 107
Bowyer, Edmund, Kt.1633, II. 201, lxii.
Bower, Graham J., K.C.M.G.1892, I. 376
Bowyer, Henry, Kt.1603, II. 118
Bowyer, Henry, Kt.1609, II. 149
Bowyer, John, Kt.1604, II. 132
Bowyer, John, Kt.1607, II. 142
Bowyer, Rauf, Kt.1482, II. 20
Bowyer, William, Kt.1603, II. 107
Bowyer, William, Kt.1617, II. 165
Bowes, Edward, Kt.1596, II. 93
Bowes, George, Kt.1544, II. 54
Bowes, George, Kt.1560, II. 70
Bowes, George, Kt.1617, II. 164
Bowes, Jerome, Kt.1570, II. 74
Bowes, Martin, Kt.1538, II. 51
Bowes (Bowyer), Rauf, Kt. or Banneret, 1482, II. 20
Bowes, Rauf, Kt.1513, II. 37
Bowes, Robert, Kt.1538, II. 51
Bowes, Talbot, Kt.1617, II. 162
Bowes, Thomas, Kt.1630, II. 198
Bowes, William, Kt.1586, II. 84
Bowes, William, Kt.1684, II. 259

BOWLES, BOWLE, BOLLES, BAILLES
Bowles (Bolles), Charles, Kt.1616, II. 160
Bowles (Bolles), George, Kt.1618, II. 168
Bowles, George, K.C.B.1851, I. 239; G.C.B.1873, I. 196

BOWLES

Bowlles (Bailles, Bolles), John, Kt. 1596, II. 93
Bowle, Paul, Kt.1622, II. 179
Bowles, Thomas, Kt.1482, II. 18
Bowles (Bolles), Thomas, Kt.1607, II. 141
Bowles, William, K.C.B.1862, I. 248

Bowmer. See Bulmer
Bowring, Charles C., Kt.1900, II. 408
Bowring, John, Kt.1854, II. 350
Bowser, Rauf, Kt.1584, II. 82
Bowser, Robert, Kt.1347, II. 8
Bowser, Thomas, K.C.B.1827, I. 230
Bowser. See Bourchier
Bowthe. See Booth
Bowyer. See Bower
Box, Ralph, Kt.1689, II. 265
Boxall, Charles G., K.C.B.1902, I. 299
Boxall, William, Kt.1871, II. 363
Boxer, Edward, K.C.B.1855, I. footnote 241
Boxstead, Peter de, K.B.1324, I. 123
Boy, Randal McD., Kt.1602, II. 100
Boyce, John, Kt.1727, II. 284
Boyd, Andrew, Kt.1620, II. 175
Boyd, John, Kt.1891, II. 389
Boyd, John A., Kt.1899, II. 405; K.C.M.G.1901, I. 391
Boyd, Robert, K.B.1785, I. 173
Boyd, Thomas J., Kt.1881, II. 373
Boyd, William, Kt.1787, II. 300
Boyer, Turtliff, K.H.1837, I. 476
Boyer. See Bowyer
Boyland, John de, K.B.1306, I. 116
Boylden (Baldwine, Balden, Bayldon), Francis, Kt.1603, II. 116
Boyle, Cavendish, K.C.M.G.1897, I. 382
Boyle, Charles, earl of Orrery, K.T.1705, I. 76
Boyle, Courtenay, K.C.H.1832, I. 459; Kt.1832, II. 333
Boyle, Courtenay, K.C.B.1892, I. 292
Boyle, David, earl of Glasgow, G.C.M.G. 1892, I. 343
Boyle, Edmund, earl of Cork, K.P.1835, I. 100
Boyle, George, Kt.1624, II. 186

Boyle, George, 4th earl of Glasgow, G.C.H.1830, I. 450
Boyle, Henry, earl of Shannon, K.P. 1808, I. 98
Boyle, Lewis, viscount Kinalmeakie, Kt. 1628, II. 194
Boyle, Richard, Kt.1603, II. 127
Boyle, Richard, viscount of Dungarvan, Kt.1624, II. 186
Boyle, Richard, earl of Burlington, K.G. 1730, I. 43
Boyle, Richard, earl of Shannon, K.P. 1783, I. 96
Boyle, Richard E. St. L., earl of Cork and earl of Orrery, K.P.1860, I. 102
Boyle, Roger, lord Boyle, Kt.1628, II. 194
Boynton. See Baynton
Boynton, Francis, Kt.1603, II. 101
Boynton, Henry, Kt.1497, II. 31
Boynton, John, Kt.1678, II. 253
Boynton, Matthew, Kt.1618, II. 168
Boynton, Thomas, Kt.1578, II. 78
Boys, Edward, Kt.1604, II. 132
Boys, John (Edward), Kt.1604, II. 130
Boys, John, Kt.1644, II. 218
Boys, William, Kt.1717, II. 281
Boyville, John de, K.B.1306, I. 118
Boyville, Thomas de, K.B.1306, I. 115
Brabant, Edward Y., K.C.B.1900, I. 273
Brabazon, Anthony, Kt.1626, II. 190
Brabazon, Edward, Kt.1595, II. 91
Brabazon, Edward, Kt.1626, II. 190
Brabazon, John C., earl of Meath, K.P. 1821, I. 99
Brabazon, William, K.B.1306, I. 115
Brabazon, William, Kt.1546, II. 58
Brabazon, William, Kt.1603, II. 129
Brace, Edward, K.C.B.1834, I. 233
Bracken (Bracking), John, Kt.1629, II. 195
Brackenbury, Edward, Kt.1836, II. 338
Brackenbury, Henry, K.C.B.1894, I. 265; K.C.S.I.1896, I. 325; G.C.B.1900, I. 203
Brakenbury, John M., Kt.1845, II. 346
Brackenbury, M., K.H.1836, I. 475
Brackenbury, Robert, Kt.1485, II. 22
Brackley, lord. See Egerton, J.
Bradburne. See Braidburie

Braddon, Edward N. C., K.C.M.G.1891, I. 376
Bradeston, Thomas de, K.B.1330, I. 125
Bradford, Edward R. C., K.C.S.I.1885, I. 323; K.C.B.1890, I. 291; G.C.B. 1897, I. 215; G.C.V.O.1902, I. 420
Bradford, Henry H., K.C.B.1815, I. 224
Bradford, John F., K.C.B.1871, I. 252
Bradford, Thomas, K.C.B.1815, I. 221; G.C.H.1831, I. 451; G.C.B.1838, I. 188
BRADSHAW, BRADSHAIGH
Bradshaw, Cornwall, Kt.1682, II. 258
Bradshaw, George P., K.H.1837, I. 476
Bradshaw, James, Kt.1673, II. 248
Bradshaigh, Roger, Kt.1660, II. 228
Bradshaw, Roger, Kt.1679, II. 253
Brady, Antonio, Kt.1870, II. 362
Brady, Francis, Kt.1860, II. 354
Brady, Nicholas W., Kt.1821, II. 323
Brady, Thomas F., Kt.1886, II. 380
Braham (Bream, Breym), Richard, Kt. 1645, II. 219
Brahams, Arnold, Kt.1660, II. 226
Braiboef, Hugh, K.B.1306, I. 114
Braidburie (Bradbourne), Humfry (Thomas), Kt.1544, II. 56
Braila, Pietro A., K.C.M.G.1855, I. 353; G.C.M.G.1864, I. 335
BRAITHWAITE, BRATHWAITE, BRAYTHWAITE
Braithwaite, Strafford, Kt.1672, II. 247
Braythwaite, Thomas, Kt.1616, II. 158
Brakenbury. See Brackenbury
Brampton, —, Kt.1500, II. 32
BRAMSTON, BRAMPSTON
Bramston, Francis, Kt.1678, II. 253
Brampston, John, K.B.1661, I. 166
Bramston, John, Kt.1634, II. 203
Bramston, John, K.C.M.G.1897, I. 381; G.C.M.G.1900, I. 346
Bramston (Brampston), Mundeford, Kt.1661, II. 234
Bramwell, Frederick J., Kt.1881, II. 372
Bramwell, George W. W., Kt.1856, II. 351
Branch, Alexander B., K.H.1836, I. 475
Branche, John, Kt.1581, II. 81

Brancker (Branker), Thomas, Kt.1831, II. 330
BRAND, BRENT
Brand, Christoffel J., Kt.1860, II. 355
Brand, Henry B. W., viscount Hampden, G.C.B.1881, I. 211
Brand, Henry R., viscount Hampden, G.C.M.G.1899, I. 346
Brand (Brent), John, Kt.1553, II. 66
Brand, John, Kt.1617, II. 163
Brand, John H., G.C.M.G.1882, I. 339
Brand, Joseph, Kt.1679, II. 253
Brand, Mathew, Kt.1622, II. 178
Brent, Nathaniel, Kt.1629, II. 196
Brente, Robert, K.B.1327, I. 124
Brand, Thomas, Kt.1718, II. 281
Brent, Timothy, K.H.1828, I. 465
Brandenburg, Frederick W., Margrave of, K.G.1654, I. 35
Brandenburg-Anspach, Charles W. F., margrave of, K.G.1749, I. 44
Brandis, Dietrich, K.C.I.E.1887, I. 399
BRANDLYN, BRANLYN, BRANDLING
Brandlyn (Brandling), Francis, Kt. 1617, II. 164
Branlyn, Robert, Kt.1547, II. 62
Brandon, Charles, Kt.1512, II. 35
Brandon, Charles, duke of Suffolk, K.G. 1513, I. 20
Brandon, Charles, Kt.1545, II. 56
Brandon, Charles, duke of Suffolk, K.B.1547, I. 150
Brandon, Henry, duke of Suffolk, K.B. 1547, I. 150
Brandon, Robert, Kt.1487, II. 25
Brandon, Robert, Kt.1513, I. 36
Brandon, Thomas, Kt.1497, II. 29
Brandon, Thomas, K.G.1507, I. 19
Brandon, William, Kt.1471, II. 15
Brandon, William, Kt.1485, II. 22
Brandreth, Thomas, K.C.B.1887, I. 261
Branham. See Barnham
Branscomb, James, Kt.1807, II. 308
Brase. See Brewse
Brassey, Thomas, lord Brassey, K.C.B. 1881, I. 287
Brathwaite. See Braithwaite
Brattle, John, Kt.1682, II. 257
Brawn. See Brown

INDEX

Bray, Charles (Giles), Kt.1607, II. 144
Bray, Edmond, Kt.1513, II. 41
Bray, Edmund (Edward), Kt.1646, II. 221
Bray, Edward, Kt.1560, II. 71
Bray, John, lord Bray, Kt.1544, II. 56
Bray, John C., K.C.M.G.1890, I. 375
Bray, Reginald, K.B.(1485), I. 142; Kt.1497, II. 28; K.G.1501, I. 19
Bray, Reginald M., Kt.1904, II. 419
Braye, Richard, Kt.1553, II. 68
Braythwaite. See Braithwaite
Brazier (afterwards Arundel), John, Kt. 1800, II. 305
Brazil, Pedro II. of, K.G.1871, I. 65
Breadalbane, earl and marquess of. See Campbell
Bream. See Braham
Bredon, Robert E., K.C.M.G.1904, I. 395
Breedon, Robert, Kt.1714, II. 279
Bremer, James J. G., K.C.H.1836, I. 461; Kt.1836, II. 337; K.C.B.1841, I. 237
Brenchesley, William, K.B.1400, I. 128
Brent. See Brand
Brenton, Jahleel, K.C.B.1815, I. 222; Kt.1822, II. 323
BREOUSA, BREHUS, BREUS, BRUSE, BRASE, BRUCE, BREWSE
Breousa, Giles de, K.B.1306, I. 112
Bruse (Brewse), John, Kt.1553, II. 68
Brewse (Bruse, Brase), John, Kt.1618, II. 170
Brewese, Peter de, Kt.1346, II. 6
Breousa, Richard de, K.B.1306, I. 116
Breus, Robert de, K.B.1327, I. 124
Brewce, or Bruce, Thomas, K.B. (1465), I. 134
BRERETON, BREERTON, BRUERTON, BRERTON
Breerton, —, Kt.1492, II. 28
Bruerton, Andrew, Kt.1497, II. 31
Brereton, Andrew (Randolph), Kt. 1533, II. 49
Breerton, George (Roger), Kt.1544, II. 55
Bruerton (Brereton), John, Kt.1497, II. 30
Brereton, John, Kt.1624, II. 184

BRERETON
Bruerton, Randolph, Kt.1497, II. 31
Brereton, Randolf, Kt.1513, I. 36
Breerton, Rauf, Kt.1577, II. 78
Breereton, Richard, Kt.1523, II. 43
Brereton, Thomas, Kt.1611, II. 150
Breerton, Evrynge (Uryan), Kt.1544, II. 55
Brereton, Uryan, Kt.1547, II. 60
Brerton, William, Kt.1513, II. 39
Breerton, William, Kt.1544, II. 54
Brereton, William, Kt.1588, II. 86
Brereton, William, K.H.1837, I. 477; K.C.B.1861, I. 247
Brerewood, Robert, Kt.1643, II. 217
Breteuil, marquis Henry C. J. de, K.C.V.O.1904, I. 443
BRETT, BRET
Brett, Alexander, Kt.1603, II. 110
Brett, Alexander, Kt.1624, II. 187
Brett, Edward R., Kt.1644, II. 218
Bret, Gerard de la, K.B.1327, I. 124
Brett, Percy, Kt.1753, II. 288
Brett, Reginald B., viscount Esher, K.C.V.O.(1901), I. 433; K.C.B.1902, I. 299
Brett, Robert, Kt.1603, II. 102, 131
Brett, Wilfred, K.C.M.G.1864, I. 354
Brett, William B., Kt.1868, II. 359
BRETTON, BRETON, BRITTON
Britton, Henry, Kt.1617, II. 161
Breton, Peter, K.B.1327, I. 124
Breton, Thomas le, Kt.1825, II. 325
Breton, Thomas le, Kt.1847, II. 347
Bretton, William, Kt.1761, II. 290
Brewesa. See Breousa
Brewster, David, K.H.1831, I. 466; Kt. 1832, II. 332
Brewster, Francis, Kt.1670, II. 244
Briane, Guy de, Kt.1346, II. 6
Brice. See Bryce
Brickwood, John, Kt.1904, II. 417
Bridge, Cyprian A. G., K.C.B.1899, I. 271; G.C.B.1903, I. 204
Bridge, Frederick, Kt.1897, II. 400
Bridge, John, Kt.1890, II. 386
Bridge. See Bridger
Bridgeman, Francis, Kt.1673, II. 248
Bridgeman, James, Kt.1646, II. 220
Bridgeman, John, Kt.1623, II. 183

INDEX 31

Bridgeman, Orlando, Kt.1643, II. 216
Bridger (Bridge), John, Kt.1761, II. 290
Bridgewater, earl of. See Egerton
Bridgford, Robert, K.C.B.1902, I. 299
Bridport, viscount. See Hood
Brierly, Oswald W., Kt.1885, II. 378
Briggs, James, K.H.1837, I. 477
Briggs, John F., K.H.1837, I. 479
Briggs, John H., Kt.1870, II. 362
Briggs, John T., Kt.1851, II. 348
Briggs, Thomas, G.C.M.G.1833, I. 333
Bright, Charles T., Kt.1858, I. 353
Bright, Robert O., K.C.B.1881, I. 257; G.C.B.1894, I. 200
Brikenel. See Brudenel
Brind, James, K.C.B.1869, I. 252; G.C.B.1884, I. 198
Brisbane, Charles, Kt.1807, II. 308; K.C.B.1815, I. 222
Brisbane, James, Kt.1816, II. 318
Brisbane (afterwards Makdougall-Brisbane), Thomas, K.C.B.1815, I. 220; G.C.H.1831, I. 451; G.C.B. 1837, I. 187
Briscoe. See Bristow
Brise, Evelyn J. R., K.C.B.1902, I. 300
Brise, Samuel B. R., K.C.B.1897, I. 296
Bristol, earl of. See Digby
BRISTOW, BRISCOE, BRISTOWE
Brisco, John, Kt.1683, II. 259
Bristow, James, Kt.1787, II. 300
Bristowe, Henry F., Kt.1887, II. 382
Bristow, James, Kt.1787, II. 300
Brito Capello, Guilherme, K.C.V.O.1902, I. 440
Brito Capello, Hermengilde de, K.C.V.O. 1903, I. 440; G.C.V.O.1904, I. 431
Britton. See Bretton
Broadbent, William H., K.C.V.O.(1901), I. 434
Brocas (Brockhurst), Pecksall, Kt.1603, II. 107
Brocas, Richard, Kt.1729, II. 284
Brock, Isaac, K.B.1812, I. 178
Brock, Saumarez, K.H.1836, I. 473
BROCKETT, BROCKET
Brokett, John, Kt.1547, II. 60
Brocket, John, Kt.1577, II. 78
Brockett, John, Kt.1599, II. 97
Brockhurst. See Brocas
Brockman, William, Kt.1633, II. 200
BRODRICK, BRODERICK, BRODERY, BORDERY
Broderick, Allen, Kt.1660, II. 230
Brodrick, St. John, Kt.1661, II. 233
Broderick (Bordery, Brodery), Thomas, Kt.1625, II. 189
Brodnax (Broadnix), William, Kt.1664, II. 240
Brograve. See Blagrave
Broke. See Brooke
Bromfield, Edward, Kt.1637, II. 205
Bromfield, Laurence, Kt.1660, II. 226
Bromley, Edward, Kt.1604, II. 134
Bromley, Edward, Kt.1610, II. 149
Bromley, George, Kt.1580, II. 80
Bromley, Henry, Kt.1592, II. 89
Bromley, Richard M., K.C.B.1858, I. 280
Bromley, Thomas, Kt.1545, II. 58
Bromley, Thomas, Kt.1579, II. 79
Bromley, Thomas, Kt.1603, II. 126
Bromley, William, K.B.1661, I. 165
Brompton, Thomas de, K.B.1306, I. 119
Bromsell (Bromsall), Thomas, Kt.1704, II. 274
Broome, Frederick N., K.C.M.G.1884, I. 367
BROOKE, BROOKS, BROOK, BROKE, BROOKES
Brooke, Arthur, K.C.B.1833, I. 232
Brook, Basil, Kt.1603, II. 103, 132
Brooke, Basil, Kt.1617, II. 160
Brooke, Calistenes, Kt.1597, II. 94
Broke, Charles, K.C.B.1815, I. 225
Brooke, Charles J., G.C.M.G.1888, I. 341
Broke, David, Kt.1553, II. 67
Brooke, lord and earl. See Greville
Brooke, Edward, Kt.1599, II. 98
Brooke, George, lord Cobham, K.G. 1549, I. 24
Brooke, George, K.C.B.1867, I. 251
Brooke, alias Cobham, Henry, Kt.1575, II. 76
Brooke, Henry, lord Cobham, Kt.1598, II. 95; K.G.1599, I. 29
Brooke (Brookes), Henry, Kt.1664, II. 239
Brooke, James, K.C.B.1848, I. 277

BROOKE

Brooke, John, 7th lord Cobham, Kt. 1471, II. 14
Brooks, John Cotterell, Kt.1761, II. 291
Brook, Peter, Kt.1660, II. 230
Broke, Philip B. V., K.C.B.1815, I. 222
Brook, Richard, Kt.1621, II. 176
Broke, Robert, Kt.1555, II. 69
Brooke, Robert, Kt.1599, II. 97
Brooke, Robert, Kt.1609, II. 147
Brooke, Robert, Kt.1615, II. 157
Brooke, Robert, Kt.1660, II. 228
Brooke, Thomas, K.B.(1483), I. 140
Brooke, Thomas, lord Cobham, Kt. 1513, II. 38
Brooke, Thomas, Kt.1606, II. 139
Brook (Brookes), Thomas, Kt.1613, II. 153
Brooke, William, K.B.1626, I. 162
Brooke, William (Edward), Kt.1591, II. 89
Brooke, William, lord Cobham, K.G. 1584, I. 27
Brooke, William R., K.C.I.E.1895, I. 408
Brooke-Hitching, Thomas H., Kt.1902, II. 413
Brotherton, Thomas W., K.C.B.1855, I. 241; G.C.B.1861, I. 193
Broughton, Brian, Kt.1660, II. 228
Broughton, Edward, Kt.1618, II. 167
Broughton, lord. See Hobhouse.
Broughton, Robert, K.B.1478, I. 138
Broughton, Robert, Kt.1487, II. 25
Broughton, Robert [Edward], Kt.1497, II. 29
Broughton, Thomas, Kt.1482, II. 18

BROUNKER, BROUNCKER, BRUNKARD, BRINKERD

Brounker, Henry, Kt.1597, II. 94
Brinkerd (Brunkard), William, Kt. 1592, II. 89
Brouncker, William, Kt.1615, II. 157

BROWN, BROWNE, BRAWN

Browne, Anthony, Kt.1487, II. 25
Browne, Anthony, Kt.1523, II. 44
Browne, Anthony, K.G.1540, I. 23
Browne, Anthony, K.B.1547, I. 151

BROWNE

Browne, Anthony, viscount Montagu, K.G.1555, I. 25
Browne, Anthony, Kt.1567, II. 72
Browne, Anthony, Kt.1624, II. 187
Browne, Anthony, Kt.1603, II. 119, 129
Browne, Benjamin C., Kt.1887, II. 381
Brown, Charles, Kt.1818, II. 320
Brown, Charles G., K.C.M.G.1897, I. 382
Browne, Christopher, Kt.1566, II. 72
Browne, Dominick, Kt.1635, II. 203
Browne, Francis, Kt.1619, II. 173
Browne, George, Kt.1471, II. 15
Browne, George, Kt.1591, II. 88
Browne, George, Kt.1660, II. 229
Browne, George, K.B.1661, I. 165
Browne, George, Kt.1683, II. 259
Brown, George, K.H.1831, I. 465; K.C.B.1852, I. 239; G.C.B.1855, I. 191
Brown, George, K.C.M.G.1879, I. 361
Browne, George S., K.C.B.1815, I. 227
Brown, George T., Kt.1898, II. 402
Browne, Howe P., marquess of Sligo, K.P.1810, I. 98
Brawn, Hugh, Kt.1603, II. 125
Browne, Humfrey, Kt.1538, II. 51
Browne, James, K.C.S.I.1888, I. 324
Browne, James F. M., K.C.B.1894, I. 265
Browne, James. See Crichton-Brown
Brown, John, K.B.(1483), I. 139, 141
Browne, John, Kt.1486, II. 23
Browne, John, Kt.1549, II. 65
Brown, John, Kt.1603, II. 116
Brown, John, Kt.1608, II. 145
Browne, John, Kt.1630, II. 197
Browne, John, Kt.1664, II. 239
Browne, John, Kt.1814, II. 313
Brown, John, K.C.H.1831, I. 456
Brown, John, Kt.1867, II. 359
Brown, John C., K.C.B.1875, I. 255
Browne, John D., earl of Altamont, K.P. 1800, I. 97
Browne, Matthew, K.B.(1489), I. 143
Browne, Mathew, Kt.1596, II. 93
Brown, Nicholas, Kt.1604, II. 129
Brown, Peter, Kt.1644, II. 218
Brown, Richard, Kt.1603, II. 127

INDEX

BROWN
Brown (Brawn), Richard, Kt.1619, II. 173
Brown, Richard, sen. and jun., Kt. 1660, II. 227
Brown, Robert, Kt.1603, II. 125
Brown, Robert, Kt.1616, II. 160
Brown, Robert, H., K.C.M.G.1902, I. 393
Browne, Samuel, Kt.1660, II. 232
Brown, Samuel, Kt.1838, II. 340
Browne, Samuel J., K.C.S.I.1876, I. 320; K.C.B.1879, I. 256; G.C.B. 1891, I. 200
Brown Samuel W., K.H.1835, I. 472
Browne, Thomas, Kt.1576, II. 77
Browne, Thomas, Kt.1603, II. 113
Browne, Thomas, Kt.1607, II. 143
Browne, Thomas, Kt.1671, II. 246
Brown, Thomas, K.C.B.1823, I. 229
Browne Thomas, K.C.H.1832, I. 459; Kt.1832, II. 333
Brown, Thomas, Kt.1903, II. 415
Browne, Thomas G., K.C.M.G.1869, I. 354
Browne, Thomas H., K.H.1818, I. 463; K.C.H.1821, I. 455; Kt.1826, II. 326
Browne, Valentyne, Kt.1570, II. 74
Brown, Valentine, Kt.1603, II. 102, 116
Browne, Valentine A., earl of Kenmare, K.P.1872, I. 104
Browne, Walter, Kt.1546, II. 58
Browne, Weston (Wystan), Kt.1511, II. 35
Brown, Weston, Kt.1603, II. 126
Browne, William, Kt.1492, II. 28
Browne, William, K.B.1603, I. 156
Brown, William, Kt.1604, II. 129
Brown, William, Kt. 1623, II. 182
Browne, William, Kt.1747, II. 288
Brown, William, Kt.1870, II. 362
Brown, William R., Kt.1893, II. 392
Brownless, Anthony C., K.C.M.G.1893, I. 378
Brownlow, Charles, baron Lurgan, K.P. 1864, I. 102
Brownlow, Charles H., K.C.B.1872, I. 253; G.C.B.1887, I. 199
Brownlow, earl. See Cust

Brownlow, John, 1st viscount Tyrconnell, K.B.1725, I. 168
Brownlow, William, Kt.1622, II. 180
Brownlow, William, lord Lurgan, K.C.V.O.(1903), I. 436
Brownrigg, Henry J., Kt.1858, II. 353
Brownrigg, Robert, G.C.B.1815, I. 182
BRUCE, BRUSE, and see Breousa
Bruce, Alexander C., Kt.1903, II. 415
Bruce, Alexander H., lord Balfour of Burghley, K.T.1901, I. 89
Bruce, Charles, K.C.B.1831, I. 231
Bruce, Charles, K.C.M.G.1889, I. 374; G.C.M.G.1901, I. 348
Bruce, Edward, lord Kinlosse, K.B. 1610, I. 158
Bruce, Frederick W. A., K.C.B.1862, I. 282; G.C.B.1865, I. 209
Bruce, Gainsford, Kt.1892, II. 390
Bruce, George B., Kt.1888, II. 384
Bruce, Henry A., lord Aberdare, G.C.B.1885, I. 211
Bruce, Henry Le G., K.C.B.1897, I. 267
Bruce, Henry W., K.C.B.1861, I. 247
Bruce, James, earl of Elgin, K.T.1847, I. 83; G.C.B.1858, I. 208; K.S.I. 1862; I. 307; Grand Master, Star of India, I. 305
Bruce, James A. T., K.C.M.G.1900, I. 388
Bruce, James L. K., Kt.1842, II. 344
Bruce, Robert, Kt.1594, II. 91
Bruce, Robert, earl of Elgin, Kt.1638, I. 163
Bruce, Thomas, earl of Elgin, Kt. 1638, II. 205
Bruce, Thomas C., Kt.1880, II. 371
Bruce, Victor A., earl of Elgin, G.C.I.E.1894, I. 402; G.C.S.I.1894, I. 313; Grand Master, Star of India, G.C.S.I., I. 305; K.G.1899, I. 70
Bruce, William, K.H.1837, I. 477

BRUDENEL, BRUDENELL, BRUDENALL, BRIKENELL, BRYKENELL
Brudenell, Edmond, Kt.1565, II. 72
Brudenell, James T., earl of Cardigan, K.C.B.1855, I. 240

34   INDEX

BRUDENEL
  Brikenell, John, Kt.1485, II. 23
  Brykenell (Brudenall), Thomas, K.B. 1547, I. 151
  Brudenell, Thomas, Kt.1612, II. 151
  Brudenell-Bruce, Charles, marquess of Ailesbury, K.T.1819, I. 81
  Brudenell-Bruce, George W. F., marquess of Ailesbury, K.G.1864, I. 62
  Brudenell-Bruce, Thomas B., earl of Ailesbury, K.T.1786, I. 80
Bruen, John, Kt.1619, II. 174
Bruerton. See Brereton
Bruges. See Brydges
Bruguing (Bruyeninck, Brunning), Albertus, Kt.1621, II. 176
Brunlees, James, Kt.1886, II. 379
Brunel, Isambert M., Kt.1841, II. 343
Brunswick, William, duke of, K.G.1450, I. 12
Brunswick-Bevern, Ferdinand, prince of, K.G.1759, I. 45
Brunswick-Wolffenbüttel, Augustus, etc., duke of, K.G.1831, I. 54
Brunswick-Wolffenbüttel, Charles W. F., duke of, K.G.1765, I. 46
Brunswick-Wolffenbüttel, Christian, duke of, K.G.1624, I. 31
Brunton, Thomas L., Kt.1900, II. 406
Brusati, Ugo, G.C.V.O.1903, I. 426
Bruse. See Breousa
Bryan, Barnaby, Kt.1615, II. 156
Bryan, Francis, Kt.1523, II. 44
Bryan, Francys, Kt.1547, II. 61
Bryan, Guy, lord Bryan, K.G.1369, I. 4
Bryan, Thomas, K.B.(1475), I. 136
Bryan, Thomas, Kt.1497, II. 30
Bryant, Jeremiah, Kt.1829, II. 328
BRYCE, BRICE, BRYSE
  Bryce, Alexander, Kt.1816, II. 318; K.H.1819, I. 463; K.C.H.1830, I. 456
  Brice (Bryse), Hugh, K.B.(1485), I. 142
BRYDGES, BRIDGES, BRUGES, A BRUGES, BRUGYS
  Bruges, Charles a, Kt.1497, II. 29
  Bruges, Edmond (Edward), Kt.1547, II. 61

BRYDGES
  Brydges, Edmund, lord Chandos, K.G.1572, I. 27
  Bridges (Bruges), Giles, Kt.1616, II. 159
  Brydges, Grey, lord Chandos, K.B. 1605, I. 156
  Bridges (Brydges), Henry, Kt.1814, II. 313
  Brydges, Henry, duke of Chandos, K.B.1732, I. 168
  Bruges, John, Kt.1513, II. 40
  Bridges, John, Kt.1663, II. 239
  Brydges, John W. H., Kt.1822, II. 323
  Bridges, Matthew, Kt.1688, II. 264
  Bruges (Brugys), Richard, Kt.1553, II. 68
  Bridges, Thomas, Kt.1603, II. 115
  Bridges, Thomas, Kt.1641, II. 210
  Bridges, Thomas, K.B.1661, I. 165
  Bridges (Bergyll), Thomas (John), Kt.1482, II. 18
  Bridges, William, Kt.1592, II. 89
  Bridges, William, Kt.1645, II. 219
Bryers, William, Kt.1627, II. 192
Bryson, Alexander, K.C.B.1865, I. 283
Buccleuch, duke of. See Scott; see Montagu-Scott; see Montagu-Douglas-Scott
Buchan, earl of. See Erskine
Buchan, John, Kt.1816, II. 318; K.C.B. 1831, I. 231
Buchanan, Andrew, K.C.B.1860, I. 281; G.C.B.1866, I. 209
Buchanan, Ebenezer J., Kt.1901, II. 409
Buchanan, Francis J., Kt.1776, II. 295
Buchanan, George, Kt.1892, II. 389
Buchanan (Buckhannon), James, Kt.1619, II. 173
Büchsel, William G. C., G.C.V.O., 1904, I. 430
BUCK, BUCKE
  Buck, Edward C., Kt.1886, II. 379; K.C.S.I., 1897, I. 326
  Buck, George, Kt.1603, II. 119
  Bucke, John, Kt.1596, II. 93
  Buck, John, Kt.1603, II. 119
  Buck, John, Kt.1617, II. 161
  Buck, Peter, Kt.1604, II. 134

INDEX

Buckhurst, lord. See Sackville
Buckingham, duke of. See Stafford; see Villiers; see Sheffield; see Temple-Nugent-Brydges-Chandos-Grenville
Buckinghamshire, earl of. See Hobart
Buckingham, marquess of. See Nugent-Temple-Granville
Buckingham (Bokenham), Henry, Kt. 1603, II. 124
Buckingham, Owen, Kt.1695, II. 268
Buckle, Christopher, Kt.1617, II. 167
Buckle, Christopher, Kt.1681, II. 256
Buckle, Claude H. M., K.C.B.1875, I. 255
BUCKLEY, BULKELEY, BUNCKLY, BULCKLEY, BANCKLEY
Bulkeley, Dewey, Kt.1696, II. 269
Buckley, Henry B., Kt.1900, II. 406
Buckley (Bunckle, Bunckly), George, Kt.1645, II. 219
Buckley (Bunkley, Bulckley, Banckley), John, Kt.1605, II. 138
Bulkeley, John, Kt.1795, II. 303
Buckley, Patrick A., K.C.M.G.1892, I. 377
Buckley, Richard, Kt.1547, II. 63
Bulkeley (Barkley), Richard, Kt.1577, II. 78
Bulkleigh (Buckley), Richard, Kt. 1604, II. 135
Buckmore, —, Kt.1603, II. 127
BUCKNALL, BUCKNELL, BUCKNILL
Bucknell (Bucknall), John, Kt.1686, II. 261
Bucknill, John C., Kt.1894, II. 393
Bucknill, Thomas T., Kt.1899, II. 404
Bucknell, William, Kt. 1670, II. 244
Bucknall-Estcourt, James B., K.C.B. 1855, footnote, I. 241
Buckworth, John, Kt.1681, II. 256
Buckworth, John, Kt.1693, II. 268
Bugg (Bugges), Anthony, Kt.1618, II. 169
Bugges, Thomas, Kt.1603, II. 127
Buggin, George, Kt.1797, II. 304
Bulgari, count S. V., K.C.M.G.1833, I. 352; G.C.M.G.1833, I. 333
Bulgaria, Alexander Joseph of, G.C.B. 1886, I. 199
Bulgaria, Ferdinand, etc., of, G.C.V.O. 1904, I. 430

Bulkeley. See Buckley
Bull, John, Kt.1717, II. 281
Bull, Robert, K.H.1833, I. 468
Bullard, Harry, Kt.1887, II. 382
Bullen, Charles, K.C.H.1835, I. 460; Kt.1835, II. 335; K.C.B.1839, I. 236; G.C.B.1852, I. 190
Buller, Alexander, K.C.B.1896, I. 266; G.C.B.1902, I. 203
Buller, Anthony, Kt.1816, II. 317
Buller, Arthur W., Kt.1848, II. 347
Buller, George, K.C.B.1855, I. 240; G.C.B.1869, I. 195
Buller, Redvers H., K.C.M.G.1882, I. 365; K.C.B.1885, I. 259; G.C.B.1894, I. 201; G.C.M.G.1901, I. 347
Buller (Ballary), Richard, Kt.1608, II. 145
Buller, Walter L., K.C.M.G.1886, I. 370
Bullock, Edward, Kt.1609, II. 148
Bullough, George, Kt.1901, II. 409
BULMER, BULLMER, BOWMER, BOULMER
Bulmer, Bertram, Kt.1603, II. 100
Bulmer, Fenwick, Kt.1821, II. 322
Bulmer, John, Kt.1513, II. 38
Bulmer, Rauf, Kt.1482, II. 20
Boulmer, Rafe, Kt.1523, II. 44
Bullmer, Rafe, Kt.1544, II. 54
Bulmer, William, Kt.1497, II. 31
Bowmer, William, Kt.1523, II. 44
Bülow, count Bernard von, G.C.V.O. 1899, I. 423
Bulrampoor, Dig Bijye Singh of, K.C.S.I.1866, I. 316
Bulstrode, Richard, Kt.1676, II. 251
Bulwer, Edward G., K.C.B.1886, I. 260
Bulwer, Henry E. G., K.C.M.G.1874, I. 357; G.C.M.G.1883, I. 339
Bulwer, William H. L. E., lord Dalling and Bulwer, K.C.B.1848, I. 277; G.C.B.1851, I. 208
Bulwer-Lytton, Edward G. E. L., lord Lytton, G.C.M.G.1869, I. 336
Bulwer-Lytton, Edward R. L., earl of Lytton, G.C.S.I.1876, I. 310; Grand Master, Star of India, I. 305
Bulzo, Dionizio, K.C.M.G.1818, I. 350
Bunbury, Henry, Kt.1603, II. 124
Bunbury, Henry E., K.C.B.1815, I. 222

INDEX

Bunbury, Thomas, K.H.1835, I. 471
Bunce, James, Kt.1660, II. 225
Bunckly. See Buckley
Bundey, William H., Kt.1904, II. 420
Bundi, Raja Ram Singh of, G.C.S.I. 1877, I. 311
Bundi, Raja Ranghubir Singh of, K.C.I.E.1894, I. 408; K.C.S.I.1897, I. 326; G.C.I.E.1901, I. 403
Burchinshaw (Birkenshawe), Ralph, Kt. 1618, II. 168
Burdett, Henry C., K.C.B.1897, I. 296
Burdett, John, Kt.1512, II. 35
Burdon, Thomas, Kt.1817, II. 319
Burford, baron of. See Cornwall
Burford, earl of. See Beauclerk
Burford-Hancock, Henry J. B., Kt.1882, II. 374
Burgate, Peter de, K.B.1306, I. 119
Burgh. See Bourke
Burgchier. See Bourchier
Burghersh, Bartholomew, lord Burghersh, K.G.1348, I. 1
Burghersh, lord. See Fane
Burghersh, Stephan de, K.B.1306, I. 112
Burghley, lord. See Cecil
Burgman, George, Kt.1813, II. 313
BURGOYNE, BURGOYN
  Burgoyne, John J., Kt.1810, II. 310
  Burgoyne, John F., K.C.B.1838, I. 235
  Burgoyne, John F., K.C.B.1838, I. 235; G.C.B.1852, I. 190
  Burgoyn, Roger, Kt.1641, II. 210
BURGUNDY
  Charles the Bold of, K.G.1468 I. 15
  Philip II. of, K.G.1422, I. 10
Burke. See Bourke
Burkitt, William R., Kt.1904, II. 418
BURLACY, BURLACIE, BORLACE
  Burlacy, John, Kt.1606, II. 140
  Borlace, John, Kt.1641, II. 211
  Burlacy, William, Kt.1603, II. 111
  Burlacie, William, Kt.1617, II. 166
Burland, John, Kt.1774, II. 294
Burley, John, K.G.1377, I. 5
Burley, Simon, K.G.1381, I. 5
Burlington, earl of. See Boyle
Burlton, George, K.C.B.1815, I. 221
Burnaby. See Barnby

Burnand, Francis C., Kt.1902, II. 411
Burne, Owen T., K.C.S.I.1879, I. 322; G.C.I.E.1897, I. 402
Burnell, Edward, Kt.1617, II. 164
Burnell, Hugh, lord Burnell, K.G.1406, I. 8
Burnell, Robert, Kt.(1450), II. lx.
Burnes, Alexander, Kt.1838, II. 341
BURNETT, BURNET
  Burnett, Robert, Kt.1795, II. 302
  Burnet, Thomas, Kt.1745, II. 287
  Burnett, William, K.C.H.1831, I. 457; Kt.1831, II. 330; K.C.B.1850, I. 239
Burns, James, K.H.1837, I. 479
Burney, William, K.H.1837, I. 477
Burnside, Bruce L., Kt.1884, II. 376
Burrell, John, Kt.1642, II. 213
Burrell, Peter, Kt.1781, II. 296
BURROW, BURROWS, BURROWES, BURROUGH, BURROUGHES, BOUROUGH, BOROUGH, BORRUGH, BORROWES, BORROUGH, BOROUGHS, also see Bourke
  Burroughes, James, Kt.1759, II. 289
  Burrow, James, Kt.1773, II. 294
  Burrough, James, Kt.1816, II. 317
  Borrugh (Borrowes), John, Kt.1586, II. 85
  Borrough (Boroughs), John, Kt.1624, II. 185
  Burrows, John C., Kt.1873, II. 365
  Burrowes, Robert E., K.H.1836, I. 474
  Borough, Thomas, Kt.1538, II. 51
  Bourough (Borough), Thomas, Kt. 1513, II. 38
Burslem, Nathaniel, K.H.1836, I. 472
Burt, Archibald P., Kt.1873, II. 366
Burt, John M., Kt.1902, II. 413
Burton, baron. See Bass
Burton, Charles, Kt.1750, II. 288
Burton, Fowler, K.C.B.1903, I. 275
Burton, Francis N., K.C.H.1822, I. 455; G.C.H.1824, I. 449
Burton, Frederick W., Kt.1884, II. 376
Burton, George W., Kt.1898, II. 403
Burton, Henry (Thomas), K.B.1603, I. 156
Burton, James R., K.H.1837, I. 475
Burton, John, Kt.1513, II. 42
Burton, John, Kt.1805, II. 308

INDEX

Burton, Richard, Kt.1831, II. 330
Burton, Richard F., K.C.M.G.1886, I. 368
Burton, Robert, Kt.1800, II. 305
Burton, Roger de, K.B.1306, I. 118
Burton, Thomas, Kt.1605, II. 139
Burton, Thomas, Kt.1660, II. 232
Burwell, Jeffry, Kt.1663, II. 237
Bury. See Berry
Busby, John, Kt.1661, II. 235
Bush, William, K.H.1835, I. 471
Bushell, Edward, Kt.1604, II. 136
Busk, Edward H., Kt.1901, II. 408
Busk, Wadsworth, Kt.1781, II. 296
BUSSY, BUSSEY, BUSHEY
Bussy (Bushey), Edward (Edmund), Kt.1603, II. 103
Bussy, Miles, Kt.1504, II. 34; K.B. 1504, I. 147
Bussey (Bushey), Rawlyn, Kt.1618, II. 169
Bustie, Laurence de, Kt.1672, II. 247
Bute, earl of. See Stuart
Bute, marquess of. See Crichton-Stuart
BUTLER, BOTELER, BOTELLER, BOTYLAR, BOTILLER, BUCLER
Butler, Allen, Kt.1646, II. 220
Boteller, Edmund le, Kt.(1330), II. lix.
Butler, Edmund, Kt.1560, II. 70
Butler [Edmund], Kt.1643, II. 216
Butler, Edward, Kt.1603, II. 122
Butler, Edward, Kt.1619, II. 174
Butler, Edward, Kt.1840, II. 342
Butler, Francis, Kt.1642, II. 213
Boteler, Henry, Kt.1577, II. 78
Butler (Botylar), Henry, Kt.1603, II. 104
Butler, Henry, Kt.1616, II. 159
Boteler, James, K.B.1326, I. 123
Butler, James, K.B.(1426), I. 131
Butler, *alias* Ormond, James, earl of Ormond, K.B.(1426), I. 130
Butler, James, earl of Wiltshire, K.G. 1459, I. 13
Butler, James, Kt.1598, II. 95
Butler, James, duke of Ormonde, K.G. 1649, I. 34
Butler, James, Kt.1672, II. 247
Butler, James, duke of Ormonde, K.G.1688, I. 38

BUTLER
Butler, James, duke of Ormonde, K.T., Jacobite, 1716, I. footnote 75
Butler, James, earl of Ormonde and Ossory, K.P.1821, I. 99
Butler, James, K.H.1836, I. 475
Butler, James E. W. T., marquess of Ormonde, K.P.1888, I. 105
Butler (Boteler), John, Kt.1372, II. 10
Butler (Boteler), John, K.B.(1426), I. 131
Butler, John, Kt.1547, II. 59
Butler (Boteler), John, Kt.1607, II. 143
Boteler (Butler), John, Kt.1622, II. 178
Butler, John, K.B.1626, I. 162
Boteler, John, Kt.1677, II. 251
Butler, John, marquess of Ormonde, K.P.1845, I. 101
Butler, Nicholas, Kt.1682, II. 257
Butler (Boteler), Oliver, Kt.1604, II. 135
Butler, Peter, Kt.1555, II. 69
Butler, Philippe, Kt.1529, II. 47
Boteller, Philip, Kt.1583, II. 82
Butler, Phillip, Kt.1586, II. 85
Butler, Philip, K.B.1661, I. 165
Butler, Pierce, Kt.1615, II. 155
Butler, Piers, earl of Newcastle, K.G., Jacobite, 1714, I. footnote 38
Boteler, Ralph, baron Sudeley, K.G. 1440, I. 12
Butler, Richard, Kt.1547, II. 63
Butler, Richard, Kt.1605, II. 137
Butler, Richard, Kt.1627, II. 192
Butler, Robert, Kt.1607, II. 141
Boteler (Butler), Stephen, Kt.1616, II. 158
Butler, Theobald, Kt.1567, II. 73
Butler, Theobald, Kt.1689, II. 265
Butteler, Thomas, K.B.(1483), I. 139
Butler, Thomas, K.B.(1487), I. 142
Butteler, Thomas, Kt.1533, II. 49
Butler, Thomas, Kt.1541, II. 52
Butler, Thomas, 11th earl of Ormond, Kt.(1546), II. lvi.; K.B.1547, I. 150
Butler, Thomas, earl of Ormonde, K.G.1588, I. 28
Butler, Thomas, Kt.1608, II. 146

INDEX

BUTLER
    Butler, Thomas, earl of Ossory, K.G. 1672, I. 36
    Bucler, Walter (William), Kt.1547, II. 60
    Butler, Walter, Kt.1598, II. 94
    Butler, Walter, earl of Ormonde and Ossory, K.P.1798, I. 97
    Butler, William, K.B.1400, I. 128
    Botteller, William, Kt.1471, II. 14
    Butler (Boteler), William, Kt.1515, II. 43
    Butler, William, Kt.1561, II. 71
    Butler, William, Kt.1641, II. 208, 209
    Boteler, William, Kt.1653, II. 223
    Butler, William F., K.C.B.1886, I. 260
Butora, prince of (1816). See Wilding, G.
Butt, Charles P. Kt.1883, II. 375
BUTTES, BUTTS
    Butts, Augustus de, K.C.H.1837, I. 461; Kt.1837, II. 338
    Butts (Bucke), John, Kt.1596, II. 93
    Buttes, William, Kt.1545, II. 58, 62
Button, Ambrose, Kt.1605, II. 138
Button, Thomas, Kt.1616, II. 159
Button (Hutton), William, Kt.1605, II. 138, 141
Buxhull, Alan, K.G.1372, I. 4
Buxton, Thomas Fowell, K.C.M.G.1895, I. 380; G.C.M.G.1899, I. 346
Byam, Ashton W., Kt.1789, II. 301
Byam, William, Kt.1859, II. 354
Byard, Thomas, Kt.1789, II. 300
Byde, Thomas, Kt.1661, II. 233
Byles, John B., Kt.1858, II. 353
BYLISBY, BYLESBY
    Bylisby, Andrew, Kt.1513, II. 41
    Bylesby, Andrew, Kt. after 1529, II. 48
Byng, George, viscount Torrington, Kt. 1704, II. 274; K.B.1725, I. 167
Byng, Henry W. J., earl of Strafford, K.C.V.O.(1897), I. 432
Byng, John, earl of Strafford, K.C.B.1815, I. 220; G.C.H.1826, I. 450; G.C.B. 1831 I. 186
Byngham. See Bingham
Bynne. See Binns
Byrne, Edmund W., Kt.1897, II. 399

Byrd. See Bird
BYRON, BIRON, BERON
    Byron, John, Kt.1347, II. 9
    Beron, John, K.B.(1483), I. 139
    Byron, John, Kt.1486, II. 23
    Byron, John, Kt.1580, II. 80
    Biron, John, Kt.1603, II. 102
    Byron, John, K.B.1626, I. 162
    Byron, Nicholas, Kt.1449, II. 12
    Byron, Nicholas, K.B.(1461), I. 133
    Biron, Nicholas, Kt.1630, II. 197
    Biron, Nicholas, K.B.1501, I. 146
    Byron, Richard, Kt.1642, II. 214
    Byron, Robert, Kt.1644, II. 217
    Biron, Thomas, Kt.1642, II. 214
    Byron, William, Kt.1646, II. 220
Bysshe, Edward, Kt.1661, II. 234
Byster, Martin, Kt.1625, II. 188
Bythell. See Bethell

C

Cade, William, Kt.1617, II. 165
Cadell, Charles, K.H.1837, I. 476
Caddell, Robert, Kt.(1397), II. lx.
Cadell, Robert, K.C.B.1894, I. 265
Cadman, Alfred J., K.C.M.G.1903, I. 394
Cadogan, George, K.C.B.1875, I. 255
Cadogan, George H., earl Cadogan, K.G.1891, I. 69; Grand Master, K.P.1895, I. 95
Cadogan, William, baron Cadogan, K.T. 1716, I. 77
Caerlion (Carlion), Lewys, Kt.1492, II. 27
Cæsar, Charles, Kt.1613, II. 153
Cæsar, Charles, Kt.1671, II. 246
Cæsar, Henry, Kt.1660, II. 229
Cæsar, John, Kt.1617, II. 163
Cæsar, Julius, Kt.1603, II. 109
Caffin, James C., K.C.B.1868, I. 284
Cage, Anthony, Kt.1634, II. 202
Cage, John, Kt.1609, II. 148
Cage, Toby, Kt.1627, II. 192
Cailliard, Vincent H. P., Kt.1896, I. 398
Caird, James, K.C.B.1882, I. 288
Cairncross, Alexander, K.H.1837, I. 476
Cairns, Hugh MacC., Kt.1858, II. 353
Cairnes, John E., K.H.1834, I. 470

INDEX

Cairns, William W., K.C.M.G.1877, I. 358
Calcraft, Henry G., K.C.B.1890, I. 291
Calder, Robert, Kt.1797, II. 304; K.C.B. 1815, I. 217
Calderwood. See Henderson
Caldwell, Alexander, K.C.B.1837, I. 233; G.C.B.1838, I. 188
Caldwell, Benjamin, G.C.B.1820, I. 184
Caldwell, James L., K.C.B.1837, I. 233; G.C.B.1848, I. 190
Caledon, earl of. See Alexander
Caley. See Cayley
Calfield. See Caulfield
Calichiopulo, Altavilla V., K.C.M.G. 1840, I. 352
Calichiopulo, Angiolo, K.C.M.G.1842, I. 352
Calichiopulo, Stamo, G.C.M.G.1818, I.331
Calicut, Mana Vikrama of, K.C.S.I. 1892, I. 325
Callan, viscount. See Feilding
Callcott, Augustus W., Kt.1837, II. 339
Caley, Calley, Cawley. See Cawley
Calmady, Shilston, Kt.1618, II. 170
CALTHORP, CALTHORPE, CALTHROPP
Calthorpe, Charles, Kt.1605, II. 137
Calthorpe, Christopher, K.B.1661, I. 165
Calthorp, Henry, Kt.1636, II. 204
Calthorpe, Henry, K.B.1744, I. 169
Calthropp, James, Kt.1603, II. 121
Calthorp, James, Kt.1656, II. 223
Calthorpe, Lestrange, Kt.1675, II. 250
Calthorpe, Martin, Kt.1588, II. 87
Calthorpe, Philip, K.B.(1483), I. 139
Calthorpe, Philippe, Kt.1497, II. 30
Calthorpe, Philippe, Kt.1547, II. 59
Calthorp, William, K.B.(1465), I. 134
Calton, Francis, Kt.1605, II. 137
CALVELEY, CALVERLEY
Calveley, George, Kt.1533, II. 49
Calveley (Calverley), George, Kt.1571, II. 75
Calvely (Calverley), George, Kt.1617, II. 165
Calverley, Henry, Kt.1675, II. 250
Calvely, Hugh, Kt.1544, II. 55
Calveley, Hugh, Kt.1642, II. 214
Calverley, John, Kt.1617, II. 163

CALVERLEY
Calverley, Richard, Kt.1497, II. 32
Calveley, Richard, Kt.1618, I. 169
Calverley, Walter, Kt.1513, II. 42
Calverley, William, Kt.1497, II. 32
Calverley, William, Kt.1545, II. 57
Calvert, George, Kt.1617, II. 166
Calvert, Harry, G.C.B.1815, I. 183; G.C.H.1817, I. 448
Calvert, William, Kt.1744, II. 286
Cambon, Paul, G.C.V.O.1903, I. 427
Cambray, Charles de, Kt.1605, II. 139
CAMBRIDGE
Adolphus F., duke of, K.G.1786, I. 48; G.C.H.1815, I. 447; G.C.B.1815, I. 182; G.C.M.G. Grand Master, etc., 1825, I. 332; Grand Master and Principal G.C.M.G.1825, I. 331
George W. F. C., duke of, G.C.H.1825, I. 449; K.G.1835, I. 55; G.C.M.G. 1845, I. 334; K.P.1851, I. 101; Grand Master of St. Michael and St. George, 1851, I. 331, 337; G.C.B.1855, I. 191; G.C.S.I.1877, I. 311; K.T.1881, I. 88; G.C.I.E.1887, I. 401; G.C.V.O.1897, I. 417
James, duke of, K.G.1666, I. 36
Cambridge, John de, K.B.1329, I. 125
Camden, earl and marquess. See Pratt
Camerlyn. See Chamberlain
Cameron, Alan, K.C.B.1815, I. 219
Cameron, Alexander, K.C.B.1838, I. 235
Cameron, Charles A., Kt.1885, II. 377
Cameron, Duncan A., K.C.B.1864, I. 248; G.C.B.1873, I. 196
Cameron, Ewen, K.C.M.G.1900, I. 388
Cameron, Hector C., Kt.1900, II. 407
Cameron, John, K.C.B.1815, I. 223
Cameron, Matthew C., Kt.1887, II. 381
Cameron, Roderick W., Kt.1883, II. 375
Cameron, William G., K.H.1834, I. 470
Cameron, William G., K.C.B.1893, I. 264; G.C.B.1904, I. 204
Camou, Jacques, K.C.B.1856, I. 241
Camoys, —, Kt.1380, II. 10
Camoys, Hugh de, lord Camoys, K.B. (1426), I. 131
Camoys, Ralph de, K.B.1306, I. 114
Camoys, Richard, K.B.1399, I. 128

INDEX

Camoys, Thomas de, lord Camoys K.G. 1414, I. 9
Campbell, Alexander, Kt.1812, II. 311
Campbell, Alexander, K.C.B.1817, I. 228
Campbell, Alexander, K.H.1831, I. 466
Campbell, Alexander, K.C.M.G.1879, I. 361
Campbell, Archibald, K.B.1785, I. 173
Campbell, Archibald, Kt.1814, I. 313; K.C.B.1815, I. 224; G.C.B.1826, I. 185
Campbell, Colin, K.C.B.1815, I. 224
Campbell, Colin, lord Clyde, K.C.B.1849, I. 238; G.C.B.1855, I. 191; K.S.I. 1861, I. 306
Campbell, Duncan, Kt.1633, II. lxiii.
Campbell, Duncan, Kt.1714, II. 278
Campbell, Edward A., Kt.1838, II. 341
Campbell, Frederick A., K.C.B.1880, I. 257
Campbell, Gavin, marquess of Breadalbane, K.G.1894, I. 69
Campbell, George, K.C.B.1815, I. 217; G.C.B.1820, I. 185
Campbell, George, Kt.1832, II. 332
Campbell, George, K.C.S.I.1873, I. 319
Campbell, George D., duke of Argyll, K.T.1856, I. 84; K.G.1884, I. 67
Campbell, George W., 6th duke of Argyll, G.C.H.1833, I. 452
Campbell, George W. R., K.C.M.G.1891, I. 376
Campbell, Henry F., K.C.B.1815, I. 218; G.C.H.1818, I. 448
Campbell, Hugh, earl of Londoun, K.T. 1706, I. 76
Campbell, James, Kt.1630, II. 197
Campbell, James, Kt.1724, II. 283
Campbell, James, K.B.1743, I. 169
Campbell, James, Kt.1788, II. 300
Campbell, James, G.C.H.1817, I. 448
Campbell, James, K.C.B.1822, I. 229
Campbell, James, Kt.1831, II. 329; K.C.H.1831, I. 456
Campbell, James, K.H.1836, I. 473
Campbell, James, Kt.1842, II. 344
Campbell, James MacN., K.C.I.E.1897, I. 409
Campbell, John, duke of Argyll, K.T.1704, I. 76; K.G.1710, I. 40
Campbell, John, earl of Breadalbane, K.B.1725, I. 167
Campbell, John, duke of Argyll, K.T.1765, I. 79
Campbell, John, Kt.1815, II. 315
Campbell, John, Kt.1832, II. 333
Campbell, John, K.H.1835, I. 472
Campbell, John, marquess of Breadalbane, K.T.1838, I. 83
Campbell, John, K.C.B.1855, footnote, I. 241
Campbell, John, K.C.S.I.1869, I. 318
Campbell, John, Kt.1871, footnote, II. 363
Campbell, John D. S., duke of Argyll, K.T.1871, I. 86; G.C.M.G.1878, I. 338; G.C.V.O.1901, I. 418
Campbell, John L., Kt.1902, II. 411
Campbell, John N. R., K.C.H.1836, I. 461; Kt.1832, II. 333
Campbell, Neil, Kt.1814, II. 314
Campbell, Patrick, K.C.B.1836, I. 233
Cambell, Thomas, Kt.1603, II. 128
Campbell, William, Kt.1829, II. 328
Campbell-Bannerman, Henry, G.C.B. 1895, I. 214
Camperdown, earl. See Duncan
Campion. See Champion
Campsfield (Cansfield), John, Kt.1644, II. 218
Cammell, John, Kt.1615, II. 156
Candy, Edward T., Kt.1904, II. 417
Candyshe, John, Kt.1542, II. 53
Candyshe, Richard, Kt.1545, II. 57
Cane, Charles Du, K.C.M.G.1875, I. 357
Cane, Edmund F. Du, K.C.B.1877, I. 286
Canford, Edmond, K.B.1426, I. 132
Canhauser, Balthezar, Kt.1487, II. 27

CANNE, CANN
 Canne, Robert, Kt.1662, II. 236
 Cann, Thomas, Kt.1680, II. 254
 Cann, William, Kt.1663, II. 238
Canning, Charles J., viscount Canning, G.C.B.1859, I. 208; K.S.I.1861, I. 306; Grand Master Star of India, I. 305; K.G.1862, I. 61
Canning, Samuel, Kt.1866, II. 358

INDEX   41

Canning, Stratford, viscount Stratford de Redcliffe, G.C.B.1829, I. 206; K.G.1869, I. 64
Cannon, Thomas, Kt.1623, II. 182
Canrobert, François C., G.C.B.1855, I. 191
Cansfield. See Campsfield
Canterbury, archbishop of. See Davidson
Canterbury, viscount. See Sutton; see Manners-Sutton

CANTILUPE, CANTELEWE
Cantilupe, —, Kt.1471, II. 16
Cantilupe, George de, baron of Bergavenny, Kt.1272, II. 5
Cantilupe, Nicholas de, K.B.1326, I. 123
Cantelewe, William, K.B.(1461), I. 133
Cantley, Proby T., K.C.B.1854, I. 279
Canto e Castro, viscount M. do, K.C.M.G., 1902,, I. 393
Cantrell, Ralph, Kt.1624, II. 184
Cantwell, Thomas, Kt.(1333), II. lix.

CAPEL, CAPELL
Capell, Arthur, Kt.1617, II. 166
Capell, Arthur, lord Capel, Kt.1645, II. 219
Capell, Edward, Kt.1560, II. 71
Capel, Edward, Kt.1603, II. 121
Capel, Gamaliel, Kt.1603, II. 104
Capell, Gamaliel, Kt.1613, II. 153
Capell, Gaudensius de, Kt.1700, II. 272
Capell, Gyles, Kt.1513, II. 39
Capell, Henry (Arthur), Kt.1603, II. 104
Capell, Henry, K.B.1661, I. 164
Capel, Thomas B., K.C.B.1832, I. 232; G.C.B.1852, I. 190
Capell, William, Kt.1486, II. 23
Capell, William, earl of Essex, K.T. 1725, I. 77; K.G.1738, I. 43
Cappel, Albert J. L., K.C.I.E.1887, I. 400
Capellen, Theodorus F. van, K.C.B.1816, I. 228
Capello. See Brito-Capello
Capello, Franciscus de, Kt.1502, II. 33
Capon, David, K.C.B.1862, I. 248

Cappadoca, Giovanni, K.C.M.G.1820, I. 350; G.C.M.G.1832, I. 333
Cappadoca, Paolo, C.M.G.(1820), I. xxviii.
Caradoc, John H., 2nd lord Howden, K.H.1830, I. 465; K.C.B.1852, I. 278; G.C.B.1858, I. 208
Carazia, Marco, C.M.G.(1821), I. xxviii.
Carbery, earl of. See Vaughan
Carbone, Guiseppe, K.C.M.G.1891, I. 376; G.C.M.G.1901, I. 348
Carbone, Joseph, K.C.V.O.(1903), I. 435
Carbonell, Richard, K.B.(1426), I. 132
Carden, Robert W., Kt.1851, II. 348
Carden (Coordenne), Thomas, Kt.1545, II. 56
Cardew, Frederic, K.C.M.G.1897, I. 382
Cardiff, lord. See Herbert
Cardigan, earl of. See Brudenell; see Montagu

CAREW, CAREY, CARY, CARIE, CARUE, CARU
Carew. See Crew
Carew, Adolphus (Rodolphus Carie), Kt.1604, II. 132
Carew, Benjamin H., G.C.B.1831, I. 186
Carew, Edmund, Kt.1485, II. 23
Cary, Edward, Kt.1628, II. 194
Cary, Edward (Edmond), Kt.1586, II. 85
Carey, Ferdinando, Kt.1630, II. 197
Carew, Francis, Kt.1576, II. 77
Carew, Francis, K.B.1626, I. 162
Carew (alias Throgmorton), Francis, K.B.1626, I. 163
Carey, George, Kt.1527, II. 46
Cary, George, Kt.1570, II. 74
Carewe, George, Kt.1587, II. 84
Carey, George, lord Hunsdon, K.G. 1597, I. 29
Cary, George, Kt.1598, II. 95
Carew, George, Kt.1603, II. 114
Carey, George, Kt. 1632, II. 200
Carey, Henry, baron Hunsdon, Kt.1558, II. 70; K.G.1561, I. 26
Cary, Henry, Kt.1599, II. 96, 97
Carey, Henry, earl of Dover, K.B.1610, I. 158
Carey, Henry, viscount of Falkland, K.B. 1616, I. 160

INDEX

CAREW.
Carey, Henry, Kt.1644, II. 218
Cary, John, Kt.1547, II. 60
Carew, John, Kt.1603, II. 108
Carew, John, Kt.1625, II. 189
Carey, John, earl of Dover, K.B.1626, I. 161
Cary, Lorenzo, Kt.1634, II. 202
Cary, Lucius, Kt.1626, II. 190
Cary, Lucius B., viscount of Falkland, G.C.H.1831, I. 451
Carew, Mathew, Kt.1603, II. 114
Carew, Mathew, Kt.1611, II. 151
Carew, Nicholas, K.G.1536, I. 22
Carey, Octavius, Kt.1830, II. 329; K.C.H.1835, I. 461
Cary, Pelham, Kt.1633, II. 201
Carue, Peter, Kt.1579, II. 80
Carey, Peter, Kt.1863, II. 357
Carew, Philip, Kt. 1605, II. 137
Cary, Richard, Kt.1460, II. 13
Carewe, Richard [John], Kt.1497, II. 30
Carew, Richard, Kt.1513, I. 36
Carew, Robert, Kt.1624, II. 183
Cary, Robert, Kt.1660, II. 231
Carew, Robert S., baron Carew, K.P. 1851, I. 102
Carew, Robert S., baron Carew, K.P. 1872, I. 103
Cary, Rosse, Kt.1629, II. 196
Carewe, Thomas, Kt.1536, II. 50
Cary, Thomas, Kt.1628, II. 194
Carew, Thomas, Kt.1671, II. 246
Carey, Thomas, K.H.1816, I. 463
Carew, Thomas, Kt.1836, II. 337
Carey, Thomas G., Kt.1900, II. 407
Carew, William, Kt.1487, II. 25
Carey, William, Kt.1523, II. 44
Carewe, Wimond, K.B.1547, I. 152
Carew, Wymond, Kt. 1604, II. 132

Carey. See Carew
Caridi, Pandasin, C.M.G.(1821), preface I. 28
Caridi, Vittor, K.C.M.G.1818, I. 350; G.C.M.G.1839, I. 334
Carington, Edward, Kt.1616, II. 159
Carington, William H. P., K.C.V.O. (1901), I. 434

CARLETON, CARLTON, and see Charlton
Carleton, Dudley, Kt.1610, II. 150
Carleton, Dudley, Kt.1630, II. 197
Carleton, Guy, lord Dorchester, K.B. 1776, I. 172
Carling, John, K.C.M.G.1893, I. 378
Carlingford, baron. See Parkinson-Fortescue
Carlisle, Anthony, Kt.1821, II. 322
Carlisle, earl of. See Hay; see Howard
Carlisle, Nicholas, K.H.1832, I. 468
Carmichael, James, Kt.1632, II. 200
Carmichael, John, earl of Hyndford, K.T.1742, I. 78
Carmichael, William, Kt.1633, II. lxii.
Carnaby, William, Kt.1619, II. 173
Carnarvon, earl of. See Dormer; see Herbert; marquess of, see Brydges
Carncross, Joseph H., K.C.B.1815, I. 226
Carne, Edward, Kt.1538, II. 52

CARNEGY, CARNEGIE
Carnegy, Alex, Kt.1633, II. lxii.
Carnegie, George, Kt.1632, II. 200
Carnegie, James, Kt.1604, II. 136
Carnegie, James, earl of Southesk, K.T.1869, I. 86
Carnegie, William, earl of Northesk, K.B.1806, I. 176; G.C.B.1815, I. 180
Carney, Richard, Kt.1684, II. 259
Carnshaw (Carveshaw, Cranshaw), John (Richard), Kt.1619, II. 174
Caron, Joseph P. R. A., K.C.M.G.1885, I. 368
Carpenter, John, K.H.1836, I. 475
Carpenter, John D., earl of Tyrconnel, G.C.H.1830, I. 450

CARR, CARRE, and see Kerr
Carre, Edward, Kt.1603, II. 103
Carre, Edward, junr., Kt.1624, II. 187
Carre, Edward, senr., Kt.1624, II. 187
Carr, George, Kt.1662, II. 237
Carr, Henry W., K.C.B.1815, I. 225
Carr, John, Kt.1806, II. 308
Carr, Ralph, Kt.1676, II. 251
Carre (Karr), Robert, Kt.1607, II. 144
Carr, Robert, earl of Somerset, K.G. 1611, I. 30

INDEX 43

CARR
Carr, Robert, 6th earl of Somerset, K.B.1603, I. 154
Carr, Thomas, Kt.1800, II. 305
Carre, William, Kt.1603, II. 103
Carr, William, Kt.1627, II. 191
Carr, William O., Kt.1854, II. 350
Carrell, Carrill. See Carroll
Carrick-Buchanan, David C. R., K.C.B. 1894, I. 293
Carrington, Charles R., lord Carrington, G.C.M.G.1885, I. 340
Carrington, Codrington E., Kt.1801, II. 306
Carrington, Frederick, K.C.M.G.1887, I. 371; K.C.B.1897, I. 267
Carrington, John W., Kt.1897, II. 399

CARROLL, CARRELL, CARYLL, CARILL
Carrell, Edward, Kt.1603, II. 107
Carroll, George, Kt.1837, II. 339
Carroll, James, Kt.1609, II. 148
Carroll, James, Kt.1903, II. 415
Carrell, John, Kt.1591, II. 88
Carrell, John, Kt.1603, II. 112
Caryll, John, baron Caryll, K.T., Jacobite, 1768, footnote I. 75
Carrell, Richard, Kt.1615, II. 155
Carrell, Thomas, Kt.1603, II. 107
Carell, William, Kt.1603, II. 105
Carroll, William, Kt.1868, II. 360
Carroll, William F., K.C.B.1852, I. 239
Carroll (Carrol), William P., Kt.1816, II. 317; K.C.H.1832, I. 458
Carson, Edward H., Kt.1900, II. 406
Carswell, John de, Kt.1377, II. 10
Carswell, Robert, Kt.1850, II. 348
Carter, Frederick B. T., K.C.M.G.1878, I. 360
Carter, Gilbert T., K.C.M.G.1893, I. 378
Carter, James, Kt.1859, II. 354
Carter, John, Kt.1658, II. 224, 227
Carter, John, Kt.1773, II. 294
Carter, John, K.H.1837; I. 476
Carter, Lawrence, Kt.1724, II. 283
Carter, Richard, Kt.1714, II. 278

CARTERET, CARTWRIGHT
Carteret, Charles, Kt.1687, II. 263

CARTWRIGHT
Cartwright, Henry E., Kt.1887, II. 381
Cartwright, Hugh, Kt.1644, II. 217
Cartwright, John, Kt.1761, II. 291
Carteret, John, earl Granville, K.G. 1749, I. 44
Cartwright (Carteret), Philip, Kt. 1617, II. 161
Carteret, Philip, Kt.1667, II. 242
Cartwright, Richard J., K.C.M.G. 1879, I. 361; G.C.M.G.1897, I. 345
Cartwright, Thomas, G.C.H.1834, I. 452
Cartwright. See Carteret
Carty, James, Kt.1785, II. 298
Carus (Carowse), John, Kt.1603, II. 120
Caruso, count Demetrio, G.C.M.G.1852, I. 335
Carvell, Henry, Kt.1620, II. 176
Cary. See Carew
Caryll. See Carroll
Carysfoot, baron and earl. See Proby
Casault, Louis E. N., Kt.1894, II. 393
Casement, William, K.C.B.1837, I. 234
Cashmere, Runbeer Sing, maharaja of, K.S.I.1861, I. 306; G.C.S.I.1866, I. 308
Casolani, Vincenzo, C.M.G. (1822), preface I. 28; K.C.M.G.1833, I. 351; G.C.M.G.1853, I. 335
Cason, Henry, Kt.1629, II. 196
Cass, John, Kt.1712, II. 277
Cass, John, Kt.1896, II. 398
Cassel, Ernest G., K.C.M.G.1899, I. 387; K.C.V.O.(1901), I. 434
Cassillis, earl of. See Kennedy
Castello, George de, K.B.1306, I. 121
Castenskiold, Ludwig, G.C.V.O.1901, I. 425
Castile, Ferdinand V. of, K.G.1479-80, I. 16
Castile, Philip I. of, K.G.1503, I. 19
Castilion, Francis, Kt.1603, II. 109
Castlereagh, viscount. See Stewart
Castleton, John, Kt.1687, II. 262

CASWALL, CASWELL
Caswell, George, Kt.1718, II. 281
Caswall, John, Kt.1631, II. 199
Catcher, John, Kt.1619, II. 174

CATCHMAY, CATCHMAYD, CATSMAY
  Catchmayd (Catsmay), Richard, Kt. 1608, II. 145
  Catchmay, William, Kt.1628, II. 195
CATELYNE, CATLYNE, CATLYN
  Catlyne, Nathaniel, Kt.1635, II. 203
  Catelyne, Nevill, Kt.1662, II. 237
  Catelyne (Catlyn), Robert, Kt.1559, II. 70
Catena, Strickland G., count Della, K.C.M.G.1897, I. 382
Cater, Edward, Kt.1660, II. 232
Cater [or Kendall-Cater], Robert K., Kt.1738, II. 285
CATESBY, CATISBY
  Catisby (Catesby), Humfrey, Kt. 1501, II. 33
  Catesby, Richard, Kt.1542, II. 53
  Catesby, William, K.B.(1449), I. 132
  Catesby, William, Kt.1483, II. 21
  Catesby, William, Kt.1575, II. 76
Cathcart, Charles M., earl Cathcart, K.C.B.1838, I. 234; G.C.B.1859, I. 192
Cathcart, Charles S., lord Cathcart, K.T. 1763, I. 79
Cathcart, George, 1660, Kt. II. 226
Cathcart, George, K.C.B.1853, I. 240; G.C.B.1855, I. 191
Cathcart, William S., earl Cathcart, K.T. 1805, I. 80
Catherlough, earl of. See Knight
Cator, William, K.C.B.1865, I. 249
Cats, Vere a, Kt.1623, II. 181
CAULFIELD, CALFIELD
  Caulfield, Francis W., earl of Charlemont, K.P.1831, I. 100
  Caulfield, James, earl of Charlemont, K.P.1783, I. 97
  Caulfield, James M., earl of Charlemont, K.P.1865, I. 102
  Calfield, Toby, Kt.1603, II. 127
  Caulfield, William, Kt.1618, I. 168
Causton, Joseph, Kt.1869, II. 362
Cavagnari, Pierre L. N., K.C.B.1879, I. 287
Cavan, earl of. See Lambart
Cave, Alexander, Kt.1603, II. 115
Cave, Brian, Kt.1609, II. 148
Cave, Lewis W., Kt.1881, II. 372
Cave, Stephen, G.C.B.1880, I. 211
Cave, Thomas, Kt.1553, II. 67
Cave, Thomas, Kt.1603, II. 103
Cave, Thomas, Kt.1603, II. 112
Cave, Thomas, Kt. 1615, II. 156
Cave, Thomas, Kt.1616, II. 159
Cave, Thomas, Kt.1641, II. 209
Cave, William, Kt.1603, II. 113
Cavenagh, Orfeur, K.C.S.I.1881, I. 322
Cavendish, Charles, Kt.1582, II. 81
Cavendish, Charles, Kt.1619, II. 173
Cavendish, Charles C. W., lord Chesham, K.C.B.1900, I. 273
Cavendish, Henry, duke of Newcastle, K.G.1677, I. 37
Cavendish, John, K.B.1616, I. 160
Cavendish, Spencer C., duke of Devonshire, K.G.1892, I. 69
Cavendish, William, Kt.1545, I. 57
Cavendish, William, Kt.1580, II. 81
Cavendish, William, Kt.1609, II. 147
Cavendish, William, duke of Newcastle, K.B.1610, I. 158
Cavendish, William, earl of Devonshire, K.B.1626, I. 161
Cavendish, William, duke of Newcastle, K.G.1650, I. 34
Cavendish, William, duke of Devonshire, K.G.1689, I. 39
Cavendish, William, duke of Devonshire, K.G.1710, I. 40
Cavendish, William, duke of Devonshire, K.G.1733, I. 43
Cavendish, William, duke of Devonshire, K.G.1756, I. 45
Cavendish, William, duke of Devonshire, K.G.1782, I. 47
Cavendish, William G. S., duke of Devonshire, K.G.1827, I. 53
Cavendish, William, duke of Devonshire, K.G.1858, I. 60
Cavendish-Bentinck, William H., duke of Portland, K.G.1794, I. 49
Cavendish-Bentinck, William J. A. C. J., duke of Portland, G.C.V.O.1896, I. 417; K.G.1900, I. 70
Caw, John, Kt.1671, II. 245
Caw (Cau, Cawe), John, Kt.1674, II. 249

INDEX

CAYLEY, CALEY, CALLEY, CALLWEY, CAWLEY
Cayley, Arthur, Kt.1660, II. 228
Cayley, Richard, Kt.1882, II. 374
Callwey, William, K.B.1501, I. 146
Calley, William, Kt.1629, II. 196
Cawley (Caley), William, Kt.1642, II. 212
Caley (Calley), William, Kt.1661, II. 235
Cayzer, Charles W., Kt.1897, II. 400
Cazzaiti, Georgio, K.C.M.G.1844, I. 353
CECIL, CECILL, SCISSALL
Cecil, Brownlow, marquess of Exeter, K.G.1827, I. 53
Cecil, Charles, viscount Cranborne, K.B.1626, I. 160
Cecil, Edward, Kt.1601, II. 99
Cecil, James, earl of Salisbury, K.G. 1680, I. 37
Cecil, James, marquess of Salisbury, K.G.1793, I. 49
Cecil, Richard, Kt.1616, II. 159
Cecil, Robert, Kt.1591, II. 88
Cecil, Robert, earl of Salisbury, K.G. 1606, I. 30
Cecil (Siksalt, Scissall), Thomas, Kt. 1575, II. 76
Cecil, Thomas, earl of Exeter, K.G. 1601, I. 29
Cecil, Thomas, Kt.1623, II. 182
Cecil, William, Kt.1549, II. 65
Cecil, William, lord Burghley, K.G. 1572, I. 27
Cecil, William, earl of Exeter, Kt. 1603, II. 100; K.G.1630, I. 32
Cecil, William, earl of Salisbury, K.B. 1605, I. 157; K.G.1624, I. 31
Cesar, Thomas, Kt.1610, I. 149
Chabannes-Curton, Octave P. A. de, K.C.B.1857, I. 244
Chabot, Louis W., viscount, K.C.H.1822, I. 455
Chabot. See Neublanche
Chads, Henry, K.C.B.1887, I. 260
Chads, Henry Ducie, K.C.B.1855, I. 240; G.C.B.1865, I. 194
Chadwick, Andrew (Ambrose), Kt.1710, II. 277

Chadwick, Edwin, K.C.B.1889, I. 291
CHALK, CHAULKE
Chaulke, Alexander, Kt.1621, II. 176
Chalk, James J., Kt.1871, II. 363
CHALLENOR, CHALONER, CHALLONER
Chaloner, Edward, Kt.1672, II. 247
Challoner, John, Kt.1557, II. 70
Chaloner, Thomas, Kt.1547, II. 62
Challoner, Thomas, Kt.1591, II. 88
Challenor, Thomas, Kt.1762, II. 291
Chalmers, —, K.H.1832, I. 468
Chalmers, David P., Kt.1876, II. 368
Chalmers, John M., K.C.B.1815, I. 227
Chalmers, William, K.H.1832, I. 467; Kt.1844, II. 345
Chalmers. See Chambers
Chalons, Robert, K.B.(1400), I. 129
CHAMBERLAIN, CHAMBERLAINE, CAMBERLYN CHAMBERLEYN, CHAMBERLAYN
Chamberlain, Crawford T., G.C.I.E. 1897, I. 403
Chamberlaine, John, Kt.1599, II. 97
Chamberleyn, John, Kt.1603, II. 113, 118
Camberlyn, John, Kt.1621, II. 176
Chamberlyn, Leonard, Kt.1553, II. 66
Chamberlain, Neville, F. F., K.C.B. 1903, I. 301
Chamberlain, Neville B., K.C.B.1863, I. 248; K.C.S.I.1866, I. 316; G.C.S.I. 1873, I. 310; G.C.B.1875, I. 197
Chamberlayn, Rauf (Edward), Kt. 1513, II. 39
Chamberlain, Raufe, Kt.1553, II. 66
Chamberlaine, Robert, K.B.1603, I. 156
Chamberlaine, Thomas, Kt.1616, II. 158
Chamberlaine, Thomas, K.B.1660, I. 226
Chamberlaine, William, K.G.1461, I. 14
Chamberlayne, Willoughby, Kt.1696, II. 269
Chambers, Charles H., Kt.1823, II. 324
Chambers, George H., Kt.1880, II. 372
Chambers [Robert] Newman, Kt.1897, II. 398
Chambers, Robert, Kt.1777, II. 295
Chambers, Samuel, Kt.1800, II. 305

F F

INDEX

Chambers, Thomas, Kt.1666, II. 242
Chambers, Thomas, Kt.1872, II. 364
Chambers, William F., K.C.H.1837, I. 462
Chambers. See Chalmers
Chambre, Alan, Kt.1800, II. 305
Chambre, Laurence de La, Kt.1630, II. 197
Chamoun, John, Kt.1529, II. 47
Champagné, Josiah, Kt.1832, II. 331; G.C.H.1832, I. 451
Champante, John, Kt.1674, II. 249
Champernoun, Arthur, Kt.1549, II. 64
Champernoun, Arthur, Kt.1599, II. 96
Champernoun, John, Kt.1501, II. 33
Champernon, Richard, Kt.1599, II. 98
CHAMPION, CAMPION, CHAMPTON
 Champion, George, Kt.1737, II. 285
 Campion, Henry, Kt.1621, II. 177
 Campion, William, Kt.1618, II. 169
 Champyon, Richard, Kt.1566, II. 72
 Campion, William, Kt.1644, II. 219
CHANCY, CHAUNCY, CHAUNCIE
 Chauncy, Henry, Kt.1681, II. 256
 Chancy (Chauncie), Tobie, Kt.1603, II. 125
 Chancy, William, Kt.1603, II. 125
Chandée, Philibert de, earl of Bath, Kt. 1485, II. 22
Chandos, John, K.B.1306, I. 115
Chandos, John, K.G.1348, I. 2
Chandos, duke of. See Brydges
Chandos, lord. See Brydges
Chandos, marquess of. See Temple-Nugent-Brydges, etc.
Chandos, Roger de, K.B.1306, I. 112
Chang yen Hoon, G.C.M.G.1897, I. 345
Channell, Arthur M., Kt.1897, II. 402
Channell, William F., Kt.1857, II. 352
Chantrey, Francis, Kt.1835, II. 336
Chao Phya Bhanuwongse, K.C.M.G.1880, I. 362
Chapell (Chapple), William, Kt.1729, II. 284
Chapleau, Joseph A., K.C.M.G.1896, I. 381
Chaplin, Francis, Kt.1670, II. 245
Chapman, Frederick E., K.C.B.1867, I. 251; G.C.B.1877, I. 197
Chapman, John, Kt.1618, II. 169
Chapman, John, Kt.1678, II. 253

Chapman, John, Kt.1823, II. 324
Chapman, Peter, Kt.1617, II. 167
Chapman, Stephen R., K.H.1817, I. 463; K.C.H.1831, I. 457; Kt.1831, II. 330
Chapman, Thomas, Kt.1780, II. 296
Chapman, William, Kt.1714, II. 279
Chardin, John, Kt.1682, II. 257
Charem. See Chater
Charkhari, Mulkhan Singh, K.C.I.E. 1902, I. 411
Charlemont, earl of (1783). See Caulfield, J.
Charles I., K.B.1605, I. 156; K.G.1611, I. 30
Charles II., Kt.1638, II. 205; K.B.1638, I. 163; K.G.1638, I. 33
Charles, prince, K.G., Jacobite, 1742, footnote I. 38; K.T., Jacobite, 1742, footnote I. 75
Charles, Arthur, Kt.1887, II. 384
CHARLETON, CHARLTON, CARLTON, and see Carleton, Cherleton
 Charleton, Edward, K.H.1836, I. 474
 Charlton, Job, Kt.1662, I. 236
 Charleton, Richard, K.B.(1475), I. 136
 Charleton, Robert, K.B.1389, I. 127
 Carlton (Charlton), Thomas, Kt.1630, II. 198
Charley, William T., Kt.1880, II. 371
Charner, Leonard V. J., K.C.B.1857, I. 243
Charnock, Robert, Kt.1619, II. 173
Chase, Richard, Kt.1744, II. 286
Chastillion, Jean de Foix, vicomte de, K.G.1446, I. 12
Chater, Catchick P., Kt.1902, II. 412
Chater (Chator, Charem), William, Kt. 1617, II. 162
Chatham, earl of. See Pitt
Chatterton, James C., K.H.1832, I. 467; K.C.B.1862, I. 247; G.C.B.1873, I. 196
Chaulke. See Chalk
Chaworth, Christopher de, Kt.1347, II. 9
Chaworth, George, Kt.1584, II. 82
Chaworth, George, Kt.1605, II. 138
Chaworth, George, Kt.1608, II. 146
Chaworth, John, Kt.1533, II. 49
Chaworth, Richard, Kt.1663, II. 239

INDEX

Chaworth, Thomas de, K.B.1306, I. 121
Cheape, John, K.C.B.1849, I. 238; G.C.B. 1865, I. 194
Chebborne. See Chibborne
Chedle, Roger de, K.B.1306, I. 120
Chedle (Cheddle), Thomas, Kt.1644, II. 217
Cheek. See Cheke
Cheere, Henry, Kt.1760, II. 289
Cheetwood. See Chetwood

CHEKE, CHEEK
 Cheek, Hatton, Kt.1603, II. 106
 Cheke, John, Kt.1549, II. 65
 Cheek, Thomas, Kt.1603, II. 105
Chelmsford, lord. See Thesiger
Chenow, Connor, king of, K.B.1394, I. 127
Cherif, Pasha, G.C.S.I.1878, I. 311
Cherleton, Edward, lord Cherleton, K.G.1407-8, I. 8
Chermside, Herbert C., K.C.M.G.1897, I. 383; G.C.M.G.1899, I. 346
Chermside, Robert A., K.H.1831, I. 465; Kt.1835, II. 336
Chernstone, John de, K.B.1327, I. 124
Cherry, Francis, Kt.1604, II. 134
Chesham, lord. See Cavendish
Cheshire, John, Kt.1713, II. 278
Chesnall. See Chisnall
Chesney, George T., K.C.B.1890, I. 263
Chester, Anthony, Kt.1603, II. 111
Chester, Edward, Kt.1643, II. 215
Chester, Henry, K.B.1661, I. 166
Chester, Robert, Kt.1603, II. 118
Chestre, Robert, Kt.1549, II. 65
Chester, Robert, Kt.1603, II. 123
Chester, Robert, Kt.1818, II. 320
Chester, William, Kt.1557, II. 70
Chester. See Chichester
Chesterfield, earl of. See Stanhope
Chetham (afterwards Chetham-Strode), Edward, Kt.1837, II. 338; K.C.H. 1837, I. 462; K.C.B.1845, I. 238
Chetwood (Cheetwood), Richard, Kt.1603, II. 111
Chetwynd, George, Kt.1787, II. 300
Chetwynd, Walter, Kt.1604, II. 134
Chetwynd, William, Kt.1604, II. 134

Chetwynd-Talbot, Charles C., earl Talbot, Grand Master K.P.1817, I. 93; K.P. 1821, I. 99; K.G.1844, I. 57
Chetwynd-Talbot, Wellington P. M., K.C.B.1897, I. 295
Chevedon (Chiverton), Richard, Kt.1678, II. 224
Chevers, Christopher, Kt.1556, II. 69
Chevers, Walter, Kt.1541, II. 52.
Chevreuse, Claude de Lorraine, duc de, K.G.1625, I. 32
Chewte. See Chute
Cheyffelde, Robert, Kt.1529, II. 47

CHEYNE, CHENEY, CHEYNY, CHEINY, CHEINEY, CHEYNEY, SHEYNE, CHENAY
 Cheyney, Francis, K.B.1509, II. 148
 Cheyney, Francis, Kt.1603, II. 111
 Cheyney, Henry, Kt.1563, II. 71
 Cheyney, Henry, Kt.1606, II. 140
 Cheyney, John, son of, Kt.1409, II. 11
 Cheney, John, K.B.(1465), II. 135
 Cheney (Cheiny), John, Kt.1485, II. 22
 Cheyne, John, lord Cheyne, K.G.1486, I. 17
 Cheyney, John, Kt.1487, II. 24
 Cheyne, John, Kt.1897, II. 402
 Cheiney, Robert, Kt.1487, II. 25
 Cheyney, Thomas, K.G.1539, I. 22
 Cheney, Thomas, K.B.(1489), II. 143
 Cheney, Thomas (John), Kt.1608, II. 145
 Cheyney (Sheyne, Cheyne), William, K.B.(1426), I. 132
 Cheyney, William, K.B.1327, I. 124
 Cheney William, K.B.(1483), I. 140

Chibborne (Chyborn, Chebborne), Charles Kt.1619, II. 171
Chicele-Plowden, Trevor J. C., K.C.S.I. 1898, I. 326
Chicheley, Thomas, Kt.1670, II. 244
Chichester, Arthur, Kt.1596, II. 93
Chichester, Arthur, Kt.1660, II. 231
Chichester, Charles, Kt.1840, II. 343
Chichester, earl of. See Leigh
Chichester, Edward, Kt.1616, II. 158
Chichester, George A., marquess of Donegall, K.P.1821, I. 99

48 INDEX

Chichester, George H., marquess of Donegall, G.C.H.1831, I. 451; K.P. 1857, I. 102
Chichester, John, Kt.1553, II. 67
Chichester, John, Kt.1580, II. 80
Chichester, John, Kt.1597, II. 94
Chichester, John, Kt.1625, II. 189
Chichester, Robert, K.B.1603, I. 154
Chichester (Chester), Robert, Kt.1603, II. 118
Chichester, Thomas, Kt.1607, II. 143
Chichley, Henry, Kt.1645, II. 219
Chichley, Thomas, Kt.1607, II. 142
Chidioke, John, K.B.(1426), I. 132
Chidley. See Chudleigh
Chiesley, John, Kt.1646, II. 221
Chiffinch, William, Kt.1676, II. 251
Child, Francis, Kt.1689, II. 265
Child, Francis, Kt.1732, II. 284
Child, Josiah, Kt.1692, II. 267
Child, Lacon W., Kt.1673, II. 248
Child, Robert, Kt.1714, II. 279
Child, William, Kt.1661, II. 234
Child-Villiers, George, earl of Jersey, G.C.H.1834, I. 452
Child-Villiers, Victor A. G., earl of Jersey, G.C.M.G.1890, I. 342; G.C.B. 1900, I. 215
Chirkingham, Walter de, Kt.1347, II. 9
Chisnall (Chesnall, Chesenall), Edward, Kt.1671, II. 245
Chisselme (Chishealme), James, Kt.1619, II. 172
Chitty, Joseph W., Kt.1881, II. 373
Chitty, Thomas, Kt.1759, II. 289
Chiverton, Richard, Kt.1663, II. 239
Chiverton. See Chevedon
CHOCK, CHOKE, CHOOKE, CHEOKE
  Chock (Choke), Francis, Kt.1643, II. 216
  Chooke or Cheoke, John (William), K.B.(1494), I. 144
  Choke, Richard, K.B.(1465), I. 134

CHOLMONDELEY, CHOLMLEY, CHOLMELEY, CHOMLEY
  Cholmondeley, George, earl of Cholmondeley, K.B.1725, I. 167

CHOLMONDELEY
  Cholmondeley, George J., marquess of Cholmondeley, G.C.H.1816, I. 448; K.G.1822, I. 52
Cholmley, Henry, Kt.1603, II. 101, 120
Cholmley, Henry, Kt.1641, II. 211
Cholmley, Hugh, Kt.1544, II. 54
Cholmeley, Hugh, Kt.1587, II. 86
Cholmondeley, Hugh, Kt.1626, II. 190
Cholmondeley, Richard, Kt.1497, II. 32
Chomley, Richard, Kt.1544, II. 55
Cholmley, Richard, Kt.1603, II. 113
Chomley, Richard (Henry), Kt.1643, 216, 218
Cholmeley, Roger, Kt.1538, II. 51
Choloniewski-Myszka, count Edouard, K.C.V.O.1903, I. 441
Chowne, George, Kt.1603, II. 117
Christie, Archibald, K.H.1817, I. 463; Kt.1820, II. 321; K.C.H.1831, I.457
Christie, William H. M., K.C.B.1904, I. 301
Christofero, Don, Kt.1596, II. 92
Christian, Hugh C., K.B.1796, I. 174
Christopher, Robert, Kt.1661-2, II. 236
Chubb, George H., Kt.1885, II. 377
CHUDLEIGH, CHIDLEY
  Chidley (Chidleigh), John, Kt.1625, II. 190
  Chudley, Roger (Richard), Kt.1553, II. 68
Church, Richard, Kt.1822, II. 323; K.C.H.1822, I. 455; G.C.H.1837, I 453
Church, William S., K.C.B.1902, I. 299
Churchill, John, Kt.1670, II. 244
Churchill, John, duke of Marlborough, K.G.1701-2, I. 40
Churchill, Winston, Kt.1664, II. 239
Churchill, viscount. See Spencer
Churchman, John, Kt.1683, II. 258
Churchman, Thomas, Kt.1761, II. 290
CHUTE, CHEWTE
  Chewte, George, Kt.1608, II. 146
  Chute, George, Kt.1660, II. 229
  Chute, Trevor, K.C.B.1867, I. 251
  Chute, Walter, Kt.1603, II. 103
Ciantar-Paleologo, Serafino Georgio, count, K.C.M.G.1882, I. 364

INDEX

Cipriani, Henry, Kt.1831, II. 330
Clackson. See Claxton
Clahull, Robert de, Kt.(1312), preface to Irish Kuts II. lviii.
Clanbrassill, earl of. See Hamilton
Clancarty, earl of. See Le-Poer Trench
Clanrickarde, earl and marquess of. See De Burgh
Clanvowe, Thomas, Kt.1399, II. 11
Clanwilliam, earl of. See Meade
Clapham, Christopher, Kt.1660, II. 228
Clapham, Sheffield (John), Kt.1625, II. 190

CLARE, CLEERE, CLEARE, CLERE, CLEIR, CLEER
Clare, earl of. See FitzGibbon
Cleere, Edward, Kt.1578, II. 79
Cleare, Edward, Kt.1603, II. 104
Cleer (Cleare), Francis, Kt.1603, II. 121
Clare, Francis, Kt.1604, II. 136
Clare, Gilbert de, K.B.1306, II. 111
Clare (Cleere), Henry, Kt.1603, II. 106
Clare, Michael B., Kt.1822, II. 324
Clere, Robert, K.B.(1494), I. 144
Cleir (Clere), Thomas, Kt.1544, II. 55
Clarence, Albert V. C. E., duke of, K.G. 1883, I. 67; K.P.1887, I. 105
Clarence, George, duke of, K.B.(1461), I. 133; K.G.1461, I. 14
Clarence, Lionel, duke of, K.G.1360, I. 3
Clarence, Thomas, duke of, K.B.1399, I. 127; K.G.1399, I. 7
Clarendon, earl of. See Hyde; see Villiers
Clarges, Richard G. H., K.C.B.1856, I. 242
Clarges, Thomas, Kt.1660, II. 225
Claridge, John T., Kt.1825, II. 325
Clark. See Clerk
Claverhouse, Richard, Kt.1900, II. 408
Clavering, John, Kt.1614, II. 154
Clavering, John, K.B.1776, I. 172

CLAXTON, CLACKSON
Claxton, John (Edward), Kt.1603, II. 123
Claxton (Clackson), William, Kt.1702, II. 272
Clay, John, Kt.1471, II. 14

Clayborne (Cleyborne), Edward, Kt. 1603, II. 123
CLAYPOLE, CLAYPOOLE
Claypoole, John, Kt.1604, II. 133
Claypole, John, Kt.1657, II. 223
CLAYTON, CLEYTON
Clayton, Jasper, Kt.1660, II. 229
Clayton, John, Kt.1664, II. 240
Clayton, Oscar M. P., Kt.1882, II. 374
Cleyton, Randall, Kt.1622, II. 178
Clayton, Robert, Kt.1671, II. 246
Clayton, Thomas, Kt.1661, II. 233
Cleare, Cleere, Clere, Cleir, Cleer. See Clare
Cleasby, Anthony, Kt.1868, II. 360
Cleaver, Charles, Kt.1660, II. 227
Clement, Richard, Kt.1529, II. 48
Clements, Nathaniel, earl of Leitrim, K.P.1834, I. 100
Clenck, John, Kt.1660, II. 231
CLERK, CLERKE, CLARK, CLARKE
Clerk, Alex., Kt.1633, II. lxii.
Clerke, Alexander, K.H.1836, I. 474
Clark (afterwards Clark-Kennedy), Alexander K., K.H.1831, I. 466
Clarke, Alured, K.B.1797, I. 175; G.C.B.1815, I. 180
Clarke, Andrew, K.H.1837, I. 477
Clarke, Andrew, K.C.M.G.1873, I. 356; G.C.M.G.1885, I. 340
Clarke, Arthur, Kt.1811, II. 310
Clark, Bouverie F., K.C.B.1900, I.
Clarke, Campbell, Kt.1897, II. 39?
Clarke, Caspar P., Kt.1902, II. 4?
Clarke, Charles M., K.C.B.1896, I. G.C.B.1900, I. 203; G.C.V.O.190?, I. 420
Clerk, Edward, Kt.1625, II. 188
Clark, Edward, Kt.1627, II. 192
Clark, Edward, Kt.1646, II. 221
Clark, Edward, Kt.1689, II. 265
Clarke, Edward G., Kt.1886, II. 380
Clarke, Ernest, Kt.1898, II. 402
Clarke, Fielding, Kt.1894, II. 392
Clarke, Francis, Kt.1608, II. 144*
Clarke, Francis, Kt.1624, II. 185
Clark, Francis, Kt.1627, II. 191
Clarke, Francis, Kt.1660, II. 227
Clarke, Francis, Kt.1665, II. 241

CLERK
　Clark, George, Kt.1641, II. 211
　Clerke, George R., K.C.B.1848, I. 277;
　　K.S.I.1861, I. 306; G.C.S.I.1866, I.
　　308
　Clarke, George S., K.C.M.G.1893, I. 378
　Clerke (Clark), Gilbert, Kt.1671, II. 245
　Clerk, Godfrey, K.C.V.O.(1902), I. 435
　Clarke, Henry, Kt.1615, II. 156
　Clarke, James, Kt.1681, II. 256
　Clarke, James, Kt.1708, II. 276
　Clark, James, K.C.B.1866, I. 284
　Clerke, John, Kt.1529, II. 47
　Clarke, John, Kt.1619, II. 172
　Clerke, John, Kt.1684, II. 260
　Clerke, John, Kt.1772, II. 293
　Clarke, John, K.H.1833, I. 469; K.H.
　　1837, I. 477
　Clarke, Justinian, Kt.1608, II. 146
　Clarke, Marshall J., K.C.M.G.1886, I.
　　368
　Clarke, Robert, Kt.1578, II. 79
　Clark, Robert, Kt.1603, II. 114
　Clarke, Robert, Kt.1613, II. 153
　Clarke, Robert, Kt.1684, II. 260
　Clarke, Robert B., Kt.1840, II. 342
　Clerke, Rowland, Kt.1547, II. 62
　Clarke, Rowland, Kt.1578, II. 79
　Clerke, St. John A., K.H.1832, I. 466
　Clarke, Samuel, Kt.1673, II. 248
　Clarke, Samuel, Kt.1712, II. 277
　Clarke, Stanley de A. C., K.C.V.O.
　　(1897), I. 432; G.C.V.O.1902, I. 420
　Clarke, Thomas, Kt.1618, II. 170
　Clerk, Thomas, Kt.1706, II. 275
　Clarke, Thomas, Kt.1754, II. 288
　Clerke, Thomas H. S., K.H.1831, I. 466
　Clarke, Thomas, Kt.1603, II. 116, 119
　Clerk, William le, K.B.1305, I. 111
　Clarke, William, Kt.1578, II. 79
　Clarke, William, Kt.1594, II. 91
　Clark, William, Kt.1642, II. 213
　Clarke, William, Kt.1792, II. 301
　Clark, William O., Kt.1903, II. 414
　Clark, William S., Kt.1840, II. 342
Clerk-Rattray, James, K.C.B.1897, I. 267
Clermont, baron. See Parkinson-
　Fortescue
Clermont, earl of. See Fortescue

Clervaux, Richard, Kt.1487, II. 26
Clery, Cornelius F., K.C.B.1899, I. 271;
　K.C.M.G.1901, I. 389
Clethero. See Clitherow
Cleve, Cleive, Cleeve. See Clive
Cleveland, duke of. See Fitzroy; see
　Vane
Cleveland, earl of. See Wentworth
Cleveland, Robert, Kt.1603, II. 109
CLIFFORD, CLYFFORDE, CLYFORD
　Clifford, Alexander, Kt.1596, II. 92
　Clifford, Augustus, Kt.1830, II. 329
　Clifford, Charles, Kt.1858, II. 353
　Clifford, Conyers, Kt.1591, II. 88
　Clifford Francis, earl of Cumberland,
　　K.B.1605, I. 157
　Clifford, George, earl of Cumberland,
　　Kt.1588, II. 87; K.G.1592, I. 28
　Clifford, Henry, 10th lord Clyfford,
　　K.B.(1494), I. 144
　Clyfford, Henry, earl of Cumberland,
　　K.B.1509, I. 148
　Clyfforde, Henry, Kt.1513, II. 36
　Clifford, Henry, earl of Cumberland,
　　K.B.1533, I. 149; K.G. 1537, I. 22
　Clifford, Henry, earl of Cumberland,
　　K.B.1610, I. 157
　Clifford, Henry H., K.C.M.G.1879, I.
　　362
　Clyfforde, Ingram, Kt.1545, II. 56
　Clifford, John de, lord de Clifford,
　　K.G.1421, I. 10
　Clifford, lord [John] Kt.1460, II. 12
　Clifford, John, K.B.(1465), I. 135
　Clifford, Lewis, K.G.1377, I. 5
　Clifford, Miller, K.H.1836, I. 473
　Clifford, Nicholas, Kt.1591, II. 89
　Clifford, Richard, Kt.1603, II. 104
　Clyfford, Robert, Kt.1487, II. 24
　Clifford, Roger, Kt.1460, II. 13
　Clyfforde, Thomas, Kt.1523, II. 43
CLIFTON, CLYFTON, CLIFDEN, CLIVEDON
　Clifton, Arthur B., K.C.H.1832, I. 458;
　　K.C.B.1838, I. 234; G.C.B.1861, I.
　　193
　Clifton, Clifford, Kt.1661, II. 236
　Clyfton, Gervase, Kt.1483, II. 21
　Clyfton, Gervase [Denys], K.B.(1483),
　　I. 140, 141

INDEX

CLIFTON
Clifton, Gervase, K.B.(1494), I. 144
Clyfton, Gervase, Kt.1538, II. 51
Clifton, Gervase or William, K.B.1603, I. 154
Clifton, Gilbert (Gervas), Kt.1617, II. 165
Clivedon, John de, Kt.1347, II. 8
Clifton, John, Kt.1574, II. 76
Clifton, Robert, K.B.1725, I. 168
Clifden or Clifton, Robert, K.B.(1461), I. 133

CLINTON, CLYNTON
Clinton, earl. See Fortescue
Clinton, Edward, lord Clinton, Kt. 1544, II. 54
Clinton, Edward, earl of Lincoln, K.G. 1551, I. 24
Clinton, Edward, earl of Lincoln, K.B. 1661, I. 163
Clinton, Francis, Kt.1661, II. 235
Clinton, Henry, lord Clinton, K.B.1553, I. 152
Clinton, Henry, earl of Lincoln, K.G. 1721, I. 42
Clinton, Henry, K.B.1777, I. 172
Clinton, Henry, K.B.1813, I. 179; G.C.B.1815, I. 182; G.C.H.1816, I. 447
Clinton, John de, K.B.1306, I. 115
Clinton, John, lord Clinton, K.B.1501, I. 145
Clinton, Theophilus, earl of Lincoln, K.B.1616, I. 159
Clynton, Thomas, Kt.1513, II. 40
Clinton, William Henry, G.C.B.1815, I. 183
Clitheroe (Clethero), Christopher, Kt. 1637, II. 205

CLIVE, CLYVE, CLEIVE, CLEEVE, CLEVE
Cleve (Cleive), Christopher, Kt.1605, II. 137
Clive, Edward, Kt.1753, II. 288
Cleeve, Frederick, K.C.B.1902, I. 274
Clyve, George, Kt.1588, II. 86
Clive, Robert, lord Clive, K.B.1754, I. 171
Cleeve, Thomas H., Kt.1900, II. 407
Clivedon. See Clifton

Clobery, John, Kt.1660, II. 227
Cloete, Abraham J., K.H.1836, I. 475; Kt.1854, II. 350; K.C.B.1862, I. 248
Clonbrock, baron. See Dillon
Clopton, Hugh, Kt. 1733 I. 284
Clopton, John, K.B.(1483), I. 139
Clopton, John, Kt.1662, II. 237
Clopton, Walter, K.B.1389, I. 127
Clopton, William, Kt.1501, II. 33
Clopton, William, Kt.1614, II. 154
Clotworthy, Hugh, Kt.1618, II. 167
Clotworthy, John, Kt.1626, II. 191
Clovell, William, Kt.1599, II. 97
Clowes, William L., Kt.1902, II. 411
Clutterbuck, Thomas, Kt.1669, II. 243
Clutterbuck, William, Kt.1683, II. 259
Clux, Hertong von, K.G.1421, I. 10
Clyde, lord. See Campbell

COATS, COTES, COOTE, COOTS
Cotes, John, Kt.1542, II. 54
Cotes (Coote), Nicholas, Kt.1603, II. 117
Cotes (Coots), Raphael, Kt.1682, II. 257
Coats, Peter, Kt.1869, II. 361

COBBE, COB, COBB
Cobbe, Alexander H., K.C.B.1898, I. 270
Cob, Francis, Kt.1642, II. 213
Cobb, James, Kt.1644, II. 218
Cob, William, Kt.1603, II. 121
Cobbe, William, Kt.1624, II. 184
Cobb, William, Kt.1661, II. 232
Cobham, George, Kt.1523, II. 45
Cobham, lord. See Brooke
Cobham, Reginald de, lord Cobham, K.G.1352, I. 2
Cobham, Reginald, K.B.(1426), I. 131
Cobham, Stephen de, K.B.1306, I. 116
Cobham, Thomas, lord, Kt.1513, II. 38
Cobham, William, Kt.1548, II. 63
Cobham, William, Kt.1605, II. 138
Cochin, rajah of, K.C.S.I.1869, I. 318
Cochin, Rama Varma, of, K.C.S.I.1897, I. 326; G.C.S.I.1903, I. 314
Cochin, Vinakerala, of, K.C.I.E.1888, I. 405
Cochrane, Alexander F. I., K.B.1806, I. 176; G.C.B.1815, I. 180

52 INDEX

Cochrane, Arthur A. L. P., K.C.B.1889, I. 262
Cochrane, Henry, Kt.1887, II. 383
Cochrane, James, Kt.1845, II. 346
Cochrane, Thomas, lord Cochrane, Kt. 1809, II. 309
Cochrane, Thomas, earl of Dundonald, K.B.1809, I. 177; G.C.B.1847, I. 190
Cochrane, Thomas J., Kt.1812, II. 311
Cochrane, Thomas J., Kt.1825, II. 325; K.C.B.1847, I. 238; G.C.B.1860, I. 193
Cochraine-Baillie, Charles W. A. N. R., lord Lamington, K.C.M.G.1895, I. 381; G.C.M.G.1900, I. 346; G.C.I.E. 1903, I. 404
Cock, Henry, Kt.1577, II. 78
Cock, Henry, Kt.1603, II. 127
Cock, Robert, Kt.1625, II. 190
COCKAINE, COCKAYN, COKAYN, COKEYN, COKIN, COKER
Cockayn, Edmond, Kt.1603, II. 102
Cokayn, Thomas, Kt.1513, II. 42
Cokin (Coker, Cokeyn), Thomas, Kt. 1544, II. 55
Cockaine, William, Kt.1616, II. 158
Cockburn, Alexander J. E., Kt.1850, II. 348; G.C.B.1873, I. 210
Cockburn, Francis, Kt.1841, II. 344
Cockburn, Geo., Kt.1633, II. lxii.
Cockburn, George, K.C.B.1815, I. 220; G.C.B.1818, I. 184
Cockburn, George, K.C.H.1821, I. 455; Kt.1831, II. 331; G.C.H.1831, I. 451
Cockburn, James, K.C.H.1831, I. 457; G.C.H.1835, I. 453
Cockburn, John A., K.C.M.G.1900, I. 387
Cockett, Edmond, Kt.1613, II. 153
Cockle, James, Kt.1869, II. 361
Cocks. See Cox
Codington, John de, Kt.1347, II. 9
Codony, Henry, Kt.1665, II. 241
Codrington, Edward, K.C.B.1815, I. 221; G.C.M.G.1827, I. 332; G.C.B.1827, I. 185
Codrington, Henry J., K.C.B.1867, I. 250
Codrington, William J., K.C.B.1855, I. 240; G.C.B.1865, I. 194
Coell. See Cowell

Coey, Edward, Kt.1861, II. 356
Coffin, Edward P., Kt.1846, II. 346
Coffin, Isaac, G.C.H.1832, I. 452
Coffin, Isaac C., K.C.S.I.1866, I. 316
Coffyn, William, Kt.1537, II. 50
Cogeshale, Jo de, Kt.1336, II. 5
Coghill, Coell, Coghil. See Cowell
Coghlan, William M., K.C.B.1864, I. 283
Coidan, Pietro, K.C.M.G.1825, I. 351; G.C.M.G.1840, I. 334
Coimbra, Peter, duke of, K.G.1427, I. 11
Cokayn. See Cockaine
COKE, COOKE, COOK, COOKES
Cook, Anthony, K.B.1547, I. 151
Cooke, Anthony, Kt.1596, II. 92
Cooke, Charles, Kt.1717, II. 281
Coke, Edward, Kt.1603, II. 110
Cooke (Coke), Edward, Kt.1603, II. 115
Cooke, Francis, Kt.1611, II. 151
Cook, Francis, Kt.1619, II. 173
Cooke, George, Kt.1715, II. 280
Cooke, George, K.C.B.1815, I. 228
Cook, Henry, Kt.1904, II. 419
Cooke, Henry F., K.C.H.1821, I. 455; Kt.1825, II. 325
Cook, John, Kt.1624, II. 187
Coke, John, Kt.1633, II. 201
Cooke, John, Kt.1701, II. 272
Coke, John, K.C.B.1881, I. 258
Cooke, John H., Kt.1867, II. 359
Cooke, Miles, Kt.1674, II. 249
Cooke, Philippe, Kt.1497, II. 30
Cook, Richard, Kt.1603, II. 129
Cook, Robert, Kt.1607, II. 144
Cook, Robert, Kt.1621, II. 177
Cooke, Samuel, Kt.1713, II. 278
Cooke, Thomas, K.B.(1465), I. 135
Cook, Thomas, Kt.1690, II. 266
Coke, Thomas, earl of Leicester, K.B. 1725, I. 168
Coke, Thomas W., earl of Leicester, K.G.1873, I. 65
Coke, Walsingham, Kt.1630, II. 193
Cooke, William, Kt.1603, II. 104
Coke, William, Kt.1815, II. 316
Cooke, William F., Kt.1869, II. 361
Cookes, Thomas, Kt.1662, II. 236
Coker, Reginald de, K.B.1253, I. 110
Coker, Thomas, Kt.1544, II. 55

INDEX 53

Cokesy, Cokesay, Cokesey
  Cokesy, Hugh, Kt.(1419), II. lx.
  Cokesay, Thomas, K.B.(1485), I. 142
  Cokesey, alias Grevell, Thomas, Kt. 1487, II. 24
Colawarth. See Cosworth
Colbatch, John, Kt.1716, I. 281
Colborne, Francis, K.C.B.1876, I. 255
Colborne, John, lord Seaton, K.C.B.1815, I. 224; G.C.H.1836, I. 453; G.C.B. 1838, I. 188; G.C.M.G.1843, I. 334
Colby, Huntingdon, Kt.1616, II. 160
Colchester, Duncombe, Kt.1674, II. 249
Colclough, Anthony, Kt.1582, II. 81
Cole, Christopher, Kt.1812, II. 311; K.C.B.1815, I. 222
Cole, Galbraith, L., K.B.1813, I. 179; G.C.B.1815, I. 181
Cole, Henry, K.C.B.1875, I. 285
Cole, John W., earl of Enniskillen, K.P. 1810, I. 98
Cole, Lowry E., earl of Enniskillen, K.P. 1902, I. 106
Cole, Michael, Kt.1673, II. 248
Cole, Nicholas, Kt.1641, II. 208
Cole, Robert, Kt.1671, II. 245
Cole, Thomas, Kt.1706, II. 275
Cole, William, Kt. 1617, II. 166
Cole (Coles), William, Kt.1694, II. 268
Cole, William J., K.H.1837, I. 476
Colebrooke, H. C., K.H.1833, I. 469
Colebrooke, William M. G., K.H.1834, I. 471; Kt.1837, II. 338
Coleclough, Thomas, Kt.1591, II. 89
Colepeper. See Culpeper
Coleridge, John D., Kt.1868, II. 360
Coleridge, John T., Kt.1835, II. 337
Coles, Jenkin, K.C.M.G.1894, I. 379
Coles. See Cole
Colet. See Collett
Colgrave, George, Kt., Jacobite, 1710, footnote, II. 266
Coll, Patrick, Kt.1896, II. 396; K.C.B. 1903, I. 301

Colladon, Collydon
  Colladon, John, Kt.1664, II. 240
  Collydon, Theodore, Kt.1700, II. 271
Collard, George, Kt.1903, II. 414

Collen, Edwin H. H., K.C.I.E.1893, I. 407; G.C.I.E.1901, I. 403
Collett, Colet
  Colet, Henry, K.B.(1483), I. 140
  Collett, Henry, Kt.1486, II. 23
  Collett, Henry, K.C.B.1891, I. 264
  Collett, James, Kt.1697, II. 270
Colley, Anthony, Kt.1621, II. 177
Colley, George, Kt.1593, II. 90
Colley, George P., K.C.S.I.1879, I. 322
Colley (Coulke), Henry, Kt.1576, II. 77
Colley, William, Kt.1615, II. 156
Collier, Collyer, and see Colyear
  Collier, Edward, K.C.B.1865, I. 250
  Collier, Francis A., Kt.1830, II. 329; K.C.H.1833, I. 459
  Collier, George, Kt.1775, II. 294
  Collier, George R., Kt.1807, II. 308; K.C.B.1815, I. 222
  Collier, Robert P., Kt.1863, II. 357
  Collyer, William, Kt.1584, II. 83
Collingbourne, Cuthbert, Kt.1570, II. 75
Collins, Collings
  Collins, Arthur J. H., Kt.1885, II. 378
  Collins, John, Kt.1681, II. 256
  Collins, John, Kt.1783, II. 298
  Collins, Richard H., Kt.1891, II. 389
  Collins, Robert H., K.C.B.1884, I. 288; K.C.V.O.(1904), I. 437
  Collings, William, Kt.1838, II. 340
  Collins, William, Kt.1881, II. 373
  Collins, William J., Kt.1902, II. 411
Collinson, Richard, K.C.B.1875, I. 255
Collonel. See Coronel
Collymore, John, Kt.1604, II. 130
Colnaghi, Dominic E., Kt.1888, II. 384
Colne, Baldwin de, K.B.1306, I. 120
Colomb, John C. R., K.C.M.G.1888, I. 373
Colonna. See Sonnino
Colpoys, John, K.B.1798, I. 175; G.C.B. 1815, I. 180
Colpoys, Edward G., K.C.B.1831, I. 230
Colquhoun, Patrick M. de, Kt.1861, II. 356
Colquhoun, Robert G., K.C.B.1865, I. 283
Colston, Joseph, Kt.1669, II. 243
Colt, George, Kt.1578, II. 78
Colt, Henry, Kt.1605, II. 137
Colt (Coult), John, Kt.1633, II. 200

Colt, William D., Kt.1684, II. 260
Coltman, Thomas, Kt.1837, II. 338
Colton, John, K.C.M.G.1892, I. 377
COLVILLE, COLVILL, COLEVILLE, COLVILE
  Colville, Charles, K.C.B.1815, I. 219;
    G.C.B.1815, I. 183; G.C.H.1816, I.
    448
  Colville, Charles H., Kt.1812, II. 311
  Colville, Charles J., viscount Colville,
    K.T.1874, I. 86; G.C.V.O.1896, I. 417
  Coleville, Geoffry de, K.B.1306, I. 118
  Colville, Henry E., K.C.M.G.1895, I.
    381
  Colvile, James W., Kt.1848, II. 347
  Colvile, John (James), Kt.1607, II. 144
  Colvill, Robert, Kt.1676, II. 251
  Colville, William J., K.C.V.O.(1896),
    I. 432
Colvin, Auckland, K.C.M.G.1881, I. 364;
  K.C.S.I.1892, I. 324
Colvin, Walter M., Kt.1904, II. 417
Colvin-Smith, Colvin, K.C.B.1903, I. 276
Colyear, Charles, earl of Portmore, K.T.
  1732, I. 77
Colyear, David, earl of Portmore, K.T.
  1712-3, I. 76
Colyngwod, Robert, Kt.1513, II. 38
Combarieu, Abel, G.C.V.O.1903, I. 427
Combermere, viscount. See Cotton
COMBES, COMBE
  Combes, Emile, G.C.V.O.1903, I. 427
  Combes, John, Kt.1695, II. 268
  Combe, Richard, Kt.1656, II. 223, 233
Commerell, John E., K.C.B.1874, I. 254;
  G.C.B.1887, I. 199
Compton, Charles, Kt.1643, II. 217
Compton, Francis, Kt.1661, II. 236
Compton, (Corupton), Henry, Kt.1567,
  II. 73
Compton, Henry, K.B.1603, I. 154
Compton, Herbert A. D., Kt.1831, II. 330
Compton, John, Kt.1622, II. 180
Compton, John W., Kt.1816, II. 317
Compton, Spencer, earl of Northampton,
  K.B.1616, I. 160
Compton, Spencer, Kt.1643, II. 217
Compton, Spencer, earl of Wilmington,
  K.B.1725, I. 167; K.G.1733, I. 43
Compton, Thomas, Kt.1603, II. 111

Compton, William, Kt.1643, II. 217
Compton, William, Kt.1513, II. 39, 42
Compton, William, earl of Northampton,
  K.B.1605, I. 156; K.G.1628, I. 32
Compton, William, marquess of North-
  ampton, K.G.1885, I. 67
Compton. See Crompton
Comuto, Antonio count, G.C.M.G.1818, I.
  331

COMYN, COMYNS
  Comyn, John, K.B.1306, I. 117
  Comyns, John, Kt.1726, II. 283
  Comyn, Nicholas, Kt.1650, II. 221
  Comyn, Robert B., Kt.1825, II. 325
Conant, Nathaniel, Kt.1813, II. 313
Condari, Angiolo, C.M.G.(1822), I. xxviii.;
  K.C.M.G.1825, I. 351; G.C.M.G.1832,
  I. 333
Conesby. See Coningsby
Congreve, William, K.C.H.1816, I. 454
Coningham. See Cunningham

CONINGSBY, CONESBY, CONINGESBY,
  CONYSBY, CONISBY, CONNISBY,
  CONESBIE, CONNESBIE, CONISBYE
  Coningesby, Francis, Kt.1616, II. 159
  Coningesby, Henry, Kt.1585, II. 83
  Coningsby, Henry, Kt. 1660, II. 227
  Conisby, Humfrey, Kt.1603, II. 104
  Connisby, Philip, Kt.1603, II. 121
  Conesbie, Ralph, Kt.1603, II. 101
  Cunnisby, Richard, Kt.1603, II. 114
  Conisbye, Thomas, Kt.1591, II. 89
Connal, Michael, Kt.1885, II. 377
Connaught, Arthur W. P. A., duke of,
  K.G.1867, I. 64; K.P.1869, I. 103;
  K.T.1869, I. 86; G.C.M.G.1870, I.
  336; G.C.S.I.1877, I. 311; G.C.I.E.
  1887, I. 401; G.C.V.O.1896, I. 417;
  K.C.B.1890, I. 263; G.C.B.1898, I.
  202; Grand Master of the Bath
  (1901), I. 109; Victorian Chain 1902,
  I. 415
Connaught, prince Arthur F. P. A. of,
  G.C.V.O.1899, I. 418; K.G.1902, I. 72
Connell, John, Kt.1820, II. 321
Connemara, lord. See Bourke
Connisby. See Coningsby

CONNY, CONY, CONEY, CUNNYE, CONNEY, COUNY, and see Conway
Cony, George, Kt.1661, II. 234
Coney (Conny, Cunnye), Sutton, Kt. 1619, II. 173
Coney (Conney), Thomas, Kt.1603, II. 119
Couny (Cunny), Thomas, Kt.1624, II. 184
Coney (Conny), William, Kt.1642, II. 213
Connock, Timon, Kt. Jacobite, 1707, footnote, II. 266

CONNOR, CONNER
Connor, C. C., Kt.1889, II. 386
Connor, Henry, Kt.1880, II. 371
Conner, Richard, Kt.1617, II. 161
Conquest, Edmund, Kt.1603, II. 110, 112
Conquest, John, K.B.1306, I. 118
Conquest, Richard, Kt.1603, II. 111, 124
Conquest, Richard, Kt.1607, II. 146
Conroy, John, K.C.H.1827, I. 456; Kt. 1827, II. 326
Considine, James, K.H.1832, I. 466
Constable, Henry, Kt.1586, II. 84
Constable, Henry, Kt.1604, II. 130
Constable, John, Kt.1347, II. 9
Constable, John, Kt.1482, II. 20
Constable, John, Kt.1504, II. 34
Constable, John, Kt.1533, II. 49
Constable, John, Kt.1544, II. 54
Constable, John, Kt.1553, II. 68
Constable, John, Kt.1607, II. 143
Constable, Marmaduke, Kt.1482, II. 20
Constable, Marmaduke, Kt.1513, II. 37
Constable, Marmaduke, Kt.1523, II. 44
Constable, Marmaduke, Kt.1547, II. 62
Constable, Philip, Kt.1603, II. 100
Constable, Rafe, Kt.1603, II. 128
Constable, Robert le, K.B.1306, I. 116
Constable, Robert, Kt.1497, II. 30
Constable, Robert (Thomas), Kt.1544, II. 56
Constable, Robert, Kt.1570, II. 74
Constable, Robert, Kt.1599, II. 96
Constable, Robert, Kt.1701, II. 272
Constable, Thomas, K.B.1426, I. 132
Constable, William, Kt.1599, II. 96
Constable, William, of Carethorp, Kt. 1513, II. 38
Constable, William, of Hatfield, Kt.1513, II. 38
Constantine, William, Kt.1668, II. 243
CONWAY, CONNYE, CONNER, and see Conny
Conway, Edward, Kt.1596, II. 92
Conway, Edward, Kt.1618, II. 168
Conway, Fulke, Kt.1599, II. 97
Conway, Hugh, K.B.(1487), I. 142
Conway, John, Kt.1560, II. 71
Conway, John (Thomas), Kt.1603, II. 115
Conway, John, Kt.1604, II. 130
Conway, Richard, Kt.1547, II. 61
Conway (Connye, Conner), Richard, Kt.1617, II. 161
Conway, Thomas, senr., Kt.1624, II. 185
Conway, Thomas, junr., Kt.1624, II. 185
Conway, William M., Kt.1895, II. 396
CONYERS, COGNIERS, CONIERS, COIGNERS, COGNYERS, COMMES, COMINES
Conyers, Christopher, Kt.1523, II. 44
Conyers (Commes, Comines), Edward, Kt.1603, II. 104
Cogniers, George, Kt.1533, II. 49
Conyers, George, Kt.1604, II. 131
Coniers (Conyers), Gerard, Kt.1714, II. 279
Conyers, John, K.G.1483, I. 17
Conyers, John, 3rd lord Conyers, Kt. 1544, II. 54
Conyers, John, Kt.1595, II. 91
Conyers, John, Kt.1603, II. 100
Conyers, John, Kt.1624, II. 185
Conyers, Ralph, Kt.1617, II. 163
Coigners, Richard, Kt.1482, II. 20
Cognyers (Connyers), William, Kt. 1497, II. 31
Conyngham. See Cunningham
Conysby. See Coningsby
Cooch Behar, Nripendra, of, G.C.I.E. 1888, I. 401
Cooche, Thomas, Kt.1603, II. 127
Coode, John, Kt.1872, II. 363; K.C.M.G. 1886, I. 368
Coode, John Henry, K.C.B.1855, I. 241

Cook, Cooke, Cookes. See Coke
Cookson, Charles A., K.C.M.G.1888, I. 373
Cooper. See Cowper
Coorden. See Carden
Coote, Charles, Kt.1616, II. 160
Coote, Charles, Kt.1626, II. 190
Coote, Charles, Kt.1660, II. 228
Coote, Charles, 5th earl of Bellamont, K.B.1764, I. 171; Kt.1764, II. 292
Coote, Eyre, K.B.1770, I. 171
Coote, Eyre, K.B.1802, I. 175; G.C.B. 1815, I. 180
Coote, Eyre, Kt.1903, II. 415
Coote, Phillips, Kt.1680, II. 255
Coote. See Coats
Coots. See Coats
COPE, COAPE
  Cope, Anthony, Kt.1547, II. 63
  Cope, Anthony, Kt.1591 (1592), I. 88
  Cope, Edward, Kt.1605, II. 138
  Cope, John, Kt.1696, II. 269
  Cope, John, K.B.1743, I. 169
  Cope, Walter, Kt.1603, II. 102
  Cope (Coape), William, Kt.1603, II. 106
Copley, John S., Kt.1819, II. 320
Coppin (Coppen), George, Kt.1603, II. 114
COPPINGER, COPYNGER
  Coppinger Ambrose (Henry), Kt.1603, II. 117
  Coppinger, John, Kt.1624, II. 187
  Copynger, Rauf, Kt.1547, II. 62
  Coppinger, Walter, Kt.1624, II. 187
Coppleston, John, Kt.1655, II. 223
CORBET, CORBETT, COURBET
  Corbet, Andrew, Kt.1547, II. 63
  Corbet, Andrew, Kt.1617, II. 165
  Corbet, Edward (Richard), K.B.1603, I. 154
  Courbet, Fouke, Kt.1380, II. 10
  Corbett, John, K.C.B.1886, I. 260
  Corbet, Miles, Kt.1596, II. 92
  Corbett, Richard, Kt. 1523, II. 45
  Corbett, Richard, Kt.1548, II. 63
  Corbet, Robert, K.B.1501, I. 145
  Corbet, Roger, K.B.1306, I. 120
  Corbet, Roger, Kt.1347, II. 8
  Corbet, Roger, K.B.(1465), I. 135
  Corbett, Stuart, K.C.B.1862, I. 247

CORBET
  Corbet, Thomas, K.B.1306, I. 118
  Corbet, Thomas, Kt.1635, II. 204
  Corbet, Vincent, Kt.1607, II. 143
  Corbet, Vincent, Kt.1641, II. 209
  Corbet, William, K.B.1306, I. 115
Corby. See Crosby
Cordell, John, Kt.1641, II. 211
Cordell William, Kt.1557, II. 70
Cork, earl of (1835). See Boyle, E.
Cormack, John R., Kt.1872, II. 363
Cormeilles, John de, K.B.1303, I. 110
Cornerd, Ric, Kt.1347, II. 6
Corntcall. See Cornwall
Cornwall, Edmund, duke of, Kt.1272, II. 5
Cornwall, Edmund de, K.B.1306, I. 112
Cornwall, Edmund de, K.B.1330, I. 125
Cornewall, Edmund, lord of Burford, K.B.(1483), I. 139, 141
Cornwall, Francis, Kt.1604, II. 133
Cornwall, George, Kt.1546, II. 58
Cornwall, Gilbert, Kt.1620, II. 176
Cornwall, Henry of, Kt.1257, II. 7
Cornwall, John, lord Fanhope, K.G.1410, I. 9
Cornwall, John, K.B.(1426), I. 131
Cornwall [Corntcall], Ric, Kt.1347, II. 8
Cornwall, Thomas, Kt.1471, II. 15
Cornewall, Thomas, baron of Burford, Kt.1497, II. 29
Cornwall, Thomas, Kt.1513, II. 36
Cornwall, Thomas, Kt. after 1524, II. 46
Cornwall, Thomas, Kt.1603, II. 107

CORNWALLIS, CORNWALLYS
  Cornwallis, Charles (Thomas), Kt.1603, II. 105
  Cornwallis, Charles, 2nd lord Cornwallis, K.B.1661, I. 164
  Cornwallis, Charles, marquess Cornwallis, K.G.1786, I. 48; Grand Master K.P.1798, I. 93
  Cornwallis, Frederick, Kt.1630, II. 198
  Cornwallis, John, Kt.1523, II. 45
  Cornwallis, Thomas, Kt.1548, II. 63
  Cornwallis, Thomas, Kt.1605, II. 137
  Cornewallys, William, Kt.1599, II. 97
  Cornwallis, William, G.C.B.1815, I. 182

INDEX

Coronel or Collonel, Augustine, Kt.1661, II. 235
Corranza y de Echevarria, Jose de, K.C.M.G.1893, I. 378
Corrario, Angelo, Kt.1638, II. 206
Corry, Armar Lowry, K.C.B.1855, footnote, I. 241
Corry, Trevor, Kt.1776, II. 295
Corsellis, Thomas, K.C.B.1838, I. 235
Corupton. See Compton
Cosby, Henry A. M., Kt.1784, II. 298
Cosington, William de, K.B.1306, I. 115
Costa, Michael, Kt.1869, II. 361
Costa Ferreira, Cornelius Alvaro da, K.C.M.G.1902, I. 393
Cosway, William R, Kt.1829, II. 328
Cosworth (Colawarth), Samuel, Kt.1643, II. 216
Cotes. See Coats
Cotgreave, John, Kt.1816, II. 317
Cottel (Cutteal), Thomas, Kt.1609, II. 148
Cotter, Ludlow, Kt.1874, II. 366
COTTERELL, COTTRELL
Cotterel, Charles, Kt.1645, II. 219
Cottrell, Charles, Kt.1687, II. 263
Cotterell, Clement, Kt.1620, II. 176
Cotterell, Clement, Kt.1710, II. 277
Cottrell, Stephen, Kt.1796, II. 303
Cotton, —, Kt.1503, II. 33
Cotton, Allen, Kt.1626, II. 190
Cotton, Arthur, Kt.1861, II. 355
Cotton, Arthur T., K.C.S.I.1866, I. 316
Cotton, Dodmore, Kt.1626, II. 190
Cotton, George, Kt.1542, II. 53
Cotton, George, Kt.1603, II. 121
Cotton, George, Kt.1897, II. 401
Cotton, Henry, Kt.1877, II. 369
Cotton, Henry J. S., K.C.S.I.1902, I. 327
Cotton, John, Kt.1553, II. 67
Cotton, John, Kt.1603, II. 115
Cotton, John, Kt.1623, II. 183
Cotton, Joh., Kt.1641, II. 209
Cotton, John, Kt.1685, II. 261
Cotton, Richard, Kt.1547, II. 59
Cotton, Robert, Kt.1603, II. 106, 125
Cotton, Robert, Kt.1660, II. 229
Cotton, Robert, Kt.1663, II. 238
Cotton, Roger, Kt.1482, II. 18
Cotton, Rowland, Kt.1608, II. 146

Cotton, Stapleton, viscount Combermere, K.B.1812, I. 178; G.C.B.1815, I. 181; G.C.H.1817, I. 448; K.S.I. 1861, I. 307
Cotton, Sidney J., K.C.B.1858, I. 244; G.C.B.1873, I. 196
Cotton, William J. R., Kt.1892, II. 390
Cotton, Willoughby, K.C.H.1830, I. 456; Kt.1830, II. 328; K.C.B.1838, I. 234; G.C.B.1840, I. 188
Cottysmore, John, Kt.1501, II. 32
Couch, Richard, Kt.1866, I. 358
Couci, Ingelram de, Sire de Couci, earl of Bedford, K.G.1365, I. 3
Coudenhove, count Charles, G.C.V.O. 1904, I. 431
Coulke, Henry, Kt.1576, II. 77
Coult. See Colt
Couper. See Cowper
Courbet. See Corbet
Courcy, Gerald, lord Courcy, Kt.1567, II. 73
Courcy, Michael, Kt.1541, II. 52
Courcy-Perry, Gerald R. de, Kt.1900, II. 406
Courteen. See Curteen

COURTENAY, COURTENEY, COURTNEY
Courtenay, —, K.B.1399, I. 127
Courteney, —, Kt.1492, II. 28
Courtenay, Edward, K.B.(1483), I. 138
Courteney, Edward, earl of Devonshire, Kt.1485, II. 22; K.G.1491, I. 18
Courtenay, Edward, earl of Devon, K.B.1553, I. 152
Courtenay, Henry, marquess of Exeter, K.G.1521, I. 21
Courtenay, Hugh de, K.B.1327, I. 124
Courtney, Hugh, Kt.1347, II. 7; K.G. 1348, I. 1
Courtenay, Hugh, earl of Devon, K.B. 1399, I. 127
Courteney, John, Kt.1460, II. 12
Courtenay, John, Kt.1471, II. 15
Courtenay, Peter, K.G.1388, I. 6
Courtney, Peter, Kt.1642, II. 213
Courtenay, Philip de, K.B.1306, I. 113
Courteney, Philippe, Kt.1471, II. 14

COURTENAY
Courtenay, Thomas, earl of Devon, K.B.(1426), I. 130
Courtenay, William de, K.B.1253, I. 110
Courteney, William, Kt.1485, II. 23
Courtenay, William, earl of Devon, K.B.(1487), I. 142
Courtney, William, Kt.1553, II. 67
Courteney, William, Kt.1576, II. 77
Courtney, William, Kt.1599, II. 96
Courtney, William, Kt.1625, II. 189
Courtenay, William, Kt.1641, II. 211
Courtney, William, Kt.1644, II. 217

COURTHOPE, COURTHOP
Courthope, George, Kt.1641, II. 209
Courthorpe, George, Kt.1661, II. 234
Courthop, Peter, Kt.1661, II. 233

Courtown, earl of. See Stopford
Courtpeny, —, Kt.1549, II. 65
Couteur, John le, Kt.1872, II. 364
Coventry, John, K.B.1661, I. 165
Coventry, Thomas, Kt.1617, II. 161
Coventry, William, Kt.1665, II. 240
Covert, John, Kt.1660, II. 228
Covert, Walter, Kt.1591, II. 88
Covert, Walter, Kt.1624, II. 183

COWAN, COWEN
Cowan, Edward P., Kt.1881, II. 373
Cowan, Robert, Kt.1736, II. 285
Cowen, Joseph, Kt.1872, II. 363

COWELL, COGHILL, COELL
Coell, John, Kt.1665, II. 241
Coghill, John, Kt.1686, II. 262
Cowell, John C., K.C.B.1865, I. 283
Cowell, Stepney, K.H.1832, I. 468
Coghil, Thomas, Kt.1633, II. 202

Cowen. See Cowan
Cowley, Henry, Kt.161⁵. II. 156
Cowley, lord and earl. See Wellesley
Cowlings, Alfred S., Kt.1904, II. 420

COWPER, COOPER, COUPER
Cooper, Alfred, Kt.1901, II. 408
Cooper, Alfred, Kt.1902, II. 411
Cooper, Anthony A., earl of Shaftesbury, K.G.1862, I. 61
Cooper, Arthur (John), Kt.1603, II. 105
Cooper, Astley P., G.C.H.1836, I. 453
Cooper, Charles, Kt.1857, II. 352

COWPER
Cowper, Charles, K.C.M.G.1872, I. 356
Cooper, Daniel, Kt.1857, II. 352; K.C.M.G.1880, I. 363; G.C.M.G. 1888, I. 341
Cooper, Edmund, Kt.1642, II. 212
Cooper, Edward, Kt.1645, II. 220
Cowper, Francis T. de G., earl Cowper, K.G.1865, I. 63; Grand Master K.P.1880, I. 95
Cooper, George, Kt.1816, II. 317
Couper, George, K.H.1831, I. 465
Couper, George E. W., K.C.S.I.1877, I. 321
Cooper, Henry, Kt.1854, II. 350
Cowper, John, Kt.1622, II. 179
Cooper, Maurice, Kt.1603, II. 121
Cooper, Pope A., Kt.1904, II. 418
Cooper (Coop, Roper), Richard, Kt. 1603, II. 118
Cooper, Roger, Kt.1624, II. 186
Cooper, William, Kt.1642, II. 212
Cooper, William E., Kt.1903, II. 414
Cooper, William W., Kt.1886, II. 379

COX, COXE, COCKS
Cox, Charles, Kt.1709, II. 277
Cox, Charles, K.C.M.G.1887, I. 370
Coxe, James, Kt.1863, II. 357
Cocks, John, Kt.1671, II. 246
Cox, John, K.H.1832, I. 466
Cocks, Richard, Kt.1603, II. 127
Cox, John W., K.C.B.1896, I. 266
Cox, Lawrence, Kt.1786, II. 299
Cox, Richard, Kt.1692, II. 267
Cox, William, Kt.1816, II. 318
Cox, William, K.H.1835, I. 472
Cox, William H. L., Kt.1896, II. 398

Coxhead, Thomas, Kt.1793, II. 301
Coyet, Peter J., Kt.1656, II. 223
Cozans. See Cusins
Cozens-Hardy, Herbert H., Kt.1899, II. 405
Crabbe, Eyre, J., K.H.1837, I. 477
Craddock, John F., K.B.1803, I. 175; G.C.B.1815, I. 180
Cradock, Joseph, Kt.1661, II. 234
Cragge, James, Kt.1616, II. 159
Craggs, John G., Kt.1903, II. 416
Craig, James H., K.B.1797, I. 175

Craigie, Peter E., K.C.B.1867, I. 250
Craik, Henry, K.C.B.1897, I. 295
Crampton, John F. T., K.C.B.1856, I. 280
Cranborne, viscount. See Cecil, C.
Cranbrook, viscount. See Gaythorne-Hardy
Crane, Francis, Kt.1617, II. 166
Crane, Richard, Kt.1642, II. 214
Crane, Robert, Kt.1605, II. 137
Cranfield, Lyonel, Kt.1613, II. 153
Cranfield, Randall, Kt.1623, II. 182
Cranley, William, Kt.1603, II. 128
Cranmer, Cæsar, Kt.1677, II. 252
Cranmer, William, Kt.1689, II. 265
Cranshaw. See Carnshaw
Cranston, Robert, Kt.1903, II. 414
Crape, Walter, Kt.1603, II. 101
Craven, Anthony, Kt. 1661, II. 235
Craven, Robert M., Kt.1896, II. 397
Craven, William, Kt.1603, II. 128
Craven William, lord Craven, Kt.1627, II. 191
Craven, William, Kt.1639, II. 207
Craven, William, Kt.1662, II. 236
CRAWFORD, CRAUFORD, CRAYFORD, CRAFFORD, CRAFORD
Crauford, Charles C., G.C.B.1820, I. 185
Crawford, earl of. See Lindsay
Crayford (Crafford), George, Kt.1619, II. 172
Crawford, Henry, Kt. Jacobite, 1716, footnote, II. 266
Crawford (Henry), Homewood, Kt. 1900, II. 407
Crauford, Philip (? Patrick), Kt.1777 II. 295
Crayford (Craford), Robert, Kt.1624, II. 185
Crawford, Thomas, K.C.B.1885, I. 259
Craford (Crayford), William, Kt.1603, II. 125
Crawford (Crayford), William, Kt. 1621, II. 177
Crawley, Francis, Kt.1632, II. 200
Crayford. See Crawford
Creagh, Michael, Kt.1686, II. 262
Creagh, Michael, K.H.1832, I. 467; Kt. 1832, II. 332
Creagh, O'Moore, K.C.B.1903, I. 276
Creagh, William, Kt.1685, II. 260
Crease, Henry P. P., Kt.1896, II. 397
Crease, John F., K.C.B.1902, I. 274
Creasy, Edward S., Kt.1860, II. 354
Creed, James, Kt.1744, II. 286
Cremer, John, Kt.1660, II. 229
Cremorne, baron. See Dawson
Crenequer, Robert de, K.B.1253, I. 110
Cressemere, Alexander, K.B.(1483), I. 139
Cressenor, John, Kt.1513, II. 42
Cressfield, Ralph, Kt.1713, II. 278
Cressie, Robert, Kt.1621, II. 178
Cressy, Bertrandus de, K.B.1253, I. 110
Cresswell, Cresswell, Kt.1842, II. 344
Creswick, Henry, Kt.1663, II. 238
Crew, Clipsby, Kt.1620, II. 175
Crew, John, Kt.1673, II. 248
Crew, Randolph, Kt.1614, II. 154
Crew, Thomas, Kt.1623, II. 183
Crew, Thomas, Kt.1660, II. 231
Crew. See Carew
Crew. See Crowe
Crewes, Jo, Kt.1347, II. 6
CRICHTON, CRIGHTONE
Crichton, Alexander, Kt.1821, II. 322
Crichton, Archibald W., Kt.1817, II. 319
Crightone, David, Kt.1633, II. lxiii.
Crichton, John, earl Erne, K.P.1868, I. 103
Crichton, John H., earl Erne, K.P. 1889, I. 105
Crichton, William, lord, Kt.1484, II. 22
Crichton-Browne, James, Kt.1886, II. 378
Crichton-Stuart, John, marquess of Bute, K.T.1843, I. 83
Crichton-Stuart, John P., marquess of Bute, K.T.1875, I. 87
Crimes. See Grimes
Crioll, Nicholas, K.B.1306, I. 113
CRIPPS, CRIPPES, CRISP, CRISPE, CRIPS
Crippes (Crispe), Edmond, Kt.1604, II. 132
Cripps, Henry, Kt.1553, II. 67
Cripps (Crispe), Henry, Kt.1603, II. 107
Crispe, Nicholas, Kt.1640, II. 207
Crisp, Thomas, Kt.1703, II. 273

Crisp. See Cripps
Critchett, Anderson, Kt.1901, II. 409
Crocker, Hugh, Kt.1644, II. 218
CROFT, CROFTS, CROFTES, CROFTE
  Croft, Alfred W., K.C.I.E.1887, I. 400
  Crofts, Charles, Kt.1628, II. 194
  Croft, Edward, Kt.1513, II. 41
  Croft, Edward, Kt.1522, II. 43
  Croftes, Henry, Kt.1603, II. 128
  Crofts, Henry, Kt.1611, II. 150
  Croft (Crofts), Herbert, Kt.1603, II. 104
  Crofte, Hugh de, K.B.1305, I. 111
  Croftes, James, Kt.1547, II. 63
  Croft (Croftes), James, Kt.1603, II. 120
  Croft, James, Kt.1644, II. 219
  Crofts, John, Kt.1553, II. 68
  Croftes, John, Kt.1599, II. 97
  Crofte, Richard, Kt.1471, II. 14
  Crofts, Richard, Kt.1487, II. 24
  Croft (Crofts), Thomas, Kt.1668, II. 243
  Croft, William, Kt.1614, II. 154
  Croft, Crofts. See Cross
  Crofts. See Croft
Crofton, Walter F., Kt.1862, II. 356
Croix. See De la Croix
CROKE, CROOKE, CROOK
  Croke, Alexander, Kt.1816, II. 318
  Crook (Croke), George, Kt.1623, II. 182
  Crooke, George, Kt.1660, II. 232
  Crook, Henry, Kt.1615, II. 157
  Crook (Croke), John, Kt.1603, II. 110, 111
  Crook (Croke), John, Kt.1609, II. 147
  Croke, Richard, Kt.1681, II. 255
  Crook, Robert, Kt.1641, II. 210
  Crooke, Thomas, Kt.1624, II. 184
Croker, Gerard, Kt.1575, II. 77
Croker, John, Kt.1471, II. 15
CROMER, CROWMER
  Cromer, earl of. See Baring
  Crowmer, James, Kt.1471, II. 15
  Cromer, James, Kt.1603, II. 105
Crowmer, William, K.B.1509, I. 148
Cromie, Michael, Kt.1773, II. 294
Cromp. See Crump
Crompton, Charles, Kt.1852, II. 349
Crompton, John, Kt.1608, II. 144

Crompton, Robert, Kt.1642, II. 212
Crompton (Compton), Thomas, Kt.1603, II. 111
Crompton, Thomas, Kt.1603, II. 114
Crompton (Compton), Thomas, Kt.1607, II. 141
Crompton, William, Kt.1608, II. 144
Cromwell, Edward, lord Cromwell, Kt. 1599, II. 96
Cromwell, Gregory, lord Cromwell, K.B. 1547, II. 150
Cromwell, Gregory, Kt.1603, II. 102
Cromwell, Oliver, K.B.1603, I. 154
Cromwell, Philip, Kt.1604, II. 135
Cromwell, Richard, Kt.1523, II. 45
Cromwell, Richard, Kt.1538, II. 51
Cromwell, Thomas, Kt.1471, II. 15
Cromwell, Thomas, earl of Essex, Kt. 1536, II. 50; K.G.1537, I. 22
Crook. See Croke
Crookes, William, Kt.1897, II. 400
Crookshanks, Chichester W., K.H.1835, I. 471
Croom (John), Halliday, Kt.1902, II. 411
Cropley, Edward, Kt.1660, II. 231
CROSBY, CROSBIE, CORBY
  Crosby, John, Kt.1471, II. 16
  Crosby, John, Kt.1628, II. 195
  Crosbie, John G., G.C.H.1837, I. 453; Kt.1837, II. 339
  Crosbie, Maurice, Kt.1712, II. 277
  Crosbie (Corby), Peirce, Kt.1616, II. 158
  Crosby, Thomas, Kt.1677, I. 252
Crosland, Jordan, Kt.1642, II. 213
Crosland, Joseph, Kt.1889, II. 385
Crosley, Charles D., Kt.1855, II. 351
CROSS, CROSSE
  Cross, John, Kt.1831, II. 331
  Cross, John, K.H.1834, I. 470
  Cross, Richard A., viscount Cross, G.C.B.1880, I. 211; G.C.S.I.1892, I. 313
  Crosse, Robert, Kt.1596, II. 92
  Crosse, Robert N., K.H.1837, I. 477
  Crosse (Croft, Crofts), William, Kt. 1614, II. 154
Crossman, William, K.C.M.G.1884, I. 366

INDEX 61

Crosthwaite, Charles H. T., K.C.S.I.1888, I. 324
Crosthwaite, Robert J., K.C.S.I.1897, I. 326
Crowder, John, K.H.1837, I. 476
Crowder, Richard B., Kt.1854, II. 350
Crowe, Arthur de C., Kt.1892, II. 390
Crowe, John, K.H.1837, I. 477
Crowe, John R., Kt.1874, II. 366
Crowe, Joseph A., K.C.M.G.1890, I. 375
Crowe, Thomas, Kt.1603, II. 127
Crowe. See Crew
Crowley, Ambrose, Kt.1707, II. 275
Crowmer. See Cromer
Crozier, Philippe M., K.C.V.O.1898, I. 439
Cruise, Francis R., Kt.1896, II. 398
CRUMP, CROMP, CRUMPE
Crumpe (Cromp), Richard, Kt.1681, II. 257
Crump, William J., Kt.1902, II. 413
Crundall, William H., Kt.1889, II. 385
Cubbledike (Cobledyl), Alexander de, K.B.1327, I. 125
Cubbon, Mark, K.C.B.1856, I. 279
CUBITT, COUBETT
Coubett, Roger, Kt.1471, II. 15
Cubitt, William, Kt.1851, II. 349
Cuddon (Cudden), Thomas, Kt.1697, II. 270
Cuffe, Hamilton, J. A., viscount Desart, K.C.B.1898, I. 297
Cuffe, James, Kt.1660-1, II. 233
Cuffe, Thomas, Kt.1787, II. 300
Cuffe. See Cutte
Cullinan, Frederick F., Kt.1897, II. 400
Cullum, Hugh, Kt.1623, II. 183
Culme-Seymour, Michael, K.C.B.1893, I. 265; G.C.B.1897, I. 202; G.C.V.O. 1901, I. 419
CULPEPER, CULPEPPER, COLEPEPER
Colepeper, Alexander, Kt.1573, II. 75
Culpeper, Alexander, Kt.1621, II. 178
Culpeper (Colepeper), Anthony, Kt. 1603, II. 118
Culpepper, Cheyney, Kt.1628, II. 195
Culpeper, John, Kt.1617, II. 166
Culpeper, John, Kt.1622, II. 178
Culpepper, Martin, Kt.1604, II. 132

CULPEPER
Culpeper, Nicholas, K.B.(1465), I. 135
Culpepper, Thomas (Edward), Kt. 1603, II. 118; Kt.1604, II. 130
Cupeper, Thomas, Kt.1619, II. 174
Culpeper, Thomas, Kt.1625, II. 188
Culpepper, Thomas, Kt.1628, II. 195

CUMBERLAND
Ernest Augustus, duke of, king of Hanover, K.G.1786, I. 48; G.C.B. 1815, I. 182; G.C.H.1815, I. 447, 450; K.P.1821, I. 99
Ernest Augustus, duke of, K.G.1878, I. 65
George, duke of, K.G.1684, I. 37
George, etc., duke of, king of Hanover, G.C.H.1827, I. 450; K.G.1835, I. 55
Henry Frederick, duke of, K.G.1767, I. 46
William Augustus, duke of, K.B.1725, I. 167; K.G.1730, I. 43
Earl of. See Clifford
Cumming, Arthur, K.C.B.1887, I. 261
Cumming, Henry J., K.C.H.1833, I. 459; Kt.1833, II. 333
Cumming, John, Kt.1780, II. 296
Cunha, Manuel A. P. da, K.C.V.O., 1903, I. 441
Cunliffe, Ellis, Kt.1756, II. 289
Cunliffe, Robert H., Kt.1829, II. 328
Cunliffe-Owen, Francis P., K.C.B.1886, I. 289
Cunnesbie. See Coningsby
Cunny. See Conny

CUNNINGHAM, CONYNGHAM, CONINGHAM
Conyngham, Albert, Kt.1670, II. 245
Conyngham, Albert, Kt.1829, II. 328
Conyngham, Albert D., lord Londesborough, K.C.H.1829, I. 456
Cunningham, Alexander, K.C.I.E.1887, I. 399
Cunningham, Alexander F. D., K.C.I.E. 1901, I. 410
Cunynghame, Arthur A. T., K.C.B.1869, I. 252; G.C.B.1878, I. 197
Cunningham, Charles, K.C.H.1832, I. 459; Kt.1832, II. 333
Coningham, David, Kt.1604, II. 131

GG

INDEX

CUNNINGHAM
Conyngham, lord Francis N., marquess Conyngham, K.C.H.1821, I. 455; G.C.H.1823, I. 449; K.P.1833, I. 100
Conyngham, Henry, marquess Conyngham, K.P.1801, I. 98; G.C.H.1821, I. 449
Cunningham, Henry S., K.C.I.E.1889, I. 406
Coningham, John, Kt.1482, II. 18
Cunningham, John, Kt.1622, II. 180
Cunningham, William, Kt.1627, II. 192
Conyngham, William F. L., K.C.B.1881, I. 287
Cuningham, William J., K.C.S.I.1897, I. 326
Cuppage, Burke, K.C.B.1875, I. 255
Curcumelli, Demetrio, K.C.M.G.1857, I. 353
Cureton, Charles, K.C.B.1891, I. 263
Currey, Edmund, K.C.H.1834, I. 460
Currie, Donald, K.C.M.G.1881, I. 363; G.C.M.G.1897, I. 345
Currie, Edmund H., Kt.1876, II. 367
Currie, Philip H. W., lord Currie, K.C.B.1885, I. 289; G.C.B.1892, I. 213
Currie, Walter, Kt.1860, II. 355
Curson. See Curzon

CURTIS, CURTES, CURTEIS, CURTEYS
Curtes, George, Kt.1667, II. 242
Curtis Lucius, K.C.B.1862, I. 248
Curtis, Roger, Kt.1782, II. 297; G.C.B.1815, I. 182
Curteys, Thomas, Kt.1557, II. 70
Curteis, Thomas I. H., Kt.1833, II. 334

CURTEEN, COURTEEN, CURTON
Curteen (Courteen), Peter, Kt.1624, II. 183
Curton, Thomas de, Kt.1529, II. 47
Courteen, William, Kt.1622, II. 179

CURWEN, CURWYN
Curwen, Christopher, Kt.1482, II. 21
Curwen, Henry, Kt.1570, II. 74
Curwen, Nicholas, Kt.1603, II. 100
Curwyn, Thomas, K.B.1501, I. 146

CURZON, CURSON
Curson, Francis, Kt.1603, II. 111, 123
Curson, George, Kt.1604, II. 133

CURZON
Curzon, George N., lord Curzon of Kedleston, G.C.S.I.1899, I. 314; Grand Master Star of India I. 305; G.C.I.E.1899, I. 403; Victorian Chain 1903, I. 415
Curson, John, Kt.1641, II. 210
Curzon, Richard W., earl Howe, G.C.H. 1830, I. 450
Curzon-Howe, Richard G. P., earl Howe, G.C.V.O.1903, I. 421
Curzon-Howe, Richard W. P., earl Howe, G.C.V.O.1897, I. 417
Curson, Robert, Kt.1492, II. 28
Curson, Robert, Kt.1547, II. 63
Cusack, Ralph S., Kt.1873, II. 365
Cusack, Thomas, Kt.1541, II. 52
Cusack, Walter, Kt.(1361), II. lx.
Cusack-Smith, Thomas B., K.C.M.G.1898, I. 385

CUSINS, COZANS
Cozans, William, Kt.1347, II. 7
Cusins, William G., Kt.1892, II. 390
Cust, Edward, Kt.1831, II. 330; K.C.H.1831, I. 457
Cust, John, earl Brownlow, G.C.H.1834, I. 452
Cust, Pury, Kt.1690, II. 265
Cust, Reginald J., Kt.1890, II. 387
Custance, Hambleton F., K.C.B.1881, I 287
Custance, Reginald N., K.C.M.G.1904, I. 395
Cutch, Khengarji of, G.C.I.E.1887, I. 403
Cutch, Rao Pragmuljee, of, G.C.S.I.1871, I. 310
Cuthbert, Henry, K.C.M.G.1897, I. 383
Cuthbertson, John N., Kt.1887, II. 383
Cutler, Gervaise, Kt.1624, II. 186
Cutler, Jervase, Kt.1662, II. 236
Cutler, John, Kt.1660, II. 228
Cutler, Thomas, Kt.1681-2, II. 257
Cutliffe, John M., K.H.1816, I. 463
Cutseus, James, Kt.1628, II. 193

CUTTE, CUT, CUYT, CUTTS, CUTTES, and see Cutseus
Cutte, John, Kt.1504, II. 34
Cutt (Cuff or Cuyt), John, K.B.1547, I. 152

INDEX

CUTTE
Cut, John, Kt.1549, II. 63
Cutte (Cuttes), John, Kt.1571, II. 75
Cutts, John, Kt.1603, II. 107
Cutts, William, Kt.1608, II. 145
Cuttings, Roger, Kt.1665, II. 241

D

Dabridgecourt. See Abrichecourt
Dacca, Abdul Ghani, of, K.C.S.I.1886, I. 323
Dacca, Khwaja of, K.C.I.E.1897, I. 409
Dacombe, John, Kt.1616, II. 158
DACRES, DACRE, DACERS, DAKERS
Dacres, Christopher, Kt.1513, II. 37
Dacre (Dacres, Dacers), Henry, Kt. 1677, II. 252
Dacre, lord. See Fiennes
Dacres, Philip, Kt.1523, II. 43
Dacres, Richard, G.C.H.1836, I. 453
Dacres, Richard J., K.C.B.1855, I. 240; G.C.B.1869, I. 195
Dacres, Sydney C., K.C.B.1865, I. 250; G.C.B.1871, I. 196
Dacre, Thomas, lord Dacre of the North, Kt.1504, II. 34; K.B.1504, I. 147; K.G.1518, I. 20
Dacres, Thomas, Kt.1545, II. 57, 61
Dacres, Thomas, Kt.1604, II. 135
Dacres (Dakers), Thomas, Kt.1617, II. 161
Dakers, Thomas, Kt.1633, II. 201
Dacton. See Acton
D'Aguilar. See Aguilar
Dagworth, John de, K.B.1303, I. 110
Daines. See Danes
Dakin, Thomas, Kt.1872, II. 364
Dakyns, Arthur, Kt.1604, II. 135
Dalbiac, James Charles, K.C.H.1831, I. 456; Kt.1831, II. 329
Dalby, William B., Kt.1886, II. 378
Dalberg-Acton, John E. A., lord Acton, K.C.V.O.(1897), I. 432
Dale, Langham, K.C.M.G.1889, I. 374
Dale, Theodore, Kt.1355, II. 9
Dale, Thomas, Kt.1606, II. 140
Dales, Samuel, K.H.1833, I. 468

Dalesme, Jean B. C., K.C.B.1856, I. 242
Dalhousie, earl of. See Ramsey; see Maule
Dalington. See Dallington
Dalison. See Dallison
Dalkeith, earl of. See Scott; see Montagu-Douglas-Scott
Dallas, Robert, Kt.1813, II. 312
Dallas, Thomas, K.C.B.1815, I. 227; G.C.B.1833, I. 187
Dalling and Bulwer, lord. See Bulwer
DALLINGTON, DALINGTON
Dalington, Robert, Kt.1604, II. 130
Dallington, Robert, Kt.1624, II. 187
DALLISON, DALISON, DALYSON
Dallison, Charles, Kt.1642, II. 213
Dalison, Maximilian, Kt.1603, II. 106
Dalyson, Roger, Kt.1603, II. 103
Dallison, Thomas, Kt.1603, II. 122
Dalrymple, Charles, Kt.1814, II. 315
Dalrymple, Hew W., Kt.1779, II. 296
Dalrymple, John, earl of Stair, K.T. 1710, I. 76
Dalrymple, John H., earl of Stair, K.T. 1847, I. 83
Dalrymple-Crichton, William, earl of Dumfries, K.T.1752, I. 78
DALSTON, DAULSTON, and see Dalton
Dalston, Christopher, Kt.1617, II. 164
Dalston, George, Kt.1664, II. 239
Dalston, John, Kt.1664, II. 239
Dalston, William, Kt.1641, II. 210
Daulston, William, Kt.1760, II. 290
Dalton, Charles, Kt.1727, II. 283
Dalton (Dalston), George, Kt.1607, II. 142
Dalton, John, Kt.1636, II. 204
Dalton, Marmaduke, Kt.1676, II. 251
Dalton, William, Kt.1629, II. 196
Dalton, William, Kt.1660, II. 227
Daly, Dominick, Kt.1856, II. 351
Daly, Henry, G.C.B.1889, I. 200
Daly, Henry D., K.C.B.1875, I. 255
Daly, Malachy B., K.C.M.G.1900, I. 387
Dalyell, John G., Kt.1836, II. 338
Dalyell, Robert A., K.C.I.E.1887, I. 399
Damaschino, Alesandro, K.C.M.G.1849, I. 353; G.C.M.G.1855, I. 335
Dammory, Ric, Kt.1336, II. 5

64 INDEX

Dampier, Henry, Kt.1813, II. 313
Damport. See Davenport
Damsell, William, Kt.1553, II. 67
Danby, Abstrupus, Kt.1691, II. 266
Danby, Christopher, Kt.1513, II. 38
Danby, Christopher, Kt.1533, II. 49
Danby, earl of. See Danvers; see Osborne
Danby, James, Kt.1482, II. 17, 20
Danby, Robert, K.B.(1461), I. 133
Danby, Thomas, Kt.1547, II. 61
Danby, Thomas, Kt.1633, II. 202

DANCE, DAUNCE
Dance, Charles W., Kt.1821, II. 322; K.H.1836, I. 472
Daunce, John, Kt.1513, II. 40
Dance, Nathaniel, Kt.1805, II. 308

Dane (Dave), A. P., Kt.1502, II. 33
Danes (Daines), William, Kt.1694, II. 268
D'Angain. See Engaine
Dangervile (Daungerville), Roger, Kt. 1336, II. 5
Daniel, Francis C., Kt.1821, footnote II. 322
Daniel, Ingleby, Kt.1603, II. 122
Daniel, Peter, Kt.1684, II. 259
Daniel, Richard, K.B.1306, I. 117
Daniel, Samuel, Kt.1709, II. 276
Daniell, Thomas, Kt.1662, II. 236
Daniel, William, Kt.1603, II. 114
Daniel, William, Kt.1836, II. 337
Danneskjold-Samsöe, count Christian F., G.C.V.O.1904, I. 429
Danneskjold-Samsöe, Christian C. S., K.C.V.O.1904, I. 442

DANVERS, DAVERS
Danvers, Charles, Kt.1588, II. 87
Danvers, Henry, Kt.1591, II. 89
Danvers, Henry, earl of Danby, K.G. 1633, I. 33
Danvers, John, Kt.1501, II. 32
Danvers, John, Kt.1574, II. 76
Davers (Danvers), John, Kt.1609, II. 147
Danvers, John, Kt.1624, II. 184
Danvers, Juland, K.C.S.I.1886, I. 323
Danvers, Robert, K.B.(1465), I. 134
Danvers, Thomas, Kt.1501, II. 33
Danvers, William, Kt.1501, II. 33

DANVERS
Danvers (Davers), William, Kt.1607, II. 143
Darbhanga, Lachmessur Singh, of, K.C.I.E.1887, I. 400; G.C.I.E.1897, I. 402
Darbhanga, Rameshwar Singh, of, K.C.I.E.1902, I. 411
Darby, Henry D'E., K.C.B.1820, I. 229
Darcus (Darus), *alias* Denys, Thomas, Kt.1513, II. 36
Darcy, Arthur (Anthony), Kt.1523, II. 43
Darcy, Christopher, Kt.1623, II. 182
Darcy, Conyers, Kt.1603, II. 119
D'Arcy, Coniers, K.B.1725, I. 168
Darcy, Edward, Kt.1603, II. 105
Darcy, Francis, Kt.1591, II. 88
Darcy, George, Kt.1513, II. 37
Darcy, Henry, Kt.1565, II. 71
Darcy or Ducie, Hugh, K.B.1661, I. 166
Darcy, John, Kt.1336, II. 5
Darcy, John, Kt.1347, II. 8
Darcy, John, lord Darcy of Chiche, K.B. 1559, I. 153
Darcy, John, 2nd lord Darcy of Darcy and Mainhill, K.B.1559, I. 153
Darcy, Norman, Kt.1347, II. 6
Darcy, Robert, K.B.(1465), I. 135
Darcy, Thomas, K.B.(1483), I. 140
Darcy, Thomas, K.B.(1489), I. 143
Darcy, Thomas, Kt.1497, II. 31
Darcy, Thomas, lord Darcy de Darcy, K.G.1509, I. 20
Darcy, Thomas, Kt.1532, II. 48
Darcy, Thomas, lord Darcy of Chiche, K.G.1551, I. 24
Darcy, William, Kt.1482, II. 20
Darcy, William, Kt.1639, II. 206
Darell. See Darrell
Darley, Frederick M., Kt.1887, II. 381; K.C.M.G.1897, I. 382; G.C.M.G. 1901, I. 347
Darley, Richard, Kt.1617, II. 162
Darling, Charles H., K.C.B.1862, I. 282
Darling, Charles J., Kt.1897, II. 402
Darling, Ralph, Kt.1835, 336; G.C.H. 1835, I. 453
Darling, Robert, Kt.1766, II. 292
Darnell, John, Kt.1699, II. 271

INDEX

Darnell, John, Kt.1724, II. 283
DARRELL, DARELL, DAREL, DORRELL, DOREL, DAYRELL, DAYREL, DARELLE
Darell, Edward, Kt.1487, II. 25
Darrell, Edward, Kt.1544, II. 54
Dayrell (Dorrel), Francis, Kt.1672, II. 247
Darelle, George, K.B.(1465), I. 134
Darell, George, Kt.1465, II. 14
Darell, George, Kt.1492, II. 28
Darell, James, Kt.1513, II. 40
Darrell, John, Kt.1482, II. 18
Darell (Barrel), John, Kt.1497, II. 29
Dorrel (Darel), John, Kt.1642, II. 212
Darrell, John, Kt.1670, II. 244
Dayrell, Marmaduke, Kt.1685, II. 261
Darrell (Dorrel), Marmaduke, Kt. 1603, II. 127
Darrell (Dorrell), Robert, Kt.1614, II. 154
Darrell (Dorrell), Sampson, Kt.1619, II. 172
Darrell, Thomas, Kt.1603, II. 118, 121
Darrell (Dayrell, Dorrell), Thomas, Kt.1607, II. 143
Dayrel (Darrell), Thomas, Kt.1634, II. 202
Dartmouth, earl of. See Legge
Dartnell, John G., K.C.B.1900, I. 273
Dartrey, earl of. See Dawson
Darvall, John B., K.C.M.G.1877, I. 359
Darvill, Henry, Kt.1883, II. 375
Darwin, Francis S., Kt.1820, II. 321
Dasent, George W., Kt.1876, II. 367
Daschkoff, count Dmitri, K.C.V.O.1901, I. 440
Dashkov, count H. V., G.C.V.O.1896, I. 422
Dashwood, Charles, Kt.1825, II. 325; K.C.B.1840, I. 236
Dashwood, Francis, Kt.1702, II. 273
Dashwood, Robert, Kt.1682, II. 257
Dashwood, Samuel, Kt.1684, II. 260
Datia, Bhawani, Singh, of, K.C.S.I. 1898, I. 326
DAUBENEY, DAWBENEY
Daubeney, Giles, K.B.1400, I. 128
Dawbeney, Giles, K.B.(1477-8), I. 138
Daubeney, Giles, Kt.1481, II. 17

DAUBENEY
Daubeney, Giles, lord Daubeney, K.G. 1487, I. 17
Daubeney, Henry, lord Daubeney, K.B.1509, I. 148
Daubeney, Henry, K.H.1832, I. 467
Daubeney, Henry C. B., K.C.B.1871, I. 253
Daubeney, Henry C. B., G.C.B.1884, I. 198
Dawbeney, John, Kt.1347, II. 9
Daubeney, Ralph, K.B.1327, I. 124
Daubeney, William, K.B.1327, I. 124
Daulston. See Dalston
Daunce. See Dance
Daunet, John, Kt.1529, II. 47
Dauney [De Launey], John, K.B.1306, I. 120
DAUNTSEY, DAUNSEY, DAUNCIE, DANNSEY
Dauntsey, John, Kt.1399, II. 11
Dannsey (Dauncie), John, Kt.1603, II. 122
Dautre, William, K.B.1306, I. 120
Davall (De Vall), Thomas, Kt.1683, II. 258
Davall, Thomas, Kt.1713, II. 278
Dave. See Dane
Davell (Dovalle), M., Kt.1603, II. 129
Davenant, William, Kt.1643, II. 216
DAVENPORT, DAMPORT
Davenport, Francis, Kt.1603, II. 101
Davenport, Humphrey, Kt.1624, II. 184
Davenport, John, Kt.1617, II. 165
Davenport, Peter, Kt.1744, II. 287
Davenport, Salusbury P., K.C.H.1834, I. 460; Kt.1834, II. 334
Davenport, Samuel, Kt.1884, II. 376; K.C.M.G.1886, I. 369
Davenport, Thomas, Kt.1783, II. 298
Damport (Davenporte), William, Kt. 1544, II. 55
Davenport (Damport), William, Kt. 1603, II. 102
Daventry, John de, K.B.1306, I. 122
Davey, Horace, Kt.1886, II. 378
DAVIES, DAVIS, DAVYS
Davies, David, K.C.H.1837, I. 462; Kt.1837, II. 339

INDEX

DAVIES
  Davies, Edward, Kt.1619, II. 171
  Davies, Henry, Kt.1610, II. 149
  Davies, Horatio D., K.C.M.G.1898, I. 385
  Davies, James A., Kt.1903, II. 414
  Davys, John, Kt.1599, II. 96
  Davis, John, Kt.1603, II. 129
  Davies, John, Kt.1608, II. 144
  Davies, John, Kt.1662, II. 237
  Davys, John, Kt.1673, II. 248
  Davis, John, Kt.1778, II. 295
  Davis, John, K.C.B.1898, I. 270
  Davis, John F., K.C.B.1854, I. 279
  Davies, Lewis H., K.C.M.G.1897, I. 383
  Davies, Matthew H., Kt.1890, II. 386
  Davies, Paul, Kt.1636, II. 204
  Davies, Robert H., K.C.S.I.1874, I. 320
  Daveys, Roland, Kt.1355, II. 9
  Davies, Thomas, Kt.1667, II. 242
  Davis, William, Kt.1662, II. 237
  Davies, William, Kt.1893, II. 392
  Davies, William G., K.C.S.I.1887, I. 324
Davidson, David, Kt.1812, II. 311
Davidson, David, K.C.B.1897, I. 295
Davidson, Randall T., K.C.V.O.(1902), I. 434; G.C.V.O.1904, I. 421
Davill. See Delavale
Davis. See Davies
Davison, Alexander, Kt.1639, II. 206
Davison, Henry, Kt.1856, II. 352
Davison, Thomas, Kt.1660, II. 230
Davison, William, K.H.1822, I. 464
Davison, William, Kt.1824, II. 325; K.H.1824, I. 464
Davison. See Davidson
Davson, Henry K., Kt.1903, II. 416
Davy, Humphry, Kt.1812, II. 310
Davy, William G., K.C.H.1836, I. 461; Kt.1836, II. 337
Davys. See Davies
Dawbeney. See Daubeney
DAWES, DAWS
  Dawes, Abraham, Kt.1633, II. 200
  Dawes, Edwyn S., K.C.M.G.1894, I. 380
  Dawes, Jonathan, Kt.1671, II. 246
  Daws, Thomas, Kt.1639, II. 207
  Dawkins, Clinton E., K.C.B.1902, I. 299

DAWNAY, DAWNEY
  Dawney, Guy, Kt.1513, II. 38
  Dawnay, Hugh R., viscount Downe, K.C.V.O.(1902), I. 435
  Dawney, John, Kt.1542, I. 53
  Dawnay, John, Kt.1580, II. 81
  Dawney, John, Kt.1660, II. 227
  Dawney, Thomas, Kt.1553, II. 67
  Dawney, Thomas, Kt.1603, II. 101
Dawson (Lawson), John, Kt.1604, II. 136
Dawson, John W., Kt.1884, II. 376
Dawson, Richard, earl of Dartrey, K.P. 1855, I 102
Dawson, William, Kt.1680, II. 255
Dawson-Damer, Henry J. R., earl of Portarlington, K.P.1879, I. 104
DAWTREY, DAWTRIE
  Dawtrey, Henry, Kt.1630, II. 198
  Dawtrey, John, Kt.1513, II. 42
  Dawtrie, John, Kt.1545, II. 58
  Dawtrey (Hawtry), William, Kt.1591, II. 89
Day, Henry, Kt.1603, II. 117
Day, John, Kt.1777, II. 295
Day, John C., Kt.1882, II. 374
Day, Thomas, Kt.1694, II. 268
Daynwell, John, Kt.1347, II. 9
Dayrell. See Darrell
Deacon, Charles, K.C.B.1837, I. 233
DEANE, DEAN, DENIE, DENE
  Deane, Charles, K.H.1837, I. 477
  Dean, Drew, Kt.1627, II. 192
  Dene, Henry de, K.B.1306, I. 114
  Dean, James, Kt.1604, II. 134
  Deane, James P., Kt.1885, II. 377
  Dene, John de, K.B.1306, I. 112
  Deane (Denie), John, Kt.1603, II. 109
  Deane, Mathew, Kt.1680, II. 255
  Dean, Richard, Kt.1629, II. 196
  Deane, Robert T., lord Muskerry, Kt.1783, II. 297
  Deane, Thomas, Kt.1830, II. 329
  Deane, Thomas N., Kt.1890, II. 387
Deas, David, K.C.B.1867, I. 251
Deas, George, Kt.1858, II. 352
Dease, Gerald R., Kt.1897, II. 400; K.C.V.O.(1903), I. 436
DEBENHAM, DEBBENHAM
  Debenham, Gilbert, K.B.(1426), I. 131

INDEX

DEBBENHAM
Debbenham, Gilbert, Kt.1503, II. 33
Debono, Guiseppe C., G.C.M.G.1832, I. 332
Deckham, Philip, Kt.1617, II. 161
Degge, Simon, Kt.1669-70, II. 244
De Grey. See Grey
Deinhard, Carl A., K.C.B.1890, I. 263
D'Eivil. See Delavale
Delabere, Richard, Kt.1362, II. 10
Delabere, Richard, K.B.1478, I. 138
Delabere, Richard, Kt.1487, II. 24
De la Croix, Henri, G.C.V.O.1903, I. 427
Della Decima, count Demetrio, K.C.M.G. 1840, I. 352; G.C.M.G.1842, I. 334
Delafaye, Louis V., Kt.1901, II. 409
De la Mare. See Mare
Delaune (De Laune), William, Kt.1664, II. 239
DELAVALL, DALLIVALL, DALEVAL, DAVILL D'EIVIL
Delaval, Francis B., K.B.1761, I. 170
Delavall, John, Kt.1617, II. 163
Delavall, Ralph, Kt.1690, II. 266
Delavall (Dallivall), Ralph, Kt.1608, II. 144
Delavall, Robert, Kt.1603, II. 100
Delavale (Davill, D'Eivil), Roger, Kt. 1605, II. 137
Delawarre, Delaware, De la Warr. See Warre
Delcassé, Theophile, G.C.V.O.1903, I. 427
De L'Isle, lord. See Sidney
De Lisle. See Lisle
Delme, Peter, Kt.1714, II. 279
Deloraine, earl of. See Scott
Delves, George, Kt.1591, II. 88
Delves, Thomas, Kt.1609, II. 148
Delvin, lord. See Nugent
Delyne (De Ligne), Daniel, Kt.1620, II. 175
Demarias, Anthony, Kt.1659, II. 225
Demsturt. See Dewhurst
Denbigh, earl of. See Fielding
Dengayne. See Engaine
Denham, Henry M., Kt.1867, II. 358
Denham, John, Kt.1609, II. 148
Denham, John, Kt.1616, II. 159
Denham, John, K.B.1661, I. 165
Denham, William, Kt.1542, II. 53
Denham, William de, K.B.1332, I. 125
Denham. See Dinham
Denia, Alphonso, son of count of, K.B. 1390, I. 127
Denie. See Dean
Denman, Thomas, Kt.1830, II. 329
DENMARK
Christiern IV. of, K.G.1603, I. 29
Christiern, V. of, K.G.1662, I. 36
Christian IX. of, K.G.1865, I. 63; G.C.B.1863, I. 209; Victorian Chain 1904, I. 415
C. Frederick W. C., crown prince of, G.C.B.1888, I. 212; K.G.1896, I. 70; G.C.V.O.1901, I. 424; Victorian Chain 1902, I. 415
C. F. Charles G. W. A., prince of, G.C.B.1896, I. 214; G.C.V.O.1901, I. 424; Victorian Chain 1902, I. 415
Christian C. F. A. A. W., prince of, G.C.V.O.1901, I. 424
Eric IX. of, K.G.1404, I. 8
Frederick II. of, K.G.1578, I. 27
Frederick VI. of, K.G.1822, I. 52
John, king of Denmark, Sweden, and Norway, K.G.1493, I. 18
Harold Christian Frederick of, G.C.V.O.1901, I. 425
Waldemar, prince of, G.C.B.1901, I. 216
Dennehy, Thomas, K.C.I.E.1896, I. 409
Dennet, John, Kt.1523, II. 44
DENNEY, DENIE, DENNY, and see Deane
Denny, Anthony, Kt.1545, II. 56
Denny, Arthur, Kt.1661, II. 233
Denny, Edward, Kt.1586, II. 84
Denny, Edward, Kt.1589, II. 87
Denny, Edward, Kt.1626, II. 191
Denny, Thomas, Kt.1744, II. 286
Denney, William, Kt.1627, II. 193
DENNIS, DENIS, DENNYS, DENYS, and see Darcus
Dennis, Edward, Kt.1607, II. 143
Dennis, James, K.C.B.1844, I. 238
Denys, Mauryce, Kt.1547, II. 59
Denys, Robert, Kt.1555, II. 69
Dennys, Thomas, Kt.1586, II. 85
Denis, Walter, K.B.(1489), I. 143

DENNIS
   Denys, William, Kt.1520, II. 43

DENNISON, DENISON
   Dennison, Thomas, Kt.1745, II. 287
   Denison, William T., Kt.1846, II. 346;
      K.C.B.1856, I. 279
   Denre, John, K.B.1306, I. 114
   Densell (Damsell), William, Kt.1553,
      II. 67
   Dent, Alfred, K.C.M.G.1888, I. 373
   Dent, Digby, Kt.1778, II. 295
   Denton, Alexander, Kt.1617, II. 166
   Denton, Anthony, Kt.1603, II. 120
   Denton, George C., K.C.M.G.1900, I. 387
   Denton, Thomas, Kt.1603, II. 111
   Derby, earl of. See Stanley; see Smith-Stanley

DEREHAM, DERHAM, DEERHAM
   Derham (Dereham), Richard, Kt.1680,
      II. 254
   Derham (Deerham), Thomas, Kt.1618,
      II. 170
   Dereham, Thomas, Kt.1681, II. 255
   Dering, Anthony, Kt.1603, II. 108
   Dering, Edward, Kt.1619, II. 170
   Dering, Edward, Kt.1680, II. 254
   Dering, Henry, Kt.1687, II. 264
   Dering, Henry N., K.C.M.G.1901, I. 388
   Dering, Thomas, Kt.1471, II. 16
   Derinzy Bartholomew V., K.H.1834, I.
      470
   Derlyngham, Walter de, K.B.1306, I. 115
   Desanges. See Anges
   Desbouverie. See Bouverie
   Descurs. See Scures
   Desmond, earl of. See Preston; see
      Feilding, G.
   Despencer, Edward le, lord le Despencer,
      K.G.1361, I. 3
   Despenser, Hugh le, K.B.1306, I. 113
   Despenser, Richard le, K.B.(1413), I. 129
   Despencer, Thomas, Kt.1360, II. 10
   Despencer, Thomas le, earl of Gloucester,
      K.G.1388, I. 6
   Desse, William, Kt.1771, II. 293
   D'Este. See Este
   Des Voeux. See Voeux

DETHICK, DETHIKE
   Dethike, Gilbert, Kt.1549, II. 65
   Dethick, John, Kt.1656, II. 223
   Dethick, John, Kt.1661, II. 234
   Dethick, William, Kt.1603, II. 109
   Deuntzer, Johan Henrik, G.C.V.O.1904,
      I. 429
   Devenishe, John, Kt.1487, II. 25
   De Vere. See Vere

DEVEREUX, DEVEREULX
   Devereux, Edward, Kt.1612, II. 152
   Devereux, George, Kt.1596, II. 92
   Devereux, George, Kt.1632, II. 199
   Devereux, James, Kt.1599, II. 95
   Devereux, John, lord Devereux, K.G.
      1388, I. 6
   Devereux, John, Kt.1471, II. 15
   Devereux, John, lord Ferrers of
      Chartley, K.B.(1475), I. 137
   Devereux, Joseph, Kt.1883, II. 376
   Devereux, Nicholas, Kt.1555, II. 69
   Devereux, Nicholas, Kt.1591, II. 88
   Devereux, Richard, K.B.1547, I. 151
   Devereux, Robert, earl of Essex, Kt.
      1586, II. 84; K.G.1588, I. 28
   Devereux, Robert, earl of Essex, Kt.
      1638, II. 205; K.B.1638, I. 163
   Devereux, Walter, Kt.1461, II. 13
   Devereux, Walter, lord Ferrers, K.G.
      1472, I. 15
   Devereux, Walter, viscount Hereford,
      K.G.1523, I. 21
   Devereux, Walter, earl of Essex, K.G.
      1572, I. 27
   Devereux, Walter, Kt.1603, II. 123
   Devereux, Walter, Kt.1617, II. 165
   Devereulx, William, Kt.1565, II. 72

DEVILLE, DEYVILLE
   Deville, Alphonse, G.C.V.O.1903, I. 427
   Deyville, Bartholomew, K.B.1305, I.
      111
   Devon, Thomas B., K.H.1820, I. 464;
      K.C.H.1837, I. 462
   Devonshire, duke of. See Cavendish;
      see Courtenay; see Blount; earl of,
      see Cavendish
   Devonshire, John F., K.C.H.1834, I. 460;
      Kt.1834, II. 335

INDEX

Dewa, Singh, K.C.S.I.1880, I. 322
Dewar, James, Kt.1829, II. 327
Dewar, James, Kt.1904, II. 417
Dewar, Thomas R., Kt.1902, II. 413
Dewas, Jeypercash Singh, of, K.C.S.I. 1866, I. 315
D'Ewes, Simonds, Kt.1626, II. 191
Dewhurst (Dias, Dyose, Demsturt), Bernard, Kt.1611, II. 150
Deymer, Edward, Kt.1520, II. 43
Deyncourt, John, lord Deyncourt, K.B. 1399, I. 128
Deyncourt, Roger, K.B.1326, I. 124
Dhar, Rao Puar, K.C.S.I.1877, I. 321
Dholpur, Rana of, G.C.S.I.1869, I. 309
Dhrangadra, Rajah of, K.C.S.I.1866, I. 316
Dhrangadra, Man Singjee of, K.C.S.I. 1877, I. 321
Dhuleep Singh, K.S.I.1861, I. 306; G.C.S.I.1866, I. 308
Dias, Bernard, Kt.1611, II. 150
Dias, Henry, Kt.1893, II. 391
Dibbs, George R., K.C.M.G.1892, I. 377
Dibdin, Lewis T., Kt.1903, II. 415
Dick, James N., K.C.B.1895, I. 266
Dick, Robert H., Kt.1831, II. 331; K.C.H.1832, I. 458; K.C.B.1838, I. 235
Dickens, Samuel T., K.C.H.1834, I. 459; Kt.1834, II. 334

DICKINSON, DICKENSON
Dickinson, Drury J., Kt.1833, II. 334
Dickinson, John N., Kt.1860, II. 355
Dickenson, Thomas, Kt.1657, II. 223

DICKSON, DICKESON, DIXON
Dickson, Alexander, K.C.H.1817, I. 454; G.C.B.1838, I. 188
Dickson, Alexander J., K.C.B.1815, I. 225
Dickson, Collingwood, K.C.B.1871, I. 253; G.C.B.1884, I. 198
Dixon, Daniel, Kt.1892, II. 390
Dickson, David J. H., Kt.1834, II. 335
Dixon, Henry G., K.C.B.1902, I. 274
Dickson, James R., K.C.M.G.1901, I. 388
Dickson, Jeremiah, K.C.B.1815, I. 224
Dickson, John F., K.C.M.G.1888, I. 373

DICKSON
Dickson, Joseph R. L., Kt.1873, II. 365
Dixon, Manley, K.C.B.1819, I. 229
Dixon, Raylton, Kt.1890, II. 386
Dixon, Richard, Kt.1684, II. 259
Dickeson, Richard, Kt.1884, II. 376
Dixon, Robert, Kt.1634, II. 202
Dixon, William, Kt.1661, II. 234
Dietrichstein, prince Hugo, etc., von, K.C.V.O.1904, I. 443
Digby, Everard, Kt.1603, II. 103
Digby, George, Kt.1586, II. 85
Digby, George, earl of Bristol, K.G. 1653, I. 34
Digby, Henry, K.C.B.1831, I. 230; G.C.B.1842, I. 189
Digby, John, Kt.1487, II. 25
Digby, John, Kt.1606, II. 139
Digby, John, Kt.1642, II. 213
Digby, John, Kt.1635, II. 203
Digby, Kenelm, Kt.1623, II. 183
Digby, Kenelm E., K.C.B.1893, I. 297
Digby, Robert, Kt.1599, II. 97
Digby, Robert, Kt.1617, II. 167
Digby, Thomas, Kt.1497, II. 29
Diggle, Charles, K.H.1831, I. 466
Diggs, Dudley, Kt.1607, II. 142
Dike (Dyke), Thomas, Kt.1641, II. 209
Dilkes, Thomas, Kt.1604, II. 132
Dilkes, Thomas, Kt.1704, II. 274

DILLON, DE LION
Dillon, Arthur, earl Dillon, K.T., Jacobite, 1722, footnote, I. 75
Dillon, Charles, viscount Dillon, K.P. 1798, I. 97
Dillon, Christopher, Kt.1615, II. 155
Dillon, James, Kt.1640, II. 207
Dillon, James, Kt.1600, II. 98
Dillon, James, Kt.1626, II. 191
Dillon, John, Kt.1620, II. 176
Dillon, John, Kt.1677, II. 252
Dillon, Lucas, Kt.1624, II. 184
Dillon (De Lion), Lucas, Kt.1575, II. 77
Dillon, Luke G., baron Clonbrock, K.P.1900, I. 106
Dillon, Martin, K.C.B.1887, I. 262; G.C.B.1902, I. 203
Dillon (De Lion), Robert, Kt.1567, II. 73

DILLON
Dillon, Robert, Kt.1581, II. 81
Dillon, Robert, Kt.1615, II. 155
Dillon, Theobald, Kt.1599, II. 96
Dillon, William, Kt.1607, II. 142
Dillon, William, Kt.1793, II. 302
Dillon, William H., K.C.H.1835, I. 460; Kt.1835, II. 336
Dimmock. See Dymocke
Dimsdale, John, Kt.1726, II. 283
Dimsdale, Joseph C., Kt.1894, II. 393; K.C.V.O.(1902), I. 435
Dingley, Edward, Kt.1681, II. 256
Dingley, John, Kt.1615, II. 156
Dingli, Adriano, K.C.M.G.1860, I. 354; G.C.M.G.1868, I. 336
Dingli, Paolo, K.C.M.G.1856, I. 353; G.C.M.G.1860, I. 335
DINHAM, DYNHAM, and see Denham
Dinham, John, lord Dinham, K.G. 1487, I. 17
Dinham, Oliver, Kt.1347, II. 7
Dynham, Thomas, Kt.1518, II. 43
Dinkur, Rao, K.C.S.I.1866, I. 316
Dinley (Dynley), Robert, Kt.1603, II. 122
Disbrowe, Edward C., G.C.H.1831, I. 451
Disbrowe, George, K.H.1835, I. 472
Disney, Henry, Kt.1603, II. 121
Disney, Moore, K.C.B.1815, I. 226
D'Israeli, Benjamin, earl of Beaconsfield, K.G.1878, I. 66
Dive. See Dyve
Dixie, Wolstan, Kt.1586, II. 84
Dixie, Wolston, Kt.1604, II. 132
Dixon. See Dickson
Dixwell, Basil, Kt.1628, II. 194
Dobbes, Richard, Kt.1549, II. 65
Dobbin, Alfred G., Kt.1900, II. 407
Dobson, Benjamin A., Kt.1897, II. 400
Dobson, Richard, Kt.1831, II. 330
Dobson, William L., Kt.1886, II. 380; K.C.M.G.1897, I. 382
Docwra, Theodore, Kt.1623, II. 180
Dod, Samuel, Kt.1714, II. 279
DODDINGTON, DORRINGTON, DODINGTON
Dorrington (Doddington, Carrington), Edward, Kt.1616, II. 159
Doddington (Dorrington), Francis, Kt.1625, II. 189

DODDINGTON
Dorrington (Dodington), John, Kt. 1603, II. 120
Dorrington, William, Kt.1603, II. 118
Dorrington, William, Kt.1623, II. 181
Dodds, John S., Kt.1900, II. 405; K.C.M.G.1901, I. 389
Dodmere, Rauf, Kt.1529, II. 47
Dodgson, David S., K.C.B.1896, I. 266
Dodridge, John, Kt.1607, II. 142
Dodson, John, Kt.1834, II. 335
Dodson, William, Kt.1680, II. 254
Dodsworth, Edward, Kt.1628, II. 195
Dodwell, William, Kt.1709, II. 276
Doe, Charles, Kt.1665, II. 241
Doe, Mullmore M., Kt.1599, II. 96
Doherty, George, K.H.1833, I. 469
Doherty, Patrick, K.C.H.1835, I. 461
Doherty, Richard, Kt.1841, II. 344
Dolben, William, Kt.1677, II. 251
DOLEMAN, DOLMAN
Doleman, Humphrey, Kt.1674, II. 249
Dolman, Robert, Kt.1604, II. 131
Doleman, Thomas, Kt.1661, II. 232
Doleman, Thomas, Kt.1703, II. 273
Dollins, Daniel, Kt.1722, II. 282
Dolgorouky, prince Alexis, G.C.V.O. 1896, I. 422
Dollyffe (Doliff, D'Olive), James Kt. 1714, II. 279
Dolman. See Doleman
Dombrain, James, Kt.1843, II. 345
Domenichini, Giulio, C.M.G.(1820), I. xxviii.
Domett, William, K.C.B.1815, I. 217; G.C.B.1820, I. 184
Domraon, Bux Singh, of, K.C.S.I.1881, I. 322
Domraon, Prosad Sing, of, K.C.I.E. 1888, I. 405
Domvile, Compton E., K.C.B.1898, I. 270; G.C.V.O.1903, I. 420; G.C.B.1904, I. 204
Domvill, William, Kt.1685, II. 260
Domville, William, Kt.1660, II. 231
DON, DONNE, DOON, DONE, DUN, and see Dunn
Doon (Dun), Edward, Kt.1513, II. 39

INDEX

DON
Don, George, G.C.H.1816, I. 448; G.C.B.1820, I. 185
Done, John, Kt.1461, II. 13
Done (Donne), John, Kt.1471, II. 14
Done, John, Kt.1617, II. 165
Done, Ralph, Kt.1624, II. 185
Donaldson, George, Kt.1904, II. 417
Donaldson, Stuart A., Kt.1860, II. 355
Donalt, Robert, Kt.1603-4, II. 131
Done. See Don
Donegall, marquess of. See Chichester
Donellan, James, Kt.1661, II. 234
Dongola, Moustapha B. Y., mudir of, K.C.M.G.1884, I. 367
Donkin, Rufane S., K.C.B.1818, I. 228; G.C.H.1825, I. 449
Donne. See Done
Donnelly, John F. D., K.C.B.1893, I. 293
Donnelly, Ross, K.C.B.1837, I. 233
Donnet, James J. L., K.C.B.1897, I. 269
Donoughmore, earl of. See Hely-Hutchinson
Donovan, Henry, Kt.1874, II. 366
Doran, John, K.C.B.1893, I. 265
Doratt, John, Kt.1838, II. 339
Dorchester, lord. See Carleton
Dorion, Antoine A., Kt.1877, II. 369
Dormer, Charles C., Kt.1758, II. 289
Dormer, Clement C., Kt.1779, II. 296
Dormer, Fleetwood, Kt.1603, II. 124
Dormer, Fleetwood, Kt.1678, II. 253
Dormer, James C., K.C.B.1889, I. 263
Dormer, John (William), Kt.1603, II. 107, 122
Dormer, John, Kt.1661, II. 235
Dormer, Michael, Kt.1538, II. 52
Dormer, Michael, Kt.1604, II. 131
Dormer, Robert, Kt.1537, II. 50
Dormer, Robert, Kt.1591, II. 88
Dormer, Robert, Kt.1617, II. 166
Dormer, Robert, earl of Carnarvon, Kt. 1642, II. 212
Dormer, William, K.B.1553, I. 153
Dormond, lord, K.B.(1483), I. 139
Dornberg, Wilhelm de, K.C.B.1815, I. 226
Dorrell. See Darrell
Dorrington. See Doddington

Dorset, duke of. See Sackville; see Sackville-Germaine; earl of, see Sackville; marquess of, see Beaufort, see Grey, T.
Dorward, Arthur R. F., K.C.B.1901, I. 273
Doughty, George, Kt.1904, II. 417
Dougherty, James B., Kt.1902, II. 410
Douglas. See Thorpe-Douglas
Douglas, —, Kt.1639, II. 207
Douglas, Andrew S., Kt.1789, II. 300
Douglas, Archibald, Kt.1624, II. 187
Douglas, Archibald, Kt.1633, II. lxiii.
Douglas, Archibald, Kt.1651, II. 222
Douglas, Archibald L., K.C.B.1902, I. 273
Douglas, Arthur, Kt.1633, II. lxii.
Douglas, Charles, marquess of Queensberry, K.T.1821, I. 81
Douglas, Charles E., Kt.1832, II. 333; K.C.M.G.1859, I. 353
Douglas, George, Kt.1607, II. 143
Douglas, George, Kt.1633, II. 200
Douglas, George, earl of Dumbarton, K.T.1687, I. 75
Douglas, George, earl of Morton, K.T. 1797, I. 80
Douglas, Howard, G.C.M.G.1835, I. 333; K.C.B.1840, I. 237; G.C.B.1841, I. 207
Douglas, James, earl of Douglas, K.G. 1463, I. 14
Douglas, James, Kt.1635, II. 203
Douglas, James, duke of Queensberry, K.G.1701, I. 40
Douglas, James, earl of Morton, K.T. 1738, I. 78
Douglas, James, Kt.1759, II. 289
Douglas, James, Kt.1765, II. 292
Douglas, James, Kt.1785, II. 298
Douglas, James, K.C.B.1863, I. 283
Douglas, James D., K.C.B.1815, I. 224; G.C.B.1860, I. 193
Douglass, James N., Kt.1882, II. 374
Douglas, Jo, Kt.1633, I. lxii.
Douglas, John, Kt.1800, II. 305
Douglas, John, K.C.B.1859, I. 245; G.C.B.1877, I. 197
Douglas, John, K.C.M.G.1883, I. 365
Douglas, Joseph, Kt.1841, II. 343

Douglas, Neil, K.C.H.1831, I. 457; Kt. 1831, II. 330; K.C.B.1838, I. 235
Douglas, Patrick, Kt.1633, I. lxiii.
Douglas, Robert, Kt.1609, II. 147
Douglas, Robert K., Kt.1903, II. 416
Douglas, William, Kt.1633, II. lxii.
Douglas, William, earl of Morton, K.G. 1633, I. 33
Douglas, William, duke of Queensberry, K.T.1763, I. 79
Douglas, William, K.C.B.1815, I. 224
Douglas, William, K.C.H.1832, I. 459
Douglas, William F., Kt.1882, II. 373
Douglas-Hamilton, James, duke of Hamilton, K.T.Jacobite,1723, footnote I. 75; K.G.Jacobite,1723, footnote I. 38
Douglas-Hamilton, James, duke of Hamilton, K.T.Jacobite,1740, footnote, I. 75
Douglas-Hamilton, William, duke of Hamilton, K.G.1682, I. 37
Douglas-Hamilton, W. A. L. S., duke of Hamilton, K.T.1878, I. 87
Douglas-Home, Charles A., earl of Home, K.T.1899, I. 88
Doulton, Henry, Kt.1887, II. 382
Dovalle. See Davell
Dove, William, Kt.1624, II. 184
Dover, earl of. See Carey; lord, see Yorke
Doveton, John, K.C.B.1819, I. 229; G.C.B.1837, I. 187
Doveton, John, K.C.B.1838, I. 236
Doveton, William W., Kt.1819, II. 320
Dovigni, Nicholas, Kt.1720, II. 282
Dowdall, James, Kt.1541, II. 52
Dowdall, James (? William), Kt.1583, II. 82, 83
Dowdall, John, Kt.1594, II. 90
Dowdall, John, Kt.1618, II. 167
Dowdall, Luke, Kt.1665, II. 241
Dowell, William M., K.C.B.1882, I. 258 G.C.B.1895, I. 201
Dowling, James E., Kt.1838, II. 341
Downe, earl of. See Pope
Downe, viscount. See Ducie; see Dawnay
Downer, John W., K.C.M.G.1887, I. 370

Downes, Joseph, Kt.1900, II. 406
Downes, lord. See Burgh
Downie, Alexander M., Kt.1840, II. 342
Downie, John, Kt.1813, II. 312
Downing, George, Kt.1660, II. 226
Downing, George, K.B.1732, I. 168
Downman, Thomas C. F., Kt.1831, II. 331; K.C.H.1831, I. 457; K.C.B. 1852, I. 239
Downshire, marquess of. See Hill
Downton, Richard, Kt.1681, II. 257
Dowse, Edward (Edmund), Kt.1610, II. 149
Dowse, Francis, Kt.1603, II. 118
Dowse, Gabriell, Kt.1617, II. 167
Doxford, William T., Kt.1900, II. 406
Doyle, Arthur C., Kt.1902, II. 411
Doyle, Bentinck C., Kt.1825, II. 325
Doyle, Charles H., K.C.M.G.1869, I. 354
Doyle, Charles W., Kt.1815, II. 316; K.C.H.1821, I. 455; G.C.H.1837, I. 453
Doyle, Henry, Kt.1547, II. 60
Doyle, John, K.B.1813, I. 178; G.C.B. 1815, I. 181
Doyle, John M., Kt.1814, II. 314; K.C.B. 1815, I. 224
Doyle. See Doyly
DOYLY, D'OYLY, DOYLEY, DOYLEE, and see Doyle
Doyley, Cope, Kt.1627, II. 192
D'Oyley, Francis, K.C.B.1815, I. 225
Doyley, Henry, Kt.1616, II. 158
Doylee, Robert, Kt.1576, II. 77;
Doyly (Doyle), William, Kt.1641, II. 209
D'Oyly, William Kt.1664, II. 239
Doyle, William H., Kt.1873, II. 366
Drake, Bernard, Kt.1586, II. 84
Drake, Francis, Kt.1581, II. 81
Drake, James (? John), Kt.1660, II. 227
Drake, John, Kt.1616, II. 159
Drake, William, Kt.1641, II. 209
Drake, William, Kt.1668, II. 243
Drake, William, Kt.1685, II. 260
Drake, William H., K.C.B.1871, I. 253
Drake, William R., Kt.1869, II. 361
Draper, Christopher, Kt.1567, II. 73
Draper, William, K.B.1765, I. 171

INDEX

Drax, James, Kt.1658, II. 224, 228
Drax, James, Kt.1663, II. 239
Draycott, John, Kt.1599, II. 97
Dresnay, marquis de, Kt.1713, II. 278
Drew, Thomas, Kt.1603, II. 125
Drew, Thomas, Kt.1900, II. 407
Drewell, Humfry, Kt.1596, II. 93
Driby, Ralph de, K.B.1306, I. 118
Drinir, Ochemach, Kt.1596, II. 93
Drinkwater, George, Kt.1830, II. 328
Drinkwater, William L., Kt.1877, II. 369
Drogheda, earl and marquess of. See Moore

DRUMMOND, DROMMOND, DROMOND
Drummond, Adam, K.C.H.1837, I. 462; Kt.1837, II. 338
Dromond, David, Kt.1617, II. 164
Drummond, Edmund, K.C.I.E.1887, II. 399
Drummond, George A., K.C.M.G.1904, I. 394
Drummond, Gordon, K.C.B.1815, I. 218; G.C.B.1817, I. 183
Drummond, James, Kt.1651, II. 222
Drummond, James, earl and duke of Perth, K.T.1687, I. 75; K.G.1706, Jacobite, footnote I. 38
Drummond, James, marquess of Drummond, K.T.1705, Jacobite, footnote I. 75
Drummond, James, duke of Perth, K.T.1739, Jacobite, footnote I. 75
Drummond, James R., K.C.B.1873, I. 253; G.C.B.1880, I. 197
Drommond, John, Kt.1603, II. 115
Drummond, lord. See Dormond
Drummond, John, duke of Melfort, K.T.1687, I. 75; K.G.1692, Jacobite, footnote I. 38
Drummond, Morris, Kt.1625, II. 188
Drummond, Patrick, Kt.1625, II. 187
Drummond, Patrick, Kt.1642, II. 212
Drummond, Victor A. W., K.C.M.G. 1903, I. 394
Drummond-Hay, John H., Kt.1859, II. 354; K.C.B.1862, I. 282; G.C.M.G. 1884, I. 340

DRURY, DREWRY, DRURIE
Drury, Anthony, Kt.1603, II. 125
Drury, Charles C., K.C.S.I.1903, I. 327
Drewry, Drewe, Kt.1579, II. 79
Drury, Drew, Kt.1603, II. 120
Drury, Henry, Kt.1603, II. 111
Drury, Henry, Kt.1603, II. 117
Drury, John, Kt.1604, II. 136
Drury, Robert, Kt.1497, II. 29
Drury, Robert, Kt.1591, II. 89
Drury, Robert, Kt.1603, II. 125
Drury, William (Thomas), K.B.(1426), I. 132
Drury, William, Kt.1547, II. 60
Drury, William, Kt.1570, II. 74
Drury, William, Kt.1574, II. 76
Drury, William, Kt.1576, II. 77
Drurie (Drewry), William, Kt.1618, II. 170
Drury-Lowe, Drury C., K.C.B.1882, I. 258; G.C.B.1895, I. 201
Dry Richard, Kt.1858, II. 352
Dryden, John T., Kt.1793, II. 302
Drysdale, William, Kt.1842, II. 344
Drysdale, William, K.C.B.1893, I. 264
Duarte, e Silva Antonio, K.C.V.O.1903, I. 441
Duberly, James, Kt.1803, II. 307
Dubois, Emile, G.C.V.O.1903, I. 427

DUCIE, DUCY, and see Darcy
Ducy, Robert, Kt.1631, II. 199
Ducie, William, viscount Downe, K.B. 1661, I. 164
Ducket, Francis, Kt.1603, II. 102
Duckett, Lionel, Kt.1573, II. 75
Duckett, Thomas, Kt.1603, II. 118
Duckworth, Dyce, Kt.1886, II. 379
Duckworth, John T., K.B.1801, I. 175; G.C.B.1815, I. 180
Duddleston, John, Kt.1690, II. 266
Dudgeon, Charles J., Kt.1903, II. 415
Dudley, Ambrose, earl of Warwick, Kt. 1549, II. 64; K.G.1563, I. 26
Dudley, Andrew, Kt.1547, II. 62; K.G. 1552, I. 24
Dudley, earl of. See Ward
Dudley, Gamaliel, Kt.1646, II. 221
Dudley, Henry, Kt.1545, footnote II. 56

Dudley, John, duke of Northumberland, Kt.1523, II. 45; K.G.1543, I. 23
Dudley, John, earl of Warwick, K.B. 1547, I. 150
Dudley or Sutton de, lord. See Sutton, *alias* Dudley, E.
Dudley, Robert, earl of Leicester, K.G. 1559, I. 26
Dudley, Robert, Kt.1596, II. 93
Dudley, Robert, Kt.1603, II. 100
Duff, Alexander, G.C.H.1833, I. 452; Kt.1834, II. 335
Duff, Alexander W. G., duke of Fife, K.T.1881, I. 87; G.C.V.O.1901, I. 418; Victorian Chain 1902, I. 415
Duff, James, Kt.1779, II. 296
Duff, James, earl Fife, G.C.H.1823, I. 449; K.T.1827, I. 82
Duff, James, earl of Fife, K.T.1860, I. 85
Duff, Robert W., G.C.M.G.1893, I. 343
Duffe, Thady, Kt.1623, II. 183
Dufferin, marquess of (1861). See Hamilton-Temple-Blackwood, F. T.
Duffy, Charles G., Kt.1873, II. 365; K.C.M.G.1877, I. 359
Duffey, George F., Kt.1897, II. 400
Dugdale, William, Kt.1677, II. 252
Duke (Ducke), Edward, Kt.1607, II. 143
Duke, Edward, Kt.1641, II. 209
Duke, Henry, Kt.1588, II. 86
Duke, James, Kt.1837, II. 338
Dulac, Joseph, K.C.B.1856, I. 242
Dulton, Hugh de, K.B.1306, I. 120
Dumaresq, John, Kt.1803, II. 307
Dumbell, Alured, Kt.1899, II. 404
Dumbarton, earl of. See Douglas
Dumfries, earl of. See Dalrymple-Crichton
Dunbar, earl of (1608). See Home, G.; see Murray, J.
Dunbar, James, Kt.1810, II. 310
Dumbreck, David, K.C.B.1871, I. 253
Duncan, Henry, K.C.H.1834, I. 460; Kt.1834, II. 335
Duncan, Robert D., earl of Camperdown, K.T.1848, I. 84
Dunche, William, Kt.1603, II. 111
Duncombe, Charles, Kt.1699, II. 271
Duncombe, Edmond, Kt.1642, II. 213

Duncombe, Francis, Kt.1619, II. 174
Duncomb, John, Kt.1646, II. 221
Duncombe, Sanders, Kt.1617, II. 163
Duncomb. See Dunton
Dundas, David, K.B.1803, I. 176; G.C.B. 1815, I. 180
Dundas, David, Kt.1847, II. 347
Dundas, Henry, viscount Melville, K.C.B. 1849, I. 238; G.C.B.1865, I. 194
Dundas, James W. D., G.C.B.1855, I. 191
Dundas, Jo, Kt.1633, II. lxii.
Dundas, Lawrence, marquess of Zetland, Grand Master K.P.1889, I. 95; K.T. 1900, I. 88
Dundas, Richard S., K.C.B.1856, I. 243
Dundas, Robert L., K.C.B.1815, I. 224
Dundas, Thomas, K.C.B.1831, I. 231
Dundas, Thomas, earl of Zetland, K.T. 1861, I. 85; K.G.1872, I. 65
Dundas, Walter, Kt.1594, II. 91
Dundee, earl of. See Gualterio
Dundonald, earl of. See Cochrane
Dunfermline, lord. See Abercromby
Dungarvan, viscount. See Boyle, R.
Dunham, John, Kt.1497, II. 30
Dunke (Danck), Thomas, Kt.1710, II. 277
Dunkin, William, Kt.1791, II. 301
Dunkley, Robert, Kt.1708, II. 276
DUNN, DUNNE, DUNE, and see Don
Dunne, Daniel, Kt.1603, II. 114
Dunn, David, Kt.1835, II. 336; K.C.H. 1837, I. 462
Dunne, John, Kt.1897, II. 401
Dune, Hugh O'C., Kt.1599, II. 96
Dun (Dunn), Patrick, Kt.1697, II. 270
Dunning, Edwin H., Kt.1904, II. 417
Dunraven, earl of. See Wyndham-Quin
Dunstall, Thomas, K.B.1426, I. 132
Dunton (Duncombe), Edward, Kt.1603, II. 116
Dunton, William de, K.B.1323, I. 122
Duppa, Thomas, Kt.1683, II. 258
Dupree, William T., Kt.1902, II. 413
Dupuis, John E., K.C.B.1865, I. 249
Durand, Henry M., K.C.S.I.1867, I. 317
Durand, Henry M., K.C.I.E.1889, I. 406; K.C.S.I.1894, I. 325; G.C.M.G. 1900, I. 347
Durando, Giovanni, K.C.B.1857, I. 244

INDEX

Durant, Raymond, K.B.1323, I. 122
Duras, Lewis de, earl of Feversham, K.G.1685, I. 38
Duras, Durefort, Galeard de, Seigneur de, K.G.1463, I. 14
Duras, lord, K.B.(1465), I. 135
D'Urban, Benjamin, K.C.B.1815, I. 223; K.C.H.1818, I. 454; G.C.B.1840, I. 188
Durbin, John, Kt.1778, II. 295
Durham, earl of. See Lambton
Durham, James, Kt.1651, II. 222
Durham, Philip C. H., K.C.B.1815, I. 219
Durie, William, K.H.1837, I. 478
Durno, James, Kt.1799, II. 304
Durston, Albert J., K.C.B.1897, I. 296
Durward, John, K.B.(1465), I. 135
Dusmani, count A. L., K.C.M.G.1849, I. 353
Dussen. See Vandreduffen
Dutton, Ralph, Kt.1624, II. 186
Dutton, Robert, Kt.1608, II. 144
Dutton, Thomas, Kt.1603, II. 118
Dwarris, Fortunatus, Kt.1838, II. 340
Dyal, Missar, K.C.S.I.1866, I. 316
Dyer, Edward, Kt.1596, II. 93
Dyer, James, Kt.1549, II. 65
Dyer, John, K.C.B.1815, I. 226
Dyer, Richard, Kt.1585, II. 83, 85
Dyer, Thomas, Kt.1547, II. 59
Dyer, William, Kt.1603, II. 108
Dyer, William T. T., K.C.M.G.1899, I. 386
Dyes, Christopher, Kt.1547, II. 62
Dyett, Richard, Kt.1635, II. 203
DYMOCK, DYMOCKE, DYMMOCK, DIMMOCK, DYMOKE, DYMMOKE
Dimmock (Dymocke), Charles Kt.1603, II. 116
Dymock, Charles, Kt.1673, II. 248
Dymoke, Edward, Kt.1584, II. 83
Dymmock, Edward, Kt.1605, II. 137
Dymock, Edward, Kt.1661, II. 233
Dymoke, Lyonell, Kt.1513, II. 40
Dymmoke, Robert, Kt.1483, II. 21
Dymoke, Robert, Kt.1513, II. 36
Dymock, Thomas, K.B.(1400), I. 129
Dymoke, Thomas, Kt.1460, II. 12
Dynham. See Dinham

Dyose, Bernard, Kt.1611, II. 150
Dysart, earl of. See Tollemash
DYVE, DYVES, DIVE
Dyve (Dyves), John, Kt.1603, II. 111
Dyve, Lewis, Kt.1587, II. 85
Dive, Lewis, Kt.1620, II. 175

E

Eade, Peter, Kt.1885, II. 377
Eady, Charles S., Kt.1901, II. 409
Eam, Henry, K.G.1348, I. 2
Eamer, John, Kt.1795, II. 302
Eames, William, K.C.B.1902, I. 274
Earle, James, Kt.1800, II. 305
Earle, Thomas, Kt.1681, II. 257
Earle, Walter, Kt.1616, II. 158
Earle. See Erle
Earnley, Michael, Kt.1639, II. 207
East, Cecil J., K.C.B.1897, I. 269
East, Edward H., Kt.1813, II. 312
Eastlake, Charles L., Kt.1850, II. 348
EATON, EYTON
Eyton, James, Kt.1702, II. 273
Eyton, Kendrick, Kt.1675, II. 250
Eaton, Peter, Kt.1715, II. 280
Eaton, Philip, Kt.1619, II. 173
Eaton, Robert, Kt.1612, II. 152
Eaton, Robert, Kt.1630, II. 198
Eaton (Eyton), Thomas, Kt.1642, II. 214
Ebrington, viscount. See Fortescue
Eccles, John, Kt.1714, II. 280
Echingham, Edward, Kt.1513, II. 37
Echingham, Osburne, Kt.1529, II. 47
Echlin, Henry, Kt.1692, II. 267
Eckersley, Nathaniel, K.H.1818, I. 463
Eckhardstein, baron Hermann von, K.C.V.O.1902, I. 440
Eckley (Ecclye), Samuel, Kt.1702, II. 272
Eden, Ashley, K.C.S.I.1878, I. 321
Eden, Charles, K.C.B.1873, I. 253
Eden, George, earl of Auckland, G.C.B. 1835, I. 206
Eden, Morton, lord Henley, K.B.1791, I. 174; G.C.B.1815, I. 205
Eden, Thomas, Kt.1603, II. 124, 133
Edgar, James D., K.C.M.G.1898, I. 384

INDEX

Edgar, John W., K.C.I.E.1889, I. 406
EDGCUMBE, EDGECOMBE
Edgecumbe, Edward R. P., Kt.1895, II. 395
Edgecombe, Piers, K.B.(1494), I. 144; Kt.1513, II. 36
Edgcombe, Richard, Kt.1485, II. 23
Edgecombe, Richard, Kt.1542, II. 53
Edgecombe, Richard, Kt.1603, II. 121
Edgecumbe, Richard, K.B.1661, I. 165
Edgcumbe, William H., earl of Mount Edgcumbe, G.C.V.O.1897, I. 418
Edge, John, Kt.1886, II. 379
Edgeworth, John, Kt.1672, II. 247
Edlin, Peter H., Kt.1888, II. 385
Edmarker (Egmorles), monsieur, Kt. 1596, II. 92
Edmonds, Christopher, Kt.1592, II. 89
Edmonds, Clement, Kt.1617, II. 166
Edmonds, Henry, K.B.1626, I. 162
Edmondes, Thomas, Kt.1603, II. 109
Edmonstone, George F., K.C.B.1863, I. 283
Edolfe, Robert, Kt.1603, II. 123
Edolph, Thomas, Kt.1609, II. 147
Edridge, Frederick T., Kt.1897, II. 399
Edridge, Thomas R., Kt.1887, II. 383
Edward II., K.B.1306, I. 111
Edward III., K.B.1327, I. 125
Edward V., K.B.(1475), I. 136; K.G. 1475, I. 16
Edward VI., Kt.1547, II. 58
Edward VII., K.G.1841, I. 56; K.G.1858, I. 60; K.S.I.1861, I. 306; G.C.B. 1865, I. 194; G.C.S.I.1866, I. 308; K.T.1867, I. 86; K.P.1868, I. 103; G.C.M.G.1877, I. 337; G.C.I.E.1887, I. 401; G.C.V.O.1896, I. 417; grand master of the Bath (1897), I. 109

EDWARDES, EDWARDS
Edwards, Bryan, Kt.1859, II. 354
Edwards, Fleetwood I., K.C.B.1887, I. 290; G.C.V.O.1901, I. 419
Edwards, George W., Kt.1887, II. 381
Edwards, Henry, Kt.1885, II. 378
Edwardes, Herbert B., K.C.B.1860, I. 281; K.C.S.I.1866, I. 317
Edwards, James, Kt.1670, II. 245
Edwards, James B., K.C.M.G.1891, I. 376

EDWARDES
Edwards, John, Kt.1680, II. 254
Edwards, Robert, Kt.1603, II. 115
Edwards, Robert B., K.H.1835, I. 472
Edwardes, Stanley de B., K.C.B.1898, I. 270
Edwyn, Humphry, Kt.1687, II. 264
Eeles, Thomas, K.H.1832, I. 467
Effingham, earl of (1820). See Howard, K.A.
Egeock, Francis, Kt.1603, II. 122
Egerton (Everton), Charles, Kt.1604, II. 132
Egerton, Charles, Kt.1607, II. 142
Egerton, Charles B., K.C.H.1832, I. 458; Kt.1832, II.331; G.C.M.G.1837, I.334
Egerton, Charles C., K.C.B.1903, I. 275; G.C.B.1904, I. 204
Egerton, Edwin H., K.C.B.1897, I. 295; G.C.M.G., 1902, I. 348
Egerton, John, earl of Bridgewater, Kt. 1599, II. 95; K.B.1603, I. 154
Egerton, John, earl of Bridgewater, K.B. 1661, I. 163
Egerton, Philip, Kt.1544, II. 55
Egerton, Philip, Kt.1660, II. 229
Egerton, Rauf, Kt.1513, II. 39
Egerton, Rauf, Kt.1553, II. 68
Egerton, Richard, Kt.1544, II. 55
Egerton, Richard, Kt.1603, II. 122
Egerton, Robert, K.C.S.I.1879, I. 322
Egerton, Rowland, Kt.1617, II. 161
Egerton, Thomas, Kt.1597, II. 94
Egerton, Thomas, earl of Wilton, G.C.H. 1835, I. 452
Egerton, William, K.B.1661, I. 164
Eggebaston, Richard de, K.B.1306, I. 121
Eggleton, Charles, Kt.1744, II. 286
Eglandby. See Aglionby
Eglintoun, earl of (1812). See Montgomerie, H.
Egmorles, monsieur, Kt.1596, II. 92

EGYPT
Abbas Pasha, khedive of, G.C.M.G.1891, I. 342; G.C.B.1892, I. 213; G.C.V.O. 1900, I. 424
Ismail Pacha, viceroy of, G.C.B.1866, I. 210; G.C.S.I.1868, I. 309
Mohamed Ali, of, G.C.M.G.1900, I. 347

EGYPT
 Tewfik Pasha, khedive of, G.C.S.I.1875, I. 310; G.C.B.1887, I. 212
Eisendecker, Charles J. G. von, G.C.V.O. 1904, I. 430
Ekins, Charles, K.C.B.1831, I. 230; G.C.B.1852, I. 190
Elder, George, Kt.1813, I. 313; K.C.B. 1831, I. 232
Elder, Thomas, Kt.1878, II. 370; G.C.M.G.1887, I. 341
ELDERTON, ELDRETON
 Elderton (Eldrington, Etherington), Richard, Kt.1603, II. 118
 Eldreton, Thomas, Kt.1460, II. 12
Eldrecare, William, Kt.1523, II. 44
Elgar, Edward, Kt.1904, II. 417
Elgin, earl of. See Bruce
Eliot. See Elliot
Ellenborough, earl of. See Law
ELLERCAR, ELLERKER, ILLERKER
 Ellercar, Raulf, Kt.1497, II. 32
 Ellercar, Rauf, Kt.1544, II. 54
 Ellerkar, Rauf, Kt.1513, II. 37
 Ellerker (Illerker), Ralph, Kt.1603, II. 101
Elles. See Ellis
Ellet, Gilbert, Kt.1651, II. 222
Ellesmere, earl of. See Leveson-Gower
Elley, John, K.C.B.1815, I. 223; K.C.H. 1819, I. 454
Ellice. See Ellis
Ellicombe, Charles G., K.C.B.1862, I. 247
ELLIOT, ELLIOTT, ELIOT, ELYOTT
 Elliott, Alexander J. H., K.C.B.1897, I. 268
 Elliot, Charles, K.C.B.1856, I. 280
 Elliott, Charles A., K.C.S.I.1887, I. 323
 Elliott, Charles B., K.C.M.G.1901, I. 390
 Elliot, Charles G. J. B., K.C.B.1881, I. 257
 Eliot, Charles N. E., K.C.M.G.1900, I. 387
 Elliott, Daniel, K.C.S.I.1867, I. 317
 Eliot, Edward G., earl of St. Germans, Grand Master K.P.1853, I. 94; G.C.B.1857, I. 208
 Elliot, Edward L., K.C.B.1902, I. 275

ELLIOTT
 Elliot, Francis E. H., K.C.M.G.1904, I. 395
 Elliott, George, K.C.B.1862, I. 248
 Elliot, George, K.C.B.1877, I. 255
 Elliott, George A., lord Heathfield, K.B. 1783, I. 173
 Elliot, Henry G., G.C.B.1869, I. 210
 Elliot, Henry G., K.C.M.G.1899, I. 386
 Elliot, Henry M., K.C.B.1849, I. 278
 Eliot, J., Kt.1609, II. 147
 Eliot, John, Kt.1618, II. 168
 Elliott, John, Kt.1776, II. 295
 Eliot, John, K.C.I.E.1903, I. 411
 Elyott, Thomas, Kt.1527, II. 46
 Elliot, Thomas, Kt.1603, II. 126
 Elliott, Thomas, Kt.1615, II. 156
 Elliott, Thomas F., K.C.M.G.1869, I. 355
 Elliott, Thomas H., K.C.B.1902, I. 299
 Elliot, Walter, K.C.S.I.1866, I. 316
 Elliot, William, Kt.1621, II. 176
 Eliot (Elliot), William, Kt.1681, II. 256
 Elliott, William, K.C.H.1835, I. 460; Kt.1837, II. 339
 Elliott, William, K.H.1837, I. 476
 Eliot, William G., K.H.1834, I. 470
 Elliott, William H., K.H.1837, I. 477; K.C.B.1862, I. 248; G.C.B.1873, I. 196
 Elliot-Murray-Kynynmound, Gilbert, earl of Minto, G.C.B.1834, I. 206
 Elliot-Murray-Kynynmound, Gilbert J., earl of Minto, G.C.M.G.1898, I. 346
 Elliot-Murray-Kynynmound, William H., earl of Minto, K.T.1870, I. 86
ELLIS, ELLICE, ELLES, ELLYS, ELVES, ELWYS, ELWES
 Ellis, Adam G., Kt.1882, II. 374
 Ellis, Alfred B., K.C.B.1894, I. 266
 Ellis, Arthur E. A., K.C.V.O.(1897), I. 432; G.C.V.O.1902, I. 420
 Ellis, Barrow H., K.C.S.I.1875, I. 320
 Ellis, Charles A., lord Howard de Walden, G.C.B.1838, I. 207
 Ellice, Charles H., K.C.B.1873, I. 254; G.C.B.1882, I. 198
 Elles, Edmond R., K.C.B.1898, I. 269; K.C.I.E.1904, I. 412

INDEX

ELLIS
Ellys (Elvis, Elwys, Elwes), Gervase, Kt.1603, II. 104
Ellis, George, Kt.1618, II. 170
Ellis, Henry, K.H.1832, I. 468; Kt. 1833, II. 333
Ellis, Henry, K.C.B.1848, I. 277
Ellis, Henry W., K.C.B.1815, I. 223
Elwes, Jeffery, Kt.1744, II. 286
Elwis (Elwes), Jervis, Kt.1629, II. 196
Elwes, John, Kt.1665, II. 241
Ellis, John, Kt.1705, II. 274
Lilis, Samuel B., K.C.B.1860, I. 246
Ellis, Thomas, Kt.1617, II. 162
Elways (Elwiss), William, Kt.1615, II. 156
Ellis, William, Kt.1617, II. 162
Ellis, William, Kt.1658, II. 224
Ellis, William, Kt.1671, II. 245
Ellis, William, Kt.1688, II. 264
Ellis, William C., Kt.1835, II. 336
Elles, William K., K.C.B.1891, I. 264
Ellys. See Ellis

Elmer. See Aylmer
Elmes, Thomas, Kt.1688, II. 264
Elphingston, George, Kt.1594, II. 91
Elphingstone, George K., viscount Keith, K.B.1794, I. 174; G.C.B.1815, I. 180
Elphinstone, Howard C., K.C.B.1871, I. 285
Elphinstone, John, lord Elphinstone, G.C.H.1836, I. 453; G.C.B.1859, I. 208
Elrington, John, K.B.1478, I. 138
Elrington, John, Kt.1482, II. 17
Elrington. See Elderton
Elverton (Elveston), William, Kt.1637, II. 205

Elves. See Ellis
Elvey, George, Kt.1871, II. 363
Elwes. See Ellis
Elwill, John, Kt.1696, II. 269
Elwys. See Ellis
Ely, earl and marquess of. See Loftus
Emerson, William, Kt.1902, II. 411
Emerton (Emmerson or Erneston), John Kt.1729, II. 284

Emson, Richard, Kt.1504, II. 34
Enderby, William, K.B.(1483), I. 141

Enfield, Bartholomew de, K.B.1306, I. 111
ENGAINE, DENGAYNE
Dengaine, Henry, Kt.1346, II. 6
Engaine, Jo de, Kt.1347, II. 8
D'Angain, Thomas, Kt.1380, II. 10
Engaine, Tho de, Kt.1347, II. 8
Engelbrechten, Maximilian G. F. C. von, K.C.V.O.1904, I. 443
Engham. See Ingham
Engleby. See Ingleby
ENGLEFIELD, INGLEFIELD, INGELFIELD, ENGLEFEILDE
Inglefield, Edward A., Kt.1877,, II. 369; K.C.B.1887, I. 261
Englefeilde, Francys, Kt.1547, II. 60
Inglefield (Englefield), Francis. Kt. 1622, II. 180
Englefield, Roger de, K.B.1306, I. 114
Ingilfield, Thomas, K.B.1501, I. 146
England, George, Kt.1671, II. 246
England, Richard, K.H.1836, I. 473; K.C.B.1843, I. 237; G.C.B.1855, I. 191
Engleheart, John G. D., Kt.1892, II.390; K.C.B.1897, I. 295
English, John H., Kt.1815, II. 315
Enniskillen, earl of. See Cole
Ent, George, Kt.1665, II. 240
Epernon, Nogaret de Foix, duc d', K.G.1645, I. 33
Erbach-Schoenberg, count Gustavus E., K.C.V.O.1898, I. 438; G.C.V.O.1900, I. 423
Ercedekne, John le, Kt.(1342), II. lx.
Ercedekne, Richard Fitz-R., Kt.(1342), II. lx
Erdington, Henry de, K.B.1306, I. 120
Erle, William, Kt.1845, II. 346
Erle. See Earle
Ermyne (Ayrmine), William, Kt.1603, II. 103
Erne, earl. See Crichton
Ernle, John, Kt.1665, II. 241
Erpyngham, Thomas, K.G.1401, I. 8
Erroll, earl of. See Hay
Erskine, Alexander, master of Fenton or viscount of Fenton, K.B.1616, I. 159
Erskine, David, Kt.1830, II. 329

INDEX

Erskine, George, Kt.1606, II. 140
Erskine, James C. C., lord Erskine, afterwards 18th earl of Buchan, K.B.1610, I. 157
Erskine, James E., K.C.B.1897, I. 269
Erskine, John, 19th earl of Mar, K.G. 1603, I. 30
Erskine, John, afterwards 20th earl of Mar, K.B.1603, I. 154
Erskine, John, earl of Mar, K.T.1706, I. 76
Erskine, John, duke of Mar, K.G.1716, Jacobite, I. note 38
Erskine, John K., K.C.H.1830, I. 456
Erskine, Thomas, Kt.1611, II. 150
Erskine, Thomas, baron Erskine, K.T. 1815, I. 81
Erskine, Thomas, earl of Kellie, K.G. 1615, I. 31
Erskine, William, Kt.1609, II. 147
Erskine, William, Kt.1763, II. 292
Ervillé, Charles d' A., K.C.B.1856, I. 242
Escott. See Estcourt
Esdaile, James, Kt.1766, II. 292
Esdaile, Joseph, Kt.1801, II. 306
Esher, viscount. See Brett
Esmond, Laurence, Kt.1603, II. 127
Esmond (Ismond), Thomas, Kt.1628,II.195
Essex, earl of. See Bourchier; see Cromwell; see Devereux; see Capell
Essex, Edward, Kt.1599, II. 97
Essex, Thomas, Kt.1549, II. 64
Essex, William, Kt.1513, II. 39
Essington, William, K.C.B.1815, I. 217
ESTCOURT, ESCOTT, ESTCOURTE, ESCOURT, ERESCOURT
  Estcourt (Estocke, Escott), Edward, Kt.1607, II. 143
  Estcourte, Giles, Kt.1622, II. 180
  Estcourt (Erescourt), Thomas, Kt.1607, II. 143
  Estcourt, Thomas, Kt.1661, II. 233
  Estcourt, Thomas, Kt.1674, II. 249
D'Este, Augustus F., K.C.H.1830, I. 456; Kt.1830, II. 329
Esterhazy, Paul Anthony, prince, G.C.B. 1837, I. 206
Esterhazy, Louis, G.C.V.O.1902, I. 425
Estfield, William, Kt.1439, II. 12
Etheredge, George, Kt.1680, II. 255

Etheridge, James, Kt.1682, II. 257
Etherington. See Elderton
Etherington, George, Kt.1619, II. 171
Ethiopia, Menelik II. of, G.C.M.G.1897, I. 345; G.C.B.1902, I. 204
Euan-Smith, Charles B., K.C.B.1890, I. 291
Eulenberg, count August zu, G.C.V.O. 1899, I. 423
Eure, Sampson, Kt.1641, II. 210
Eure, William, lord Eure, K.B.1603, I. 153
Eustace, John, Kt.1663, II. 237
Eustace, John R., Kt.1816, II. 316; K.H.1835, I. 472
Eustace, Maurice, Kt.1639, II. 206
Eustace, Maurice, Kt.1663, II. 237
Eustace, William C., K.C.H.1832, I. 459
EVANS, EVENS, EVANCE
  Evans, David, K.C.M.G.1892, I. 377
  Evans, Francis H., K.C.M.G.1893, I. 378
  Evans, Frederick J. O., K.C.B.1881, I. 288
  Evans, Griffith H. P., K.C.I.E.,1892, I. 407
  Evans, Herbert, Kt.1674, II. 249
  Evans, John, Kt.1817, II. 319
  Evans, John, K.C.B.1892, I. 292
  Evans, De Lacy, K.C.B.1838, I. 234; G.C.B.1855, I. 191
  Evens (Evers), Peter, Kt.1603, II. 106
  Evance, Stephen, Kt.1690, II. 266
  Evans, William D., Kt.1820, II. 321
Evelyn, Edward, Kt.1676, II. 251
Evelyn, John, Kt.1623, II. 182
Evelyn, John, Kt.1641, II. 209
Evelyn, Thomas, Kt.1617, II. 164
Everard, Anthony, Kt.1603, II. 117
Everard, John, Kt.1605, II. 136
Everard, Mathias, K.H.1831, I. 465
Everard (Evered), Michael, Kt.1614, I. 154
Evercy, Peter de, K.B.1306, I. 119
Everest, George, Kt.1861, II. 356
EVERETT, EVERITT, and see Everard
  Everitt (Everett), John, Kt.1800, II. 305

EVERETT
Everett, William, K.C.M.G.1898, I. 385
Evereux, William de, K.B.1327, I. 125
Everingham, Adam de, K.B.1306, I. 121
Everingham, John, Kt.1482, II. 18, 21
Everingham, John, Kt.1504, II. 34
EVERS, EWERS
Evers, —, Kt.1492, II. 28
Evers (Ewers), Francis, Kt.1604, II. 132
Evers, Rauf, Kt.1497, II. 31
Evers, Rauf, Kt.1538, II. 51
Evers, William, Kt.1482, II. 17
Evers, William, Kt.1513, II. 39
Eversfield, Thomas, Kt.1603, II. 112
Eversfield, Thomas, Kt.1621, II. 177
Eversfield, Thomas, Kt.1641, II. 210
Eversley, viscount. See Shaw-Lefevre
Everton, baron d'. See Sebright
Everton, Charles, Kt.1604, II. 132
Every, Simon, Kt.1641, II. 209
Evington, James, Kt.1617, II. 161
Ewart, Henry P., K.C.B.1885, I. 259; K.C.V.O.(1897), I. 432; G.C.V.O. 1902, I. 420
Ewart, John A., K.C.B.1887, I. 261; G.C.B.1904, I. 204
Ewart, Joseph, Kt.1895, II. 396
Exeter, duke of. See Holand, see Beaufort, see Holand
Exeter, earl of. See Cecil
Exeter, marquess of. See Courtenay, see Cecil
Exmew, Thomas, Kt.1518, II. 43
Exmouth, lord. See Pellew
Exton, Thomas, Kt.1675, II. 250
Eyles, John, Kt.1687, II. 263
Eyles, Joseph, Kt.1724, II. 283
Eyles, Joseph, Kt.1795, II. 303
Eynden, Jacob van der, Kt.1610, II. 150
Eyre, Charles, Kt.1699, II. 271
Eyre, Christopher, Kt.1664, II. 240
Eyre, George, Kt.1812, II. 310; K.C.B. 1815, I. 222; G.C.M.G.1838, II. 334
Eyre, Giles, Kt.1689, II. 265
Eyre, James, Kt.1772, II. 294
Eyre, James, Kt.1830, II. 329
Eyre, Jervis (Jacob), Kt.1639, II. 207

Eyre, John, Kt.1605, II. 137
Eyre, Robert, Kt.1710, II. 277
Eyre (Eyres), Samuel, Kt.1694, II. 268
Eyre, Vincent, K.C.S.I.1867, I. 318
Eyre, William, Kt.1592, II. 89
Eyre, William, Kt.1633, II. 201
Eyre, William, Kt.1663, II. 237
Eyre, William, K.C.B.1855, I. 240
Eyton. See Eaton

F

Fahie, William C., K.C.B.1825, I. 230
Fair, Robert, K.H.1834, I. 470
FAIRBAIRN, FAIRBORNE
Fairbairn, Andrew, Kt.1868, II. 360
Fairborne, Palmes, Kt.1675, II. 250
Fairbairn, Peter, Kt.1858, II. 353
Fairborne, Stafford, Kt.1701, II. 272
FAIRFAX, FAYREFAX, FAIREFAX, FAYRFAX
Fairfax, Charles, Kt.1603, II. 107
Fairfax, Ferdinando, Kt.1608, II. 144
Fairfax, George, Kt.1797, II. 304
Fairfax, Guy, K.B.1478, I. 138
Fairfax, Henry, K.C.B.1896, I. 267
Fairfax, James R., Kt.1898, II. 403
Fayrefax, Nicholas, Kt.1531, II. 48
Fairfax, Philip, Kt.1608, II. 146
Fairfax, Thomas, K.B.(1494), I. 144
Fairefax, Thomas, Kt.1513, II. 38
Fayrfax, Thomas, Kt.1579, II. 79
Fairfax, Thomas, Kt.1591, II. 89
Fairfax, Thomas (Charles), Kt.1603, II. 101, 107
Fairfax, Thomas, Kt.1641, II. 208
Fayrfax, William, Kt.1527, II. 46
Fayrfax, William, Kt.1560, II. 71
Fairfax, William, Kt.1603, II. 104
Fairfax, William, Kt.1630, II. 197
Fairmadow, Cornelius, Kt.1628, II. 195
Faiz, Ali Khan, K.C.S.I.1875, I. 320
Fakhry, Hussein, K.C.M.G.1902, I. 393
Falconar, Falkiner. See Faulkener
Falkland, viscount of. See Carey under Carew
FANE, VANE, and see Vane
Fane, Charles G., K.C.B.1901, I. 273
Fane, Edmund D. V., K.C.M.G.1899, I. 386

INDEX 81

Fane, Francis, afterwards 7th earl of Westmorland, K.B.1603, I. 154
Fane, Francis, K.B.1626, I. 161
Fane, Francis, K.B.1661, I. 164
Fane, George, Kt.1603, II. 120
Fane (Vane), Henry, Kt.1611, II. 150
Fane, Henry, K.B.1661, I. 164
Fane, Henry, K.C.B.1815, I. 219
Fane, John, 16th earl of Westmorland, Grand Master K.P.1790, I. 93; Kt.1792, II. 301; K.G.1793, I. 49
Fane, John, earl of Westmorland, G.C.H. 1817, I. 448; K.C.B.1838, I. 234; G.C.B.1846, I. 207
Fane, Mildmay, earl of Westmorland, K.B.1626, I. 161
Fane, Vere, earl of Westmorland, K.B. 1661, I. 164
Fanhope, lord. See Cornwall
Fanning, Rowland F. N., Kt.1886, II. 380

FANSHAWE, FANSHAW
Fanshawe, Arthur, K.C.B.1860, I. 246
Fanshawe, Arthur D., K.C.B.1904, I. 276
Fanshawe, Arthur U., K.C.I.E.1903, I. 411
Fanshawe, Edward G., K.C.B.1881, I. 257; G.C.B.1887, I. 199
Fanshaw, Henry, Kt.1603, II. 104
Fanshaw, Richard, Kt.1660, II. 225
Fanshaw, Simon, Kt.1641, II. 208
Fanshaw, Thomas, Kt.1624, II. 187
Fanshawe, Thomas, K.B.1626, I. 163
Fanshawe, Thomas, Kt.1660, II. 232
Fanshawe, Thomas, K.B.1661, I. 165
Fardell, Thomas G., Kt.1897, II. 400
Farington. See Farrington

FARMER, FARMOUR, FERMOR, FERMOUR, and see Farrer
Farmer, Edward, Kt.1660, II. 230
Farmer, George, Kt.1586, II. 85
Farmour, Henry, Kt.1529, II. 47
Fermor (Farmer), Hatton, Kt.1603, II. 111
Fermour, Henry, Kt.1531, II. 48
Farmer, James, Kt.1887, II. 382
Farmour (Fermour), John, Kt.1553, II. 68

FARMER
Farmer (Farwell, Farewell), John, Kt.1617, II. 164
Farmer (Fermer), John, Kt.1624, II. 186
Farmer (Fermor), Richard, Kt.1603, II. 107
Fermor, Thomas, earl of Pomfret, K.B.1725, I. 167
Fermor, William, Kt.1540, II. 52, 58
Farmer, William, Kt.1891, II. 389
Farnaby, Charles, Kt.1715, II. 280
Farnborough, lord. See Long; see May
Farnfield. See Fernefold
Farnham, Clement, Kt.1665, II. 241
Farnham, baron. See Maxwell
Farquhar, Arthur, K.H.1816, I. 463; K.C.H.1832, I. 459; Kt.1833, II. 334; K.C.B.1841, I. 237
Farquhar, Arthur, K.C.B.1886, I. 260
Farquhar, Horace B. T., 1st lord Farquhar, K.C.VO.(1901), I. 434; G.C.V.O.1902, I. 420
Farquhar, Robert, Kt.1651, II. 222
Farquharson, John, K.C.B.1899, I. 297
Farran, Charles F., Kt.1896, II. 397
Farrant, George, Kt.1822, II. 323
Farrant, Richard, Kt.1897, II. 399

FARRAR, FARRER
Farrer (Farmour), George, Kt.1586, II. 85
Farrar, George, Kt.1902, II. 412
Farrer, Robert, Kt.1634, II. 202
Farrer, William J., Kt.1887, II. 382
Farrell, Thomas, Kt.1894, II. 393
Farren, Richard T., K.C.B.1893, I. 264
Farrer. See Farrar

FARRINGTON, FARINGTON
Farington, Henry, Kt.1533, II. 49
Farrington, John, Kt.1661, II. 235
Farington, John, Kt.1681, II. 256
Farrington, William, Kt.1482, II. 19
Farrington, William, Kt.1761, II. 290
Farwell, George, Kt.1610, II. 149
Farwell, George, Kt.1899, II. 405
Farwell, John, Kt.1617, II. 164
Farewell, Roger, Kt.1513, II. 38
Fastolf, John, K.G.1426, I. 11

Fathullah, Khan H. A., governor of Enzeli, K.C.M.G.1903, I. 393
Fauconberge, lord. See Nevill
Fauconberg, Walter de, K.B.1306, I. 120
Fauconberge, Walter de, K.B.1326, I. 123

FAULKENER, FALCONAR, FAWKENER, FALKINER
Faulkener (Faulkner), Arthur B., Kt. 1815, II. 315
Falconar, Chesborough G., K.H.1837, I. 476
Fawkener, Everard, Kt.1735, II. 284
Falkiner, Frederick R., Kt.1896, II. 398
Faudel-Phillips, George, G.C.I.E.1897, I. 403
Faudon, Robert de, K.B.1306, I. 120
Faunce, Robert, Kt.1666, II. 242
Faure, Pieter H., K.C.M.G.1898, I. 384
Fawcett, John H., K.C.M.G.1887, I. 372
Fawcett, William, K.B.1786, I. 173
Fawcett-Lynar, William W., Kt.1833, II. 334
Fawkes, Wilmot H., K.C.V.O. (1903), I. 436; and see Fowke
Fawkner. See Faulkener
Fawnt (Faunt), William, Kt.1603, II. 103
Fayrer, Joseph, K.C.S.I.1876, I. 321
Fazakerly, William, Kt.1706, II. 275
Fearne. See Ferne
Feast, Felix, Kt.1723, II. 282
Featherston (Featherstonhalgh), Timothy, Kt.1628, II. 194
Felbrigge, Roger, Kt.1347, II. 9
Felbrigge, Simon, K.G.1397, I. 7

FELLOWES, FELLOWS
Fellows, Charles, Kt.1845, II. 346
Fellowes (Fellows), James, Kt.1809, II. 309
Fellowes, John, K.C.B.1903, I. 276
Fellowes, Thomas (Edward), Kt.1828, II. 327
Felton, Anthony, K.B.1603, I. 156
Felton, John de, K.B.1303, I. 110
Felton, Thomas, K.G.1381, I. 5
Fencotes, Thomas de, K.B.1347, I. 125
Fenes, Ingeram de, K.B.1253, I. 110
Fenkell (Fenkyll), John, Kt.1486, II. 23

FENN, FEN
Fenn, John, Kt.1787, II. 300
Fen, Richard, Kt.1638, II. 206
Fen, Robert, Kt.1641, II. 210

FENNER, FENNOR
Fenner, Edmund (Edward), Kt.1619, II. 174
Fennor, Edward, Kt.1603, II. 113
Fenner, Gregory (George), Kt.1618, II. 170
Fenner, John, Kt.1621, II. 177
Fenouilhet, Peter, Kt.1761, II. 290
Fenton, Geffery, Kt.1589, II. 87
Fenton, Maurice, Kt.1658, II. 224
Fenton, Myles, Kt.1889, II. 385
Fentoun, viscount. See Erskine

FENWICK, FENWYKE, FENWICKE
Fenwick, John, Kt.1605, II. 136
Fenwyke, Rauf, Kt.1523, II. 44
Fenwick, Robert, Kt.1683, II. 259
Fenwyke, Roger, Kt.1545, II. 57
Fenwicke, William, Kt.1603, II. 100
Fenwick, William, Kt.1617, II. 163
Ferby (Feerby), Leonard, Kt.1629, II.197
Feres, John, Kt.1471, II. 15
Ferguson, Adam, Kt.1822, II. 324
Ferguson, James, K.C.B.1855, I. 241; G.C.B.1860, I. 193
Ferguson, James, K.C.M.G.1874, I. 357; G.C.S.I.1885, I. 312
Ferguson, Ronald C., K.C.B.1815, I. 218; G.C.B.1831, I. 186
Ferguson, Samuel, Kt.1878, II. 370
Fermer, Fermor. See Farmer
Ferne (Feron, Fearne), John, Kt.1603, II. 128, 133
Fernefold (Fernefoll, Farnfield), Thomas, Kt.1621, II. 178
Ferns, John, Kt.1801, II. 306
Ferrato, Symon de, Kt.1513, II. 41
Ferrers, Edward, Kt.1513, II. 39
Ferrers, Edward, Kt.1591, II. 88
Ferrers, Henry, Kt.1471, II. 14
Ferrers, Humfrey, Kt.1533, II. 49
Ferrers, Humphrey, Kt.1617, II. 166
Ferrers, Humphry, Kt.1671, II. 245
Ferrers (Ferres), John, Kt.1497, II. 29
Ferrers, John, Kt.1603, II. 103, 104
Ferrers, lord. See Devereux

INDEX

83

Ferrers, Robert, Kt.1347, II. 7
Ferrers, Thomas de, K.B.1306, I. 111
Ferrers, William, Kt.1347, II. 7
Ferrier, Alexander, K.H.1834, I. 471; Kt.1835, II. 336
Festetics De Tolna, count T. de, G.C.V.O. 1904, I. 430
Festing Benjamin, M., K.H.1837, I. 476
Festing, Francis W., K.C.M.G.1874, I. 357

FETTIPLACE, FETYPLACE, FETTEPLACE, FETIPLACE
Fetyplace, Edmond, Kt.1575, II. 77
Fetteplace, Edmund, Kt.1603, II. 127
Fettiplace, Edward, Kt.1601, II. 99
Fetyplace, John, Kt.1575, II. 77
Fettiplace, John, Kt.1663, II. 237
Fetiplace, Richard, Kt.1599, II. 98, 126
Fetyplace, Thomas, Kt.1504, II. 34
Feversham, earl of. See Duras
Fevre, George le, Kt.1841, II. 343
Ficalho, count of, G.C.V.O.1901, I. 424
Field, Charles V., Kt.1778, II. 295
Field, John, K.C.B.1891, I. 263
Field, Thomas, Kt.1681, II. 256
Field, William V., Kt.1875, II. 367

FIELDING, FEILDINGES, FYLDINGE, FELDYNGE
Fielding, Basil, earl of Denbigh, K.B. 1626, I. 161
Fielding, Charles, Kt.1673, II. 248
Fylding, Everard, Kt.1509, II. 35
Fyldenge, George or Gerard [?Edward], K.B.1501, I. 146
Fielding, George, earl of Desmond, K.B.1626, I. 160
Fielding, John, Kt.1761, II. 290
Fielding, Percy R. B., K.C.B.1893, I. 264
Fielding, Roger, Kt.1641, II. 209
Feldynge, William, Kt.1533, II. 49
Fielding, William, Kt.1603, II. 103, 141
Fielding, William B. P., earl of Denbigh, G.C.H.1833, I. 452

FIENNES, FYNES, FENYS, FINNIS, FYENS
Fiennes, Edward, Kt.1617, II. 161
Fenys, Richard, Kt.1452, II. 12

FENYS
Fenys (Fynes), Richard, Kt.1568, II. 74
Fynes, Richard, Kt.1592, II. 90
Fiennes, Thomas, lord Dacre, K.B. (1494), I. 144
Fenys or Finnis, Thomas, K.B.1501, I. 145
Fyens, William, Kt.1399, II. 11
Fife, Aubone G., Kt.1902, II. 411
Fife, duke and earl of. See Duff
Fife, John, Kt.1840, II. 342

FILMER, FILMORE, and see Phillimore
Filmore, Edward, Kt.1603, II. 126
Filmer, Robert, Kt.1619, II. 170

FINCH, FYNCHE, FINCHE
Finch, Daniel, earl of Winchilsea, K.G.1752, I. 45
Finch, George, earl of Winchilsea, K.G.1805, I. 50
Finch, Heneage, Kt.1623, II. 182
Finch, Henry, Kt.1616, II. 158
Finch, John, Kt.1625, II. 188
Finch, John, Kt.1661, II. 235
Fynche, Moyle, Kt.1585, II. 83
Finch, Nathaniel, Kt.1640, II. 207
Finch, Theophilus, Kt.1599, II. 96
Finche, Thomas, Kt.1553, II. 68
Finch, Thomas, Kt.1609, II. 147
Fynche, William, Kt.1513, II. 40
Findlay, Alexander, K.H.1836, I. 473
Findlay, George, Kt.1892, II. 390
Findlater, earl of. See Ogilvy
Findlater, William H., Kt.1897, II. 398
Finett, John, Kt.1616, II. 157
Fingall, earl of. See Plunkett
Finlay, Robert B., Kt.1895, II. 396; G.C.M.G.1904, I. 349
Finlay, Thomas, Kt.1837, II. 338
Firbank, Joseph T., Kt.1902, II. 411
Firebrace, Basil, Kt.1687, II. 263
Firth, Charles H., Kt.1868, II. 360
Fischel, Max, K.C.V.O.1904, I. 443

FISHER, FYSHER
Fysher, Clement, Kt.1604, II. 136
Fisher, Edward, Kt.1603, II. 129
Fisher, Edward, Kt.1608, II. 144
Fisher, Ferdinando, Kt.1645, II. 220

FISHER
  Fisher, George B., K.C.H.1831, I. 457; Kt.1831, II. 331
  Fisher, Henry C., Kt.1898, II. 403
  Fisher, James H., Kt.1860, II. 355
  Fisher, John, Kt.1503, II. 33
  Fisher, John A., K.C.B.1894, I. 266; G.C.B.1902, I. 203
  Fisher, John W., Kt.1853, II. 353
  Fisher, Robert, Kt.1609, II. 148
  Fisher, Thomas, Kt.1617, II. 161
FITCH, FYTCH, FITZ, FITCHE, FISH
  Fitch, Barrow, Kt.1670, II. 244
  Fitche (Fitz), Francis, Kt.1604, II. 131
  Fitch, Joshua G., Kt.1896, II. 398
  Fitch, Thomas, Kt.1679, II. 254
  Fish (Fitch), William, Kt.1617, II. 167
  Fytch (Fitch), William (Ferdinando), Kt.1608, II. 144
FITTON, FYTTON
  Fytton, Edward, Kt.1533, II. 49
  Fitton, Edward, Kt.1553, II. 68
  Fitton, Edward, Kt.1579, II. 80
Fitz-Alan, Henry, son of the earl of Arundel, Kt.1439, II. 12
Fitz-Alan, Henry, earl of Arundel, K.G. 1544, I. 23
Fitz-Alan, Henry, lord Maltravers, K.B. 1547, I. 150
Fitz-Alan, John, earl of Arundel, K.B. (1426), I. 131; K.G.1432, I. 11
Fitz-Alan, John, lord Maltravers, K.B. (1465), I. 134
Fitz-Alan, Richard, earl of Arundel, K.G.1386, I. 6
Fitz-Alan, Thomas, earl of Arundel, K.B. 1399, I. 127; K.G.1400, I. 7
Fitz-Alan, Thomas, earl of Arundel, K.B. (1461), I. 133; K.G.1474, I. 15
Fitz-Alan, William, earl of Arundel, K.G.1471, I. 15
Fitz-Alan, William, earl of Arundel, K.B. (1489), I. 143; K.G.1525, I. 21
Fitzalan-Howard, Henry, duke of Norfolk, K.G.1886, I. 68; G.C.V.O. 1902, I. 419
Fitz-Clarence, lord Adolphus, G.C.H. 1832, I. 451
Fitz-Clarence, lord Frederick, G.C.H. 1831, I. 451

Fitz-Conan, Henry, K.B.1306, I. 118
FitzGeorge, Adolphus A. F., K.C.V.O. (1904), I. 437
FitzGeorge, Augustus C. F., K.C.V.O. (1904), I. 437
Fitzgerald, Edmond F., Kt.1606, II. 141
Fitzgerald, Edward, Kt.1593, II. 90
Fitzgerald, Edward T., K.H.1833, I. 468
Fitzgerald, Gerald, earl of Kildare, K.G.1504, I. 19
Fitzgerald, alias MacShane, Gerald F., Kt. before 1541, II. 52
Fitzgerald, Gerald F., Kt. before 1541, II. 53
Fitzgerald, Gerald, earl of Desmond, Kt.1558, II. 70
Fitzgerald, Gerald, K.C.M.G.1885, I. 367
Fitzgerald, James, Kt.1560, II. 70
Fitzgerald, James, Kt.1573, II. 75
Fitzgerald, James F., Kt.1600, II. 98
Fitzgerald, John, Kt.1567, II. 73
Fitzgerald, John, Kt.1602, II. 99
Fitzgerald, John, Kt.1617, II. 163
Fitzgerald, John F., Kt.1602, II. 99
Fitzgerald, John F., K.C.B.1831, I. 231; G.C.B.1862, I. 194
Fitzgerald, Luke, Kt.1624, II. 185
Fitzgerald, Maurice, Kt.1553, II. 66
Fitzgerald, Maurice, Kt.1556, II. 69
Fitzgerald, Maurice, Kt.1558, II. 70
Fitzgerald, Pierce F., Kt.1585, II. 84
Fitzgerald, Robert L., K.C.H.1835, I. 461; Kt.1835, II. 337
Fitzgerald, alias O'Desmond, Thomas, Kt.1564, II. 71
Fitzgerald, Thomas, Kt.1569, II. 74
Fitzgerald, Thomas N., Kt.1897, II. 399
Fitzgerald, William, Kt.1669, II. 244
Fitzgerald, William G. S. V., K.C.I.E. 1887, I. 405
Fitzgerald, William R., duke of Leinster, K.P.1783, I. 96
Fitzgerald, William R. S. V., K.C.S.I. 1867, I. 318; G.C.S.I.1868, I. 309
Fitzgerald-de-Ros, Dudley C., lord de Ros, K.C.V.O.(1897), I. 432; K.P. 1902, I. 106
FitzGibbon, John, earl of Clare, G.C.H. 1835, I. 453; K.P.1845, I. 101

INDEX

FitzGuy, Robert, K.B.1306, I. 119
Fitzhardinge, lord. See Berkeley
Fitz Henry, Aucher, K.B.1306, I. 111
FitzHenry, Henry, Kt.1347, II. 8
FitzHenry, Hugh, K.B.1306, I. 121
FitzHerbert, —, Kt.1525, II. 46
FitzHerbert, Alleyne, lord St. Helens, G.C.H.1819, I. 449
FitzHerbert, John, Kt.1624, II. 186
FitzHerbert, Matthew, K.B.1326, I. 123
FitzHerbert, Thomas, Kt.1547, II. 60
FitzHerbert, William, K.C.M.G.1877, I. 358
Fitz-Hugh, George, lord Fitz-Hugh, K.B.1509, I. 148
Fitz-Hugh, Henry, lord Fitz-Hugh, K.G. 1408, I. 8
Fitz-Hugh, Richard, lord Fitz-Hugh, Kt. 1482, II. 19
Fitz Hughs (Fitz Hews), Richard, Kt. 1487, II. 25
Fitz Humfrey, Walter, K.B.1306, I. 121
FitzJames, —, Kt.1525, II. 46
FitzJames, James, Kt.1553, II. 68
FitzJames, James, duke of Berwick, K.G. 1688, I. 38
FitzJames, James, duke of Liria, K.G. Jacobite 1727, I. 38
FitzJames, John, Kt.1615, II. 156
FitzJames, John, 1660, II. 229
FitzJeffrey (Fitz-Geffrey), George, Kt. 1607, II. 141
Fitz, John, Kt.1603, II. 126
Fitz Lewes (Fitz Hews), Richard, Kt. 1487, II. 25
Fitz-Maurice, George W. H., earl of Orkney, K.C.M.G.1875, I. 358
Fitzmaurice, John, K.H.1833, I. 469
Fitzmaurice, Nicholas, Kt.(1312), II. lviii.
Fitzmaurice, Thomas, lord of Kerry, Kt. 1567, II. 73
Fitzmayer, James W., K.C.B.1871, I. 253
Fitzpatrick, Bernaby, Kt.1560, II. 71
Fitzpatrick, Dennis, K.C.S.I.1890, I. 324
Fitzpatrick, James P., Kt.1902, II. 412
Fitzpatrick, Jerome, Kt.1782, II. 297
Fitz Payn, Robert, K.B.1306, I. 113
Fitz Randall, Rauf, Kt.1482, II. 20

Fitz Ralph, Simon, K.B.1327, I. 124
Fitz Richard, Simon, K.B.1333, I. 125
Fitz Richard, Symon, Kt.1513, II. 41
Fitz-Roy, Augustus H., duke of Grafton, K.G.1769, I. 46
Fitz-Roy, Augustus C. L., duke of Grafton, K.G.1883, I. 67
Fitz Roy, Charles, duke of Cleveland, K.G.1673, I. 37
Fitz-Roy, Charles, duke of Grafton, K.G. 1721, I. 42
Fitzroy, Charles A., K.H.1837, II. 479; Kt.1837, II. 339; K.C.B.1854, I. 279
Fitz Roy, George, duke of Northumberland, K.G.1684, I. 37
Fitz-Roy, George H., duke of Grafton, K.G.1834, I. 54
Fitzroy, Henry, duke of Richmond, K.G.1525, I. 21
Fitz-Roy, Henry, duke of Grafton, K.G. 1680, I. 37
Fitz Roy, Robert O'B., K.C.B.1895, I.266
Fitzroy, lord William, K.C.B.1840, I. 236
Fitz Simon, James, Kt.1541, II. 52
Fitz Simon, Nicholas, Kt.1841, II. 344
Fitz-Simon, Richard, K.G.1348, I. 2
Fitzsymond, John, Kt.1347, II. 9
Fitz Thomas, Maurice, K.B.1347, I. 125
Fitz-Urian, Rhys ap T., K.G.1506, I. 19
Fitzwalter, —, Kt.1347, II. 6
Fitz Walter, John, Kt.1360, II. 10
Fitz-Walter, lord. See Radcliff
Fitz Waryn, —, Kt.1492, II. 28
Fitz Warine, Fulk, K.B.1306, I. 112
Fitz Warine, John, K.B.1306, I. 114
Fitz Warin, lord. See Bourchier
Fitzwaryne, William, K.G.1348, I. 2
Fitzwilliam, earl. See Wentworth Fitzwilliam
Fitzwilliam(Fitzwilliams),John(William), Kt.1553, II. 67
Fitzwilliam, Richard, viscount Fitzwilliam, K.B.1744, I. 169
Fitzwilliam, Thomas, Kt.1482, II. 20
Fitzwilliam, Thomas, Kt.1487, II. 26
Fitzwilliam, Thomas, Kt.1566, II. 72
Fitzwilliam, William, Kt.1482, II. 20
Fitzwilliam, William, Kt.1513, II. 39
Fitzwilliam, William, Kt.1515, II. 43

INDEX

Fitzwilliam, William, Kt.1549, II. 65
Fitzwilliam, William, Kt.1572, II. 75
Fitzwilliam, William, earl of Southampton, 1526, I. 22
Fitzwilliam, William, earl Fitzwilliam, Grand Master K.P.1795, I. 93
Fitzwilliams, —, Kt.1603, II. 126
Fitzwilliams, George, K.B.1533, I. 150
Fitzwilliams, George, Kt.1607, II. 141
Fitzwilliams, John, Kt.1605, II. 138
Fitzwilliams, Thomas, Kt.1605, II. 138
Fitzwilliams, William, Kt.1603, II. 105
Flamburiari, count Dionisio, K.C.M.G.1844, I. 353 : G.C.M.G.1857, I. 335
Flamocke (Flemok), Andrew, Kt.1545, II. 57
Flannery, James F., Kt.1899, II. 404
Fleet, John, Kt.1688, II. 264
Fleetwood, Edward, Kt.1618, II. 167
Fleetwood, George, Kt.1603, II. 106
Fleetwood, George, Kt.1632, II. 200
Fleetwood, George, Kt.1656, II. 223
Fleetwood, Gerrard, Kt.1603, II. 112
Fleetwood, Myles, Kt.1602, II. 100, 106
Fleetwood, Paul, Kt.1623, II. 181
Fleetwood, Thomas, Kt.1619, II. 171
Fleetwood, William (Miles), Kt.1603, II. 106, 110
Fleetwood, William, Kt.1624, II. 185
Fleetwood-Wilson. See Wilson

FLEMING, FLEMYNGE, FLEMYNG, FLAMING, FLEMINGE
Fleming, Christopher, lord Slane, Kt.1494, II. 28
Fleming, Daniel, Kt.1681, II. 255
Flemynge, Francys, Kt.1547, II. 61
Fleming, Francis, Kt.1583, II. 82
Fleming, Francis, K.C.M.G.1892, I.376
Flemyng, Gerald, Kt.1541, II. 53
Flaming, John, Kt.1606, II. 141
Fleming, John, Kt.1686, II. 261
Fleming, Sandford, K.C.M.G.1897, I. 382
Fleminge, Thomas, baron of Slane, Kt.1583, II. 82
Flemyng, Thomas, Kt.1603, II. 114, 137
Fleming, Valentine, Kt.1856, II. 351
Fleming, William, Kt.1761, II. 291

Fletcher, Richard, Kt.1617, II. 164
Fletcher, Richard, Kt.1812, II. 310
Fletcher, Robert, Kt.1763, II. 292
Fletcher, William A., Kt.1811, II. 310
Flint, Charles W., Kt.1812, II. 311
Floswick, John, Kt.1661, II. 235

FLOWER, FLOURE
Flower, Ernest, Kt.1903, II. 416
Flower, George, Kt.1605, II. 137
Floure, William, Kt.1660, II. 231
Flower, William H., K.C.B.1892, I. 293

Floyd, Fluid. See Lloyd
Floyer, Augustus, K.C.B.1815, I. 227
Floyer, John, Kt.1685, II. 260
Floyer, Peter, Kt.1701, II. 272
Fludyer, Samuel, Kt.1755, II. 288
Fludyer, Thomas, Kt.1761, II. 291
Foche, John, Kt.1692, II. 267
Fogge, John, Kt.1461, II. 13
Fogge (Foog), John, Kt.1501, II. 33
Fogge, John, Kt.1543, II. 54
Foix, Peter de la, K.B.1303, I. 110
Foley, St. George G., K.C.B.1886, 1. 260
Foley, Thomas, K.C.B.1815, I. 218; G.C.B.1820, I. 184

FOLJAMB, FOULCHAMPE, FOULGIAM, FOLJAMBE
Foulgiam (Fouliambe), Geoffrey, Kt.1580, II. 80
Foulchampe, James, Kt.1538, II. 52
Foljambe, Thomas, Kt.1605, II. 137
Follett, Charles J., Kt.1902, II. 413
Follett, William W., Kt.1834, II. 335

FOLLIOTT, FOLIOTT, FOLIOT
Folliott, Henry, Kt.1599, II. 97
Foliott, (Talbot) John, Kt.1603, II. 110
Foliot, Richard, K.B.1306, I. 121
Fonblanque, Thomas de Grenier, afterwards viscount, K.H.1821, I. 464
Foote, Edward J., K.C.B.1831, I. 230
Foote, Thomas, Kt.1657, II. 224
Forbes, Charles F., K.H.1837, I. 479 ; Kt.1844, II. 345
Forbes, Francis, Kt.1713, II. 278
Forbes, Francis, Kt.1837, II. 338
Forbes, George A. H., earl of Granard, K.P.1857, I. 102
Forbes, James, Kt.1689, II. 265

INDEX

Forbes, John, Kt.1853, II. 350
Forbes, John, K.C.B.1881, I. 258; G.C.B. 1899, I. 202
FORD, FORTH, FOORTH
Foord (Forth), Ambrose, Kt.1604, II. 135
Ford, Edward, Kt.1643, II. 216
Ford, Francis C., K.C.M.G.1885, I.368; G.C.M.G.1886, I. 341; G.C.B.1889, I. 213
Ford, Henry, Kt.1672, II. 247
Ford, John, Kt.1610, II. 149
Ford, Richard, Kt.1660, II. 226
Ford, Richard, Kt.1801, II. 306
Ford, Theodore T., Kt.1888, II. 385
Forth, Robert, Kt.1628, II. 193
Ford (Forth), William, Kt.1604, II. 133, 134
Ford, William, Kt.1618, II. 169
Fordyce, John, K.C.B.1873, I. 254
Fordyce, William, Kt.1782, II. 297
FORESTER, FORRESTER, and see Foster
Forester, James, Kt.1594, II. 91
Forrester, John, Kt. Jacobite 1714, footnote, II. 266
Forester, William, Kt.1689, II. 265
Foresti (Forester), Spiridion, Kt.1817, II. 319
Forestier-Walker, Edward W., K.C.B. 1871, I. 252
Forestier-Walker, Frederick W. E., K.C.B.1894, I. 265; G.C.M.G.1901, I. 347
Forlong, James, K.H.1835, I. 472
Forman, Nicholas, Kt.1538, II. 51
Forrest, Anthony, Kt.1604, II. 135
Forrest, Diggory, Kt.1815, II. 315
Forrest, John, K.C.M.G.1891, I. 376; G.C.M.G.1901, I. 347
Forstal, Mark, Kt. Jacobite 1734, footnote, II. 266
Forster. See Foster
Forsyth, John, K.C.S.I.1881, I. 322
Forsyth, Thomas Douglas, K.C.S.I.1874, I. 320
FOSTER, FORSTER, and see Forrester
Foster, Balthazar W., Kt.1886, II. 380
Foster, Charles J., K.C.B.1893, I. 265
Forster, Christopher, Kt.1630, II. 198

FOSTER
Foster (Forster), (Nicholas) Claudius, Kt.1615, II. 155
Foster, Clement Le N., Kt.1903, II.416
Forster, George, Kt.1603, II. 121, 125
Forster, Humfrye, Kt.1527, II. 46, 48
Foster, Humfrey, Kt.1592, II. 89
Foster (Forster), Humphrey, Kt.1704, II. 274
Foster, John (George), K.B.1501, I. 146
Forster, John, Kt.1567, II. 61
Forster, Matthew, Kt.1617, II. 163
Foster, Michael, Kt.1745, II. 287
Foster, Michael, K.C.B.1899, I. 298
Forster, Nicholas, Kt.1603, II. 100
Forster, Robert, Kt.1640, II. 207
Foster, Thomas, Kt.1523, II. 44
Forster, Thomas, Kt.1604, II. 134
Foster, Thomas, Kt.1665, II. 240
Forster, William, K.B.1603, I. 156
Foster (Forster), William, Kt.1603, II. 112
Forster, William, Kt.1660, II. 232
Forster, William F., K.H.1833, I. 469
Foster-Skeffington, John S., viscount Massareene, K.P.1851, I. 101
Fortescue, Adrian, Kt.1504, II. 34
Fortescue, Chichester, Kt.1788, II. 300
Fortescue, Edmond, Kt.1642, II. 213
Fortescue, Edmond, Kt.1664, II. 239
Fortescue, Francis, K.B.1603, I. 154
Fortescue, Hugh, earl Clinton, K.B.1725, I. 167
Fortescue, Hugh, earl Fortescue, Grand Master K.P.1839, I. 94; K.G.1856, I. 59
Fortescu, John, Kt.1485, 1487, II. 22, 24
Fortescue, John, Kt.1592, II. 89
Fortescue, John, Kt.1642, II. 212
Fortescue, Nicholas, Kt.1619, II. 171
Fortescue, Thomas, Kt.1663, II. 238
Fortescue, Walter H., earl of Clermont, K.P.1795, I. 97
Fortescue, William, Kt.1600, II. 98
Fortescue-Aland, John, Kt.1717, II. 281
Forth. See Ford
Fortick, William, Kt.1782, II. 296
Forward, William B., Kt.1883, II. 375

Foscardi, Demetrio, count, K.C.M.G.1821, I. 351
Fossad, Amaricus de, K.B.1306, I. 112
Fotherby, John, Kt.1628, II. 194
Fotherby, Thomas, Kt.1681, II. 256
Fotherby, Thomas, Kt.1640, II. 207
FOULIS, FOWLIS, and see Fowle
Fowlis, David, Kt.1603, I. 109
Foulis, David, K.C.B.1838, I. 236
Foulke. See Fowke
Fountaine, Andrew, Kt.1699, II. 271
Fountain, Erasmus de la, Kt.1623, II. 181
Fourneaux, Fourneys. See Furness
Fournier, Francois E., G.C.V.O.1903, I. 427
Fowell. See Vowell
FOWKE, FOULKE, FOOKES, FULKS, FOULXE, and see Fawkes
Fulks (Fowkes), Bartholomew, Kt.1603, II. 127
Fookes (Foulxe), Henry, Kt.1599, II. 97
Foulke, Francis, Kt.1661, II. 233
Fowke, Sydenham, Kt.1723, II. 282
Fowke, Thomas, Kt.1779, II. 296
Fowle, John, Kt.1619, II. 174
Fowle, Thomas, Kt.1686, II. 262; and see Foulis
Fowler, Edward, Kt.1617, II. 163
Fowler, Henry H., G.C.S.I.1895, I. 313
Fowler, Jasper, Kt.1623, II. 183
Fowler, John, K.C.M.G.1885, I. 368
Fowler, John D., Kt.1818, II. 320
Fowler, Richard, K.B.1501, I. 147
Fowler, Thomas, Kt.1603, II. 108, 124
Fowlis. See Foulis
Fownes, William, Kt.1709, II. 276
Fox, FOXE, and see Fawkes, Vaux
Fox, Charles, Kt.1851, II. 349
Fox, Charles D., Kt.1886, II. 378
Fox, Charles R., K.C.H.1830, I. 456
Foxe, Edward (Edmond), Kt.1603, II. 102
Fox, Henry, Kt.1616, II. 158
Fox, Patricke, Kt.1616, II. 158
Fox, Stephen, Kt.1665, II. 241
Fox, William, K.C.M.G.1879, I. 361
Fox-Strangways, Thomas, K.C.B.1855, footnote, I. 241

Foxen, Samuel, Kt.1678, II. 253
Foxley, John de, K.B.1306, I. 114
Framingham, Haylett, K.C.B.1815, I. 223; K.C.H.1819, I. 454
Framlingham, Charles, Kt.1581, II. 81
Fremlingham (Framlingham), James, Kt.1513, II. 40
FRANCE
Charles IX. of, K.G.1564, I. 26
Charles X. of, K.G.1825, I. 53
Francis I., king of, K.G.1527, I. 22
Henry II. of, K.G.1551, I. 24
Henry III. of, K.G.1575, I. 27
Henry IV. of, K.G.1590, I. 28
Louis XVIII. of, K.G.1814, I. 51
Louis Philippe of, K.G.1844, I. 57
Napoleon III. of, K.G.1855, I. 59
FRANCIS, FRAUNCIS
Francis, Edward, Kt.1603, II. 106, 137
Francis, Philip, K.B.1806, I. 176; G.C.B.1815, I. 205
Francis, Philip, Kt.1868, II. 360
Francis, Richard, K.B.1400, I. 128
Fraunces, William, Kt.1547, II. 62
Franck, Leventhorpe, Kt.1609, II. 147
Francks. See Franks
Frankland, Edward, K.C.B.1897, I. 296
Frankland, Henry, Kt.1636, II. 204; and see Franklin
FRANKLIN, FRANKLYN, FRANKLAND
Franklin, Benjamin, K.C.I.E.1903, I. 411
Franklin (Frankland), Henry, Kt.1607, II. 142
Franklin, John, Kt.1614, II. 154
Franklin, John, Kt.1675, II. 250
Franklin, John, Kt.1786, II. 299
Franklin, John, Kt.1829, II. 328; K.C.H.1836, I. 461
Franklin, Richard, Kt.1840, II. 343
Franklyn, William, Kt.1675, II. 250
Franklin, William, Kt.1823, II. 324; K.C.H.1832, I. 458
Franklin, Willingham, Kt.1822, II. 323
FRANKS, FRANCKS
Franks, Augustus W., K.C.B.1894, I. 293
Franks, John, Kt.1825, II. 325
Franks, John H., Kt.1902, II. 410

INDEX 89

FRANKS
Franks, Kendall M. S., Kt.1904, II. 418
Franks, Thomas H., K.C.B.1858, I. 245
Francks, William, Kt.1347, II. 8
FRASER, FRAZER
Fraser, Alexander, Kt.1594, II. 91
Fraser, Alexander G., lord Saltoun, G.C.H.1837, I. 453; K.C.B.1842, I. 237; K.T.1852, I. 84
Fraser, Andrew H. L., K.C.S.I.1903, I. 327
Frazer, Augustus S., K.C.B.1815, I. 226
Fraser, Charles C., K.C.B.1891, I. 263
Fraser, David M., K.C.B.1889, I. 263
Fraser, Hugh, K.C.B.1832, I. 232
Fraser, James, K.C.B.1886, I. 289
Fraser, John, Kt.1826, II. 326; G.C.H. 1832, I. 451
Fraser, John, K.C.M.G.1853, I. 353
Fraser, Malcolm, K.C.M.G.1887, I. 371
Fraser, Robert, K.H.1837, I. 477
Fraser, Thomas, K.C.B.1900, I. 271
Fraser, Thomas A., lord Lovat, K.T. 1865, I. 85
Fraser, Thomas R., Kt.1902, II. 411
Fraser, William, K.C.B.1887, I. 290
Fraser-Tytler, James M. B., K.C.B. 1887, I. 260
Frator (Vaire), William, Kt.1347, II. 8
Frazer. See Fraser
Freak, Thomas, Kt.1603, II. 124
Freckleton, Ferdinando, Kt.1603, II. 127
Frederick, Charles, K.B.1761, I. 170
Frederick, John, Kt.1660, II. 229;
Frederick, Thomas, Kt.1721, II. 282
Frederiks, baron Vladimir, K.C.V.O. 1896, I. 438
Freeling, Sanford, K.C.M.G.1878, I. 360
Freeman, Francis, Kt.1607, II. 142
Freeman, George, K.B.1661, I. 166
Freeman, Ralph, Kt.1617, II. 166
Freeman-Mitford, Algernon B., lord Redesdale, K.C.V.O.(1903), I. 436
Freer, William G., K.H.1834, I. 469
Freestun, William L., Kt.1860, II. 355
Freeth, James, K.H.1833, I. 468; K.C.B. 1862, I. 247
Fremantle, Arthur J. L., K.C.M.G.1894, I. 379; G.C.M.G.1898, I. 345

Fremantle, Charles H., K.C.B.1857, I. 243; G.C.B.1867, I. 195
Fremantle, Charles W., K.C.B.1890, I. 291
Fremantle, Edmund R., K.C.B.1889, I. 263; G.C.B.1899, I. 202
Fremantle, Thomas F., K.C.B.1815, I. 219; G.C.H.1818, I. 448; G.C.B. 1818, I. 183; G.C.M.G.1819, I. 332
Fremantle, William H., Kt.1827, II. 327; G.C.H.1827, I. 450
French, Cudbert, K.H.1836, I. 474
French, George A., K.C.M.G.1902, I. 393
French, John D. P., K.C.B.1900, I. 272; K.C.M.G.1902, I. 393
French, Oliver, Kt.1650, II. 221
French, Peter, Kt.1623, II. 182
French, Somerset R., K.C.M.G.1901, I. 390
FRENE, FREIGNE
Frene, Fulk de la, Kt.(1335), II. lix.
Freigne, John de la, Kt.(1361), II. lx.
Frene, Matthew F. de la, Kt.(1335), II. lix.
Freigne, Patrick de la, Kt.(1361), II. lx.
Freigne, Robert de la, Kt.(1361), II. lx.
Freigne, William de, K.B.1306, I. 112
Frere, Henry B. E., K.C.B.1859, I. 281; K.C.S.I.1866, I. 315; G.C.S.I.1866, I. 309; G.C.B.1876, I. 210
FRESCHVILE, FRETCHWELL, FRECHEVILLE
Fretchwell (Frecheville), Peter, Kt. 1544, II. 55
Freschvile (Freshwell), Peter, Kt.1603, II. 102
Freston, Richard, Kt.1553, II. 66; and see Freestun
Frevil (Frewil), George, Kt.1603, II. 101
Frewen, Edward, Kt.1685, II. 260
Friend, John, Kt.1685, II. 261
Frigerio, Giovanni G., G.C.V.O.1903, I. 426
Fripp, Alfred D., Kt.1903, II. 414
Friville, Johannes de, K.B.1306, I. 112
Frizelle, Joseph, Kt.1899, II. 405
Frobisher, Martin, Kt.1588, I. 86
Fropier, Gabriel P. J., Kt.1862, II. 356

INDEX

Frost, John, K.C.M.G.1904, I. 394
Gawler, George, K.H.1837, I. 476
Frowde, Philip, Kt.1665, II. 240

FROWICK, FROWECK, FROWYKE
    Frowick, Henry, K.B.1501, I. 147
    Froweck, Thomas, K.B.1478, I. 138
    Frowyke, Thomas, Kt.1502, II. 33
Fruges, Warin de, K.B.1253, I. 110
Fry, Edward, Kt.1877, II. 369
Fryer, Frederick W. R., K.C.S.I.1895, I. 325
Fryer, John, K.C.B.1903, I. 275
Fryer, Thomas, Kt.1627, II. 192
Fryer, William, Kt.1617, II. 164
Fuchs, Thomas, Kt.1513, II. 41
Fukushima, maj. gen., K.C.B.1902, I. 275
Fulks. See Fowke
Fulford, Francis, Kt.1605, II. 137
Fulford, Humphrey, K.B.(1494), I. 144
Fulford, Thomas, Kt.1460, II. 13
Fullarton, J., K.H.1832, I. 467
Fuller, Dowse, Kt.1663, II. 238
Fuller, Joseph, Kt.1826, II. 326; G.C.H. 1827, I. 450
Fuller, Nicholas, Kt.1619, II. 172
Fuller, Thomas E., K.C.M.G.1904, I. 395
Fullerton, John R. T., K.C.V.O.(1899), I. 433; G.C.V.O.1901, I. 418
Fulmerston, Richard, Kt.1560, II. 71
Fulnetby (Fownetby), Vincent, Kt.1603, II. 122
Fulton, James F., K.H.1837, I. 476
Fulton, Forrest, Kt.1892, II. 391
Fulwood, George, Kt.1606, II. 141
Furley, John, Kt.1899, II. 404

GERARD, GERRARD, GARRETT, GARRET,
    Furness, Christopher, Kt.1895, II. 396
    Fournes (Furnace), Henry, Kt.1691, II. 266
    Fourneaux (Fourneys), John, Kt.1347, II. 6
Fyers, William A., K.C.B.1889, I. 263
Fylloll, William, K.B.1501, I. 146
Fynes. See Fiennes
Fyneulx (Fyneux), John, Kt.1497, II. 30
Fysh, Philip O., K.C.M.G.1896, I. 381
Fytch, Fytton. See Fitch, Fitton

G

Gabelline, —, Kt.1612, II. 152
Gabriel, James W., K.H.1837, I. 475
Gabriel, Robert B., K.H.1834, I. 470
Gage, Edward, Kt.1555, I. 69
Gage, Henry, Kt.1644, II. 218
Gage, John, K.G.1541, I. 23
Gage, William, Kt.1660, II. 232
Gage, William, K.B.1725, I. 168
Gage, William H., G.C.H.1834, I. 452; G.C.B.1860, I. 193
Gahan, Daniel, Kt.1704, II. 273
Gainsforth, Thomas, Kt.1609, II. 147
Gainsford, William, Kt.1603, II. 126
Gairdner, William T., K.C.B.1898, I. 296
Galbraith, William, K.C.B.1897, I. 269
Galhardo, Eduardo A. R., K.C.I.E.1901, I. 410
Galiace, Christopher, Kt.1509, II. 35
Galitzin, prince Dmitri, G.C.V.O.1896, I. 422
Galloway, Archibald, K.C.B.1848, I. 238
Galloway, earl of. See Stewart
Gallwey, Michael H., K.C.M.G.1888, I.373
Gallwey, Thomas J., K.C.M.G.1901, I. 389
Gallwey, Thomas L. J., K.C.M.G.1889, I. 374
Galsworthy, Edwin E., Kt.1887, II. 382
Galt, Alexander T., K.C.M.G.1869, I.355; G.C.M.G.1878, I. 338
Galt, Thomas, Kt.1888, II. 384
Galton, Douglas, K.C.B.1887, I. 290
Galway, viscount. See Monckton-Arundell
Galwey, Michael, K.C.B.1877, I. 256
Gamage, Thomas, Kt.1513, II. 41
Gambier, Edward J., Kt.1834, II. 335
Gambier, James, Kt.1808, II. 309
Gambier, James, lord Gambier, K.C.B. 1815, I. 217; G.C.B.1815, I. 183
Gamble, David, K.C.B.1904, I. 301
Gamble, John, Kt.1603, II. 119
Gamble, Mathew, Kt.1603, II. 119
Gambow, Peter, Kt.1546, II. 58
Gammes, John, Kt.1603, II. 113
Gammon, Martin, Kt.1603, II. 113
Gamull, Francis, Kt.1644, II. 217, 218
Gangadi, Stamo, K.C.M.G.1839, I. 352

INDEX

GARDINER, GARDNER, GARDENER
Gardner, Alan H., lord Gardner, K.C.B.1815, I. 218
Gardner (Gardiner), Edmund, Kt. 1686, II. 262
Gardiner, Henry L., K.C.V.O.(1897), I. 432
Gardiner, John, K.C.B.1838, I. 234
Gardiner, Robert, Kt.1591, II. 88
Gardiner, Robert W., K.C.B.1815, I. 226; K.C.H.1820, I. 455; G.C.B. 1859, I. 193
Gardner (Gardener, Goodnes), Thomas, Kt.1603, II. 110
Gardner, Thomas, Kt.1641, II. 211
Gardner, Thomas, Kt.1644, II. 217
Gardiner, Thomas, Kt.1660, II. 230
Gardner, William, Kt.1603, II. 109
Gardner, William, Kt.1626, II. 191
Gardiner, William, K.B.1661, I. 164

Gargrave, Clopton, Kt.1582, II. 81
Gargrave, Cotton, Kt.1585, II. 83
Gargrave, Richard, Kt.1603, II. 101
Gargrave, Thomas, Kt.1549, II. 64
Garland, John, K.H.1833, I. 469
Garlington. See Girlington.
Garneys, Christopher, Kt.1513, II. 39
Garrard. See Gerrard
Garraunt, William, K.B.(1483), I. 139
Garret, Garrett. See Gerrard
Garrick, James F., K.C.M.G.1886, I. 369
Garrod, Alfred B., Kt.1887, II. 382
Garrow, William, Kt.1812, II. 312
Garroway, Henry, Kt.1640, II. 207
Garstin, William E., K.C.M.G.1897, I. 383; G.C.M.G.1902, I. 348
Garth, Richard, Kt.1875, II. 367
Garth, Samuel, Kt.1714, II. 279

GARTON, GERTON
Garton, Henry, Kt.1553, II. 66
Garton, Peter, Kt.1604, II. 130
Garton (Gerton), Thomas, Kt.1618, II. 168

Garvey, Christopher, Kt.1628, II. 194
Garvock, John, K.C.B.1864, I.249; G.C.B. 1875, I. 196
Garway (Garraway), William, Kt.1615, II. 156

GASCOIGNE, GASCOIGN, GASCON, GASCOYN, GASCOYNE
Gascoigne, —, Kt.1492, II. 28
Gascoigne, Crispe, Kt.1752, II. 288
Gascon (Gascoigne, Gaston), Henry, Kt.1553, II. 66
Gascoigne, John, Kt.1538, II. 52
Gascoyne, John or William, K.B.(1487), I. 142
Gascoyne, Nicholas, Kt.1603, II. 119
Gascoigne, William, Kt.1460, II. 12
Gascoigne, William, K.B.1478, I. 138
Gascoigne, William, Kt.1482, II. 17
Gascoign, William, Kt.1497, II. 31
Gascoigne, William, Kt.1513, II. 38
Gascoigne, William, Kt.1520, II. 43
Gascoigne, William, Kt.1599, II. 97
Gascoigne, William J., K.C.M.G.1901, I. 390
Gascoyne-Cecil, James B., marquess of Salisbury, K.G.1842, I. 57
Gascoyne-Cecil, Robert A. T., marquess of Salisbury, K.G.1878, I. 66; G.C.V.O.1902, I. 419
Gaselee, Alfred, K.C.B.1898, I. 269; G.C.I.E.1901, I. 403
Gazelee, Stephen, Kt.1825, II. 325
Gatacre, William F., K.C.B.1898, I. 270
Gatehouse, Thomas, Kt.1762, II. 291
Gates, Geoffrey, Kt.1513, II. 39
Gates, Henry, Kt.1547, II. 61
Gates, John, K.B.1547, II. 151
Gates, Thomas, Kt.1596, II. 93
Gathorne - Hardy Gathorne, viscount Cranbrook, G.C.S.I.1880, I. 311
Gatty. See Scott-Gatty
Gatty, Stephen H., Kt.1904, II. 420
Gauden, Dennis, Kt.1667, II. 242
Gaunt, Edwin, Kt.1887, II. 382
Gaunt, John of, K.G.1360, I. 3
Gavaston, Peter de, K.B.1306, I. 112
Gawdy, Anthony, Kt.1609, II. 148
Gawdy, Bassingbourne, Kt.1597, II. 94
Gawdy, Charles, Kt.1613, II. 154
Gawdy, Charles, Kt.1639, II. 206
Gawdy, Clipesby, Kt.1603, II. 122
Gawdy, Francis, Kt.1603, II. 113
Gawdy, Henry, K.B.1603, I. 155
Gawdy, Thomas, Kt.1578, II. 79

Gawdy, Thomas, Kt.1629, II. 197
Gawler, George, K.H.1837, I. 476
Gawsell (Gowshill), Edmund, Kt.1616, II. 158; and see Gousehill
Gawyn, John, Kt.1505, II. 34
Gaydon, Richard, Kt. Jacobite 1719, footnote, II. 266
GAYER, GAYRE, GAIR
　Gayer (Gair), John, Kt.1641, II. 211
　Gayer, John, Kt.1693, II. 268
　Gayre, Robert, K.B.1661, I. 166
Gear (Gere), Michael, Kt.1625, II. 190
Geary, Henry le Guay, K.C.B.1900, I.271
Gebhart, Paul, K.C.V.O.1898, I. 438
Geddes, John, K.H.1836, I. 473
Geddes, William D., Kt.1892, II. 389
Gee, Orlando, Kt.1682, II. 258
Gee, Thomas, Kt.1622, II. 178
Gee, William, Kt.1604, II. 132
Geikie, Archibald, Kt.1891, II. 388
Gelder, William A., Kt.1903, II. 414
Gell, James, Kt.1877, II. 369
Gell, William, Kt.1814, II. 313
Genoa, Tommaso, duke of, G.C.V.O.1903, I. 426
Genouilly, Charles R. de, K.C.B.1856, I. 242
Genville, Nicolas de, K.B.1306, I. 117
Geoffrey. See Jeffery
George I., K.G.1701, I. 40
George II., K.G.1706, I. 40
George III., K.G.1749, I. 44
George IV., K.G.1765, I. 46
George, Rupert, Kt.1803, II. 307
George, Thomas, Kt.1586, II. 85
George. See Gorge
GERRARD, GERARD, GARRETT, GARRET, JARRET, GARRARD
　Gerard (Garrett), Charles, Kt.1617, II. 164
　Garret (Gerard), Eaton, Kt.1642, II. 214
　Garret (Jarret), Edward), Kt.1642, II. 213
　Garret, lord Fitzgerald, Kt.1553, II. 66
　Gerard, Francis, Kt.1660, II. 228
　Garret, George, Kt.1641, II. 211
　Garrett, George, Kt.1820, II. 321

GERARD
　Gerard, Gilbert, Kt.1579, II. 79
　Gerard, Gilbert, lord Gerard, K.B.1610, I. 158
　Gerard, Gilbert, Kt.1661, II. 233
　Gerrard, Jacob, Kt.1641, II. 211
　Garrett (Garrard), John, Kt.1615, II. 155
　Gerard, Mark A., Kt.1809, II. 309
　Gerard, Montagu G., K.C.S.I.1897, I. 326; K.C.B.1902, I. 274
　Garrett, Robert, K.H.1836, I. 474; K.C.B.1857, I. 243
　Gerard, Samuel, Kt.1688, II. 264
　Gerrard, Thomas, Kt.1591, II. 89
　Gerrat (Gerard), Thomas, Kt.1544, II. 55
　Gerrard, Thomas, Kt.1553, II. 67
　Gerrard, Thomas, Kt.1603, II. 101
　Gerrard (Garret), Thomas, Kt.1628, II. 194
　Gerrard, Thomas, Kt.1615, II. 155
　Garret [Gerard], William, Kt.1555, II. 69
　Gerard (Gerald), William, Kt.1579, II. 80
　Gerrard (Garrard, Garrett), William, Kt.1603, II. 116
Gerbier, Balthazar, Kt.1638, II. 206
Gerdeston, William de, Kt.1347, II. 8

GERMANY
　Charles V., emperor of, K.G.1508, I. 19
　Ferdinand, emperor of, K.G.1522, I. 21
　Frederick III., emperor of, K.G.1457, I. 13
　Frederick III. of, K.G.1858, I. 60; G.C.B.1883, I. 198
　Maximilian I., emperor of, K.G.1489, I. 18
　Maximilian II., emperor of, K.G.1567, I. 26
　Rodolphus II. of, K.G.1578, I. 27
　Sigismund, emperor of, K.G.1415, I. 9
　William I. of, K.G.1861, I. 61; G.C.B. 1857, I. 192

INDEX

GERMANY
William II. of, K.G.1877, I. 65; G.C.V.O.1899, I. 423; Victorian Chain 1902, I. 415
Frederick W. V. A. E., crown prince of, K.G.1901, I. 71
Gernon, James, Kt.1548, II. 63
Gernon, Patrick, Kt. before 1541, II. 53
Gerton. See Garton
Gery, Thomas, Kt.1666, II. 242
Gery, Thomas, Kt.1712, II. 277
Gex, John P. de, Kt.1882, II. 374
Ghaly, Boutros, K.C.M.G.1899, I. 386
Gholam, Hussan Khan, K.C.S.I.1879, I. 322
Gholam, Mahomed, K.C.S.I.1870, I. 319
Giallina, Spiridion, C.M.G.(1822), I. 28
Gianotti, Cesare, G.C.V.O.1903, I. 426
Gib, William A., K.C.B.1897, I. 268
Gibb, George S., Kt.1904, II. 417
Gibb (Gill), Henry, Kt.1624, II. 187
Gibbon. See Guibon
Gibbons, John, K.B.1761, I. 170
GIBBS, GIPPS, GIBBES
  Gibbs, Ben T. B., Kt.1878, II. 370
  Gibbs, Edward, K.C.B.1838, I. 235
  Gipps, George, Kt.1835, II. 336
  Gibbes (Gibbs), George S., Kt.1820, II. 321
  Gibbes, Henry, Kt.1617, II. 166
  Gibbs, Ralph, Kt.1603, II. 122
  Gipps, Reginald, K.C.B.1888, I. 262; G.C.B.1902, I. 203
  Gipps, Richard, Kt.1676, II. 251
  Gipps (Gibbs), Richard, Kt.1682, II. 258
  Gibbs, Samuel, K.C.B.1815, I. 221
  Gibbs, Vicary, Kt.1805, II. 308
Gibethorpe (Gilethorpe), William, K.B. (1400), I. 129
Gibney, John, Kt.1832, II. 332
GIBSON, GYBSON
  Gibson, Isaac, Kt.1674, II. 249
  Gibson, James Brown, K.C.B.1865, I. 250
  Gybson, John, Kt.1603, II. 114
  Gibson, John, Kt.1607, II. 142
  Gibson, John, Kt.1625, II. 190
  Gibson, John, Kt.1636, II. 204
  Gibson, John, Kt.1705, II. 275

Gidhaur, Prasad Singh, of, K.C.I.E. 1895, II. 408
Gidhaur, Jymungul Singh, of, K.C.S.I. 1866, I. 316
Giffen, Robert, K.C.B.1895, I. 294
GIFFARD, GIFFORD, GEFFORD, GYFFORDE, JEFFORD
  Gifford (Gefford), George, Kt.1553, II. 67
  Gifford, George, Kt.1596, II. 92
  Giffard, George, K.C.B.1875, II. 255
  Giffard, George M., Kt.1868, II. 359
  Giffard, Hardinge, Kt.1819, II. 321
  Giffard, Hardinge S., earl of Halsbury, Kt.1875, II. 367
  Giffard, Henry A., Kt1903, II. 416
  Giffard, John, K.B.1303, I. 110
  Gifford, John, K.B.(1483), I. 140
  Gyfford, John, K.B.1501, I. 145
  Gyfforde, John, Kt.1513, II. 39
  Gyfford, John, Kt.1636, II. 204
  Gifford, Maurice R., KC.M.G.1896, I. 381
  Giffard, Nicholas, K.B.1333, I. 125
  Gifford, Robert, Kt.1817, II. 319
  Gyfforde, Roger, Kt.1547, II. 59
  Gyfforde (Gilford), Thomas, Kt.1547, II. 59
  Gifford (Jefford), Thomas, Kt.1688, II. 264
  Gyfforde, William, Kt.1504, II. 34
  Gyfford, William, Kt.1522, II. 43
  Gifford, William, Kt.1705, II. 275
Gifford. See Giffard
Gilbert, George, Kt.1662, II. 237
Gilbert, Humphrey, Kt.1570, II. 74
Gilbert, Jeffery, Kt.1725, II. 283
Gilbert, John, Kt.1571, II. 75
Gilbert, John, Kt.1596, II. 93
Gilbert, John, Kt.1603, II. 115, 121
Gilbert, John, Kt.1872, II. 364
Gilbert, John T., Kt.1897, II. 398
Gilbert, Joseph H., Kt.1893, II. 392
Gilbert, Otes, K.B.(1483), I. 138
Gilbert, Walter R., K.C.B.1846, II. 238; G.C.B.1849, I. 190
Gilbert, William, Kt.1629, II. 196
Gilborn, Edward, Kt.1617, II. 164
Gilborne, Nicholas, Kt.1603, II. 115

94 INDEX

Gilby (Selbee), George, Kt.1603, II. 125
Gilby, Theophilus, Kt.1645, II. 220
Gildea, James, Kt.1902, II. 414
Gildenshorne, Conrad, Kt.1660, II. 230
Giles, Edward, Kt.1603, II. 118
Gill, David, K.C.B.1900, I. 298
Gill, George, Kt.1603, II. 122
Gill, John, Kt.1613, II. 154
Gill (Gyll), Robert, Kt.1831, II. 330
Gill, Henry. See Gibb
Gillespie, John, Kt.1883, II. 375
Gillespie, Robert, Kt.1891, II. 389
Gillespie, Robert R., K.C.B.1815, I. 220

GILLOTT, GYLLOT
  Gyllot, John, K.B.1501, I. 147
  Gillott, Samuel, Kt.1901, II. 409

Gillman, John St. L., Kt.1793, II. 302
Gilman, Charles R., Kt.1897, II. 401
Gilmour, Dugald L., K.C.B.1831, I. 231
Gilpin, Joseph, Kt.1815, II. 315
Gilzean-Reid, Hugh, Kt.1893, II. 392
Gipps. See Gibbs.
Girlington (Garlington), John, Kt.1642, II. 213
Girouard, Edward P. C., K.C.M.G.1901, I. 389
Gise, John de, K.B.1306, I. 116
Glanvile, Francis, Kt.1621, II. 176
Glanvile, John, Kt.1641, II. 210
Glanville, John, Kt.1755, II. 288
Glasgow, earl of. See Boyle
Glass, Richard A., Kt.1866, II. 358
Glasscock, William, Kt.1661, II. 234
Glasscock, William, Kt.1682, II. 258
Glastinbur, Henr, Kt.1347, II. 8
Gledstanes, Albert, Kt.1814, II. 314
Gleen (Glean), Peter, Kt.1624, II. 184
Glegg, William, Kt.1690, II. 266

GLEMHAM, GLENHAM, GLEYMHAM
  Glemham, Charles, Kt.1625, II. 188
  Glemham, Henry, Kt.1591, II. 88
  Gleymham, John, Kt.1513, II. 40
  Glenham (Glemham), Sackvil, Kt.1644, II. 218
  Glenham (Glemham), Thomas, Kt.1617, II. 166

Glenlyon, lord. See Murray
Glode, Richard, Kt.1795, II. 303

GLOUCESTER
  Henry, duke of, K.G.1653, 1. 34
  Humphrey, duke of, K.G.1399, I. 7; K.B.1399, I. 127
  Richard of, Kt.1483, II. 21
  Thomas, duke of, K.G.1380, I. 5
  William, duke of, K.G.1696, I. 39
  William F., duke of, K.G.1794. I. 49; G.C.B.1815, I. 182; G.C.H.1815, I. 447
  William, H., duke of, K.G.1762, I. 46
  Earl of. See Despenser

Glover, John, Kt.1900, II. 407
Glover, John H., G.C.M.G.1874, I. 337
Glover, Thomas, Kt.1605, II. 137, 140
Glover, William, Kt.1603, II. 128
Glyn, Julius R., K.C.B.1886, I. 260
Glynn, John, Kt.1660, II. 232
Glynn, Richard, Kt.1752, II. 288
Glynn, Richard C., Kt.1790, II. 301
Glynn, William, Kt.1606, II. 140
Goch (Gooche), John de, Kt.1619, II. 172
Goddard, Richard, Kt.1603, II. 128

GODFREY, GODFRAY
  Godfrey, Edmond B., Kt.1666, II. 242
  Godfray, James, Kt.1891, II. 387
  Godfrey, Peter, Kt.1641, II. 210
  Godfrey, Thomas, Kt.1641, II. 210

Godley, Arthur, K.C.B.1893, I. 293
Godmanston, Robert de, K.B.1306, I. 121
Godolphin, Francis, Kt.1580, II. 80
Godolphin, Francis, Kt.1621, II. 178
Godolphin, Francis, K.B.1661, I. 165
Godolphin, John, Kt.1579, II. 80
Godolphin, Sidney, earl of Godolphin, K.G.1704, I. 40
Godolphin, William, Kt.1599, II. 96
Godolphin, William, Kt.1644, II. 217
Godolphin, William, Kt.1668, II. 243
Godsalve, John, Kt.1547, II. 59
Godschall, Robert, Kt.1735, II. 284
Godshall, John, Kt.1660, II. 229
Godsell, William, Kt.1903, II. 415
Godson, Augustus F., Kt.1898, II. 403

GODWIN, GOODWIN, GOODWYNE
  Goodwin, Edwin, Kt.1601, II. 99
  Godwin, Henry, K.C.B.1853, I. 240
  Goodewyne, John, Kt.1570, II. 74
  Goodwin, Robert, Kt.1658, II. 224

INDEX 95

Gofton, Francis, Kt.1619, II. 171
Gold. See Gould
Goldfinch, Henry, K.C.B.1852, I. 239
Goldie, brig. gen. [Andrew], K.C.B.1855, footnote, I. 241
Goldie, George L., K.C.B.1861, I. 246
Goldie-Taubman, John S., Kt.1896, II. 397
Goldington, William de, K.B.1306, I. 119
Goldney, John T., Kt.1893, II. 391
Goldsborough, John, Kt.1692, II. 267
Goldsmid, Frederick J., K.C.S.I.1871, I. 319
Goldsmith, Francis, Kt.1603, II. 126
Goldsmith, William B., Kt.1897, II. 401
Goldsworthy, Roger T., K.C.M.G.1889, I. 374
Goldynge, Thomas, Kt.1549, II. 64
Gollan, Alexander, K.C.M.G.1898, I. 385
Goltz, baron von der, G.C.M.G.1891, I. 342
Goluchowski, Agenor M. A., count von, G.C.V.O.1903, I. 428
Gomarcyn, Gaucher de, K.B.1253, I. 110
Gomm (Gomme), William M., K.C.B.1815, I. 225; G.C.B.1859, I. 193
Gondal, Bhagwut Singh, of, K.C.I.E.1887, I. 399; G.C.I.E.1897, I. 402
Gonning. See Gunning
Gonson, John, Kt.1722, II. 282
Gontherant (Guntherope, Gounthrout), Henry, Kt.1607-8, II. 144
Goodenough, William H., K.C.B.1897, I. 268
Goodman, George, Kt.1852, II. 349
Goodman, Stephen A., K.H.1836, I. 473
Goodman, William M., Kt.1902, II. 413
Goodnes, Thomas, Kt.1603, II. 110
GOODRICK, GOODERICK
  Goodrick, Francis, Kt.1661-2, II. 236
  Gooderick (Goodrike), Henry, Kt.1603, II. 106
Goodwin. See Godwin
GOODYEAR, GOODEARE, GOODYERE
  Goodyear, Henry, Kt.1586, II. 85
  Goodeare, Henry, Kt.1599, II. 97
  Goodyeere, Henry Kt.1608, II. 145
  Goodyere, Robert, Kt.1762, II. 291
  Goodyere, William, Kt.1603, II. 120

Gookin, Vincent, Kt.1631, II. 199
Goold. See Gould
Goold-Adams, Hamilton J., K.C.M.G. 1902, I. 391
Gordon, Alexander, duke of Gordon, K.T. 1775, I. 80
Gordon, Alexander, Kt.1800, II. 305
Gordon, Alexander, K.C.B.1815, I. 225
Gordon, Arthur H., K.C.M.G.1871, I. 355
Gordon, Benjamin L., K.C.B.1899, I. 271
Gordon, Charles, Kt.1812, II. 311
Gordon, Charles, Kt.1837, II. 338
Gordon, Charles A., K.C.B.1897, II. 267
Gordon, Cosmo G., duke of Gordon, K.T. 1748, I. 78
Gordon, George, marquess of Huntley, K.B.1610, I. 157
Gordon, George, duke of Gordon, K.T. 1687, I. 75
Gordon, George, duke of Gordon, G.C.B. 1820, I. 185
Gordon, George, marquess of Huntley, K.T.1827, I. 82
Gordon, George, earl of Aberdeen, K.T. 1808, I. 80; K.G.1855, I. 59
Gordon, Henry W., K.C.B.1877, I. 286
Gordon, James A., K.C.B.1815, I. 222; G.C.B.1855 I. 191
Gordon, James D., K.C.S.I.1881, I. 322
Gordon, James W., K.C.B.1815, I. 221; G.C.H.1825, I. 450; G.C.B.1831, I. 186
Gordon, John, earl of Sutherland, K.T. 1716, I. 77
Gordon, John, Kt.1855, II. 351
Gordon, lord John F., G.C.H.1836, I. 453
Gordon, John J. H., K.C.B.1898, I. 270
Gordon, John W., Kt.1850, II. 348
Gordon, John W., K.C.B.1865, I. 250
Gordon, Robert, G.C.H.1829, I. 450; G.C.B.1829, I. 206
Gordon, Samuel, Kt.1761, II. 290
Gordon, Thomas E., K.C.I.E.1893, I. 407; K.C.B.1900, I. 271
Gordon, William, K.B.1775, I. 172
Gordon-Lennox, Charles, duke of Richmond, K.G.1829, I. 53
Gordon-Lennox, Charles H., duke of Richmond, K.G.1867, I. 63

Gordon-Lennox, Charles H., duke of Richmond and Gordon, G.C.V.O. 1904, I. 421
Gore. See Gower
Gore, Arthur S., earl of Arran, K.P.1783, I. 97
Gore, Arthur S. W. C. F., earl of Arran, K.P.1898, I. 106
Gore, Charles S., K.H.1836, I. 473; K.C.B.1860, I. 246; G.C.B.1867, I. 195
Gore, Francis, Kt.1661, II. 234
Gore, Francis C., Kt.1903, II. 414
Gore, George, KH.1836, I. 473
Gore, Humphry, Kt.1660, II. 230
Gore, John, Kt.1626, II. 190
Gore, John, Kt.1641, II. 208, 210
Gore, John, Kt.1660, II. 231
Gore, John, Kt.1805, II. 308; K.C.B. 1815, I. 221; G.C.H.1835, I. 453
Gore, Philip Y., earl of Arran, K.P.1841, I. 101
Gore, Robert, Kt.1679, II. 253
Gore, Thomas, Kt.1663, II. 237
Gore, Walter, Kt.1604, II. 134
Gore, William, Kt.1692, II. 267
GORGES, GORGE
  Gorges, Arthur, Kt.1597, II. 94
  Gorges, Arthur, Kt.1621, II. 178
  Gorges, Edmund, K.B.(1489), I. 143
  Gorge, Edward, Kt.1513, II. 37
  Gorge, Edward, Kt.1515, II. 42
  Gorges, Edward, Kt.1603, II. 110, 118
  Gorge, Ferdinand, Kt.1591, II. 89
  Georges, George (?William), Kt.1579, II. 80
  Gorges (George), Robert, Kt.1616, II. 158, 172
  Gorges (George), Theobald, Kt.1616, II. 158
  Gorges, Thomas, Kt.1586, II. 84
  Gorges, Thomas, Kt.1603, II. 110
Goring, Edward, Kt.1617, II. 163
Goring, George, Kt.1608, II. 145
Goring, Henry, Kt.1591, II. 88
Goring, Henry, Kt.1603, II. 106
Goring, Robert, Kt.1678, II. 253
Gorjao, R., K.C.B.1902, I. 275
Gormanston, viscount. See Preston

Gorrequer, Gideon, K.H.1818, I. 463
Gorrie, John, Kt.1882, II. 373
Gorst, John E., Kt.1885, II. 377
Gorst, John L. E., K.C.B.1902, I. 299
Goschen, William E., K.C.M.G.1901, I. 390; K.C.V.O.(1904), I. 437
Gosford, earl of. See Acheson
GOSLING, GOSLYN
  Gosling, Audley C., K.C.M.G.1901, I. 391
  Gosling, Francis, Kt.1760, II. 289
  Goslyn (Gosling), William), Kt.1684, II. 260
Goss, John, Kt.1872, II. 364
Gosselin, Martin, Le M. H., K.C.M.G. 1898, I. 385; K.C.V.O.(1903), I. 435; G.C.V.O.1904, I. 421
Gosset, Ralph A., K.C.B.1885, I. 289
Gosset, William, K.C.H.1831, I. 456; Kt. 1831, II. 330
Gostery (Gostry, Gostro), Henry, Kt. 1609, II. 148
GOSTWICK, GOSTWYKE
  Gostwick, Edward, Kt.1607, II. 142
  Gostwyke, John, Kt.1538, II. 52
  Gostwick, William, Kt.1668, II. 243
Gott, Henry T., Kt.1784, II. 298
Gough, Charles J. S., K.C.B.1881, I 257; G.C.B.1895, I. 201
Gough, Edward, Kt.1602, II. 100
Gough, Henry, Kt.1678, II. 252
Gough, Hugh, Kt.1815, II. 316
Gough, Hugh, viscount Gough, K.C.B. 1831, I. 231; G.C.B.1841, I. 189; K.P.1857, I. 102; K.S.I.1861, I. 306; G.C.S.I.1866, I. 308
Gough, Hugh, viscount Gough, K.C.V.O. (1904), I. 436
Gough, Hugh H., K.C.B.1881 I. 257; G.C.B.1896, I. 201
Gough (Goghe), James, Kt.1603, II. 129
Gough, John B., K.C.B.1867, I. 250; G.C.B.1875, I. 196
Gough, Richard, Kt.1715, II. 280
Gough, Thomas, Kt.1627, II. 193
GOULD, GOOLD, GOLD
  Gould, Charles, Kt.1779, II. 296
  Gould, Davidge, K.C.B.1815, I. 228; G.C.B.1833, I. 186

INDEX

GOULD
Gould, Edward, Kt.1709, II. 276
Gould (Goold, Gold), Henry, Kt.1694, II. 268
Gould, Henry, Kt.1761, II. 291
Gould, Nathaniel, Kt.1721, II. 282
Gold, Thomas, Kt.1675, II. 250
Gourdon, George, Kt.1699, II. 271
Gourdon, William, Kt.1624, II. 187, 188
Gourley, Edward T., Kt.1895, II. 395
Gourley, Thomas, Kt.1651, II. 222
Gourney, Thomas, Kt.1613, II. 153
Gousehill, Thomas de, K.B.1326, I. 123; and see Gawsell
Gowans, James, Kt.1886, II. 380

GOWER, GOWRE, GAWRE, and see Gore
Gower, earl. See Leveson-Gower
Gower, Edward, Kt.1527, II. 46
Gower, Erasmus, Kt.1792, II. 301
Gowre (Gawre), Fitzwilliam, Kt.1347, II. 7
Gower, John, Kt.1497, II. 32
Gower, Samuel, Kt.1744, II. 287
Gowre, Thomas, Kt.1482, II. 18
Gower, Thomas, Kt.1630, II. 198
Gowers, William R., Kt.1897, II. 400
Gowshill. See Gawsell

GRAS, GRACE
Gras, John de, K.B.1326, I. 123
Grace, John, Kt.1541, II. 52
Grace, Sheffield, K.H.1837, I. 479
Gracedieu, Bartholomew, Kt.1697, II. 270
Grafton, duke of. See Fitz-Roy

GRAHAM, GREAME, GRYMES, GREIME
Graham, Douglas B. M. R., duke of Montrose, K.T.1879, I. 87
Graham, Fortescue, K.C.B.1865, I. 249
Greame (Grymes), George, Kt.1603, II. 127
Graham, Gerald, K.C.B.1882, I. 258; G.C.M.G.1885, I. 340; G.C.B.1896, I. 201
Graham, Henry J. L., K.C.B.1902, I. 300
Graham, James, marquess of Montrose, K.G.1650, I. 34
Graham, James, duke of Montrose, K.T.1793, I. 80; K.G.1812, I. 50

GRAHAM
Graham, James, duke of Montrose, K.T.1845, I. 83
Graham, James, Kt.1901, II. 409
Graham, James R. G., G.C.B.1854, I. 208
Graham (Greime, Greame), Richard, Kt.1600, II. 98
Graham (Grimes), Richard, Kt.1629, II. 195
Graham, Ro, Kt.1633, II. lxiii.
Graham, Robert, Kt.1800, II. 305
Graham, Samuel J., K.C.B.1902, I. 274
Graham, Thomas, lord Lynedoch, K.B. 1812, I. 177; G.C.B.1815, I. 181; G.C.M.G.1837, I. 333
Graham, William, K.C.B.1887, I. 261; G.C.B.1902, I. 203
Grailly, John de, vicomte de Benanges, K.G.1348, I. 1
Grainger-Stewart, Thomas, Kt.1894, II. 394
Grampe (Grampy), William, Kt.(1468), II. lxi.
Granado, Jaques, Kt.1547, II. 62
Granard, earl of. See Forbes
Grandison, viscount. See Villiers
Granger, John, Kt.1603, II. 118
Granson, Thomas de, K.G.1369, I. 4
Grant, Alexander, K.H.1837, I. 477
Grant, Charles, K.C.S.I.1885, I. 323
Grant, Colquhoun, K.C.B.1815, I. 221; K.C.H.1816, I. 454; G.C.H.1831, I. 451
Grant, Francis, Kt.1866, II. 358
Grant, James A., K.C.M.G.1887, I. 371
Grant, James H., K.C.B.1858, I. 244; G.C.B.1860, I. 193
Grant, James R., K.H.1816, I. 463; Kt. 1819, II. 320
Grant, John P., Kt.1827, II. 326
Grant, John P., K.C.B.1862, I. 282; G.C.M.G.1874, I. 337
Grant, John T., K.C.B.1881, I. 257
Grant, Lewis, K.C.H.1831, I. 457; Kt. 1831, II. 331
Grant, Maxwell, K.C.B.1815, I. 226

Grant, Patrick, K.C.B.1857, I. 243;
G.C.B.1861, I. 193; G.C.M.G.1868, I.
336
Grant, Richard, Kt.1820, II. 321
Grant, Robert, G.C.H.1834, I. 452; Kt.
1834, II. 335
Grant, Robert, K.C.B.1896, I. 267;
G.C.B.1902, I. 203
Grant, Thomas T., K.C.B.1858, I. 280
Grant, William, Kt.1799, II. 304
Grant, William K., K.C.H.1821, I. 455;
K.C.B.1822, I. 229; G.C.H.1835, I.
453
Grant-Duff, Mountstuart E., G.C.S.I.1886,
I. 312
Grantham, lord. See Robinson
Grantham, Thomas, Kt.1603, II. 103
Grantham, William, Kt.1886, II. 378
GRANVILLE, GRANVILE, GRENFIELD
Granville. See Grenvile
Granville, Beville, Kt.1686, II. 262
Granville, earl. See Carteret; see
Leveson-Gower
Granvile (Grenfield), John, Kt.1643, II.
216
Grattan, Edmund A., Kt.1889, II. 386
Grattan, Richard, Kt.1736, II. 285
Gratwicke (Greatwick), William, Kt.1604,
II. 132
Gravener, Thomas, Kt.1547, II. 60
Graves (Greeves), Richard, Kt.1604, II.
133
Graves, Thomas, K.B.1801, I. 175
Graves, Thomas N., lord Graves, Kt.
1821, II. 322
Gravière, Pierre E. J. J. de la, K.C.B.
1857, I. 244
Gravile, —, K.B.(1483), I. 139
Graville, comte de, K.G.1658, I. 35
Gray. See Grey
Graydon, George, K.H.1832, I. 467
Greame. See Graham
Greathed, Edward H., K.C.B.1865, I. 250
Greaves, George R., K.C.M.G.1881, I. 363;
K.C.B.1885, I. 259; G.C.B.1896, I.
201
Greaves, William H., Kt.1904, II. 418

GREECE
George I. of, K.G.1876, I. 65; G.C.V.O.
1901, I. 424
Prince Andrew of, G.C.V.O.1902, I. 425
Constantine, crown prince of, duke of
Sparta, G.C.B.1895, I. 214; Victorian
Chain 1902, I. 416
Prince George of, G.C.B.1900, I. 215
Prince Nicolas of, G.C.V.O. 1901, I.
424
GREEN, GREENE, GRENE
Green, —, Kt.1617, II. 163
Grene, —, K.B.(1483), I. 140
Green, —, Kt.1617, II. 163
Green, Andrew P., K.H.1818, I. 463;
K.C.H.1832, I. 459; Kt.1832, II. 333
Greene, Anthony, Kt.1644, II. 218
Greene, Benjamin, Kt.1707, II. 275
Green, Charles, Kt.1803, II. 307
Greene, Edward, Kt.1553, II. 67
Green, Edward, K.C.B.1867, I. 251
Green, George W. G., K.C.B.1877, I.
256
Greene, Jonas, Kt.1821, II. 322
Greene, John, Kt.1497, II. 30
Green, John, Kt.1874, II. 366
Greene, John B., Kt.1885, II. 377
Green, Michael, Kt.1603, II. 113
Green, Richard, Kt.1617, II. 163
Greene, Robert, Kt.1471, II. 14
Green (Grey), Thomas, Kt.1487, II. 24
Greene, Thomas, Kt.1497, II. 29
Green, Thomas, Kt.1578, II. 79
Green, Thomas, Kt.1622, II. 180
Greene, William, Kt.1603, II. 113
Green, William, K.H.1837, I. 477
Green, William, K.C.B.1894, I. 266
Greene, William C., K.C.B.1900, I. 298
Green, William H. R., K.C.S.I.1866, I.
317
Green, William K., K.C.M.G.1887, I.
372
Greenacre, Benjamin W., Kt.1901, II. 409
Greenfield, Grenfield. See Granville,
Grevile, Grenvile
Greenock, lord. See Cathcart
Greenville. See Grenvile
Greenway, Oliver, Kt.1727, II. 284
Greenway, Richard, Kt.1604, II. 131

INDEX

Greenwell, Leonard, K.C.H.1832, I. 458; Kt.1832, II. 332; K.C.B.1838, I. 235
Greeve. See Greve
Gregory, Augustus C., K.C.M.G.1903, I. 394
Gregory, Charles H., K.C.M.G.1883, I. 365
Gregory, William, Kt.1679, II. 253
Gregory, William H., K.C.M.G.1875, I. 385
Greig, Hector, K.C.M.G.1839, I. 352
Greknecke, Adryan van, Kt.1487, II. 27
Grenfell, Francis W., lord Grenfell, K.C.B.1886, I. 260; G.C.M.G.1892, I. 343; G.C.B.1898, I. 202
Grenier, John C. S., Kt.1892, II. 389
Grenn, Paul de, Kt.1621, II. 176
GRENVILE, GREENFEILD, GREENVILLE, and see Granville
Grenvile (Greenefeilde), Barnard, Kt. 1608, II. 146
Grenvile, Bevil, Kt.1639, II. 206
Greenfield, alias Grenvile, Christopher, Kt.1693, II. 268
Grenvile (Greinfeld), George, Kt.1603, II. 125
Greenfeilde, Richard, Kt.1529, II. 47
Greneville, Richard, Kt.1577, II. 78
Greenville (Grenvyle), Richard, Kt. 1627, II. 192
Grenefield or Grenville, Thomas, K.B. 1501, I. 145
Grenville-Temple, Richard, earl Temple, K.G.1760, I. 45
Gresham, Edward, Kt.1617, II. 167
Gresham, John, Kt.1538, II. 51
Gresham, John, Kt.1547, II. 61
Gresham, John, Kt.1617, II. 160
Gresham, Richard, Kt.1538, II. 51
Gresham, Thomas, Kt.1559, II. 70
Gresham, Thomas, Kt.1603, II. 123
Gresham, William (Richard), Kt.1603, II. 120

GRESLEY, GRELLEY, GREISLEY, GRISLE, GRYSLEY, GREDISLEY, GRYSELEY
Gresley, George, Kt.1533, II. 49
Greisley, John, K.B.(1400), I. 129
Grisle, Peter de, K.B.1306, I. 117

GRESLEY
Gresley (Gredisley), Robert (George), Kt.1612, II. 152
Grelley, Thomas de, K.B.1306, I. 111
Gresley, Thomas, Kt.1603, II. 102
Grysley (Grisle), William, Kt.1513, II. 42
Gryseley (Gresley), William, Kt.1553, II. 67
Greve (Greeve, Green), Thomas, Kt.1622, II. 180

GREVILLE, GREVILE, GREVILL
Greville, Charles J., K.C.B.1815, I. 223
Greville, Edward, Kt.1513, II. 41
Grevile, Edward, Kt.1553, II. 68
Grevill, Edward, Kt.1603, II. 104
Greville, Francis, earl of Warwick, K.T.1753, I. 78
Grevill, Fowke, Kt.1525, II. 46
Grevell, Foulke, Kt.1544, II. 54
Grevill, Foulke, Kt.1565, II. 72
Greville, Fulke, lord Brooke, K.B.1603, I. 154
Grevile, Fulke, Kt.1615, I. 155
Greville, Henry R., earl Brooke, K.T. 1827, I. 82
Grevill, John, Kt.1547, II. 60
Grevill, Lodovick, Kt.1597, II. 94

GREY, GRAY, GRAYES, and see Guy
Grey, Albert H. G., earl Grey, G.C.M.G. 1904, I. 349
Grey, Ambrose, Kt.1605, II. 139
Grey, Andrew, Kt.1616, II. 159
Grey, Arthur, lord Grey of Wilton, Kt.1560, II. 70; K.G.1572, I. 27
Gray (Grey), Arthur, Kt.1617, II. 162
Gray, Bastard, Kt.1347, II. 6
Grey, Charles, earl Grey, K.B.1783, I. 173
Grey, Charles, earl Grey, K.G.1831, I. 54
Grey, Charles E., Kt.1820, II. 321; G.C.H.1837, I. 453
Grey of Wrest, earl de. See Weddell; see Robinson
Gray, Edmund (Edward), Kt.1617, II. 163
Grey, Edward, Kt.1513, II. 40
Grey, Edward, Kt.1523, II. 44

INDEX

Grey

Grey, Edward, lord Powis, Kt.1523, II. 45
Grey, lord Edward, Kt.1544, II. 56
Grey, Edward, Kt.1557, II. 70
Grey, Frederick W., K.C.B.1857, I. 243; G.C.B.1865, I. 194
Grey, George, K.B.(1465), I. 134
Grey, George, earl of Kent, K.B.(1483), I. 140, 141
Grey, George, K.C.B.1820, I. 229
Grey, George, K.C.B.1848, I. 277
Grey, George, G.C.B.1849, I. 208
Grey, Henry, earl of Tankerville, K.B. —(1426), I. 131
Grey, Henry, Kt.1471, II. 15
Grey, Henry, marquess of Dorset, K.B. 1533, I. 149
Grey, Henry, duke of Suffolk, K.G. 1547, I. 24
Gray, Henry, Kt.1570, II. 74
Grey, Henry, Kt.1587, II. 86
Grey, Henry, Kt.1603, II. 101
Grey, Henry, duke of Kent, K.G.1712, I. 40
Grey, Henry G., G.C.H.1831, I. 450; G.C.B.1831, I. 186
Grey, Henry G., earl Grey, K.G.1863, I. 62; G.C.M.G.1869, I. 336
Gray, James, K.B.1761, I. 170
Gray, Jeoffrey de, Kt.1347, II. 8
Grey, John, lord Grey de Rotherfield, K.G.1348, I. 1
Grey, John, earl of Tankerville, K.G. 1419, I. 10
Gray, John, Kt.1461, II. 13
Grey, John, lord Powis, K.B.1478, I. 137
Grey, John [*sic* for George], earl of Kent, K.B.(1483), I. 141
Grey, John, of Wilton, Kt.1482, II. 18
Grey, John, viscount Lisle, Kt.1504, II. 34; K.B.1504, I. 147
Grey, lord John, Kt.1544, II. 56
Gray, John, Kt.1596, II. 93
Grey (Grayes), John, Kt.1606, II. 140
Grey, John, K.C.B.1844, I. 238
Gray, John, Kt.1863, II. 356
Gray, Joseph, Kt.1785, II. 298

Grey

Grey, Rauf, K.B.(1426), I. 131
Grey, Rauf, Kt.1504, II. 34; K.B.1504, I. 147
Grey, Rafe, Kt.1603, II. 100
Grey, Richard, K.B.1305, I. 111
Grey, Richard, lord Grey de Codnor, K.G.1403, I. 8
Grey (Gray), Richard de, K.B.(1426), I. 131
Grey, Richard, K.B.(1475) I,. 137
Grey, Richard, earl of Kent, K.B. (1489), I. 143; K.G.1505, I. 19
Grey, lord Richard, Kt.1513, II. 38
Grey, Richard, Kt.1709, II. 276
Grey, Robert, lord Grey, K.B.1377, I. 126
Grey, Robert de, Kt.1641, II. 209
Grey, Roger, Kt.1513, II. 38
Grey (Gray), Roger, Kt.1617 ,II. 163
Gray, Samuel B., Kt.1901, II. 409
Grey, Thomas de, K.B.1306, I. 118
Grey, Thomas, Kt.1471, II. 14, 15
Grey, Thomas, marquess of Dorset, K.B.(1475), I. 136; K.G.1476, I. 16
Grey, Thomas, of Warke ,Kt.1482, II. 18
Grey, Thomas, Kt.1482, II. 20
Grey, Thomas, of Horton, Kt.1482, II. 21
Grey, Thomas, marquess of Dorset, K.B.(1494), I. 144; K.G.1501, I. 19
Grey, Thomas, of Horton, Kt.1545, II. 57
Grey, lord Thomas, Kt.1547, II. 59
Grey, Thomas, lord Grey of Wilton, Kt.1599, II. 96
Grey, Thomas, Kt.1819, II. 321
Grey, Thomas P. de, earl de Grey, Grand Master K.P.1841, I. 94
Gray, Walter, Kt.1902, II. 413
Grey, William, lord Grey of Wilton, Kt.1547, II. 61; K.G.1557, I. 25
Grey (Gray), William de, Kt.1603, II. 122
Grey, William de, Kt.1771, II. 293
Grey, William, K.C.S.I.1870, I. 319
Gray, William, Kt.1890, II. 387

INDEX 101

Greystoke, —, Kt.1482, II. 19
Greystoke, Herbert, Kt.1482, II. 17
Grey-Wilson, William, K.C.M.G.1904, I. 395
Griffin, Edward, K.B.1603, I. 155
Griffin, Edward, Kt.1608, II. 146
Griffin, Edward, Kt.1625, II. 188
Griffin, John G., lord Howard de Walden, K.B.1761, I. 170
Griffin, Lepel H., K.C.S.I.1881, I. 322
Griffin, Nicholas, K.B.1501, I. 146
Griffin, Rice, Kt.1605, II. 137
Griffin, Thomas, Kt.1603, II. 105
GRIFFITH, GRYFFITH, GRYFFYTHE
Griffith, George, Kt.1532, II. 48
Griffith, Henry, Kt.1603, II. 101
Griffith, John, Kt.1665, II. 240
Griffith, Maurice, Kt.1619, II. 174
Griffith, Morris, Kt.1603, II. 121
Gryffythe, Res, Kt.1547, II. 60
Griffith, Samuel W., K.C.M.G.1886, I. 370; G.C.M.G.1895, I. 344
Griffith, Thomas, Kt.1682, II. 257
Gryffith, Walter, K.B.(1494), I. 144
Gryffith, Walter, Kt.1497, II. 31
Griffith, William, K.B.(1489), I. 143
Gryffyth, William, Kt.1513, II. 39
Griffith, William B., K.C.M.G.1887, I. 371
Griffith, William B., Kt.1898, II. 402
Grills, John, Kt.1644, II. 218
Grimani, —, Kt.1713, II. 278
GRIMES, GRYMES, CRIMES, and see Graham
Grimes (Crimes), George, Kt.1628, II. 195
Grymes, Richard, Kt.1604, II. 133
Grimes, Richard, Kt.1629, II. 195
Grymes (Crimes, Gorges), Thomas, Kt. 1603, II. 110
GRIMSTON, GRYMSTONE
Grimston, Henry, Kt.1619, II. 174
Grymston, Harbottle, Kt.1604, II. 130
Grimston, Marmaduke, Kt.1603, II. 101
Grimstone, Roger de, K.B.1306, I. 120
Grindall, Richard, K.C.B.1815, I. 217
Grinlinton, John J., Kt.1894, II. 393
Grise (Le Gris), Robert, Kt.1628, II. 195

Grobham (Grubham), Richard, Kt.1604, II. 131
Grose, Nash, Kt.1787, II. 300
Grosse, Charles le, Kt.1616, II. 160
Grosse (Legrosse), Thomas, Kt.1603, II. 108
Grosvenor, Hugh L., duke of Westminster, K.G.1870, I. 64
Grosvenor, John, Kt.1727, II. 283
Grosvenor, Richard, Kt.1617, II. 165
Grosvenor, Richard, marquess of Westminster, K.G.1857, I. 60
Grosvenor, Robert, marquess of Westminster, K.G.1841, I. 56
Grove, —, K.H.1837, I. 477
Grove, Coleridge, K.C.B.1898, I. 270
Grove, George, Kt.1883, II. 375
Grove, William R., Kt.1872, II. 363
Groves, John, Kt.1900, II. 407
Grubb, Howard, Kt.1887, II. 383
Gryffyth, Gryffith. See Griffith
Grymes. See Grimes and Graham
Grymstone. See Grimstone
Grubham. See Grobham
Gualterio, John B., earl of Dundee, K.T. Jacobite, 1708, footnote, II. 75
Gudenus, baron Leopold, K.C.V.O.1903, I. 442
Guelders, William I., duke of, K.G.1390, I. 6
Guest, Lyonell, Kt.1604, II. 132
Guevara, John, Kt.1605, II. 137
Guibon, Francis, Kt.1682, II. 257
Guibon (Gibbon), Thomas, Kt.1641, II. 209
GUILDFORD, GUYLFORDE, GUILDEFORDE, GUILFORD
Guilford —, Kt.1596, II. 93
Guilford, earl of. See North
Guylforde, Edward, Kt.1513, II. 39
Guildeforde, Henry, Kt.1511, II. 35, bis
Guildford, Henry, Kt.1513, II. 36
Guildford, Henry, K.G.1526, I. 22
Guildford, Henry, Kt.1591, II. 88
Guildeforde, John, Kt.1542, II. 53
Guildford, Richard, Kt.1485, 1497, II. 22, 28; K.G.1500, I. 19
Guilford, Thomas, K.B.1547, II. 59
Guildeforde, Thomas, Kt.1573, II. 75

INDEX

Guinness, Edward C., baron Iveagh, K.P.1896, I. 105
Guinness, Reginald R. B., Kt.1897, II. 400
Guise, John W., K.C.B.1831, I. 231; G.C.B.1862, I. 194
Guise, William, Kt.1619, II. 174
Gulston (Goulston), William, Kt.1680, II. 254
Gunbert. See Gunter

GUNN, GUN
Gunn, John, Kt.1898, II. 403
Gun, William, Kt.1639, II. 207

GUNNING, GONNING
Gonning, John, Kt.1666, II. 242
Gunning, Robert, K.B.1773, I. 172; G.C.B.1815, I. 205
Gunston, Thomas, Kt.1762, II. 292

GUNTER, GUNBERT
Gunter, George, Kt.1604, II. 131
Gunbert (Gunter), John, Kt.1603, II. 122
Gurdon, William B., K.C.M.G.1882, I. 364
Gurney, Goldsworthy, Kt.1863, II. 357
Gurney, John, Kt.1832, II. 331
Gurney, Richard, Kt.1641, II. 211
Guson, Otes de, Kt.1347, II. 8
Guthrie, James, Kt.1903, II. 414
Guy, Philip M. N., K.C.B.1873, I. 254
Guy [Grey], Richard, Kt.1709, II. 276
Guyon, Mark, Kt.1675, II. 250
Guyse, John, K.B.(1489), I. 143
Gwalior, Kirkee Shamshir, of, K.C.S.I. 1875, I. 320
Gwalior, Rao Sindhia, maharaja of, K.S.I.1861, I. 306; G.C.S.I.1866, I. 308; G.C.B.1877, I. 197
Gwalior, Maharaja Sindhia, of, G.C.S.I. 1895, I. 313; K.C.B.1901, I. 273; G.C.V.O.1903, I. 420
Gwillim, Henry, Kt.1801, II. 306
Gwydott, Anthony, Kt.1549, II. 65
Gwyn, Rowland, Kt.1680, II. 254
Gyll. See Gill
Gzowski, Casimir S., K.C.M.G.1890, I. 375

H

Haast, John F. J. von, K.C.M.G.1886, I. 369
Haberfield, John K., Kt.1851, II. 348
Habrda, ritter John von, K.C.V.O.1904, I. 443
Hacker, John, Kt.1603, II. 120
Hackett, Andrew, Kt.1671, II. 245
Hacket, Cuthbert, Kt.1627, II. 192
Hackett, Ja, Kt.1633, II. lxii.
Hackett, John, Kt.1612, II. 152
Hackett, John W., Kt.1902, II. 412
Hackett, Robert, Kt.1677, II. 252
Hackett, Thomas, Kt.1687, II. 263
Hackett, William, Kt.1866, II. 358
Hackett, Wililam B., Kt.1852, II. 349
Haddington, earl of. See Hamilton; see Baillie-Hamilton-Arden
Haddock, Richard, Kt.1675, II.. 250
Haddon, Richard, Kt.1497, II. 30
Haden, Francis S., Kt.1894, II. 394
Hagan, Robert, Kt.1835, II. 336
Hagarty, John H., Kt.1897, II. 402
Hagron, Alexis A. R., K.C.V.O.1898, I. 439
Hailes. See Hales
Haines, Frederick P., K.C.B.1871, I. 253; G.C.B.1877, I. 197; G.C.S.I.1879, I. 311
Hakelut, Walter, K.B.1306, I. 112
Haldane, Jo, Kt.1633, II. lxiii.
Haldimand, Frederick, K.B.1785, II. 173
HALES, HALE, HALSE, HALLES, HAILES, and see Hall
Hales (Hale), Bartholomew, Kt.1619, II. 173
Hale, Bernard, Kt.1726, II. 283
Halles (Hales), Edward, Kt.1603, II. 112
Hale, Frank von, K.G.1359, I. 3
Hailes, Harris C., K.H.1836, I. 473
Hales (Hailes or Halles), James, K.B. 1547, I. 151
Hales, James, Kt.1573, II. 75
Hales, James, Kt.1581, II. 81
Hales (Halles), James, Kt.1618, II. 167
Hales, John, Kt.1617, II. 164
Hales, John, Kt.1625, II. 188

INDEX

HALES
Hale, John, Kt.1660, II. 229
Hale, Mathew, Kt.1662, II. 236
Halse, Nicholas, Kt.1605, II. 138
Hales, Stephen, K.B.1661, I. 166
HALFORD, HOLFORD, HOLFORDE, HALLFORTH
Holforde, George, Kt.1482, II. 19
Holforde (Hallforth), George, Kt.1513, II. 36
Halford, Henry, K.C.H.1825, I. 455; G.C.H.1830, I. 450
Holforde, John, Kt.1513, II. 42
Halford (Holford), Richard, Kt.1642, II. 211
Holford, Richard, Kt.1695, II. 269
Halford, William, Kt.1673, II. 248
Halford, William, Kt.1673, II. 248
Holford (Halford), William, Kt.1683, II. 259
Halghton (Haluton), Tho de, Kt.1347, II. 8
Halibruntone, George, Kt.1633, II. lxiii.
Haliburton, Arthur L., lord Haliburton, K.C.B.1885, I. 289; G.C.B.1897, I. 215
HALIFAX, HALLIFAX
Halifax, earl of. See Montague; see Montague-Dunk; see Wood, C.
Hallifax, Thomas, Kt.1773, II. 294
Haliwel. See Hallowell
Halkett, Alexander, K.C.H.1837, I. 461; Kt.1837, II. 338
Halkett, Colin, K.C.H.1815, I. 454; K.C.B.1815, I. 222; G.C.H.1820, I. 449; G.C.B.1847, I. 190
Halkett, Hugh, K.C.H.1815, I. 454
Halkett, Peter, G.C.H.1832, I. 452
Hall, Alexander, Kt.1633, II. 200
Hall, Angus W., K.C.B.1904, I. 301
Hall, Charles, Kt.1873, II. 365
Hall, Charles, K.C.M.G.1890, I. 376
Hall, John, Kt.1604, II. 130
Hall, John, Kt.1632, II. 200
Hall, John, K.H.1823, I. 464
Hall, John, K.C.H.1831, I. 456; Kt.1831, II. 330; K.C.B.1856, I. 243
Hall, John, K.C.M.G.1882, I. 364
Hall, Philip, Kt.1727, II. 283

Hall (Halse), Nicholas, Kt.1605, II. 138
Hall, Robert, Kt.1816, II. 318
Hall, Samuel, Kt.1902, II. 411
Hall, William, Kt.1604, II. 133
Hall, William H., K.C.B.1867, I. 251
Hall, William K., K.C.B.1871, I. 253
Hallé, Charles, Kt.1888, II. 384
Halles. See Hales
Hallett, James, Kt.1707, II. 275
Hallforth. See Halford
Halliburton, Brenton, Kt.1859, II. 353
HALLIDAY, HALIDAY, HOLIDAY
Halliday, Andrew, K.H.1820, I. 464; Kt.1821, II. 322
Halliday, Frederick J., K.C.B.1860, I. 281
Haliday (Holiday), Leonard, Kt.1603, II. 128
HALLOWELL, HALIWEL
Hallowell(afterwardsCarew),Benjamin, K.C.B.1815, I. 220
Haliwel (Halwyn), John, Kt.1485, II. 22
HALSALL, HALSELL
Halsell, Cuthbert, Kt.1599, II. 96
Halsall, Henry, Kt.1497, II. 32
Halsall, Henry, Kt.1513, II. 36
Halsall, Thomas, Kt.1533, II. 49
Halsbury, earl of. See Giffard
Halse. See Hales
Halsey, John, Kt.1670, II. 244
Halsted, Lawrence W., K.C.B.1815, I. 218; G.C.B.1837, I. 187
Halswell or Haslewell, Nicholas, Kt. 1603, II. 107
Halton, Robert (Roger), Kt.1603, II. 122
Halton (Houghton, Haughton), William, Kt.1618, II. 168
Halton. See Hatton
Halwton. See Halghton
Halwyn, John, Kt.1485, II. 22
Haly, John, Kt.1785, II. 298
Haly, William O'G., K.C.B.1875, I. 255
Hambleton. See Hamilton
Hamby, John, Kt.1669, II. 243
Hamdaine, Hamden. See Hampden, Holmden
Hamelin, Ferdinand A., G.C.B.1857, I. 192

Hamer. See Hanmer
Hamerton, Stephen, Kt.1482, II. 17, 20
Hamilton, Alexander, Kt.1633, II. lxiii.
Hamilton, Alexander, Kt.1786, II. 299
Hamilton, Alexander, duke of Hamilton, K.G.1836, I. 55
Hamilton, Bruce M., K.C.B.1902, I. 275
Hamilton, Charles, Kt.1662, II. 236
Hamilton, Charles, K.C.B.1833, I. 232
Hamilton, David, Kt.1703, II. 273
Hamilton, Douglas, duke of Hamilton, K.T.1786, II. 80
Hamilton, duke of. See Douglas-Hamilton
Hamilton, Edward, Kt.1800, II. 305; K.C.B.1815, I. 222
Hamilton, Edward W., K.C.B.1894, I. 293; K.C.V.O.(1901), I. 434
Hamilton, Frederick W., K.C.B.1873, I. 253
Hamilton (Hambleton), George, Kt.1616, II. 159
Hamilton, George, earl of Orkney, K.T. 1704, I. 76
Hamilton, George B., K.C.H.1831, I.457; Kt.1831, II. 330
Hamilton, lord George F., G.C.S.I.1903, I. 314
Hamilton, Hans, Kt.1661, II. 235
Hamilton, Ian S. M., K.C.B.1900, I. 272
Hamilton, James, Kt.1609, II. 149
Hamilton, James, marquess of Hamilton, K.G.1623, I. 31
Hamilton, James, duke of Hamilton, K.G.1630, I. 32
Hamilton, James, Kt.1633, II. lxiii.
Hamilton, James, duke of Hamilton, K.T.1687, I. 75; K.G.1712, I. 40
Hamilton, James, duke of Hamilton, KT.1726, I. 77
Hamilton, James, duke of Hamilton, K.T.1755, I. 78
Hamilton, James, earl of Clanbrassill, K.P.1783, I. 96
Hamilton, James, Kt.1786, II. 299
Hamilton, James, duke of Abercorn, K.G.1844, I. 57; Grand Master K.P. 1866, I. 94
Hamilton, James, Kt.1872, II. 364

Hamilton, James, duke of Abercorn, K.G.1892, I. 69
Hamilton, John, Kt.1813, II. 313
Hamilton, John, Kt.1845, II. 346
Hamilton, John J., marquess of Abercorn, K.G.1805, I. 50
Hamilton, John P., K.H.1836, I. 473
Hamilton, Nicholas, K.H.1836, I. 473
Hamilton, Patrick, Kt.1633, I. lxii.
Hamilton, Patrick, Kt.1761, II. 291
Hamilton, Ralph, Kt.1829, II. 327
Hamilton, Richard V., K.C.B.1887, I. 261; G.C.B.1895, I. 201
Hamilton, Robert, Kt.1670, II. 245
Hamilton, Robert G. C., K.C.B.1884, I. 288
Hamilton, Robert M., lord Belhaven, K.T.1861, I. 85
Hamilton, Robert N. C., K.C.B.1860, I. 281
Hamilton, Thomas, earl of Haddington, K.T.1717, I. 77
Hamilton, Thomas, earl of Haddington, Grand Master K.P.1835, I. 94; K.T.1853, I. 84
Hamilton, William, duke of Hamilton, K.G.1650, I. 34
Hamilton, William, K.B.1772, I. 171
Hamilton, William, Kt.1873, II. 365
Hamilton, William O., Kt.1815, II. 316
Hamilton, William R., Kt.1835, II. 336
Hamilton-Dalrymple, John, earl of Stair, K.T.1865, I. 85
Hamilton-Gordon, Alexander, K.C.B. 1873, I. 254
Hamilton-Gordon, Arthur, G.C.M.G. 1878, I. 338
Hamilton-Gordon, John C., earl of Aberdeen, Grand Master K.P.1886, I. 95; G.C.M.G.1895, I. 344
Hamilton-Temple-Blackwood, Frederick T., marquess of Dufferin, K.C.B. 1861, I. 282; K.P.1864, I. 102; G.C.M.G.1876, I. 337; G.C.B.1883, I 211; G.C.S.I.1884, I. 312; Grand Master Star of India, I. 305; G.C.I.E.1887, I. 401
Hamley, Edward B., K.C.M.G.1879, I. 362; K.C.B.1882, I. 258

INDEX

Hammersley, Hugh, Kt.1628, II. 194
Hammersley, Thomas, Kt.1641, II. 210
Hammett, Benjamin, Kt.1786, II. 299
HAMMOND, HAMOND, HEYMAN, HAYMAN
Hamond (Hammond), Andrew S., Kt. 1779, II. 296
Hammond, Arthur G., K.C.B.1903, I. 275
Hamond, Charles F., Kt.1896, II. 397
Hammond, Francis T., K.C.H.1819, I. 454; Kt.1819, II. 321; G.C.H.1827, I. 450
Hamond, Graham E., K.C.B.1831, I. 231; G.C.B.1855, I. 191
Hamond (Heyman, Hayman), Henry, Kt.1641, II. 210
Hammond, John, Kt.1603, II. 115
Hamond (Hayman), William, Kt.1607, II. 144
Heyman, William, Kt.1685, II. 260
Hammond William, Kt.1717, II. 281
Hammys, Symond, Kt.1461, II. 13
Hamnare. See Hanmer
HAMPDEN, HAMDEN
Hampden, Alexander, Kt.1603, II. 112
Hampden, Edmond, Kt.1504, II. 34
Hampden, John, Kt.1513, II. 40
Hamden, John, Kt.1604, II. 130
Hamden, Thomas, Kt.(1483), II. 140
Hampden, Thomas T., viscount Hampden, G.C.H.1816, I. 447
Hampden, viscount. See Brand
Hambden (Harpden, Humdaine), William, Kt.1604, II. 136
Hampet, John, Kt.1838, II. 339
Hampson, Robert, Kt.1603, II. 128
Hampson, Robert A., Kt.1904, II. 418
Hampton, lord. See Pakington
Hampton, William, Kt.1471, II. 16
Hanagan, Richard D., K.H.1817, I. 463
Hanbury, James A., K.C.B.1882, I. 258
Hanbery, John, Kt.1627, II. 192
Hanbury, John, K.C.H.1832, I. 458; Kt. 1832, II. 332; K.C.B.1862, I. 247
Hanbury, Thomas, K.C.V.O.(1901), I.434
Hancock, Samuel, Kt.1841, II. 343
Handcock, William, Kt.1700, II. 271
Handford, Humphrey, Kt.1622, II. 179
Hanel, Friedrich A., K.C.V.O.1900, I.439

Hanger, George, Kt.1696, II. 269
Hankey, Frederick, K.C.M.G.1818, I. 350; G.C.M.G.1833, I. 333
Hankey, Henry, Kt.1732, II. 284
Hankey, Joseph, Kt.1737, II. 285
Hankey, Richard, Kt.1803, II. 307
Hankey, Thomas, Kt.1745, II. 287
Hankford, William, K.B.1400, I. 128
Hankin, Thomas P., Kt.1822, II. 324
HANMER, HANMORE, HAMNARE, HAMER, and see Harman
Hanmore, Edward, Kt.1497, II. 32
Hanmer, Henry, K.H.1833, I. 468
Hanmer, John, Kt.1660, II. 231
Hanmer (Hamer), Thomas, Kt.1513, II. 41
Hamnare (Hanmer), Thomas, Kt.1547, II. 60
Hanmer (Hammond), Thomas, Kt. 1603, II. 115, 125
Hanmer, Thomas, Kt.1676, II. 251
Hannam. See Hunnam
Hannen, James, Kt.1868, II. 360
Hannen, Nicholas J., Kt.1895, II. 396
Hannes, Edward, Kt.1705, II. 274
Hanover, king of. See Cumberland
Hansard, Richard, Kt.1604, II. 135
Hansard, Thomas, Kt.1487, II. 25
Hansarde, William, Kt.1513, II. 39
Hansby, Ralph, Kt.1619, II. 173
Hansler, John J., Kt.1837, II. 339
Hanson (Ansam, Awnsham), Julian (Gideon), Kt.1603, II. 120
Hanson, Reginald, Kt.1882, II. 374
Hanson, Richard D., Kt.1869, II. 361
Hanson, Robert, Kt. 1666, II. 241
Hants, John de, K.B.1306, I. 113
Hanybal, Matthew, K.B.1255, I. 110
Harben, Henry, Kt.1897, II. 400
Harbert. See Herbert and Harbord
Harbord, Charles, lord Suffield, K.C.B. 1876, I. 286; G.C.V.O.1901, I. 419
Harbord, William M., K.B.1744, I.169
Harbord. See Herbert
Harbottell, Rauf, Kt.1482, II.21
Harby. See Harvey
HARCOURT, HARECOURT
Harcourt, John de, K.B.1306, I. 113

HARCOURT
Harcourt, Philip, Kt.1660, II. 227
Harecourt, Richard, K.B.(1465), I. 135
Harcourt, Robert, K.G.1463, I.14
Harcourt or Hardecourt, Robert, K.B. (1494), I. 144
Harecourt, Robert, Kt.1497, II. 28
Harcourt, Symon, Kt.1513, II. 40
Harcourt (Harecourt), Simon, Kt. 1627, II. 192
Harcourt, Simon, Kt.1702, II. 272
Harcourt, Walter, Kt.1591, II. 88
Harcourt, William, earl Harcourt, G.C.B.1820, I. 184
Harcourt. See Venables - Vernon Harcourt
Harden, William de, K.B.1306, I. 114
HARDINGE, HARDING
  Hardinge, Arthur, K.C.M.G.1897, I. 383
  Hardinge, Arthur E., K.C.B.1886, I. 259
  Hardinge, Arthur H., K.C.B.1904, I. 301
  Hardinge, Charles, K.C.V.O.(1904), I. 437; K.C.M.G.1904, I. 394
  Harding, George J., K.C.B.1860, I. 246
  Hardinge, Henry, viscount Hardinge, K.C.B.1815, I.224; G.C.B.1844, I. 207
  Harding, John D., Kt.1852, II. 349
  Hardinge, Richard, K.H.1825, I.465
  Hardinge, Robert, Kt.1675, II. 249
  Harding, Robert P., Kt.1890, II.386
Hardman, William, Kt.1885, II.378
Hardres (Hardes), Thomas, Kt.1603, II. 120
Hardresse (or Hardy), Thomas, Kt.1676, II. 251
Hardwicke, earl of. See Yorke
Hardy, Charles, Kt.1732, II. 284
Hardy Charles, Kt.1755, II.288
Hardy Thomas, Kt.1702, II. 273
Hardy, Thomas D., Kt.1869, II. 361
Hardy, Thomas M., K.C.B.1815, I. 222; G.C.B.1831, I. 186
Hardy, William, Kt.1883, II. 376

Hardy. See Hardresse
Hare, John, Kt.1618, II. 170
Hare, John, K.H.1834, I. 469
Hare, John, Kt.1840, II. 342
Hare, Nicholas, Kt.1538, II. 51
Hare, Ralph, Kt.1603, II. 156
Hare, William, earl of Listowel, K.P. 1839, I. 100
Hare, William, earl of Listowel, K.P. 1873, I. 104
Harewell. See Hartwell
Harewood, Thomas, Kt.1603, II. 126
Harfleet, Charles (Christopher), Kt.1619, II. 171
Harfleet, alias Septuans, Thomas, Kt. 1603, II. 118
Hargood, William, K.C.B.1815, I. 218; G.C.H.1831, I. 451; G.C.B.1831, I. 186
Harington. See Harrington
Harley, Edward, Kt.1660, II. 232; K.B. 1661, I. 165
Harley, John, Kt.1471, II. 14
Harley, Robert, K.B.1603, I. 155
Harley, Robert, earl of Oxford, K.G. 1712, I. 41
Harley, Robert, K.C.M.G.1883, I. 365
Harman, George B., K.C.B.1887, I. 262
Harman, Thomas, Kt.1664, II. 239
Harman (Hanmer), William, Kt.1603, II. 116, 119
Harne. See Herne
Harness, Henry D., K.C.B.1873, I. 254
Harnhull, Henry de, K.B.1326, I. 123
Harpden, William, Kt.1604, II. 136
Harpeden, William de, K.B.1306, I. 117
HARPER, HARPUR
  Harper, George, Kt.1547, II. 60
  Harper, John, Kt.1603, II. 102
  Harper, John, Kt.1630, II. 198
  Harper (Harpur), Richard, Kt.1608, II. 146
  Harper, Richard, Kt.1617, II. 162
  Harper, Sebastian, Kt.1616, II. 158
  Harper, William, Kt.1561, II. 71
Harpesfeld, John de, K.B.1306, I. 118
Harpole, William, Kt.1603, II. 129
Harrel, David, Kt.1893, II. 391; K.C.B. 1895, I. 294; K.C.V.O.(1900), I. 433

INDEX 107

HARRINGTON, HARINGTON, HARYNGTON
Harrington, earl of. See Stanhope
Haryngton, lord. See Grey
Harrington, Edward, Kt.1603, II. 108
Harrington, Edward, Kt.1795, II. 302
Harrington, Henry, Kt.1578, II. 78
Harrington, Henry B., K.C.S.I.1866, I. 315
Harington, James, K.B.1413, II. 11
Harrington, James, Kt.1487, II. 26
Harington, James, Kt.1565, II. 71
Harrington, James, Kt.1603, II. 101
Harrington, James, Kt.1628, II. 195
Harington, John, Kt.1542, II. 53
Harington, John, lord Harington of Exton, Kt.1584, II.82
Harrington, John, Kt.1599, II. 97
Harrington, John, Kt.1603, II. 108
Harrington, John, lord Harrington of Exton, K.B.1605, I. 157
Harrington, John L., K.C.V.O.(1903), I. 436
Harington, Robert, lord Harington, K.B.1377, I. 126
Harrington, Robert, Kt.1471, II. 14
Harrington, Robert, Kt.1482, II. 18
Haryngton, William, K.G.1415, I. 9
Harington, William, Kt.1615, II. 157
Harris, Arthur, Kt.1606, II. 140
Harris, Augustus H. G., Kt.1891, II. 389
Harris, Christopher, Kt.1607, II. 142
Harris, Cranmer, Kt.1629, II. 196
Harris (Davies), Edward, Kt.1618, II. 171
Harris, Edward A. J., K.C.B.1872, I. 285
Harris, Francis, Kt.1603, II. 112
Harris, Francis, Kt.1608, II. 145
Harris, George, lord Harris, G.C.B.1820, I. 185
Harris, George D., Kt.1888, II. 384
Harris, George F. R., lord Harris, K.S.I. 1861, I. 306; G.C.S.I.1866, I. 308
Harris, George R. C., lord Harris, G.C.I.E.1890, I. 401; G.C.S.I.1895, I. 313
Harris, Harry B., K.H.1834, I. 470
Harris, James, earl of Malmesbury, K.B. 1779, I. 172; G.C.B.1815, I. 205

Harris, James C., Kt.1896, II. 397; K.C.V.O.(1902), I. 434
Harris, James H., earl of Malmesbury, G.C.B.1859, I. 209
Harris, John, Kt.1603, II. 114
Harris, Matthew, Kt.1899, II. 405
Harris, Paul, Kt.1625, II. 188
Harris, Richard, Kt.1691, II. 267
Harris, Robert H., K.C.M.G.1898, I. 384; K.C.B.1900, I. 271
Harris, Thomas, Kt.1603, II. 126
Harris, Thomas, Kt.1626, II. 191
Harris, Thomas, Kt.1765, II. 292
Harris, Thomas N., K.H.1830, I. 465; Kt.1841, II. 343
Harris, William, Kt.1603, II. 122, 125
Harris, William C., K.B.1844, II. 345
Harris, William G., lord Harris, K.C.H. 1833, I. 459
Harris, William S., Kt.1847, II. 347
Harrison, Edmund, Kt.1698, II. 271
Harrison, Edmund S., Kt.1880, II. 371
Harrison, (Charles) Frederick, Kt.1902, II. 413
Harrison, George, K.C.H.1831, I. 456; Kt.1831, II. 330
Harrison, George, Kt.1884, II. 376
Harrison, Henry L., Kt.1887, II. 380
Harrison, John, Kt.1641, II. 208
Harrison, John C., K.H.1836, I. 473
Harrison, Richard, Kt.1621, II. 177
Harrison, Richard, K.C.B.1889, I. 263; G.C.B.1903, I. 204
Harrison, Robert, Kt.1689, II. 264
Harrison, Thomas, Kt.1640, II. 208
Harrison, Thomas, Kt.1752, II. 288
Harrowby, earl of. See Ryder
HART, HARTE
Hart, Andrew S., Kt.1886, II. 378
Hart, Anthony, Kt.1827, II. 326
Hart, Christopher (Eustace), Kt.1603, II. 118
Hart, George, Kt.1581, II. 81
Hart, Henry, Kt.1626, II. 163
Hart, Henry, K.C.H.1836, I. 461; Kt. 1836, II. 337
Hart, Israel, Kt.1895, II. 395
Hart, John, Kt.1591, II. 88
Harte, Percyvall, Kt.1538, II. 51

INDEX

HART
  Hart, Percivall, Kt.1601, II. 99
  Hart, Percival, Kt.1672, II. 247
  Hart, Reginald C., K.C.B.1899, I. 270;
    K.C.V.O.(1904), I. 437
  Hart, Richard, Kt.1680, II. 255
  Harte, Richard, Kt.1807, II. 308
  Hart, Robert, K.C.M.G.1882, I. 364;
    G.C.M.G.1889, I. 342
  Hart, William, Kt.1760, II. 289
  Hartgill, Thomas, Kt.1603, II. 126
  Hartlewe, —-, Kt.1347, II. 9
  Hartley, Charles A., Kt.1862, II. 356;
    K.C.M.G.1884, I. 366
  Hartmann, Julius, K.C.B.1815, I. 226
  Hartop, Edward, Kt.1634, II. 202
  Hartop, Thomas, Kt.1624, II. 186
  Hartop, William, Kt.1617, II. 165
  Hartopp, William, Kt.1660, II. 228
  Hartpole, Robert, Kt.1668, II. 243

HARTWELL, HAREWELL, HARWELL,
    HORWOLL
  Harwell, Edward, K.B.1603, I. 155
  Hartwell, Francis J., Kt.1803, II. 307
  Harewell (Hartwell), Robert, Kt.1603,
    II. 111
  Harwell (Hartwell, Horwoll), Thomas,
    Kt.1603, II. 123
  Hartwell, William, K.B.1501, I. 146
  Harty, Joseph M., K.H.1837, I. 477
  Harwell. See Hartwell
  Harwood, Busic. Kt.1806, II. 308
  Harwood, John J., Kt.1888, II. 384

HARVEY, HERVEY, HARBY, HARVY
  Harvey, Bissell, K.H.1837, I. 477
  Harby, Clement, Kt.1669, I. 243
  Harvey, Daniel, Kt.1660, II. 226
  Harvey, Edward, K.C.B.1861, I. 246;
    G.C.B.1865, I. 194
  Harvey, Eliab, Kt.1660, II. 226
  Harvey, Eliab, K.C.B.1815, I. 217;
    G.C.B.1825, I. 185
  Hervey, Felton E. B., K.H.1818, I. 463
  Harvey, Francis, Kt.1626, II. 191
  Harvey, Gawen, Kt.1604, II. 136
  Harvey, George, Kt.1513, II. 40
  Harvy (Hervey), George, Kt.1603, II. 107

HARVEY
  Harvey, George, Kt.1867, II. 358
  Harvey, George F., K.C.S.I.1867, I. 318
  Harvy, Gerrat, Kt.1596, II. 93
  Harvey, Henry, K.B.1800, I. 175
  Hervy, James, Kt.1582, II. 81
  Harvey, James, K.H.1835, I. 471
  Harvey (Harbey), Job, Kt.1637, II. 205
  Harbey, John, Kt.1523, II. 44
  Harvey, John, Kt.1628, II. 195
  Harvey, John, K.C.H.1824, I. 455; Kt.
    1824, II. 325; K.C.B.1838, I. 235
  Harvey, John, K.C.B.1833, I. 232
  Harvey, Ludford, Kt.1813, II. 312
  Harvey, Peter, Kt.1664, II. 240
  Hervey, Raymond, viscount Frankfort
    de Montmorency, K.C.B.1898, I. 270
  Harvey, Robert, Kt.1901, II. 408
  Harvey, Robert J., Kt.1817, II. 318
  Harvy (Harper), Sebastian, Kt.1616,
    II. 158
  Harvy, Simon, Kt.1623, II. 182
  Harvey, Stephen, K.B.1626, I. 163
  Harvey, Thomas, K.C.B.1833, I. 232
  Harvy, William, Kt.1596, II. 93
  Harvey, William, Kt.1608, bis, II. 145
  Haryngton. See Harrington
  Hassam, Assem, K.C.M.G.1900, I. 388
  Hasan Khan, styled Etimad-us-Sultaneh,
    K.C.M.G.1889, I. 374
  Haselrig, Thomas, Kt.1608, II. 145

HASELWOOD, HASLEWOOD
  Haselwood, Anthony, Kt.1621, II. 177
  Haselwood (Halswell, Haselwell),
    Nicholas, Kt.1603, II. 107
  Haslewood, Thomas, Kt.1681, II. 256
  Haslewood, William, Kt.1669, II. 244
  Haslam, Alfred S., Kt.1891, II. 388
  Hasler, John, Kt.1772, II. 293
  Haslett, James H., Kt.1887, II. 383
  Hassard, Francis J., Kt.1809, II. 309
  Hassard, John, Kt.1888, II. 384; K.C.B.
    1897, I. 296

HASSEL, HASEL
  Hasel, Edward, Kt.1699, II. 271
  Hassell, Leonard, Kt.1603, II. 120

INDEX

HASTINGS, HASTINGES, HASTYNGS
Hastings, Bryan, Kt.1533, II. 49
Hastings, Charles, G.C.H.1819, I. 449
Hastings, Charles, Kt.1850, II. 348
Hastings, Charles H., K.H.1833, I. 468; K.C.H.1835, I. 461; Kt.1835, II. 336
Hastinges, Edmond, Kt.1482, II. 17
Hastings, Edward, K.B.(1400), I. 129
Hastings, Edward, lord Hastings, K.B. (1475), I. 137
Hastinges, Edward, lord Hastings, Kt. 1547, II. 62; K.G.1555, I. 25
Hastings, Edward, Kt.1570, II. 74
Hastinges, Edward, Kt.1591, II. 89
Hastings, Francis, earl of Huntingdon, K.B.1533, I. 149; K.G.1549, I. 24
Hastinges, Francis, Kt.1592, II. 90
Hastings, George, earl of Huntingdon, K.B.1501, I. 145
Hastings, George, K.B.1509, I. 148
Hastings, George, Kt.1565, II. 72
Hastings, George, Kt.1575, II. 77
Hastings, George, Kt.1615, II. 157
Hastings, George, Kt.1619, II. 174
Hastings, Henry, earl of Huntingdon, K.B.1547, I. 150; K.G.1570, I. 26
Hastings, Henry, Kt.1603, II. 102, 105
Hastings, Hugh, Kt.1482, II. 17
Hastings, John, earl of Pembroke, K.G.1369, I. 4
Hastings, John, K.B.(1489), I. 143
Hastinges, John, Kt.1497, II. 31
Hastings marquess of. See Rawdon-Hastings
Hastings, Ralph, Kt.1347, II. 7
Hastinges, Rauf, Kt.1471, II. 14, 16
Hastinges, Richard, lord Wells, Kt. 1471, II. 14, 15
Hastings, Richard, lord Willoughby de Eresby, K.B.1501, I. 145
Hastings, Roger, Kt.1497, II. 32
Hastinges, Thomas, Kt.1553, II. 66
Hastings, Thomas, Kt.1835, II. 336
Hastings, Thomas, Kt.1839, II. 341; K.C.B.1859, I. 280
Hastings, William, lord Hastings, Kt. 1461, II. 13; K.G.1461, I. 14

Hatsell, Henry, Kt.1697, II. 270
Hatton, Christopher, Kt.1577, II. 78; K.G.1588, I. 28
Hatton, Christopher, K.B.1603, I. 155
Hatton, Christopher, K.B.1625, I. 162
Hatton, Henry, Kt.1660, II. 232
Hatton (Halton), Richard, Kt.1645, II. 219
Hatton, Robert, Kt.1617, II. 161
Hatton, Robert, Kt.1677, II. 252
Hatton, Thomas, Kt.1616, II. 159
Hatton, William, Kt.1586, II. 84
Hatton, William, Kt.1605, II. 138
Hatton. See Hutton
Haudlo, John de, K.B.1306, I. 116
Haughton. See Houghton
Haughton. See Halton
Haultain, Charles, K.H.1833, I. 469
Haundesacre, William de, K.B.1306, I. 117
Havelock, Arthur E., K.C.M.G.1884, I. 367; G.C.M.G.1895, I. 344; G.C.I.E. 1896, I. 402; G.C.S.I.1901, I. 314
Havelock, Henry, K.C.B.1857, I. 244
Havelock, William, K.H.1816, I. 463
Havelock-Allan, Henry M., K.C.B.1887, I. 261; G.C.B.1897, I. 202
Haverington, John de, K.B.1306, I. 120
Haviland (Havilland), Peter de, Kt.1817, II. 318
Hawaii, king of, G.C.M.G.1881, I. 339
Haward. See Howard, Hayward
Hawes, Benjamin, K.C.B.1856, I. 279
Hawes, James, Kt.1575, II. 76
Hawke, Edward, lord Hawke, K.B.1747, I. 169
Hawker, Samuel, K.C.H.1831, I. 457 G.C.H.1836, I. 453
Hawker, Thomas, K.C.H.1837, I. 461; Kt.1837, II. 338
Hawkesworth, Stephen (Richard), Kt. 1621, II. 177
HAWKINS, HAWKYNS
Hawkins, Henry, Kt.1876, II. 368
Hawkins, John, Kt.1588, II. 86
Hawkins, John, Kt.1702, II. 273
Hawkins, John, Kt.1772, II. 294
Hawkins, John S., K.C.M.G.1881, I. 363

HAWKYNS
Hawkyns, Richard, Kt.1603, II. 116
Hawkins, Richard, Kt.1687, II. 263
Hawkins, Stephen, Kt.1645, II. 219
Hawkins, Thomas, Kt.1608, II. 145
Hawkins, Thomas, Kt.1618, II. 168
Hawkins, William, Kt.1783, II. 297
Hawkmore (or Hockmore), Gregory (George), Kt.1676, II. 251
Hawks, Robert S., Kt.1817, II. 319
Hawkshaw, John, Kt.1873, II. 365
Hawles (Hawlis), John, Kt.1695, II. 269
Hawley, Edward, Kt.1624, II. 184
Hawte, Richard, Kt.1482, II. 18
Hawte, Thomas, K.B.1501, I. 146
Hawte, William, K.B.(1465), I. 135
Hawte, William, Kt.1492, II. 28
Hawtry. See Dawtrey
Hawtry, William, Kt.1591, II. 89

HAYDEN, HAYDON, HEYDON, HAIDON
Heydon, Christopher, Kt.1549, II. 64
Haidon (Heydon), Christopher, Kt. 1596, II. 92
Hayden, Henry, K.B.(1483), I. 139
Heydon, Henry, K.B.(1485), I. 142
Haydon (Heydon), James, Kt.1603, II. 111
Haydon, John, Kt.1599, II. 97
Heydon, John, K.B.1509, I. 149
Heydon, John, Kt.1620, II. 175
Heydon, John, Kt.1629, II. 195
Heydon, Nicholas, Kt.1513, II. 40
Haydon, William, Kt.1583, II. 82

HAY, HAYE
Hay, Andrew, Kt.1633, II. lxiii.
Hay, Andrew L., K.H.1834, I. 469
Hay, Charles, earl of Errol, K.T. Jacobite 1705, footnote, I. 75
Hay, Charles, earl of Erroll, K.T.1901, I. 89
Hay. See Drummond-Hay
Hay, Frank R. D., Kt.1891, II. 388
Hay, George, jun., Kt.1651, II. 222
Hay, George, Kt.1773, II. 294
Hay, George, marquess of Tweeddale, K.T.1820, I. 81; K.C.B.1862, I. 247; G.C.B.1867, I. 195
Hay, James, lord Hay of Yester, K.B. 1603, I. 154
Hay, James, earl of Carlisle, K.B.1610, I. 157; K.G.1624, I. 31
Hay, James, earl of Carlisle, K.B.1626, I. 160
Hay, James, Kt.1651, II. 222
Hay, James, earl of Inverness, K.T. Jacobite 1725, footnote, I. 75
Hay, James, K.C.H.1832, I. 457; Kt.1832, II. 331
Hay, James S., K.C.M.G.1889, I. 374
Haye, John de la, K.B.1323, I. 122
Hay, John, K.C.M.G.1878, I. 360
Hay, lord John, K.C.B.1881, I. 258; G.C.B.1886, I. 199
Hay, John C. D., K.C.B.1885, I. 259; G.C.B.1902, I. 203
Hay, Patrick, Kt.1621, II. 177
Hay, Patrick, Kt.1633, II. lxii.
Haye, Peter, Kt.1621, II. 177
Hay, Peter, Kt.1633, II. lxii.
Hay, Robert J., K.C.B.1894, I. 266
Hay, William G., earl of Erroll, G.C.H. 1830, I. 450; K.T.1834, I. 82
Hay, William M., marquess of Tweeddale, K.T.1898, I. 88
Hayes, Alexander, Kt.1608, II. 145
Hayes, George, Kt.1622, II. 178
Hayes, George, Kt.1868, II. 360
Hayes, Henry B., Kt.1790, II. 301
Hayes, James, Kt.1670, II. 244
Hayes (Hays), John, Kt.1829, II. 328
Hayes, Joseph, Kt.1619, II. 172
Hayes, Nicholas, Kt.1606, II. 140
Hayes, Thomas, Kt.1603, II. 123, 128
Hayman. See Hamond
Hayter, George, Kt.1842, II. 344
Haythorne, Edmund, K.C.B.1873, I. 254

HAYWARD, HEYWARD, HAYWARDE, HAWARD
Hayward, and see Howard
Heyward (Haward, Haywood), George, Kt.1604, II. 135
Heyward (Hayward), John, Kt.1609, II. 148
Hayward (Heyward), John, Kt.1619, II. 174

HAYWARD
  Haywarde, Rowlande, Kt.1570, II. 75
  Hayward, Thomas, Kt.1799, II. 304
  Hayward, William W., Kt.1897, II. 399
Head, Edmund W., K.C.B.1860, I. 282
Head, Francis B., K.H.1834, I. 470; K.C.H. 1835, I. 461; Kt.1831, II. 330
Head, George, Kt.1831, II. 331
Head, Thomas, Kt.1744, II. 286
Headfort, marquess of. See Taylour
Heale. See Hele
Heard, Isaac, Kt.1786, II. 299
Hearsay, John B., K.C.B.1857, I. 244
Heath, Edward, K.B.1661, I. 166
Heath, John, Kt.1664, II. 239
Heath, Leopold G., K.C.B.1868, I. 251
Heath, Richard, Kt.1686, II. 262
Heath, Robert, Kt.1621, II.176
Heath, Thomas, Kt.1677, II. 252
Heath, Thomas, Kt.1715, II. 280
Heathcote, Gilbert, Kt.1702, II. 273
Heathcote, Henry, Kt.1819, II. 320
Heathcote, John E., Kt.1784, II. 298
Heathfield, lord. See Elliott
HEBBURN, HEYBRON, HEBRON
  Hebburn, Ferdinando, Kt.1611, II. 151
  Heybron (Hebron), John, Kt.1627, II. 193
Hebdon, John, Kt.1663, II. 238
Heblethwayt, Thomas, Kt.1660, II. 228
Hector, James, K.C.M.G.1887, I. 371
Hedges, Charles, Kt.1689, II. 264
Hedges, alias Lacy, William, Kt.1688, II. 264
Hedley. See Hetley
Hedworth, John, Kt.1604, II. 130
Hedworth, Ralph, Kt.1523, II. 44
Hegarty, Daniel J., Kt.1900, II. 406
Hekyn, Richard, Kt.1347, II. 7
HELE, HEALE
  Heale, Francis, Kt.1608, II. 146
  Hele, John, Kt.1603, II. 114
  Hele (Heal), John, Kt.1639, II. 206
  Hele, Warwick, Kt.1603, II. 110

Hely, Henry, Kt.1643, II. 215
Hely, James P., K.H.1837, I. 477
Hely, John, Kt.1692, II. 267
Hely, John, Kt. Jacobite 1728, footnote, II. 266
Hely-Hutchinson, John, earl of Donoughmore, K.B.1801, I.175; G.C.B.1815, I. 180
Hely-Hutchinson, John, earl of Donoughmore, K.P.1834, I. 100
Hely-Hutchinson, John L. G., earl of Donoughmore, K.C.M.G.1879, I. 361
Hely-Hutchinson, Walter F., K.C.M.G. 1888, I. 373; G.C.M.G.1897, I. 345
Hellier, Samuel, Kt.1762, II. 291
Helmes, Henry, Kt.1603, II. 121
Helps, Arthur, K.C.B.1872, I. 285
Hemming, Augustus W. L., K.C.M.G. 1890, I. 375; G.C.M.G.1900, I. 346
Henden, John, Kt.1641, II. 210
Henderson, Edmund Y. W., K.C.B.1878, I. 286
Henderson (Hindersham), Francis, Kt. 1616, II. 157
Henderson, George A., K.H.1836, I. 473
Henderson, James, K.H.1836, I. 474
Henderson, James, Kt.1899, II. 404
Henderson, John W., K.H.1837, I. 477
Henderson, William, Kt.1893, II. 392
Henderson, William W., K.H.1835, I. 471
Henderson-Durham, Philip C., G.C.B. 1830, I. 186
Hene, Henry, Kt.1642, II. 215
Heneage, Algernon C. F., K.C.B.1892, I. 264; G.C.B.1902, I. 203
Heneage, George, Kt.1583, II. 82
Heneage, George, Kt.1607, II. 142
Heneage, Michael, Kt.1664, II. 239
Heneage, Thomas, Kt.1537, II. 50
Heneage, Thomas, Kt.1577, II. 78
Heneage, Thomas, Kt.1603, II. 117
Henle, Guyot de, sieur de la Mote, Kt. 1512, II. 35
Henley, Andrew, Kt.1660, II. 230
Henley, lord. See Eden
Henley, Robert, Kt.1663, II. 238
Henley, Robert, earl of Northington, Kt. 1756, II. 289

Henley, Robert, earl of Northington, K.T.1773, . 79 ;Grand Master K.P. 1783, I. 93
Henley (Hendley), Thomas, Kt.1605, II. 138
Hennell, Reginald, Kt.1902, II. 411
Hennessy, George R., K.C.B.1903, I. 276
Hennessy, John P., K.C.M.G.1880, I. 362
Henry IV., K.G.1377, I. 5
Henry V., Kt.(1399), I. lx; K.G.1399, I. 7
Henry VI., Kt.1426, II. 11; K.B.(1426), I. 130
Henry VIII., K.B.(1494), I. 144; K.G. 1495, I. 18
Henry Arsène, G.C.V.O.1896, II. 422
Henry, Thomas, Kt.1864, II. 357
Hensley, Robert M., Kt.1902, II. 413
Henslow, John, Kt.1793, II. 302
Henton (Fenton), William, Kt.1616, II. 159
Henyngham. See Heveningham

HERBERT, HARBERT, HARBORD, and see Harbord
 Herbert, Arnold, Kt.1617, II. 164
 Herbert, Arthur J., K.C.B.1882, I. 258
 Harbert (Herbert), Charles, Kt.1622, II. 180
 Herbert, Charles, commonly called lord Herbert of Shurland, K.B.1625-6, I. 160
 Herbert (Harbord), Charles, Kt.1636, II. 204
 Herbert, Charles L., Kt.1836, II. 338
 Herbert, Edward, Kt.1574, II. 76
 Herbert, Edward, Kt.1593, II. 90
 Herbert, Edward, lord Herbert of Chirbury, K.B.1603, I. 154
 Herbert, Edward, Kt.1641, II. 208
 Herbert, Edward, Kt.1684, II. 259
 Herbert, Edward H., earl of Powis, K.G.1844, I. 57
 Harbert, Francis, Kt.1550, II. 65
 Herbert, George, Kt.1487, II. 26
 Herbert, George, Kt.1630, II. 197
 Herbert, George A., earl of Pembroke, K.G.1805, I. 50
 Harbert, Gerrard, Kt. 1613, II. 153
 Herbert, lord Henry, Kt.1523, II. 45

HERBERT
 Herbert, Henry, earl of Pembroke, K.B.1553, I. 152; K.G.1574, I. 27
 Herbert, Henry, Kt.1617, II. 162
 Herbert, Henry, Kt.1623, II. 182
 Herbert, Henry H. M., earl of Carnarvon, Grand Master K.P.1885, I. 95
 Herbert, James, Kt.1680, II. 255
 Herbert, Jasper, Kt.1618, II. 167
 Harbert (Herbert), John, Kt.1617, II. 160
 Harbert, John, Kt.1662, II. 236
 Herbert, lord. See Somerset W.
 Herbert, Michael H., K.C.M.G.1902, I. 392; G.C.M.G.1903, I. 349
 Herbert, Percy, Kt.1622, II. 180
 Herbert, Percy E., K.C.B.1869, I. 252
 Herbert, Philip, earl of Pembroke, K.B.1603, I. 153; K.G.1608, I. 30
 Herbert, Philip, earl of Pembroke, K.B.1661, I. 163
 Herbert, Richard, Kt.1513, II. 41
 Herbert, Robert G. W., K.C.B.1882, I. 288; G.C.B.1892, I. 213
 Herbert, Sidney, earl of Pembroke, G.C.V.O.1896, I. 417
 Herbert, Thomas (John), Kt.1573, II. 75
 Herbert, Thomas, Kt.1658, II. 224
 Herbert, Thomas, earl of Pembroke, K.G.1700, I. 39
 Herbert, Thomas, K.C.B.1841, I. 237
 Herbert, Walter, K.B.(1475), I. 136
 Herbert, Walter, Kt.1482, II. 17
 Herbert, Walter, Kt.1542, II. 53
 Herbert, Walter, Kt.1549, II. 64
 Herbert, William, earl of Pembroke, K.B.(1449), I. 132; K.G.1461, I. 14
 Herbert, William, 1516, II. 43
 Herbert, William, earl of Pembroke, Kt.1543, II. 54; K.G.1549, I. 24
 Herbert, William, Kt.1549, II. 64
 Herbert William, Kt.1576, II. 77, 79
 Herbert, William, lord Herbert, earl of Pembroke, Kt.1596, II. 92; K.G. 1603, I. 30
 Herbert, William, lord Powis, K.B. 1603, I. 154

INDEX

HERBERT
Herbert, William, duke of Powis, K.G.
Jacobite 1692, footnote, I. 38
Herbillon, Emile, K.C.B.1856, I. 242
Hereford, earl of. See Bohun
Hereford, viscount. See Devereux
Hereford, James, Kt.1760, II. 289
Herham, Roger, Kt.1347, II. 6
Herne. See Heron

HERON, HERNE, HARNE, HEYRON
Heron (Herne), Edward, Kt.1603, II. 114
Heron, Edward, K.B.1603, I. 156
Heron, Henry, K.B.1661, I. 165
Heyron (Heron), John, Kt.1518, II. 43
Heron, John, Kt.1523, II. 44
Herne, Joseph, Kt.1690, II. 266
Heron, Joseph, Kt.1869, II. 361
Herne, Nathaniel, Kt.1674, II. 249
Heron, Nicholas, Kt.1566, II. 72
Heron, Roger, Kt.1482, II. 20
Hern (Harne), Thomas, Kt.1608, II. 145, 148
Heron, William, Kt.1623, II. 44
Herne, William, Kt.1797, II. 304
Herrick, Edmond, Kt.1603, II. 110
Herrick, William, Kt.1605, II. 137
Herries, Charles J., K.C.B.1880, I. 287
Herries (Heryk), John de, K.B.1306, I. 119
Herries, Robert, Kt.1774, II. 294
Herries, William L., K.C.H.1826, I. 455; Kt.1826, II. 326
Herriott, Frederick G., Kt.1822, II. 323
Herron, Robert, Kt.1887, II. 383; and see Heron
Herschell, Farrer, lord Herschell, Kt. 1880, II. 371; G.C.B.1893, I. 214
Herschel, John F. W., K.H.1831, I. 466; Kt.1831, II. 331
Herschell, William, K.H.1816, I. 463
Hersey (Hercy), John, Kt.1547, II. 60
Hertford, earl of. See Seymour E., marquess of; see Seymour W.; see Seymour - Conway; see Ingram-Seymour-Conway
Hertoghe, William de, lord of Ormaele, Kt.1615, II. 157

Hertslet, Edward, Kt.1878, II. 370; K.C.B.1892, I. 292
Hertzberg, Frederick A. de, K.C.B.1815, I. 226
Hervey. See Harvey
Herwick, John, Kt.1641, II. 210
Hesketh, Thomas, Kt.1603, II. 110
Heskett, Thomas, Kt.1553, II. 68

HESSE
Alexandre L. G. F. E., prince of, G.C.B.1885, I. 198
Ernest L. C. A. W., grand duke of, G.C.B.1887, I. 212; K.G.1892, I. 69; Victorian Chain 1902, I. 415
Frederic C. L. C., prince of, G.C.B. 1897, I. 214
Louis III. of, K.G.1865, I. 63
Louis IV. of, K.G.1862, I. 61
Henry L. W. A. W. A., prince of, G.C.B.1892, I. 200

HESSE-CASSEL
Frederick of, K.G.1740-1, I. 43
William of, K.G.1786, I. 48

HESSE-HOMBURG
Louis W. F. of, G.C.B.1836, I. 187

HESSE-PHILIPPSTHAL-BARCHFELD
Ernest F. F. C. W. P. L., prince of, G.C.B.1835, I. 187
Hetchetter (Hochstetter, Hechstetter), David, Kt. 1714, II. 279

HETLEY, HEDLEY
Hetley, Richard, Kt.1800, II. 305
Hedley (Hetley), Thomas, Kt.1623, II. 183
Heward, Simon, Kt.1837, II. 339

HEVENINGHAM, HENYNGHAM, HEYGHAM, HEVENYNGHAM, HENNINGHAM
Henyngham, Anthony, Kt.1547, II. 59
Heveningham (Heygham), Arthur, Kt. 1578, II. 78
Hevenyngham, John, Kt.1414, II. 11
Henningham, John, Kt.1471, II. 16
Henyngham, John, K.B.(1465), I. 135
Heveningham, John, Kt.1603, II. 107
Heveningham, Walter, Kt.1619, II. 170
Heveningham, William, Kt.1674, II. 249
Hewer. See Haward

HEWETT, HEWITT, HEWET, HEWYTT, HUET
  Hewett, George, G.C.B.1820, I. 185
  Huet (Hewett), John, Kt.1605, I. 136
  Hewitt, Thomas, Kt.1904, II. 417
  Hewet, Thomas, Kt.1613, II. 154
  Hewit, Thomas, Kt.1641, II. 209
  Hewet, Thomas, Kt.1719, II. 281
  Hewet, William, Kt.1559, I. 70
  Hewet, William, Kt.1606, II. 140
  Hewytt, William, Kt.1660, II. 232
  Hewett, Wiliam N. W., K.C.B.1874, I. 254; K.C.S.I.1882, I. 323
Hewley, John, Kt.1663, II. 238; and see Howley
Hewson, John, Kt.1657, II. 224; and see Howson
Hext (Hex), Edward, Kt.1604, II. 132
Hext, John, K.C.I.E.1897, I. 409
Heybron. See Hebburn
Heyden, Louis, count von, K.C.B.1828, I. 230
Heydon. See Haydon
Heygham. See Heveningham
Heyman. See Hamond
Heytesbury, lord. See A'Court
Heyward. See Hayward
Hibbert, Henry F., Kt.1903, II. 414
Hibbert, John T., K.C.B.1893, I. 293
Hibbotts, Thomas, Kt.1618, II. 170
Hickford (Higford), John, Kt.1591, II. 88, 89
HICKMAN, HYCKMAN
  Hickman, Alfred, Kt.1891, II. 388
  Hyckman, William, Kt.1603, II. 103
Hicks, Baptist, Kt.1603, II. 127
Hicks, Elias (Ellis), Kt. 1635, II. 204
Hicks, Francis, Kt.1871, II. 363
Hicks, Henry, Kt.1734, II. 284
Hicks, Michael, Kt.1604, II. 135
Hickson, Joseph, Kt.1890, II. 386
Hide. See Hyde
Higeton, John de, K.B.1306, I. 121
HIGGINS, HIGGONS
Higgins, Samuel G., K.H.1830, I. 465; K.C.H.1834, I. 460
Higgins (Higgons), Thomas, Kt.1663, II. 238
Higgons, Thomas, Kt. Jacobite 1713, footnote, II. 266

Higgins, Warner W., K.H.1834, I. 470
Higginson, George W. A., K.C.B.1889, I. 262; G.C.B.1903, I. 204
Higginson, James M., K.C.B.1857, I. 280
HIGHAM, HYGHAM
  Hygham (Higham), Clement, Kt.1554, II. 69
  Higham, Clement (John), Kt.1591, II. 88
  Higham, John, Kt.1579, II. 80
  Higham, Richard, Kt.1623, II. 181
  Higham, Thomas, K.C.I.E.1902, I. 411
Higs, Roger, Kt.1633, II. 201
Hilditch, Edward, Kt. 1865, II. 358
HILDYARD, HILLYARD, HYLYARD, HILLYAR, HILLIER, HELYARDE, HILLARD
  Hylyarde, Christopher, Kt.1533, I. 49
  Hylyard (Hillyard), Christopher, Kt. 1578, II. 78
  Hillyard (Haward, Hellyard), Christopher, Kt.1603, II. 100
  Hillyar, Charles F., K.C.B.1887, II. 261
  Hildyard, Henry J. T., K.C.B.1900, I. 272
  Hillyar, James, K.C.H.1834, I. 460
  Hillyar, John, K.C.B.1840, I. 236
  Hildeyard, Robert de, K.B.1306, I. 119
  Hilyard (Helyarde), Robert, Kt.1482, II. 20
  Hillyar, Robert P., K.H.1837, I. 479
  Hillier, Walter C., K.C.M.G.1897, I. 383
  Hillard (Hilliard), William, Kt.1603, II. 113
HILL, HYLL
  Hill, Adam, Kt.1617, II. 163
  Hill, Arthur B. S. T., marquess of Downshire, K.P.1831, I. 100
  Hill, Arthur W. B. S. T. W., marquess of Downshire, K.P.1859, I. 102
  Hill, Clement L., K.C.M.G.1887, I. 372
  Hill, Dudley St. L., Kt.1816, II. 318; K.C.B.1848, I. 238
  Hill, Edward, Kt.1722, II. 282
  Hill, Edward S., K.C.B.1892, I. 292
  Hill, Hugh, Kt.1859, II. 354
  Hill, James, Kt.1873, II. 365

HILL
  Hill John, Kt.1831, II. 330
  Hill, John E. G., Kt.1904, II. 417
  Hill, Moses, Kt.1616, II. 160
  Hill, Robert C., Kt.1812, II. 311
  Hill, Roger, Kt.1668, II. 243
  Hyll, Rowland, Kt.1542, II. 53
  Hill, Rowland, viscount Hill, K.B. 1812, I. 178; G.C.B.1815, I. 181; G.C.H.1816, I. 448
  Hill, Rowland, K.C.B.1860, I. 281
  Hill, Stephen J., K.C.M.G.1874, I. 357
  Hyll, Thomas, Kt.1484, II. 22
  Hyll (Hill), Thomas, Kt.1603, II. 112
  Hill, Thomas N., Kt.1814, II. 314; K.C.B.1815, I. 225
  Hill, Wiliam, Kt.1604, II. 134
  Hill, Wiliam, Kt.1619, II. 174
  Hill, William, Kt.1682, II. 258
  Hill, William, K.C.S.I.1867, I. 318
  Hillary, Roger Kt.1336, II. 5
HILLERSDEN, HILDERSTON
  Hilderston (Hillersdon), James, Kt. 1623, II. 182
  Hillersden, Thomas, Kt.1622, II. 180
  Hillesley, Francis, Kt.1603, II. 124
  Hillier. See Hildyard
  Hillman, William, Kt.1786, II. 299
  Hills, James, K.C.B.1881, I. 257
  Hills, John, K.C.B.1900, I. 271
  Hills-Johnes, James, G.C.B.1893, I. 200
HILTON, HYLTON
  Hilton, Thomas, Kt.1523, II. 44
  Hylton, William, Kt.1570, II. 74
  Hime, Albert H., K.C.M.G.1900, I. 387
  Hincks, Francis, K.C.M.G.1869, I. 354

HINDE, HYNDE
  Hinde, Edward, Kt.1615, II. 157
  Hynde, Francys, Kt.1578, II. 78
  Hinde (Hynde), John, Kt.1545, II. 58
  Hinde, Samuel V., K.C.B.1831, I. 231
  Hynde, Wiliam, Kt.1603, II. 105
  Hindmarsh, John, K.H.1836, I. 475; Kt.1851, II. 348
  Hingston, Wiliam H., Kt.1895, II. 395
  Hinrich, Henry B., Kt.1831, II. 330
  Hintley (Huntley), Richard, Kt.1603, II. 111

HINTON, HYNTON
  Hynton, Anthony, Kt.1620, II. 175
  Hinton, John de, K.B.1306, I. 116
  Hinton, Thomas, Kt.1619, II. 172
  Hinuber, Henry de, K.C.B.1815, I. 226
  Hippesley (Hepsley), John, Kt.1617, II. 162
  Hislop, Thomas, K.C.B.1818, I. 228; G.C.B.1818, I. 184
  Hitchins, Edward, Kt.1812, II. 311
  Hitchman (Hitcham), Robert, Kt.1604, II. 133
  Hoare, Richard, Kt.1702, II. 273
  Hoare, Richard, Kt.1745, II. 287
  Hobart, Henry, Kt.1671, II. 246
  Hobart, John, Kt.1611, II. 151
  Hobart, John, earl of Buckinghamshire, K.B.1725, I. 168
  Hobart (Hoberd), Miles, Kt.1623, II.182; K.B.1626, I. 163
  Hobart, Nathaniel, Kt.1661, II. 235
  Hobart, Richard, Kt.1633, II. 202
  Hobart, Robert H., K.C.V.O.(1902), I. 435

HOBBY, HOBY
  Hobby, Charles, Kt.1705, II. 274
  Hobby, Edward, Kt.1582, II. 81
  Hobby, Philippe, Kt.1545 II. 56
  Hobby, Thomas, Kt.1566, II. 72
  Hoby, Thomas P., Kt.1594, II. 91
  Hobby, William, Kt.1622, II. 179
  Hobhouse, Arthur, lord Hobhouse, K.C.S.I.1877, I. 321
  Hobhouse, John C., lord Broughton, G.C.B.1852, I. 208
  Hobson, Thomas, Kt.1702, II. 273
  Hochstetter. See Hetchetter
  Hocking, Henry H., Kt.1895, II. 396
  Hodeston. See Holdiston
  Hodge, Edward C., K.C.B.1873, I. 254; G.C.B.1887, I. 199
  Hodges, George L., K.C.B.1860, I. 281
  Hodges, James, Kt.1759, II. 289
  Hodges, Nathaniel, Kt.1727, II. 283
  Hodges, William, Kt.1858, II. 352
  Hodgkinson, George E., Kt.1851, II. 348

HODGSON, HODSON, and see Hudson
  Hodgson, Arthur, K.C.M.G.1886, I. 369
  Hodson, Christopher, Kt.1603, II. 125
  Hodgson, Edward M., Kt.1901, II. 408
  Hodgson, Frederick M., K.C.M.G.1899, I. 386
  Hodgson, Richard, Kt.1795, II. 303
  Hodgson, Robert, Kt.1869, II. 361
  Hodgson. See Hudson
Hodie, William, Kt.1487, II. 23
Hodleston, Richard, Kt.1482, II. 18
Hoffman, Cornelius, Kt.1609, II. 148, 150; Kt.1610-11, II. 150
Hoffmeister, Wiliam C., Kt.1884, II. 376
Hogan, —, Kt.1545, II. 58
Hogg, Adam G. F., K.C.B.1904, I. 276
Hogg, Frederick R., K.C.I.E.1888, I. 405
Hogg, Stuart S., Kt.1876, II. 367
Hogg. See McGarel-Hogg
Hogge, John, K.H.1837, I. 476

HOHENLOHE-LANGENBURG
  Ernest C. C., prince of, G.C.B.1848, I. 208
  Ernest W. F. C. M., prince of, G.C.B.1897, I. 215
  Herman E. F. B., prince of, K.C.B.1866, I. 283; G.C.B.1867, I. 210
  Victor, F., &c., of, G.C.B.1887, I. 212
Holand. See Holland
Holbeech, Laurence de, K.B.1306, I. 115
Holborn, Robert, Kt.1644, II. 217
Holcroft, Henry, Kt.1622, II. 178
Holcroft, John, K.B.1847, I. 152
Holcroft, John, Kt.1547, II. 62
Holcroft, Thomas, Kt.1544, II. 54
Holcroft, Thomas, Kt.1603, II. 100
Holder, Frederick W., K.C.M.G.1902, I. 392
Holdich, Edward A., K.C.B.1875, I. 255; G.C.B.1904, I. 204
Holdich, Thomas H., K.C.I.E.1897, I.409; K.C.M.G.1902, I. 393
Holdilston (Hodeston), John, Kt.1489, II. 27
Holford. See Halford
Holker, John, Kt.1874, II. 366
Hollams, John, Kt.1831, II. 331
Hollams, John, Kt.1902, II. 413

HOLLAND, HOLAND
  William VI., count of, K.G.1390, I. 6
  Holland, earl of. See Rich
  Holand, Edmond de, earl of Kent, K.G. 1403, I. 8
  Holand, Henry, son of the earl of Huntington, Kt. 1439, II. 12
  Holland, Henry T., viscount Knutsford, K.C.M.G.1877, I. 358; G.C.M.G.1886, I. 340
  Holand, John, duke of Exeter, K.G. 1381, I. 5
  Holand, John, duke of Exeter, K.B. (1413), I. 129; K.G.1415, I 9
  Holand, Otho, K.G.1348, I. 2
  Holand, Richard, K.B.(1413), I. 129
  Holland, Richard, Kt.1544, II. 55
  Holand, Thomas, earl of Kent, K.G. 1344, I. 1
  Holand, Thomas de, earl of Kent, K.G. 1376, I. 4
  Holand, Thomas de, duke of Surrey, K.G.1397, I. 7
  Holland, Thomas, Kt.1608, II. 145
  Holland, Thomas, Kt.1622, II. 179
  Holland, William de, K.B.1306, I. 118
  Holland, William H., Kt.1902, II. 411
HOLLES, HOLLIS, HOLES, HALES, HOLLEYS
  Hollis (Holes, Hales), Charles, Kt.1604, II. 133
  Hollis, George (John), Kt.1609, II. 148
  Hollis, Jervis, Kt.1621, II. 176
  Holles, John, Kt.1593, II. 90
  Holles, John, duke of Newcastle, K.G. 1698, I. 39
  Holleys, Thomas, Kt.1547, II. 60
  Hollyes, William, Kt.1538, II. 51
  Holleys, William, Kt.1547, II. 60
Holloway, Charles, Kt.1803, II. 306
Holloway, Richard, Kt.1683, II. 259
Holloway, Thomas, K.C.B.1867, I. 251
Holman, Constantine, Kt.1904, II. 417
Holmeden (Hamdaine), Edward, Kt. 1603, II. 128
Holmeden (Hamsden), Thomas, Kt.1622, II. 180
Holmes, George, K.C.B.1815, I. 227
Holmes, Robert, Kt.1666, II. 242
Holmes, Robert W. A., K.C.B.1902, I. 300
Holmes, Stephen, K.H.1832, I. 468
Holmes, William H., Kt.1856, II. 351

INDEX

Holmes, William R., Kt.1877, II. 369
Holroyd, Charles, Kt.1903, II. 416
Holroyd, Edward D., Kt.1903, II. 416
Holroyd, George S., Kt.1816, II. 317

HOLSTEIN
   Adolphus, duke of, K.G.1560, I. 26
   Ulric, duke of, K.G.1605, I. 30
Holt, John, K.B.1385, I. 126
Holt, John, Kt.1686, II. 261
Holt, Thomas, Kt.1544, II. 55
Holt, Thomas, Kt.1603, II. 101
Holt, Thomas, Kt.1680, II. 254
Holworthy, Matthew (Martin), Kt.1665, II. 241
Holywood, Robert, Kt.(1361), II. lx.
Holzmann, Maurice, K.C.V.O.(1901), I. 433
Homan, William J., Kt.1799, II. 305
Home, Anthony D., K.C.B.1874, I. 255
Home, earl of. See Douglas-Home
Home, George, earl of Dunbar, K.G.1608, I. 30
Home, John, earl Home, Kt.1623, II. 182
Homfray, Jeremiah, Kt.1809, II. 309
Hompesch, Graf, K.C.H.1821, I. 455
Honner, Robert W., K.C.B.1865, I. 250

HONYWOOD, HONIWOOD
   Honywood, John, Kt.1619, II. 172
   Honywood, Philip, K.B.1743, I. 169
   Honiwood, Robert, Kt.1625, II. 188, 192
   Honywood, Thomas, Kt.1604, II. 133
   Honiwood, Thomas, Kt.1632, II. 200
Hoo, Robert de, K.B.1306, I. 119
Hoo, Thomas, baron of Hoo, K.G.1445, I. 12
Hood, Alexander, Kt.1812, II. 311
Hood, Alexander, viscount Bridport, K.B.1788, I. 174
Hood, Alexander N., viscount Bridport, K.C.B.1885, I. 289; G.C.B.1891, I. 213
Hood, Arthur W. A., K.C.B.1885, I. 259; G.C.B.1889, I. 200
Hood, Samuel, K.B.1804, I. 176
Hood, Samuel, viscount Hood, G.C.B. 1815, I. 182

Hood, William C., Kt.1868, II. 360
Hoode. See Hoord
Hoody, Alexander, Kt.1460, II. 13
Hooke (Hookes), Humphrey, Kt.1661, II. 233
Hooker, Joseph D., K.C.S.I.1877, I. 321; G.C.S.I.1897, I. 314
Hooker, William, Kt.1666, II. 241
Hooker, William J., K.H.1836, I. 475; Kt.1836, II. 337
Hooper, Edward, Kt.1665, II. 241
Hooper, Nicholas, Kt.1713, II. 278
Hooper, Thomas, Kt.1644, II. 218
Hooper, William R., K.C.S.I.1903, I. 328
Hoord (Hoode), Thomas, Kt.1619, II. 174
Hope, Alexander, K.B.1813, I. 179; G.C.B.1815, I. 182
Hope, Charles, earl of Hopetoun, K.T. 1728, I. 78
Hope, George, K.C.B.1815, I. 220
Hope, Henry, K.C.B.1855, I. 241
Hope, James, K.C.B.1860, I. 246; G.C.B. 1865, I. 194
Hope, James A., K.C.B.1815, I. 225; G.C.B.1861, I. 193
Hope, John, G.C.H.1820, I. 449; Kt.1821, II. 322
Hope, John, earl of Hopetoun, K.B.1809, I. 177; G.C.B.1815, I. 181
Hope, John A. L., marquess of Linlithgow, G.C.M.G.1889, I. 342; G.C.V.O.1900, 418; K.T.1900, I. 88
Hope, John C., K.H.1833, I. 469
Hope, Roger, Kt.1622, II. 179
Hope, Theodore C., K.C.S.I.1886, I. 323
Hope, Thomas, Kt.1628, II. 194
Hope, Thomas, Kt.1633, II. lxiii.
Hope, William, K.C.B.1897, I. 267
Hope, William J., K.C.B.1815, I. 220; G.C.B.1825, I. 185
Hopkins, John, Kt.1792, II. 301
Hopkins, John O., K.C.B.1892, I. 264; G.C.B.1899, I. 202
Hopkins, John P., K.H.1836, I. 474; Kt. 1867, II. 359
Hopkins, Richard, Kt.1660, II. 231
Hopkins, Richard, Kt.1722, II. 282
Hopkins, Thomas, Kt.1605, II. 139

Hopkins, William, Kt.1628, II. 194
Hopkinson, Charles, Kt.1837, II. 338
Hopson, Charles, Kt.1709, II. 276
Hopton, Arthur, Kt.1513, II. 41
Hopton, Arthur, K.B.1603, I. 155
Hopton, Arthur, Kt.1638, II. 205
Hopton, Edward, Kt.1645, II. 220
Hopton, Edward, K.C.B.1900, I. 271
Hopton, George, Kt.1487, II. 24
Hopton, Ingram, Kt.1642, II. 213
Hopton, Owen, Kt.1561, II. 71
Hopton, Ralph, Kt.1626, II. 162
Hopton, Rauf, Kt.1545, II. 57
Hopton, Richard, Kt.1604, II. 136
Hopton, Roger, Kt.1497, II. 31
Hopton, Thomas, Kt.1633, II. 201
Hopton, William, Kt.1483, II. 21
Hopetoun, earl of. See Hope
Hopwood, Francis J. S., K.C.B.1901, I. 298

HORN, HORNE
  Horn, Frederick, K.C.B.1869, I. 252; G.C.B.1889, I. 199
  Horne, John de, K.B.1303, I. 110
  Horne, Thomas, Kt.1609, II. 148
  Horn, William, Kt.1487, II. 26
  Horne, William, Kt.1830, II. 329
  Horne, William C. van, K.C.M.G.1894, I. 380

Hornby, Edmund G., Kt.1862, II. 356
Hornby, Geoffrey T. P., K.C.B.1878, I. 256; G.C.B.1885, I. 198
Hornby, Phipps, G.C.B.1861, I. 193; K.C.B.1852, I. 239
Hornby, William W., K.C.B.1892, I. 292
Horner, George, Kt.1660, II. 229
Horner, John, Kt.1574, II. 76
Horner, John, Kt.1614, II. 154
Horrell, Edmund, Kt.1603, II. 112
Horse, Peter de la, K.B.1324, I. 123
Horsey, Algernon F. R. de, K.C.B.1903, I. 276
Horsey, Edward, Kt.1577, II. 78
Horsey, George, Kt.1619, II. 171
Horsey, Jerom (Jeremy), Kt.1603, II. 126
Horsey, John, Kt.1547, II. 60
Horsey, John, Kt.1574, II. 76
Horsey, Ralph, Kt.1591, II. 88
Horsey, Thomas, Kt.1586, II. 85
Horsfall, Cyprian, Kt.1628, II. 194
Horsford, Alfred H., K.C.B.1860, I. 246; G.C.B.1875, I. 197
Horsford, John, K.C.B.1815, I. 227
Horsford, Robert M., Kt.1841, II. 343
Horseley, John, Kt.1547, II. 61
Horsley, Victor A. H., Kt.1902, II. 411
Horsman, Thomas, Kt.1604, II. 130
Horton, John, Kt.1610, II. 149
Horton (Halton), Robert (Roger), Kt. 1603, II. 122
Horton, Robert W., G.C.H.1831, I. 451; Kt.1831, II. 330
Horwolle (Horwood), Thomas, Kt.1603, II. 121
Horwoll. See Hartwell
Horwood William, Kt.1604, II. 134
Horwood, William H., Kt.1904, II. 420
Horwood. See Whorwood
Hose, Hugh, K.B.1306, I. 119

HOSKINS, HOSKYNS
  Hoskins, Anthony H., K.C.B.1882, I. 258; G.C.B.1893, I. 200
  Hoskins, Edmund, Kt.1662, II. 236
  Hoskyns (Hoskins), John, Kt.1676, II. 251
  Hoskins (Hopkins), Thomas, Kt.1605, II. 139
  Hoskyns, William, Kt.1668, II. 243

Hoste, George, Kt.1830, II. 329
Hoste, William, K.C.B.1815, II. 222

HOTHAM, HOTHOME, HOTHOM
  Hotham, Beaumont, lord Hotham, Kt. 1775, II. 294
  Hotham, Charles, K.C.B.1846, I. 238
  Hotham (afterwards Hotham-Thompson), Charles, K.B.1772, I. 171
  Hotham, Charles F., K.C.B.1895, I. 266; G.C.V.O.1901, I. 419; G.C.B. 1902, I. 204
  Hothome, Francis, Kt.1544, II. 56
  Hotham, Henry, K.C.B.1815, I. 221, G.C.M.G.1831, I. 332
  Hotham, John de, K.B.1327, I. 125
  Hothom, John, Kt.1497, II. 31
  Hothom, John, Kt.1513, II. 37
  Hothom, John, Kt.1617, II. 162
  Hotham, Richard, Kt.1769, II. 293

INDEX

HOTHAM
Hotham, William, K.C.B.1815, I. 221; G.C.B.1840, I. 189
Hotham, William, K.H.1836, I. 475
Houblethorne, Henry, Kt.1546-7, II. 58
Houblon, James, Kt.1692, II. 267
Houblon, John, Kt.1689, II. 265
Houblon, Richard, Kt.1715, II. 280
HOUGHTON, HAUGHTON
Houghton. See Halton
Houghton, Alexander, Kt.1482, II. 18
Houghton, baron. See Milnes
Houghton (Haughton), Gilbert, Kt. 1604, II. 134
Haughton, Graves C., K.H.1833, I. 469; Kt.1833, II. 334
Haughton, Richard, Kt.1600, II. 98
Houghton, Robert, Kt.1613, II. 153
Houghton, William, Kt.1482, II. 18
Houlton, Edward V. L., K.C.M.G.1860, I. 354; G.C.M.G.1868, I. 336
Houlton George (William C.), Kt.1838, II. 340
Houstoun, Robert, K.C.B.1837, I. 233
Houstoun, William, K.C.B.1815, I. 218; G.C.H.1827, I. 450; G.C.B.1831, I. 186
Hovell, William, Kt.1660, I. 227
HOWARD, HAWARD, HOWARDE, HAYWARD
Howard, Andrew C., K.C.B.1902, I. 300
Howard, Bernard E., duke of Norfolk, K.G.1834, I. 54
Howard, Cecil, Kt.1651, II. 222
Howard, Charles, Kt.1544, II. 55
Howard, Charles, earl of Nottingham, K.G.1575, I. 27
Howard (Haward), Charles, Kt.1603, II. 105
Howard, Charles, Kt.1611, II. 150, 152
Howard, Charles (son of the earl of Nottingham), Kt.1623, II. 181, 184
Howard, Charles, earl of Berkshire, K.B.1626, I. 161
Howard, Charles, Kt.1635, II. 203
Howard, Charles (son to William, lord Howard), Kt.1639, II. 206
Howard, Charles, K.B.1749, I. 169
Howard (Andrew), Charles, Kt.1897, II. 401

HOWARD
Haward, Christopher, Kt.1603, II. 100
Howard, Edmund, Kt.1513, II. 37
Howard, Edward, Kt.1497, II. 31; K.G.1513, I. 20
Howard (Haward), Edward, Kt.1603, II. 105
Howard, Edward, K.B.1616, I. 159
Howard, Francis, Kt.1604, II. 133
Howard, Francis, Kt.1617, II. 160
Howard, Francis, K.C.B.1900, I. 272
Howard, Frederick, earl of Carlisle, K.T.1767, I. 79; K.G.1793, I. 49
Howard, Frederick, Kt.1895, II. 395
Howarde, George, Kt.1547, II. 62
Howard, George, K.B.1774, I. 172
Howard, George, earl of Carlisle, K.G. 1837, I. 55
Howard, George W. F., earl of Carlisle, K.G.1855, I.59; Grand Master K.P. 1855, I. 94
Howard, Henry, earl of Surrey, Kt. 1538, II. 51; K.G.1541, I. 23
Howard, Henry, earl of Northampton, K.G.1605, I. 30
Howard, Henry, duke of Norfolk, K.G.1685, I. 38
Howard, Henry, earl of Carlisle, K.G. 1756, I. 45
Howard, Henry, earl of Berkshire, K.G.1778, I. 47
Howard, Henry, K.C.M.G.1899, I. 386
Howard, Henry C., duke of Norfolk, K.G.1848, I. 58
Howard, Henry F., earl of Arundel, K.B.1616, I. 159
Howard, Henry F., K.C.B.1863, I. 283; G.C.B.1872, I. 210
Howard, James, lord Maltravers, K.B. 1616, I. 159
Howard, James, earl of Suffolk, K.B. 1625-6, I. 161
Howard, John, duke of Norfolk, K.B. 1461, II. 13; K.G.1472, I. 15
Howard, Kenneth A., earl of Effingham, K.C.B.1815, I.219; G.C.B.1820, I.184
Howard, Philip, Kt.1604, II. 134
Howard, Philip, Kt.1660, II. 226
Howard, Richard N., Kt.1886, II. 379

INDEX

HOWARD
Howard, Robert, K.B.1616, I. 159
Howard, Robert, Kt.1644, II. 218
Howard, Thomas, earl of Surrey, duke of Norfolk, Kt.1477, II. 17; K.B. 1478, I. 138; K.G.1483, I. 16
Howard, lord Thomas, duke of Norfolk, Kt.1497, II. 31; K.G.1510, I. 20
Howard, lord Thomas, Kt.1547, II. 61
Howard, Thomas, earl of Surrey, duke of Norfolk, K.B.1553, I. 152; K.G. 1559, I. 26
Howard, Thomas, lord Howard, earl of Suffolk, Kt.1588, II. 86; K.G.1597, I. 29
Haward, alias Hewer, Thomas, Kt. 1605, II. 139
Howard, Thomas, earl of Berkshire, K.B.1605, II. 157; K.G.1625, I. 32
Howard, Thomas, viscount Howard of Bindon, K.G.1606, I. 30
Howard, Thomas, earl of Norfolk, K.G.1611, I. 30
Howard, Theophilus, earl of Suffolk, K.G.1627, I. 32
Howard, Thomas P., K.H.1837, I. 476
Howard, lord William, Kt.1523, II. 44
Howard, William, lord Howard of Effingham, K.G.1554, I. 25
Howard, William, Kt.1596, II. 92
Howard, William, K.B.1616, I. 159
Howard, William (son of lord William), Kt.1623, II. 183
Howard, William, K.B.1626, I. 161
Howard, William, Kt.1637, II. 205
Howard (Hayward), William, Kt.1643, II. 216
Howard, William, earl of Wicklow, K.P.1842, I. 101
Howard de Walden. See Griffin; see Ellis
Howden, lord. See Caradoc

HOWE, How
Howe, earl. See Curzon; see Curzon-Howe
How, Richard, Kt.1678, II. 253
Howe, Richard, earl Howe, K.G.1797, I. 49
Howe, Scrope, Kt.1663, II. 237

HOWE
Howe, Thomas G., Kt.1660, II. 232
Howe, William, viscount Howe, K.B. 1776, I. 172
HOWELL, HOWEL
Howell, George, Kt.1719, II. 281
Howell, Hugh, K.B.1306, I. 116
Howell, John, Kt.1619, II. 172
Howell, John, Kt.1668, II. 243
Howel, Richard, Kt.1641, II. 208
Howell, Thomas, Kt.1876, II. 367
Howland, Giles, Kt.1603, II. 124
Howland, John, Kt.1617, II. 161
Howland, Matthew, Kt.1633, II. 201
Howland, William P., K.C.M.G.1879, I. 361
Howlett, Arthur, K.C.B.1896, I. 266
Howley, John, Kt.1865, II. 357
Howse, Henry G., Kt.1902, II. 411
Howson, William, Kt.1603, II. 125; and see Hewson
Howth, earl of. See St. Lawrence
Howth, lord Nicholas, Kt.1494, II. 28
HOWORTH, HOWARTH
Howorth, Edward, K.C.B.1815, I. 219; G.C.H.1817, I. 448
Howorth, Henry H., K.C.I.E.,1892, I. 407
Howarth (Howorth), Humphry, Kt. 1715, II. 280
Howycheke, Richard, Kt.1523, II. 44
Hoy, James, Kt.1902, II. 413
Hoye, John, Kt.1641, II. 211
Hoyles, Hugh W., Kt.1869, II. 360
Hozier, Henry M., K.C.B.1903, I. 300
HUBBERT, HUBERT, HOBART, HUBBERD, HUBARD, HUBBARD, HUBAND
Huband (Hubbert), John, Kt.1574, II. 76
Hubert (Hobart), Henry, Kt.1603, II. 114
Hubert, James, Kt.1504, II. 34; K.B. 1504, I. 147
Hubert, John, Kt.1574, II. 76
Hubert (Hubbert), John, Kt.1603, II. 124
Hubert (Hobart, Hubart, Hubbarde), Thomas, Kt.1603, II. 109
Hubberd, Walter, Kt.1536, II. 50

INDEX

Hubblethorne. See Houblethorne
Huddart, Joseph, Kt.1821, II. 322
HUDDLESTON, HUDLESTON
Hudleston, Henry (Edmond), Kt.1579, II. 80
Hudleston, John, K.B.1533, II. 149
Huddleston, John, Kt 1553, II. 66
Huddleston, John W., Kt.1875, II. 367
HUDSON, HODGSON, and see Hodgson
Hudson, James, K.C.B.1855, I. 279; G.C.B.1863, I. 209
Hudson, John, K.C.B.1885, I. 259
Hudson (Hodgson), Robert, Kt.1624, II. 187
Hudson, Roger, Kt.1721, II. 282
Hudson, Thomas, Kt.1677, II. 252
Hudson, Walter, Kt.1787, II. 300
Hudson, William, Kt.1603, II. 123
Hudson, William B., K.C.I.E.1893, I. 407
Huet. See Hewett
Hügel, baron von, K.C.B.1827, I. 230
Hugeson, William, Kt.1660, II. 230
Hugford, Walter de, K.B.1306, I. 112
Huggins, William, K.C.B.1897, I. 296
Huggon, Thomas, Kt.1605, II. 137
Hughes, Edward, Kt.1773, II. 294; K.B. 1778, I. 172
Hughes, Edwin, Kt.1902, II. 414
Hughes, Frederic, Kt.1858, II. 353
Hughes, Robert J., K.C.B.1894, I. 265
Hughes, Thomas (George), Kt.1619, II. 174
Hughes, Thomas, Kt.1898, II. 402
Hughes, Walter W., Kt.1880, II. 372
Hughes, William B., Kt.1803, II. 307
Hughes, William T., K.C.B.1891, I. 263
Huish, Richard, K.B.1306, I. 119
Huizon (Husseyn), John, Kt.1624, II. 184
Hulett, James L., Kt.1902, II. 411
Hull, Edward, K.G.1453, I. 13
Hull, Richard, Kt.1678, II. 253
Hull, William, Kt.1621, II. 176
Hullock, John, Kt.1812, II. 310
Hullock, John, Kt.1823, II. 324
Hulse, Samuel, G.C.H.1819, I. 449; Kt. 1821, II. 323
Hulsteyn, Willem van, Kt.1902, II. 411

Hume, Alexander, Kt.1619, II. 172
Hume, Andrew, Kt.1618, II. 168
Hume, Gustavus, Kt.1880, II. 372
Hume, Robert, K.C.B. 1887, I. 261; G.C.B.1902, I. 203
Hume, Thomas, Kt.1665, II. 241
Hume-Campbell, Alexander, earl of Marchmont, K.T.1725, I. 77
HUMPHERY, HUMPHREY, HUMPHRY
Humphry, George M., Kt.1891, II. 388
Humfrey, Thomas, Kt.1581, II. 81
Humphrey, Thomas, Kt.1603, II. 115
Humphery, William H., K.C.B.1892, I. 292
Humphreys, John, Kt.1881, II. 373
Humphreys, Salusbury P., Kt.1834, II. 334
Humphreys, William, Kt.1704, II. 274
HUNCKES, HUNCKS
Huncks, Henry, Kt.1643, II. 215
Hunckes, Thomas, Kt.1605, II. 139
Huncks, Thomas, Kt.1626, II. 191
Hungate, Henry, Kt.1619, II. 171
Hungate, William, Kt.1617, II. 162
HUNGERFORD, HUNGERFORDE
Hungerford, —, Kt.1492, II. 28
Hungerforde, Anthony, Kt.1513, II. 40
Hungerforde, Anthony, Kt.1606, II. 141; Kt.1608, II. 144
Hungerford, Edmond [? Robert], K.B. 1426, I. 131
Hungerforde, Edward, Kt.1513, II. 39
Hungerford, Edward, Kt.1601, II. 99
Hungerford, Edward, K.B.1626, I. 162
Hungerford, Edward, K.B.1661, I. 165
Hungerforde, Giles, Kt.1676, II. 251
Hungerforde, John, Kt.1497, II. 30
Hungerforde, John, Kt.1574, II. 76
Hungerford, John, Kt.1591, II. 88
Hungerford, Thomas, K.B.(1487), I. 142
Hungerford, Walter, lord Hungerford, K.B.(1400), I. 129; K.G.1420, I. 10
Hungerforde, Walter, Kt.1485, II. 22
Hunlock (Hunloke), Henry, Kt.1643, II. 215

Hunnam (Hannam, Hamman), John, Kt.1603, II. 105
Hunsdon, lord. See Carey
HUNTE, HUNT
  Hunt, George Le, Kt.1609, II. 147
  Hunte, George R. Le, K.C.M.G.1903, I. 394
  Hunt, Henry A., Kt.1876, II. 368
  Hunt, John, Kt.1611, II. 151
  Hunt, Thomas, Kt.1603, II. 119
  Hunt-Grubbe, Walter J., K.C.B.1882, I. 258; G.C.B.1899, I. 202
  Hunter, Archibald, K.C.B.1898, I. 270
  Hunter, David, K.C.M.G.1901, I. 390
  Hunter, John, Kt.1813, II. 313
  Hunter, Martin, G.C.H.1832, I. 451; Kt.1832, II. 332; G.C.M.G.1837, I. 334
  Hunter, Richard, Kt.1826, II. 326
  Hunter, Robert, Kt.1894, II. 393
  Hunter, William G., K.C.M.G.1884, I. 366
  Hunter, William W. K.C.S.I.1887, I. 323
  Huntingdon, earl of. See D'Angle; see Holand; see Grey; see Hastings
  Huntingfield, William de, K.B.1306, I. 113
  Huntley, Henry, Kt.1841, II. 344
  Huntley, marquess of. See Gordon
  Huntley, Richard, Kt.1603, II. 111
  Huntley. See Hintley
  Hurdle, Thomas, K.C.B.1877, I. 256
  Husbands, Samuel, Kt.1684, II. 259
  Hussein, Khan, G.C.S.I.1873, I. 310
  Hussein, Kuli Khan, K.C.I.E.1902, I. 410
HUSSEY, HUSSY, HUSSEE, HUSE, HUYSSEY, HUSSE, HUSEE
  Hussy (Hussey), Charles, Kt.1603, II. 117
  Hussey, Charles, Kt.1617, II. 167
  Hussey, Edward, Kt.1608, II. 144
  Hussey, George, Kt.1901, II. 409
  Hussey, Giles, Kt.1523, II. 45
  Hussee (Hussey), Henry, Kt.1547, II. 62, 65
  Hussey, James, Kt.1619, II. 174
  Hussee, John, Kt.(1316), II. lix.
  Hussey, John, Kt.1347, II. 8
  Hussee (Huse), John, Kt.1497, II. 29

HUSSEY
  Husee (Hussey), John, Kt.1513, II. 36
  Huyssey, John, lord of Catterdyke, Kt. 1616, II. 157
  Hussey, Patrick, baron of Galtrim, Kt. 1548, II. 63
  Hussey, Richard, Kt.1604, II. 136
  Hussey, Richard H., K.C.B.1833, I. 232; G.C.M.G.1837, I. 334
  Husse (Husee), William, Kt.1513, II. 39
  Hussee, William, Kt.1529, II. 47
  Hussey, William, Kt.1690, II. 265
  Hussey-Montagu, Edward, earl of Beaulieu, K.B.1753, I. 170
  Hussey-Vivian. See Vivian
  Hustler, William, Kt.1673, II. 248
  Hutchins, George, Kt.1689, II. 265
  Hutchins, Philip P., K.C.S.I.1891, I. 324
  Hutchinson, Joseph T., Kt.1895, II. 395
  Hutchinson, Michael, Kt.1641, II. 210
  Hutchinson, Richard, Kt.1708, II. 276
  Hutchinson (Huchenson), Thomas, Kt. 1617, II. 161
  Hutchinson, William, Kt.1820, II. 321; K.C.H.1831, I. 457
  Huthwaite, Edward, K.C.B.1869, I. 252
  Hutt, George, K.C.B.1887, I. 262
  Hutt, William, K.C.B.1865, I. 283
  Hutton, Edward T. H., K.C.M.G.1901, I. 389
  Hutton, John, Kt.1894, II. 394
  Hutton, Richard, Kt.1617, II. 162
  Hutton, Richard, Kt.1625, II. 189
  Hutton (Hatton), Thomas, Kt.1617, II. 164
  Hutton, Timothy, Kt.1606, II. 139
  Hutton, William, Kt.1604, II. 133
  Hutwa, Partab Sahi, of, K.C.I.E.1889, I. 406
  Huxley, John, Kt.1663, II. 237
  Hyckman. See Hickman

HYDE, HIDE
  Hyde, Arthur, Kt.1624, II. 186
  Hyde, Bernard, Kt.1661, II. 234
  Hyde, Edward, Kt.1643, II. 215
  Hyde, Frederick, Kt.1663, II. 238
  Hyde, George, K.B.1603, I. 156

HYDE
Hyde, Henry earl of Clarendon, K.B. 1661, I. 164
Hide, James de la, Kt.(1361), II. lx.
Hyde, Lawrence, Kt.1614, II. 154
Hyde, Lawrence, earl of Rochester, K.G.1685, I. 38
Hyde, Leonard, Kt.1603, II. 120
Hide, Nicholas, Kt.1627, II. 191
Hyde, Richard, Kt.1604, II. 131
Hyde, Robert, Kt.1603, II. 118
Hyde, Robert, Kt.1660, II. 227
Hyde, Rowland de la, Kt.1628, II. 195
Hyde, Walter de la, Kt.(1397), II. lx.
Hyde, Walter de la, Kt.1541, II. 52

HYDERABAD
Asaf Jah, nizam of, G.C.S.I.1884, I. 312; G.C.B.1903, I. 216
Nizam-Ool-Moolk, nizam of, K.S.I. 1861, I. 306; G.C.S.I.1866, I. 308
Secundar Jung of, K.C.I.E.1896, I. 409
Sharf-ul-Omrah, bahadoor of, K.C.S.I. 1866, I. 316

Hylston, John, Kt.1545, II. 58
Hylyard. See Hildyard
Hynde. See Hinde
Hylton. See Hilton
Hyndford, earl of. See Carmichael
Hyngham, —, K.B.(1465), I. 134
Hynton. See Hinton

I

Ibbetson, Denzil C. J., K.C.S.I.1903, 1. 327

IDAR
Keshri Singhji of, K.C.S.I.1887, I. 323
Pratab Singhji of, G.C.S.I.1897, I. 314
Sree Jowan, chief of, K.C.S.I.1867, I. 317

Iddlesleigh, earl of. See Northcote
Iguin, admiral, K.C.B.1902, I. 275
Ilbert, Courtenay P., K.C.S.I.1895, I. 325
Ilderton, Thomas, Kt.1497, II. 32
Illingworth, Richard, K.B.(1465), I. 134
Imam, Baksh Khan, K.C.I.E.1888, I. 406
Imhoff, Charles, Kt.1807, II. 309
Impey, Elijah, Kt.1774, II. 294
Inchiquin, baron and earl of. See O'Brien

INDORE
Rao Holkar, maharaja of, K.S.I.1861, I. 306; G.C.S.I.1866, I. 308
Rao Holkar, of, K.C.S.I.1875, I. 320; G.C.S.I.1887, I. 312

Ingham (Engham), Edward, Kt.1619, I. 172
Ingham, James T., Kt.1876, II. 368
Ingham, Thomas, Kt.1603, II. 127
Ingham, Thomas, Kt.1660, II. 226

INGLEBY, INGILBY, ENGELBY, INGOLDSBY
Ingleby, Charles, Kt.1688, II. 264
Ingoldsby, George, Kt.1671, II. 246
Ingolsby (Ingleby), Richard, Kt.1604, II. 132
Ingoldsby, Richard, Kt.1617, II. 166
Ingoldsby, Richard, K.B.1661, I. 166
Ingleby (Engelby), William, Kt.1482, II. 18
Ingleby, William, Kt.1545, II. 57
Ingleby, William, Kt.1603, II. 100
Ingilby, Wiliam B., K.C.B.1867, I.251
Inglefield. See Englefield
Inglis, John E. W., K.C.B.1858, I. 244
Inglis, John M., Kt.1900, II. 407
Inglis, William, K.C.B.1815, I. 227
Inglott, Ferdinando V., K.C.M.G.1892, I. 377
Ingoldsby. See Ingleby
Ingram, Arthur, Kt.1613, II. 153
Ingram, Arthur, Kt.1621, II. 177
Ingram, Arthur, Kt.1664, II. 240
Ingram, Thomas, Kt.1636, II. 204
Ingram, William, Kt.1617, II. 162
Ingram, William, Kt.1624, II. 184
Ingram-Seymour-Conway, Francis, marquess of Hertford, K.G.1807, I. 50
Innes, James R., K.C.M.G.1901, I. 390
Innes, John H. K., K.C.B.1887, I. 261
Innes, Joseph G. L., Kt.1875, II. 367
Innes-Ker, H. J., duke of Roxburghe, K.T.1902, I. 89
Innes-Ker, James H R., duke of Roxburghe, K.T.1840, I. 83

INDEX

Inverness, earl of. See Hay
Inwood, William, Kt.1684, II. 259

IRBY, IREBY

Ireby, Anthony, Kt.1603, II. 124
Irby, Anthony, Kt.1624, II. 184
Ireland, duke of. See Vere
Ireland, Francis, Kt.1622, II. 179
Ireland, George, Kt.1471, II. 16
Ireland, Gilbert, Kt.1617, II. 165
Ireland, Gilbert, Kt.1660, II. 228
Ireland, John, Kt.1497, II. 32
Ireland, Thomas, Kt.1617, II. 165
Ireton, John, Kt.1658, II. 224
Irvin, Frederick C., K.H.,1836, I. 475
Irvine, George C. D'A., K.C.B.1902, I. 273
Irving, Henry B., Kt.1895, II.396
Irving, Henry T., K.C.M.G.1878, I. 360; G.C.M.G.1888, I. 341
Irwin, George, Kt.1892, II. 391
Irwine, John, K.B.1775, I. 172
Isaac, Charles, Kt.1697, II. 270
Isaacs, Henry A., Kt.1887, II. 382
Isham, Eusebius, Kt.1603, II. 105
Ishom (Isham), John, Kt.1608, II. 144
Isle. See Lisle
Ismond. See Esmond
Ispania, Roderick de, K.B.1306, I. 112

ITALY

Humbert of, K.G.1878, I. 65
Victor Emmanuel II. of, K.G.1855, I. 59
Victor Emmanuel III., K.G.1891, I. 68; Victoria Chain 1903, I. 416

Ito, the marquess, G.C.B.1902, I. 216
Ive, George, Kt.1605, II. 137
Ive (Ives), Mark, Kt.1603, II. 121
Iveagh, baron. See Guinness
Ivernois, Francis, D', Kt.1796, II. 303
Ivers. See Jarvis
Ivory, James, K.H.1831, I. 466
Ivory, John, Kt.1683, II. 259
Ivy (Ivey), Thomas, Kt.1661, II. 235
Iwardby (Inwardby), John (George), K.B.1501, I. 147

J

Jacob, Abraham, Kt.1683, II. 259
Jacob, George le G., K.C.S.I.1869, I. 318
Jacob, John, Kt.1633, II. 200
Jacob, Robert, Kt.1607, II. 143
Jacob, Samuel S., K.C.I.E.1902, 411
Jacobson, Jacob, Kt.1718, II. 281
Jackson, Anthony, Kt.1650, II. 222
Jackson, Charles R. M., Kt.1852, II. 349
Jackson, Edward, K.H.1835, I. 471
Jackson, George, K.C.H.1832, I. 459; Kt. 1832, I. 333
Jackson, Henry M., K.C.M.G.1899, I. 386
Jackson, James, K.H.1837, I. 476; K.C.B. 1856, I. 243; G.C.B.1865, I. 194
Jackson, John, Kt.1604, II. 132
Jackson, John, Kt.1619, II. 171
Jackson, John, Kt.1895, II. 395
Jackson, Louis S., Kt.1880, II. 372
Jackson, Philip, Kt.1714, II. 279, 281
Jackson, Richard D., K.C.B.1815, I. 224
Jackson, Robert, Kt.1617, II. 163
Jackson, Robert W., Kt.1882, II. 374
Jackson, Thomas, Kt.1899, II. 405
Jackson, Thomas S., K.C.V.O.(1902), I. 434
Jacques, Roger, Kt.1639, II. 206
Jaffé, Otto, Kt.1900, II. 406

JAIPUR

Jaipur, Madhu Singh, maharaja of, G.C.S.I.1888, I. 313; G.C.I.E.1900, I. 403; G.C.V.O.1903; I. 420
Jyepore, Ram Sing, maharaja of, K.S.I.1863, I. 307; G.C.S.I.1866, I. 309

James I., K.G.1590, I. 28
James II., Kt.1642, II. 212; K.G.1642, I. 33
James I. of Scotland, K.B.(1421), II. 130
James V., king of Scotland, K.G.1535, I. 22
James, Bartholomew, Kt.1471, II. 16
James, Demetrius, Kt.1665, II. 240
James, Henry, Kt.1553, II. 68
James, Henry, Kt.1603, II. 125
James, Henry, Kt.1860, II. 354
James, Henry, lord James of Hereford, Kt.1873, II. 365; G.C.V.O.1902, I. 419

INDEX 125

James, Henry E. M., K.C.I.E.1901, I. 410
James (MacJames), Hugh, Kt.1597, II. 94
James, John, Kt.1665, II. 241
James, John, Kt.1670, II. 244
James, John K., Kt.1821, II. 323
James, John K., Kt.1854, II. 350
James (Jeames), Roger, Kt.1613, II. 153
James, William M., Kt.1869, II. 360
Jameson, George I., K.C.S.I.1871, I. 319
Jamieson (Jamison), John, Kt.1813, II. 312
Jammu and Kashmir, Partab Singh, of, G.C.S.I.1892, I. 313
Japan, Arisugawa, prince of, G.C.B.1902, I. 216
Jan, Saddozai, K.C.I.E.1904, I. 412
Janjira, Ahmad Khan, of, K.C.I.E.1895, I. 408
Janson, Brian, Kt.1624, II. 187
Janssen, Theodore, Kt.1696, II. 269

JARDINE, JARDEN, JURDEN
Jardine, Henry, Kt.1825, II. 325
Jardine, John, K.C.I.E.1897, I. 409
Jarden (Jurden), Sandy, Kt.1482, II. 18
Jarret. See Garret

JARVIS, JERVIS, JERVOIS, IVERS
Jervis, Humphrey, Kt.1681, II. 257
Jervis, John, Kt.1846, II. 346
Jervis, John, earl of St. Vincent, K.B. 1782, I. 173; G.C.B.1815, I. 180
Jarvis, Lewis W., Kt.1878, II. 370
Jarvis, Samuel R., Kt.1834, II. 335
Jarvis (Jervois, Ivers), Thomas, Kt. 1607, II. 143
Jervois, William, K.H.1835, I. 471
Jervois, William F. D., K.C.M.G.1874, I. 357; G.C.M.G.1878, I. 338
Jaudrell, Robert, Kt.1604, II. 134
Jaures, Jean L C., K.C.B.1865, I. 249
Jay, James, Kt.1763, II. 292
Jay, Thomas, Kt.1625, II. 190
Jebb, Henry, Kt.1782, II. 297
Jebb, Joshua, K.C.B.1859, I. 281
Jedina, ritter Leopold von, K.C.V.O. 1903, I. 442

Jeejeebhoy, Jamsetjee, Kt.1842, II. 344
Jeffcott, John W., Kt.1833, II. 333
Jeffcott, William, Kt.1849, II. 348

JEFFERY, GEOFFREY, GEFFERY
Geoffrey (Jeffery), John, Kt.1577, II. 78
Geffery (Jeffery), John, Kt.1603, II. 129

JEFFERIES, JEFFREYS
Jefferies, George, Kt.1677, II. 252
Jeffreys, Griffith, Kt.1687, II. 263
Jefferies, Jeffry, Kt.1699, II. 271
Jefferies, Robert, Kt.1673, II. 248
Jeffreys, Thomas, Kt.1686, II. 262

Jefford. See Gifford
Jeffreyson, John, Kt.1692, II. 267
Jehanghier, Jehanghier Cowasjee, Kt. 1895, II. 395
Jekyll, Herbert, K.C.M.G.1901, I. 389
Jekyll, Joseph, Kt.1697, II. 270
Jelf, Arthur, Kt.1901, II. 409
Jelf, James, Kt.1814, II. 314

JENKINS, JENKYNS
Jenkins, Francis H., K.C.B.1897, I. 268
Jenkins, George H., Kt.1904, II. 420
Jenkyns, Henry, K.C.B.1892, I. 292
Jenkins, James, K.C.B.1887, I. 262
Jenkins, John (Henry), Kt.1603, II. 122
Jenkins, John J., Kt.1882, II. 373
Jenkins, Lawrence H., Kt.1899, II. 405; K.C.I.E.1903, I. 411
Jenkins, Leoline, Kt.1670, II. 244
Jenkins, Richard, G.C.B.1838, I. 207
Jenkinson, Charles C. C., earl of Liverpool, G.C.B.1845, I. 207
Jenkinson, Edward R., K.C.B.1888, I. 291
Jenkinson, Henry, Kt.1604, II. 130
Jenkinson, Robert, Kt.1618, II. 168
Jenkinson, Robert B., earl of Liverpool, K.G.1814, I. 51
Jenner (Jenner-Fust), Herbert, Kt.1828, II. 327
Jenner, Thomas, Kt.1683, II. 259
Jenner, William, K.C.B.1872, I. 285; G.C.B.1889, I. 213

L L

INDEX

JENNINGS, JENYNS, JENNYNS
Jennings (Jenyns), John, Kt.1544, II. 55
Jennings, John, Kt.1603, II. 107
Jennings, John, K.B.1626, I. 163
Jennings, John, Kt.1704, II. 274
Jennings, John R., Kt.1887, II. 381
Jennings, Jonathan, Kt.1678, II. 252
Jennings, Patrick, K.C.M.G.1880, I. 363
Jennings, Robert, Kt.1660, II. 230
Jennyns (Jenyns), Roger, Kt.1700, II. 271
Jennyns, Stephen, Kt.1509, II. 35; K.B. 1509, I. 149

JENNISON, JENISON
Jennison, Mathew, Kt.1683, II. 259
Jenison, Ralph, Kt.1677, II. 252
Jenny, Edmond, Kt.1501, II. 33
Jeynes (Joynes), Edwin, Kt.1799, II. 304

JENNET, JENNY, JERMY, JENNEY
Jermy (Jenny), Arthur, Kt.1639, II. 206
Jermey, Henry (John), K.B.1533, I.150
Jennet (Jenny, Jermy), John, Kt.1642, II. 212
Jenney, William, Kt.1483, II. 21
Jephson, Alfred, Kt.1891, II. 389
Jephson, John, Kt.1603, II. 129
Jepson, William, Kt.1603, II. 103
Jeremie, John, Kt.1840, II. 343
Jermey, Jermy. See Jennet

JERMYN, JERMIN, JERMAYNE
Jermin, Ambrose, Kt.1553, II. 66
Jermyn, Henry, earl of St. Albans, K.G.1672, I. 36
Jermyn, Isaac, Kt.1604, II. 136
Jermyn, John, Kt.1547, II. 63
Jermayne, John, Kt.1698, II. 270
Jermyn, Robert, Kt.1578, I. 78
Jermin, Robert, Kt.1604, II. 136
Jermyn, Thomas, Kt.1591, II. 89
Jermyn, Thomas, K.B.1603, I. 156

JERNINGHAM, JERNYNHAM, JERMINGHAM
Jerningham, George, Kt.1717, footnote, II. 266
Jerningham, Henry, K.B.1553, I. 153

JERNINGHAM
Jerningham, Hubert E. H., K.C.M.G. 1893, I. 378
Jernynham (Jermingham), Richard, Kt.1513, II. 39
Jerningham, Robert, Kt.1523, II. 45
Jersey, earl of. See Child-Villiers
Jervis, Jervois. See Jarvis
Jessel, George, Kt.1872, II. 363
Jesson, William, Kt.1669, II. 243
Jetté, Louis A., K.C.M.G.1901, I. 391
Jeune, Francis H., lord St. Helier, Kt. 1891, II. 388; K.C.B.1897, I. 296; G.C.B.1902, I. 216

JIND, JHEEND
Rugbir Sing, bahadur of, G.C.S.I. 1875, I. 310
Suroop Sing, maharaja of, K.S.I.1863, I. 307
Joackimy, Albert, Kt.1610, II. 149
Jobson, Francys, Kt.1549, II. 64
Jocelyn, Robert, earl of Roden, K.P.1806, I. 98
Jocelyn, Robert, earl of Roden, K.P. 1821, I. 99

JODHPUR
Maharaja of, K.C.S.I.1866, I. 315; G.C.S.I.1866, I. 309
Jeswnt Sing, bahadur of, G.C.S.I.1875, I. 310
Jodrell, Paul, Kt.1787, II. 300
John, Lewis, Kt.1439, II. 12
Johnson, Allen B., K.C.B.1889, I. 263
Johnson, Charles C., K.C.B.1881, I. 258; G.C.B.1900, I. 202
Johnson, Edward, Kt.1838, II. 340
Johnson, Edwin B., K.C.B.1875, I. 255; G.C.B.1887, I. 199
Johnson, Francis G., Kt.1890, II. 387
Johnson, George, Kt.1892, II. 390
Johnson, Henry, Kt.1680, II. 254
Johnson, Henry, Kt.1685, II. 260
Johnson, Henry, G.C.B. 1820, I. 184
Johnson, James, Kt.1671, II. 246
Johnson, John, Kt.1696, II. 269
Johnson, John, Kt.1765, II. 292
Johnson, John H., Kt.1874, II. 366
Johnson, Nathaniel, Kt.1680, II. 255
Johnson, Robert, Kt.1604, II. 134
Johnson, Robert, Kt.1719, II. 281

INDEX 127

Johnson, Samuel G., Kt.1893, II. 392
Johnson, Thomas, Kt.1708, II. 276
Johnson, William G., Kt.1849, II. 347

JOHNSTON, JOHNSTONE
Johnston, Alexander, Kt.1809, II. 309
Johnston, Henry H., K.C.B.1896, I. 294; G.C.M.G.1901, I. 348
Johnstone, James, K.C.S.I.1887, I. 324
Johnston, John B., Kt.1899, II. 404
Johnston, William, Kt.1715, II. 280
Johnston, William, K.C.B.1837, I. 234
Johnston, William, Kt.1851, II. 349
Johnstone, William J. H., K.C.B.1862, I. 248
Johnston, William, marquess of Annandale, K.T.1703-4, I. 76

JOHORE
Datu, maharajah of, K.C.S.I.1866, I. 317; G.C.M.G.1876, I. 337
Ibraham, sultan of, K.C.M.G.1897, I. 383

Joliffe, William, Kt.1714-5, II. 280
Jolles (Jowles), John, Kt.1606, II. 140
Jones, Alfred L., K.C.M.G.1901, I. 391
Jones, Arthur, Kt.1674, II. 249
Jones, Baptista, Kt.1619, II. 172
Jones, Charles, Kt.1610, II. 149
Jones, Charles T., Kt.1809, II. 309
Jones, Daniel, Kt.1836, II. 337
Jones, Elias, Kt.1604, II. 129
Jones, Francis, Kt.1617, II. 161
Jones, George E., K.H.1832, I. 468
Jones, Harry D., K.C.B.1855, I. 240; G.C.B.1861, I. 194
Jones, Henry, Kt.1603, II. 116
Jones (Joanes, James), Henry, Kt.1553, II. 68
Jones, Henry, Kt.1586, II. 85
Jones, Henry, Kt.1591, II. 89
Jones, Henry, Kt.1642, II. 214, 221
Jones, Henry, Kt.1658, II. 224
Jones, Horace, Kt.1886, II. 379
Jones, Howard S., K.C.B.1897, I. 268
Jones, James, K.H.1831, I. 465
Jones, John, Kt.1677, II. 251
Jones, John, K.C.B.1858, I. 245
Jones, John S., K.H.1836, I. 475
Jones, John T., K.C.B.1838, I. 235

Jones, Lewis T., K.C.B.1861, I. 247; G.C.B.1873, I. 196
Jones, Owen, Kt.1761, II. 290
Jones, Pryce, Kt.1887, II. 381
Jones, Rice, K.H.1834, I. 470
Jones, Richard, Kt.1809, II. 309
Jones, Richard, K.C.B.1817, I. 228
Jones, Roger, Kt.1604, II. 134
Jones, Roger, Kt.1607, II. 141
Jones, Roger, Kt.1624, II. 184
Jones, Samuel, Kt.1660, II. 231
Jones, Theophilus, Kt.1644, II. 217
Johanes, Thomas, Kt.1542, II. 53
Jones, Thomas, Kt.1584, II. 83, 86
Jones, Thomas, Kt.1671, II. 246
Jones, Thomas, Kt.1715, II. 280
Jones, Thomas, Kt.1760, II. 289
Jones, Thomas A., Kt.1880, II. 371
Jones, Thomas H., viscount Ranelagh, K.C.B.1881, I. 287
Jones, William, Kt.1617, II. 161
Jones, William, Kt.1671, II. 246
Jones, William, Kt.1783, II. 297
Jones, William, K.C.B.1869, I. 252; G.C.B.1886, I. 198
Jones, William H. Q., Kt.1892, II. 389

JORDAN, JORDAIN
Jordan, John, K.H.1835, I. 471
Jordan, John N., K.C.M.G.1904, I. 395
Jordan, Joseph, Kt.1665, II. 241
Jordain, Thomas, Kt.1606, II. 140

JOSSELYN, JOSELYNE, JOSSELYNE, JOSSELING
Josselyne, Ralph, K.B.(1465), I. 134
Joselyne, Robert, Kt.1621, II. 177
Josselyn, Thomas, K.B.1547, I. 151
Josseling, Thomas, Kt.1603, II. 106
Jotindra, Mohan T., K.C.S.I.1882, I. 322
Jourdain, Henry J., K.C.M.G.1900, I. 387
Joyce, Matthew I., Kt.1900, II. 408
Joynes. See Jeynes
Judde, Andrew, Kt.1549, II. 65
Julyan, Penrose G., K.C.M.G.1874, I. 357
Jumper, William, Kt.1704, II. 274

JUNAGAR
Mohubut Khan, nawab of, K.C.S.I. 1871, I. 319
Nawab of, G.C.I.E.1890, I. 401
Rasul Khanji of, K.C.S.I.1898, I. 327

INDEX

June (Juen), John K.B.(1426), I. 132
Jung, Bahadoor Kunwar Ranajee, G.C.S.I.1873, I. 310
Jurden. See Jardine
Justinianus, George, Kt.1608, II. 146
Juta, Henry H., Kt.1897, II. 399
Juxon, George, Kt.1663, II. 238
Juxon, William, Kt.1661, II. 232

K

Kahlur, Khem Singh of, K.C.I.E.1898, I. 409
Kane, Robert J., Kt.1846, II. 346
Kapos-Mére, Kajetan M. von, K.C.V.O. 1903, I. 442
KAPURTHALA
  Harnam Singh of, K.C.I.E.1898, I. 410
  Jagatjit Singh of, K.C.S.I.1897, I. 326
  Rundheer Sing, bahadoor of, K.S.I. 1864, I. 307; G.C.S.I.1866, I. 309
KARAULI
  Maharaja of, K.C.S.I.1866, I. 315; G.C.S.I.1866, I. 309
  Maharaja of, K.C.I.E.1894, I. 408; G.C.I.E.1897, I. 402
Karr. See Carr, Kerr
Karslake, John B., Kt.1866, II. 358
Karslake, William W., Kt.1895, II. 396
KAY, KAYE
  Kay, Edward E., Kt.1881, II. 372
  Kaye, John W., K.C.S.I.1871, I. 319
  Kaye, William S. B., Kt.1885, II. 377
  Kay. See Key
KEANE, KEENE, KEEN
  Keene, Benjamin, K.B.1754, I. 170
  Keen, Frederick J., K.C.B.1900, I. 271
  Keane, John, lord Keane, K.C.B.1815, I. 222; G.C.H.1831, I. 451; G.C.B. 1839, I. 188
Kearles. See Kyrle
Kearney, James, K.C.H.1834, I. 459; Kt. 1834, II. 334
Keating, Henry S., K.C.B.1836, I. 233
Keating, Henry S., Kt.1857, II. 352

Keats, Richard G., K.B.1808, I. 177; G.C.B.1815, I. 181
Keck, Anthony, Kt.1689, II. 264
Kedah, Ahmed Taj Udin, &c., the raja of, K.C.M.G.1879, I. 360
Keedham, John, Kt.1603, II. 121
Keenan, Patrick J., K.C.M.G.1881, I. 363
Keen, Keene. See Keane
Keer. See Kerr
KEIGHLEY, KIGHLEY, KYGHLEY
  Kyghley, Henry, Kt.1482, II. 19
  Keighley Kighley), Philip, Kt.1603, II. 122
Keith, Alexander, Kt.1819, II. 320
Keith, Basil, Kt.1772, II. 293
Keith, George, earl marischal, K.T.1725, footnote, I. 75
Keith, Robert M., K.B.1772, I. 172
Keith, viscount. See Elphinstone
Keith, William, earl marischal, K.T. 1705, footnote, I. 75
Keith-Falconer, Algernon H. T., earl of Kintore, G.C.M.G.1889, I. 342
Kekewich, Arthur, Kt.1886, II. 380
Kekewich, George W., K.C.B.1895, I. 293
Kele, Ralph de, K.B.1306, I. 121
Keling, John, Kt.1662, II. 236
Keling, John, Kt.1679, II. 254
Kelk, Charles, Kt.1603, II. 124
Kellaway, William, Kt.1553, II. 66
Kellett, Henry, K.C.B.1869, I. 252
Kellett, Richard, Kt.1785, II. 298
Kelleyon (Kellion, Kelley), Thomas, Kt. 1627, II. 192
Kellie, earl of. See Erskine
Kellner, George W., K.C.M.G.1879, I. 361
KELLY, KELLEY
  Kelly, Fitz Roy, Kt.1845, II. 346
  Kelley, George, Kt.1762, II. 291
  Kelly, Richard D., K.C.B.1860, I. 246
  Kelly, William F., K.C.B.1900, I. 272
  Kelly. See Kelleyon
Kelly-Kenny T., K.C.B.1902, I. 274; G.C.B.1904, I. 204
Kelvin, lord. See Thompson
Kemball, Arnold B., K.C.S.I.1866, I. 317; K.C.B.1878, I. 256

INDEX 129

KEMP, KEMPE
Kemp, George, Kt.1627, II. 191
Kemp, George (Garret), Kt.1604, II. 129
Kemp, Nicholas, Kt.1617, II. 166
Kemp, Robert, Kt.1641, II. 210
Kemp, Robert, Kt.1618, II. 170
Kemp, Thomas, K.B.1501, I. 147
Kempe, Thomas, Kt.1547, II. 60
Kemp, Thomas, Kt.1603, II. 106
Kempt, James, K.C.B.1815, I. 220; G.C.H.1816, I. 448; G.C.B.1815, I. 183
Kempthorne, John, Kt.1670, II. 244
KEMYS, KEMEYS, KEMISH, KEMIS, KEYMICH
Kemish, Charles, Kt.1643, II. 216
Kemis, Nicholas, Kt.1641, II. 208
Kemeys, Robert J. A., Kt.1617, II. 318
Kenah, Thomas, K.C.B.1865, I. 249
Kenart. See Kinnaird
Kendal, earl of. See Foix, J. de
Kendal, Robert de, K.B.1306, I. 114
Kendall-Cater. See Cater
Kenmare, earl of. See Browne
Kennedy, Alex., Kt.1633, lxiii.
Kennedy, Alexander K. C., K.C.B.1862, I. 247
Kennedy, Archibald, marquess of Ailsa, K.T.1821, I. 81
Kennedy, Archibald, marquess of Ailsa, K.T.1859, I. 84
Kennedy, Arthur E., Kt.1867, II. 359; K.C.M.G.1871, I. 356; G.C.M.G. 1881, I. 339
Kennedy, Charles M., K.C.M.G.1893, I. 379
Kennedy, James S., K.C.B.1861, I. 246
Kennedy, John G., K.C.M.G.1901, I. 389
Kennedy, Michael K., K.C.S.I.1878, I. 321
Kennedy, Richard, Kt.1660, II. 231
Kennedy, Robert H., Kt.1812, II. 310; K.C.H.1834, I. 460
Kennedy, William R., Kt.1892, II. 391
Kennedy, William R., K.C.B.1897, I. 269
Kennet (Knevitt), William, Kt.1617, II. 163
Kennett-Barrington, Vincent H. B., Kt. 1886, II. 379

Kenny, Edward, Kt.1870, II. 362
Kent, Edward A., duke of, K.P.1783, I. 96; K.G.1786, I. 47; G.C.H.1815, I. 447; G.C.B.1815, I. 182
Kent, duke of. See Grey
Kent, earl of. See Holand; see Nevill; see Grey
Kent, Thomas, Kt.1771, II. 293
Keppel, Arnold J. van, earl of Albemarle, K.G.1700, I. 39
Keppel, George, earl of Albemarle, K.G. 1765, I. 46
Keppel, Henry, K.C.B.1857, I. 244; G.C.B.1871, I. 195
Keppel, William, K.B.1813, I. 178; G.C.B.1815, I. 181
Keppel, William A. van, earl of Albemarle, K.B.1725, I. 167; K.G.1749, I. 44
Keppel, William C., earl of Albemarle, G.C.H.1833, I. 452
Keppel, William C., earl of Albemarle, K.C.M.G.1870, I. 355
Kerdeston, Roger de, K.B.1306, I. 122
Kerit. See Knyvet
Kern, John, Kt.1604, II. 130
KERR, KER, KEER, and see Carr
Ker, Charles, Kt.1822, II. 323
Keer, George, Kt.1604, II. 134
Ker, John, Kt.1651, II. 222
Ker, John, duke of Roxburghe, K.G. 1722, I. 42
Kerr, John, duke of Roxburghe, K.T. 1768, I. 79; K.G.1801, I. 49
Ker, Mark, Kt.1633, II. lxiii.
Kerr, lord Mark, K.C.B.1881, I. 257; G.C.B.1893, I. 200
Kerr, lord Robert, K.H.1835, I. 471
Kerr, Schomberg H., marquess of Lothian, K.T.1878, I. 87
Ker, Thomas, Kt.1633, II. lxii.
Kerr, lord Walter T., K.C.B.1896, I. 267; G.C.B.1902, I. 203
Kerr, William, marquess of Lothian, K.T.1705, I. 76
Kerr, William, marquess of Lothian, K.T.1734, I. 78
Kerr, William, marquess of Lothian, K.T.1820, I. 81

KERR

Kerr, William H., marquess of Lothian, K.T.1768, I. 79
Kerr, William J., marquess of Lothian, K.T.1776, I. 80
Kerrison, Edward, Kt.1815, II. 315; K.C.H.1821, I. 455; G.C.H.1831, I. 451; K.C.B.1840, I. 236
Kerrison, Roger, Kt.1800, II. 305
Kershaw, Louis A., Kt.1898, II. 403
Kessel, Gustav von, G.C.V.O.1901, I. 424
Kettelby, Francis, Kt.1606, II. 139
Kettle, Rupert A., Kt.1880, II. 372
Kevit. See Knyvet
Key, Astley C., K.C.B.1873, I. 254; G.C.B.1882, I. 198
Key (Kay), John, Kt.1641, II. 208
Key. See Kay

KEYES, KAYES

Keyes, Charles P., K.C.B.1880, I. 257; G.C.B.1891, I. 200
Keyes (Kayes), John, Kt.1607, II. 142
Keymich. See Kemis
Keyser, Polydore de, Kt.1888, II. 385

KHAIRPUR

Faiz Muhammad of, G.C.I.E.1897, I. 402
Murad Khan of, G.C.I.E.1891, I. 402
Kharan, Naoroz Khan of, K.C.I.E.1888, I. 406

KHELAT

Mir Khodadad, khan of, G.C.S.I.1879, I. 311
Mir Mahmud of, G.C.I.E.1894, I. 402
Khushed, Jah, K.C.I.E.1888, I. 405
Kid, John, Kt.1685, II. 261
Kiderminster (Kederminster), John, Kt. 1609, II. 145
Kidson (Ritson), Thomas, Kt.1578, II. 79
Kielmansegg, count Erich L. F. C., K.C.V.O.1903, I. 442; G.C.V.O.1904, I. 431
Kildare, earl of. See Fitz-Gerald
Kilmorey, earl of. See Needham

KILLEGREW, KILLIGREW, KILLIGREWE, KELLIGREW

Killegrew, Henry, Kt.1591, II. 88
Killigrew, Henry, Kt.1625, II. 189
Kelligrewe, John, Kt.1576, II. 77

KILLIGREW

Killigrew, John, Kt.1617, II. 165
Killegrew, Joseph, Kt.1613, II. 152
Killigrew, Peter, Kt.1625, II. 190
Kelligrew, Robert, Kt.1603, II. 127
Killegrew, Robert, Kt.1650, II. 222
Killigrew, William, Kt.1603, II. 104
Killigrew, William, Kt.1626, II. 190
Kimberley, earl of. See Wodehouse
Kinaston. See Kynaston
Kincaid, John, Kt.1852, II. 349
Kincaidine, earl of. See Bruce
Kindersley, Richard T., Kt.1851, II. 349
King, Andrew, Kt.1660, II. 228
King, Anthony, Kt.1770, II. 293
King, Charles, K.H.1833, I. 468
King, Edward (Edmund), Kt.1686, II. 261
King, Edward D., K.C.H.1833, I. 459; Kt.1833, II. 333
King, George St, V., K.C.B.1873, I. 253
King, George, K.C.I.E.1898, I. 409
King, Henry, K.C.H.1834, I. 460; Kt. 1834, II. 335
King, Henry, K.C.B.1835, I. 233
King, Henry S., K.C.I.E.1892, I. 407
King, James, Kt.1887, II. 381
King, John, Kt.1609, II. 148
King, John, Kt.1658, II. 224, 227
King, John, Kt.1674, II. 249
King, Patrick, Kt.1776, II. 295
King, Peter, lord King, Kt.1708, II. 276
King, Richard, Kt.1784, II. 298
King, Richard, K.C.B.1815, I. 220
King, Robert, Kt.1621, II. 177
King, Robert, Kt.1682, 258
King, William, Kt.1661, II. 233
King, William D., Kt.1887, II. 381
King-Harman, Charles A., K.C.M.G.1900, I. 387
Kingcome, John, K.C.B.1865, I. 249
Kingscote, Robert N. F., K.C.B.1889, I. 291; G.C.V.O.1902, I. 420
Kingshemede, Walter de, K.B.1306, I. 122
Kingsmill, Francis, Kt.1604, II. 129
Kingsmill, George, Kt.1603, II. 114
Kingsmill, Henry, Kt.1611, II. 150
Kingsmill, John, Kt.1617, II. 163

INDEX

Kingsmill, John, Kt.1830, II. 329
Kingsmill, Richard, Kt.1623, II. 182
Kingsmill, W., Kt.1601, II. 99
Kingsmill, William, Kt.1603, II. 106
Kingsmill, William, Kt.1680, II. 255
Kingesmyth, William, Kt.1569, II. 74

KINGSTON, KYNGESTON

Kyngeston, —, K.B.(1483), I. 140
Kyngeston, Anthony, Kt.1538, II. 51
Kingston, duke of. See Pierrepont
Kingston, George S., Kt.1870, II. 362
Kingston (Kniveton, Knighton, Knifton), Gilbert, Kt.1605, II. 138
Kingeston, William, Kt.1513, II. 40
Kingston, William, K.G.1539, I. 22

Kinlosse, lord. See Bruce
Kinnaird (Kenart), George, Kt.1660, II. 226
Kinnaird, George W. F., lord Kinnaird, K.T.1857, I. 84
Kinneir. See Macdonald, J.
Kinsey, Thomas, Kt.1685, II. 261
Kintore, earl of. See Keith-Falconer
Kirby, Alfred, Kt.1887, II. 382
Kirby, Richard C., Kt.1861, II. 356
Kirby, Walter, K.H.1835, I. 472
Kiriell, Thomas, K.G.1461, I. 13
Kirk, David, Kt.1633, II. 201
Kirk, John, K.C.M.G.1881, I. 364; G.C.M.G.1886, I. 340; K.C.B.1890, I. 291
Kirk, Lewis, Kt.1643, II. 215
Kirk, William, Kt.1787, II. 300
Kirkeby, John de, K.B.1306, I. 119
Kirkelots, —, Kt.1347, II. 7
Kirkham (Kirtham), William, Kt.1605, II. 138
Kirkland, John, Kt.1838, II. 340
Kirkpatrick, George A., K.CM.G.1897, I. 382
Kirkton, John de, K.B.1326, I. 123
Kirkwall, viscount. See Fitz-Maurice
Kirton, James, Kt.1618, II. 169
Kirwan, John, Kt.1690, II. 266
Kirwood, Mathew, Kt.1715, II. 280
Kishangarh, Sardul Singh, of, G.C.I.E.1892, I. 402

Kitchener, Horatio H., viscount Kitchener, K. C. B. 1896, I. 267; K.C.M.G.1894, I. 379; G.C.B.1898, I. 202; G.C.M.G.1901, I. 347
Kite, Robert, Kt.1760, II. 289
Knatchbull, Norton, Kt.1604, II. 131
Knatchbull, Norton, Kt.1641, II. 210
Kneller, Godfrey, Kt.1692, II. 267
Knesebeck, Bodo von den, K.C.V.O.1899, I. 439
Knevit. See Knyvet, Kennet
Knight, Arnold J., Kt.1841, II. 343
Knight, Christopher, Kt.1785, II. 298
Knight, Christopher, K.H.1837, I. 475
Knight, Frederick W., K.C.B.1886, I. 289
Knight, Henry E., Kt.1883, II. 376
Knight, John, Kt.1663, II. 238
Knight, John, Kt.1682, II. 257
Knight, John, K.C.B.1815, I. 217
Knight, Joseph, Kt.1773, II. 294
Knight, Richard, Kt.1668, II. 243
Knight, Robert, earl of Catherlough, K.B.1770, I. 171
Knight, Thomas, Kt.1501, II. 33

KNIGHTLEY, KNYGHTLEY

Knightley, Edmond, Kt.1538, II. 52
Knightley, Ferdinando, Kt.1616, II. 160
Knightley, Francis, Kt.1617, II. 164
Knightley de Falwesley, Richard, K.B.(1494), I. 144
Knyghtley, Richard, Kt.1510, II. 35
Knightley, Richard, Kt.1565, II. 71
Knightley, Richard, K.B.1661, I. 165
Knightley, Robert, Kt.1676, II. 251
Knightley, Seymour, Kt.1608, II. 146
Knightley, Valentine, K.B.1547, I. 151
Knightley, Valentine, Kt.1603, II. 105

KNIGHTON, KNIVETON, KNIFTON

Knighton, George, Kt.1603, II. 116
Knighton (Kniveton), Gilbert, Kt. 1605, II. 138
Knighton, William, K.C.H.1821, I. 455; G.C.H.1823, I. 449
Knipe, Randolph, Kt.1708, II. 276
Kniveton. See Knighton

Knocker, Edward W., Kt.1901, II. 408
KNOLLYS, KNOLLES, KNOWLES, KNOWLIS
Knowles, Charles B., K.C.B.1903, I. 275
Knowles, Charles H., G.C.B.1820, I. 184
Knollys, Clement C., K.C.M.G.1897, I. 382
Knolles, Francys, Kt.1547, II. 62
Knolles, Francys, Kt.1587, II. 86
Knollys, Francis, K.G.1593, I. 28
Knollys, Francis, lord Knollys, K.C.M.G.1886, I. 369; K.C.B.1897, I. 295; G.C.V.O.1901, I. 419
Knolles, Henry, Kt.1605, II. 137
Knowlis (Knolles), Henry, Kt.1633, II. 200
Knowles, James T., K.C.V.O.(1903), I. 436
Knowles, Robert, K.B.1603, I. 154
Knolles (Knowles), Robert, Kt.1613, II. 152
Knolles (Knowles), Robert, Kt.1619, II. 171
Knowles (Knolles), Thomas, Kt.1588, II. 87
Knowles, William, Kt.1586, II. 85
Knollys, William, earl of Banbury, K.G.1615, I. 31
Knollys, William T., K.C.B.1867, I. 284
Knot. See Nott
Knotsford. See Knutsford
Knovill. See Nowell
Knowill. See Nowell
Knowles. See Knollys
Knox, Alexander, K.C.B.1831, I. 232
Knox, Charles E., K.C.B.1900, I. 272
Knox, Edward, Kt.1898, II. 403
Knox, John, Kt.1686, II. 261
Knox, Ralph H., K.C.B.1895, I. 294
Knox, Thomas G., K.C.M.G.1880, I. 362
Knox, Uchter J. M., earl of Ranfurly, K.C.M.G.1897, I. 382; G.C.M.G. 1901, I. 348
Knox, William G., K.C.B.1900, I. 272

KNUTSFORD, KNOTSFORD
Knotsford, John, Kt.1644, II. 218
Knutsford, lord and viscount. See Holland
Knuydyt, Franciscus, Kt.1687, II. 262
KNYVET, KNEVIT, KNYVETT, KNEVET, KNIVETT
Knyvet, Anthony, Kt.1538, II. 51
Knyvett, Carey J., K.C.B.1899, I. 297
Knevit (Cenit, Kevitt, Keritt), George, Kt.1626, II. 191
Knyvett, Henry, Kt.1538, II. 50
Knyvet, Henry, Kt.1574, II. 76
Knyvett (Revet), Henry, Kt.1578, II. 79
Knyvet, John, K.B.1661, I. 165
Knevet, Thomas, K.B.1509, I. 148
Knivett, Thomas, Kt.1553, II. 67
Knyvet, Thomas, Kt.1578, II. 79
Knivett, Thomas, Kt.1603, II. 106, 131
Knyvett, William, K.B.(1475), I. 137
Knevitt, William, Kt.1617, II. 163
Koester, Hans L. R. von., G.C.V.O.1904, I. 430
Kohat, Khwajah Muhammed, of, K.C.S.I.1873, I. 319
KOLHAPUR
Shahu Chatrapati, raja of, G.C.S.I. 1895, I. 313; G.C.V.O.1903, I. 420
Shivaji Chatrapati, of, K.C.S.I.1877, I. 321
Shreemun, maharaja of, K.C.S.I.1866, I. 315
König, Charles, K.H.1831, I. 466
Korea, emperor of, G.C.I.E.1900, I. 403
Kortright, Charles E. K., Kt.1886, II. 380
Kortright, Cornelius H., K.C.M.G.1882, I. 364
Kota, Umaid-Singh, of, K.C.S.I.1900, I. 327
Kotz von Dobrz, freiherr Wenzel, G.C.VO.1904, I. 429
Krag Juel, count Julius B., K.C.VO. 1904, I. 442
Krag Juel, count Magers Christian, K.C.V.O.1904, I. 442
Krus, John, Kt.1635, II. 203

INDEX

Kunwar Ranajee, G.C.B.1858, I. 192
Kuper, Augustus L., K.C.B.1864, I. 249; G.C.B.1869 I. 195
Kydwell, Morgan, K.B.1501, I. 147
Kyffen, Thomas, Kt.1782, II. 296
Kykenell, John, Kt.1485, II. 23
KYNASTON, KINASTON
  Kynaston, Edward, Kt.1593, II. 90
  Kynaston, Francis, Kt.1619, II. 170
  Kynaston, Francis, Kt1660, II. 231
  Kinaston, Roger, Kt.1471, II. 14
Kynardeston, Thomas, Kt.1513, II. 42
Kynsey, William R., Kt.1897, II. 399
Kyrle (Kearles), Richard, Kt.1661, II. 235

L

Lacaita, James P., K.C.M.G.1859, I. 353
Lack, Henry R., Kt.1891, II. 388
Lackey, John, K.C.M.G.1894, I. 379
Lacon, Edmund, Kt.1792, II. 301
Lacon, Francis, Kt.1599, II. 96
Lacoste, Alexandre, Kt.1892, II. 390
Lacy, Henry de, earl of Lincoln, Kt. 1272, II. 5
Lacy, Hugh de, Kt.(1308), II. lviii.
Lacy, John de, K.B.1306, I. 117, 119
Lacy, Robert de, K.B.1306, I. 116
Lacy, Robert (John), Kt.1619, II. 170
Lacy, Rowland, Kt.1603, II. 120
Lacy, Rowland, Kt.1685, II. 261
Lacy, Walter de, Kt.(1308), II. lviii.
Lacy. See Lucy
Ladbrooke, Robert, Kt.1744, II. 286
Laffan, Joseph de C., K.H.1836, II. 475
Laffan, Robert M., K.C.M.G.1877, I. 359
Laforey, Francis, K.C.B.1815, I. 219
Lagden, Godfrey Y., K.C.M.G.1897, I. 383
Lahej, Ahmad bin Fadthl, of, K.C.S.I. 1901, I. 327
Laing, James, Kt.1897, II. 399
Laird, William, Kt.1897, II. 399
Lajatico, marchese Pier J. C. di, K.C.V.O. 1903, I. 441
Lake, Arthur, Kt.1617, II. 164
Lake, Henry A., K.C.B.1875, I. 285
Lake, Lancelot, Kt.1660, II. 227
Lake, Thomas, Kt.1617, II. 163

Lake, Thomas, Kt.1670, II. 245
Lake, Willoughby T., K.C.B.1830, I. 230
Lake. See Leake
Lakeman, Stephen B., Kt.1853, II. 350
LAKING, LAKYN
  Laking, Francis H., Kt.1893, II. 391; K.C.V.O.(1898), I. 433; G.C.V.O. 1902, I. 419
  Lakyn, Richard, K.B.1478, I. 138
  Lakyn, Thomas, Kt.1532, II. 48
  Lakyn, Warren, Kt.1347, II. 8
Lalaing, count Jacques H. E. de, K.C.M.G.1890, I. 376
Lamb, Frederick J., viscount Melbourne, G.C.B.1827, I. 206
Lamb, John, Kt.1619, II. 170, 177
Lambard (Lambert), Molton, Kt.1608, II. 144
Lambard, Multon, Kt.1727, II. 284
Lambart, Frederick E. G., earl of Cavan, K.P.1894, I. 105
Lambermont, Francois A., G.C.B.1890, I. 213
Lambert, Cary, Kt.1622, II. 180
Lambert, Daniel, Kt.1743, II. 286
Lambert, George R., K.C.B.1853, I. 240; G.C.B.1865, I. 194
Lambert, George T., Kt.1903, II. 415
Lambert, John, K.C.B.1815, I. 221; G.C.B.1838, I. 188
Lambert, John, K.C.B.1879, I. 286
Lambert, John, K.C.I.E.1893, I. 408
Lambert, Oliver, Kt.1596, II. 92
Lambert, Thomas, Kt.1603, II. 124
Lambert, Thomas, Kt. 1620, II. 175
Lambert, William, Kt.1603, II. 103
Lambton, John G., earl of Durham, G.C.B.1837, I. 206
Lamburn, James de, K.B.1306, I. 117
Lamington, lord. See Cochraine-Baillie
Lamont, Norman, K.H.1837, I. 478
Lamotte, lt.-gen., K.C.B.1819, I. 229
LAMPLOUGH, LAMPLEY, LAMPELOWE
  Lampley, Richard, Kt.1529, II. 48
  Lamplough, George, Kt.1616, II. 160
  Lampelowe, Roger, Kt.1527, II. 46
  Lamplough, Thomas, Kt.1615, II. 155

Lampton, William, Kt.1615, II. 155
Lamvill, John, Kt.1615, II. 156
Lancaster, Henry, duke of, K.G.1348, I. 1
Lancaster, James, Kt.1603, II. 129
Lancastre, Antonio M. de, K.C.V.O.1904, I. 443
Lancastre, Thomas de, Kt.(1346), II. 6
Lancey, William H. de, K.C.B.1815, I. 223
Landaff, earl of. See Mathew
Lando, Jeronimo (Sercomius), Kt.1622, II. 179
Landseer, Edwin, Kt.1850, II. 348
Lane, George, Kt.1657, II. 225
Lane (Lamm, Lambe), John, Kt.1619, II. 170
Lane, Parr, Kt.1604, II. 132
Lane, Raphe, Kt.1593, II. 90
Lane, Rauf, Kt.1538, II. 52
Lane, Richard, Kt.1644, II. 217
Lane, Richard, Kt.1661, II. 233
Lane, Richard, Kt.1714, II. 279
Lane, Robert, Kt.1553, II. 67
Lane, Robert, Kt.1603, II. 115
Lane, Ronald B., K.C.V.O.(1904), I. 437
Lane, Thomas, Kt.1688, II. 264
Lane, William, Kt.1597, II. 94
Lanesque, John, Kt.1494, II. 28
LANG, LANGE
   Lange, Daniel A., Kt.1870, II. 362
   Lang, John de, Kt.1729, II. 284
   Lang, Robert H., K.C.M.G.1897, I. 383
Langdale, Marmaduke, Kt.1628, II. 193
Langdale, William, Kt.1660, II. 232
Langdon. See Langton
Langevin, Hector L., K.C.M.G.1881, I. 363
LANGFORD, LANGFORTH, LANGFORDE
   Langford, Christopher de, Kt.1347, II.6
   Langford, Hercules, Kt.1621, II. 177
   Langford, John, Kt.1497, II. 30
   Langford, lord. See Rowley
   Langford, Nicholas, Kt.1347, II. 6
   Langford, Nicholas, Kt.1471, II. 15
   Langford [Sanford], Rauf, K.B.(1483), I. 140
   Langforth, Rauf, Kt.1487, II. 26
   Langforde, Rauf, Kt.1529, II. 47
   Langford, Roger, Kt.1630, II. 198

Langham, James, Kt.1660, II. 226
Langham, John, Kt.1660, II. 225
Langham, Stephen, Kt.1672, II. 247
Langham, William, Kt.1671, II. 246
Langley, George C., K.C.B.1881, I. 257
Langley, Henry, Kt.1681, II. 255
Langley, John, Kt.1577, II. 78
Langley, Richard, Kt.1673, II. 248
Langley, Robert, Kt.1547, II. 60
Langstone, Stephen, Kt.1796, II. 303
LANGTON, LANGDON
   Langton, —, Kt.1347, II. 9
   Langton, John de, K.B.1306, I. 122
   Langton, John, Kt.1603, II. 111, 112
   Langdon (Langton), Philip, Kt.1630, II. 197
   Langton, Richard, Kt.1482, II. 19
   Langton, Thomas, K.B.1603, I. 155
   Langton, Thomas, Kt.1666, II. 242
   Langdon, Walter, Kt.1628, II. 194
Langworth, John, Kt.1628, II. 195
Lannoy, Timothy, Kt.1717, II. 281
Lansdowne, marquess of. See Petty; see Petty-Fitzmaurice
Lanyon, Charles, Kt.1868, II. 359
Lanyon, William O., K.C.M.G.1880, I.362
Larcom, Thomas A., K.C.B.1860, I. 281
Las Bela, Ali Khan, K.C.I.E.,1893, I. 407
Lasher (Lusher), Nicholas, Kt.1603, II. 118
LASCELLES, LASSELLS
   Lassells, Brian, Kt.1603, II. 102
   Lascelles, Frank C., K.C.M.G.1886, I. 368; G.C.M.G.1892, II. 343; G.C.B. 1897, I. 214; G.C.V.O.1904, I. 421
   Lassells, Richard (Thomas), Kt.1600, II. 98
Laten (Latyne), Warrein, Kt.1347, II. 9
Lathom, earl of. See Bootle-Wilbraham
LATIMER, LATYMER
   Latymer, —, Kt.1460, II. 12
   Latimer, lord. See Nevill; see Willoughby, J.
   Latymer, Nicholas, Kt.1471, II. 15
   Latymer, Thomas D., K.B.1305, I. 111
   Latimer (Latyne), Warrein, Kt.1347, II. 8
   Latimer, William, lord Latimer, K.G. 1361, I. 3

INDEX 135

Lau d'Allemand, marquess Alfred T. A. du, K.C.V.O.1904, I. 443
Lauchlan (Lachlan), Maclean, Kt.1812, II. 312
Lauderdale, earl and duke of. See Maitland

LAUNDE, LAWNE, LOUNDRES
Loundres, Edmund, Kt.(1397), I. lx.
Launde, Gregory de la, Kt.(1335), I. lix.
Loundres, John, Kt.(1397), I. lx.
Lawne (de la Launde), Thomas, Kt. 1497, II. 30

Launey, John de. See Dauney
Laurie, Peter, Kt.1824, II. 324
Laurie, Robert, K.C.B.1831, I. 231
Laurent, Peter F., Kt.1768, II. 293
Laurier, Wilfrid, G.C.M.G.1897, I. 345
Lautour, Peter A., K.H.1816, I. 463
Lauzan, Francis N. de C., duke of, K.G. 1692, I. 38
Lavie, Thomas, K.C.B.1815, I. 222
Lavington, lord. See Payne
Lavins, Monsieur, Kt.1596, II. 92
Law, Edward, lord Ellenborough, Kt. 1801, II. 305
Law, Edward, earl of Ellinborough, G.C.B.1844, I. 207
Law, Edward F., K.C.M.G.1898, I. 385
Law, Robert, K.H.1837, I. 478
La Warr. See Warr
Lawes, Nicholas, Kt.1717, II. 281
Lawford, John, K.C.B.1838, I. 234
Lawley, Arthur, K.C.M.G.1901, I. 389
Lawley, Beilby, lord Wenlock, G.C.I.E. 1891, I. 402; G.C.S.I.1896, I. 314; K.C.B.1901, I. 299
Lawley, Edward, Kt.1619, II. 175
Lawne. See Launde
Lawrance, John C., Kt.1890, II. 387

LAWRENCE, LAURENCE
Lawrence, Alfred T., Kt.1904, II. 419
Lawrence, Arthur J., K.C.B.1869, I. 252
Lawrence, Edward, Kt.1619, II. 174
Laurence, Edward, Kt.1643, II. 216
Laurence, Edward, Kt.1701, II. 272
Lawrence, Edward, Kt.1899, II. 404

LAWRENCE
Lawrence, George St. P., K.C.S.I.1866, I. 316
Lawrence, Henry M., K.C.B.1848, I. 277
Lawrence, James, Kt.1482, II. 19
Lawrence, John, Kt.1610, II. 149
Laurence, John, Kt.1660, II. 228
Lawrence, John J. T., K.C.V.O.(1902), II. 435
Lawrence, John L. M., lord Lawrence, K.C.B.1856, I. 279; G.C.B.1857, I. 208; K.S.I.1861, I. 306; G.C.S.I. 1866, I. 308; Grand Master S.I., I. 305
Laurence, Joseph, Kt.1714, II. 279
Lawrence, Joseph, Kt.1902, II. 411
Lawrence, Nicholas, Kt.1471, II. 15
Lawrence, Olyver, Kt.1547, II. 61
Lawrence, Soulden, Kt.1794, II. 302
Laurence, Thomas, K.B.1501, II. 145
Lawrence, Thomas, Kt.1815, II. 315
Lawrence, Walter R., K.C.I.E.1903, I. 411
Lawrence, William, Kt.1887, II. 382
Lawrie, Archibald C., Kt.1901, II. 409

LAWSON, LUSON, and see Dawson
Lawson, Charles A., Kt.1887, II. 381
Lawson, George, Kt.1527, II. 46
Lawson, George, K.C.B.1897, I. 295
Lawson, John, Kt.1604, II. 136
Lawson, John, Kt.1660,II. 231
Lawson, Rafe, Kt.1603, II. 115
Lawson, Richard, Kt.1553, II. 67
Lawson (Luson), Walter (Wilfred), Kt. 1603, II. 117
Lawson, Wilford, Kt.1604, II. 131
Lawson, Wilfrid, Kt.1641, II. 208
Lawson, William, Kt.1553, II. 68

Laxton, William, Kt.1545, II. 57
Layard, Charles P., Kt.1903, II.415
Layard, Henry A., G.C.B.1878, I. 210
Layard, Peter, K.C.M.G.1876, I. 358
Layborne. See Leybourne
Layton. See Leighton
Lea. See Leigh

INDEX

Leach, Leech
  Leech, Bosdin T., Kt.1894, II. 394
  Leach, Edward, Kt.1621, II. 178
  Leach, George A., K.C.B.1892, I. 292
  Leach, John, Kt.1817, II. 318
  Leach, John, K.C.V.O.(1904), I. 437
  Leech, Simon, Kt.1625, II. 189
  Leech, Simon, K.B.1661, I. 166
  Leech, Walter, Kt.1626, II. 191
  Leech, William, Kt.1660, II. 228
Leader (Leder), Oliver, Kt.1555, II. 69
Leake, Leyke, Luke, Lake, Leek
  Leake (Luke), Andrew, Kt.1703, II. 273
  Leyke, Francis, Kt.1545, II. 58
  Leake, Francis, Kt.1604, II. 98, 131
  Leeke, Henry J., Kt.1835, II. 336; K.H.1836, I. 475; K.C.B.1858, I. 245
  Leyke, John, Kt.1513, II. 41
  Leake, John, Kt.1704, II. 273
  Leake, Luke S., Kt.1876, II. 368
  Leake (Lake), Thomas, Kt.1603, II. 109
  Leek (Leake), William, Kt.1603, II.108
Leamore, Joseph, Kt.1643, II. 216
Lechford, Richard, Kt.1603, II. 118
Lechford, Richard, Kt.1623, II. 182
Lechmere, Nicholas, Kt.1689, II. 265
Lecky, Thomas, Kt.1887, II. 383
Léclezio, Eugene P. J., Kt.1887, II. 381
Lee. See Leigh
Leech. See Leach
Leeds, Leedes
  Leeds, duke of. See Osborne
  Leedes, John, Kt.1611, II. 150
  Leeds, Thomas, K.B.1603, I. 155
Lees, Charles C., K.C.M.G.1883, I. 365
Lees, Edward S., Kt.1821, II. 323
Lees, John C., Kt.1865, II. 358
Leese, Joseph F., Kt.1895, II. 396
Leeson, Edward N., earl of Milltown, K.P.1890, I. 105
Leeson, Joseph, earl of Milltown, K.P. 1841, I. 101
Leeson, William E., Kt.1838, II. 340
Le Fevre. See Fevre
Lefroy, John H., K.C.M.G.1877, I. 359
Legard, Robert, Kt.1682, II. 258
Legge, Arthur K., K.C.B.1815, I. 219
Legge, George, earl of Dartmouth, K.G. 1805, I. 50

Legh. See Leigh
Le Gris. See Grise
Le Grosse. See Grosse

Leicester, Leycester, Layster, Lester
  Leicester, —, Kt.1603, II. 126
  Leicester, earl of. See Dudley; see Sydney; see Coke
  Lester (Leycester), George, Kt.1599, II. 97
  Lester, John, Kt.1802, II. 306
  Layster (Leycester), Rauff, Kt.1544, II. 55

Leigh, Lee, Legh, Ley, Lea, Leight
  Leigh, —, Kt.1601, II. 99
  Leghe, Anthony, Kt.1538 ,II. 51
  Lee (Leigh), Charles, Kt.1645, II. 220
  Leigh, Daniel, Kt.1622, II. 178
  Lee, Edward, Kt.1603, II. 111
  Lee, Edward, Kt.1872, II. 364
  Leigh, Edward C., K.C.B.1901, I. 298
  Legh (Leigh), Ferdinando, Kt.1617, II. 162
  Leigh, Francis, earl of Chichester, K.B.1603, I. 155
  Leigh, Francis (Olave), Kt.1613, II. 152
  Leigh, Francis, Kt.1618, II. 170
  Leigh, Francis, Kt.1671, II. 246
  Lee, Francis G. G., Kt.1832, II. 333
  Lee, George, Kt.1752, II. 288
  Lee, George P., Kt.1844, II. 345
  Lee (Ley), Henry, Kt.1553, II. 66; K.G.1597, I. 29
  Lea, Henry, Kt.1561, II. 71
  Leigh, Henry, Kt.1603, II. 101
  Legh (Lee), Henry, Kt.1607, II. 142
  Lee (Leigh), Henry, Kt.1611, II. 151
  Lee, Henry, Kt.1614, II. 154
  Ley (Leigh), Henry Kt.1617 II. 165
  Lee, Henry, Kt.1618, II. 168
  Lee, Henry A., K.C.M.G.1902, I. 393
  Lea (Ley), James, Kt.1603, II. 129
  Leigh, James, Kt.1683, II. 258
  Lee, John, K.B.1501, I. 146, 147
  Lee (Legh), John, Kt.1544, II. 55
  Lee (Lye, Leigh), John à, Kt.1553, II. 67
  Lea, John, Kt.1596, II. 93
  Lee (Leigh), John, Kt.1603, II.104, 116

INDEX

LEE
Lee (Leigh), John, Kt.1605, II. 138
Leigh, John, Kt.1606, II. 140
Leigh, John, Kt.1616, II. 157
Leigh, John, Kt.1628, II. 195
Lee, John, Kt.1629, II. 196
Leigh, John, Kt.1685, II. 261
Leigh, John, Kt.1702, II. 272
Lee, John T., Kt.1827, II. 327
Leigh, Joseph, Kt.1894, II. 394
Lee, Joseph C., Kt.1882, II. 374
Lee, Peter, Kt.1544, II. 54
Lee, Peter (Pierre), Kt.1599, II. 92, 98
Legh, Piers A., Kt.1482, II. 18
Lee, Richard, Kt.1471, II. 16
Lee, Richard, Kt.1544, II. 55
Lee, Richard, Kt.1599, II. 98
Lea, Richard, Kt.1611, II. 150
Lee, Richard, K.C.B.1815, I. 220
Leghe, Robert, Kt.1529, II. 47
Lee (Leigh), Robert, Kt.1603, II. 108, 109
Lee, Robert, Kt.1608, II. 146
Leigh, Robert, Kt.1616, II. 157
Leigh, Robert, Kt.1642, II. 214
Leight (Lee), alias Doctor, Thomas, Kt.1544, II. 54
Leigh, Thomas, Kt.1558, II. 70
Lee (Leigh), Thomas, Kt.1608, II. 146
Leigh, Thomas, Kt.1616, II. 160
Leigh, Thomas, Kt.1642, II. 214
Leigh, Thomas, Kt.1661, II. 234
Leigh, Thomas, Kt.1669, II. 243
Leigh, William, Kt.1589, II. 87
Leigh, William (John or Pierre), Kt. 1596, II. 92
Leigh, William, Kt.1624, II. 185
Lee, William, Kt.1737, II. 285
Lee-Warner, William, K.C.S.I.1898, I. 326

LEIGHTON, LAYTON
Layton, Brian, Kt.1544, II. 54
Leyton, Christopher de, Kt.1347, II. 8
Leighton, David, K.C.B.1837, I. 233
Layton, Edward, Kt.1591, II. 88
Leighton, Ellis, Kt.1659, II. 225
Leighton, Frederick, Kt.1878, II. 370
Leighton, James, Kt.1830, II. 329
Leighton, Thomas, Kt.1513, II. 36

LEIGHTON
Layton (Leighton), Thomas, Kt.1579, II. 79
Leighton, Thomas (John), Kt.1615, II. 157
Layton (Laton, Leighton), William, Kt.1603, II. 121
Layton, William, Kt.1645, II. 220
Leighton, William, Kt.1800, II. 305

LEININGEN
Charles W. F. E., prince of, K.G.1837, I. 55
Edward E. C., prince of, G.C.V.O.1898, I. 418
Edward F. M. J., prince of, K.C.V.O. 1898, I. 438
Ernest L., etc., prince of, K.C.B.1863, I. 283 ; G.C.B.1866, 1887, I. 209, 199
Leinster, Arthur, king of, K.B.1394, I. 127
Leinster, duke of. See FitzGerald
Leisure. See Lisures
Leith, Alexander, K.C.B.1815, I. 224
Leith, James, K.B.1813, I. 178 ; G.C.B. 1815, I. 181
Leitrim, earl of. See Clements
Lekeborn, Peter de, K.B.1306, I. 121
Lely, Peter, Kt.1680, II. 254
Leman, John, Kt.1617, II. 161
Le Marchant, John G., Kt.1838, II. 340 ; G.C.M.G.1860, I. 335 ; K.C.B.1865, I. 283
Lemvigh, Waldemar E., K.C.V.O.1904, I. 442
Leng, John, Kt.1893, II. 392
Leng, William C., Kt.1887, II. 381
Lennox, Charles, duke of Richmond, K.G.1681, I. 37
Lennox, Charles, duke of Richmond, K.B.1725, I. 167 ; K.G.1726, I. 42
Lennox, Charles, duke of Richmond, K.G.1782, I. 47
Lennox, Charles, duke of Richmond, Grand Master K.P.1807, I. 93 ; K.G. 1812, I. 50
Lennox, duke of. See Stuart
Lennox, Wilbraham O., K.C.B.1891, I. 263
Lentaigne, John, Kt.1880, II. 371
Lenthall, Edward, Kt.1608, II. 146

Lenthall, John Kt.1616, II. 160
Lenthall, John, Kt.1658, II. 224
Lenthall, John, Kt.1678, II. 252

LEONARD, LENNARD
　Leonard, Henry, Kt.1596, II. 92
　Lennard, Samuel (Sampson), Kt.1603, II. 126
Lépine, Louis, G.C.V.O.1903, I. 427
Le Poer Trench, Richard, viscount Clancarty, G.C.B.1815, I. 183; G.C.H. 1821, I. 449
Le Poer Trench, Robert, K.C.B.1815, I. 223
Lequesne, John, Kt.1737, II. 285
Lere, Banco de, K.B.1329, I. 125
Lerment (Larmant), John, Kt.1604, II. 136
Le Scrope. See Scrope

LESLEY, LESLIE
　Lesley, Alexander, Kt.1627, II. 193
　Leslie, Bradford, K.C.I.E.1887, I. 400
　Leslie, Charles, K.H.1836, I. 473
　Lesley, James (John), Kt.1625, II. 188
　Leslie, John, earl of Rothes, K.T.1753, I. 78
　Leslie, John, K.H.1831, I. 466; Kt. 1832, II. 332
　Leslie, John, K.H.1837, I. 476
　Lesley, Patrick, Kt.1651, II. 222
　Leslie. See Lesley
Lesseps, Ferdinand de, G.C.S.I.1870, I. 310
Lester. See Leicester

L'ESTRANGE, LESTRANGE, LE STRANGE, and see STRANGE
　L'Estrange, George B., Kt.1860, II. 355
　Le Strange, Hamon, Kt.1604, II. 129
　Le Strange, John, lord Strange of Knokyn, K.B.(1461), I. 133
　Lestrange, Nicholas, Kt.1589, II. 87
　Lestrange, Thomas, Kt.1584, II. 83
Letchworth, Edward, Kt.1902, II. 413
Lethbridge, Alfred S., K.C.S.I.1896, I. 325

Lethbridge, Roper, Kt.1885, II. 378; K.C.I.E.1890, I. 406
Lethieullier, Christopher, Kt.1689, II. 265
Lethieullier, John, Kt.1674, II. 249
Leuthold, von, K.C.V.O.1901, I. 439
Levaillant, Charles, K.C.B.1856, I. 242
Levens (Lewens), Fabian, Kt.1607, II. 143
Leventhorp, John,, Kt.1603, II. 104
Lever, Ashton, Kt.1778, II. 296
Lever, James D., Kt.1737, II. 285
Lever, Richard, Kt.1596, II. 94

LEVESON, LEWSON
　Leveson, John, Kt.1589, II. 87
　Leveson, John (James), Kt.1611, II. 151
　Lewson (Lawson, Lasen), Richard, Kt. 1553, II. 67
　Lewson (Leveson), Richard, Kt.1596, II. 92
　Lewson, Richard, K.B.1626, I. 162
　Leveson, Thomas, Kt.1621, II. 177
　Lewson (Leveson), Walter, Kt.1587, II. 85
　Leveson-Gower, Francis, earl of Ellesmere, K.G.1855, I. 59
　Leveson-Gower, Granville, earl Granville, G.C.B.1825, I. 206
　Leveson-Gower, Granville, earl Granville, K.G.1857, I. 60
　Leveson-Gower, Granvile, marquess of Stafford, K.G.1771, I. 47
　Leveson-Gower, George Granville, duke of Sutherland, K.G.1806, I. 50
Levesque (Lanesque), John, Kt.1494, II. 28
Leveston, Henry, Kt.1616, II. 158
Levet, Richard, Kt.1691, II. 266
Levinge, Charles, K.H.1837, I. 478
Levinge, Creswell, Kt.1678, II. 253
Levinge, Richard, Kt.1692, II. 267
Levingston, George, Kt.1594, II. 91
Levingston, William, Kt.1594, II. 91
Lewens. See Levens

LEWIN, LEWYN, LEWEN, LOWEN
Lewin, Gregory A., Kt.1820, II. 321
Lewen (Lowen), Justinian, Kt.1604, II. 130
Lewyn (Lewen), Justinian, Kt.1661, II. 234
Lewen (Lewyn), William, Kt.1712, II. 277
LEWIS, LEWES, LOYS, LOUIS
Lewis, Edward, Kt.1603, II. 104
Lewes (Lewis), Edward, Kt.1608, II. 145
Lewis (Loys), Henry, Kt.1460, II. 12
Lewis, George H., Kt.1893, II. 392
Lewis, John, Kt.1604, II. 134
Lewis, John, Kt.1660, II. 226
Lewis, Neil E., K.C.M.G.1902, I. 392
Lewis (Fitz-Lewes), Richard, Kt.1497, II. 29
Lewis, Samuel, Kt.1896, II. 397
Lewes, Samuel W. S., Kt.1886, II. 379
Lewis, Simon, Kt.1679, II. 254
Lewis, Thomas, Kt.1628, II. 194
Lewis, Walter W., Kt.1904, II. 420
Lewes (Lewis), Watkin, Kt.1773, II. 294
Lewis, William, Kt.1619, II. 174
Lewis (Louis), William, Kt.1703, II. 273
Lewis, William T., Kt.1885, II. 378
LEWKENOR, LEWKNOR, LEWKENORE
Lewkenor, Christopher, Kt.1644, II. 219
Lewkenor, Edward, Kt.1603, II. 106, 140, 144
Lewkenor, John, K.B.1661, II. 165
Lewknor, Lewis, Kt.1603, II. 102
Lewkenor, Lewis, Kt.1644, II. 219
Lewkenor, Richard, Kt.1600, II. 98
Lewkner, Robert, Kt.1608, II. 144
Lewknor, Roger, K.B.(1449), I. 132
Lewkenor, Roger, K.B.(1485), I. 142
Lewkenore, Thomas de, K.B.1306, I. 119
Lewkenor, Thomas (James), K.B. (1483), I. 139, 141
Lewsey, Thomas, Kt.1604, II. 130
Lewson. See Leveson
Ley. See Leigh

LEYBOURNE, LAYBORNE
Layborne, —, Kt.1347, II. 9
Leybourne, James, Kt.1529, II. 48
Leyborne, John de, Kt.1347, II. 8
Leylonde, William, Kt.1513, II. 42
Li Ching Fong, K.C.V.O.1896, I. 438
Li Hung Chang, G.C.V.O.1896, I. 422
Liang-Chêng, Chêntung, K.C.M.G.1897, I. 384
Libreto (d'Albret), lord de, Kt.(1355), II. 9
Lidcott. See Lytcott
LIDDELL, LIDDALL
Liddell, Adolphus F. O., K.C.B.1880, I. 287
Liddell, John, Kt.1848, II. 347; K.C.B.1864, I. 248
Liddall, Richard, Kt.1617, II. 165
Liddell (Lydall), Thomas, Kt.1621, II. 178
Liechtenstein, prince Rudolf von, G.C.V.O.1903, I. 428
Lien (Linn, Lyn), Thomas, Kt.1487, II. 25
Light, Henry, K.C.B.1848, I. 277
Ligonier, Edward, earl Ligonier, K.B. 1781, I. 173
Ligonier, John L., earl Ligonier, K.B. 1743, I. 169
Lile. See Lisle
Lille. See Lisle
Lilley, Charles, Kt.1881, I. 373
Lillie, John S., Kt.1816, II. 316, 318; Kt.1817, II. 318
Lima, Wenceslau de, G.C.V.O.1903, I. 426
Limerick, earl of. See Pery
Limond, James, Kt.1835, II. 335
Limri, Thakur of, K.C.I.E.1887, I. 405
Linch. See Lynch
Lincoln, earl of. See Lacy; see Pole; see Clinton; see Pelham-Clinton
Lind, James, Kt.1805, II. 308; K.C.B. 1815, I. 222
Lindequist, gen. von, G.C.V.O.1901, I. 425
Lindley, Henrie, Kt.1599, II. 96
Lindley, Nathaniel, Kt.1875, II. 367

LINDSAY, LINDESAY
  Lindsay, Alexander, KC.B.1862, I. 247
  Lindsay, James, K.C.M.G.1870, I.355
  Lindsay, James L., earl of Crawford, K.T.1891, I. 88
  Lindsay, John, Kt.1594, II. 91
  Lindesay, John, K.B.1603, I. 154
  Lindsay, John, K.B.1770, I. 171
  Lindsay, John, Kt.1764, II. 292
  Lindesay, Patrick, K.C.H.1834, I.460; Kt.1836, II. 338; K.C.B.1838, I. 234

LINDSEY, LYNDSEY
  Lindsey, earl. See Bertie
  Lyndsey, Thomas, Kt.1482, II. 18

LINGEN, LYNGEYN, LYNGEYNE, LINGAIN
  Lingen, Henry, Kt.1645, II. 220
  Lingain, John de, K.B.1306, I. 118
  Lyngeyne, John, Kt.1471, II. 14
  Lyngeyn, John, Kt.1486, II. 23
  Lyngeyn, John, Kt.1504, II. 34
  Lingen, Ralph R. W., K.C.B.1879, I. 286

Linlithgow, marquess of. See Hope
Linsingen, Charles, count, K.C.B.1815, I. 226
Linton, James D., Kt.1885, II. 377
Linton, William, K.C.B.1865, I. 250
Linwray, John, Kt.1604, II. 134
Lipton, Thomas J., Kt.1898, II. 402; K.C.V.O.(1901), I. 433
Liria, duke of. See Fitzjames
Lisgar, lord. See Young

LISLE, L'ISLE, LILLE, LILE, LYLE, LISLEY, DE INSULA, LYSLEY, LYSLE
  Lille (Lisle), Arnold de, Kt.1642, II. 214
  Lisle (Lyle), George, Kt.1645, II. 220
  Lisle, Gerard, K.B.1377, I. 126
  Lisle, Gerard de, lord Lisle of Kingston Lisle, K.B.1327, I. 124
  Lille (Lillo), Henry, Kt.1608, II. 144
  Lysley (Lyll), Humphrey, Kt.1497, II. 32
  L'Isle, John de, lord Lisle of the Isle of Wight, K.B.1306, I. 114

LISLE
  Lisle, John de, lord Lisle de Rougemont, Kt.1336, II. 5; banneret1346, II. 5; K.G.1348, I. 1
  Lisle, John de, Kt.1347, II. 8
  Lisle, John, K.B.1400, I. 128
  Lysle, John, Kt.1504, II. 34
  Lisle and Dudley, lord. See Sidney, P.
  Lile, Nicholas, K.B.(1483), I. 140, 142
  Lisle, Robert, Kt.1406, II. 11
  Lisle, viscount. See Talbot; see Grey; see Dudley; see Sydney
  L'Isle, Walter de, K.B.1306, I. 119
  Lisle, Warren de, Kt.1347, II. 8
  Lysle, William, Kt.1513, II. 42
  Lisle (Lisley), William, Kt.1606, II.139
  Lisle, William, Kt.1665, II. 241
  Lislebone, Walter, K.B.1306, I. 111
  Lisley. See Lisle
  Lismore, earl of. See O'Brien; see O'Callaghan

LISTER, LYSTER
  Lyster, John, Kt.1628, II. 194
  Lyster (Bister), Martin, Kt.1625, II. 188
  Lyster, Matthew, Kt.1636, II. 204
  Lyster, Michael, Kt.1537, II. 50
  Lister, Thomas, Kt.1642, II. 214
  Lister, Thomas V., K.C.M.G.1885, I. 368
  Lister, William Kt.1615, II. 156
  Liston, Robert, G.C.B.1816, I. 205
  Listowel, earl of. See Hare
  Lisures (Leesures, Leisure), Stephen, Kt. 1608, II. 144
  Littebon (Villabon), William, K.B.1306, I. 122
  Little, Archibald, K.C.B.1869, I. 252; G.C.B.1889, I. 200
  Little, James, Kt.1816, II. 318
  Little, Joseph I., Kt.1901, II. 409
  Littledale, Joseph, Kt.1824, II. 325
  Littlejohn, Henry D., Kt.1895, II. 396
  Littler, John H., K.C.B.1844, I. 238; G.C.B.1848, I. 190
  Littler, Ralph D. M., Kt.1902, II. 411
  Littleton, Litleton, Littilton. See Lyttleton
  Litton. See Lytton

INDEX 141

Liverpool, earl of. See Jenkinson
Livesey, George T., Kt.1902, II. 411
Llewelyn, Robert, B., K.C.M.G.1898, I. 384

LLOYD, FLOYD, LLOYDE, FLUDD
Lloyd, Charles Kt.1644 II. 218
Lloyd Charles, Kt.1693, II. 268
Lloyd, Edward, Kt.1630, II. 198
Lloyd, Edward, K.H.1834, I. 470
Lloyd, Evan, Kt.1586, II. 85
Lloyd, Evan, K.C.H.1834, I. 459; Kt. 1834, II. 334
Lloyd, Francis, Kt.1643, II. 215
Lloyd, Godfrey, Kt.1657, II. 225
Lloyd, Horatio, Kt.1890, II. 387
Lloyd (Floyd), John, Kt.1586, II. 85
Lloyd (Fluid), John, Kt.1624, II. 183
Lloyd, John, Kt.1678, II. 253
Lloyd, Marmaduke, Kt.1622, II. 178
Lloyd, Nathaniel, Kt.1710, II. 277
Lloyd, Philip, Kt.1674, II. 249
Lloyd, Richard, Kt.1642, II. 214
Lloyd, Richard, Kt.1674, II. 249
Lloyd, Richard, Kt.1677, II. 251
Lloyd, Richard, Kt.1745, II. 287
Lloyd, Robert, Kt.1616, II. 159
Lloyde, alias Fludd, Thomas, Kt.1589, II. 87
Lloyd, Walter, Kt.1643, II. 215
Lloyd, William, Kt.1838, II. 340
Lluellyn, Richard, K.C.B.1862, I. 247
Lobos (Loges), Ferdinand de Villa, Kt. 1501, II. 33
Loch, Henry B., lord Loch, K.C.B.1880, I. 287; G.C.M.G. 1887, I. 341; G.C.B.1892, I. 214
Lock, John, Kt.1717, II. 281
Lock, Joseph, Kt.1814, II. 314
Locke, William, Kt.1549, II. 63
Lockhart, William Kt.1656, II. 223
Lockhart, William S. A., K.C.B.1887, I. 262; K.C.S.I.1895; I. 325; G.C.B. 1898, I. 202
Lockrane. See Lorayn
Lockton, John, Kt.1603, II. 125
Lockwood, Frank, Kt.1894, II. 394
Lockwood, George H., K.C.B.1867, I. 250

Lockyer, Henry F., K.H.1837, I. 478
Lockyer, Joseph N., K.C.B.1897, I. 295
Loder. See Lowther
Lodge, Edmund, K.H.1832, I. 468
Lodge, Oliver J., Kt.1902, II. 411
Lodge, Thomas, Kt.1563, II. 71
Lodovick, count, Kt.1596, II. 92
Loewenfeld, Alfred von, K.C.V.O.1902, I. 440
Loftus, Adam, Kt.1604, II. 136
Loftus, Adam, Kt.1611, II. 150
Loftus, Arthur, Kt.1634, II. 202
Loftus, lord Augustus W. F. S., K.C.B. 1862, I. 282; G.C.B.1866, I. 209
Loftus, Charles, earl of Ely, K.P.1794, I. 97
Loftus, Dudley, Kt.1593, II. 90
Loftus, Dudley, Kt.1630, II. 197
Loftus, Edward, Kt.1599, II. 98
Loftus, Edward, Kt.1623, II. 180
Loftus, Henry, earl of Ely, K.P.1783, I. 97
Loftus, John, marquess of Ely, K.P.1807, I. 98
Loftus, Nicholas, Kt.1662, II. 237
Loftus, Robert, Kt.1619, II. 174
Loftus, Thomas, Kt.1599, II. 98
Logan, Charles B., Kt.1899, II. 405
Logan, Thomas G., K.C.B.1869, I. 252
Logan, William E., Kt.1856, II. 351
Login, John S., Kt.1854, II. 351
Loh-Feng-Luh, K.C.V.O.1896, I. 438
Loharu, Amir-ud-din, of, K.C.I.E.1897, I. 409
Lombe, Thomas, Kt.1727, II. 283
Londesborough, lord. See Conyngham
Londonderry, marquess of. See Stewart; see Vane; see Vane-Tempest; see Vane-Tembest-Stewart
Lonsdale, earl of. See Lowther

LONG, LONGE
Long, Charles, lord Farnborough, G.C.B.1820, I. 205
Longe, Edward, Kt.1578, II. 78
Long, George H., Kt.1897, II. 399
Longe, Henry, Kt.1513, II. 38
Long, Lislebone, Kt.1656, II. 223
Longe, Richard, Kt.1537, II. 50
Long, Thomas, K.B.1501, I. 146

INDEX

Long
  Longe, Walter, Kt.1589, II. 87
  Long, Walter, Kt.1625, II. 188
  Long, William, Kt.1814, II. 314
  Longchamp, Henry, K.B.1323, I. 122
  Longden, Henry E., K.C.B.1886, I. 260
  Longden, James R., K.C.M.G.1876, I. 358; G.C.M.G.1883, I. 339
  Longespée, William, K.B.1233, I. 109
  Longfeild. See Longueville
  Longhurst, Henry B., Kt.1902, II. 412
  Longley, Henry, K.C.B.1889, I. 291
  Longmore, Thomas, Kt.1886, II. 379
  Longford, —, Kt.1533, II. 50
  Longford, earl of. See Pakenham
  Longford (Alonghford), Rauf, K.B. (1426), I. 132
Longueville, Longvile, Longfeild, Longville, Longeville
  Longueville, Gaston de Foix, count of, K.G.1438, I. 11
  Longfeild (Longvile), Henry, Kt.1603, II. 111, 116
  Longeville, John de, K.B.1306, I. 118
  Longville, John, Kt.1487, II. 26
  Longevill, Michael, Kt.1618, II. 167
  Longvill, Thomas, Kt.1623, II. 183
  Longueville, Thomas, Kt.1646, II. 221
Loosse (Losse), Hugh, Kt.1603, II. 108
Lopes, Henry C., Kt.1876, II. 368
Lorayn (Lockrane), Edward, Kt.1603, II. 101
Lord, Riley, Kt.1900, II. 408
Lorimer, James, K.C.M.G.1887, I. 370
Loring, Loryng
  Loring, John W., K.C.H.1837, I. 462; Kt.1837, II. 339; K.C.B.1840, I. 236
  Loryng, Nele, K.G.1348, I. 2
  Loring, William, K.C.B.1875, I. 255
Lorne, marquess of. See Campbell
Lort, John, Kt.1662, II. 236
Lotbinière, Henri G. J. de, K.C.M.G. 1895, I. 380
Lothian, marquess of. See Kerr
Loudoun, earl of. See Campbell
Louis. See Lewis
Loundres. See Launde
Louther. See Lowther

Lovat, lord. See Fraser
Love, James F., K.H.1831, I. 465; K.C.B. 1856, I. 243; G.C.B.1865, I. 194
Love, Thomas, Kt.1625, II. 190
Lovel, Lovell
  Lovell, Francis, Kt.1603, II. 101
  Lovell, Frauncys, viscount Lovel, Kt.1482, II. 19 K.G.1483, I. 16
  Lovell, Francis H., Kt.1900, II. 405
  Lovell, Gregory, Kt.1487, II. 24, 25
  Lovell, Henry, Kt.1607 II. 143
  Lovel, Henry, lord Morley, K.B.1478, I. 137
  Lovel, John, lord Lovel of, K.G.1405, I. 8
  Lovell, Lovell B., K.H.1835, I. 471; K.C.B.1856, I. 243
  Lovel, Richard, K.B.1306, I. 112
  Lovel, Robert, K.B.1306, I. 116
  Lovell, Robert, Kt.1497, II. 29
  Lovell, Robert, Kt.1596, II. 93
  Lovel, Salathiel, Kt.1692, II. 267
  Lovell, Stanhope, K.H.1836, I. 475
  Lovell, Thomas, Kt.1487, II. 24; Kt. 1497, II. 28; K.G.1498, I. 19
  Lovell, Thomas, Kt.1513, II. 38
  Lovell, Thomas, Kt.1553, II. 67
  Lovell, William, Kt.1347, II. 7
  Lovelace, Richard, Kt.1497, II. 30
  Lovelace, Richard, Kt.1599, II. 97
  Lovelace, William, Kt.1599, II. 97
  Lovelace, William, Kt.1609, II. 148
  Lovet (Lovertt), Robert, Kt.1606, II. 141
  Lovet. See Lovel
Lowe, Low
  Low, Alexander, K.C.B.1904, I. 276
  Lowe, Edward, Kt.1673, II. 247
  Lowe, Gabriell, Kt.1618, II. 167
  Lowe, Gabriel, Kt.1660, II. 231
  Lowe, Hudson, Kt.1814, II. 313; K.C.B.1816, I. 228; G.C.M.G.1837, I. 334
  Low, Hugh, K.C.M.G.1883, I. 366; G.C.M.G.1889, I. 342
  Low, James, Kt.1895, II. 396
  Lowe, John, Kt.1661, II. 234
  Low, John, K.C.B.1862, I. 247; G.C.S.I.1873, I. 310
  Low, Philip le, K.B.1306, I. 116

INDEX

LOWE
Lowe, Robert, viscount Sherbrooke, G.C.B.1885, I. 211
Low, Robert C., K.C.B.1887, I. 262; G.C.B.1896, I. 201
Low, Sigismund, baron, K.C.B.1815, I. 226
Lowe, Timothy, Kt.1603, II. 120
Lowe, Thomas, Kt.1603, II. 128
Lowen, Pierce, K.H.1837, I. 478
Lowen. See Lewin
Lower, Francis, Kt.1622, II. 179
Lower, Nicholas, Kt.1619, II. 171
Lower, William, Kt.1603, II. 107, 134
Lowreston (Loweston), Robert, Kt.1604, II. 136

LOWTHER, LODER, LOUTHER, LOWDER
Lowther, Christopher, Kt.1603, II. 100, 113
Lowther, Garret, Kt.1618, II. 168
Lowther, Gerrard, Kt.1631, II. 199
Loder, Hugh, K.B.1501, I. 147
Lowther (Loder), John, Kt.1626, II. 190
Lowther, Lancelot, Kt.1631, II. 199
Louther, Richard, Kt.1603, II. 101, 113
Lowther, William, Kt.1661, II. 236
Lowther, William, earl of Lonsdale, K.G.1807, I. 50
Lowthrop, William, Kt.1840, II. 342
Lowry-Corry, Montagu W., lord Rowton, K.C.V.O.(1897), I. 432
Lowry-Corry, Somerset R., earl of Belmore, K.C.M.G.1872, I. 356; G.C.M.G.1890, I. 342
Loyd-Lindsay, Robert J., lord Wantage, K.C.B.1881, I. 287
Loys. See Lewis
Luard, William G., K.C.B.1897, I. 267
Lubbock, Neville, K.C.M.G.1899, I. 386
Lucan, earl of. See Bingham
Lucas, Alfred W., K.C.B.1893, I. 264
Lucas, Charles, Kt.1639, II. 207
Lucas, John, Kt.1638, II. 205
Lucas, Thomas, Kt.1571, II. 75
Lucas, Thomas, Kt.1628, II. 194
Luchana, Baldomero E., count of, G.C.B. 1840, I. 189

LUCK, LUKE
Luck, George, K.C.B.1897, I. 268
Luke (Luck), John, Kt.1603, II. 107
Luke, Oliver, Kt.1603, II. 106
Luke, Samuel, Kt.1624, II. 185
Luckyn, Capell, Kt.1660, II. 227

LUCY, LACY
Lucy, Edmond, Kt.1503, II. 33
Lucy (Lacy), Edmond, Kt.1603, II. 102
Lucy, Richard, Kt.1618, II. 167
Lucy, Robert, Kt.1603, II. 108
Lucy, Thomas de, K.B.1306, I. 114
Lucy, Thomas, Kt.1512, II. 35
Lucy, Thomas, Kt.1565, II. 72
Lucy, Thomas, Kt.1592, II. 90
Lucy, William de, K.B.1306, I. 120
Lucy, William, K.B.(1487), I. 142
Ludlam, George, Kt.1719, II. 281

LUDLOW, LUTLOW
Ludlow, Christopher de, Kt.1347, II. 7
Ludlow (Lutlow), Edmund, Kt.1601, II. 99
Ludlow, George J., earl Ludlow, K.B. 1804, I. 176; G.C.B.1815, I. 180
Ludlow, Henry, Kt.1890, II. 387
Ludlow, Richard, K.B.(1475), I. 137
Ludlow, Thomas de, K.B.1306, I. 113
Ludlow, William de, K.B.1306, I. 113
Lugard, Edward, K.C.B.1858, I. 244; G.C.B.1867, I. 195
Lugard, Frederick J. D., K.C.M.G.1901, I. 388
Lugeol, Jean, K.C.B.1857, I. 244
Luke. See Luck

LUMLEY, LOMLEY
Lomley, George, Kt.1461, II. 13
Lumley, George de, lord Lumley, Kt. 1482, II. 20
Lumley, James R., K.C.B.1844, I. 238
Lumley, John, lord Lumley, K.B.1553, I. 152
Lumley, John S., K.C.B.1878, I. 286; G.C.B.1885, I. 211
Lumley, Martin, Kt.1624, II. 184
Lumley, Martin, Kt.1641, II. 208
Lumley, Richard, Kt.1616, II. 159
Lumley, Richard, earl of Scarborough, K.G.1724, I. 42

LUMLEY
  Lumley, William, K.C.B.1815, I. 218; G.C.B.1831, I. 186
  Lumley-Saunderson, Thomas, earl of Scarborough, K.B.1725, I. 168
  Lumsden, Harry B., K.C.S.I.1873, I. 319
  Lumsden, Henry (Harry) N., Kt.1816, II. 317
  Lumsden, James, Kt.1868, II. 360
  Lumsden, Peter S., K.C.B.1879, I. 256; G.C.B.1885, I. 198
  Lunawara, Wakhtsinghji, of, K.C.I.E. 1889, I. 406
  Lüneburg, duke of, Kt.1549, II. 64
  Lunsford, Henry, Kt.1645, II. 220
  Lunsford, John, Kt.1610, II. 149
  Lunsford, Thomas, Kt.1641, II. 211
  Lurgan, baron. See Brownlow
  Luscombe, John H., Kt.1902, II. 412
  Lush, Robert, Kt.1865, II. 358
  Lushington, Franklin, Kt.1899, II. 405
  Lushington, Godfrey, K.C.B.1892, I. 292; G.C.M.G.1899, I. 346
  Lushington, James L., K.C.B.1837, I. 234; G.C.B.1838, I. 188
  Lushington, Stephen, K.C.B.1855, I. 241; G.C.B.1867, I. 195
  Luson. See Lawson
LUTTRELL, LUTTERELL
  Luttrell, Hugh, K.B.(1487), I. 142
  Lutterell, James, Kt.1460, II. 12
  Luterele, Jo, Kt.(1336), II. 5
  Luttrell, John, K.B.1400, I. 128
  Lutterell, John, Kt.1544, II. 54
  Luttrell, Thomas, Kt.1541, II. 53
  Lutwiche, Edward, Kt.1684, II. 260
  Lützow, count Heinrich J. R. G., K.C.V.O. 1903, I. 442
  Lyall, Alfred C., K.C.B.1881, I. 288; K.C.I.E.1887, I. 399; G.C.I.E.1896, I. 402
  Lyall, Charles J., K.C.S.I.1897, I. 326
  Lyall, James B., K.C.S.I.1888, I. 324; G.C.I.E.1892, I. 402
  Lycett, Francis, Kt.1867, II. 359
  Lydcote. See Lytcot
  Lyell, Charles, Kt.1848, II. 347
  Lygon, Arnold, Kt.1603, II. 119
  Lygon, Edward, Kt.1603, II. 108
  Lygon, Richard, Kt.1533, II. 49
  Lygon, William, Kt.1603, II. 108
  Lygon, William, Kt.1610, II. 149
  Lygon, William, earl Beauchamp, K.C.M.G.1899, I. 386
  Lyle. See Lisle
  Lymburne, John, Kt.1347, II. 7
  Lynch (Linch), Thomas, Kt.1670, II. 245
  Lynch, William, K.B.1771, I. 171
  Lyndon, John, Kt.1692, II. 267
  Lynedoch, lord. See Graham
  Lyngeyn. See Lingen
LYNE, LYNNE, LYNDE
  Lynne (Hame), George, Kt.1604, II. 134
  Lyne (Lynde), Humphrey, Kt.1613, II. 153
  Lyne, John, Kt.1599, II. 98
  Lyne, William J., K.C.M.G.1900, I. 387
  Lynes (Liens), Joachim, Kt.1619, II. 172
  Lyon, James, K.C.B.1815, I. 227 K.C.H. 1815, I. 454; G.C.H.1817, I. 448
  Lyon (Lyons), John, Kt.1555, II. 69
  Lyons, Algernon McL., K.C.B.1889, I. 262; G.C.B.1897, I. 202
  Lyons, Edmund, lord Lyons, K.C.H.1835, I. 460; Kt.1835, II. 335; G.C.B. 1844, I. 207; G.C.B.1855, I. 191; G.C.M.G.1858, I. 335
  Lyons, Richard B. P., viscount Lyons, K.C.B.1860, I. 281; G.C.B.1862, I. 209; G.C.M.G.1879, I. 338
  Lyons, William, Kt.1849, II. 347
  Lysley. See Lisle
  Lysons, Daniel, K.C.B.1877, I. 255; G.C.B.1886, I. 198
  Lyster. See Lister
LYTCOTT, LIDCOTT, LYDCOTE
  Lydcote, Christopher, Kt.1591, II. 89
  Lidcott, John, Kt.1609, II. 148
  Lytcott, John, Kt.1686, II. 262
  Lyte, Henry C. M., K.C.B.1897, I. 295
LYTTLETON, LITTLETON, LYTTELTON, LITLETON, LITILTON
  Littleton, Edward, Kt.1553, II. 67
  Litleton, Edward, Kt.1560, II. 71
  Littleton, Edward, Kt.1603, II. 103
  Littleton, Edward, Kt.1621, II. 177

INDEX

LYTTLETON
Littleton, Edward, Kt.1635, II. 203
Littleton, Edward, Kt.1699, II. 271
Lyttleton, George W., baron Lyttleton, K.C.M.G.1869, I. 354
Litleton, John, Kt.1565, II. 72
Lyttelton, Neville G., K.C.B.1902, I. 275
Lyttelton, Richard, K.B.1753, I. 170
Lyttelton, Thomas, K.B.(1475), I. 136
Littleton, Thomas, Kt.1618, II. 170
Littleton, Timothy, Kt.1671, II. 246
Littleton, Walter, Kt.1662, II. 236
Littilton William, Kt.1487, II. 25
Lyttelton-Annesley, Arthur L., K.C.V.O. (1903), I. 436
LYTTON, LITTON, LITTEN
Lytton, earl of. See Bulwer-Lytton
Lytton, Edward R., earl of Lytton, G.C.B.1878, I. 210
Lytton or Litten, Robert, K.B.(1494), II. 144
Lytton, Robert, K.B.1547, I. 151
Litton, Robert, Kt.1641, II. 209
Litton, Rowland, Kt.1603, II. 104
Lytton, Rowland, Kt.1660, II. 229
Lytton, William, Kt.1624, II. 185
Lytton, William, Kt.1677, II. 252
Lyveden, lord. See Smith

M

Maasdorp, Andries F. S., Kt.1904, II. 418
McAdam, James N., Kt.1834, II. 335
McAdam, William, K.H.1834, I. 469
Macalister, Charles A., K.H.1833, I. 468
Macan, Arthur V., Kt.1903, II. 417
MacAndrew, Henry C., Kt.1887, II. 384
Macandrew, John, K.C.B.1859, I. 245
Macara, Robert, K.C.B.1815, II. 225
Macarthur, Edward, K.C.B.1862, I. 282
Macarthur, William, Kt.1856, II. 351
McArthur, William, K.C.M.G.1882, I.365
Macartney, George, earl Macartney, Kt. 1764, II. 292; K.B.1772, I. 172
Macartney, Halliday, K.C.M.G.1885, I. 368

Macartney, John, Kt.1796, II. 303
Macauley, James B., Kt.1859, II. 353
MacBain, James, Kt.1886, II. 379; K.C.M.G.1889, I. 374
MacBean, Frederick, K.H.1835, I. 472
Macbean, William, K.C.B.1831, I. 231
MacCabe, Francis X. F., Kt.1892, II. 390
McCallum, Henry E., K.C.M.G.1898, I. 385; G.C.M.G.1904, I. 349
McCalmont, Hugh, K.C.B.1900, I. 271
McCammond, William, Kt.1895, II. 396
McCarty, Charles, Kt.1620, II. 175
MacCarthy, Charles J., Kt.1857, II. 352
MacCarthy, Charles L., Kt.1820, II. 322
MacCartie, Cormac MacTeig, Kt.1573, II. 75
MacCartie, Dermot, lord of Muskerry, Kt.1567, II. 73
McCaskill, John, K.H.1836, I. 473; K.C.B.1842, I. 237
McCausland, Richard B., Kt.1856, II. 351
McCleverty, Robert, K.C.H.1837, I. 462
McClintock, Francis L., Kt.1860, II. 354; K.C.B.1891, I. 263
McClure, Robert J. le M., Kt.1855, II. 351
MacCoghlan, John, Kt.1570, II. 75
MacCoghlan, John, Kt.1599, II. 96
MacCormac, William, Kt.1881, II. 373; K.C.V.O.(1898), I. 433 K.C.B.1900, I. 298
McCostly, John, Kt.1584, II. 83
McCoy, Frederick, K.C.M.G.1891, I. 376
McCreagh, Michael, K.C.H.1831, I. 457; Kt.1831, II. 331
McCraith, John L., Kt.1904, II. 419
MacCullagh [James] Acheson, Kt.1896, II. 397
MacCulloch, Edgar, Kt.1886, II. 379
McCulloch, James, Kt.1870, II. 362; K.C.M.G.1874, I. 356
McDermot, Terence, Kt.1690, II. 266

MCDONALD, MACDONALD, MACDONNELL, MACDONALD, MACDONELL, MACDONNELL, MCDONNEL, MACDONELL
Macdonell, Alexander, Kt.1628, II. 194

MACDONALD
  Macdonell, Alexander, K.C.B.1881, II. 258
  McDonald, Andrew, Kt.1897, II. 402
  Macdonnell, Anthony P., K.C.S.I.1893, I. 325; G.C.S.I. 1897, I. 314; K.C.V.O.(1903), I. 436
  Macdonald, Archibald, Kt.1788, II. 300
  McDonald, Archibald, K.H.1819, I. 464
  MacDonald, Claude M., K.C.M.G.1892, 378; K.C.B.1898, I. 297; G.C.M.G. 1900, I. 347; K.C.B.1901, I. 273
  MacDonell, Donald, Kt.1557, II. 70
  McDonnel, Edward, Kt.1849, II. 347
  MacDonnell, Francis, Kt.1827, II. 327
  Macdonald, Hector A., K.C.B.1900, I. 272
  MacDonnell, Hugh G., K.C.M.G.1892, I. 377; G.C.M.G.1899, I. 346
  Macdonald, James, G.C.M.G.1832, I. 333
  Macdonnell, James, K.C.H.1837, I. 462; Kt.1837, I. 339; K.C.B.1838, I. 234; G.C.B.1855, I. 191
  Macdonald, John, K.C.B.1815, I. 227
  McDonald (afterwards Kinneir), John, Kt.1829, II. 328
  Macdonald, John, K.C.B.1831, I. 231; G.C.B.1847, I. 190
  McDonald, John, K.C.B.1856, I. 242
  Macdonell, John, Kt.1903, II. 416
  Macdonald, John A., K.C.B.1867, I. 284; G.C.B.1884, I. 211
  Macdonald, John D., K.C.B.1902, I. 274
  Macdonald, John H. A., K.C.B.1900, I. 298
  MacDonell, Randall, earl of Antrim, Kt.1639, II. 206
  MacDonnell, Randall W., marquess of Antrim, K.B.1779, I. 173; K.P. 1796, I. 96.
  Macdonald, Reginald J., K.C.S.I.1877, I. 321; K.C.B.1887, I. 261
  MacDonnell, Richard G., Kt.1856, I. 351; K C.M.G.1871, I. 356

MACDONALD
  Macdonald, Ronald R., K.H.1833, I. 469
  MacDonnell, Schomberg K., K.C.B. 1902, I. 300
  Macdonald, William C., Kt.1899, II. 403
  Macdowall, Andrew, K.C.B.1831, I. 232
  MACDOWGALL, MACDOUGALL, MACDOWGAL, M'DOUGALL, and see Brisbane
  MacDowgall, Andrew, Kt.1683, II. 259
  MacDougall, Duncan, Kt.1838, II. 340
  MacDowgal, John, Kt.1615, II. 156
  McDougall, John, K.C.B.1862, I. 248
  McDougall, John, Kt.1902, II. 412
  M'Dougall, Patrick L., K.C.M.G.1877, I. 359
  McEacharn, Malcolm D., Kt.1900, II. 406
  Macewen, William, Kt.1902, II. 412
  Macfarlane, Donald H., Kt.1894, II. 392
  Macfarlane, Robert, G.C.H.1816, I. 448; K.C.B.1817, I. 228
  Macfarren, George A., Kt.1883, II. 375
  McGarel-Hogg (formerly Hogg), James M., lord Magheramorne, K.C.B.1874, I. 285
  McGlashan, James, K.H.1816, I. 463
  MacGregor, Charles M., K.C.B.1881, I. 257
  McGregor, Duncan, K.C.B.1848, I. 277
  MacGregor, Evan, K.C.B.1892, I. 293
  McGregor, Evan J. M., K.H.1821, I. 464; K.C.H.1831, I. 457; K.C.B.1838, I. 235
  Macgregor, George H., K.C.B.1861, I. 282
  MacGregor, William, K.C.M.G.1889, I. 374
  McGrigor, Charles, K.H.1834, I. 470
  McGrigor (Gregor), James, Kt.1814, II. 314; K.C.B.1850, I. 239
  MAGUIRE, MCGUIRE, MACGWIRE, MAGWIER
  Maguire, Brian, Kt.1626, II. 190
  Macgwire, Conor, Kt.1616, II. 158
  Maguire (McSkrine), Cuconaght, Kt. 1585, II. 83
  Magwier, Hughe, Kt.1591, II. 88
  McGuire, Richard, Kt.1785, II. 298
  Machado, Joaquim, J., K.C.M.G.1902, I. 393

INDEX 147

McIlwraith, Thomas, K.C.M.G.1882, I. 365
Macintosh, Alexander F., K.H.1833, I. 468
McIntyre, John, Kt.1895, II. 394
Mackay, Donald J., lord Reay, G.C.I.E. 1887, I. 401; G.C.S.I.1890, I. 313
Mackay, James L., K.C.I.E.1894, I. 408; G.C.M.G.1902, I. 348
McKenna, Joseph N., Kt.1867, II. 359
MACKENZIE, McKENZIE, MACKENZIE
Mackenzie, Alexander, Kt.1802, II. 306
Mackenzie, Alexander, G.C.H.1817, I. 448
Mackenzie, Alexander, K.C.S.I.1891, I. 324
Mackenzie, Alexander C., Kt.1895, II. 395
Mackenzie, Felix C., Kt.1897, II. 401
Mackenzie, George S., K.C.M.G.1902, I. 392
McKenzie, John, K.C.M.G.1901, I. 390
Mackenzie, Kenneth, earl of Seaforth, K.T.1687, I. 75
MacKenzie, Kenneth A. M., K.C.B. 1898, I. 297
Mackenzie, Morell, Kt.1887, II. 384
Mackenzie, Stephen, Kt.1903, II. 414
Mackenzie, William, K.C.B.1887, I. 262
McKerlie, John G., K.C.B.1883, I. 288
Mackey, James W., Kt.1874, II. 366
Mackie, James, K.C.M.G.1897, I. 383
Mackie, William, K.H.1834, I. 469
Mackinnon, William A., K.C.B.1891, I. 264
Mackintosh, James, Kt.1803, II. 307
Maclagan, Douglas, Kt.1886, II. 379
Maclaine, Archibald, Kt.1831, II. 331; K.C.B.1852, I. 239
Macklarand (Maickland, Mackland, Markeham), Robert, Kt.1603, II. 109
MacLaurin, Henry N., Kt.1902, II. 410
MACLEAN, MACLEAN, McLEAN, M'LEAN
Maclean, Andrew, Kt.1887, II. 382
Maclean, Donald, K.C.M.G.1874, I. 357

MACLEAN
Maclean, Fitzroy D., K.C.B.1904, I. 301
Maclean, Francis W., Kt.1896, II. 398; K.C.I.E.1898, I. 409
Maclean, George, Kt.1854, II. 350; K.C.B.1856, I. 243
McLean, Hector, K.C.B.1815, I. 227
McLean, John, K.C.B.1815, I. 223
Maclean, John, Kt.1871, II. 362
MacLean, Joseph, Kt.1834, II. 335; K.C.H.1834, I. 460
Maclean, kaid Harry, K.C.M.G.1901, I. 390
Maclear, Thomas, Kt.1860, II. 355
M'Learn, William, Kt.1900, II. 406
Macleay, George, K.C.M.G.1875, I. 357
Macleay, William, Kt.1889, II. 386
Mcleod, Alexander, Kt.1827, II. 326
McLeod, Charles, K.C.B.1852, I. 239
Macleod, Donald, K.C.B.1838, I. 234
McLeod, Donald F., K.C.S.I.1866, I. 315
Macleod, George H. B., Kt.1887, II. 382
Macleod, Henry G., K.H.1836, I. 474; Kt.1837, II. 338
Macleod, John, G.C.H.1820, I. 449
Macleod, John, K.C.H.1832, I. 458; Kt. 1832, II. 332
McLeod, John C., K.C.B.1874, I. 254; G.C.B.1891, I. 200
McLeod, John M., K.C.S.I.1866, I. 316
MACMAHON, McMAHON, McMAHOUNE
McMahoune, Bryan M. O., Kt.1604, II. 135
MacMahon, Charles, Kt.1875, II. 367
MacMahon, Marie E. P. M. de, duc de Magenta, G.C.B.1856, I. 192
MacMahon, Rosse, Kt.1585, II. 83
MacMahon, Tegue, Kt.1628, II. 195
McMahon, Thomas, K.C.B.1827, I. 230; G.C.B.1859, I. 192
McMair, James, K.H.1834, I. 470
McMillan, Daniel H., K.C.M.G.1902, I. 391
McMillan, William, K.C.M.G.1901, I. 388
McMurdo, William M. S., K.C.B.1881, I. 257; G.C.B.1893, I. 200
MacMurrogh, king of Leinster, Kt.(1394), II. lx.

McNab, Allan N., Kt.1838, II. 340
Macnabb, Donald C., K.C.I.E.1887, I. 400

MACNAGHTEN, MACNAUGHTEN
Macnaghten, Edward, lord Macnaghten, G.C.M.G.1902, I. 348
Macnaughten (Macnaghten), Francis, Kt.1809, II. 309
Macnaghten, Steuart, Kt.1890, II. 387
Macnamara, Burton, Kt.1839, II. 341
Macnamara, John, Kt.1603, II. 129
Macnee, Daniel, Kt.1876, II. 368
McNeill, John, G.C.B.1839, I. 207
MacNeill, John, Kt.1844, II. 345
McNeill, John C., K.C.M.G.1880, I. 363; K.C.B.1882, I. 259; G.C.V.O.1901, I. 419
McOnie, William, Kt.1888, II. 385
Maconochie, Alexander, K.H.1836, I. 475
Macpherson, Arthur G., K.C.I.E.1889, I. 406
Macpherson, David L., K.C.M.G.1884, I. 367
Macpherson, Donald, K.H.1837, I. 476
Macpherson, Herbert T., K.C.B.1881, I. 257; K.C.S.I.1882, I. 323
Macpherson, James D., K.C.B.1873, I. 254
Macpherson, Robert B., K.H.1835, I. 471
Macpherson, William, Kt.1900, II. 406
McQueen, Donald J., K.H.1835, I. 472
McQueen, John W., K.C.B.1889, I. 262
Macra, John, K.C.H.1827, I. 456; Kt. 1828, II. 327
Macrae, Colin G., Kt.1900, II. 408
Mackreth, Robert, Kt.1795, II. 302
MacTurk, Michael, Kt.1839, II. 342
McVicker, Robert, Kt.1885, II. 378
Mackworth, Digby, K.H.1832, I. 466
Mackworth, Humphry, Kt.1683, II. 258
Madden, Frederick, K.H.1832, I. 468; Kt.1833, II. 333
Madden, George A., Kt.1816, II. 317
Madden, John, Kt.1893, II. 391; K.C.M.G.1899, I. 385
Madden, Monson M., K.H.1837, I. 478

MADISON, MADESON, MADDISON
Madeson, Edward, Kt.1533, II. 49
Madison (Wadeson), John, Kt.1622, II. 180

MADDISON
Maddison (Matteson), Lionel, Kt.1633, II. 201
Maddison, Ralph, Kt.1603, II. 123
Maddock, Thomas H., Kt.1844, II. 345
Madox, Henry, K.H.1832, I. 467

MAGENIS, MAGENNIS, MAKENYCE, MACAMICE
Makenyce [Magenis], Arthur, Kt.1542, II. 53
Magennis, Arthur, Kt.1604, II. 135
Magenis, Arthur C., K.C.B.1856, I. 280; G.C.B.1866, I. 210
Magenis, Con, Kt.1627, II. 192
Macamyce [Magenis], Donugans, Kt. 1542, II. 53
Magenis (Maginniss), John, Kt.1821, II. 323
Magill, John, Kt.1680, II. 255
Magnus, James, lord of Amers, Kt.1615, II. 157
Magnus, Philip, Kt. 1886, II. 380
Magrath, George, Kt.1831, II. 331; K.H. 1834, I. 471
Mahmudabad, Amir Hassan of, K.C.I.E. 1893, I. 407
Maigret, comte de, K.C.V.O.1899, I. 439
Mailly, Hugh de, K.B.1306, I. 114
Main. See Mayney
Maine, Henry S., K.C.S.I.1871, I. 319

MAINWARING, MANWARING, MANNERING, MANWERYNGE, MAYNWERINGE
Manwerynge, Arthur, Kt.1547, II. 63
Manwaring (Mannering), Arthur, Kt. 1603, II. 106
Mannering, George, Kt.1595, II. 91
Manwaring, Henry, Kt.1618, II. 167
Mainwaring, John, Kt.1513, II. 39, 42
Manneringe, Peter, Kt.1565, II. 72
Mainwaring, Philip, Kt.1634, II. 202
Mannering, Randolfe, Kt.1602, II. 100
Manwaring, Richard, Kt.1603, II. 123
Manwaring, Thomas, Kt.1642, II. 215
Manwaring, William, Kt.1644, II. 217

MAIR, MAIER, MAJOR, and see Major
Mair, John H., K.H.1831, I. 465
Maier, Peter Le, Kt.1624, II. 185
Major (Majon, Mayon, Mason), William, Kt.1624, II. 187
Maisters. See Masters

INDEX 149

MAITLAND, MAICKLAND
  Maitland, Anthony, earl of Lauderdale, K.C.M.G.1820, I. 350; K.C.B.1852, I. 239; G.C.B.1862, I. 194
  Maitland, Frederick L., K.C.B.1830, I. 230
  Maitland, James M. H., K.C.B.1897, II. 268
  Maitland, James, earl of Lauderdale, K.T.1821, I. 81
  Maitland, John, duke of Lauderdale, K.G.1672, I. 36
  Maitland, Peregrine, K.C.B.1815, I. 228; G.C.B.1852, I. 190
  Maickland, Robert, Kt.1603, II. 109
  Maitland, Thomas, G.C.B.1815, I.183; G.C.H.1817, I.448; Grand Master and Principal G.C.M.G.1818, I. 331
  Maitland, Thomas, earl of Lauderdale, Kt.1843, II. 345; K.C.B.1865, I. 249; G.C.B.1873, I. 196
Majendie, Vivian D., K.C.B.1895, I. 294
Majo, Pio C. di, K.C.V.O.1903, I. 441
Major. See Mair
Major, Alfred, Kt.1904, II. 419
Makenyce. See Magenis
Malakoff duc de. See Pélissier
Malaussena, comte Alzcary de, K.C.V.O. 1896, I. 438
Malby, George, Kt.1625, II. 188
Malby, Nicholas, Kt.1576, II. 77
Malcolm, Charles, Kt.1826, II. 326
Malcolm, George, K.C.B.1868, I. 251; G.C.B.1886, I. 198
Malcolm, James, K.C.B.1815, I. 225
Malcolm, John, Kt.1812, II. 312; K.C.B. 1815, I. 227; G.C.B.1819, I. 184
Malcolm, Ormond D., Kt.1898, II. 403
Malcolm, Pulteney, K.C.B.1815, I. 221; G.C.M.G.1829, I. 332; G.C.B.1833, I. 187
Malemains, Nicholaus, K.B.1306, I. 113

MALEVERER, MAULEVERER, MALYVERER, MALIVERY, MALEVER, MALEVERY, MALEVERAY, MAULIVERER
  Malyverer, Alnathe, K.B.1501, I. 146
  Mauleverer (Malevery), Edward (Edmond), Kt.1553, II. 68

MAULEVERER
  Mauleverer, John, K.B.1306, I. 120
  Malever, John, Kt.1460, II. 12
  Mauleverer, Richard, Kt.1513, II. 38
  Malivery (? Molineux), Richard, Kt. 1553, II. 68
  Maliverer, Richard, Kt.1584, II. 82
  Maleverer (Malevery), Richard, Kt. 1645, II. 219
  Maleveray (Malyverer), Thomas, Kt. 1544, II. 55
  Malyverer, Thomas, Kt.1482, II. 17, 20
  Mauliverer, William, Kt.1513, II. 37

MALET, MALLET
  Malet, Alexander, K.C.B.1866, I. 284
  Malet, Edward B., K.C.B.1881, I. 288; G.C.M.G.1885, I. 340; G.C.B.1886, I. 212
  Mallet, John, K.B.1603, I. 155
  Malet, John, Kt.1667, II. 242
  Mallet, Louis, Kt.1868, II. 360
  Mallet, Thomas, Kt.1641, II. 209
Mallet. See Malet
Malmesbury, earl of. See Harris
Malins, Richard, Kt.1867, II. 358
Malise, earl of Strathherne, K.B.1306, I. 111

MALORY, MALLORY
  Mallory, Henry, Kt.1605, II. 138
  Mallory, John, Kt.1603, II. 100
  Mallory, John, Kt.1641, II. 211
  Mallory, Richard, Kt.1565, II. 71
  Malory, Richard, Kt.1586, II. 84
  Malory, Thomas, K.B.1306, I. 117
  Malory, William, Kt.1482, II. 20
  Mallory, William, Kt.1560, II. 71
  Mallory, William, Kt.1643, II. 215
Malpas, viscount. See Cholmondeley

MALTRAVERS, MAUTRAVERS
  Mautravers, John, K.B.1306, I. 113
  Mautravers, John, K.B.1306, I. 118
  Maltravers, lord. See Fitz-Alan; see Howard
Man. See Mann
Manby, Alan R., Kt.1903, II. 416
Manby, Thomas, Kt.1686, II. 262
Manby, Wiliam de, K.B.1306, I. 119
Mance, Henry C., Kt.1885, II. 377

Manchester, earl and duke of. See Montagu
Manduca, count Vincenzo, K.C.M.G.1833, I. 352
MANEY, MAYNEY, MANE, MAIN
  Maney, Anthony, Kt.1588, II. 87
  Maney (Mane), Anthony, Kt.1593, II. 90
  Mayney, Anthony, Kt.1609, II. 148
  Mayney (Main), John, Kt.1641, II. 209
Manfield, Philip, Kt.1894, II. 394
Manington. See Manyngton
Manipur, Kirtee Sing, of, K.C.S.I.1880, I. 322
Manisty, Henry, Kt.1876, II. 368
Manmaker, Adrian, Kt.1609, II. 148
Manley, Richard, Kt.1629, II. 196
MANN, MAN
  Man, Christopher, Kt.1625, II. 188
  Mann, Horatio, K.B.1768, I. 171
  Mann, Horatio, K.B.1772, II. 293
  Man, William, Kt.1642, II. 212
Mannering. See Mainwaring
Manning, William H., K.C.M.G.1904, I. 395
Manning, William M., Kt.1858, II. 352; K.C.M.G.1892, I. 377
Manning, William P., Kt.1894, II. 392
Manningham, Richard, Kt.1722, II. 282
Manns, August, Kt.1903, II. 416
Manny [Mauny], Walter de, K.B.1331, I. 125
Manny, Walter, lord Manny, K.G.1359, I. 3
MANNERS, MANNORS, MANERS
  Mannors, Charles, Kt.1599, II. 97
  Manners, Charles, duke of Rutland, K.G.1782, I. 47; Grand Master K.P. 1784, I. 93
  Manners, Charles C. J., duke of Rutland, K.G.1867, I. 63
  Manners, lord Charles H. S., K.C.B. 1838, I. 234
  Manners, Edward, earl of Rutland, K.G.1584, I. 27
  Manners, Francis, earl of Rutland, K.B.1605, I. 157; K.G.1616, I. 31
  Manners, George, Kt.1497, II. 31
  Manners, George, Kt.1599, II. 96, 102

MANNERS
  Manners, Henry, earl of Rutland, Kt. 1544, II. 56; K.G.1559, I. 26
  Manners, Henry H., K.H.1836, I. 474
  Manners, John, Kt.1587, II. 85
  Manners, John, Kt.1603, II. 101
  Manners, John, duke of Rutland, K.G.1714, I. 41
  Manners, John, duke of Rutland, K.G.1722, I. 42
  Manners, John H., duke of Rutland, K.G.1803, I. 49
  Manners, John J. R., duke of Rutland, G.C.B.1880, I. 211; K.G. 1891, I. 68
  Maners, Olyver, Kt.1523, II. 45
  Manners, Oliver, Kt.1603, II. 102
  Manners, Richard, Kt.1538, II. 51, 54
  Manners, Roger, earl of Rutland, Kt. 1599, II. 95
  Manners, Roger, Kt.1615, II. 155
  Manners, Thomas, earl of Rutland, K.G.1525, I. 21
  Manners, Thomas, Kt.1560, II. 70
  Manners, Thomas, Kt.1570, II. 74
  Manners-Sutton, John H. T., viscount Canterbury, K.C.B.1866, I. 284; G.C.M.G.1873, I. 336
MANSELL, MANSEL, and see Mansfield, Maunsell
  Mansel, Anthony, Kt.1629, II. 196
  Mansell, Robert C., K.H.1832, II. 467
  Mansell, Thomas, K.C.H.1837, I. 462; Kt.1837, II. 338
MANSFIELD, MANSELL, MAUNSELL, and see Mansell, Maunsell
  Mansfield, Charles E., K.C.M.G.1887, I. 372
  Mansfield, earl of. See Murray
  Mansfield (Mansell), Edward, Kt.1604, II. 130
  Mansfield, James, Kt.1804, II. 307
  Mansfield (Mansell, Maunsell), Lewis, Kt.1603, II. 116
  Mansfield (Mansell), Robert, Kt.1596, II. 93
  Mansfield, William, lord Sandhurst, G.C.I.E.1895, I. 402; G.C.S.I.1900, I. 314

MANSFIELD
Mansfield, William R., lord Sandhurst, K.C.B.1858, I. 245; K.C.S.I.1866, I. 315; G.C.S.I.1866, I. 309; G.C.B. 1870, I. 195
Mansford, George, Kt.1607, II. 142
Manson, Patrick, K.C.M.G.1903, I. 394
Mantell, John I., Kt.1867, II. 359
Mantell, Thomas, Kt.1820, II. 321
Mantell (Martell), William, Kt.1523, II. 45
Manwaring. See Mainwaring
MANWOOD, MANWOODE
Manwood, John, Kt.1618, II. 168
Manwood, Peter, Kt.1603, II. 127; K.B.1603, I. 155
Manwoode, Roger, Kt.1578, II. 79
Manyngton, Thomas, Kt.1487, II. 26
Manzaro, Giacomo C., K.C.M.G.1821, I. 351
Maple, John B., Kt.1892, II. 391
Mar, earl and duke of. See Erskine
Marbury, Edward, Kt.1603, II. 122
Marbury, Anthony, Kt.1616, II. 157
Marbury (Merbury), George, Kt.1606, II. 140
March, earl of. See Mortimer; see Douglas
Marchant. See Le Marchant
Marchmont, earl of. See Hume-Campbell
Marcoran, Georgio, K.C.M.G.1853, I. 353; G.C.M.G.1867, I. 336
Mare, John, lord de la, K.B.1306, I. 111, 115
Mare, Martin, of the sea (de la Mare), Kt.1482, II. 19
Mare, Reginald de la, K.B.1327, I. 124
Mare, Robert de la, K.B.1306. I, 118
Mare, Thomas de la, K.B.1377, I. 126
Marett, Robert R., Kt.1880, II. 372
Mareyn (Marnia, Marian, Marina), Angell, K.B.1547, I. 151
Marindin, Francis A., K.C.M.G.1897, I. 383
Marischal, earl. See Keith
Mark, John, Kt.1901, II. 408
Markby, William, K.C.I.E.1889, I. 406
Markham, Albert H., K.C.B.1903, I. 276

Markham, Anthony, Kt.1603, II. 103
Markham, Clements R., K.C.B.1896, I. 294
Markham, Edwin, K.C.B.1897, I. 269
Markham (Martham), George, Kt.1603, II. 109
Markham, Griffin, Kt.1591, II. 89
Markham, John, K.B.(1461), I. 133
Markham, John, Kt.1513, II. 38
Markham, Robert, K.B.(1461), I. 133
Markham, Robert, Kt.1603, II. 109
Markynfeld, Vyvyan, Kt.1513, II. 37
Marlborough, duke of. See Churchill; see Spencer; see Spencer-Churchill
Marlborough, Thomas de, K.B.1324, I. 123
Marmion, William, K.B.1306, I. 122
Marmora, Alfonso F., della, G.C.B.1855, I. 191
MARNY, MARNEY
Marney, Henry, lord Marny, K.B. (1494), I. 144; K.G.1510, I. 20
Marny (Merry), Henry, Kt.1621, I. 177
Marney, John, Kt.1513, II. 38
Marr, Henry, Kt.1785, II. 298
Marrable, Thomas, Kt.1840, II. 342
Marriott, Charles H., Kt.1904, II. 419
Marrett, Christopher, Kt.1821, II. 323
Marriott, James, Kt.1778, II.295
Marriott, William T., Kt.1888, II.384
Marrow, Samuel, Kt.1669, II. 244
Marsh, Charles, Kt.1786, II. 299
Marsh, William H., K.C.M.G.1887, I. 371
Marshall, Anthony, Kt.1894, II. 393
Marshall, Arthur W., Kt.1898, II. 403
Marshall, Chapman, Kt.1831, II. 329
Marshall, Charles, Kt.1832, II. 332
Marshall, Dyson, K.C.B.1818, I. 228
Marshall, Frederick, K.C.M.G.1897, I. 383
Marshall, George, Kt.1615, II. 157
Marshall, George, K.H.1837, I. 478
Marshall, George H., K.C.B.1900, I. 272
Marshall, Henry, Kt.1745, II. 287
Marshall, Horace B., Kt.1902, II. 411
Marshall, James, Kt.1882, II. 374
Marshall (Mashall), John, Kt.1603, II. 109
Marshall, John, Kt.1681, II. 256

Marshall, John, K.H.1832, I. 468; Kt. 1832, II. 332
Marshall, John, W. P., Kt.1822, II. 323; K.C.H.1832, I. 458
Marshall, Robert, Kt.1603, II. 109
Marsham, John, Kt.1660, II. 229
Marsin, Gasper, count, Kt.1658, II. 225
Marten, Alfred G., Kt.1896, II. 397
Marten, Thomas, K.H.1837, I. 476
Martimprey, Edmond C. de, K.C.B.1856, I. 241

MARTIN, MARTYN
  Martyn, Christopher, Kt.1604, II. 130
  Martin, George, Kt.1814, II. 314; K.C.B.1815, I. 217; G.C.B.1821, I. 185; G.C.M.G.1837, I. 334
  Martin, George C., Kt.1897, II. 401
  Martin, Henry, Kt.1616, II. 160
  Martin, Henry, Kt.1683, II. 258
  Martin, Henry B., K.C.B.1855, I. 241
  Martin, James, Kt.1574, II. 76
  Martin, James, Kt.1869, II. 361
  Martin, James R., Kt.1860, II. 355
  Martin, John, K.B.1306, I. 116
  Martin, Joseph, Kt.1712, II. 277
  Martin, Nicholas, Kt.1625, II. 188
  Martin, Richard, Kt.1589, II. 87
  Martin, Richard E. R., K.C.M.G.1895, I. 380; K.C.B.1898, I. 297
  Martin, Roger, Kt.1568, II. 73
  Martin, Roger, Kt.1625, II. 188
  Martin, Samuel, Kt.1850, II. 348
  Martin, Theodore, K.C.B.1880, I. 287; K.C.V.O.(1896), I. 432
  Martin, Thomas, Kt.1642, II. 211
  Martin, Thomas A., Kt.1895, II. 396
  Martin, Thomas B., K.C.B.1815, I. 220; G.C.B.1830, I. 185
  Martin, William de, Kt.1494, II. 28
  Martyn, William, K.B.1501, I. 146
  Martin, William, Kt.1617, II. 160
  Martin, William, Kt.1860, II. 354
  Martin, William F., K.C.B.1861, I. 247; G.C.B.1873, I. 196
  Martin-Holloway, George, Kt.1887, II. 383

Martineau, Thomas, Kt.1887, II. 380
Martindale, Arthur H. T., K.C.S.I.1904, I. 328
Martindell, Gabriel, K.C.B.1815, I. 227
Martino, De, K.C.M.G.1900, I. 388
Martins, William, Kt.1840, II. 342
Marvyn, Edmund, Kt.1542, II. 53
Marvyn (Mervine), Henry, Kt.1619, II. 171
Marvin, Thomas, Kt.1603, II. 126
Marwick, James D., Kt.1888, II. 385
Marwood. See Merwood
Maryborough, lord. See Wellesley-Pole
Marzials, Frank T., Kt.1904, II. 417
Mash, Thomas B., Kt.1837, II. 338
Mashall. See Marshall
Massareene, viscount. See Foster-Skeffington

MASSEY, MASSY
  Massey, Edward, Kt.1660, II. 226
  Massey, Edward, Kt.1671, II. 246
  Massy, George, Kt.1778, II. 295
  Massey, Hugh, Kt.1808, II. 309
  Massey, John, Kt.1544, II. 56
  Massey, William, Kt.1617, II. 165
Massingberd, Draymer, Kt.1662, II. 236
Mason, Francis, K.C.B.1841, I. 237
Mason, George C., Kt.1895, II. 396
Mason, John, Kt.1547, II. 59
Mason, John, Kt.1698, II. 270
Mason, Josiah, Kt.1872, II. 364
Mason, Richard, Kt.1661, II. 233
Mason, Robert, Kt.1661, II. 233
Mason, William, Kt.1624, II. 187
Mason, William, Kt.1645, II. 219
Masson, David P., Kt.1904, II. 419

MASTER, MASTERS, MAISTERS
  Master, Edward, Kt.1666, II. 242
  Masters, Edward, Kt.1630, II. 197
  Masters, Harcourt, Kt.1714, II. 279
  Master, Streynsham, Kt.1698, II. 271
  Masters, Thomas, Kt.1725, II. 283
  Maisters (Master), William, Kt.1622, II. 180
Masterson, Richard, Kt.1599, II. 96
Masterson, Thomas, Kt.1588, II. 86
Mather, William, Kt.1902, II. 412
Matheson, Donald, K.C.B.1887, I. 290; and see Maddison

INDEX 153

MATTHEW, MATHEW, MATHIEU
Mathew, Francis J., earl of Llandaff, K.P.1831, I. 100
Mathieu (Mathew), George, Kt.1553, II. 67
Matthew, George B., K.C.M.G.1879, I. 361
Mathew, James C., Kt.1881, II. 372
Mathew, Toby, Kt.1623, II. 183
Mathew, Wiliam, Kt.1513, II. 41
Mathews, George, Kt.1704, II. 274
Mathews, John, Kt.1677, II. 252
Mathews, Lloyd W., K.C.M.G.1894, I. 379
Mathews, William, Kt.1704, II. 273
Matthias, Henry, Kt.1816, II. 317
Matsukata, count, G.C.M.G.1902, I. 348
Maude, Frederick F., K.C.B.1879, I. 256; G.C.B.1886, I. 198
Maude, George A., K.C.B.1887, I. 290
Maude, James A., K.C.H.1836, I. 461; Kt.1836, II. 337
Mauduit, John, K.B.1306, I. 115
Maule, Fox, earl of Dalhousie, K.T.1853, I. 84; G.C.B.1855, I. 208
Maule, Francis, K.H.1833, I. 469
Maule, James, earl of Panmure, K.T. 1716, I. footnote 75
Maule, John B., Kt.1882, II. 374
Maule, Robert de, Kt.(1346), I. 6
Maule, William H., Kt.1839, II. 341
Mauleverer, Mauliverer. See Malleverer
Mauley, Peter de, K.B.1306, I. 114
Mauley, Peter de, lord Mauley, K.B. 1399, I. 128
MAUNSELL, MAUNCELL, MANSFIELD, and see Mansell, Mansfield
Mauncell (Mansfield), Edward, Kt. 1572, II. 75
Maunsell, Frederick R., K.C.B.1897, I. 267
Mauncel, John, K.B.1306, I. 117
Monsell, John, Kt.(1330), II. lix.
Mauntelle, Walter, K.B.(1465), I. 135
Maureward, Thomas, Kt.1401, II. 11
Maurice, John F., K.C.B.1900, I. 271
Mautravers. See Maltravers
Maxey, Arthur (William), Kt.1617, II. 166

Maxey, Henry, Kt.1603, II. 124
Maxim, Hiram S., Kt.1901, II. 408
Maxse, Henry F. B., K.C.M.G.1877, I. 358
Maxwell, Archibald M., K.H.1836, I. 474
Maxwell, Charles W., K.C.H.1836, I.461; Kt.1836, II. 337
Maxwell, George V., K.C.B.1881, I. 257
Maxwell, Henry, baron Farnham, K.P. 1845, I. 101
Maxwell, John G., K.C.B.1900, I. 273
Maxwell, Murray, Kt.1818, II. 320
Maxwell, Patrick, Kt.1887, II. 383
Maxwell, Peter B., Kt.1856, II. 351
Maxwell, William, earl of Nithsdale, K.T. 1725, footnote, I. 75
Maxwell, William E., K.C.M.G.1896, I. 381
May, Humphrey, Kt.1613, II. 152
May, John, Kt.1670, II. 244
May, John, K.C.B.1815, I. 225; K.C.H. 1822, I. 455
May, Richard, Kt.1681, II. 256
May, Stephen E., Kt.1816, II. 317
May, Thomas, Kt.1603, II. 117, 119
May, Thomas, Kt.1697, II. 270
May, Thomas E., lord Farnborough, K.C.B.1866, I. 284
May, William, Kt.1753, II. 288
Mayart, Samuel, Kt.1631, II. 199
Maycott (Macott), Cavallero, Kt.1604, II. 130
Mayhern, Theodore, Kt.1624, II. 185
Maynard, Boyle, Kt.1661, II. 233
Maynard, Henry, Kt.1603, II. 104
Maynard, Henry, Kt.1660, II. 228
Maynard, John, K.B.1626, I. 162
Maynard, John, Kt.1660, II. 227, 232
Maynard, William, Kt.1609, II. 147
Maynard, William, Kt.1628, II. 194
Mayne, Richard, K.C.B.1851, I. 278; and see Maney
Maynors, Roger, Kt.1527, II. 46
Maynweringe. See Mainwaring
Mayo, earl of. See Bourke
MEADE, MEAD, MEDE
Meade, John, Kt.1622, II. 178, 181
Meade, John, Kt.1678, II. 253
Meade, John, Kt.1816, II. 318; K.H. 1825, I. 464

MEADE

Mead, Nathaniel, Kt.1715, II. 280
Meade, Richard, C. F., earl of Clanwilliam, G.C.H.1826, I. 450
Meade, Richard J., earl of Clanwilliam, K.C.M.G.1882, I. 364; K.C.B.1887, I. 261; G.C.B.1895, I. 201
Meade, Richard J., K.C.S.I.1874, I. 320
Meade, Robert H., K.C.B.1894, I. 293; G.C.B.1897, I. 214
Meade, Roche, K.H.1825, I. 464
Meade, Thomas, Kt.1600, II. 98, 105

MEADOWES, MEDOWES, MEDOWS

Medowes, Philip, Kt.1662, II. 237
Medowes, Philip, Kt.1700, II. 272
Meadows (Medowes), Thomas, Kt.1660, II. 231
Medows, William, K.B.1792, I. 174

Measom, George S., Kt.1891, II. 388
Meath, earl of. See Brabazon
Meautis, Thomas, Kt.1641, II. 208
Meaux, Godfrey de, K.B.1306, I. 118

MECKLENBURG-STRELITZ

Adolphus F., duke of, K.G.1764, I. 46
Adolphus F., duke of, G.C.B.1877, I. 210
Friedrich W., duke of, G.C.B.1848, I. 208; K.G.1862, I. 61

Meene. See Mennes
Medcalf. See Metcalf
Medhi Kuli Khan, K.C.M.G.1889, I. 374
Medhurst, Walter H., Kt.1877, II. 369
Medina, Solomon de, Kt.1700, II. 272
Medkir (Medkerke, Methkirk), Baldwin, Kt.1596, II. 93
Medlicot, John, Kt.1624, II. 186
Medowes. See Meadows
Meek, James, Kt.1851, II. 348
Meek, James, Kt.1869, II. 361
Meerpur, Shere Mahomed, of, K.C.S.I. 1866, I. 316

MEERES, MERES, MEERS

Meres (Meeres), John, Kt.1603, II. 116
Meeres (Meres), John, Kt.1700, II. 272
Meers, Thomas, Kt.1660, II. 228

Meggott, George, Kt.1690, II. 266
Mehedi, ben el Arbi, G.C.M.G.1901, I. 348

Meiklejohn, William H., K.C.B.1898, I. 269
Melbourne, viscount. See Lamb
Melbourne. See Milbourn
Meldahl, Ferdinand, G.C.V.O.1904, I. 429

MELDRUM, MELDROM

Meldrum, David, Kt.1594, II. 91
Meldrom, John, Kt.1622, II. 180

Melfort, duke and earl of. See Drummond
Mellinet, Emile, K.C.B.1856, I. 242
Mellish, George, Kt.1870, II. 362
Mellish, Richard, K.H.1832, I. 467
Melliss, Howard, K.C.S.I.1897, I. 326
Melissino, Giovanni, C.M.G.(1820), I. xxviii.
Meller. See Miller
Mellor, John, Kt.1862, II. 356
Melton, John, Kt.1482, II. 20
Melton, John, Kt.1632, II. 200

MELVILLE, MELVILL

Melville, George, K.C.M.G.1900, I. 387
Melvill, James C., K.C.B.1853, I. 279
Melville, John, Kt.1859, II. 354
Melvill, Maxwell, K.C.I.E.1887, I. 399
Melvill, Peter M., K.C.B.1860, I. 281
Melville, viscount. See Saunders-Dundas
Melville, viscount. See Dundas
Melvill, William H., Kt.1888, II. 384

Mence. See Mennes
Mends, Robert, Kt.1815, II. 316
Mends, William, K.C.B.1817, I. 253; G.C.B.1882, I. 198

MENNES, MINNES, MENCE, MINNE, MEENE, MYNN, MYNNES, MINGS, MENY

Mence, —, Kt.1492, II. 28
Minnes (Mynnes, Mings), Christopher, Kt.1665, II. 241
Minne (Meene, Mynn), Henry, Kt 1609, II. 148
Meny (Minnes, Mennes), John, Kt. 1642, II. 212
Mynne, John, Kt.1671, II. 246
Mynne, William, Kt.1603, II. 121

Mensdorf-Pouilly, count Alexander, prince of Dietrichstein-Nicolsburg, K.C.B.1847, I. 277
Mensdorff-Pouilly, count Arthur A. von, G.C.V.O.1897, I. 423

INDEX 155

Mensdorff-Pouilly, count Emanuel, G.C.B.1842, I. 189
Mensdorff-Pouilly-Dietrichstein, count Albert Victor von, K.C.V.O.1897, I. 438; G.C.V.O.1901, I. 425
Meny. See Mennes
Menymrate (Momyrate), William de, K.B.1306, I. 116
Menzies, Charles, K.H.1831, I. 466; K.C.B.1865, I. 250
Menzies, Paul, Kt.1623, II. lxii.
Menzies, Thomas, Kt.1620, II. 175
Menzies, William J., Kt.1903, II. 414
Mere, Joh de, Kt.(1336), II. 5
MEREDITH, MEREDYTH
  Meredith, Charles, Kt.1669, II. 243
  Meredith, James C., Kt.1899, II. 404
  Meredyth (Meredith), John, Kt.1762, II. 291
  Meredyth, John, Kt.1783, II. 297
  Meredith, Joshua C., Kt.1794, II. 302
  Meredith, Robert, Kt.1635, II. 203
  Meredyth, Thomas, Kt.1630, II. 198
  Meredith, William, Kt.1603, II. 115
  Meredith, William C., Kt.1886, II. 379
  Meredith, William R., Kt.1896, II. 397
Meres. See Meeres
Merewether, William L., K.C.S.I.1868, I. 318
Mereworth, John de, Kt.1347, II. 8
Meriet, John de, K.B.1306, I. 114
MERINGE, MERYNGE
  Meringe Rauf (William), Kt.1553, II. 68
  Merynge, William, Kt.1497, II. 29
Merrick. See Meyrick
Merry, Thomas, Kt.1617, II. 162
Merry. See Marny
Merton. See Morton
Merttins, George, Kt.1713, II. 278
MERVYN, MERVIN
  Mervin, Audley, Kt.1660, II. 230
  Mervin (Martin), James, Kt.1574, II. 76
  Mervyn, John, Kt.1547, II. 62
Merwood (Marwood), Richard, Kt.1608, II. 146

Merynge. See Meringe
METCALFE, METCALF, MEDCALFE
  Metcalfe, Charles T., G.C.B.1835, I. 206
  Metcalf, Christopher, Kt.1545, II. 57
  Medcalfe, Francis, Kt.1618, II. 169
  Metcalfe, Gilbert, Kt.1695, II. 269
  Metcalfe, James, Kt.1527, II. 46
  Medcalfe, Thomas, Kt.1603, II. 104
Metham, George M., Kt.1756, II. 289
Metham, Jordan, Kt.1642, II. 213
Metham, Thomas, Kt.1460, II. 12
Metham, Thomas, K.B.1509, I. 148
Metham, Thomas, Kt.1533, II. 49
Metham (Mettam), Thomas, Kt.1553, II. 67
Metham (Mettame), Thomas, Kt.1603, II. 108
Methuen, Paul, K.B.1725, II. 168
Methuen, Paul S., lord Methuen, K.C.V.O.(1897), I. 432; K.C.B.1900, I. 272; G.C.B.1902, I. 204
Methwold, William, Kt.1612, II. 151
Metternich, count Paul W., G.C.V.O. 1901, I. 424
MEUX, MEWSE, MEWS, MEWES
  Meux (Mewse, Monox), John, Kt.1605, II. 138
  Mews (Mewes), Peter, Kt.1712, II. 277
  Mewes (Meux), William, Kt.1607), II. 142
Mewtas, Peter, Kt.1544, II. 56
Mewtas (Meutis), Thomas, Kt.1611, II. 150
Mexborough, earl of. See Savile
Meyer, Peter, Kt.1714, II. 279
Meyer, Samuell, Kt.1714, II. 279
MEYRICK, MERRICK, MERRICKE, MERICK
  Merricke, Francis, Kt.1599, II. 97
  Merrick, Gillam, Kt.1639, II. 206
  Merrick, John, Kt.1614, II. 154
  Meyrick, Samuel R., K.H.1832, I. 466; 1832, II. 332
  Merrick (Gellian), William, Kt.1596, II. 93
  Merick, William, Kt.1661, II. 235
  Merrick, William, Kt.1686, II. 262

Mewar (Udaipur), Fateh Singh Bahadur, maharana of, G.C.S.I.1887, I. 312
Micallef, Antonio, K.C.M.G.1860, I. 353; G.C.M.G.1879, I. 338
Michel. See Mitchell
Michelborne, Edward, Kt.1599, II. 97
Michelborne, Richard, Kt.1603, II. 125
Michie, Archibald, K.C.M.G.1878, I. 360
Micks, Robert, Kt.1892, II. 390
Mico (Micault), Samuel, Kt.1665, II. 240
MIDDLETON, MIDLETON, MIDDELTON
  Middleton, Frederick D., K.C.M.G. 1885, I. 368
  Middleton, George, Kt.1642, II. 213
  Middleton, Henry, Kt.1606, II. 140
  Middleton, John, Kt.1642, II. 214
  Midleton, Peter, Kt.1617, II. 162
  Middelton, Piers, Kt.1482, II. 20, 17
  Middelton, Robert, Kt.1482, II. 20
  Middleton, Thomas, Kt.1603, II. 128
  Midleton, Thomas, Kt.1617, II. 160
  Middleton, Thomas, Kt.1675, II. 250
  Middleton, William, Kt.1513, II. 37
Miéville, Walter F., K.C.M.G.1898, I. 384
Milan, Sforza, Francis, duke of, K.G. 1462-3, I. 14
MILBOURN, MILBORN
  Milbourn, —, K.B.(1483), I. 139
  Milborn (Melbourne), Thomas, Kt. 1485, II. 22
MILDMAY, MYLDMAY
  Mildmay, Henry, Kt.1605, II. 138
  Mildmay, Henry, Kt.1607, II. 142
  Mildmay, Henry, Kt.1617, II. 164
  Mildmay, Humphrey, Kt.1616, II. 158
  Myldmay, Thomas, Kt.1567, II. 73
  Mildmay, Thomas, Kt.1603, II. 115, 120
  Mildmay, Thomas, Kt.1616, II. 158
  Myldmay, Walter, Kt.1547, II. 60
  Mildmay, Walter, Kt.1603, II. 106
MILES, MYLES
  Miles, Edward, Kt.1826, II. 326
  Miles, Jonathan, Kt.1807, II. 308
  Myles, Thomas, Kt.1902, II. 410
Mill, Richard, Kt.1601, II. 99
Millard. See Mylord
Miller, Alexander E., Kt.1889, II. 385
Miller (Francis), Henry, Kt.1902, II. 410
Miller, Henry J., Kt.1901, II. 408
Miller, John, Kt.1619, II. 170
Miller (Meller), John, Kt.1625, II. 188
Miller, Nicholas, Kt.1641, II. 208
Miller, Nicholas, Kt.1681, II. 256
Miller, Robert, Kt.1603, II. 124
Miller, Thomas, Kt.1689, II. 265
Miller, William, K.H.1837, I. 478
Miller, William, Kt.1876, II. 368
Millet. See Myllet
Millington, Thomas, Kt.1680, II. 254
Millisent, John, Kt.1607, II. 141
Millisent, Roger (George), Kt.1607, II. 141
Milman, Archibald J. S., K.C.B.1902, I. 299
Milman, William, Kt.1705, II. 275
Mills, Charles, K.C.M.G.1885, I. 367
Mills, John, Kt.1628, II. 194
Mills, Richard, K.C.B.1901, I. 298; K.C.V.O.(1903), I. 435
Mills, Thomas, Kt.1772, II. 293
Milltown, earl of. See Leeson
Milne, Alexander, K.C.B. civil 1858, I. 280; K.C.B. mil. 1864, I. 248; G.C.B.1871, I. 195
Milne, Archibald B., K.C.V.O.(1904), I. 437
Milne, David, K.C.B.1816, I. 228; G.C.B. 1840, I. 189
Milne, William, Kt.1876, II. 368
Milner, Alfred, viscount Milner, K.C.B. 1895, I. 294; G.C.M.G.1897, I. 345; G.C.B.1901, I. 215
Milnes, Robert O. A., baron Houghton, Grand Master K.P.1892, I. 95
Milton, Christopher, Kt.1686, II. 262
Milton, John, Kt.1529, II. 47
Milton, John, Kt.1878, II. 370
Milton, William H., K.C.M.G.1903, I. 394
Milward, Christopher A., Kt.1897, II. 401
Milward (Mildward), Thomas, Kt.1638, II. 205
Minnes, Minne, Mings. See Mennes
Minshull, Edward, Kt.1660, II. 231
Minshull (Minshal), Richard, Kt.1626, II. 191
Minto, earl of. See Elliot-Murray-Kynynmound

INDEX

Miraj, Gangadhar Rao, of, K.C.I.E.1903, I. 412
Mirfield. See Myrfeilde
Mirza, Mohamed Khan, G.C.M.G.1903, I. 349
Missett, John, Kt. Jacobite 1719, II. 266
Misson, James, Kt.1715, II. 280

MITCHELL, MICHEL, MICHIL, MYCHIL
Mitchell, Andrew, K.B.1765, I. 171
Mitchell, Andrew, K.B.1800, I. 175
Mitchell, Arthur, K.C.B.1887, I. 290
Michel, Bartholomew, Kt.1604, II. 132
Mitchell, Charles, Kt.1796, II. 303
Mitchell, Charles B. H., K.C.M.G.1883, I. 366; G.C.M.G.1895, I. 344
Michell, Charles C., K.H.1836, I. 474
Mitchell, David, Kt.1698, II. 271
Michill (Mychill), Francis, Kt.1620, II. 176
Mitchell, Frederick T., K.C.B.1867, I. 251
Mitchell, Henry, Kt.1887, II. 383
Michell, John, Kt.1619, II. 174
Michel, John, K.C.B.1859, I. 245; G.C.B.1871, I. 195
Mitchell, John, K.C.B.1861, I. 247
Michell, Lewis L., Kt.1902, II. 412
Mitchell, Michael, Kt.1692, II. 267
Mitchell, Thomas L., Kt.1839, II. 341
Mitchell, William, K.C.B.1815, I. 218
Mitchell, William, Kt.1867, II. 359
Mitchell, William H. F., Kt.1875, II. 367
Mitchell, William W., Kt.1900, II. 407

Mitford, John, Kt.1793, II. 301
Mitter, Romesh C., Kt.1890, II. 387
Mocler, James, Kt.1690, II. 266
Modena, Hercules d'Este, duke of, K.G. 1480, I. 16
Moeles, John de, K.B.1327, I. 124
Moffett, Thomas W., Kt.1896, II. 397
Mohamed, Sultan Pasha, K.C.M.G.1882, I. 365
Mohun, Charles, Kt.1643, II. 216
Mohun, John, lord Mohun, K.G.1348, I. 1
Mohun, Renald, Kt.1599, II. 95
Mohun, William, Kt.1583, II. 82

MOINE, MOYNE, MOIGNE, LE MOINE
Moigne, Henry le,, K.B.1306, I. 116
Moine, James McP. Le, Kt.1897, II. 399
Moyne, Reynold, Kt.1347, II. 8
Moira, earl of. See Rawdon-Hastings
Moleston, Adam de, K.B.1326, I 123
Molesworth, Guilford L., K.C.I.E.1888, I. 405
Molesworth, John, Kt.1675, II. 250
Molesworth, Robert, Kt.1886, II. 379
Molesworth, Walter de, K.B.1306, I. 112

MOLINES, MOLINE, MOLLIN, MOLYN
Molines, Barentine, jun., Kt.1594, II. 94
Molines, Michael, Kt.1592, II. 89
Mollin (Moline), Nicholas de, Kt.1606, II. 139
Molyn. See Mont-Hermer
Mollard, Armand, K.C.V.O.1903, I. 441
Molloy, Charles, Kt.1743, II. 285
Moloney, Cornelius A., K.C.M.G.1890, I. 375
Molteno, John C., K.C.M.G.1882, I. 365
Moltkè, count Joachim, G.C.V.O.1896, I. 422
Moltke, count von, K.C.V.O.1901, I. 440
Molyn. See Molines

MOLYNEUX, MOLINEUX, MOLYNEULX, MULLENEUX
Molyneux, Edmund, K.B.1547, I. 151
Molyneux, Francis, Kt.1765, II. 292
Molineux, John, Kt.1608, II. 146
Molyneux, John, Kt.1612, II. 151
Molyneux, Moore, Kt.1724, II. 283
Molyneulx, Richard, Kt.1586, II. 84
Molineux, Richard, Kt.1553, II. 68
Molyneux, Richard, Kt.1613, II. 153
Molyneux, Robert H. M., K.C.B.1885, I. 259; G.C.B.1902, I. 204
Molyneux, Thomas, Kt.1482, II. 18
Molineux, Thomas, Kt.1715, II. 280
Molineux (Mulleneux), Vivian, Kt. 1639, II. 206
Molyneux, William P., earl of Sefton, K.G.1885, I. 67
Molyneux-Williams, Thomas, K.H. 1836, I. 474
Mompesson, Giles, Kt.1616, II. 160

Mompesson, Richard, Kt.1603, II. 102
Monpesson, Thomas, Kt.1662, II. 236

MONCK, MONK, MONKE
  Monck, Charles S., viscount Monck, G.C.M.G.1869, I. 336
  Monck, Christopher, duke of Albemarle, K.G.1670, I. 36
  Monck, George, duke of Albemarle, K.G.1660, I. 35
  Monk, James, Kt.1825, II. 325
  Monke, Thomas, Kt.1603, II. 112

MONCKTON, MONKTON
  Monkton, Francis, Kt.1642, II. 213
  Monckton, John B., Kt.1880, II. 371
  Monckton, Philip, Kt.1617, II. 164
  Monckton-Arundell, Robert, viscount Galway, K.B.1786, I. 173

MONCRIEFF, MUNCRIFE
  Moncrieff (Muncrife), Alexander, Kt. 1615, II. 157, 171
  Moncrieff, Alexander, K.C.B.1890, I. 292
  Moncrieff, Colin C. S., K.C.S.I.1903, I. 328

Mondeford. See Mountford
Money, Alonzo, K.C.M.G.1898, I. 384
Money, William T., K.H.1831, I. 465
Moneypeny, Ja, Kt.1633, I. lxii.
Moneypenny, Patrick, Kt.1616, II. 160
Monins, Edward, Kt.1595, II. 91
Monins, Matthew, K.B.1626, I. 163
Monk. See Monck
Monkton. See Monckton
Monmouth, duke of. See Scott
Monox, John, Kt.1605, II. 138
Monro, Monroe. See Munro.
Monsell. See Maunsell

MONSON, MOUNSON, MUNSON
  Monson, Edmund J., K.C.M.G.1886, I. 369; G.C.M.G.1892, I. 343; G.C.B. 1896, I. 214; G.C.V.O.1903, I. 421
  Monson, John, Kt.1586, II. 84
  Munson (Monson), John, K.B.1626, I. 162
  Monson, John, K.B.1661, I. 164
  Monson, John, lord Monson, K.B.1725, I. 168

MONSON
  Monson, Robert, Kt.1603, II. 117
  Mounson, William, Kt.1596, II. 93
  Monson, William, Kt.1623, II. 181
  Mont-Hermer, alias Molyn, Edward, Kt. 1347, II. 6

MONTACUTE, DE MONTE ACUTO, and see Montague
  Montacute, John de, earl of Salisbury, K.G.1397, I. 7
  Montacute, Thomas de, earl of Salisbury, K.G.1414, I. 9
  Montacute, William de, K.B.1306, I. 113
  Montacute, William de, earl of Salisbury, K.B.1326, I. 123; K.G.1348, I. 1
  Montacute, William de, earl of Salisbury, Kt.(1346), II. 6

MONTAGU, MONTAGUE
  Montague, Charles, Kt.1603, II. 101
  Montague, Charles, earl of Halifax, K.G.1714, I. 41
  Mountagu, Charles, K.B.1771, I. 171
  Mountague (Montacute), Edward de, Kt.(1336), II. 5
  Montagu, Edward, Kt.1538, II. 51
  Montagu, Edward, Kt.1568, II. 73
  Montagu, Edward, lord Montagu of Boughton, K.B.1603, I. 155
  Montagu, Edward, earl of Manchester, K.B.1626, I. 161; K.G.1661, I. 35
  Montagu, Edward, earl of Sandwich, K.G.1660, I. 35
  Montague, George, earl of Halifax, K.B.1725, I. 167
  Montagu, George, duke of Montagu, K.G.1752, I. 45
  Montagu, George, G.C.B.1815, I. 182
  Montague, Henry, Kt. 1603, II. 114
  Montagu, Henry, lord Rokeby, K.C.B. 1856, I. 243; G.C.B.1875, I. 196
  Montagu, James, Kt.1705, II. 274
  Montagu, John, duke of Montagu, K.G.1718, I. 41; K.B.1725, I. 167; Grand Master of the Bath, I. 109
  Montagu, lord and marquess of. See Nevill
  Montagu, Sidney, Kt.1616, II. 159

INDEX

MONTAGU
Montagu, viscount. See Browne
Montagu, Walter, Kt.1603, II. 108
Montagu, William, duke of Manchester, K.B.1725, I. 167
Montague, William A., K.H.1830, I. 465; K.C.H.1832, I. 458; Kt.1832, I. 331
Montagu, William D., duke of Manchester, K.P.1877, I. 104
Montagu-Douglas-Scott, lord Charles T., K.C.B.1898, I. 270; G.C.B.1902, I. 204
Montagu-Douglas-Scott, Walter F., duke of Buccleuch, K.T.1830, I. 82; K.G.1835, I. 54
Montagu-Douglas-Scott, William H. W., duke of Buccleuch, K.T.1875, I. 87; K.G.1897, I. 70
Montague-Dunk, George, earl of Halifax, K.G.1764, I. 46
Montague-Scott, Charles W. H., duke of Buccleuch, K.T.1812, I. 80
Monteagle, lord. See Stanley; see Parker; see Rice

MONTEATH, MONTEITH
Monteath, James, K.C.S.I.1903, I. 327
Monteith, William, Kt.1594, II. 91
Monteath-Douglas, Thomas, K.C.B. 1865, I. 249
Monte Odorisio, count de, K.G.1347, I. 15
Montecuccoli, count Rudolph G.C.V.O. 1904, I. 429
Montefiore, Joseph S., Kt.1896, II. 398
Montefiore, Moses, Kt.1837, II. 339
Montenegro, prince Danilo, K.C.V.O. 1898, I. 438
Montenegro, Nicholas I. of, G.C.V.O. 1897, I. 422
Montenuovo, prince Alfred, &c., von, G.C.V.O.1903, I. 428

MONTFORD, MOUNTFORD
Montford, Edmond (Edward), Kt.1603, II. 117
Mountford, Edward, Kt.1629, II. 197
Montford, John de, earl of Richmond, K.G.1375, I. 4
Montford, John, Kt.1603, II. 117

MONTFORD
Mountford, Symon, Kt.1471, II. 16
Montford, Thomas, Kt.1604, II. 131

MONTGOMERIE, MONTGOMERY
Montgomerie, Archibald W., earl of Eglintoun, Grand Master of St. Patrick 1852, I. 94; K.T.1853, I. 84
Montgomery, earl of. See Herbert
Montgomery, Hugh, Kt.1605, II. 138
Montgomerie, Hugh, earl of Eglintoun, K.T.1812, I. 81
Montgomery, James, Kt.1630, II. 197
Montgomery, John, K.B.(1418), I. 130
Montgomery, John, Kt.1497, II. 29
Montgomery, Nicholas, K.B.(1483), I. 140
Montgomery, Nicholas, K.B.(1489), I. 143
Montgomery, Patrick, K.C.B.1865, I. 249
Montgomery, Robert, K.C.B.1859, I. 281; K.C.S.I.1866, I. 315; G.C.S.I. 1866, I. 309
Montgomery, Thomas, Kt.1461, II. 13; K.G.1476, I. 16
Montgomery, Thomas, Kt.1686, I. 262
Montgomery, Walter de, K.B.1306, I. 113
Montmorency, Anne, duc de, K.G.1532, I. 22
Montmorency, Francis, duc de, K.G.1572, I. 27
Montmorency, viscount de. See Hervey
Montresor, Henry T., G.C.H.1817, I. 448; Kt.1818, II. 320; K.C.B.1820, I. 229
Montresor, Thomas G., K.C.H.1834, I. 459; Kt.1834, II. 334
Montrose, duke and marquess of. See Graham
Moody, Henry, Kt.1606, II. 139

MOORE, MOOR, MORE
Moore, Alexander G. M., K.C.B.1900, I. 271
Moore, Arthur W., K.C.B.1902, I. 274
Moore, Charles, Kt.1623, II. 181
Moore, Charles, earl of Drogheda, K.P. 1783, I. 96
More, Christopher, Kt.1538, II. 52
More, Donal MacCartie, Kt.1558, I. 70

MOORE

Moore, Edward, Kt.1579, II. 80
More, Edward, Kt.1600, II. 98
Moore, Edward, Kt.1613, II. 153
More, Francis (Robert), Kt.1603, II. 110
Moore, Francis, Kt.1617, II. 161
More, George, 1598, II. 95
Moore, George, Kt.1781, II. 296
Moore, George M. J., Kt.1897, II. 401
Moore, Gerratt, Kt.1599, II. 97
Moore, Graham, K.C.B.1815, I. 220; G.C.M.G.1820, I.332; G.C.B.1836, I. 187
More, Henry, Kt.1523, II. 45
Moore, Henry, K.C.B.1897, I. 268
Moore, Henry F. S., marquess of Drogheda, K.P.1868, I. 103
Moore, James, Kt.1630, II. 198
Moore, Jasper, Kt.1603, II. 125
More (Moore), John, Kt.1549, II. 64
More, John, Kt.1607, II. 141
Moore, John, Kt.1672, II. 247
Moore, John, K.B.1770, I. 171
Moore, John, K.B.1804, I. 176
Moore, John, K.H.1837, I. 476
Moore, John, Kt.1894, II. 393
Moore, John W., Kt.1900, II. 407
Moore, Jonas, Kt.1673, II. 247
Moore, Jonas, Kt.1680, II. 255
Moore, Lorenzo, K.C.H.1834, I. 460; Kt.1834, II. 335
More, Fineen (Florence) O'Driscoll, Kt.1585, II. 83
Moor, Ralph D. R., K.C.M.G.1897, I. 383
Moor (More), Richard, Kt.1619, II. 172
Moore, St. John, Kt.1661, II. 236
More, Thom del, Kt.(1336), II. 5
Moore, Thomas, Kt.1593, II. 90
Moore, Thomas, Kt.1617, II. 167
Moore, Thomas, Kt.1715, II. 280
Moore, William, Kt.1576, II. 77
Moore, William G., K.C.B.1856, I. 243
Moore, William J., K.C.I.E.1888, I. 406
Moorsom, Robert, K.C.B.1815, I. 218
Moran (Morgan), John, Kt.1596, II. 93
Morant, George D., K.C.B.1901, I. 273

Moray, earl of. See Stuart

MORDAK, MORDAKE

Mordake, John, Kt.1347, II. 7
Mordak, Thomas, K.B.1306, I. 122

MORDAUNT, MORDANT, MORDEN, MORDANTE

Morden (Mordant), Charles, Kt.1608, II. 145
Mordant, Charles, Kt.1637, II. 205
Mordaunt, Charles, earl of Peterborough, K.G.1713, I. 41
Mordaunt, Henry, Earl of Peterborough, K.G.1685, I. 38
Mordaunt, John, K.B.1504, I. 147; Kt. 1504, II. 34
Mordaunt, John, lord Mordaunt, K.B. 1533, I. 149
Mordaunt, John, earl of Peterborough, K.B.1616, I. 159
Mordaunt, John, Kt.1669, II. 244
Mordaunt, John, K.B.1749, I. 169
Mordant, Lewes, Kt.1568, II. 73
Mordante, Nicholas, Kt.1604, II. 133
Mordant, Robert, Kt.1619, II. 170
More. See Moore
Morel, Thomas, Kt.1899, II. 405
Moresby, Christopher, Kt.1471, II. 14
Moresby, Fairfax, K.C.B.1855, I. 241; G.C.B.1865, I. 194
Moreton. See Morton
Morgan, Anthony, Kt.1642, II. 214
Morgan, Anthony, Kt.1656, II. 223, 224, 232
Morgan, Charles, Kt.1603, II. 120
Morgan, Charles T., Kt.1811, II. 310
Morgan, John, Kt.1596, II. 93
Morgan, John, Kt.1658, II. 224
Morgan, Lewis, Kt.1629, II. 196
Morgan, Mathew, Kt.1591, II. 89
Morgan, Morgan, Kt.1887, II. 383
Morgan, Richard, Kt.1553, II. 67
Morgan, Richard (Edward), Kt.1599, II. 97
Morgan, Richard F., Kt.1874, II. 366
Morgan, Rowland, Kt.1603, II. 120
Morgan, Thomas, Kt.1545, II. 57
Morgan, Thomas, Kt.1587, II. 86
Morgan, Thomas, Kt.1623, II. 182
Morgan, Walter, Kt.1866, II. 358
Morgan, William, Kt.1513, II. 41

Morgan, William, Kt.1574, II. 76
Morgan, William, Kt.1603, II. 126
Morgan, William, Kt.1646, II. 221
Morgan, William, K.B.1725, I. 168
Morgan, William, K.C.M.G.1883, I. 366
Moriarty, Thomas, Kt.1810, II. 310
Morice. See Morris
Morichi, Giovanni, C.M.G.(1822), I. xxviii.
Morier, Robert, B. D., K.C.B.1882, I. 288; G.C.M.G.1886, I. 340; G.C.B.1887, I. 212
Morin, Enrico C., G.C.V.O.1903, I. 426
Morison. See Morrison
Morland, Henry, Kt.1887, II. 381
Morland, Samuel, Kt.1660, II. 225
Morley, Charles, Kt.1696, II. 269
Morley, Edward, Kt.1618, II. 169
Morley, Francis B., K.C.B.1886, I. 289
Morley, Isaac, Kt.1841, II. 343
Morley, John, Kt.1603, II. 119
Morley, John, Kt.1630, II. 197
Morley, John, Kt.1639, II. 207
Morley, John, Kt.1661, II. 234
Morley, lord. See Lovel
Morley, Thomas D., lord Morley, K.G. 1411, I. 9
Morley, William, Kt.1625, II. 189
Morley, William, K.B.1661, I. 166
Mornington, earl of. See Wellesley; see Wellesley-Pole
Morocco, Moulaï Abdul-el-Aziz, sultan of, G.C.B.1901, I. 216
Morphett, John, Kt.1870, II. 362
Morres. See Morris
Morrice. See Morris
MORRIS, MORICE, MORRICE, MORRYS, MORYS, MORRES, and see Norris
Morris, Benjamin, Kt.1836, II. 337
Morrys, Christopher, Kt.1538, II. 51
Morris, Daniel, K.C.M.G.1903, I. 394
Morris, Edmund F., K.C.B.1867, I. 250
Morys, Edward, Kt.1487, II. 24
Morris, Edward, K.C.B.1882, I. 258
Morris, Edward P., Kt.1904, II. 418
Morris, Evan, Kt.1889, II. 386
Morice, Ferik G., K.C.M.G.1898, I. 384
Morris, George, Kt.1841, II. 343

MORRIS
Morris, George, K.C.B.1898, I. 297
Morris, James N., K.C.B.1815, I. 220
Morrys (Norrys, Norris), John, Kt. 1603, II. 110
Morris, John, Kt.1866, II. 358
Morris, John H., K.C.S.I.1883, I. 323
Morris, Lewis, Kt.1895, II. 396
Morris, Louis M., G.C.B.1856, I. 192
Morice, Thomas H., K.H.1835, I. 472
Morris, William, Kt.1603, II. 121
Morrice, William, Kt.1660, II. 226
Morres, William E., Kt.1755, II. 288

MORRISON, MORISON, MORYSON
Moryson, —, Kt.1587, II. 86
Morison, Alexander, Kt.1838, II. 341
Morison (Moryson), Charles, K.B.1603, I. 155
Morrison, George W., Kt.1885, II. 378
Morison, Henry, Kt.1627, II. 193
Morrison, James W., Kt.1851, II. 348
Morison, Richard, Kt.1599, II. 97
Morrison, Richard, Kt.1841, II. 343
Morison, William, K.C.B.1848, I. 277
Morrys. See Morris
Morteign, count of. See Beaufort

MORTIMER, MORTEMER
Mortimer, Edmund de, K.B.1327, I. 124
Mortimer, Edmond, earl of March, K.B.(1413), I. 129
Mortimer, Geoffrey de, K.B.1327, I. 124
Mortimer, John, Kt.(1317), I. lix.
Mortemer, John (Roger), Kt.1485, II. 22
Mortemer, John, Kt.1487, II. 24
Mortimer, Roger, K.B.(1413), I. 129
Mortimer, Roger de, earl of March, K.B.1306, I. 112
Mortimer, Roger de, K.B.1306, I. 113
Mortimer, Roger de, K.B.1327, I. 124
Mortimer, Roger de, earl of March, Kt.(1346), II. 6; K.G.1348, I. 1
Mortimer, Roger, earl of March, K.B. 1390, I. 127
Mortimer, William, Kt.1347, II. 7
Mortlock, John C., Kt.1816, II. 317

INDEX

MORTON, MORETON, MOURTON, MERTON
  Morton, Albert, Kt.1617, II. 166
  Morton, earl of. See Douglas
  Morton, Francis, Kt.1679, II. 253
  Morton (Moreton, Norton), George, Kt.1603, II. 109
  Morton, Gerald de, K.C.I.E.1898, I. 410
  Morton, James, Kt.1671, II. 246
  Morton, John de, K.B.1306, I. 119
  Morton, John, Kt.1574, II. 76
  Morton (Mutton), Peter, Kt.1622, II. 179
  Morton, Robert, Kt.1512, II. 35
  Morton, Robert, Kt.1628, II. 194
  Moreton (Mourton), Rowland, Kt. 1547, II. 59
  Morton, Thomas, Kt.1625, II. 189
  Morton (Merton), William, Kt.1643, II. 216
  Moreton, William, Kt.1755, II. 288
Morvi, Thakore of, K.C.I.E.1887, I. 405; G.C.I.E.1897, I. 403
Morys. See Morris
Moryson. See Morrison
Moseley, Edward, Kt.1614, II. 155
Moseley (Mosley), Edward, Kt.1689, II. 265
Moseley, Nicholas, Kt.1600, II. 98
MOSTON, MOSTYN, MOSTEN
  Moston, Roger, Kt.1606, II. 140
  Mostyn, Roger, Kt.1660, II. 227
  Mosten, Thomas, Kt.1599, II. 95
  Moston (Moiston), Thomas, Kt.1623, II. 183
Mote, William de la, K.B.1306, I. 121
MOTTON, MOTON
  Moton, William, K.B.1306, I. 116
  Motton, William, Kt.1471, II. 15
Mottram, Richard, Kt.1897, II. 401
Moubray. See Mowbray
Moulford (Mondeford, Mountford), Edmond, Kt.1629, II. 197
Moulson, Thomas, Kt.1634, II. 202
Mounson. See Monson
Mount Charles, earl of. See Conyngham
Mount Edgcumbe, earl of. See Edgcumbe
Mountford. See Montford

Mountjoy, lord. See Blount
MOUNTNEY, MOUNTENEY
  Mountney, John de, K.B.1306, I. 116
  Mounteney (Monckton), Philip, Kt. 1617, II. 164
MOWATT, MOWAT, MOUAT
  Mowat, —, Kt.1650–1, II. 222
  Mowatt, Francis, K.C.B.1893, I. 293; G.C.B.1901, I. 215
  Mouat, James, K.C.B.1894, I. 265
  Mowat, Oliver, K.C.M.G.1892, I. 377; G.C.M.G.1897, I. 345
MOWBRAY, MOUBRAY
  Mowbray, John, lord Mowbray, K.B. 1306, I. 111
  Mowbray, John, K.B.1360, I. 125
  Mowbray, John de, duke of Norfolk, K.G.1421, I. 10
  Mowbray, John de, duke of Norfolk, K.B.(1426), I. 130; K.G.1451, I. 12
  Mowbray, John de, duke of Norfolk, K.B.(1461), I. 133; K.G.1472, I. 15
  Mowbray, Robert, Kt.1825, II. 325; K.H.1833, I. 468
  Mowbray, Thomas, duke of Norfolk, K.G.1383, I. 5
Mowne, John, Kt.1549, II. 64
Moyers, George, Kt.1887, II. 383
Moyle (MacMahon), Patrick M., Kt.1604, II. 135
Moyle, Robert, Kt.1660, II. 226
Moyle, Thomas, Kt.1542, II. 53
Moyle, Walter, K.B.(1465), I. 134
Moyle, Walter, Kt.1664, II. 239
Moyne. See Moine
Moyte, —, de la, Kt.1537, II. 50
Mudaliyar, Ramaswami, Kt.1887, II. 380
Mudie, Thomas, Kt.1651, II. 222
Muffling, Frederick F. K., baron de, K.C.B.1815, I. 228
Muggeridge, Henry, Kt.1855, II. 351
Muir, William, K.C.S.I.1867, I. 317
Muir, William M., K.C.B.1873, I. 254
Mulcaster, Frederick W., K.C.H.1832, I. 458; Kt.1832, II. 332
Mulcaster, William H., K.C.H.1831, I. 457; Kt.1831, II. 330
Mulgrave, earl of. See Sheffield; see Phipps

INDEX

Mulgrave, Edward, Kt.1646, II. 221
Mulledy, Anthony, Kt.1688, II. 264
Mullen, Robert, K.H.1835, I. 472
Müller, Robert von, G.C.V.O.1897, I. 423
Müller, Ferdinand von, K.C.M.G.1879, I. 361
Mullyns, Thomas, Kt.1604, II. 130
Mulock, William, K.C.M.G.1902, I. 392
Multon, John de, K.B.1306, I. 118
Multon, Thomas de, K.B.1306, I. 113
Munden, John, Kt.1701, II. 272
Munden (Mundy), Richard, Kt.1673, II. 248

MUNDY, MUNDAY, and see Munden
Mundy, George, K.C.B.1837, I. 233
Mundy, George R., K.C.B.1862, I. 248; G.C.B.1877, I. 197
Mundy, John, Kt.1529, II. 47
Mundy, Robert M., K.C.M.G.1877, I. 359
Munday, Thomas, Kt.1761, II. 290

MUNRO, MONRO, MONROE
Munro, Alexander, Kt.1783, II. 297
Munro, Alexander, K.H.1836, I. 473
Munro (Monro), David, Kt.1866, II. 358
Munro, David, Kt.1904, II. 417
Monroe, George, Kt.1649, II. 221
Munro, George, Kt.1779, II. 296
Munro, George G., Kt.1842, II. 344
Monro, Hector, K.B.1779, I. 173
Munro, Thomas, K.C.B.1819, I. 229

Munson. See Monson
Munster, count Ernest F. H., G.C.B.1831, I. 186
Murch, Jerom, Kt.1894, II. 394
Murchison, Roderick I., Kt.1846, II. 346; K.C.B.1863, I. 283
Murden, Jeremiah, Kt. 1726, II. 283
Murdoch, Thomas W. C., K.C.M.G.1870, I. 355
Mure, Andrew, Kt.1899, II. 404
Murphy, Francis, Kt.1860, II. 355
Murphy, James, Kt.1902, II. 410
Murphy, Shirley F., Kt.1904, II. 419

MURRAY, MURREY
Murray, —, Kt.1610, II. 150
Murrey, Adam, Kt.1482, II. 18
Murray, Andrew, Kt.1633, II. lxiii.
Murray, Charles A., K.C.B.1866, I. 284
Murray, David, Kt.1605, II. 138
Murray, David, earl of Mansfield, K.T. 1768, I. 79
Murray, David W., earl of Mansfield, K.T.1835, I. 82
Murray, George, K.B.1813, I. 179; G.C.B.1815, I. 182; G.C.H.1816, I. 448
Murray, George, K.C.B.1815, I. 217
Murray, George A. F. J., duke of Atholl, K.T.1853, I. 84
Murray, George H., K.C.B.1899, I. 297
Murray, Henry, K.C.B.1860, I. 246
Murray, Herbert H., K.C.B.1895, I. 293
Murray, James, Kt.1603, II. 128
Murray, Ja, Kt.1633, I. lxiii., bis
Murray, James, Kt.1643, II. 216
Murray, James, earl of Dunbar, K.T. Jacobite 1725, footnote, I. 75
Murray, James, duke of Atholl, K.T. 1734, I. 78
Murray, James, lord Glenlyon, K.C.H. 1820, I. 455
Murray, James, Kt.1833, II. 334
Murray, James W., K.C.B.1900, I. 273
Murray, John, Kt.1594, II. 91
Murray, John, marquess of Atholl, K.T.1687, I. 75
Murray, John, duke of Atholl, K.T. 1704, I. 76
Murray, John, duke of Atholl, K.T. 1767, I. 79
Murray, John, duke of Atholl, K.T. 1800, I. 80
Murray, John, G.C.H.1817, I. 448
Murray, John, K.C.B.1898, I. 297
Murray, John A., Kt.1839, II. 341
Murray, John I., K.C.B.1897, I. 267
Murray, Patrick, earl of Tullibardine, K.B.1603, I. 154
Murray (Marrey), Patrick, Kt.1615, II. 157
Murray, Robert, Kt.1643, II. 215

INDEX

MURRAY
Murray, Robert, Kt.1697, H. 270
Murray, Terence A., Kt.1869, II. 361
Murray, Thomas K., K.C.M.G.1901, I. 391
Murray, William D., earl of Mansfield, K.T.1843, I. 83
Murshidabad, nawab of, K.C.I.E.1887, I. 400; G.C.I.E.1890, I. 402
Murton, Walter, Kt.1899, II. 405
Muskat, Saiyid Faisal, of, K.C.I.E.1903, I. 412; G.C.I.E.1903, I. 404
Muskat, Syud Toorkee, sultan of, G.C.S.I. 1886, I. 312
Muschamp, Thomas, Kt.1605, II. 136
Muschamp, Thomas, Kt.1627, II. 193
Muschamp, William, Kt.1617, II. 163
Musgrave, Anthony, K.C.M.G.1875, I.358
Musgrave, Anthony, G.C.M.G.1885, I. 340
Musgrave, Cuthbert, Kt.1568, II. 74
Musgrave, Edward, Kt.1604, II. 134
Musgrave, James, Kt.1889, footnote, II. 386
Musgrave, John, Kt.1487, II. 24
Musgrave, Richard, Kt.1603, II. 101
Musgrave, Richard, K.B.1603, I. 155
Musgrave, Simon, Kt.1570, II. 74
Musgrave, Thomas, Kt.1619, II. 171
Musgrave, William, Kt.1523, II. 44
Musgrave, William, Kt.1617, II. 164
Mustapha, Fehmy Pasha, K.C.M.G.1887, I. 372; G.C.M.G.1898, I. 345
Musters, John, Kt.1663, II. 238
Mustoxidi, Andrea, C.M.G.(1820), preface, I. 28; K.C.M.G.1857, I. 353
Muthuswami, Aiyar, K.C.I.E.1892, I. 407
Mutton. See Motton, Morton
Muzzan, Francesco, K.C.M.G.1823, I.351; G.C.M.G.1840, I. 334
Myers, Francis W., Kt.1824, II. 325
Myles. See Miles
Mylord (Millard), William, Kt.1696, II. 269
Myllet, Nicholas, Kt.1667, II. 242
Mynnes, Mynn. See Mennes
Myrfeilde, Richard, Kt.1497, II. 32
MYSORE
Chama Rajendra, maharajah of, G.C.S.I.1884, I. 312

MYSORE
Krishnah Raj Wadyar, maharaja of, G.C.S.I.1867, I. 309
Narasingharao of, K.C.I.E.1903, I.412
Sheshadri Aiyar, of, K.C.S.I.1893, I. 325

N

Nabha, Raja Hira Singh, G.C.S.I.1879, I. 311; G.C.I.E.1903, I. 404
Nadown, Jodhbir Chund, of, K.C.S.I. 1867, I. 318
Nagel, Edmund, K.C.H.1821, I. 455
Nagle, Edmund, Kt.1795, II. 303; K.C.B. 1815, I. 217; G.C.H.1817, I. 448
Nagle, Richard, Kt.1687, II. 263
Nahun, Shamshir Prakash, rajah of, K.C.S.I.1875, I. 320
NAIRNE, NEARNE
Nairne, Charles E., K.C.B.1897, I. 268
Nearne (Nairn), David, Kt.1704, II. 273
Namur, Robert de, K.G.1369, I. 4
Nanfant, Richard, Kt.1488, II. 27
Nangle, Thomas, baron of Navan, Kt. 1555, II. 69
Nanpara, Jang, of, K.C.I.E.1901, I. 410
NAPIER, NAPPER, NAPER, NAPPIER

Napper, Archibald, Kt.1616, II. 159
Napier, Charles, K.C.B.1840, I. 237
Napier, Charles J., K.C.B.1838, I. 235; G.C.B.1843, I. 189
Napier, Francis, lord Napier, K.T. 1864, I. 85
Napper, George (Gerard), Kt.1641, II. 209
Napier, George T., K.C.B.1838, I. 235
Napier, James, Kt.1778, II. 295
Napper, Nathaniel, Kt.1618, II. 170
Napier, Nathaniel, Kt.1662, II. 236
Napper, Richard, Kt.1641, II. 209
Napper (Napier), Robert, Kt.1612, II. 152
Napper (Napier), Robert, Kt.1623, II. 181
Napier (Neppier, Naper), Robert, Kt. 1681, II. 255

INDEX 165

NAPIER
  Napier, Robert C., lord Napier of Magdala, K.C.B. 1858, I. 245; G.C.S.I.1867, I. 309; G.C.B.1868, I. 195
  Napper, Thomas, Kt.1593, II. 90
  Napier, Thomas E., K.C.B.1860, I. 246
  Napier, William F. P., K.C.B.1848, I. 238
NAPLES
  Alphonsus II., king of, K.G.1493, I. 18
  Ferdinand I., king of, K.G.1462-3, I. 14
Napoleon, prince, G.C.B.1855, I. 191
Napper. See Napier
Narborough, John, Kt.1673, II. 248
Narendra, Krisna, K.C.I.E.1888, I. 406
Nares, George, Kt.1771, II. 293
Nares, George S., K.C.B.1876, I. 286
Nash, Nathaniel, Kt.1761, II. 291
Nash, Stephen, Kt.1786, II. 299
Nash, Vincent, Kt.1902, II. 410
Nassau de Zulestein, William H., earl of Rochford, K.G.1778, I. 47
Nathan, Gustavus, Kt.1891, II. 388
Nathan, Matthew, K.C.M.G.1902, I. 391
Nathan, Nathaniel, Kt.1903, II. 416
Nathoobhoy, Munguldass, Kt.1874, II. 367
Nation, John L., K.C.B.1900, I. 271
Naudi, Salvatore, Kt.1878, II. 370
Naunton, Robert, Kt.1615, II. 156
Navanagar, Jam Shri Vibhajee, of, K.C.S.I.1877, I. 321
Nawazish Ali Khan, K.C.I.E.1888, I. 405
Nayler, George, Kt.1813, II. 313; K.H. 1816, I. 463
Naz, Virgile, K.C.M.G.1880, I. 363
Nearne. See Nairne
NEALE, NIEL, NEILL, NEILE, NEELLS, NEAL
  Neil, Adolphe, K.C.B.1856, I. 241
  Neale, Charles, Kt.1678, II. 253
  Neale, Francis, Kt.1609, II. 146
  Neale, Harry, K.C.B.1815, I. 219; G.C.B.1822, I. 185
  Neale, Harry B., G.C.M.G.1824, I. 332

NEALE
  Neale, Henry J. V., K.C.B.1902, I. 300
  Neill, James G., K.C.B.1857, I. footnote, 244
  Neells, John, Kt.1640, II. 207
  Neile, Paul, Kt.1633, II. 201
  Neale, Richard, Kt.1686, II. 262
  Neal, Thomas, Kt.1604, II. 131
  Neal, William, Kt.1643, II. 215
Need, Arthur, Kt.1881, II. 372
Needham, Francis, Kt.1617, II. 167
Needham, Francis C., earl of Kilmorey, K.P.1890, I. 105
Needham, John, K.B.(1465), I. 134
Needham (Keedham), John, Kt.1603, II. 121
Needham, Joseph, Kt.1873, II. 365
Nedham, Robert, Kt.1533, II. 49
Needham, Robert, Kt.1594, II. 91
Needham, Robert, Kt.1630, II. 197
Negrier, François de, G.C.V.O.1898, I. 423
Negro, Peter, Kt. 1547, II. 62
Neile. See Neale
Neill. See Neale
Neligan, John C., Kt.1899, II. 404
Nelson, Alexander A., K.C.B.1891, I. 264
Nelson, Edward M., K.C.M.G.1897, I. 383
Nelson, Horatio, viscount Nelson, K.B. 1797, I. 175
Nelson, Hugh M., K.C.M.G.1896, I. 381
Nelson, Thomas J., Kt.1880, II. 371
Nemours, Julian de Medicis, duke of, K.G.1514, I. 20
Nepal, Runnodeep Sing, of, K.C.S.I.1875, I. 320
Nepean, Evan C., Kt.1891, II. 389
Neppier. See Napier
Neteof (Neetens, Neetese), —, Kt.1617, II. 160

NETHERLANDS
  William F., king of the, K.G.1814, I. 52; K.B.1814, I. 179; G.C.B.1815, I. 182
  William III. of the, K.G.1882, I. 66
Nethersole, Francis, Kt.1619, II. 174

Netterville, John, Kt.1625, II. 190
Neublanche, Philip de Chabot, comte de, K.G.1532, I. 22
Neurath, freiherr Constantin von, G.C.V.O.1904, I. 429
Neufville, Noefville. See Neville
Neve, William Le, Kt.1634, II. 202
Neveson, Roger, Kt.1604, II. 133
NEVILLE, NEVILL, NEVILE, NEVIL
Nevill, —, Kt.1492, II. 27
Nevill, Anthony, Kt.1544, II. 55
Neville, Christopher, K.B.1626, I. 162
Nevill, Christopher, Kt.1674, II. 249
Nevile, Edward, Kt.1513, II. 39
Nevill, Edward, Kt.1671, II. 246
Nevill, Edward, Kt.1681, II. 256
Neville, Garrett, Kt.1820, II. 321
Nevill, George [William or Henry], lord Abergavenny, K.B.(1483), I. 141
Nevill, George, Kt.1487, II. 25
Nevill, George, lord Bergavenny, Kt. 1471, II. 14
Nevill, George, lord Abergavenny, K.B. (1483), I. 139; K.G.1513, I. 20
Neville, Henry, Kt.1400, II. 11
Nevill, Henry, earl of Westmorland, Kt.1544, II. 56; K.G.1552, I. 24
Nevill, Henry, Kt.1549, II. 65
Nevill, Henry, lord Abergavenny, K.B. 1553, I. 152
Nevill, Henry, Kt.1596, II. 92
Nevill, Henry, Kt.1609, II. 147
Nevill, Henry, earl of Abergavenny, K.T.1814, I. 81
Neville, Hugh de, K.B.1325, I. 123
Nevil, Jervis, Kt.1628, II. 195
Neville, John de, K.B.1305, I. 111
Neville, John de, K.B.1306, I. 114
Neville, John de, K.B.1327, I. 124
Nevill, John de, lord Nevill de Raby, Kt.1360, II. 10; K.G.1369, I. 4
Nevill, John, lord Latimer, K.B.1399, I. 128
Neville, John [George], lord Latimer, K.B.(1426), I. 131
Nevill, John, marquess of Montagu, K.B.(1449), I. 132; K.G.1461, I. 14
Nevill, John (of Liverseege), Kt.1482), II. 20

NEVILLE
Nevill, John, Kt.1497, II. 31
Nevill, John (of Liverseege), Kt.1513, II. 39
Nevill, John, Kt.1513, II. 41
Nevill, John, Kt.1544, II. 56
Nevill, John, lord Latimer, Kt.1545, II. 57
Neville, Philip de, K.B.1303, I. 110
Nevil, Ralph de, earl of Westmorland, Kt.1380, II. 10; K.G.1402, I. 8
Nevill, Ralph de, earl of Westmorland, K.B.(1426), I. 130
Neville, Ralph, earl of Westmorland, K.B.(1475), I. 136
Nevill, Rauf, earl of Westmorland, Kt.1523, II. 44; K.G.1525, I. 21
Nevill, Richard, earl of Salisbury, K.G.1438, I. 11
Nevill, Richard, earl of Warwick, K.G. 1461, I. 13
Nevill, Richard, lord Latimer, K.B. 1478, I. 137
Nevyll, Robert, Kt.1513, II. 42
Nevill, Robert, Kt.1538, II. 51
Nevill, Thomas, K.B.(1449), I. 132
Nevill, Thomas, Kt.1547, II. 60; K.B. 1547, I. 151
Nevill, Thomas, Kt.1547, II. 63
Nevill, Thomas, Kt.1603, II. 118
Nevill, Thomas, K.B.1616, I. 160
Nevill, William, earl of Kent, K.B. (1426), I. 131; K.G.1439, I. 11
Nevill, William, Kt.1482, II. 18
Nevill, William, marquess of Abergavenny, K.G.1886, I. 68
Nevor, Robert de, Kt.1347, II. 8
Newbigging, William, Kt.1838, II. 340
Newbolt, John H., Kt.1810, II. 310
Newburgh, John de, K.B.1306, I. 119
Newburgh, Roger, K.B.(1494), I. 144
Newbury, Thomas, Kt.(1464), II. lx.
Newcastle, duke of. See Cavendish; see Holles; see Pelham-Holles; see Pelham-Clinton
Newcastle, earl of. See Butler
Newcomen, Beverley, Kt.1617, II. 161
Newcomen, Robert, Kt.1605, II. 138
Newcomen, Thomas, Kt.1670, II. 245

Newdigate, Edward N., K.C.B.1894, I. 265
Newdigate, Henry R. L., K.C.B.1897, I. 268
Newdigate, John, Kt.1603, II. 118
Newdigate, Robert (John), Kt.1603, II. 107
Newenham, Edward, Kt.1763, II. 292
Newland, Benjamin, Kt.1679, II. 254
Newland, George, Kt.1706, II. 275

NEWMAN, NEWEMAN, NEWNAM
Newman, George, Kt.1616, II. 160
Newnam (Newman), Thomas, Kt.1547, II. 59
Neweman, William, Kt.1532, II. 48
Newmarch, Oliver R., K.C.S.I.1894, I. 325
Newnam. See Newman

NEWPORT, NEWPORTE
Newport (Davenport), Francis, Kt. 1603, II. 101
Newporte, Richard, Kt.1560, II. 71
Newport, Richard, Kt.1615, II. 155
Newport, Simon, Kt.1785, II. 298
Newport, William, K.B.(1400), I. 129
Newton, Charles T., K.C.B.1887, I. 290
Newton, Edward, K.C.M.G.1887, I. 371
Newton, Henry, Kt.1592, II. 90
Newton, Henry, Kt.1715, II. 280
Newton, Isaac, Kt.1705, II. 274
Newton, Michael, K.B.1725, I. 168
Newton, Theodore, Kt.1609, II. 147
Newton, William, Kt.1513, II. 38
Newton, William H., K.H.1836, I. 474
Newton, William J., Kt.1837, II. 339
Nezam, Gaffary, Mohandes-el-Mamalek, K.C.M.G.1903, I. 393
Nias, Joseph, K.C.B.1867, I. 250

NICHOLAS, NICOLAS, and see Nichols
Nicholas, Ambrose, Kt.1576, II. 77
Nicholas, Edward, Kt.1641, II. 211
Nicholas, John, K.B.1661, I. 164
Nicolas, John T., K.H.1834, I. 470
Nicolas, Nicholas H., K.H.1831, I. 466; Kt.1831, II. 331; K.C.M.G.1832, I. 351; G.C.M.G.1840, I. 334
Nicholas, Oliver, Kt.1630, II. 197

NICHOLL, NICOLL
Nicoll, Charles G., K.B.1732, I. 169
Nicholl, John, Kt.1798, II. 304

NICHOLLS, NICOLLS, NICHOLS
Nicolls, Edward, K.C.B.1855, I. 241
Nicholls, George, K.C.B.1851, I. 278
Nicholls, Henry, K.C.B.1820, I. 229
Nicholls, Jasper, K.C.B.1826, I. 230
Nichols (Nicholas), John (Augustine), Kt.1607, II. 141
Nickalls, Patteson, Kt.1893, II. 392
Nickle, Robert, K.H.1832, I. 467; Kt. 1844, II. 345

NICHOLSON, NICOLSON
Nicolson, Arthur, K.C.I.E.1888, I. 405; K.C.B.1901, I. 298; K.C.V.O.1903, I. 435
Nicholson, Charles, Kt.1852, II. 349
Nicholson, Frederick A., K.C.I.E.1903, I. 411
Nicholson, Henry F., K.C.B.1897, I. 268
Nicholson, Humphry, Kt.1681, II. 255
Nicolson, Ja, Kt.1633, I. lxii.
Nicholson, John, K.C.B.1857, footnote, I. 244
Nicholson, Lothian, K.C.B.1887, I. 261
Nicholson, Richard, Kt.1886, II. 378
Nicolson, Thomas, Kt.1650, II. 222
Nicholson, Thomas W., K.H.1835, I. 472
Nicholson, William G., K.C.B.1898, I. 269
Nicolas. See Nicholas
Nicolay, William, K.C.H.1832, I. 458; Kt.1832, II. 332;
Nicoll. See Nicholl
Nicolson. See Nicholson
Nicolls. See Nicholls
Niddry, lord. See Hope
Niel. See Neale
Nightingale, Miles, K.C.B.1815, I. 218
Nightingale, Robert, Kt.1685, II. 261
Nihal, Sing Chachi, K.C.S.I.1866, I. 317
Nisbet, Alexander, Kt.1873, II. 365
Nithsdale, earl of. See Maxwell
Niven, William D., K.C.B.1903, I. 300
Nixon, Christopher J., Kt.1895, II. 395
Nixon, Eccles, Kt.1799, II. 304

Noble, Andrew, K.C.B.1893, I. 293
Noefville. See Neville
NOEL, NOELL, NOWELL, KNOWILL, KNOVILL
  Noel, Andrew, Kt.1586, II. 84
  Noell, Andrew, Kt.1681, II. 256
  Nowell (Noell), Charles, Kt.1615, II. 155
  Knowill, Edward, Kt.1523, II. 44
  Noell, Edward, Kt.1602, II. 100
  Noel, Gerard H. U., K.C.M.G.1898, I. 385; K.C.B.1902, I. 273
  Nowell, Henry, Kt.1587, II. 85
  Noell, Henry, Kt.1586, II. 84
  Knovill, John de, K.B.1306, I. 117
  Noell, Martin, Kt.1662, II. 237
  Noell, Martin, Kt.1665, II. 241
  Nowell, Michael, Kt.1786, II. 299
Norbury, Henry F., K.C.B.1897, I. 268
NORCLIFFE, NORCLIFF, NORTCLIFFE, NORTHCLIFFE, NOTCLIFF
  Norcliffe, Norcliffe, K.H.1836, I. 474
  Norcliffe, Thomas, Kt.1617, II. 161
  Northcliffe (Notcliff), Thomas, Kt. 1641, II. 211, 212
  Nortcliffe (Northcliffe, Norcliffe),, Thomas, Kt.1670, II. 245
Norcott, Amos G. R., K.C.H.1831, I. 457; Kt.1831, II. 330
Norcott, William S. R., K.C.B.1877, I. 255
Norfolk, duke of. See Mowbray; see Howard; see Fitzalan-Howard
Norfolk, earl of. See Howard
Norman, Francis B., K.C.B.1886, I. 260
Norman, Henry R., K.C.B.1899, I. 270
Norman, Henry W., K.C.B.1873, I. 254; G.C.M.G.1887, I. 341; G.C.B.1887, I. 199
Normanby, marquess of. See Phipps
Normanvile, John, Kt.1497, II. 32
NORRIS, NORRYS, NORREYS, NORRES, and see Morris
  Norrys (Morys), Edward, Kt.1487, II. 24
  Norris, Edward, Kt.1586, II. 85
  Norrys, Edward, Kt.1662, II. 237
  Norris, Francis, earl of Berkshire, K.B.1605, I. 156
  Norris, Francis, Kt.1633, II. 202

NORREYS
  Norreys, Henry, Kt.1566, II. 72
  Norris, Henry, Kt.1586, II. 84
  Norris, John, Kt.1601, II. 99
  Norrys, John, Kt.1586, II. 84
  Norris, John, Kt.1646, II. 221
  Norris, John, Kt.1705, II. 275
  Norres, Lyonell, Kt.1529, II. 47
  Norrys, Thomas, Kt.1588, II. 86
  Norris, William, Kt.1460, II. 12
  Norrys, William, Kt.1487, II. 25
  Norris, William, K.B.1603, I. 156
Nortcliffe. See Norcliffe
North, Charles, Kt.1618, II. 169
North, Dudley, lord North, K.B.1616, I. 160
North, Dudley, Kt.1683, II. 258
North, Edward, Kt.1542, II. 53
North, Ford, Kt.1881, II. 373
North, Francis, Kt.1671, II. 245
North, Frederick, earl of Guilford, K.G. 1772, I. 47
North, Frederick, earl of Guilford, G.C.M.G.1819, I. 332
North, Henry, Kt.1586, II. 85
North, John, Kt.1596, II. 92
North, John, K.B.1616, I. 160
North, Roger, K.B.1559, I. 153
North, Roger, Kt.1618, II. 168
Northampton, earl of. See Bohun; see Howard; see Compton
Northampton, marquess of. See Parr; see Compton
Northbrook, earl of. See Baring
Northcliffe. See Norcliffe
Northcote, Henry S., lord Northcote, G.C.I.E.1900, I. 403; G.C.M.G.1904, I. 349
Northcote, Stafford H., earl of Iddlesleigh, G.C.B.1880, I. 211
Northesk, earl of. See Carnegie
Northey, Edward, Kt.1702, II. 272
Northington, earl of. See Henley
Northumberland, duke of. See Dudley; see Fitz-Roy; see Percy
Northumberland, earl of. See Percy
Northwood, James de, K.B.1306, I. 112
Norton, Alexander, Kt.1620, II. 176
Norton, Charles, Kt.1714, II. 280

INDEX 169

Norton, Daniel, Kt.1603, II. 122
Norton, Daniel, Kt.1627, II. 192
Norton, Dudley, Kt.1615, II. 155
Norton, Fletcher, Kt.1762, II. 291
Norton, George, K.B.1547, I. 151
Norton, George, Kt.1603, II. 109
Norton, George, Kt.1660, II. 227
Norton, George, Kt.1671, II. 246
Norton, James de, K.B.1306, I. 122
Norton, John, K.B.1501, I. 146
Norton, John, Kt.1547, II. 60
Norton (Morton), John, Kt.1574, II. 76
Norton, John D., Kt.1842, II. 344
Norton, lord. See Adderley
Norton, Richard, Kt.1601, II. 99
Norton, Richard, Kt.1611, II. 150
Norton, Sampson, Kt.1489, II. 27
Norton, Thomas, Kt.1607, II. 143
Norton, William, Kt.1603, II. 110

NORWICH, NORWYCH, NORWECHE, NORWYCHE
Norwych, Charles, Kt.1604, II. 131
Norweche, John de, Kt.1347, II. 8
Norwich (Herwich), John, Kt.1641, II. 210
Norwyche, Robert de, Kt.1529, II. 47
Norwich, Simon, Kt.1618, II. 167
Notcliff. See Norcliffe
NOTT, KNOT, and see Nutt
Knot (Nott), Thomas, Kt.1639, II. 207
Nott, William, G.C.B.1842, I. 189
Nottingham, earl of. See Mowbray; see Howard
Nourse, Charles, Kt.1786, II. 299
Nouyon, William de, Kt.1513, II. 41
Nowell. See Noel
Nozim, Nabob, G.C.H.1837, I. 453
Nubar, Pasha, G.C.M.G.1879, I. 339; G.C.S.I.1896, I. 314
Nuce, William, Kt.1621, II. 177
Nugent, Charles B. P. N. H., K.C.B.1882, I. 258
Nugent, Charles E., G.C.H.1834, I. 452; Kt.1834, II. 334
Nugent, Christopher, Kt.1566, II. 72
Nugent, Christopher, Kt.1604, II. 136
Nugent, count, K.C.B.1815, T. 226
Nugent, Edmond, Kt.1828, II. 327

Nugent, George, K.B.1813, I. 178; G.C.B. 1815, I. 181
Nugent, Gerald, Kt.1553, II. 66
Nugent, John, Kt.1890, II. 386
Nugent, Oliver, Kt.1555, II. 69
Nugent, Oliver, Kt.1872, II. 363
Nugent, Richard, lord Delvin, Kt.1603, II. 128
Nugent, Robert, Kt.1606, II. 139
Nugent, Thomas, Kt.1546, II. 58
Nugent, Thomas, Kt.1622, II. 178
Nugent, Thomas, earl of Westmeath, K.P. 1783, I. 96
Nugent, William, Kt.(1397), II. lx.
Nugent-Temple-Grenville, George, marquess of Buckingham, K.G.1786, I. 48; Grand Master K.P.1787, I. 93
Nugent-Temple-Grenville, George, lord Nugent, G.C.M.G.1832, I. 333
Nulls (? Neells), John, Kt.1639-40, II. 207
Nurrotumdas, Hurkisondas, Kt.1903, II. 414
Nutt, Thomas, Kt.1660, II. 229
Nutt, William, Kt.1660, II. 230
Nuttall, James M., K.C.B.1894, I. 265

O

Oakeley, Henry E., Kt.1899, II. 405
Oakeley, Herbert S., Kt.1876, II. 368
Oakes, Hildebrand, G.C.B.1820, I. 185
Oakley, Henry, Kt.1891, II. 388
Oates, James P., K.H.1837, I. 476
Oatley. See Otley
Obeidullah Khan, K.C.I.E.1900, I. 410

O'BRIEN, O'BRYEN
O'Brien, king of Munster, Kt.(1394). I. lx.
O'Brien, Daniel, Kt.1604, II. 133
O'Brien, Daniel, earl of Lismore, K.G. 1747, I. footnote, 38
O'Brien, Donal, Kt.1541, II. 53
O'Brien, Edward D., baron Inchiquin, K.P.1892, I. 105
O'Brien, George T. M., K.C.M.G.1894, I. 379

170 INDEX

O'BRIEN
  O'Bryen, James, marquess of Thomond, G.C.H.1831, I. 451
  O'Brien, John T. N., K.C.M.G.1887, I. 371
  O'Brien, Murrough, marquess of Thomond, K.P.1783, I. 96
  O'Brian, Teque (Tirlaugh), Kt.1602, II. 99
  O'Brien, Turlogh, Kt.1541, II. 53
  O'Brian, Tyrlow (Tyrelagh), Kt.1583, II. 82
  O'Brien, William, earl of Inchiquin, K.B.1725, I. 168
  O'Bryen, William, marquess of Thomond, K.P.1809, I. 98
O'Callaghan, Francis L., K.C.M.G.1902, I. 392
O'Callaghan, George P., viscount Lismore, K.P.1864, I. 102
O'Callaghan, Robert W., K.C.B.1815, I. 221; G.C.B.1838, I. 188
O'Carroll, Charles, Kt.1585, II. 83
O'Carroll, Mulrony, Kt.1603, II. 127
O'Carroll, Thady (Teige), Kt.1551, II. 66
O'Carroll (Ockervill), William, lord of Ely, Kt.1567, II. 73
O'Cathan, Donell, Kt.1607, II. 142
OCHTERLONY, OUCHTERLONY
  Ochterlony, David, K.C.B.1815, I. 227; G.C.B.1816, I. 183
  Ouchterlony, James, Kt.1603, II. 129
O'Connell, Maurice C., K.C.H.1835, I. 461; Kt.1835, II. 337
O'Connell, Maurice C., Kt.1871, II. 363
O'CONNOR, O'CONOR
  O'Conor, king of Connaught, Kt. (1394), I. lx.
  O'Connor, Charles, Kt.1622, II. 179
  O'Connor, Donal S., Kt.1567, II. 73
  O'Connor, Donnogh S., Kt.1604, II. 131
  O'Conor, Nicholas R., K.C.B.1895, I. 294; G.C.M.G.1896, I. 344; G.C.B. 1897, I. 215
  O'Conor, Patrick, Kt.1795, II. 302
  O'Conor, Richard, K.C.H.1836, I. 461; Kt.1836, II. 338

O'Dempsie, Christopher, Kt.1624, II.185
O'Dempsy, Terence, Kt.1599, II. 95
Odet-Pellion, Marie J. A., K.C.B.1857, I. 244
Odner. See Oldner
O'DOGHERTY, O'DOGHERTIE, O'DOHERTY
  O'Doghertie, Cahire, Kt.1602, II. 100
  O'Doherty, John, Kt.1585, II. 83
  O'Dogherty, William, Kt.1787, II. 300
O'DONNELL, ODONELL, O'DONNEL, O'DONELL
  O'Donnell, Charles R., Kt.1835, II. 336
  O'Donnell, George C., Kt.1865, II. 357
  Odonell, Hugh, Kt.1511, II. 35
  O'Donnel, Hugh, Kt.1567, II. 73
  O'Donell, Neale G., Kt.1602, II. 100
  O'Donnell, Roderick (Rorey), earl of Tyrconnel, Kt.1603, II. 128
O'Donohoe, James, Kt.1903, II. 415
O'Dowd, James C., Kt.1900, II. 408
O'Farrell, Connell, Kt.1657, II. 225
O'Farrell, George P., Kt.1899, II. 404
OFFLEY, OFFELEY
  Offley, John, Kt.1615, II. 155
  Offley, Robert, Kt.1616, II. 157
  Offeley (Offley), Thomas, Kt.1557, II 69
Officer, Robert, Kt.1869, II. 361
O'Flaherty, Morogh ne doe, Kt.1585, II. 83
Oflard, Murthowne do, Kt.1588, II. footnote, 86
O'Gallagher, Owen MacToole, Kt.1575, II. 77
Ogborne, William, Kt.1727, II. 283
Ogg, William A., Kt.1882, II. 374
Ogilby, David, Kt.1804, II. 307
OGILVY, OGILVEY
  Ogilvy, David G. D., earl of Airlie, K.T.1862, I. 85
  Ogilvy, James, earl of Findlater, K.T.1704, I. 76
  Ogilvey, Pat, Kt.1633, II. lxii.
  Ogilvie-Grant, John C., earl of Seafield, K.T.1879, I. 87

INDEX

Oglander, John, Kt.1615, II. 157
Oglander, William, Kt.1606, II. 140
Oglander, William, Kt.1665, II. 241
Ogle, Challoner, Kt.1723, II. 282
Ogle, Chaloner, Kt.1768, II. 293
Ogle, John, Kt.1646, II. 220
Ogle, Richard, Kt.1603, II. 103
Ogle, Robert, lord Ogle, Kt.1513, II. 42
Ogle, Thomas, Kt.1660, II. 230
Ogle, William, Kt.1523, II. 44
Oglethorpe, Owen, Kt.1603, II. 119
Oglethorpe, Robert, Kt.1609, II. 147
O'Hagan, Thomas, baron O'Hagan, K.P.1882, I. 104
O'Halloran, Joseph, Kt.1835, II. 335; K.C.B.1837, I. 233; G.C.B.1841, I. 189
O'Hanlon, Oghy, Kt.1587, II. 86
O'Hara, Charles, Kt.1689, II. 265
O'Kelly, St. George, Kt.1794, II. 302
Okeover, Rowland, Kt.1665, II. 241
Oldenbarnevelt, Helias ab, Kt.1610, II. 149
Oldenburg, Waldemar, K.C.V.O.1904, I. 442
Oldes (Owlds), William, Kt.1710, II. 277
Oldfield, John, K.H.1836, I. 473
Oldfield, Philip, Kt.1628, II. 193
Oldfield, Richard C., Kt.1889, II. 385
Oldfield (Owfield), Samuel, Kt.1641, II. 208
Oldham, Henry H., Kt.1897, II. 401
Oldknow, James, Kt.1878, II. 370
Oldmixon, John M., Kt.1782, II. 297
Oldner (Odner), Richard, Kt.1713, II. 278

OLIPHANT, OLLIVANT
Oliphant, Anthony, Kt.1839, II. 341
Ollivant, Edward C. K., K.C.I.E.1892, I. 407
Oliphant, Lawrence, Kt.1651, II. 222
Olive d'. See Dollyffe, Olliffe
Oliver, Benjamin, Kt.1671, II. 246
Oliver, Donough, Kt.1583, II. 82
Oliver, Robert, Kt.1843, II. 345
Olivey, Walter R., K.C.B.1887, I. 290

Olivier, Giuseppe B., G.C.M.G.1818, I. 331
Olliffe, Joseph F., Kt.1853, II. 350
Ollivant. See Oliphant
Olphert, John Kt.1902, II. 410
Olpherts, William, K.C.B.1886, I. 260; G.C.B.1900, I. 202
O'Magenis, Hugh, Kt.1575, II. 77
O'Malley, Edward L., Kt.1891, II. 388
O'Malley, William, Kt.1835, II. 336
Omar, Lutfi, G.C.B.1854, I. 191
Ommanney, Erasmus, Kt.1877, II. 369; K.C.B.1902, I. 273
Ommaney, Francis M., Kt.1820, II. 321
Ommanney, John A., Kt.1835, II. 336; K.C.B.1838, I. 235
Ommanney, Montagu F., K.C.M.G.1890, I. 375; K.C.B.1901, I. 298; G.C.M.G.1904, I. 349
O'Neale. See O'Neill
Oneby, John, Kt.1672, II. 247
O'NEILL, O'NEALE, O'NELE
O'Neill, king of Ulster, Kt.(1394), I. lx.
O'Neale, king of Meath, K.B.1394, I. 127
O'Nele, Kt.(1520), I. lvi.
O'Neill (Nele), Arthur, Kt.1585, II. 83
O'Neale, Brian MacP., Kt.1567, II. 73
O'Neill, Charles H., earl O'Neill, K.T. 1809, I. 98
O'Neill, Con oge, Kt.1585, II. 83
O'Neale, Cormack McB., Kt.1605, II. 138
O'Neale, Henry oge, Kt.1604, II. 135
O'Neale, Henry, Kt.1624, II. 183
O'Neale, Phelim, Kt.1639, II. 206
O'Nele, Tirlough L., Kt.1588, II. 87
O'Neale, Tirloghe M., Kt.1604, II. 131
Ongley, Samuel, Kt.1713, II. 278
Onley, Edward, Kt.1603, II. 121
Only, Roger, K.B.1326, I. 123
ONSLOW, ONSLOWE
Onslow, Alexander C., Kt.1895, II. 395
Onslow, Henry, Kt.1664, II. 239
Onslowe, Richard, Kt.1624, II. 184
Onslow, Richard, lord Onslow, K.B. 1752, I. 169

ONSLOW
  Onslow, Richard, G.C.B.1815, I. 182
  Onslow, William, K.H.1832, I. 468
  Onslow, William H., earl of Onslow, K.C.M.G.1887, I. 371; G.C.M.G. 1889, I. 342
Oporto, Alphonso, duke of, G.C.V.O. 1903, I. 426
Oppenheimer, Charles, Kt.1892, II. 391
ORANGE
  Henry F. de Nassau, prince of, K.G. 1627, I. 32
  Maurice de Nassau, prince of, K.G. 1612, I. 31
  William, prince of, K.G.1645, I. 33
  William V. of, K.G.1752, I. 44
  William C. H. F., prince of, K.G.1733, I. 43
Orbaston, Alexander, Kt.1513, II. 42
Orchha, Pratab Singh, maharaja of, K.C.I.E.1894, I. 408; G.C.I.E.1900, I. 403
Ord, Harry St. G., Kt.1867, II. 359; K.C.M.G.1877, I. 358; G.C.M.G. 1881, I. 339
Orde, Robert H., K.H.1822, I. 464
O'Regan, Teigue, Kt.1690, II. 266
Orell, Lewis, Kt.1513, II. 40
O'Reilly, Hugh C., Kt.1579, II. 79
Orelly, John, Kt.1583, II. 82
Orford, earl of. See Walpole
Orkney, earl of. See Hamilton; see Fitz-Maurice
Orme, Humfrey, Kt.1604, II. 135
Ormeston, Roger, K.B.1501, I. 146
ORMONDE, ORMOND
  Ormonde, duke, earl, and marquess of. See Butler
  Ormond, Thomas, K.B.(1483), I. 141
Ormsby, Charles M., Kt.1806, II. 308
Ormsby, Edward, Kt.1666, II. 242
Ormsby, Lambert H., Kt.1903, II. 416
O'RORKE, O'ROURKE
  O'Rorke, Brian, Kt.1579, II. 79
  O'Rorke, George M., Kt.1880, II. 372
  O'Rourke, Teige, Kt.1604, II. 131
Orpen, Richard J. T., Kt.1868, II. 359
Orr, Andrew, Kt.1858, II. 352
Orrery, earl of. See Boyle

OSBALDSTON, OSBALDESTON
  Osbaldston (Osbaston, Osberston), Edward, Kt.1617, II. 165
  Osbaldeston, Richard, Kt.1637, II. 20
  Osbaldeston, Richard, Kt.1637, II. 205
  Osbaldeston, Richard, Kt.1681, II. 256
OSBORNE, OSBORN, OSBURNE, OSBOURN
  Osbourn (Osborne), Edward, Kt.1584, II. 82
  Osborne, Francis G., duke of Leeds, K.G.1790, I. 48
  Osborne, George, Kt.1772, II. 293
  Osborne, George W. F., duke of Leeds, K.G.1827, I. 53
  Osborne, Henry, Kt.1673, II. 247
  Osburne, Hewett, Kt.1599, II. 96
  Osborne, John, Kt.1604, II. 131
  Osborne, John, Kt.1619, II. 171
  Osborn, Melmoth, K.C.M.G.1893, I. 378
  Osborn, Peter, Kt.1611, II. 150
  Osburne, Robart, Kt.1599, II. 98
  Osborn, Robert, Kt.1604, II. 132
  Osborne, Thomas, Kt.1679, II. 254
  Osborne, Thomas, duke of Leeds, K.G.1677, I. 37
  Osborne, Thomas, duke of Leeds, K.G.1749, I. 44
  Osborne (? Hamilton), William, K.H. 1816, I. 463
O'SHAUGHNESSY, O'SHANASSY, O'SHAGNES, and see Shaughnessy
  O'Shaughnessy, Dermot, Kt.1650, I. 221
  O'Shanassy, John, K.C.M.G.1874, I. 357
  O'Shagnes, Roger, Kt.1617, II. 160
  O'Shaughnessy (O'Shaghnes), Rory, Kt.1567, II. 73
  O'Shaughnessy, William B., Kt.1856, II. 352
Osman Pasha Orphi, K.C.M.G.1888, I. 373
Ossory, earl of. See Butler
Osten, Rittmeister von der, K.H.1819, I. 463
Ostriche (Astry), Rauf, Kt.1494, I. 28

O'Sullivan, Daniel V., Kt.1883, II. 374
O'Sullivan, John W., Kt.1747, II. footnote, 266
Oswald, John, K.C.B.1815, I. 219; G.C.B.1824, I. 185; G.C.M.G.1837, I. 334
Oswilifant (Asswillian), Owin, Kt.1565, II. 71

OTTLEY, OTLEY, OATLEY, OTELEY
Otley, —, Kt.1643, II. 216
Ottley (Oatley), Adam, Kt.1680, II. 255
Otley (Ottley, Oatley), Francis, Kt. 1642, II. 214
Oteley, John, Kt.1603, II. 126
Ottley, John W., K.C.I.E.1904, I. 412
Ottley, Richard, Kt.1660, II. 228
Ottley, Richard, Kt.1820, II. 321

O'Toole, Edward, Kt.1719, II. footnote, 266
O'Toole, Luke, Kt.1722, II. footnote, 266
Otway, John, Kt.1673, II. 248
Otway, Loftus W., Kt.1815, II. 315
Otway, Robert W., K.C.B.1826, I. 230; G.C.B.1845, I. 189
Ouchterlony. See Ochterlony

OUDH
Ikbal-ud-Dowlah, of, G.C.S.I.1882, I. 312
Kader Mirza, of, K.C.I.E.1894, I. 408
Maun Sing, of, K.C.S.I.1867, I. 318
Mohsin-ood-Dowlah, bahadoor of, K.C.S.I.1871, I. 319

OUGAN, OWGAN
Owgan, John, Kt.1586, II. 84; Kt. 1588, II. 86

Oughton, Adolphus, Kt.1718, II. 281
Oughton, James A., K.B.1773, I. 172
Oughtred. See Ughtred
Ould, Fielding, Kᵗ.1760, II. 289
Ouley, Thomas, Kt.1487, II. 26
Ouseley, Gore, G.C.H.1831, I. 451
Ouseley, Ralph, Kt.1835, II. 336
Ouseley, William, Kt.1800, II. 305
Ouseley, William G., K.C.B.1852, I. 278
Outram, Benjamin F., Kt.1850, II. 348

Outram, James, K.C.B.1856, I. 279; G.C.B.1857, I. 192; K.S.I.1861, I. 306
Ovedale. See Uvedall
Overbury, Giles, Kt.1623, II. 183
Overbury, Nicholas, Kt.1621, II. 177
Overbury, Thomas, Kt.1608, II. 145
Overbury, Thomas, Kt.1660, II. 229
Owden, Thomas S., Kt.1878, II. 370
Owen, Andrew, Kt.1671, II. 245
Owen, Arthur D., Kt.1814, II. 314
Owen, Davy, Kt.1485, II. 22
Owen, Edward W. C. R., K.C.B.1815, I. 222; G.C.H.1832, I. 452; G.C.B. 1845, I. 190
Owen, Francis P. C., K.C.M.G.1878, I. 360
Owen, Henry, Kt.1513, II. 39
Owen, Hugh, Kt.1605, II. 139
Owen, Hugh, Kt.1641, II. 210
Owen, Hugh, Kt.1881, II. 373
Owen, Hugh, K.C.B.1887, I. 290; G.C.B. 1899, I. 215
Owen, Isambard, Kt.1902, II. 412
Owen, James Ap, Kt.1501, II. 33
Owen, John, Kt.1644, II. 219
Owen, John, K.H.1833, I. 469; K.C.B. 1852, I. 239
Owen, Richard, K.C.B.1884, I. 288
Owen, Robert, Kt.1678, II. 253
Owen, Roger, Kt.1604, II. 132
Owen, William, Kt.1617, II. 165
Owens, Charles J., Kt.1902, II. 413
Owens, George B., Kt.1876, II. 368
Ourgham, Thomas, K.B.1394, I. lx., 127
Owesley, John, Kt.1604, II. 131
Owfield. See Oldfield
Owlds. See Oldes
Owtred. See Ughtred
Oxenbridge, Edward (Godard), K.B. 1509, I. 149
Oxenbridge, Robert, Kt.1549, II. 65
Oxenbridge, Robert, Kt.1600, II. 98
Oxenbridge, Robert, Kt.1616, II. 160
Oxenden, George, Kt.1661, II. 235
Oxenden, Henry, Kt.1607, II. 141
Oxenden, Henry, Kt.1660, II. 228
Oxenden (Oxenford), James, Kt.1607, II. 143

174 INDEX

Oxenden, James, Kt.1672, II. 247
Oxenford. See Oxenden
Oxenstern, Gabriel, Kt.1635, II. 203
Oxford, earl of. See Vere; see Harley
Oxholm, Oscar S. C. O., G.C.V.O.1901, I. 425

P

Paar, count Edward M. N., G.C.V.O. 1903, I. 428
Pabenham, John de, K.B.1306, I. 122
PACK, PACKE
    Packe, Christopher, Kt.1655, II. 223
    Pack, Denis, K.C.B.1815, I. 220
Packenham. See Pakenham
Packer, Charles, Kt.1879, II. 371
Paddy, William, Kt.1603, II. 113
Pado, John, K.B.(1394), I. lx., 127
Pado, Jonathas, K.B.(1394), I. lx., 127
Page, Francis, Kt.1715, II. 280
Page, Richard, Kt.1529, II. 47
Page, Richard, Kt.1645, II. 219
Page, Thomas, Kt.1675, II. 250
Page, Thomas H., Kt.1783, II. 298
Page, William, Kt.1604, II. 134
Page, William E., Kt.1836, II. 474
Pagenham. See Pakenham
Paget, Arthur, K.B.1804, I. 176; G.C.B. 1815, I. 205
Paget, Augustus B., K.C.B.1863, I. 283; G.C.B.1883, I. 211
Paget, Charles, K.C.H.1819, I. 454; Kt. 1822, II. 324; G.C.H.1832, I. 452
Paget, lord Clarence E., K.C.B.1869, I. 252; G.C.B.1886, I. 198
Paget, Edward, K.B.1812, I. 178; G.C.B. 1815, I. 181
Paget, lord George A. F., K.C.B.1869, I. 252
Paget, George E., K.C.B.1885, I. 289
Paget, Henry, lord Paget, K.B.1553, I. 152
Paget, Henry W., marquess of Anglesey, G.C.B.1815, I. 182; G.C.H.1816, I. 447; K.G.1818, I. 52; Grand Master K.P.1828, I. 93, 94
Paget, William, lord Paget, Kt.1544, II. 54; K.G.1547, I. 24

Paget, William, lord Paget, K.B.1626, I. 161
Pagington. See Pakington
Pahang, Ahmad Maätham, sultan of, K.C.M.G.1902, I. 393
Pahlen, count Constantine, G.C.V.O. 1896, I. 422
Paine, Pain. See Payne
Painter. See Paynter
PAKENHAM, PAGENHAM, PACKENHAM
    Pakenham, Edward M., K.B.1813, I. 179; G.C.B.1815, I. 182
    Pakenham, Francis J., K.C.M.G.1898, I. 384
    Pagenham, Henry, Kt.1603, II. 103
    Pakenham, Hercules R., K.C.B.1838, I. 235
    Pakenham (Deckham), Philip, Kt. 1617, II. 161
    Pakenham, Richard, K.C.B.1848, I. 277
    Pakenham (Packenham), Thomas, Kt. 1693, II. 268
    Pakenham, Thomas, G.C.B.1820, I. 184
    Pakenham, Thomas, earl of Longford, K.P.1813, I. 98
    Pakenham, Thomas, earl of Longford, K.P.1901, I. 106
    Pakenham, William L., earl of Longford, K.C.B.1861, I. 247; G.C.B. 1881, I. 197
PAKINGTON, PACKINGTON, PAKENTON, PAGINTON
    Pakington, John, Kt.1545, II. 58
    Pagington (Packington), John, Kt. 1587, II. 86
    Pakington, John, lord Hampton, G.C.B.1859, I. 209
    Pakenton (Pakington), Thomas, Kt. 1553, II. 67
Paladines, Claude M. L. de, K.C.B.1856, I. 242
Palanpur, Mahomed, khan of, K.C.I.E. 1893, I. 407; G.C.I.E.1898, I. 403
PALATINE
    Albert, count, K.G.1397, I. 7
    Charles L., count, K.G.1633, I. 32
    Charles II., count, K.G.1680, I. 37

INDEX 175

PALATINE
Edward, count, K.G.1649, I. 34
Frederick C., elector, K.G.1612, I. 30
John C., count, K.G.1579, I. 27
Maurice, count, K.G.1649, I. 33
Rupert, count, K.G.1642, I. 33
Palgrave, Augustine, Kt.1604, II. 136
Palgrave, Francis, K.H.1832, I. 468; Kt.1832, II. 333
Palgrave, John, Kt.1641, II. 209
Palgrave, Reginald F. D., K.C.B.1892, I. 293
Palie, John de, Kt.1347, II. 9
Palikao, count Charles G. de, K.C.B. 1861, I. 246
Palitana, Mansinghji of, K.C.S.I.1896, I. 325
PALLAVICINI, PALAVICHINI, PALLAVICIN, PARAVICINI
Pallavicin, Henry, Kt.1611, II. 150
Palavichini (Palevesyn), Horatio, Kt. 1587, II. 86
Pallavicini (Paravicini), Peter, Kt. 1687, II. 263
Palliser, Charles H., K.C.B.1881, I. 257; G.C.B.1894, I. 200
Palliser, William, Kt.1873, II. 365
Palmer, Anthony, K.B.1603, I. 156
Palmer, Arthur H., K.C.M.G.1881, I. 363
Palmer, Arthur P., K.C.B.1894, I. 265; G.C.I.E.1901, I. 403; G.C.B.1903, I. 204
Palmer, Elwin M., K.C.M.G.1892, I. 377; K.C.B.1897, I. 294
Palmer, Francis, Kt.1601, II. 99
Palmer, Henry, Kt.1586, II. 84
Palmer, Henry, Kt.1618, II. 168
Palmer, Henry, Kt.1642, II. 212
Palmer, James F., Kt.1857, II. 352
Palmer, Mathew, Kt.1624, II. 186
Palmer, Ralph, Kt.1824, II. 325
Palmer, Roger, K.B.1626, I. 162
Palmer, Roundell, Kt.1861, II. 356
Palmer, Thomas, Kt.1532, II. 48
Palmer, Thomas, Kt.1546, II. 58
Palmer, Thomas, Kt.1553, II. 67
Palmer, Thomas, Kt.1573, II. 75
Palmer, Thomas, Kt.1596, II. 93
Palmer, Thomas, Kt.1603, II. 107, 116
Palmer, Thomas, Kt.1606, II. 141
Palmer, William, Kt.1641, II. 208, 214
Palmerston, viscount. See Temple
Palmes, Bryan (George), Kt.1603, II. 113
Palmes, Brian, Kt.1642, II. 212
Palmes, Guy, Kt.1603, II. 108
Palota, count Johann M. F. von, G.C.B. 1819, I. 184
Panmure, earl and lord. See Maule
Panizzi, Antony, K.C.B.1869, I. 284
Pansa, Alberto, G.C.V.O.1903, I. 427
Panton, Thomas, Kt.1607, II. 141
Pargeter, Thomas, Kt.1529, II. 47
Pargiter, William, Kt.1673, II. 247
Parham, Edward, Kt.1603, II. 124
Parish, Woodbine, K.C.H.1837, I. 462; Kt.1837, II. 338
Parisio, count Paolo, K.C.M.G.1822, I. 351; G.C.M.G.1836, I. 333
PARK, PARKE
Parke, James, Kt.1828, II. 327
Park (Parke), James A., Kt.1816, II. 317
Parke, William, Kt.1836, II. 337
Parke, William, K.C.B.1887, I. 261
Parker, Calthrop, Kt.1603, II. 122
Parker, George, K.C.B.1833, I. 232
Parker, George A., Kt.1896, II. 398
Parker (Horatio), Gilbert G., Kt.1902, II. 412
Parker, Henry, K.B.1533, I. 149
Parker, Henry, K.B.1553, I. 152
Parker, Henry, lord Monteagle, K.B. 1616, I. 160
Parker, Henry W., Kt.1858, II. 353; K.C.M.G.1877, I. 359
Parker, Henry W., Kt.1887, II. 383
Parker, Hyde, Kt.1779, II. 296
Parker (Picks), James, Kt.1487, II. 24, 25
Parker, James, Kt.1851, II. 349
Parker, John, Kt.1603, II. 102
Parker, John, Kt.1679, II. 253
Parker, Nicholas, Kt.1588, II. 87, 88
Parker, Peter, Kt.1772, II. 293
Parker, Philip, Kt.1578, II. 78
Parker, Philip, Kt.1624, II. 187

Parker, Selwin, Kt.1633, II. 202
Parker (Porter), Thomas, Kt.1617, II. 167
Parker, Thomas, Kt.1705, II. 274
Parker, Thomas, Kt.1742, II. 285
Parker, William, Kt.1482, II. 18
Parker, William, lord Monteagle, Kt. 1599, II. 96
Parker, William, K.C.B.1834, I. 232; G.C.B.1842, I. 189
Parkes, Harry S., K.C.B.1862, I. 282; G.C.M.G.1881, I. 339
Parkes, Henry, K.C.M.G.1877, I. 359; G.C.M.G.1888, I. 341
Parkhurst, Robert, Kt.1635, II. 203; Kt. 1638, II. 205
Parkhurst, Robert, Kt.1660, II. 228
Parkhurst, William, Kt.1619, II. 172
Parkington, John R., Kt.1902, II. 413
Parkins (Perkins), Christopher, Kt.1603, II. 114
Parkins, George, Kt.1603, II. 123
Parkinson-Fortescue, Chichester S., lord Clermont, K.P.1882, I. 104

PARR, PARRE, A PARRE
Parr (a Parre), John, Kt.1471, II. 14, 17
Parre, Thomas, K.B.1509, I. 148
Parre, William, K.G.1474, I. 15
a Parre, William, lord Parr, Kt.1513, 39, 51, note
Parr, William, marquess of Northampton, Kt.1538, II. 51; K.G.1543, I. 23

PARRATT, PARRETT, PERROTT
Parrett, John, Kt.1594, II. 64
Parrett (Perrott), James, Kt.1603, II. 112
Parratt, Walter, Kt.1892, II. 390

PARRY, PARREY
Parry, Charles H. H., Kt.1898, II. 403
Parrey, George, Kt.1644, II. 217
Parry, Love P. J., Kt.1835, II. 337; K.H.1836, I. 472
Parry, Thomas, Kt.1558, II. 70
Parry, William E., Kt.1829, II. 328
Parrys (Paris), Philip, Kt.1553, II. 67
Parsons, Charles S. B., K.C.M.G.1899, I. 387
Parson, John, Kt.1622, II. 178

Parsons, John, Kt.1687, II. 263
Parsons, Lawrence, Kt.1620, II. 176
Parsons, Lawrence, earl of Rosse, K.P. 1890, I. 105
Parsons, William, Kt.1620, II. 175
Parson, William, Kt.1795, II. 303
Parsons, William, earl of Rosse, K.P. 1845, I. 101
Parton, Thomas, Kt.1603, II. 109

PARTRIDGE, PARTRICHE
Partriche, —, Kt.1538, I. 52
Partridge, Edward, Kt.1641, II. 210
Partrige, Miles, Kt.1547, II. 61
Paschall, Andrew, Kt.1603, II. 121

PASLEY, PASHLEY, PASLEU
Pasley, Charles W., K.C.B.1846, I. 238
Pasheley (Pasleu), John, K.B.(1426), I. 132
Pasley, Thomas S., K.C.B.1873, I. 253
Paston, John, Kt.1487, I. 25
Paston (Payton or Paynton), John, Kt. 1586, II. 85
Paston, Robert, Kt.1660, II. 226
Paston, Thomas, Kt.1545, II. 56
Paston, William, Kt.1578, II. 79
Paston, William (Edmund), Kt.1609, II. 147
Paté, Charles, K.C.B.1856, I. 242
Paterson, William, K.C.H.1832, I. 458; Kt.1832, II. 331
Patey, James, Kt.1784, II. 298
Paty, George W., K.H.1832, I. 467; K.C.B.1861, I. 246

PATIALA
Nurendur Singh, maharaja of, K.S.I. 1861, I. 306
Mohender Sing, maharaja of, G.C.S.I. 1870, I. 309
Maharaja of, G.C.S.I.1898, I. 314
Ranbir Singh, of, K.C.S.I.1903, I. 328
Paton, Joseph N., Kt.1867, II. 358
Patteson, John, Kt.1830, II. 329
Pattison, Alexander H., K.H.1834, I. 470
Patterson, James B., K.C.M.G.1894, I. 379
Patterson, Robert L., Kt.1902, II. 410

INDEX

PAUL, PAULE, PAULLE
Paule, George, Kt.1607, II. 142
Paul, Gregory C., K.C.I.E.1888, I. 406.
Paul, James B., Kt.1900, II. 406
Paulle, Jehan, Kt.(1380), II. 10
Paule, lord of, K.B.1399, I. 128
Paul, Onesiphorus, Kt.1760, II. 289
Paul, William, Kt.1671, II. 246
Paulet. See Powlett
Pauncefote, Julian, Kt.1874, II. 366; K.C.M.G.1879, I. 362; G.C.M.G. 1885, I. 340; K.C.B.1888, I. 291 G.C.B.1892, I. 213
Pavely, John, Kt.1347, II. 8
Pavely, Walter, K.G.1348, I. 2; Kt.1347, II. 8
Pawel-Rammingen, Luitbert A. G. L. A., Freiherr von, K.C.B.1880, I 287; K.C.V.O.(1897), I. 432
Pawlet. See Powlett
Paxton, Joseph, Kt.1851, II. 349
Paxton, William, Kt.1803, II. 306
PAYNE, PAYN, PAINE, PAIN
Payne, Charles, Kt.1728, II. 284
Payne, John, Kt.1663, II. 238
Payn, Joseph, Kt.1660, II. 230
Payne, Ralph, lord Lavington, K.B 1771, I. 171
Payn, Robert, Kt.1605, II. 138
Pain, Robert, Kt.1632, II. 200
Paine, Thomas, Kt.1882, II. 374
Payn, William, K.C.B.1886, I. 260
PAYNTER, PAINTER, PEINTER
Peinter (Painter), Edward, Kt.1603, II. 116
Paynter, Paul, Kt.1664, II. 240
Payton. See Peyton
Peace, Walter, K.C.M.G.1897, I. 382
Peachey. See Peche
PEACOCK, PECOCKE
Peacock, Alexander J., K.C.M.G.1902, I. 392
Peacock, Barnes, Kt.1859, II. 354
Peacock, Edward, Kt.1603, II. 120
Pecocke, Stephen, Kt.1538, II. 50
Peacock, Warren M., Kt.1815, II. 316; K.C.H.1832, I. 458
Peake, Henry, Kt.1814, II. 314
Peake, John, Kt.1676, II. 251

Peake, Robert, Kt.1645, II. 219
Peake, William, Kt.1663, II. 238
PEARCE, PEIRCE, PEERS, PIERS
Peers, Charles, Kt.1707, II. 275
Peirce, Edmond, Kt.1645, II. 220
Pearce, Edward L., Kt.1732, II. 284
Peirce, Henry, Kt.1622, II. 180
Piers, Henry, Kt.1658, II. 224
Piers, Ric, Kt.1347, II. 7
Piers, William, Kt.1632, II. 199
Pearce, William, K.H.1835, I. 471
Pearl, James, K.H.1836, I. 475
Pears, Thomas T., K.C.B.1871, I. 285
PEARSON, PIERSON
Pearson, Charles J., Kt.1887, II. 384
Pearson, Charles K., K.C.M.G.1879, I. 362
Pearson, Edwin, Kt.1836, II. 337
Pearson, Hugo L., K.C.B.1904, I. 276
Pearson, John, Kt.1882, II. 374
Pierson, Mathew (Martin), Kt.1669, II. 243
Pierson, Richard, K.B.1780, I. 173
Pearson, Richard, Kt.1780, II. 296
Pearson, Thomas, K.C.H.1835, I. 460; Kt.1835, II. 335
Pierson, William H., Kt.1836, II. 338
Pearson, William H., Kt.1838, II. 340
Pease, Thales, K.C.B.1901, I. 273
Peasley. See Peisley
PECHE, PEACHEY, PECHAY
Peche, Edmund, K.B.1306, I. 121
Peachey, Henry, Kt.1696, II. 269
Peche, John, Kt.1497, II. 29
Peche (Peachey), John, Kt.1513, II. 36
Pechay, Walter, Kt.1347, II. 9
Pechell, John S. B., K.C.H.1833, I. 459
PECKHAM, PEKHAM
Peckham, Edmond (Richard), Kt.1542, II. 53
Pekham, Edmond, Kt.1604, II. 133
Peckham, George, Kt.1570, II. 74
Peckham, George, Kt.1617, II. 162
Peckham, Henry, Kt.1662, II. 236
Peckham, Robert, Kt.1553, II. 66
Peckham, Thomas, Kt.1722, II. 282
Pecknell. See Picknell
Pedder, John L., Kt.1838, II. 341
Peddie, John, K.H.1832, I. 467

Pedley, Nicholas, Kt.1672, II. 246
Pedotti, Ettore, G.C.V.O.1903, I. 426
Peel, Bartholomew, Kt.1619, II. 170
Peel, Charles L., K.C.B.1890, I. 291; G.C.B.1899, I. 215
Peel, Frederick, K.C.M.G.1869, I. 355
Peel, Laurence, Kt.1842, II. 344
Peel, Robert, G.C.B.1866, I. 209
Peel, William, K.C.B.1858, I. 244
Peers. See Pearce
Pegge, Christopher, Kt.1799, II. 304
Peile, James B., K.C.S.I.1888, I. 324
Peinter. See Paynter
Peirce. See Pearce
Peisley (Peasley), Francis, Kt.1664, II. 239
Pekham. See Peckham
Pelham, Anthony, Kt.1603, II. 124
Pelham, Edmond, Kt.1604, II. 133
Pelham, John, Kt.1573, II. 75
Pelham, Nicholas, Kt.1549, II. 64
Pelham, Nicholas, Kt.1661, II. 234
Pelham, Thomas, K.B.1400, I. 128
Pelham, William, Kt.1579, II. 80
Pelham, William, Kt.1603, II. 102
Pelham, William, Kt.1616, II. 160
Pelham-Clinton, Edward W., K.C.B.1896, I. 294; G.C.V.O.1901, I. 418
Pelham-Clinton, Henry, duke of Newcastle, K.G.1752, I. 45
Pelham-Clinton, Henry P., duke of Newcastle, K.G.1812, I. 51
Pelham-Clinton, Henry P., duke of Newcastle, K.G.1860, I. 61
Pelham-Holles, Thomas, duke of Newcastle, K.G.1718, I. 42
Pélissier, Aimable J. J., duc de Malakoff, G.C.B.1855, I. 191
Pell, Albert, Kt.1831, II. 331
Pell, Anthony, Kt.1608, II. 145
Pell, Richard, Kt.1603, II. 124
Pell, Valentine, Kt.1641, II. 209
Pell, Watkin O., Kt.1837, II. 339
Pellet, Benjamin, Kt.1603, II. 121
Pelletier, Charles A. P., K.C.M.G.1898, I. 384
Pellew, Edward, viscount Exmouth, Kt. 1793, II. 302; K.C.B.1815, I. 217; G.C.B.1816, I. 183

Pellew, Fleetwood B. R., K.C.H.1836, I. 461; Kt.1836, II. 337
Pellew, Israel, K.C.B.1815, I. 219
Pelly, Lewis, K.C.S.I.1874, I. 320; K.C.B. 1877, I. 286
Pelsant, Euseby, Kt.1642, II. 213
Pemberton, Edward L., K.C.B.1898, I. 297
Pemberton, Francis, Kt.1675, II. 250
Pemberton. (Pempton), Goddard, Kt 1603, II. 108
Pemberton, James, Kt.1603, II. 128
Pemberton, Lewis, Kt.1617, II. 165
Pembroke, earl of. See Hastings; see Tudor, J.; see Herbert, W.
Pemery. See Pomerey
Penaud, Charles, K.C.B.1856, I. 242
Penbridge, John de, K.B.1306, I. 116
Pendarves, William, Kt.1713, II. 278
PENDAR, PINDER
Pender, John, K.C.M.G.1888, I. 372; G.C.M.G.1892, I. 343
Pender, John D., K.C.M.G.1901, I. 391
Pindar (Pendar), Paul, Kt.1620, II. 175
Pendlebury, Ralph, Kt.1840, II. 342
Pengelly, Thomas, Kt.1719, II. 281
PENN, PEN, PENNE
Penne, John de la, K.B.1306, I. 115
Pen, William, Kt.1658, II. 224, 228
Pennant, Samuel, Kt.1745, II. 287
Pennefather, John L., K.C.B.1855, I. 240; G.C.B.1867, I. 195
Pennell, Charles H., Kt.1867, II. 358
Pennethorne, James, Kt.1870, II. 362
PENNINGTON, PENYNGTON, PENINGTON
Pennington, Isaac, Kt.1649, II. 221
Pennington, Isaac, Kt.1795, II. 303
Penyngton, John, Kt.1482, II. 19
Pennington, John (Thomas), Kt.1634, II. 202
Penington, William, Kt.1513, II. 37
Penyngton, William, Kt.1523, II. 46
Pennycuick, John, K.H.1837, I. 478
Pennyman, James (Thomas), Kt.1642, II. 213
Penrice, Henry, Kt.1715, II. 280
Penrose, Charles V., K.C.B.1816, I. 228; G.C.M.G.1818, I. 331

INDEX 179

Penrose, George D., Kt.1876, II. 368
Penrose, Penrose C., K.C.B.1887, I. 261
PENRUDDOCKE, PENRODOCKE, PENRUDDOK
Penruddocke, Edward, Kt.1603, II. 126
Penrodocke, George, Kt.1568, II. 73
Penruddock, John, Kt.1643, II. 215
Penruddok, Manwood, Kt.1603, II.123
Penruddok, Robert, Kt.1603, II. 126
Penruddock, Thomas, Kt.1603, II. 115
Penshurst, lord. See Smythe, P. C. S.
Pepper, Cuthbert, Kt.1604, II. 132
Pepys, Charles C., Kt.1834, II. 334
Perak, sultan of, K.C.M.G.1892, I. 376; G.C.M.G.1901, I. 347
PERCEVAL, PERCIVAL, PERSEVALL, PERCIVALL
Percival, Anthony, Kt.1641, II. 211
Persevall, John, Kt.1487, II. 26
Percivall, John, Kt.1658, II. 224
Percival, Philip, Kt.1636, II. 204
Perceval, Westby B., K.C.M.G.1894, I. 379
PERCY, PERSAY, PERCYE
Percy, Algernon, earl of Northumberland, K.B.1616, I. 159; K.G.1635, I. 33
Percy, Algernon, duke of Northumberland, K.G.1853, I. 58
Percy, Algernon, duke of Northumberland, K.G.1886, I. 68
Percy, Allan, K.B.1605, I. 157
Percy, Anthony, Kt.1700, II. 271
Percy, Charles, Kt.1591, II. 89
Percy, Henry, K.B.1322, I. 122
Percy, Henry, earl of Northumberland, K.G.1366, I. 3
Percy, Henry ("Hotspur"), K.G.1388, I. 6
Percy, Henry, K.B.(1400), I. 129
Percy, Henry, earl of Northumberland, K.B.(1426), I. 130
Percy, Henry, earl of Northumberland, K.G.1474, I. 16
Percy, Henry, Kt.1482, II. 17
Percy, Henry, earl of Northumberland, K.G.1531, I. 22
Percy, Henry, earl of Northumberland, Kt.1557, II. 70

PERCY
Percy, Henry, earl of Northumberland, K.G.1593, I. 28
Percy, Henry A., earl of Northumberland, K.B.(1489), I. 143; K.G.1495, I. 18
Percy, Henry G., duke of Northumberland, K.G.1899, I. 70
Percy, lord Henry H. M., K.C.B.1873, I. 254
Percy, Hugh, duke of Northumberland, K.G.1756, I. 45
Percy, Hugh, duke of Northumberland, K.G.1788, I. 48
Percy, Hugh, duke of Northumberland, K.G.1819, I. 52; Grand Master K.P.1829, I. 93
Percy, Jocelin, Kt.1599, II. 96
Percy, Richard, Kt.1460, II. 12
Percy, Richard, Kt.1598, II. 95
Persay (Percye), Robert, Kt.1483, II. 21
Percy, Thomas, earl of Northumberland, Kt.1557, II. 70; K.G.1563, I. 26
Percy, Thomas, earl of Worcester, K.G.1376, I. 4
Percy, William de, K.B.1327, I. 124
Percy, William, Kt.1513, II. 37
Percy, William H. J. C., earl of Limerick, K.P.1892, I. 105
PERIAM, PERYENT
Periam, George, Kt.1605, II. 138
Peryent (Perriant), Thomas, Kt. 1615-6, II. 157
Periam, William, Kt.1592, II. 90
Perkins, Æneas, K.C.B.1897, I. 268
Perkins, Christopher, Kt.1603, II. 114
Perkins, Frederick, Kt.1873, II. 365
Perkins, William, Kt.1681, II. 256
Perkins, William, Kt.1714, II. 279
Perny (Berney), Thomas, Kt.1603, II. 119
Perrier, Anthony, Kt.1809, II. 309
Perrier, Anthony, Kt.1843, II. 345
Perrier, David, Kt.1795, II. 303
PERROTT, PERROT
Perrott, Herbert, Kt.1660, II. 231
Perrot, James, Kt.1603, II. 112

INDEX

PERROTT
Perrott, John, Kt.1561, II. 71
Perrot, Owen, Kt.1513, II. 39
Perrot, Thomas, Kt.1579, II. 80
Perot, William, K.B.1306, I. 116
Perot, William, Kt.1501, II. 33
Perry, Allan, Kt.1904, II. 419
Perry, Edwin C., Kt.1903, II. 415
Perry, Thomas E., Kt.1841, II. 343
Perry, William, Kt.1872, II. 364
Perryn, Richard, Kt.1776, II. 295

PERSALL, PERSHALL
Pershall, Charles, Kt.1603, II. 127
Persall, Hugh, Kt.1485, II. 23
Pershete, Nicholas de, K.B.1306, I. 115

PERSIA
Moayyed - ed - Dowleh (H.R.H.), of, G.C.M.G.1903, I. 349
Muzaffer-ed-Din, shah of, K.G.1903, I. 72
Nasir-ed-din, shah of, K.G.1873, I. 65
Pert, Thomas, Kt.1643, II. 217
Pertab Singh, K.C.S.I.1886, I. 323; K.C.B.1901, I. 273
Perth, earl and duke of. See Drummond
Peryent. See Periam
Peshall, John, Kt.1629, II. 196
Peshal (Pelshull), William, Kt.1627, II. 191; Kt.1628, II. 194
Peshkar, Kishn Parshad, K.C.I.E.1903, I. 412
Peter, Peters. See Petre
Peterborough, earl of. See Mordaunt
Petersen, Eugen, K.C.V.O.1904, I. 442
Petheram, William C., Kt.1884, II. 376
Petit, Dinshaw M., Kt.1887, II. 380
Petit, Gerald, Kt.1556, II. 69
Petit, John, K.B.1333, I. 125

PETRE, PETER, PETERS
Peter (Peeters), George, Kt.1603, II. 119
Petre, George G., K.C.M.G.1890, I. 375
Peter, John, Kt.1576, II. 77
Peter (Peters), William, Kt.1603, II. 104
Peter, William, Kt.1543, II. 54
Petrie, Charles, Kt.1903, II. 415
Petrides, Plato, K.C.M.G.1844, I. 352

Petrizzopulo, Pietro, C.M.G.(1820), I. xxviii.; K.C.M.G.1833, I. 352; G.C.M.G.1838, I. 334
Pets. See Potts
Pett, Peter, Kt.1663, II. 238
Pett, Phineas, Kt.1680, II. 255
Pettesworth (Bettesworth), Peter, Kt. 1609, II. 147
Petto, Jonathan, Kt.1599, II. 97
Pettus (Pethouse), Augustine, Kt.1611, II. 151
Pettus (Pethouse), John, Kt.1607, II. 142
Pettus, John, Kt.1641, II. 211
Petty, Henry, marquess of Lansdowne, K.G.1836, I. 55
Petty, William, Kt.1661, II. 234
Petty, William, marquess of Lansdowne, K.G.1782, I. 47
Petty-Fitzmaurice, Henry, marquess of Lansdowne, K.G.1864, I. 62
Petty-Fitzmaurice, Henry C. K., marquess of Lansdowne, G.C.M.G. 1884, I. 339; G.C.I.E.1888, I. 401; G.C.S.I.1888, I. 313; Grand Master Star of India, I. 305; K.G.1895, I. 70
Peveril, William, K.B.1326, I. 124
Pexall, Richard, Kt.1550, II. 65
Peyto, Edward, Kt.1611, II. 150

PEYTON, PAYTON
Peyton, Henry, Kt.1606, II. 139
Payton, John, Kt.1586, II. 85
Peyton, John, Kt.1596, II. 94
Peyton (Payton), John, Kt.1603, II. 100
Peyton, John, Kt.1608, II. 146
Peyton, John S., K.C.H.1836, I. 461; Kt.1836, II. 337
Payton, Robert, Kt.1497, II. 30
Payton, Robert, Kt.1529, II. 47
Peyton, Robert, Kt.1670, II. 244
Payton, Samuel (Thomas), Kt.1608, II. 145
Peyton (Parton), Thomas, Kt.1603, II. 109
Phayre, Arthur P., K.C.S.I.1867, I. 318; G.C.M.G.1877, I. 337
Phayre, Robert, K.C.B.1881, I. 257; G.C.B.1894, I. 200
Phear, John B., Kt.1877, II. 369

Phelip. See Phillips
Phelps, James H., K.H.1837, I. 478
Philip. See Phillips
Philipps, Philips. See Phillips
Philipson. See Phillipson
PHILLIMORE, PHILMER, FILMER
  Phillimore, Augustus, K.C.B.1887, I. 261
  Philmer (Filmer), Edward, Kt.1642, II. 212
  Phillimore, John, Kt.1821, II. 323
  Phillimore, Robert, J., Kt.1862, II. 356
PHILLIPS, PHILIPPE, PHELIP, PHELIPP, PHILLIPPS, PHILIPS, PHILIP
  Phillips, Ambrose, Kt.1686, II. 261
  Phillips, Benjamin S., Kt.1866, II. 358
  Phillips, Benjamin T., Kt.1858, II. 352
  Phillips, Charles, Kt.1817, II. 319
  Phillips (Philips), Clifford W., Kt. 1744, II. 287
  Philippe, Davy, Kt.1504, II. 34
  Philipps, Edward, Kt.1603, II. 114
  Phillipps, George, Kt.1882, II. 374
  Phillips, Henry L., Kt.1880, II. 371
  Phelip, John, K.B.(1413), I. 129
  Phillipps, Jonathan, Kt.1786, II. 299
  Philips, Joseph, K.C.B.1897, I. 268
  Philip, Mathew, K.B.(1465), I. 135
  Philip, Matthew, Kt.1471, II. 16
  Phillips, Richard, Kt.1808, II. 309
  Phillipps, Robert, Kt.1603, II. 118
  Philipps, Thomas, Kt.1513, II. 41
  Phillips, Thomas, Kt.1603, II. 127
  Phillips, Thomas, Kt.1607, II. 141
  Phillips, Thomas, Kt.1839, II. 342
  Phelipp, William, lord Bardolf, K.G. 1418, I. 10
PHILLIPSON, PHILIPSON
  Phillipson (Phillopson), Christopher, Kt.1681, II. 256
  Philipson, George H., Kt.1900, II. 407
Philmer. See Phillimore
Philpot, George, Kt.1606, II. 140
Philpot, John, K.B.1501, I. 146
Philpot, John, Kt.1603, II. 118
Philpot, John, Kt.1631, II. 199
Phipard, William, Kt.1699, II. 271
Phipps, Charles B., K.C.B.1858, I. 280

Phipps, Constantine, Kt.1710, II. 277
Phipps, Constantine H., marquis of Normanby, G.C.H. 1832, I. 452; Grand Master K.P.1835, I. 94; G.C.B.1847, I. 207; K.G.1851, I. 58
Phipps, Edmund C. H., K.C.M.G.1902, I. 392
Phipps, George A. C., marquis of Normanby, K.C.M.G. 1874, I. 356; G.C.M.G.1877, I. 337; G.C.B.1885, I. 211
Phipps, Henry, earl of Mulgrave, G.C.B. 1820, I. 184
Phipps, Paul. K.H.1836, I. 473
Phipps, William, Kt.1687, II. 263
Phirozshah Merwanji Mehta, K.C.I.E. 1904, I. 412
Pichard, Roger, K.B.1306, I. 116
Pick, Vesian, Kt.1797, II. 304
PICKERING, PYKERINGE, PUCKERING
  Pickering, —, Kt.1492, II. 28
  Pickering, Christopher, Kt.1607, II. 142
  Pykeringe, Edward, Kt.1487, II. 24
  Pykeringe, Edward, Kt.1497, II. 31
  Pykeringe, Edward, Kt.1529, II. 47
  Pickering, Gilbert, Kt.1611, II. 151
  Pickering, Henry, Kt.1658, II. 224
  Puckeringe, John, Kt.1592, II. 90
  Pickering, John, Kt.1619, II. 174
  Puckering, Thomas, Kt.1612, II. 151
  Pickering, Thomas, Kt.1795, II. 302
  Pykeringe, William, Kt.1547, II. 60
Picknell (Pecknell), George, Kt.1795, II. 302
Picks, James, Kt.1487, II. 24
Picton, James A., Kt.1881, II. 372
Picton, Thomas, K.B.1813, I. 179; G.C.B.1815, I. 181
Pickworth, Hugh de, K.B.1306, I. 120
PIERREPONT, PERPOINT, PERPOUNT, PERPENT
  Pierrepont, Evelyn, duke of Kingston, K.G.1719, I. 42
  Pierrepont, Evelyn, duke of Kingston, K.G.1740-1, I. 44
  Perpont, Henry, Kt.1471, II. 14
  Perpoint (Pierrepont), Henry, Kt. 1603, II. 101

PIERREPONT
    Perpent, John, Kt.1545, II. 58, 60
    Perpoynt, William, Kt.1504, II. 34
    Perpount, William, Kt.1513, II. 36
Piers. See Pearce
Pierson See Pearson
PIGOTT, PIGOT, PYGOTT, PIGGOTT
    Pigott (Piggott), Arthur, Kt.1806, II. 308
    Pigot, Christopher, Kt.1604, II. 135
    Pigott, Gillery, Kt.1863, II. 357
    Pigot, Henry, Kt.1660, II. 232
    Pigot, Henry, G.C.M.G.1837, I. 333
    Pigot, Hugh, K.C.H.1834, I. 460; Kt. 1834, II. 335; K.C.B.1847, I. 238
    Pigott, Paynton, Kt.1902, II. 412
    Pygott, Randolf, Kt.1482, II. 18
    Pigot, Richard, Kt.1630, II. 198
    Pigott (Pygott), Richard, Kt.1666, II. 242
    Pigott, Robert, Kt.1609, II. 148
    Pigott, Thomas, Kt.1604, II. 131
Pikard, John, K.B.1306, I. 122
Pike, Richard, K.B.1324, I. 123
Pile (Pille), Gabriel, Kt.1607, II. 143
Pile, George C., Kt.1892, II. 390
PILKINGTON, PILKYNTON
    Pilkington Andrew, K.C.B.1838, I. 234
    Pilkington, Charles, Kt.1482, II. 20
    Pilkington, George A., Kt.1893, II. 392
    Pilkington, Henry, K.C.B.1902, I. 299
    Pilkington, John, Kt.1471, II. 14
    Pilkynton, John, K.B.1475, I. 136
    Pilkington, Thomas, Kt.1482, II. 20
    Pilkington, Thomas, Kt.1689, II. 264
    Pilkington, William H., Kt.1904, II. 417
Pinching, Horace H., K.C.M.G.1902, I. 392
Pinder. See Pendar
Pine, Benjamin C. C., Kt.1856, II. 352; K.C.M.G.1871, I. 356
Pine. See Pyne
Pinfold, Thomas, Kt.1686, II. 262
Pinha, vice-admiral, K.C.V.O.1901, I. 439
Pinhorn, John, Kt.1802, II. 306
Pink, Thomas, Kt.1904, II. 419
Pink, William, Kt.1891, II. 388
Pinsent, Robert J., Kt.1890, II. 387
Pinson (Pylson), Edmond, Kt.1553, II. 68
Pipe, Richard, Kt.1578, II. 79
Pipon, George, K.H.1836, I. 474
Pippe, Raoul de, Kt.(1380), II. 10
Piro, Guiseppe M., baron de, K.C.M.G. 1842, I. 352; G.C.M.G.1856, I. 335
Pitcairn, James, Kt.1837, II. 339
Pitches, Abraham, Kt.1782, II. 296
Pitman, Henry A., Kt.1883, II. 375
Pitman, Isaac, Kt.1894, II. 394
PITT, PITTS, PYTTS, PYTT
    Pytts (Pitts), Edward, Kt.1603, II. 116
    Pitt, George D., K.H.1836, I. 473
    Pitts, James, Kt.1603, II. 117
    Pitt, John, earl of Chatham, K.G.1790, I. 49
    Pytt (Pittes), Oliver, Kt.1608, II. 145
    Pitt (Pitts), William, Kt.1619, II. 171
    Pitt, William, A., K.B.1792, I. 174
Pittfield, Charles, Kt.1676, II. 251
Pittis, Francis, Kt.1887, II. 383
Pitts. See Pitt
Planta, Joseph, G.C.H.1837, I. 453
Plantagenet, Arthur, viscount Lisle, Kt. 1513, II. 40; K.G.1524, I. 21
Plasket, Richard, K.C.M.G.1818, I. 350
Plater (Plaiters), William, Kt.1623, II. 182
Platers (Playter), Thomas, Kt.1606, II. 140
Plat, Charles T. du, K.C.B.1896, I. 294
Plat, Gustavus du, K.H.1831, I. 466
Platt, Hugh, Kt.1605, II. 138
Platt, John, Kt.1672, II. 247
Platt, Thomas J., Kt.1845, II. 346
Playfair, Hugh L., Kt.1856, II. 351
Playfair, Lyon, lord Playfair, K.C.B. 1883, I. 288; G.C.B.1895, I. 214
Playfair, Patrick, Kt.1897, II. 401
Playfair, Robert L., K.C.M.G.1886, I. 369
Player, Thomas, jun., Kt.1660, II. 229
Player, Thomas, sen., Kt.1660, II. 229
Playz (Plessis), Edmunde de, K.B.1306, I. 118
Playz, Hugh de, K.B.1324, I. 123

INDEX 183

Playz, John de, K.B.1306, I. 118
Plessen, Hans von, G.C.V.O.1899, I. 423
Plestov, Thomas B., Kt.1818, II. 320
Pleydell, Charles, Kt.1618, II. 169
Plomer. See Plumer
Plomley, Richard, Kt.1633, II. 202
Plompton (Plumpton), Edward, Kt.1603, II. 113
Plompton, Robert, Kt.1482, II. 19
Plowden, Edmund, Kt.1630, II. 198
Plowden, Henry M., Kt.1887, II. 380
Plowden, William C., K.C.S.I.1886, I. 323
Plunkenet, Alan, K.B.1306, I. 111
PLUMER, PLOMER, PLUMMER
   Plomer, John, K.B.(1465), I. 135
   Plumer (Plomer), Thomas, Kt.1807, II. 308
   Plomer (Plumer), William, Kt.1616, II. 159
   Plomer, William, Kt.1782, II. 296
   Plomer, William, Kt.1809, II. 309
   Plummer, Walter R , Kt.1904, II. 417
Plumpton. See Plompton
Plumridge, James H., K.C.B.1855, I. 240
PLUNKETT, PLUNKET, and see Plukenet
   Plunkett, Arthur J., earl of Fingall, K.P.1821, I. 99
   Plunkett, Arthur J., earl of Fingall, K.P.1846, I. 101
   Plunkett, Christopher, Kt.1597, II. 94
   Plunkett, Francis R., K.C.M.G.1886, I. 368; G.C.M.G.1894, I. 344; G.C.B. 1901, I. 216; G.C.V.O.1903, I. 421
   Plunkett, Horace C., K.C.V.O.(1903), I. 436
   Plunket, John, Kt.1541, II. 52
   Plunket, John, Kt.1567, II. 73
   Plunket, Oliver, Kt.1541, II. 52
   Plunket, Oliver, Kt.1557, II. 69
   Plunket, Thomas, Kt.1541, II. 52
   Plunket, Thomas, baron of Louth, Kt. 1566, II. 72
   Plunkett, Walter, Kt.1660, II. 232
   Plunkett, William L., lord Plunkett, K.C.V.O. (1903), I. 436
Pocklington, R., Kt.1801, II. 306
Pocock, George, K.B.1761, I. 170
Pocock, George B., Kt.1821, II. 322
Pocock, Isaac, Kt.1786, II. 299

POER, POWER, and see Power
   Power, Piers, lord Le, Kt.1544, II. 56
   Poer, Walter le, K.B.1306, I. 121
Poille, John de la, K.B.1306, I. 119
Pointz. See Poyntz
Poitiers, Ernomville de, K.B.1327, I. 124
Poland, Casimir IV. of, K.G.1450, I. 12
Poland, Harry B., Kt.1895, II. 396
Poland, William H., Kt.1831, II. 330
POLE, POOLE, POULE, POLLE, POALL
   Poole, —, Kt.1471, II. 15
   Poole, Arthur, Kt.1523, II. 45
   Poole (Poule), Benjamin, Kt.1701, II. 272
   Pole, Charles M., K.C.B.1815, I. 217; G.C.B.1818, I. 183
   Poole, Devereux, Kt.1591, II. 89
   Pole, Edmund de la, duke of Suffolk, K.B.(1483), I. 141; K.G.1496, I. 19
   Poole, Geoffrey, Kt.1529, II. 47
   Pole, Griffin de la, K.B.1306, I. 113
   Poole, Gyles, Kt.1547, II. 61
   Poole, Henry, Kt.1513, II. 38
   Poole, Henry, Kt.1587, II. 85
   Poole, Henry, Kt.1603, II. 111
   Poole, James, Kt.1603, II. 101
   Poole, James, Kt.1887, II. 382
   Pole, John de la, duke of Lincoln, K.B. (1475), I. 136; K.G.1473, I. 15
   Pole, Michael de la, lord de la Pole, K.B.1377, I. 126
   Poole, Nevill, Kt.1613, II. 152
   Poole (Polle), Richard, Kt.1487, II. 25
   Pole, Richard, K.G.1499, I. 19
   Poole (Poall), Thomas, Kt.1487, II. 24
   Pole, William de la, duke of Suffolk, K.G.1421, I. 10
   Poole, William de la, Kt.1497, II. 29
   Poole, William, Kt.1513, II. 42
   Poole, William (John), Kt.1607, II.141
   Pole (Pool), William, Kt.1641, II. 208
Pole-Carew, Reginald, K.C.B.1900, I. 272
Poley. See Pooley
Pohhill (Polley), Thomas, Kt.1619, II. 171
Pollard (Pawlett, alias Pollard), George (John), Kt.1553, II. 67

Pollard, Hugh, Kt.1536, II. 50
Pollard, Hugh, Kt.1605, II. 137
Pollarde, John, Kt.1549, II. 64
Pollard, Richard, Kt.1538, II. 52
Pollexfen, Henry, Kt.1689, II. 264
Pollock, Charles E., Kt.1873, II. 365
Pollock, David, Kt.1846, II. 346
Pollock, Frederick R., K.C.S.I.1873, I. 319
Pollock, George, G.C.B.1842, I. 189; K.S.I.1861, I. 307; G.C.S.I.1866, I. 308
Pollock, Jonathan F., Kt.1834, II. 335
Polley. See Polhill, Pooley
Pollitt, William, Kt.1899, II. 405

POMEREY, POMERY, PEMERY
  Pomerey, Edward, Kt.1504, II. 34; K.B.1504, I. 147
  Pemery (Pomerey), Thomas (Richard), K.B.(1487), I. 142
  Pomerey, Thomas, Kt.1549, II. 64
  Pomeroy, William de, K.B.1330, I. 125

Pomfret, earl of. See Fermor
Pondre, William, Kt.1529, II. 47
Ponsonby, Frederick C., G.C.M.G.1828, I. 332; K.C.H.1831, I. 456; K.C.B. 1831, I. 231
Ponsonby, Henry, Kt.1679, II. 254
Ponsonby, Henry F., K.C.B.1879, I. 286; G.C.B.1887, I. 212
Ponsonby, John, Kt.1661, II. 233
Ponsonby, John, viscount Ponsonby, G.C.B.1834, I. 206
Ponsonby, John W., earl of Bessborough, Grand Master K.P.1846, I. 94
Ponsonby, William, K.C.B.1815, I. 220
Ponsonby-Fane, Spencer C. B., K.C.B. 1884, I. 288; G.C.B.1897, I. 214
Pontifex, Charles, K.C.I.E.1892, I. 407
Poole. See Pole

POOLEY, POLEY, POLY
  Pooley, Edmund, Kt.1646, II. 220
  Pooley, John, Kt.1588, II. 87
  Pooley (Poley), John, Kt.1599, II. 96, 98
  Poly (Pooley), John, Kt.1660, II. 232, 239

POOLEY
  Poley (Pooley), Wiliam, Kt.1596, II. 93
  Poley (Pooley), William, Kt.1631, II. 199
Pooney, Francis, Kt.1622, II. 180
Pope, Thomas, Kt.1538, II. 51
Pope, Thomas, Kt.1625, II. 189
Pope, William, earl of Downe, K.B. 1603, I. 155
Pope, William, Kt.1616, II. 159
Popely, Derrick, Kt.1671, II. 246
Popham, Francis, Kt.1596, II. 92
Popham, Francis, K.B.1661, I. 165
Popham, Home R., K.C.B.1815, I. 221; K.C.H.1818, I. 454
Popham, John, Kt.1592, II. 90
Popham, Stephen, Kt.1427, II. 12
Porchester, —, Kt.1347, II. 9
Pordage, William, Kt.1613, II. 152
Pore, John, Kt.1588, II. 87
Portarlington, earl of. See Dawson-Damer
Porte, John, Kt.1527, II. 46
Porte, John, K.B.1547, II. 151
Portal, Gerald H., K.C.M.G.1892, I. 377
Portelli, Agostino, K.C.M.G.1850, I. 353
Porten, Francis, Kt.1726, II. 283
Porten, Stanier, Kt.1772, II. 293
Porter, —, Kt.1615, II. 156
Porter, Alfred de Bock, K.C.B.1902, I. 300
Porter, Arthur, Kt.1603, II. 112
Porter, Charles, Kt.1686, II. 261
Porter, George H., Kt.1883, II. 376
Porter, James, Kt.1763, II. 292
Porter, Neale, K.C.M.G.1894, I. 379
Porter, Robert K., Kt.1813, II. 312; K.C.H.1836, I. 461
Porter (Parler), Thomas, Kt.1574, II. 76
Porter, Thomas, Kt.1617, II. 167
Porter, William, K.B.1409, II. 11
Portington, Roger, Kt.1603, II. 124
Portland, duke of. See Bentinck; see Cavendish-Bentinck
Portland, earl of. See Weston; see Bentinck
Portman, Henry, Kt.1574, II. 76
Portman, John, Kt.1547, II. 58
Portman, John, Kt.1605, II. 136

INDEX

Portman (Potman), Richard, Kt.1603, II. 118
Portman, William, K.B.1661, I. 164
Portmore, earl of. See Colyear
Portsea, Richard de, K.B.1306, I. 112
PORTUGAL
  Alphonsus V. of, K.G.1447, I. 12
  Charles I. of, K.G.1895, I. 70;
    Victorian Chain 1902, I. 416
  Edward, king of, K.G.1435, I. 11
  Emanuel, king of, K.G.1510, I. 20
  John I. of, K.G.1400, I. 8
  John II. of, K.G.1482, I. 16
  John VI. of, K.G.1822, I. 52
  Louis I. of, K.G.1865, I. 62
  Louis Philippe, etc., crown prince of, K.G.1902, I. 72
  Pedro V. of, K.G.1858, I. 60
Potter, John, Kt.1851, II. 349
Potter, Thomas, Kt.1840, II. 342
Pottinger, Henry, G.C.B.1842, I. 207
Potts (Pets), John, Kt.1641, II. 210
Poule. See Pole
Poulet. See Powlett
Poultney. See Pulteney
Pounde, John, Kt.1501, II. 33
Pountney. See Pulteney
Povey, Edward, Kt.1629, II. 197
Povey, John, Kt.1673, II. 248
POWELL, POWEL, POWLE
Powell, Alexander, Kt.1762, II. 291
Powel, Edward, Kt.1631, II. 199
Powell, Francis, Kt.1893, II. 392
Powell, Francis, K.C.M.G.1902, I. 392
Powell, Gabriel, Kt.1800, II. 305
Powell (Pownall), George, Kt.1796, II. 303
Powell, John, Kt.1603, II. 123
Powell, John, Kt.1686, II. 262
Powell, John, Kt.1691, II. 266
Powell, Nathaniel, Kt.1660, II. 230
Powle, Richard, K.B.1661, I. 166
Powell, Richard D., K.C.V.O.(1901), I. 433
Powle, Stephen, Kt.1604, II. 135
Powell, Thomas, Kt.1687, II. 263
Powell, Thomas, K.H.1837, I. 476
Powell, William, Kt.1607, II. 144
Powell, William, Kt.1619, II. 173

Power, Alfred, K.C.B.1873, I. 285
Power, James A., Kt.1904, II. 417
Power, Manley, K.C.B.1815, I. 221
Power (Gower), Thomas, Kt.1604, II. 132
Power, Thomas, Kt.1625, II. 188
Power, William, Kt.1610, II. 149
Power, William G., K.H.1834, I. 469; K.C.B.1862, I. 247
Power, William J. T., K.C.B.1865, I. 250
Power. See Poer
Powerscourt, viscount. See Wingfield
Powis, Powys
Powis, duke and earl of. See Herbert
Powis, lord. See Grey; see Herbert
Powys, Littleton, Kt.1692, II. 267
Powys, Thomas, Kt.1686, II. 262
Powle. See Powell
POWLETT, POULET, PAWLETT, PAULET, POWLET, PAWLET
Powlett, —, Kt.1536, II. 50
Poulet, Amyas, Kt.1487, II. 25
Powlett, Amyas, Kt.1575, II. 77
Pawlet, Amyas, Kt.1625, II. 189
Powlett, Charles, duke of Bolton, K.G. 1714, I. 41
Powlett, Charles, duke of Bolton, K.G. 1722, I. 42
Powlett, Charles, duke of Bolton, K.B. 1753, I. 170
Powlett, Charles A., K.B.1749, I. 169
Pawlett, George (John), Kt.1553, II. 67
Pawlett, George, Kt.1607, II. 142
Paulet, Hamden, Kt.1601, II. 99
Pawlet, Hector, Kt.1619, II. 173
Paulet, lord Henry, K.B.1626, I. 161
Paulet, lord Henry, K.C.B.1815, I. 220
Pawlett, Hercules, Kt.1618, II 169
Powlet, Hugh, Kt.1538, II. 50
Pawlet, John, K.B.(1483), I. 140
Paulet, John, K.B.1501, I. 145
Powlett, John, marquess of Winchester, Kt.1545, II. 57
Pawlett, John, Kt.1603, II. 111, 125
Poulett, John, lord Poulett, Kt.1635, II. 203
Poulett, John, Kt.1635, II. 203
Pawlet, John, Kt.1639, II. 206
Poulett, John, earl Poulett, K.G.1712, I. 41

INDEX

POWLETT
  Poulett, John, earl Poulett, K.T.1794, I. 80
  Paulet, lord Nassau, K.B.1725, I. 167
  Pawlett, Richard, Kt.1591, II. 88
  Pawlet, Thomas (Amyas), Kt.1625, II. 189
  Poulett, Thomson C. E., lord Sydenham, G.C.B.1841, I. 207
  Paulet, William, marquess of Winchester, K.G.1543, I. 23
  Paulet, William, marquess of Winchester, K.B.1553, I. 152
  Pawlet, William, Kt.1603, II. 112, 125
  Paulet, William, K.C.B.1865, I. 250; G.C.B.1871, I. 196
Powney, John, K.H.1837, I. 476
POYNINGS, POYNINGES, PONINGS
  Poyninges, Adryan, Kt.1563, II. 71
  Poyninges, Christopher de, Kt.1347, II. 7
  Ponyinges, Edward, Kt.1485, II. 22; K.G.1493, I. 18
  Poyninges, Edward, Kt.1513, II. 36
  Poyninges, Jo, Kt.1347, II. 7
  Poynings, Richard, lord Poynings, K.B.1377, I. 126
  Poynings, Thomas, K.B.1533, I. 149
  Ponings, Thomas de, K.B.1306, I. 114
Poynter, Edward J., Kt.1896, II. 398
POYNTZ, POINTZ, POYNES
  Pointz, Charles, Kt.1630, II. 198
  Poyntz, Gabriel, Kt.1604, II. 132
  Pointz, Hugh de, K.B.1323, I. 122
  Pointz (Pore), John, Kt.1588, II. 87
  Poyntz (Poynes), John (James), Kt. 1617, II. 161
  Poyntz, John, Kt.1666, II. 242
  Poynes (Pointz), Nicholas, K.B.1559, I. 153
  Poyntz, Nicholas, Kt.1603, II. 119
  Pointz, Robert, Kt.1485, II. 23
  Poyntz, Robert, K.B.1626, I. 163
  Poyntz, Toby, Kt.1662, II. 237
Pratt, Charles, Kt.1761, II. 291
Pratt, Charles, K.C.B.1815, I. 223
Pratt, George C., marquess of Camden, K.G.1846, I. 58
Pratt, Henry, Kt.1641, II. 210
Pratt, John, Kt.1714, II. 279
Pratt, John J., marquess of Camden, Grand Master K.P.1795, I. 93; K.G. 1799, I. 49
Pratt, Roger, Kt.1668, II. 243
Pratt, Thomas S., K.C.B.1861, I. 247
Preece, William H., K.C.B.1899, I. 298
Preissac, Bermond A. de, K.G.1379, I. 5
Prendergast, Harry N. D., K.C.B.1885, I. 259; G.C.B.1902, I. 203
Prendergast, James, Kt.1881, II. 373
Prendergast, Jeffery, Kt.1838, II. 341
PRESCOTT, PRESCOT
  Prescott, Henry, K.C.B.1856, I. 242; G.C.B.1869, I. 195
  Prescot, John, Kt.1622, II. 179
  Prescott, John, Kt.1660, II. 228
Pressly, Charles, K.C.B.1866, I. 284
Preston, —, Kt.1622, II. 179
Preston, Amyas, Kt.1596, II. 93
Preston, Christopher, Kt.(1397), II. lx.
Preston, George, Kt.1833, II. 334
Preston, Isaac, Kt.1695, II. 268
Preston, Jenico W. J., viscount Gormanston, K.C.M.G.1887, I. 371; G.C.M.G. 1897, I. 344
Preston, John, Kt.1878, II. 370
Preston, Richard, earl of Desmond, K.B. 1603, I. 154
Preston, Robert, Kt.(1361), II. lx.
Preston, Thomas, Kt.1603, II. 107, 113
Prestwich, Joseph, Kt.1896, II. 397
Prestwich, Thomas, Kt.1644, II. 218
PRETTYMAN, PRETYMAN
  Prettyman, George, Kt.1660, II. 231
  Pretyman, George T., K.C.M.G.1901, I. 389
  Pretyman, John, Kt.1603, II. 125
PRICE, PRYCE, APRICE, AP RES, AP RICE
  Price (Pryce), Charles, Kt.1761, II. 290
  Price, Jarvis, Kt.1607, II. 143
  Aprice (ap Res, Deprice), John, Kt. 1547, II. 60
  Price, John, Kt.1618, II. 169
  Price, John F., K.C.S.I.1898, I. 326
  Pryce, Richard, Kt.1603, II. 111
  Ap Rice, William, Kt.1603, II. 123
Prichard. See Pritchard
Pride, Thomas, Kt.1656, II. 223

INDEX 187

Prideaux, Edward, Kt.1646, II. 221
Prideaux, Nicholas, Kt.1606, II. 141
Prideaux, Robert, Kt.1603, II. 126
Prideaux, Thomas, Kt.1603, II. 124
Prideaux, Walter S., Kt.1891, II. 388
Pridgean (Prugean, Privian), Francis, Kt.1661, II. 233
Priest, William O., Kt.1893, II. 392
Priestley, Edward J., K.H.1837, I. 478
Prime (Prince), Richard, Kt.1632, II. 200
Prime, Samuel, Kt.1745, II. 287
Primrose, Archibald J., earl of Rosebery, K.T.1840, I. 83
Primrose, Archibald P., earl of Rosebery, K.G.1892, I. 69; K.T.1895, I. 88
Primrose, Henry W., K.C.B.1899, I. 297
Primrose, Neil, earl of Rosebery, K.T.1771, I. 79
Prince, Francis, Kt.1611, II. 150
Prince, Richard, Kt.1632, II. 200
Prince, William (Gilbert), Kt.1604, II. 132
Pringle, George, Kt.1882, II. 374
Pringle, William H., K.C.B.1815, I. 220; G.C.B.1834, I. 187
Prinsep, Henry T., Kt.1894, II. 393; K.C.I.E.1904, I. 412;
Prior, James, Kt.1858, II. 353
PRITCHARD, PRICHARD
   Pritchard, Charles B., K.C.I.E.1891, I. 407
   Prichard, William, Kt.1672, II. 247
Pritzler, Theophilus, K.C.B.1822, I. 229
Privian. See Pridgean
Probat, George, Kt.1646, II. 221
Probert. See Roberts
Proby, Granville L., earl of Carysfort, K.P.1869, I. 103
Proby, Henage, Kt.1640, II. 208
Proby, John, Lord Carysfort, K.B.1761, I. 170
Proby, John J., baron Carysfort, K.P.1784, I. 97
Proby, Peter, Kt.1623, II. 181
Proby, William, earl of Carysfort, K.P.1874, I. 104
Probyn, Dighton M., K.C.S.I.1876, I. 320; K.C.B.1887, I. 290; G.C.V.O.1896, I. 417; G.C.B.1902, I. 216

Probyn, Edmund, Kt.1726, II. 283
Proctor, Stephen, Kt.1604, II. 130
Proctor, William B., K.B.1761, I. 170
Prossalendi, Paolo, C.M.G.(1820), I. xxviii.
Prothero, Henry, Kt.1803, II. 306
Proud, John, Kt.1623, II. 181
Provis, Samuel B., K.C.B.1901, I. 299
Prugean. See Pridgean
PRUSSIA
   Augustus William, etc., prince of, G.C.V.O.1904, I. 430
   Eitel Fritz, prince of, G.C.V.O.1904, I. 430
   Frederick I. of, K.G.1690, I. 39
   Frederick C. N., prince of, G.C.B.1878, I. 197
   Frederick Leopold, prince of, G.C.V.O.1899, I. 423
   Frederick William III. of, K.G.1814, I. 51
   Frederick William IV. of, K.G.1842, I. 56
   Frederick W. C., prince of, G.C.B.1843, I. 189
   Henry, prince of, G.C.B.1881, I. 211; K.G.1889, I. 68; Victorian Chain 1902, I. 416
   Joachim Francis, prince of, G.C.V.O.1904, I. 430
   Oscar Charles, etc., prince of, G.C.V.O.1904, I. 430
   Waldemar, prince of, G.C.B.1846, I. 190
   William, crown prince of, Victorian Chain 1904, I. 416
Pryce. See Price
Puckering. See Pickering
Pudsey, George, Kt.1681, II. 255
Pudsey (Puesey), Richard, Kt.1497, II. 29
Puleston, John H., Kt.1887, II. 383
Puleston, Roger, Kt.1617, II. 165
Puleston, Roger, Kt.1680, II. 255
Pullar, Robert, Kt.1895, II. 396
Puller, Christopher, Kt.1823, II. 324
Pullyson, Thomas [Edward], Kt.1585, II. 83
PULTENEY, POULTNEY, POUNTNEY
   Pulteney, James M., Kt.1803, II. 307

PULTENEY

Pulteney, Joh de, Kt.(1336), II. 5
Poultney (Pountney), John, Kt.1603, II. 105
Pulteney, Thomas, K.B.(1487), I. 142
Pulteney, Thomas, Kt.1527, II. 46
Pulteney, William, Kt.1660, II. 227
Punnah, Pertab Sing, maharajah of, K.C.S.I.1875, I. 320

PURCELL, PURSELL, PURSLEY

Purcell, John, Kt.1811, II. 310
Purcell, John S., K.C.B.1900, I. 298
Pursell (Pursley), Robert, Kt.1606, II. 139

Purdon, Nicholas, Kt.1661, II. 233
Putnam, George, K.B.1501, I. 146
Pycroft, Thomas, K.C.S.I.1866, I. 316
Pye, Edmund (Edward), Kt.1641, II. 208
Pye, Robert, Kt.1621, II. 177
Pye, Thomas, Kt.1773, II. 294
Pye, Walter, Kt.1630, II. 198
Pygott. See Pigott
Pykeringe. See Pickering
Pylson, Edmond, Kt.1553, II. 68
Pylston, Roger, Kt.1497, II. 32
Pym, Charles, Kt.1663, II. 237
Pym, Samuel, K.C.B.1839, I. 236
Pym, William, Kt.1830, II. 328; K.C.H.1831, I. 457
Pynchon, Edward, Kt.1603, II. 112, 123
Pyne, Richard, Kt.1692, II. 267
Pyne, Thomas S., Kt.1894, II. 393
Pyne. See Pine
Pynn, Henry, Kt.1815, II. 315
Pytt, Pytts. See Pitt

Q

Quadring, William, Kt.1628, II. 195
Quain, John R., Kt.1872, II. 364
Quarles, George, Kt.1624, II. 185
Quarles, Robert, Kt.1608, II. 144
Queensberry, duke and marquess of. See Douglas
Quentin, George A., K.C.H.1821, I. 455; Kt.1821, II. 323
Querini, Tomaso, Kt.1768, II. 293
Quick, John, Kt.1901, II. 409

R

Rachese, Tho de, Kt.1347, II. 7

RADCLYFF, RATCLIFFE, RADCLIFFE, RADCLYFFE, RADCLIFF, RATCLIFF, RADCLIF

Radclyff, Alexander, Kt.1513, II. 42
Ratcliffe, Alexander, K.B.1626, I. 162
Radclyff, Cuthbert, Kt.1530, II. 48
Radcliffe, David, Kt.1886, II. 379
Radclyff, Edward, Kt.1501, II. 32
Ratclyffe, Edward, earl of Sussex, Kt. 1594, II. 90
Radcliffe, Edward, Kt.1605, II. 136
Ratcliff, Francis, Kt.1628, II. 193
Radclyffe, George, Kt.1545, II. 57
Radcliffe, George, Kt.1633, II. 202
Ratcliffe, Henry, earl of Sussex, K.B. 1533, I. 149; K.G.1554, I. 25
Radclyffe, Henry, earl of Sussex, Kt. 1553, II. 66; K.G.1589, I. 28
Ratcliffe, Henry, lord Fitzwalter, K.B. 1610, I. 157
Ratcliffe, Jeremiah, K.H.1833, I. 469
Radcliffe, John, K.G.1429, I. 11
Radcliff, John, lord Fitzwalter, K.B. (1485), I. 142
Radclyffe, John, Kt.1547, II. 59
Radcliff, John, Kt.1578, II. 78
Ratcliff, John, Kt.1599, II. 98
Ratcliff, John (William), Kt.1645, II. 219
Ratcliff, John, Kt.1858, II. 353
Radclif, Rauf, K.B.(1426), I. 132
Ratcliffe, Ralph, Kt.1668, II. 243
Radclyffe, Richard, Kt.1471, 1482, II. 15, 17; K.G.1483, I. 17
Radclyffe, Robert, earl of Sussex, K.G. 1524, I. 21
Radcliffe, Robert, lord Fitzwalter, K.B.1509, I. 148
Radclyffe, Robert, earl of Sussex, Kt. 1596, II. 92; K.G.1599, I. 29
Radcliffe, Thomas, earl of Sussex, Kt. 1544, II. 56; K.G.1557, I. 25
Ratcliffe, Thomas, K.B.1610, I. 158
Ratcliff (Radcliffe), William, Kt.1544, II. 55
Ratcliff, William, Kt.1644, II. 218

INDEX

RADCLYFF
Radcliffe, William P., K.C.B.1886, I. 260
Radford, Samuel, K.H.1836, I. 475
Radley (Rodley), Henry, Kt.1616, II. 160
Radstock, lord. See Waldegrave
Rae, William, Kt.1858, II. 353
Raeburn, Henry, Kt.1822, II. 324
Raffles, Thomas S., Kt.1817, II. 319
Raglan, lord. See Somerset
Raglande, John, Kt.1513, II 39
Rainals, Harry T. A., Kt.1887, II. 383
Rainals. See Reynolds

RAINES, REYNES
Raines, Julius A. R., K.C.B.1893, I. 264
Reynes (Raines), Richard, Kt.1686, II. 262

Rainey, Henry, K.H.1832, I. 466
Rainey (Rayney), John, Kt.1642, II. 212

RAINSFORD, RAYNSFORD, RAYNSFORDE, RANSFORD, REYNFORD, REYNSFORD
Rainsford, Francis, Kt.1632, II. 200
Rainsford, Garret, Kt.1627, II. 193
Rainsford (Raynsford), George, Kt. 1681, II. 257
Raynsford, Henry, Kt.1603, II. 118
Rainsford, Henry, Kt.1624, II. 186
Raynsforde, John, Kt.1497, II. 30
Reynsford, John, Kt.1513, II. 36
Raynsford, John, Kt.1523, II. 45
Reynford, Lawrence, Kt.1466, II. 14
Ransford, Mark, Kt.1701, II. 272
Rainsford, Richard, Kt.1685, II. 260
Raynsforde, William, Kt.1547, II. 60
Rainton, Nicholas, Kt.1633, II. 200

RALEIGH, RAWLEIGH, RALEE, RAWLEY, RAWGHLEY
Rawleigh, Carew, Kt.1601, II. 99
Rawley, Charles, Kt.1681, II. 256
Raleigh, Edward, Kt.1603, II. 121
Rawley (Rawghley), George, Kt.1603, II. 107
Raleigh (Ralee), John de, K.B.1327, I. 124
Raleigh, Thomas, K.C.S.I.1904, I. 328
Rawley, Walter, Kt.1585, II. 83
Rawleigh, Walter, Kt.1660, II. 228

Ram, Abell, Kt.1684, II. 260
Ram Singh, K.C.B.1895, I. 266

RAMPUR
Furzund, nawab of, G.C.S.I.1875, I. 310
Yoosuf, nawab of, K.S.I.1861, I. 307; G.C.S.I.1866, I. 308

RAMSAY, RAMSEY
Ramsey, —, Kt.1620, II. 175
Ramsey, Andrew, Kt.1660, II. 230
Ramsay, Andrew, Kt.1881, II. 373
Ramsay, George A., K.H.1834, I. 470
Ramsay, George D., Kt.1900, II. 406
Ramsey, George, earl of Dalhousie, K.B.1813, I. 179; G.C.B.1815, I. 182
Ramsay, Henry, K.C.S.I.1875, I. 320
Ramsay, James A., marquess of Dalhousie, K.T.1848, I. 84
Ramsay, John, Kt.1633, II. 200
Ramsay, John W., earl of Dalhousie, K.T.1881, I. 87
Ramsay, N., K.H.1834, I. 471
Ramsey, Thomas, Kt.1578, II. 78
Ramsay, William, K.C.B.1869, I. 251
Ramsay, William, K.C.B.1902, I. 300
Ramsden, James, Kt.1872, II. 364
Ramsden, John, Kt.1619, II. 173
Ramsey. See Ramsay
Randall, Edward, Kt.1603, II. 111
Randall (Randel), Morgan, Kt.1625, II. 189
Randall (Ruddall), Richard, Kt.1596, II. 93
Randolph, George G., K.C.B.1897, I. 267
Randolph, John, Kt.1732, II. 284
Randon, Agostino, K.C.M.G.1839, I. 352; G.C.M.G.1842, I. 334
Rands, Robert, Kt.1676, II. 251
Ranelagh, viscount. See Jones
Ranfurly, earl of. See Knox
Rant, Thomas, Kt.1660, II. 230
Rant, William, Kt.1671, II. 245
Raper, Robert G., Kt.1886, II. 378
Ras Makunan, K.C.M.G.1902, I. 392
Ratcliffe, Ratcliff. See Radclyff
Ratlam, Ranjit Singh, of, K.C.I.E.,1887, 400
Rattigan, William H., Kt.1895, II. 395

Ravenesholm, John de, Kt.(1346), II. 6
Rawdon (Roydon), Marmaduke, Kt.1643, II. 217
Rawdon-Hastings, Francis, marquess of Hastings, K.G.1812, I. 51; G.C.H. 1818, I. 449; G.C.B.1818, I. 184
Rawleigh, Rawley, Rawghley. See Raleigh
Rawlins, Benjamin, Kt.1737, II. 285
Rawlins, William, Kt.1802, II. 306
Rawlinson, Christopher, Kt.1847, II. 347
Rawlinson, Henry C., K.C.B.1856, I. 279; G.C.B.1889, I. 213
Rawlinson, John, Kt.1604, II. 134
Rawlinson, Robert, Kt.1883, II. 376; K.C.B.1888, I. 291
Rawlinson, Thomas, Kt.1686, II. 262
Rawlinson, Thomas, Kt.1760, II. 289
Rawlinson, Walter, Kt.1774, II. 294
Rawlinson, William, Kt.1689, II. 264
Rawson, Harry H., K.C.B.1897, I. 267
Rawson, William, Kt.1814, II. 313
Rawson, William R., K.C.M.G.1875, I. 358
Rawstorme (Royston), William, Kt.1677, II. 252
Raymond, Jemmett, Kt.1680, II. 254
Raymond, Jonathan, Kt.1679, II. 254
Raymond (Raymund), Robert, Kt.1710, II. 277
Raymond, Thomas, Kt.1679, II. 253
Rayner, William, Kt.1603, II. 129
Rayner, Thomas C., Kt.1899, II. 405
Rayney. See Rainey
Raynoldes. See Reynolds
Raynsford. See Rainsford
Rea, John, Kt.1663, II. 238
Reade, Read. See Reid
Readymoney, Cowasjee J., Kt.1872, II. 364
Reagh, Owen MacCartie, Kt.1579, II. 79
Reagh, Donogh MacCartie, Kt.1567, II. 73
Reay, lord. See Mackay
Rebow (Reboes), Isaac, Kt.1693, II. 268
Réchad, Pacha, K.C.M.G.1879, I. 360
Rede. See Reid
Redesdale, lord. See Freeman-Mitford
Redhakanth, Deb, K.C.S.I.1866, I. 316
Redhouse, James W., K.C.M.G.1888, I. 373

Redington, Thomas N., K.C.B.1849, I. 278
Redman, Mathew, Kt.1603, II. 113
Redman, William, K.B.1478, I. 138
Redman, William, Kt.1482, II. 17
Redmeyll (Redmill), William, Kt.1487, II. 25
Redmond, Peter, baron Redmond, Kt. 1717, footnote, II. 266
Reed, Reede. See Reid
Rees, Joseph, Kt.1891, II. 388
REEVES, REEVE, REVES, REVE, RYVES, RYVE, RIVES, and see Ryvet
Reve, Edmond, Kt.1639, II. 207
Reeve, George, Kt.1660, II. 227
Reeves, George J., K.H.1824, I. 464
Ryve (Reve, Reeve, Keene), Henry, Kt. 1617, II. 164
Ryves, John, Kt.1607, II. 141
Ryves, Richard, Kt.1663, II. 239
Ryves (Reves), Richard, Kt.1681, II. 255
Reeves (Rives), Thomas, Kt.1645, II. 219
Reeves (Reeve), Thomas, Kt.1736, II. 285
Reeve, Thomas, Kt.1756, II. 289
Reeve, Thomas N., Kt.1838, II. 340
Reeves, William, Kt.1619, II. 175
Reeves, William C., Kt.1889, II. 385
Reginald. See Reynolds
Regnault de Saint, Jean d'Angely, count de, G.C.B.(1856), I. 192
REID, REED, REEDE, READE, READ, REDE
Reede, gen. de, K.C.B.1819, I. 228
Reid, Alexander J. F., K.C.B.1901, I. 273
Reed, Andrew, Kt.1889, II. 385; K.C.B.1897, I. 295
Rede, Bartholomew, Kt.1503, II. 33
Reid, Charles, K.C.B.1871, I. 253; G.C.B.1886, I. 198
Reed, Charles, Kt.1874, II. 366
Reed, Charles J., K.C.B.1904, I.301
Rede, Edmund, K.B.(1465), I. 135
Read, Edward, Kt.1599, II. 97
Reid, Edward, Kt.1868, II. 360
Reed, Edward J., K.C.B.1880, I. 287
Reid, George, Kt.1891, II. 389

INDEX

REID
Reid, James, K.C.B.1895, I. 294; G.C.V.O.1901, I. 419
Reid, James J., Kt.1840, II. 343
Read, John, Kt.1603, II. 116
Read, John, Kt.1642, II. 212
Reed (Read), John, Kt.1644, II. 217
Read, John, Kt.1811, II. 310
Reed, John, K.H.1832, I. 467
Reade, John B. C., K.C.B.1903, I. 276
Reid, John W., K.C.B.1882, I. 259
Rede, Richard, Kt.1545, II. 58
Reade, Robert, Kt.1501, II. 33
Reid, Robert T., Kt.1894, II. 394; G.C.M.G.1899, I. 346
Reed, Roger, Kt.1471, II. 15
Read, Thomas, Kt.1592, II. 90
Reade, Thomas, Kt.1619, II. 172
Reade, Thomas, Kt.1815, II. 316
Reed, Thomas, K.C.B.1865, I. 249; G.C.B.1875, I. 196
Reid, Thomas W., Kt.1894, II. 394
Rede, William, K.B.1501, I. 146
Read, William, Kt.1586, II. 85
Read, William, Kt.1595, II. 91
Reade, William, Kt.1603, II. 118
Read, William, Kt.1705, II. 274
Reid, William, K.C.B.1851, I. 278; G.C.M.G.1856, I. 335
Reilly, Francis S., K.C.M.G.1882, I. 364
Reineck, Gen., K.C.V.O.1901, I. 439
Reischach, Eck, baron von, G.C.V.O.1904, I. 428
Reischach, freiherr Hugo van, K.C.V.O.1897, I. 438; G.C.V.O.1901, I. 424
Remington, Robert, Kt.1596, II. 93
Remington, Thomas, Kt.1633, II. 202
Rémono, Jean E., Kt.1860, II. 355
Rempston, Thomas, K.G.1400, I. 8
Renals, Joseph, Kt.1893, II. 391
Rendel, Alexander M., K.C.I.E.1887, I. 400
Rennie, John, Kt.1831, II. 330
Rennie, Richard T., Kt.1882, II. 374
Renouf, Peter Le P., Kt.1896, II. 398
Renton, Thomas, Kt.1723, II. 282
Renvers, —, K.C.V.O.1901, I. 440
Renwick, Arthur, Kt.1894, II. 393
Renzi, Matthew de, Kt.1627, II. 192

Renzy, Annesley C. C. de, K.C.B.1902, I. 274
REPINGTON, REPPINGTON, REPINGDON
Repingdon (Reppington), John, Kt. 1614, II. 154
Repington, John, Kt.1624, II. 186
Reresby (Risbie), George, Kt.1617, II. 162
Reresby, Thomas, Kt.1598, II. 95
Reuss, Henry XXX. of, G.C.V.O.1900, I. 424
Reves, Reve. See Reeve
Revet. See Ryvet
Rew, Skears, Kt.1815, II. 316
REWA
Prasad Singh of, G.C.S.I.1897, I. 314
Rughoo Raj Sing, of, K.S.I.1864, I. 307; G.C.S.I.1866, I. 309
Rey (Roye), James, Kt.1625, II. 187
Reynard, William, Kt.1603, II. 123
Reynardson, Abraham, Kt.1660, II. 229
Reynell, Reynel. See Reynolds
Reynes. See Raines
Reynett, James, K.H.1818, I. 464
Reynett, James H., Kt.1823, II. 324; K.C.H.1824, I. 455; K.C.B.1862, I. 247
Reynford, Reynsford. See Rainsford
REYNOLDS, RAYNOLDES, REYNELL, REGINALD, REYNEL, REYNOLL, REYNOLLES, and see Rainals
Reynolds, Alfred J., Kt.1903, II. 416
Reynolds, Barrington, K.C.B.1856, I. 243; G.C.B.1861, I. 193
Reynell (Reynodes, Reginald), Carew, Kt.1599, II. 96
Reynell, George, Kt.1603, II. 116, 117
Reynolds, James, Kt.1618, II. 168
Reynolds, James, Kt.1745, II. 287
Reynolds, John, Kt.1655, II. 223
Reynolds, Joshua, Kt.1769, II. 293
Reynell, Richard, Kt.1622, II. 179, 189
Reynell, Richard, Kt.1673, II. 248
Reynolds, Robert, Kt.1660, II. 227
Reynoll (Reynolles), Thomas, Kt.1603, II. 117
Reynel, Thomas, Kt.1625, II. 189
Reynell, Thomas, K.C.B.1826, I. 230

RHODES, RODES, and see Rolles
  Rhodes, Edward, Kt.1635, II. 203
  Rhodes, Francis, Kt.1641, II. 210
  Rodes, Godfrey, Kt.1615, II. 156
  Rhodes, John, Kt.1604, II. 131
  Rodes, Samuel, Kt.1619, II. 172

RIALL, RYALL
  Ryall, Maltis, Kt.1734, II. 284
  Riall, Phineas, K.C.H.1831, I. 457; Kt.1833, II. 334
  Riaz, Pasha, K.C.M.G.1879, I. 361; G.C.M.G.1889, I. 342
  Ribeira, Grande, count Jose, G.C.V.O. 1904, I. 431
  Ribton, George, Kt.1747, II. 288

RICAUT, RICOTT, RICKARD
  Ricott (Ricaut), Paul, Kt.1685, II. 261
  Ricaut (Ricott, Rickhard), Peter, Kt. 1641, II. 208
  Riccard, Andrew, Kt.1660, II. 229
  Rice, Edward B., K.C.B.1887, I. 261
  Rice, Ralph, Kt.1817, II. 319
  Rice, Samuel, K.H.1835, I. 471
  Rice, Stephen, Kt.1687, II. 263
  Rice, Thomas S., lord Monteagle, K.P. 1885, I. 104
  Rice, Walter, Kt.1603, II. 117
  Rich, Charles, Kt.1619, II. 171
  Rich, Edward, Kt.1670, II. 245
  Rich, Edwin, Kt.1596, II. 92
  Rich, Edwin, Kt.1666, II. 242
  Rich, George, Kt.1823, II. 324
  Rich, Henry, earl of Holland, K.B.1610, I. 158; K.G.1625, I. 32
  Rich, Hugh, K.B.1553, I. 152
  Rich, Nathaniel, Kt.1617, II. 167
  Rich, Peter, Kt.1685, II. 260
  Rich, Richard, Kt.1536, II. 50
  Riche, Robert, K.B.1559, I. 153
  Rich, Robert, earl of Warwick, K.B.1603, I. 154
  Rich, Robert, Kt.1619, II. 172
  Rich, Robert, earl of Warwick, K.B. 1626, I. 160
  Rich, Robert, Kt.1676, II. 251
  Richard II., K.G.1376, I. 5
  Richard III., K.B.(1461), I. 133; K.G. 1465-6, I. 15

RICHARDS, RICHARD
  Richards (Richard), Edward, Kt.1628, II. 194
  Richard, Franklyn, Kt.1660, II. 228
  Richards, Frederick W., K.C.B.1881, I. 258; G.C.B.1895, I. 201
  Richards, George H., Kt.1877, II. 369; K.C.B.1886, I. 260
  Richards, John, Kt.1615, II. 156
  Richards, Peter, K.C.B.1865, I. 250
  Richards, Richard, Kt.1814, II. 313
  Richards, William, K.C.B.1838, I. 235
  Richards, William B., Kt.1877, II. 369
  Richardson, Benjamin W., Kt.1893, II. 392
  Richardson, Charles, K.C.B.1841, I. 237
  Richardson, Edward, Kt.1619, II. 173
  Richardson, James, Kt.1651, II. 222
  Richardson, John, Kt.1819, II. 320
  Richardson, John, Kt.1846, II. 346
  Richardson, John L. C., Kt.1875, II. 367
  Richardson, Thomas, Kt.1621, II. 176
  Richardson, Thomas, Kt.1626, II. 191
  Richardson, Thomas, Kt.1897, II. 400
  Richardson, William, Kt.1603, II. 129
  Richardson, William, Kt.1744, II. 285
  Richardson, William H., Kt.1830, II. 329
  Richardson, Wodehouse D., K.C.B.1900, I. 272
  Richey, James B., K.C.I.E.1890, I. 406
  Richmond, David, Kt.1899, II. 404
  Richmond, duke of. See Fitzroy; see Stuart; see Lennox; see Gordon-Lennox
  Richmond, earl of. See Montfort; see Tudor
  Richmond, William B., K.C.B.1897, I. 296
  Richter, Otto de, G.C.V.O.1896, I. 422
  Richthoven, baron Oswald, etc., G.C.V.O. 1904, I. 430
  Rickhard. See Ricaut, Riccard
  Rickards, George K., K.C.B.1882, I. 288
  Ricketts, George W., Kt.1825, II. 325
  Ricketts, Henry, K.C.S.I.1866, I. 315
  Ricott. See Ricaut

RIDDELL, RIDDALL, RIDDAL, RIDELL
  Riddell, Alexander O., Kt.1904, II. 418
  Riddell, Henry J., K.H.1832, I. 467

RIDDELL
Riddall, James, Kt.1809, II. 309
Riddell, Peter, Kt.1617, II. 163
Ridell (Bedell), Thomas, Kt.1616, II. 157
Riddal, Thomas, Kt.1639, II. 206
Riddal, William, Kt.1633, II. 201, bis
Riddall, William, K.H.1832, I. 466
Riddell, William, Kt.1633, II. 201
Ridelsdon (Rydelston), Stephen (John), Kt.1604, II. 133
Rider. See Ryder
Ridge, Thomas, Kt.1746, II. 287
RIDGEWAY, RIDGWAY
Ridgeway, Joseph W., K.C.S.I.1885, I. 323; K.C.B.1891, I. 292; G.C.M.G. 1900, I. 346
Ridgeway, Robert, Kt.1608, II. 145
Ridgway, Thomas, Kt.1600, II. 98
Ridgley, Rowland, Kt.1614, II. 154
RIDLEY, RYDDELEY
Ridley, Edward, Kt.1897, II. 399
Ryddeley, Nicholas, Kt.1523, II. 44
Ridley, Thomas, Kt.1619, II. 172
Ridley, William J., K.C.M.G.1868, I. 354
Rigby, Alexander, Kt.1696, II. 269
Rigby, John, Kt.1892, II. 391
Rigden (Rigdon), William, Kt.1603, II. 117
Rigley, Edward, Kt.1523, II. 45
Rigny, Henry G., comte de, K.C.B.1828, I. 230
Riley. See Ryley
Riley. See Ryley
Ripleigh, —, Kt.1347, II. 9
Ripon, marquess of. See Robinson
Risbie. See Reresby
Rison, John de, K.B.1306, I. 120
Ritchie, James T., Kt.1897, II. 401
Ritchie, William J., Kt.1881, II. 372
Rivarola, Claude F., viscount, K.C.H. 1832, I. 458; K.C.M.G.1839, I. 352
Rivaz, Charles M., K.C.S.I.1901, I. 327
Rivers, earl. See Wydville
Rivers, George, Kt.1605, II. 139
Rivers, John, Kt.1574, II. 75
Rivers, Richard de, K.B.1306, I. 121
Rives. See Reeve

Road, Charles C., Kt.1674, II. 249
Robaire (Ribaire), Bartelot de, K.B. (1465), I. 135
Robe, William, K.C.B.1815, I. 223; K.C.H.1817, I. 454
Roberton, James, Kt.1889, II. 386
Roberts, Abraham, K.C.B.1865, I. 249; G.C.B.1873, I. 196
Roberts, Alfred, Kt.1883, II. 375
Roberts, Frederick S., earl Roberts, K.C.B.1879, I. 256; G.C.B.1880, I. 197; K.C.I.E.1887, I. 399; G.C.I.E. 1887, I. 401; G.C.S.I.1893, I. 313; K.P.1897, I. 106; K.G.1901, I. 70
Roberts (Probert), George ap, Kt.1643, II. 216
Roberts, Gabriel, Kt.1678, II. 262
Roberts, Henry G., K.C.B.1859, I. 245
Roberts, John, Kt.1641, II. 211
Roberts, Owen, Kt.1888, II. 384
Roberts, Richard, Kt.1616, II. 160
Roberts, Richard, Kt.1619, II. 175
Roberts, Richard, K.H.1835, I. 471
Roberts, Samuel, Kt.1833, II. 334
Roberts, Thomas, Kt.1603, II. 118, 121
Roberts, Walter, Kt.1624, II. 184
Roberts, William, Kt.1619, II. 173
Roberts, William, Kt.1624, II. 184
Roberts, William, Kt.1885, II. 378
Roberts-Austen, William C., K.C.B.1899, I. 297
Robertson, Daniel B., Kt.1872, II.364; K.C.M.G.1879, I. 361
Robertson, Donald, K.C.S.I.1903, I. 327
Robertson, George S., K.C.S.I.1895, I. 325
Robertson, Henry B., Kt.1890, II. 387
Robertson, John, K.C.M.G.1877, I. 359
Robertson, Robert, Kt.1674, II. 250
Robertson, William T., Kt.1888, II. 384

ROBESSART, ROBSART, ROBSERT
Robsert, —, Kt.1347, II. 9
Robessart, John, K.G.1417, I. 10
Robsart, Lewis, lord Bourchier, K.B. (1418), I. 130; K.G.1421, I. 10
Robinson, Arthur, Kt.1631, II. 199
Robinson, Bryan, Kt.1877, II. 369
Robinson, Christopher, Kt.1809, II. 309

Robinson, Christopher, Kt.1893, footnote, II. 392
Robinson, Frederic L., K.C.B.1897, I. 295
Robinson, Frederick O., earl de Grey, K.C.V.O.(1901), I. 434
Robinson, Frederick P., K.C.B.1815, I. 220; G.C.B.1838, I. 188
Robinson, George F. S., marquess of Ripon, K.G.1869, I. 64; G.C.S.I. 1880, I. 311; Grand Master and Star of India, I. 305
Robinson, Henry, Kt.1614, II. 154
Robinson, Henry, Kt.1677, II. 252
Robinson, Henry, Kt.1845, II. 346
Robinson, Henry, K.C.B.1886, I. 289
Robinson, Henry A., K.C.B.1900, I. 298
Robinson, Hercules G. R., lord Rosmead, Kt.1859, II. 354; K.C.M.G.1869, I. 355; G.C.M.G.1875, I. 337
Robinson, John, Kt.1660, II. 225
Robinson, John, Kt.1696, II. 269
Robinson, John, K.C.M.G.1889, I. 374
Robinson, John C., Kt.1887, II. 381
Robinson, John R., Kt.1893, II. 392
Robinson, Leonard, Kt.1692, II. 267
Robinson (Robertson), Robert, Kt.1675, II. 250
Robinson, Robert S., K.C.B.1868, I. 284
Robinson, Septimus, Kt.1761, II. 290
Robinson, Thomas, lord Grantham, K.B. 1742, I. 169
Robinson, Thomas, Kt.1761, II. 290
Robinson, Thomas, Kt.1894, II. 394
Robinson, Thomas W., Kt.1900, II. 407
Robinson, William, Kt.1633, II. lxii., 201
Robinson, William, Kt.1678, II. 253
Robinson, William, Kt.1702, II. 272
Robinson, William, K.C.M.G.1883, I. 365; G.C.M.G.1897, I. 345
Robinson, William C. F., K.C.M.G.1877, I. 359; G.C.M.G.1887, I. 341
Robinson, William R., K.C.S.I.1875, I. 320
Robinson, William H., Kt.1817, II. 319; K.C.H.1834, I. 460
Robison, John, K.H.1836, I. 475; Kt. 1838, II. 340
Robsart, Robsert. See Robessart
Robyns, John, K.H.1836, I. 474

Roche, Bartholomew La, Kt.1645, II. 219
Roche, Boyle, Kt.1776, II. 295
Roche, David, viscount Roche, Kt.1567, II. 73
Roche, George, Kt.1902, II. 410
Roche, Philip K., Kt.1816, II. 317; K.C.H.1817, I. 454
Roche, Theobald, Kt.1623, II. 183
Rochester, earl of. See Hyde; see Carr
Rochester, Robert, K.B.1553, I. 153; K.G.1557, I. 25
ROCHFORD, ROCHEFORD
Rochford, Bartholomew, K.B.1400, I. 128
Rochford, earl of. See Nassau
Rochfort, John de, Kt.(1336), II. lix.
Rocheford, Sayer de, K.B.1327, I. 124
Rockingham, marquess of. See Watson-Wentworth
Rockly, Thomas, Kt.1603, II. 124
Roclyff, John, Kt.1497, II. 32
Rodd, James R., K.C.M.G.1899, I. 386
Rodd, John T., K.C.B.1832, I. 232
Roden, earl of. See Jocelyn
Röder, Eugen von, K.C.V.O.1902, I. 440
Röder, freiherr Hermann R. von, K.C.V.O.1904, I. 443
Rodes. See Rhodes
Rodger, John P., K.C.M.G.1904, I. 395
Rodley. See Radley
Rodney, Edward, Kt.1614, II. 154
Rodney, George B., lord Rodney, K.B. 1780, I. 173
Rodney (Udney), John, Kt.1497, II. 29
Rodney, John, Kt.1513, II. 42
Rodney, John, Kt.1603, II. 105
Rodney, Richard de, K.B.1316, I. 122
Rodney, Walter, Kt.1513, II. 42
Roe. See Rowe
Roetiers, Gerard, Kt.1723, II. 282
Roger, John, K.B.(1483), I. 140
Rogers, Edward, Kt.1547, II. 60
Rogers, Francis, Kt.1616, II. 159
Rogers, Frederic, lord Blachford, K.C.M.G.1869, I.355; G.C.M.G.1883, I. 339
Rogers, George, Kt.1574, II. 76
Rogers, Hallewell, Kt.1904, II. 419
Rogers, Henry, K.B.1501, I. 145

INDEX

Rogers, John, Kt.1523, II. 45
Rogers, John, Kt.1603, II. 116
Rogers, John, Kt.1662, II. 236
Rogers, John G., K.C.M.G.1898, I. 385
Rogers, Richard, Kt.1576, II. 77
Rogers, Richard, Kt.1621, II. 177
Rogers, Robert G., K.C.B.1899, I. 271
Rogers, Robert H., Kt.1897, II. 401
Rogers, Roger, Kt.1471, II. 16
Rogerson, John, Kt.1693, II. 268
ROKEBY, ROOKBY
  Rokeby, lord. See Montagu
  Rokeby, Robert de, Kt.1347, II. 8
  Rookby (Rockley), Thomas, Kt.1603, II. 124
  Rokeby, Thomas, Kt.1689, II. 265
ROKELEY, ROKEL, ROCKLEY, and see Rokeby
  Rokel, Richard de la, Kt.(1330), I. lix.
  Rokeley, Thomas, Kt.1513, II. 42
Rokewood, Robert, Kt.1624, II. 187
Rolfe, Robert M., Kt.1835, II. 336
ROLLE, ROLLES, ROWLE
  Rolle, Francis, Kt.1665, II. 240
  Rolle (Rowle), Henry, Kt.1603, II. 120, bis
  Rolle (Rolles), John, Kt.1660, II. 231; K.B.1661, I. 166
  Rolles (Rodes), Samuel, Kt.1619, II. 172
Rolleston, John F. L., Kt.1897, II. 400
Rolleston, Ralph de, K.B.1306, I. 114
Rollit, Albert K., Kt.1885, II. 378
Rollock, William, Kt.1644, II. 219
Rolt, John, Kt.1641, II. 210
Rolt, John, K.C.B.1848, I. 238
Rolt, John, Kt.1866, II. 358
Roma, Candiano, count, G.C.M.G.1852, I. 335
Romer, Robert, Kt.1890, II. 387; G.C.B. 1901, I. 215
Romilly, John, Kt.1848, II. 347
Romilly, Samuel, Kt.1806, II. 308
Romney (Rumney), William, Kt.1603, II. 128
Romsey, Walter de, K.B.1306, I. 117
Ronalds, Francis, Kt.1870, II. 362
Roney, Cusac P., Kt.1853, II. 350
Rookby. See Rokeby

Rooke, George, Kt.1693, II. 268
Rooke, Giles, Kt.1793, II. 302
Rooke, Henry W., Kt.1833, II. 334; K.C.H.1834, I. 460
Rooke, William, Kt.1727, II. 283
Roose, Roos. See Rous
Rooth. See Routh
Roper, Anthony, Kt.1603, II. 115
Roper, Christopher, lord Teynham, Kt. 1603, II. 115
Roper, Henry, Kt.1839, II. 341
Roper, John, lord Teynham, Kt.1587, II. 85
Roper, John, lord Teynham, Kt.1603, II. 113; K.B.1616, I. 160
Roper, Thomas, Kt.1603, II. 128
Roper, William, Kt.1603, II. 115
Ropner (E. H. O.), Robert, Kt.1902, II. 413
Ros, John, lord Ros, K.B.1377, I. 126
Ros, lord. See Manners
Ros, lord de. See FitzGerald-de-Ros
Ros, Robert de, K.B.1306, I. 117
Ros, Thomas de, lord Ros, K.B.(1426), I. 131
Ros, William de, lord Ros, Kt.(1346), II. 6
Ros, William de, lord Ros, K.G.1403, I. 8
Roscoe, Henry E., Kt.1884, II. 377
Rose, George, Kt.1831, II. 331
Rose, George H., G.C.H.1819, I. 449; Kt. 1819, II. 321
Rose, Hugh H., lord Strathnairn, K.C.B. 1855, I. 241; G.C.B.1858, I. 192; K.S.I.1861, I. 307; G.C.S.I.1866, I. 308
Rose, John, K.C.B.1838, I. 235
Rose, John, K.C.M.G.1870, I. 355; G.C.M.G.1878, I. 338
Rose, John W., Kt.1790, II. 301
Rose, William, K.C.H.1819, I. 454
Rose, William, K.C.B.1867, I. 284
Rose, William A., Kt.1867, II. 359
Rosebery, earl of. See Primrose
Roselas, William, K.B.1306, I. 122
Rosenstand, Frants W. F., K.C.V.O. 1901, I. 440
Rosmead, lord. See Robinson
Ross, Campbell C. G., K.C.B.1880, I. 257

Ross, David, Kt.1864, II. 357
Ross, David P., Kt.1900, II. 408
Rosse, earl of. See Parsons
Ross, Edward C., Kt.1892, II. 389
Ross, Hew D., K.C.B.1815, I. 226; G.C.B.1855, I. 191
Ross, James C., Kt.1844, II. 345
Ross, James K., K.H.1837, I. 478
Ross, John, K.C.B.1831, I. 231
Ross, John, Kt.1834, II. 335
Ross, John, K.C.B.1881, I. 257; G.C.B. 1891, I. 200
Ross, Patrick, K.C.M.G.1819, I. 350; K.C.H.1834, I. 460; G.C.M.G.1837, I. 334
Ross, Robert, K.H.1832, I. 467
Ross, Robert D., Kt.1886, II. 379
Ross, Thomas, Kt.1839, II. 341
Ross, William, Kt.1513, II. 38
Ross, William, Kt.1633, II. lxiii.
Ross, William C., Kt.1842, II. 344
Ross-of-Bladensburg, John F. G., K.C.B. 1903, I. 301
Rosseter, Edward, Kt.1603, II. 103
Rossiter, Edward, Kt.1660, II. 226
Rosslyn, earl of. See St. Clair-Erskine
Roswell, Henry, Kt.1619, II. 171
Roth, John, Kt.1660, II. 231
Rothe, Robert, Kt.1646, II. 220
Rothenhale, John, K.B.(1413), I. 129
Rotherford, John, Kt.1482, II. 18
Rotherham, John, Kt.1600, II. 98
Rotherham, John, Kt.1688, II. 264
Rotherham, Thomas, Kt.1497, II. 30
Rotherham, Thomas, Kt.1605, II. 136
Rotherham, Thomas, Kt.1608, II. 145
Rothes, earl of. See Leslie
Rothschild, Nathan M., lord Rothschild, G.C.V.O.1902, I. 419
Rottenberg, Francis, baron de, K.C.H. 1817, I. 454; Kt.1818, II. 319
Rotton, John F., Kt.1899, II. 404
Rough, William H., Kt.1837, II. 339
Roult, Thomas, Kt.1682, II. 258

ROUMANIA
Charles of, K.G.1892, I. 69
Ferdinand V. A. M., prince of, G.C.B. 1892, I. 214

ROUS, ROUSE, ROWSE, ROOS, ROOSE
Rowse, Anthony, Kt.1603, II. 123
Roose, David C., Kt.1828, II. 327
Rouse, Francis, Kt.1646, II. 220
Rowse, John, Kt.1607, II. 143
Rous, John de, K.B.1306, I. 121
Rous, John de, K.B.1327, I. 124
Rouse, John, Kt.1605, II. 136
Rous, Philip le, K.B.1306, I. 117
Roos, Thomas, Kt.1461, II. 13
Rouse, Thomas, Kt.1603, II. 105
Rous, William, Kt.1737, II. 285

ROUTH, ROWTH, ROOTH, DE RUDA
Ruda, John de, K.B.1306, I. 117
Rowth, John, Kt.1628, II. 194
Routh, Randolph I., Kt.1841, II. 343; K.C.B.1848, I. 277
Rooth, Richard, Kt.1675, II. 250
Roux, Gabriel le, K.C.V.O.1898, I. 439
Rowan, Charles, K.C.B.1848, I. 278
Rowan, William, K.C.B.1856, I. 243; G.C.B.1865, I. 194

ROWE, ROE, Row
Roe, Charles A., Kt.1897, II. 399
Roe (Rowe), Francis, Kt.1603, II. 128
Roe, Frederick A., Kt.1832, II. 333
Rowe, Henry, Kt.1603, II. 128
Rowe, Henry, Kt.1617, II. 166
Rowe, Joshua, Kt.1832, II. 332
Row, Nicholas, Kt.1625, II. 189
Rowe, Samuel, K.C.M.G.1880, I. 362
Rowe, Thomas, Kt.1569, II. 74
Roe, Thomas, Kt.1603, II. 116
Rowe, Thomas, Kt.1605, II. 137
Roe, Thomas, Kt.1894, II. 393
Rowe, William, Kt.1593, II. 90
Rowe, William, Kt.1629, II. 195
Rowe, William C., Kt.1856, II. 351
Rowland, Samuel, Kt.1790, II. 301
Rowlands, Hugh, K.C.B.1898, I. 270
Rowle. See Rolle
Rowley, Charles, K.C.B.1815, I. 221; G.C.H.1835, I. 453; G.C.B.1840, I. 189
Rowley (Hawley), Henry, Kt.1603, II.117
Rowley, Hercules E., lord Langford, K.C.V.O.(1900), I. 433
Rowley, John, Kt.1661, II. 233

INDEX

Rowley, Josias, K.C.B.1815, I. 221; G.C.M.G.1834, I. 333; G.C.B.1840, I. 189
Rowley, William, K.B.1753, I. 170
Rowse. See Rous
Rowth. See Routh
Rowton, lord. See Lowry-Corry
Roxburgh, Francis, Kt.1882, II. 374
Roxburghe, duke of. See Ker; see Innes-Ker
Roydon. See Rawdon
Royds, John, Kt.1801, II. 306
Roye. See Rey
Royston. See Rawstorne
Rubens, Peter P., Kt.1630, II. 197
Rücker, Arthur W., Kt.1902, II. 412
Ruda, de. See Routh
Ruddall, Richard, Kt.1596, II. 93
Rudsdell, Joseph, K.C.M.G.1832, I. 351
Rudstone, John, Kt.1529, II. 47
RUDYERD, RUDYARD, RUDIARD
Rudyard, —, Kt.1603, II. 126
Rudiard, Benjamin, Kt.1618, II. 168
Rule, William, Kt.1794, II. 302
Rumbold, Horace, K.C.M.G.1886, I. 370; G.C.M.G.1892, I. 343; G.C.B.1897, I. 215
Rumney. See Romney
Rundle, Henry M. L., K.C.B.1898, I. 270; K.C.M.G.1901, I. 389
Runtz, John J., Kt.1903, II. 415
RUSH, RUSHE, RUSSHE
Rush, William B., Kt.1800, II. 305
Rushe, Francis, Kt.1599, II. 95
Rush, John, Kt.1724, II. 283
Russhe, Thomas, Kt.1533, II. 49
RUSSELL, RUSSEL
Russel, —, Kt.1618, II. 168
Russell, Alexander G., lord, K.C.B. 1903, I. 275
Russell, Arthur O. V., lord Ampthill, G.C.I.E.1900, I. 403; G.C.S.I.1904, I. 314
Russell, Baker C., K.C.M.G.1880, I. 362; K.C.B.1882, I. 258; G.C.B. 1900, I. 202
Russell, Charles, lord Russell, Kt.1886, II. 378; G.C.M.G.1893, I. 343
Russell, David, K.C.B.1871, I. 252

RUSSELL
Russell, Edward L., K.C.S.I.1868, I. 318
Russell, Edward R., Kt.1893, II. 392
Russell, Francis, earl of Bedford, K.B. 1547, I. 151; K.G.1564, I. 26
Russell, Francis, Kt.1570, II. 74
Russell, Francis, Kt.1607, II. 141
Russell, Francis, duke of Bedford, K.G.1847, I. 58
Russell, Francis C. H., duke of Bedford, K.G.1880, I. 66
Russel, George (John), Kt.1627, II. 192
Russell, George W., lord, G.C.B.1838, I. 207
Russel, Henry, Kt.1797, II. 304
Russell, Herbrand A., duke of Bedford, K.G.1902, I. 71
Russell, James, Kt.1672, 1676, II. 247, 250
Russell, James, K.C.B.1837, I. 233
Russell, James, Kt.1889, II. 386
Russell, James A., Kt.1894, II. 393
Russell, John, Kt.1529, II. 47
Russell, John, earl of Bedford, Kt. 1523, II. 45; K.G.1539, I. 22
Russell, John, duke of Bedford, K.G. 1749, I. 44
Russell, John, duke of Bedford, Grand Master K.P.1806, I. 93; K.G.1830, I. 54
Russell, John, earl Russell, K.G.1862, I. 61; G.C.M.G.1869, I. 336
Russell, Odo W. L., lord Ampthill, G.C.B.1874, I. 210; G.C.M.G.1879, I. 338
Russell, Peter Nicol, Kt.1904, II. 418
Russell, Thomas, Kt.1549, II. 64
Russell, Thomas, Kt.1603, II. 106
Russell, William, Kt.1579, 1581, II. 80, 81
Russell, William, Kt.1586, II. 84
Russell, William, Kt.1618, II. 168
Russell, William, duke of Bedford, K.B.1626, I. 161; K.G.1672, II. 36
Russell, William, Kt.1679, II. 254
Russell, William H., Kt.1895, II. 396
Russell, William O., Kt.1832, II. 332
Russell, William R., Kt.1902, II. 410

198 INDEX

RUSSELL
 Russell, Wriothesley, duke of Bedford, K.G.1702, I. 40
RUSSIA
 Alexander I. of, K.G.1813, I. 51
 Alexander II. of, K.G.1867, I 64
 Alexander III. of, K.G.1881, I. 66
 Michael Alexandrowich, grand duke of, G.C.B.1901, I. 215; K.G.1902, I. 71
 Michael Michaelowitch, grand duke of, G.C.V.O.1901, I. 424
 Nicholas I. of, K.G.1827, I. 53
 Nicholas II. of, K.G.1893, I. 69; Victoria Chain 1904, I. 416
 Serge Alexandrovitch, grand duke of, G.C.B.1887, I. 212
 Wladimir, grand duke of, G.C.V.O. 1903, I. 428
RUTHIN, RUTHYN
 Ruthyn, John G. de, K.G.1436, I. 11
 Ruthin, Patrick (Palmer), Kt.1627, II. 193
Ruthven, Thomas, Kt.1633, II. lxiii.
Rutland, duke and earl of. See Manners
Rutledge, Arthur, Kt.1902, II. 410
Rutzen, Albert de, Kt.1901, II. 409
Ruyter, Angell de, Kt.1675, II. 250
Ryall. See Riall
Ryan, Charles L., K.C.B.1887, I. 290
Ryan, Edward, Kt.1826, II. 326
Ryan, Thomas, K.H.1835, I. 472
Rybande, John, Kt.1547, II. 63
Rycroft, Henry, Kt.1816, II. 316
RYDER, RIDER
 Ryder, Alfred P., K.C.B.1884, I. 259
 Rider, Barnham, Kt.1714, II. 279
 Ryder, Dudley, Kt.1740, II. 285
 Ryder, Dudley, earl of Harrowby, K.G. 1859, I. 60
 Ryder, George L., K.C.B.1901, I. 299
 Rider, Ralph, K.B.(1494), I. 144
 Ryder, Rauf, Kt.1497, II. 31
 Ryder, Robert, Kt.1482, II. 20
 Ryder (Rider), Thomas, Kt.1744, II. 287
 Ryder, William, Kt.1601, II. 99
 Ryder, William, Kt.1661, II. 233
Rye, Nicholas de, K.B.1306, I. 120

Ryley (Riley), Philip, Kt.1728, II. 284
Rymer, Joseph S., Kt.1901, II. 408
Rypsford, Henry de, K.B.1306, I. 118
Ryseley, John, Kt.1485, II. 22
Ryt (Rit), William van der, Kt.1612, II. 152
Ryves, Ryve. See Reeve
RYVET, REVET
 Ryvet (Ryve), —, Kt.1580, II. 80
 Revet, Henry, Kt.1578, II. 79

S

Saadut, Ali Khan, K.C.S.I.1866, I. 317
Sabcottes (Sapcots), Edward, Kt.1547, II. 59
Sabcotts (Sappacottis), John, Kt.1487, II. 25
Sabine, Edward, K.C.B.1869, I. 284
Sabine, John, Kt.1671, II. 245
Sacheverell, Henry, Kt.1513, II. 36
Sacheverell, Ric, Kt.1513, II. 39
Sacheverell. See Sachville
Sackford. See Seckford
SACKVILLE, SACKVEYLE, SACKVIL, SAKEVILLE, SACKVILL
 Sackville, Andreas de, K.B.1306, I. 115
 Sackville, Charles, earl of Dorset, K.G.1692, I. 39
 Sackville, Edward, earl of Dorset, K.B.1616, I. 159 ;K.G.1625, I. 31
 Sackveyle (Sacheverell), Henry, K.B. 1509, I. 149
 Sackvil, John, Kt.1628, II. 194
 Sackville, John, duke of Dorset, K.G. 1788, I. 48
 Sackville, Lionel, duke of Dorset, K.G.1714, I. 41
 Sakeville, Richard, Kt.1549, II. 64
 Sackville, Thomas, earl of Dorset, Kt.1567, II. 73; K.G.1589, I. 28
 Sackvill, Thomas, Kt.1622, II. 179
 Sackville, Thomas, K.B.1625, I. 162
 Sackvill, William, Kt.1589, II. 87
 Sackville-Germaine, Charles, duke of Dorset, K.G.1826, I. 53
 Sackville-West, Charles R., earl de la Warr, K.C.B.1871, I. 253

INDEX

SACKVILLE-WEST
Sackville-West, Lionel, lord Sackville, K.C.M.G. 1885, I. 367; G.C.M.G.1888, I. 341
Sadyngton, Rob de, Kt.(1336), II. 5
Sadler, James H., K.C.M.G.1899, I. 386
Sadler, Rauf, Kt.1538, II. 51; Kt.1547, II. 61
Sadler, Thomas, Kt.1623, II. 182
Sadley, Thomas S., Kt.1849, II. 347
Safvet, Pasha, G.C.S.I.1878, I. 311
Sailana, Jaswant Singh, of, K.C.I.E. 1904, I. 412
Saint, Ailmer, K.B.(1400), I. 129
St. Albans, duke of. See Beauclerk
St. Albans, earl of. See Bourke; see Jermyn
St. Amand, Almaric de, K.B.1400, I. 128
St. Amand, lord. See Beauchamp
St. Aubyn, John de, Kt.(1330), II. lix.
St. Barbe, Henry, Kt.1604, II. 130
ST. CLAIR, SINCLAIR, ST. CLARE, ST. CLERE, ST. CLEER, SEINTCLERE
St. Cleer, —, Kt.1625, II. 187
Sinclair, Edward B., Kt.1880, II. 372
St. Clere, James, Kt.1624, II. 187
Seintclere, John, Kt.1533, II. 49
St. Clare, Ralph, K.B.1626, I. 162
St. Clair, Thomas S., K.H.1833, I. 468
St. Clere, William, Kt.1610, II. 149
Sinclair, William J., Kt.1904, II. 419
St. Clair-Erskine, James, earl of Rosslyn, G.C.B.1820, I. 185
St. Clare. See St. Clair
St. Clere. See St. Clair
St. George, George, Kt.1627, II. 192
St. George, George, Kt.1661, II. 235
St. George, Henry, Kt.1627, II. 193
St. George, Henry, Kt.1677, II. 252
St. George, John, K.C.B.1869, I. 252; G.C.B.1889, I. 199
St. George, Oliver, Kt.1659, II. 224, 230
St. George, Richard, Kt.1616, II. 159
St. George, Thomas, Kt.1669, II. 243
St. George, Thomas B., K.C.H.1835, I. 460; Kt.1835, II. 335
St. Germans, earl of. See Eliot

St. Helens, lord. See Fitzherbert
St. John, Alexander, Kt.1608, II. 146
St. John, Anthony, Kt.1608, II. 146
St. John, Beauchamp, Kt.1619, II. 173
St. John, Frederick R., K.C.M.G.1901, I. 391
St. John, Henry, Kt.1760, II. 290
St. John, Henry, Kt.1619, II. 173
St. John, John, K.B.(1489), I. 143
Seint John, John, Kt.1497, II. 29
St. John, John, Kt.1609, II. 147
Saint John, lord. See Paulet
St. John, Oliver, Kt.1600, II. 98
St. John, Oliver, earl of Bolingbroke, K.B.1610, I. 158
St. John, Oliver, lord St. John, K.B. 1626, I. 161
St. John, Oliver B. C., K.C.S.I.1882, I. 322
St. John, Pawlet, K.B.1626, I. 161
St. John, Robert W., K.H.1833, I. 469
St. John, Rowland, K.B.1616, I. 160
St. John, Spenser B., K.C.M.G.1881, I. 363; G.C.M.G.1894, I. 343
St. John, William, Kt.1607, II. 144
St. Lawrence, Christopher, Kt.1570, II. 74
St. Lawrence, Nicholas, lord Howth, Kt.1494, II. 28
St. Lawrence, Nicholas, Kt.1588, II. 86
St. Lawrence, Thomas, earl Howth, K.P. 1835, I. 100
St. Lawrence, William U. T., earl of Howth, K.P.1884, I. 104
ST. LEGER, SAINTLEGER, SELLENGER, SENTLEGER
St. Leger, Anthony, K.G.1544, I. 23
St. Leger, Anthony, Kt.1593, II. 90
St. Leger, Anthony, Kt.1627, II. 193
St. Leger (Sellenger), Anthony, Kt. 1642, II. 213
Saintleger, George, Kt.1513, II. 41
St. Leger, George, Kt.1690, II. 266
Sentleger, John, Kt.1549, II. 65
St. Leger, John, Kt.1701, II. 272
St. Leger, Thomas, K.B.1748, I. 138
St. Leger, Warham, Kt.1565, II. 71
St. Leger, Warham, Kt.1597, II. 94
St. Leger, Warham, Kt.1608, II. 145

INDEX

St. Leger
   St. Leger, William, Kt.1618, II. 168

St. Loe, Saintloe, Sentlowe, Sandelowe
   St. Low (Sandelowe), James, Kt.1619, II. 172
   St. Loe, John, Kt.1471, II. 15
   Saintloe, John, Kt.1549, II. 64
   St. Loe, John, Kt.1666, II. 242
   Sentlowe, William, Kt.1551, II. 65
Saint-Obin, Loeis de, Kt.(1380), II. 10
Sainctpoll (St. Paule, Sampole), —, Kt. 1580, II. 80
St. Peter, Urion de, K.B.1306, I. 114
St. Quintin, William, Kt.1460, II. 12
Seint Quintin, William, Kt.1545, II. 57
St. Vincent, earl of. See Jervis
Salar Jung, K.C.S.I.1866, I. 315; G.C.S.I.1870, I. 310
Salar Jung, K.C.I.E.1887, I. 400
Sale, Robert H., K.C.B.1839, I. 236; G.C.B.1842, I. 189
Sale-Hill, Rowley S., K.C.B.1902, I. 274
Salinis, Stephen de, K.B.1249, I. 109
Salisbury, earl of. See Montacute; see Nevill; see Cecil
Salisbury, marquess of. See Cecil; see Gascoyne-Cecil
Salisbury, John de, K.B.1306, I. 121
Salisbury, John, Kt.1547, II. 60
Salisbury, Robert, Kt.1593, II. 90
Salisbury, Thomas, Kt.1497, II. 30
Salkeld, Francis, Kt.1660, II. 228
Salkyld, Richard, Kt.1487, II. 26
Sall, William, K.H.1837, I. 476
Salles, comte de, G.C.B.1856, I. 192
Salmon, James, Kt.1878, II. 370
Salmon, Nowell, K.C.B.1887, I. 262; G.C.B.1897, I. 202
Salmond, William, K.C.B.1902, I. 275
Salomon, Demetrio, count, G.C.M.G. 1850, I. 335
Salomons, Julian E., Kt.1891, II. 388
Salter, Edward, Kt.1621, II. 177
Salter, John, Kt.1735, II. 284
Salter, Nicholas, Kt.1617, II. 161
Salter, William, Kt.1628, II. 195

Saltingstone, Saltonstall, Saltingstowe, Saltingstall
   Saltingston, John, Kt.1633, II. 201
   Saltonstall (Saltingstowe), Peter, Kt. 1605, II. 139
   Saltingstall (Saltingstone), Richard, Kt.1597, II. 94
   Saltonstall, Richard, Kt.1603, II. 122
   Saltonstall (Saltingstall, Saltinstone), Richard, Kt.1617, II. 167, 170
   Saltonstall (Saltingston), Thomas (Richard), Kt.1603, II. 115
Saltoun, lord. See Fraser
Salusbury, J. S. P., Kt.1817, II. 319
Salusbury, Thomas, Kt.1751, II. 288
Salveyn, Salvayn, Salveine
   Salveyn (Talboyn), Francys, Kt.1547, II. 61
   Salveyn, John, Kt.1482, II. 21
   Salvayn, Rauf, Kt.1513, II. 38
   Salveine, Roger, K.B.(1418), I. 130
Sambach, William, Kt.1639, II. 207
Sambie, John, Kt.1347, II. 7
Samborne, Bartholomew, Kt.1603, II. 124
Samborne, Henry, Kt.1609, II. 147
Sambrooke, Jeremiah, Kt.1682, II. 257
Samford (Sandford), Thomas, Kt.1603, II. 113
Samnes, Sams, Sames, and see Sandys
   Sams (Samnes), Gerrard, Kt.1616, II. 158
   Sames, John, Kt.1599, II. 97
Sampole. See Sainctpoll
Sampson, Thomas, K.B.1501, I. 147
Samuel, Samwell
   Samuel, Harry S., Kt.1903, II. 416
   Samwell (Cammell, Samrill, Lamvill), John, Kt.1615, II. 156
   Samuel, Marcus, Kt.1898, II. 403
   Samwell (Samuel), Richard, Kt.1617, II. 166
   Samuel, Saul, K.C.M.G.1882, I. 364
   Samuel, William, Kt.1603, II. 124
Sandelowe. See St. Loe
Sandelowe. See St. Loe
Sandeman, Robert, K.C.S.I.1879, I. 322
Sanders. See Saunders
Sanderson. See Saunderson

Sandes. See Sandys
SANDFORD, SANDFORDE, SANDIFORD, and see Samford
Sandforde, Bryan, Kt.1497, II. 30
Sandford, Daniel K., Kt.1830, II. 329
Sandford, Francis R. J., lord Sandford, Kt.1863, II. 356; K.C.B.1879, I. 286
Sandford, Herbert B., Kt.1877, II. 369; K.C.M.G.1889, I. 373
Sandford, Richard de, Kt.1403, II. 11
Sandford, Richard, Kt.1616, II. 160
Sandhurst, lord. See Mansfield
Sandison, Alfred, Kt.1878, II. 370
Sands. See Sandys
Sandwich, earl of. See Montagu
Sandwich, John de, K.B.1306, I. 116
Sandy, alias Napper, Robert, Kt.1612, II. 152
SANDYS, SANDES, SAUNDES, SANDS, SONDS, SAMS, SANDE
Sandes, Edwin, Kt.1599, II. 98
Sandes, Edwin, Kt.1603, II. 106
Sandes, Edwin, Kt.1617, II. 162
Sandes, George, Kt.1626, II. 163
Saundes, John, Kt.1471, II. 15
Sandes (Sams, Sands), John, Kt.1603, II. 111
Sandes, Martin, Kt.1644, II. 217
Sands (Sonds), Michill, Kt.1598, II. 95
Sands, Miles, Kt.1603, II. 106
Sandes, Miles, Kt.1619, II. 172
Sands (Sandys), Miles, Kt.1626, II. 191
Sandes, Richard, Kt.1523, II. 45
Sands, Richard (Walter), Kt.1603, II. 106
Sandys, Richard, Kt.1660, II. 230
Sands, Robert, Kt.1626, II. 191
Sandes, Samuel, Kt.1603, II. 115
Sandes (Sande), Thomas (Anthony), Kt.1583, II. 81
Sandes, Walter, Kt.1591, II. 88
Sandes (Sandalle), William, Kt.1471, II. 15
Sandes, William, Kt.1487, II. 24
Sandys, William, lord Sandys, K.G. 1518, I. 21
Sandys, Windsor E. B., Kt.1825, II. 325

Sanky, Hierome, Kt.1658, II. 224
Sankey, Richard H., K.C.B.1892, I. 292
Santiago del Castello, James de, Kt. 1689, II. 265
Sarawan, Asad Khan, of, K.C.I.E.1893, I. 408
Sargent, Charles, Kt.1860, II. 355
Sargeaunt, William C., K.C.M.G.1882, I. 365
Sargood, Frederick T., K.C.M.G.1890, I. 375
Sarle, Allen L., Kt.1896, II. 398
Sarnesfeld, Nicholas, K.G.1386, I. 6
Sarsfeild, Dominick, Kt.1605, II. 136
Sarsfield, James, Kt. Jacobite 1709, footnote, II. 266
Sarsfield, William, Kt.1566, II. 72
Sarsfield, William, Kt.1617, II. 167
Sartorius, George R., Kt.1841, II. 344; K.C.B.1865, I. 249; G.C.B.1880, I. 197
Sasiola, Gefferey de, Kt.1483, II. 21
Sassoon, Albert A. D., Kt.1872, II. 364
Satow, Ernest M., K.C.M.G.1895, I. 380; G.C.M.G.1902, I. 348
Saumarez, James, lord de Saumarez, Kt. 1793, II. 302; K.B.1801, I. 175; G.C.B.1815, I. 180
Saumarez, Thomas, Kt.1795, II. 302

SAUNDERS, SANDERS
Saunders, Charles, K.B.1761, I. 170
Saunders, Edmund, Kt.1683, II. 258
Saunders, Edward, Kt.1555, II. 69
Saunders, Edwin, Kt.1883, II. 376
Saunders, Frederick R., K.C.M.G.1897, I. 382
Saunders, George, Kt.1720, II. 282
Saunders, John, Kt.1624, II. 184
Saunders, Matthew, Kt.1617, II. 165
Sanders, Ralph, Kt.1617, II. 163
Saunders(Sanders), Richard (Nicholas), Kt.1603, II. 107
Saunders, Richard, Kt.1603, II. 112
Saunders, Sidney S., Kt.1873, II. 365
Saunders, Thomas, Kt.1549, II. 65
Sanders, Thomas, Kt.1623, II. 181
Saunders, Thomas, Kt.1714, II. 280
Sanders, William, Kt.1608, II. 145

SAUNDERS
Saunders-Dundas, Robert, viscount Melville, K.T.1821, I. 81
SAUNDERSON, SANDERSON
Sanderson (Saunderson), James, Kt. 1786, II. 299
Sanderson, Nicholas, Kt.1603, II. 103
Sanderson, Percy, K.C.M.G.1899, I. 387
Sanderson, Thomas H., K.C.M.G.1887, I. 372; K.C.B.1893, I. 293; G.C.B. 1900, I. 215
Saunderson, William, Kt.1625, II. 189
Sanderson, William, Kt.1714, II. 279
Saundes. See Sandys
Saussaye, Richard la, Kt.1841, II. 344
Sausse, Matthew R., Kt.1856, II. 351
Sauston, William de, K.B.1306, I. 120
SAVAGE, SAUVAGE
Savage, —, Kt.1492, II. 27
Savage, Arthur, Kt.1596, II. 92
Savage, Edmond, Kt.1544, II. 56
Savage, Edward, Kt.1497, II. 31
Savage, Edward, Kt.1639, II. 206
Savage, George, Kt.1681, II. 256
Sauvage, Humfrey, Kt.1487, II. 25
Savage, John, K.B.1306, I. 116
Savage, John, K.B.(1465), I. 135; K.G.1488, I. 18
Savage, John, Kt.1471, II. 15
Savage, John, Kt.1482, II. 17
Savage, John (Edward), Kt.1497, II. 29
Savage, John, Kt.1513, II. 39
Savage, John, Kt.1547, II. 60
Savage, John, Kt.1599, II. 98
Savage, John, Kt.1615, II. 155
Savage, John, Kt.1624, II. 186
Savage, John, Kt.1872, II. 364
Savage, John B., K.C.H.1833, I. 459; Kt.1833, II. 333; K.C.B.1839, I. 236
Savage, Thomas, Kt.1601, II. 99
Savage, Thomas, Kt.1617, II. 163
Savage, Thomas, Kt.1621, II. 177
Savage, William, Kt.1721, II. 282
SAVILE, SAVILL, SAVELL, SAVYLE
Savell, George, Kt.1587, II. 85
Savile, George, Kt.1603, II. 109

SAVELL
Savell, Henry, K.B.1533, I. 150
Savyle, Henry, Kt.1603, II. 116
Savile, Henry, Kt.1604, II. 135
Savell, John, Kt.1482, II. 20
Savile John, Kt.1603, II. 114
Savill, John, Kt.1627, II. 192
Savile, John, earl of Mexborough, K.B.1749, I. 169
Savile, John, baron Savile, K.C.V.O. (1904), I. 437
Savell, Robert, Kt.1583, II. 82
Savile, Thomas, Kt.1617, II. 161
Sawyer, Edmond, Kt.1625, II. 188
Sawyer, Herbert, K.C.B.1815, I. 218
Sawyer, James, Kt.1885, II. 378
Sawyer, Robert, Kt.1677, II. 252
Sawyer, William P., Kt.1904, II. 418
SAXE-COBURG-GOTHA
Albert, prince Consort. See Albert
Alfred of, K.G.1863, I. 62; K.T.1864, I. 85; G.C.M.G. 1869, I. 336; G.C.S.I.1870, I. 309; K.P.1880, I. 154; K.C.B.1886, I. 259; G.C.I.E. 1887, I. 401; G.C.B.1889, I. 199; G.C.V.O.1899, I. 418
Prince Alfred of, K.G.1894, I. 69
Charles Edward, duke of, G.C.V.O. 1901, I. 424; K.G.1902, I. 72
Ernest I., duke of, K.G.1838, I. 55
Ernest II., duke of, K.G.1844, I. 57
Prince Philippe of, G.C.B.1885, I. 212
SAXE-GOTHA
Ernest L., duke of, K.G.1790, I. 48
Frederick III., duke of, K.G.1741, I. 44
SAXE-COBURG-SAALFELD
Ferdinand G. A., prince of, G.C.B. 1839, I. 188
SAXE-MEININGEN
Bernard E. F., duke of, K.G.1830, I. 54
Bernard F. W. A. G., prince of, G.C.B.1887, I. 212
SAXE-WEIMAR
Bernard, duke of, G.C.B.1830, I. 186

SAXE-WEIMAR
  Prince Edward of, K.C.B.1881, I. 257; G.C.B.1887, I. 199; K.P.1890, I. 105; G.C.V.O.1901, I. 419
SAXE-WEISSENFELS
  John A., duke of, K.G.1745, I. 44
SAXONY, SAXE
  Albert of, K.G.1882, I. 66
  Frederick A. II. of, K.G.1842, I. 56
  John G. II. of, K.G.1668, I. 36
  John G. IV., duke of, K.G.1692, I. 39
SAVOY
  Emanuel P., duke of, K.G.1554, I. 25
Say, Geoffrey de, K.B.1306, I. 112
Say. John, K.B.(1465), I. 135
Say, William, K.B.(1483), I. 140, 141
Sayer. See Seyer
SCALES, SKALE
  Scales, lord. See Wydville
  Scales, Robert de, K.B.1306, I. 113, 120
  Scales, Thomas de, lord Scales, K.G. 1425, I. 10
Scanlen, Thomas C., K.C.M.G.1884, I. 366
Scarborough, Charles, Kt.1669, II. 243
Scarborough, earl of. See Lumley; see Lumley-Saunderson
SCARDEBURGH, SCORESBURGH
  Scardeburgh, Robert de, K.B.1333, I. 125
  Scoresburgh, Robert de, K.B.1332, I. 125
SCARGIL, SKARGYLL
  Skargyll, Robert, Kt.1527, II. 46
  Scargil, Warin de, K.B.1306, I. 119
  Skargill, William, Kt.1497, II. 32
Scarisbrick, Charles, Kt.1903, II. 416
Scarlett, James, Kt.1827, II. 326
Scarlett, James Y., K.C.B.1855, I. 240; G.C.B.1869, I. 195
Scarlett, William A., Kt.1829, II. 328
Scawen, Thomas, Kt.1714, II. 279
Scawen, William, Kt.1692, II. 267
Scharf, George, K.C.B.1895, I. 294
Schaub, Luke, Kt.1720, II. 282
SCHAUMBURG-LIPPE
  prince Adolphe George of, G.C.B.1892, I. 213

SCHLESWIG-HOLSTEIN
  prince Albert of, G.C.B.1900, I. 215; G.C.V.O.1897, I. 417
  prince Christian of, K.G.1866, I. 63; G.C.V.O.1901, I. 418; Victorian Chain 1902, I. 416
  prince Christian Victor of, G.C.B.1890, I. 213; G.C.V.O.1898, I. 418
SCHLESWIG-HOLSTEIN-SONDERBURG-GLÜCKSBURG
  prince Albert Christian of, G.C.V.O. 1904, I. 429
  prince John of, G.C.V.O.1901, I. 425
Schmiedern, Maj., K.H.1821, I. 464
Schneider, John W., K.C.B.1889, I. 262
Schœdde, James H., K.C.B.1842, I. 237
Schofield, Henry, Kt.1876, II. 368
Scholl, Friedrich von, K.C.V.O.1899, I. 439
Schomberg, Alexander, Kt.1776, II. 295
Schomberg, Charles M., K.C.H.1832, I. 459
Schomberg, Frederick A. de, duke of Schomberg, K.G.1689, I. 38
Schomberg, George A., K.C.B.1896, I. 266
Schomberg, Meinhardt, duke of Schomberg, K.G.1703, I. 40
Schomburgh, Robert, Kt.1844, II. 346
Schortales. See Shortales
Schotte, Jacob de, Kt.1621, II. 176
Schreibershofer, Maximilian von, K.C.B. 1843, I. 237
Schultz, John C., K.C.M.G.1895, I. 380
Schwartzenburg, prince Karl Philip, G.C.B.1815, I. 183
Scoble, Andrew R., K.C.S.I.1890, I. 324
Scordeck (Schoordick), James, Kt.1614, II. 154, bis
Scoresburgh. See Scardeburgh
Scory, Edmond, Kt.1618, II. 169
Scory (Story), John, Kt.1604, II. 134
Scot. See Scott
Scotland, Alexander III. of, K.B.1252, I. 110
Scotland, Colley H., Kt.1861, II. 356
SCOTT, SCOT, SCOTTE
  Scott, Benjamin, Kt.1904, II. 418
  Scott, Buchanan, K.C.I.E.1904, I. 412

INDEX

Scott

Scott, Charles S., K.C.M.G.1896, I. 381; G.C.M.G.1899, I. 346; G.C.B.1899, I. 215

Scott, David, K.H.1823, I. 464
Scot, Edmund, Kt.1630, II. 197
Scott, Edward, K.B.1626, II. 162
Scott, Francis, duke of Buccleuch, K.T.1725, I. 77
Scott, Francis C., K.C.M.G.1892, I. 378; K.C.B.1896, I. 266
Scott, George, K.C.B.1831, I. 231
Scott, George G., Kt.1872, II. 364
Scott, Gideon, Kt.1660, II. 231
Scott, Henry, duke of Buccleuch, K.T. 1767, I. 79; K.G.1794, I. 49
Scott, Henry, earl of Deloraine, K.B. 1725, I. 167
Scott, Henry H., Kt.1902, II. 413
Scott, Hopton, Kt.1782, II. 297
Scott, Hopton S., K.C.B.1831, I. 232
Scot, James (Thomas), Kt.1625, II. 189
Scott, James, duke of Buccleuch, K.G. 1663, I. 36
Scott, James, earl of Dalkeith, K.T. 1704, I. 76
Scott, James, K.C.B.1862, I. 248
Scott, James G., K.C.I.E.1901, I. 410
Scott, John, Kt.1461, II. 13
Scott, John, Kt.1588, II. 87
Scott, John, Kt.1708, II. 276
Scott, John, Kt.1788, II. 300
Scott, John, K.C.B.1865, I. 249
Scott, John, K.C.M.G.1874, I. 357
Scott, John, K.C.M.G.1894, I. 379
Scott, John H., Kt.1892, II. 390
Scott, Peter, Kt.1621, II. 176
Scotte, Reignold, Kt.1542, II. 53
Scott, Richard, Kt.1635, II. 203
Scott, Robert, Kt.1782, II. 297
Scot, Robert, K.C.B.1831, I. 232
Scot, Stephen, Kt.1630, II. 198
Scott, Thomas, Kt.1570, II. 75
Scott, Walter, Kt.1618, II. 167
Scott, Walter, Kt.1651, II. 222
Scott, William, K.B.(1489), I. 143
Scott, William, Kt.1788, II. 300
Scott-Gatty, Alfred S., Kt.1904, II. 418

Scott

Scott-Moncrieff, Colin C., K.C.M.G. 1887, I. 372
Scotter, Charles, Kt.1895, II. 395
Scovell, George, K.C.B.1815, I. 225; G.C.B.1860, I. 193
Scratchley, Peter H., K.C.M.G.1885, I. 367
Scrimshire, Thomas, Kt.1619, II. 173

Scriven, Scryven

Scriven, Nicholas, Kt.1603, II. 100
Scryven, Reynold (Reginald), Kt.1603, II. 124
Scriven, Thomas, Kt.1642, II. 214
Scroop. See Scrope

Scrope, Scroop, Le Scrope, Scroope

Scroop, Adrian, Kt.1603, II. 112
Scroope, Adrian, K.B.1661, I. 165
Scrope, Henry le, lord Scrope, K.G. 1409, I. 9
Scroope, Henry, Kt.1497, II. 31
Scrope, Henry le, lord Scrope, K.B. 1509, I. 148
Scrope, Henry, lord Scrope, K.B.1547, I. 151; K.G.1584, I. 28
Scroop, Jervis, Kt.1630, II. 198
Scrope, John le, lord Scrope, K.G. 1463, I. 14
Scrope, John, K.B.1501, I. 145
Scroope, John, Kt.1516, II. 43
Scrope, Ralph, lord, Kt.1513, II. 37
Scroop, Thomas, lord, Kt.1482, II. 19
Scroope Thomas, lord Scrope, Kt. 1585, II. 83; K.G.1599, I. 29
Scrope, William Le, earl of Wiltshire, K.G.1394, I. 6
Scroggs, William, Kt.1681, II. 255
Scryven. See Scriven
Scudamore, Barnaby, Kt.1645, II. 220
Scudamore, Charles, Kt.1829, II. 328
Scudamore, Clement, Kt.1605, II. 137
Scudamore, Clement, Kt.1624, II. 185
Scudamore, John, Kt.1596, II. 92
Scudamore, John, Kt.1643, II. 215
Scudamore, John, K.B.1661, I. 164
Scudamore, Philip, Kt.1603, II. 115
Scudamore, Walter de, K.B.1306, I. 115
Sculton, Richard de, K.B.1306, I. 117
Scures, John de, Kt.1347, II. 9

INDEX

Seabridge. See Sebright
Seafield, earl of. See Ogilvy; see Ogilvie-Grant
Seaforth, earl of. See Mackenzie
Sealy, John, K.C.M.G.1874, I. 357
Seaman, Peter, Kt.1712, II. 277
Seamore. See Seymour
Searle, Francis, Kt.1803, II. 307
Seaton. See Seton
Seaward (Seyward), Edward, Kt.1696, II. 269
SEBRIGHT, SEABRIDGE
Sebright, Charles, baron d' Everton, K.C.M.G.1864, I. 354
Seabridge (Sebright), Edward, Kt. 1627, II. 191
Seccombe, Thomas L., K.C.S.I.1877, I. 321; G.C.I.E.1892, I. 402
Seckendorff, baron Albert von, K.C.V.O. 1897, I. 438; G.C.V.O.1904, I. 430
Seckendorff, count Götz B., G.C.V.O. 1897, I. 422
Seckford (Sackford), Henry, Kt.1603, II. 106
Seckford (Sackford), Thomas, Kt.1608, II. 144
SEDLEY, SYDLEY, SIDLEY, SYDLY,, and see Sidney
Sedley, Charles, Kt.1689, II. 264
Sydley (Sedley), Isaak, Kt.1606, II. 141
Sedley (Sidley), John, Kt.1616, II. 158
Sydly, Ralphe, Kt.1603, II. 129
Sidley (Sydley), William, Kt.1605, II. 139
See, John, K.C.M.G.1902, I. 392
Seeley, John R., K.C.M.G.1894, I. 379
Sefton, earl of. See Molyneux
Segar, William, Kt.1616, II. 159
Segurus, kinsman to Henry III., K.B. 1240, I. 109
Selangore, Abdul S., sultan of, K.C.M.G. 1886, I. 369
SELBY, SELBIE, SELBEE
Selby, George, Kt.1603, II. 115, 125
Selby, Henry, Kt.1685, II. 261
Selby, John, Kt.1582, II. 81
Selby, John, Kt.1605, II. 137

SELBY
Selby, William, Kt.1603, II. 100, 110
Selbie, William, Kt.1613, II. 153
Selby, William, Kt.1639, II. 206
Selfe, William L., Kt.1897, II. 401
Sellenger. See St. Leger
Selves, Justin de, G.C.V.O.1903, I. 427
SELWYN, SELWIN
Selwyn, Charles J., Kt.1867, II. 359
Selwyn, Edward, Kt.1683, II. 258
Selwin, Nicholas, Kt.1633, II. 201
Semon, Felix, Kt.1897, II. 401
Sempill, William, Kt.1633, II. lxiii..
Sendall, Walter J., K.C.M.G.1889, I. 374; G.C.M.G.1899, I. 346
Senden-Bibran, baron Gustav von, G.C.V.O.1899, I. 423
Senhouse, Humphrey Le F., K.C.H.1832, I. 459; Kt.1834, II. 335
Senhouse, Joseph, Kt.1783, II. 297
Sennyle, Simon de, Kt.1347, II. 8
Sentleger. See St. Leger
Sentlowe. See St. Loe
Seppings, Robert, Kt.1819, II. 320
Septuans, Thomas, Kt.1603, II. 118
Serge (Seige), Alonnce de Ville, Kt.1547, II. 62
Servin, Nicholas, Kt.1633, II. 201
Serpa, Pimentel F. E. de, K.C.V.O.1903, I. 441
SETON, SEATON
Seton, Alexander, Kt.1633, I. lxiii., bis
Seton, Alexander, Kt.1651, II. 222
Settone, George, Kt.1650, II. 222
Seaton, Henry, K.C.H.1832, I. 458
Seton, Henry W., Kt.1838, II. 340
Seton, John, Kt.1633, I. lxii.
Seaton, lord. See Colborne
Seton, Tho, Kt.1633, I. lxiii.
Seaton, Thomas, K.C.B.1858, I. 245
Seton-Karr, Henry, Kt.1902, II. 414
Settle, Henry H., K.C.B.1900, I. 272
Sevestre, Thomas, Kt.1810, II. 310
Sewell, John, Kt.1815, II. 316
Sewell, Thomas,, Kt.1764, II. 292
Sewell, William H., K.C.B.1861, I. 246
Sewster, Robert, Kt.1664, II. 239
Sexton, George, Kt.1616, II. 159
Sexton, Richard, Kt.1603, II. 102

INDEX

Sexton, Robert, Kt.1892, II. 390
SEYER, SAYER
  Sayer, George, Kt.1607, II. 142
  Sayer, George, Kt.1640, II. 207
  Sayer, John, Kt.1649, II. 222
  Seyer, William, Kt.1798, II. 304
SEYMOUR, SEYMORE, SEYMER, SEAMORE, SEAMOR, SEIMORE
  Seymour, Charles, duke of Somerset, K.G.1684, I. 37
  Seymour, Edward, duke of Somerset, Kt.1523, II. 45; K.G.1541, I. 23; K.B.1547, I. 150
  Seymour, lord Edward, Kt.1547, II. 61
  Seymour, Edward, Kt.1603, II. 110
  Seymour, Edward, lord Beauchamp, K.B.1616, I. 159
  Seymour, Edward A., duke of Somerset, K.G.1837, I. 55
  Seymour, Edward A., duke of Somerset, K.G.1862, I. 61
  Seymour, Edward H., K.C.B.1897, I. 268; G.C.B.1900, I. 203; Kt.1613, II. 153
  Seymour, Francis, K.C.B.1875, I. 255
  Seymour, Francis H. G., marquess of Hertford, G.C.B.1879, I. 210
  Seymour, Frederick B. P., lord Alcester, K.C.B.1877, I. 255; G.C.B. 1881, I. 198
  Seymour, George F., K.C.H.1831, I. 456; Kt.1831, II. 330; G.C.H.1834, I. 452; K.C.B.1852, I. 239; G.C.B. 1860, I. 193
  Seymour, George H., K.C.H.1832, I. 458; G.C.H.1836, I. 453; Kt.1836, II. 337; G.C.B.1847, I. 207
  Seymour, Henry, K.B.1547, I. 151
  Seymour, Henry, lord Seymour, Kt. 1645, II. 219
  Seymour, Horace A. D., K.C.B.1902, I. 300
  Seymour, John, Kt.1497, II. 29
  Seymour, John, Kt.1513, II. 36
  Seymour, John, Kt.1591, II. 88
  Seymore, John, Kt.1605, II. 137
  Seamore (Leamore), Joseph, Kt.1643, II. 216
  Seymour, Michael, K.C.B.1815, I. 222

SEYMOUR
  Seymour, Michael, K.C.B.1855, I. 240; G.C.B.1859, I. 192
  Seymour (Seamor), Robert, Kt.1619, II. 171
  Seymour, Thomas, Kt.1520, II. 43
  Seymour, Thomas, Kt.1537, II. 50
  Seymour, Thomas, lord Seymour of Sudeley, K.G.1547, I. 24
  Seymore (Seimore), Thomas, Kt.1603, II. 121
  Seymour, William, K.B.1501, I. 145
  Seymour, William, duke of Somerset, K.B.1616, I. 159; K.G.1650, I. 34
  Seymour, William, Kt.1829, II. 328
  Seymour, lord William, F. E., K.C.V.O. 1903, I. 436
  Seymour, William H., K.C.B.1904, I. 276
Seymour-Conway Francis, marquess of Hertford, K.G.1756, I. 45
Seymour-Conway, Francis C., marquess of Hertford, G.C.H.1819, I. 449; K.G.1822, I. 53
Seymour-Conway, Richard, marquess of Hertford, K.G.1846, I. 58
Shadwell, Charles F. A., K.C.B.1873, I. 254
Shadwell, John, Kt.1715, II. 280
Shadwell, Lancelot, Kt.1827, II. 327
Shaftesbury, earl of. See Ashley-Cooper
Shafto, Cuthbert, Kt.1795, II. 303
Shafto, Robert, Kt.1670, II. 244
Shah, Aga Khan, K.C.I.E.1898, I. 410
Shahpura, Nahar Singh of, K.C.I.E.1903, I. 411
Shakerley, Charles W., K.C.B.1897, I. 296
Shakerley, Jeoffry, Kt.1662, II. 236
Shakespear, Richmond C., Kt.1841, II. 344
Shamsher, Jung, K.C.S.I.1892, I. 325; G.C.S.I.1897, I. 314
Shand, Charles F., Kt.1869, II. 361
Shane, Francis, Kt.1600, II. 98
Shane, James, Kt.1660, II. 232
Shannon, earl of. See Boyle
Shard, Abraham, Kt.1744, II. 286
Shard, Isaac, Kt.1708, II. 276

INDEX

Shardelowe, John de, K.B.1332, I. 125
SHARP, SHARPE, SHARPPE, SHAIRP
   Sharpe, Alfred, K.C.M.G.1903, I. 394
   Sharp, Cuthbert, Kt.1814, II. 314
   Sharppe, John, Kt.1513, II. 39
   Sharp, John, Kt.1604, II. 136
   Sharpe, Joshua, Kt.1713, II. 278
   Shairp, Stephen, Kt.1806, II. 308
Sharpey (Sharpeigh), Robert (John), Kt. 1622, II. 178
Shareshull, William de, K.B.1333, I. 125
Shareshull, William, Kt.1399, II. 11
Shaughnessy, Thomas G., Kt.1901, II. 409
Shaughnessy. See O'Shaughnessy
SHAW, SCHAW, SHAA, SHAWE
   Shaw, Alexander, Kt.1633, II. lxiii.
   Shaw, Charles, Kt.1838, II. 340
   Shaw, Eyre M., K.C.B.1891, I. 292
   Schaw, James, Kt.1594, II. 91
   Shaw, John, Kt.1661, II. 235
   Shaa, John, Kt.1497, II. 30
   Shaw, John, Kt.1660, II. 230
Shaw-Lefevre, Charles, viscount Eversley, G.C.B.1885, I. 211
Shaw-Lefevre, John G., K.C.B.1857, I. 280
Shea, Ambrose, K.C.M.G.1883, I. 366
Shea, Edward D'A., Kt.1902, II. 410
Shearer, John, Kt.1903, II. 414
Shee, James, Kt.1787, II. 300
Shee, Martin A., Kt.1830, II. 328
Shee, Richard, Kt.1589, II. 87
Shee, William, Kt.1864, II. 357
Sheffield, Edmund, earl of Mulgrave, Kt.1588, II. 86; K.G.1593, I. 28
Sheffield, Edward, Kt.1603, II. 122
Sheffield, Edward, K.B.1610, I. 158
Sheffield, John, lord Sheffield, K.B.1559, I. 153
Sheffield, John, Kt.1605, II. 137
Sheffield, John, duke of Buckingham, K.G.1674, I. 37
Sheffield, Robert, Kt.1497, II. 30
Sheffield, William, Kt.1617, II. 162
Sheil, John, K.C.B.1855, I. 279
Shelbourne, earl of. See Petty
SHELDON, SHELDEN, SHELTON
   Sheldon, John (Ralph), K.B.(1487), I. 142

SHELDON
   Shelton, John, Kt.1547, II. 59
   Shelton, John, Kt.1596, II. 93
   Sheldon, Joseph, Kt.1666, II. 242
   Shelton, Nicholas de, K.B.1306, I. 120
   Shelton, Ralph de, Kt.1346, II. 6
   Shelton, Rauf, Kt.1578, II. 79
   Shelton (Skelton), Ralph, Kt.1607, II. 144
   Shelden, Richard, Kt.1625, II. 190
Shelford, William, K.C.M.G.1904, I. 394
Shelley, Anthony, Kt.1591, II. 88
Shelley, John, Kt.1612, II. 151
Shelley, William, Kt.1529, II. 47
Shelley, William, Kt.1636, II. 204
Shelton. See Sheldon
Shenton, George, Kt.1893, II. 391
SHEPHERD, SHEPHARD, SHEPPARD
   Sheppard, Fleetwood, Kt.1694, II. 268
   Shephard, James, Kt.1729, II. 284
   Shepherd, Samuel, Kt.1614, II. 313
Shepstone, Theophilus, K.C.M.G.1876, I. 358
Sherbrooke, John C., K.B.1809, I. 177; G.C.B.1815, I. 181
Sherbrooke, viscount. See Lowe
SHERBURN, SHERBORNE, SHERBURNE, SHERBOURNE, SHIRBORNE
   Sherborne, —, Kt.1603, II. 126
   Sherburne, Edward, Kt.1683, II. 258
   Sherbourne, Henry, Kt.1512, II. 35
   Sherburn, John, Kt.1902, II. 413
   Shirborne, Richard, Kt.1544, II. 55
Shere, Henry, Kt.1685, II. 261
Sherer, George M., K.C.S.I.1866, I. 316
Sherer, Joseph, K.H.1836, I. 475
Sheridan, William, K.C.H.1832, I. 458
Sherley. See Shirley
Sherlock, Francis, K.H.1834, I. 470
Sherlock, George, Kt.1606, II. 141
Sherlock, John (Thomas), Kt.1631, II. 199
Sherlock, John, Kt.1636, II. 204
Sherrard, Philip, Kt.1603, II. 103
Sherrard, William, Kt.1622, II. 179
Sherrington, Henry, Kt.1574, II. 76

Sherrington (Scarrington), William, K.B.1547, I. 152
Shipley, Charles, Kt.1808, II. 309
Shippard, Sidney G. A., K.C.M.G.1887, I. 371
Shirborne. See Sherburn

SHIRLEY, SHERLEY, SHIRDELOWE, SHURLEY

Sherley (Shirley), George, Kt.1620, II. 175
Shirley, Horatio, K.C.B.1869, I. 252
Shirdelowe (Shadelowe, Shirley), John (Ralph), K.B.(1426), I. 132
Shirley (Shurley), John, Kt.1603, II. 107, 108
Shirley, Philip (George), Kt.1603, II. 103
Shirley, Rauf, Kt.1487, II. 25
Shirley, Thomas, Kt.1573, II. 75
Shirley, Thomas, Kt.1589, II. 87
Shirley, Thomas, Kt.1622, II. 179
Shirley, Thomas, Kt.1646, II. 220
Shore. See Shower
Shoreditch, John de, K.B.1333, I. 125

SHORTALES, SCHORTHALIS

Schorthalis, Geoffrey, Kt.(1336), II. lix.
Shortales, Oliver, Kt.1614-5, II. 155
Shorter, John, Kt.1675, II. 250
Shotesbrooke, John, K.B.(1418), I. 130
Shovell, Cloudesley, Kt.1689, II. 264
Shower (Shore), Bartholomew, Kt.1687, II. 263
Shrewsbury, earl and duke of. See Talbot
Shugborough, Richard, Kt.1642, II. 214
Shurley. See Shirley
Shute, Charles C., K.C.B.1889, I. 262
Shuttleworth, Richard, Kt.1684, II. 260
Siam, king of, G.C.M.G.1878, I. 338
Siam, crown prince of, G.C.V.O.1902, I. 425
Sibbald, John, Kt.1899, II. 405
Sibthorpe, Christopher, Kt.1618, II. 168
Sidenham, Sidnam. See Sydenham
Sidgreaves, Thomas, Kt.1874, II. 366
Sidley. See Sedley

SIDNEY, SYDNEY

Sydney, earl and viscount. See Townshend
Sidney, Henry, Kt.1549, II. 65; K.G. 1564, I. 26
Sidney, Henry, Kt.1603, II. 107
Sidney (Sidley), Isaac, Kt.1641, II. 210
Sidney, John, Kt.1604, II. 135
Sydney, John, earl of Leicester, K.B. 1725, I. 167
Sidney, Philip C., lord de l'Isle and Dudley, K.C.H.1830, I. 456; G.C.H.1831, I. 451
Sydney, Robert, earl of Leicester, Kt. 1586, II. 85; K.G.1616, I. 31
Sydney, Robert, earl of Leicester, K.B.1610, I. 158
Sidney, William, Kt.1512, II. 35
Sidney, William, Kt.1611, II. 150
Sydney, William R., Kt.1827, II. 327
Siemens, William, Kt.1883, II. 375
Sieveking, Edward H., Kt.1886, II. 379
Sikes, Charles W., Kt.1881, II. 372
Silbermerg, Christopher van, Kt.1487, II. 27
Silvester, Baptist J., Kt.1774, II. 294
Simmons. See Symonds
Simnevil, John de, K.B.1249, I. 110
Simon. See Symon
Simpkinson, John A. F., Kt.1845, II. 346

SIMPSON, SIMSOM, SYMPSON

Simpson, Benjamin, K.C.I.E.1887, I. 400
Simpson, Edward, Kt.1761, II. 291
Simpson, George, Kt.1841, II. 343
Simpson, Henry L., Kt.1887, II. 381
Simpson, James, G.C.B.1855, I. 191
Sympson, John, Kt.1678, II. 252
Simpson, John, Kt.1836, II. 337
Simson, Robert, K.H.1831, I. 465
Simpson, William, Kt.1697, II. 270
Sinclair. See St. Clair
Singleton, John, K.H.1837, I. 478
Sinserff, Walter, Kt.1721, II. 282
Sirmone, John de, Kt.1347, II. 9
Sirmur, Bikram Prakash, of, K.C.S.I. 1901, I. 327

Sirmur, Shamsher Prakash, of, G.C.S.I. 1887, I. 312
Sirohi, Kaishri Singh, maharaja of, K.C.S.I.1895, I. 325; G.C.I.E.1901, I. 403
Sivewright, James, K.C.M.G.1892, I. 378
Skargyll. See Scargil
Skeffington, John, Kt.1624, II. 186
Skeffington, Richard, Kt.1624, II. 186
Skeffington, William, Kt.1603, II. 103
Skelton, Charles T., Kt.1897, II. 400
Skelton, John, K.B.1509, I. 148
Skelton, John, K.C.B.1897, I. 295
Skelton, Ralph, Kt.1607, II. 144
Skerk, Peter, K.B.1305, I. 111
Skerne, —, Kt.1471, II. 15
Skerne, Edward, Kt.1619, II. 174
Skinke, Martin, Kt.1586, II. 84
SKINNER, SKYNNER
Skinner, John, Kt.1603, II. 119, 136
Skynner, John, Kt.1777, II. 295
Skinner, Mathew, Kt.1735, II. 284
Skynner, Thomas, Kt.1603, II. 120
Skinner, Vincent, Kt.1603, II. 104
Skipwith, Henry, Kt.1609, II. 148
Skipwith, John, Kt.1497, II. 30
Skipwith, Richard, Kt.1603, II. 116
Skipwith, Thomas, Kt.1673, II. 248
Skipwith, William de, K.B.1360, I. 125
Skipwith, William, Kt.1547, II. 62
Skipwith, William, Kt.1603, II. 102
SKITT, SKITTE, SKYTTE
Skittee, Jacob,(Kt.1635, II. 203
Skitt (Skept, Skeyete), John, Kt.1617, II. 167
Skittie (Skytte), John, baron of Dudeor, Kt.1635, II. 203
Skottowe, Edmund M. B., Kt.1830, II. 329
Skottowe, Nicholas B., Kt.1809, II. 309
Skrymshire (Skrymshaw), Charles, Kt. 1682, II. 257
Skynner. See Skinner
Skyppon, Philip, Kt.1675, II. 250
Slacke, Owen R., Kt.1897, II. 398
Slade, Adolphus, K.C.B.1858, I. 245
Slade, John, G.C.H.1835, I. 453
Slade, Thomas, Kt.1768, II. 292

Sladen, Charles, K.C.M.G.1875, I. 358
Sladen, Edward B., Kt.1886, II. 380
Slamnoth, Anthony, Kt.1545, II. 57
Slane, lord, Kt.1494, II. 28
Slanning, Nicholas, Kt.1632, II. 200
Slaning, Nicholas, K.B.1661, I. 166
Slatin, Rudolf C., ritter von, K.C.M.G. 1898, I. 385
Slaughter, William, K.H.1837, I. 476
Sleeman, William H., K.C.B.1856, I. 279
Sleigh, James W., K.C.B.1856, I. 242
Sleigh (Sly), Samuel, Kt.1641, II. 209
Sligo, marquess of. See Browne
SLINGSBY, SLINGSBIE, SLYNGSBY
Slingsby, Arthur, Kt.1657, II. 225
Slingsbie, Francis, Kt.1605, II. 138
Slingsby, Gilford (William), Kt.1603, II. 121
Slingsby, Henry, Kt.1602, II. 100
Slyngsby, William, Kt.1603, II. 119
Sloper, Robert, K.B.1788, I. 174
Sly. See Sleigh
Slyfield, Joseph C. S., K.H.1837, I. 478
Smale, John, Kt.1874, II. 366
Smart, George T., Kt.1811, II. 310
Smart, Joseph, Kt.1696, II. 269
Smart, Robert, K.H.1832, I. 467; K.C.B. 1865, I. 249
Smart, Tracy (Nedham), Kt.1622, II. 178
Smart, William R. E., K.C.B.1877, I. 256
Smirke, Edward, Kt.1870, II. 362
Smirke, Robert, Kt.1832, II. 332
SMITH, SMYTH, SMYTHE, SMITHE
Smythe, —, Kt.1529, II. 48
Smith, Albert, K.C.M.G.1878, I. 360
Smith, Andrew, K.C.B.1858, I. 280
Smith, Archibald L., Kt.1883, II. 375
Smith, Benjamin, Kt.1838, II. 340
Smith, Cecil C., K.C.M.G.1886, I. 368; G.C.M.G.1892, I. 343
Smith, Charles, Kt.1619, II. 172
Smith, Charles A., Kt.1903, II. 415
Smith, Charles F., Kt.1814, II. 315; K.C.B.1843, I. 237
Smith, Charles H., K.H.1834, I. 471
Smith, Charles H., K.C.M.G.1892, I. 378
Smith, Clarence, Kt.1895, II. 396
Smythe, Clement, Kt.1547, II. 60

INDEX

SMITH

Smith, Donald A., lord Strathcona, K.C.M.G.1886, I. 368; G.C.M.G. 1896, I. 344
Smyth, Edward S., K.C.M.G.1877, I. 359
Smith, Edwin T., K.C.M.G.1888, I. 372
Smyth, Francis, Kt.1603, II. 117
Smith, Francis, Kt.1862, II. 356
Smith, Francis P., Kt.1871, II. 363
Smith, Francis W., Kt.1837, II. 338
Smith, Frank, Kt.1894, II. 393
Smythe, Frederick W., K.C.M.G.1888, I. 373
Smyth, George, Kt.1604, II. 133
Smith, George, Kt.1616, II. 158
Smith, George, Kt.1660, II. 231
Smith, George, Kt.1807, II. 308
Smith, George J., Kt.1897, II. 401
Smith, Gerard, K.C.M.G.1895, I. 381
Smith, Henry, Kt.1860, II. 355
Smith, Henry, K.C.B.1873, I. 253
Smith, Henry, K.C.B.1897, I. 296
Smyth, Henry A., K.C.M.G.1890, I. 375
Smith, Henry G. W., K.C.B.1844, I. 238; G.C.B.1846, I. 190
Smith, Hugh, Kt.1603, II. 102
Smith, Hugh, K.B.1661, I. 166
Smith, James, Kt.1644, II. 218
Smith, James, Kt.1672, II. 247
Smith, James, Kt.1897, II. 401
Smythe, James C., K.C.H.1829, I. 456
Smith, James E., Kt.1814, II. 314
Smith, Jerome [Jeremiah], Kt.1665, II. 241
Smithe, John, Kt.1576, II. 77
Smith, John, Kt.1603, II. 105
Smyth, John, Kt.1605, II. 139
Smith, John, Kt.1614, II. 154
Smith, John, Kt.1617, II. 161, 169
Smith, John, Kt.1642, II. 214
Smith, John, Kt.1670, II. 244
Smith, John, G.C.H.1831, I. 451; Kt. 1831, II. 330
Smith, John, Kt.1887, II. 382
Smith, John F. S., K.C.H.1832, I. 458
Smith, John L., Kt.1870, II. 362
Smith, John M. F., K.H.1830, I. 465; Kt.1831, II. 330

SMITH

Smyth, John R., K.C.B.1867, I. 251
Smith, John S., Kt.1896, II. 397
Smith, John W., K.C.B.1863, I. 248
Smyth, Laurence, Kt.1544, II. 55
Smyth, Laurence, Kt.1660, II. 232
Smyth, Leicester, K.C.M.G.1884, I. 366; K.C.B.1886, I. 259
Smith, Lionel, K.C.B.1822, I. 229; G.C.H.1836, I. 453; G.C.B.1841, I. 207
Smith, Montague E., Kt.1865, II. 357
Smithe, Nicholas, Kt.1603, II. 126
Smith, Owen, Kt.1617, II. 160
Smith, Peter, K.C.M.G.1860, I. 354
Smith, Percy, Kt.1630, II. 197
Smythe, Percy S. C., viscount Strangford, K.B.1808, I. 177; G.C.B.1815, I. 205; G.C.H.1825, I. 449
Smith, Philip P., Kt.1880, II. 372
Smith, Richard, Kt.1603, II. 119
Smyth, Richard, Kt.1624, II. 186
Smith, Robert, Kt.1660, II. 231
Smith, Robert M., K.C.M.G.1888, I. 372
Smith, Robert V., lord Lyveden, G.C.B. 1872, I. 210
Smith, Roger, Kt.1641, II. 209
Smyth, Samuel, Kt.1622, II. 180
Smyth, Sebastian, Kt.1685, II. 261
Smith, Sigismund, Kt.1832, II. 331
Smyth, Sydney S., Kt.1750, II. 288
Smith, Swire, Kt.1898, II. 403
Smyth, Thomas, Kt.1549, II. 65
Smyth, Thomas, Kt.1596, II. 93
Smith, Thomas, Kt.1603, II. 109, bis, 115
Smith, Thomas, Kt.1615, II. 156
Smith, Thomas, viscount Strangford, K.B.1626, I. 163
Smith, Thomas, K.C.V.O.(1901), I. 434
Smith, Thurston, Kt.1625, II. 188
Smith, Walter, Kt.1616, II. 157
Smyth, Warington W., Kt.1887, II. 383
Smythe, William, Kt.1513, II. 40
Smyth, William, K.B.1547, I. 152
Smith, William, Kt.1603, II. 104, 112
Smith, William, Kt.1623, II. 183
Smyth, William, Kt.1718, II. 281

INDEX   211

SMITH
Smith, William, Kt.1744, II. 286
Smith, William, Kt.1821, II. 323
Smith, William, Kt.1892, II. 391
Smith, William A., Kt.1811, II. 310
Smith, William F. H., K.C.M.G.1890, I. 375
Smith, William J., Kt.1896, II. 397
Smith, William Sidney, Kt.1792, footnote, II. 301; K.C.B.1815, I. 217; G.C.B.1838, I. 188
Smith-Stanley, Edward, earl of Derby, K.G.1839, I. 56
Smith-Stanley, Edward G., earl of Derby, K.G.1859, I. 60; G.C.M.G.1869, I. 336
Smithes (Smithies), Arthur, Kt.1624, II. 184
Smithett, Luke, Kt.1862, II. 356
Smyly, Philip C., Kt.1892, II. 390
Smyth, Smythe. See Smith
SNAGGE, SNEGG, SNIGGE
Snigge (Snagge, Snegg), George (Thomas), Kt.1605, II. 136
Snagge, Thomas, Kt.1603, II. 111
Snagge, Thomas W., Kt.1903, II. 416
Snagg, William, Kt.1859, II. 354
Snape, Richard, K.B.1400, I. 128
Sneath (Snathe, Smyth), William, K.B. 1547, I. 152
Snegg. See Snigg
Snelgrove, Henry, Kt.1617, II. 165
Snell, Charles, Kt.1616, II. 158
Snell, Thomas, Kt.1744, II. 286
Snelling, George, Kt.1603, II. 123
Snelling, Thomas, Kt.1714, II. 279
Snigge. See Snagge
Snouckaert (Snowkart), Martin, Kt. 1627, II. 192
Snow, Jeremiah, Kt.1679, II. 253
Snowden, Arthur, Kt.1895, II. 395
SOAME, SOME, SOHAM
Soham (Soame, Some), Stephen, Kt. 1599, II. 95
Soame (Soham), Stephen, Kt.1618, II. 170
Soame, Thomas, Kt.1641, II. 211
Some, William, Kt.1614, II. 154
Soame, William, Kt.1674, II. 249

Soane, John, Kt.1831, II. 331
Soham. See Soame
Solomon, Richard, K.C.M.G.1901, I. 390
Somercotes, William de, K.B.1306, I. 121
Somerfield. See Somerville
SOMERS, SOMMERS
Sommers, George, Kt.1603, II. 118
Somers, John, Kt.1689, II. 265
Somerset, Alfred P. F. C., K.C.B.1902, I. 299
Somerset, Charles, Kt.1485, II. 22
Somerset, Charles, earl of Worcester, Kt.1485, II. 22; K.G.1496, I. 18; Kt.1497, II. 28
Somerset, Charles, Kt.1573, II. 75
Somerset, Charles, K.B.1610, I. 158
Somerset, duke of. See Beaufort; see Seymour
Somerset, earl of. See Carr
Somerset, Edward, earl of Worcester, K.G.1593, I. 28
Somerset, Edward, K.B.1610, I. 158
Somerset, Fitzroy J. H., lord Raglan, K.C.B.1815, I. 225; G.C.B.1847, I. 190
Somerset, George, Kt.1532, II. 48
Somerset, Henry, K.H.1834, I. 470; K.C.B.1853, I. 240
Somerset, Henry, duke of Beaufort, K.G.1672, I. 36
Somerset, Henry, duke of Beaufort, K.G.1712, I. 40
Somerset, Henry, duke of Beaufort, K.G.1786, I. 48
Somerset, Henry, duke of Beaufort, K.G.1842, I. 56
Somerset, Henry C., duke of Beaufort, K.G.1805, I. 50
Somerset, Henry C. F., duke of Beaufort, K.G.1867, I. 63
Somerset, John, Kt.1632, II. 199
Somerset, lord Robert E. H., K.C.B. 1815, I. 221; G.C.B.1834, I. 187
Somerset, Thomas, viscount Somerset of Cashel, K.B.1605, I. 157
Somerset, William, earl of Worcester, K.B.1547, I. 150; K.G.1570, I. 26

SOMERVILLE, SOMERVILE, SOMERFIELD
Somervell, James, Kt.1737, II. 285
Somervell, James, Kt.1(37, II. 285
Somerville, Roger de, K.B.1306, I. 120
Somerfield (Somervile), Thomas, Kt. 1603, II. 112
Somervile (Somerfield), William, Kt. 1603, II. 117
Somerfield (Somerville), William, Kt. 1617, II. 166
Somery, John de, K.B.1306, I. 118
Somester, Samuel, Kt.1616, II. 160
Sonbursa, Narajan Singh, of, K.C.I.E. 1903, I. 412
Sonds. See Sandys
Sonnino, Prospero C. P. di, G.C.V.O. 1903, I. 427
Soranzo, the Venetian ambassador, Kt.1632, II. 199
Sorenzo (Soranzo), Lorenzo, Kt.1696, II. 269
SORRELL, SORELL
Sorrell, Emanuel, Kt.1660, II. 228
Sorell (Sorrell), Thomas S., K.H. 1834, I. 470; Kt.1834, II. 335
Sotheby, Edward S., K.C.B.1875, I. 255
Sotherton, Augustin, Kt.1623, II. 182
Sotill (Satell), Gerald, K.B.(1400), I. 129
Sotomayor, duke of, G.C.V.O.1902, I. 425
Sott, Arnold H. van, Kt.1487, II. 26
Soulsby, William J., Kt. 1902, II. 412
Soundy, John T., Kt.1899, II. 404
Souter, Frank H., Kt.1875, II. 367
Souch, Sowth, Suche. See Zouche
SOUTH, SOWTHE, and see Zouch
Sowthe, Edward, Kt.1603, II. 124
South, James, Kt.1830, II. 329
South, John, Kt.1636, II. 204
South (Cutts), William, Kt.1608, II. 145
Southampton, earl of. See Fitzwilliam; see Wriothesley; see Fitzroy
SOUTHCOTT, SOUTHCOTE, SOWTHCOT
Southcot, Edward, Kt.1609, II. 148
Sowthcot, George, Kt.1603, II. 125

SOUTHCOTT
Southcote, Hamond, Kt.1603, II. 104
Southcote (Surcot), John, Kt.1646, II. 220
Southcott, John, Kt.1685, II. 260
Southcot, Popham, Kt.1629, II. 196
Southesk, earl of. See Carnegie
Southey, Richard, K.C.M.G.1891, I. 376
Southland, William, Kt.1603, II. 112
Southwell, Charles, K.H.1828, I. 465
Southwell, Henry, Kt.1615, II. 156
Southwell, Richard, Kt.1542, II. 53
Southwell, Richard, Kt.1623, II. 182
Southwell, Robert, Kt.1504, II. 34
Southwell, Robert, Kt.1538, II. 51
Southwell, Robert, Kt.1585, II. 83
Southwell, Robert, Kt.1665, II. 241
Southwell, Thomas, Kt.1603, II. 124
Southwell, Thomas, Kt.1615, II. 156
Southwell, Thomas A., viscount Southwell, K.P.1837, I. 100
Southwell, Thomas A. J., viscount Southwell, K.P.1871, I. 103
Southworthe, Christopher, Kt.1482, II. 19
Southworthe, John, Kt.1504, II. 34
Southworthe, John, Kt.1547, II. 61
Souche. See Zouche
Souza, Walter E. de, Kt.1879, II. 371
Soveral, Luiz de, G.C.M.G.1897, I. 344
Soveral, marquis de, G.C.V.O.1902, I. 426
Sowler, Thomas, Kt.1890, II. 386
Sownorth, Thomas, Kt.1523, II. 44
Soysa, Charles H. de, Kt.1892, II. 389
Spaight, James, Kt.1887, II. 383

SPAIN
Alfonso XII. of, K.G.1881, I. 66
Alfonso XIII. of, G.C.V.O.1897, I. 423; K.G.1902, I. 71
Ferdinand VII. of, K.G.1814, I. 51
Philip II. of, K.G.1554, I. 25
Sparke, William, Kt.1619, II. 175
Sparrow, John, Kt.1687, II. 263
Sparrow, John, Kt.1668, II. 242
Sparshott, Edward, K.H.1831, I. 465
Sparta, duke of. See Greece
Specot, John, Kt.1604, II. 133

SPEKE, SPEEKE
Speeke, George, Kt.1536, II. 50
Speke, George, K.B.1559, I. 153
Speke, George, K.B.1603, I. 156
Speke, John, K.B.(1483), I. 138
Speke, John, K.B.(1494), I. 144
Speke (Spoke), Thomas, Kt.1527, II. 46
SPELMAN, SPILMAN, SPILLMAN
Spillman, Anthony, Kt.1586, II. 84
Spilman, Clement, Kt.1603, II. 122, 130
Spilman, Henry, Kt.1604, II. 130
Spelman (Spilman), John, Kt.1605, II. 138
Spelman, John, Kt.1641, II. 211
Spencer, A. A., K.C.B.1865, I. 250; G.C.B.1875, I. 196
Spencer, Brent, K.B.1809, I. 177; G.C.B.1815, I. 181
Spencer, Charles, earl of Sunderland, K.G.1719, I. 42
Spencer, Charles, duke of Marlborough, K.G.1741, I. 43
Spencer, Edward, Kt.1625, II. 190
Spencer, Frederick, earl Spencer, K.G. 1849, I. 58
Spencer, George, Kt.1617, II. 164
Spencer, George, duke of Marlborough, K.G.1768, I. 46
Spencer, George J., earl Spencer, K.G. 1799, I. 49
Spencer, James, Kt.1529, II. 47
Spencer, James E., Kt.1901, II. 409
Spencer, John, Kt.1553, II. 67
Spencer, John, Kt.1588, II. 87
Spencer, John, Kt.1595, II. 91
Spencer, John P., earl Spencer, K.G. 1865, I. 62; Grand Master K.P. 1868, I. 94
Spencer, Richard, Kt.1603, II. 104
Spencer, Richard, K.C.H.1833, I. 459; Kt.1833, II. 333
Spencer, Robert, earl of Sunderland, K.G.1687, I. 38
Spencer, Robert C., K.C.H.1828, I. 456; Kt.1828, II. 327
Spencer, Thomas, Kt.1612, II. 151

Spencer, Victor A. F. C., viscount Churchill, K.C.V.O.(1900), I. 433; G.C.V.O.1902, I. 420
Spencer, William, Kt.1592, II. 90
Spencer, William, lord Spencer, K.B. 1616, I. 160
Spencer, William, Kt.1629, II. 196
Spencer-Churchill, Charles R. J., duke of Marlborough, K.G.1902, I. 71
Spencer-Churchill, John W., duke of Marlborough, K.G.1868, I. 64; Grand Master K.P.1876, I. 95
Spert (Sporte), Thomas, Kt.1529, II. 47
Spicer, Samuel, Kt.1817, II. 319
Spiller, Henry, Kt.1618, II. 169
Spiller, Robert, Kt.1622,, II. 179
Spilman. See Spelman
Spink, John, K.H.1835, I. 471
Spittal, James, Kt.1837, II. 339
Spokes, Peter, Kt.1872, II. 363
Sporte. See Spert
Spott, —, Kt.1623, II. 181
Spottesworth, Henry, Kt.1623, II. 182
Spragg, Edward, Kt.1665, II. 241
Spratling, Adam, Kt.1604, II. 133
Sprengell, Conrade J., Kt.1725, II. 283
Sprigg, John G., K.C.M.G.1886, I. 370; G.C.M.G.1902, I. 348
SPRINGE, SPRYNGE
Sprynge, John, Kt.1547, II. 60
Springe, William, Kt.1578, II. 79
Springe, William, Kt.1611, II. 150
SPRINGATE, SPRINGETT
Springett, Thomas, Kt.1621, II. 177
Springate, William, Kt.1642, II. 212
Spry, Henry, Kt.1625, II. 189
Spry, Richard, Kt.1773, II. 294
Spry, Samuel T., Kt.1834, II. 335
Sprynge. See Springe
Spurgin, John B., K.C.B.1893, I. 264
Spynola, Paule B., Kt.1549, II. 64
Staal, Georges de, G.C.V.O.1902, I. 425
Stack, George F., K.H.1837, I. 478
Stack, Maurice, K.C.B.1867, I. 251
Stafford, — de, Kt.1347, II. 8
Stafford, —, K.B.(1465), I. 134
Stafford, Edmund, earl of Stafford, K.B. 1399, I. 127; K.G.1402, I. 8
Stafford, Edmond, Kt.1583, II. 82

INDEX

Stafford, Edward, earl of Wiltshire, K.B. (1475), I. 136
Stafford, Edward, duke of Buckingham, K.B.(1485), I. 141; K.G.1496, I. 18
Stafford, Edward, Kt.1618, II. 170
Stafford, Edward W., K.C.M.G.1879, I. 361; G.C.M.G.1887, I. 341
Stafford, Francis, Kt.1599, II. 98
Stafford, Henry, Kt.1460, II. 12
Stafford, Henry, duke of Buckingham, K.B.(1465), I. 134; K.G.1474, I. 15
Stafforde, Henry, Kt.1504, II. 34
Stafford, Henry, earl of Wiltshire, K.G. 1505, I. 19
Stafford, Henry, Kt.1553, II. 68
Stafford, Hugh, earl of Stafford, K.G. 1375, I. 4
Stafford, Hugh, K.B.1399, I. 128
Stafford, Hugh, lord Bourchier, K.G. 1418, I. 10
Stafford, Humphrey, earl of Stafford, duke of Buckingham, K.B.(1421), I. 130; K.G.1429, I. 11
Stafford, Humfrey, Kt.1461, II. 13
Stafford, Humfrey, Kt.1547, II. 60
Stafford, John, earl of Wiltshire, K.B. (1461), I. 133; K.G.1472, I. 15
Stafford, John, Kt.1596, II. 93
Stafford, marquess of. See Leveson-Gower
Stafford, Ralph, earl of Stafford, K.B. 1327, I. 124; K.G.1348, I. 1
Stafford, Richard, Kt.1601, II. 99
Stafforde, Robert, Kt.1545, II. 57
Stafford, Thomas, earl of Stafford, K.B. 1390, I. 127
Stafford, Thomas, Kt.1489, II. 27
Stafford, Thomas, Kt.1611, II. 151
Stafford, William, Kt.1545, II. 57
Stafford, William, Kt.1603, II. 107
Staimford. See Stamford
Stainer, John, Kt.1888, II. 384
Stainer, Richard, Kt.1657, II. 223, 231
Staines, Thomas, Kt.1809, II. 310; K.C.B. 1815, I. 223
Staines (Staine), William, Kt.1796, II. 303
Stair, earl of. See Dalrymple; see Hamilton-Dalrymple

Stalage, Nicholas, Kt.1604, II. 132
Stalbroke, Thomas, Kt.1471, II. 16
STAMFORD, STAIMFORD, STANFORD, STAUNFORD
Stamford (Stanford), Robert, Kt.1603, II. 123
Stamford, William, Kt.1471, II. 16
Staimford (Staunford), William, Kt. 1555, II. 69
Stampe, Thomas, Kt.1676, II. 251
Standen, Anthonie, Kt.1559, II. 70
STANDIDGE, STANDISH, STANDISHE
Standishe, Alexander, Kt.1482, II. 19
Standishe, Christopher, Kt.1482, II. 19
Standish, John, Kt.1409, II. 11
Standidge, Samuel, Kt.1795, II. 303
Standish, Thomas, Kt.1603, II. 123
Stanford, Charles V., Kt.1902, II. 412
Stanford, Robert, Kt.1603, II. 125
Stanford, Robert, Kt.1850, II. 348
Stanford. See Stamford
STANHOPE, STANHOP
Stanhope, Charles, lord Stanhope, K.B. 1610, I. 158
Stanhope, Charles, earl of Harrington, G.C.H.1816, I. 448
Stanhope, Edward, Kt.1497, II. 29
Stanhop, Edward, Kt.1603, II. 114
Stanhope, Edward, K.B.1603, I. 155
Stanhope, Henry, K.B.1626, I. 161
Stanhop, John, Kt.1596, II. 94
Stanhop, John, Kt.1603, II. 102
Stanhop, John, Kt.1607, II. 142
Stanhope, John, Kt.1617, II. 162
Stanhope, Michael, Kt.1545, II. 58
Stanhop, Michael N., Kt.1603, II. 104
Stanhop, Philip, earl of Chesterfield, Kt.1605, II. 139
Stanhope, Philip, earl of Chesterfield, K.G.1805, I. 50
Stanhope, Philip D., earl of Chesterfield, K.G.1730, I. 43
Stanhop, Thomas, Kt.1575, II. 76
Stanhope, Thomas, Kt.1759, II. 289
Stanhope, Walter S., K.C.B.1904, I. 301
Stanhope, William, Kt.1683, II. 259
Stanhope, William, K.B.1725, I. 167
Stanier (Stannier), Samuel, Kt.1706, II. 275

INDEX

Stanley, —, Kt.1492, II. 28
Stanley, Charles, K.B.1661, I. 164
Stanley, Edmund, Kt.1807, II. 308
Stanley, Edward, Kt.1482, II. 18
Stanley, Edward, lord Monteagle, K.G. 1514, I. 20
Stanley, Edward, earl of Derby, K.B. 1533, I. 149; K.G.1547, I. 24
Stanley, Edward, K.B.1547, I. 150
Stanley, Edward, Kt.1560, II. 70
Stanley, Edward, Kt.1586, II. 85
Stanley, Edward, K.B.1603, I. 154
Stanley, Edward, Kt.1809, II. 309
Stanley, Edward, earl of Derby, K.G. 1884, I. 67
Stanley, Frederick A., earl of Derby, G.C.B.1886, I. 212; K.G.1897, I. 70
Stanley, George, lord Strange, K.B. (1475), I. 137; K.G.1487, I. 17
Stanley, Ger. (George), Kt.1553, II. 68
Stanley, George, Kt.1565, II. 72
Stanley, Henry, earl of Derby, K.B.1547, I. 150; K.G.1574, I. 27
Stanley, Henry M., G.C.B.1899, I. 215
Stanley, Humfrey, Kt.1485, 1487, II. 23, 24
Stanley, James, earl of Derby, K.B.1626, I. 160; K.G.1650, I. 34
Stanley, John, K.G.1404, I. 8
Stanley, John, Kt.1471, II. 16
Stanley, John, K.B.(1483), I. 139
Stanley, John, Kt.1513, II. 37
Stanley, John, Kt.1901, II. 409
Stanley, Robert, K.B.1626, I. 161
Stanley, Rowland, Kt.1553, II. 68
Stanley, Thomas, lord Stanley, K.G.1457, I. 13
Stanley, Thomas, earl of Derby, Kt.1460, II. 12; K.G.1483, II. 17
Stanley, Thomas, earl of Derby, K.B. (1494), I. 144
Stanley, Thomas, lord Monteagle, K.B. 1533, I. 149
Stanley, Thomas, Kt.1553, II. 66
Stanley, Thomas, Kt.1603, II. 102, 130
Stanley, Thomas, Kt.1622, II. 178
Stanley, Thomas, Kt.1659, II. 224
Stanley, William, K.B.(1461), I. 133
Stanley, William, Kt.1471, II. 16

Stanley, William, Kt.1482, II. 19
Stanley, William, K.G.1487, I. 17
Stanley, William, Kt.1513, II. 42
Stanley, William, Kt.1547, II. 59
Stanley, William, Kt.1579, II. 80
Stanley, William, earl of Derby, K.G. 1601, I. 29
Stannus, Ephraim, Kt.1837, II.338
Stansfeld, James, G.C.B.1895, I. 214
Stansfield, James, Kt. 1673, II. 248

STANTON, STAUNTON
Stanton, Edward, K.C.M.G. 1882, I. 364
Stanton, Francis, Kt.1621, II. 177
Staunton, John de, K.B.1306, I. 115
Staunton, Philip de, K.B.1347, I. 125
Stapeley, John, Kt.1660, II. 231
Staples, John, K.C.M.G.1886, I. 370
Staples, Thomas, Kt.1628, II. 194

STAPLETON, STAPILTON
Stapleton, Bryan, K.G.1381, I. 5
Stapilton, Bryan, K.B.(1475), I. 137
Stapleton, Bryan, Kt.1482, II. 17
Stapleton, Bryan, Kt.1504, II. 34; K.B.1504, I. 147
Stapleton, Bryan, Kt.1513, II. 37
Stapleton, Miles, K.G.1344, I. 2
Stapleton, Miles, Kt.1660, II. 229
Stapleton, Philip, Kt.1630, II. 197
Stapleton, Richard, Kt.1553, II. 67
Stapleton, Robert, Kt.1544, II. 55
Stapleton, Robert, Kt.1570, II. 74
Stapleton, Robert, Kt.1642, II. 214
Starchedell, Otto, Kt.1611, II. 151
Staresmore, Robert, Kt.1650, II. 222
Starkey, Humphrey, Kt.1483, II. 21
Starling. See Stirling
Statham, John, Kt.1714, II. 278
Staunton. See Stantor
Staveley, Charles W. D., K.C.B.1865, I. 250; G.C.B.1884, I. 198
Stavenets, —, Kt.1623, II. 181

STAWELL, STOWELL
Stowell, John, Kt.1574, II. 76
Stowell, John K.B.1603, I. 155
Stowell (Stawell,) John, K.B.1626, I. 163

STAWELL
  Stawell (Stowell), John, Kt.1663, II. 238
  Stawell, William F., Kt.1857, II. 352; K.C.M.G.1886 I. 370
Stayber, Lawrence, Kt.1520, II. 43
Stedman, Edward, K.C.I.E.1897, I. 409; K.C.B.1902, I. 274
STEDE, STEEDE, STEED
  Stede (Steed), Edwin, Kt.1693, I. 268
  Steede John Kt.1614, II. 154
  Steed, William, Kt.1603, II. 123
Steel, Scudamore W., K.C.B.1853, I. 240
Steele, Richard Kt.1715, II. 280
Steele, Robert, Kt.1817, II. 318
Steele, Thomas M., K.C.B.1871, I. 253; G.C.B.1887, I. 199
Steell, John, Kt.1876, II. 368
Steere, James G. L., Kt.1888, II. 384; K.C.M.G.1900, I. 387
Stefano, Spiridione F., G.C.M.G.1847, I. 335
Stephen, Alexander C., K.C.M.G.1894, I. 379; K.C.V.O.(1900), I. 433
Stephen, Alfred, Kt.1846, II. 346; K.C.M.G. 1874, I. 356; G.C.M.G. 1884, I. 340
Stephen, George, Kt.1838, II. 339
Stephen, Henry, Kt.1904, II. 419
Stephen, James, K.C.B.1848, I. 277
Stephen, James F., K.C.S.I.1877, I. 321
Stephen, Leslie, K.C.B.1902, I. 300
Stephens. See Stevens
Stephenson, Augustus F. W. K., K.C.B. 1885, I. 289
Stephenson, Benjamin C., K.H.1820, I. 464; Kt.1831, II. 330; K.C.H.1831, I. 456; G.C.H.1834, I. 452
Stephenson, Frederick C. A., K.C.B. 1884, I. 259; G.C.B.1886, I. 198
Stephenson, Henry, Kt.1887, II. 381
Stephenson, Henry F., K.C.B.1897, I. 269; G.C.V.O.1902, I. 420
Stephenson, Rowland M., Kt.1856, II. 352
Stephenson, William, Kt.1759, II. 289
Stephenson, William A., Kt.1753, II. 288

Stephenson, William H., Kt.1900, II. 408
Stephenson, William H., K.C.B.1871, I. 285
Sterling. See Stirling
Steuart. See Stewart
STEVENS, STEPHENS, STEEVENS, STEAVENS
  Stevens, Charles C., K.C.S.I.1898, I. 327
  Stephens, John, Kt.1658, II. 225
  Steevens, John, K.C.B.1902, I. 275
  Stephens, Richard, Kt.1679, II. 254
  Stephens, Thomas, Kt.1660, II. 229
  Steavens, Thomas, Kt.1727, II. 283
  Stevens, William, Kt.1712, II. 277
Stevenson, John A., Kt.1803, II. 307
Stevenson, Robert, K.C.B.1837, I. 234
Stevenson, Thomas, Kt.1904, II. 418
Stevenson, William, K.C.B.1862, I. 282
Stepney, John, Kt.1618, II. 169
Stepney, Thomas, Kt.1618, II. 168
Stern, Edward D., Kt.1904, II. 418
Steward. See Stewart
STEWART, STUART, STEUART, STEWARD
  Stewart, Alan, earl of Galloway, K.T. 1888, I. 88
  Steward, Alexander, Kt.1586, II. 85
  Stuart, Alexander, earl of Moray, K.T. 1687, I. 75
  Stuart, Alexander, K.C.M.G.1885, I. 367
  Stuart, Andrew, Kt.1887, II. 381
  Stewart, Archibald, K.H.1832, I. 467
  Stuart, lord Barnard, Kt.1642, II. 212
  Stuart, Charles, duke of Richmond, K.G.1661, I. 35
  Stuart, Charles, earl of Moray, K.T. 1731, I. 77
  Stuart, Charles, K.B.1799, I. 175
  Stuart, Charles, lord Stuart, K.B.1812, I. 178; G.C.B.1815, I. 205
  Stuart, Charles S., K.C.B.1859, I. 245; G.C.B.1875, I. 196
  Stuart, Charlotte, duchess of Albany, K.T. Jacobite 1784, footnote, I. 75
  Stewart, David, Kt.1896, II. 397

INDEX 217

STEWART
Stewart, Donald M., K.C.B.1879, I. 256; G.C.B.1880, I. 197; G.C.S.I. 1885, I. 312
Stewart, Donald W., K.C.M.G.1902, I. 393
Stuart, Esme, duke of Lennox, K.G. 1624, I. 31
Stuart, Francis, K.B.1610, I. 158
Stuart, Francis, earl of Moray, K.T. 1827, I. 82
Stewart, Frederick W. R., marquess of Londonderry, K.P.1856, I. 102
Stuart, George or Charles, lord Aubigny, Kt.1642, II. 212
Stewart, George, earl of Galloway, K.T.1814, I. 81
Steward, Henry, Kt.1603, II. 120
Stewart, Herbert, K.C.B.1884, I. 259
Stuart, Houston, K.C.B.1855, I. 240; G.C.B.1865, I. 194
Stuart, James, duke of Lennox, duke of Richmond, Kt.1630, II. 198; K.G. 1633, I. 32
Steuart, James, Kt.1633, II. lxii.
Stuart, James, earl of Moray, K.T. 1741, I. 78
Stuart, James, Kt.1750, II. 288
Stewart, James, G.C.H.1830, I. 450
Stewart, John, K.B.(1418), I. 130
Steward, John, Kt.1611, II. 150
Stuart, lord John, Kt.1642, II. 212
Stuart, John, earl of Bute, K.T.1738, I. 78; K.G.1762, I. 46
Stewart, John, earl of Galloway, K.T. 1775, I. 80
Stuart, John, Kt.1804, II. 308; K.B. 1806, I. 176; G.C.B.1815, I. 181
Stuart, John, Kt.1853, II. 349
Stewart, lord. See Vane
Stuart, Lodovick, duke of Richmond, K.G.1603, I. 30
Steuart, Louis, Kt.1633, I. lxiii.
Steuarte, Ludwick, Kt.1633, II. lxii.
Steward, Mark, Kt.1603, II. 119
Stuart, Patrick, G.C.M.G.1843, I. 334
Stewart, Richard C., K.C.B.1894, I. 265
Stewart, Robert, Kt.1670, II. 244

STEWART
Stewart, Robert, marquess of Londonderry, K.G.1814, I. 51; G.C.H.1816, I. 447
Stuart, Robert, Kt.1871, II. 363
Stewart, Robert M., K.C.B.1902, I. 275
Stewart, Robert P., Kt.1872, II. 363
Steward, Symon, Kt.1603, II. 119
Steuart, Thomas, Kt.1633, II. lxii.
Steward, Thomas, Kt.1604, II. 135
Stewart, Thomas, 1894. See Grainger-Stewart
Stewart, William, Kt.1594, II. 91
Stewart, William, lord Blantyre, K.B. 1610, I. 158
Steward, William, Kt.1613, II. 153
Steward, William, Kt.1619, II. 174
Stewart, William, Kt.1712, II. 277
Stuart or Stewart, William, K.B.1813, I. 179; G.C.B.1815, I. 182
Stuart, William, K.C.M.G.1886, I. 369
Stewart, William H., K.C.B.1877, I. 256; G.C.B.1887, I. 199
Steward, William J., Kt.1902, II. 413
Stewart-Murray, John J. H., duke of Atholl, K.T.1868, I. 86
Stewkly. See Stukeley
Stidolfe, Francis, Kt.1603, II. 113
STILE, STYLE, STILES
Stile, Humphrey, Kt.1544, II. 56
Stiles (Style), Humphrey, Kt.1622, II. 180
Stirley (Strelley, Shirley), Philip (George), Kt.1603, II. 103
STIRLING, STERLING, STARLING
Sterling, Anthony C., K.C.B.1860, I. 246
Stirling, James, Kt.1833, II. 333
Stirling, James, Kt.1886, II. 380
Stirling, John L., Kt.1902, II. 410
Sterling, Robert, Kt.1648, II. 221
Sterling (Starling), Samuell, Kt.1667, II. 242
Stirling, Walter, Kt.1781, II. 296
Stirling, William, K.C.B.1893, I. 265
Stirling-Maxwell, William, K.T.1876, I. 87
Stisted, Charles, K.H.1835, I. 471
Stisted, Henry W., K.C.B.1871, I. 253

Stocker, John (William), Kt.1471, II. 16
Stockton, John, Kt.1471, II. 16
STODDART, STODDER, STUDDER, STODDARD
  Stodder (Studder), Edward (Thomas), Kt.1604, II. 113, 134
  Stoddart, John, Kt.1826, II. 326
  Stodder (Stoddard), Nicholas, Kt.1603, II. 126
Stoker (William) Thornley, Kt.1895, II. 395
Stokes, Henry E., K.C.S.I.1892, I. 325
Stokes, John, K.C.B.1877, I. 286
Stokes, Robert B., Kt.1898, II. 403
Stokes, William, Kt.1886, II. 380
Stone, Edward A., Kt.1902, II. 410
Stone, John B., Kt.1892, II. 391
Stone, Richard, Kt.1642, II. 212
Stone, William, Kt.1604, II. 133
STONEHOUSE, STONHOWSE
  Stonhowse, James, Kt.1603, II. 121
  Stonehouse, John (William), Kt.1629, II. 196
STONER, STONNER, STOUNER
  Stonner, Francys, Kt.1553, II. 67
  Stoner, Francis, Kt.1601, II. 99
  Stoner (Steward), Henry, Kt.1603, II. 120
  Stonner, Walter, Kt.1513, II. 37
  Stoner, William, K.B.(1478), I. 138
  Stouner, William, Kt.1487, II. 24
Stopford, Edward, K.C.B.1815, I. 219; G.C.B.1835, I. 187
Stopford, Frederick W., K.C.M.G.1901, I. 389
Stopford, James, earl of Courtown, K.P.1783, I. 97
Stopford, James, Kt.1815, II. 315
Stopford, James G., earl of Courtown, K.P.1821, I. 99
Stopford, Montague, K.C.B.1855, I. 240
Stopford, Robert, K.C.B.1815, I. 218; G.C.B.1831, I. 186; G.C.M.G.1837, I. 333
Stopham, William de, K.B.1306, I. 118
Storey, Thomas, Kt.1887, II. 384
Story. See Scory
Storks, Henry K., K.C.B.1857, I. 243; G.C.M.G.1859, I. 335; G.C.B.1864, I. 209

Stormont, viscount. See Murray
Stormy. See Sturmy
STOTE, STOYTE, STOT
  Stoyte, Francis, Kt.1705, II. 274
  Stote, Richard, Kt.1672, II. 246
  Stot, Will, Kt.(1336), II. 5
Stothard, Coslet, Kt.1787, II. 300
Stoughton, George, Kt.1616, II. 158
Stoughton, Lawrence, Kt.1611, II. 151
Stouner. See Stoner
Stourton, Charles, lord Stourton, Kt. 1547, II. 61
Stourton, John, lord Stourton, K.B. (1475), I. 136
Stourton, William, lord Stourton, K.B. (1489), I. 143
Stourton, William, lord Stourton, Kt. 1523, II. 45
Stourton, William, lord Stourton, K.B. 1616, I. 160
Stout, Robert, K.C.M.G.1886, I. 369
Stovin, Frederick, K.C.B.1815, I. 226; K.C.M.G.1820, I. 350; G.C.B.1860, I. 193
Stowell. See Stawell
Stoyte. See Stote
Stracey, John, Kt.1748, II. 288
Strachan. See Strahan
Stracche, Joh, Kt.(1336), I. 5
Strachey, Arthur, Kt.1899, II. 404
Strachey, John, K.C.S.I.1872, I. 319; G.C.S.I.1878, I. 311
Strachey, Richard, G.C.S.I.1897, I. 314
Stradling, Edward, K.B.1327, I. 124
Stradling, Edward, Kt.1513, II. 39
Stradlinge, Edward, Kt.1544, II. 54
Stradlinge, Edward, Kt.1573, II. 75, 76
Stradling, Edward, Kt.1643, II. 216
Stradling, Henry, Kt.1620, II. 176
Stradling, Henry, Kt.1641, II. 212
Stradling, John, Kt.1608, II. 145
Stradling, Thomas, Kt.1549, II. 65
Strafford, earl of. See Wentworth; see Byng
STRAHAN, STRACHAN
  Strahan, George C., K.C.M.G.1880, I. 362; G.C.M.G.1887, I. 341
  Strahan (Strachan), Patrick, Kt.1718, II. 281

INDEX 219

STRAHAN
  Strachan, Richard J., K.B.1806, I. 176; G.C.B.1815, I. 180
Straight, Douglas, Kt.1892, II. 391
Stralley. See Strelley
STRANGE, STRAUNGE, LE STRANGE, and see L'Estrange
  Strange, —, Kt.1492, II. 28
  Strange, Ebulo, K.B.1326, I. 123
  Strange, John le, K.B.1305, I. 111
  Strange, John, Kt.1740, II. 285
  Strange, lord. See Stanley
  Strange, Nicholas, Kt.1547, II. 61
  Strange, Robert, Kt.1787, II. 299
  Strange, Roger de, K.B.1327, I. 124
  Strange, Roger, K.B.1501, I. 145
  Straunge, Thomas, Kt.1529, II. 47
  Strange, Thomas A., Kt.1798, II. 304
Strangford, viscount. See Smith or Smythe
STRANGWAYES, STRANGWAYS, STRANGWISCHE, STRANGEWAIES
  Strangwisshe, Giles, Kt.1517, II. 43
  Stranguishe, Gyles, Kt.1549, II. 64
  Strangways, James, Kt.1482, II. 20
  Strangewayes, James, Kt.1527, II. 46, 47
  Strangewaies, Richard, Kt.1553, II. 67
  Stranguishe, Thomas, Kt.1513, II. 38
Stransham, Anthony B., K.C.B.1867, I. 251; G.C.B.1897, I. 201
Stratford, John, Kt.1685, II. 260
Stratford, viscount. See Canning
Strathcona, lord. See Smith
Stratherne, earl. See Malise
Strathnairn, lord. See Rose

STRATON, STRATTON, STRETTON
  Strattone, Gilotus de, Kt.(135⁻), II. 9
  Straton, Joseph, K.C.H.1832, I. 458; Kt.1832, II. 332
  Stratton, Richard de, K.B.1303, I. 110
  Stratton, seigneur le, Kt.1347, II. 8
  Stretton, William, Kt.1529, II. 47
Straubenzee, Charles T. van, K.C.B.1858, I. 245; G.C.B.1875, I. 196
Street, Thomas, Kt.1681, II. 256
STRELLEY, STRALL, STRALLEY
  Strelley, Anthony, Kt.1547, II. 69

STRELLEY
  Strall or Stralley, William, K.B.(1400), I. 129
Strenge, Carl F. von, K.C.V.O.1899, I. 439
Stretton. See Straton
STRICKLAND, STRYKELAND
  Strickland, Edward, K.C.B.1879, I. 256
  Strickland, Robert, Kt.1603, II. 112
  Strickland, Thomas, Kt.1471, II. 15
  Strickland, Thomas, K.B.1603, I. 155
  Strickland, Walter de, K.B.1306, I. 115
  Strykeland, Walter, K.B.1501, I. 146
  Strickland, Walter, Kt.1523, II. 44
  Strickland, William, Kt.1630, II. 198
Stringer, Thomas, Kt.1669, II. 244
Strode. See Stroud
Strong, Samuel H., Kt.1893, II. 391
STROUD, STRODE, STROUDE, STROWDE, and see Chetham-Strode
  Stroude, George, Kt.1685, II. 261
  Stroud, George, Kt.1641, II. 210
  Strode, George, Kt.1676, II. 251
  Strode, John, Kt.1623, II. 183
  Strode, John, Kt.1658, II. 224
  Strode, Nicholas, Kt.1660, II. 229
  Stroude, Richard, Kt.1604, II. 130
  Stroude, Robert, Kt.1603, II. 126
  Strowde, William, Kt.1598, II. 95
  Strode, William, Kt.1660, II. 232
Struth, William J., Kt.1815, II. 315
Struthers, John, Kt.1898, II. 403
Strzelecki, Paul de, K.C.M.G.1869, I. 354
Stuart. See Stewart
Stubbs, Thomas W., Kt.1817, II. 319
Stuckey. See Stukeley
Studder. See Stoddart
STUKELEY, STUCKEY, STEWKLY, STUTELEY
  Stuckey (Stewkly), Hugh, Kt.1625, II. 188
  Stukeley, Lewis, Kt.1603, II. 126
  Stukley, Thomas, Kt.1603, II. 108
  Stewkeley (Stuteley), Thomas, Kt. 1660, II. 226
Stumpes, James, Kt.1549, II. 65
Sturmy, Jo, Kt.1347, II. 7
Sturmy (Sturi), Richard, Kt.(1360), II. 10

Sturmy, Thomas, K.B.(1204), I. 109
Sturt, Anthony, Kt.1713, II. 278
Sturt, Charles, K.C.M.G.1870, I. footnote, 355
Stuteley. See Stukeley
Stutvile, Martyn, Kt.1604, II. 134
Style. See Stile
Subramaniya, Aiyar, K.C.I.E.1900, I. 410
Suche. See Zouch
Suckling, John, Kt.1616, II. 157
Suckling, John, Kt.1630, II. 198
Sudeley, baron. See Boteler
Sudley, John de, K.B.1306, I. 113
Sudley (Sully), John de, Kt.1347, II. 9; K.G.1361, I. 3
Suffield, John, Kt.1713, II. 278
Suffield, lord. See Harbord
Suffolk, duke of. See Pole; see Brandon; see Grey
Suffolk, earl of. See Ufford; see Pole; see Howard
Sugden, Edward B., Kt.1829, II. 328
Suliard. See Sulyard
Sulivan, Bartholomew J., K.C.B.1869, I. 252
Sullivan, Arthur S., Kt.1883, II. 375
Sullivan, Benjamin, Kt.1801, II. 306
Sullivan, Francis W., K.C.B.1879, I. 256
Sully. See Sudley
Sully, John, K.G.1361, I. 3

SULYARD, SULIARD, SWYLIARD
  Suliard, Edward, Kt.1603, II. 121
  Sulyard, Edward, Kt.1618, II. 170
  Swyliard (Suliard), John, Kt.1487, II. 23
  Sulyard, John, Kt.1557, II. 70
  Suliard, John, Kt.1603, II. 121
Sunderland, earl of. See Spencer
Surawongse, Somdetch Chao Phya, K.C.M.G.1879, I. 360
Surcot. See Southcote
Surrey, duke of. See Holand
Surrey, earl of. See Howard
Surrienne, Francis, sire de Lunee, K.G. 1447, I. 12; Kt.1441, II. 12
Surtees, Stephenson V., Kt.1859, II. 354

Sussex, earl of. See Radcliffe; see Yelverton
Sussex, Augustus F., duke of, K.G.1786, I. 48; G.C.H.1815, I. 447; K.T. 1830, I. 82; Grand Master of the Bath (1837), I. 109; G.C.B.1837, I. 206
Sutherland, duke of. See Leveson-Gower; see Sutherland-Leveson-Gower
Sutherland, earl of. See Gordon
Sutherland, Thomas, K.C.M.G.1891, I. 376; G.C.M.G.1897, I. 345
Sutherland-Leveson-Gower, Cromartie, duke of Sutherland, K.G.1902, I. 72
Sutherland-Leveson-Gower, George G., duke of Sutherland, K.G.1841, I. 56
Sutherland-Leveson-Gower, George G., duke of Sutherland, K.G.1864, I. 62
Sutton, Abraham, Kt.1903, II. 415
Sutton, Charles, Kt.1814, II. 314; K.C.B. 1815, I. 224
Sutton, Charles M., viscount Canterbury, G.C.B.1833, I. 206
Sutton, alias Dudley, Edward, lord Dudley, K.B.(1483), I. 139; K.B. (1487), I. 142; K.G.1509, I. 20
Sutton, alias Dudley, Edward, lord Dudley, Kt.1553, II. 66, 68
Sutton, Ferdinando, K.B.1610, I. 158
Sutton, George M., K.C.M.G.1904, I. 394
Sutton, John de, K.B.1327, I. 124
Sutton, John de, Kt.1347, II. 8
Sutton, alias Dudley, John, lord Dudley, K.G.1459, I. 13
Sutton, John, lord Dudley, Kt.1513, II. 41
Sutton, John, K.C.B.1815, I. 217
Sutton, Richard, Kt.1619, II. 171
Sutton, Robert, Kt.1701, II. 272
Sutton, Robert, K.B.1725, I. 168
Sutton, Thomas, Kt.1504, II. 34
Sutton, Thomas M., Kt.1802, II. 306
Sutton, William, Kt.1603, II. 102
Suttor, Francis B., Kt.1903, II. 416
Swale, Richard, Kt.1603, II. 114
Swámy, Mutu Coomára, Kt.1874, II. 366

SWAN, SWANN
  Swann, Francis, Kt.1608, II. 145

INDEX 221

SWAN
  Swan, Joseph W., Kt.1904, II. 419
  Swan, Thomas, Kt.1631, II. 199
  Swann, William, Kt.1608, II. 146
  Swan, William, Kt.1649, II. 222
  Swan, William, Kt.1660, II. 227
  Swanlond, Symon de, Kt.(1336), II. 5
SWEDEN
  Charles XI. of, K.G.1668, I. 36
  Gustavus Adolphus of, K.G.1627, I. 32
  Oscar II. of, K.G.1881, I. 66
  prince Oscar Charles of, G.C.V.O.1904, I. 429
  Oscar Gustave, etc., crown prince of, G.C.B.1901, I. 216
Sweedland (Sweeland), Christopher, Kt. 1812, II. 312
Sweetapple, John, Kt.1694, II. 268
Sweet-Escott, Ernest B., K.C.M.G.1904, I. 395
Sweit, Giles, Kt.1664, II. 239
Swettenham, Frank A., K.C.M.G.1897, I. 382
Swettenham, James A., K.C.M.G.1898, I. 384
SWIFT, SWYFT
  Swyft, Edward, Kt.1603, II. 103
  Swift, Francis, Kt.1617, II. 161
  Swift, Robert, Kt.1603, II. 101
Swinburne, Thomas, Kt.1625, II. 188
SWINTON, SWYNTON
  Swinton (Swyntone, Alexander, Kt. 1633, II. lxii.
  Swynton, Roger, Kt.1347, II. 7
SWYNNERTON, SWINNERTON
  Swynerton, John, Kt.1603, II. 128
  Swinnerton, Thom de, Kt.(1336), II. 5
Swythcoat. See Whichcot
Synbald, David, Kt.1633, II. lxii.
Sydley. See Sedley
SYDENHAM, SIDENHAM, SYDNAM
  Sidenham, Edward, Kt.1642, II. 215
  Sidenham, Francis, Kt.1633, II. 201
  Sydenham, George, Kt.1584, II. 82
  Sidenham, Humphrey, Kt.1639, II. 206
  Sydenham, Humphrey, Kt.1674, II. 249
  Sydnam, John, Kt.1549, II. 64
  Sidnam (Sidenham), John, Kt.1574, II. 76

SYDENHAM
  Sydenham, John, Kt.1603, II. 105
  Sydenham, lord. See Poulett-Thomson
  Sidenham (Sanders), Ralph, Kt.1617, II. 163
Sylvius, Gabriell, Kt.1670, II. 244
Sydney. See Sidney
Symes, Edward S., K.C.I.E.1900, I. 410
Symes, Robert H., Kt.1898, II. 402
SYMON, SIMON
  Simon, John, Kt.1886, II. 380
  Simon, John, K.C.B.1887, I. 290
  Symon, Josiah H., K.C.M.G.1901, I. 388
SYMONDS, SYMONS, SIMMONS
  Symons, Thomas (John), Kt.1623, II. 181
  Symons, George, Kt.1604, II. 135
  Simmons, John L. A., K.C.B.1869, I. 252; G.C.B.1878, I. 197; G.C.M.G. 1887; I. 341
  Symonds, Thomas M. C., K.C.B.1867, I. 251; G.C.B.1880, I. 197
  Symonds, William, Kt.1836, II. 337
  Symons, William P., K.C.B.1898, I. 269
Sympson. See Simpson
Synnot, William, Kt.1606, II. 140
Synnot, William, Kt.1783, II. 297
Szlumper, James W., Kt.1894, II. 394

T

Taaffe, John, Kt.1624, II. 185
Taafe, William, Kt.1604, II. 131
Taché, Etienne P., Kt.1858, II. 353
Tacon, Thomas H., Kt.1900, II. 406
Tadema, Lawrence A., Kt.1899, II. 405
Tagor, Raja Sourindro Mohun, Kt.1884, II. 377
TAIT, TATE
  Tate, Bartholomew, Kt.1523, II. 46
  Tate, John, Kt.1497, II. 30
  Tate, John, Kt.1687, II. 263
  Tait, Melbourne McT., Kt.1897, II. 402
  Tait, Peter, Kt.1868, II. 360
  Tate, Richard, Kt.1553, II. 67
  Tate (Tatt), William, Kt.1606, II. 139
Talbor, Robert, Kt.1678, II. 255

TALBOT, TALBOTT
Talbot, Adelbert C., K.C.I.E.1895, I. 408
Talbot, Charles, duke of Shrewsbury, K.G.1694, I. 39
Talbot, Charles, K.C.B.1862, I. 248
Talbot, earl. See Chetwynd-Talbot
Talbot, Francis, earl of Shrewsbury, K.G.1545, I. 23
Talbot, George, earl of Shrewsbury, K.B.(1475), I. 136; K.G.1487, I. 17
Talbot, George, earl of Shrewsbury, K.B.1547, I. 150; K.G.1561, I. 26
Talbot, Gilbert, lord Talbot, K.G.1408, I. 8
Talbott, Gilbert, Kt.1487, II. 24
Talbot, Gilbert, Kt.1492, II. 27
Talbot, Gilbert, K.G.1495, I. 18
Talbott, Gilbert, Kt.1513, II. 41
Talbot, Gilbert, earl of Shrewsbury, K.G.1592, I. 28
Talbot, Gilbert, Kt.1645, II. 219
Talbot, Henry, Kt.1646, II. 220
Talbot, John, Kt.1347, II. 9
Talbot, John, earl of Shrewsbury, K.G. 1424, I. 10
Talbot, John, earl of Shrewsbury, K.B. (1426), I. 131; K.G.1457, I. 13
Talbott, John, Kt.1482, II. 19, 22
Talbot, John, Kt.1513, II. 40
Talbot, John, Kt.1547, II. 61
Talbot, John, Kt.1599, II. 97
Talbot, John, Kt.1603, II. 110
Talbot, John, Kt.1617, II. 165
Talbot, John, Kt.1660, II. 227
Talbot, John, K.C.B.1815, I. 222; G.C.B.1842, I. 189
Talbot, Reginald A. J., K.C.B.1902, I. 274
Talbot, Richard, lord Talbot, K.B. 1377 I. 126
Talbot, Thomas, Kt.(1361), II. lx.
Talbot, Thomas, viscount Lisle, K.B. (1465), I. 134
Talbott, Thomas, Kt.1482, II. 19
Talbot, Thomas, Kt.1539, II. 52
Talbott, Thomas, Kt.1544, II. 55
Talboyn, Francis, K.B.1547, II. 61
Talboys, George, Kt.1497, II. 30

Talboys or Tailboys, Henry, K.B.(1478), I. 138
Talboys, William, Kt.1461, II. 13
Talcarn (Tolcarn), John, Kt.1627, II. 192
Talfourd, Thomas N., Kt.1850, II. 348
Talmache. See Tollemash
Tame, Edmonde, Kt.1520, II. 43
Tancred, Henry, Kt.1610, II. 149
TANFIELD, TANFELDE
Tanfield, Francis, Kt.1603, II. 122
Tanfield, Lawrence, Kt.1604, II. 129
Tanfelde, Robert, Kt.1501, II. 33
Tangye, Richard, Kt.1894, II. 394
Tankard, Richard, Kt.1642, II. 213
Tankerville, earl of. See Grey, J.; see Bennet
Tanner, Henry, Kt.1904, II. 418
Tanner, Oriel V., K.C.B.1882, I. 258
Tappin. See Tipping
TARBOCK, TERBUKE
Tarbock (Turbocke), Edward, Kt.1606, II. 140
Tarbock, Henry, Kt.1482, II. 19
Terbuke, William, Kt.1497, II. 32
Tarent, H. C. de la Tremouille, prince of, K.G.1653, I. 35
Tarleton, Banastre, G.C.B.1820, I. 185
Tarleton, John W., K.C.B.1873, I. 254
Tarouca, count, G.C.V.O.1903, I. 426
Tasborough, John, Kt.1603, II. 107
Tasborough, Thomas, Kt.1599, II. 95
Taschereau, Henri E., Kt.1902, II. 410
Tash, John, Kt.1719, II. 281
Tate. See Tait
Taubman-Goldie, George D., K.C.M.G. 1887, I. 372
Taunton, William E., Kt.1814, II. 314
Taunton, William E., Kt. 1830, II. 329
Tawney, Richard, Kt.1786, II. 299
Tay, Henry, Kt.1497, II. 29
TAYLOR, TAYLOUR
Taylor, Abraham B., K.H.1837, I. 478
Taylor, Alexander, Kt.1865, II. 357
Taylor, Alexander, K.C.B.1877, I. 256; G.C.B.1889, I. 200
Taylor, Brook, G.C.H.1822, I. 449
Taylor, David, Kt.1884, II. 376
Taylor, Henry, K.C.M.G.1869, I. 355

INDEX 223

TAYLOR
Taylor, Henry G. A., K.C.B.1862, I. 247; G.C.B.1873, I. 196
Taylor, Herbert, K.C.H.1819, I. 454; G.C.H.1825, I. 450; G.C.B.1834, I. 187
Taylor, James, Kt.1765, II. 292, lviii.
Taylor, John, Kt.1727, II. 284
Taylor, John, K.C.B.1834, I. 233
Taylor, John, K.C.B.1897, I. 296
Taylor, Pringle, K.H.1835, I. 472
Taylor, Richard C. H., K.C.B.1882, I. 258; G.C.B.1902, I. 203
Taylor, Robert, Kt.1783, II. 297
Taylor, Robert A., Kt.1899, II. 404
Taylour, Simon, Kt.1684, II. 260
Taylour, Thomas, earl of Bective, K.P. 1783, I. 97
Taylour, Thomas, marquess of Headfort, K.P.1806, I. 98
Taylour, Thomas, marquess of Headfort, K.P.1839, I. 100
Taylour, Thomas, marquess of Headfort, K.P.1885, I. 105
Taylor, Thomas W., Kt.1897, II. 402
Taylor, William, Kt.1471, II. 16
Taylor, William, K.C.B.1902, I. 275
Taynt. See Tinte
Tebbs, Benjamin, Kt.1792, II. 301
Teck, Adolphus, duke of, K.C.V.O. (1897), I. 432; G.C.V.O.1901, I. 418
Teck, prince Alexander A. of, K.C.V.O. (1898), I. 433; G.C.V.O.1904, I. 421
Teck, Francis, duke of, G.C.B.1866, I. 209; G.C.V.O.1897, I. 417
Teck, H.S.H. prince Francis J. of, K.C.V.O.(1898), I. 433
Teddiman, Thomas, Kt.1665, II. 241
Teesdale, Christopher C., K.C.M.G.1887, I. 372
Teesdale, George, K.H.1833, I. 468; Kt. 1833, II. 333
Tehri, Kirti Sah, of, K.C.S.I.1903, I. 328
Tempest, John, Kt.1545, II. 57
Tempest, Nicholas, Kt.1604, II. 129
Tempest, Nicholas, Kt.1621, II. 177

Tempest, Rafe (Richard), Kt.1603, II. 111
Tempest, Richard Kt.1460, II. 13
Tempest, Ric, Kt.1513, II. 39
Tempest, Stephen (Richard), Kt.1603, II. 113
Tempest, Stephen, Kt.1660, II. 231
Tempest, Thomas, Kt.1482, II. 17, 21
Tempest, Thomas, Kt.1523, II. 44
Tempest, Thomas (Nicholas, Richard), Kt.1603, II. 113
Tempest, Thomas, Kt.1640, II. 208
Temple, Alexander, Kt.1604 II. 130
Temple, earl. See Grenville-Temple
Temple, earl. See Nugent-Temple-Grenville
Temple, Henry J., viscount Palmerston, G.C.B.1832, I. 206; K.G.1856, I. 59
Temple, John, Kt.1613, II. 153
Temple, John, Kt.1633, II. 201
Temple, John, Kt.1663, II. 238
Temple, Peter, Kt.1641, II. 209
Temple, Purbeck, Kt.1660, II. 231
Temple, Richard, K.B.1661, I. 164
Temple, Richard, K.C.S.I.1867, I. 318; G.C.S.I.1878, I. 311
Temple, Thomas, Kt.1603, II. 112
Temple, William, Kt.1622, II. 179
Temple, William, K.C.B.1851, I. 278
Temple-Nugent, &c., Richard, duke of Buckingham, K.G.1820, I. 52
Temple-Nugent, &c., Richard, duke of Buckingham, G.C.H.1835, I. 453; K.G.1842, I. 56
Temple-Nugent, &c., Richard, duke of Buckingham, G.C.S.I.1876, I. 310
Templetown, viscount. See Upton
TENNANT, TENNENT, TENANT
Tennant, David, Kt.1877, II. 369; K.C.M.G.1892, I. 377
Tennant, James, K.C.B.1852, I. 239
Tennent, James E., Kt.1845, II. 346
Tenant, Mathew, Kt.1603, II. 113
Tennent. See Tennant
Tenniel, John, Kt.1893, II. 392
Tennyson, Hallam, lord Tennyson, K.C.M.G. 1899, I. 386; G.C.M.G 1903, I. 349
Tenterden, lord. See Abbott

Terbuke. See Tarbock
Terrill. Tyrrell
Terringham (Tiringham), William, K.B.1661, I. 165
Terry, Joseph, Kt.1887, II. 381
Terry (Tirrey), William, Kt.1624, II. 187
Testaferrata, Guiseppe, marquis, C.M.G. (1822), I. preface, xxviii.; K.C.M.G.1833, I. 351
Teynham, lord. See Roper
Teynt. See Tinte
Thackeray, Edward T., K.C.B.1897, I. 295
Thackwell, Joseph, K.H.1834, I. 470; K.C.B.1839, I. 236; G.C.B.1849, I. 190
Theam. See Thynne
Thekeston (Checkstone, Sexton), Richard, Kt.1603, II. 102
Theckston, William, Kt.1624, II. 184
Thelwall, Bevis, Kt.1623, II. 182
Thelwall, Ewball, Kt.1619, II. 172
Theobald, Francis, Kt.1669, II. 243
Theobalds, George, Kt.1633, II. 201
Theotoky, Antonio, count, K.C.M.G. 1818, I. 350; G.C.M.G.1844, I. 334
Theotoky, Emanuel, baron, G.C.M.G. 1818, I. 331
Therry, Roger, Kt.1869, II. 361
Thesiger, Frederic, lord Chelmsford, Kt.1844, II. 345
Thesiger, Frederick A., lord Chelmsford, K.C.B.1878, I. 256; G.C.B. 1879, I. 197; G.C.V.O.1902, I. 420
Thimbilby, John, Kt.1513, II. 41
Thimbleby, John, Kt.1624, II. 186
Thimblethorp (Themilthorp), Edmond (Edward), Kt.1603, II. 117
Thinn. See Thynne
Thiry, François A., K.C.B.1856, I. 241
Tholozan, Joseph D., K.C.M.G.1889, I. 374
Thomas, Alfred, Kt.1902, II. 412
Thomas, Anthony, Kt.1619, II. 174
Thomas, Dalby, Kt.1703, II. 273
Thomas, Edmund, Kt.1686, II. 262
Thomas, Gryffithe ap Rys, K.B.1501, I. 145

Thomas, Griffith, Kt.1904, II. 419
Thomas, John, Kt.1859, II. 354
Thomas, John W., K.C.B.1904, I. 276
Thomas, Leon E. C., K.C.I.E.1893, I. 408
Thomas, Noah, Kt.1775, II. 294
Thomas, Res Ap, Kt.1497, II. 29
Thomas, William, Kt.1513, II. 40
Thomas, William (James), Kt.1603, II. 121
Thomason, Edward, Kt.1832, II. 332
Thomkins. See Tomkins
Thomlinson, Mathew, Kt.1657, II. 224
Thomond, Brian, king of, K.B.1394, I. 127
Thomond, marquess of. See O'Brien, O'Bryen

THOMPSON, THOMSON, TOMPSON

Thompson (Thomson), Alexander, Kt. 1787, II. 300
Thompson, Augustus R., K.C.S.I.1885, I. 323
Thompson, Benjamin, Kt.1784, II. 298
Thomson, Charles W., Kt.1876, II. 367
Thomson, Edward D., K.C.M.G.1874, I. 357
Thompson, Edward M., K.C.B.1895, I. 294
Thomson, George, K.C.B.1898, I. 269
Thompson, Harry L., K.C.M.G.1900, I. 388
Thompson, Henry, Kt.1665, II. 240
Tompson, Henry, Kt.1668, II. 243
Thompson, Henry, Kt.1867, II. 359
Thomson, James, K.C.B.1850, I. 239
Thompson, James, Kt.1897, II. 401
Thomson, James, K.C.S.I.1904, I. 328
Thompson, John, Kt.1607, II. 144
Thompson, John, Kt.1727, II. 283
Thompson, John D., K.C.H.1832, I. 459; Kt.1832, II. 332
Thompson, John S. D., K.C.M.G.1888, I. 373
Thompson, Peter, Kt.1745, II. 287
Thompson, Ralph W., K.C.B.1882, I. 288
Thompson, Ronald F., K.C.M.G.1884, I. 367; G.C.M.G.1888, I. 341
Thompson, Samuel, Kt.1692, II. 267

INDEX

THOMPSON
Thompson, Stephen, Kt.1673, II. 248
Thomson, S., Kt.1688, II. 264
Thompson, Thomas B., Kt.1799, II. 304; K.C.B.1815, I. 218; G.C.B.1822, I. 185
Thompson, William, Kt.1660, II. 225
Thompson, William, Kt.1689, II. 265
Thompson, William, Kt.1715, II. 280
Thomson, William, lord Kelvin, Kt. 1866, II. 358; G.C.V.O.1896, I. 417
Thomson, William, Kt.1897, II. 400
Thomson, William T., K.C.M.G.1879, I. 360
Thon, —, K.C.V.O.1901, I. 440
Thorburn, Robert, K.C.M.G.1887, I. 370
Thorburn, Walter, Kt.1900, II. 406

THORN, THORNE
Thorn, Nathaniel, K.H.1832, I. 467; K.C.B.1857, I. 243
Thorne, Peregrine F., K.H.1837, I. 478
Thorne, Richard T., K.C.B.1897, I. 295
Thorn, William, K.H.1832, I. 466
Thorne, William, Kt.1904, II. 418

THORNBROUGH, THORNBORROW, THORNBERY
Thornborrow, Benjamin, Kt.1618, II. 170
Thornbrough, Edward, K.C.B.1815, I. 217; G.C.B.1825, I. 185
Thornborowe (Thornbery), John, Kt. 1603, II. 117
Thornborough, Thomas, Kt.1630, II. 197
Thorneborough, William, Kt.1547, II. 62
Thorne. See Thorn

THORNEY, THORNHAUGH, THORNY, THORNEGH, THORNIX, THORNHURST
Thorney, Francis, Kt.1615, II. 156
Thornhaugh (Thorney, Thornix), John, Kt.1603, II. 103, 116, 127
Thornehurst, Stephen, Kt.1594, II. 91
Thornix (Thornhurst), Thomas, Kt. 1625, II. 189
Thorny (Thornegh), William (John), Kt.1603, II. 116
Thornhill, James, Kt.1720, II. 281
Thornhill, James B., K.H.1837, I. 478
Thornhill, John, Kt.1619, II. 175
Thornhill, Robert, Kt.1715, II. 280
Thornhill, Timothy, Kt.1614, II. 154
Thornhill, William, K.H.1816, I. 463
Thornhaugh, Thornhurst, Thornix. See Thorney

THORNTON, THORNETON, THORNTON
Thornton, Charles, G.C.H.1837, I. 453
Thornton, Charles W., K.H.1819, I. 464; K.C.H.1831, I. 456; Kt.1831, II. 329
Thornton, Edward, G.C.B.1822, I. 205
Thornton, Edward, K.C.B.1870, I. 285; G.C.B.1883, I. 211
Thornton, George, Kt.1599, II. 95
Thornton, Gregory de, K.B.1306, I. 115
Thornton, Isaac, Kt.1661, II. 233
Thornton, James H., K.C.B.1904, I. 276
Thorntone, Peter de, K.B.1329, I. 125
Thorneton, Piers de, Kt.1347, II. 9
Thorneton, Roger, Kt.1482, II. 18, 21
Thornton, Roger, Kt.1625, II. 188
Thornton, Thomas, Kt.1894, I. 394
Thornton, William, Kt.1707, II. 275
Thornton, William, K.C.B.1836, I. 233
Thornton, William H., K.C.M.G.1856, I. 353
Thornycroft, John I., Kt.1902, II. 412
Thorold, Anthony, Kt.1585, II. 83
Thorold, Charles, Kt.1704, II. 273
Thorold, Edward (Edmund), Kt.1603, II. 117
Thorold (Thorald), George, Kt.1708, II. 276
Thorold, John, Kt.1603, II. 103
Thorold, Robert, Kt.1641, II. 209
Thorold, William, Kt.1604, II. 130
Thorold, William, Kt.1617, II. 164
Thorold, William, Kt.1660, II. 230
Thoroton, John, Kt.1614, II. 313
Thorowgood, Benjamin, Kt.1685, II. 261
Thorowgood, John, Kt.1630, II. 198, 201
Thorowgood, Thomas, Kt.1761, II. 290
Thorpe, George de, K.B.1305, I. 110
Thorpe, Samuel, K.H.1835, I. 472
Thorpe, Thomas, Kt.1460, II. 12
Thorpe-Douglas, Adye, Kt.1902, II. 410
Thouthorp, John de, K.B.1306, I. 117

Thring, Henry, lord Thring, K.C.B. 1873, I. 285
THROGMORTON, THROCKMORTON
Throgmorton, Arthur, Kt.1596, II. 92
Throckmorton, Baynham, Kt.1660, II. 227
Throgmarton, Christopher, Kt.1489, II. 27
Throckmorton, Clement, Kt.1660, II. 231
Throckmorton, George, Kt.1604, II. 132
Throckmorton, Gerrard, Kt.1603, II. 111
Throgmorton, John, Kt.1565, II. 72
Throgmorton, John, Kt.1606, II. 139
Throckmorton, Joseph, Kt.1661, II. 232
Throckmorton, Nicholas, Kt.1547, II. 62
Throgmorton, Nicholas, Kt.1603, II. 110
Throgmorton, Robert, K.B.1501, I. 145
Throgmorton, Thomas, Kt.1553, II. 68
Throgmorton, Thomas, Kt.1587, II. 85
Throckmorton, William, Kt.1661, II. 235
Throgmorton. See Carew
Thuillier, Henry E. L., Kt.1879, II. 371
Thuillier, Henry R., K.C.I.E.1895, I. 408
Thurland, Edward, Kt.1665,, II. 240
Thurstan, John, B., K.C.M.G.1887, I. 371
THWAITES, THWAYTES
Thwaites, John, Kt.1865, II. 357
Thwaites, Samuel, Kt.1619, II. 174
Thwaytes, Thomas, 1483, II. 21
THYNNE, THINN, THEAM, THEIN, THIN, THYNE
Thinn, Egremont, Kt.1624, II. 183
Thynne (Theam, Theim), George, Kt. 1642, II. 213
Thynne, Henry Kt.1603, II. 122
Thynne, Henry, Kt.1898, II. 402

THYNNE
Thin (Thynne) James, Kt.1639, II. 206
Thyne (Boteville alias Thynne), John, Kt.1547, II. 61
Thinne, John, Kt.1603, II. 105
Thynne, Reginald T., K.C.B.1902, I. 274
Thinne, Thomas, Kt.1604, II. 135
Thynne, Thomas, marquess of Bath, K.G.1778, I. 47
Thynne, Thomas, marquess of Bath, K.G.1823, I. 53
Thyrkyll, Lancelot, K.B.1501, I. 146
Tibetot. See Tiptoft
TICHBOURNE, TICHBORNE, TITCHBORNE
Tichbourne, Benjamin, Kt.1601, II. 99
Tichborne, Benjamin, Kt.1618, II. 169
Tichborne, Benjamin, Kt.1670, II. 244
Tichborne, Henry, Kt.1623, II. 182
Titchbourne, Henry, Kt.1694, II. 268
Tichborne, Richard, Kt.1603, II. 107
Titchborne, Robert, Kt.1656, II. 223
Tichborne, Walter, Kt.1603, II.107,136
Titchborne, William, Kt.1661, II. 234
Tierney, Matthew, K.C.H.1831, I. 457
Tildesley, Thomas, Kt.1616, II. 158
Tileswick, Thomas, Kt.1661, II. 235
Tillard, Isaac, Kt.1722, II. 282
TILLY, TILLEY, TILLIE, TYLEY
Tilly, Henry, K.B.1323, I. 122
Tilley (Tillie), James, Kt.1687, II. 263
Tilley, John, K.C.B.1880, I. 287
Tyley, Joseph, Kt.1696, II. 269
Tilley, Samuel L., K.C.M.G.1879, I.361
Tilney, Philippe, Kt.1501, II. 33
Tilson, Thomas, Kt.1868, II. 360
TIMPERLEY, TYMPERLEY
Timperley, —, Kt.1347, II. 9
Tymperley, John, Kt.1501, II. 33
Timperley, Thomas, Kt.1618, II. 169
Tindal. See Tyndall
TINTE, TEYNT, TYNTE
Teynt (Tynte, Taynt), Henry, Kt.1660, II. 232
Tinte, Robert, Kt.1620, II. 175
TIPTOFT, TIBETOT
Tiptoft, John, K.B.1400, I. 128

INDEX

TIPTOFT
Tiptoft, John de, earl of Worcester, K.G.1461, I. 14
Tibetot, Pain de, K.B.1305, I. 110

TIPPING, TIPPIN, TAPPIN, TYPPIN
Tippin (Typpin, Tapin), George, Kt. 1605, II. 139
Tipping, Thomas, Kt.1660, II. 228

Tirpitz, Alfred von, G.C.V.O.1904, I. 430
Tirrell. See Tyrrell
Tirrey. See Terry

TIRRINGHAM, TYRRINGHAM
Tirringham, Anthony, Kt.1603, II. 111
Tirringham, Arthur, Kt.1617, II. 163
Tyrringham, John, Kt.1642, II. 215
Tirringham, Thomas, Kt.1603, II. 110

Tirwhit. See Tyrwhitt
Tite, William, Kt.1869, II. 361
Tittoni, Tommaso, G.C.V.O.1903, I. 428
Tobin, John, Kt.1820, II. 321
Tobin, Thomas, Kt.1855, II. 351
Todd, Charles, K.C.M.G.1893, I. 378
Todd, D'Arcy, K.H.1822, I. 464
Todde, Richard, Kt.1487, II. 26
Toke, Nicholas, Kt.1681, II. 257
Toketts, Roger, Kt.1471, II. 16
Tolcorn. See Talcarn
Tolly, Barclay de, G.C.B.1815, I. 183

TOLLEMASH, TALMACHE
Talmache, Lyonall, Kt.1612, II. 151
Tollemash, Lionel, earl of Dysart, K.T. 1743, I. 78

Toller, Samuel, Kt.1812, II. 310
Tombs, Henry, K.C.B.1868, I. 251
Tomes, John, Kt.1886, II. 379
Tomkins (Thompkins), Thomas, Kt. 1662, II. 236
Tomlins, Thomas E., Kt.1814, II. 314
Tompson. See Thompson.
Tonge, George, Kt.1617, II. 162
Tonk, Nawab of, G.C.I.E.1890, I. 401
Tonkin, Warwick H., Kt.1836, II. 337
Toone, William, K.C.B.1819, I. 229
Topan, Tharia, Kt.1890, II. 387
Topham, John, Kt.1679, II. 253
Topham, William, Kt.1858, II. 352
Torrens, Arthur W. K.C.B.1853, I. 240
Torrens, Henry, K.C.B.1815, I. 222

Torrens, Henry D'O., K.C.B.1887, I. 261; K.C.M.G.1889, I. 374
Torrens, Robert R., K.C.M.G.1872, I. 356; G.C.M.G.1884, I. 339
Torriano, John, Kt.1755, II. 288
Torrington, viscount. See Byng
Totty, John, Kt.1672, II. 247
Touche, James J. D. La, K.C.S.I.1901, I. 327

TOUCHET, TUCHET
Touchet, Ferdinando, K.B.1610, I. 158
Tuchet, George, lord Audley, Kt.1586, II. 84
Tuchet, James, lord Audley, K.B.(1475), I. 136
Tuchet, John, lord Audley, Kt.1513, II. 38
Touchet, alias Audley (Dudley), Mervyn, Kt.1608, II. 144

Townley, Charles, Kt.1761, II. 290
Townley, John, Kt.1497, II. 32
Townley, Richard, Kt.1482, II. 19
Towneley, Richard, Kt.1547, II. 62

TOWNSHEND, TOWNSEND, TOWNESEND
Townshend, Charles, viscount Townshend, K.G.1724, I. 42
Townsend, Edmond, K.C.B.1904, I. 276
Townsend, Henry, Kt.1604, II. 133
Townshend, Horatio G. P., K.C.H. 1835, I. 461; Kt.1835, II. 336
Townsend, Isaac, Kt.1722, II. 282
Townshend, lord James, K.C.H.1835, I. 461
Townsend, John, Kt.1596, II. 92
Townsend, John, Kt.1603, II. 110
Townshend, John R., earl Sydney, G.C.B.1863, I. 209
Townshende, Robert, Kt.1545, II. 57
Townesend, Robert, Kt.1603, II. 109
Townsend, alias Agborough, Robert, Kt.1660, II. 227
Townesende, Roger, Kt.1486, II. 23
Townsend, Roger, Kt.1588, II. 86
Tozer, Horace, K.C.M.G.1897, I. 383

TRACEY, TRACY
Tracey, John, Kt.1347, II. 6
Tracey, John, Kt.1574, II. 76
Tracy, John, Kt.1591, II. 89

INDEX

TRACY
Tracy, John (Richard), Kt.1603, II. 115
Tracy, John, Kt.1618,' II. 168
Tracy, Richard, Kt.1603, II. 115, 123, 133
Tracey, Richard E., K.C.B.1898, I. 270
Tracy, Robert, Kt.1616, II. 159
Tracy, Thomas, Kt.1609, II. 148
Tracy, William, K.B.1306, I. 113

TRAFFORD, TRAFORD
Trafford, Cecil, Kt.1617, II. 164
Trafford, Clement, Kt.1760, II. 289
Trafford, Edmond, Kt.1603, II. 100
Trafford (Canford), Edmond, K.B. (1426), I. 132
Trafford, Edmund, Kt.1532, II. 48
Trafford, Edmond, Kt.1544, II. 55
Trafford, Edmond, Kt.1578, II. 78
Traford, Edward (Edmond), K.B. (1494), I. 144

Traile, John, Kt.1787, II. 300
Traill-Burroughs, Frederick W., K.C.B. 1904, I. 276
Trappes, Francis, Kt.1603, II. 113
Trautmansdorff-Weinsberg, prince Charles, &c., of, G.C.V.O.1904, I. 430
Travancore, Bala Rama Varma, of, G.C.S.I.1888, I. 313; G.C.I..E1903, I. 404
Travancore, Madava Rao, dewan of, K.C.S.I.1866, I. 317
Travancore, maharaja of, K.C.S.I.1866, I. 315; G.C.S.I.1866, I. 309
Travancore, maharaja of, G.C.S.I.1882, I. 312
Travell, Thomas, Kt.1684, II. 260
Travers, Eaton, K.H.1834, I. 471
Travers, Eaton S., Kt.1834, II. 334
Travers, James, K.H.1837, I. 478
Travers, John, Kt.1550, II. 65
Travers, Patrick, Kt.(1330), I. lix.
Travers, Robert, Kt.(1330), I. lix.
Travers, Robert, Kt.1625, II. 188
Travers, Robert, K.C.M.G.1823, I. 351
Treacher, John, Kt.1785, II. 298

Treacher, William H., K.C.M.G.1904, I. 394
Treadway, Walter, Kt.1603, II. 116
Treby, George, Kt.1681, II. 255
Tredenham, William, Kt.1660, II. 230
Tredway, Robert, Kt.1642, II. 213
Tregonnell, John, Kt.1553, II. 66
Treiagu, John de, K.B.1306, I. 121
Treise, Christopher, Kt.1761, II. 290
TRELAWNEY, TRELANY
Trelany, Jonathan, Kt.1598, II. 95
Trelawney, John, Kt.1628, II. 194
Treloar, William P., Kt.1900, II. 406
Tremain, John, Kt.1689, II. 265
TREMAYLE, TRENAYLL
Tremayle, John, Kt.1513, II. 42
Tremayle, Thomas, Kt.1501, II. 33
Trenayll, William, Kt.1523, II. 44
Tremenheere, Walter, K.H.1832, I. 467
Trenayll. See Tremayle
Trench, Frederick W., K.C.H.1832, I. 458; Kt.1832, II. 332
Trench. See Le Poer Trench
Trenchard, George, Kt.1588, II. 87
Trenchard, George, Kt.1603, II. 110
Trenchard, John, Kt.1589, II. 265
Trenchard, Thomas, Kt.1504, II. 34
Trenchard, Thomas, Kt.1613, II. 154
Trendell, Arthur J. R., Kt.1900, II. 407
Trentham, Christopher, Kt.1627, II. 191
Trentham, Thomas, Kt.1617, II. 165
Tresham, —, Kt.1461, II. 13
Tresham, Lewis, Kt.1612, II. 151
Tresham, Thomas, Kt.1575, II. 76
Tresham, Thomas, Kt.1608, II. 145
Tresham, William, Kt.1613, II. 152
Tress, Thomas, Kt.1633, II. 201
Treury (Terury), John, Kt.1485, II. 22
TREVANYON, TREVANION, TREVANIAN
Trevanion, Charles, Kt.1644, II. 218
Trevanion, Hugh, Kt.1532, II. 49
Trevanyon, John, K.B.1509, I. 148
Trevanion, Nicholas, Kt.1710, II. 277
Trevanyon, William, Kt.1508, II. 34
TREVELYAN, TREVELLIAN
Trevelyan, Charles E., K.C.B.1848, I 277
Trevellian, George, Kt.1617, II. 164
Trevelyan, John, K.B.1501, I. 146

INDEX

Treves, Frederick, K.C.V,O.(1901), I. 434
Trevisano, Andrew de, Kt.1497, II. 31
Trevor, Arthur C., K.C.S.I.1898, I. 326
Trevor, Arthur H., K.H.1835, I. 472
Trevor, Charles C., Kt.1896, II. 398
Trevor, Edward, Kt.1617, II. 166
Trevor (Treavor, Traver), John, Kt.1603, II. 109
Trevor, John, Kt.1619, II. 171, 172
Trevor, John, Kt.1671, II. 245
Trevor, Richard, Kt.1597, II. 94
Trevor, Seckford, Kt.1604, II. 133
Trevor, Thomas, Kt.1619, II. 171, 172
Trevor, Thomas, Kt.1641, II. 211
Trevor, Thomas, K.B.1661, I. 164
Trevor, Thomas, Kt.1692, II. 267
Trigge, Thomas, K.B.1801, I. 175
Trigona, baron Pasquale S., K.C.M.G. 1868, I. 354
Trilby, Joseph, Kt.1697, II. 270
Trollope, Andrew, Kt.1461, II. 13
Trollope, Charles, K.C.B.1873, I. 254
Trollope, Henry, Kt.1797, II. 304; K.C.B.1820, I. 229; G.C.B.1831, I. 186
Tromp, Martin van, Kt.1642, II. 212
Trot, Nicholas, Kt.1619, II. 172
Trotter, Henry, Kt.1617, II. 164
Trotter, Henry, K.C.V.O.(1901), I. 433; G.C.V.O.1902, I. 420
Trotti, Ardingo, K.C.B.1857, I. 244
Trousiaus, Guillaume de, Kt.(1360), II. 10
Trowtbek, William, K.B.(1483), I. 139; Kt.1487, II. 24; Kt.1487, II. 25
Trumbull, William, Kt.1634, II. 260
Truman (Trueman), Benjamin, Kt.1761, II. 290
Truscott, Francis W., Kt.1872, II. 364
Truscott, George W., Kt.1902, II. 413
Trussell, —, Kt.1347, II. 8
Trussel, Jo, Kt.1347, II. 7
Trussel, William, K.B.1306, I. 113
Trutch, Joseph W., K.C.M.G.1889, I. 374
Trüter, Johannes A., Kt.1823, II. 324
Tryon, George, K.C.B.1887, I. 262
Tryon, Samuel, Kt.1615, II. 155
Tuchet. See Touchet
Tucker, Charles, K.C.B.1900, I. 272

Tucker, Edward, Kt.1813, II. 312; K.C.B.1815, I. 223; G.C.B.1862, I. 194
Tudor, Edmund, earl of Richmond, K.B.(1449), I. 132
Tudor, Jasper, earl of Pembroke, K.B. (1449), I. 132; K.G.1459, I. 13
Tufton, Charles, Kt.1666, II. 242
Tufton, Humphrey, Kt.1614, II. 154
Tufton, John, Kt.1603, II. 105
Tufton, John, Kt.1627, II. 193
Tufton, John, Kt.1641, II. 211
Tufton, Nicholas, Kt.1603, II. 100
Tufton, Richard, Kt.1681, II. 255
Tuite, Edmund, Kt.1619, II. 174
Tuite, Richard, Kt.1555, II. 69
Tuke, John B., Kt.1898, II. 402
Tuke, Samuel, Kt.1664, II. 239
Tullibardine, earl of. See Murray
Tulloch, Alexander B., K.C.B.1902, II. 274
Tulloch, Alexander M., K.C.B.1857, I. 280
Tulp, Didrigh, Kt.1674, II. 249
Tulse, Henry (William), Kt.1673, II. 248
Tunis, Bey of, G.C.B.1865, I. 209
Tunstall, John, Kt.1619, II. 172
Tunstall, Marmaduke, Kt.1533, II. 49
Tunstall, Richard, K.G.1483, I. 17
Tunstall (Dunstall, Constable), Thomas, K.B.(1426), I. 132
Tupper, Charles, K.C.M.G.1879, I. 361; G.C.M.G.1886, I. 340
Tupper, Charles H., K.C.M.G.1893, I. 379
Tupper, Charles L., K.C.I.E.1903, I. 411
TURBERVILLE, TURBERVILL, and see Turville
  Turbervill, Gervase, K.H.1836, I. 473
  Turberville, John, Kt.1485, II. 23
  Turberville, Thomas, Kt.1665, II. 240
Turbock. See Tarbock
Turin, Vittorio E., count of, G.C.V.O. 1903, I. 426
TURKEY
  Abdul Aziz, sultan of, K.G.1867, I. 64

INDEX

TURKEY
Abdul Medjid, sultan of, K.G.1856, I. 59

TURNER, TURNOR, TOURNER, TOURNEUR, TOURNOUR
Turner, Alfred E., K.C.B.1902, I. 275
Turner, Barnard, Kt.1784, II. 298
Turnor (Turner), Charles, Kt.1696, II. 269
Turner, Charles A., Kt.1879, II. 370; K.C.I.E.1888, I. 405
Turner, Charles B., K.H.1832, I. 467
Turner, Charles R., Kt.1871, II. 362
Turnor, Christopher, Kt.1660, II. 230
Turner, Edmund, Kt.1664, II. 239
Turnor, Edward, Kt.1660, II. 229
Turnor, Edward, Kt.1664, II. 239
Turner, Frank, K.C.B.1886, I. 260
Turner, George, K.C.B.1862, I. 247
Turner, George, K.C.M.G.1897, I. 381
Turner, George J., Kt.1851, II. 348
Turner, Jeremiah, Kt.1604, I. 134
Turner, John, Kt.1684, II. 260
Turner, John C., Kt.1786, II. 299
Turner, Llewellyn, Kt.1870, II. 362
Turner, Montagu C., Kt.1903, II. 414
Tourner (Tourneur, Turnour), Timothy, Kt.1670, II. 244
Turner, Tomkyns H., Kt.1814, II. 314; K.C.H.1819, I. 454; G.C.H. 1827, I. 450
Turner, William, Kt.1662, II. 237, 239
Turnor, William, Kt.1686, II. 262
Turner, William, Kt.1886, II. 379; K.C.B.1901, I. 298
Turner, William W., K.C.S.I.1867, I. 318
Turney, John, Kt.1889, II. 385

TURPIN, TURPYN
Turpyn, George, Kt.1565, II.. 72
Turpin, William, Kt.1603, II. 103
Turpington, John, K.B.(1400), I. 129
Turton, John, Kt.1689, II. 265
Turton, John, Kt.1782, II. 296

TURVILLE, TURVILE, and see Turberville
Turvile (Turwell), Ambrose, Kt.1603, II. 107

TURVILLE
Turville, Francis F., K.C.M.G.1875, I. 358
Tuson, Henry B., K.C.B.1895, I. 266
Tuthill, George L., Kt.1820, II. 321
Tutt, Alexander, Kt.1604, II. 131
Tuyll, Henry a, Kt.1623, II. 181
Tuyll, Philibert a, Kt.1623, II. 181, bis
Tuyll, William, baron de Tuyll, K.H. 1827, I. 465; K.C.H.1831, I. 457; Kt.1831, II. 331
Tweeddale, marquess of. See Hay
Twisden, Roger, Kt.1620, II. 175
Twisden, Thomas, Kt.1660, II. 229
Twisden, William, Kt.1603, II. 106
Twisleton, Philip, Kt.1658, II. 224
Twiss, Travers, Kt.1867, II. 359
Twyford, John de, K.B.1306, I. 116
Twynam, William C., K.C.M.G.1896, I. 381
Tyas (Tyers), Daniel, Kt.1644, II. 217
Tyes, Theodoric le, K.B.(1205), I. 109
Tyke, Bryan, Kt.1529, II. 47
Tylden, John M., Kt.1812, II. 311
Tylden, William B., K.C.B.1855, footnote, I. 241
Tyler, Charles, K.C.B.1815, I. 218; G.C.B. 1833, I. 187
Tyler, George, K.H.1833, I. 469; Kt. 1838, II. 341
Tyler, Henry W., Kt.1877, II. 369
Tyler, James, Kt.1851, II. 348
Tyler, John, K.H.1835, I. 472
Tyler, John W., Kt.1888, II. 384
Tyler, William, Kt.1485, II. 22
Tyler, William, Kt.1497, II. 31
Tyler, William, Kt.1513, II. 39
Tyley. See Tilly

TYNDALL, TINDAL, TYNDALE
Tyndall, John, K.B.1533, I. 150
Tyndall, John, Kt.1603, II. 114
Tindal, Nicholas C., Kt.1826, II. 326
Tyndall, Thomas, Kt.1553, II. 68
Tyndale, Thomas, Kt.1561, II. 71
Tyndall, William, K.B.(1489), I. 143
Tynte. See Tinte
Tyrconnel, earl of. See Carpenter
Tyrconnell, viscount. See Brownlow
Tyrone, earl of. See Beresford

TYRRELL, TERRILL, TIRRELL, TYRELL,
TERRIL
Terrill, Anthony, Kt.1609, II. 149
Tirrell (Terrill), Edward, Kt.1603, II.
  106
Tyrrell, Edward, Kt.1607, II. 143
Tyrell (Terrell), Henry, K.B.1547, I.
  152
Tyrell, James, Kt.1471, 1482, II. 14, 17
Tyrrell, John, Kt.1586, II. 84
Tirrell, John, Kt.1553, II. 66
Tyrell, John, Kt.1603, II. 104, 127
Terril (Tirrell), John, Kt.1628, II. 193
Tyrell (Tyrett, Terell), Robert, Kt.1497,
  II. 29
Tirrell, Robert, Kt.1607, II. 141
Tyrell (Terell), Thomas, Kt.1487, II.26
Tyrell (Tyrett, Tyrwhit, Thomas, Kt.
  1497, II. 29
Tirrell, Thomas, of Gyppynge, Kt.1513,
  II. 38
Tyrrell, Thomas, of Heron, Kt.1513,
  II. 38
Tyrell, Thomas, Kt.1557, II. 69
Tyrrell, Thomas, Kt.1607, II. 141
Tyrrell, Thomas, Kt.1660, II. 230
Tirrell, Timothy, Kt.1624, II. 186
Tirrel, Timothy, Kt.1643, II. 216
Tyrrell, Walter, Kt.(1428), II. lx.
Tyrell, William, Kt.1460, II. 12
TYRWHITT, TYRWHITE, TYRWHYT, TIRWHIT,
TIRWHITT, and see Tyrrell
Tirwhit, Edward, Kt.1603, II. 103
Tirwhitt, Philip, Kt.1603, II. 102
Tyrwhyt, Rob, Kt.1513, II. 39
Tyrwhite, Robert, Kt.1543, II. 54
Tyrwhitt, Thomas, Kt.1812, II. 311
Tyrwhit, William, Kt.1487, II. 24
Tyrwhite, William, Kt.1497, II. 29
Tyrringham. See Tirringham

U

Udaipur, Sujjun Singh, maharana of,
  G.C.S.I 1881, I. 312
Udaipur, Sumbho Sing, maharana of,
  G.C.S.I.1871, I. 310
Udall. See Uvedall
Udney, John, Kt.1497, II. 29

Udny, Richard, K.C.S.I.1897, I. 326
Ufford, Robert de, K.B.1303, I. 110
Ufford, Robert de, earl of Suffolk, K.G.
  1348, I. 2
Ufford, Thomas, K.G.1360, I. 3
Ufford, William de, earl of Suffolk, K.G.
  1375, I. 4
UGHTRED, OUGHTRED, OWTRED, UTRIGHT,
UTREIGHT
Utreight [Ughtred], Anthony, Kt.1512,
  1513, II. 35, 36
Owtred, Henry, K.B.1509, I. 148
Oughtred, Henry, Kt.1593, II. 90
Utreight, Robert, Kt.1523, II. 45
Ughtred, Thomas, lord Ughtred K.G.
  1358, I. 3
UMFREVILLE, UMFRAVILLE
Umfrevill, Charles, Kt.1661, II. 234
Umfraville, Robert, K.G.1408, I. 9
UMPTON, UNTON
Umpton, Alexander, K.B.1547, I. 151
Umpton (Unton), Edward), K.B.1559,
  I. 153
Umpton (Unton), Henry, Kt.1586, II.
  84
Umpton, Thomas, Kt.1533, II. 49
Underhill, Edward, Kt.1613, II. 152
Underhill, Hercules, Kt.1617, II. 166
Underhill, John, Kt.1626, II. 191
Unton. See Umpton
Upington, Thomas, K.C.M.G.1887, I. 370
Upton, George F., viscount Templetown,
  K.C.B.1869, I. 251; G.C.B.1886, I.
  198
Urbino, Frederick Ubaldi, duke of, K.G.
  1474, I. 16
Urbino, Guido Ubaldi de Montefeltre,
  duke of, K.G.1503-4, I. 19
Urling (Urlin), Simon, Kt.1744, II. 286
Urmston, James B., Kt.1824, II. 324
Urrey (Verrey), John, Kt.1643, II. 216
Urswick, Thomas, Kt.1471, II. 16
Usedom, Ernest A. J. G. von, K.C.M.G.
  1902, I. 391
Usfleet, Gerard de, K.B.1306, I. 119
USSHER, USHER
Ussher, Thomas, K.C.H.1831, I. 457;
  Kt.1831, II. 331
Ussher, William, Kt.1603, II. 127

USSHER
Usher, William, Kt.1636, II. 204
Utreight. See Ughtred
UVEDALL, UDALL, UVEDALE, OVEDALE
Uvedall (Udall), Edmond, Kt.1607, II. 143
Uvedall, Edward, Kt.1588, II. 87
Uvedale, John de, K.B.1305, I. 110
Uvedale, Richard, Kt.1618, II. 169
Uvedale, Thomas, Kt.1465, II. 14; K.B.(1465), I. 135
Ovedale, William, K.B.1483, I. 140
Uvedall, William, K.B.(1489), I. 143
Udall, William, Kt.1601, II. 99
Uvedall (Udall), William, Kt.1613, II. 153
Uvedall, William T., Kt.1605, II. 137
Uxbridge, earl of. See Paget

V

Vache, Philip de la, K.G.1399, I. 7
Vache, Richard de la, K.G.1356, I. 2
Vachill. See Vaschell
Vaglia, Emilio Ponzio, G.C.V.O.1903, I. 426
Vaillant, Jean B. P., comte, G.C.B.1855, I. 191
Vaire. See Frator
Valaoriti, Spiridione, K.C.M.G.1862, I. 354
VALE, VALL, VALLE, and see Davall
Vale, Geoffrey de la, K.B.1389, I. 126
Vale, Gustavus du, Kt.1656, II. 223
Valle, Henry de, Kt.(1337), preface, II. lix.
Valeresso, —, Kt.1624, II. 187
Valiant, Thomas, K.H.1836, I. 473; K.C.B.1844, I. 238
Vall, Valle. See Vale
Vallack, James, K.H.1834, I. 470
Vallentin, James, Kt.1869, II. 362
Valsamachi, Demetrio, count, C.M.G. (1820), preface, I. xxviii.; K.C.M.G. 1844, I.352; G.C.M.G.1857, I. 335
Valsamachi, Spiridione, K.C.M.G.1855, I. 353
Vampage, William, Kt.1487, II. 25
Vanaker, Nicholas, Kt.1701, II. 272
Vanbrugh, John, Kt.1714, II. 279

Vance, Horatio P., Kt.1897, II. 401
Vanchelin, Cornelius, Kt.1619, II. 173
Vandeleur, John O., K.C.B.1815, I. 219; G.C.B.1833, I. 187
Vandeput, Peter, Kt.1684, II. 260
Vanderduffin, Ewald (Edmund), Kt.1619, II. 172
Vandyke, Anthony, Kt.1632, II. 200
Vane, Charles W., marquess of Londonderry, K.B.1813, I. 179; G.C.B.1815, I. 181; G.C.H.1816, I. 447; K.G. 1853, I. 59
Vane, George, Kt.1640, II. 208
Vane (Powlett), Harry G., duke of Cleveland, K.G.1865, I. 62
Vane, Henry, Kt.1640, II. 207
Vane, Henry, duke of Cleveland, K.G. 1842, I. 57
Vane, Henry F., G.C.B.1826, I. 185
Vane, Henry M., Kt.1883, II. 376
Vane, Rauf, Kt.1545, 1547, II. 56, 61
Vane, Thomas, Kt.1573, II. 75
Vane, Thomas, Kt.1598, II. 95
Vane, William H., duke of Cleveland, K.G.1839, I. 56
Vane-Tempest, George H. R. C. W., marquess of Londonderry, K.P.1874, I. 104
Vane-Tempest-Stewart, Charles S., marquess of Londonderry, Grand Master K.P.1886, I. 95; K.G.1888, I. 68; G.C.V.O.1903, I. 421
Vane. See Fane
Vanhatten, John, Kt.1761, II. 290
Van Keppel. See Keppel
Vanlore, Peter, Kt.1621 II. 178
Varlett, Edward, Kt.1588, footnote, II. 86
Varnam. See Vernon
Varnbuler, baron Axel, G.C.V.O.1904, I. 429
Varney. See Verney
VASCHELL, VACHILL
Vachill (Vacathell), Thomas, Kt.1603, II. 108
Vaschell, William, Kt.1809, II. 309
Vassall, Spencer L. H., K.H.1837, I. 479; Kt.1838, II. 340
Vatchope, Jo, Kt.1633, I. lxii.
Vaudry, Edward, Kt.1687, II. 263

Vaughan (Wangham), Charles, Kt.1608, II. 146
Vaughan, Charles R., G.C.H.1833, I.452; Kt.1833, II. 333
Vaughan, Edward, Kt.1643, II. 217
Vaughan, George, Kt.1643, II. 215
Vaughan, Henry, Kt.1603, II. 105
Vaughan, Henry, Kt.1643, II. 215
Vaughan, Henry, Kt.1662, II. 236
Vaughan, Hugh, Kt.1504, II. 34
Vaughan, James, Kt.1897, II. 400
Vaughan, John, Kt.1547, II. 59
Vaughan, John, Kt.1599, II. 96
Vaughan, John, Kt.1617, II. 160
Vaughan, John, K.B.1661, I.164
Vaughan, John, Kt.1668, II. 243
Vaughan, John, K.B.1792, I. 174
Vaughan, John, Kt.1828, II. 327
Vaughan, John L., K.C.B.1887, I. 261
Vaughan, Richard, Kt.1513, II. 41
Vaughan, Richard, Kt.1603, II. 121
Vaughan, Richard, earl of Carbery, K.B. 1626, I. 161
Vaughan, Richard, Kt.1815, II. 315
Vaughan, Robert, Kt.1619, II. 172
Vaughan, Roger, II. 1549, II. 64
Vaughan, Rowland, Kt.1618, II. 167
Vaughan, Thomas, K.B.1475, I. 137
Vaughan, Walter, Kt.1603, II. 111
Vaughan, William, Kt.1542, II. 53
Vaughan, William, Kt.1628, II. 194
Vaux, Nicholas, Kt.1487, II. 25; Kt. 1497, II. 29
Vaux, Theodore de, Kt.1665, II. 240
Vaux, Thomas, lord Vaux, K.B.1533, I. 149
VAVASOUR, VAVASOR, LE VAVASOUR, VAVAZOR
Vavasour, Henry le, K.B.1326, I. 123
Vavasour, John, Kt.1501, II. 33
Vavasor, John, Kt.1617, II. 162
Vavasour, Mauger, Kt.1603, II. 101
Vavasour, Peter, Kt.1513, II. 40
Vavazor, Philip, Kt.1761, II. 290
Vavasor, Thomas, Kt.1597, II. 94
Vavasour, William, Kt.1544, II. 55
Veel. See Veil
Veiga, Francisco M. da, K.C.V.O.1903, I. 441

VEIL, VEEL
Veel, John, Kt.1629, II. 196
Veil, Thomas de, Kt.1744, II. 287
Veja, Marino, K.C.M.G.1820, I. 350; G.C.M.G.1825, I. 332
Venetian ambassador, Kt.1611, II. 151
Venables, Thomas, Kt.1544, II. 54
Venables, William, baron of Kynderton, Kt.1533, II. 50
Venables-Vernon, William H., Kt.1903, II. 416
Venables-Vernon-Harcourt, William G. G., Kt.1873, II. 365
Venkatagiri, Velugoti of, K.C.I.E.1888, I. 406
Ventrice, Francis, Kt.1603, II. 124
Ventris, Peyton, Kt.1689, II. 265
Verdoen, Pieter, Kt.1730, II. 284
Verdon, Christofer, Kt.1347, II. 8
Verdon, George F., K.C.M.G.1872, I. 356
Verdon, John, Kt.1347, II. 8
Verdon, Thomas de, K.B.1306, I. 112
Vere, —, Kt.1492, II. 28
Vere, Albert de, Kt. 1610, II. 149
Vere, Aubrey de, earl of Oxford, K.G. 1660, I. 35
Vere, Charles B., K.C.B.1815, I. 225
Vere, Edward, Kt.1607, II. 142
Vere, Francis, Kt.1588, II. 87
Vere, Henry de, earl of Oxford, K.B. 1610, I. 157
Vere, Horatio, Kt.1596, II. 92
Vere, Hugh de, earl of Oxford, K.B. 1233, I. 109
Vere, John de, earl of Oxford, K.B. (1426), I. 130
Vere, John de, earl of Oxford, K.B. (1465), I. 134; K.G.1486, I. 17
Vere, John, earl of Oxford, Kt.1513, II. 38; K.G.1527, I. 22
Vere, John de, earl of Oxford K.B. 1547, I. 150
Vere, John, Kt.1607, II. 142
Vere, Richard de, earl of Oxford, K.G. 1415, I. 9
Vere, Robert de, duke of Ireland, K.G. 1384, I. 6
Vere, Robert, K.B.(1426), I. 131

INDEX

Vere, Robert de, earl of Oxford, Kt. 1629, II. 196
Vere, Thomas de, K.B.1306, I. 113
Verley, Philip de, K.B.1306, I. 116
Vermuyden, Cornelius, Kt.1629, II. 195
Vernam. See Vernon
VERNEY, VARNEY
 Verney, Edmund, Kt.1643, II. 217
 Verney, Edward (Edmund), Kt.1611, II. 150
 Verney, Francis, Kt.1604, II. 130
 Verney, Grevill, Kt.1617, II. 166
 Verney, Grevill, K.B.1661, I. 165
 Verney, John, K.B.(1485), I. 142
 Verney, Ralph, Kt.1471, II. 16
 Verney, Ralph, Kt.1641, II. 208
 Verney, Rauf, Kt.1501, II. 33
 Verney, Rauf, Kt.1513, II. 40
 Verney, Rauf, Kt.1538, II. 51
 Verney, Richard, Kt.1603, II. 105
 Varney, Richard, Kt.1685, II. 261
 Verney, Robert, Kt.1604, II. 131
 Verney, Thomas, Kt.1553, II. 68
 Verney, Thomas, Kt.1603, II. 127
VERNON, VERNAM, VARNAM, VARNON, and see Venables
 Vernon, Charles, Kt.1717, II. 281
 Vernon, Charles H., Kt.1799, II. 305
 Vernon, Edward, Kt.1624, II. 186
 Vernon, Edward, Kt.1773, II. 294
 Vernon, George, K.B.1547, I. 151
 Vernon, George, Kt.1627, II. 193
 Vernon, George, Kt.1681, II. 257
 Vernon, Henry, K.B.(1483), I. 140
 Vernon, Henry, K.B.(1489), I. 143
 Vernon, John, Kt.1538, II. 51
 Vernon, Robert, Kt.1599, II. 96
 Varnam (Varnon), Robert, Kt.1603, II. 115, 127
 Vernon, Robert, Kt.1615, II. 155
 Varnam (Vernan), Thomas, Kt.1603, II. 125
 Vernon, Thomas, Kt 1685, II. 260
Verrey. See Urry
Versturme, Dr., K.H.1821, I. 464
Verteuil, Louis A. A. de, K.C.M.G.1895, I. 381
Verver (Vervon), Frederick de, Kt.1621, II. 176
Veulle, John de, Kt.1831, II. 329
Veylleville, Rouland de, Kt.1497, II. 30
Vicars, Arthur E., Kt.1896, II. 398; K.C.V.O.1903, I. 436
Victoria, duke de la. See Espartero
Vigliani, Paul H., G.C.M.G.1897, I. 344
Villaca, Antonio E., G.C.V.O.1904, I. 431
VILLIERS, VILLERS, WILLERS
 Villiers, Edward, Kt.1616, II. 159
 Villiers, Edward, Kt.1680, II. 254
 Villiers, Edward H., earl of Clarendon, G.C.B.1902, I. 216
 Villiers (Willers), George, Kt.1593, II. 90
 Villiers, George, duke of Buckingham, Kt.1615, II. 155; K.G.1616, I. 31
 Villiers, George, Kt.1644, II. 217
 Villiers, George, duke of Buckingham, K.G.1649, I. 34
 Villiers, George W. F., earl of Clarendon, G.C.B.1837, I. 206; Grand Master K.P.1847, I. 94; K.G.1849, I. 58
 Villers (Villiers), John, Kt.1501, II. 33
 Villiers, John, Kt.1531, II. 48
 Villiers (Villers), John, Kt.1616, II. 158
 Villiers, John H. de, Kt.1877, II. 369; K.C.M.G.1882, I. 364
 Villiers, William, viscount Grandison, Kt.1638, II. 205; K.B.1638, I. 163
Vincent, Andrew A., K.H.1831, I. 465
Vincent, Arthur (Anthony), Kt.1617, II. 166
Vincent, Charles E. H., Kt.1896, II. 397; K.C.M.G.1899, I. 386
Vincent, Edgar, K.C.M.G.1887, I. 372
Vincent, Francis, Kt.1603, II. 115
Vincent, Mathias, Kt.1684-5, II. 261
Vincent, Nicholas C. B., K.C.B.1819, I. 228
Vincent, William, Kt.1660, II. 226
Vine, John R. S., Kt.1886, II. 380
Viner, Vinor. See Vyner
Viney, James, K.C.H.1834, I. 460
Viseu, Henry, duke of, K.G.1442, I. 12
VIVIAN, VIVYAN, VYVYAN
 Vivian, Arthur P. K.C.B.1902, I. 299
 Vivyan, Francis, Kt.1619, II. 170

INDEX 235

VYVYAN
Vyvyan, George R., K.C.M.G.1902, I. 392
Vivian, Hussey C., lord Vivian, K.C.M.G.1886, I. 369
Vivian, Richard, Kt.1636, II. 204
Vivian, Richard H., K.C.B.1815, I. 222; K.C.H.1816, I. 454; G.C.H. 1831, I. 451; G.C.B.1837, I. 138
Vivian, Robert J. H., K.C.B.1857, I. 244; G.C.B.1871, I. 195
Vizagapatam, Gajapati Rao of, K.C.I.E. 1903, I. 412
Vizianagram, Maharaja Pasupati, K.C.I.E.1887, I. 400; G.C.I.E.1892, I. 402
Vizianagram, Raz Maune, of, K.C.S.I. 1866, I. 315
Voeux, George W. Des, K.C.M.G.1883, I. 365; G.C.M.G.1893, I. 343
Vogel, Julius, K.C.M.G.1875, I. 358
Volkousky, prince, G.C.B.1819, I. 184
Vowell (Fowell), Edward, Kt.1619, II.174
VYNER, VYNOR, VINER, VINOR
Vinor, George, Kt.1663, II. 238
Viner (Vinor, Vyner), Robert, Kt.1665, II. 241
Viner, Thomas, Kt.1653, II. 223, 230
Vyvyan. See Vivian

W

Wachesham, John de, K.B.1306, I. 115
Waddam, Nicholas, Kt.1504, II. 34
Waddington, Henry, Kt.1662, II. 237
Waddy, Richard, K.C.B.1877, I. 255
Wade, Claude M., Kt.1839, II. 342
Wade, Thomas F., K.C.B.1875, I. 286; G.C.M.G.1889, I. 342
Wade (Waad), William, Kt.1603, II. 109
Wade, Willoughby F., Kt.1896, II. 397
Wadeson. See Madeson
Wadham, Edward, Kt.1513, II.40
Waechter, Max L., Kt.1902, II. 413
Wafyr (Waver), Henry, K.B.(1465), I. 135
Wager, Charles, Kt.1709, II. 277
Wagstaff, Combe, Kt.1660, II. 230
Wagstaff, Joseph, Kt.1644, II. 218

Wagstaff, Thomas, Kt.1693, II. 268
Waite, Nicholas, Kt.1699, II. 271
Wake, Isaack, Kt.1619, II. 171
Wakering, Gilbert, Kt.1604, II. 129
Walcott, John, Kt.1646, II. 221
Walcott, Stephen, K.C.M.G.1877, II. 359
Wallcott, Thomas, Kt.1681, II. 257
Waldeck, lord, Kt.1547, II. 61
Waldeck and Pyrmont, Frederic, prince of, G.C.B.1904, I. 204
Waldeck, George V., prince of, G.C.B. 1882, I. 211
WALDEGRAVE, WALGRAVE, WALDGRAVE
Waldegrave, Edward, Kt.1553, II. 66
Walgrave, Edward, Kt.1607, II. 143
Walgrave (Mulgrave), Edward, Kt.1646, II. 221
Waldegrave, George, Kt.1603, II. 119
Waldgrave, Henry, Kt.1683, II. 259
Waldegrave, James, earl Waldegrave, K.G.1738, I. 43
Waldegrave, James, earl Waldegrave, K.G.1757, I. 45
Walgrave, Thomas, Kt.1461, II. 13
Walgrave, William, K.B.1501, I. 145
Walgrave, William, Kt.1533, II. 49
Waldegrave, William, Kt.1576, II. 77
Waldegrave, William, Kt.1595, II. 91
Waldegrave, William, Kt.1688, II. 264
Waldegrave, William, lord Radstock, G.C.B.1815, I. 182
Walden, Humfrey de, K.B.1306, I. 112
Walden, Richard, Kt.1513, II. 40
Waldencourte, Lewes de, Kt.1513, II. 40
Waldersee, count von, G.C.B.1901, I. 203
Walderton, William, Kt.1549, II. 65
Waldo, Edward, Kt.1677, II. 252
Waldo, Timothy, Kt.1769, II. 293
Waldron. See Walrond
Wale, Charles, K.C.B.1815, I. 219
Wale, Thomas, K.G.1344, I. 2
Wale, William, Kt.1660, II. 226
WALES
Arthur, prince of, K.B.(1489), I. 143; K.G.1491, I. 18
Edward, prince of, K.G.1348, I. 1; Kt. 1346, II. 6
Edward, prince of, Kt.1461, II. 13

INDEX

WALES
 Frederic L., prince of, K.G.1717, I. 41
 George F. E. A., prince of, K.G.1884, I. 67; K.T.1893, I. 88; K.P.1897, I. 106; G.C.V.O. 1897, I. 417; G.C.M.G.1901, I. 347; Victorian Chain 1902, I. 416
 Henry F., prince of, Kt.1594, II. 91; K.G.1603, I. 29
 James, prince of, K.G.1692, I. note, 38
Waleys, Roger, K.B.1306, I. 116
Walker, Andrew B., Kt.1877, II. 369
Walker, Baldwin W., K.C.B.1841, I. 237
Walker, Chamberlain, Kt.1721, II. 282
Walker, Charles P. B., K.C.B.1881, I. 258
Walker, Edward, Kt.1645, II. 219
Walker, Edward, K.H.1832, I. 467
Walker, Edward N., K.C.M.G.1888, I.373
Walker, Edward S., Kt.1841, II. 343
Walker, George, Kt.1676, II. 251
Walker, George G., K.C.B.1892, I. 292
Walker, George T., K.C.B.1815, I. 219; G.C.B.1817, I. 183
Walker, Hovenden, Kt.1711, II. 277
Walker, James, K.C.M.G.1869, I. 354
Walker, James L., Kt.1903, II. 414
Walker, Leslie, K.H.1832, I. 467
Walker, Mark, K.C.B.1893, I. 265
Walker, Patrick, Kt.1814, II. 314
Walker, Thomas, Kt.1681, II. 256
Walker, Walter, Kt.1661, II. 234
Walker, William, Kt.1685, II. 260
Walker, William H., Kt.1871, II. 362
Walker, William S., K.C.B.1886, I. 289
Walkingham, John de, K.B.1306, I. 114
Walkington, William, Kt.1347, II. 6
Walkinshaw, John, Kt.1717, footnote, II. 266
Wallace, Arthur R., Kt.1901, II. 408
Wallace, Donald M., K.C.I.E.1887, I.400; K.C.V.O.(1901), I. 434
Wallace, James, Kt.1777, II. 295
Wallace, James M., K.H.1830, I. 465; Kt.1831, II. 331
Wallace, John A., K.C.B.1833, I. 232
Wallace, Richard, K.C.B.1878, I. 286
Wallace, Robert, K.H.1837, I. 476
Wallace, Robert, K.C.S.I.1866, I. 317

Waller, Hardresse, Kt.1629, II. 196
Waller, James W. S., K.H.1832, I. 467
Waller, Johnathan W., K.H.1824, I. 464; K.C.H.1827, I. 456; G.C.H.1830, I. 450
Waller, Thomas, Kt.1597, II. 94
Waller, Walter, Kt.1572, II. 75
Waller, Walter, Kt.1622, II. 180
Waller, William, Kt.1622, II. 179
Wallington, John W., K.C.B.1898, I. 297
Wallis, Provo W. P., K.C.B.1860, I. 246; G.C.B.1873, I. 196
Wallop, Henry, Kt.1569, II. 74
Wallop, Henry, Kt.1599, II. 97
Wallop, John, K.G.1543, I. 23
Wallop, Oliver, Kt.1547, II. 62
Wallum, John, Kt.1347, II. 9
Wallwyn, Richard, Kt.1553, II. 69
Walmoden-Gimborn, Ludwig G. T., count of, K.C.B.1815, I. 226; G.C.B.1834, I. 187
Walmesley, Joshua, Kt.1840, II. 342
Walmesley, Thomas, Kt.1603, II. 114
Walmesley, Thomas, Kt.1617, II. 164
Walmore. See Wilmore
Walpole, Charles G., Kt.1897, II. 402
Walpole, Edward, K.B.1661, I. 165
Walpole, Edward, Kt.1663, II. 238
Walpole, Edward, K.B.1753, I. 169
Walpole, Horace G., K.C.B.1892, I. 293
Walpole, John, Kt.1645, II. 220
Walpole, Robert, earl of Orford, K.B. 1725, I. 168; K.G.1726, I. 42
Walpole, Robert, earl of Orford, K.B. 1725, I. 167
Walpole, Robert, K.C.B.1859, I. 245
Walpole, Spencer, K.C.B.1898, I. 297
WALROND, WALRON, WALDRON, WALRAN
 Walran, Adam, K.B.1306, I. 116
 Waldron, Alexander, Kt.1672, II. 247
 Waldron, Charles, Kt.1644, II. 218
 Waldron, Richard, Kt.1616, II. 160
 Waldron, Thomas, Kt.1621, II. 177
 Walrond (Waldron), William, Kt.1671, II. 245
Walsh. See Welsh
Walsham, John, K.C.M.G.1895, I. 380
Walsingham, —, Kt.1513, II. 42
Walsingham, Edmond, Kt.1513, II. 42

INDEX

Walsingham, Francis, Kt.1577, II. 78
Walsingham, Thomas, Kt.1573, II. 75
Walsingham, Thomas, Kt.1613, II. 154
Walter, Edward, Kt.1885, II. 377; K.C.B.1887, I. 290
Walter, John, Kt.1619, II. 171
Walter, Richard, Kt.1700, II. 271
Walter, Robert, Kt.1603, II. 101
Walter, William, Kt.1603, II. 108
Walters, George, Kt.1727, II. 284
Walton, Adam de, K.B.1306, I. 120
Walton, George, Kt.1604, II. 135
Walton, George, Kt.1721, II. 282
Walton, Joseph, Kt.1901, II. 409
Walton, Thomas of, Kt.1487, II. 25
Walton (Wolton), William, Kt.1347, II. 7
Walton, William H., Kt.1875, II. 367
WANDESFORD, WANDISFORD, WANDSFORD
Wandesford, Christopher, Kt.1586, II. 84
Wandesford, (Mansford), George, Kt. 1607, II. 142
Wandisford, John, Kt.1497, II. 32
Wandsford, Rowland, Kt.1638, II. 205
Wannerville, Adam de, K.B.1306, I. 121
Wantage, lord. See Loyd-Lindsay
Wanton, Thomas, Kt.1603, II. 120
WARBURTON, WARBLETON, WERBERTON, WARBRETON, WARBERTON
Warbleton, George (John), Kt.1513, II. 36
Warbreton, John, Kt.1497, II. 31
Werberton, John, Kt.1553, II. 67
Warberton, Peter, Kt.1603, II. 114
Warburton, Richard, Kt.1603, II. 102
Warburton, Robert, K.C.I.E.1898, I. 410
Warcop. See Warcup
WARDE, WARD
Warde, Charles, K.H.1837, I. 475
Warde, Christopher, Kt.1482, II.17, 20
Ward, Edward, Kt.1657, II. 223
Ward, Edward, Kt.1693, II. 268
Warde, Edward C., K.C.B.1869, I. 252
Ward, Edward W. D., K.C.B.1900, I. 272
Ward, Edward W., K.C.M.G.1879, I. 361
Warde, Francis, K.C.B.1873, I. 253

WARDE
Warde, Henry, K.C.B.1815, I. 218; G.C.B.1831, I. 186
Ward, Henry G., G.C.M.G.1849, I. 335
Ward, Humble, Kt.1643, II. 216
Ward, James (Lamer), Kt.1683, II. 258
Ward, John, Kt.1714, II. 279
Ward, Joseph G., K.C.M.G.1901, I. 390
Ward, Patience, Kt.1675, II. 250
Warde, Richard, Kt.1601, II. 99
Ward, Robert, Kt.1670, II. 245
Ward, Thomas, Kt.1761, II. 291
Ward, William, Kt.1900, II. 407
Ward, William E., K.C.S.I.1896, I. 325
Ward, William H., earl of Dudley, Grand Master K.P.1902, I. 95; G.C.V.O.1903, I. 421
Wardeler (Wardlaw), Henry, Kt.1613, II. 153
Wardle, Thomas, Kt.1897, II. 399
Wardour, Edward, Kt.1618, II. 169
Ware. See Warre
Waren. See Warren
WARHAM, WARRAM
Warham, George, Kt.1523, II. 45
Warram (Warham), William, Kt.1553, II. 69
WARING, WAREING
Wareing, Arnold, Kt.1633, II. 200
Waring, Henry J., Kt.1891, II. 388
Warneford, Edmund, Kt.1681, II. 257
Warner, Edward, Kt.1544, II. 56
Warner, Henry, Kt.1603, II. 123
Warner, Joseph H., Kt.1892, II. 391
Warner, Thomas, Kt.1629, II. 196
Warner, Thomas, Kt.1675, II. 250
WARRE, WARR, WARE, DE LA WARR
Warr, de la, earl. See Sackville-West
Warre, Henry J., K.C.B.1886, I. 260
Ware, James, Kt.1616, II. 159
Ware, James, Kt.1630, II. 197
Warre, John, Kt.1660, II. 227
Warr, lord de la. See West
Ware, Piers de la, Kt.1347, II. 7
Were, Ric de, Kt.1347, II. 8
Warr, Richard de la, K.B.1501, I. 146
La Warr, Roger, sire de la Warr, Kt. (1360), II. 10

INDEX

WARR
Warr, Thomas de la, lord la Warr, K.B.1377, I. 126
Warre, William de la, Kt.1347, II. 8
Warre, William, Kt.1839, II. 341
WARREN, WAREN, WARRENNE
Warren, Charles, K.C.B.1865, I. 250
Warren, Charles, K.C.M.G.1883, I. 366; G.C.M.G.1885, I. 340; K.C.B. 1888, I. 291
Warren, Edward, Kt.1544, II. 54
Warren, Edward, Kt.1599, II. 96
Warren, George, K.B.1761, I. 170
Warren, Henry, Kt.1596, II. 92
Warrenne, John de, earl of Surrey, K.B.1306, I. 111
Waren, John, Kt.1487, II. 26
Warren, John B., K.B.1794, I. 174; G.C.B.1815, I. 180; G.C.H.1819, I. 449
Warren, Pelham L., K.C.M.G.1902, I. 392
Warren, Peter, K.B.1747, I. 169
Warren, Rauf, Kt.1538, II. 51
Warren, Samuel, K.C.H.1835, I. 461; Kt.1835, II. 336; K.C.B.1839, I. 236
Warren, William, Kt.1599, II. 96
Warren, William, Kt.1661, II. 234
Warrington, Thomas R., Kt.1904, II. 417
Warton. See Wharton
Warwick, earl of. See Beauchamp; see Nevill; see Dudley; see Rich; see Greville
Washington, John, Kt.1623, II. 181
Washington, Laurence, Kt.1627, II. 192
Washington, William, Kt.1622, II. 178
Washington, William, K.C.B.1843, I. 237
Waspayl, William, Kt.(1284), II. lviii.
Watenald, William de, Kt.1347, II. 6
Waterfield, Henry, K.C.S.I.1893, I. 325; G.C.I.E.1902, I. 404
Waterfleet, Cornelius, Kt.1616, II. 157
Waterfleet, Giles, Kt.1616, II. 157
Waterford, marquess of. See Beresford
Waterhouse, Edward, Kt.1603, II. 106
Waterhowes, Edward, Kt.1584, II. 83

Waterlow, Ernest A., Kt.1902, II. 412
Waterlow, Sydney H., Kt.1867, II. 359; K.C.V.O.(1902), I. 435
Waterman, George, Kt.1665, II. 241
Waters, John, K.C.B.1832, I. 232
Waterton, Robert, Kt.1482, II. 20
Waterton, Robert, K.B.1501, I. 145
Waterton, Thomas, Kt.1544, II. 55
Waterville, John de, K.B.1305, I. 111
Waterville, Robert de, K.B.1306, I. 122
Wathen. See Baghott, Paul
Wathen, Charles, Kt.1889, II. 385
Wathen, Samuel, Kt.1803, II. 306
Watkin, Edward W., Kt.1868, II. 360
Watkins, David, Kt.1620, II. 176
Watney, John, Kt.1900, II. 407
Watson, Edward, Kt.1603, II. 105
Watson, Edward, Kt.1619, II. 173
Watson, Francis, Kt.1678, II. 252
Watson, Frederick, K.H.1819, I. 464; Kt. 1819, II. 320
Watson, Frederick B., K.C.H.1827, I. 455; Kt.1827, II. 326
Watson, George W., K.C.B.1891, I. 263
Watson, Henry, Kt.1817, II. 318
Watson, Henry E., Kt.1886, II. 378
Watson, James, Kt.1795, II. 302
Watson, James, K.C.B.1839, I. 236
Watson, James, Kt.1874, II. 366
Watson, James M., K.C.M.G.1878, I. 360
Watson, John, K.C.B.1886, I. 260; G.C.B. 1902, I. 203
Watson, Lewis, Kt.1608, II. 146
Watson, Patrick H., Kt.1903, II. 414
Watson, Thomas, Kt.1617, II. 161, 169
Watson, William, Kt.1786, II. 299
Watson, William, Kt.1796, II. 303
Watson, William, Kt.1897, II. 400
Watson, William H., Kt.1856, II. 352
Watson, William R., Kt.1892, II. 391
Watson-Wentworth, Charles, marquess of Rockingham, K.G.1760, I. 45
Watson-Wentworth, Thomas, marquess of Rockingham, K.B.1725, I. 168
Watt, George, Kt.1903, II. 414
Watts, James, Kt.1857, II. 352
Watts, John, Kt.1603, II. 128
Watts, John, Kt.1625, II. 190
Watts, John, Kt.1645, II. 220

INDEX 239

Waugh, Andrew S., Kt.1860, II. 355
Wauton, George, Kt.1604, II. 135
Wauton, Thomas, Kt.1603, II. 120
Wauton, Thomas, Kt.1622, II. 180
Wautor, alias Aches, William, Kt.1347, II. 6
Way, Gregory H. B., Kt.1814, II. 314
Way, Samuel J., Kt.1900, II. 406
Wayll, John de la, Kt.1523, II. 44

WAYNEMAN, WAINEMAN, WEYNMAN, WAYNMAN
Wayneman, Edmond, Kt.1605, II. 138
Waineman, Francis, Kt.1618, II. 168
Wayneman, Richard, Kt.1566, II. 72
Waynman, Richard, Kt.1596, II. 93
Wayneman, Thomas, Kt.1553, II. 68
Waynman, Thomas, Kt.1603, II. 108
Wayneman, Thomas, Kt.1617, II. 166
Weare, Henry E., K.C.B.1891, I. 264
Weare, Thomas, K.H.1836, I. 474
Wearge Clement, Kt.1724, II. 283

WEBB, WEBBE
Webb, Aston, Kt.1904, II. 420
Webb, Daniel, Kt.1714, II. 279
Webbe, John, Kt.1604, II. 130
Webb, John, Kt.1821, II. 322
Webb, John, K.H.1832, I. 458
Webb, John S., K.C.M.G.1889, I. 374
Webb, William, Kt.1592, II. 90
Webbe, William, Kt.1604, II. 130
Webb, William, Kt.1609, II. 147
Weber, Hermann, Kt.1899, II. 404
Webster, Godfrey, Kt.1708, II. 276
Webster, Henry V., Kt.1843, II. 345
Webster, Richard E., Kt.1885, II. 377; G.C.M.G.1893, I. 343
Weddell, Thomas P., earl de Grey, K.G. 1844, I. 57
Wedderburn, James, Kt.1822, II. 323
Wedel, count von, K.C.V.O.1901, I. 439; G.C.V.O.1901, I. 425
Wedon, Ralph de, K.B.1306, I. 114
Weede, jonkheer Rudolf E. W. de, K.C.V.O.1904, I. 442
Welby, Reginald E., lord Welby, K.C.B. 1882, I. 288; G.C.B.1892, I. 214
Welby, William, K.B.1603, I. 155

WELCH, WEALCH, WELCHE, WELSH, WALSH, WALSHE
Walsh, Aubrey, Kt.1889, II. 386
Walsh, Edmond, Kt.1606, II. 140
Walsh, John, Kt.1649, II. 221
Walshe, Nicholas, Kt.1597, II. 94
Walsh, Nicholas, Kt.1623, II. 183
Walshe, Patricke, Kt.1579, II. 80
Welche, Richard, Kt.1591, II. 88
Welsh (Wealch), Richard, Kt.1605, II. 137
Welch, Richard, Kt.1803, II. 306
Welsh, Robert, Kt.1603, II. 123
Welch, Robert, Kt.1642, II. 214
Welsh, William, Kt.1603, II. 110, 112

WELD, WILDE, and see Wild
Weld, Frederick A., K.C.M.G.1880, I. 362; G.C.M.G.1885, I. 340
Weld (Wilde), Humphrey, Kt.1603, II. 128
Weld, John, Kt.1683, II. 258
Weldon, Anthony, Kt.1617, II. 163
Weldon, Rafe, Kt.1603, II. 127
Wellesley, Arthur, duke of Wellington, K.B.1804, I. 176; K.G.1813, I. 51; G.C.B.1815, I. 180; G.C.H.1816, I. 447
Wellesley, Arthur C., duke of Wellington, GC.V.O.1902, I. 419; K.G. 1902, I. 72
Wellesley, Arthur R., duke of Wellington, K.G.1858, I. 60
Wellesley, Henry, lord Cowley, K.B. 1812, I. 178; G.C.B.1815, I. 205
Wellesley, Henry R. C., earl Cowley, K.C.B.1851, I. 278; G.C.B.1853, I. 208; K.G.1866, I. 63
Wellesley, George G., K.C.B.1880, I. 257; G.C.B.1887, I. 199
Wellesley, Richard, marquess Wellesley, K.P.1783, I. 97; K.G.1810, I. 50; Grand Master St. Patrick, I. 93, 94
Wellesley-Pole, William, earl of Mornington, G.C.H.1830, I. 450
Wellington, duke of. See Wellesley
Wellisbourne, John, Kt.1545, II. 57

WELLS, WELLES
Wells, John, K.C.B.1820, I. 229; G.C.B.1834, I. 187
Wells, John, viscount Welles, Kt. 1485, II. 22; K.G.1488, I. 18
Welles, Lionel de, lord Welles, K.B. (1426), I. 131; K.G.1457, I. 13
Wells, Mordaunt L., Kt.1858, II. 353
Wells, Richard, K.C.B.1896, I. 267
Welsh. See Welch
WENDY, WINDY
Windy (Wendy), Thomas, K.B.1661, I. 166
Wendy, William, Kt.1618, II. 169
Wenlock, John, lord Wenlock, K.G.1461, I. 13
Wenlock, lord. See Lawley
Wentworth, George, Kt.1630, II. 197
Wentworth, George, Kt.1633, II. 202
Wentworth, Henry, K.B.1478, I. 138
Wentworth, John, Kt.1547, II. 59
Wentworth, John, Kt.1603, II. 103, 108, 119
Wentworth, John, Kt.1667, II. 242
Wentworth, Michael, Kt.1681, II. 256
Wentworth, Nicholas, Kt.1545, II. 56
Wentworth, Peter, K.B.1626, I. 162
Wentworth, Richard, K.B.1478, I. 138
Wentworth, Richard, K.B.1509, I. 148
Wentworth, Richard, Kt.1513, II. 36
Wentworth, Roger, Kt.1497, II. 30
Wentworth, Thomas, Kt.1513, II. 42
Wentworth, Thomas, lord Wentworth, Kt.1523, II. 45
Wentworth, Thomas, lord Wentworth, Kt.1547, II. 62
Wentworth, Thomas, earl of Cleveland, K.B.1610, I. 157
Wentworth, Thomas, earl of Strafford, Kt.1611, II. 151; K.G.1640, I. 33
Wentworth, Thomas, Kt.1616, II. 160
Wentworth, Thomas, lord Wentworth, K.B.1626, I. 161
Wentworth, Thomas, Kt.1660, II. 229
Wentworth, Thomas, earl of Strafford, K.G.1712, I. 41
Wentworth, William, Kt.1603, II. 108
Wentworth, William, earl of Strafford, Kt.1635, II. 203; K.G.1661, I. 35

Wentworth, William, Kt.1637, II. 205
Wentworth-Fitzwilliam, Charles W., earl Fitzwilliam, K.G.1851, I. 58
Wentworth-Fitzwilliam, William, earl Fitzwilliam, K.G.1862, I. 61
Were. See Warre
West, Algernon E., K.C.B.1886, I. 290; G.C.B.1902, I. 216
West, Augustus, Kt.1824, II. 325
West, Edward, Kt.1822, II. 323
West, John, earl De la Warr, K.B.1725, I. 167
West, John, K.C.B.1840, I. 236; G.C.B. 1860, I. 193
West, Raymond, K.C.I.E.1888, I. 405
West, Thomas, K.B.1326, I. 123
West, Thomas, K.B.(1413), I. 130
West, Thomas, lord de la Warr, K.B. 1478, I. 137; K.G.1510, I. 20
West, Thomas, lord De La Warr, K.B. (1489), I. 143; K.G.1549, I. 24
West, Thomas, Kt.1513, II. 36, 42
West, Thomas, lord de la Warr, Kt.1587, II. 86
West, Thomas, Kt.1591, II. 88
West, Thomas, lord de la Warr, Kt.1599, II. 96
West William, Kt.1536, II. 50
West, William, lord de la Warr, Kt.1570, II. 74
Westbrooke, William, Kt.1844, II. 345
Westland, James, K.C.S.I.1895, I. 325
Westley, Robert, Kt.1744, II. 286
Wesley, Samuel R., K.C.B.1862, I. 248
Westmacott, Richard, Kt.1837, II. 339
Westmacott, Richard, K.C.B.1898, I. 269
Westmeath, earl of. See Nugent
Westminster, duke and marquess of, See Grosvenor
Westmorland, earl of. See Nevil; see Fane
Weston, Brown, Kt.1511, II. 35
Weston, Francis, K.B.1533, I. 149
Weston, Henry, K.B.1559, I. 153
Weston, James, Kt.1631, II. 199
Weston, Jerom, Kt.1603, II. 107
Weston, John de, K.B.1306, I. 114
Weston, Joseph D., Kt.1886, II. 380
Weston, Richard, Kt.1518, II. 43

INDEX 241

Weston, Richard, Kt.1596, II. 93
Weston, Richard, earl of Portland, Kt. 1603, II. 119; K.G.1630, I. 32
Weston, Richard, Kt.1622, II. 179
Weston, Richard, Kt.1635, II. 204
Weston, Richard, Kt.1679, II. 253
Weston, Simon, Kt.1599, II. 97
Weston, Thomas de, K.B.1326, I. 123
Weston, William, Kt.1593, II. 90
Westphall, George A., Kt.1824, II. 324
Westropp, Michael R., Kt.1870, II. 362
Wet, Jacobus A. de, K.C.M.G.1890, I. 375
Wet, Jacobus P. de, Kt.1883, II. 375
Wetherall, Charles, Kt.1824, II. 324
Wetherall, Edward R., K.C.S.I.1867, I. 318
Wetherall, Frederick A., G.C.H.1833, I. 452; Kt.1833, II. 333
Wetherall, George A., K.H.1833, I. 468; K.C.B.1856, I. 243; G.C.B.1865, I. 194
Wetherall, J., K.H.1832, I. 468
Wetheryngton. See Widdrington
Wetwang, John, Kt.1680, II. 255
Weyland, William de, K.B.1306, I. 120
Weymes, Henry, Kt.1678, II. 253
Weymes, James, Kt.1662, II. 237
Weymes, Patrick, Kt.1641, II. 211
Weymouth, viscount. See Thynne
Whale, John, Kt.1829, II. 327
Whaley, Herbert, Kt.1684, II. 259
Whalley, Samuel St. S. B., Kt.1827, II. 326

WHARTON, WARTON

Wharton, George, K.B.1603, I. 153
Wharton, Henry, Kt.1548, II. 63
Warton, Michael, Kt.1617, II. 162
Wharton, Miles (Michael), Kt.1666, II. 242
Wharton, Philip, duke of Wharton, K.G. Jacobite, 1726, note, I. 38
Warton, Ralph, Kt.1669, II. 243
Wharton, Thomas, Kt.1527, II. 46
Wharton, Thomas, Kt.1545, II. 57
Wharton, Thomas, Kt.1611, II. 151
Wharton, Thomas, K.B.1626, I. 162
Wharton, William J. L., K.C.B.1897, I. 296

Whatley, Joseph, K.C.H.1831, I. 457; Kt. 1831, II. 330
Whatton, John, Kt.1662, II. 237
Wheatley, Henry, K.C.H.1831, I. 456; Kt.1831, II. 330; G.C.H.1834, I. 452
Wheatstone, Charles, Kt.1868, II. 359
Wheeler, Edmond, Kt.1615, II. 155
Wheeler, Francis, Kt.1688, II. 264
Wheeler, George, Kt.1682, II. 258
Wheeler, Hugh M., K.C.B.1850, I. 239
Wheeler, William, Kt.1657, II. 223
Wheeler-Denny-Cuffe, Richard, Kt.1782, II. 297
Wheelhouse, William St. J., Kt.1882, II. 374
Whelan, Thomas, Kt.1821, II. 323
Whetbrook (Whitbroke), John, Kt.1604, II. 133
Whetham, Charles, Kt.1874, II. 366
Whethill, Richard, Kt.1513, II. 40
Whetstone, Barnard, Kt.1603, II. 119
Whetstone, William, Kt.1705, II. 274
Whettenhall, Henry, Kt.1609, II. 147
Whichcot (Swythcoate), Hugh, Kt.1603, II. 103
Whichcote, Paul, Kt.1665, II. 241
Whish, William S., K.C.B.1849, I. 238
Whorwood (Horwood, Harwood), Edward, Kt.1611, II. 151
Whorwood, Thomas, Kt.1624, II. 185
Whyche. See Wyche
Whiddon, John, Kt.1555, II 69
Whinyates, Edward C., K.H.1823, I.464; K.C.B.1860, I. 246
Whitaker, Edward, Kt.1704, II. 274
Whitaker, Frederick, K.C.M.G.1884, I. 366
Whitbrook. See Whetbrook
Whitburne, Richard, Kt.1625, II. 189
Whitcombe, Samuel, Kt.1812, II. 312
White, Arnold W., Kt.1887, II. 382
White, Charles A., Kt.1900, II. 407
White, Dominick, Kt.1637, II. 205
White, George S., K.C.B.1886, I. 260; K.C.I.E.1890, I. 406; G.C.I.E.1893, I. 402; G.C.B.1897, I. 201; G.C.S.I. 1898, I. 314; G.C.V.O.1900, I. 418; G.C.M.G.1901, I. 347
White, Henry, Kt.1814, II. 314

White, Henry, K.C.B.1815, I. 227
White, Henry A., Kt.1898, II. 402
White, Henry D., K.C.B.1877, I. 255
White, Herbert T., K.C.I.E.1903, I. 411
White, John, Kt.1541, II. 52
White, John, Kt.1563, II. 71
White, John, Kt.1619, II. 172
White, John, Kt.1801, II. 306
White, John, C., K.C.B.1841, I. 237
White, Luke, baron Annaly, K.P.1885, I. 104
White, Michael, K.C.B.1862, I. 248
White, Nicholas, Kt.1584, II. 83
White, Nicholas, Kt.1609, II. 148
White, Patrick, Kt.1541, II. 53
White, Richard, Kt.1601, II. 99, 128, 139
White, Robert, K.B.(1483), I. 140
White, Robert, K.C.B.1893, I. 265
White, Sampson, Kt.1661, II. 234
White, Stephen, Kt.1660, II. 230
White, Thomas, Kt.1553, 67, 69
White, Thomas, Kt.1615, II. 155
White, Thomas, Kt.1873, II. 365
White, William, Kt.1835, II. 336
White, William A., K.C.M.G.1885, I. 367; G.C.M.G.1886, I. 340; G.C.B.1888, I. 212
White, William H., Kt.1882, II. 373
White, William H., K.C.B.1895, I. 294
White-Thomson, Robert T., K.C.B.1897, I. 296
Whitechurch, Marmaduke, Kt.1626, II. 191

WHITEFORD, WHITEFOORD, WHITFORD
Whitford, George, Kt.1821, II. 322
Whiteford, John, K.H.1832, I. 466
Whitefoord, John R., Kt.1811, II. 310

Whitehead, Henry, Kt.1603, I. 124
Whitehead, Thomas, K.C.B.1838, I. 235
Whitehouse, George, K.C.B.1902, I. 300
Whitelock. See Whitlock
Whiteway, William V., K.C.M.G.1880, I. 362
Whitfield, Henry, Kt.1641, II. 209
Whitfield, Ralph, Kt.1635, II. 204
Whitford. See Whiteford
Whitgrave, Thomas, Kt.1658, II. 224
Whitla, William, Kt.1902, II. 410

WHITELOCK, WHITLOCK
Whitlock, George C., K.C.B.1859, I. 245
Whitlock, James, Kt.1620, II. 175
Whitelock, James, Kt.1657, II. 223
Whitlock, William, Kt.1689, II. 264
Whitmore, Edmund A., K.C.B.1882, I. 258
Whitmore, George (William), Kt.1632, II. 200
Whitmore, George, K.C.H.1832, I. 458, Kt.1832, II. 332
Whitmore, George S., K.C.M.G.1882, I. 364
Whitmore, Thomas, Kt.1641, II. 209
Whitmore, Thomas, K.B.1661, I. 166
Whitmore, Thomas, K.B.1744, I. 169
Whitmore, William, Kt.1621, II. 177

WHITNEY, WHITENAY, WYTNEY
Whitney, Benjamin, Kt.1897, II. 400
Whitenay, Eustace de, K.B.1306, I. 113
Whitney, Everard, Kt.1608, II. 145
Whitney, James, Kt.1578, II. 79
Wytney, Robert, Kt.1553, II. 68
Whitney, Robert, Kt.1570, II. 74
Whitshed, James H., K.C.B.1815, I. 217; G.C.B.1830, I. 186
Whittall, James W., Kt.1898, II. 403

WHITTINGHAM, WHYTYNGHAM
Whytyngham, —, Kt.1461, II. 13
Whittingham, Robert, Kt.1460, II. 12
Whittingham, Samuel F., Kt.1815, II. 315; K.C.H.1821, I. 455; K.C.B. 1826, I. 230
Whittingham, Timothy, Kt.1604, II. 129
Whitton (Whiddon), John, Kt.1603, II. 115
Whitwell, Nathaniel, Kt.1715, II. 280
Whitworth, Charles, Kt.1768, II. 293
Whitworth, Charles, earl Whitworth, K.B.1793, I. 174; Grand Master of St. Patrick 1813, I. 93; G.C.B.1815, I. 205
Whitworth, Francis, Kt.1803, II. 307
Whitworth-Aylmer, Matthew, lord Aylmer, G.C.B.1836, I. 187
Whymper, William, Kt.1833, II. 333
Wiche. See Wych

INDEX

Wickens, John, Kt.1871, II. 363
Wickham. See Wykeham
Wicklow, earl of. See Howard
WIDDRINGTON, WETHERYNGTON, WYDERINGTON, WIDERINGTON, WITHERINGTON, WODERINGTON
  Widdrington, David L. T., K.C.H. 1833, I. 459; Kt.1833, II. 333
  Wyderington, Henry, Kt.1504, II. 34
  Woderington (Widdrington, Wetheryngton), Henry, Kt.1580, II. 80
  Widerington, Henry, Kt.1603, II. 100
  Woderington (Widrington), John, Kt. 1482, II. 18
  Woderington, Rauf, Kt.1482, II. 18, 21
  Widdrington, Thomas, Kt.1639, II. 206
  Wytherington, William, Kt.1603, II. 122
  Witherington, William, Kt.1632, II. 199
Widmarkter, Gasper, Kt.1611, II. 151
Widnall (Wignall), Edward, Kt.1619, II. 172
Widvile. See Wydville
Wied, prince William, &c., of, G.C.V.O. 1904, I. 428
Wier. See Wyer
Wigan, Fredcrick, Kt.1894, II. 394
Wightman, William, Kt.1841, II. 343
Wigley, Edward, Kt.1683, II. 259
Wignall. See Widnall
Wigram, Charles H., Kt.1902, II. 413
Wigram, James, Kt.1842, II. 344
Wigram, Robert, Kt.1818, II. 320
Wigstone, William, Kt.1553, II. 68
Wilbraham, Richard, Kt.1603, II. 128
Wilbraham, Richard, K.C.B.1873, I. 254
Wilbraham, Roger, Kt.1603, II. 109
WILCOCKS, WILLCOCKS
  Wilcocks, James, K.C.M.G.1900, I. 388
  Wilcocks, Richard, Kt.1827, II. 327
  Willcocks, Robert H., K.H.1837, I. 478
  Willcocks, William, K.C.M.G.1902, I. 393
WILDE, WYLD, WYLDE
  Wilde, Alfred T., K.C.B.1869, I. 252
  Wyld, Edmond, Kt.1613, II. 152

WILDE
  Wilde, James P., Kt.1860, II. 354
  Wylde, John, Kt.1607, II. 142
  Wild (Weld), John, Kt.1617, II. 167
  Wilde, John, Kt.1641, II. 210, 214, bis
  Wylde, John, Kt.1827, II. 326
  Wilde, Thomas, Kt.1840, II. 342
  Wilde, William, Kt.1660, II. 225
  Wilde, William R. W., Kt.1864, II. 357
Wilder, Francis J., Kt.1817, II. 319
WILDGOOSE, WILDEGOS, WILDGOSE
  Wildegos, Annesley (Anselm), Kt.1605, II. 138
  Wildgose, John, Kt.1603, II. 119
  Wildgoose, Robert, Kt.1641, II. 208
Wilding, George, prince of Butora, K.C.H.1816, I. 454
WILDMAN, WYLDMAN
  Wildman, Edward, K.H.1836, I. 473
  Wyldman, John, Kt.1692, II. 267
WILFORD, WYLFORDE
  Wylforde, James, Kt.1547, II. 62
  Wilford, James, Kt.1661, II. 234
  Wilford, Thomas, Kt.1588, II. 87
  Wilford, Thomas, Kt.1607, II. 143
Wilkes, Thomas, Kt.1591, II. 89
Wilkie, David, Kt.1836, II. 337
Wilkin, Walter H., Kt.1893, II. 391; K.C.M.G.1896, I. 381
Wilkins, Charles, K.H.1833, I. 469; Kt. 1833, II. 334
Wilkins, George, K.H.1837, I. 478
Wilkinson, Henry, Kt.1790, II. 301
Wilkinson, Henry C., K.C.B.1897, I. 268
Wilkinson, Hiram S., Kt.1903, II. 414
Wilkinson, John G., Kt.1839, II. 342
Wilkinson, Joseph L., Kt.1902, II. 412
Wilkinson, Thomas, K.C.S.I.1866, I. 317
Wilkinson, William, G.C.M.G.1837, I. 334
Willcocks. See Wilcocks
Willers. See Villiers
William III., K.G.1653, I. 35
William IV., K.T.1770. I. 79; K.G.1782, I. 47; G.C.B.1815, I. 182; G.C.H. 1815, I. 447; Grand Master of the Bath (1827), I. 109
Williams, Abraham, Kt.1625, II. 188
Williams, Albert H. W., K.C.V.O.(1904), I. 437

Williams, Charles, Kt.1621, II. 176
Williams, Charles F., Kt.1838, II. 340
Williams, Charles H., K.B.1744, I. 169
Williams, Daniel, Kt.1802, II. 306
Williams, David, Kt.1603, II. 114
Williams, Edmund K., K.C.B.1815, I. 226
Williams, Edmund, Kt.1639, II. 206
Williams, Edward C. S., K.C.I.E.1893, I. 407
Williams, Edward E., Kt.1878, II. 370
Williams, Edward L., Kt.1894, II. 393
Williams, Edward V., Kt.1847, II. 346
Williams, George, Kt.1894, II. 394
Williams, Hartley, Kt.1894, II. 392
Williams (alias Cromwell), Henry, Kt. 1564, II. 71
Williams, Henry, Kt.1603, II. 118
Williams, James (Thomas), Kt.1553, II. 68
Williams James, Kt.1824, II. 324
Williams, John, Kt.1497, II. 30
Williams, John, Kt.1538, II. 50
Williams, John, Kt.1604, II. 130
Williams, John, Kt.1713, II. 278
Williams, John, Kt.1771, II. 293
Williams, John, Kt.1834, II. 335
Williams, John, K.C.V.O.(1902), I. 435
Williams, John B., Kt.1837, II. 339
Williams, John W., Kt.1840, II. 342
Williams, John W. C., K.C.B.1892, I. 264
Williams, Monier, Kt.1886, II. 378
Williams, Morrice, Kt.1638, II. 205
Williams, Rice, Kt.1676, II. 251
Williams, Richard, K.C.B.1815, I. 225
Williams, Roger, Kt.1586, II. 85
Williams, Roland L. V., Kt.1890, II. 387
Williams, Thomas, Kt.1587, II. 86
Williams, Thomas, Kt.1603, II. 127
Williams, Thomas, Kt.1796, II. 303; K.C.B.1815, I. 218; G.C.B.1831, I. 186
Williams, Thomas M., Kt.1904, II. 418
Williams, Watkin, Kt.1880, II. 372
Williams, William, Kt.1687, II. 264
Williams, William, K.C.B.1815, I. 224

Williams, William F., K.C.B.1856, I. 243; G.C.B.1871, I. 195
Williams, William F., K.H.1835, I. 472
Williams, William J., K.C.B.1891, I. 263
Williams-Wynn, Henry W., K.C.B.1851, I. 278
Williamson, Adam, K.B.1794, I. 174
Williamson, Francis, Kt.1641, II. 210
Williamson, James, Kt.1900, II. 407
Williamson, Joseph, Kt.1672, II. 246
Williamson, Richard, Kt.1604, II. 132
Williamson, Thomas, Kt.1642, II. 213
Willes. See Wills
Willis. See Wills
Willock, Henry, Kt.1827, II. 326
Willox, John A., Kt.1897, II. 400
WILLOUGHBY, WILUGHBY, WILOUGHBY, WYLUGHBY, WILLOUGHBIE, WILLOWBY
Willoughby, —, K.B.1399, I. 128
Willoughby, Ambrose, Kt.1603, II. 105
Willoughby, Anthony, Kt.1646, II. 220
Willoughby, Christopher, K.B.1483, I. 139, 141
Willoughby, Christopher, Kt.1513, II. 39
Wylughby, Francys, Kt.1575, II. 76
Willoughby, Francis, Kt.1583, II. 81
Willoughbie, Francis, Kt.1610, II. 150, 190
Willoughby, George, Kt.1686, II. 262
Wiloughby, Henry, Kt.1487, 1497, II. 24, 29
Willoughby, Henry, Kt.1625, II. 190
Wylloughby, Hew, Kt.1544, II. 56
Willoughby, John de, K.B.1327, I. 124
Willoughby, John, lord Latimer, Kt. 1471, II. 15
Willoughby, John, Kt.1513, II. 37
Wilughby, John, Kt.1533, II. 49
Willoughby, John, Kt.1603, II. 115
Willoughby de Eresby, lord. See Bertie; see Hastings
Willoughby, Nesbit J., Kt.1827, II. 326; K.C.H.1832, I. 459
Willoughby, Percivall, Kt.1603, II. 102
Willowby, Robert, Kt.1347, II. 8
Willoughby, Robert, lord Willoughby de Eresby, K.G.1416, I. 9

INDEX

WILLOUGHBY
Willoughby, Robert, Kt.1480, II. 17
Willoughby, Robert, lord Willoughby de Broke, K.G.1488, I. 18
Willoughby, Robert, lord Willoughby de Broke, K.B.1509, I. 148
Willoughbie, Robert, Kt.1618, II. 170
Willoughby, Rotherham, Kt.1608, II. 145
Willoughby, Thomas, Kt.1603, II. 102
Willoughby, Thomas, Kt.1617, II. 161
Willoughby, William de, K.B.1327, I. 124
Willoughby, William, lord Willoughby de Eresby, K.G.1400, I. 7
Wyloughby, William, Kt.1485, II. 23
Wiloughby, William, Kt.1542, II. 53
Willoughby, William, Kt.1603, II. 102, 112

WILLS, WILLES, WILLIS, WILES, WYLLIS
Wills, Alfred, Kt.1884, II. 376
Wills (Willis), Charles, K.B.1725, I. 168
Wills (Wiles), Edward, Kt.1695, II. 268
Wills, Edward P., K.C.B.1899, I. 298
Willes, Francis, Kt.1784, II. 298
Willis, Frederick, A., K.C.B.1899, I. 270
Willis, George H. S., K.C.B.1882, II. 258; G.C.B.1895, I. 201
Willes, George O., K.C.B.1884, I. 259; G.C.B.1892, I.. 200
Willes, James S., Kt.1855, II. 351
Willes, John, Kt.1757, II. 285
Wyllis, Richard, Kt.1642, II. 214
Willis, William, Kt.1885, II. 377
Willshire. See Wiltshire
Willson. See Wilson
Wilmington, earl of. See Compton

WILMORE, WALMORE, WOLMORE, WILMER, WILLMORE
Wilmore (Walmore), George, Kt.1603, II. 119
Wilmore (Wolmore), Gregory, Kt.1603, II. 119
Wilmer (Willmore), William, 1617, II. 162

WILMOT, WILLMOTE, WILLIMOT
Willmote, Charles, Kt.1599, II. 97

WILMOT
Wilmot, George (John), Kt.1628, II. 195
Wilmot, Henry, K.C.B.1897, I. 296
Wilmot, John E., Kt.1755, II. 288
Wilmot, Nicholas, Kt.1674, II. 249
Wilmot, Robert, Kt.1739, II. 285
Willimott, Robert W., Kt.1744, II. 286
Wilmot, Stafford, Kt.1620, II. 175

WILSON, WILLSON
Wilson, Adam, Kt.1887, II. 384
Wilson, Alexander, Kt.1813, II. 312
Wilson, Alexander, Kt.1887, II. 380
Wilson, Archdale, K.C.B.1857, I. 244; G.C.B.1867, I. 195
Wilson, Arthur, K.C.I.E.1898, I. 409
Wilson, Arthur K., K.C.B.1902, I. 273; K.C.V.O.(1903), I. 436
Wilson, Belford H., K.C.B.1852, I. 279
Wilson, Charles R., K.C.M.G.1879, I. 362; G.C.M.G.1895, I. 344
Wilson, Charles W., K.C.M.G.1881, I. 363; K.C.B.1885, I. 259
Wilson, David, K.C.M.G.1899, I. 386
Wilson, Daniel, Kt.1888, II. 385
Wilson, Erasmus, Kt.1881, II. 373
Wilson, Giffin, Kt.1823, II. 324
Wilson, Guy D. A. F., Kt.1902, II. 412
Wilson (Wright-Wilson), Henry, Kt. 1794, II. 302
Wilson, Isaac, Kt.1838, II. 340
Wilson, Jacob, Kt.1889, II. 386
Wilson, James., K.C.B.1815, I. 225
Wilson, James M., Kt.1873, II. 365
Wilson, John, Kt.1629, II. 196
Wilson, John, Kt.1786, II. 299
Wilson, John, Kt.1814, II. 313; K.C.B. 1837, I. 233
Wilson, John, K.H.1836, I. 474
Wilson, John C., K.C.S.I.1872, I. 319
Wilson, John M., K.H.1831, I. 465; Kt. 1838, II. 341
Wilson, Nathan, K.H.1834, I. 470
Wilson, Nicholas, K.H.1836, I. 474
Willson, Mildmay W., K.C.B.1902, I. 275
Wilson, Ralph, Kt.1661, II. 233
Wilson, Samuel, Kt.1875, II. 367
Wilson, Thomas, Kt.1618, II. 169

WILSON

Wilson, Thomas, Kt.1760, II. 289
Wilson, William, Kt.1682, II. 257
Wilson, William D., K.C.M.G.1901, I. 389
Wilson, Wiltshire, K.C.H.1836, I. 461; Kt.1836, II. 337

WILTSHIRE, WILLSHIRE

Wiltshire, earl of. See Scrope; see Stafford; see Boleyn; see Egerton
Wiltshire, John, Kt.1504, II. 34
Wiltshire, Thomas, K.C.B.1839, I. 236 G.C.B.1861, I. 194
Winchester, bishop of. See Davidson
Winchester, marquess of. See Paulet
Winchester, Robert, K.H.1834, I. 469
Winchilsea, earl of. See Finch
Winde. See Wynde

WINDEBANK, WYNYBANKE

Windebank, Francis, Kt.1632, II. 200
Wynybanke, Richard, Kt.1545, II. 56
Windebanck, Thomas, Kt.1603, II. 115
Windeyer, William C., Kt.1891, II. 388

WINDHAM, WYNDHAM

Windham, Charles A., K.C.B.1865, I. 249
Wyndham, Charles, Kt.1902, II. 412
Wyndham, Edmund, Kt.1549
Wyndham, Edward, Kt.1538, II. 51
Windham, George, Kt.1633, II. 201
Wyndham, George H., K.C.M.G.1894, I. 379
Windham, Henry, Kt.1603, II. 125
Wyndham, Henry, K.C.B.1859, I. 245
Windham, Hugh, Kt.1641, II. 210
Windham, Hugh, Kt.1670, II. 244
Wyndham, John, Kt.1487, II. 25
Wyndham, John, Kt.1547, II. 59
Windham, John, Kt.1603, II. 126
Windham, Thomas, Kt.1631, II. 199
Windham, Wadham, Kt.1660, II. 232
Wyndham-Quin, Edwin R. W., earl of Dunraven, K.P.1866, I. 103
Wyndham-Quin, Windham T., earl of Dunraven, K.P.1876, I. 104

WINDSOR, WYNDESORE

Windsor, Andrew, lord Windsor, K.B. 1509, I. 148; Kt.1513, II. 36

WINDSOR

Wyndesore, Anthony, Kt.1533, II. 49
Wyndesore, Edmonde (Edward), lord Windsor, Kt.1553, II. 66
Windsor, Edmond (Edward), Kt.1621, II. 177
Windsor, Thomas, K.B.1547, I. 151
Wyndesore, Thomas, K.B.(1483), I. 140
Windsor, Thomas, lord Windsor, K.B.1610, I. 157
Windsor, William, lord Windsor, K.B.1533, I. 149
Windsor, William, Kt.1603, II. 128
Windy. See Wendy
Winford, John, Kt.1643, II. 215
Winford, Thomas, Kt.1702, II. 272
Wingate, Andrew, K.C.I.E.1898, I. 410
Wingate, Francis, Kt.1672, II. 247
Wingate, Francis R., K.C.M.G.1898, I. 385; K.C.B.1900, I. 271
Wingate, George, K.C.S.I.1866, I. 317
Wingareden, Jacob de, Kt.1621, II. 176

WINGFIELD, WINGEFELDE, WINGFEILD, WYNGEFEILDE, WYNKEFELD

Wingefelde, Anthony, Kt.1513, II. 38; K.G.1541, I. 23
Wingfield, Anthony, Kt.1597, II. 94
Wingfield, Charles J., K.C.S.I.1866, I. 317
Wingfield, Edward, Kt.1471, II. 16
Wingfield, Edward, Kt.1586, II. 84, 86
Wingfeild, Edward, Kt.1603, II. 126
Wingfield, Edward, Kt.1623, II. 183
Wingfield, Edward, K.C.B.1899, I. 297
Wingfield, Henry, Kt.1471, II. 14
Wyngefeilde, Humfrey, Kt.1538, I. 52
Wingfield, James, Kt.1604, II. 135
Wingefield, John, K.B.(1461), I. 133
Wynkefeld, John, K.B.(1483), I. 139
Wingfield, John, Kt.1586, II. 85
Wingfeild, John, Kt.1619, II. 171
Wingfield, Mervyn, viscount Powerscourt, K.P.1871, I. 103
Wingfield, Richard, K.G.1522, I. 21

INDEX

WINGFIELD
Wyngefeilde, Richard, Kt.1545, II. 57
Wingfield, Richard, Kt.1595, II. 91
Wingfield, Richard, Kt.1642, II. 213
Wingfield, Robert, K.B.(1426), I. 131
Wingfield, Robert, Kt.1553, II. 67
Wingfield, Robert, Kt.1603, II. 106
Wingfield, Robert, Kt.1613, II. 152
Wingfield, Thomas, Kt.1471, II. 14
Wingfeild, Thomas, Kt.1606, II. 140
Wingfield, Thomas M., Kt.1597, II. 94
Winkfield. See Wingfield
Winne. See Wynne
Winniett, William, Kt.1849, II. 347
Winnington, Francis, Kt.1672, II. 247
Winston, Henry, Kt.1592, II. 90
WINTER, WINTOUR, WYNTER
Winter (Winton), Charles, Kt.1686, II. 262
Winter, Edward, Kt.1595, II. 91
Winter (Wintour), Edward, Kt.1662, II. 236
Winter, Francis P., Kt.1900, II. 408
Winter, George (Gregory), Kt.1624, II. 185
Winter, George, Kt.1641, II. 209
Winter, James S., K.C.M.G.1888, I. 373
Winter, John, 1624, II. 186
Wynter, William, Kt.1573, II. 75
Winton, earl of. See Montgomerie
Winterbotham, Henry M., K.C.S.I.1903, I. 327
Winton, Francis W. de, K.C.M.G.1884, I. 366; G.C.M.G.1893, I. 343
Winton. See Winter
Wintringham, Clifton, Kt.1762, II. 291
Wisdom, Robert, K.C.M.G.1887, I. 371
WISE, WYSE
Wise, Edward, K.B.1661, I. 165
Wise, Thomas, K.B.1603, I. 156
Wyse, Thomas, K.C.B.1857, I. 280
Wise, William, Kt.1670, II. 244
Wise, William L., Kt.1904, II. 418
WISEMAN, WYSEMAN
Wiseman, Charles, Kt.1629, II. 196
Wiseman, Edmund, Kt.1681, II. 256
Wyseman, John, Kt.1513, II. 40

WISEMAN
Wiseman, Rafe, Kt.1603, II. 105
Wiseman, Richard, Kt.1619, II. 171
Wiseman, Richard, Kt.1660, II. 229
Wiseman, Robert, Kt.1616, II. 158
Wiseman, Robert, Kt.1661, II. 234
Wiseman, Thomas, Kt.1604, II. 131
Wiseman, Thomas, Kt.1616, II. 158
Wiseman, William, Kt.1604, II. 135
Wiseman, William, Kt.1660, II. 229
Wiseman, William S., K.C.B.1867, I. 251
Wishart, James, Kt.1704, II. 274
Witham, Charles, Kt.1830, II. 329
Withens. See Wythens
WIHEPOLE, WYTHIPOLE
Withepole, Edm., Kt.1600, II. 98
Wythipole, William, Kt.1617, II. 167
Witherington. See Widdrington
Withers, Charles S., Kt.1788, II. 300
Withers, William, Kt.1699, II. 271
Wittenoom, Edward H., K.C.M.G.1900, I. 388
Witterong, John, Kt.1641, II. 208
WIVELL, WYVELL, WIVILLE
Wyvell, Marmaduke, Kt.1603, II. 110
Wivell, Marmaduke, Kt.1617, II. 162
Wiville, Robert de, K.B.1306, I. 117
Wodehouse. See Woodhouse
Woder, Nicholas, Kt.(1453), II. lx.
Woellwarth-Lauterburg freiherr August von, G.C.V.O.1900, I. 423
Wogan, John, K.B.1501, I. 145
Wogan, John, Kt.1603, II. 113
Wogan, William, Kt.1603, II. 113
Wogan (Wogham), William, Kt.1689, II. 265
WOLFF, WOLFE, WOOLFE
Wolff, Henry D., K.C.M.G.1862, I. 354; G.C.M.G.1878, I. 338; K.C.B.1879, I. 287; G.C.B.1889, I. 212
Wolfe (Woolfe), John, Kt.1696, II. 269
Wolfe (Woolfe), Joseph, Kt.1704, II. 273
Wollaston, John, Kt.1641, II. 211
WOLLEY, WOOLEY
Wolley, Francis, Kt.1603, II. 106
Woolley, John, Kt.1592, II. 90

Wolseley, Garnet J., viscount Wolseley, K.C.M.G.1870, I. 355; K.C.B.1874, I. 254; G.C.M.G. 1874, I. 337; G.C.B.1880, I. 197; K.P.1885, I. 105
Wolseley, George B., K.C.B.1891, I. 264
Wolseley, Thomas, Kt.1617, II. 165
Wolstan, Guy of, K.B.(1487), I. 142
Wolstenholm, John, Kt.1617, II. 161
Wolstenholm, John, Kt.1633, II. 200
Wolton. See Walton
Wolveridge. See Wooldridge

WOOD, WOODE
Wood, Alexander, Kt.1820, II. 321; K.C.M.G.1820, I. 351
Wood, Charles, viscount Halifax, G.C.B.1856, I. 208
Wood, Charles A., Kt.1874, II. 366
Wood, David, Kt.1604, II. 133
Wood, David E., K.C.B.1859, I. 246; G.C.B.1877, I. 197
Wood, Elliott, K.C.B.1900, I. 272
Wood, Gabriel, Kt.1825, II. 325
Wood, George, Kt.1807, II. 309
Wood, George, K.C.B.1815, I. 227
Wood, George A., Kt.1812, II. 311; K.C.H.1816, I. 454
Wood, Henry, Kt.1644, II. 217
Wood, Henry, Kt.1671, II. 246
Wood, Henry E., K.C.B.1879, I. 256; G.C.M.G.1882, I. 339; G.C.B.1891, I. 200
Wood, Henry H. A., K.C.B.1894, I. 265
Wood, Henry T., Kt.1890, II. 387
Wood, James A., Kt.1809, II. 309
Wood, John, Kt.1483, II. 21
Wood, John, Kt.1603, II. 109, 116
Wood, John S., K.C.B.1870, I. 285
Wood, Richard, K.C.M.G.1877, I.359; G.C.M.G.1879, I. 339
Woode, Robert, Kt.1578, II. 79
Wood, Robert, Kt.1633, II. 201
Woode, Thomas, Kt.1501, II. 33
Wood, William, K.H.1835, I. 471
Wood, William, K.C.B.1865, I. 249
Wood, William L., K.H.1837, I. 478
Wood, William P., Kt.1851, II. 348

Woodburn, John, K.C.S.I.1897, I. 326; G.C.I.E.1903, I. 404
Woodcock, Thomas, Kt.1660, II. 225
Woderington. See Widdrington
Woodford, Alexander, K.C.B.1831, I. 231; G.C.M.G.1832, I. 333; G.C.B. 1852, I. 190
Woodford, John G., K.C.H.1832, I. 458; Kt.1832, II. 332; K.C.B.1838, I. 234
Woodgate, Edward R. P., K.C.M.G.1900, I. 387
Woodhead, John, Kt.1897, II. 399
WOODHOUSE, WODEHOUSE, WOODHOWSE
Woodhouse, Edward, Kt.1471, II. 15
Woodhouse, Henry, Kt.1578, II. 79
Woodhouse, James T., Kt.1895, II. 395
Wodehouse, John, earl of Kimberley, Grand Master K.P.1864, I. 94; K.G.1885, I. 67
Woodhouse, Michael, Kt.1643, II. 216
Woodhouse, Philip, Kt.1596, II. 92
Wodehouse, Philip E., K.C.B.1862, I. 282; G.C.S.I.1876, I. 310
Woodhowse (Wodowse), Roger, Kt. 1553, II. 67
Woodhouse, Roger, Kt.1578, II. 79
Woodhouse, Thomas, K.B.1501, I. 147
Woodhouse, Thomas, Kt.1549, II. 64
Woodhouse, Thomas, Kt.1603, II. 111
Woodhouse, Thomas, Kt.1666, II. 242
Woodhowse, William, Kt.1544, II. 55
Woodhowse, William, Kt.1591, II. 89
Woodiwiss, Abraham, Kt.1883, II. 375
WOODROFFE, WOODRUFFE, WOODROFE
Woodroffe, David, Kt.1603, II. 123
Woodruffe, George, Kt.1681, II. 256
Woodroffe, Nicholas, Kt.1580, II. 80
Woodrofe, Richard, Kt.1497, II. 32
Woodroff, Roger (Robert), Kt.1604, II. 132
Woods, Albert W., Kt.1869, II. 361; K.C.M.G.1890, I. 375; K.C.B.1897, I. 295; G.C.V.O.1903, I. 421
Woods, Henry F., K.C.V.O.(1902), I. 434
Woods, William, Kt.1832, II. 332; K.H. 1834, I. 471
Woodville. See Wydville

INDEX 249

Woodward, John, Kt.1613, II. 152
Wooley. See Wolley
Woolfe. See Wolfe
Woolfryes, John A., K.C.B.1902, I. 274
WOOLMORE, WOLMORE, and see Wilmore
  Woolmore, John, K.C.H.1834, I. 460;
    Kt.1834, II. 335
  Woolnough, Joseph C., K.H.1834, I. 470
WOOLDRIDGE, WOOLRIDGE, WOLVERIDGE,
  WOOLRICH
  Wolveridge (Wolrich), James, Kt.1619,
    II. 172
  Woolridge, Thomas, Kt.1641, II. 210
  Wooldridge, Thomas T., K.H.1836, I.
    473
  Woolrich, Toby, Kt.1661, II. 235
Wools-Sampson, Aubrey, K.C.B.1902, I.
  275
Wootton. See Wotton
Worcester, earl of. See Percy; see
  Tiptoft; see Somerset
Worcester, marquess of. See Somerset
Worcup (Warcop), Edmund, Kt.1684, II.
  260
Worley. See Wortley
Worlington. See Worthington
Woronzow, count, G.C.B.1819, I. 184
Worrall. See Wyrall
WORSLEY, WORSELEY
  Worsley, Bowyer, Kt.1607, II. 143
  Worsley (Worseley), Edward, Kt.1744,
    II. 286
  Worsley, Henry, K.C.B.1831, I. 232;
    G.C.B.1838, I. 188
  Worsley, James, Kt.1669, II. 243
  Worseley, Richard, Kt.1611, II. 150
  Worseley, Robert, Kt.1544, II. 55
  Worsley, Robert, Kt.1664, II. 240
Worsop (Worssop), Thomas, Kt.1664, II.
  240
Worth. See Wroth
WORTHINGTON, WORLINGTON
  Worlington (Worthington), William,
    Kt.1603, II. 120
  Worthington, William, Kt.1796, II.
    303
WORTLEY, WORLEY, WYRLEY, WORTELEY
  Wortley, Edward, Kt.1621, II. 177
  Wortley, Francis, Kt.1611, II. 150

WORTLEY
  Worley (Wyrley), John, Kt.1641, II.
    209
  Wortley, Richard, Kt.1603, II. 101
  Wortley, Thomas, Kt.1482, II. 20
  Wortley, Thomas, Kt.1497, II. 31
  Worteley, Thomas, Kt.1629, II. 196
WOTTON, WOOTTON
  Wotton, Edward, Kt.1592, II. 90
  Wootton, James, Kt.1596, II. 93
  Wootton, John, Kt.1591, II. 89
  Wotton, Thomas, Kt.1608, II. 145
Wragg, Walter T., Kt.1891, II. 388
WRAY, WREY
  Wrey (Wray), Bourchier, K.B.1661, I.
    164
  Wray, Christopher, Kt.1574, II. 76
  Wray, Christopher, Kt.1623, II. 183
  Wray, Christopher, Kt.1643, II. 216
  Wray, Daniel, Kt.1708, II. 276
  Wray, John, Kt.1612, II. 152
  Wray, William, Kt.1596, II. 94
  Wray, William, Kt.1603, II. 125
  Wray, William, Kt.1660, II. 227
  Wray, William, Kt.1617, II. 163
Wrede, Charles P., prince von, G.C.B.
  1815, I. 183
WREN, WRENNE, WRINNER
  Wrenne (Wrinner), Charles, Kt.1607
    II. 142
  Wren, Christopher, Kt.1673, II. 248
  Wren, William, Kt.1685, II. 261
Wrench, Benjamin, Kt.1720, II. 281
Wrenfordsley, Henry T., Kt.1883, II. 375
Wrey. See Wray
Wright, Charles, K.H.1831, I. 465
Wright, Edmund, Kt.1641, II. 209
Wright, George, Kt.1604, II. 134
Wright, James, Kt.1766, II. 292
Wright, James, Kt.1887, II. 381
Wright, John, K.H.1833, I. 469
Wright, Martin, Kt.1745, II. 287
Wright, Nathan, Kt.1697, II. 270
Wright, Robert, Kt.1605, II. 138
Wright, Robert, Kt.1680, II. 254
Wright, Robert S., Kt.1891, II. 388
Wright, Sampson, Kt.1782, II. 297
Wright, Thomas, Kt.1893, II. 392
Wright, Thomas, K.C.B.1893, I. 265

Wright, William, Kt.1606, II. 140
Wright, William, Kt.1869, II. 361
Wright, William P., K.C.B.1904, I. 276
Wright-Wilson. See Wilson, Henry
Wrightington, Thomas, Kt.1640, II. 207
Wrinner. See W·en
WRIOTHESLEY, WROTTESLEY, WROTESLEY, WRYOTHESLEY
  Wriothesley, Henry, earl of Southampton, Kt.1597, II. 94; K.G.1603, I. 30
  Wrottesley, Hugh, K.G.1348, I. 2
  Wrotesley, Hugh, Kt.1617, II. 165
  Wriothesley, James, lord Wriothesley, K.B.1616, I. 159
  Wryothesley, Thomas, Kt.1524, II. 46
  Wryothesley, Thomas, earl of Southampton, Kt.1538, II. 51; K.G.1545, I. 23
  Wriothesley, Thomas, earl of Southampton, K.G.1650, I. 34
  Wrottesley, Walter, Kt.1642, II. 214
  Wrottesley, William de, K.B.1306, I. 119
Wrixon, Henry J., K.C.M.G.1892, I. 377
WROTH, WROTHE, WORTHE
  Wroth, Henry, Kt.1645, II. 220
  Wrothe, Peter, Kt.1619, II. 171
  Wrothe (Worthe), Robert, Kt.1603, II. 110
  Wrothe, Thomas, Kt.1547, II. 60
  Wroth, Thomas, Kt.1613, II. 153
Wrottesley. See Wriothesley
Wroughton, Christopher, Kt.1487, II. 25
Wroughton, George, Kt.1618, II. 169
Wroughton, Thomas, Kt.1574, II. 76
Wroughton, Thomas, K.B.1780, I. 173
Wroughton, William, Kt.1544, II. 54
WÜRTEMBERG
  Charles, king of, K.G.1890, I. 68
  Frederick, duke of, K.G.1597, I. 29
  William I. of, G.C.B.1815, I. 183; K.G.1830, I. 54
  William II. of, K.G.1904, I. 72
WYATT, WYAT, WYOTTE
  Wyatt, —, Kt.1603, II. 126
  Wyatt, Dudley, Kt.1645, II. 220
  Wyatt, Francis, Kt.1618, II. 169
  Wyatt, Henry, K.B.1509, I. 148; Kt. 1513, II. 36

WYATT
  Wyatt, Matthew, Kt.1848, II. 347
  Wyatt, Matthew D., Kt.1869, II. 360
  Wyatt, Richard H., Kt.1883, II. 375
  Wyatt, Thomas, Kt.1537, II. 50
  Wyatt, Thomas, Kt.1549, II. 65
  Wyatt, William H., Kt.1876, II. 368
Wyatville, Jeffery, Kt.1828, II. 327
WYCH, WHYCHE, WICHE
  Wych, Cyril, Kt.1660, II. 226
  Whyche, Hugh, K.B.(1465), I. 135
  Wiche, Peter, Kt.1626, II. 191
Wycherley, George J., Kt.1885, II. 377
Wyderington. See Widdrington
WYDVILLE, WIDVILE, WYDVILE, WOODVILLE
  Wydville, Anthony, earl Rivers, K.G. 1466, I. 15
  Wydville, Edward, lord Wydville, K.B.(1475), I. 137; Kt.1482, II. 17; K.G.1487, I. 17
  Wydvile, John, K.B.(1465), I. 134
  Wydvill, Richard, earl Rivers, K.B. (1426), I. 132; K.G.1450, I. 12
  Wydvile, Richard, K.B.(1465), I. 134
Wyer (Wier), Lodowick, Kt.1645, II. 219
Wygmore, Richard, Kt.1603, II. 102
Wyke, Charles L., K.C.B.1860, I. 281; G.C.M.G.1879, I. 338
WYKEHAM, WICKHAM
  Wickham, Robert de, K.B.1306, I. 117
  Wykeham, Thomas, Kt.1416, II. 11
  Wickham, William, K.B.1323, I. 122
Wylde. See Wilde
Wyldman. See Wildman
Wylforde. See Wilford
Wylie, James, Kt.1614, II. 315
Wylie, William H. C., K.C.I.E.1902, I. 411
Wylington, Edmund de, K.B.1306, I. 114
Wylington, Ralph de, K.B.1327, I. 124
Wyllie, James, Kt.1843, II. 345
Wyllie, William, K.C.B.1865, I. 249; G.C.B.1877, I. 197
Wyllis. See Wills
Wymer, George P., K.C.B.1857, I. 243
Wymondesold, Dawes, Kt.1672, II. 247

INDEX 251

Wymondesold, Robert, Kt.1685, II. 260
Wynde (Windey, Winde), Robert, Kt. 1603, II. 123
Wyndham. See Windham
WYNNE, WYNN, WINNE
 Wynn, Henry W. W., G.C.H.1831, I. 451
 Wynn, John, Kt.1606, II. 139
 Wynn, John, Kt.1613, II. 153
 Wynn, John, Kt.1663, II. 237
 Wynne, Richard, Kt.1616, II. 158
 Wynne, Richard, Kt.1719, II. 281
 Winne, Thomas, Kt.1615, II. 156
 Wynne, William, Kt.1727, II. 284
 Wynne, William, Kt.1788, II. 300
 Wynn, William, Kt.1810, II. 310
Wynneve (Wynyeve), George, Kt.1663, II. 238
Wynwood, Ralph, Kt.1607, II. 142
Wyrall (Worrall), Hugh, Kt.1603, II. 122
Wyrley. See Wortley
Wyse. See Wise
Wyseman. See Wiseman
Wythens (Withens), Francis, Kt.1680, II. 254
Wythens, William, Kt.1603, II. 122
Wythipole. See Withepole
Wyvell. See Wivell
Wyver, Richard, Kt.1603, II. 123

X

Xerri, Raffaele C., G.C.M.G.1818, I. 332
Xidian, Anastasio T., K.C.M.G.1849, I. 353
Ximenes, David, K.C.H.1832, I. 458; Kt. 1832, II. 332
Ximenes, Moris, Kt.1806, II. 308

Y

Yallop, John H., Kt.1832, II. 331
Yallop, Robert, Kt.1664, II. 239
Yarborough, Thomas, Kt.1663, II. 238
YARDLEY, YARTLEY
 Yardley, George, Kt.1618, II. 170
 YARDLEY
 Yartley, Henry, Kt.1586, II. 85
 Yardley, William, Kt.1847, II. 347
Yarford. See Yerforde
Yarmouth, earl of. See Seymour-Conway
Yarner, Abraham, Kt.1670, II. 245
Yartley. See Yardley
YATES YATE, YEATES
 Yate (Yates), John, Kt.1629, II. 196
 Yates, Joseph, Kt.1763, II. 292
 Yeates, Thomas C., Kt.1827, II. 327
Yaxeley, Robert, Kt.1599, II. 97
Yeates. See Yates
Yelverton, Charles, Kt.1603, II. 120
Yelverton, Christopher, Kt.1603, II. 114, 120
Yelverton, Christopher, Kt.1623, II. 181
Yelverton, Hastings R., K.C.B.1869, I. 252; G.C.B.1875, I. 196
Yelverton, Henry, Kt.1613, II. 153
Yelverton, Henry, Kt.1618, II. 167, 176
Yelverton, Robert, Kt.1631, II. 199
Yelverton, Talbot, earl of Sussex, K.B. 1725, I. 167
Yelverton, William, K.B.(1461), I. 133
Yelverton, William, Kt.1620, II. 176
Yemin-ed-Dowlah, G.C.S.I.1887, I. 313
Yeo, James L., Kt.1810, II. 310; K.C.B. 1815, I. 223
Yeomans, Robert, Kt.1663, II. 238
Yerforde (Yarford), James, Kt.1519, II. 43
Yonge, Yong. See Young
YORK
 Edmund, duke of, K.G.1360, I. 3
 Edward, duke of, K.B.1377, I. 126; K.G.1387, I. 6
 Edward Augustus, duke of, K.G.1752, I. 44
 Ernest Augustus, duke of, K.G.1717, I. 41
 Frederick, duke of, K.B.1767, I. 171; Grand Master of the Bath (1767), I. 109; K.G.1771, I. 47; G.C.B.1815, I. 180; G.C.H.1815, I. 447
 Richard, duke of, K.B.(1426), I. 130; K.G.1433, I. 11
 Richard, duke of, K.B.1475, I. 136; K.G.1475, I. 16

YORK, YORKE
Yorke, Charles, K.C.B.1856, I. 243; G.C.B.1860, I. 193
Yorke, Edward (Edmond), Kt.1591, II. 89
Yorke, Henry F. R., K.C.B.1902, I. 300
Yorke, John, Kt.1549, II. 64
York, John, Kt.1603, II. 113
Yorke, John, Kt.1660, II. 228
Yorke, Joseph, lord Dover, K.B.1761, I. 170
Yorke, Joseph S., Kt.1805, II. 308; K.C.B.1815, I. 219
Yorke, Philip, earl of Hardwicke, Kt. 1720, II. 282
Yorke, Philip, earl of Hardwicke, Grand Master of St. Patrick 1801, I. 93; K.G.1803, I. 50
Yorke, Richard, Kt.1487, II. 26
York, Rowland, Kt.1586, II. 85
York, Thomas, Kt.1625, II. 189
Yorke, William, Kt.1674, II. 249
Youl, James A., K.C.M.G.1891, I. 376
YOUNG, YONGE, YOUNGE, YONG
Young, Allen, Kt.1877, II. 368
Young, Aretas W., Kt.1834, II. 335
Young, Charles G., Kt.1842, II. 345

YOUNG
Young, Frederick, K.C.M.G.1888, I. 372
Young, George, Kt.1603, II. 119, 129
Younge, George, Kt.1781, II. 296
Yonge, George, K.B.1788, I. 174
Young, Henry E. F., Kt.1847, II. 347
Yonge, John, Kt.1471, II. 16
Yonge, John, Kt.1574, II. 76
Yong (Young), John, Kt.1625, II. 189
Younge, John, Kt.1685, II. 260
Young, John, lord Lisgar, G.C.M.G. 1855, I. 335; K.C.B.1859, I. 245; G.C.B.1868, I. 210
Young, Peter, Kt.1605, II. 137
Yong, Peter, Kt.1627, II. 193
Young, Plomer, K.H.1836, I. 474
Young, Richard, Kt.1618, II. 167
Young, Richard, Kt.1604, II. 131
Young, William, Kt.1608, II. 145
Yonge, William, K.B.1725, I. 168
Young, William, K.B.1814, I. 179
Young, William, Kt.1869, II. 360
Young, William M., K.C.S.I.1897, I. 326
Yule, George U., K.C.S.I.1866, I. 317
Yule, Henry, K.C.S.I.1889, I. 324

INDEX

Z

Zammit, Guiseppe N., K.C.M.G.1818, I. 350
Zacharie, George H. R., K.C.V.O.1901, I. 440
Zanardelli, Giuseppe, G.C.V.O.1903, I. 426

ZANZIBAR
  Hamud bin Mahomed, sultan of, G.C.S.I.1898, I. 314
  Hamad - bin - Thowani, sultan of, G.C.S.I.1894, I. 313
  Ali bin Saeed, &c., sultan of, G.C.M.G. 1889, I. 342; G.C.S.I.1890, I. 313
  Seyyid Barghash-bin-Said, sultan of, G.C.M.G.1883, I. 339

Zavo, Basilio, K.C.M.G.1820, I. 351
Zeal, William A., K.C.M.G.1895, I. 380
Zedesen, Thomas de, K.B.1306, I. 118
Zelle, George W., duke of, K.G.1690, I. 39
Zeroudacchi, Constantine G., K.C.M.G. 1883, I. 366
Zetland, earl and marquess of. See Dundas
Zieten, Ernst K., count von, G.C.B.1819, I. 184
Zohrab, pasha Edward, K.C.M.G.1885, I. 368

ZOUCHE, ZOUCH, SOUCH, SOWTH, SUCHE, ZOUSCH, SOUWCHE
Zouche, Adam de la, Kt.(1355), II. 9
Souche (Souck), Albertus, Kt.1621, II. 176
Zouch, Allan, Kt.1620, II. 175
Zouch, Allen, Kt.1646, II. 221
Zouche (Sowth), Francis, Kt.1603, II. 117
Zouche, John de la, Kt.1513, II. 41
Zouche, John de la, Kt.1549, II. 64
Souwche, John de la, K.B.1559, I. 153
Zouche, John, Kt.1603, II. 103
Zouche, Simon la, Kt.1347, II. 7
Zouche, William le, K.B.1306, I.112
Zousch, Will de, Kt.(1336), II. 5
Zouche, William le, K.B.1347, II. 8
Zouche, William la, lord Zouche, K.G. 1415, I. 9
Zouche, William, K.B.(1483), I. 141
Zouch, William, Kt.1579, II. 80
Zouche, William, Kt.1615, II. 156
Zowkett, John, Kt.1513, II. 40
Zulfikar, pasha, K.C.M.G.1888, I. 373

www.ingramcontent.com/pod-product-compliance
Lightning Source LLC
Chambersburg PA
CBHW051105230426
43667CB00014B/2453